Frommer's®

England 2012 & the Best of Wales

by Nick Dalton & Deborah Stone

WILEY

John Wiley & Sons, Inc.

Published by:

JOHN WILEY & SONS, INC.

Copyright © 2011 John Wiley & Sons, Ltd, The Atrium, Southern Gate, Chichester, West Sussex PO19 8SQ, UK

Telephone (+44) 1243 779777

Email (for orders and customer service enquiries): cs-books@wiley.co.uk. Visit our Home Page on www.wiley.com

Editorial Director: Kelly Regan
Project Manager: Daniel Mersey
Commissioning Editor: Mark Henshall
Development Editor: Matthew Brown
Content Editor: Erica Peters
Cartography: Andrew Murphy
Photo Editor: Jill Emeny
Front Cover Photo: Whitby, Yorkshire / © Ingram Publishing / PhotoLibrary
Back Cover Photo: British Museum / © Mariano Pozo / Robert Harding Picture Library

British Library Cataloguing in Publication Data

A catalogue record for this book is available from the British Library

ISBN 978-1-119-99304-9 (pbk)
ISBN 978-1-119-99454-1 (ebk)
ISBN 978-1-119-97257-0 (ebk)
ISBN 978-1-119-99471-8 (ebk)

Typeset by Wiley Indianapolis Composition Services

Printed and bound in the United States of America

5 4 3 2 1

CONTENTS

LIST OF MAPS

ABOUT THE AUTHORS

Nick Dalton and **Deborah Stone** work as a team (generally helped on research trips by children Georgia and Henry). Using the knowledge garnered from writing about England and Wales for newspapers, magazines, and books, they were lead writers here, uniting a team despatched to the countries' far reaches.

They co-wrote Kent, Surrey & Sussex, Cambridge & East Anglia, and Cardiff & South Wales, along with Suggested Itineraries, and much of The Best of . . . , In Depth (in which history graduate Deborah revelled in the "Today" and "Making of . . . " sections), and Planning Your Trip.

Together they have written *Frommer's Wales With Your Family,* and have worked on Frommer's editing projects for destinations from Vienna to Iceland.

Nick writes on travel for U.K. newspapers such as the *Daily Telegraph,* the *Times* and the *Daily Express.* He also, for his sins, covers skiing and cruises worldwide, and is a regular visitor to the U.S., where he has written travel guides for Colorado and other states. He has also written *Frommer's Salzburg Day By Day.*

Deborah has written prolifically for the *Daily Telegraph* and *Daily Express,* on U.K. and family travel, having spent her childhood camping all over Britain, but particularly in East Anglia and Wales. She is a leading cruise writer, and is Online Gardening Editor at the *Daily* and *Sunday Express.*

Donald Strachan is a Scottish journalist, writer, and editor who has lived most of his life "down south" in England. He has written about the country, and wider European travel, for newspapers worldwide, including the *Sydney Morning Herald* and the *Independent on Sunday,* and is the U.K. *Sunday Telegraph's* regular contributor on travel-related new technology. He's also authored or co-authored several recent guidebooks to European destinations, including *Frommer's London 2012* and *Frommer's Tuscany, Umbria & Florence With Your Family.* Donald was responsible for the sections on London, North Wales, Hampshire, Dorset, Wiltshire, and southern Somerset.

Stephen Keeling is a journalist and writer who lives in New York but returns to his native England several times a year. He usually visits Bristol to deliver Hershey bars to his nephews, before making an annual pilgrimage through the Cotswolds to the RSC in Stratford (Stephen wrote the Cotswolds and Heart of England chapters in this guide, and the Bristol, Bath and west Somerset sections of chapter 8). Stephen also wrote the Thames Valley and Chilterns chapter, allowing him to re-visit his old college haunts in Oxford. He's authored or co-authored several recent guidebooks to European destinations, including *Frommer's Florence, Tuscany & Umbria With Your Family.*

Rhonda Carrier, who hails from the East Midlands, has lived in London, Paris, Vienna, and Hong Kong, and is now based in Manchester, writes widely about travel in the U.K. and abroad for Frommer's and frommers.com, Rizzoli, takethefamily.com, *The Guardian* and *The Observer, The Mail Online,* P&O Ferries, and others. A family travel expert, she has authored three editions of *Frommer's London with Kids* as well as the guidebooks *Frommer's Brittany With Your Family* and *Frommer's Normandy With Your Family,* and edited several other titles in the 'With Your Family' series. Rhonda wrote the chapters East Midlands, The Northwest, and Yorkshire & the Northeast.

Louise McGrath is a freelance travel writer and editor. Born in England, she lived in the U.S., Colombia, and Spain before moving to Northern Ireland in 2006. Since 2000 she has worked as an editor for Whatsonwhen (now Frommer's Unlimited) writing destination guides, and has authored several guide books, including *Frommer's Lisbon Day by Day, Frommer's Lake District Day by Day,* and co-authored *Frommer's England 2012 & the Best of Wales,* for which she worked on the Lake District chapter. Louise speaks Spanish and Portuguese, has an MA in Latin American Literature & Culture and is currently studying for the CIM Diploma in Digital Marketing.

Christi Daugherty has written for newspapers and wire services around the world on subjects ranging from politics to murder. She's also written numerous books for Frommer's, including *Frommer's Ireland 2011* and *Frommer's Ireland Day by Day.* Her first novel, *Night School,* will be published in 2012. She lives in a small town in southeast England, where she wrote the Devon chapter for this book.

Rebecca Ford is an award-winning travel writer and journalist who contributes to a wide range of national newspapers and magazines, writing about subjects as varied as wildlife watching in Peru and walking in Italy. She has authored and co-authored many guidebooks, including ones to U.K. destinations such as Scotland, Wales, and London, as well as *Frommer's England 2012 & the Best of Wales.* Rebecca wrote the chapter on Cornwall, which is fitting as she's part Cornish and has been visiting this fascinating corner of the country since she was a child.

HOW TO CONTACT US

In researching this book, we discovered many wonderful places—hotels, restaurants, shops, and more. We're sure you'll find others. Please tell us about them, so we can share the information with your fellow travelers in upcoming editions. If you were disappointed with a recommendation, we'd love to know that, too. Please email frommers@wiley.com or write to:

England 2012 & the Best of Wales
John Wiley & Sons, Inc. • 111 River St. • Hoboken, NJ 07030-5774

ADVISORY & DISCLAIMER

Travel information can change quickly and unexpectedly, and we strongly advise you to confirm important details locally before traveling, including information on visas, health and safety, traffic and transport, accommodation, shopping, and eating out. We also encourage you to stay alert while traveling and to remain aware of your surroundings. Avoid civil disturbances, and keep a close eye on cameras, purses, wallets, and other valuables.

While we have endeavored to ensure that the information contained within this guide is accurate and up-to-date at the time of publication, we make no representations or warranties with respect to the accuracy or completeness of the contents of this work and specifically disclaim all warranties, including without limitation warranties of fitness for a particular purpose. We accept no responsibility or liability for any inaccuracy or errors or omissions, or for any inconvenience, loss, damage, costs, or expenses of any nature whatsoever incurred or suffered by anyone as a result of any advice or information contained in this guide.

The inclusion of a company, organization, or website in this guide as a service provider and/or potential source of further information does not mean that we endorse them or the information they provide. Be aware that information provided through some websites may be unreliable and can change without notice. Neither the publisher nor author shall be liable for any damages arising herefrom.

FROMMER'S STAR RATINGS, ICONS & ABBREVIATIONS

Every hotel, restaurant, and attraction listing in this guide has been ranked for quality, value, service, amenities, and special features using a star-rating system. In country, state, and regional guides, we also rate towns and regions to help you narrow down your choices and budget your time accordingly. Hotels and restaurants are rated on a scale of zero (recommended) to three stars (exceptional). Attractions, shopping, nightlife, towns, and regions are rated according to the following scale: zero stars (recommended), one star (highly recommended), two stars (very highly recommended), and three stars (must-see).

In addition to the star-rating system, we also use **seven feature icons** that point you to the great deals, in-the-know advice, and unique experiences that separate travelers from tourists. Throughout the book, look for:

special finds—those places only insiders know about

fun facts—details that make travelers more informed and their trips more fun

kids—best bets for kids and advice for the whole family

special moments—those experiences that memories are made of

overrated—places or experiences not worth your time or money

insider tips—great ways to save time and money

great values—where to get the best deals

The following **abbreviations** are used for credit cards:

AE	American Express	DISC	Discover	V	Visa
DC	Diners Club	MC	MasterCard		

TRAVEL RESOURCES AT FROMMERS.COM

Frommer's travel resources don't end with this guide. Frommer's website, **www.frommers. com**, has travel information on more than 4,000 destinations. We update features regularly, giving you access to the most current trip-planning information and the best airfare, lodging, and car-rental bargains. You can also listen to podcasts, connect with other Frommers. com members through our active-reader forums, share your travel photos, read blogs from guidebook editors and fellow travelers, and much more.

THE BEST OF ENGLAND & WALES

by Nick Dalton & Deborah Stone

Below is the best of the best: the things we love and that we think you will, too. From the teeming streets of modern, cosmopolitan London to the far-flung, unspoiled green and pleasant land that hasn't changed for centuries, England and Wales, is greater than the sum of its parts. A respect for the past, rubs along with a vibrant and innovative outlook, evident in experiences such as Hadrian's Wall, Stonehenge, the Eden project and Tate Modern. In cities such as Manchester, Cardiff and Brighton you will find tremendous diversity and a dynamic cultural life.

CITIES & TOWNS Start with **London,** treasure of treasures—its beautiful buildings going back hundreds of years, its classic sights (the Tower of London, St. Paul's Cathedral), plus its **British Museum** (free, like most museums and galleries), its expansive parks, and its even more expansive shopping. Then move on to places such as **Manchester,** the cradle of industry; **Liverpool,** with its docks and Beatles history; and small, more esoteric cities such as classical **Bath,** quaint **Chichester,** and tiny **St. Davids** in the west of Wales. Each will inspire you in a different way.

THE COUNTRYSIDE England and Wales have it all, from the mountains of the **Peak District** and **Snowdonia** to the flat fenlands of the **East Coast,** from the rolling hills of the **South Downs** to the fantastic scenery of the **Lake District.** And amid all that are 13 National Parks, taking in the undulating openness of the **North York Moors** and the ancient woodlands of the **New Forest.** And the backdrop changes quickly; a day's journey can take you across several different landscapes.

EATING & DRINKING The cuisine here has really come on. There are now more than 120 restaurants with the esteemed **Michelin star.** Even more important, Britons have started respecting their food again. Whether it's a top **London** restaurant or somewhere modest in the **countryside** you'll find that the accent is on local, often organic, seasonal produce; fresh seafood or estate-reared game; just-picked vegetables; even salt dried from buckets of seawater (for example, at the **Sportsman** at

Whitstable in Kent). And beer has never been better, with small breweries producing top ales, while English vineyards produce decent wines.

THE COAST   The coastline of England and Wales is exceptional. You will find beautiful sandy beaches (**West Wittering** in Sussex, **Newgale** in Pembrokeshire, whole swathes of **North Norfolk**), strangely bleak stretches (**Dungeness** in Kent), looming white cliffs (much of England's south coast, from **Dover** to **Devon**), estuaries in **Essex,** and countless little bays around **Wales.** The variety is astonishing for what is basically a small island.

THE most unforgettable
TRAVEL EXPERIENCES

- **Standing at the top of Snowdon (Wales):** And, even better, finding it's so clear a day that you can see the sea both to the west and, in the haze, to the north. It's the highest mountain in England and Wales, and feels like it. You might have walked up, but you probably took the clattery steam cog railway. Walking down the grassy, rocky slopes will take several hours, but it's worth it. See p. 722.
- **Seeing Buckingham Palace for the first time (London):** Enter the Mall under Admiralty Arch and you can see the palace at the end of The Mall; the grandeur of the Queen's home increases step by step until it fills your vision, dotted with the bright red tunics of the ceremonial guardsmen. See p. 86.
- **Having a pint:** It could be at a centuries-old pub on the Yorkshire Moors or a little place in the backstreets of London; it might be a famous inn or somewhere unassuming in any town or city. But there's nothing that helps you appreciate the scenery quite like a glass of good British beer.
- **Viewing the sea for the first time:** Coming over the crest of a hill, or around a bend, and finding that great, twinkling expanse, fringed by beaches, maybe cliffs: Everyone has their own perfect memory, but the excitement never fades. You'll pull over, stroll onto the sands… and you can do it all around the country.
- **Looking over the city from the top of St. Paul's (London):** You really can climb up to that glorious dome, which offers 360-degree views over the capital, giving the feeling that you're at the heart of where modern London began. If that's uplifting, the view down is deliciously dizzying. See p. 111.
- **Riding an old train:** Waiting for the whistle and the blast of steam is magical. There are dozens of "heritage lines" around the country, more than 20 in Wales alone. Old locomotives chug across idyllic countryside, along the coast, and up Welsh mountains. The National Railway Museum in York (p. 644) pays homage.

THE most unforgettable
CITY EXPERIENCES

- **Finding yourself in the city of the Beatles (Liverpool):** The childhood homes of Paul and John might be underwhelming (in a nice way), but there's still the Magical Mystery Tour (taking in Penny Lane), the Beatles Story (full of memorabilia), a reborn Cavern Club, and the Beatle Week in August. See p. 583.
- **Having a bath in Bath (Somerset):** The stunning, steaming Roman Baths are there to visit, with lunch in the Pump Room restaurant; then you can sample the

waters at the modern Thermae Bath Spa with its open-air pool and views across the Georgian, UNESCO World Heritage site rooftops. See p. 335.

o **Seeing the backstreets of Manchester:** Britain's inner-city regeneration is summed up by Castlefield, a once-blighted area of warehouses and canals that is now full of restaurants, bars, museums, and art galleries. The world's first railway station, from 1830, is the free Museum of Science & Industry. See p. 562.

o **Crisscrossing the Tyne (Newcastle):** Sixties art-rockers The Nice once performed the "Five Bridges Suite" to celebrate the city crossings, but there's now also the Millennium Footbridge, a curving, modernistic affair that looks like a blinking eye when it tilts to let boats past. On one side are the city streets, on the other the arts venues of Gateshead. See p. 661.

o **Wandering across London:** Sure, it's a big place. But there's no better way to see it than on foot. Start, maybe, in Kensington and meander across Hyde Park, down Piccadilly, into Soho and Covent Garden, up Fleet Street, past St. Paul's, and into the City, spotting tiny churches and other gems on the way. See p. 73.

o **Wondering whether you're actually in a city (South Wales):** Yes, you are; it's St. Davids, Britain's smallest city, in the far west. It's hardly a small town but the population of barely 2,000 is bolstered by the thousands of tourists who come for the nearby countryside and beaches, and the elegant cathedral. See p. 711.

THE most unforgettable
FOOD & DRINK EXPERIENCES

o **Tasting snail porridge at the Fat Duck (Berkshire):** Nothing shows England's emergence as a culinary innovator more than this multi-Michelin-starred restaurant, a window into the singularly creative mind of Heston Blumenthal. The earthy porridge (snails, oats, ham, almonds) is genius, and dishes such as salmon poached in licorice gel are a whimsical treat. See p. 201.

o **Sampling oysters in Whitstable (Kent):** Slurp on a single bivalve as you walk the seafront, or have a dozen in a relaxed waterside restaurant. This old fishing town has transformed itself into the home of the oyster, and the quayside is awash with stalls, takeout options, and a fish market. See p. 249.

o **Browsing at Borough Market (London):** The sight and smell of fresh produce (and grilling meat) are heaven at this focal point for the real food movement. Tucked under the railway near London Bridge Station, there's a feel of the past, combined with the eco-friendly ethics that are so very now. See p. 151.

o **Giving yourself up to a restaurant with rooms:** They're all the rage in Wales, where you can spend a weekend in boutique luxury while eating splendid food. Tyddyn Llan (p. 743), off the beaten track in Denbighshire in the north, won a Michelin star in 2010, while Patrick's With Rooms (p. 702) is a family delight facing the sea in Mumbles, near Swansea.

o **Going bulb crazy at the Garlic Farm (Isle of Wight):** The U.K.'s leading garlic grower is a pungent paradise, with a shop selling many varieties, including smoked garlic, as well as garlic to grow, and a restaurant serving dishes featuring the farm's own game, produce, and, of course, garlic. See p. 308.

o **Dining with a celebrity chef:** Try Restaurant Gordon Ramsay in Chelsea (p. 139), or a whole menu of the outrageous chef's other places in London; his former protégé Marcus Wareing at the Berkeley has also blossomed and serves some of the best food in the capital (p. 137). Giorgio Locantelli creates innovative Italian cuisine at Michelin-starred Locanda Locatelli (p. 134).

THE most unforgettable
LOCAL EXPERIENCES

o **Finding the road over Hardknott and Wrynose Passes (Cumbria):** It's dizzying as you round a hairpin and look into the deep valley between the two passes, but that's only one moment in a switchback experience on steep, narrow roads in a remote area. Late-summer sun gives the burned orange and ocher landscape a golden glow. See p. 621.

o **Taking the cliff train from Lynmouth (Devon):** When the old pullies creak and the big tanks fill, this century-old, water-powered train climbs 183m (600 ft.) from the North Devon fishing village up to cliff-top Lynton. The views are extraordinary, but the experience is both breathtaking and kind of scary. See p. 368.

o **Sipping homemade wine in the countryside (Isle of Wight):** You'll often find locals at the Rosemary Vineyard on the edge of Ryde, sitting on the terrace outside the Vineleaf cafe, enjoying views across the fields and hills, with a glass of wine, or maybe even a blackberry liqueur. See p. 308.

o **Stumbling over a field of bluebells (Surrey):** The flowers herald spring all over the place, but there's nowhere finer than Surrey Hills (p. 281). Potter about the little roads that dive into the woods, see a footpath sign, and just walk. Or aim for Leith Hill (p. 282), with one of the best spots near the parking lot at the bottom.

o **Finding a bargain at London's best street market:** A jumble of open-air stalls and warrens of indoor arcades combine to make Portobello Road the quintessential West London market. Haggle hard and you'll likely get 15% off the asking price. Saturday is the best day, when even the crowds can't ruin the fun. See p. 152.

o **Experiencing winter in the garden (Cambridge):** Cambridge University Botanic Garden is lovely year-round, but few visitors explore during the winter, when the intelligent planting reveals a wealth of multihued stems and bark, plus winter-flowing plants, giving way to Lenten roses and early wild daffodils. See p. 499.

THE best FAMILY EXPERIENCES

o **Sitting on Southwold beach (Suffolk):** This is old-school seaside in a nicely gen-teel way, with ice creams and good waves (and not far to walk to get to them). And for grown-ups, there's a pub (the Lord Nelson) to slip off to at the top of the steps, and beguiling individual shops not much farther. See p. 521.

o **Riding the coasters (Surrey):** Chessington World of Adventures is a theme park that proves England can do it as well as the U.S. Scare yourself silly on the big roller coasters, but there are also rides for youngsters, as well as nice grassy areas, and a zoo full of animals (*real* ones such as lions and tigers). See p. 285.

o **Being a right Charlie (Buckinghamshire):** There's nothing quite like painting your own diddly design onto a phizz-whizzing plate. The Roald Dahl Museum, in the village where the late author lived and wrote *Charlie and the Chocolate Factory* and other children's classics, is as irreverent as his books. See p. 229.

o **Going back in time (Warwickshire):** The crashing and banging of ancient battles fought turns Warwick Castle from simply a castle into a whole medieval theme park. You'll find yourself on a quest to fit everything in amid the princesses, kings, towers, dungeons, gardens, and more. See p. 462.

- **Playing Robin Hood (Nottingham):** The bow-carrying outlaw comes alive at the medieval-themed Robin Hood Festival (Aug) with its jugglers and jesters, at Nottingham Castle's Robin Hood Pageant (Oct), and simply from running around ancient Sherwood Forest. See p. 544.
- **Staying at Portmerion (North Wales):** This Italianate holiday village (where 1960s' TV series *The Prisoner* was set) makes children want their friends to come and live here with them. They love the fairytale surroundings, with beach and woodland. And no one tells them to stop splashing in the fountains. See p. 727.

THE best HISTORIC EXPERIENCES

- **Seeing the world's first indoor tennis court (Surrey):** No, it's not at Wimbledon, it's at Hampton Court Palace, the Thames-side home of Henry VIII. The court dates from 1625, and is still used today although it's rather different from the ones Roger Federer plays on. See p. 285.
- **Walking in King Harold's footsteps (East Sussex):** There's something quite eerie but exciting about walking on the grassy spot where English history changed forever. The site of the Battle of Hastings, and the Norman Conquest, is quietly impressive, with an excellent visitor center. See p. 262.
- **Standing on Hadrian's Wall (Northumberland):** It leaves you speechless, the breathtaking scale of this Roman monument, which weaves off in either direction, across hill and dale, coast to coast. Walking all 73 miles is the ultimate achievement, but pop into the remains of its forts if you can't. See p. 669.
- **Watching the donkeys work (Devon):** The coastal town of Clovelly's precipitous cobblestone streets make driving all but impossible. Supplies for the village stores are carried on sleds, pulled by donkeys as they have been for centuries. No rides, though: You have to walk. See p. 370.
- **Marveling at Stonehenge (Wiltshire):** Okay, it might be hemmed in by roads, but this monolithic stone circle will still be here when the traffic is history. With stones weighing 50 tons and more than 2 millennia old, it really does give you a creepy feeling in this windswept spot. See p. 328.
- **Exploring Welsh castles:** There's a whole hatful here, and they're all different. Don't miss Conwy (p. 736) with its eight towers; rugged Harlech (p. 724); Caernarfon (p. 729), overlooking the Isle of Anglesey; and Pembroke (p. 707), with its huge town walls. And the wild fantasy of Cardiff Castle (p. 680) is a must.

THE best OUTDOOR EXPERIENCES

- **Wandering along the Thames (Surrey):** No sooner do you get out of London proper than you're in a leafy, countryside idyll, little craft put-putting past and grass under foot as you tread the Thames Path. There are riverside pubs, historic sites, and the disbelief that the city is just a 20-minute train ride away. See p. 286.
- **Taking the Ullswater Steamer (Cumbria):** There's nothing like being huddled up against the mist as the little Victorian boat sails the length of the Lake District's pristine showpiece. Stand on deck, taking photos as the scenery changes around every bend, and hop off halfway back for a hike. See p. 627.

o **Getting lost on Dartmoor (Devon):** The landscape in the National Park constantly changes, rising to steep hills, then plunging into deep gorges. The roads are narrow and winding, and often unmarked. It's when you get lost that you'll end up alone at the top of a hill as a herd of wild ponies runs by, a storm hard on their heels. Heaven. See p. 376.

o **Walking the South Downs Way (Hampshire/West Sussex):** Fill your lungs as you follow the chalk downland that sweeps along the south coast some 99 miles. It crosses windswept cliffs, climbs open hills, and ducks into valleys and then up again. It's a week's experience for serious hikers, although you can dip in for a Sunday afternoon stroll. See p. 276.

o **Gardening at Wisley (Surrey):** Gardens bloom across the country but you have to start somewhere, and this home of the Royal Horticultural Society (less frenetic than London's Kew Gardens) is the biggest and the best. There are flowers, woods, hills, cathedral-like glasshouses, show gardens, plant trials, and good food. See p. 280.

o **Spending a day on the Blue Flag Beach at Westward Ho! (Devon):** Two divine miles of broad, golden sand earned this beach the name "Golden Crescent." Compacted sand and perfect blue waters are prized by kite-surfers, swimmers, surfers, and those who just want to lounge and watch them work. See p. 368.

THE best FREE EXPERIENCES

o **Entering another world in Richmond Park (Surrey):** Go through big gates in high walls and you find deer grazing in flank-high ferns and swans lording it over a host of other waterbirds on the Pen Ponds. This great Royal Park's hills, woods, and grassland look as they might have in Henry VIII's time. Go in Spring to see Isabella Plantation in bloom with azaleas and rhododendrons. See p. 285.

o **Admiring the world's souvenirs (London):** The British Museum has artifacts from around the world, including Greece's Elgin Marbles and a wealth of Egyptian treasures. For kids, it's an incredible space to fire their imaginations. And no matter how many times you come, you'll find something different (and you'll never have time to see it all). See p. 86.

o **Waking at the foot of Scafell Pike (Cumbria):** It's a summer's morn and you leave your tent to conquer England's highest peak. The stone steps are seemingly endless, but you forget the thigh-burn as you take in the panoramic views of Wastwater behind you, then push onto the peak-top plateau for a satisfying 360-degree view of mountains and tarns below. See p. 622.

o **Doing the National Gallery (London):** One of the world's greatest collections of Western art, packed with artists from da Vinci to Rembrandt to Picasso. It's also incredibly well thought out, so straightforward to navigate the areas in chronological order. As if that's not enough, next door is the National Portrait Gallery, featuring works by everyone from Warhol to Rossetti to George Bernard Shaw. See p. 89.

o **Cycling the Mawddach Trail (North Wales):** The scenery is breathtaking as you leave the seaside town of Barmouth, in the shadow of Snowdon; this path on an old rail line crosses the Mawddach Estuary then follows the waters along the beautiful, deep valley to Dolgellau, almost 10 miles. See p. 724.

THE best CONTEMPORARY EXPERIENCES

- **Seeing what Turner saw (Kent):** Turner Contemporary opened in spring 2011. The simplistic but stunning white building sits on the seafront in the fast-rejuvenating resort town of Margate, on the spot where J. M. W. Turner stayed when he used to paint his mesmeric seascapes. The light here, on the eastern tip of England, is sensational and illuminates the building at sunset. See p. 251.
- **Getting fresh air on Cardiff Bay (South Wales):** It's hard to believe this was once the grubby docks; it really has cleaned up well. The extraordinary Barrage circles the now calm Bay, while the quay is a riot of restaurants and bars under the eye of the Millennium Centre, a copper-roofed arts complex. See p. 682.
- **Feeling small in Tate Modern (London):** Enter this former power station on the Thames and your jaw drops at the size of the cathedral-like piston hall, which usually houses outrageous art installations, from twisting metal slides to monstrous spiders. Delve deeper and you find a wealth of Dalis, Warhols, Picassos, and a restaurant with one of London's best views. See p. 109.
- **Finding a hidden garden (Cornwall):** The Eden Project is not quite what you'd expect in a lush Cornish valley. The huddle of huge geodesic domes looks like a moonbase—and well it could be: It's a garden of the future, an Amazon rain forest under glass. See p. 406.
- **Heading for space (Leicestershire):** Calling Houston: We have a rival. A futuristic tower signals the National Space Centre, which has space rockets, moon rock, a landing simulator, interactive displays, and a galaxy of jaw-dropping facts. All that in a place where they really do study comets—Leicester. See p. 555.
- **Seeing with a different eye (London):** The London Eye, on the South Bank, is a giant ferris wheel with glass pods, with views over the city. It's great to ride (aim for twilight), but the gleaming white wheel is awesome just to look at; it pops into view between buildings, particularly from across the river, near Westminster Abbey. See p. 107.

THE best ARTS EXPERIENCES

- **Going to a festival:** They're big business, attract all ages, and feature everyone from the latest acts to venerable megastars playing Glastonbury (Somerset) and the Isle of Wight as well as lesser-known gems such as Guilfest (Surrey) and the Rhythm Festival (Bedfordshire).
- **Seeing Shakespeare in his hometown (Warwickshire):** Well, seeing one of his plays, anyway. The Royal Shakespeare Theatre in Stratford-upon-Avon is the place for powerful, up-to-the-minute interpretations, and you'll have the chance to visit all the Shakespeare sights, including his birthplace. See p. 452.
- **Learning to love panto:** England's traditional Christmas fare, pantomime is great slapstick fun, often with top TV names and, increasingly, U.S. stars: In the past several seasons, Wimbledon Theatre has had Henry (The Fonz) Winkler, David Hasselhoff, and even Pamela Anderson, all dressed up and falling over.

- **Reveling on the South Bank (London):** England's arts quarter takes in both the 1950s' beauty of the Royal Festival Hall (RFH) and the brutal modernism of the National Theatre. Street theatre rubs shoulders with classic productions, and there's usually something free in the grand foyer of the RFH. See chapter 4.

- **Discovering Discover Another Place (Lancashire):** A hundred figures cast in iron from sculptor Antony Gormley's own body rise from the sand for 2 miles along the coast at Crosby between Formby and Liverpool, and gaze eerily out to sea. See p. 585.

- **Being enchanted by the Aldeburgh Festival (Suffolk):** You stand on the lawn outside the Snape Maltings concert hall, looking over the swaying rushes of the fens, boat masts bobbing; then you pop inside for the finest classical music, possibly conducted by the master, Simon Rattle. Spellbinding. See p. 522.

ENGLAND & WALES IN DEPTH

by Nick Dalton & Deborah Stone

The last decade has seen a transformation in the major cities of England and Wales. Never have they been so proud of their history and artistic achievements, as visitors will see in stylish new museums, galleries, and attractions.

The castles, palaces, and stately homes that distinguish England and Wales from other countries continue to present world-beating experiences as tradition and innovation combine to cultivate national life. And the countryside, ever changing and often stunning, increasingly offers challenging activities for those who love the outdoors. You'll also find hotels, restaurants, and tourist facilities are better equipped to offer what travelers need: comfortable rooms, excellent food, and a welcoming ambience.

Exploring England and Wales is like climbing a mountain—you always want to carry on to see what's over the next peak or around the next corner. The character of every region is as diverse as its countryside. The north of England has more dramatic scenery than the gently rolling south, and west Wales is green and hilly while East Anglia is flat with big skies. Yet every region is connected with the whole, and once you've explored one you can't help wanting to experience another. It's addictive, and there's no shame in carrying around a sightseeing wishlist—as long as you take your time ticking things off. England and Wales may not be big countries but they're crammed full of incredible sights. And not just historic sights, either. Sport, music, theatre, fashion, and even food here are among the best in the world. You might be visiting a region for the first time but be warned: Once you've seen one part of England and Wales you'll want to see more.

ENGLAND & WALES TODAY

The most obvious sign of Britain's bright new future is The Shard, the shimmering, glassy tower near London Bridge that is now Europe's tallest building. It soars 350m (1,107 ft.) above the city and provides a fitting backdrop for both the medieval Tower of London and the Victorian masterpiece of Tower Bridge. It is England pushing forward, regaining her crown as one of the world's major powers and destinations, while looking over her sovereign past.

The Shard, by architect **Renzo Piano,** is the pinnacle, literally, of the postmodern architecture that has swept Britain. Other examples in London include the **Lloyd's building** by **Richard Rogers,** 30 St. Mary Axe, dubbed the **"Gherkin"** by Sir Norman Foster, and **Canary Wharf Tower (One Canada Square)**, by **César Pelli.**

It's not the only way that England and Wales have changed dramatically in recent years. Once they were known for drab hotels and even drabber food, but the invention and imagination—always evident in art, music, and design—have now spread into where we stay and what we eat. A hotel will be opening high in The Shard, and it will look down over Borough Market, London's trendiest spot dealing in posh, organic, locally sourced food. The hotel will also have views over the City, the country's financial heart, which has caused more than a few heartaches for its role in the global financial crash.

The economic downturn has seriously affected employment, lifestyle, and attitudes. The government, a coalition between the right-wing Conservatives and the marginally less-so Liberal Democrats, is cutting services, from health to road-mending, while increasing taxes. The vibrant cultural life enjoyed is being pressurised as, for example, the arts, humanities, and education struggle for funding. The English and Welsh are practical people— empiricists; however, as the cuts bite, their frustration at how this affects their daily life, infrastructure, and creative freedom is beginning to manifest itself. The riots in England of August 2011 have been the cause of much national soul-searching. Meanwhile, the previous political governing party is happy to lie low, given that Prime Minister David Cameron is never going to be popular and could lead his party out of power as soon as the next election (likely in 2014). The implications of News International's phone-hacking scandal—forcing the closure of the *News of the World* after 168 years—could yet prove far reaching, and change the political and media landscape.

Abnormal weather in parts of the world on which Britain depends for staples, such as flour and grain, has pushed shop prices higher. And the cost of gas (petrol), already at record levels because of huge levels of taxation (more than $7 for a U.S. gallon), is soaring due to unrest in the Middle East.

The Shard

But life goes on, and 2012 will be a summer of celebration with the Olympics coming to London (July 27–Aug 12), and events being held as far from the capital as the south coast. There also continues to be a lot to shout about, as a dynamic cultural milieu of independent thinking, eccentricity and verve, mean talent is often appreciated. From the Academy-award winning *The King's Speech* and Adele's record breaking 2nd album *21* to Carol Ann Duffy becoming the first woman Poet Laureate and Hillary Mantel's critically acclaimed historic novel *Wolf Hall,* these are lands that revel in diversity.

Britain began believing it was great again in the 1990s. It was the decade of Cool Britannia. A wave of music—Britpop—from bands such as Blur, Oasis, and Pulp, was followed by the optimism prompted by the 1997 landslide General Election victory by Tony Blair's New Labour Party. After nearly 20 years of Conservative governments it felt like a new era of opportunity. In London, the Millennium Dome opened in 1999 and thousands visited the Millennium Experience, a modern-day Festival of Britain. It is now a concert venue called the O2—although to most people it is still the Dome. The **Tate Modern** (p. 109) art museum opened in May 2000 in a former power station, and the **London Eye** (p. 107) was also built to celebrate the new millennium.

OUR LOVE OF A royal WEDDING

We do adore a royal wedding. Prince Charles and Lady Diana Spencer were married at St. Paul's Cathedral in London on July 29, 1981, a ceremony watched by an estimated global television audience of 750 million. The fairytale wedding came 5 months after Charles, 32, had presented Diana with a memorable sapphire and diamond engagement ring. The wedding day was declared a national holiday and 600,000 people lined the wedding procession route to see 20-year-old Diana arrive for the ceremony in the royal family's glass coach with her father, Earl Spencer. Diana's wedding dress was a fashion hit, made from ivory taffeta and antique lace with a spectacular 7.62-m (25-ft.) train. After the drive to Buckingham Palace in an open-topped State Landau the couple appeared on the palace balcony to the cheers of thousands.

Prince William was born less than a year later, on June 21, 1982, and Prince Harry came along on September 15, 1984. However, 9 years later Charles and Diana had separated, and they divorced in August 1996.

Tragically, Diana died after a car crash in Paris on August 31, 1997. Her death prompted an unprecedented public outpouring of grief, which many say has changed the British national psyche forever. The Queen and Prince Charles came under unaccustomed public criticism, accused of not caring about Diana's death.

Around 1 million people were on the streets to see the funeral cortege on its way to Westminster Abbey on September 6, and many watched it continue to the Spencer family's estate at Althrop in Northamptonshire, where Diana was buried. An award-winning exhibition at the stately home displays Diana's wedding dress and many childhood mementos.

Now there is a new generation: Prince William gave Diana's sapphire and diamond engagement ring to his fiancée, Kate Middleton (now known as Catherine) when they became engaged on November 16, 2010. They were married at Westminster Abbey on April 29, 2011, in a ceremony viewed by an estimated 2 billion people around the world. The public, it seems, never tires of royal weddings.

Lots was also happening elsewhere. Manchester was transformed after the 1996 IRA bombing; Birmingham's **Bull Ring shopping center** (p. 473) was rebuilt in sensational style in 2003, and the city's regeneration continues. Newcastle, Liverpool, Cardiff, and most recently Swansea have all benefitted from major overhauls.

But care has been taken with this 21st-century makeover, and England and Wales continue to offer an unbeatable mix of beautiful countryside, a culture rich in history and the arts, plus modern cities that cater to discerning visitors.

THE MAKING OF ENGLAND & WALES

Prehistory & the Romans (3600 B.C.–ca. A.D. 400)

England and Wales have several prehistoric sites, but the most famous is **Stonehenge** near Salisbury (p. 328), which experts believe was a temple, possibly started in 3600 B.C. and added to over subsequent centuries. Hadrian's Wall is the most dramatic piece of architecture to survive from the Roman period, although there are also **Roman baths** at Bath (p. 339) and the remains of Roman walls, villas, temples, and forts elsewhere.

England, Wales, and the rest of the British Isles became detached from continental Europe at the end of the Ice Age when sea levels rose and the English Channel and Irish Sea were formed. The islands have been inhabited for 500,000 years, and it was these prehistoric inhabitants who built Stonehenge. The Britons were joined by the Celtic tribes who arrived in about 800 B.C. from mainland Europe, bringing variants of the Welsh, Cornish, and Celtic languages still spoken by a minority in the U.K. today.

There were constant clashes between the tribes over territory, which is why they failed to unite to prevent the first Roman invasion by Julius Caesar, the Roman governor of Gaul (France and Belgium), in 55 B.C.

Bad weather damaged Caesar's ships, and trouble in France meant he returned to the mainland despite landing at Deal, in Kent. But he returned the next year and defeated the Britons, imposing trade treaties and tax-like tributes. He didn't stay long, and the tribal Britons continued fighting among themselves without any Roman Legions to keep order.

That all changed in A.D. 43–44, when Emperor Claudius invaded, pushing farther than the south coast and capturing the Southeast's capital, present-day Colchester. You can still see parts of the Roman walls in **Colchester** (p. 512) and the castle that was built with bricks taken from the Roman temple that lies beneath it. Although Colchester remained the capital for a while, by A.D. 47 the Romans had founded Londinium as a garrison with a trading settlement. Remains of Roman London are still being discovered as new developments are built, and you can see part of London's original Roman wall near the **Tower of London** (p. 112).

What They Say

"We have really everything in common with America nowadays except, of course, language."
—Oscar Wilde

"The British are special. The world knows it. In our innermost thoughts we know it. This is the greatest nation on earth."
—Tony Blair

England's Historical Highlights

1. Stonehenge
2. Hastings
3. Runnymede
4. Tower of London
5. Windsor Castle
6. Pembroke Castle
7. Plymouth
8. Ironbridge
9. The Big Pit
10. Home of the Beatles

There was little resistance to the Roman fighting machine, although there was one well-known uprising, led by Queen Boudicca of the Iceni tribe who ruled parts of East Anglia. The Romans had tried to force their will on Boudicca by publicly whipping her, and she subsequently led a rebellion that razed Colchester. Then she marched on London (there's a statue of Boudicca in Parliament Square) and rampaged through St. Albans, then known as Verulamium—70,000 people were killed.

The Romans moved north and west, conquering tribes as they went, but they were stopped by the ferocious Picts in Scotland, and did not get far into Wales because of the mountainous countryside, although a Roman Legion was stationed at **Caerleon,** where the remains of an impressive amphitheatre and baths can still be seen (p. 683). In A.D. 122, **Hadrian's Wall** was built across northern England from Wallsend on the east coast to Bowness-on-Solway, on the west coast (p. 669); meantime, the Welsh tribes—well, they were just left to their fighting. Then, after 350 years of rule, the Romans went home, abandoning the Romano-Britons.

By 410, the Germanic Saxons, Jutes, and Angles had carved out settlements in southern and eastern England, and the Saxons went on to dominate all but the far north and Wales, where the Romano-Britons were forced to flee. The Saxons had neatly divided England into Northumbria in the north, East Anglia in the east, Wessex in the south, and Mercia in the west and Midlands by the 600s. Subsequently, King Offa of Mercia had the 177-mile **Offa's Dyke** earthworks built (p. 692) from **Chepstow** in South Wales to **Prestatyn** in North Wales, to keep the Celtic Welsh tribes out of England in 787.

The Saxon kings reigned supreme until the Vikings, forced from their settlements in Scandinavia, started taking an interest in England. They were driven from southern England by King Alfred the Great of Wessex, whose headquarters were at **Winchester** (p. 290), but the Vikings remained in the north and east, evidenced by astonishing burial mounds at **Sutton Hoo** in Suffolk (p. 523). The Vikings were even stronger in the Northeast, as the **Jorvik Viking Centre** in York (p. 644) illustrates. By 924, the rest of England was united behind King Athelstan of Wessex, but this

DATELINE

55 B.C.	Julius Caesar invades England.
A.D. 43	Romans conquer England.
410	Jutes, Angles, and Saxons form small kingdoms in England.
470	Romans found Londinium.
500–1066	Anglo-Saxon kingdoms fight off Viking warriors.
1066	William, Duke of Normandy, invades England, defeats Harold II at the Battle of Hastings.
1154	The Plantagenets launch their rule (which lasts until 1399) with the crowning of Henry II.
1215	King John signs the Magna Carta at Runnymede.
1215	Hadrian's Wall is built.
1337	Hundred Years' War between France and England begins.
1485	Battle of Bosworth Field ends the Wars of the Roses between the houses of York and Lancaster; Henry VII launches the Tudor dynasty.
1534	Henry VIII brings the Reformation to England and dissolves the monasteries.

Historian Simon Schama's BBC series *A History of Britain* (available on DVD) begins around 3100 B.C., finishing in 1965. There are three BBC books from the series, all called *A History of Britain*, subtitled *At the Edge of the World?: 3000 B.C.–A.D. 1603*; *The British Wars: 1603–1776*; and *The Fate of Empire: 1776–2001*. Journalist and television broadcaster Andrew Marr has produced a DVD called *A History of Modern Britain* as well as the book *The Making of Modern Britain*, while broadcaster David Dimbleby has written a book to accompany his BBC documentary series *Seven Ages of Britain*. Also excellent is Terry Deary's series of *Horrible Histories* children's books, with all the facts plus some delightful gore.

Anglo-Saxon period of peace was ruptured by the Viking King Sweyn and his son Cnut, who were given gold—Danegeld in fact—to leave the Anglo-Saxons alone.

By 1013 Sweyn had thrown out King Ethelred (the Unready), and even when Ethelred returned from Normandy King Sweyn remained in charge. Several Viking (or Danish) kings followed, hence the influx of Viking words into what became the English language. Tuesday, Wednesday, Thursday, and Friday are all named after Viking gods, and the Viking word for village, "by," led to names such as **Grimsby** and **Whitby** (p. 648).

The Saxons maintained control of some southern regions, which is why the Saxon king Edward the Confessor assumed the throne in 1042. Childless, he promised the crown to William, Duke of Normandy. Later his adviser, Harold Godwinson, swore to support William's claim to the throne. When Edward died in 1066 and Harold succeeded him, he surely knew trouble lay ahead. William invaded **Pevensey,** in Sussex, while Harold was fighting a Viking invasion in the northeast. He had to march south to meet the Normans at **Battle,** near **Hastings,** in Sussex. Harold lost and died—the end of an era.

1558 The accession of Elizabeth I ushers in an era of exploration and a renaissance in science and learning.

1588 Spanish Armada defeated.

1603 James VI of Scotland becomes James I of England, thus uniting the crowns of England and Scotland.

1620 Pilgrims sail from Plymouth on the *Mayflower* to found a colony in the New World.

1629 Charles I dissolves Parliament, ruling alone.

1642–49 Civil war between Royalists and Parliamentarians; the Parliamentarians win.

1649 Charles I beheaded, and England is a republic.

1653 Oliver Cromwell becomes Lord Protector.

1660 Charles II restored to the throne with limited power.

1665–66 Great Plague and Great Fire decimate London.

1688 James II, a Catholic, is deposed, and William and Mary come to the throne, signing a bill of rights.

continues

Norman rule was to change everything in England and Wales, but already the tribal rivalries that still trouble Great Britain—between the Celts in Wales, Scotland, and Ireland, and the Anglo-Saxons in England—were well established.

The Middle Ages (1066–1599)

White Tower, London

Among the most impressive legacies of these unstable ages are the medieval castles and cathedrals, which have stood the test of time. See William the Conqueror's Tower of London with its sublime **White Tower** (p. 112).

Other examples are the impregnable Conwy and Caernarfon castles in Wales. Visit remarkable Ely Cathedral near Cambridge and the incomparable Canterbury Cathedral.

The Normans descended from another branch of the Viking tribes who had left the cold, wet, infertile islands of Scandinavia to seek a better life. Although they had changed their name, they hadn't changed their ways. They quickly colonized England and, unlike the Romans, tamed the more fertile (and therefore profitable) parts of South Wales.

William's success came partly from his building impregnable castles wherever they were needed. In 1078, for example, he built the White Tower at the Tower of London and used it as a palace and fortress, and he built the original castle at **Windsor** (p. 199).

William was crowned King William I at **Westminster Abbey** (p. 103) in 1067, and his supporters went on to build simple motte and bailey castles on the land William

1727	George I, the first of the Hanoverians, assumes the throne.	1914–18	England enters World War I and emerges victorious on the Allied side.
1756–63	In the Seven Years' War, Britain wins Canada from France.	1936	Edward VIII abdicates to marry an American divorcée.
1775–83	Britain loses its American colonies.	1939–45	In World War II, Britain stands alone against Hitler from the fall of France in 1940 until the U.S. enters the war in 1941. Dunkirk is evacuated in 1940; bombs rattle London during the Blitz.
1795–1815	The Napoleonic Wars lead, finally, to the Battle of Waterloo and the defeat of Napoleon.		
1837	Queen Victoria begins her reign as Britain reaches the zenith of its empire.		
1901	Victoria dies, and Edward VII becomes king.	1945	Germany surrenders. Churchill is defeated; the Labour government introduces the welfare state and begins to dismantle the Empire.

gave them. The mottes—mounds of earth—still survive in many places; some were incorporated into the stone castles that replaced the original wooden baileys, or keeps.

William is also remembered for *The Domesday* (or Doomsday) *Book* of 1086, a survey of all his newly conquered land and possessions. The feudal system of the time meant that the King owned all the land but divided it between the Church and his supporters. The Domesday survey was an efficient way to assess the financial and military resources available to him, as well as enabling him to levy taxes and ensure an oath of allegiance from all landlords and tenants. It was known as *The Domesday Book* because—like Judgment Day—there was no escape from it. The original is still kept in the National Archives, and it's been used to settle property arguments and trace family trees for centuries.

The Normans are also renowned for their religious architecture, with **Ely Cathedral** in Cambridgeshire (p. 504) among the most glorious examples of their work, although the abbey and original church was founded by a Saxon princess.

The French Gothic style of architecture invaded in the late 12th century, trading rounded arches for pointy ones—an engineering discovery that freed churches from the heavy Norman walls and allowed ceilings to soar and windows to proliferate. The style can be divided into three overlapping periods: Early English (1150–1300), Decorated (1250–1370), and Perpendicular (1350–1550). The best example of Early English is **Salisbury Cathedral** (p. 327). The first to use pointy arches was **Wells Cathedral** (p. 355).

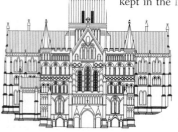

Salisbury Cathedral

1952	Queen Elizabeth II ascends the throne.
1973	Britain joins the European Union.
1979	Margaret Thatcher becomes prime minister.
1982	Britain defeats Argentina in the Falklands conflict.
1990	Thatcher is ousted; John Major becomes prime minister.
1991	Britain fights with Allies to defeat Iraq.

1992	Royals are jolted by fire at Windsor Castle and marital troubles of their two sons. Britain joins the European Single Market. Deep recession signals the end of the booming 1980s.
1994	England is linked to the Continent by rail via the Channel Tunnel, or Chunnel. Tony Blair elected Labour Party leader.
1996	The IRA breaks a 17-month cease-fire with a truck bomb at the Docklands that claims two lives. Charles and Diana divorce.

continues

William died in 1087, succeeded by his son William II who died in a hunting accident in 1100. The next significant king was Henry II, the first of the Plantagenet family, who came to the throne in 1154. This French nobleman had made strategic marriages and, when he married Eleanor of Aquitaine, he owned more of France than the French king. Eleanor was a formidable character, as portrayed in the 1968 film *The Lion in Winter*. Together they had eight children, among them Richard the Lionheart and his younger brother King John.

Richard I, who came to the throne in 1189, is regarded as a romantic hero in the stories of Robin Hood and his merry men, who were said to have lived in **Sherwood Forest** near Nottingham. Hollywood films have portrayed Richard as much loved by his subjects—ironic because he didn't like cold, wet England and preferred to fight for Christianity in the Crusades. When he died in 1199, John succeeded him, but Bad King John was so unpopular that the Norman barons, whose families had been given their land by William I after the conquest, forced him to sign the Magna Carta in 1215 to limit his power. The Magna Carta gave all freemen (barons) rights and liberties, but, more importantly, meant English monarchs were no longer above the law. This became the basis of the English Constitution, and later the American Bill of Rights.

The Plantagenets ruled for the next 200 years, with King John's son Henry III succeeding him in 1216, aged 9, and setting up the first English Parliament in 1258. He rebuilt **Westminster Abbey** and built the first Palace of Westminster where Parliament still sits today (p. 103). This was the period when the nobility started to consider themselves English rather than French, although they still spoke French. (Only the Saxon peasants spoke English.) Henry III died in 1272, and his son Edward I was a much stronger monarch. He marched into Wales, defeated Llewelyn ap Gruffydd, the Prince of Wales, and incorporated Wales into England in 1284.

He built the superb Welsh medieval castles of **Beaumaris,** on Anglesey (p. 732; **Conwy,** which still has its town walls (p. 735); **Caernarfon** (p. 729), which is where Prince Charles was invested as the present Prince of Wales in 1969; and Harlech. All were built as a response to the second Welsh rebellion of

1997 London swings again. The Labour Party ends 18 years of Conservative rule with a landslide election victory. The death of Diana, Princess of Wales.

1998 Prime Minister Tony Blair launches "New Britain"—young, stylish, and informal.

1999 England rushes toward the 21st century with the Millennium Dome at Greenwich.

2000 London presides over millennium celebration; gays allowed to serve openly in the military.

2002 Queen Elizabeth, the Queen Mother, dies at age 101.

2005 Suicide bomb attacks devastate London.

2007 Tony Blair steps down; Gordon Brown becomes prime minister.

2009 England suffers economic slowdown.

2010 Conservative David Cameron narrowly becomes prime minister thanks to a coalition with the Liberal Democrats.

2011 Prince William marries Kate Middleton.

2012 Summer Olympic Games in London.

What They Say

"When a man is tired of London, he is tired of life; for there is in London all that life can afford."

—Samuel Johnson

"There'll always be an England ... even if it's in Hollywood."

—Bob Hope

1282 and were significantly more imposing than the castles at **Aberystwyth** (p. 714), Flint, and Rhuddlan, which followed the first rebellion a decade before.

In 1307 Edward II came to the throne, but, an ineffectual king, he was deposed by his wife Eleanor of Castille in 1327. She put their 14-year-old son, Edward, on the throne so she could in effect rule the country. When he turned 18, though, Edward III took control and tried to claim the French throne. When he was rebuffed, he started what turned out to be the Hundred Years' War in 1337. This kept him, his son the Black Prince, and successive monarchs occupied abroad until 1453.

At home, the ordinary people were having a hard time. The Black Death, or plague, which had ravaged Europe reached England in 1348. It killed one-third of the European population and half of the people of England and Wales, and returned in 1361, 1374, and regularly thereafter until about 1670. Richard II, aged 10, succeeded his grandfather, Edward III, and became one of the most unpopular kings. His poll tax of 1381 sparked the Peasants' Revolt. Richard met leaders Wat Tyler and Jack Straw in London and agreed to the abolition of serfdom, but then joined in the suppression of the revolts.

One of Richard's courtiers was Geoffrey Chaucer, who wrote *The Canterbury Tales*—stories told by a group of pilgrims as they journeyed from London to Canterbury where Thomas Becket, Henry II's Archbishop, had been murdered by Henry's knights. The *Tales* were written in English, unusual at the time because Latin and French dominated the written word. At about the same time John Wycliffe translated the Bible into English. Both were signs of social unrest, and in 1399 Richard II was deposed by his cousin Henry of Bolingbroke. Richard died in captivity at Pontefract Castle, Yorkshire, in 1400 while Bolingbroke was crowned Henry IV and made a coronation speech in English. For a fun, erudite, and engaging guide to how daily life must have been in the Middle Ages check out Ian Mortimer's *The Time Traveller's Guide to Medieval England: A Handbook for Visitors to the Fourteenth Century* (Vintage).

Henry IV was the first of a new dynasty called the House of Lancaster and spent much of his reign fighting off rebellious nobles, such as Owain Glyndwr, the last native Prince of Wales. The Welsh nobles were still sympathetic to Richard II, and Glyndwr led a rebellion against Henry IV helped by his cousins the Tudors. Henry IV, having failed to defeat the rebellion, decreed that the Welsh could not hold public office or marry anybody English. Not surprisingly, this didn't garner him any support in Wales, which by 1404 was mostly controlled by Glyndwr, who held a Parliament at Machynlleth and made alliances with France and Scotland.

England gradually regained control of Wales. Henry V, crowned in 1417, restored land and titles to the nobility who had fought his father, ensuring relative domestic peace. He was successful in the continuing One Hundred Years' War, notably at the battle of Agincourt, and ended up owning much of France. He died in 1422, when his heir was 9 months old. Although his son succeeded him, he wasn't crowned Henry VI until 1429. Two years later, he also became the King of France. Henry VI's poor choice of advisers left him vulnerable to power struggles. He lost all of France (except Calais), much of it to Joan of Arc, and in 1453 he had a breakdown.

By 1455 there was civil war—the War of the Roses—between Henry VI's House of Lancaster and the House of York. It was messy: In 1461 the dead Duke of York's son crowned himself Edward IV, causing Henry VI to flee—but he returned, was captured, and then restored to the throne in 1471. Then it was Edward's turn to flee, but he returned to destroy the Lancastrian army at Tewkesbury and Henry was murdered shortly afterward.

Edward IV appointed his brother Richard to be Protector when he was succeeded by his 12-year-old son, Edward V, in 1483. It was a bad decision. Richard put the boy king and his younger brother (also Richard) in the Tower of London and crowned himself Richard III. The Princes in the Tower, as they became known, were murdered. But things didn't work out well for Richard III, either. In 1485 Henry Tudor, born in **Pembroke Castle** (p. 707) and part of the House of Lancaster, killed Richard in the Battle of Bosworth Field, between Coventry and Leicester, and claimed the throne to become Henry VII, the first of the Tudor dynasty.

The Tudors (1485–1603)

There's now a Bosworth **Battlefield Heritage Centre** (p. 554) at the spot where Henry VII won the crown. But it's fair to say Henry Tudor is responsible for far more of England's and Wales's heritage than that. His reign is considered to be the close of the Middle Ages, and he ended rivalry between the Houses of Lancaster and York by marrying Elizabeth of York, the eldest child of King Edward IV.

He was a clever king: Avoiding costly wars, forging trade alliances to create more wealth, setting up councils in Wales and the north to bring them into the administrative fold, and reforming the judicial system by introducing the Court of Star Chamber. Flamboyant Henry VIII inherited a fortune from his father in 1509, and a wife from his elder brother Arthur. Arthur had married the King of Spain's eldest daughter, Catherine of Aragon, at London's old St. Paul's Cathedral in 1501, but the sickly heir to the throne died 5 months later. Catherine came with a huge dowry so Henry VII petitioned the Pope to have the marriage annulled so that his new heir, Henry, could marry her and keep the money.

The marriage went forth and Catherine gave birth to several children, but only daughter Mary survived—and Henry wanted a son. By now he also wanted Anne Boleyn, born at **Blickling Hall** in Norfolk (p. 525) and a member of his wife's court. The 2008 film *The Other Boleyn Girl* portrays Henry's affair with Anne's sister Mary, but Anne was more ambitious and demanded to be queen.

Henry petitioned the Pope in 1530 for an annulment to his marriage with Catherine, but the Pope didn't want to upset the Spanish king. A few years later, Anne gave in to Henry's lust, and when she became pregnant, he secretly married her in 1533. When the Pope declared the marriage invalid, Henry announced himself Head of the Church of England, confirmed by an Act of Parliament in 1534. The Reformation had begun.

Henry still considered himself a Catholic and persecuted Protestants, but he was also suspicious of those loyal to the Pope, particularly monks and nuns. So in 1535 he executed several as a warning to others, then sent out officials to investigate the monasteries. In 1538 he was excommunicated from the Catholic Church and eventually closed all monasteries and nunneries and sold off their land.

By this time Henry had already executed Anne Boleyn for alleged adultery and, within days, married Anne's lady-in-waiting Jane Seymour. Anne had given birth to a girl—Elizabeth—but Jane finally gave Henry a male heir, Prince Edward, then died shortly afterward.

Henry was advised to marry a Protestant princess to create a new alliance against the Catholic monarchs, so artist Hans Holbein was sent to Saxony to paint a portrait of Anne of Cleeves. Henry married her in January 1540 on the strength of the painting but later found he didn't like her much. The marriage was annulled in July 1540, and he subsequently married Catherine Howard, cousin of Anne Boleyn. That didn't end well either: 2 years later she was executed for having lovers *before* their marriage (and the three alleged lovers were executed with her).

The sixth and final wife of Henry VIII was Katherine Parr, a well-educated widow who had hoped to marry Jane Seymour's brother Thomas. However, she was obliged to marry Henry, at **Hampton Court Palace** (p. 122 and 285) in 1543. She nursed Henry through various ailments, though he died in 1547 and was buried in St. George's Chapel at **Windsor Castle** (p. 199) next to Jane Seymour.

If Henry's life was dramatic, what happened next was extraordinary. His sickly son succeeded him as Edward VI, aged 10. During Edward's 5-year reign, the Church of England finally became Protestant and adopted an English Book of Common Prayer. Although Edward was devout, he obviously couldn't have made those decisions himself, and that atmosphere of religious fervor intensified when Edward was succeeded by his Catholic elder sister in 1553.

Before Mary I gained the crown, though, there was an attempt to put Lady Jane Grey on the throne. Jane was Henry VIII's niece, and married to the Duke of Northumberland's son. The Duke was fiercely Protestant and a powerful adviser to Edward VI. When it was obvious Edward was dying, Northumberland made the king denounce his half-sisters as illegitimate and declare Jane his heir. Jane was queen for 9 days, until Mary arrived in London to take the throne.

Mary was supported over Lady Jane Grey because she promised not to challenge the religious status quo, and she did not have Jane executed—at least not initially. That came when Mary started reintroducing Catholicism, which didn't please many of the noble families now living on monastery land. After another attempt to put Jane on the throne, Mary had her beheaded in 1554.

Mary also reintroduced Catholic bishops, revived heresy laws, and pronounced Protestantism a treasonable offense punishable by death. And that was just the start. She had 300 Protestants burned at the stake during her 4-year reign. That's 75 a year, compared with the 81 people in 38 years that her father had burned! It's no wonder she was called Bloody Mary.

Her marriage to Catholic Philip II of Spain had already made her unpopular, and she lost England's last French possession—Calais—when Spain dragged England into a war with France. Not surprisingly, few mourned her death in 1558.

Her sister Elizabeth was under house arrest at **Hatfield House** in Hertfordshire (p. 237) when the news of Mary's death arrived. She was crowned Queen in 1559 at Westminster Abbey. The Virgin Queen had many suitors but, sensibly, managed to play one against another so she could retain her own power.

Elizabeth reversed Mary's Catholic laws and worked with Parliament to create an Anglican form of Protestantism that tolerated Catholicism, but she was often the target of Catholic plots, many involving her cousin Mary Queen of Scots. Mary was forced to abdicate by Scotland's nobility and her 1-year-old son, James VI, was put on the Scottish throne. She escaped to England, only to be imprisoned by Elizabeth for nearly 20 years and eventually executed, in 1587.

The most famous Catholic plot against Elizabeth was the King of Spain's attempt to invade England to claim his dead wife's—Mary I's—throne. King Philip II of Spain sent the Spanish Armada of 130 ships in July 1588 to invade England. When it was spotted off Cornwall, beacons were lit all the way to London to warn of the danger. Enter one of England's greatest heroes—Sir Francis Drake—who was in Plymouth (p. 393) when the alarm went up.

The English Navy followed the Armada, which was on its way to Spanish-owned Netherlands to pick up troops. The Armada anchored at Gravelines, in France—the nearest suitable port to the troops—and at nightfall Drake sent eight burning ships into the middle of the wooden fleet. With the route to the English Channel blocked by Drake's ships, the Spanish were forced to sail through storms around Scotland to Ireland, where they stopped for supplies. But the Irish thought they were being invaded and drove them off. Only about half the Armada returned to Spain.

It added to Drake's heroic reputation—and to Elizabeth's image as a strong, unbeatable leader. Drake had already been knighted and lived comfortably at **Buckland Abbey** in Devon (p. 378), today owned by the National Trust, and made his fortune by attacking and looting Spanish bullion ships on their way from South America back to Europe.

Elizabeth's reign was also a time of major exploration, mainly to find a new route to the East to break the Spanish hold on the lucrative spice trade. The attempted colonization of Newfoundland, by Sir Martin Frobisher, and North Carolina, by Sir Walter Raleigh, laid the foundation for the British Empire.

Elizabeth I died in 1603, aged a remarkable 69. Ironically, she was succeeded by Mary Queen of Scots' son, who became James I of England and Wales while remaining James VI of Scotland. Although he hadn't been much help to his mother when she was alive, one of the first things he did was have the remains of Mary Queen of Scots moved to **Westminster Abbey** (p. 103), to an exceptionally fine tomb, which is still there today.

This was also a time of some of England's finest literature. Shakespeare (1564–1616) was creating his vast body of work, with his plays being performed in London at the Globe theatre, which opened on the south bank of the Thames in 1599. A re-creation today sits just along the river (p. 163). Also at work was Ben Jonson (1572–1637)—a playwright, poet, and actor, and a competitor to Shakespeare, best known for his satirical plays such as *Volpone*.

The Stuarts (1603–88)

James I was the first of the Stuart kings, but although he effectively united the crowns of England and Scotland, they still had separate governments and were not politically united until 1707 (interestingly in May 2011 a Scottish National Party—SNP— parliamentary majority election result means a Scottish independence referendum in the next few years is possible). He was welcomed to England because people did not want continued fighting over the crown, but he broke promises to be lenient to Catholics and upset some Protestants by not introducing the more extreme rules of Scottish Presbyterianism.

The Gunpowder Plot, in 1605, was the most dramatic consequence: Disaffected Catholics plotted to blow up the House of Lords while James I was in it, neatly disposing of him and the pro-Protestant nobility, clergy, and judges at the same time. Guy Fawkes, a Catholic convert who had fought for the Spanish in the Netherlands, was put in charge of the explosives. However, the plot was leaked, and Guy Fawkes was discovered in the building's cellar. He was tortured until he betrayed his co-conspirators, and was executed at the **Tower** (p. 112).

Bonfire Night is still celebrated on November 5 with effigies of Guy Fawkes burned on fires throughout the land, often in people's backyards. There are large events, too, where the town turns out for parades, public bonfires, and fireworks.

James I is also remembered for ordering a definitive English translation of the Bible. The *Authorized King James Bible* of 1611 remained the standard text until it was revised in the 1880s. When James died in 1625 he was succeeded by his son Charles I, who attempted to bypass Parliament, taxed people to the hilt, and—his worst mistake—favored high-church Anglicanism (closely aligned to his French wife's Catholicism) while remaining deeply suspicious of Puritan Protestants. He alienated politicians and subjects of every persuasion. Then he tried to take control of the army. No wonder civil war broke out.

The English Civil War was in fact a series of wars from 1642–46, with the Royalist supporters mainly in the north and west, and the Parliamentary supporters in the south and east. Ironically, they also had the backing of the Scots because of his anti-Puritanism. Charles eventually tried to make an alliance with the Scots, but they handed him to the Parliamentarians who decided the only way to prevent more war was to execute him. In 1649 he was beheaded outside the Banqueting House in London's **Whitehall** (p. 83).

The Civil War is often referred to as the English Revolution. Certainly the following 11 years make up the only period in which England and Wales have been republics. The decision to execute Charles came after "purging" Parliament of his sympathizers, but it shocked the public and many of the nobility—in fact it shocked most of Europe.

Oliver Cromwell, a Member of Parliament and gentleman farmer from Cambridgeshire, had created a New Model Army during the Civil War and remained at the head of the new Commonwealth's army. He crushed all rebellions, notably in Ireland. The Scottish were furious with England for executing their king, and when his son Charles arrived from Europe, they crowned him Charles II and sent him with an army to invade England. Charles II got all the way to **Worcester** (p. 476) before Cromwell defeated his troops, but Charles famously escaped by hiding in a hollow tree and fleeing to France.

Many people in England and Wales wanted Charles as their king, too, but in 1653 Cromwell dismissed Parliament and became Lord Protector, a military dictator with puritan leanings. He shut theatres, closed inns to discourage drinking, and banned most sports—outlawing them completely on Sundays. He is even accused of "killing Christmas" by sending soldiers out to prevent celebrations involving raucous eating and drinking.

So it was a relief to most people when Cromwell died in 1658, even though his son Richard succeeded him. Richard didn't last long, though, and by 1660 Charles II was king of England and Wales, as well as Scotland. One of the first things he did was order that Cromwell should be dug up and his corpse put on trial. It was found guilty and hanged, with his head cut off and put on display.

The Restoration (1660–89)

Among the still-extant legacies of Cromwell's Commonwealth are a deep-seated unease about military rule and a religious tolerance colored by a suspicion of extremism. But the Restoration was notable primarily for its revelry, and at times shocking, licentiousness.

Sports and theatres were high on Charles's agenda. He had a house built in **Newmarket** (p. 505) so he could live there during the racing season, as did his most famous mistress, the actress Nell Gwynne. He was also patron of two theatre companies, and Restoration comedy became known for its bawdy plots and use of satire, poking fun at political figures and topical events. William Wycherley's 1675 play *The Country Wife* is often performed today.

This was also a period of scientific expansion. Mathematician Isaac Newton studied the composition of light, invented a reflecting telescope, and, most famous of all, set out his theory of gravity and the laws of motion in 1687—2 years after Charles II's death.

Architect Christopher Wren was also a mathematician, and in 1661 was made Professor of Astronomy at Oxford University. His knowledge of physics and engineering led to his being commissioned to design the **Sheldonian Theatre** in Oxford (p. 217) in 1664. But it was the Great Fire of London, in 1666, that really gave him the opportunity to shine.

London at the time was still a medieval city of half-timbered buildings, which had grown from the walled Roman city. Shops and houses were built very close together in a maze of alleys and narrow streets. The city was filthy, with open sewers and little access to clean water, and plague was a recurring problem. The Great Plague of 1665 was spread by rats' fleas, although nobody knew that at the time. By July, during a hot summer, more than 1,000 Londoners were dying every week. Theatres, markets, and taverns were closed by order of the Privy Council, and the king and his entourage moved to **Salisbury** (p. 325).

Possibly the most famous plague village in England is Eyam, in Derbyshire (p. 534), where about 260 of 350 villagers died. The clergyman had persuaded them to remain in quarantine, helping to stop the spread of the disease. Now the victims are remembered each year with a church service on Plague Sunday, the last Sunday in August.

Back in London, in 1666 the plague continued to pick off occasional victims, but in September a fire started at the king's baker's shop in Pudding Lane, in the old city. The baker's ovens had not been put out properly overnight, sparks escaped, and fire spread through the wooden buildings. It was so intense that the lead roof of the old St. Paul's Cathedral melted before the building burned down along with 84 other churches.

The fire is commemorated by the **Monument** (p. 110), a 61.5-m (202-ft.) tower topped by an urn of golden flames. It was designed by Sir Christopher Wren, and if you climb the 311 spiral steps you can see many of the other buildings Wren built after the fire, when modern London was created. Wren's greatest triumph was the new **St. Paul's Cathedral** (p. 111). But Wren also designed 51 other new churches, as well as the **Royal Observatory** at Greenwich (p. 120), through which the Prime Meridian line runs. This is the internationally agreed official starting point for each day, year, and millennium, and the longitude of every place on earth is measured from here, as explained in the Dava Sobel novel *Longitude* (Walker & Co.). Wren also designed the Royal Hospital for retired soldiers, where the RHS Chelsea Flower Show takes place each May, and **Trinity College Library** in Cambridge (p. 498).

Charles II was succeeded by his brother James II in 1685, an unpopular heir because he was openly Catholic (Charles was a secret Catholic). He appointed Catholics to key posts and dismissed Parliament so he could rule without interference. In 1688 his wife gave birth to a son, which was the last straw for England's

Protestant nobility. They invited James's Protestant daughter from his first marriage and her Dutch husband William of Orange to take the throne.

Glorious Revolution (1689)

William of Orange arrived with a small army and was supported by the English military chiefs who James had alienated, marching on London in what became known as the Glorious Revolution. James fled, and a new Parliament declared his abdication in 1689, leaving the throne free for the joint monarchs William III and Mary II. Their reign brought the end of a monarch's divine right to rule England and Wales. Parliament passed the Bill of Rights, preventing the throne from passing laws or raising taxes without Parliament's consent, so a monarch could never dismiss Parliament. The Bill also prevented Catholics from taking the throne.

Mary died of smallpox in 1694 and William died in 1702. They had no surviving children so Mary's sister, Anne, succeeded William. Anne attended Parliament regularly, restored the income from tithes to the Church, and it was during her reign that England and Wales became politically united with Scotland to create the United Kingdom of Great Britain with the 1706 Act of Union.

One of the greatest legacies of Anne's reign was architecture. Queen Anne buildings are particularly notable, and among the best known is **Blenheim Palace** (p. 226) in Woodstock, Oxfordshire. It was built for the Churchill family by Queen Anne to reward the first Duke of Marlborough (John Churchill) for leading British troops to victory over the French in the 1704 Blenheim Battle (part of the Spanish Succession wars). Sir Winston Churchill was born there in 1874.

Anne had 17 children but only one survived birth—and he died at age 11. Parliament had already passed the Act of Succession to ensure the Protestant heirs of Sophia of Hanover (James I's granddaughter) could claim the throne, rather than James II's Catholic heirs, so Anne was succeeded by George of Hanover in 1714.

The Georgians (1714–1830)

George I and his son George II never learned to speak English, sticking to their native German. Unsurprisingly they were disliked by the people. George III was the first English-born king in the Hanover line, and although he is chiefly remembered for losing the American colonies and going mad (as portrayed in Alan Bennett's 1991 play and the subsequent film *The Madness of King George*), at least he could speak English.

Georgian England was a cruel and lawless period. This was the era of Dick Turpin, the highway robber who brought terror to Essex until his death in 1739. It was also a time of piracy: Blackbeard was born in Bristol in 1718 and looted ships off North Carolina. There were at least 200 hanging offenses—from murder to stealing fish—while bear-baiting, badger-baiting, cock fights, and goose-riding were regarded as entertainment.

The Georgians were pretty stylish, though, as we can see from the period's architecture. In London, architect John Nash was responsible for **Regent Street** and remodeled **Buckingham Palace** (p. 86). The London churches of Nicholas Hawksmoor are also revered—and, according to Peter Ackroyd's 1985 novel *Hawksmoor*, built under the influence of Freemasonry—while architect John Soane designed the Bank of England in the City. The churches (and Jack the Ripper) also feature in Alan Moore's graphic novel *From Hell*, and the subsequent film of the same name starring Johnny Depp. Ackroyd, a poet, novelist, and biographer, is London to

THE GEORGIAN arts SCENE

The arts flourished during the Georgian era: *Robinson Crusoe* author Daniel Defoe visited the east of England and wrote about **East Anglia** (p. 491) in *Tour Through the Eastern Counties of England 1722*, noting Colchester's "fair and beautiful" streets. In 1726 *Gulliver's Travels* was published by Jonathan Swift, an Anglo-Irish clergyman, and the artist William Hogarth created satirical illustrations of the country's low morals. Among his most famous work was *A Rake's Progress,* a series of eight prints based on paintings now at **Sir John Soane's Museum** in London (p. 93). They track a wealthy young man's descent from a life of pleasure to debtor's prison and madness. His work was in sharp contrast to the genteel portraits by Joshua Reynolds and Thomas Gainsborough, which are in London's **Tate Britain** (p. 102).

William Blake, born in 1757, brought a vision of heaven and hell with his illustrations and engravings for books and poetry, and his epic Jerusalem. John Constable, born in the flat Suffolk countryside in 1776, was starting to make waves with his landscapes, which he continued to produce until his death in 1837. J.M.W. Turner was a landscape painter, whose work flourished well into the Victorian era. His depictions of light, particularly at the east coast, were remarkable; the new **Turner Contemporary** museum opened at Margate in Kent, where he spent time, in April 2011 (p. 251).

The mid-18th century to the early 19th century was also a time for the Romantic Poets, generally regarded as Percy Bysshe Shelley, Lord Byron, John Clare, Samuel Taylor Coleridge, and William Wordsworth (as well as William Blake). Wordsworth's *Daffodils* is perhaps the most oft-quoted for its simple sentiments, but much of the group's work combined a romantic view of England with a social conscience.

the core; his retelling of novels and history to bring a gripping new conclusion is one of British literature's finest forces.

George I overcame a rebellion by supporters of the Catholic descendants of James II (Jacobites) but left most of the governing of England, Wales (and now Scotland) to Parliament. He was succeeded by George II in 1727, who overcame a second Jacobite rebellion—this time led by Bonnie Prince Charlie, last of the Stuart line—in 1745.

George II was the last British king to lead his troops into battle, taking on the French in 1743. However, it was William Pitt, essentially foreign affairs minister, who masterminded Britain's victory in the Seven Years' War (1756–63), a series of colonial conflicts between Britain, France, and Spain that left Britain with control over India and North America.

Ten years after George III came to the throne in 1760, Captain Cook claimed Australia for Britain during his HMS *Endeavour* voyage to find the fabled southern continent. He claimed parts of New Zealand in 1769 before reaching Australia, and his story is told at the **Captain Cook Memorial Museum** (p. 648), in his hometown of Whitby in Yorkshire.

The 1801 Act of Union led to the creation of the United Kingdom of Britain and Ireland, with far-reaching consequences. Irish Catholics were promised equality with Protestants by Prime Minister William Pitt, but George III was against Catholic emancipation and appointed another prime minister. Equality did not come until 1829 and by then civil war in Ireland was a constant threat.

Royal Crescent, Bath

George III's more famous ill-advised policy was to excessively tax the North American colonies to pay for his grandfather George II's wars. This, of course, led to war with America in 1771 and defeat in 1781. The loss of the American colonies ruined the king's health, and from 1811 his son the Prince Regent took control. He was crowned George IV in 1820.

The **Regency style** covers the years 1811 to 1820, the period before the Prince Regent's became king. It is best illustrated in Brighton's **Royal Pavilion** (p. 266), the Prince's exotic India-inspired summer house on England's South Coast. Many of Bath's beautiful Georgian buildings were also Regency haunts.

Bath became the most fashionable city outside London during the **Regency period** thanks to its ancient spa. Novelist Jane Austen included the city's Assembly Rooms (p. 338) in two of her novels—*Persuasion* and *Northanger Abbey*. There's now a Jane Austin Centre at the handsome **Royal Crescent** (p. 336), built between 1767 and 1774 and regarded as the pinnacle of Palladian architecture in Britain. The whole city is a UNESCO World Heritage site.

With the British defeat of Napoleon at Waterloo in 1815, Britain was emerging as the most powerful country in Europe. The Industrial Revolution had started around the town of Ironbridge in Staffordshire, where the award-winning **Ironbridge Gorge Museums** can be found (p. 486), and the world's first steam-driven passenger railway was opened between Stockton and Darlington in 1825. A carriage from the line is on display at the **National Railway Museum Shildon,** in County Durham (p. 655) and the **National Railway Museum** in York has possibly the world's greatest railways collection (p. 644).

The Victorians (1837–1901)

England and Wales are still largely defined by the Victorian Age. Britain became the most industrialized country in the world, fueled mainly by coal from Wales and Northeast England. You can see these old mines work at the **Blaenavon World**

HOW THE georgians BECAME victorians

George IV died in 1830 and was succeeded by his brother, William IV, who ruled during a time of social unrest caused by the appalling working conditions of the industrial revolution. Although he tried for social reforms at the start of his reign, he had second thoughts during the riots before the 1832 Reform Act was passed. This gave the vote to male householders where the house was worth more than £10, which did nothing for the angry working classes and left the popularity of the monarchy dangerously low. William had 10 illegitimate children by his mistress but no surviving children with his wife Queen Adelaide, so when he died in 1837 his crown (and the resentment of the increasingly vocal industrial workers) was inherited by his niece, **Victoria.**

Heritage Site (p. 690) near Abergavenny (p. 691), where there are iron works, workers cottages, a heritage railway, and the elevator below ground at the fantastic Big Pit.

Alexander Cordell wrote about Blaenavon in his novels, notably his trilogy *Rape of the Fair Country* (1959), *The Hosts of Rebecca* (1960), and *Song of the Earth* (1969). These moving accounts of working life in the 19th century dealt with the social unrest at the time, much arranged by the Chartist Movement, which held protests in many industrial towns. Chartism shaped modern politics, despite it being rejected over the next 60 years. Workers won the right to vote in elections (previously only a landowner's privilege).

In 1848, when there were revolutions all over Europe, the Chartist Movement was waning because political rights in England and Wales were ahead of other countries. Employment was rising and living standards improving, thanks partly to the building of railways, which provided work and transported agricultural products to towns and manufactured products to ports for export. Many of the industrial railways are now heritage lines popular with tourists, for instance the Llanberis Lake Railway, which takes visitors to the **National Slate Museum** in Snowdonia (p. 723).

The most influential Victorian writer was Charles Dickens who knew from first-hand experience the misery of poverty: His father's financial problems landed them in a debtor's prison in 1824. By Victoria's time he had established himself as a journalist and wrote *Oliver Twist* (1837–39), *David Copperfield* (1849–50), and *Great Expectations* (1860–61) in monthly installments. Go to Kent to find out more about Dickens's life in **Rochester** (p. 247), although families might prefer **Dickens World,** in Chatham (p. 248).

Another major writing talent of the Victorian age was Oscar Wilde. Although he was born and educated in Dublin, Ireland, he won a scholarship to Magdalen College, Oxford (p. 215), and moved to London after graduation to write poetry. He eventually became a journalist and published children's stories such as *The Happy Prince,* producing his only novel, *The Picture of Dorian Gray,* in 1891. He is best known, though, for his plays: *Lady Windermere's Fan, A Woman of No Importance, An Ideal Husband,* and *The Importance of Being Earnest.* Wilde was jailed for homosexuality in 1895 and sentenced to hard labor at Reading Gaol (the subject of his 1898 poem *The Ballad of Reading Gaol*). He died, impoverished and broken, in Paris, in 1900.

The Pre-Raphaelite movement transformed painting in the Victorian era. There are fabulous collections at **Tate Britain** in London (p. 102) and the **Birmingham Museums & Art Gallery** (p.469). The art critic John Ruskin had greatly promoted the work

Houses of Parliament, London

of the Pre-Raphaelite Brotherhood (notably its founder William Holman Hunt, John Everett Millais, and D. G. Rossetti), but he was also a poet, conservationist (influencing the founders of the National Trust), and social revolutionary—campaigning for free schools and libraries. His home, **Brantwood,** near Coniston in the Lake District (p. 618) was visited by luminaries such as Charles Darwin.

The fairytale version of the Middle Ages by the pre-Raphaelite painters led to Gothic Revival architecture. Gothic "Revival" is a bit misleading, as its practitioners usually applied Gothic features at random. The best example is the **Houses of Parliament** in London (1835–52). **Charles Barry** designed the wonderful seat of government and his clock tower, usually called **Big Ben** after its biggest bell, has become an icon.

Victoria was only 18 when she became queen in 1837, and married her cousin Prince Albert of Saxe-Coburg-Gotha 3 years later. Contrary to Victoria's image as a gloomy killjoy, she was lively and independent when young, and very much in love with Albert. The couple was not popular, though, until Prince Albert began to win public recognition for his work on behalf of Britain.

His most impressive triumph was the Great Exhibition of 1851 in the huge glass-built Crystal Palace in London's **Hyde Park** (p. 94). This showcased Britain's industrial and technological achievements, but exhibits from colonized countries were invited to make it an even more important global event. The exhibition's profits funded the construction of the **Natural History Museum** (p. 100), **Science Museum** (p. 101), and **Victoria & Albert Museum** (p. 102) in London. Albert was finally given a title, Prince Consort, in 1857 in recognition of his growing popularity. Tragically, 4 years later he was dead from typhoid.

Victoria never recovered from his death and retired to their favorite family home, **Osborne House** on the Isle of Wight (p. 308), which is still full of the personal presents they bought each other. She wore black for the rest of her life, and withdrew from public life. Her increasing unpopularity was only reversed by her new interest in the British Empire—particularly India.

By the beginning of the 20th century Britain had the world's largest Empire, a booming economy, and a growing middle class.

The Edwardians (1901–10)

The end of the Victorian era coincided with the start of the 20th century. Victoria died in 1901 and was succeeded by her son Edward VI who, now 60, had spent most of his adult life as the leading light of London society. He married Princess Alexandra of Denmark in 1863 but had many mistresses, notably the actress Lily Langtry. The Edwardian era was a glittering period of modernization: **Harrods** department store (p. 158) moved into its building in Knightsbridge in 1901, and the American-inspired **Selfridges** (p. 159) opened in Oxford Street.

Since the 1880s Art Nouveau had been gaining popularity and was the forerunner of Art Deco, which emerged in about 1908 to crystallize the modern style of the 20th century. London's **Victoria & Albert Museum** (p. 102) and Eltham Palace in south London are among the best examples of Art Deco interiors in England.

Although Britain was booming, the struggle for social equality continued, not least by the Suffragette Movement—or Women's Social and Political Union—founded by Emmeline Pankhurst in 1903 to win the right to vote for women. By the time Edward

RULE OF THE railways

There are more "heritage railways" in Wales (well over 20) than in any other country in the world, and England is not far behind. These nostalgic train trips were all working railway lines once. Some are former passenger railways, but many were used by industries such as coal and slate mines to transport materials to iron and steelworks, factories, or the docks. The railways were a product of the Industrial Revolution and ensured that Britain's manufacturing industries led the world. Many were narrow-gauge tracks that ran through valleys and around mountains where there were no roads. In some places, that's still the case, so you're seeing countryside that might only otherwise be accessible to hardened walkers.

James Watt invented the rotary steam engine in 1783. By 1804 Richard Trevithick had built the first steam locomotive to run on rails for the Pennydarren Ironworks in Merthyr Tydfil, South Wales. The Brecon Mountain Railway now runs from Merthyr along the old Brecon and **Merthyr Railway Line** (p. 698), opened in 1859 and closed in 1964. There are views of Pen-y-Fan, the highest peak in South Wales, and the Taf Fechan Reservoir. By 1811, 150 miles of rail track had been built in South Wales, the powerhouse of the Industrial Revolution.

George Stephenson, son of a colliery fireman in Northumberland, became an engineer after working on James Watt's engine. He was appointed engineer of the Liverpool to Manchester Line in 1826—the first passenger railway line in Britain. Stephenson's locomotive—The Rocket—reached 30mph, and the line was opened for business in 1830. You can still see **Stephenson's Rocket** in London's Science Museum (p. 153).

By the 1840s, railway lines were built by private companies all over the country. There were 8,000 miles of track in Britain by 1855, which allowed the iron and coal industries to expand. Ports grew to deal with exports and fishing towns benefited from being able to sell to a wider market. The same was also true of agricultural products, increasing the farmers' markets and making food cheaper for people in urban areas. Manufactured goods also reached their markets more easily, bringing down prices and increasing demand and therefore creating jobs.

Railways helped to shape the national character: Trains led to nationwide developments such as newspapers, trade unions, and even a time zone.

VII was succeeded by his son George V in 1910, the movement was known for women chaining themselves to railings and going on hunger strikes in jail. However, with the advent of World War I, the Suffragettes threw themselves behind the war effort—many women did men's jobs in munitions factories. They were rewarded in 1918, when Parliament gave women property owners over the age of 30 the vote.

On April 10, 1912, RMS *Titanic* left Southampton and 5 days later sunk after hitting an iceberg in the Atlantic. Most of those on board died, including many of the crew from Southampton, in Hampshire. The city's **Maritime Museum,** a 15th-century wool warehouse (p. 301), tells their story and has one of the world's best collections of maritime history.

In 1913, news arrived of the death of Captain Scott of Antarctica in his bid to reach the South Pole. He and his team had reached the pole on January 18, 1912, only to find a Norwegian team led by Roald Amundsen had beaten them to it. On the way back to their ship, Captain Oates—suffering from frostbite and virtually unable to

Previously, every region had a slightly different time, based on the local sunrise and sunset. Now everybody in Britain kept the same time, so that rail timetables would work.

After World War I, there were 120 rail companies in Britain, which were reduced to four: the Great Western Railway; London, Midland, and Scottish Railway (LMS); London and North Eastern Railway (LNER); and the Southern Railway. This created an efficient, golden age of rail travel. The LNER's Mallard still holds the world steam speed record, reaching 126mph in 1938. This beautiful blue engine is now at **Locomotion: The National Railway Museum** at Shildon (p. 644), where you can see many other historic trains including the streamlined Duchess of Hamilton—a 1938 Art Deco masterpiece.

The railways were nationalized in 1948, including industrial lines such as the Ffestiniog Railway in North Wales. You can travel on the Ffestiniog and **Welsh Highland Railways** (p. 730) from the coast at Porthmadog to Blaenau Ffestiniog (where you can visit the **slate mine**—p. 723—or from Porthmadog to **Caernarfon** with its mighty castle; p. 729). Both branches take you past Snowdonia's spectacular scenery.

By 1955 the railways were losing so much money that the network was "modernized." Steam trains had largely already been replaced by diesel engines, and now some lines were electrified. But it was the 1963 report by Dr. Richard Beeching, chairman of the British Railways Board, that changed the rail network forever. He recommended closing 5,000 miles of line and more than 2,000 stations—throwing thousands out of work and cutting off remote areas. Among the lines that went was the West Somerset Railway (p. 361). Before it closed in 1971 it was used to film the train carriage scenes in the Beatles' film *A Hard Day's Night*. Reopened by enthusiasts in 1976, it is now the longest heritage railway in Britain.

Another victim was the Severn Valley Railway, which is now a heritage line. Its Bradley Manor station appeared in the 2005 movie *The Chronicles of Narnia: The Lion, the Witch and the Wardrobe*, while Keighley and Worth Valley Railway in West Yorkshire was where 1970's *The Railway Children* was filmed. The line now has steam trains and Railway Children events. For details of more than 250 rail museums and tourist lines see the **Heritage Railway Association** website **www.heritagerailways.com**.

carry on—left their tent and walked to his death so he would no longer be a burden, uttering the immortal words: "I am just going outside and may be some time." Scott and the rest of his team were discovered in their tent in November 1912, with the last entry in Scott's diary dated March 29. The **Scott Polar Research Institute** in Cambridge (p. 500) has Scott's letters home and many other exhibits from his expeditions.

World Wars I & II (1914–45)

Britain joined World War I in August 1914 when Germany refused to withdraw from Belgium. Among the soldiers who chronicled the horror of trench warfare was Rupert Brooke, a Cambridge graduate who wrote the 1912 war poem *The Old Vicarage, Grantchester*. Many people visit **Grantchester** (p. 497) to see the village church mentioned in his poem, where the clock has been stopped at "ten to three"—and where there's honey still for tea.

The coalition wartime prime minister was Liberal Party leader Lloyd George, who was put in charge of the war effort and given much of the credit for the Allies' military success. Lloyd George said he wanted to create "a land fit for heroes," but recession following the war delivered only unemployment—particularly in the industrial heartlands, which had produced coal, iron, steel, and ships for the war.

In 1926 the coal miners walked off the job because pit owners wanted to increase hours and reduce wages. It led to a General Strike, but there was significant opposition owing to a fear of Communisim after the 1918 Russian Revolution. It was a time of social unrest, particularly in Ireland. In 1916 the Easter Week Rebellion in Dublin by republicans started a civil war, which ended in 1922 with an Irish Free State breaking away from Northern Ireland and the U.K. after Prime Minister Lloyd George signed the Irish Agreement in 1921.

Work started in 1922 on the Stadium of the British Empire Exhibition, which was to take place in 1924, but the first event at what was to be called simply **Wembley Stadium** was the 1923 Football Association Cup—or FA Cup—between West Ham and Bolton. It was dubbed the White Horse Cup Final when police on horses had to control the 200,000-plus spectators who had forced their way into the stadium, which had a capacity of 127,000. Bolton won 2–0 and the FA Cup was held there every year until 2000, when the stadium was demolished and a new one built.

The Wall Street Crash of 1929 ushered in an even more chaotic decade, with the Great Depression causing massive unemployment in the old industrial areas, although the Midlands and the Southeast were less affected. There were high points, though, despite the Depression. Sir Malcolm Campbell beat his own world land speed record at Daytona Beach in Florida in 1932, driving his distinctive Bluebird car at 241.773mph. You can see the Bluebird at the **National Motor Museum** in Beaulieu, Hampshire (p. 303), as well as other famous exhibits including several James Bond vehicles and the flying Ford Anglia from *Harry Potter and the Chamber of Secrets*.

King George V died in 1936, and was succeeded by Edward VIII. But Edward's plan to marry divorced American Wallace Simpson caused a constitutional crisis. As head of the Church of England he could not marry a divorcée, so he abdicated after 327 days and the crown passed to his brother George VI.

By September 1939, Britain was at war again, and Oscar-winning film *The King's Speech* tells the story of how George VI announced the start of World War II. However, the emerging national hero was Winston Churchill (knighted by the present Queen Elizabeth in 1953). As prime minister Churchill became the symbol of Britain's fighting spirit during World War II. In May and June 1940, during the Dunkirk evacuation, 338,000 British and allied troops were rescued against all odds from the beaches of Normandy in northern France and brought safely back to England. They were saved by hundreds of little boats as well as Royal Navy ships as the nation famously "pulled together." It prompted one of Churchill's most famous Parliamentary speeches: "We shall fight on the beaches, we shall fight on the landing grounds, we shall fight in the fields and in the streets, we shall fight in the hills. We shall never surrender." The **Churchill War Rooms** (p. 97) in London's King Charles Street brings the conflict to life for visitors of all ages.

In June 1940 Churchill announced: "… the Battle of France is over. I expect that the Battle of Britain is about to begin." France surrendered 4 days later and by July German fighter planes were attacking shipping in the English Channel and coastal towns. By August, RAF airfields were under attack and in September London and other important cities were targeted. There are several Battle of Britain museums in England, but by far the most important is the **Imperial War Museum Duxford** (p. 508) near Cambridge. The fight for air supremacy was over by fall 1940 with the RAF on top. "Never in the field of human conflict, was so much owed by so many to so few," was Churchill's famous tribute. However, the Luftwaffe continued to bomb British cities until the end of the war.

These blitzes were aimed at factories and transport but inevitably hit residential areas and historic buildings too. In London 30,000 people were killed and countless buildings bombed. Birmingham, Liverpool, Manchester, Sheffield, Southampton, and Hull were among the major targets, as was Coventry where the medieval **St. Michael's Cathedral** (p. 465) was destroyed in 1940. The ruins remain, but a new cathedral was built after the war as a symbol of hope, and it has attracted tourists ever since its consecration in 1962.

Classic Authors for a Taste of England

Graham Greene
W. Somerset Maugham
H. G. Wells
C. P. Snow
Sir Arthur Conan Doyle
Charles Dickens
Jane Austen

For a better idea of how the people of England and Wales coped from 1939 to 1945, you can also visit the **Imperial War Museum** in London (p. 107), and **Imperial War Museum North** in Manchester (p. 567). The hospital in tunnels at Dover Castle in Kent (p. 254) is also a revelation.

Post-War England & Wales (1945–Present Day)

The war ended in Europe in May 1945, with Britain heavily in debt and the economy ruined. Many towns and cities needed to be rebuilt. Rationing, introduced in 1940, became even stricter. It wasn't completely lifted until 1954.

One of the bright spots of the 1940s was Princess Elizabeth's wedding to Prince Philip of Greece and Denmark, who had served in the Royal Navy during the war as a lieutenant. The couple became secretly engaged in 1946, and Philip had to give up his Greek citizenship and title to become a British citizen. He used the surname Mountbatten, a version of his mother's German family name Battenburg. The couple were married at **Westminster Abbey** (p. 103) in November 1947, and moved into Clarence House at St. James's Palace in London, now the official residence of Prince Charles.

After the war, the British Empire became the Commonwealth of Nations. One of the most significant events was the partition of India and Pakistan into two countries in 1947, when the king's title of Emperor of India ceased. Many other countries were granted independence in the following decades.

The postwar break-up of the British Empire was reflected in domestic social reforms. Free secondary school education had only been introduced in 1944, and after the war the Labour Party won the 1945 General Election by a landslide vote. It nationalized the coal industry in 1947, and in 1948 the National Health Service (NHS) was established to provide free hospital and medical provision.

The 1948 Olympic Games were held in London, the first since the Berlin Games of 1936, and were known as the "Austerity Games" because rationing was still in force. The Olympics took place largely in the old Wembley Stadium, with 59 nations participating. The new Wembley Stadium is a venue for the 2012 Olympic Games, and tours are available. You can also see international sport and the world's biggest bands there.

George Orwell's novel *Nineteen Eighty-Four* was published in 1949, warning about the perils of centralized government and coining the phrase "Big Brother," but the 1950s brought a new optimism. The 1951 Festival of Britain celebrated British industry, arts, and sciences on London's **South Bank** (p. 104), a bomb site from World War II. The Royal Festival Hall is now a concert hall with regular free foyer events. It is part of the South Bank Centre, which includes the Queen Elizabeth Hall music venue, the Hayward Gallery, the British Film Institute's BFI Southbank, and the National Theatre.

King George VI died unexpectedly of lung cancer in 1952 and Queen Elizabeth came to the throne, the symbol of a new era. This is illustrated by the "kitchen sink" novels of the period focusing on the new social mobility. John Braine's 1957 novel, *Room at the Top,* about a young man's attempt to escape the working class, became the first of Britain's "New Wave" films in 1959. Braine was one of a dozen or so writers and novelists labeled "angry young men" after the 1956 John Osborne play *Look Back in Anger*, which was filmed in 1959. Find out more at the **National Media Museum** in Bradford (p. 636).

The Great Train Robbery of 1963, when £2.6 million was stolen in used bank notes from the Glasgow-to-London mail train, is as much a part of English folklore now as the Hole in the Wall gang of the American Wild West. Numerous books and television documentaries have been made about the robbery, including the 1988 film *Buster,* starring Phil Collins and Julie Walters.

Also in 1963, the Profumo Affair (Secretary of War John Profumo's affair with model Christine Keeler, a friend of a Soviet naval attaché) caused a scandal. Assignations took place at Lord Astor's **Cliveden House** in Taplow, Buckinghamshire. It was once the home of high society and visited by British monarchs since the early 18th century. It's now a hotel, but the grandiose gardens and beautiful woodlands, owned by the National Trust, are open year-round (p. 205).

The rock-and-roll music of the 1950s was falling out of fashion by the mid-1960s, but motor bike-riding rockers were still going strong and in 1964 they fought with

A Great British Top 10

"England Swings"	Roger Miller (1965)
"Scarborough Fair"	Simon and Garfunkel (1966)
"Penny Lane/Strawberry Fields Forever"	The Beatles (1967)
"Waterloo Sunset"	The Kinks (1967)
"Streets of London"	Ralph McTell (1969)
"Grantchester Meadows"	Pink Floyd (1970)
"Solsbury Hill"	Peter Gabriel (1977)
"(I Don't Want To Go To) Chelsea"	Elvis Costello and the Attractions (1978)
"London Calling"	The Clash (1979)
"(Waiting For You and) England to Return"	Stackridge (2009)

SWINGING sixties

In the 1960s, England was at the heart of the world. Recovering from the battering it had received during World War II, a new generation was emerging. Youngsters, who hadn't seen war, and who wanted something new. They craved music, and found it, mostly, through the r 'n' b and soul records imported for American servicemen who were still based here. **The Beatles** weren't the first homegrown act to entrance teenagers (they'd already had Adam Faith and Cliff Richard), but they were the first with a new attitude, and who wrote their own music. Others followed, **The Rolling Stones, The Zombies, Downliners Sect, The Pretty Things, The Kinks, The Yardbirds, The Who**... the list was endless. The Beatles, with their lovable mop-tops, had their first number 1, "Please Please Me," in 1963. The Beatles and Merseybeat conquered the world but there were more and more bands from the south. The Stones were marketed as the bad boys of cool, with their first show at London's Marquee Club in 1962. Meanwhile Tom Jones, son of a miner from Pontypridd in South Wales, had his first number 1 in 1965 with "It's Not Unusual." Other outsiders moved in, such as American Jimi Hendrix who, between 1968 and 1969, lived in a flat on Brook Street, next door to the house occupied by composer Handel in 1723–59 (it's now the **Handel House Museum;** p. 88). Venues like the Marquee (now closed) and the 100 Club hosted gigs and parties that have become legendary. As the decade wore on, psychedelic and progressive acts emerged: Cambridge's **Pink Floyd,** Canterbury's **Soft Machine,** and many others.

Clothing was an essential ingredient in the '60s' mix. The mod fashions and miniskirts of designer **Mary Quant** defined the era. Models **Jean Shrimpton** (b. 1942) and **Twiggy** (b. 1949) were the faces of Swinging London. Chelsea's **King's Road** (p. 74) and **Carnaby Street** (p. 72) were the places to be.

Many films define the era. *Performance,* starring The Rolling Stones' lead singer Mick Jagger, the Beatles' *Hard Day's Night,* and Michelangelo Antonioni's *Blowup* (with a live cameo by the Yardbirds) all capture the spirit of the era.

gangs of mods (style-conscious youngsters who listened to ska and English, rather than American, music) at south-coast seaside resorts such as **Margate** (p. 250) and **Brighton** (p. 264) during the May bank holiday weekend. Movies such as 1979's *Quadrophenia,* starring Sting, capture the mood of the era.

By contrast, Churchill's death in 1965 at the age of 90 seemed to herald the end of an era. His funeral at St. Paul's Cathedral was attended by heads of state from all over Europe. He was buried at the parish church in Bladon, near his **Blenheim** estate (p. 226) in Woodstock, Oxfordshire. At one stage, the public line to file past his coffin was more than 1 mile long.

The 1966 Football World Cup final was won by England, in a 4–2 victory over West Germany at Wembley Stadium. It's an achievement that has never been repeated, although the nation lives in hope. The warm glow of this summer success was swept away that October, however, with one of the most heart-breaking disasters ever to affect these islands. A coal-tip slide at Aberfan near Merthyr Tydfil in South Wales engulfed the village school and nearby houses, killing 144 people, including 116 children. *Cider With Rosie* novelist Laurie Lee visited the village in 1967 and was moved to write about "The Village That Lost Its Children" in his 1975 collection of essays, *I Can't Stay Long.*

Meanwhile, Francis Chichester sailed into Plymouth, in Devon (p. 392) in May 1967 to become the first man to sail single-handedly around the world—an incredible achievement in an age before electronic navigation systems. Aged 65, he had stopped only at Sydney on his epic voyage, and was rewarded with a knighthood from the Queen a few months later, in a public ceremony at the Royal Naval College in Greenwich. The college was designed by Christopher Wren and built between 1696 and 1712. It is now part of the UNESCO World Heritage site of **Maritime Greenwich** (p. 120).

The 1970s was a troubled decade of shortages and strikes. The oil crisis of 1973–74 led to regular power cuts and the 3-day working week to save fuel. In February 1974 an all-out strike by the National Union of Miners was enough to bring Prime Minister Edward Heath's Conservative government down, and by March there was a new Labour government led by Harold Wilson. A recession from 1975 prompted years of strike and unrest, culminating in the Labour government's Winter of Discontent in 1978, when the country ground to a halt, a combination of public services strikes and heavy snow. Punk music, a response to the decade's dire prospects, peaked in 1977 with the release of The Sex Pistols' notorious "God Save the Queen," originally called "No Future."

The Tate Gallery (now **Tate Britain;** p. 102) hit the headlines in February 1976 with its brick sculpture by American artist Carl Andre. The sculpture, 120 firebricks laid out in a two-deck oblong, had been bought more than 3 years before but caught the public imagination when the Tate's director refused to say how much the sculpture had cost.

Then in 1977 the nation's most-loved racehorse, Red Rum, won the **Grand National** at Aintree (p. 580) for an unprecedented third time. The **National Horseracing Museum** at Newmarket (p. 506) near Cambridge has items associated with Red Rum, as well as other legendary racehorses and jockeys.

A General Election put Margaret Thatcher and the Conservatives into power in 1979, and her economic policies divided the nation as unemployment dramatically increased. Her popularity was only assured by the 1982 Falklands "War" (officially only a "conflict") and victory, when Britain defended its South Atlantic islands against Argentina. Thatcher's political success was cemented by free-market agreements with the United States, and her domestic success was underlined by the growing prosperity of Britain's new homeowners and shareholders after council houses were sold off and nationalized industries were privatized.

The 1984 miners' strike, over the closure of pits that were no longer producing enough coal to be economic, was a bitter struggle and did much to cause the hostility toward Mrs. Thatcher, which still exists today in the areas where job losses were severe. The movie *Billy Elliot*, released in 2000 and now a West End musical, is set in 1984–85 with the strike as its backdrop. By the late 1980s, divisions within the Conservatives led to a leadership challenge, and Mrs. Thatcher resigned in 1990 to make way for Conservative leader John Major to become prime minister. But among her lasting legacies is the **Docklands** area of East London (p. 76), where London's love affair with high-rise buildings began.

"New Labour" took power in 1997, under the leadership of the youngest prime minister in over 180 years, Tony Blair (43 years old). This was an age of optimism and Blair became Labour's longest-serving prime minister, but his tenure in the U.K. became increasingly shrouded in his support for the "War on Terror" and actions in Iraq. Gordon Brown succeeded his long-term sparring partner Blair in 2007 but by 2010 had resigned as prime minister and Leader of the Labour Party.

Compared to Thatcher's '80's, today—despite the economic climate—the country is a very different place; just juxtapose some of the gloomy New Town Brutalist architecture—that seemed to resonate with Thatcher's government—to contemporary architecture's refreshing new buildings: Eric Parry's extension to the Holburne Museum in Bath, the new Hepworth Wakefield museum in West Yorkshire, and the Turner Contemporary museum in Margate, Kent.

It also *feels* different, an invigorating environment where a cutting-edge cultural environment exists happily alongside the ever-present pop culture of the past.

The 60s still rule, as shown by the 2010 movie *Brighton Rock,* Graham Greene's 1950s' gangster tale reset in the following decade. The music from that era (and from the 1970s) is acquiring a new lease of life, as the stars are treated with the reverence that used to be accorded old bluesmen; **Paul McCartney** has never been bigger and younger generations are as keen to watch him at a festival as they are new-found idols such as rapper Tinie Tempah. One of the biggest draws is Damon Albarn's post-Blur electro-pop extravaganza **Gorillaz,** which features two ex-members of The Clash, comic book artwork, and a host of stars from down the years. And **Elvis Costello** even hosts his own U.S. chat show.

The first U.K. rock festival was on the **Isle of Wight** (p. 306) in 1968, and starred Marc Bolan's band Tyrannosaurus Rex. Bob Dylan played in 1969 and **Jimi Hendrix** (who'd made his home in Britain) in 1970, although that was the last **Isle of Wight Festival** until it was revived in 2002. The **Glastonbury Festival** (p. 358) in Somerset took up the baton in 1970. Both are still going strong. There is no festival in 2012.

Yet there is still an irrepressible surge of new bands; some explode swiftly while others stay the course. Of the latter, the **Editors, Kasabian, White Lies,** and **Arctic Monkeys** are some of the best known.

Wales has long had its own music: The infectious rock 'n' roll of **Andy Fairweather Low** (once the singer in '60s chart toppers Amen Corner, a long-time guitarist in Eric Clapton's band, and now splendidly solo) and **Dave Edmunds,** and the experimental angst of the Velvet Underground's **John Cale** (who played major shows in summer 2011), while more recent acts such as **Duffy** with her rich soul music, and art rockers **Super Furry Animals** (and their solo frontman **Gruff Rhys**) are major stars.

Comic books used to be a particularly American thing, but a host of Brits have crossed the Atlantic and many have their work made into big-budget films, not least **Neil Gaiman** (the novels *Coraline* and *Stardust*) and **Alan Moore** (*Watchmen, V For Vendetta, League of Extraordinary Gentlemen, From Hell*).

Literature in Britain has never been stronger. Erudite fantasy has become bigselling reality for Philip (*Golden Compass*) Pullman and J.K. (Harry Potter) Rowling, but there are far more esoteric novels that have become bestsellers. Read almost anything by A.S. Byatt, Hillary Mantel, Ian McEwan (whose *Atonement* was turned into the movie starring Keira Knightley), Martin Amis, Jeanette Winterson, Zadie Smith, and Will Self and it is possible to see the anger, introspection, and inventiveness of modern Britain, with some, such as Byatt and Winterson, spilling over into young people's fiction. Meanwhile, author Niall Griffiths' edgy novels have put Aberystwyth on the map as much as Irvine Welsh and Ian Rankin's books did for Edinburgh.

What They Say

"Now that I own the BBC/What am I supposed to make of this thing/All this power/All this glory/All these DJs/And all these lorries."

—Sparks, *Now That I Own The BBC* (1994)

EATING & drinking

There are now more than 100 restaurants in England with one Michelin star. There are another dozen-plus with two stars, and four with that ultimate accolade of three stars. One of them is the home of Gordon Ramsay, who seems to be on American TV more than President Obama; another, the Fat Duck at Bray, is the masterwork of another TV star, Heston Blumenthal and his molecular cooking style. Oh, and a handful of restaurants in Wales also have stars.

It says a lot about British cuisine, once so derided, where an emphasis on locally sourced produce is now king. Even high-street chain restaurants are largely of a decent standard (you can never go wrong with a Pizza Express), and you'd have to be extremely unlucky not to stumble on a good curry house. Add to that the plethora of Chinese, Thai, and Italian places, plus growing numbers of French and Spanish tapas restaurants, as well as all those fish-and-chips shops and coffee shops (a Starbucks is as much an English institution now as a chippie), and you'll never want for food.

There are few things visitors won't be familiar with these days, as even the most remote U.S. brewpub, Canadian bar, or New Zealand eatery sometimes features a menu heavy in Englishness (cottage pie, bangers and mash). What you will find is increasingly good pub grub, with gastropubs offering fare that would outstrip that of many restaurants. There are seafood delights around the country (Morecambe Bay prawns, Whitstable oysters, Cromer crabs, jellied eels in London's East End, kippers and other smoked fish around the land). Local lamb, estate-raised beef and venison, eclectic gourmet sausages and pies are all increasingly on the menu. Wales has all these, too, plus its own treats... flat, sugary Welsh cakes, and (more of an acquired taste) laverbread, a type of seaweed.

In the 1960s and 1970s real ale was being replaced with trouble-free gassy kegs of Watney's Red Barrel; a people's revolution followed with small brewers popping up, traditional methods being praised, and something that was declared dead reborn, better than ever before. The revolution even swept America, brewpubs appearing in every town offering dark beers instead of the pale yellow fizz that was the norm.

Nowadays in Britain there's a regional variety of beers, from the divine Hop Back from Salisbury, Wiltshire, with its award-winning White Lightning to the Whitstable Brewery, making Oyster Stout, in a shed in the Kent seaside town. But England has wine, too, with a number of vineyards in southern England, including the Adgestone on the Isle of Wight.

Stage plays are also another British success story, with a wealth of erudite offerings, often dealing with difficult subjects, from Alan Bennett, David Hare, Harold Pinter, Tom Stoppard, Michael Frayn, and others.

British movies are still taking on the world, such as *The King's Speech*, which won four 2011 Oscars, including best film, and *Archipelago* (2010), a gripping tale of family breakdown and isolation. Yet it is not just the arty films that are crossing the Atlantic successfully; Simon Pegg and Nick Frost are now U.S. stars with their films *Shaun of the Dead*, *Hot Fuzz*, and *Paul*. British directors (who are often also writers) are also big business: Paul Greengrass (*Green Zone*, *The Bourne Ultimatum*), Christopher Nolan (*Batman Begins*, *The Dark Knight*, plus 2012's *The Dark Knight Rises*, as well as the story for 2012's Superman rebirth *Man of Steel*), Stephen Daldry (*The Reader*, for which Kate Winslet won the best actress Oscar, and the 2012 drama *Extremely Loud and Incredibly Close*, starring Sandra Bullock and Tom Hanks), Edgar Wright (*Shaun of the Dead*, *Scott Pilgrim vs. the World*), and Andrea Arnold, whose 2009 movie *Fish Tank* was named Outstanding British Film in the BAFTA awards.

And TV just grows, with perhaps more choice on dozens of cable and satellite channels than even in the U.S., a far cry from the dark days of 1982 when the country celebrated the launch of its 4th TV station, Channel 4. Yet still the BBC reigns supreme, the world's greatest broadcaster, feted for its news reporting, its drama, and its comedy. And on U.S. TV, the biggest star of the moment is Englishman Hugh Laurie, for *House*, a veteran of BBC comedy and drama series.

Wales is making its mark in the entertainment world, with BBC Wales making the revamped *Dr. Who* science fiction series (now becoming a transatlantic hit, filming in the U.S. and with Neil Gaiman among the writers), along with hard-hitting, alien-hunting spin-off *Torchwood*. Welsh comedy is on the up, too, with performers such as Rob Brydon, and the award-winning BBC series *Gavin and Stacey*. Welsh actors Rhys Ifans (*Notting Hill*, *Enduring Love*, *Mr Nice*, *Harry Potter and the Deathly Hallows*) and Michael Sheen (*Wilde*, *Frost/Nixon*, *The Twilight Saga: New Moon*, and even *Dr. Who*) are male leads in the footsteps of Anthony Hopkins and Richard Harris. Even Mr. Fantastic in the *Fantastic Four* movies is Welshman Ioan Gruffudd.

WHEN TO GO

Climate

You don't come to England and Wales for the weather, but it's nowhere near as bad as many visitors expect. You can't be an island on the edge of the Atlantic Ocean without experiencing some rain brought over by westerly winds, but while the west coast of Wales and England get the worst of this you'll enjoy warm, sunny, summer days all over England and Wales (and mild, wet ones).

Like all countries, mountainous areas can have local cloud and drizzle so North Wales, the Lake District, and other rugged areas in the north have their own weather trends. Particularly enjoyable are the light summer evenings, when daytime stretches until at least 10pm at the summer solstice in June (although in winter it can be dark before 4pm). Rain is most likely in the latter part of the year, but there's no "dry season" here, hence Wimbledon's famous tennis in late June and early July being regularly disrupted.

Daytime temperatures can range from 30° to 95°F (−1° to 35°C), but they rarely stay below 36°F (2°C) or above 79°F (26°C) for too long. Evenings are usually cool, even in summer, but hot July and August days can be muggy—particularly on London's Tube network (also known as the Underground), which is not air-conditioned. Note that the British like to keep hotel thermostats about 10°F (6°C) below the American comfort level.

London's Average Daytime Temperatures & Rainfall

	JAN	FEB	MAR	APR	MAY	JUNE	JULY	AUG	SEPT	OCT	NOV	DEC
TEMP. (°F)	39	39	45	48	55	61	61	64	59	52	46	43
TEMP. (°C)	4	4	7	9	13	16	16	18	15	11	8	6
RAINFALL (IN.)	2.1	1.6	1.5	1.5	1.8	1.8	2.2	2.3	1.9	2.2	2.5	1.9

Cardiff's Average Daytime Temperatures & Rainfall

	JAN	FEB	MAR	APR	MAY	JUNE	JULY	AUG	SEPT	OCT	NOV	DEC
TEMP. (°F)	40	40	43	46	52	57	61	61	57	52	44	42
TEMP. (°C)	4	4	6	8	11	14	16	16	14	11	7	6
RAINFALL (IN.)	4.2	3.0	2.9	2.5	2.7	2.6	3.1	4.0	3.8	4.6	4.3	4.6

CURRENT WEATHER CONDITIONS The best place to head online for a detailed weather forecast is **www.bbc.co.uk/weather**.

WHEN YOU'LL FIND BARGAINS In short, summer's warmer weather gives rise to many outdoor music and theatre festivals. But winter offers savings pretty much across the board.

The cheapest time to fly to Britain is usually during the off season: from late October to mid-December and from January to mid-March. In the last few years, the long-haul airlines in particular have offered some irresistible fares during these periods. Remember that weekday flights are often cheaper than weekend fares.

Rates generally increase between March and June, then hit their peak in high travel seasons between late June and September, and in December for the run-up to Christmas and New Year. July and August are also when most Europeans take their holidays, so besides higher prices, there's more crowds and more limited availability of the best hotel rooms.

You can avoid crowds, to some extent, by planning trips for November or January through March. Sure, it may be rainy and cold—but the country doesn't shut down when the tourists thin out (although many countryside attractions such as National Trust properties do close for the winter). Often you'll find city arts festivals during the off season, and hotel prices can drop by 20%. By arriving after the winter holidays, you can also take advantage of post-Christmas sales, which these days start on December 26 or 27. There's usually another major sales period in stores in mid-summer.

Calendar of Events

JANUARY

London's **New Year's Day Parade** crowns the capital's festive season with 3 hours of pomp and frivolity. More than 10,000 dancers, acrobats, cheerleaders, musicians, and performers assemble in the heart of the city every year for a "celebration of nations." Over 400,000 people regularly descend on central London to admire the floats and entertainers that appear in the parade—be sure to arrive early to secure a good space. www.londonparade.co.uk.

London's large Chinese community welcomes the **Chinese New Year** with a colorful bang. Discover cultural events throughout the city center and catch splendid lion dances and performances in Trafalgar Square and Leicester Square. The New Year celebrations are one of the biggest in the world outside of China and as dusk sets in the day the crowds descend on Chinatown to continue the celebrations into the night. www.londonchinatown.org.

FEBRUARY

York, most often associated historically with the Romans, was in fact ruled by Viking kings as Jorvik between A.D. 866 and A.D. 952. These age-old leaders are remembered each year during the **Jorvik Viking Festival.** Would-be adventurers and wannabe Vikings from all over the world gather in the city to watch Norse warriors fight to the (mock) death with their enemies, the Saxons, as well as to enjoy dozens of specially organized arts, music, drama, and action events throughout the city. www.jorvik-viking-centre.co.uk.

As a preview to its annual **Food and Drink Festival,** Chester hosts its famous **Cheese**

Rolling Championships. Locals cheer on the Cheshire team as they take on their Lancashire and Stilton rivals over a creative obstacle course, in what has become a charmingly curious celebration of Chester's cheese-making tradition. www.visitchester.com.

MARCH

The **Newcastle Science Festival** sees venues throughout the city fizzle with amazing robots, incredible inventions, and the occasional fireball. With plenty of activities for kids and adults, the program appeals to aspiring academics and skeptic scientists alike. www.newcastlesciencefest.co.uk.

St. Patrick's Day may have started in Ireland but nowadays it's celebrated throughout the world, not least in Manchester which hosts one of Europe's biggest celebrations of all things Irish. Lasting roughly 2 weeks, the **Manchester Irish Festival** pays tribute to the Emerald Isle with parties, music, comedy, theatre, sport, and dance throughout the city. It all culminates in the city's own St. Patrick's Day parade, which regularly attracts crowds of up to 150,000 people. www.irishfestival.co.uk.

APRIL

It's not just the pretty timber-framed houses that lure tourists to Stratford-upon-Avon. As Shakespeare's birthplace this small town carries real cultural clout, and the Royal Shakespeare Company celebrates "the Bard" with performances of his works throughout the year. It's in April, the month of Shakespeare's birth (and death), that the latest program is released and the **Shakespeare Season** begins afresh. www.rsc.org.uk.

More than just a sporting event, the **London Marathon** is the world's longest street party. Roads along the route come alive with bands, cheering crowds, entertainers, and 36,000 pairs of feet hitting the tarmac along the 26.2 mile course. www.virginlondonmarathon.com.

The **Grand National** at Aintree Racecourse in Liverpool is widely regarded as the greatest steeplechase in the world. The atmosphere is compelling, with punters exchanging tips and form and almost as much to see off track as on it. Scan the stands and look out for the ladies who make up Liverpool's high society and soccer players' wives sorority—their attire has a reputation for being reliably lavish, frequently lurid, and occasionally ludicrous. www.aintree.co.uk.

The **Oxford and Cambridge University Boat Race,** in London on a Saturday in early April, is another great tradition. Rowers battle it out on the Thames between Putney and Chiswick bridges with the riverbanks inbetween taking on a festival atmosphere. www.theboatrace.org.

MAY

The **Hay Festival** is among the largest literary get-togethers in the English-speaking world. The event annually attracts up to 50,000 people to Hay-on-Wye in Wales for a program of interviews, lectures, readings, and performances featuring distinguished authors. This is a festival that will leave you flushed with enthusiasm and brimming with inspiration rather than stressed out and exhausted. www.hayfestival.com.

Bohemian, beach-front Brighton comes into its own every summer and not just due to the much-anticipated good weather. In May, the city's **Brighton Festival** returns with 3 weeks of energetic arts-themed performances and eclectic occurrences, the development of which is heavily influenced by whichever illustrious creative is awarded the role of Guest Artistic Director. www.brightonfestival.org.

London's **Chelsea Flower Show** is Europe's premier gardening event. Some of the greatest exponents of the art exhibit imaginative garden designs over an 11-acre site at the Royal Hospital in Chelsea, creating a floral wonderland for the public to explore. Visitors can roam through scores of gardens and exhibitions, with the displays showcasing some of the world's finest examples of horticultural excellence. www.rhs.org.uk/chelsea.

The country house of Glyndebourne, near Lewes, draws crowds to its manicured lawns and pristine interiors with the return of the **Glyndebourne Festival.** A celebration of opera, its productions can range from Mozart to modern but some things retain a cute, anachronistic flourish. Gentlemen typically gather for performances in tuxedos, while ladies in evening dresses sip champagne in the gardens. www.glyndebourne.com.

JUNE

The Royal Academy of Arts' **Summer Exhibition** in London is the world's largest open contemporary art exhibition. Paintings, sculptures, drawings, and models by many distinguished artists jostle with works by unknown and emerging artists. The exhibition is spread over themed rooms, with separate spaces for invited artists and open submissions, so visitors can easily deduce if a canvas of blotched figures or indistinguishable squiggles is from a supposed master or overenthusiastic novice. www.royalacademy.org.uk.

Trooping the Colour is a quintessentially English experience of pomp and ceremony that celebrates Queen Elizabeth II's birthday and sees central London bedecked in flags and regaled by pageantry. Troupes of troops form a procession along St. James's Park and the Queen herself can be glimpsed enjoying the spectacle at the head of the parade—by those lucky enough to secure a good viewing spot. www.royal.gov.uk.

The town of Ascot becomes the focal point of horseracing each June with the return of the **Royal Ascot** meeting. The most famous meeting in the series is the **Gold Cup,** which takes place on Thursday. The Queen herself occasionally enters horses in the race but betting fervor isn't limited to the action on course. Bookies also routinely take bets on what color hat Her Majesty will wear on the day. www.ascot.co.uk.

Whether Londoners are right to claim it, the world's greatest tennis tournament is one thing, but the top-seed players, traditional strawberries and cream, and the infamous rain delays definitely distinguish **Wimbledon** from other Grand Slams. Some of the greatest matches of all time have been fought on Centre Court, a short distance from central London. www.wimbledon.org.

Glastonbury is the festival-goers festival. It's been going since 1970 and features stars now whose parents weren't even born then, as well as the likes of Paul McCartney and, in 2011, U2. The Somerset site becomes its own city, which is as much effete slumming as hippie chic. And there's usually mud. No festival 2012. www.glastonburyfestivals.co.uk.

JULY

The Proms concerts at London's Royal Albert Hall take over the capital's classical musical calendar every summer and, with some justification, can claim to be the greatest classical music festival in the world. Over 8 weeks, the majestic Royal Albert Hall resounds to the sound of dozens of perhaps unexpectedly experimental concerts, all amid a staple diet of symphony orchestra performances. www.bbc.co.uk/proms.

The **Cardiff Festival** offers a program of outstanding events each summer featuring the best in street theatre, live music, family entertainment, fun fairs, and drama. Events take place throughout the city, mostly at weekends, and to make the festival even more accessible many events are entirely free. www.cardiff-festival.com.

Dozens of performances in venues throughout Birmingham attract thousands of visitors each year to the **Birmingham International Jazz Festival.** The event includes impromptu performances and lively sessions hosted everywhere from department stores to parks and restaurants, and winds down with late-night, lounge-style performances from top jazz stars in more intimate venues. www.bigbearmusic.com/bijf.

The event's logo proved controversial, while its collection of new stadia has drawn praise. Now after years of debate and development London finally hosts the **Olympics** in summer 2012. With the eyes of the world on the city once again, records will be broken, history will be made, and visitors for years to come will remember "I was there." www.london2012.com.

AUGUST

Liverpool's **International Beatle Week** celebrates the music and lives of one of the most innovative, inspirational, and influential pop groups of all time: The Beatles. Although the band broke up decades ago, they're still proudly celebrated in Liverpool, and fans can rest assured the week's conventions, tours, and music performances are all top quality. www.beatlesfestival.co.uk.

Around a million people throng the pastel-hued streets of west London for the **Notting Hill Carnival,** Europe's biggest carnival. Fabulous floats make a colorful circuit of the area and sound systems blast out music all day. Sample delicious Caribbean jerk chicken as you savor a soundtrack of calypso, soul, funk, and reggae. www.nottinghill-carnival.co.uk.

Manchester stages one of the biggest **Pride** events in Europe, offering a host of parties, parades, and celebrations as the city sways in a fiesta of fun. The program varies immensely but is reliably colorful, chaotic, and endearingly cheeky—much like Manchester itself. www.manchesterpride.com.

SEPTEMBER

It's absolutely vital to get your quiff and sideburns just right at the annual **Porthcawl Elvis Festival** in Wales, the largest Elvis event in Europe. Revel in Elvis-themed activities around Porthcawl among like-minded fans of the King of Rock 'n' Roll. www.elvies.co.uk.

Gentle giants fill the sky over Ashton Court Estate every year for Bristol's **International Kite Festival.** The aerial extravaganza is the U.K.'s leading showcase for designers, operators, and manufacturers of inflatables, play structures, and air sculptures. www.kite-festival.org.uk.

The U.K.'s largest festival of contemporary art takes place not in London but in Liverpool. Held for the seventh time in 2012, the **Liverpool Biennial** is getting more eclectic and ambitious with every incarnation. Venues throughout the city are transformed into impromptu creative spaces for its duration, with seemingly every other street

the setting for an artistic extravaganza. www.biennial.com.

Peek inside some 700 of the English capital's most famous buildings and best-kept architectural secrets at the **London Open House Weekend.** Explore the Foreign Office, the Bank of England, and other landmark buildings that are normally obscured from public view. www.london openhouse.org.

OCTOBER

Exemplifying just how provocative and precocious the British art world can be, the **Turner Prize** is awarded to a British artist under 50 and can be relied upon to court controversy and collect commendations year after year. Previous winners have included Chris Ofili and Martin Creed. The works of this year's nominees are displayed at London's Tate Britain gallery. www.tate.org.uk.

NOVEMBER

Foiled in his attempt to blow up London's Houses of Parliament and murder King James I on November 5, 1605, Guy Fawkes was executed and the safety of the king celebrated with the lighting of bonfires throughout the country. The tradition continues to this day with towns throughout the country celebrating **Bonfire Night** around November 5. As darkness descends families gather around a blazing pyre, with a smouldering effigy of Fawkes its centerpiece. Children are distracted from the more macabre connotations of the ceremony by sugary candyfloss (cotton candy) and toffee apples, and the huge fireworks display that ends the evening.

DECEMBER

The **New Year's** celebrations in the village of Allendale are more adrenaline-fuelled than most. In the approach to midnight, costumed men balance flaming whisky barrels filled with hot tar—and weighing up to 15kg (33 lb)—on their heads and then toss them onto an unlit bonfire. The bonfire explodes into flames, and at the stroke of midnight everyone joins to dance around the fire and sing Auld Lang Syne. www.visitnorthumberland.com.

Public Holidays

England has **eight public holidays:** New Year's Day (Jan 1); Good Friday/Easter Monday (usually Apr); May Bank Holiday (first Mon in May); Spring Bank Holiday (last Mon in May, or first in June); August Bank Holiday (last Mon in Aug); Christmas Day (Dec 25); Boxing Day (Dec 26). In 2012, there is an extra holiday on June 5, to mark the Queen's Diamond Jubilee (60 years). If a date such as Christmas Day falls on a Saturday or Sunday, the public holiday rolls over to Monday.

RESPONSIBLE TOURISM

It's difficult to talk about the rights and wrongs of tourism if you're flying several thousand miles to get somewhere. However, there are everyday things you can do to minimize the impact—and especially the carbon footprint—of your travels. Remove chargers from cellphones, PSPs, laptops, and anything else that draws from the mains, once the gadget is fully charged. Turning off all hotel room lights (plus the TV and air-conditioning) can have a massive effect; it really is time all hotels had room card central power switches.

If you're shopping, consider buying seasonal fruit and vegetables or local cheeses from farmers' markets rather than produce sourced by supermarkets from the far side of the globe. Tap water in Britain is always drinkable, and far preferable to a plastic bottle of water that has been pumped out of the earth hundreds of miles away and transported by truck; and although we all need bottled water occasionally when we travel, it makes sense to reuse the bottle. British supermarkets still offer free grocery bags, but are encouraging customers to reuse them, or bring their own bags. Use public transportation to get around cities. And don't rent a car any bigger than you need (apart from anything else, gas/petrol is so expensive in England these days that as well as saving fossil fuel, you'll also be saving yourself from bankruptcy).

Green trips also extend to where you eat and stay. Vegetarian foods tend to have a much smaller impact on the environment because they eschew energy- and resource-intensive meat production. Most hotels now offer you the choice to use your towels for more than 1 night before they are re-laundered—laundry makes up around 40% of an average hotel's energy use. Turning down the air conditioning whenever you go out obviously also makes a difference. The **Green Tourism Business Scheme** (www.green-business.co.uk) was set up in 1997 and covers the whole of the U.K. It awards grades to hotels that meet various sustainability criteria—businesses that are "actively engaged in reducing the negative environmental and social impacts of their tourism operations." Gold, silver, and bronze award-winners are expected to manage energy effectively, promote public transport and green spaces, and support local cultural activities—and are listed on their website. Properties are assessed every 2 years against strict criteria covering areas such as energy efficiency, waste minimization and recycling, use of local produce, and support of public transport.

Another source for environmentally sensitive hotels is **It's a Green Green World** (www.itsagreengreenworld.com), which lists green places to stay, including "eco cottages" that are powered by the wind and sun. **Responsible Travel** (www.responsible travel.com, www.responsiblevacation.com in U.S.) is one among a growing number of environmentally aware travel agents. They offer a number of "green holidays" across the U.K., including in London. Newspaper green travel sections like **www.guardian.co. uk/travel/green** and **www.telegraph.co.uk/travel/hubs/greentravel** are good places to keep up with the issues and get inspiration. **Vision on Sustainable Tourism** (www.tourism-vision.com) is another excellent news hub. Carbon offsetting (not uncontroversial) can be arranged through, among others, **ClimateCare** (www.climate care.org). In the U.K., **Tourism Concern** (www.tourismconcern.org.uk) works to reduce social and environmental problems connected with tourism.

For flexible **volunteering** opportunities that you can build into your city itinerary, see "Voluntourism & Slow Travel," p. 49.

Getting Back to Basics

There are more than three dozen places in England that have been designated as areas of natural beauty; England also has 10 national parks, 12 national trails, and a protected coastline that stretches for miles and miles, including all of Cornwall. If you're looking for green spaces, there are rolling hills, moorland, vast parks (such as the Peak District in Derbyshire), and even huge green areas in London and other cities. Wales also has three National Parks: Brecon Beacons, Snowdonia, and Pembrokeshire Coast. For general information, go to **www.enjoyengland.com** or call ℂ **020/7678-1400.**

If you'd like to explore the National Parks in particular, the best source of information is the **Association of National Park Authorities,** 126 Bute St., Cardiff CF10 5L3, in Wales (ℂ **029/2049-9966;** www.nationalparks.co.uk). It provides information for both Wales and England, from the Yorkshire Dales to Snowdonia in the north of Wales.

A trio of National Parks in Wales covers around 20% of the land mass of the country. With the addition of the South Downs (which in 2010 became England's 10th National Park), 10% of the landmass in England and Wales will be part of the National Park system.

Leave No Trace (www.lnt.org) has drawn up a code for outdoor visitors to unspoiled landscapes, such as those found in the English countryside. Park officials can also offer advice on hiking and camping, and will also steer you to festivals or special events being staged.

Those who want to further reduce the size of their carbon footprint can travel on bike. For details on cycling through England (including some escorted tours), contact the U.K.'s **National Cyclists Organisation** at CTC, Parklands, Railton Road, Guildford, Surrey GU2 9JX (ℂ **0844/736-8450;** www.ctc.org.uk). Membership is £37.

If you don't want to explore green England on your own, you can take part in an eco-friendly tour. Ranging from canoeing to kayaking, mountain climbing to archeological digs, the best clearing house for organized adventure trips is **Specialty Travel Index** (ℂ **888/624-4030;** www.specialtytravel.com).

The **Association of Independent Tour Operators** (www.aito.co.uk) is a group of specialist operators leading the field in making U.K. holidays sustainable. The **Association of British Travel Agents** (**ABTA;** www.abta.com) acts as a focal point for the U.K. travel industry, and is one of the leading groups spearheading responsible tourism in Britain.

SPECIAL INTEREST TOURS

Cycling

The **National Cycle Network** ★★ covers 10,000 miles throughout the country, running from Dover on the south coast to Inverness in the Scottish Highlands. Most routes use old railway lines, canal towpaths, and riversides. The **C2C (Coast to**

Coast or Sea to Sea) Cycle Route runs 140 miles linking the Irish Sea with the North Sea across the Pennines, Dales, and Lake District. The **Essex Cycle Route** covers 250 miles of countryside, through some of England's most charming villages. The **Devon Coast to Coast Route** runs 90 miles across the southwest peninsula, skirting Dartmoor. The **West Country Way** links the Cornish coast to Bath and Bristol for 248 miles. And the **Severn & Thames Cycle Route** runs 100 miles linking two of Britain's major rivers.

Sustrans (© 0845/113-0065; www.sustrans.org.uk) has full information and free online maps of the Network. The **Cyclists Touring Club** (© 0844/736-8450; www.ctc.org.uk) can suggest routes and provide information and maps for tours. Membership in the U.K. costs £37 a year and includes a bi-monthly magazine, maps, and cycle shop discounts.

For a free copy of *Britain for Cyclists,* with information on these routes, call the **British Tourist Authority** (© 800/462-2748 in the U.S., or 888/847-4885 in Canada), or contact U.S. operator **Euro-Bike & Walking Tours** (© 800/575-1540 in the U.S. and Canada; www.eurobike.com).

Fishing

Fly-fishing was born here, and it's an art form. Local fishing guides are available to lead you to waters that are well stocked with trout, perch, grayling, sea bream, Atlantic salmon, and such lesser-known species as rudd and roach. The **Salmon & Trout Association,** Fishmonger's Hall, London Bridge, London EC4R 9EL (© 020/7283-5838; www.salmon-trout.org), has information about British fishing regulations.

Golf

Golf has been around in Britain since Edward VII first began stamping over the greens of such courses as Royal Lytham & St. Annes, in the Northwest, and Royal St. Georges, near London. Yet, despite its huge popularity, golf in Britain remains a clubby sport where some of the most prestigious courses are reserved for members. Rules at most British golf courses tend to be stricter in matters of dress code and protocol than their equivalents in the United States.

Golf International, 14 E. 38th St., New York, NY 10016 (© 800/833-1389 or 212/986-9176; www.golfinternational.com), can open doors with packages from 7 to 14 days, including as much or as little golf, on as many different courses, as a participant wants.

Adventures in Golf, 22 Greeley St., Ste. 7, Merrimack, NH 03054 (© 877/424-7320 or 603/424-7320; www.adventures-in-golf.com); and **Jerry Quinlan's Celtic Golf,** 1129 Rte. 9 South, Cape May Courthouse, NJ 08210 (© 800/535-6148 or 609/465-0600; www.celticgolf.com), also arrange tours, during which you can stay anywhere from guesthouses to deluxe manors.

Sailing

Britain has a rich maritime heritage and there are plenty of opportunities to get afloat. There are sailing schools and charter operations all round the coast, as well as on inland lakes and rivers. **The Royal Yachting Association,** RYA House, Ensign Way, Hamble, Hants, SO31 4YA (© 023 8060 4100; www.rya.org.uk) can provide a list of suitable companies. There is also a wealth of advice and instruction among the books published by Wiley Nautical (www.wileynautical.com).

Hiking, Walking & Other Activities

England and Wales alone have some 100,000 miles of trails and footpaths. The **Ramblers' Association,** Camelford House, 87–90 Albert Embankment, 2nd Floor, London SE1 7TW (℃ **020/7339-8500,** or 029/2064-4308 in Wales; www.ramblers. org.uk), has several books and maps on hiking and walking in Great Britain. Prices range from free to £15.

Visit Wales has a comprehensive file of active options on www.visitwales.com/ active, from fishing to climbing, caving to repelling (abseiling), plus alternative activities such as bushcraft and archery. In Wales there are many companies offering activities, such as **Black Mountain Adventure** (℃ **01497/84897;** www.black mountain.co.uk) in Brecon Beacons National Park, with whitewater rafting, whitewater kayaking, and wet and dry gorge adventure walking.

There are many companies across England and Wales with tours focused on an individual area. For the mountain terrain of Wales's Snowdonia National Park, **Pathfinder,** Clynnog Fawr, Tan-yr-allt, Caernarfon, Gwynedd LL54 5NS, in North Wales (℃ **01286/660202;** www.pathfindersnowdonia.co.uk), offers walks of the summits, as well as rock climbing, kayaking, and rafting, among other activities.

Walking Holidays (℃ **01761/233807;** www.bathwestwalks.com) has guided tours through the West Country and the Cotswolds, taking in such attractions as the Wiltshire Downs and the Mendip Hills, as well as the coastal scenery of Exmoor.

One of Britain's leading specialist companies, **Headwater** (℃ **01606/720199;** www.headwater.com) has several self-guided tours, with classy accommodations: There's Wye Valley cycling, which includes bikes and baggage transfers between hotels (including a Regency coaching inn in Hay-on-Wye) for 5 nights, while you make your own way, crisscrossing between England and Wales. There are also 5-night independent walking tours, in the Cotswolds and from Oxford to Stratford-upon-Avon, which again include luggage transfers and luxury hotels and inns. The tours cost about £500.

Discovery Travel (℃ **01904/632226;** www.discoverytravel.co.uk) has a number of self-guided walking holidays in England and Wales.

Wilderness Travel (℃ **800/368-2794** or 510/558-2488; www.wildernesstravel. com) has treks and inn-to-inn hiking tours, including a 2-week coast-to-coast ramble across England.

English Lakeland Ramblers (℃ **800/724-8801** or 703/680-4276; www. ramblers.com) offers 7- or 8-day walking tours for the average active person in places such as the Lake District. A minibus takes hikers and sightseers daily to trails and sightseeing points. Experts tell you about the area's culture and history and highlight its natural wonders. There are also tours of the Cotswolds, as well as inn-to-inn tours and privately guided tours.

Country Walkers (℃ **800/464-9255** or 802/244-1387; www.countrywalkers. com) has "walking vacations" that last 7 days in the Cotswolds and the Lake District.

For a refreshingly different take on hiking the countryside, the website **www. walkinganddrinkingbeer.blogspot.com**, by American writer Rich Grant, features engaging features for walkers who hope to encounter good English beer around every corner.

The **British Activity Holiday Association** (℃ **01244/301342;** www.baha.org. uk) has details of activity camps, family holidays, day camps, and adult breaks.

Horseback Riding

There are a number of companies in Britain offering horse-riding holidays. **Equestrian Escapes** (© **01829/781133**; www.equestrian-escapes.com) is a good example, with breaks including beach riding in Cornwall, spa and ride in the Brecon Beacons (both from 2 nights), to family holidays in Berkshire, just an hour from London.

Various U.S. companies, such as **Equitour** (© **800/545-0019** or 307/455-3363; www.ridingtours.com), offer horseback-riding package tours of Britain. Two types of 7-day trips can be arranged: One based at a stable beside the Bristol Channel, or on the fields of Dartmoor, with instruction in jumping and dressage, and tours in Wales, with a 7-day trek. On the latter, riders spend nights at different B&Bs or inns and keep their mount at nearby stables.

Eastern Trekking Associates (© **888/836-6152** or 706/541-2450) leads small groups of around six riders each on tours of the Exmoor region, arguably the most beautiful district of England. Horseback-riding trips are also arranged in Wales.

Literary Tours

Lynott Tours (© **800/221-2474**; www.lynotttours.com) has a number of tours, including "Jane Austen, Beatrix Potter, and the Brontës" (taking in the Lake District and Yorkshire) and "Literary Cotswolds." Hotels, guide, and most meals are included. The **British Connection** (© **404/373-1420**; www.thebritishconnection.com) offers literary tours with a focus on Shakespeare, Jane Austen, Agatha Christie, and even mystery writers.

Rail Tours

Great Rail Journeys (© **01904/734154**; www.greatrail.com) offers luxury escorted tours by rail (mostly aboard steam train and all involving steam journeys) throughout England and Wales. **UK Railtours** (© **01438/715050**; www.ukrail tours.com) has a large number of day-trips on railways, mostly historic, although some involving modern trains on unusual goods routes, which include travel from several stops en route. The **Railway Touring Company** (© **01553/661500**; www.railway touring.co.uk) puts together wonderful days out on steam trains (the Cumbrian Mountain Express, the Sussex Belle) which set off from various points around the U.K.

University Study Programs

You can study British literature at renowned universities such as Oxford and Cambridge during the week and then take weekend excursions to the countryside of Shakespeare, Austen, Dickens, and Hardy. While doing your coursework, you can live in dormitories with other students and dine in elaborate halls or the more intimate Fellows' clubs. Study programs in England are not limited to the liberal arts, or to high school or college students. Some programs are designed specifically for teachers and seniors.

Affiliated with Richmond College in London, the **American Institute for Foreign Study** (© **866/906-2437** or 203/399-5000; www.aifs.com) offers 4 weeks or more for high school students, as well as internships and academic programs for college students. There are also courses leading to an MBA.

The **Institute of International Education (IIE)** (📞 212/883-8200; www.iie.
org), administers a variety of academic, training, and grant programs for the U.S.
Information Agency (USIA), including Fulbright grants. It is especially helpful in
arranging enrollment for U.S. students in summer school programs. **Worldwide
Classrooms,** P.O. Box 1166, Milwaukee, WI 53201 (📞 **414/224-3476;** www.
worldwide.edu), produces an extensive listing of schools offering study-abroad programs in England.

Escorted Tours

Escorted tours are structured group tours, with a group leader. The price usually
includes everything from airfare to hotels, meals, tours, admission costs, and local
transportation.

Abercrombie & Kent (📞 **800/554-7016;** www.abercrombiekent.com) offers
extremely upscale escorted tours that are loaded with luxury. They're perhaps the best
in the business.

Martin Randall Travel (📞 **800/988-6168;** www.martinrandall.com) features
cultural tours led by expert lecturers in archeology, architecture, art, history, music,
and so on. Its tours focus on everything from English country houses and gardens to
Hadrian's Wall to the Welsh National Opera in Cardiff. It also has all-inclusive classical music holidays timed for international festivals.

Other U.S. contenders in the upscale package-tour business include **Maupintour**
(📞 **800/255-4266;** www.maupintour.com) and **Tauck World Discovery** (📞 **800/
788-7885;** www.tauck.com).

But not all escorted tours are pricey. One of the U.K.'s leading tour operators, **Wallace Arnold,** and its sister brand, **Shearings,** have a number of tours lasting
between 5 and 10 days, including decent hotels and most meals.

The trips available from **www.coachholidays.com** (📞 **0845/3303747**) bring
together a number of other operators.

U.S.-based **Trafalgar Tours** (📞 **866/544-4434;** www.trafalgartours.com) offers
affordable packages, with lodgings in unpretentious hotels. Seven-day itineraries start
from a little over $1,000, not including flights. One of Trafalgar's leading competitors,
with similar tours, is **Globus & Cosmos Tours** (📞 **866/755-8581;** www.globus
andcosmos.com).

There are a number of companies within the U.K. offering tours. **Travelsphere**
(📞 **0844/567-9960;** www.travelsphere.co.uk) is one of the leading escorted operators, putting together trips that take in castles and gardens, and particularly scenic
railways in England and Wales.

For more information on escorted tours, see www.frommers.com/planning.

Voluntourism & Slow Travel

If you have an interest in giving something back, try volunteering while you're here.
Conservation charity **BTCV** (📞 **020/7278-4294;** www.btcv.org) is always looking
for people to help with projects such as clearing ponds and coppicing woodland.
Anyone can volunteer via the website, and it's free to take part. There are many sessions that are part of the charity's Green Gym, which makes sure you stay fit as you
help. It's also worth keeping an eye on **Timebank** (www.timebank.org.uk). This
online resource helps you match your location and availability with volunteering
opportunities nearby—although most are more suited to a long stay or residency.

Volunteering England (© 020/7520-8900; www.volunteering.org.uk), is a charity that works with groups such as Friends of the Earth to find volunteers for projects; many of them are conservation-minded, although it also works in other areas, such as helping with those who want to be part of London's 2012 Olympics voluntary team. Before you commit to voluntary work, it's important to make sure of its aims, who will benefit, and whether the work will suit you. **Volunteer International** (www.volunteerinternational.org) has a helpful list of questions to ask to determine the intentions and nature of a project.

USEFUL TERMS & LANGUAGE

There are dialects and language variations across England and Wales, far too many to give a full breakdown (and language changes rapidly these days), but here are a selection of words that you might encounter, and which pretty much transcend local barriers.

bangers   sausages; usually paired with mashed potato for "bangers and mash"

banging   good; usually applied to music

barking   crazy or mad; coined from a former asylum in the eastern suburb of Barking

barney   an argument or disagreement

bedlam   madness; as in "the roads are bedlam today"; a corruption of "Bethlehem," an asylum formerly at the corner of Moorgate and London Wall, in the City

black cab   an official black taxi, as opposed to a private hire "minicab"; only black cabs are permitted to tout for fares curbside

butcher's   a look (from Cockney "butcher's hook"); as in "can I have a butcher's?"

BYO   short for "bring your own"; a restaurant that doesn't have a licence to sell alcoholic drinks but will happily open any you bring along, sometimes for a small corkage fee

circus   a (usually circular) coming together of streets, as at Piccadilly Circus and Finsbury Circus

clink   a prison; after the former Clink Prison, on the South Bank

damage   the cost or bill; as in "what's the damage?"

dodgy   not to be trusted, suspect; as in "that £20 note looks dodgy"

dosh   money; also "bread" or "dough"

gaff   home; "back to my gaff" means "back to my place"

G 'n' T   gin and tonic; served with "ice and a slice," i.e. an ice cube (two if you're lucky) and a lemon wedge

greasy spoon   a basic cafe known for fried food

gutted   extremely disappointed; as in "I'm gutted that Arsenal beat Spurs last night"

IPA   India Pale Ale; a type of hoppy, light, English ale first brewed in the 18th century

lager   straw-hued, fizzy beer such as Budweiser and Foster's, served colder than traditional ales (although it's a myth that English beers are served "warm", lager should appear at cool cellar temperature)

naff   cheap looking, or unfashionable

Porter type of dark, strong ale; London brewers Fuller's and Meantime both brew contemporary versions

pint both a measure of beer and a general term for having a drink; as in "do you fancy going for a pint later?"

quid one pound; "10 quid" or "a tenner" is £10

subway pedestrian underpass; the underground railway is "the Tube"

How to Speak Welsh

To the novice, it's quite extraordinary just how *Welsh* Wales is. Signs, addresses, place names, and menus are mostly in both Welsh and English, which can be baffling in itself. Road signs are in both languages, which leads the unwary to suspect there are two different towns ahead. And then sometimes there's a lone sign that's just Welsh, making you think you've missed the road to Cardiff. Because, unlike many other languages, there's rarely a translation obvious to the untrained eye. Pembrokeshire becomes Dyfed while Cardigan comes in slightly closer as Cerdigion. *Llan* (which seems to be the start of half the place names) means "church," while *aber* (which seems to start the other half) is "river mouth."

Several words it is handy to know are *gwesty* (hotel), *siôp* (shop), *gorsaf* (station), *traeth* (beach), *ffordd* (road), and *cawl cennin* (leek soup).

And while we're on the subject we shouldn't forget the classic Llanfairpwllgwyngyllgogerychwyrndrobwllllantysiliogogogoch, the village in Anglesey, which (roughly) is translated as: "The Church of St. Mary by the pool with the white hazel near the rapid whirlpool by St. Tysilio's church and the red cave." On the road signs you'll see it as Llanfair PG, which isn't half as much fun.

aber	river mouth	**ffordd**	road
afon	river	**gorsaf**	station
araf	slow	**gwesty**	hotel
bach/fach	small	**heddlu**	police
bont/pont	bridge	**llan**	church lands
bwlch	gap, pass	**llyn**	lake
carreg	stone	**llwybr cyhoeddus**	public footpath
cefn	ridge	**lôn**	lane
coed	wood	**marched**	ladies
croes/groes	cross	**mynydd**	mountain
cwm	valley	**pen**	top
dim	no	**rhyd**	ford
dim mynediad	no entry	**siôp**	shop
dinas	fort, city	**Swyddfa'r Post**	Post Office
dynion	gentlemen	**toiledau**	toilets
eglwys	church	**traeth**	beach
fawr/mawr	big	**ysbyty**	hospital
felin/melin	mill		

SUGGESTED ITINERARIES

by Nick Dalton & Deborah Stone

You want to get the most out of your trip in the short time that you have available. Here are some ideas for using your time wisely. The first itinerary is a general highlights tour, the second gives you an in-depth look at a region you might otherwise bypass, and the others are for those with special interests: gardens and families.

Each itinerary can be enjoyed in a single week, but they are designed so that you can, by and large, fit two or more together.

REGIONS IN BRIEF

England is a part of the United Kingdom, which comprises England, Wales, Scotland, and Northern Ireland. Only 130,347 sq. km (50,327 sq. miles)—about the size of New York State—England has an amazing amount of countryside and wilderness and an astonishing regional, physical, and cultural diversity. See the map in the insert at the beginning of this book for the regions outlined below.

England

LONDON   Around 7 million Londoners live here, although "London" extends to cover more than 1,577 sq. km (609 sq. miles). The City of London is rather different, just 2.5 sq. km (1 sq. mile). The rest is the city (as opposed to the City, the financial hub), which gives way to towns and boroughs. London's outlying areas are described in chapter 4.

THE THAMES VALLEY   England's most famous river continues westward from Kew to its source in the Cotswolds. A land of meadows, woodlands, attractive villages, market towns, and rolling hillsides, this is one of England's most scenic areas. Highlights include **Windsor Castle** (Elizabeth II's chosen residence) and nearby **Eton College,** founded by a young Henry VI in 1440. **Henley-on-Thames,** site of the Royal Regatta, is one of the best Thames-side towns; and at the university city of **Oxford,** you can tour the colleges.

THE SOUTHEAST (KENT, SURREY & SUSSEX)   This is the land of Admiral Nelson and Virginia Woolf, Sir Winston Churchill and Turner. It's where you'll find the boisterous seaside city of **Brighton;** and **Canterbury,** famed for its religious pilgrimages and cathedral. Kent is blessed with many castles and stately homes (exquisite **Leeds Castle, Chartwell,** where Churchill lived) but also the dockyards that Nelson sailed from. Sussex has many coastal beauty spots (such as West Wittering beach) and lovely towns, including Chichester. Beyond all of these is the South Downs Way, a wild walk across the chalk hills that lie just inland. Surrey, on the edge of London, is often overlooked by visitors, yet has Thames-side towns, the wonderful Surrey Hills (with Leith Hill, the highest point in the Southeast), the city of Guildford and a spread of forest and heathland that offers splendid walks.

HAMPSHIRE & WILTSHIRE   Southwest of London, these counties possess two of England's greatest **cathedrals,** Winchester and Salisbury, and Europe's most significant prehistoric monument, **Stonehenge.** Hampshire is bordered on its western side by the woodlands and heaths of the **New Forest.** The towns of **Portsmouth** and **Southampton** loom large in naval heritage; the former's historic dockyard is where you can see Nelson's flagship, HMS *Victory*. The **Isle of Wight,** once Queen Victoria's favorite retreat, is a seaside haven trapped in time. Wiltshire is the beginning of the **West Country;** here you'll find Wilton House, the 17th-century home of the earls of Pembroke, and Old Sarum, the remains of what is believed to have been an Iron Age fortification.

THE SOUTHWEST (DORSET, SOMERSET, DEVON & CORNWALL)
These four counties are the country's great trip getaways. Dorset, associated with Thomas Hardy, is a land of rolling downs, rocky headlands, well-kept villages, and rich farmlands. Somerset—the Somerset of King Arthur and Camelot—offers such magical towns as **Glastonbury.** Devon has both **Exmoor** and **Dartmoor national parks,** and its northern and southern coastlines are peppered with famous resorts such as Lyme Regis and villages such as Clovelly. In Cornwall, you're never more than 20 miles from the rugged coastline, which terminates at **Land's End.** Among the cities worth visiting in these counties are **Bath,** with its impressive Roman baths and Georgian architecture; **Plymouth,** the departure point of the *Mayflower;* and **Wells,** the site of a great cathedral.

THE COTSWOLDS   A wonderful region to tour, this is a pastoral land of honey-hued limestone villages where rural England unfolds before you like a storybook. In the Middle Ages, wool made the Cotswolders prosperous, but now they put out the welcome mat for visitors, with famously lovely inns and pubs. Start at Burford, the traditional gateway to the region, continuing on to Bourton-on-the-Water, Lower and Upper Slaughter, and Stow-on-the-Wold. **Cirencester** is the uncrowned capital of the south Cotswolds, and **Cheltenham** is still an elegant Regency spa town.

STRATFORD & WARWICK   This region encompasses both Shakespeare country and the Midlands. The Midlands was the birthplace of the Industrial Revolution. Its foremost tourist town is **Stratford-upon-Avon,** but also drawing visitors are **Warwick Castle,** one of England's great castles, and the ruins of **Kenilworth Castle.**

BIRMINGHAM & THE WEST MIDLANDS   The area known as the West Midlands embraces the so-called "Black Country." **Birmingham,** nicknamed "Brum," is Britain's largest city after London. This sprawling metropolis was once known for its overpass jungles and grubby suburbs, but is becoming the heart of new Britain with its urban makeover. The English marshes cut through **Shropshire** and

Herefordshire. The **Ironbridge Gorge** was at the heart of the Industrial Revolution (and should be on everyone's must-see list), and the famous **Potteries** are in Staffordshire.

EAST ANGLIA (ESSEX, CAMBRIDGESHIRE, NORFOLK & SUFFOLK)

East Anglia is a geographic bulge northeast of London, comprising four very flat counties. The land of John Constable is still filled with the landscapes he painted. The **Fens**—a broad expanse of fertile, black soil north of Cambridge—is quite mystical in its openness. Go there to see **Ely Cathedral. Cambridge,** with its colleges, is a big attraction, and everyone should have a go at punting on the River Cam. The coast of Essex is startlingly attractive, while farther north is Suffolk (with the genteel seaside town of Southwold), and Norfolk, where the north-facing coast is windswept, bleak, and beautiful.

THE EAST MIDLANDS (DERBYSHIRE, LEICESTERSHIRE, LINCOLN-SHIRE, NORTHAMPTONSHIRE & NOTTINGHAMSHIRE)

Derbyshire's Peak District is one of Britain's rugged charms; here you'll find **Chatsworth House,** the seat of the dukes of Devonshire. Northamptonshire has **Sulgrave Manor,** the ancestral home of George Washington; and **Althorp House,** the childhood home of Diana, Princess of Wales. **Lincoln** has one of England's great cathedrals. **Nottingham** recalls Robin Hood, though Sherwood Forest is not what it was in the outlaw's heyday.

THE NORTHWEST

Here you'll find the magnificent port city of Liverpool, once a major gateway to the U.S., and childhood home to the most famous pop group of all, the Beatles. There's also Manchester, Britain's one-time industrial heart, and now a hip, happening place. Along with those you've got the charming walled Roman city of **Chester,** and the brash but unmissable seaside resort of **Blackpool** with its Coney Island-style fun by the sea.

THE LAKE DISTRICT

Here is some of England's most dramatic scenery: A lake around every bend, hemmed in by ominous peaks (snow-tipped until early summer), with tiny roads and little towns. It's a place of poetry and literature, home to, among others, Wordsworth, Samuel Taylor Coleridge, John Ruskin, and Beatrix Potter. **Windermere** is perhaps the best location for touring the area, but there are many other charming towns, including **Grasmere** and **Ambleside.**

YORKSHIRE & NORTHUMBRIA

Yorkshire will be familiar to fans of the Brontës and James Herriot. **York,** with its immense cathedral and medieval streets, is the city to visit, though more and more visitors are calling on rejuvenated **Leeds** and **Bradford.** Northumbria comprises **Northumberland, Cleveland, Durham,** and **Tyne and Wear** (the area around **Newcastle,** a city that's now a throbbing arts and culture destination). The whole area echoes the ancient border battles between the Scots and English. **Hadrian's Wall,** built by the Romans, is a highlight. The **cathedral** at Durham is one of Britain's finest examples of Norman church architecture, and **Fountains Abbey** is among the country's greatest ecclesiastical ruins. Country homes abound; here you find **Harewood House** and **Castle Howard.**

Wales

CARDIFF & SOUTHERN WALES

The capital of Wales, **Cardiff** is a city reborn, the docks where coal and slate were once shipped out turned into Cardiff Bay, a tourist attraction of arts, food, watersports, and leisure. In the old heart are the vast **National**

Museum of Wales, with everything from a huge collection of Impressionist paintings to an animatronic woolly mammoth, as well as the quite astonishing Victoria decorative arts delight of **Cardiff Castle.** It's only a short journey to the **Big Pit,** with its mining history (and mine tour). Southern Wales is full of other delights, from the mountainous beauty of **Brecon Beacons National Park** to the wild coastline of Pembrokeshire and the west. West of Cardiff is **Swansea,** birthplace of Dylan Thomas; you'll also find places he lived as you travel farther west.

NORTH WALES This is where you'll find Snowdonia National Park, a massive area of mountains, rivers, lakes, and rugged coast; at its heart is Snowdon, the highest point in England and Wales at 1,085m (3,560 ft). Once you've done this, it's time to move on to see historic castles such as **Harlech, Caernarfon,** and especially **Conwy Castle,** ordered by Edward I and a masterpiece of medieval architecture. The playful Italianate coastal village of Portmeirion is a delight, and you'll find more historic railways than you could do in one trip.

ENGLAND IN 1 WEEK

If you're coming to England for a short time, you want to make the most of it. And our week-long tour does just that. It might seem packed, but that's what you're here for. If you'd like to slow down for a bit then feel free to drop a place or two to save a day to relax. This tour gives you a good dip into London (the **Tower of London, British Museum**), and then takes you on an edited highlights trip of all those places you could name without hardly thinking (**Windsor Castle, Stratford-upon-Avon, Oxford, Hampton Court**).

Days 1 & 2: London Calling

Start on the banks of the Thames, the mighty river that flows through London. A ride on the **London Eye** (p. 107), near Westminster Bridge, the world's largest observation wheel, is the way to get your bearings. The ride takes 30 minutes. Afterwards, check out Westminster Bridge with its wonderful view of the **Houses of Parliament** and the clock tower **Big Ben** (although the name is actually that of the bell; p. 100). Walk past them and you're immediately at **Westminster Abbey** (p. 103), where most of England's queens and kings have been crowned and where they lie at rest. Check out the fan-vaulted Henry VII's Chapel (one of the loveliest in all of Europe), the shrine to Edward the Confessor, and Poets' Corner, where the literati (Chaucer, Dickens, Tennyson) are buried. Allow 1 hour here.

Now it's time for a stroll up **Whitehall,** passing **10 Downing Street,** the official residence of the prime minister (you can join the crowd gawking at the gates), to **Trafalgar Square** (p. 93). Towering over the pedestrianized square is Nelson's Column, a tribute to Admiral Nelson. It's the thing to have your photo taken in front of one of the stone lions at the base. On one side of the square is the **National Gallery** (p. 89), where you can do a highlights tour of the gallery's 30 must-see paintings, which include Van Gogh's sunflowers and works by Gainsborough, Monet, and Vermeer. You could easily spend 1½ hours here, but it's worth nipping next door to the **National Portrait Gallery** (p. 90) with everything from Old Masters to pop art by David Oxtoby and Andy

Warhol. Head up Long Acre to **Covent Garden** (p. 71), the former fruit and vegetable market, now full of shops, cafes, sandwich bars, and, often, street entertainers. Treat yourself to a swift lunch break.

Wander along the **Strand** back to Trafalgar Square, and straight across and up the **Mall** all the way to **Buckingham Palace** (p. 86). Stare at the guardsmen, and maybe even pose with one for a photo. Turn around and head into St. James's Park where you can walk by the lake, coming out near Parliament Square. Head across Westminster Bridge again, and walk along the river, past the London Eye, and onto the South Bank arts area. Here is the 1950s grand **Royal Festival Hall** where you may be able to pick up good-priced tickets for a play (which is likely to feature top stars). Whether you do or not, there may well be free music in the foyer (which has a bar), or there are a number of other places, mostly with outside tables, where you can relax with a glass of wine.

On **Day 2,** start at the world's most impressive city castle, the **Tower of London** (p. 112). There's an hour-long guided tour by a Yeoman (a "Beefeater") plus exhibitions of Royal treasures, so allow 2 hours here. Afterward, walk out onto Tower Bridge and marvel at the Victorian engineering feat. Turn back and head down onto the embankment, past the Tower Hotel, and into St. Katherine Docks. The old dock is now full of yachts and gin palaces, plus coffee houses and restaurants. From St. Katherine's Pier hop aboard a river bus for the short ride past the Tower, the South Bank, and the Savoy Hotel to Embankment Pier. Hop off and walk up Charing Cross Road, full of old bookshops, and to the **British Museum** (p. 86). This is the mammoth home of one of the world's greatest treasure-troves—much of it plundered from other parts of the globe when Britannia ruled the waves. The most exciting of these treasures are the Elgin Marbles, taken from Greece, and the Rosetta Stone, taken from Egypt. You'll need at least 2 hours for the most cursory of visits.

Now walk east along Holborn and veer off into London's legal quarter, taking in placid Lincoln's Inn Fields. Drop down onto Fleet Street, once home to Britain's newspaper industry, which has gorgeous views of St. Paul's Cathedral up Ludgate Hill. This whole walk may take an hour. To bolster your energy levels, pop into El Vino, a dark, old wine bar, once the Fleet Street haunt of journalists, who are now outnumbered by lawyers. **St. Paul's,** masterpiece of architect Sir Christopher Wren, is your next stop (p. 111). And you can get up to the dome, for London views and nerve-jangling looks down to the ground.

Your work's almost done. Just wander down the footpath to the river and onto the Millennium Bridge, a narrow footbridge, which has terrific views up and down the river. On the other side is the **Tate Modern** (p. 154), a vast, brick power station converted into one of the world's most exciting art museums. If you have the energy you can have a walk around (it's free); if not, just poke your nose in and retire to the riverfront cafe-bar for a drink, or maybe to the 7th-floor restaurant for dinner with one of the best views in London.

Day 3: Windsor Castle

This is a perfect day trip, and calmer than the previous 2 days. Windsor and **Windsor Castle** (p. 199) are just half an hour's train ride from London's Waterloo or Paddington. Windsor is a place the Queen loves, and she spends lots of time here. There's pageantry to rival the Changing of the Guard ceremony at

Suggested England Itineraries

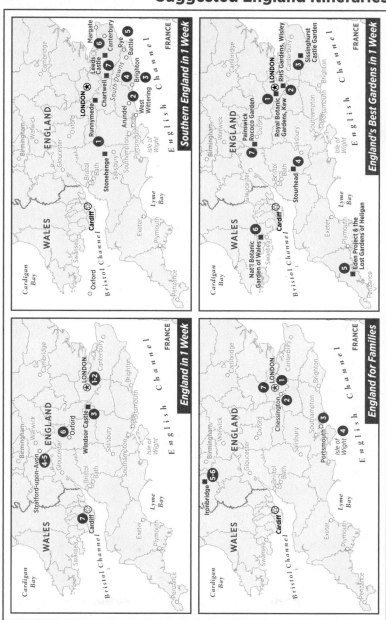

Southern England in 1 Week

England's Best Gardens in 1 Week

England in 1 Week

England for Families

Buckingham Palace, from April to July, Monday to Saturday at 11am (off-season hours differ slightly—see p. 199). Wander through **St. George's Chapel,** where some monarchs are entombed; and stroll through **Jubilee Gardens.** You'll need at least 2 hours, and maybe a bit more as you should have a quick look around the riverside town.

Head back to London, probably in the late afternoon, and you might want to have a quiet walk in **Hyde Park** (p. 94). It's a tranquil spot at any time of year, with the long lake, the Serpentine, cutting across the middle like a rural river. It's an easy walk into **Kensington Gardens** (basically it's the same park, the other side of the road) for a look at the Albert Memorial, Queen Victoria's monumental tribute to her late husband. Now you're in the Kensington/Knightsbridge area and it's not finding a restaurant that's the problem, it's the choosing.

Days 4 & 5: Stratford-upon-Avon

From Paddington Station, you can be in the lovely riverside town of **Stratford-upon-Avon** in 2 hours. After checking into a hotel for 2 nights, head for the **Shakespeare Birthplace Trust** (p. 452), which owns five Shakespeare-related properties, and buy a global ticket. Start with **Shakespeare's Birthplace** (p. 456); pop into **Holy Trinity Church** (p. 454), where he is buried; and then move onto **Hall's Croft** (p. 454), where his daughter Susanna lived. At some point you might want a spot of lunch—the riverside terrace at the **Royal Shakespeare Theatre** (p. 452) is a good spot. While at the theatre, see if there are tickets available for tomorrow. Later, for dinner, you don't need to head farther than the **Black Swan,** generally called the **Dirty Duck** (p. 458). The old riverside pub is the place for a drink, and you can either eat in the bar or in its Conservatory restaurant.

On the morning of **Day 5,** continue with the Shakespeare theme, visiting **Anne Hathaway's Cottage** (p. 454), the thatched, childhood home of his wife, and **Mary Arden's House (Glebe Farm) & Palmer's Farm** (p. 454), his mother's childhood home.

Don't stop for lunch; instead, grab a sandwich, and get the train to Warwick, 8 miles away. Here is **Warwick Castle** (p. 462), one of England's most perfect castles. It's now a full-fledged medieval theme zone, but walking around the place is a singular experience itself.

Return to Stratford, where the glass-walled, Art Deco-tinged rooftop restaurant in the 1930s' Royal Shakespeare Theatre serves pre-performance dinners beginning at 4:30pm. Then you can see the Shakespeare production we know you managed to get tickets for...

Day 6: Oxford

You can get to Oxford by train in a little over 1½ hours, changing at Banbury or Leamington Spa, so you'll be at the university city by mid-morning. Head straight for the **Oxford Tourist Information Centre** (p. 212), a 5-minute walk from the station, and sign up for one of the regular 2-hour walking tours. You'll get a knowledgeable view of the city, and often your small group will go inside otherwise-closed college gates.

Have lunch at the 17th-century **Turf Tavern** (p. 223), tucked away down an alleyway; it's where Bill Clinton used to drink while at university.

Refreshed, walk around the corner to the **Ashmolean** (p. 214), one of Britain's finest museums, which rivals the British Museum in its hoard of ancient things; it's Egypt galleries reopened in 2011, the latest phase of a huge revamp. Around the corner again is the quirky **Pitt Rivers Museum** (p. 216), based around the collection of early archeologist and anthropologist General Pitt-Rivers.

Relax over dinner at the **Cherwell Boathouse** (p. 218), a summertime punt station on the Cherwell, and an acclaimed year-round restaurant with terrace.

Day 7: Cardiff

It may seem unlikely, but heading off to Wales for the day can be done; the hourly train takes only 1¾ hours (changing at Didcot, in the Cotswolds). You'll arrive mid-morning and should walk straight to the **National Museum and Gallery** (p. 681), where you can get a nice coffee in the foyer cafe before browsing the collection of Impressionists, archeological finds, and geographical exhibits. Don't spend too long because you need to dart around the corner to **Cardiff Castle** (p. 680). This isn't a sensible castle at all but a Victorian Arts & Crafts folly on a medieval base, the work of a Welsh coal baron—the richest man in the world—who could pretty much do as he wished. Have a bite at the cafe, with views from the terrace across the grounds and up at the castle on its mound while you're waiting for your tour to start.

Afterward, it's time to hop on the Baycar bendy-bus outside to nip over to **Cardiff Bay** (p. 682); it only takes a few minutes. Once there, you can see how much time you've got, and how late you feel like getting back to London. You'll find yourself by Roald Dahl Plass, the big open space, with iconic water sculpture, between the copper-topped Millennium Centre and the Bay. Wander out past the old Pierhead Building, the Senedd (the Welsh parliament), and back. Treat yourself to one of the country's best ice creams at **Cadwaladers Ice Cream Café** (p. 685) on the waterfront, and think about getting the train back.

SOUTHERN ENGLAND IN 1 WEEK

It's all very well tearing around a country, but sometimes there are great bits on your doorstep that you ignore, or don't even know about. Southern England can be a bit like that. It doesn't quite have the scenery of farther-flung locales but, make no mistake, this is a place that will fill your time more than adequately. This tour, which requires a car, is delightful in itself, a relaxing swing through the byways and along the coast, but it also makes a perfect second week after you've seen England's iconic highlights (see itinerary, above).

Day 1: Runnymede & Stonehenge

You're heading for Stonehenge, but first an added attraction: Drive out of London heading west onto the M3, turn on the M25, then come off at junction 13 onto the A308. On the rural banks of the Thames (6 miles from the frenetic activity of Windsor) is **Runnymede** (p. 205). It was in a meadow here in 1215 that King John sealed the Magna Carta, the document that made all men equal under the law. There is an impressive monument erected by the American Bar

Association, and you can walk through the meadows, take the Thames Path, and even go on a boat ride. There's a little cafe here facing the river, or you might want to plan ahead and bring a picnic.

Get back onto the M3 and head southwest, turning onto the A303. If you're lucky with the traffic you may get to **Stonehenge** (p. 328) in 90 minutes. The monumental stone circle in the middle of Salisbury Plain is a must-see site, even though, with main roads running past, it can be a disappointment. You walk around the circle, at a distance, on paths, so while you'll be glad to have done it, you won't spend as long here as you might have anticipated. You can get up close to the stones at **Avebury** (p. 333), the biggest stone circle in the world, about 25 miles north, and you can visit for free (although the museum is worth paying for). You can get in until dusk, so it's worth trying for a sunset. There are many country hotels near here, particularly in the picturesque town of **Marlborough** (p. 333) several miles away.

Day 2: West Wittering & Arundel

Head south past Salisbury, and southeast past Southampton and Portsmouth to **Chichester** (p. 274); you might do it in a couple of hours. This is a pretty town—stop if you have time—but you're looking for signs to The Witterings, then **West Wittering** (p. 277), several miles away. This is one of Britain's most divine beaches, privately owned and splendidly maintained. The pure sands, backed by dunes, stretch into the distance and there are views across to the **Isle of Wight** (p. 306). This is a place that's as loved by adults as by children: There are walks onto East Head, a sand dune spit that protects Chichester harbor. There's a cafe, ice-cream shops, and the big grassy parking lot behind the dunes doubles as a picnic and games area.

A few miles east of Chichester is **Arundel** (p. 274), an ancient Sussex town on the River Arun. Have a wander (outside town there are walks through the water meadows), but concentrate on **Arundel Castle** (p. 274). Take an hour or so to explore the rooms filled with paintings by Old Masters, the walled gardens, and grounds. You don't want to be too late leaving as you'll have surely booked in at **Amberley Castle** (p. 278), a real castle several miles away that is now a luxury hotel. Here you can explore among the medieval weaponry, the clipped yew hedges, the gardens, lawns, and ponds knowing that at the end of the day the portcullis comes down with you inside.

Day 3: Brighton

You won't want to leave Amberley, but less than half an hour away is Brighton, the capital of the south coast, a city by the sea. You'll want to stay on the seafront, and the Hilton Metropole (p. 272) is a good choice, a grand hotel from the past that's part of the resort's history. Check in, then hit the seafront; you've got the day so you can relax. Head toward the pier; you can walk above the beach, or you can drop down to beach level where under the arches there are pubs, seafood bars, shops, cafes, and other seaside fun. Close together are the **Fishing Museum** (p. 267) and **Brighton Smokehouse** (p. 267), where you can join the line for a hot mackerel sandwich. Head out onto the pier for the views back onto the Regency seafront.

Opposite the pier is the **SeaLife Centre** (p. 269), the world's oldest aquarium, and worth an hour's visit. A few minutes' walk away is the **Royal Pavilion,** a royal holiday home from the Regency era, a must-see extravagance of Oriental design. In the grounds is **Brighton Museum** (p. 266), a decidedly modern collection of furniture, art, and local history; it's free, so pop in at the very least to see Salvador Dali's *Lips* sofa, which is near the entrance.

For lunch, head down to the seafront near your hotel, to the **Regency** (p. 270), a superb fish restaurant without little fanfare; get an outside table and a whole crab salad, or grilled Dover sole, or the wonderful fish and chips.

The rest of the day you can wander the streets. **The Lanes** and **North Laine** are little streets filled with quirky designer shops, which cross the main shopping area that is full of mainstream brands.

For the evening, have a drink at the traditional **Fortune of War** pub (p. 267), spilling out from the beachfront arches. There are plenty of restaurants in the area, too. **Due South** (p. 269), also under the arches, is casual in a smart, organic way, while the **Windsor** (p. 272) in the Hilton Metropole—big, white, chandeliered, and with huge sea-view windows—is more refined.

Day 4: The South Downs

A short drive east and you come to **Charleston** (p. 268), the farmhouse home of Vanessa Bell, sister of Virginia Woolf, and Duncan Grant. The house is a place to love whether you're into the Bloomsbury Set of arty intellectuals or not; it's imaginatively, even crazily decorated from walls to furniture to garden. Aim to spend an hour or so here (the garden is particularly striking) before getting your walking boots on. The farmhouse is in the lee of the **South Downs,** the rolling hills that follow the coast, and just off the **South Downs Way** (p. 276), the phenomenal walk that goes from Eastbourne to Winchester. If you've set off promptly this morning, you should still have a good half-day's hike, topping bare, windy Firle Beacon 217m (712 ft.) in one direction, or passing through the pretty village of Alfriston in the other. There are plenty of inns and hotels in the area.

Day 5: Battle & Rye

Just along the coast is a place that was at the turning point of British history. In the Battle of Hastings, King Alfred was defeated by the Normans, marking the end of English rule and the start of French. The battlefield is still an emotional spot and now the site of an award-winning exhibition. It's easy to spend the morning here, looking round **Battle** (p. 262), the market town that grew up around the Abbey that William the Conqueror founded to celebrate his victory. There are various choices for lunch in the medieval streets. For the afternoon, **Rye** is a charming spot. This town used to be a leading sea port until the harbor silted up; it's now several miles from the sea but still has a river and hostelries that reflect its history as a place where smugglers gathered. Rye is a place to walk around and appreciate (you don't come here for any specific attraction). You could end your day at **The George** (p. 264), one of southern England's most charming hotels.

Day 6: Margate & Canterbury

Keep following the coast around to Dover, and keep going until you reach **Margate** (p. 250), one of England's easternmost points. It may take around 1½ hours. This is a classic English seaside town, a place that fell into disrepair as people went abroad for their holidays, but which is now back on its feet. Explore the seafront and jolly beach, but you're here for the **Turner Contemporary** (p. 251) the country's newest major art museum. The stark, white building on the seafront celebrates J. M. W. Turner, whose iconic seascapes were painted at this very spot when there was a lodging house here. Grab a coffee and a snack at one of the trendy places on the **Harbour Arm** pier, and then make the 30-minute drive to **Canterbury** (p. 240). Check into your hotel and then head for the **cathedral; St. Augustine's Abbey** next door; and the fascinating, subterranean **Roman Museum.** You might even fancy **The Canterbury Tales** (p. 243), a lively, garish attraction devoted to Chaucer's classic tale. There are a number of good places for dinner but the **Goods Shed** (p. 245), a farmers' market and restaurant, showcases the food of this area, known as the Garden of England.

Day 7: Leeds Castle & Chartwell

You've got less than an hour's drive to get to **Leeds Castle** (p. 259), England's most perfect castle, which is in the middle of a serene lake, in rolling grounds. Some castles you can get away with simply looking around the outside, but this one, with its royal apartments, demands to be explored further. The gardens are an attraction in themselves.

Half an hour away, just off the M25 (your route back to London), is **Chartwell** (p. 256), the long-time home of war-time prime minister Winston Churchill. Not only do you get to see his papers, you also see the gardening work he did in his spare time. From here, allow 2 hours to get to London.

ENGLAND FOR FAMILIES

England's offerings may appeal as much to your children as to you. Let them experience sights they've seen on TV, great buildings, and history. London can be quite tiring, so this tour begins and ends there, cutting a happy swath across the countryside in between.

Day 1: London

The heart of England's history and culture is the **Tower of London** (p. 112), and this is the place to start. The megafortress is not only a splendid castle, it also has enough *Horrible Histories* about it to please the pickiest youngster: Traitors' Gate, where miscreants were unloaded from barges, never to be seen again until their heads popped up on spikes at London Bridge, is one example. The tour, led by a Yeoman, has an air of timelessness about it. Allow 2 hours.

Afterward, cross **Tower Bridge** and take a stroll from here to the South Bank, passing the warship HMS *Belfast*. From London Bridge, take the Tube to Hampstead (the journey is less than 30 min.), a village-like northern suburb that opens onto **Hampstead Heath.** This vast area of open space has ponds, woods, and hills, not least Parliament Hill with its views across the City, with St. Paul's Cathedral looking like a toy below.

Day 2: Chessington

A big trip isn't just about ticking off the sights; it's about relaxing and having fun. Drive the few miles to London's southwestern outskirts and check into the Holiday Inn Chessington, a big, stylishly modern hotel with a safari lodge theme at **Chessington World of Adventures** (p. 285), one of the country's top theme parks; you get free entry if you stay. Head straight into the park, which has rides for all ages, from tots to teenagers, and is the only park to have an impressive collection of animals, too. It started as a zoo, and still has tigers and lions in big, grassy, junglelike enclosures (which you can see from all sides), along with gorillas, birds of prey, and the new Wanyama Reserve safari-like area with zebras, gazelles, and giraffes roaming. The reserve is right near the hotel, so you can look at the animals from the terrace of the African-themed Zafari Bar and Grill. The large indoor pool has views of monkeys and birds. The family rooms are cool (and that's our children's view) with a separate sleeping area and their own TV.

Day 3: Portsmouth

Chessington is not far from the A3, which will take you all the way to Portsmouth in 1½ hours. Here the **Historic Dockyard** (p. 297) is a fantastic place for youngsters. It's home to Admiral Nelson's flagship, **HMS *Victory*,** which you can walk around. They'll also love HMS *Warrior*, from 1860, the iron-hulled, steam-powered warship, which also involves ladders, hatches, and other gymnastics. There are docks to run around on, harbor boat rides, and exhibitions. Just across the road is the ferry to the Isle of Wight; it's a tiny ship that takes less than half an hour, and has great views of both the island and Portsmouth. You dock in Ryde and it's a 15-minute drive to **Seaview,** and the **Seaview hotel** (p. 310), a boutique family hotel, where the food (including inventive children's menus) is excellent.

Day 4: The Isle of Wight

Drive to the island's south coast (about 20 min.), and the resort of **Sandown.** This is one of the best areas for finding fossils, which pour out of the chalk cliffs, and the modern **Dinosaur Isle Museum** (p. 307), on the coast road, has a collection going back almost 2 centuries, plus lots of child-friendly fun. Join one of the museum's fossil walks out onto the beach and under the cliffs—children love the combination of fossil-hunting and splashing in rock pools. Then spend the afternoon swimming and playing. Plan to leave around teatime, as your next stop, the following day, is a bit of a journey to an exceptional place. Plan to stay near **Oxford.**

Days 5 & 6: Ironbridge

It's about 80 miles (2 hr.) by car from Oxford to **Ironbridge** (p. 486), site of the world's first iron bridge. It was at the heart of the Industrial Revolution, at one time a raging place of foundries and smoke. Now, however, it is a family delight, which needs to be explored over 2 days. Start with the gorge itself, where children love running across the bridge and throwing sticks into the River Severn below; just up the hill is **Enginuity** (p. 487), a hands-on science and energy museum. Ironbridge's little high street has cute stores and coffee shops, and there are plenty of pretty places to stay locally.

On the following day, head about a mile out of town to **Blists Hill Victorian Town,** a collection of old buildings turned into a townscape on the site of old blast furnaces. It's a wealth of industrial history turned into a world of wonder and fun with a steam train, shops, horse and cart rides, a fairground, and an old-time fish-and-chips shop. There's a carnival atmosphere, and its hillside setting means country walks and clambering along the Hay Incline Plane, a fantastical contraption that lowered barges to river level. When you've finished, drive down the river to the **Tar Tunnel,** a spot where natural bitumen was collected and used for pitch; children love donning hard hats for the short, dark exploration. Then walk across the footbridge and along the river to **Jackfield Tile Museum,** where even youngsters find the Edwardian extravagance interesting.

Day 7: London

Head back to London (several hr.), and use the rest of the day for exploring **London Zoo** (p. 119). Both you and the children will love it as there's plenty of "London" in the zoo, with park-like gardens and views over the Regent's Park Canal. It's also good for any age, with interactive displays, up-close enclosures, and a children's zoo, as well as all the big animals and a rainforest.

ENGLAND'S BEST GARDENS IN 1 WEEK

England's gardens grow beautifully, and in some cases they have been doing so for centuries. This tour takes you to those that are at the very pinnacle of horticulture and beauty. You'll need a car, and your travels will take you across some wonderful countryside. You might naturally expect this to be a summer tour, but while these gardens are at their best from June to September, they are designed to be year-round spectacles, with winter foliage, spring bulbs, and rich late-season hues.

Day 1: Royal Botanic Gardens, Kew

London's great garden, **Kew** (p. 123), is a fantastic world tucked away behind high walls, one that has been developing for 250 years and which lays claim to containing more than one in eight of all known plant species. You can generally find parking, but there is a Kew Gardens stop on the District Line Tube. This is a full day out at any time of year as there are 121 hectares (300 acres), which vary from clipped formal gardens to wild woodland areas. The ornate Palm House is massive and dates from the 1840s, while the Princess of Wales Conservatory is modernistic. Kew was long a prim, traditional garden but now boasts the Rhizotron (an underground look at tree roots) and the Xstrata Treetop Walkway, which runs 18m (60 ft.) high through the tops of oaks and other trees. There are also museums, an art gallery, a Chinese pagoda (from 1762), and the Orangerie, a lovely restaurant that serves everything from sandwiches to table-service meals. There is a gate directly on the Thames, so this is also a good excuse for a riverside walk, or you can cross Kew Bridge to the pubs at Strand on the Green (the Bell & Crown, Bull's Head, and City Barge) for a post-Kew riverside drink.

Day 2: RHS Gardens, Wisley

Off the A3 (itself a picture in spring, lined with gorse bushes), just past the M25, is **Wisley** (p. 280), the home of the Royal Horticultural Society. Whereas Kew is first and foremost a scientific institution, Wisley is just as concerned with the nuts and bolts of everyday gardening. You'll find fields where there may be dozens of varieties of sweet peas on trial, or vegetables, and there are vast areas of fruit trees. But that's beyond the extravagantly planted borders, the exquisite rose garden, the wild gardens (where you'll find toads the size of dinner plates croaking madly in the summer), woodland, lake, and the modern, cathedral-like Glasshouse, with its tropical and temperate collections. Like Kew, this is very much a destination, with its sophisticated Conservatory restaurant (which also does afternoon teas), less formal Conservatory cafe, and the little Orchard Cafe, where you'll find the Honest Sausage selling posh hot dogs. The county town of Guildford is nearby and a good place to stay; you might also be able to fit in a walk in the formal gardens in the castle grounds or in Stoke Park.

Day 3: Sissinghurst Castle Garden

An hour or so from Guildford, across the heart of Surrey into Kent, is **Sissinghurst** (p. 260). This is perhaps the most romantic garden of your tour, and a contrast to your previous days. Set in the grounds of a ruined Elizabethan manor, Sissinghurst was created by garden designer and writer Vita Sackville-West and her husband, novelist and diplomat Harold Nicholson, in the 1930s. The pair turned around 300 years of neglect and created a year-round delight; the dreamlike White Garden, with its silver and white foliage, is perhaps the highlight, but there's also a spring garden full of daffodils and a vegetable garden that shows how it should be done, in style and execution, all with the surviving tower looming over them. It's a good several-hour drive to your next stop, but a charming one, and for much of it you can use the A272 directly west, which follows the line of the chalky South Downs to Winchester.

Day 4: Stourhead

Stourhead (p. 335) is near Salisbury in Wiltshire. The huge lake, which reflects the temples, grottos, and trees lining its banks, leaves you breathless, but it is only the heart of the 1,072-hectare (2,650-acre) estate. This landscaped garden is much the same as when it was created in 1740; flowering shrubs are everywhere (try for the rhododendrons in late spring) and rare trees thrive. There are endless walks to enjoy, and the restaurant serves vegetables from the walled garden, and beef from the estate. The next couple of days are hectic, but worth it. It's a significant drive (3–4 hr.) to Cornwall, so we recommend traveling this evening and staying in the St. Austell or St. Mawes area at Hotel Tresanton or Idle Rocks Hotel.

Day 5: Eden Project & the Lost Gardens of Heligan

These two gardens are different again from anything you've seen so far, and both a great contrast to one another. The **Lost Gardens of Heligan** (p. 406), near the fishing village of Mevagissey, were part of a Victorian estate that fell into disrepair over a period of 70 years. Rediscovered in 1990, the sub-tropical jungle that has been protected by Cornwall's warm climate has been gradually restored.

Equally extraordinary is the **Eden Project** (p. 406), a former clay mine in a lush Cornish valley that's been covered with a series of huge geodesic domes, like something from a science-fiction film. Inside are more than a million plants from around the world, including the planet's largest "captive" rainforest. Afterward, hit the road for 3 or so hours and you can be in Wales for dinner, in a little hotel just across the Severn Bridge.

Day 6: National Botanic Garden of Wales

From your hotel it should take less than 2 hours to get to this relatively new garden (opened 2000), near **Swansea.** The **National Botanic Garden** (p. 701), however, was created on 400-year-old parkland, which still peeps out in places such as the walled garden. At the garden's heart is the Great Glasshouse, a low, wide dome that seems a continuation of the hill (and which features warmth-loving plants from many locations, including California); around the edge are woods and parkland; and in between are lawns and formal gardens. Lunch should be taken in the **Seasons** restaurant, in an old stable block, which uses produce from the walled garden and lamb and beef from the garden's own organic farm. Stay in one of the many little hotels that dot the countryside.

Day 7: Painswick Rococo Garden

The drive here shouldn't take more than a couple of hours, as it's almost all motorway (M4/M5). **Painswick** (p. 436), near Stroud, in the Cotswolds, is a great example of gardens at their most ornate. It was created in the early 1700s and rescued late last century. The garden's flamboyance (including a maze) is in contrast to the views across the valley in which it sits. The **Coach House** restaurant uses produce from the kitchen garden and is a nice spot for lunch before your drive back to London, which will take a little over 2 hours.

LONDON

by Donald Strachan

London never seems to get tired. It's perhaps the greatest paradox of a city with a history spanning 2 millennia that it stays forever young and energetic. Britain's capital is home to the great art collections of the National Gallery, architectural icons like Tower Bridge, and a rich royal heritage, but it also spawns underground design and musical innovation. It is a city of independent villages—Chelsea or Greenwich have little in common with Shoreditch or Soho—and a conurbation of green spaces as well as great buildings.

4

SIGHTSEEING   The old sits alongside the new—nowhere more than at Wren's great baroque dome of **St. Paul's Cathedral,** framed by 21st-century skyscrapers—and London is rightly famed for its museums and galleries. Prized collections, ancient and contemporary—from Bloomsbury's **British Museum** to the South Bank's **Tate Modern**—share top billing with small spaces like the **Sir John Soane's Museum** that could only exist here. Ride the **London Eye** observation wheel to get to grips with the layout.

EATING & DRINKING   Whatever your favorite flavor, you'll find it somewhere in this global culinary city. As London's center of gravity moves east, so does the dining scene: **Viajante** is the latest, and most creative, eatery to grace an eastside hotel. The institutions **Rules** and **J. Sheekey** are as good as ever, and 2011 saw superstar chef Heston Blumenthal reinvent **Dinner** in Knightsbridge. Areas with lower rents continue to attract skillful chefs to destination gastropubs, cool cafes, and a new breed of tapas bar.

SHOPPING   The sheer variety of shops and shopping districts can be bewildering, even for a regular visitor. **Knightsbridge** and **Chelsea** have the chi-chi boutiques, **Mayfair** the finest men's tailors, and the latest in street-style springs up from the hip shops of **Shoreditch** and the East End. This is a city that has something for every taste or budget, and best buys remain collectables, vintage fashions, and accessories. Street markets as diverse as **Columbia Road** and **Portobello** are also experiencing a mini-renaissance.

ENTERTAINMENT & NIGHTLIFE   If you do your relaxation after dark, you've chosen the right city. When the sun sets, the historic monuments and grand museums fade into the inky night, and a whole new London comes to life. The **West End's** bright lights draw the crowds with long-running mega-musicals and big-name dramas. **Soho** is still buzzing—and the streets of **Shoreditch, Hoxton,** and **Dalston** are jumping well into the small hours.

THE best LONDON TRAVEL EXPERIENCES

- o **Taking afternoon tea at the Ritz Palm Court:** The traditional tea ritual lives on in 21st-century London. The pomp and circumstance of the British Empire continue at the Ritz—only the Empire is missing these days. See p. 147.

- o **Hanging out on the hip streets of the "New" East End:** London's fashionable folk haunt the streets and alleyways of "New" East London. Shop the designer boutiques and vintage stores of Shoreditch (p. 151), dine out on French cuisine at Les Trois Garçons (p. 143), drink elegant cocktails at Loungelover (p. 166), and dance till the small hours at Plastic People (p. 173).

- o **Spending an evening at a West End theatre:** London is the theatrical capital of the world. The live stages of Theatreland, around Covent Garden and Soho, offer a unique combination of variety, accessibility, and economy—and programs have everything from serious drama to marquee musicals. See p. 161.

- o **Watching the sunset from Waterloo Bridge:** This famous river crossing is perfectly positioned to watch the embers of the day dissipate behind the Houses of Parliament. The view is so memorable that it moved the Kinks to write a chart-topping song in 1967: *"As long as I gaze on / Waterloo sunset / I am in paradise."* See p. 75.

- o **Walking in the footsteps of Sir Christopher Wren:** The architect who rebuilt so much of London after the Great Fire of 1666 is most known for his churches. Walk from St. Bride's, on Fleet Street, past his icon, St. Paul's Cathedral, to St. Mary-le-Bow and beyond to appreciate his genius. See "Saints & the City," p. 114.

ORIENTATION

Arriving

BY PLANE

London's flagship airport for arrivals from across the globe is **London Heathrow** (LHR; www.heathrowairport.com), 17 miles west of the center and boasting five hectic, bustling terminals (named imaginatively, Terminals 1 to 5, although Terminal 2 is closed until 2014). This is the U.K. hub of most major airlines, including British Airways, Virgin Atlantic, Qantas, and the North American carriers. **London Gatwick** (LGW; www.gatwickairport.com) is the city's second major airport, with two terminals (North and South), 31 miles south of central London in the Sussex countryside. As with Heathrow, you can fly direct, or with a connection to or from pretty much anywhere on the planet.

Increasingly, however, passengers are arriving at London's smaller airports—particularly since the recent proliferation of budget airlines, which now dominate many short-haul domestic and international routes. **London Stansted** (STN; www.stanstedairport.com), 37 miles northeast of the center, is the gateway to a vast array of short-haul destinations in the U.K., Continental Europe, and parts of the Middle East. It's also a hub for Ryanair. **London Luton** (LTN; www.london-luton.co.uk)

anchors a similarly diverse short-haul network, and lies 34 miles northwest of the center. Ryanair and easyJet are regular visitors. **London City** (LCY; www.london city airport.com), the only commercial airport actually in London itself, is frequented mainly by business travelers from nearby Docklands and the City, but does have some key intercity links with regular direct flights to New York, Paris, Edinburgh, Florence, and Madrid. British Airways and Cityjet are the two major airlines at London City.

For information on getting into London from each of the major airports, see p. 744.

BY CAR

To anyone thinking of arriving in the capital by car, our most important piece of advice would be: "Don't." Roads in and around the city are clogged with traffic, and the M25 highway that rings the city is prone to major traffic jams at any time of day—but especially between 7:30 and 9am, or 4 and 7pm on weekdays, and on Sundays from mid-afternoon onward. On top of that, and despite the complaints and grumbles of Londoners, the public transportation system is pretty efficient.

From the north, roads converge at London's **North Circular Road** (the A406), then proceed in a fairly orderly fashion into the center, with the occasional bottleneck and inevitable jam. It's horribly clogged at peak traffic hours, but otherwise a reasonable route into the north of the city. From the west, both the M40/A40 and M4/A4 routes into the city are similarly efficient. (Remember, we're talking in *relative* terms here; no one averse to sitting in stationary traffic should attempt any of these routes at peak times.) From Kent and the Channel ports, the A2 usually clips along satisfactorily outside rush hour, although the bottleneck at the Blackwall Tunnel creates long lines every weekday. From the Southwest, it's usually quicker to head clockwise around the M25 to enter London via the M4 or M40 (see above), unless you're heading for a southwestern suburb like Richmond, Kew, or Twickenham.

BY TRAIN

Precisely which of London's many mainline stations you arrive at depends on where you started your journey. **Paddington Station** serves Heathrow Airport, and also destinations west of London—including Oxford, Reading, and Bristol—as far as South Wales. **Marylebone Station** is used mostly by commuters, but also serves Warwick. **Euston Station** serves North Wales and major cities in northwest England, including Liverpool and Manchester; trains also depart from here to the Lake District and Glasgow, Scotland, via the West Coast Mainline. **King's Cross Station** is the endpoint of the East Coast Mainline—trains arrive here from York, Newcastle, and Edinburgh. **Liverpool Street Station** is the City's main commuter hub, but also links London with Stansted Airport, Cambridge, and Norwich. The City's other mainline stations—Cannon Street, Moorgate, Blackfriars, and Fenchurch Street— are also heavily used by commuters from the neighboring counties of Hertfordshire, Essex, Kent, Surrey, and Sussex, as is **Charing Cross Station,** close to Trafalgar Square. **Waterloo Station** serves the southwest of England: Trains from Devon, Dorset, and Hampshire terminate here, as do Salisbury services. **Victoria Station** serves Gatwick Airport, as well as cities and towns across southern England, including Brighton. South of the River Thames, **London Bridge Station** is another busy commuter hub, and also serves Brighton and Gatwick Airport. Each of London's mainline train stations is connected to the city's vast bus and Tube networks (see below), and each has phones, sandwich bars, fast-food joints, luggage storage areas, and somewhere to ask for transport information.

Missing from the list above is **St. Pancras Station,** the London hub for high-speed Eurostar services to Paris and Brussels, as well as some domestic services to the East Midlands and South Yorkshire. Restored and reopened in 2007, it connects England with Belgium and France through the multibillion-pound **Channel Tunnel.**

Visitor Information

The official **Visit London** online home is the excellent **www.visitlondon.com**. You can download PDF brochures and maps, or have them mailed to a U.K. or U.S. address, or ask any question about the city by filling out the online contact form at **www.visitlondon.com/contact-us**.

Once in the city, the **Britain and London Visitor Centre,** 1 Lower Regent Street, London SW1 4XT (℃ **08701/566-366;** Tube: Piccadilly Circus), can help you with almost anything, from the superficial to the most serious queries. Located just downhill from Piccadilly Circus, it deals with procuring accommodations in all price categories through an on-site travel agency, and you can also book bus or train tickets throughout the U.K. It's open year-round Monday 9:30am to 6pm, Tuesday to Friday 9am to 6pm, and Saturday and Sunday 9am to 4pm. Between April and September, weekday closing is a half-hour later. There are further helpful central information points at: **King's Cross, St. Pancras,** LUL Western Ticket Hall, Euston Road; **Holborn Station,** Kingsway; **Victoria Railway Station,** opposite Platform 8; **Piccadilly Circus Tube Station; Liverpool Street Tube Station; Euston Rail Station,** opposite Platform 8; **Greenwich,** Pepys House, Cutty Sark Gardens (℃ **0870/608-2000**).

The Square Mile (see below) has its own visitor information center, the striking **City of London Tourist Information Centre,** St. Paul's Churchyard (℃ **020/7332-1456**). Opening hours are Monday to Saturday 9:30am to 5:30pm, Sunday 10am to 4pm.

London is such a web-savvy city that almost as soon as we recommend a news source or blog, it is immediately matched or superseded by another. However, there are some phenomenally useful London resources on the Internet. You'll find the latest local news and weather at **www.bbc.co.uk/london** and **www.thisislondon.co.uk. LDN** (www.ldn.in) does a great job of aggregating information about all kinds of events, deals, and trivia. The **Visit London Blog** (http://blog.visitlondon.com) manages to combine officialdom with an eye for the offbeat. **Londonist** (http://londonist. com) remains the best source for street-level coverage of arts, events, food, drink, and London trivia. The **Great Wen blog** (http://greatwenlondon.wordpress.com) is loaded with London miscellany. For the latest on London's theater scene, consult **www.officiallondontheatre.co.uk**. If you wish to attend Christian worship, **www. cityevents.org.uk** has a regularly updated calendar of services at all the City's churches. The Museum of London's **Streetmuseum** iPhone app uses augmented reality and the inbuilt camera to superimpose historic images of London onto a view of the modern streets. For regular features and updates, visit **www.frommers.com/ destinations/London**.

London's Neighborhoods in Brief

WEST END

Bloomsbury & Fitzrovia Bloomsbury, a world within itself, is bounded roughly by Euston Road to the north, Tottenham Court Road to the west, New Oxford Street to the south, and Clerkenwell to the east. It is, among other things, the academic heart of London. There are several colleges here, including University College London, one of the main branches of the University of London. Writers such as Virginia Woolf, who lived in the area, have fanned the neighborhood's reputation as a place devoted to liberal thinking, arts, and "sexual frankness." However, Bloomsbury is a now fairly staid neighborhood of neat garden squares, with most of the students actually living outside the area.

The heart of Bloomsbury is **Russell Square,** where the outlying streets are lined with moderately priced to expensive hotels and B&Bs. It's a noisy but central place to stay. Hotel prices have risen here in the past decade but are still nowhere near the levels of those in Mayfair and St. James's, and there are still bargains to be found, particularly on busy Gower Street. In general, Bloomsbury's hotels are comparable in price to what you'll find in Marylebone to the west, but Bloomsbury is arguably more convenient—at its southern doorstep lie the restaurants and nightclubs of Soho, the theatre district, and the markets of Covent Garden. If you stay here, it's a 5-minute Tube ride to the heart of the West End.

To the west across Tottenham Court Road is **Fitzrovia,** a rather forgotten stretch of the West End, somewhat overshadowed by its more glamorous neighbors. To those in the know it offers a welcome respite from the crowds and madness along Oxford Street, with many good shops and pubs, particularly on Charlotte Street.

Covent Garden & the Strand The flower, fruit, and "veg" market is long gone (since 1970), but memories of Professor Higgins and his "squashed cabbage leaf," Eliza Doolittle, linger on. Covent Garden contains the city's busiest group of restaurants, pubs, and cafes outside of Soho, as well as some of the city's hippest shops, particularly along and around Neal Street and Seven Dials. The restored market buildings here represent one of London's more successful examples of urban recyling. The main building is now home to a number of shops, as well as a small arts and crafts market, while the former flower market holds the **London Transport Museum** (p. 89).

The area attracts professional street performers, who do their juggling and unicycling on the piazza by **St. Paul's Church** (p. 111) in front of thronging crowds in summer—and just a few shivering souls in winter. Appropriately enough, London's theatre district starts around Covent Garden and spills westward over to Leicester Square, Piccadilly Circus, and Soho (see below).

You'll probably come to the Covent Garden area for the theatre or dining rather than for a hotel room. There are only a few hotels—although among those few are some of London's smartest. We recommend our favorites, beginning on p. 179.

Running east from Trafalgar Square, parallel to the River Thames, the Strand forms the southern border of Covent Garden. Most of the grand mansions and fine houses that once lined its length have—with the honorable exceptions of **Somerset House** (p. 88) and the **Savoy Hotel** (p. 180)—been replaced by nondescript offices and chain restaurants.

Leicester Square & Piccadilly Piccadilly Circus and Leicester Square are two of the capital's most famous locations, and yet you can't help feeling that if all London's attractions were of this quality, the city wouldn't receive any visitors at all. A barely-there square, Piccadilly Circus is more the confluence of major streets—Regent Street, Shaftesbury Avenue, and Piccadilly—than it is a venue in its own right. It is a small, partly pedestrianized junction with relentless traffic and crowds; some interesting, if rather overshadowed Regency architecture (which can be seen to better effect on Regent Street); and one small, albeit undeniably pretty statue known to most Londoners as Eros (although trivia fans should note that it was meant to be his brother, Anteros, the Greek god of requited love).

Leicester Square, just to the east, is larger and fully pedestrianized, and has a bit more going on, but is perhaps even more tawdry—a hub of theatres, restaurants, movie palaces, and mainstream nightlife. It's convenient for those who want to be at the center of the action. The downside is the noise, congestion, and pollution. Perhaps the 2011 arrival of the **St. John Hotel** (p. 180) will herald the green shoots of a renaissance.

Much more inviting than either is **Piccadilly** itself, the grand avenue running west from Piccadilly Circus, which was once the main western road out of London. It was named for the "picadil," a ruffled collar created by Robert Baker, a 17th-century tailor. If you want to do some shopping with a bit of added grandeur, retreat to a Regency promenade of exclusive shops, the **Burlington Arcade** (p. 149), designed in 1819.

Soho & Chinatown Just south of the international brands and off-the-peg glamor of Oxford Street—the capital's über-high street—is somewhere altogether more distinctive: Soho, London's louche dissolute heart. It's a place where high and low living have gone hand in hand since the 19th century, and where today the gleaming offices of international media conglomerates and Michelin-starred restaurants sit next to tawdry clip joints and sex shops. In the '50s and '60s, its smoky clubs helped give birth to the British jazz and rock 'n' roll scenes. There are dozens of great places to eat, drink, and hang out, ranging from chic, high-end gastrofests to cheap, late opening stalwarts like **Bar Italia** (p. 148). Many of the best are found on Dean, Frith, and Greek Streets.

Soho is bordered by Regent Street to the west, Oxford Street to the north, Charing Cross Road (lined with secondhand bookstores) to the east, and the Theatreland of Shaftesbury Avenue to the south. At its northeastern corner is Soho Square, where the central stretch of grass is usually packed with sunbathing workers during sunny lunchtimes, while close to its southern end is Old Compton Street, the longtime home of the capital's gay scene. Carnaby Street—a block from Regent Street—was the epicenter of the universe during the swinging '60s. It's recently become a bit of a schlocky tourist trap, although a few quality, independent stores have begun to emerge again.

South of Shaftesbury Avenue is London's **Chinatown**... although "town" is a slightly grand way of describing what essentially amounts to one-and-a-bit streets lined with restaurants. The main street, Gerrard Street, is rather kitsch, with giant oriental-style gates and pagodaesque phone boxes. However, this is a genuine, thriving community, and one of the most dependable areas for Chinese food.

Marylebone Pretty much every town in the country has a high street, a collection of shops and businesses aimed at the surrounding community. **Oxford Street** could be regarded as London's high street, where the biggest chains have flagship branches and where several of the capital's most prestigious department stores, including Selfridges and John Lewis, are found. It can be a brutal place, particularly on weekends and the weeks before Christmas, when it is choked with people, traffic, and noise.

North of Oxford Street, the district of Marylebone (pronounced *Mar*-lee-bone) was once the poor relation of Mayfair to the south, but has become much more fashionable of late—certainly more so than when it was the setting for public executions at the Tyburn gallows (although those did at least attract the crowds). The last executions took place here in the late 18th century. Marylebone has emerged as a major "bedroom" district for London, competing with Bloomsbury to its east. It's not as convenient as Bloomsbury, but the hub of the West End's action is virtually at your doorstep if you stay here. Once known only for its townhouses turned into B&Bs, the district now offers accommodations in all price ranges, catering to everyone from rock stars to frugal family travelers.

Mayfair Once a simple stretch of fields outside the main part of the city where an annual party was held at the start of summer (the "May Fair" that gave the area its name), this is now one of the most exclusive sections of London, filled with luxury hotels, Georgian townhouses, and swanky shops—hence its status as the most expensive property on the U.K. version of the board game Monopoly. Sandwiched between Regent Street and Hyde Park, it's convenient for London's best shopping and reasonably close to the West End theatres, yet removed from the peddlers and commerce of Covent Garden and Soho.

One of the curiosities of Mayfair is **Shepherd Market**, a micro-village of pubs, two-story inns, restaurants, and book and food stalls, nestled within Mayfair's grandness. At the center of Mayfair, **Grosvenor Square** (pronounced *Grove*-nor) is nicknamed "Little America" because it's home to a statue of Franklin D. Roosevelt and the U.S. Embassy.

St. James's   The neighborhood begins at Piccadilly Circus and moves southwest, incorporating the south side of Piccadilly, Pall Mall, The Mall, St. James's Park, and Green Park. Often called "Royal London," St. James's basks in its associations with everybody from the "merrie monarch" King Charles II to the current Queen Elizabeth II and Prince Charles. Be sure to stop in at **Fortnum & Mason** (p. 158), on Piccadilly itself, the grocer to the Queen. Hotels in this neighborhood tend to be expensive, but if the Queen should summon you to Buckingham Palace, you won't have far to walk.

Trafalgar Square (p. 93) lies at the opposite end of the Mall to Buckingham Palace, marking the district's eastern boundary. Its north side is taken up by the neoclassical facade of the **National Gallery** (p. 89), while in the middle stands Nelson's Column, erected in honor of the country's victory over Napoleon at the Battle of Trafalgar, in 1805.

WEST LONDON

Kensington   The Royal Borough lies west of Kensington Gardens and Hyde Park and is traversed by two of London's major shopping streets, Kensington High Street and Kensington Church Street. Since 1689, when asthmatic William III fled Whitehall Palace for Nottingham House (where the air was fresher), the district has enjoyed royal associations. In time, Nottingham House became **Kensington Palace** (p. 96), and the royals grabbed a chunk of Hyde Park to plant their roses. Kensington Palace was home to the late princesses Margaret and Diana, and is still home to Prince and Princess Michael of Kent, and the Duke and Duchess of Gloucester. With all those royal associations, Kensington is a wealthy neighborhood with some very well-to-do hotels and shops. Although it can feel like you've left central London behind on its quiet residential streets, it's just a few Tube stops from High Street Kensington Station to the heart of the action.

Paddington & Bayswater   Paddington radiates out from Paddington Station, north of Hyde Park and Kensington Gardens. It's one of the major B&B centers in London, attracting budget travelers who fill the lodgings along Sussex Gardens and Norfolk Square. Just south of Paddington, north of Hyde Park, and abutting more fashionable Notting Hill to the west, is Bayswater, also filled with budget B&Bs.

Paddington and Bayswater are "in-between" areas. Stay here for moderately priced lodgings (there are expensive hotels, too) and for convenience to **Hyde Park** (p. 94) and transportation. Pick your hotel with care; you'll find our favorites starting on p. 185.

Notting Hill   Fashionable Notting Hill is bounded on the east by Bayswater and on the south by Kensington. Hemmed in on the north by the elevated road known as the Westway and on the west by the Shepherd's Bush roundabout, it has many turn-of-the-20th-century mansions and small houses sitting on quiet, leafy, recently gentrified streets, plus a number of hot restaurants and clubs. In the 1950s the area welcomed a significant influx of Caribbean immigrants, whose cultural heritage is vibrantly celebrated each year at the **Notting Hill Carnival,** Europe's largest street party. Hotels are few, but often terrifyingly chic. Notting Hill is also home to **Portobello Road,** the site of London's most famous street market (p. 152). Adjacent **Holland Park,** an expensive residential neighborhood spread around the park of the same name, is a little more serene, but also more staid. Just to the west, the increasingly fashionable area of **Shepherd's Bush** is attracting a slew of artists and photographers, and in their wake a number of trendy new hangouts, while Europe's largest shopping center—upscale **Westfield**—can be found on the northeastern flank of Shepherd's Bush Green.

SOUTHWEST LONDON

Westminster Westminster has been the seat of first English, then British government since the days of Edward the Confessor (1042–66). Dominated by the Houses of Parliament and **Westminster Abbey** (p. 103), the area runs along the Thames to the east of St. James's Park. Whitehall is the main thoroughfare, linking Trafalgar Square with Parliament Square.

Westminster also encompasses Victoria, an area that takes its name from bustling Victoria Station. Many B&Bs and hotels have sprouted up here because of the neighborhood's proximity to the rail station, which provides the main fast link with Gatwick Airport. If you've arrived without a hotel reservation, you'll find decent pickings on the streets off Belgrave Road; we've selected our local favorites starting on p. 187. Things are a bit pricier to the southwest in Pimlico, the area bordering the river, which is filled with fine Regency squares.

Belgravia South of Knightsbridge, this area has long been one of the main aristocratic quarters of London, rivaling Mayfair in grandeur. Although it reached its pinnacle of prestige during the reign of Queen Victoria, the Duke of Westminster—the country's third-richest man—still maintains one of his many houses at Eaton Square (where both the 1970s' and 2010 versions of BBC drama *Upstairs, Downstairs* were set). Packed with grand, formal, and often startlingly expensive hotels, Belgravia is a haven of upmarket tranquility. If you lodge here, no one will ever accuse you of staying on the "wrong side of the tracks."

Chelsea Beginning at Sloane Square, this stylish Thames-side district lies south and to the west of Belgravia. The area has always been a favorite of writers and artists, including Oscar Wilde, George Eliot, James Whistler, J. M. W. Turner, Henry James, and Thomas Carlyle. The main drawback to Chelsea as a base is inaccessibility. Except for Sloane Square, there's a dearth of Tube stops, and unless you like to take a lot of buses or expensive taxis, you may find getting around a chore.

Chelsea's major boulevard is **King's Road,** where Mary Quant launched the miniskirt in the 1960s, Vivienne Westwood devised the punk look in the 1970s, and where today Charles Saatchi's eponymous **Saatchi Gallery** (p. 101) makes the running in the contemporary art world.

Knightsbridge & Brompton One of London's swankiest neighborhoods, Knightsbridge is a top residential, hotel, and shopping district just south of Hyde Park. Its defining feature and chief attractions are **Harrods** (p. 158) on the Brompton Road, "the Notre Dame of department stores," and nearby Beauchamp Place (pronounced *Bee*-cham), a Regency-era, boutique-lined street with a scattering of restaurants. Knightsbridge, and the equally well-to-do Brompton to the south, make up one of the most convenient areas of western London, ideally located if you want to head east to the theatre district or the Mayfair shops, or west to Chelsea or Kensington's restaurants and museums. However, staying here will come at a price.

South Kensington If you want to be in the vicinity of the shops, boutiques, and restaurants of Knightsbridge and Chelsea, but don't have the resources for a hotel there, head for South Kensington, where the accommodations are more moderately priced. Southeast of Kensington Gardens, primarily residential South Kensington is often called "museumland" because it's dominated by a complex of museums and colleges, including the **Natural History Museum** (p. 100), **Victoria & Albert Museum** (p. 102), and **Science Museum** (p. 153). South Kensington boasts some fashionable restaurants and townhouse hotels, and is just a couple of stops along the Tube's Piccadilly Line from Green Park.

Earl's Court Earl's Court lies south of Kensington and just west of South Kensington. For decades the favored haunt of visiting Australians (hence its nickname, "Kangaroo Valley"), the area is still home to many immigrants—mainly eastern Europeans these days—and is also a popular base for budget travelers, thanks to its wealth of B&Bs, inexpensive hotels, and hostels, and its convenient access to central London: A 15-minute Tube ride takes you into the heart of the West End. Littered with fast-food joints, pubs, and cafes, it provides a cheap, cheerful base, but little in the way of refinement and no major sights.

SOUTH BANK

Lying south across the Thames from Covent Garden, this is where you'll find the **London Eye** (p. 107), **National Theatre** (p. 162), and **Southbank Arts Centre** (p. 165; the largest arts center in Western Europe, and still growing). It's reached from the south via Waterloo Station, and from the north by crossing any one of Westminster Bridge, Hungerford Bridge, or Waterloo Bridge.

Although the area's time as a top hotel district may yet come, that day certainly hasn't arrived yet. A few interesting accommodations aside, the South Bank is, however, a popular evening destination for culture and dining. To the east the South Bank bleeds into Bankside, the site of **Tate Modern** (p. 109), **Shakespeare's Globe** (p. 163), and **HMS *Belfast*** (p. 106), and today the two areas are generally regarded as forming a single riverside zone linked by a cheery riverside path taking you all the way—via a couple of inland detours at London Bridge—from Westminster Bridge to Tower Bridge.

THE CITY

The Square Mile When Londoners speak of "the City," they mean the original Square Mile that's now Britain's main financial district. The City was the original site of "Londinium," the first settlement of the Roman conquerors. Although it retains some of its medieval character, much of the City was swept away by the Great Fire of 1666, the Blitz of 1940, and the zeal of modern developers. Landmarks include Sir Christopher Wren's masterpiece, **St. Paul's Cathedral** (p. 111), which stood virtually alone in the surrounding rubble after the Blitz, and the curvy glass skyscraper 30 St. Mary Axe, better known as the "Gherkin." Some 2,000 years of history unfold at the City's **Museum of London** (p. 114). Most of the hotels are set up for business travelers, not sightseers. However, that can sometimes mean weekend bargains at upscale establishments; see p. 192 for our favorite City hotels.

Holborn & the Inns of Court The old borough of Holborn (pronounced *Ho*-burn), which abuts the Square Mile southeast of Bloomsbury, and Temple, south of Holborn across the Strand, represents the heart of legal London—this is where you'll find the city's barristers, solicitors, and law clerks, operating out of four Inns of Court (legal associations that are part college, part club, and part hotel): Gray's Inn, Lincoln's Inn, Middle Temple, and Inner Temple. Still Dickensian in spirit, the Inns are otherworldly places to explore, away from London's traffic, with ancient courtyards, mazy passageways, and gas lamps.

Clerkenwell This neighborhood, north and a little west of the City, was the site of London's first hospital, and is the home of several early churches. In the 18th century, Clerkenwell declined into a muck-filled cattle yard, home to cheap gin distilleries and little else. A handful of hot restaurants and clubs have sprung up, and art galleries line St. John's Square and the fringe of Clerkenwell Green. The area is a good base for young and fashionable visitors, just a couple of stops on the Tube away from Oxford Street and a short walk from the Square Mile itself.

EAST LONDON

The East End, Hoxton & Dalston A multitude of slums formed east of the old city walls during the intense industrialization and urbanization of the 19th century, many of which were bombed out of existence during World War II. Cheap rents have attracted a certain type of young, design-savvy entrepreneur to some parts, and you'll now find lots of trendy bars, clubs, restaurants, and vintage clothing outlets. Much of the most fashionable life is found just north of the Square Mile, around **Hoxton Square** and its periphery, including the "Shoreditch Triangle," formed by Old Street, Great Eastern Street, and Shoreditch High Street. There's always plenty going on, making it a place to base yourself if you want to take advantage of the intense, fluid nightlife, but perhaps a little hectic if you prefer your 8 hours and an early start. Options for accommodations have grown (p. 193) and there are plenty of good, affordable places to eat, particularly in **Shoreditch** and **Dalston.**

Immediately east of the City, the redeveloped Spitalfields area boasts a number of great (and historic) markets, including a craft market still trading in the old **Spitalfields Market** (p. 152) building.

Brick Lane is the heart of London's Bangladeshi community, and still a great place for a curry. Farther east, the shiny stadia of **Olympic Park** (p. 176) represents the area's biggest development for a generation.

Docklands   In 1981, in the most ambitious scheme of its kind in Europe, the London Docklands Development Corporation (LDDC) was formed to redevelop the then-moribund dockyards of Wapping, the Isle of Dogs, the Royal Docks, and Surrey Docks. The area is bordered roughly by Tower Bridge to the west and London City Airport to the east. Despite some early setbacks and a couple of ill-timed recessions, the plan was ultimately successful. Many businesses have moved here; Thames-side warehouses have been converted to Manhattan-style lofts and museums, entertainment complexes, shops, and an ever-growing list of restaurants has popped up at this 21st-century river city in the making.

Canary Wharf, on the Isle of Dogs, is the heart of Docklands. This 28-hectare (69-acre) site is dominated by a 240-m (787-ft.) tower, One Canada Square, which remains the tallest building in the U.K. until the "Shard" is completed at London Bridge.

NORTH & NORTHWEST LONDON

King's Cross & St. Pancras   Long a seedy area on the fringe of central London, King's Cross is in the midst of a massive regeneration program. Millions of pounds are being ploughed into its decaying infrastructure. Six Tube lines convene underneath King's Cross Station, and it also provides direct links with airports at Gatwick (via regular rail services) and Heathrow (via the Tube). Adjacent St. Pancras International is the new transport hub for Eurostar services to Paris and Brussels, and one of the finest architectural icons of the Age of Steam, with a huge single-span roof—the largest in the world when it was built—gargoyles, and Gothic revival towers. Once pretty much the last place you'd want to base yourself, King's Cross is now no more (or less) dangerous than anywhere else in central London.

Camden   London's alternative heart lies just east of Regent's Park. Since the 1960s, its thicket of clubs and pubs have been at the forefront of a succession of—usually short-lived—musical scenes: Punk, Brit-pop, alt-folk, the embers of which often continue smoldering here some time after the wider blaze has died down. Camden's various sprawling markets (p. 152), which occupy a number of venues north of the Tube stop and sell a vast abundance of arts, crafts, and fashions, have turned the area into one of London's major tourist destinations, with tens of thousands pitching up here each weekend. It's a noisy, vibrant, crowded, and intense place, and for all those reasons, perhaps not the best area to base yourself unless you're here to party. In any case, Camden doesn't really have much of a hotel scene, although there are some good restaurants. Adjacent **Primrose Hill** is a pretty urban village of Victorian terrace houses rolling up a hill on the north side of Regent's Park. From the hill, some 78m (256 ft.) up, you have a panoramic sweep of central London to the southeast.

Hampstead   This residential suburb of north London, beloved by Keats and Hogarth, is a favorite excursion for Londoners. Everyone from Sigmund Freud and D. H. Lawrence to Anna Pavlova and John Le

Carré have lived here, and it's still one of the most desirable districts in the city. It has a few hotels and B&Bs, although it is quite far from central London. Hampstead's calling card is **Hampstead Heath** (p. 118), nearly 320 hectares (791 acres) of meadows, ponds, and woodland; it maintains its rural atmosphere despite being surrounded by cityscapes on all sides.

Highgate Along with Hampstead, Highgate is another choice north London residential area, particularly on or near Pond Square and along Highgate High Street. Once celebrated for its "sweet salutarie airs," Highgate has long been a desirable place for Londoners to live. Today most visitors come to see Highgate Cemetery (p. 119), the final resting place of Karl Marx and George Eliot.

SOUTHEAST LONDON—GREENWICH

In the southeast of London, this suburb, which contains the prime meridian—"zero" for the reckoning of terrestrial longitudes—enjoyed its first heyday under the Tudors. King Henry VIII and both of his daughters, Queens Mary I and Elizabeth I, were born here. Greenwich Palace, Henry's favorite, is long gone, though, replaced by a hospital for sailors during its second great age, which saw it emerge in the 18th and 19th centuries as one of the country's main naval centers. Today's visitors come to this lovely port village for nautical sights, including the **National Maritime Museum** (p. 120), and some niche shopping opportunities (p. 152).

GETTING AROUND
By Public Transportation

The first London word that any visitor needs to learn is "Oyster." The **Oyster Card** is a plastic smartcard that is your gateway to pretty much every form of London public transport. You can still pay to use all these services with cash, but an Oyster offers substantial savings on just about every journey. The pay-as-you-go card costs £5 for adults from any Tube or major rail station—a charge that's refundable if you return the card after use. As well as these significant discounts, your daily bill for using an Oyster is capped at the price of an equivalent 1-Day Travelcard (see below), so there's no longer any need to calculate in advance whether to buy a discounted multi-trip travel ticket. Basically, if you're staying more than a day or so, and plan to use London's public transport network, then investing in an Oyster is a no-brainer. It saves you time and money.

To use an Oyster, simply swipe it over the yellow card-reader that guards the entry/exit gates at Tube and rail stations. You should always swipe your Oyster card as you leave the station, even if the gate is open, otherwise you will get charged maximum fare next time you use your card because you haven't "completed" your previous journey. On the bus you'll find the reader next to the driver, or opposite any of the sets of doors on London's long "bendy buses." If you're caught traveling without having swiped your Oyster, you're liable for an on-the-spot fine.

You can order an Oyster in advance, preloaded with as much credit as you like, from **www.tfl.gov.uk/oyster**. Postage to the U.K. is free, but worldwide delivery costs £4. It's cheaper for overseas residents to wait and purchase from the first Tube station they encounter. To top-up your balance, use cash or a credit card at any Oyster machine, which you'll find inside most London rail stations, at any of a network of around 4,000 newsagents citywide (see http://ticketstoplocator.tfl.gov.uk), or online if you register your card in advance.

Central London

LONDON | Getting Around

NW3

PRIMROSE HILL

PRIMROSE HILL

Camden Town

Camden High St.

Regent's Canal

CAMDEN TOWN

Regent's Park Road

Prince Albert Rd.

Avenue Rd.

Abbey Road

London Zoo

Albany St.

Mornington Crescent

St. Pancras Station

British Library

KILBURN

NW8

St. John's Wood

Wellington Rd.

ST. JOHN'S WOOD

Regent's Canal

REGENT'S PARK

NW1

Hampstead Rd.

Eversholt St.

Euston

Euston Station

Maida Vale

Lord's Cricket Ground

Boating Lake

QUEEN MARY'S GARDENS

Albany St.

Euston Sq.

Woburn Pl.

PICCADILLY

MAIDA VALE

W9

Warwick Avenue

St. John's Wood Rd.

Maida Vale Rd.

Park Rd.

Church St.

METROPOLITAN JUBILEE

CIRCLE. METRO. HAMMERSMITH

Euston Rd.

Gower St.

WC1

Russell Sq.

BLOOMSBURY

ST. MARY'S CHURCHYARD

Edgware Rd.

Marylebone Station

Baker St.

Marylebone Rd.

Regent's Park

Great Portland St.

Tottenham Court Rd.

Goodge St.

British Museum

Harrow Rd.

Paddington

Edgware Rd.

Marylebone

Marylebone

MARYLEBONE

Portland Pl.

Gt. Portland St.

FITZROVIA

Goodge St.

New Oxford St.

HAMMERSMITH & CITY

Paddington Station

Praed St.

PADDINGTON

WESTMINSTER

Edgware Rd.

Baker St.

Marylebone High St.

Wigmore St.

W1

Regent St.

Oxford St.

Tottenham Court Rd.

Charing Cross Rd.

Monmouth St.

W2

Spring St.

Paddington

Westbourne Terr.

Edgware Rd.

Seymour St.

Orchard St.

Bond St.

Oxford St.

Oxford Circus

CENTRAL

Oxford St.

BAKERLOO

SOHO

WC2

BAYSWATER

CENTRAL

Bayswater Rd.

Marble Arch

JUBILEE

VICTORIA

Regent St.

Piccadilly Circus

Shaftesbury Ave.

Leicester Sq.

National Gallery

Charing Cross

Bayswater Rd.

Lancaster Gate

The Long Water

HYDE PARK

Park Ln.

MAYFAIR

PICCADILLY

Trafalgar Square

KENSINGTON GARDENS

Round Pond

The Serpentine

PICCADILLY

Green Park

Piccadilly

ST. JAMES'S

Pall Mall

The Mall

Whitehall

Kensington Palace

W8

Albert Memorial

Hyde Park Corner

GREEN PARK

St. James's Palace

ST. JAMES'S PARK

10 Downing Street

Kensington Gore Rd.

Knightsbridge

Hyde Park Corner

Constitution Hill

Queen Victoria Memorial

Birdcage Walk

Westminster

Royal Albert Hall

Exhibition Rd.

Knightsbridge

Buckingham Palace

St. James's Park

CIRCLE. DISTRICT

Westminster Abbey

KENSINGTON

Science Museum

KNIGHTS-BRIDGE

Brompton Rd.

Harrods

PALACE GARDENS

Queen Victoria Memorial

WESTMINSTER

Natural History Museum

Imperial College

Victoria & Albert Museum

Pont Street

Belgrave Pl.

Buckingham Palace Rd.

Westminster Cathedral

SW1

Gloucester Rd.

Cromwell Rd.

South Kensington

BROMPTON

Sloane St.

Eaton Sq.

BELGRAVIA

Victoria

Victoria Station

VICTORIA

Tate Britain

Gloucester Rd.

South Kensington

Old Brompton Rd.

CIRCLE. DISTRICT

Sloane Sq.

Ebury St.

Victoria Coach Station

Vauxhall Bridge Rd.

SW7

SOUTH KENSINGTON

SW5

KENSINGTON & CHELSEA

King's Rd.

Pimlico Rd.

Warwick Way

Belgrave Rd.

PIMLICO

Pimlico

EARL'S COURT

CHELSEA

SW3

Sutherland St.

Lupus St.

Fulham Road

Beaufort St.

King's Rd.

Oakley St.

Royal Hospital Rd.

Chelsea Bridge Rd.

Grosvenor Rd.

Vauxhall Bridge

SW10

Albert Bridge

Chelsea Embankment

River Thames

BATTERSEA PARK

Chelsea Bridge

Nine Elms Lane

0 — 1/2 mi

0 — 1/2 km

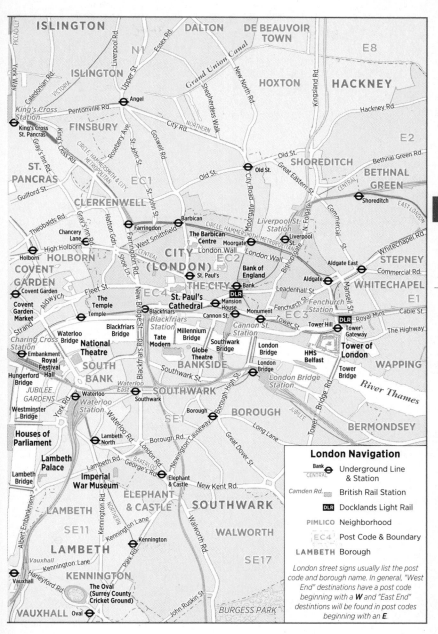

London Navigation

Bank CENTRAL	Underground Line & Station
Camden Rd.	British Rail Station
DLR	Docklands Light Rail
PIMLICO	Neighborhood
EC4	Post Code & Boundary
LAMBETH	Borough

*London street signs usually list the post code and borough name. In general, "West End" destinations have a post code beginning with a **W** and "East End" destinations will be found in post codes beginning with an **E**.*

THE TUBE & DOCKLANDS LIGHT RAILWAY The **"Tube"** is the quickest and easiest way to move around the capital. All Tube stations are clearly marked with a red circle and blue crossbar. There are 10 extensive lines, plus the short Waterloo & City line linking Waterloo and Bank, all of which are conveniently color-coded and clearly mapped on the walls of every Tube station. The Tube generally operates Monday to Saturday 5am to 12:30am, Sunday 7:30am to 11:30pm. The above-ground extension of the Tube that links the City with points around the East End and Docklands, including London City Airport, is known as the **Docklands Light Railway,** or "DLR." This metro system is, to all intents and purposes, integrated with the Tube.

Tickets for the Tube operate on a system of six fare zones. The fare zones radiate in concentric rings from the central Zone 1, which is where most visitors spend the majority of their time. Zone 1 covers the area from Liverpool Street in the east to Notting Hill in the west, and from Waterloo in the south to Baker Street, Euston, and King's Cross in the north. Tube maps should be available at any Tube station. You can also download one before your trip from the excellent Transport for London (TfL) website, at **www.tfl.gov.uk/assets/downloads/standard-tube-map.pdf** or download one of the many London Tube apps from the appropriate app store. A 24-hour information service is also available at ✆ **0843/222-1234.** The best planning tool is the TfL Journey Planner, online at **www.tfl.gov.uk/journeyplanner.**

If you don't have an Oyster (see above), you can get your ticket at a vending machine or a ticket window. But note the prices: The cash fare for travel across up to three zones is £4, rising to £5 to travel across six zones. A journey from anywhere in zones 1 or 2 to anywhere else in zones 1 or 2 using Oyster pay-as-you-go costs £1.90 outside peak hours, £2.50 before 9:30am. Oyster will get you across all six zones for £2.70 after 9:30am. On all ticketed journeys, you can transfer as many times as you like as long as you stay on the Tube or DLR network.

THE BUS NETWORK London's buses can be a delightful way to navigate the city. Not only are they regular, efficient, and—late nights aside—comfortable, but also cheap compared to the Tube system. Buses also have the distinct advantage of allowing you to see where you're going—no need for an open-topped bus tour when you can ride the upper deck of an old-fashioned heritage **Routemaster** from Knightsbridge to Trafalgar Square on route no. 9, or Regent Street to St. Paul's and the Tower of London on the no. 15. Other excellent "sightseeing" routes include the no. 8 (from Oxford Circus to the Bank of England) and the no. 11 (from Victoria Station, through Parliament Square and Trafalgar Square to Bank).

Unfortunately, the bewildering array of services and routes deters many visitors—and even some locals. If you plan to keep largely to the center, the excellent "Key bus routes in central London" map borrows a few design tricks from the Tube map to help first-timers out. It's also available to download from **www.tfl.gov.uk/assets/downloads/visitor-bus-route-map.pdf**.

Unlike on the Tube, fares do not vary according to distance traveled—but if you transfer buses, you must pay again. A single journey from anywhere to anywhere costs £2.20 with cash, £1.30 with an Oyster Card. You can travel on buses all day with an Oyster for £4.

Buses generally run from 5am to just after midnight. Some run 24 hours, but other popular routes are served by **night buses,** running once every half-hour or so during the night, and with service numbers prefixed by an "N." For **open-top bus tours** of the city, see "Special Interest Tours," p. 45.

KIDS' travel DISCOUNTS

As long as they're accompanied by an adult, children under 10 travel free on just about everything public, including Tube, Overground, DLR, bus, and regular rail services. Children in this age bracket who look older than 10 should carry photo ID. Children aged 11 to 15 carrying an **11–15 Zip Oyster photocard** travel free on buses and trams, and pay child fare on Tube, Overground, DLR, and regular rail services—up to a maximum of £1.30 for unlimited off-peak journeys in

one day. To obtain a Zip Oyster photocard, apply online at **www.tfl.gov.uk/zip**. There's an administration fee of £10, and you'll need to upload a photo. Postage is free to U.K. addresses, and overseas visitors can arrange to collect their card at any Travel Information Centre. It's a similar drill for anyone aged 16 to 18. The **16+ Zip Oyster photocard** gets you single tickets at half the adult price on bus, Tube, tram, and Overground services, as well as child-fare Travelcards.

THE OVERGROUND & OTHER RAIL SERVICES   The remarkable improvements in London's surface rail network have been the big transport story of recent years. Especially useful for visitors to south and east London is the **London Overground** (marked in orange on most transport maps). The Overground connects Kew in southwest London with Highbury in North London, Stratford in East London adjacent to the Olympic Park, as well as Whitechapel and Wapping in the East End, and then points south of the river as far as Croydon. The new, air-conditioned carriages and upgraded track ensure an efficient, comfortable ride. Oyster Cards are valid on Overground services. See **www.tfl.gov.uk/overground** for more. Oyster Cards are also valid on the remainder of London's surface rail network—encompassing a vast web of commuter and local services.

TRAVELCARDS   For the **1-Day Off-Peak Travelcard,** valid for travel anywhere within zones 1 and 2 after 9:30am, the cost is £6.60 for adults or £3 for children aged 5 to 15. **One-Week Travelcards** cost adults £27.60 for travel in zones 1 and 2. For more Travelcard prices, visit **www.tfl.gov.uk/tickets**.

By Taxi

London "black cab" taxi drivers must pass a series of tests known as "the Knowledge," and cabbies generally know every London street within 6 miles of Charing Cross. You can pick up a taxi either by heading for a cab rank—stations, marquees of West End hotels and department stores, and major attractions all have them—or by hailing one in the street. The taxi is available if the yellow taxi sign on its roof is lit.

Black-taxi meters start at £2.20, with increments of £2 or more per mile thereafter, based on distance and elapsed time. Surcharges are imposed after 8pm and on weekends and public holidays. Expect a mile-long journey to average around £6 to £8, a 2-mile journey around £8 to £12, and so on. There's no need to tip, although you may like to round the fare upward if you receive friendly service. To book a black cab, phone **One-Number Taxi** on ℂ **0871/871-8710.** There's a £2 booking fee.

Minicabs are also plentiful, and are useful when regular taxis are scarce, as is often the case in the suburbs or late at night. These cabs are usually meterless, so do discuss the fare in advance. If you text CAB to ℂ **60835,** TfL's Cabwise service will text you back with the telephone number of the nearest two licensed minicab offices.

By Boat

Once London's watery highway, the River Thames is these days more suited to a sightseeing trip than an A-to-B journey. However, it is used by some Docklands commuters, and that commuter service is as fun a way as any to get to the maritime sights of Greenwich (p. 120). **Thames Clippers** (www.thamesclippers.com) runs a year-round fleet of catamarans between the London Eye Pier and North Greenwich Pier, stopping at Embankment Pier, Bankside Pier, Tower Millennium Pier, Canary Wharf Pier, and Greenwich Pier, among others. Services run every 20 to 30 minutes for most of the day; journey time from Embankment to Greenwich is 35 minutes. An adult single costs £5.50, £5 with an Oyster Card, £3.70 if you hold a valid Travelcard, and £2.80 for children aged 5 to 15. A **River Roamer,** allowing unlimited travel after 10am through the day—or all-day at weekends—costs £12.60, £8.40 for Travelcard holders, and £6.30 for children. A Family River Roamer costs £26.50. Buy online, on board, or at any of the piers. There's also a separate **Tate-to-Tate** service that connects Tate Modern, in Bankside, with Tate Britain, in Pimlico. Tickets cost £5, and boats depart each end at least hourly, all day between 10am and 5pm.

For trips upriver to Hampton Court and Kew, see "River Cruises Along the Thames," p. 123.

By Bicycle

The **Barclays Cycle Hire scheme** (www.tfl.gov.uk/barclayscyclehire) was launched with great fanfare in 2010. Anyone can rent a so-called "Boris Bike"—jocularly named after incumbent mayor, Boris Johnson—from any of the hundreds of docking stations dotted around the center from Whitechapel to Olympia, and Hoxton to the Oval. Stations are scheduled to spread farther east during early 2012. There's no need to return the bike to the same docking station you collected it from, making the scheme ideal for short-range, spontaneous tourism. Charges are made up of a fixed access fee—£1 per day or £5 per week—and a usage fee—it's free to rent a bike for 30 minutes, £1 for an hour, £6 for 2 hours. Buy access with a credit or debit card at the docking station or join online. The bikes are suited to anyone aged 14 or over.

You should always ride London's roads with extreme care. For more on cycling in London, see **www.tfl.gov.uk/cycling**.

[FastFACTS] LONDON

Area Codes The country code for Great Britain is **44**. The area code for London is **020** (omit the initial "0" if calling from overseas). The full telephone number is then usually eight digits long. As a general rule, businesses and homes in central London have numbers beginning with a **7;** those farther out begin with an **8**.

Doctors If you need a non-emergency doctor, your hotel can recommend one, or you can contact your embassy or consulate. Failing that, try the G.P. (General Practitioner) finder at **www.nhsdirect.nhs.uk**. North American members of the **International Association for Medical Assistance to Travelers (IAMAT;** ℂ **716/754-4883,** or

416/652-0137 in Canada; www.iamat.org) can consult that organization for lists of local approved doctors. *Note:* U.S. and Canadian visitors who become ill while they're in London are eligible only for free *emergency* care. For other treatment, including follow-up care, you'll be asked to pay.

Emergencies Dial ℂ **999** for police, fire, or

ambulance. Give your name and state the nature of the emergency. Dialing ⓒ **112** also connects you to the local emergency services anywhere in the E.U.

Hospitals There are 24-hour, walk-in Accident & Emergency departments at the following central hospitals: **University College London Hospital,** 235 Euston Road, London NW1 2BU (ⓒ **020/3456-7890;** www.uclh.nhs.uk; Tube: Warren St.); **St. Thomas' Hospital,** Westminster Bridge Road (entrance on Lambeth Palace Road), London SE1 7EH (ⓒ **020/7188-7188;** www.guysand stthomas.nhs.uk; Tube: Westminster or Waterloo).

The **NHS Choices** website (www.nhs.uk) has a search facility that enables you to locate your nearest Accident & Emergency department wherever you are in the U.K. In a medical emergency, you should dial ⓒ **999.**

Maps If you plan to explore London in any depth, you'll need a detailed street map with a street index. We use and recommend the *London A to Z,* available in various sizes at newsagents and bookstores citywide.

Police London has two official police forces, the City of London police (www.cityoflondon.police. uk) whose remit covers the

"Square Mile" and its 8,600 residents; and the Metropolitan Police ("the Met"), which covers the rest of the capital and is split into separate borough commands for operational purposes. Non-emergency contact numbers and opening hours for all the Met's local police stations are listed at **www. met.police.uk/local**. Losses, thefts, and other criminal matters should be reported at the nearest police station immediately. You will be given a crime number, which your travel insurer will request if you make a claim against any losses. Dial ⓒ **999** or 112 if the matter is serious.

EXPLORING LONDON

In the listings below, children's prices generally apply to those 15 and under. To qualify for a senior discount, you must be 60 or older. Students must present a student ID to get discounts. In addition to closing on public holidays, many attractions close between Christmas and New Year, so always check ahead if visiting at that time. All museums are closed Good Friday, December 25 and 26, and New Year's Day.

The West End

Banqueting House ★ HISTORIC SITE   This sumptuous dining chamber is the only remaining part of the once-mighty Whitehall Palace. Its commission in the early 17th century by James I marked both the arrival of Renaissance architecture in England and a particular high point for the Stuart Dynasty, which had recently become the first royal family to rule both England and Scotland. However, just a few decades later, in 1649, Banqueting House would provide the setting for the dynasty's lowest ebb when James's successor, Charles I, fresh from his defeat in the English Civil Wars, was executed in front of the building.

Today the main attraction of this great feasting hall is not the food—which you won't be able to sample unless you're a visiting head of state—but the ceiling paintings by Rubens that imagine James I crowned amid a swirling mass of cherubic flesh. The house often closes on short notice for official events, so it's best to call in advance. *Insider tip:* Classical concerts are held here on the first Monday of each month (Aug excepted). The website lists the upcoming program; book by calling ⓒ **020/3166-6153.**

Whitehall Palace, Horse Guards Ave., SW1. ⓒ **0844/482-7777.** www.hrp.org.uk/banquetinghouse. Admission £4.80 adults, £4 seniors and students, free children 15 and under. Mon–Sat 10am–5pm (last admission 4:30pm). Tube: Westminster or Embankment.

Attractions, Hotels & Restaurants in the West End

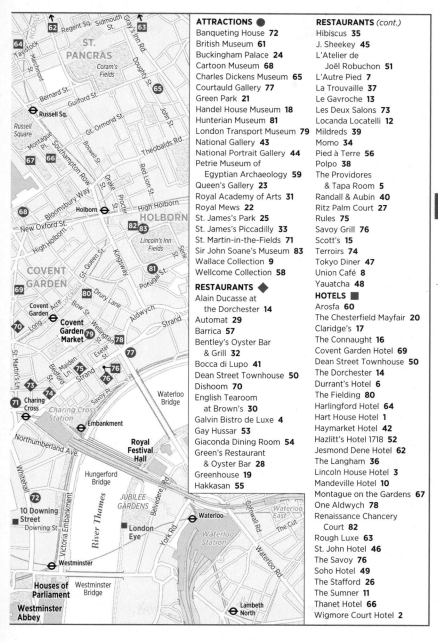

ATTRACTIONS ●

Banqueting House **72**
British Museum **61**
Buckingham Palace **24**
Cartoon Museum **68**
Charles Dickens Museum **65**
Courtauld Gallery **77**
Green Park **21**
Handel House Museum **18**
Hunterian Museum **81**
London Transport Museum **79**
National Gallery **43**
National Portrait Gallery **44**
Petrie Museum of
    Egyptian Archaeology **59**
Queen's Gallery **23**
Royal Academy of Arts **31**
Royal Mews **22**
St. James's Park **25**
St. James's Piccadilly **33**
St. Martin-in-the-Fields **71**
Sir John Soane's Museum **83**
Wallace Collection **9**
Wellcome Collection **58**

RESTAURANTS ◆

Alain Ducasse at
    the Dorchester **14**
Automat **29**
Barrica **57**
Bentley's Oyster Bar
    & Grill **32**
Bocca di Lupo **41**
Dean Street Townhouse **50**
Dishoom **70**
English Tearoom
    at Brown's **30**
Galvin Bistro de Luxe **4**
Gay Hussar **53**
Giaconda Dining Room **54**
Green's Restaurant
    & Oyster Bar **28**
Greenhouse **19**
Hakkasan **55**

RESTAURANTS *(cont.)*

Hibiscus **35**
J. Sheekey **45**
L'Atelier de
    Joël Robuchon **51**
L'Autre Pied **7**
La Trouvaille **37**
Le Gavroche **13**
Les Deux Salons **73**
Locanda Locatelli **12**
Mildreds **39**
Momo **34**
Pied à Terre **56**
Polpo **38**
The Providores
    & Tapa Room **5**
Randall & Aubin **40**
Ritz Palm Court **27**
Rules **75**
Savoy Grill **76**
Scott's **15**
Terroirs **74**
Tokyo Diner **47**
Union Café **8**
Yauatcha **48**

HOTELS ■

Arosfa **60**
The Chesterfield Mayfair **20**
Claridge's **17**
The Connaught **16**
Covent Garden Hotel **69**
Dean Street Townhouse **50**
The Dorchester **14**
Durrant's Hotel **6**
The Fielding **80**
Harlingford Hotel **64**
Hart House Hotel **1**
Haymarket Hotel **42**
Hazlitt's Hotel 1718 **52**
Jesmond Dene Hotel **62**
The Langham **36**
Lincoln House Hotel **3**
Mandeville Hotel **10**
Montague on the Gardens **67**
One Aldwych **78**
Renaissance Chancery
    Court **82**
Rough Luxe **63**
St. John Hotel **46**
The Savoy **76**
Soho Hotel **49**
The Stafford **26**
The Sumner **11**
Thanet Hotel **66**
Wigmore Court Hotel **2**

British Museum ★★★ ☺ MUSEUM The "BM" was born in the age of Enlightenment and Empire, the progeny of two great British desires—the desire for knowledge and the desire for other people's possessions. In the 18th and 19th centuries, the British upper classes traveled across the globe, uncovering the artifacts of distant civilizations, packing them in crates, and shipping them home. Their acquisitions formed the basis of the museum's collection, which has since been built into one of the world's largest and finest.

The collection is arranged along roughly geographical lines, so you could order your tour accordingly, taking in the **Rosetta Stone** from Egypt (the object that finally enabled scholars to decipher hieroglyphics), the **Elgin (or Parthenon) Marbles** from Ancient Greece, or the treasures of a 7th-century Saxon ship burial from **Sutton Hoo,** in nearby Suffolk. But there's so much more—Babylonian astronomical instruments, giants heads from Easter Island, totem poles from Canada, mummies from Egyptian tombs, Chinese sculptures, Indian texts, Roman statues, African art . . . the list goes on. In fact, the museum has more objects in storage than it ever does on display.

And if that wasn't enough, the BM hosts a succession of blockbuster temporary exhibitions, which are often staged in the **Reading Room,** the former home of the British Library. It lies at the center of the **Great Court,** the building's central courtyard, which is topped by a giant glass roof designed by Foster and Partners, and boasts various cafes and picnic areas.

Of course you could always take the easy option, and let someone else decide what you should see. Free half-hour tours (known as "Eye Opener Tours") to different sections of the museum are given every 15 to 30 minutes from 11am to 3:45pm. The museum also provides plenty of extra fun for younger visitors, mostly free, including activity backpacks (free), trail leaflets (free), handling sessions (free), multimedia guides (£3), and drop-in family events.

Great Russell St., WC1. ☎ **020/7323-8299.** www.britishmuseum.org. Free admission. Sat–Wed 10am–5:30pm; Thurs–Fri 10am–8:30pm. Tube: Holborn, Tottenham Court Rd., Goodge St., or Russell Sq.

Buckingham Palace ★ ☺ ♛ ROYAL BUILDING The setting is glorious, sat between two great sweeping parks (Green and St. James's) at the end of an elegant tree-lined boulevard (The Mall), but the palace itself is a little… *meh*. It's big, certainly and clearly expensive, but it's also a touch boxy and uninspiring. There's little fantasy here. For generations brought up on Disney, it doesn't really look like a palace; more like a very large Georgian-Victorian home, which essentially is what it is. Windsor (p. 199), just outside the city, is much more fairytale like. But this is the principal London home of the monarch, and has been since the accession of Queen Victoria in the mid-19th century, which is what draws the crowds.

The first house to stand on this site was built by the Duke of Buckingham in 1702. It was acquired by George II in 1761 and expanded and renovated throughout the 19th century, first by the flamboyant John Nash for George IV, and later by the more dour Edward Blore (dubbed "Blore the Bore") for Victoria. A new facade—including the famous balcony from which the royal family waves to the masses on major royal occasions—was added in 1913.

Although the exterior is no great shakes, the interior has a lot more going on. For 8 weeks in August and September, while the royals are holidaying elsewhere, you can look for yourself. Tours visit a small selection of the palace's 600-plus rooms, including the Grand Staircase, the Throne Room, the Picture Gallery (which displays masterpieces by Van Dyck, Rembrandt, Rubens, and others) and the lavish State Rooms, where the Queen entertains heads of government with grand formal banquets. You can also take a walk along a 3-mile path through 40 acres of landscaped gardens.

Outside of the summer months, the only parts of the palace open to the public are the **Queen's Gallery** (p. 91) and the **Royal Mews** (p. 91).

Buckingham Palace is also the setting for a daily dose of public pageantry, the **Changing of the Guard.** Pretty much every guidebook says the same thing about the ceremony—it's terribly British and a bit dull, and who are we to buck the trend? The needlessly elaborate ceremony for changing the 40 men guarding Buckingham Palace with another contingent from Wellington Barracks only exists for the benefit of visitors these days. It's actually interesting for about 5 minutes—with bearskin-wearing, red-coated soldiers, music from the marching band, shouted orders, complicated marching patterns. The trouble is the whole thing lasts for around 40 minutes—and if you want a decent vantage point, you'll need to turn up at least 1 hour early.

A much more accessible piece of pageantry can be seen at nearby **Horse Guards Parade** (p. 97) in Whitehall.

At end of The Mall. ✆ **020/7766-7300.** www.royalcollection.org.uk. Palace tours £17.50 adults, £16 seniors and students, £10 children 5–16, £46 family ticket, free for ages 4 and under; Changing of the Guard free. Aug 1–Sept 25 (dates can vary), and additional dates may be added. Daily 9:45am–6pm. Changing of the Guard daily May–July at 11:30am and alternating days for the rest of the year at 11am. Tube: St. James's Park, Green Park, or Victoria.

Cartoon Museum ★★ 🎒 MUSEUM Just around the corner from the British Museum, this is the capital's first and only museum dedicated to the great British traditions of cartooning, caricaturing, and comics. Displays are arranged chronologically, beginning in the early 18th century with the first British attempts at the new art form of "*caricatura*," recently imported from Italy. From here it traces the development of the great cartoonists of the age, such as William Hogarth and George Cruikshank, whose work helped shine a light on the political and social hypocrisies of the day. The displays then take in the great magazine boom of the 19th and 20th centuries, which saw publications such as *Punch* setting the

The Guard Doesn't Change Every Day

The ceremony begins at 11:30am sharp every day between May and July, and on alternate days for the rest of the year—in theory, anyway. However, it's often canceled in bad weather, which shows just what an unnecessary ceremony it is. If it looks like it's going to rain, it's probably best to head somewhere else instead.

standard for political cartooning, and onto the works of modern satirists, including Steve Bell and Gerald Scarfe.

35 Little Russell St., WC1. ✆ **020/7580-8155.** www.cartoonmuseum.org. Admission £5.50 adults, £4 seniors, £3 students, free for children 17 and under. Tues–Sat 10:30am–5:30pm; Sun noon–5:30pm. Tube: Tottenham Court Rd. or Holborn.

Charles Dickens Museum ★ MUSEUM   This is the great novelist's only surviving London address. Although he lived here for just a few years, from 1837 until 1840, this most prolific of authors still found the time to churn out several classics, including *Nicholas Nickleby, Oliver Twist, Pickwick Papers, The Old Curiosity Shop,* and *Barnaby Rudge.* Revamped and expanded to celebrate the bicentenary of Dickens' birth in 2012, the museum's reconstructed interiors contain his study, manuscripts, and personal effects. On Wednesday afternoons you can, under careful supervision, handle some of his possessions and even write with his (presumably reinforced) quill pen.

48 Doughty St., WC1. ✆ **020/7405-2127.** www.dickensmuseum.com. Admission £6 adults, £4.50 students and seniors, £3 children, £15 family ticket. Mon–Sat 10am–5pm; Sun 11am–5pm. Tube: Russell Sq., Chancery Lane, or Holborn.

Courtauld Gallery ★ GALLERY   Like a mini-National Gallery, the Courtauld is one of the capital's finest small art museums. It holds an intense collection of works, covering all periods from the Renaissance to the 20th century, although the focus is very much on **Impressionism** and **Post-Impressionism** with works by Monet, Renoir, Gaugin, Van Gogh (including his *Self-Portrait with Bandaged Ear*), and Manet (it holds his final painting, *A Bar at the Folies-Bergère*). The Kandinskys on the top floor are also well worth seeking out. *Insider tip:* If money is a bit tight, try to visit on Monday morning when entry is free (until 2pm); if you stick around there's also a free lecture about the collection at 1:15pm.

Somerset House, Strand, WC2. ✆ **020/7872-0220.** www.courtauld.ac.uk. Admission £6 adults, £4.50 seniors and international students, free for children 17 and under, UK students, and for all Mon till 2pm. Daily 10am–6pm. Tube: Covent Garden, Temple, or Waterloo.

Green Park ★ ☺ PARK   This most basic of London's great Royal Parks has an almost zen-like simplicity to it. There are no statues, water features, or adventure playgrounds here, just acres of rolling green lawns and tall trees—plus, in summer, scores of local workers sunning their lunch hour away either on the grass or on the stripy **deckchairs** (£1.50) that are the park's only formal facility. In spring the park's color scheme broadens slightly, when hosts of bright yellow daffodils pop into bloom.

Piccadilly, SW1. ✆ **020/7930-1793.** www.royalparks.org.uk/parks/green_park. Free admission. Open 24 hours. Tube: Green Park.

Handel House Museum ★ HISTORIC HOME   Two musicians, separated by a couple of hundred years, and with profoundly different approaches to their art—albeit both hugely influential in their own way—made their homes on Brook Street, in the heart of Mayfair. The first was George Frederic Handel (1685–1759), the German composer who moved to Britain aged 25 and settled at this address in 1723. He remained here for the rest of his life, creating the scores for many of his most famous works, including the Messiah and Music for Royal Fireworks. He was followed in 1968 by the American guitarist, **Jimi Hendrix,** who lived (some of the time) next door at number 23 with his English girlfriend until his death in 1970.

Both properties are now owned by the Handel House Museum, although only Handel's former home is currently open to the public. It's been meticulously restored to its Georgian prime with period fixtures, fittings, and fabrics. Exhibits include two antique harpsichords, various scores, and a canopied bedroom from 1720.

Classical recitals are given every Thursday (plus the occasional Tues), between 6:30 and 7:30pm and cost £9 (£5 for students). The program is mainly Handel favorites played by harpsichordists, baroque quartets, and the like, although Hendrix tunes (done in a classical style) crop up occasionally.

25 Brook St., W1. *C* **020/7495-1685.** www.handelhouse.org. Admission £5 adults, £4.50 students and seniors, £2 children 5–15. Free for children 4 and under, and all children on Sat and Sun. Tues–Sat 10am–6pm (until 8pm Thurs); Sun noon–6pm. Tube: Bond St.

Hunterian Museum ★ MUSEUM   The shiny cases and cabinets of the Hunterian may give it a superficially modern, antiseptic feel, but this is a collection with its roots firmly in the past—and gore very much at its heart. It's made up of medical oddities and curiosities, most of them assembled in the late 18th century by John Hunter, the physician to "mad" King George III, for the purposes of instructing medical students. Bizarre highlights include various body parts pickled in jars (both human and animal), gruesome-looking teaching models (such as the lacquered systems of arteries and veins stuck onto wooden boards), skeletons of "dwarfs" and "giants," and some horror-inducing items of surgical equipment. Its grimly fascinating stuff. Free guided tours of the collection take place every Wednesday at 1pm.

Royal College of Surgeons, Lincoln's Inn Fields, WC2. *C* **020/7869-6560.** www.rcseng.ac.uk. Free admission. Tues–Sat 10am–5pm. Tube: Holborn.

London Transport Museum ★★ ☺ MUSEUM   Arranged more or less chronologically, this museum, housed in the swish glass-and-iron confines of Covent Garden's former flower market, traces the history of the capital's transport network from the days of steam and horse power to the green technologies of today. There are some wonderful old contraptions on display, including a reconstruction of an 1829 omnibus, a steam locomotive that ran along the world's first underground railway, and London's first trolleybus.

In addition to all the impressive hardware, the museum has displays on the often-overlooked aesthetics of public transport, particularly the signs, posters, and logos that together provided London Transport with such a clear graphic sensibility in the early 20th century. Perhaps the finest example of this is Harry Beck's 1931 London Tube map, one of the most distinctive and user-friendly pieces of public design ever created.

There's lots of great stuff for kids here, too, including a hands-on gallery where they can climb aboard miniature buses, trams, trains, and tubes, and trails to pick up at the front desk. *Insider tip:* The £13.50 entrance fee entitles you to unlimited visits over a 12-month period—hang on to your ticket.

Covent Garden Piazza, WC2. *C* **020/7379-6344.** www.ltmuseum.co.uk. Admission £13.50 adults, £10 seniors and students, free for children 15 and under. Sat–Thurs 10am–6pm; Fri 11am–6pm (last admission 5:15pm). Tube: Covent Garden.

National Gallery ★★★ ☺ GALLERY   Its collection may not be of quite the same monumental scale as some of Europe's other great galleries, such as the Louvre, the Prado, or the Uffizi, but for the sheer skill of its display and arrangement, the

National surpasses its counterparts. And the gallery's 2,300-plus paintings would still take some considerable time to view in their entirety—certainly a good deal longer than the gallery's original collection, which consisted of just 38 works. It was founded in 1824 by the British government, and gradually built up via a combination of private bequests and purchases.

Today the collection provides a comprehensive overview of the development of Western art from the mid-1200s to 1900, with most major artists and movements of the period represented.

The layout is straightforwardly chronological. Passing through the sturdy neoclassical facade on Trafalgar Square, you turn left to find the gallery's oldest works, housed, by way of contrast, in its newest section, the 1990s-built **Sainsbury Wing.** It covers the period from 1250 to 1500, including paintings by such Renaissance and pre-Renaissance greats as Giotto, Piero della Francesca, Botticelli, Leonardo da Vinci, and Van Eyck (including his famed *Arnolfini Portrait*).

The chronology then moves onto the West Wing, covering 1500 to 1600 and filled with European Old Masters, such as Titian, Raphael, El Greco, and Hans Holbein. Next in line is the North Wing (1600–1700), where highlights include a Rembrandt self-portrait and works by Caravaggio and Velázquez, with things culminating in the East Wing (1700–1900), with a celebrated selection of Impressionist and Post-Impressionist paintings, including various water-lilies by Monet, Van Gogh's *Sunflowers*, and Renoir's *Les Parapluies* (The Umbrellas)—some of the gallery's most popular (not to say most valuable) paintings.

If you can't decide where to begin, try joining a free 1-hour taster tour of the collection given every day at 11:30am and 2:30pm. Children's trails are available for £1 from the front desk (or can be downloaded for free in advance from the website).

Trafalgar Sq., WC2. ℰ **020/7747-2885.** www.nationalgallery.org.uk. Free admission; fee charged for temporary exhibitions. Sat–Thurs 10am–6pm; Fri 10am–9pm. Tube: Charing Cross or Leicester Sq.

National Portrait Gallery ★★ ☺ GALLERY Most galleries acquire their collections according to some notion of quality, with the aim of displaying the finest works of a particular artist, movement, or period. Not so the "NPG," where the collection is based not so much on ability as identity. Pictures have been chosen on the basis of who the subject is, not how well they've been captured by the artist. As a result, the works vary hugely in quality, and have been rendered in a great mish-mash of styles and mediums, including oil paintings, photographs, and collages. The result is rather jolly and exuberant, like a giant scrapbook of the nation.

You'll pass Tudor kings and queens (including a study of Henry VIII by Holbein), great writers and thinkers (look out for Shakespeare sporting a natty gold earring, a portly looking Samuel Johnson by Sir Joshua Reynolds, and the Brontë sisters as captured by their brother, Bramwell), as well as the musicians, movie stars, politicians, and sporting royalty of today. However, if you need a little help working out who's who, free "Portrait of the Day" talks are given every Saturday at midday. This is a great place to hang out on Thursdays and Fridays, when the gallery (as well as its cafe, bar, and restaurant) stays open till 9pm, laying on art workshops and concerts—typically classical, jazz, or blues. *Insider tip:* The NPG's **Portrait Restaurant** has one of London's great "secret" views, out over Trafalgar Square toward the Houses of Parliament.

St. Martin's Place, WC2. ℰ **020/7306-0055.** www.npg.org.uk. Free admission; fee charged for temporary exhibitions. Sat–Wed 10am–6pm; Thurs–Fri 10am–9pm. Tube: Charing Cross or Leicester Sq.

Petrie Museum of Egyptian Archaeology ★ 🎁📷 MUSEUM   Tucked away on the University College London campus, this dusty, musty collection of miniature treasures from Ancient Egypt makes the perfect companion exhibition to the rather larger and grander items on display in the Egyptian galleries of the nearby British Museum (see above). Built up by the famed 19th-century Egyptologist, Flinders Petrie, the museum boasts a wonderfully evocative array of finds from the land of the pharaohs, including jewelry, pots, papyrus documents, frescoes, carvings, and some of the world's oldest-surviving clothes. Pick up a torch from the front desk and get exploring—the lighting is kept to a minimum to help conserve the delicate items.

University College London, Gower St., WC1. ℂ **020/7679-2884.** www.ucl.ac.uk/museums/petrie. Free admission. Tues–Sat 1–5pm. Tube: Goodge St. or Euston Sq.

Queen's Gallery ★ GALLERY   This 19th-century chapel is the only part of Buckingham Palace (aside from the Royal Mews; see p. 91) that welcomes visitors year round. Today it's a gallery dedicated to rotating exhibitions of the wide-ranging treasure trove that is the **Royal Collection.** You'll find special showings of paintings, prints, drawings, watercolors, furniture, porcelain, miniatures, enamels, jewelry, and other works of art. At any given time, you may see such artistic peaks as Van Dyck's equestrian portrait of Charles I; a dazzling array of gold snuffboxes; paintings by Monet; studies by Leonardo da Vinci; or perhaps even the recent and less-than-flattering portrait of the current Queen, by Lucian Freud.

Buckingham Palace, Buckingham Palace Rd., SW1. ℂ **020/7766-7301.** www.royalcollection.org.uk. Admission £8.75 adults, £7.75 students and seniors, £4.50 children 5–16, free for children 4 and under. Daily 10am–5:30pm (last admission 4:30pm). Tube: Victoria.

Royal Academy of Arts ★ GALLERY   Established in 1768, the country's first professional art school counted painters Sir Joshua Reynolds and Thomas Gainsborough among its founding members. Each member has had to donate a work of art, and so, over the years, the Academy has built up a sizable collection. Ever-changing highlights are displayed in the **John Madejski Fine Rooms,** which can be visited as part of a free guided tour at 1pm on Tuesday, 1 and 4pm Wednesday to Friday, and 11:30am on Saturday. The Academy's annual **Summer Exhibition** has been held for more than 200 years. Today, however, the main focus of the gallery, and the principal draw for visitors, are its temporary exhibitions (costing upward of £12), which are usually blockbuster affairs—"Aztecs," "Turks," and "Monet in the Twentieth Century" have been recent hits.

Burlington House, Piccadilly, W1. ℂ **020/7300-8000.** www.royalacademy.org.uk. Admission for temporary shows varies from £7–£12. Free admission to guided tours of John Madejski Fine Rooms depending on the exhibition. Sat–Thurs 10am–6pm (last admission 5:30pm); Fri 10am–10pm (last admission 9:30pm). Tube: Piccadilly Circus or Green Park.

Royal Mews HISTORIC SITE   This is where the British royal family's grandest forms of road transport are stored, including their fleet of Rolls Royces, their carriages, and the horses that pull them, who enjoy luxurious stables adorned with tile walls and gleaming horse brasses. Pride of place goes to the **Gold State Coach,** built in 1761. Decorated with a riotous assortment of gold leaf, painted panels, and sculptures of cherubs, lions' heads, and dolphins, it's the sort of thing that only a monarch could get away with. It's also absolutely huge—3.6m (12 ft.) high, 7m (23 ft.) long, weighing 4 tonnes (4.4 tons), and requiring eight horses to pull it.

Buckingham Palace, Buckingham Palace Rd., SW1. ℂ **020/7766-7302.** www.royalcollection.org.uk. Admission £7.75 adults, £7 seniors and students, £5 children 5–17, free for children 4 and under. Mar

26–July 26 and Sept 26–Oct 31 Mon–Thurs and Sat–Sun 11am–4pm; Aug 1–Sept 25 daily 10am–5pm; Nov 1–March 25 Mon–Fri 11am–4pm; closed during state visits and last week in Dec. Tube: Victoria.

St. James's Park ★★ ☺ PARK   With its scenic central pond, tended flowerbeds, and picnic-friendly lawns, it's difficult to believe that this Royal Park was once a swamp near a leper colony. Today it's as elegant a green space as London can muster, and one of the best places in the center of town to watch wildfowl. Its pond is home to more than 20 species, including ducks, geese, and even pelicans—the descendants of a pair presented to Charles II by a Russian ambassador in 1662—which are all fed daily at 2:30pm.

Great as the park is for just lazing about, if you want to get a bit more active, the park office offers guided walks throughout the year—including to **Duck Island** in the center of the pond, on the hunt for the park's bats, and following the course of the River Tyburn, which flows beneath the park. See the website for times and frequencies.

The Mall, SW1. ℂ **020/7930-1793.** www.royalparks.org.uk/parks/st_james_park. Free admission. Open 24 hr. Tube: St. James's Park.

St. James's Piccadilly CHURCH   This late 17th-century Anglican church doesn't so much provide a respite from the bustle and commerce of Piccadilly, as form a vibrant part of it. A market is held in the churchyard every day except Monday (it's antiques on Tues and general arts and crafts from Wed to Sun) and classical concerts are put on at lunchtime on Mondays, Wednesdays, and Fridays. They're nominally free, although a donation of £3.50 is requested.

The church formed part of the post-Great Fire London skyline created by Sir Christopher Wren. But unlike almost all his other commissions, this was a new church, not a rebuild, first consecrated in 1684. Diarist John Evelyn wrote of the interior, "There is no altar anywhere in England, nor has there been any abroad, more handsomely adorned." Wren's master carver Grinling Gibbons created the reredos (a screen decorated with religious icons and placed behind the altar), organ case, and font.

197 Piccadilly, W1. ℂ **020/7734-4511.** www.st-james-piccadilly.org. Free admission. Lunchtime concerts are held on Mon, Wed, and Fri at 1:10pm. Suggested donation £3.50. Evening concerts are on an irregular schedule; check at the church for a poster listing the current slate of evening concerts. Tickets cost £10–£22. Tube: Piccadilly Circus.

St. Martin-in-the-Fields ★ CHURCH   Although its setting at the edge of one of London's busiest squares makes the church's name seem almost willfully ironic, St. Martin's was indeed surrounded by fields when first founded in the 13th century. But these had already long gone by the time the current grand 18th-century building was constructed, the work of James Gibbs, a disciple of Christopher Wren. Today, following a £36 million makeover, it looks as good as ever, with an interior adorned with fine Italian plasterwork. A full program of classical concerts (plus the odd bit of jazz) is laid on here. Those performed at lunchtime, typically on Mondays, Tuesdays, and Fridays are free (although a £3.50 donation is "suggested"), while evening tickets cost £7 to £26. A craft market is held during the week at the back of the church.

Inside, the excellent **Café in the Crypt** enjoys one of the most atmospheric locations in London, its floor made up numerous gravestones (including the highwayman Jack Sheppard and Nell Gwynne, Charles II's mistress). The crypt is also home to the **London Brass Rubbing Centre** ★ ☺, where children can rub a wide selection of replica brasses (from £4.50), open Monday to Wednesday 10am to 7pm, Thursday to Saturday 10am to 10pm, and Sunday noon to 7pm.

Trafalgar Sq., WC2. ℗ **020/7766-1100.** www.stmartin-in-the-fields.org. Mon–Fri 9am–6pm; Sat–Sun 8:45am–7:30pm as long as no service is taking place. Concerts Mon, Tues, and Fri 1:05pm; Tues and Thurs–Sat 7:30pm. Tube: Charing Cross.

Sir John Soane's Museum ★★ MUSEUM   Perhaps the finest small museum in London, this is the former home of Sir John Soane (1753–1837), the architect who built the Bank of England (although not most of the present structure). With his multiple levels, fool-the-eye mirrors, flying arches, and domes, Soane was a master of perspective and a genius of interior space—his picture gallery, for example, is filled with three times the number of paintings that a room of similar dimensions would normally hold. One prize of the collection is William Hogarth's satirical series *The Rake's Progress,* a satire on mid-18th-century politics. Soane also filled his house with classical sculpture: The sarcophagus of Pharaoh Seti I, found in a burial chamber in the Valley of the Kings, is here.

Insider tip: On the first Tuesday evening of every month, this most evocative of collections ups the ante by giving visitors the chance to explore its labyrinthine confines by candlelight. Expect to wait in line for at least 1 hour.

13 Lincoln's Inn Fields, WC2. ℗ **020/7405-2107.** www.soane.org. Free admission (donations invited). Tues–Sat 10am–5pm; 1st Tues of each month also 6–9pm. Tours given Sat at 11am; £5 tickets distributed at 10:30am, first-come, first-served (group tours by appointment only). Tube: Holborn.

Wallace Collection ★★ GALLERY   Located in a palatial setting (the modestly described "townhouse" of the late Lady Wallace), this collection, built up over 2 centuries by one of London's leading aristocratic families, is a contrasting array of art and armaments. (The collection is similar in many ways to those of the Frick Museum in New York and the Musée Jacquemart-André in Paris.) The artworks include such classics as Frans Hals's *Laughing Cavalier* and Rembrandt's portrait of his son Titus. The paintings of the Dutch, English, Spanish, and Italian schools are outstanding. It's best visited as one of the free guided tours given at 1pm Monday to Friday, 11:30am Wednesday and Saturday, and 3pm Sunday.

💬 TRAFALGAR: LONDON'S most famous SQUARE

London is a city full of landmark squares. Without a doubt, the best known is **Trafalgar Square ★★** (www.london.gov.uk/trafalgarsquare; Tube: Charing Cross), which has been significantly remodeled over the past decade, with parts pedestrianized and most of the former swarms of pigeons sent on their way. It boasts numerous landmarks, including the **National Gallery** (p. 89) on the north side, **St. Martin-in-the-Fields** (p. 92) on the east, and at the center, **Nelson's Column**—a 44m (144 ft.) granite column topped with a statue of Horatio Viscount Nelson (1758–1805), one of the country's most celebrated naval heroes.

The square is also the site of a few unusual attractions, including an equestrian statue of Charles I, from where all distances from London are measured, and in the southwest corner, the **world's smallest police station**—it has room for just one, rather lonely, officer. The square is also cornered by four plinths, three of which bear statues, while the **"Fourth Plinth"** plays host to a succession of temporary, often sensationalist artworks.

Manchester Sq., W1. ✆ **020/7563-9500.** www.the-wallace-collection.org.uk. Free admission (some exhibits charge). Mon–Sat 10am–5pm; Sun noon–5pm. Tube: Bond St. or Baker St.

Wellcome Collection ★★ ☺ MUSEUM   The capital's finest museum of medicine was born out of the personal compulsion of Sir Henry Wellcome, a renowned 19th-century pharmacist and collector of historical medical artifacts from around the world. It's divided into two sections. The first, "Medicine Man," comprises Henry's original collection, and is wonderfully strange, an extraordinary assortment of medical oddities, including Ancient Egyptian canopic jars, Roman phallic amulets, South American mummies, a medieval leper clapper, and "secondhand" guillotine blades, as well as a number of "celebrity" items, such as Napoleon's toothbrush, Nelson's razor blade, and Darwin's walking stick. The second section, "Medicine Now" is slightly less bonkers, but no less interesting, focusing on modern medical trends and developments, with plenty of hi-tech stuff on genomes, vaccines, nanotechnology, and the like. Free tours of the museum are given on Saturdays (11:30am and 2:30pm) and Sundays (2:30pm).

183 Euston Rd., NW1. ✆ **020/7611-2222.** www.wellcomecollection.org. Free admission. Tues–Wed and Fri–Sat 10am–6pm; Thurs 10am–10pm; Sun 11am–6pm. Tube: Euston Sq., Euston, or Warren St.

West London

Hyde Park ★★★ & Kensington Gardens ★★ ☺ PARK   Once a favorite deer-hunting ground of Henry VIII, Hyde Park is central London's largest park. With the adjoining Kensington Gardens it forms a single giant open space, made up of 246 hectares (608 acres) of velvety lawns interspersed with ponds, flowerbeds, and trees. The two parks are divided by a 17-hectare (42-acre) lake known as the **Serpentine.** Paddleboats and rowboats can be rented from the **boathouse** (open Mar–Oct) on the north side (✆ **020/7262-1330**) costing £9 per hour for adults, £3 per hour for children. Part of the Serpentine has also been set aside for use as a **lido,** where you can swim, provided you don't mind the often rather challenging water temperature.

Near the Serpentine bridge is the **Princess Diana Memorial Fountain,** the somewhat (perhaps appropriately) troubled monument to the late princess. When first opened in 2004, its slippery granite surfaces proved singularly unsuited for something intended as a swimming and paddling venue, leading to its almost instant closure. It was later reopened, but you're no longer allowed to swim, although you can put your hands and feet into the fountain.

At the northeastern tip of Hyde Park, near Marble Arch, is **Speakers' Corner,** where people have the right to speak (and more often shout) about any subject that takes their fancy. In the past you might have heard Karl Marx, Lenin, or George Orwell trying to convert the masses; today's speakers tend to be less well known, if no less fervent, and heckling is all part of the fun.

Blending with Hyde Park to the west of the Serpentine, and bordering the grounds of Kensington Palace (see below), are the well-manicured **Kensington Gardens.** They contain numerous attractions including the **Serpentine Gallery** (p. 96), a famous statue of **Peter Pan** erected by J. M. Barrie himself (secretly, in the middle of the night), and the **Diana, Princess of Wales Memorial Playground,** a pirate-themed fun area that has proved a more successful tribute to the late Princess of Wales than Hyde Park's fountain. At the park's southern edge is the **Albert Memorial,** a gloriously over-the-top, gilded monument erected by Queen Victoria in honor of her late husband.

Hyde Park, W2. ✆ **020/7298-2100.** www.royalparks.org.uk/parks/hyde_park. Free admission. Open 24 hours. Tube: Hyde Park Corner, Marble Arch, or Lancaster Gate.

Attractions, Hotels & Restaurants in West London

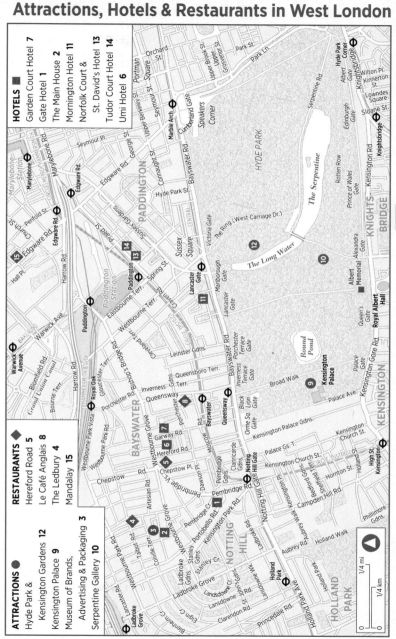

ATTRACTIONS ●

Hyde Park &
Kensington Gardens **12**
Kensington Palace **9**
Museum of Brands,
Advertising & Packaging **3**
Serpentine Gallery **10**

RESTAURANTS ◆

Hereford Road **5**
Le Café Anglais **8**
The Ledbury **4**
Mandalay **15**

HOTELS ■

Garden Court Hotel **7**
Gate Hotel **1**
The Main House **2**
Mornington Hotel **11**
Norfolk Court &
St. David's Hotel **13**
Tudor Court Hotel **14**
Umi Hotel **6**

LONDON | Exploring London

4

95

Kensington Palace ★ HISTORIC SITE   This grand palace started life as a much simpler (relatively speaking) Jacobean mansion. It was acquired in the late 17th century by the new Dutch king of England, William III, who wanted a residence away from the damp air of central London. Expanded and extended under the guidance of Sir Christopher Wren, it remained the official home of the reigning monarch until 1760 when George II died and his successor George III decided he preferred Kew Palace. Since then it has been the home of various royals, including Victoria (who in 1837, aged just 17, was woken to be told that her uncle, William IV, had died and she was now Queen), Princess Margaret (the late sister of the current Queen), and perhaps most famously, Diana, Princess of Wales—it was at the palace's gates that the great carpet of flowers was laid in the weeks following her death in 1997.

At the time of writing, the palace is undergoing renovation due for completion in June 2012, which will see new cafes, courtyards, and educational facilities added, and the palace gardens connected to Kensington Gardens (see above) for the first time since the 19th century. The interior will be reorganized into four "story zones" focusing on the lives of William and Mary, George II, Victoria, and Margaret and Diana. Although some sections will close while the building work takes place, the palace's magnificent 18th-century **Orangery** (p. 147) will remain open throughout, and is a fine venue for afternoon tea.

The Broad Walk, Kensington Gardens, W8. ℂ **0844/482-7777.** www.hrp.org.uk/KensingtonPalace. Admission £12.50 adults, £11 seniors and students, £6.25 children 5–15, £34 family ticket. Mar–Sept daily 10am–6pm; Oct–Feb daily 10am–5pm. Tube: Queensway or Notting Hill Gate; High St. Kensington on south side.

Museum of Brands, Advertising & Packaging ★ 🏛 MUSEUM   A museum
dedicated not so much to things, as the packets the things come in. These days people are pretty savvy as to the value and appeal of packaging. However, back when the museum's founder, Robert Opie, began his collection—according to legend, in 1963 at the age of 16 with a chocolate wrapper—the idea of appreciating packaging for its own sake was still in its infancy (that great art hymn to packaging, Andy Warhol's *Campbell's Soup Cans* had been produced just the year before). The collection has since grown to vast proportions, comprising some 12,000 items from the past 120 years, including everything from magazine advertisements and washing powder boxes to cereal packets and milk bottles, as well as assorted toys and household appliances.

2 Colville Mews, Lonsdale Rd., W11. ℂ **020/7908-0880.** www.museumofbrands.com. Admission £6.50 adults, £4 seniors and students, £2.25 children 5–15, £15 family ticket. Tues–Sat 10am–6pm, Sun 11am–5pm. Closed Fri–Mon last weekend in August. Tube: Notting Hill Gate.

Serpentine Gallery ★ GALLERY   Just southwest of the Serpentine (see above),
from which it takes its name, Kensington Gardens' Serpentine Gallery is one of London's leading contemporary art spaces—not to mention a good place to retire to should the British weather curtail your plans for a day of sunbathing or boating. It plays host to a rolling succession of shows, each displayed for a couple of months. Notable exhibitions have featured Henry Moore, Andy Warhol, and Damien Hirst. Over the past decade the Serp has perhaps become best known for commissioning a temporary **pavilion** each summer from one of the world's leading architects (in the Jean Nouvel, Frank Gehry, Daniel Libeskind league), the more avant-garde and "out there," the better.

Kensington Gardens, W2. ℂ **020/7402-6075.** www.serpentinegallery.org. Free admission. Daily 10am–6pm. Tube: Knightsbridge or Lancaster Gate.

Southwest London

Chelsea Physic Garden ★ GARDEN   Founded in 1673 by the Worshipful Society of Apothecaries, this is the second-oldest surviving botanical garden in England. Sir Hans Sloane, doctor to King George II, required the apothecaries of the Empire to develop 50 plant species a year for presentation to the Royal Society. The objective was to grow plants for medicinal study. Plant specimens and even trees arrived at the gardens by barge from all over the world, many to grow in English soil for the first time. Some 7,000 plants still grow here, including everything from pomegranate to exotic cork oak, and the garden also houses England's earliest rock garden.

66 Royal Hospital Rd., SW3. ℂ **020/7352-5646.** www.chelseaphysicgarden.co.uk. Admission £8 adults, £5 children 5–15 and students. Apr–Oct Wed–Fri noon–5pm, Sun and bank holiday Mon noon–6pm. Tube: Sloane Sq.

Churchill War Rooms ★★ MUSEUM/WWII SITE   These cramped subterranean rooms were the nerve center of the British war effort during the final years of World War II, where Winston Churchill and his advisors planned what they hoped would be an Allied victory. In August 1945, with the conflict finally won, the rooms were abandoned exactly as they were, creating a time capsule of the moment of victory.

You can see the **Map Room** with its huge wall maps; the Atlantic map is a mass of pinholes (each hole represents at least one convoy). Next door is Churchill's bedroom-cum-office, which has a bed and a desk with two BBC microphones on it, via which he tried to rally the nation. Other rooms include Churchill's kitchen and dining room, and the Transatlantic Telephone Room that is little more than a broom closet housing the special scrambler phone with which Churchill conferred with U.S. President Roosevelt.

Also in the war rooms is the **Churchill Museum,** the world's first major museum dedicated to the life of Sir Winston Churchill.

Clive Steps, at end of King Charles St., SW1. ℂ **020/7930-6961.** http://cwr.iwm.org.uk. Admission £14.95 adults, £12 seniors and students, free for children 15 and under. Daily 9:30am–6pm (last admission 5pm). Tube: Westminster or St. James's Park.

Horse Guards HISTORIC SITE   North of Downing Street, on the site of the guard house of Whitehall Palace (which burned down in 1698) stands the 18th-century Horse Guards building, the headquarters of the **Household Cavalry Mounted Regiment,** a combination of the oldest and most senior regiments in the British Army—the **Life Guards,** and the **Blues and Royals.** Today these regiments have two principal duties: To protect the sovereign and to provide photo opportunities for tourists—their dandy uniforms of red tunics and white plumed helmets for the Life Guards, blue tunics and red plumed helmets for the Blues and Royals, take a great shot.

The **ceremony** ★ for changing the two mounted guards here is a good deal more accessible than the more famous one just down the road at Buckingham Palace. It takes place at 11am and 4pm from Monday to Saturday, and at 10am and 4pm on Sunday, and lasts around 30 minutes.

If you pass through the arch at Horse Guards, you'll find yourself at **Horse Guards Parade,** formerly the tiltyard (jousting area) of Whitehall Palace, which leads onto St. James's Park. It is here that the Household Cavalry help celebrate the Queen's birthday in June with a military pageant known as **"Trooping the Colour"** (p. 42).

Most of the building is usually closed to visitors, although a small section has been turned into the **Household Cavalry Museum** (ℂ **020/7930-3070;** www.householdcavalrymuseum.co.uk); admission costs £6 for adults, £4 for children.

Whitehall, SW1. ℂ **020/7414-2479.** Free admission. Tube: Charing Cross, Westminster, or Embankment.

Attractions, Hotels & Restaurants in Southwest London

ATTRACTIONS ●

Chelsea Physic Garden **17**
Churchill War Rooms **42**
Horse Guards **43**
Houses of Parliament & Big Ben **41**
Natural History Museum **12**
Saatchi Gallery **20**
Science Museum **11**
Tate Britain **37**
Victoria & Albert Museum **13**
Westminster Abbey **40**
Westminster Cathedral **36**

RESTAURANTS ◆

Amaya **27**
Bar Boulud **25**
Cambio
  de Tercio **10**
Cinnamon Club **39**
Dinner by Heston
  Blumenthal **25**
Gordon Ramsay **18**
The Goring **34**

Jenny Lo's Teahouse **33**
Marcus Wareing at
  the Berkeley **26**
The Orange **30**
The Orangery **1**
Palm **28**
Pig's Ear **16**
Tom Aikens **14**
Tom's Kitchen **15**
Zaika **2**

HOTELS ■

B&B Belgravia **32**
Baglioni Hotel **4**
Base2Stay **7**
The Capital **23**
Diplomat Hotel **29**
Draycott Hotel **21**

Easyhotel **8**
41 Hotel **35**
The Goring **34**
Henley House **6**
Knightsbridge Hotel **22**
The Milestone **3**
Mint Hotel **38**

Morgan House Hotel **31**
Parkcity Hotel **9**
The Rockwell **5**
Royal Horseguards
  Hotel **44**
San Domenico House **19**
30 Pavilion Road **24**

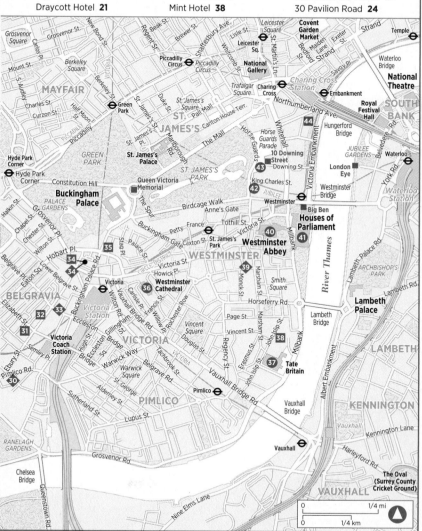

4

LONDON | Exploring London

Houses of Parliament & Big Ben ★ HISTORIC SITE   The image of the **Palace of Westminster** (the official name for the building containing the Houses of Parliament) and its clocktower known as **Big Ben** (to everyone except pedants, who will tell you that Big Ben is in fact the name of the bell, not the tower) has become an icon of icons. It is the scene most evocative of the capital's timeless nature, and yet all is not as it seems. Although the site has been in use for almost 1,000 years—first as a royal palace, and then from the 16th century onward as the seat of Parliament—most of what you see dates only from the mid-19th century. It was designed in a deliberately medieval-looking, "Gothic Revival" style to replace an earlier structure that burned down in 1834. There are, however, much older sections hidden within, including the 11th-century **Westminster Hall,** which still boasts its 14th-century hammerbeam roof, and the 14th-century Jewel Tower (see below).

You can take a guided tour of the buildings on Saturdays throughout the year and during the summer recess (when the politicians are on vacation), which takes in various places of interest in the vast 1,000-room complex, including Westminster Hall, the Royal Gallery, and the Queen's Robing Room, where the monarch gets ready for her annual speech to parliament. You are also allowed to pop into the **House of Commons** chamber itself, where the country's 650 elected MPs (Members of Parliament) come to argue over the latest legislation, as well as the secondary chamber, the **House of Lords.** To see British democracy in (for want of a better word) action, will probably involve a fair bit of waiting around. When the House is sitting—Monday to Thursday and some Fridays during the parliamentary seasons—line up outside the Cromwell Green visitor entrance, usually for a couple of hours (generally less for the Lords). Tickets are allocated on a first-come, first-served basis. Don't go expecting any great rhetorical fireworks, however. Most debates are sparsely attended and jargon-heavy.

Across the street is the **Jewel Tower** ★, Abingdon Street (© **020/7222-2219;** www.english-heritage.org.uk), one of only two surviving buildings from the medieval Palace of Westminster. Although originally built in 1365 to house Edward III's treasure-trove, the tower today holds only an exhibition on the history of Parliament. It is open daily from 10am to 5pm April to October and 10am to 4pm November to March. Admission is £3.20 for adults, £2.70 for students and seniors, and £1.60 for children.

Old Palace Yard, SW1. House of Commons © **020/7219-4272;** House of Lords © **020/7219-3107.** www.parliament.uk. Free admission. Guided tours take place Sat 9:15am–4:30pm; Aug–Sept Mon–Tues and Fri–Sat 9:15am–4:30pm, Wed–Thurs 1:15pm–4:30pm. Tours last 75 min. To attend debates, the House of Commons sits at the following times Mon–Tues 2:30–10:30pm, Wed 11:30am–7:30pm, Thurs 10:30am–6:30pm, Fri 9:30am–3pm. Join the line at Cromwell Green entrance. Tube: Westminster.

Natural History Museum ★★★ ☺ MUSEUM   It seems fitting that one of London's great museums should be housed in such a grand building, a soaring Romanesque structure that provides a suitably reverent setting for what is often described as a "cathedral of nature." The museum's remit is to cover the great diversity of life on Earth in all its myriad forms, although that coverage is by no means uniform. One group of life forms gets a lot more attention lavished on it than any others, much to the delight of visiting 8-year-olds—**dinosaurs.** As you arrive, your first vision will be the giant cast of a diplodocus looming down above you. If you want to see more of these great prehistoric beasts—but with added rubbery skin and jerky movements—then turn left where you'll find a hall filled with fossils and finds, as well as displays of animatronic dinosaurs permanently surrounded by gaggles of wide-eyed children.

The dinosaurs form part of the Blue Zone, one of the four color-coded sections that make up the museum. This zone is primarily concerned with animals, both past and present, and has plenty of other showstoppers, including a 40-m (90-ft.) model of a blue whale hanging from the ceiling, a saber-tooth tiger skeleton, and an adult-size model of a fetus.

The Green Zone's galleries focus on plants, insects, and ecology. Highlights include giant models of insects, a cross-section of a sequoia (the world's largest tree), a leaf-cutter ant colony, and a life-size termite mound.

The Earth's interior processes are explored in the Red Zone, where you can try and stay upright on an earthquake simulator, see plastercasts of victims preserved in ash by the volcanic eruption at Pompeii, and explore a gallery of minerals, rocks, and gemstones.

The final zone, the Orange Zone, is the museum's latest pride and joy, comprising the eight-story glass-and-steel **Darwin Centre,** the most significant addition to the museum since it opened in 1881. Constructed in 2008 in time for the 150th anniversary of Darwin's *Origin of the Species*, the center is primarily a research institute, but also boasts a number of hi-tech attractions for the public, including Cocoon, which has a transparent table filled with insect and plant specimens. The museum offers a wealth of resources for younger visitors, including free discovery guides, explorer backpacks, and family workshops.

Cromwell Rd., SW7. © **020/7942-5000.** www.nhm.ac.uk. Free admission. Mon–Sat 10am–5:50pm; Sun 11am–5:50pm. Tube: S. Kensington.

Saatchi Gallery ★ GALLERY   The capital's largest gallery of contemporary art recently decamped to the grand three-story surrounds of the Duke of York's HQ building, a former military school. The man behind it, British mega-collector Charles Saatchi, is known for upsetting mainstream opinion with his willfully avant-garde exhibitions. The constantly changing temporary displays are often of the "challenging" variety. If you think you're going to be offended by a Madonna with elephant dung or one of Damien Hirst's pickled sharks, then it's probably best to go look at a Rembrandt in the **National** (p. 89) instead.

Duke of York's Headquarters, King's Rd., SW3. © **020/7811-3070.** www.saatchi-gallery.co.uk. Free admission. Daily 10am–6pm. Tube: Sloane Sq.

Science Museum ★★★ ☺ MUSEUM   The country's pre-eminent museum of science, this is one of the capital's great interactive experiences, filled with buttons to press, levers to pull, and experiments to absorb you. It aims to provide a complete overview of technological progress, beginning, just after the entrance, in the **Energy Hall,** where you can meet the great clunking behemoths of the Industrial Revolution, including steam locomotives and giant beam engines. From here, things shoot ahead a couple of hundred years to the **Exploring Space** gallery, where you can see one of the great icons of the U.S. space program, the Apollo 10 command module, as well as lots of fascinating space paraphernalia (including space food). Beyond is the shiny **Wellcome Wing,** where the "Who Am I?" exhibit whisks us off into the future to explore what it means to be human—computers let you experiment with your appearance, changing your facial features and even your gender. There's also an IMAX cinema showing spectacular nature- and space-related epics on a giant screen.

And that's just the start of the museum. Elsewhere you'll find galleries dedicated to medicine, telecommunications, computers, and flight—the last now with state-of-the-art flight simulators—as well as the ever popular **Launchpad,** where there are more than 50 hands-on experiments for kids to try.

Exhibition Rd., SW7. ☎ **0870/870-4868.** www.sciencemuseum.org.uk. Free admission. Daily 10am–6pm. Closed Dec 24–26. Tube: S. Kensington.

Tate Britain ★★ MUSEUM   Fronting the Thames near Vauxhall Bridge, the Tate looks like a smaller and more graceful relation of the British Museum. Within is the country's finest collection of domestic art, dating from the 16th century to the present, with most of the country's leading artists represented, including such notables as Gainsborough, Reynolds, Stubbs, Blake, and Constable; William Hogarth, and the incomparable William Blake, as well as such modern greats as Stanley Spencer, Francis Bacon, and David Hockney. The collection of works by J. M. W. Turner is the Tate's largest by a single artist, spread over seven rooms. Turner himself willed most of his paintings and watercolors to the nation.

And, just to show the young ones that it can still swing with the best of them, Tate Britain is also the host each autumn of the annual **Turner Prize,** the media-baiting, controversy-seeking competition for the best contemporary British art.

Free tours of parts of the collection are offered Monday to Friday (at 11am, noon, and 3pm) and on Saturdays and Sundays at noon and 3pm, and the first Friday of each month sees the "Late at Tate" event, which involves extended opening hours and free events, such as talks, film screenings, or live music.

If you want to make an art-filled day of it, the **Tate to Tate boat service** departs from just out front to **Tate Modern** all day (p. 109).

Millbank, SW1. ☎ **020/7887-8888.** www.tate.org.uk/britain. Free admission; special exhibitions incur a charge of £5–£15. Daily 10am–6pm (last admission 5:15pm). Tube: Pimlico.

Victoria & Albert Museum ★★★ ☺ MUSEUM   Of the three great South Kensington collections, the "V&A" is perhaps the least ostentatious, which might seem strange for a museum dedicated to all that is most eye-catching in the visual arts. That's not to say it doesn't provide a feast for the eyes—this is perhaps the world's greatest collection of applied arts—more that it relies less on gizmos, gadgets, and touchscreens to get its point across. The wonders on display here need no sexing up.

The museum comprises seven floors split into 150 galleries, in which are displayed, at a rough estimate, around four million items of decorative art from across the world and throughout the ages—sculptures, jewelry, textiles, clothes, paintings, ceramics, furniture, architecture, and more. Many of the collections are among the finest found anywhere. The V&A has the largest collection of Renaissance sculptures outside Italy, the greatest collection of Indian art outside India (in the Nehru Gallery), and the country's most comprehensive collection of antique dresses (in the Fashion Gallery). The Photography Gallery can draw on some 500,000 individual images, the recently added William & Judith Bolling Gallery holds one of the world's largest (and most glittering) collections of European jewelry, while the British Galleries can offer perhaps the greatest diversity of British design available anywhere, with all the great names of the past 400 years represented, including Chippendale, Charles Rennie Mackintosh, and William Morris.

To help you plot your path, your first stop should be the front desk where you can pick up leaflets, floor plans, and themed family trails. If you'd rather somebody else made the decisions for you, free guided tours leave from the grand entrance daily, hourly between 10:30am and 3:30pm. Art-based drop-in events are laid on for families on weekends.

Cromwell Rd., SW7. ☎ **020/7942-2000.** www.vam.ac.uk. Free admission. Temporary exhibitions often £12. Sun–Thurs 10am–5:45pm; Fri 10am–10pm. Tube: S. Kensington.

Westminster Abbey

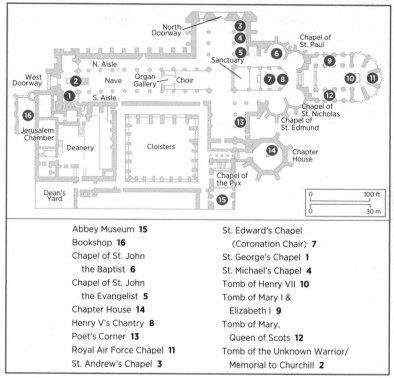

Abbey Museum **15**

Bookshop **16**

Chapel of St. John
the Baptist **6**

Chapel of St. John
the Evangelist **5**

Chapter House **14**

Henry V's Chantry **8**

Poet's Corner **13**

Royal Air Force Chapel **11**

St. Andrew's Chapel **3**

St. Edward's Chapel
(Coronation Chair) **7**

St. George's Chapel **1**

St. Michael's Chapel **4**

Tomb of Henry VII **10**

Tomb of Mary I &
Elizabeth I **9**

Tomb of Mary,
Queen of Scots **12**

Tomb of the Unknown Warrior/
Memorial to Churchill **2**

Westminster Abbey ★★★ ABBEY   The Abbey is not just one of the finest examples of ecclesiastical architecture in Europe, it's also the shrine of the nation where monarchs are anointed before their god and memorials to the nation's greatest figures fill every corner. From the outside, it's a magnificently earnest-looking structure, its two great square towers and pointed arches the very epitome of medieval Gothic. The building was begun in 1245 under the reign of Henry II and finally completed in the early 16th century. This replaced an earlier structure commissioned in 1045 by Edward the Confessor (which itself had replaced a 7th-century original) and was consecrated in 1065, just in time to play host to Edward's funeral and (following a brief tussle in Hastings) the coronation of William the Conqueror. It has been, with a couple of exceptions, the setting for every coronation since, and it is here on April 29, 2011, that Prince William married Kate Middleton.

More or less at the center of the Abbey stands the shrine of Edward the Confessor, while scattered around are the tombs of various other royals, including Henry V, Elizabeth I, and Richard III. Splendid as they are, they are all rather overshadowed by the tomb of Henry VII. This elaborately carved, gilded structure, the work of the Italian artist Torrigiano (a contemporary and sometime rival of Michelangelo), introduced Renaissance lushness to the Abbey's otherwise overwhelmingly austere, Gothic confines.

Nearby is the surprisingly shabby **Coronation Chair,** on which almost every monarch since Edward II, including the current one, has sat during their coronation.

In **Poet's Corner** you'll find a great assortment of memorials to the country's greatest men (and a few women) of letters, clustered around the grave of Geoffrey Chaucer, who was buried here in 1400. These include a statue of Shakespeare, his arm resting on a pile of books, Jacob Epstein's bust of William Blake, as well as tributes to Jane Austen, Samuel Taylor Coleridge, John Milton, Dylan Thomas, and D. H. Lawrence.

Statesmen and men of science—Disraeli, Newton, Charles Darwin—are also interred in the Abbey or honored by monuments. Near to the west door is the 1965 memorial to Sir Winston Churchill and the tomb of the **Unknown Warrior,** commemorating the British dead of World War I.

Broad Sanctuary, SW1. ⒸⒻ **020/7222-5152.** www.westminster-abbey.org. Admission £15 adults, £12 students and seniors, £6 children 11–18, £30 family ticket, free for children 10 and under. Mon–Tues and Thurs–Fri 9:30am–3:30pm; Wed 9:30am–5pm; Sat 9:30am–1:30pm. Tube: Westminster or St. James's Park.

Westminster Cathedral ★ CATHEDRAL This spectacular brick-and-stone church (1903) is the headquarters of the Roman Catholic Church in Britain. Adorned in retro-Byzantine style, it's massive: 108m (354 ft.) long and 47m (154 ft.) wide. One hundred different marbles compose the richly decorated interior, and mosaics emblazon the chapels and the vaulting of the sanctuary. If you take the elevator to the top of the 82-m (269-ft.) campanile, you'll be rewarded with sweeping views that take in Buckingham Palace, Westminster Abbey, and St. Paul's Cathedral. The cathedral's renowned choir usually performs daily: Download a timetable from the website.

Ashley Place, SW1. ⒸⒻ **020/7798-9055.** www.westminstercathedral.org.uk. Cathedral free. Tower £5. Cathedral services Mon–Sat 7am–7pm; Sun 8am–8pm. Tower Mon–Sat 9:30am–5pm; Sat–Sun 9:30am–6pm. Tube: Victoria.

The South Bank

Florence Nightingale Museum ★ ☺ MUSEUM The museum celebrates the life and work of one of the great Victorian British women, best known for nursing soldiers during the Crimean War (1853–56). However, you'll learn that her greatest achievement was probably as a statistician. She used then revolutionary techniques for presenting data, such as pie charts, to prove the importance of sanitation and good hygiene in lowering the death rate of wounded soldiers.

The museum holds many objects owned or used by Nightingale, including clothes, furniture, letters, and even her pet stuffed owl. There are also audio-visual displays on her life and a reconstruction of a Crimean ward scene.

The museum is very much slanted toward families and schoolchildren—parties of whom arrive regularly during term time—and free family events, such as storytellings, art workshops, and trails are put on most weekends.

St. Thomas' Hospital, 2 Lambeth Palace Rd., SE1. ⒸⒻ **020/7620-0374.** www.florence-nightingale.co.uk. Admission £5.80 adults, £4.80 seniors, students, children ages 5–15, and persons with disabilities, free for children 4 and under; £16 family ticket. Daily 10am–5pm. Tube: Westminster, Waterloo, or Lambeth North.

Garden Museum ★ MUSEUM Housed in a small medieval church, St. Mary-Lambeth, next door to Lambeth Palace (the official residence of the Archbishop of Canterbury), this offers a celebration of that most British of pastimes—gardening. Its focus is unashamedly domestic, concentrating less on the Capability Browns of the world with their grand landscaped parks, than on the various unsung heroes of suburbia carefully

Attractions, Hotels & Restaurants in South Bank & the City

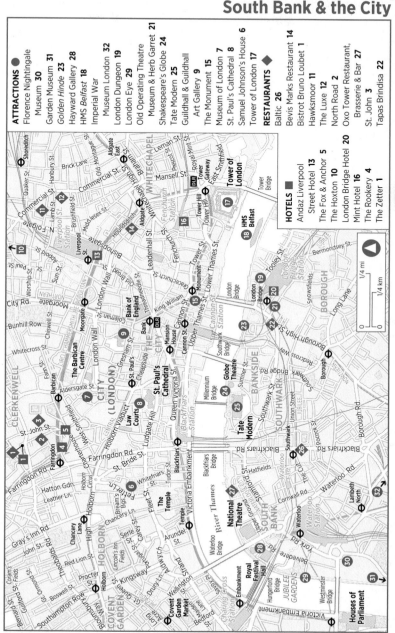

ATTRACTIONS ●

Florence Nightingale Museum **30**
Garden Museum **31**
Golden Hinde **23**
Hayward Gallery **28**
HMS *Belfast* **18**
Imperial War Museum London **32**
London Dungeon **19**
London Eye **29**
Old Operating Theatre Museum & Herb Garret **21**
Shakespeare's Globe **24**
Tate Modern **25**
Guildhall & Guildhall Art Gallery **9**
The Monument **15**
Museum of London **7**
St. Paul's Cathedral **8**
Samuel Johnson's House **6**
Tower of London **17**

RESTAURANTS ◆

Baltic **26**
Bevis Marks Restaurant **14**
Bistrot Bruno Loubet **1**
Hawksmoor **11**
The Luxe **12**
North Road **2**
Oxo Tower Restaurant, Brasserie & Bar **27**
St. John **3**
Tapas Brindisa **22**

HOTELS ■

Andaz Liverpool Street Hotel **13**
The Fox & Anchor **5**
The Hoxton **10**
London Bridge Hotel **20**
Mint Hotel **16**
The Rookery **4**
The Zetter **1**

4

LONDON | Exploring London

tending backyard plots. Inside is an assortment of antique gardening implements, a collection of gardening-related art, and a treasure trove of gardening memorabilia.

Outside, the museum's own garden is filled with historic plants that thrive in the microclimate within the church's walls. The churchyard contains two notable memorials from the history of horticulture: The tomb of **Captain Bligh,** whose journey aboard the *Bounty* to Tahiti in the late 18th century to obtain breadfruit trees prompted the famous mutiny against him; and the tomb of John Tradescant, a gardener and plant hunter for King Charles II. *Insider tip:* Free guided tours are given on the last Tuesday of each month at 2pm. First come, first served.

Lambeth Palace Rd., SE1. ℂ **020/7401-8865.** www.gardenmuseum.org.uk. Admission £6 adults, £5 seniors, free students and children 15 and under. Sun–Fri 10:30am–5:30pm, Sat 10:30am–4pm; closed 1st Mon of month (except bank holidays). Tube: Lambeth North.

Golden Hinde ☺ HISTORIC SITE   By the river, just around the corner from Southwark Cathedral, is this full-size replica of the ship on which Sir Francis Drake became the first Englishman to circumnavigate the globe in the 16th century. It may seem a touch cozy, but the proportions are accurate—it has even been sailed around the world to prove it. On board it's all very yo-ho-ho, with actors in period costume entertaining you with Tudor maritime tales as you explore the five levels. Understandably, it's very popular with children, and at weekends is usually given over to private birthday parties where everyone dresses up as pirates and buccaneers.

If you really want to get a feel for life at sea (or rather, in dry dock), then you could sign up for an "Overnight Living History Experience," which runs from 5pm till 10am the next day, when you join a crew of Tudor sailors, tending to the ship's needs, eating Tudor food and drink, and sleeping in the (somewhat cramped) cabins in the lower deck.

Pickford's Wharf, Clink St., SE1. ℂ **020/7403-0123.** www.goldenhinde.com. Admission £6 adults, £4.50 seniors, students, and children 15 and under; £18 family. Mon–Sat 10am–5:30pm; sleepovers cost £39.95 per person—bring sleeping bag. Tube: London Bridge.

Hayward Gallery GALLERY   Opened in 1968, and forming the arts wing of the **Southbank Centre** (p. 165), which also includes the Royal Festival Hall, the Queen Elizabeth Hall, and the Purcell Room, the Hayward is perhaps the epitome of the concrete brutalist style of architecture for which the Southbank is so derided (or occasionally, admired). But, while the outside might not grace that many postcards, the interior is a superior art space that presents a changing program of major contemporary exhibits. The gallery closes between exhibitions, so call before making your way here.

Belvedere Rd., South Bank, SE1. ℂ **0871/663-2500.** www.southbankcentre.co.uk/venues/hayward-gallery. Admission varies but usually £10 adults, £8 students, seniors, and children 12–17; free for children 11 and under. Hours subject to change, depending on the exhibit: Mon–Wed and Sat–Sun 10am–6pm; Thurs–Fri 10am–8pm. Tube: Waterloo or Embankment.

HMS *Belfast* ★ ☺ HISTORIC SITE   An 11,500-ton cruiser, the HMS *Belfast* is a World War II ship that's now preserved as a floating museum run by the Imperial War Museum (see below). It's moored opposite the Tower of London, between Tower Bridge and London Bridge. Its guns have a range of 14 miles, which means it could take out Hampton Court Palace if staff felt so inclined.

It's particularly popular with kids, who love climbing between its seven levels of clunking metal decks, exploring the cramped living quarters that once housed up to 950 sailors, and taking aim behind the (unloaded, obviously) naval guns and antiaircraft weaponry. Exhibits above and below show how sailors have lived and fought over the past 50 years. An audio guide is included in the admission price, and activity trails are available at the entrance (and from the website). Children under 16 must be accompanied by an adult.

Morgan's Lane, Tooley St., SE1. ✆ **020/7940-6300.** http://hmsbelfast.iwm.org.uk. Admission £12.95 adults, £10.40 seniors and students, £6.50 unemployed, free for children under 16. Mar–Oct daily 10am–6pm (last admission 4pm); Nov–Feb 10am–5pm (last admission 4pm). Tube: London Bridge.

Imperial War Museum London ★★★ ☺ MUSEUM   From 1814 to 1930, this deceptively elegant, domed building was the Bethlehem Royal Hospital, an old-style "madhouse," where the "patients" formed part of a Victorian freak show—visitors could pay a penny to go and stare at the lunatics. (The hospital's name since entered the language as "Bedlam," a slang expression for chaos and confusion.) Thankfully, civilization has moved on in its treatment of the mentally ill, although as this museum shows, nations are still as capable of cruelty and organized madness as they ever were.

The great, gung-ho 38-cm (15-in.) naval guns parked outside the entrance give an indication of what you can expect in the main hall. This is the boys' toys section with a whole fleet of tanks, planes, and missiles on display (including a Battle of Britain Spitfire, a V2 rocket, and a German one-man submarine), and plenty of interactivity for the kids, with cockpits to climb into and touch-screen terminals to explore.

After the initial bombast, however, comes a selection of thoughtful, sobering exhibits, focusing on the human cost of war. These include galleries exploring life during World Wars I and II—both on the battlefield and at home—a new gallery celebrating exploits of supreme valor, "Extraordinary Heroes," and the "Secret War" exhibition which looks at the use of duplicity, subterfuge, and spying in wartime.

On the upper floors, things become more thoughtful still. The third floor provides an intense account of the Holocaust, examining the first attempt to apply modern industrial techniques to the destruction of people. And, just to remind you that this is not an evil that has been permanently consigned to history, the "Crimes against Humanity" exhibition explores modern genocides. Its central exhibit is a harrowing 30-minute film. These two galleries are not recommended for children under 14.

Lambeth Rd., SE1. ✆ **020/7416-5000** (info line). http://london.iwm.org.uk. Free admission. Daily 10am–6pm. Tube: Lambeth North or Elephant and Castle.

London Dungeon ★ ☺ MUSEUM   Set beneath the arches of London Bridge Station, this is a sort of hi-tech haunted house aimed squarely at children and teenagers to whom it delivers a series of "safe" shocks, themed (very loosely) on events and legends from London's history. A list of some of the dungeon's current "scenes" should give you an idea of what to expect: "Great Plague & Surgery: Blood & Guts," "Jack the Ripper," and "Extremis: Drop Ride to Doom."

You'll find it either a terrible piece of kitsch, overpriced nonsense, or a glorious exercise in Grand Guignol-lite—probably depending on your age. It's certainly all very tongue-in-cheek, although you should use discretion with very young children.

28–34 Tooley St., SE1. ✆ **020/7403-7221.** www.the-dungeons.co.uk. Admission £23 adults (£13 online, off-peak price), £21 students and seniors (£11 online, off-peak price), £17 children 5–14 (£11 online, off-peak price), free for children 4 and under. Times vary; the dungeon is open daily, typically 10am–5pm, but stays open later (till 6:30 or 7pm) during the school holidays. Tube: London Bridge.

London Eye ★★ ☺ OBSERVATION POINT   The largest observation wheel in Europe, the London Eye has become, just over a decade after it opened, a potent icon of the capital, as clearly identified with London as the Eiffel Tower is with Paris. And indeed, it performs much the same function—giving people the chance to observe

The **London Eye (p. 107)** is the most obvious of the attractions offering a "bird's eye" view of the capital, but it's by no means the only vantage point. For centuries before the Eye was built, **St. Paul's Cathedral (p. 111)** has been letting Londoners willing to climb its 500 plus steps gaze out over their city, spread out before them like a great 3-D map. Worthy, albeit slightly less elevated, panoramas are also offered from the top of **Westminster Cathedral (p. 104)**, the **Monument (p. 110)**, the **National Portrait Gallery** restaurant **(p. 90)**, and the **Oxo Tower**—this last one is particularly recommended, because it's free.

The number of views is set to increase in the future as London is currently witnessing the development of a glut of skyscrapers, some of which have promised to operate viewing galleries.

the city from above. Passengers are carried in 32 glass-sided "pods," each representing one of the 32 boroughs of London (which lucky travelers get Croydon?), that make a complete revolution every half-hour. Along the way you'll see bird's-eye views of some of London's most famous landmarks, including the Houses of Parliament, Buckingham Palace, the BT Tower, St. Paul's, the "Gherkin," and of course, the River Thames itself. You're free to move around inside the pod, during its voyage, although everyone tends to congregate in the northern half to look out over the river and the heart of sightseeing London. "Night flights," when you can gaze at the twinkling lights of the city are available in winter.

Millennium Jubilee Gardens, SE1. ℂ **0870/5000-600.** www.ba-londoneye.com. Admission £18 adults, £14 seniors and students, £9.50 children 4–15. Times vary, but the Eye is open daily from 10am, usually till 9pm in summer (9:30pm in July–Aug) and till 8pm in winter..Tube: Waterloo or Westminster.

Old Operating Theatre Museum & Herb Garret ★★ ☺ MUSEUM Next
time you find yourself moaning about a trip to the family doctor, remember it could be *much* worse, as this antique operating theatre shows. Although less than 200 years old, it might as well be from the Stone Age, such have been the advances in medical science. It was once part of St. Thomas' Hospital, but was sealed over and forgotten about for more than a century when the hospital relocated in 1861. Now restored, it provides a grim window into the past. At its center is a table on which operations—mainly amputations—were performed without anesthetic or antiseptic. Patients were bound to prevent them struggling free, a box of sawdust was placed beneath them to collect the blood, and then the surgeon got to work, the aim being to sever the limb as quickly as possible to prevent the patient from bleeding to death. The grisly spectacle was watched by medical students in the surrounding seating—this really was a "theatre"—as you can do every Saturday at 2pm, when a demonstration of 19th-century "Speed Surgery" is staged.

The **herb garret,** located above the theatre, was used for drying medicinal plants. It was rediscovered at the same time, and provides a more peaceful, aromatic second act.

9a St. Thomas St., SE1 .(ℂ **020/7188-2679.** www.thegarret.org.uk. Admission £5.80 adults, £4.80 seniors and students, £3.25 children 15 and under, £13.75 family. Daily 10:30am–5pm. Tube: London Bridge.

Shakespeare's Globe ★ HISTORIC SITE/THEATRE This is a recent re-
creation of one of the most important public theatres ever built, Shakespeare's Globe, where the Bard premiered many of his most famous plays. The new Globe isn't an

exact replica: It seats 1,500 patrons, not the 3,000 who regularly squeezed in during the early 1600s, and this thatched roof has been specially treated with a fire retardant—just as well, as a shot from a stage cannon fired during a performance of *Henry VIII* provided the ultimate finale, setting the roof alight and burning the original theatre to the ground.

Insider tip: Guided tours of the facility are offered throughout the day in the theatre's winter off-season. From May to September, however, Globe tours are only available in the morning. In the afternoon, when matinee performances are taking place, alternative tours to the rather scanty remains of the **Rose Theatre,** the Globe's precursor (which was torn down in the early 17th century), are offered instead.

See p. 163 for details on attending a play here.

21 New Globe Walk, SE1. ℂ **020/7902-1400.** www.shakespeares-globe.org. Admission and Globe Tour/Rose Tour £11.50/7.50 adults, £10/6.50 seniors and students, £7/4.50 children 5–15, free children 4 and under. Oct–Apr daily 10am–5pm; May–Sept daily 9am–noon and 12:30–5pm. Tube: Mansion House or London Bridge.

Tate Modern ★★★ GALLERY   Welcoming more than four million visitors a year, Tate Modern is the world's most popular modern art gallery (the free admission helps), and one of the capital's very best attractions. From the day it opened in 2000, the gallery has received almost as many plaudits for its setting as for its contents. It's housed in a converted 1940s' brick power station, the brooding industrial functionalism of the architecture providing a fitting canopy for the often challenging art within. Through the main entrance you enter a vast space, the **Turbine Hall,** where a succession of giant temporary exhibitions are staged—the bigger and more ambitious, the better.

The permanent collection encompasses a great body of modern art dating from 1900 to the present. Spread over three levels, it covers all the big hitters, including Matisse, Rothko, Pollock, Picasso, Dali, Duchamp, and Warhol, and is arranged according to movements—surrealism, minimalism, cubism, expressionism, and so on. Free 45-minute guided tours of the collection are given daily at 11am, noon, 2, and 3pm. The gallery stays open late on Friday and Saturday, when events, such as concerts and talks, are often put on.

Such has been the gallery's success that a new extension is being built. It will take the form of a giant asymmetrical, brick-and-glass pyramid, which should be completed in 2012.

Bankside, SE1. ℂ **020/7887-8888.** www.tate.org.uk/modern. Free admission. Sun–Thurs 10am–6pm; Fri–Sat 10am–10pm. Tube: Southwark or London Bridge.

The City

Guildhall & Guildhall Art Gallery ★ HISTORIC SITE   The headquarters of the City of London Corporation, the administrative body that has overseen the City's affairs for the past 800 years, the Guildhall's original medieval framework has endured significant repairs following the 1666 Great Fire and World War II (as well as the addition of a rather incongruous concrete wing in the 1970s). Today its Great Hall has a touch of the medieval theme park about it, filled with colorful livery banners and with a (reconstructed) minstrel's gallery from where 3-m (9-ft.) statues of mythical giants Gog and Magog gaze down on proceedings.

East across Guildhall Yard, the **Guildhall Art Gallery** displays a constantly updated selection from the Corporation's 4,000-plus works relating to the capital. The main attraction (there's certainly no missing it) is John Singleton Copley's *The Defeat of the Floating Batteries at Gibraltar, September 1782,* which at 42.5 sq m (458 sq ft.)

is Britain's largest independent oil painting, and takes up two whole storys. Fridays are the best time to visit, when admission is free, and you can join a free tour of the collection at 12:15, 1:15, 2:15, and 3:15pm.

Head down beneath the gallery to visit the scant remains of **London's Roman amphitheatre,** which dates from the 2nd century A.D., but remained undiscovered until 1988 (and didn't go on display until 2003). Images of spectators and missing bits have been added to give visitors a better idea of what it once looked like.

Guildhall Yard, Gresham St., EC2. ℂ **020/7332-3700.** www.guildhall-art-gallery.org.uk. Admission £2.50 adults, £1 seniors and students, free for children 15 and under. Free Fri and after 3:30pm on all other days. Mon–Sat 10am–5pm; Sun noon–4pm. Tube: Bank, St. Paul's, or Moorgate.

The Monument ★ ☺ OBSERVATION POINT   Once upon a time, the Monument towered above the city, a proud and defiant reminder of London's revival following the destructive Great Fire of 1666. At 61.5m (202 ft.), the Sir Christopher Wren-designed column was then the world's tallest free-standing stone column, a record it continues to hold—largely because they don't really make free-standing stone columns any more.

It's 311 steps to the top, from where the views are among the finest in the city. Those who baulk at either heights or energetic climbs can enjoy them from the live feed shown at the bottom. Apparently, if the Monument fell over, it would, providing it fell in the right direction, land on the exact spot in Pudding Lane where the Great Fire started.

Fish Street Hill, EC3. ℂ **020/7626-2717.** www.themonument.info. Admission £3 adults, £2 seniors and students, £1 children. Daily 9:30am–5:30pm. Tube: Monument or London Bridge.

Museum of London ★★ ☺ MUSEUM   Although the location is rather grim, in the center of a particularly unappealing roundabout in London's Barbican district, this museum is a joy. It traces the history of the capital from prehistoric times to the 20th century. Exhibits are arranged so that you can begin and end your chronological stroll through 250,000 years at the main entrance to the museum. Upstairs you'll find sections devoted to "London before London" (with flint arrow heads and bronze age weapons); Roman London (mosaics, statues, coins, and more); Medieval London (Viking battleaxes and knights' armor); and War, Plague, and Fire (a model of Shakespeare's Rose Theatre, Cromwell's death mask, and paintings of the Great Fire). The recently revamped downstairs galleries bring the story up to date with displays on the

 A money-saving **PASS**

The **London Pass** provides admission to more than 55 attractions in and around London, "timed" admission at some attractions (bypassing the line ups), plus free travel on public transport (buses, Tubes, and trains) and a pocket guidebook. It costs £40 for 1 day, £55 for 2 days, £68 for 3 days, and £90 for 6 days (children 5–15 pay £27, £41, £46, or £64, respectively), and includes admission to St. Paul's Cathedral, HMS *Belfast,* the Jewish Museum, and the Thames Barrier Visitor Centre—and many other attractions. This rather pricey pass is useful if you're trying to cram 2 days' worth of sightseeing into a single day. But if you're a slow-moving visitor, who likes to stop and smell the roses, you may not get your money's worth. See **www. londonpass.com**.

St. Paul's Cathedral

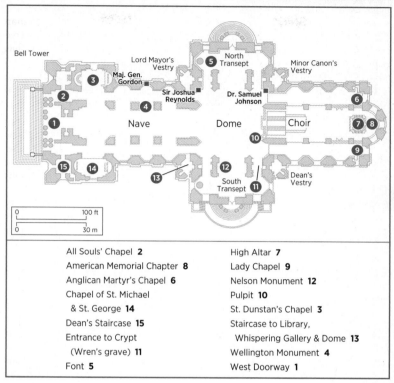

Bell Tower

Lord Mayor's Vestry

5 North Transept

Minor Canon's Vestry

3 Maj. Gen. Gordon

2

Sir Joshua Reynolds

Dr. Samuel Johnson

6

1

Nave

Dome

Choir

7 **8**

4

10

9

15 **14**

12

13 **11**

South Transept

Dean's Vestry

0 ————— 100 ft

0 ————— 30 m

All Souls' Chapel **2**	High Altar **7**
American Memorial Chapter **8**	Lady Chapel **9**
Anglican Martyr's Chapel **6**	Nelson Monument **12**
Chapel of St. Michael	Pulpit **10**
& St. George **14**	St. Dunstan's Chapel **3**
Dean's Staircase **15**	Staircase to Library,
Entrance to Crypt	Whispering Gallery & Dome **13**
(Wren's grave) **11**	Wellington Monument **4**
Font **5**	West Doorway **1**

"Expanding City: 1666–1850" (including a re-created 18th-century prison and a 240-year-old printing press); "People's City: 1850s–1940s" (walk a replica Victorian street); and "World City: 1950s–Today" (explore an interactive model of the Thames), as well as perhaps the museum's most eye-catching exhibit, the **Lord Mayor's Coach,** a gilt-and-scarlet fairytale carriage built in 1757.

London Wall, EC2. ✆ **020/7001-9844.** www.museumoflondon.org.uk. Free admission. Daily 10am–6pm. Tube: St. Paul's or Barbican.

St. Paul's Cathedral ★★★ ☺ CATHEDRAL   London's skyline has changed dramatically during the past three centuries. Buildings have come and gone, architectural styles have waxed and waned, but throughout there has been one constant—the great plump dome of St. Paul's Cathedral gazing beatifically down upon the city. Despite the best intentions of the Luftwaffe and modern skyscraper designers, Sir Christopher Wren's masterpiece is still the defining landmark of the City skyline—and it's never looked so good. Preparations for its 300th anniversary (in 2008) saw the cathedral scrubbed and swabbed inside and out until it positively gleamed.

The interior is a neck-craningly large space. Dotted around at ground level are tombs and memorials to various British heroes, including the Duke of Wellington,

Lawrence of Arabia, and in the South Quire Aisle, an effigy of John Donne, one of the country's most celebrated poets and a former dean of St. Paul's. It's one of the few items to have survived from the previous, medieval cathedral, which was destroyed by the Great Fire in 1666; you can still see scorch marks on its base.

The cathedral offers some of the capital's best views, although you'll have to earn them by undertaking a more than 500-step climb up to the **Golden Gallery.** Here you can enjoy giddying 360° panoramas of the capital, as well as perhaps equally stomach-tightening views down to the floor 111m (364 ft.) below.

Down in the crypt is a bumper crop of memorials, including those of Alexander Fleming, Admiral Lord Nelson, William Blake, and Wren himself—the epitaph on his simple tombstone reads: "Reader, if you seek a monument, look around you."

St. Paul's Churchyard, EC4. ℂ **020/7246-8350.** www.stpauls.co.uk. Cathedral and galleries £12.50 adults, £11.50 seniors, £9.50 students, £4.50 children 6–16, £29.50 family ticket, free for children 5 and under. Cathedral (excluding galleries) Mon–Sat 8:30am–4pm; galleries Mon–Sat 9:30am–4pm. No sightseeing Sun (services only). Tube: St. Paul's.

Samuel Johnson's House ★ HISTORIC HOME   Poet, lexicographer, critic, biographer, and above all, quotation machine, Dr. Samuel Johnson lived in this Queen Anne house between 1748 and 1759. It was here that he compiled his famous dictionary—not as is commonly supposed, the first of the English language, but certainly the most influential to that date. His house has been painstakingly restored to its mid-18th-century prime and is well worth a visit. Guided walks taking in many of the local sites associated with Johnson's life, including Temple Bar and Fleet Street, take place on the first Wednesday of the month, leaving from the entrance of the house at 3pm. They cost £3. No booking is required.

17 Gough Sq., EC4. ℂ **020/7353-3745.** www.drjohnsonshouse.org. Admission £4.50 adults, £3.50 students and seniors, £1.50 children, £10 family ticket, free for children 10 and under. Oct–Apr Mon–Sat 11am–5pm; May–Sept Mon–Sat 11am–5:30pm. Tube: Chancery Lane.

Tower of London ★★★ ☺ HISTORIC SITE   On a sunny summer afternoon, the Tower, one of the best preserved medieval castles in the world, can be a cheerful buzzing place, filled with happy swarms of tourists being entertained by costumed actors and historically themed events. At such times it can be easy to forget that beneath all the kitschy tourist trappings lies a very real castle with a very brutal and bloody history.

The Tower is actually a compound of structures built at various times for varying purposes. The oldest is the **White Tower,** begun by William the Conqueror in 1078 to keep London's native Saxon population in check. Later rulers added towers, walls, and fortified gates, until the buildings became like a small town within a city. Although it began life as a stronghold against rebellion, the tower's main role eventually became less about keeping people out, than making sure whoever was inside couldn't escape. It became the favored prison and execution site for anyone who displeased the monarch. Notable prisoners served their last meals here include the "princes in the tower," Lady Jane Grey (who reigned as queen for just 9 days before being toppled by Mary I in 1553), and Anne Boleyn, one of several unfortunates who thought that marrying that most unforgiving of monarchs, Henry VIII, was a good idea. A plaque on Tower Green marks the spot where they met their grisly ends.

Displays on some of the Tower's captives can be seen in the **Bloody Tower,** including a reconstruction of the study of Sir Walter Raleigh, the great Elizabethan adventurer who is generally credited with having introduced tobacco smoking to

England. A favorite of Elizabeth I, he was executed by James I, a fervent anti-smoker, having spent 13 years as a prisoner here.

In addition to being a prison, the Tower has also been used as a royal palace, a mint, and an armory. Today, however, it's perhaps best known as the keeper of the **Crown Jewels,** the main ceremonial regalia of the British monarch, which—when not being used—are displayed in the tower's **Jewel House.** It's probably best to tackle this soon after your arrival, as the lines seem to build exponentially over the course of the day. You hop aboard a travelator for a slow glide past some of the Queen's top trinkets, including the Imperial State Crown (as modeled each year at the State Opening of Parliament), which looks like a child's fantasy of a piece of royal headwear, set with no fewer than 3,000 jewels, including the fourth-largest diamond in the world.

After the jewels, the tower's next most popular draw is probably the **Royal Armory** located in the White Tower, where you can see various fearsome-looking weapons, including swords, halberds, and morning stars, as well as bespoke suits of armor made for kings. The complex also boasts the only surviving medieval palace in Britain, dating back to the 1200s. It stands in the riverside wall above **Traitors' Gate,** through which prisoners were brought to the Tower. You can see reconstructed bedrooms, a throne room, and chapel.

Be sure to take advantage of the free hour-long tours offered by the iconic guards, the Yeoman Warders—more commonly known as **Beefeaters.** They'll regale you with tales of royal intrigue, and introduce you to the Tower's current most famous residents, the six ravens who live on Tower Gardens. According to legend, if the ravens ever leave the Tower, the monarchy will fall—the birds' wings are kept clipped, just to make sure. The tours take place every half-hour from 9:30am until 3:30pm in summer (2:30pm in winter) and leave from the Middle Tower near the entrance.

Tower Hill, EC3. ℂ **0844/482-7777.** www.hrp.org.uk/TowerOfLondon. Admission £18.70 adults, £15.95 students and seniors, £10.45 children 5–15, family ticket £51.70, free for children 4 and under. Mar–Oct Tues–Sat 9am–5:30pm, Sun–Mon 10am–5:30pm; Nov–Feb Tues–Sat 9am–4:30pm, Sun–Mon 10am–4:30pm. Tube: Tower Hill/DLR: Tower Gateway.

East London

Geffrye Museum ★ MUSEUM   If you'd like an overview of British interiors and lifestyles of the past 4 centuries, head to this museum, housed in a series of restored 18th-century almshouses. Period rooms are arranged chronologically, allowing you to follow the changing tastes in furnishings in English middle-class homes over the generations. The collection is rich in Jacobean, Georgian, and Victorian interiors. In the 20th-century rooms, you'll see the luxuriant Art Deco styles giving way to the bleakness of the utilitarian designs that followed in the aftermath of World War II.

Tower Tips

Tickets are cheaper if booked online: £16 for adults, £9 for children. If buying your ticket at the venue, pick them up at the kiosk at Tower Hill Tube station before emerging above ground—the lines should be shorter. Even so, choose a day other than Sunday—crowds are at their worst then—and arrive as early as you can in the morning, or late in the afternoon.

SAINTS & THE city: A WALK

For somewhere so unashamedly dedicated to Mammon, the financial center of London also offers plenty of spiritual comfort (which no doubt comes in handy when stocks start tumbling). Our favorite historic churches can be comfortably toured in a day—or an afternoon, if you're quick.

Beginning at Temple Tube, turn left out of the station, and head north up Arundel Place. Turn right onto the Strand, and stroll east along Fleet Street till you reach **Prince Henry's Room,** 17 Fleet St. (✆ **020/7332-1097**), one of London's only surviving houses to predate the Great Fire of 1666. Turn right through the stone arch by the house, down Inner Temple Lane to **Temple Church** ★, King's Bench Walk, EC4 (✆ **020/7353-3470;** www.temple church.com), a round church founded in the late 12th century by the **Knights Templar,** one of the most powerful religious military orders during the Crusades. Much restored and rebuilt in subsequent centuries, it has enjoyed a resurgence of interest since being featured in *The Da Vinci Code*. Admission is free. Opening hours are Monday, Tuesday, and Friday 11am to 12:30pm and

1–4pm, Wednesday 2 to 4pm, Thursday 11am to 12:30pm and 2 to 3:30pm, Saturday 11am to 12:30pm and 1 to 3pm, and Sunday 1 to 3:30pm.

Back on Fleet Street continue east. Take a right down Salisbury Court, then a left onto St. Bride's Passage for **St. Bride's,** Fleet Street, EC4 (✆ **020/7427- 0133;** www.stbrides.com), perhaps the city's oldest church, founded back in the 6th century. Rebuilt by Sir Christopher Wren after the Great Fire, its distinctive multistep spire was said to have inspired the design of modern wedding cakes. It's known as the "Journalists' Church," owing to its proximity to Fleet Street, the old home of the British press. It's free to enter. Hours are Monday through Friday 8am to 6pm, Saturday 11am to 3pm, and Sunday 10am to 1pm and 5 to 7:30pm.

Return to Fleet Street and head east along Ludgate Hill. A diversion north up Old Bailey will take you past the Central Criminal Court (also more commonly known as the **Old Bailey**). If you crane your neck you should just about be able to make out the statue of Lady Liberty holding a sword and a set of scales perched upon its roof. Carry on north, along Giltspur Street and West Smithfield,

---

Outside the chronological theme is continued with a series of four period gardens dating from the 17th to the 20th centuries. The Geffrye is especially charming around Christmas, when each room is dressed in authentic festive style.

136 Kingsland Rd., E2. ✆ **020/7739-9893.** www.geffrye-museum.org.uk. Free admission to period rooms; £2 to Almshouses (free for children 15 and under). Tues-Sat 10am–5pm; Sun and bank holidays noon–5pm. Gardens Apr-Oct only. Tube: Liverpool St., then bus 149 or 242; or Old St., then bus 243/ Train: Hoxton.

Museum of London Docklands ★ ☺ MUSEUM   This East London outpost of the Museum of London looks at the history of the capital's river, and in particular the growth and demise of the trading industry that once flourished upon it. Housed in a relic of that industry, a Georgian sugar warehouse, the museum tells the story of the docks from the beginnings of river commerce under the Romans through the glory days of Empire, when London was the world's busiest port, to the closure of the central London docks in the 1970s. It also takes a look at the subsequent regeneration of the area, of which this museum forms a part. The displays focus on both local

bearing right until you reach **St. Bartholomew-the-Great**, 6–9 Kinghorn St., EC1 (ℂ **020/7606-5171;** www.great stbarts.com). Begun in 1123, this is one of the best examples of large-scale Norman architecture in the city. Admission is £4, and it's open Monday through Friday 8:30am to 5pm, Saturday 10:30am to 4pm, and Sunday 8:30am to 8pm. Opposite, **St. Bartholomew's Hospital** ("Barts") has a small **Hospital Museum** of medical curiosities (North Wing, West Smithfield, EC1; ℂ **020/3465-5798;** www.barts andthelondon.nhs.uk). It's free, and open Monday through Friday 10am to 4pm. Guided tours of the collection are given at 2pm on Fridays (£5).

Retrace your steps back down to Ludgate Hill and continue east until the glorious facade of **St. Paul's Cathedral ★★★** (p. 111), surely the city's finest church, looms into view. Pass through the cathedral's churchyard onto New Change, site of a major new shopping center, **One New Change** (p. 151), then right on Cheapside for **St. Mary-le-Bow** (ℂ **020/7248-5139;** www. stmarylebow.co.uk), otherwise known as the "Cockney Church"; to be a "true Cockney," you must be born within the

sound of its bells. First erected around 1,000 years ago, it was rebuilt by Sir Christopher Wren following the Great Fire and again, in the style of Wren, after World War II. It's open Monday through Friday 6:30am till 6pm; admission is free.

Continue east, then southeast down King William Street, and finally east along Eastcheap and Great Tower Street to **All-Hallows-by-the-Tower ★**, Byward Street, EC3 (ℂ **020/7481-2928;** www. allhallowsbythetower.org.uk), just down the road from (and providing elevated views over) the Tower of London. When the first church was built here in the 7th century, the site had already been in use for several centuries. You can see Roman, Saxon, and medieval remains at its small museum. The famous diarist **Samuel Pepys** supposedly watched the progress of the Great Fire from the church's spire. Admission to the church is free; a crypt museum tour costs £6. Museum hours are Monday through Friday 10am to 5:30pm, Saturday 10am to 5pm, and Sunday 1 to 5pm. The church is open Monday to Friday 8am to 6pm, Saturday and Sunday 10am till 5pm,

From here it's a short walk east to the nearest Tube station, Tower Hill.

social aspects—you can walk through "Sailor Town," a reconstructed Victorian community—and the global implications of London's rise as a major trading city. The more unsavory aspects of the subject are examined in "London: Sugar and Slavery," and there's also a dedicated hands-on kids' section by the entrance, "Mudlarks." West India Quay, E14. ℂ **020/7001-9844.** www.museumindocklands.org.uk. Free admission. Daily 10am–6pm. Tube: Canary Wharf/DLR: West India Quay.

V&A Museum of Childhood ★ ☺ MUSEUM This branch of the Victoria & Albert Museum specializes in historic toys. The variety of dolls alone is staggering; some have such elaborate period costumes that you don't even want to think of the price tags they would carry today. With the dolls come dollhouses, from simple cottages to miniature mansions, complete with fireplaces, grand pianos, and kitchen utensils. You'll also find optical toys, marionettes, puppets, board games from throughout the ages, a considerable exhibit of soldiers and war toys, trains, and aircraft, and a display of clothing and furniture relating to the social history of childhood. Of course, looking at toys, but not touching them, can prove frustrating for

Attractions, Hotels & Restaurants in East London

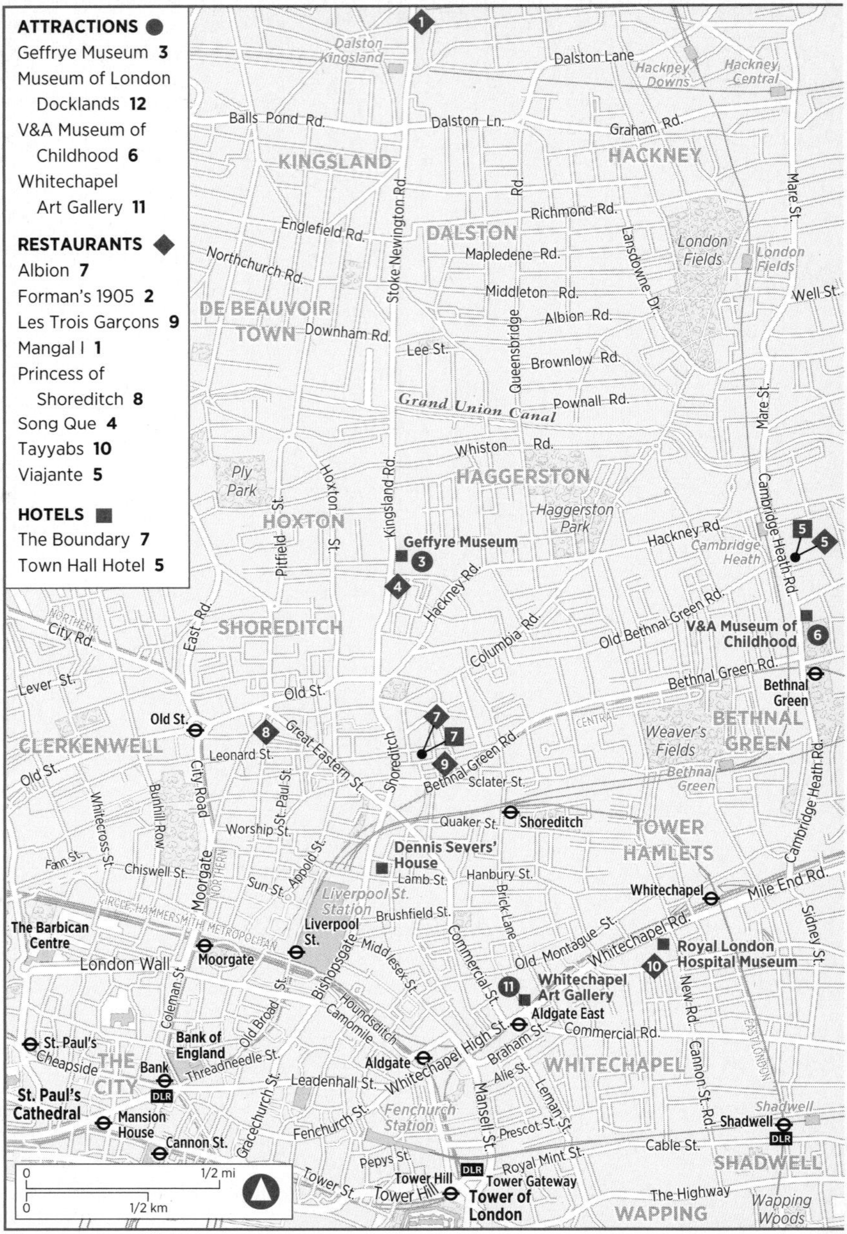

ATTRACTIONS ●

Geffrye Museum **3**
Museum of London
    Docklands **12**
V&A Museum of
    Childhood **6**
Whitechapel
    Art Gallery **11**

RESTAURANTS ◆

Albion **7**
Forman's 1905 **2**
Les Trois Garçons **9**
Mangal I **1**
Princess of
    Shoreditch **8**
Song Que **4**
Tayyabs **10**
Viajante **5**

HOTELS ■

The Boundary **7**
Town Hall Hotel **5**

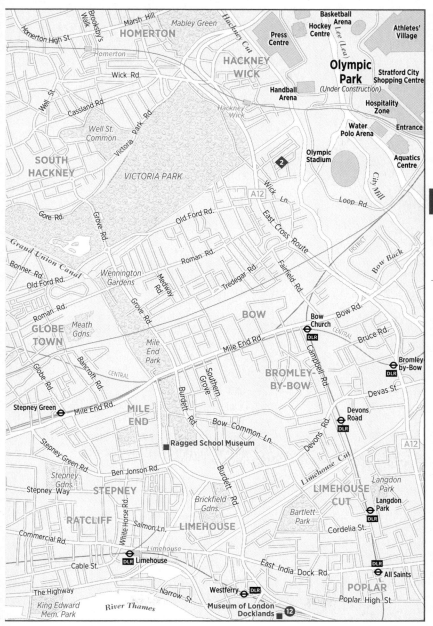

younger visitors. Thankfully, the museum also boasts a hands-on "Creative Gallery" and organizes free activities and workshops for children on weekends and during the school holidays.

Cambridge Heath Rd., E2. ℂ **020/8983-5200.** www.vam.ac.uk/moc. Free admission. Daily 10am–5:45pm. Tube: Bethnal Green.

Whitechapel Art Gallery ★★ GALLERY   In 2009 East London's premier art gallery reopened following the most significant revamp since its foundation in 1901. Throughout its history the gallery has often played a leading role in the development of artistic movements. In the 1930s, it hosted Britain's first showing of Picasso's *Guernica,* as part of an exhibition protesting the Spanish Civil War. It then shocked postwar audiences by introducing them to Jackson Pollock's abstracts, and pioneered Pop Art in the 1960s. Expect further revelations in the future. It also offers regular free talks, as well as cheap film screenings and concerts.

77-82 Whitechapel Rd., E1. ℂ **020/7522-7888.** www.whitechapelgallery.org. Free admission. Tues–Sun 11am–6pm. Tube: Aldgate East.

4 North & Northwest London

British Library ★ ☺ MUSEUM   One of the world's great repositories of books, the British Library receives a copy of every single title published in the U.K., which are stored on 400 miles of shelves. In 1996, the whole lot (14 million books, manuscripts, sound recordings, and other items) was moved from the British Museum to the library's new home in St. Pancras. The current building may be a lot less elegant than its predecessor, but the bright, roomy interior is far more inviting than the rather dull, redbrick exterior suggests. Within are a number of permanent galleries, the highlight being the "Treasures of the British Library", where some of the library's most precious possessions are displayed, including a copy of the *Magna Carta* (1215), a Gutenberg Bible, and the journals of Captain Cook.

96 Euston Rd., NW1. ℂ **0843/208-1144.** www.bl.uk. Free admission. Mon and Wed–Fri 9:30am–6pm; Tues 9:30am–8pm; Sat 9:30am–5pm; Sun 11am–5pm. Tube: King's Cross or Euston. ·

Hampstead Heath ★★★ ☺ PARK   This 320-hectare (791-acre) expanse of high heath is made up of a great mixture of formal parkland, woodland, heath, meadowland, and ponds. One of the few places in the big city that feels properly wild, it's a fantastic place to lose yourself on a rambling wander. On a clear day, you can see St. Paul's Cathedral, the Houses of Parliament, and even the hills of Kent from the prime viewing spot atop Parliament Hill, 98m (322 ft.) up. For years Londoners have come here to sun-worship, fly kites, fish the ponds, swim, picnic, or jog.

Much of the northern end is taken up by the more manicured grounds of **Kenwood House,** a great spot for a picnic, where concerts are staged on summer evenings. Along its eastern end are a group of ponds set aside for bathing (there's a ladies' pool, a men's pool, and a mixed pool), sailing model boats, and as a bird sanctuary—the heath is one of London's best **birdwatching** locations.

South of the heath is the leafy, well-to-do **Hampstead Village,** a longtime favorite haunt of writers, artists, architects, musicians, and scientists. Keats, D. H. Lawrence, Shelley, Robert Louis Stevenson, and Kingsley Amis all lived here. The village's Regency and Georgian houses offer a quirky mix of historic pubs, toy shops, and chic boutiques, as exemplified by **Flask Walk.**

Hampstead, NW3. ℂ **020/7482-7073.** www.cityoflondon.gov.uk. Free admission. Open 24 hours. Tube: Hampstead/Train: Hampstead Heath or Gospel Oak.

Highgate Cemetery CEMETERY   A stone's throw east of Hampstead Heath, this beautiful cemetery is laid out around a huge 300-year-old cedar tree and is laced with serpentine pathways. The cemetery was so popular and fashionable in the Victorian era that it was extended on the other side of Swain's Lane in 1857. The most famous grave is that of **Karl Marx,** who died in Hampstead in 1883; his grave, marked by a gargantuan bust, is in the eastern cemetery. In the old western cemetery—accessible only by guided tour, given hourly in summer—are scientist Michael Faraday and poet Christina Rossetti.

Swain's Lane, N6. ✆ **020/8340-1834.** http://highgate-cemetery.org. Western Cemetery guided tour £7 adults, £5 students, £3 children 8–15 (cash only). Eastern Cemetery admission £3 adults, £2 students, free children 15 and under (cash only). Western Cemetery: Mar–Oct tours Mon–Fri 2pm, Sat–Sun hourly 11am–4pm; Nov–Feb tours Sat–Sun hourly 11am–3pm. Eastern Cemetery: Apr–Oct Mon–Fri 10am–4:30pm, Sat–Sun 11am–4:30pm; Nov–Mar Mon–Fri 10am–3:30pm, Sat–Sun 11am–3:30pm. Both cemeteries closed at Christmas and during funerals. Tube: Archway, then bus 143, 210, 271, or C11.

Jewish Museum ★ MUSEUM   Reopened to the public in 2010, following a £10 million improvement, this Camden museum retells the often difficult history of Britain's Jewish communities from the Middle Ages to the present, as well as illuminating aspects of Jewish ritual and belief. Most of the items date from after the English Civil Wars, when Oliver Cromwell changed the law to allow Jews to settle in Britain. You can explore a recreated Victorian Jewish Quarter from East London, see a variety of historical artifacts, including a 17th-century synagogue ark, and, in the most affecting section, learn about the Holocaust as experienced by a single Auschwitz survivor, Leon Greenman, whose story is cleverly (and movingly) used to represent the plight of an entire people.

129-131 Albert St., NW1. ✆ **020/8371-7373.** www.jewishmuseum.org.uk. Admission £7 adults, £6 seniors and students, £3 children 5–15, free for children 4 and under. Sun–Wed 10am–5pm, Thurs 10am–9pm, Fri 10am–2pm. Tube: Camden Town.

London Zoo (ZSL) ★★ ☺ ZOO   When London Zoo—one of the finest big city zoos in the world—was founded back in 1820, it was purely for the purposes of scientific research. Highlights of the modern London Zoo include the "Clore Rainforest Lookout," a steamy indoor replica jungle inhabited by sloths, tamarin monkeys, and lemurs; "B.U.G.S," which apparently stands for Biodiversity Underpinning Global Survival, but does also contain plenty of bugs, including leaf-cutter ants, brightly colored beetles, and giant, scary bird-eating spiders; and, the current flagship, "Gorilla Kingdom," a moated island resembling an African forest clearing, which provides a naturalistic habitat for gorillas and colobus monkeys. There are always plenty of activities going on here, including keeper talks, feeding times, and "meet the animals" displays. A day-planner is handed out at the front gate, or you can download one from the website.

   Insider tip: Savings of around 10% can be made if you book a family ticket online; these are not available at the front gate.

Outer Circle, Regent's Park, NW1. ✆ **020/7722-3333.** www.zsl.org/zsl-london-zoo. Admission winter season/mid-season/peak-season including donation: £18/19/19.80 adults, £16.50/17.50/18.30 students and seniors, £15/15.50/16 children 3–15. Mar–Oct daily 10am–5:30pm; Nov–Feb daily 10am–4pm. Tube: Regent's Park or Camden Town/Bus: C2 or 274.

Regent's Park ★★ ☺ PARK   Designed by 18th-century genius John Nash to surround a palace for the Prince Regent (the palace never materialized), this is the most classically beautiful of all London's parks, and featured briefly in the film, *The*

King's Speech. Its core is a rose garden planted around a small lake alive with waterfowl and spanned by Japanese bridges; in early summer, the rose perfume is heady in the air. Rowboats and sailing dinghies are available from the **Boathouse Café** (✆ **020/7724-4069**) for £6.50 per adult and £4.40 per child for 1 hour.

Regent's Park, NW1. ✆ **020/7486-7905.** www.royalparks.org.uk/parks/regents_park. Free admission daily 5am–dusk. Tube: Baker St., Great Portland St., or Regent's Park.

Southeast London—Greenwich

With the great skyscrapers of Canary Wharf to the north, and waves of faceless suburbia to the south, Greenwich seems almost out of place—a royal theme park smuggled into London's backwaters. It makes a great escape from the center of town, with a look and ambience all its own. For the full effect, arrive by **Thames Clipper** boat (p. 82), which shows off the riverside architecture to its best effect.

National Maritime Museum ★★ ☺ MUSEUM   From the days of early seafarers to 20th-century naval power, the National Maritime Museum illustrates the glory that was Britain at sea. The cannon, relics, ship models, and paintings tell the story of 1,000 naval battles and 1,000 victories (plus the odd defeat). The lower two floors are divided into themed sections, including "Explorers," "Maritime London," and "Atlantic Worlds," and are filled with nautical oddities—everything from the dreaded cat-o'-nine-tails used to flog sailors until 1879, to Nelson's Trafalgar coat, with the fatal bullet hole in the left shoulder clearly visible.

Romney Rd., SE10. ✆ **020/8858-4422.** www.nmm.ac.uk. Free admission. Daily 10am–5pm. DLR: Cutty Sark.

Old Royal Naval College ★ HISTORIC SITE   The great baroque waterfront facade of this wonderfully grand structure offers perhaps the clearest distillation of Greenwich's charms. UNESCO certainly thought so, describing it as the "finest and most dramatically sited architectural . . . ensemble in the British Isles." It's the work of England's holy trinity of 17th-century architects: Wren, Hawksmoor, and Vanbrugh (mostly Wren, in truth), and was designed in 1694 as a hospital for veteran sailors. The pensioners moved out in 1873, when the complex became the Royal Naval College. The Royal Navy finally ended its association with the building in 1998, since when it has been home to part of the University of Greenwich. Just three sections are open to the public: The Georgian chapel of **St. Peter and St. Paul,** where organ recitals are often given; the magnificent **Painted Hall ★** by Sir James Thornhill, where the body of Nelson lay in state in 1805; and the new **Discover Greenwich Centre,** which contains an intriguing and interactive exhibition on the history of Greenwich as well as the suburb's tourist information service.

Old Royal Naval College, SE10. ✆ **020/8269-4747.** www.oldroyalnavalcollege.org. Free admission. Daily 10am–5pm. DLR: Cutty Sark.

Royal Observatory ★★ ☺ HISTORIC SITE   The home of **Greenwich Mean Time,** the Observatory was designed by Sir Christopher Wren in the early 18th century and boasts the country's largest refracting telescope (reserved for the use of professional astronomers only, unfortunately), as well as a small collection of historic timekeepers and astronomical instruments (which you're more than welcome to browse). The highlight, however, is the **Planetarium** (opened in 2007, it's the only one in the country), where effects-laden star shows are projected onto its ceiling.

Outside, overlooking Greenwich's serene park, you can enjoy one of London's most popular photo opportunities, standing across the **Prime Meridian,** the line of 0°

Greenwich

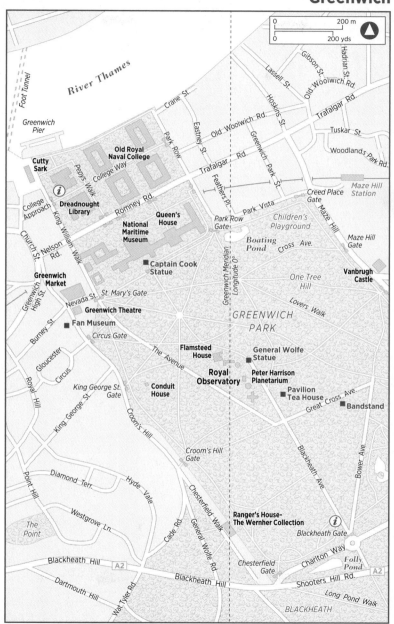

River Thames

Foot Tunnel

Greenwich Pier

Cutty Sark

Old Royal Naval College

Pepys Walk

College Way

(i)

Dreadnought Library

College Approach

Romney Rd.

King William Walk

Church St.

Nelson Rd.

National Maritime Museum

Queen's House

Captain Cook Statue

Greenwich Market

Greenwich High St.

Nevada St.

St. Mary's Gate

Greenwich Theatre

Fan Museum

Burney St.

Circus Gate

Gloucester

Circus

Royal Hill

King George St. Gate

King George St.

Conduit House

The Avenue

Flamsteed House

Royal Observatory

Peter Harrison Planetarium

General Wolfe Statue

Pavilion Tea House

Great Cross Ave.

Bandstand

Croom's Hill

Point Hill

Diamond Terr.

Hyde Vale

Westgrove Ln.

The Point

Croom's Hill Gate

Cade Rd.

Chesterfield Walk

General Wolfe Rd.

Ranger's House-The Wernher Collection

(i)

Blackheath Gate

Blackheath Hill A2

Dartmouth Hill

Wat Tyler Rd.

Blackheath Hill

Chesterfield Gate

Charlton Way

Folly Pond A2

Shooters Hill Rd.

Long Pond Walk

BLACKHEATH

Crane St.

Eastney St.

Park Row

Old Woolwich Rd.

Trafalgar Rd.

Feathers Pl.

Greenwich Park St.

Park Vista

Park Row Gate

Boating Pond

Greenwich Meridian

Longitude O°

GREENWICH PARK

Lassell St.

Hoskins St.

Gibson St.

Old Woolwich Rd.

Hadrian St.

Trafalgar Rd.

Tuskar St.

Woodlands Park Rd.

Maze Hill Station

Creed Place Gate

Children's Playground

Maze Hill

Cross Ave.

Maze Hill Gate

One Tree Hill

Lovers Walk

Vanbrugh Castle

Blackheath Ave.

Bower Ave.

0   200 m
0   200 yds

121

longitude marked in the courtyard, with one foot in the Earth's eastern hemisphere and one foot in the western. At lunch you can set your watch precisely by watching the red **"time ball"** atop the roof, which has dropped at exactly 1pm since 1833, to enable passing shipmasters to set their chronometers accurately.

Blackheath Ave., SE10. ✆ **020/8858-4422.** www.nmm.ac.uk/places/royal-observatory. Free admission to observatory; planetarium £6.50 adults, £5.20 children, £18.70 family. Daily 10am–5pm. Train: Greenwich/DLR: Cutty Sark.

Outlying Attractions

Dulwich Picture Gallery ★★ GALLERY   Just 12 minutes by train from Victoria Station, this houses one of the country's most significant collections of European Old Masters from the 17th and 18th centuries. The core of the collection was assembled by a pair of London art dealers in the 1790s on behalf of King Stanislaus Augustus of Poland, who thought a royal art collection would be just the thing to enhance his prestige. Unfortunately, he'd rather overestimated his standing and his kingdom was partitioned out of existence before the shipment could be made, and the paintings remained in London. The dealers bequeathed the collection to the independent school, Dulwich College, which commissioned the great **Sir John Soane** (p. 93) to create the world's first public art gallery to display them; it opened in 1817. Soane's cunningly positioned skylights beautifully illuminate the pieces from such figures as Rembrandt, Rubens, Canaletto, Gainsborough, Watteau, and Pousin. Indeed, the *Sunday Telegraph* hailed Dulwich as "the most beautiful small art gallery in the world." Free guided tours of the collection are given at 3pm on Saturdays and Sundays.

Gallery Rd., SE21. ✆ **020/8693-5254.** www.dulwichpicturegallery.org.uk. Admission £5 adults, £4 seniors, free for students, the unemployed, and children 17 and under. Tues–Fri 10am–5pm; Sat–Sun 11am–5pm. Train: W. Dulwich.

Hampton Court Palace ★★★ ☺ HISTORIC SITE   The 16th-century palace of Cardinal Wolsey can teach us a lesson: Don't try to outdo your boss, particularly if he happens to be Henry VIII. The rich cardinal did just that, and he eventually lost his fortune, power, and prestige, and ended up giving his lavish palace to the Tudor monarch. Henry's additions include the Anne Boleyn gateway, and the aptly named Great Hall, with its hammerbeam ceiling, as well as a Tiltyard (where jousting competitions were held) and a "real tennis" court.

Although the palace enjoyed prestige in Elizabethan days, it owes much of its present look to William and Mary—or rather, to Sir Christopher Wren. You can parade through the apartments today, filled with porcelain, furniture, paintings, and tapestries. The **King's Dressing Room** is graced with some of the best art, mainly paintings by Old Masters on loan from Queen Elizabeth II. Also, be sure to inspect the **Royal Chapel** (Wolsey wouldn't recognize it), and the **kitchens** where great Tudor feasts are regularly prepared.

The 24-hectare (59-acre) **gardens**—including Tudor and Elizabethan Knot Gardens—are open daily year-round. The most popular section is the serpentine shrubbery **Maze,** also the work of Wren, and accounting for countless lost children every year. A garden **cafe** and restaurant are located in the Tiltyard. *Insider tip:* Tickets are considerably cheaper if bought online.

East Molesey, Surrey. ✆ **0844/482-7777.** www.hrp.org.uk/HamptonCourtPalace. Palace admission £15.95 adults, £13.20 students and seniors, £8 children 5–15, £43.45 family ticket, free for children 4 and under; gardens admission £5.30 adults, £4.60 students and seniors, free children without palace ticket during summer. Maze: £3.85 adults, £2.75 children 5–15, free children 4 and under. Cloisters, courtyards, state apartments, great kitchen, cellars, and Hampton Court exhibition Mar–Oct daily 10am–6pm; Nov–Feb daily 10am–4:30pm. Gardens year-round daily 7am–dusk (no later than 9pm). Train: Hampton Court (30 min. from Waterloo).

Horniman Museum ★★ ☺ MUSEUM   This early 20th-century museum set in 6.5 hectares (16 acres) of landscaped gardens in the suburban depths of South London is quirky, funky, and fun. The collection was accumulated by Frederick Horniman, a Victorian tea trader, and amounts to 350,000 objects made up of all sorts and everything, from African tribal masks to a gigantic, overstuffed walrus, and from musical instruments (it holds one of the country's most important collections) to oversized model insects, as well as a small aquarium constructed in waterfall-like tiers. It's divided into three broad categories: natural history, music, and world cultures. There's a full range of events and activities, including storytelling and craft sessions for kids.

100 London Rd., Forest Hill, SE23. © **020/8699-1872.** www.horniman.ac.uk. Free admission except for temporary exhibitions. Museum daily 10:30am–5:30pm. Gardens Mon–Sat 7:30am–dusk; Sun 8am–dusk. Train: Forest Hill (13 min. from London Bridge Station; 24 min. from Shoreditch High St.).

Royal Botanic Gardens, Kew ★★★ ☺ GARDEN   These world-famous gardens are home to thousands of elegantly arranged plants, but Kew Gardens, as it's more commonly known, is no mere pleasure garden—it's essentially a vast scientific research center that also happens to be extraordinarily beautiful. The gardens' 121-hectare (299-acre) site encompasses lakes, greenhouses, walks, pavilions, and museums. Among the 50,000 plants are notable collections of ferns, orchids, aquatic plants, cacti, mountain plants, palms, and tropical water lilies.

No matter what season you visit, Kew always has something to see, with species of shrubs, flowers, and trees from every part of the globe, from the Arctic Circle to tropical rainforests. If the weather's chilly, you can keep warm in the three great hothouses: the **Palm House** (the warmest, with a thick, sweaty mass of jungle plants); the slightly cooler **Temperate House;** and the **Princess of Wales Conservatory,** which encompasses 10 climatic zones, from arid to tropical. But when the sun is out, head to the garden's newest attraction, a 200-m (656-ft.) Treetop Walkway taking you up into the canopy, some 20m (59 ft.) in the air, for a stroll through chestnut, lime, and oak trees.

Kew, Surrey. © **020/8332-5655.** www.rbgkew.org.uk. Admission £13.50 adults, £11.50 students and seniors, free for children 15 and under. Apr–Aug Mon–Fri 9:30am–6pm, Sat–Sun 9:30am–7pm; Sept–Oct daily 9:30am–5:30pm; Nov–Jan daily 9:30am–3:45pm; Feb–Mar daily 9:30am–5pm. Tube: Kew Gardens.

Organized Tours
RIVER CRUISES ALONG THE THAMES
A trip up or down the river will give you an entirely different view of London. You'll see how the city grew along and around the Thames, and how many of its landmarks turn their faces toward the water. The Thames was London's first highway.

Thames River Services, Westminster Pier, Victoria Embankment, SW1 (© **020/7930-4097;** www.westminsterpier.co.uk; Tube: Westminster), concerns itself with downriver traffic from Westminster Pier to such destinations as Greenwich, St. Katharine's Dock, and the Thames Barrier. The most popular excursion departs for Greenwich (a 50-min. ride) at half-hour intervals between 10am and 4pm daily in April, May, September, and October, and between 10am and 5pm from June to August; from November to March, boats depart from Westminster Pier at 40-minute intervals daily

WHERE TO EAT

London is one of the world's great dining capitals. Here you can experience a global range of cuisines, anything from a traditional English feast to the regional cooking of countries from Italy to India. The last few years have been momentous for the restaurant scene. Top-end places can no longer rest on their laurels; they are dealing with educated, well-traveled, and opinionated customers who know the value of a meal. Prices have stayed the same and even lowered in some cases, and every major restaurant now offers good-value set meals.

On top of that, the "gastropub" has become a force to be reckoned with. Young chefs have taken over moribund pubs, filled them with odd pieces of furniture, and now offer top cooking at less-than-top prices. Some are in the center, but you'll find many gastropubs in residential neighborhoods outside the usual tourist areas. Another big change in the last few years is the geographic shift from the West End to East London, where new cafes and small restaurants have emerged in what is now a dynamic part of the capital. It's all good news for restaurant-goers: Eating out in London offers more choice, more value, and more fun than ever.

Look to the Internet for occasional impressive discounts on London dining. Websites promoting special deals include **Lastminute.com** and **Squaremeal.co.uk**. It's also worth subscribing to regular newsletters like those e-mailed weekly by **Lovefoodlovedrink.co.uk** and **Travelzoo.com**, and signing up to deals websites like **KGB Deals** (www.kgbdeals.co.uk/london), **LivingSocial** (www.livingsocial.com), or **Groupon** (www.groupon.com). For a top meal at reasonable prices, many destination restaurants offer set-price lunch deals, as well as limited, but top-quality pre- and post-theatre menus; see details in the reviews below.

The West End
MAYFAIR
Very Expensive

Alain Ducasse at the Dorchester ★★★ FRENCH   Alain Ducasse is the name here, but it's talented Jocelyn Herland who earned three Michelin stars in 2010. The plush room centers around a circular table for six, hidden behind a translucent curtain and lit with fiber-optic cables. It's better to sit in the pretty front room overlooking Hyde Park. This is French haute cuisine, but with a nod toward London's more relaxed style. The cooking is superb; the quality of the seasonal ingredients shining through in starters like Scottish crab with coral jus and mains of halibut in a celeriac, shellfish, and squid broth; or the rich venison from the Limousin. Desserts are great set-pieces, although the cheeseboard is lacking the range such a restaurant should offer. And the wine list? Splendid, but splendidly priced too.

Inside the Dorchester Hotel, Park Lane, W1. ✆ **020/7629-8866.** www.alainducasse-dorchester.com. Reservations required 2 weeks in advance. Set-price menus 2 courses £55, 3 courses £75, 4 courses £95, 7 courses £115. AE, DC, MC, V. Tues–Fri noon–2pm; Tues–Sat 6:30–10pm. Tube: Green Park, Hyde Park Corner, or Marble Arch.

Le Gavroche ★★★ FRENCH   There may be new kids on the block, new cuisines, and new young chefs, but Le Gavroche remains the number-one choice in London for classical French cuisine from Roux, Jr., son of the chef who founded the restaurant in 1966. The famous cheese soufflé is still there, alongside hot foie gras on a crisp duck pancake with cinnamon. Also on a masterly menu: rich loin of venison with walnut gnocchi and bitter chocolate sauce; and desserts like apricot and Cointreau soufflé. It's beautifully presented and served with style by the faultless staff. The wine list is a masterclass in top French wines, and is kind to the purse as well on lesser- known varieties. It all takes place in a comfortable, conventional basement dining room which may be too old-fashioned for some, but which perfectly sets the scene for a truly classic meal.

43 Upper Brook St., W1. ℂ **020/7408-0881.** www.le-gavroche.co.uk. Reservations required as far in advance as possible. Main courses £26.90–£54.80; set lunch £48.90; *Le Menu Exceptionnel* (whole table) £100. AE, MC, V. Mon–Fri noon–2pm; Mon–Sat 6:30–11pm. Tube: Marble Arch.

Expensive

Greenhouse ★★ CONTEMPORARY EUROPEAN   The secret garden and fountain comes as a surprise to first-time visitors. Tucked away in Mayfair, the Greenhouse's pretty dining room looks out onto the greenery. Lyon-born head chef Antonin Bonnet is an inspired master, producing first-class dishes without destroying the natural flavors of his ingredients. His skill in mixing unusual combinations shines through in dishes like a cleverly assembled autumn salad with black olive powder, Iberico ham, and balsamic dressing, followed by roast pigeon breast with pomegranate, turnip purée, almonds, and a jus of giblets and pancetta. Vegetarians are well treated with a separate menu so tempting it might convert carnivores.

27a Hays Mews, W1. ℂ **020/7499-3331.** www.greenhouserestaurant.co.uk. Reservations required. Set lunch 2 courses £25, 3 courses £29; 3-course fixed-price dinner or vegetarian menu £70; tasting menu £85;. AE, DC, MC, V. Mon–Fri noon–2:30pm; Mon–Sat 6:30–11pm. Tube: Green Park.

Hibiscus ★★★ CONTEMPORARY EUROPEAN   The cooking is spectacular—with enough culinary fireworks to satisfy the most adventurous—while the setting is elegant and understated. Claude Bosi made his name and reputation at his Hibiscus restaurant in Ludlow in Shropshire, then came to London in 2007 with his wife Claire, who runs front of house. His style of cooking includes ingredients that you wouldn't expect in classic French dishes: Pork pie sauce appears in a starter of scallops along with pink grapefruit and sorrel; roast goose is paired with smoked eel. This is one to save for—put yourself into the hands of the master and appreciate an exceptional and different eating experience.

29 Maddox St., W1. ℂ **020/7629-2999.** www.hibiscusrestaurant.co.uk. Reservations required. Lunch 3 courses £29.50–£53.50, 6-course tasting menu (whole table only) £85–£97.50. A la carte 2 courses £60, 3 courses £80. Fri and Sat evenings 4 courses £77.50, 6 courses £87.50, 8 courses £97.50. AE, DC, MC, V. Tues–Fri noon–2:30pm and 6:30–10pm; Sat 6–10pm. Tube: Green Park.

Scott's ★★ SEAFOOD   Scott's is glamorous and glitzy, a seafood restaurant that is on every celebrity's speed dial. Opened as an oyster warehouse in 1851 by a young fishmonger, John Scott, the restaurant moved to Mayfair in 1968. The dining room is drop-dead gorgeous, oak-paneled with art on the walls and a show-stopping crustacean display in the central bar. Meat eaters are taken care of, as are vegetarians and vegans, but fish is the raison d'être; it seems perverse to ignore the freshest of oysters, caviar that starts at £80, octopus carpaccio, smoked haddock with colcannon, or a simple, perfectly cooked sea bass. The owners have opened the **Mount Street Deli,** 100 Mount St., W1 (ℂ **020/7499-6843;** www.themountstreetdeli.co.uk) opposite, a perfect place for breakfast, a light lunch, or afternoon tea.

20 Mount St., W1. ℂ **020/7495-7309.** www.scotts-restaurant.com. Reservations required. Main courses £17.50–£42. AE, DC, MC, V. Mon–Sat noon–10:30pm; Sun noon–10pm. Tube: Green Park or Bond St.

Moderate

Automat AMERICAN   The famous faces who flocked to this Mayfair eatery when it opened aren't seen too much anymore, but there's still a steady clientele of

Londoners and homesick expat Americans who appreciate this glamorous diner with its tiled floors and banquette seating. The menu covers all tastes, from smoked chicken and mango salad to steak tartare, from macaroni and cheese to excellent U.S. beef including a 10-oz New York strip that weighs in at £30. If prices appear high, remember this is Mayfair, and portions are generous, American-style sizes.

33 Dover St., W1. ℂ **020/7499-3033.** www.automat-london.com. Reservations recommended. Main courses £12–£30. AE, DC, MC, V. Mon–Fri 7–11am and noon–3pm; Sat–Sun 10am–4pm; Mon–Sat 6pm–midnight. Tube: Green Park.

Momo ★ MOROCCAN/NORTH AFRICAN   Entering, you step into a colorful fantasy of Moroccan life: Stucco walls, wooden screens, rugs, brass lanterns, and low tables take you straight to Marrakech. The menu is pretty authentic as well, built around couscous and tagines bursting with chicken or lamb, preserved lemons, and olives. You might start with a *briouat* of cheese, mint, and potatoes served with quince marmalade, or the chef's specialty of *pastille*—filo pastry parcels filled with sweet-tasting wood pigeon, almonds and cinnamon, and an orange confit. Informal, on-site **Mô Café** serves all-day meze (£4.50 per dish or meze selections £13.50–£21).

25 Heddon St., W1. ℂ **020/7434-4040.** www.momoresto.com. Reservations required. Main courses £17–£36; fixed-price lunch £15–£19; set menu £49. AE, DC, MC, V. Mon–Sat noon–2:30pm and 6:30–11:30pm; Sun 6:30–11pm. Tube: Piccadilly Circus or Oxford Circus.

ST. JAMES'S
Moderate

Green's Restaurant & Oyster Bar ★ SEAFOOD/TRADITIONAL BRITISH   Clubby, comfortable, and definitely part of the Establishment, Green's has been serving its brand of traditional British cooking for over 30 years. Wood-paneled walls hung with cartoons, a central bar, and seemingly soundproof booths with leather banquettes make Green's a safe bet for its political and power-broking customers. This is the place for roasted parsnip soup with apple crisps; their famous salmon fishcakes; oysters in season; very upscale fish and chips; filet of beef with horseradish; or the occasional discreet foray into contemporary cooking like monkfish with butternut squash ravioli and hazelnut sage butter. Game is a strength, as are the fish dishes and the wine list is superb. It could all be rather stuffy but it's not.

36 Duke St., St. James's, SW1. ℂ **020/7930-4566.** www.greens.org.uk. Reservations required. Main courses £15–£42.50. AE, DC, MC, V. Mon–Sat 11:30am–3pm and 5:30–11pm. Tube: Green Park. Also at 14 Cornhill, EC2 (ℂ **020/7220-6300**).

PICCADILLY CIRCUS & LEICESTER SQUARE

All the choices below (along with those under "Covent Garden & the Strand" and "Soho," elsewhere in this section) are candidates for dining before or after a show in London's Theatreland.

Expensive

Bentley's Oyster Bar & Grill ★★ SEAFOOD/TRADITIONAL BRITISH   Bentley's is a London institution that opened in 1916 and went through various ups and downs, before being rescued by the highly talented and charming Irish chef, Richard Corrigan. Under his expert guidance, Bentley's (according to its many fans) now serves the best fish in London. The ground-floor Oyster Bar, vaguely Arts and Crafts in feel, is a great place for watching the guys shucking oysters behind the bar and dining off the likes of dressed crab, smoked salmon, or smoked eel. In the more formal upstairs Grill, the menu includes stalwarts like the rich Bentley's fish soup, but it's worth being more adventurous and trying dishes such as roast cod with chorizo sausage and rocket. It's all conducted in a genuinely friendly atmosphere, though high-ish prices and occasionally slow service put off some people.

11–15 Swallow St., W1. ℂ **020/7734-4756.** www.bentleysoysterbarandgrill.co.uk. Oyster Bar: Main courses £10.50–£19.50. Grill: Main courses £18.50–£27.90. AE, MC, V. Oyster Bar: Mon–Sat noon–midnight; Sun noon–10pm. Restaurant: Mon–Fri noon–3pm and 6–11pm; Sat 6–11pm. Tube: Piccadilly Circus.

Inexpensive

Tokyo Diner ✒ JAPANESE This Japanese interloper into prime Chinatown territory is cheap and friendly, refuses tips, takes £1 off dishes between 3 and 6pm, and is open every day of the year from noon to midnight. No wonder it's so popular. Donburi rice dishes pull in students and the impecunious to fill up on beef and onion braised in sweet Japanese sauce with ginger. Others go for their popular bento box set meals: £14.80 gets you a chicken teriyaki box, in which chicken flambéed in teriyaki sauce is served with rice, vegetables, and pickles. Sushi and soup noodles complete the picture.

2 Newport Place, WC2. ℂ **020/7287-8777.** www.tokyodiner.com. Main courses £8.50–£13.70. Bento box set meals £11.50–£16.40. MC, V. Daily noon–midnight. Tube: Leicester Sq.

COVENT GARDEN & THE STRAND

The restaurants in and around Covent Garden and the Strand are convenient choices for West End theatre-goers.

Very Expensive

L'Atelier de Joël Robuchon ★★★ FRENCH The London Atelier of Robuchon (who, incidentally, has 26 Michelin stars and restaurants around the world) is based on his concept of an informal restaurant. There are three areas: the first floor, which is the most conventional; the top floor Le Salon bar; and the moody red and black "Atelier." For the most dramatic effect, eat here and book at the counter. Here you can watch the theatre of the chefs producing tapas-style dishes—small bombshells of taste as in beef and foie gras mini-burger; pig's trotter on parmesan toast; and egg cocotte with wild mushroom cream, all wildly inventive and beautifully presented. The a la carte menu follows the conventional three-course approach, using superb ingredients. The pre-theatre menu represents stunning value.

13–15 West St., WC2. ℂ **020/7010-8600.** www.joel-robuchon.com. Reservations essential. Main courses £19–£34; small tasting dishes £13–£21; Menu Découverte 8 courses £125; Vegetarian Découverte 8 courses £80; lunch and pre-theatre 2-course menu £25, 3 courses £29. AE, MC, V. Daily noon–2:30pm and 5:30–10:30pm. Tube: Leicester Sq.

Expensive

J. Sheekey ★★ SEAFOOD Tucked into a small alleyway off St. Martin's Lane, J. Sheekey has long been a Theatreland favorite for both the famous (Laurence Olivier and Vivien Leigh) and the not-so-famous. It's a charming dining room with pictures of theatrical greats lining the walls. You can opt for the favorites—Atlantic prawns, the famous Sheekey's fish pie—but it's worth trying more unusual dishes. Monkfish and tiger prawn curry comes topped with crispy fried shallots and basmati rice. The more casual **J. Sheekey Oyster Bar,** 33–34 St Martin's Court (ℂ **020/7240-2565**), is next door, has the same look, and offers Sheekey classics and smaller dishes.

28–32 St. Martin's Court, WC2. ℂ **020/7240-2565.** www.j-sheekey.co.uk. Reservations recommended. Main courses £14.75–£42. AE, DC, MC, V. Mon–Sat noon–3pm and 5:30pm–midnight; Sun noon–3:30pm and 6–11pm. Tube: Leicester Sq.

Les Deux Salons ★★ FRENCH/BRASSERIE   The third venture from Michelin-starred Anthony Demetre and Will Smith is the kind of smart brasserie that will have the French reaching for their smelling salts. It's large, bustling, decorated with the requisite amount of polished brass, mirrors, and dark wood, evokes the Belle Epoque, and offers a standard of cooking that is now rare in Parisian brasseries. The upper floor is more intimate; the ground floor swings along in style. A well-drilled kitchen produces impeccable dishes like snail and Herefordshire bacon pie; ravioli stuffed with veal; bavette of beef; daily specials like rabbit in mustard, plus such tongue-in-cheek desserts as rum baba, and floating islands. Service is spot on; prices are reasonable; Les Deux Salons is a palpable hit.

40–42 William IV St., WC2. ✆ **020/7420-2050.** www.lesdeuxsalons.co.uk. Reservations recommended. Main courses £14.50–£23.95. AE, MC, V. Daily noon–11pm. Tube: Charing Cross.

Rules ★ TRADITIONAL BRITISH   This is the place for a genuine taste of traditional London. Established in 1798 as an oyster bar, the gorgeous, red plush Edwardian interior with drawings and cartoons covering the walls is much as it was when feeding the great and good of the theatrical and literary world—like Charles Dickens, H. G. Wells, Laurence Olivier, and Clark Gable. What keeps Rules alive today is its devotion to top, traditional British cooking. Native Irish or Scottish oysters; the best game only served in season—wild Highland Red deer; grouse; snipe; pheasant and woodcock; and beef from the owner's estate, skillfully prepared and cooked. Puddings (not desserts in this most British of restaurants) might be a rib-stickingly good Golden Syrup sponge pudding, a winter blackberry and apple crumble, or even rice pudding, bringing back childhood memories.

35 Maiden Lane, WC2. ✆ **020/7836-5314.** www.rules.co.uk. Reservations recommended. Main courses £18–£32. AE, DC, MC, V. Mon–Sat noon–11:45pm; Sun noon–10:45pm. Tube: Covent Garden.

Savoy Grill ★★★ TRADITIONAL BRITISH   Opened a few months after the glorious Savoy Hotel reclaimed its place among London's icons of discreet luxury, the Savoy Grill, run by Gordon Ramsay, is everything we hoped for. The Art Deco-inspired interior is a real gem, with sparkling chandeliers, walls that gleam a deep amber, and black-and-white photographs of past stars like Bogart and Bacall. The menu balances the classics with a touch of the modern: Cornish crab mayonnaise with apple salad, wild celery, and wafer-thin Melba toast, scallops with leeks and shrimp butter; or go for a grilled venison chop. This is a return to past glories.

In the Savoy Hotel, Strand, WC2. ✆ **020/7592-1600.** www.gordonramsay.com. Reservations required. Main courses £18–£39. AE, DC, MC, V. Mon–Sat noon–3pm and 5:30–11pm; Sun noon–4pm and 6–10pm. Tube: Charing Cross.

Moderate

Giaconda Dining Room ★ 🍴 CONTEMPORARY EUROPEAN   Tucked among the guitar shops of Denmark Street, just off Tottenham Court Road, the Giaconda comes as a surprise. Run by husband and wife Australians, Paul and Tracey Merrony, its bistro-like atmosphere, good cooking, and down-to-earth pricing set it apart. Dishes like salad of baked beetroot and leeks vinaigrette with goat curd to start followed by sautéed duck breast with celeriac purée and beetroot with a cherry sauce have Giaconda regulars purring with pleasure. A reasonably priced wine list, relaxed atmosphere, and pleasant staff complete the attractive package.

9 Denmark St., WC2. ✆ **020/7240-3334.** www.giacondadining.com. Main courses £11.75–£31.50. AE, MC, V. Mon–Fri noon–2:15pm and 6–9:15pm. Tube: Tottenham Court Rd.

Terroirs ★ FRENCH Hearty rustic French food, good wines (including "natural" wine from small artisan growers, unfiltered and unrefined), and a vibrant atmosphere is what gives Terroirs the edge over other Covent Garden restaurants. The ground-floor wine bar is a great meeting place for pre-theatre drinks, charcuterie that takes in pork and pistachio terrine, rillettes, and Bigorre saucisson, properly kept French cheeses, and tapas-style snacks. The basement restaurant is the place for a longer meal, although it has a similar menu of small plates like potted shrimps on toast, herring and warm potato salad, and whole Dorset crab with mayonnaise.

5 William IV St., WC2. © **020/7036-0660.** www.terroirswinebar.com. Reservations recommended. Small plates £3.50–£12. AE, MC, V. Mon–Sat noon–midnight. Tube: Charing Cross. Also at Brawn, 49 Columbia Rd., E2 (© **020/7729-5629**).

Inexpensive

Dishoom ★ INDIAN India has provided so much inspiration for London dining that it's difficult to imagine a new experience. Then up pops this wonderful place, modeled on the Bombay cafes of the 1960s. It looks great, with a geometrically tiled floor, marble-topped tables, odd lights and pictures, and its blackboard of rules at the door: "No water to outsiders" and "All castes served." It's clearly hit the spot with the kind of vibe that has attracted London's trendsetters in droves. It swings along from breakfasts of sausage or bacon naan rolls through all-day dining on lightly spiced soups, salads, small plates of vegetable or lamb samosas, fish fingers, or calamari to dinner grills of chicken tikka, sheekh kebab, spicy lamb chops, or one-pot biryani dishes. Finish off with *kulfi* (Indian ice cream) on a stick or a lassi.

12 Upper St. Martin's Lane, WC2. © **020/7420-9320.** www.dishoom.com. No reservations. Main courses £6.50–£9.70. AE, MC, V. Mon–Fri 8am–11pm; Sat 10am–11pm; Sun 10am–10pm. Tube: Leicester Sq.

SOHO

Soho's restaurants offer more options for dining before a show at a West End theatre.

Expensive

Hakkasan ★ CHINESE/CANTONESE Opened by the restaurateur Alan Yau (who has done so much to transform London's dining scene), this sexy, moody, subtly lit basement venue serves top-notch modern Cantonese cuisine. During the day, the dim sum is among the best in London—delicate, exquisitely fresh, and beautifully cooked. In the evening top-end ingredients are cooked with subtle skill. Sweet-and-sour Duke of Berkshire pork with pomegranate takes the concept to new heights; stir-fry ostrich comes in yellow bean sauce; from the seafood section, the Chilean sea bass with Szechuan pepper, sweet basil, and spring onion is perfectly treated, the sauce complementing, not overpowering the fish. Even desserts, often the poor relation in Chinese restaurants, are superb. The wine list is a lesson in matching food and wine; ask the knowledgeable waiting staff for advice.

8 Hanway Place, W1. © **020/7927-7000.** www.hakkasan.com. Reservations recommended. Main courses £10–£68. AE, MC, V. Mon–Fri noon–3:15pm, Sat–Sun noon–4:15pm; Sun–Wed 6–11:30pm, Thurs–Sat 6pm–12:15am. Tube: Tottenham Court Rd. Also at 17 Bruton St., W1 (© **020/7907-1888**).

Moderate

Bocca di Lupo ★★ ITALIAN The hugely popular "mouth of the wolf" is a smart restaurant with an open kitchen, tiled floors, wooden tables, and large paintings of food on the walls. The downside of its popularity is that it's busy, cramped, and noisy—and you must book in advance. Chef Jacob Kenedy has toured Italy in his search for genuine regional dishes, and the result is a glorious trot around the country. If you want the full tour, go for the small plates and share as many as possible, perhaps blood salami with toast from Tuscany, and the Venetian fried eel, prawns, and squid with polenta. More substantial dishes include roast teal with polenta and *guanciale* (unsmoked bacon from pig's cheek) made with herbs, and Ligurian sea bream baked in salt. The all-Italian wine list offers a good selection by the carafe or the glass, but beware: Drinking will up your bill.

12 Archer St., W1. ℂ **020/7734-2223.** www.boccadilupo.com. Main courses £10.50–£28. AE, MC, V. Mon–Sat 12:30–3pm and 5:30–11pm; Sun noon–4pm. Tube: Piccadilly Circus.

Dean Street Townhouse ★ TRADITIONAL BRITISH   Part of the achingly fashionable hotel (p. 181), Dean Street Townhouse dining room fits perfectly into Soho, with a clubby ambience, fashionable Brit-art on the walls, crystal chandeliers, and a long bar, all housed in a four-story Georgian townhouse. The food is thoroughly British, a wonderful exercise in nostalgia for those brought up on pressed ham and piccalilli (a pickle of chopped vegetables, mustard, and turmeric), or fish and chips. There are forays into more sophisticated modern dishes—try pollock (a fish which we used to feed to cats, but is now a sustainable alternative to cod) with borlotti beans and black cabbage. A return to the cooking of the past, inside one of the hippest venues in London, is another nice touch of (typically British) irony.

69-71 Dean St., W1. ℂ **020/7434-1775.** www.deanstreettownhouse.com. Reservations required. Main courses £11.50–£32.50; pre-theatre, 5–7:30pm 2 courses £16.50, 3 courses £19.50. AE, MC, V. Mon–Thurs 7am–midnight; Fri 7am–1am; Sat 8am–1am; Sun 8am–midnight. Tube: Tottenham Court Rd.

Gay Hussar ★ HUNGARIAN   This much-loved, well-established Soho institution (it was founded in 1953) is as close to the restaurants of the "good old days" as you'll find. It may not be quite the hotbed of political and journalistic intrigue that it once was, but the wood-paneled walls covered in political caricatures, and the sight of the odd Member of Parliament indulging in (yes) a long, boozy lunch, are still refreshingly politically incorrect. A loyal waiting staff has been serving pretty much the same dishes for decades from a thoroughly traditional Hungarian menu of goulash soup; smoked salmon and blinis; roast goose with red cabbage and Hungarian-style potatoes (i.e. well spiced); venison goulash; poppy seed strudel; and Eszterhazy chocolate and raspberry gateau. And don't forget to try the Hungarian wines.

2 Greek St., W1. ℂ **020/7437-0973.** www.gayhussar.co.uk. Reservations recommended. Main courses £11.75–£16.95; set lunch 2 courses £18.50, 3 courses £21.50. AE, DC, MC, V. Mon–Sat 12:15–2:30pm and 5:30–10:45pm. Tube: Tottenham Court Rd.

La Trouvaille ★ 🛉 FRENCH   Rather surprisingly tucked off Carnaby Street—known for its high-street names rather than for independent businesses—La Trouvaille has a charming wine bar on the ground floor (old floorboards, brown paper covers, and candles in bottles) and a formal restaurant on the first floor (black-and-white decor and crisp white table linen). The wine bar is the place for excellent platters of charcuterie or cheese, salads, and small casseroles. The dining room offers classic French fare, perhaps a foie gras and apple roulade with truffle brioche and sherry vinegar, followed by a rack of lamb with a carrot and cumin purée, apricot, Swiss chard, and thyme jus. It's all beautifully cooked—cod with just the right firmness, a duck breast tastefully rich.

12a Newburgh St., W1. ℂ **020/7287-8488.** www.latrouvaille.co.uk. Main courses £13–£21.50. Set lunch 2 courses £23, 3 courses £28. AE, MC, V. Mon–Sat noon–3pm; Tues–Sat 5:45–10:30pm. Tube: Oxford Circus.

Randall & Aubin ★ SEAFOOD   Randall & Aubin began as a butcher's shop in 1911 selling top-quality meat from Paris, so it's appropriate that it was turned into a restaurant in 1996 by restaurateurs Ed Baines and James Poulton. It's a genuinely lovely setting; its marble surfaces, white tiles, and old wooden furniture fit perfectly into its new incarnation as a restaurant—albeit one that specializes in fish and seafood. Caviar might weigh in at £90 to £150 a serving, but it's the well-priced dishes like fried sole with beans and sautéed potatoes (£14), and grilled sea bass with scallions, chives, and rosemary salsa and potatoes (£15.50) that please the crowds of loyal fans. Or do as we like to do: Sit at the bar, order champagne, and toy with an oyster.

16 Brewer St., W1. ✆ **020/7287-4447.** www.randallandaubin.com. No reservations. Main courses £7.10–£27. AE, DC, MC, V. Mon–Sat noon–11pm; Sun noon–10pm. Tube: Piccadilly Circus or Leicester Sq.

Inexpensive

Mildreds ★ 🎁 VEGETARIAN   Mildreds may sound like a 1940s' Joan Crawford movie, but it's one of London's most enduring vegetarian and vegan dining spots. The large, airy room with a bar at the front can get very crowded, and you'll probably find yourself sharing a table. The food always hits the spot, and correctly uses organically grown, seasonal produce. The menu changes daily, but always includes homemade soups, pastas, and salads. There are dishes like sundried tomato and buffalo mozzarella risotto cake; Sri Lankan sweet potato and cashew nut curry; and unusual sides.

45 Lexington St., W1. ✆ **020/7494-1634.** www.mildreds.co.uk. No reservations. Main courses £7.25–£9.75. No credit cards. Mon–Sat noon–11pm. Tube: Tottenham Court Rd.

Polpo ★★ 🎁 ITALIAN   Modeled on a *baraco* (Venetian wine bar), the decor here is perfect, with stripped brick walls, Victorian tiles, wooden floors, and leather banquettes. A menu of small dishes of regional specialties includes *cicchetti* (Venetian bar snacks) of asparagus, taleggio cheese, and prosciutto ham or salt cod on grilled polenta, all costing between £1 and £3. Breads are excellent—try the broad bean, ricotta, and mint bruschetta for something different. More substantial tapas-style dishes run from cotechino (warm, thick-sliced salami) with lentils and salsa verde to a *fritto misto* (mixed fried fish) or *linguine vongole* (pasta with clams), and there are plenty of vegetarian choices too. Alas, a no-bookings policy at dinner can mean long waits. A sister "Venetian osteria" **Polpetto,** opened in 2010 above the **French House** pub (p. 167) in the heart of Soho, at 49 Dean St. (✆ **020/7734-1969;** www.polpetto.co.uk; Tube: Leicester Sq.).

41 Beak St., W1. ✆ **020/7734-4479.** www.polpo.co.uk. No reservations for dinner; reservations recommended for lunch. Dishes £1.50–£11. AE, MC, V. Mon–Sat noon–3pm and 5:30–11pm; Sun noon–4pm. Tube: Piccadilly Circus.

Yauatcha ★ ASIAN   This Asian eatery, describing itself as a modern reinterpretation of the old Chinese teahouse, is the brainchild of Alan Yau, who won Britain's first Michelin star for Chinese cooking at his top-of-the-range restaurant, Hakkasan (see above). At this informal dim sum outlet service is casual, although it's so popular you're unfortunately rushed through your meal to make way for new arrivals. The ground floor is quiet; the basement buzzes. Dim sum, among London's finest, is served for both lunch and dinner, and often takes unusual ingredients like scallops, Wagyu beef, venison, or king crab.

15 Broadwick St., W1. ✆ **020/7494-8888.** www.yauatcha.com. Dim sum £3–£12. Set meal for 2 £28.88. AE, MC, V. Mon–Sat noon–11:45pm; Sun noon–10:30pm. Tube: Oxford Circus.

BLOOMSBURY & FITZROVIA
Very Expensive

Pied à Terre ★★★ FRENCH   You could easily walk past the entrance to one of London's best restaurants without a second glance. And once inside, the dark decor is as unassuming as the exterior. But persevere, for Australian chef Shane Osborn has two well-deserved Michelin stars. The set lunch is one of London's greatest bargains. Where else could you get tuna tartare with avocado crème fraîche, quail eggs, and fennel dressing, then roast pork with its braised cheek, potato fondant, and spicy sauce perfectly balanced with pickled apples and apple purée for £23.50? Cheese or dessert (including pre-dessert) might be a smooth mango velouté with coconut mousse and Thai basil for an extra £6. The a la carte dinner menu is more ambitious producing superb dishes that look as beautiful as they taste. Save up for Pied à Terre; you won't regret it.

34 Charlotte St., W1. © **020/7636-1178.** www.pied-a-terre.co.uk. Set-price 2-course lunch £23.50; set-price 2-course dinner £57.50 (desserts £14, cheeses £16.50 per person); 10-course dinner £90; vegetarian £80. AE, MC, V. Mon–Fri 12:15–2:30pm; Mon–Sat 6–11pm. Tube: Goodge St. or Tottenham Court Rd.

Inexpensive

Barrica ★ SPANISH/TAPAS   Barrica looks the part—blackboards chalked up with daily specials, tiled floor, jars of colored pickled vegetables, Spanish posters, hanging hams, and a wall of wine bottles. This excellent tapas bar has an authentic feeling of Spain. The menu offers a tempting selection of dishes from around the country, served in proper small proportions at proper small prices. Those famous hams are here, of course, but also on offer are pork and oxtail meatballs, ham croquettes, and more, plus a substantial dish of the day. They take their wine list seriously, so try an unusual variety or go for their sherry suggestions.

62 Goodge St., W1. © **020/7436-9448.** www.barrica.co.uk. Tapas £1.75–£15. AE, MC, V. Mon–Fri noon–11:30pm, Sat 1–11pm. Tube: Goodge St. or Tottenham Court Rd.

MARYLEBONE
Very Expensive

Locanda Locatelli ★★ ☺ ITALIAN   The setting is sexy with beige leather seating and etched-glass dividers—it's a great place for spotting the A-list of celebrities who love the restaurant. But chef Giorgio is a family man and children are just as welcome, particularly at Sunday brunch. The cooking is superb and portions are generous with pastas scoring particularly highly. Pan-fried red mullet comes with Parma ham and warm fennel salad; roast partridge with Swiss chard, chestnut, and grape is meltingly tender and gutsy. Panettone bread-and-butter pudding has to be the best in London. The all-Italian wine list is superb, with many bottles under £30 and a Sicilian at £12, surely the best value in town.

8 Seymour St., W1. © **020/7935-9088.** www.locandalocatelli.com. Reservations required. Main courses £26.50–£32.50. AE, MC, V. Mon–Fri noon–3pm; Sat–Sun noon–3:30pm; Mon–Thurs 6:45–11pm; Fri–Sat 6:45–11:30pm; Sun 6:45–10:15pm. Tube: Marble Arch.

Expensive

L'Autre Pied ★★ CONTEMPORARY EUROPEAN   The younger sister of the successful **Pied à Terre** (p. 133), this is the domain of young chef Marcus Eaves, who gained his first Michelin star in 2009 soon after opening. The dark red seating, hand-painted walls, and wooden tables make a cozy ambience, ideal for the well-heeled shoppers of Bond Street. The cooking is skillful, with intense flavors brought to the fore in dishes that range from a starter of ravioli of confit pheasant with savoy cabbage and a nutmeg and chestnut cream, to a deeply satisfying main dish of roasted partridge breast and confit leg coming with its own mini-game pie, *choucroûte*, and a mustard sauce. It's expensive, but the set lunch and pre-theatre dinner is a steal.

5–7 Blandford St., W1. ⓒ **020/7486-9696.** www.lautrepied.co.uk. Reservations required. Main courses £26.95–£32.95; fixed-price lunch or pre-theatre (6–7pm) set menu 2 courses £18.95, 3 courses £22.50; tasting menu £59.50. AE, MC, V. Mon–Fri noon–2:45pm; Sat noon–2:30pm; Sun noon–3:30pm; Mon–Sat 6–10:45pm (Sun until 9:30pm). Tube: Bond St.

The Providores & Tapa Room ★★ PACIFIC RIM/FUSION   If you've wondered what fusion cooking is all about, book at Peter Gordon's Providores for a sublime example. For more than 10 years, the New Zealander has been showing how combinations of often relatively unknown ingredients can be fused together to produce a truly gourmet experience. It's the masterly combinations that make each dish such a wonderful discovery. Squid with papaya, pickled carrot, and pomelo (Asian citrus fruit) salad with tamarind caramel and coriander is a glorious explosion of sweet and sour tastes. Grilled scallops come with a dumpling of quinoa and crab, purée of celeriac and tomato sambal (chili-based sauce), and lotus crisps. Lunch is a la carte, but dinner is a set menu with the savory dishes starter-sized to encourage you to taste as many as possible. The main **Providores** restaurant is upstairs. The downstairs, low-key **Tapa Room** offers all-day dining, and is a perfect place for breakfast.

109 Marylebone High St., W1. ⓒ **020/7935-6175.** www.theprovidores.co.uk. Tapa Room: tapas £2.40–£16.40. The Providores: Main courses lunch £15–£24; set dinner 2/3/4/5 courses £30/£43/£53/£60. Tapa Room Mon–Fri 9–11:30am and noon–10:30pm; Sat 10am–3pm and 4–10:30pm; Sun 10am–3pm and 4–10pm. The Providores Mon–Fri noon–2:45pm and 6–10:30pm; Sat noon–2:45pm and 6–10:30pm; Sun noon–2:45pm and 6–10pm. AE, MC, V. Tube: Baker St. or Bond St.

Moderate

Galvin Bistro de Luxe ★★ FRENCH   The Galvin brothers, Chris and Jeff, opened Galvin Bistro de Luxe in 2005, considered at the time a brave venture because the site had seen off several hopefuls. But their formula of producing some of the best rustic French food to be found in London *and* Paris at reasonable prices in an elegant, buzzing brasserie has proved a winner. Tastes shine through in well-loved dishes like fish soup with rouille and cheese; sautéed veal kidneys with chanterelle mushrooms and a mustard sauce; and those staples of bistro cooking, *tarte au citron* and apple *tarte tatin*.

6 Baker St., W1. ⓒ **020/7935-4007.** www.galvinrestaurants.com. Reservations required. Main courses £14.50–£26; fixed-price menu lunch £17.50, dinner £19.50. AE, MC, V. Mon–Sat noon–2:30pm; Sun noon–3pm; Mon–Wed 6–10:30pm; Thurs–Sat 6–11pm; Sun 6–9:30pm Tube: Baker St. Also at 35 Spital Sq., E1 (ⓒ **020/7299-0400**).

Union Café CONTEMPORARY EUROPEAN   We find this place a real haven after shopping in Oxford Street or Marylebone. The buzzing restaurant, part of the upmarket Brinkley's group, is chic with wooden floors, industrial air vents, and an open kitchen. The menu goes the global path: Deep-fried brie with cranberry jelly; tempting meze plates; linguine with tiger prawns, mussels, and chili; but it's the juicy, tender Union burger with chips that seems to go down best with the punters.

96 Marylebone Lane, W1. ⓒ **020/7486-4860.** www.brinkleys.com/unioncafe.asp. Reservations recommended. Main courses £12–£23. AE, MC, V. Mon–Fri noon–3:30pm and 6–10:30pm; Sat 11am–4pm and 6:30–11pm; Sun 11am–4pm. Tube: Bond St.

West London

PADDINGTON & BAYSWATER
Moderate

Hereford Road ★★ MODERN BRITISH   Once a butcher's shop, now a restaurant in the St. John mode of British no-fuss, no-fancy cooking. Chef Tom Pemberton's time at **St. John Bread & Wine** (p. 143) shows in a menu that takes in potted crab as well as grilled ox heart and roast quail with that most British (but underused) meddler jelly for starters, and moves onto mains of pot-roast duck leg and fennel, or devilled lamb's kidneys and mash. The regulars of Notting Hill have taken this offal-heavy restaurant to their heart.

13 Hereford Rd., W2. ℂ **020/7727-1114.** www.herefordroad.org. Reservations recommended. Main courses £10–£14.20; set lunch, 2 courses Mon–Fri £13.60, 3 courses £15.50. AE, MC, V. Daily noon–3pm and 6-10:30pm; Sun 6-10pm. Tube: Bayswater.

Inexpensive

Mandalay 🍴 BURMESE   This cramped, family-run cafe is still the only Burmese restaurant in London, drawing a mix of students, locals, and those in the know. The menu takes in influences from China, India, and Thailand too, so you can combine shrimp and vegetable spring rolls; samosas and fritters; as well as spicy lamb curry, sweet-and-sour chicken, and shrimps with bamboo shoots. The small kitchen turns out the dishes with remarkable skill, particularly given the size of the menu. The drinks list is short.

444 Edgware Rd., W2. ℂ **020/7258-3696.** www.mandalayway.com. Reservations required at dinner. Main courses £4.40–£7.90; set lunch £3.90-£5.90. AE, MC, V. Mon–Sat noon-2:30pm and 6-10:30pm. Tube: Edgware Rd.

NOTTING HILL
Expensive

The Ledbury ★★ EUROPEAN   Australian-born Brett Graham has now earned two Michelin stars at this sophisticated neighborhood restaurant. With an inventive approach to ingredients and taste combinations that show true Aussie innovation, he produces dishes like flamegrilled mackerel with smoked eel, mustard, and shiso (Japanese mint) as a starter and grouse in season cooked in lapsang souchong tea with prunes, walnut milk, and mushrooms for a main dish. This is adventurous stuff—and in lesser hands could be a disaster. Here it is some of the best cooking around, and he's just as good at the desserts.

127 Ledbury Rd., W11. ℂ **020/7792-9090.** www.theledbury.com. Reservations recommended. Main courses (lunch) £24–£26; set lunch Mon–Fri 2 courses £27.50, 3 courses £33.50; set lunch Sat–Sun £40; set dinner £70. AE, MC, V. Mon 6:30-10:30pm; Tues–Sat noon-2:30pm and 6:30-10:30pm; Sun noon-3pm and 7-10pm. Tube: Westbourne Park.

Moderate

Le Café Anglais ★★ 😊 MODERN BRITISH   This is a grand brasserie in feel with huge windows, high ceilings, and banquette seating, located in Whiteleys shopping center. There's also a glamorous all-day cafe and oyster bar, ideal for those seeking an elegant light snack between buying posh frocks. There are plenty of classics on the menu, like Parmesan custard and anchovy toast for a starter and any of the excellent game dishes. With its long menu, set menus, children's meals and parties, and friendly welcome, Le Café Anglais works hard to create the atmosphere of a neighborhood restaurant and succeeds; this is a restaurant that pleases everyone.

8 Porchester Gardens, W2. ℂ **020/7221-1415.** www.lecafeanglais.co.uk. Reservations required. Main courses £12.50–£30; set lunch Mon–Fri 2 courses £18.50, 3 courses £22.50; Sun lunch 2 courses £21.50, 3 courses £25. AE, MC, V. Daily noon-3pm; Mon–Thurs 6:30-11pm; Fri–Sat 6:30-11:30pm; Sun 6:30-10:15pm. Tube: Bayswater or Queensway.

Southwest London
BELGRAVIA
Expensive

Amaya ★★ INDIAN Theatrical, with its chefs working at the open kitchen and charcoal grill; beautiful, with pink sandstone black granite worktops, chandeliers of cascading crystals, and colorful modern art; and seductive, with its rosewood and red bar—it's not surprising that Amaya is such a hit. And that's before you taste the food. Chef Karunesh Khanna not only has a Michelin star, he also specializes in tapas-style Indian food, so go in a group to share as many of the wonderful array of dishes as possible. Try prawns with tomato and ginger; marinated leg of lamb; lamb seasoned with cardamom, mace, and ginger cooked over charcoal; and a range of vegetarian dishes like tandoor-cooked broccoli in yogurt sauce.

Halkin Arcade, Motcomb St., SW1. ☎ **020/7823-1166.** www.amaya.biz. Reservations required. Main courses £11.50–£24; set-price lunch £19.50–£29, set-price dinner £38.50–£70. AE, DC, MC, V. Mon–Sat 12:30–2:15pm and 6:30–11:30pm; Sun 12:45–2:45pm and 6–10:30pm. Tube: Knightsbridge.

Palm ★ ☺ AMERICAN/STEAK Walk into the long buzzing bar and you'll find a TV at one end showing North American sports. Two adjacent dining rooms follow the decor of the other Palms in this American group: casual yet smart, with wooden floors and walls covered in caricatures of famous or faithful customers. The menu goes beyond the normal steakhouse, with classic Italian dishes (Palm's founders were Italian immigrants) like veal marsala, and fresh seafood and burgers, but steak is what Palm is all about. It's expensive, but go for the Prime New York Strip—12 oz, for £39.50. The welcome is as big as the portions; there's a good children's menu and a reasonably priced wine list.

1 Pont St., SW1. ☎ **020/7201-0710.** www.thepalm.com/london. Reservations recommended. Main courses £17–£49. AE, DC, MC, V. Mon–Sat noon–11pm, Sun noon–9pm. Tube: Knightsbridge or Sloane Sq.

KNIGHTSBRIDGE
Very Expensive

Dinner by Heston Blumenthal ★★ TRADITIONAL BRITISH This restaurant opened in 2011 by one of the world's great chefs, Heston Blumenthal of the Fat Duck in Bray, was one of London's most eagerly expected openings in recent memory. Dishes are based on Britain's culinary past, from savory porridge (c.1660) and broth of lamb (c.1730) to powdered duck (c.1670) and beef royal (c.1720). Finish with a sublime dessert—tipsy cake from 1810 perhaps? Don't worry; this is an extremely serious, profoundly satisfying re-rendering of historic recipes with modern cooking techniques. A unique experience in a crowded marketplace.

Inside Mandarin Oriental Hyde Park, 66 Knightsbridge, SW1. ☎ **020/7201-3833.** www.dinnerbyheston.com. Reservations required. Main courses £20–£32; 3-course set lunch Mon–Fri £28. Daily noon–2:30pm and 6:30–10:30pm. AE, DC, MC, V. Tube: Knightsbridge.

Marcus Wareing at the Berkeley ★★★ FRENCH Diners at this claret-colored, cosseting restaurant are treated to all the goodies expected from one of London's top venues. Marcus Wareing began as a protégée of Gordon Ramsay but then took over the restaurant independently and blossomed. The three-course, fixed-price lunch menu at £38 is relatively inexpensive, but the dishes—wood pigeon with tomato, black pudding, and lettuce followed by perhaps chicken with root vegetables—don't stretch the kitchen. So if you can, blow the budget and go a la carte. Start with foie gras with prunes, walnuts, apple, and celery, then follow with sweet Cornish lamb, offset with a pink peppercorn yogurt. The kitchen delivers dishes that are beautifully constructed in looks and full of rich flavors that never overpower. Don't expect a quick meal; delicious extras—smooth velouté as a pre-starter, lip-tingling granitas between courses, and pre-desserts keep you guessing as to what might come your way next.

Inside Berkeley Hotel, Wilton Place, SW1. ℂ **020/7235-1200.** www.marcus-wareing.com. Reservations required. Lunch menu £38; a la carte menu £80; prestige menu or vegetarian menu £98; weekend menus £85 and £120. AE, MC, V. Mon–Fri noon–2:30pm; Mon–Sat 6–11pm. Tube: Knightsbridge.

Moderate

Bar Boulud ★★ FRENCH   French-born, U.S.-raised, superstar chef Daniel Boulud opened the doors of his first London venture to universal approval in 2009. It's in the Mandarin Oriental, but with its own entrance, and has an attractive decor of red banquette seating, an open kitchen, and a real buzz. You won't encounter the Michelin three-star cuisine of his New York restaurant, but hearty, rustic cooking. A charcuterie counter rightly takes pride of place—Daniel Boulud was born in Lyon. Feast on classic French bistro fare like a *petit aioli* of seafood and vegetables with a perfect garlic mayonnaise; a coq au vin that had us rushing home to dig out the French recipe books; homemade sausages; and for dessert, a rich dark chocolate and raspberry gâteau. Prices are very reasonable for this part of London and level of glamor.

In the Mandarin Oriental Hyde Park, 66 Knightsbridge, SW1. ℂ **020/7201-3899.** www.barboulud.com. Reservations recommended. Main courses £12.50–£18.75. AE, MC, V. Daily noon–2:30pm and 6–11pm. Tube: Knightsbridge.

KENSINGTON & SOUTH KENSINGTON
Very Expensive

Tom Aikens ★★★ FRENCH   Chef Tom Aikens has a remarkable capacity to shrug aside life's mishaps (an abrupt departure from his first restaurant, Pied à Terre, economic woes, and the rapid closure of one of his recent restaurants). His signature dining room is quietly chic, a discreet background for a meal that delivers real punch. His style is a modern interpretation of haute French cuisine, produced with flourish and skill. A roast scallop soup comes with black pudding and parsnip purée; poached lobster tail with English asparagus and an asparagus mousse. Despite contrasting ingredients, the cooking shows harmony and cohesion, as exemplified by John Dory with chestnut ravioli, chestnut sauce, cabbage, and bacon.

43 Elystan St., SW3. ℂ **020/7584-2003.** www.tomaikens.co.uk. Reservations required. Set lunch 2 courses £45; dinner main courses £30–£40; tasting menu £55. AE, DC, MC, V. Mon–Fri noon–2:30pm; Mon–Sat 6:45–11pm. Tube: S. Kensington.

Expensive

Cambio de Tercio ★★ CONTEMPORARY SPANISH   Vibrantly colored in blood reds, deep pinks, and bright yellows, and adorned with equally vibrant stylized paintings of bull fighting, this is not the place for the shy and retiring. But it is the place for exciting, modern Spanish cooking. The menu has wide appeal. It offers conventional dishes like fried squid; prawns with garlic-parsley oil; and the classic, and beautifully cooked, crisp suckling pig with rosemary. But it also takes you on a different journey. With many of the dishes available tapas size, you'll be tempted to forgo the straight three-course route for a series of small dishes, perhaps foie gras cream with sherry, roast corn, and Manchego cheese; hake with baby squid cooked in its own ink and roast green pepper; and, naturally, superb Iberico pata negra ham.

163 Old Brompton Rd., SW5. ℂ **020/7244 8970.** www.cambiodetercio.co.uk. Main courses £17.50–£23; 7-course tasting menu £37. AE, DC, MC, V. Mon–Fri noon–2:30pm; Sat–Sun noon–3pm; Mon–Sat 7–11:30pm; Sun 7–11pm. Tube: Gloucester Rd. or S. Kensington. Also at 174 Old Brompton Rd., SW7 (ℂ **020/7370-3685**) and 108–110 New King's Rd., SW6 (ℂ **020/7371-5147**).

Moderate

Zaika ★★ INDIAN   Zaika's name translates as "sophisticated flavors." The cooking is complex but the final tastes meld together. It was one of the first Indian restaurants to get a Michelin star; the original innovative chef, Vineet Bhatia has gone, but Zaika still hits the spot. Start with a platter of salmon marinated in orange and ginger, smoked in the tandoor with salmon cured with lemon, and a lemon and smoked salmon pancake; follow with our favorite, duck breast masala delicately cooked in a jus with cloves and cardamom with garlic and chili mash and okra. For a true feast, order the tasting menu, *Jugalbandi,* or if you're fish lovers, go for the seafood tasting menu.

1 High St., Kensington, W8. ℂ **020/7795-6533.** www.zaika-restaurant.co.uk. Reservations required. Main courses £13.50–£25; fixed-price lunch 2/3 courses £20/£25. Tasting menus £42–£45. Tues–Sun noon–2:45pm; Mon–Sat 6–10:45pm; Sun 6–9:45pm. Tube: High St. Kensington.

CHELSEA
Very Expensive

Gordon Ramsay ★★★ FRENCH   Whatever may be happening in the fiery chef's empire elsewhere, a meal here remains one of London's great pleasures. From the moment you walk in the door, you are cosseted, and made to feel special. The menu is changing under head chef Clare Smyth—a chef to take note of—while retaining the subtlety and delicacy of the master. Try, for example, ravioli of lobster, langoustine, and salmon with a lemongrass and chervil velouté, or sautéed foie gras with roasted veal sweetbreads. The emphasis is on retaining the essential flavors of top ingredients while delivering exquisite tastes. A rare experience.

68 Royal Hospital Rd., SW3. ℂ **020/7352-4441.** www.gordonramsay.com. Reservations essential (1 month in advance). A la carte menu 3 courses £90; fixed-price 3-course lunch £45, 7-course dinner £120. AE, DC, MC, V. Mon–Fri noon–2:30pm and 6:30–11pm. Tube: Sloane Sq.

Moderate

Pig's Ear ★ 🎀 MODERN BRITISH/GASTROPUB   The ground floor bar serves excellent traditional beers, and dishes like risotto or roast guinea fowl in the packed back dining room. The Blue Room serves more sophisticated meals: smoked salmon mousse; a good charcuterie plate for starters; wild duck with buttered Savoy cabbage, miso-glazed turnips, and sour cherries as a typical main. It's a posh gastropub, befitting its posh location in Chelsea, but it's friendly and casual and you're always made to feel welcome.

35 Old Church St., SW3. ℂ **020/7352-2908.** www.thepigsear.info. Reservations required in restaurant. Main courses £12–£15.50. AE, DC, MC, V. Mon–Sat noon–11pm; Sun noon–10:30pm. Tube: Sloane Sq.

Tom's Kitchen ★ TRADITIONAL BRITISH   High octane, hugely busy, and wildly popular, this former pub has been turned into a brasserie from top chef **Tom Aikens** (p. 138), and is a great all-day venue. The menu is a rundown of all that is good in London's more casual venues: full English breakfast, butternut squash soup; mackerel paté; excellent pastas and salads; mains like pork belly and lentils; and the show-stopping baked Alaska flamed at the table.

27 Cale St., SW3. ℂ **020/7349-0202.** www.tomskitchen.co.uk. Reservations required. Main courses £13–£39.50. AE, MC, V. Mon–Fri 8–11am and noon–3pm; Sat–Sun 10am–4pm; daily 6–11pm. Tube: S. Kensington. Also at Somerset House, Strand, WC2 (ℂ **020/7845-4646**).

WESTMINSTER & VICTORIA
Expensive
Cinnamon Club ★★ INDIAN   This former Victorian library is a gorgeous, stately building with wooden paneling, high ceilings, and a book-lined gallery. It's a suitably grand setting for the many Members of Parliament who seem to regard it as their club. And it's a suitably theatrical setting for the exciting modern Indian cooking from executive chef Vivek Singh. European ingredients, Indian spicing, classical cooking techniques, and Western-style presentation make for a heady mix. Such a balancing act could be disastrous in less skilled hands, but here it produces some of the most innovative Indian cooking you'll find. Try Gressingham duck breast with coconut vinegar sauce; hot sweet king prawns with curry sauce and brown rice; or saddle of lamb with sesame tamarind sauce. Go conventional at breakfast with a perfect, light kedgeree—the dish of fish, rice, eggs, parsley, and cream brought back from the Raj by British colonials.

Old Westminster Library, 30–32 Great Smith St., SW1. *②* **020/7222-2555.** www.cinnamonclub.com. Main courses £15–£32; set meal pre- and post-theatre 2 courses £24, 3 courses £28; tasting menu £75. AE, DC, MC, V. Mon–Fri 7:30–9:30am, noon–2:30pm, and 7:30–9:30pm; Sat noon–2:30pm and 7:30–9:30pm. Tube: St. James's Park or Westminster. Also at Cinnamon Kitchen, 9 Devonshire Sq., EC2 (*②* **020/7626-5000**).

Moderate
The Orange ★ ☺ GASTROPUB/CONTEMPORARY EUROPEAN   The Orange is a smart gastropub with four delightful rooms for overnight stays. There's a heaving bar downstairs, with a dining room adjoining and a second dining room upstairs. It serves a clever menu that has the wealthy nearby residents of Pimlico coming back again and again. Sautéed wild mushrooms with polenta or soup of the day might start the meal. Wood-fired pizzas, conveniently served in two sizes, are popular with the families who regularly eat here, while mains like sea bream with new potatoes, olives, and anchovies, or house-baked pies satisfy the parents. It's fun, cheerful, and the staff go about their business with great charm.

37–39 Pimlico Rd., SW1. *②* **020/7881-9844.** www.theorange.co.uk. Main courses £13–£18; set 3-course menu £30. AE, MC, V. Mon–Thurs 8–11:30pm; Fri–Sat 8am–midnight; Sun 8am–10:30pm. Tube: Sloane Sq.

Inexpensive
Jenny Lo's Teahouse 🍴 CANTONESE/SZECHUAN   This teahouse is really a small, fun cafe, ideal for inexpensive lunches. It was opened by Jenny Lo, daughter of the late Ken Lo, the tennis-playing restaurateur whose *Memories of China* brought upper-class Chinese cooking to London. Ken Lo cookbooks contribute to the dining room decor of black refectory tables set with paper napkins and chopsticks. The menu offers a good range of well-cooked dishes like vermicelli rice noodle (noodles topped with grilled chicken breast and Chinese mushrooms). Rounding out the menu are stuffed Peking dumplings; chili-garnished spicy prawns; and wonton soup with slithery dumplings.

14 Eccleston St., SW1. *②* **020/7259-0399.** Reservations not accepted. Main courses £6.95–£8.50. No credit cards. Mon–Fri noon–3pm; Mon–Sat 6–10pm. Tube: Victoria.

South Bank
BANKSIDE
Expensive
Oxo Tower Restaurant, Brasserie & Bar ★★ INTERNATIONAL   The Oxo Tower is one of London's top dining spots—literally, as it's on the 8th floor of Oxo Tower Wharf. Stunning views up and down river make the terrace one of summer's

most sought-after venues. Both the Brasserie and the Restaurant share the same chic, 1930s' liner decor, and the same contemporary ethos in the cooking. The **Brasserie** is more casual, offering all the current modish mixes of tastes, spices, and inspirations like chargrilled, Moroccan spiced quail followed by teriyaki salmon with soba noodle salad. Dishes on the **Restaurant** menu use more luxury ingredients: langoustines, foie gras, sea bass that comes with crab, samphire, a truffle beurre blanc, and fennel salad, and wild game in season. It's all seasonally led, with carefully sourced British ingredients to the fore.

22 Barge House St., SE1. *C* **020/7803-3888.** www.harveynichols.com/restaurants. Reservations recommended. Main courses £20–£32; set lunch 2 courses £22.50, 3 courses £35. AE, DC, MC, V. Mon–Sat noon–2:30pm and 6–11pm; Sun noon–3pm and 6:30–10pm. Tube: Blackfriars or Waterloo.

WATERLOO & SOUTHWARK
Moderate

Baltic ★ 🍴 EASTERN EUROPEAN   This is our favorite place after a visit to the Old Vic Theatre, particularly if the actors arrive to eat. It's cool in decor (minimalist with roof lights and upholstered chrome chairs), but hot on atmosphere—with a continuous, contented buzz and good jazz. It's owned by Jan Woroniecki who introduced his version of eastern European cuisine at Kensington's Wódka. Like its sister restaurant, the menu here mixes Polish, Russian, and Hungarian influences to great effect. Gravadlax salmon marinated in vodka with potato latkes; marinated herring; or Polish black pudding for starters, then our favorite to follow: A rich goose leg with beetroot, scallions, and redcurrant is cooked with self-confident skill. There's live jazz on Sundays, and great cocktails from the bar staff, who mix unusual ingredients like rhubarb jam or beetroot with proper Eastern European vodkas.

74 Blackfriars Rd., SE1. *C* **020/7928-1111.** www.balticrestaurant.co.uk. Main courses £11.50–£17.50; set meal 2 courses £14.50, 3 courses £17.50; Sun 2 courses £16.50, 3 courses £19.50. AE, MC, V. Daily noon–3:30pm and 5:30–11:15pm. Tube: Southwark.

Tapas Brindisa ★ SPANISH/TAPAS   Borough Market brings a steady stream of customers to the area—folk who regard good food as one of life's necessities—so Tapas Brindisa, which sources its food directly from Spain, is constantly busy. Add to that a no-bookings policy and a relatively small dining space, and you'll find yourself with a long wait at popular times. But customers agree that it's worth it, for ambitious plates like leek soup with manchego cheese; pan-fried cuttlefish with green bean salad; and clams with butter beans and bacon. Charcuterie is top class (but beware, it can push up the bill); there's also a selection of cured fish and specialty cheeses you won't find elsewhere. Partner it with a fino sherry or robust Rioja.

18-29 Southwark St., SE1. *C* **020/7357-8889.** www.brindisa.com. Tapas plates £4.95–£12.50. AE, MC, V. Fri–Sat 9–11am, noon–4pm, and 5:30–11pm; Mon–Thurs noon–3pm and 5:30–11pm. Tube: London Bridge. Also at 46 Broadwick St., W1 (*C* **020/7534-1690**); and 7-9 Exhibition Rd., SW7 (*C* **020/7590-0008**).

The City
SPITALFIELDS
Moderate

Hawksmoor ★ AMERICAN/STEAK   With its bare brick walls, wooden tables, and walls covered with photographs, Hawksmoor is every bit the New York steak joint. Its food won't disappoint steakhouse aficionados either. Hawksmoor prides itself on top-quality, perfectly aged, generous portions of beef, sourced from the famous quality London butcher, Ginger Pig, dry-aged for at least 35 days, and cooked exactly to order.

All the prime cuts are here: Porterhouse; bone-in prime rib; Chateaubriand; all perfectly seared on the outside, perfectly tender inside. Starters are pretty good too: The potted smoked mackerel with toast goes down well, and the prawn cocktail is a lovely retro number. Talking of cocktails, the bar staff mixes a mean mint julep.

157 Commercial St., E1. ℂ **020/7247-7392.** www.thehawksmoor.com. Main courses £12–£35. AE, MC, V. Mon-Fri noon–3:30pm and 6–10:30pm; Sat 11am–4pm and 6–10:30pm; Sun 11am–4pm. Tube: Liverpool St. Also at 7 Langley St., WC2 (ℂ **020/7247-7392**).

The Luxe CONTEMPORARY EUROPEAN   John Torode has expanded from his original venture, Smiths of Smithfield, into the revitalized Spitalfields Market, where restaurants sit cheek-by-jowl in the modernized Victorian structure. Torode's Luxe offers a multi-purpose restaurant experience. The noisy ground-floor cafe buzzes all day, and is a favorite of ours for breakfast or a gourmet lunchtime burger. There's a basement music and cocktail bar and an upstairs dining room, complete with open kitchen, exposed brick walls, and silk wallpaper recalling the area's Huguenot silk-weaving heritage. Start with herb and potato gnocchi with meat sauce, sage, and pecorino then move onto slow roast belly of pork with mash and green sauce.

109 Commercial St., E1. ℂ **020/7101-1751.** www.theluxe.co.uk. Main courses £13.50–£28. AE, MC, V. Restaurant Mon-Fri noon–3pm; Sun noon–4pm; Mon-Sat 6–9:30pm. Cafe-bar Mon-Sat 9am–11:30pm; Sun 9:30am–10pm. Tube: Liverpool St.

CLERKENWELL & FARRINGDON
Moderate

Bistrot Bruno Loubet ★★ FRENCH   A collective cheer went up among London's restaurant-goers when Bruno Loubet returned to the capital after 8 years in Australia. And when this star of 1990s' London opened Bistrot Bruno Loubet in the adventurous and funky **Zetter** (p. 192), nobody was disappointed. The all-day bistro hits the spot with a short, gutsy menu. Classic bistro dishes are given a twist in starters like guinea fowl boudin blanc on a pea soup, or terrine of pork and leek with pomegranate dressing, while a main dish of hare with macaroni and spinach gratin, and a classic, perfect bouillabaisse demonstrates that London restaurants are the equal of Paris's best.

St. John's Sq., 86-88 Clerkenwell Rd., EC1. ℂ **020/7324-4455.** www.thezetter.com/en/restaurant. Main courses £14.50–£19. AE, MC, V. Mon-Fri 7–10:30am, noon–2:30pm, and 6–10:30pm; Sat 7:30am–3pm and 6–10:30pm; Sun 7:30am–3pm and 6–10pm. Tube: Farringdon.

North Road ★★ CONTEMPORARY EUROPEAN/SCANDINAVIAN   Nordic cooking is notoriously under-represented in London, but this venture from Danish chef Christoffer Hruskovase should convince Londoners to look north. Suitably Scandinavian and minimal, the restaurant is both welcoming and smart. The Nordic influence comes not so much with the ingredients (which are British), as with the cooking approach, which uses less butter and cream and the *sous-vide* vacuum method (cooking in airtight plastic bags in a water bath) to keep the essentials of ingredients intact. Start with Dorset shrimp and carrot, followed by veal with celeriac, celery, and wild thyme. Norfolk deer with beetroot comes rolled in hay (a Viking preservation technique), giving a smoky taste that's enhanced by smoked bone marrow. Desserts also surprise: Try the *Flavours of Woodland*—birch bark, walnuts, chestnuts, and wild herbs. Vegetables and foraged herbs are used extensively. You'll find the clean, light tastes here refreshingly different.

60-73 St. John St., EC1. ℂ **020/3217-0033.** www.northroadrestaurant.co.uk. Reservations recommended. Main courses £10.50–£16. MC, V. Set lunch 2 courses £18, 3 courses £20; chef tasting menu

£55. Mon–Thurs noon–2:30pm and 6–10:30pm; Fri noon–2:30pm and 6–11pm; Sat 6–11pm. Tube: Barbican or Farringdon.

St. John ★★ MODERN BRITISH "Nose to tail eating" characterizes Fergus Henderson's no-nonsense approach. All parts of the animal are used—neck, tongue, trotters, tail, liver, and heart—to produce dishes that devotees travel miles for. Smoked sprats with potato and horseradish; potted beef and pickled prunes; or, for the truly dedicated, roast bone marrow and parsley salad. It's a seasonally led menu—in winter Gloucester Old Spot pork chop with bitter chard will keep out the cold. The ingredients are the best; the cooking is superb; the dish is what it says on the menu; the restaurant is a plain, whitewashed room in a former smokery. There's a sister restaurant in Spitalfields, **St. John Bread & Wine** ★, 94–96 Commercial St., E1 (✆ 020/7251-0848; www.stjohnbreadandwine.com; Tube: Liverpool St.).

26 St. John St., EC1. ✆ **020/7251-0848.** www.stjohnrestaurant.co.uk. Reservations required. Main courses £13.70–£29.50. AE, DC, MC, V. Mon–Fri noon–3pm; Mon–Sat 6–11pm. Tube: Farringdon.

TOWER HILL
Moderate
Bevis Marks Restaurant ★ JEWISH Bevis Marks is a surprising venue—a kosher restaurant attached to London's 18th-century synagogue. Stylish and very popular, it's widely recognized as the best kosher restaurant in London. The menu is an interesting mix of traditional Ashkenazi dishes and those with Asian influences. On the starter menu, chicken soup with matzo balls sits happily beside "Bevis Marks" crispy Thai salt-beef, bean shoots, sweet chili, and cilantro. Main dishes continue down the same path: English lamb chops come with new potatoes roasted in rosemary; chicken with lime leaf-scented rice and Thai green curry sauce. There's an interesting selection of Israeli bottles on a pricey wine list.

Bevis Marks, EC3. ✆ **020/7283-2220.** www.bevismarkstherestaurant.com. Main courses £14.50–£24.95. AE, MC, V. Mon–Thurs noon–3pm and 5:30–10pm; Fri noon–3pm. Tube: Aldgate or Liverpool St.

East London
SHOREDITCH
Expensive
Les Trois Garçons ★ 🎩 FRENCH Walk into Les Trois Garçons and you enter a fantasy, or possibly a nightmare, according to your taste. The interior of this former Victorian pub is full of glittering, lurid colored and crystal chandeliers, old handbags that hang from the ceiling, stuffed animals, and general bric-a-brac. The three "garçons," Hassan Abdullah, Michel Lassere, and Stefan Karlson opened the restaurant 10 years ago and have not looked back since. The menu is equally flamboyant, offering dishes that some find sublime and others just too over the top. Try their famous foie gras cured in Sauternes and cooked "*au torchon*" (in a tea towel), or perhaps a perfectly cooked tortellini of crab with bacon crisp offset with lemongrass sauce. This is an expensive restaurant, but great fun and a place to go if the culinary world seems drab and predictable.

1 Club Row, E1. ✆ **020/7613-1924.** www.lestroisgarcons.com. Reservations essential. Tasting menu £62 (whole table only); set menu 2 courses £39.50, 3 courses £45.50. AE, MC, V. Mon–Sat 7pm–midnight. Tube: Liverpool St./Train: Shoreditch High St.

Moderate
Princess of Shoreditch ★ MODERN BRITISH/GASTROPUB This handsome old pub close to Old Street has been beautifully transformed. The downstairs bar fills

up with City types at lunchtime downing pints of Wandle ale from Battersea brewery, Sambrook, and tucking into soup of the day (£5.50); fish and chips (£11.95); and pies (£10.50). Up the spiral staircase, the dining room is a more serious affair with an extended menu, and attracts more serious diners. Propose the deal over halibut with clam chowder sauce, or lamb rump with celeriac purée and crispy potatoes, then clinch it with apple crumble. At weekends it's popular with families and groups of friends.

76 Paul St., EC2. ℂ **020/7729-9270.** www.theprincessofshoreditch.com. Main courses £11.95–£18, set lunch 2 courses £14, 3 courses £18. AE, MC, V. Mon–Thurs noon–3pm and 6:30–10pm; Fri noon–3pm and 6–10:30pm; Sat–Sun 10am–4:30pm and 6–10:30pm. Tube: Old St.

Inexpensive

Albion TRADITIONAL BRITISH/CAFE   Sir Terence Conran's Boundary Project is all-embracing: Within the trendy **Boundary hotel** (p. 193) there's a smart basement restaurant, summer rooftop terrace bar, and the Albion ground-floor shop, bakery, and cafe. Don't be fooled by the retro decor with its wood and leather banquettes, industrial lights, and white tiles. Despite its description as a "caff," this is really a posh cafe where the punters wear trendy trainers rather than cloth caps. Being Sir Terence, it's all extremely well done. You can eat all day on good old British classics—omelet; potted shrimps; devilled kidneys; or rump steak. Free Wi-Fi is the icing on the steamed syrup pudding.

2-4 Boundary St., E2. ℂ **020/7729-1051.** www.albioncaff.co.uk. No reservations. Main courses £8.75–£13.50. AE, MC, V. Daily 8am–midnight. Tube: Liverpool St./Train: Shoreditch High St.

Song Que VIETNAMESE   Kingsland Road remains the headquarters of London's Vietnamese restaurants, so there is plenty of competition in the area. Song Que holds its own—although not for its decor, which is more garish cafe than chic London venue. The vast menu includes reliable *pho* noodle soups with the well-flavored, aromatic broth full of meat and herbs. Barbecued quail is another favorite for its deeply satisfying, well-cooked meat. At night the lines are long; the best time to go is at lunch.

134 Kingsland Rd., E2. ℂ **020/7613-3222.** Main courses £4.50–£6.20. MC, V. Mon–Sat noon–3pm and 5:30–11:30pm; Sun 12:30–11pm. Train: Hoxton.

WHITECHAPEL
Inexpensive

Tayyabs ★ INDIAN   This Pakistani/Punjabi-inspired restaurant goes from strength to strength. In a former Victorian pub, it's on two levels and near enough to the City for savvy bankers to make it their local lunch spot. Tayyabs' gutsy food at low prices makes it a welcome change from the more tourist-orientated Brick Lane Indian restaurants. Punjabi meat curries, flavorful kebabs, and their now well-known marinated lamb chops are the staples; or go for the daily specials.

83 Fieldgate St., E1. ℂ **020/7247-9543.** www.tayyabs.co.uk. Main courses £6–£10. AE, MC, V. Daily noon–11:30pm. Tube: Aldgate East or Whitechapel.

BETHNAL GREEN
Very Expensive

Viajante ★★ CONTEMPORARY EUROPEAN   When he was performing culinary miracles at various East London venues, Portuguese-born Nuno Mendes was the darling of diners desperately seeking the next big thing. Now he's resurfaced inside the **Town Hall Hotel** (p. 194). In a restaurant with a kitchen so open it feels like you're in somebody's living room, this El Bulli-trained chef serves dishes that will either knock your socks off or leave you scratching your head. From the first *amuse* *bouche* that is sublime—through dishes that pair skate wing topped with crisp yeast and a purée of cauliflower; slow cooked pork and tiger prawns with grated egg, anchovy purée, and deep-fried capers, the surprises keep coming. This is supremely skillful, playful, flawlessly executed cooking. Forget a long, expensive trip to Spain's El Bulli; go to the East End instead.

Inside Town Hall Hotel, Patriot Sq., E2. (*C*) **020/7871-0461.** www.viajante.co.uk. Reservations required. Menus 6 courses £60, 9 courses £75, 12 courses £85. Daily noon–2:30pm and 7–11:30pm. Tube: Bethnal Green.

HACKNEY
Moderate
Forman's 1905 🍴 TRADITIONAL BRITISH/FISH   You may not have heard of Forman's, but you've probably tasted their smoked salmon somewhere in London—perhaps at Gordon Ramsay or the Dorchester. Forman's is an established East End smokery (opened in 1905) run by generations of the same family. At the moment it's a small, casual venue where salmon reigns supreme, with a few quintessentially British dishes like rump of lamb on offer, and an all-British wine list. The present owner, Lance Forman, is a formidable character who when forced to move from his smokery due to the Olympic Park construction, struck a very good deal and built a new smokery right opposite the Stadium. Also in the large building is a gallery and event space.

Stour Rd., E3. (*C*) **020/8525-2365.** www.formansfishisland.com. Main courses £11.50–£19.50. MC, V. Restaurant Thurs–Fri 7–11pm; Sat 9am–noon and 7–11pm. Gallery and Bar Thurs–Fri 5–9pm; Sat–Sun noon–5pm. Train: Hackney Wick.

DALSTON
Inexpensive
Mangal I ★ 🍢 TURKISH   You can tell you are in prime territory for *ocakbasi* (open-coal barbecue cooking) in Stoke Newington Road from the aroma of cooking meat that wafts through the air. Follow your nose just off the main road and you come to Mangal I. The kelim-hung room might not be the greatest in looks, but it cooks and serves a succulent mound of meat and vegetables. Feast on the mixed meze while you're waiting for the herbed lamb *sis* or spicy minced kebabs to appear. You should book and expect delays in service at busy times.

10 Arcola St., E8. (*C*) **020/7275-8981.** www.mangal1.com. Main courses £9–£15. No credit cards. Daily noon–midnight. Train: Dalston Kingsland. Also at 4 Stoke Newington Rd., N16 ((*C*) **020/7254-7888**).

North & Northwest London
CAMDEN TOWN
Expensive
York & Albany ★ CONTEMPORARY EUROPEAN   Camden Town is not known as a gastronomic destination, so the locals got very excited when Gordon Ramsay reopened this derelict pub as a fine dining restaurant with rooms. Overseen by Angela Hartnett, whose credentials include Michelin stars at Murano and the Connaught Hotel, it's a relaxed place that offers the best dining in the area. Top seasonal ingredients drive the menu, as in grilled mackerel with red pepper piperade and saffron aioli; or roast partridge with a perfect smoked garlic pomme purée, spinach, and baby artichokes. Steamed treacle sponge and custard for two brings out the greedy; tiramisu is perfect. The only downsides are the sometimes slapdash service and the noise level when the place is full. The early set supper menu is a bargain. It's a wonderful breakfast place and a small courtyard makes summer dining a treat.

127-129 Parkway, NW1. ✆ **020/7388-3344.** www.gordonramsay.com/yorkandalbany. Reservations recommended. Main courses £17-£22. Set menus and early supper (3 courses) £25. AE, MC, V. Mon-Fri 7-10:30am, noon-3pm, and 6-11pm; Sat 7-11:30am, noon-3pm, and 6-11pm; Sun noon-8:30pm. Tube: Camden Town.

HAMPSTEAD
Moderate

Wells ★ CONTEMPORARY EUROPEAN/GASTROPUB   Close enough to Hampstead Heath to attract walkers with their dogs and families, this place is also the local for many of Hampstead's decidedly upmarket residents. The old Georgian building is made up of a ground-floor bar and three rooms in the 1st-floor restaurant serving the same menus. The decor is chic enough for any smart gastropub; add to that the feel of a country retreat and it's not surprising this is a winner. Dishes like rabbit and mushroom terrine, and seared scallops with pea purée, bacon, and pea shoots sit happily beside rib-eye steak and chips and smoked haddock with champ potato, poached egg, and mustard beurre blanc. It's all very well done in a charming low-key way. Sunday lunch is a family occasion, and good beers are on tap for the devoted.

30 Well Walk, NW3. ✆ **020/7794-3785.** www.thewellshampstead.co.uk. Reservations recommended. Main courses £9.95-£15.95. MC, V. Mon-Fri noon-3pm and 6-10pm; Sat noon-4pm and 7-10pm; Sun noon-4pm and 7-9:30pm. Bar open daily noon-11pm. Tube: Hampstead.

PRIMROSE HILL
Moderate

The Engineer ★ CONTEMPORARY EUROPEAN/GASTROPUB   This temple to north London chic is another of our favorite gastropubs. It's a stylish conversion named after Victorian bridge, tunnel, and railway builder Isambard Kingdom Brunel, and sits beside the Regent's Canal, one of Brunel's creations. There's a courtyard garden for summer meals and a dining area covering two floors. Vibrant floral wallpaper creates a warm ambience; the menu is chalked up on blackboards and you eat at regulation gastropub wooden tables. Ingredients, sourced from organic farms where possible, are first rate. Start with potted smoked mackerel with beetroot and horseradish relish then move onto sea bass with broccoli and chili and brown anchovies. Wash it down with a good draught beer or cocktail.

65 Gloucester Ave., NW1. ✆ **020/7722-0950.** www.the-engineer.com. Reservations recommended. Main courses £12-£24. MC, V. Mon-Fri 9-11:30am, noon-3pm, and 7:30-10:30pm; Sat 9-noon, 12:30-4pm, and 7:30-11:30pm; Sun 9am-noon, 12:30-4pm, and 7:30-9pm. Tube: Chalk Farm.

Southeast London
GREENWICH
Moderate

Old Brewery MODERN BRITISH   The handsome Old Brewery, owned and run by the Meantime Brewery and supplying some of London's restaurants and pubs with its particular amber nectar, is a cafe by day and a restaurant by night. Huge shiny vats full of brewing beer (this is a working brewery) adorn one end; large windows and wooden tables and chairs fill the main space. It has a solid, dependable menu with dishes like devilled whitebait and seared foie gras to start, and Dorset plaice and venison as mains, many coming with recommended beers to try. It's a great place for true beer buffs, who can also book the brewery tour.

Pepys Building, Old Royal Naval College, SE10. ✆ **020/3327-1280.** www.oldbbrewerygreenwich.com. Main courses £13.75-£18.25. MC, V. Cafe: Daily 10am-5pm. Bar: Daily noon-11pm. Restaurant: Daily 6-10:30pm. DLR: Cutty Sark.

Teatime

Formal afternoon tea in London is a relaxing, civilized affair. Elegantly served on delicate china, there are dainty finger sandwiches, fresh-baked scones served with jam and clotted cream, and an array of small cakes and pastries. An attentive waiter is ready to refill your pot of tea. At many places, you can gild the lily with a glass of champagne. It makes an atmospheric alternative to pre-theatre dining.

Interesting West End alternatives to top London hotels include Momo's **Mô Café** (p. 128), where you're transported to Morocco with mint tea and whichever very sweet pastry you might fancy. Or try **Chai Bazaar,** part of Indian restaurant **Chor Bizarre,** 16 Albemarle St., W1 (𝄢 **020/7629 9802;** www.chorbizarre.com; Tube: Green Park) for Indian teas matched with Indian desserts. High tea here costs £9.50.

MAYFAIR

English Tearoom at Brown's ★★   Brown's has upped the ante with not one, but two tea sommeliers who will take you through the 17-strong list of teas, and a policy of replenishing any of the delights in front of you at no extra charge. The now requisite, albeit fabulous range of sandwiches on offer in London's top hotels is augmented by some of the best fruit cake you'll find and an assortment of gluten- and nut-free items. It's all elegantly conducted in a wood-paneled room with a plaster ceiling and an open fire.

Brown's Hotel, Albemarle St., W1. 𝄢 **020/7518-4155.** www.brownshotel.com. Reservations recommended. Afternoon tea £38, with champagne £47.50–£52.50. AE, DC, MC, V. Mon–Fri 3–6pm; Sat–Sun 1–6pm. Tube: Green Park.

ST. JAMES'S

Ritz Palm Court ★★★   This remains the top place for afternoon tea in London—and the hardest to get into without reserving way in advance. It's a spectacular stage setting, complete with marble steps and columns, a baroque fountain, and little wooded gold chairs. Nibble on a smoked salmon sandwich and egg mayonnaise roll then pig out on the chocolate cake. But you're really here to feel like a duchess.

Inside Ritz Hotel, 150 Piccadilly, W1. 𝄢 **020/7493-8181.** www.theritzlondon.com. Reservations required at least 8 weeks in advance. Jeans and sneakers not accepted; jacket and tie required for men. Afternoon tea £40–£52, with champagne £62. AE, DC, MC, V. 5 seatings daily at 11:30am, 1:30, 3:30, 5:30, and 7:30pm. Tube: Green Park.

KENSINGTON

The Orangery   Just north of, but part of **Kensington Palace** (p. 96), the Orangery is a long, narrow garden pavilion built in 1704 for Queen Anne. Rows of potted orange trees bask in sunlight from soaring windows, and tea is served amid Corinthian columns, Grinling Gibbons woodcarvings, and urns and statuary. The menu includes soups, salads, and sandwiches. But it's afternoon tea that brings out the great aunts. The array of different teas is served with high style, accompanied by fresh scones with clotted cream and jam, and Belgian chocolate cake.

In the gardens of Kensington Palace, W8. 𝄢 **020/7376-0239.** Reservations not accepted. Afternoon tea £14.85, with champagne £33.75. MC, V. Daily 3–5pm. Tube: High St. Kensington.

VICTORIA

The Goring ★★   Still family owned after a century in business, this comfortable hotel offers afternoon tea in the lounge, and in the summer on the sunny terrace overlooking the private garden. It's a clubby sort of place, with regulars propping up

COFFEE & A cake

There was a time when the only cup of coffee that could pass muster with a caffeine aficionado was at the splendid survivor in Soho, **Bar Italia** ★, 22 Frith St., W1 (✆ **020/7437-4520**). Then a wave of young, well-trained baristas jetted in, mostly from Australia and New Zealand, and changed the face of London's coffee houses forever. They're all very serious, using top coffee roasts and the best techniques; there are often tasting notes to accompany the brew. Now you can get the best coffee in the world in London. It's no idle boast; try any of these below.

Flat White, 17 Berwick St., W1 (✆ **020/7734-0370**) just off Berwick Street Market, is a magnet for Antipodeans who also make up the staff. Like many, they use superior Square Mile Coffee Roaster beans. Open Monday to Friday 8am to 7pm; Saturday, and Sunday 9am to 6pm. Tube: Leicester Square, Tottenham Court Road. The same owners run **Milk Bar** ★ in Soho, at 3 Bateman St., W1 (✆ **020/7287-4796**). Go for the great welcome, coffees, sandwiches, and snacks around £4–£5 and changing art on the walls. Open Monday

to Friday 8am to 7pm; Saturday, and Sunday 9am to 6pm. Tube: Tottenham Court Road.

Another Antipodean-owned and -run place, **Kaffeine** ★, 66 Great Titichfield St., W1 (✆ **020/580-6755**) is the place for a Square Mile summer blend espresso in a smart venue. Open Monday to Friday 7:30am to 6pm; Saturday 9am to 6pm. Tube: Oxford Circus.

Monmouth Coffee House, 26 Monmouth St., WC2 (✆ **020/7379-3516**) has been serving top filter coffees for over 30 years. The original Monmouth Street venue is cozy and a great place for cakes from Paul, around £4. Monday to Saturday 8am to 6:30pm. Tube: Covent Garden. Other locations in London.

Prufrock Coffee, 140 Shoreditch High St., E1 (✆ **020/7033-0500**). The UK's first World Barista Champion, Gwylim Davies, is the hero here, serving great flat whites and espressos to go with their cakes and sandwiches. It's inside the menswear shop, Present. Open Monday to Friday 10:30am to 6pm; Saturday 11am to 5pm; Sunday 11am to 4pm. Train: Shoreditch High Street.

the very popular, convivial bar all day long. Straying a little from the format, tea has Jaffa cakes, and mulled wine and pear jelly with cinnamon cream. It's as suitable for your great aunt as it is for your next romantic interest.

Beeston Place, Grosvenor Gardens, SW1. ✆ **020/7396-9000**. www.goringhotel.co.uk. Afternoon tea £35; champagne tea £45. AE, DC, MC, V. Daily 3–5pm. Tube: Victoria.

SHOPPING

London's shopping scene is eccentric, an eclectic mix of the thrifty and the luxurious. Shopping here isn't just about the big department stores, the impressive labels, or the obvious high-street chains anymore: It's going local, it's going boutique, and it's getting more personalized, as London develops an affordable charm of its own. The shopping scene today is all about being original, whether you're buying unique glassware on Portobello Road, or haunting the vintage boutiques of the East End. It's about making your shopping personal to you, and buying something that you'll treasure forever. The chances are you've picked it up from a little-known pop-up shop that disappeared a week later. They're all over London at the moment—it's one trend that seems to be sticking around.

West End

Oxford Street is undeniably the West End's main shopping attraction. Start at Marble Arch—the westernmost end—for designer department store **Selfridges** (p. 159). As you walk the length of the famous street toward Tottenham Court Road, you'll notice that the quality of shops goes downhill, especially east of Oxford Circus. Think bargain basement tat and cheap souvenirs, and you have the idea. **Topshop** (p. 157) remains an Oxford Street must-visit (the branch here is the largest clothes shop in Europe). You're certainly very brave to attempt Oxford Street at the weekend; weekday mornings are best for your sanity.

Oxford Street is also a great starting point for hitting the more interesting shopping areas, such as affluent **Marylebone.** It's impossible not to fall in love with the quaintness of Marylebone's high street. The street's chocolate shops and interiors brands ooze luxury.

Regent Street—home of an **Apple Store**—crosses Oxford Street at Oxford Circus. Regent Street shopping is more toward the high end of "high street," typified by the affordable luxury of chain shops like **Mango** and **French Connection.** Head south from Oxford Circus for the world-famous **Liberty** (p. 158) department store. You're now at the top of **Carnaby Street,** and while it's not quite the '60s-style mecca it once was, it's worth a stroll—especially if you veer off into the **Newburgh Quarter.** The area is also home to **Kingly Court,** a gorgeous little piazza of independent shops and vintage boutiques—the cafes are generally overpriced, but do provide a great perch to sit and people-watch.

Parallel to Regent Street, the **Bond Street** area connects **Piccadilly** with Oxford Street, and is synonymous with the luxury rag trade. It's not just one street, but a whole area, mainly comprising New Bond Street and Old Bond Street. It's the hot address for international designers—**Donna Karan** has two shops here, and **Tiffany** is quite at home nestled among designer jewelry shops. A slew of international hotshots, from Chanel to Versace, have digs nearby. Make sure you stop off at **Dover Street Market**—not a market at all, but actually a designer shop housing all sorts of fashionable folk under one roof.

Burlington Arcade (Tube: Piccadilly Circus), a glass-roofed Regency passage leading off Piccadilly, looks like a period exhibition, and is lined with 35 mahogany-fronted intriguing shops and boutiques. Lit by wrought-iron lamps and decorated with clusters of ferns and flowers, its small, upscale stores specialize in fashion, gold jewelry, Irish linen, and cashmere. If you linger there until 5:30pm, you can watch the **beadles** (the last London representatives of Britain's oldest police force), in their black-and-yellow livery and top hats, ceremoniously place the iron grills that block off the arcade until 9am, at which time they remove them to start a new business day. Also at 5:30pm, the **Burlington Bell** is sounded, signaling the end of trading. Make sure to catch the clock at **Fortnum & Mason** (p. 158)—it moves on the hour in a rather lovely display.

Nearby **Jermyn Street** (Tube: Piccadilly Circus), on the south side of Piccadilly, is a tiny two-block street devoted to high-end men's haberdashers and toiletries shops; many have been doing business for centuries. A bit to the northwest, **Savile Row** is where you'll find London's finest men's tailors.

The West End theatre district borders two more shopping areas: The still-not-ready-for-prime-time **Soho** (Tube: Tottenham Court Rd. or Leicester Sq.), where the sex shops are slowly morphing into cutting-edge designer boutiques—check out clothing exchange **Bang Bang** (p. 157) for designer bargains—and **Covent Garden,** a shopping masterpiece stocked with fashion, food, books, and everything else. The original Covent Garden marketplace has overflowed its boundaries and eaten up the surrounding neighborhood; it's fun to shop the narrow streets. Just off trendy **Neal Street** and Seven Dials, **Neal's Yard** is a stunning splash of color on rainy days if you're looking to buy foodstuffs from **Neal's Yard Dairy. Monmouth Street** is somewhat of a local secret. Many shops here serve as outlets for British designers, selling both used and new clothing. In addition, stores specialize in everything from musical instruments from the Far East to palm readings. Make sure, too, to take in **Charing Cross Road** and get your nose into one of the many secondhand bookstores.

South Bank

Apart from **Gabriel's Wharf** (p. 153), the South Bank isn't really a shopping destination on its own—although the area is slowly getting a facelift. The **Oxo Tower,** Bargehouse Street (✆ **020/7021-1600;** Tube: Waterloo) now has a collection of upscale boutiques on its lower floors, and **Borough Market** (p. 151) brings foodie crowds south in their droves, as does **Tate Modern** (p. 154) with its fabulous shop for artsy visitors and locals.

Southwest London

The home of **Harrods** (p. 158), **Knightsbridge** is probably the second-most famous London retail district. (Oxford St. just edges it out.) **Sloane Street** is traditionally regarded as a designer area, but these days it's more "upscale high street," and nowhere near as luxurious as **Bond Street** (see above). This is where you can grab some aromatherapy from **Jo Malone,** 150 Sloane St. (✆ **0870/192-5121;** www. jomalone.co.uk; Tube: Sloane Square), a haven for bespoke perfumes.

Walk southwest on **Brompton Road**—toward the **V&A Museum** (p. 102)—and you'll find **Cheval Place,** lined with designer resale shops, and **Beauchamp Place** (pronounced *Bee*-cham). It's high end, but with a hint of irony. Expect to see little lapdogs in handbags.

You'll also be near **King's Road** (Tube: Sloane Square), once a beacon of '60s cool, this is now a haven for designer clothes and homewares. About a third of King's Road is devoted to independent fashion shops, another third houses design-trade showrooms and stores for household wares (Scandinavian designs are prominent), and the remaining third a mix of dress shops and shoe boutiques. The clothes shops tend to suit a more mature customer (with a more mature budget), but you'll have fun shopping here if you remain oblivious to shop assistants who can be on the snooty side.

Finally, don't forget all those museums in nearby **South Kensington.** They have fantastic and exclusive gift shops. If you're looking for jewelry and homewares, the **V&A** (p. 154) and the **Design Museum** are must-visits. The **Science Museum** (p. 153) shop is perfect for inquisitive kids. Make sure to view the collections, too. They're free, and have some world-class exhibits.

West London

If you're heading west, the first place you should find yourself in is **Notting Hill.** Of course, one of the main draws for shopping in West London is **Portobello Market** (p. 152). Every Sunday, the whole of Portobello Road turns into a sea of antiques, cool clothing (and even cooler shoppers), and maybe even a celebrity or three.

Some of the best boutiques in London are also here. The independent shopping scene thrives; this is an area where people want to be unique, but still look expensive and groomed. Expect one-off, vintage-style dresses, quirky homewares, and more than a handful of retro record shops. Stick to Portobello for the antiques, but head to **Westbourne Grove** and **Ledbury Road** for the boutiques.

The area is also full of organic and fancy food stores, with Whole Foods having its flagship home here. They take their food very seriously in West London: It does come at a price, but the quality is good so make sure you pick up a few bits.

West London is also home to two American-style shopping malls. **Westfield** takes up residence in Shepherd's Bush, and **Whiteleys** sits in Bayswater. They're huge, they have everything, and they're busy. If it's raining and you still want your high-street shops, then head here. Just don't expect to find anything special or out of the ordinary.

The City & East London

The financial district itself doesn't really offer much in the way of shopping—especially at the weekend, when everything tends to be shut. However, a new shopping center, **One New Change,** is attracting a rich crowd for its luxury goods. It's opposite the eastern end of St. Paul's Cathedral. You'll also find a handful of tailors in the area, and there are several high-end brands in the nearby **Royal Exchange** (www.the royalexchange.com; Tube: Bank). However, unless you're often suited up for work, it's really not a shopping destination by itself.

Continue your adventure farther east on **Commercial Street** (Tube: Liverpool St./Train: Shoreditch High St.). This is where you'll find the best vintage shops in the city. They're on almost every corner, and new ones seem to appear every day, alongside pop-up stores just here for the weekend. Make sure you hit **Absolute Vintage** and the smaller **Blondie** (p. 157) around the corner, on the way to the antiques market in **Spitalfields** (p. 152).

A short stroll north, **Columbia Road** is more than just a flower market; in many ways, the main attractions are the artist studios that line the street. Head up every single one of those staircases you see. If the door is open, you're allowed in. You'll find artists at work and shops like **Jessica Chorley,** 158a Columbia Rd. (© **07708/921550;** www.jessiechorley.com; Train: Shoreditch) selling handmade notebooks and jewelry. Once you're done with the studios and shops—**Ryan Town** sells fabulous papercuts—everything at the flower market will be going cheap come 3pm.

Markets

London can't quite compete with the flea markets of Paris, but it does increasingly hold its own. London's markets are smaller, more niche, and perhaps slightly too expensive—but they are lots of fun. Take cash with you (and keep it somewhere safe), as most markets are a bit of a walk from any ATMs. Then do your best not to be tempted by all the wares on offer. Do haggle. Most items can be bought for cheaper than their price tag, if you're willing to negotiate. Round things down, ask for something for nothing, and get a bargain.

Borough Market ★★★   One of the largest outdoor food markets in the world, selling a mammoth variety of delectables from across the globe. Best buys are the more unusual items and British-reared meats, rather than standard food market fare, which is aimed at tourists with money to burn. The market is open Thursday 11am to 5pm, Friday noon to 6pm, and Saturday 9am to 5pm. Try to avoid on a Saturday

Tate Modern   If you're an art lover, you should definitely swing by Tate Modern for a browse in their shop. It's a great store, full of prints and more art books than you'll ever be able to carry. Everything in their shop is inspired by the exhibitions, and if you see a piece of art you like when you're walking around, be sure to note the number so you can pick up a much more affordable postcard version to send home; it's easier than trying to sneak a Monet into your handbag. Bankside, SE1. ✆ **020/7887-8888.** www. tate.org.uk/modern. Tube: Southwark.

V&A Shop ★★   The V&A has the best museum shop in London, perfect for design lovers. It stocks everything from exotic jewelry inspired by the exhibitions to their own line of toiletries and reclaimed prints. They take design seriously, and it's celebrated in every single item in the shop. It's worth the trip to the museum just for the shop, even if you don't have much time to look around the (mostly free) exhibits. Cromwell Rd., SW7. ✆ **020/7942-2000.** www.vam.ac.uk. Tube: S. Kensington.

BEAUTY & MAKE-UP

Angela Flanders ★★   This tiny Columbia Road shop sells bespoke perfumes and home scents. Try the English Rose perfume; it's basically the countryside in a bottle. As with the rest of Columbia Road, you can only rely on finding it open on weekends. 96 Columbia Rd., E2. ✆ **020/7739-7555.** www.angelaflanders-perfumer.com. Tube: Old St./Train: Hoxton.

L'Artisan Parfumeur   Posh smells and fancy whiffs are abundant in this luscious store. The flagship Erno Laszlo salon and shop is downstairs selling skincare once approved by Audrey Hepburn herself. 13 Covent Garden Market, WC2. ✆ **020/3040-3030.** www.artisanparfumeur.com. Tube: Covent Garden.

Shu Uemera ★★★   Shu Uemera is a brand with sleek packaging, flashes of neon bright color, and a fabulous line in false eyelashes. There's something exciting about bright blue peacock feathers fluttering about your face. 25 Neal St., WC2. ✆ **020/7240-7635.** www.shuuemura.co.uk. Tube: Covent Garden.

CLOTHING & ACCESSORIES
Children

Amaia ☺   With descriptions like "easy-to-wear" and "elegant" you'd be forgiven for thinking that Amaia was a high-end designer boutique. And it is, but instead of being for adults, it's for the well-heeled kids of London used to the finer things in life. 14 Cale St., SW3. ✆ **020/7590-0999.** Tube: S. Kensington.

Elias & Grace ★★ ☺   Where do you go for the best dresses you can buy your little ones? Elias & Grace is (unsurprisingly) in the fancy "village" of Primrose Hill, and you'll find everything from designers Chloe and Marni, all perfectly sized for your mini-yous. 158 Regent's Park Rd., NW1. ✆ **020/7449-0574.** www.eliasandgrace.com. Tube: Chalk Farm.

Sasti ☺   If you're looking for something original, Sasti is an affordable children's boutique. It has one-off outfits for newborns and toddlers, so you can buy bright prints and cute outfits without spending hundreds. 281 Portobello Rd., W10. ✆ **020/8960-1125.** www.sasti.co.uk. Tube: Ladbroke Grove.

Jewelry

Comfort Station ★★   There is no jewelry brand that does quirky elegance quite like Comfort Station. From their barometer-inspired mood necklaces, to the earrings with the coordinates for Hope (a town in Devon) and Love (in Barbados), their pieces all are unique and special. Each one has a story to tell, yet the items rarely go over the £100 mark. 22 Cheshire St., E2. ☎ **020/7033-9099.** www.comfortstation.co.uk. Tube: Liverpool St./Train: Shoreditch High St.

Lazy Oaf ★   If you want something different (and well-priced), Lazy Oaf is it. Whether it's a brooch that announces that you're a lousy dancer, or a necklace with a slightly offensive slogan, Lazy Oaf will inspire you to buy something out of the ordinary and just a little bit cheeky. 19 Foubert's Place, W1. ☎ **020/7287-2060.** www.lazyoaf.co.uk. Tube: Oxford Circus.

Les Neriedes ★★   This French jewelry shop is impossible to resist. Well-priced enamel pieces are the key focus, and if you like all things floral, you'll leave laden with gift-wrapped prettiness. You can find pieces under £20, and most items are around the £60 mark, so pick your favorites and enjoy. 36 Long Lane, WC2. ☎ **020/7379-9197.** www.lesnereides.com. Tube: Covent Garden.

Tatty Devine ★★   Tatty Devine started London's acrylic jewelry trend, and is still very good at it. Everything is handmade, everything is super cool, and everything is covetable. A dinosaur skeleton around your neck might not be subtle . . . but that's a good thing, right? Cute, whimsical, and fun is what Tatty Devine do best. 236 Brick Lane, E1. ☎ **020/7739-9191.** www.tattydevine.com. Tube: Liverpool St./Train: Shoreditch High St. Also at 44 Monmouth St., WC2 (☎ 020/7836-2685).

Men

Emma Willis ★   Emma Willis is a shirt tailor to rival the best men in the industry. Expect a personal (and speedy) service and a great design, in the best silks. 66 Jermyn St., SW1. ☎ **020/7930-9980.** www.emmawillis.com. Tube: Green Park.

Folk ★★   Folk is far too cool for its own good, but that's the appeal. Trendy designers and a preppy look are the trademark style of this shop. They do a line in women's clothes too, but the focus is on the guys. 49 Lamb's Conduit St., WC1. ☎ **020/7404-6458.** www.folkclothing.com. Tube: Holborn.

Ozwald Boateng ★★   If you're after swanky threads and a suit cut better than anywhere else, Savile Row should be your first stop—and Ozwald Boateng knows his way around a pattern. Expect a perfect fit, lush fabric, and a price tag to make your eyes water. 30 Savile Row, W1. ☎ **020/7440-5231.** www.ozwaldboateng.co.uk. Tube: Piccadilly Circus.

Peckham Rye   Funky tailoring and accessories—all with a bit of a twist—are what to expect when you shop in Peckham Rye. If you can carry off yellow check, you'll have a blast. Skinny ties, woolen scarves, and a distinct Swinging Sixties vibe are all here for you to browse. 11 Newburgh St., W1. ☎ **020/7734-5181.** www.peckhamryelondon.com. Tube: Oxford Circus.

Shoes & Accessories

Accessorize ★   This high-street chain store is possibly still the best in London for easy-to-wear and well-priced accessories and jewelry. You'll find one in most main train stations, and on almost every major shopping street. Where there are people, there's an Accessorize—which is a good thing, because they have a fantastic range of items to complete an outfit. Hats, bags, and leather gloves are the best buys, and if you're in town make sure you hit their January sale, where most things are half price. 1 Piccadilly, W1. ☎ **020/7494-0566.** www.accessorize.com. Tube: Piccadilly Circus. Other locations throughout London.

James Smith & Sons ★★   This is an authentic London institution. Specializing in umbrellas, it's been open since 1830 and is still a family business. They make their own brollies, and the shop is nothing short of spectacular to look at. It's also very handy if you get caught in the rain, which is quite likely. 53 New Oxford St., WC1. ✆ **020/7836-4731.** Tube: Tottenham Court Rd.

Kate Kanzier ★★ 👜 Kate Kanzier might be the best-value shoe shop in the whole of London. The shop sells fashionable brogues in every color you could imagine, for around £30 a pair. The quality probably isn't first rank, but when you're paying so little for a favorite among London's most fashionable, you can't complain. 67–69 Leather Lane, EC1. ✆ **020/7242-7232.** www.katekanzier.com. Tube: Farringdon.

Lulu Guinness This self-taught British handbag designer launched her business in 1989. Many of the world's greatest retail outlets, including **Fortnum & Mason** (see below) sell her handbags. Her signature bags, such as the "Florist Basket" and the "House Bag," are immortalized in the fashion collection at the **V&A Museum** (p. 102)—and she's still popular with celebs like Madonna and Liz Hurley. 3 Ellis St., SW1. ✆ **020/7823-4828.** www.luluguinness.com. Tube: Sloane Sq.

Luna & Curious ★★★ 👜 Have you ever thought to yourself, "I wish I could buy sexy designer tights and false paper eyelashes shaped like horses in the same shop?" Well, strange as it sounds, it works well at Luna & Curious. The only way to describe it is as an accessory shop, but it feels more special than that. It sells beautiful things that make you feel like you're shopping in Wonderland, and doesn't (always) charge you hundreds for the privilege. 24-26 Calvert Ave., E2. ✆ **020/7033-4411.** www.shoplunaandcurious. com. Tube: Liverpool St./Train: Shoreditch High St.

The Old Curiosity Shop ★ 👜 Men are rarely well catered for in the shoe department, but this shop is one of the most special in the city. It is the very "curiosity shop" that Charles Dickens based his novel on. They stick to traditional styles and the men's selection is better than the women's, but with such a beautiful building, steeped in so much history, it's worth popping in even if you aren't planning to buy. 13–14 Portsmouth St., WC2. ✆ **020/7405-9891.** www.curiosityuk.com. Tube: Holborn.

Women

Bordello ★★ Scratchy lace is not desirable any time of the year, and Bordello has raised the bar when it comes to where the ladies of London buy their smalls. It's expensive here, but everything is sexy and screams luxury. If you're looking for very special lingerie, it should be the first place you visit—and it'll probably be the last place as well. 55 Great Eastern St., EC2. ✆ **020/7503-3334.** www.bordello-london.com. Tube: Old St./Train: Shoreditch High St.

Joy ★★ If you have a thing for dresses, this is the shop for you. Day dresses, flirty dresses, little black dresses—this shop excels in them all. They're unique, but still well priced: Apart from the odd exception that creeps into three figures, everything is around the £50 mark. They do a great range of clothes (and a frankly tacky range of homewares and gifts), but the dresses will keep you occupied. The flagship branch in Greenwich is in a stunning old public baths building. 9 Nelson Rd., SE10. ✆ **020/8293-7979.** www.joythestore.com. DLR: Cutty Sark. Other locations throughout London.

New Look You can still get great London style even if you're on a tight budget. New Look is the place to start: It's one of the best-value chains on the British high street, and stocks items that will last more than three wears. Its range is not at the cutting edge, but dresses tend to stay under £30. 502-504 Oxford St., W1. ✆ **020/7290-7860.** www.newlook.com. Tube: Marble Arch. Other locations throughout London.

Between the high-street shops, the one-off boutiques, and the department stores, lies a strange retail beast known as the "collective shop." These are the stores that grab a selection of the very best of London fashion, and spread it out over several floors—meaning you're spoilt for choice whenever you visit. U.S. chain **Urban Outfitters**, 42–56 Earlham St., WC2 (✆ **020/7759-6390**; www.urbanoutfitters.co.uk; Tube: Covent Garden) does this just right, and London has its own take on the format, with some stunning homemade shops doing the same. **My Sugarland** ★, 402–404 St. John St., N1 (✆ **020/7841-7131**; www.mysugarland.co.uk; Tube: Angel) turns to vintage inspiration and unique styling to create a one-stop lifestyle shop. They're all about dressing up, and looking darned pretty while you're doing it. Over in southwest London, the **Shop at Bluebird**, 350 King's Rd., SW3 (✆ **020/7351-3873**; www.theshopat bluebird.com; Tube: S. Kensington) is chock-full of designers, and **Dover Street Market**, 17–18 Dover St., W1 (✆ **020/7518-0680**; www.doverstreet market.com; Tube: Green Park) excels at eclectic fashion choices. It stocks apparently every fashionable designer that might take your fancy.

Topshop ★　This is the largest fashion store in the world, and remains quite affordable. Its versatile and ever-changing merchandise is aimed at younger shoppers, but that doesn't stop many fashionable women in their 30s and 40s from shopping here. The outlet was the first to release a range of designs from Kate Moss. The shop, though aimed mainly at women, also has a men's floor. Women's shoes, vintage clothing, and other designer labels are in the basement. 216 Oxford St., W1. ✆ **0844/848-7487.** www.topshop.co.uk. Tube: Oxford Circus. Other locations throughout London.

Vintage

Bang Bang ★★ 🎒　The flashy designer-clad mannequins in the window make this Goodge Street store stand out among the secondhand computer shops and lunchtime pitstops. It specializes in designer clothes and high-end high street, but all at bargain prices. You'll find cut-price Armani and cheap Topshop under the same roof, but the stock changes regularly. Best bargains are accessories and tailored items, and prices are fair. Staff can be a little surly. 21 Goodge St., W1. ✆ **020/7631-4191.** Tube: Goodge St.

Blondie ★　This is the sister store to the larger **Absolute Vintage,** 15 Hanbury St. (✆ **020/7247-3883**). Don't let the small stature of the shop put you off—it has some real gems inside. Everything is arranged by color, so you can head straight to the red polka dots or little black dresses if you like. There's also an enormous shoe collection (mostly in smaller sizes, which is always the way with vintage) and a wide selection of Dior sunglasses. 114-118 Commercial St., E1. ✆ **020/7247-0050.** Tube: Liverpool St./ Train: Shoreditch High St.

East End Thrift Store　Another vintage shop that's worth the trip to East London. This one is inside a large warehouse off the unattractive Stepney Green Road. Inside you'll find a massive array of vintage clothing, all well priced, but of varying quality and styles. Men do well here, thanks to an excellent selection of shirts, but vintage newbies might have to do a bit of hunting to find easier-to-wear items. Assembly Passage, E1. ✆ **020/7423-9700.** Tube: Stepney Green or Whitechapel.

Emporium ★★   A quick trip over the river to Greenwich takes you to this classy vintage shop. Men fare slightly better for browsing (the best stuff for women is secreted in protective covers), but the accessories cabinet is an Aladdin's cave of treasures. 330–332 Creek Rd., SE10. ✆ **020/8305-1670.** DLR: Cutty Sark.

Marshmallow Mountain   Marshmallow Mountain is pricier than most vintage boutiques—that'll be the rent for the swanky shop location—but there's some excellent buys to be found. It seems to cater better for summer wear, with funky sunglasses and cotton dresses, but it's a lively little vintage shop with friendly staff. Unit G5, Kingly Court, W1. ✆ **020/7434-9498.** www.marshmallowmountain.com. Tube: Oxford Circus.

Rokit   There are three locations for this small chain, but the most central and best stocked is in Covent Garden. The trick here is to browse at leisure, looking for that perfect item. That's when vintage shopping really becomes fun. You'll find the best buys in leather, denim, and '70s' fashions. 42 Sheldon St., WC2. ✆ **020/7836-6547.** www. rokit.co.uk. Tube: Covent Garden. Other locations throughout London.

DEPARTMENT STORES

Contrary to popular belief, **Harrods** is not the only department store in London. The British invented the department store, and have lots of them. A lot are upscale, but you can usually still find a bargain in most. They're also getting better at catering for a younger shopper, and the concessions and food halls are generally the best instore sections.

Fenwick of Bond Street ★   Fenwick (with a silent "w"), dates back to 1891. It's a stylish store that offers a large collection of (slightly conservative) designer womenswear. The perfume and toiletries are excellent if you're looking for something unique, although it comes at a price. An extensive selection of lingerie in all price ranges is also sold. 63 New Bond St., W1. ✆ **020/7629-9161.** www.fenwick.co.uk. Tube: Bond St. or Oxford Circus.

Fortnum & Mason ★★   Catering to well-heeled clients as a full-service department store since 1707, Fortnum & Mason is better than ever. Offerings include one of the most exciting delicatessens in London, as well as stationery, gift items, porcelain, and crystal. The perfume section offers unique and rare items, all available for smelling. You'll find the items here traditional, elegant, and pricey. 181 Piccadilly, W1. ✆ **020/7734-8040.** www.fortnumandmason.com. Tube: Piccadilly Circus.

Harrods   Harrods remains a London institution, but it's not as cutting edge as it once was. For the latest trends, shop elsewhere; but, it's as entrenched in English life as Buckingham Palace and racing at Ascot, and is still an elaborate emporium. Buyers are trying to become more on trend, and they've added a pet emporium so you can purchase diamond collars for your pooch and gold food dishes for your kitty (there's even a few pets to cuddle). You'll also find a traditional barber, a jewelry department, and a fashion department for younger customers. 87–135 Brompton Rd., SW1. ✆ **020/8479-5100.** www.harrods.com. Tube: Knightsbridge.

John Lewis   This department store remains one of the most trusted outlets in London. Their motto is that they have never knowingly undersold, and they mean it. There are always great bargains here, and homewares are where they excel. Whatever you're looking for, ranging from Egyptian cotton towels to clothing and jewelry, you'll find it. 278–306 Oxford St., W1. ✆ **020/7629-7711.** www.johnlewis.com. Tube: Oxford Circus. Other locations throughout London.

Liberty ★★★   This department store has a lot to thank the vintage trend for. Suddenly, it's the most popular place in town, without even needing a revamp. It's celebrated for its own line of prints: Top-echelon fabrics, often in floral patterns, prized by decorators for the way they add a sense of English tradition to a room. Chintz got big, and the trend revived Liberty along with it. It's also the prettiest store in London with a Tudor-style splendor that includes half-timbering and interior paneling. There are six floors of fashion, china, and home furnishings, including the Liberty Print fashion fabrics, upholstery, scarves, ties, luggage, gifts, and much more. 210-220 Regent St., W1. ℰ **020/7734-1234.** www.liberty.co.uk. Tube: Oxford Circus.

Selfridges ★ Those iconic yellow bags scream fashion, and Selfridges do it better than anywhere else. You'll get lost in here (that's what they want, but there's a champagne bar so don't complain). Since it was founded by an American in 1858, Selfridges has adapted to changing times. Wander the ground-floor "Wonder Room" for luxurious jewelry and their shoe choice is one of the best in London. Even if you don't care about the fashion, don't come without heading to the staggering food hall. 400 Oxford St., W1. ℰ **0800/123-400.** www.selfridges.com. Tube: Bond St.

FOOD & DRINK

Camellia Sinensis This little cafe is the perfect pitstop if you're shopping in central London. In the very top corner of Kingly Court, it's calm and quiet even on a busy Saturday. It's not just afternoon tea and cake, though; you'll also find a vast array of teas from around the world on sale. There's a tea for every mood and occasion, including teas to make you dream and to cure tummy ailments. Pick up a pretty teapot or two as well; the china here is beautiful. 212 Kingly Court, W1. ℰ **020/7734-9939.** www.camelliasteahouse.com. Tube: Oxford Circus.

Gerry's If you're a fan of interesting booze, you'll be like a kid in a tipsy candy store in Gerry's. It's a Soho institution, and houses every spirit you can think of. Some see it as just another bottle shop, but to locals it's beloved, and especially handy if you're trying to find a special gift for friends who sneer at duty-free bargains. 74 Old Compton St., W1. ℰ **020/7734-2053.** www.gerrys.uk.com. Tube: Piccadilly Circus or Leicester Sq.

Hope and Greenwood ★★ Retro candy is very trendy at the moment, and Hope and Greenwood make the sweet treats of yesteryear a pleasure to buy. The shop in Covent Garden is like a little timewarp, full of cola bottles, coconut ice, and traditional British fudge to take home. 1 Russell St., WC2. ℰ **020/7240-3314.** www.hopeandgreenwood.co.uk. Tube: Covent Garden.

La Fromagerie ★★ It's the cheese room that makes this shop special. Ignore the little grocery displays when you enter and head straight to the good stuff. Remember to close the door behind you, because the temperature is set perfect for their vast range of British and Continental cheeses. 30 Highbury Park, N5. ℰ **020/7359-7440.** www.lafromagerie.co.uk. Tube: Arsenal. Also at 2-6 Moxon St., W1 (ℰ 020/7935-0341).

Melt ★★ This chocolate shop in Notting Hill is a West London favorite. It will tempt you with caramels and sweet treats, and if you're lucky, you'll even be able to peek into the kitchen where the chocolates are made. The proprietors run workshops (must be pre-booked), and their chili chocolate is something special. It's not cheap, but if you have a sweet tooth and you're exploring West London, make this a priority stop. 59 Ledbury Rd., W11. ℰ **020/8962-0492.** www.meltchocolates.com. Tube: Notting Hill Gate.

Neal's Yard Dairy ★ Specializing in British and Irish cheeses, this shop occupies the very photogenic premises of what was originally built as a warehouse for the food stalls at Covent Garden. Today you'll see a staggering selection of artisanal cheeses, including cloth-bound cheddars and a wide selection of mild farmer's cheeses, set in big display windows behind an antique, dark-blue Victorian facade. There are also olive oils, breads, fresh produce, and many of the fixings for the perfect picnic. 17 Shorts Gardens, WC2. ℂ **020/7240-5700.** www.nealsyarddairy.co.uk. Tube: Covent Garden. Also at 6 Park St., SE1 (ℂ 020/7367-0799).

Wholefoods   The flagship Wholefoods shop in Kensington is a bit of a joy, if you have the money to enjoy it. Full of tasty (mostly organic) treats, this is a real haven for foodies. It feels like an indoor market (without the haggling) and you'll find every type of food you could wish for. You won't be able to walk past the cakes without sampling something sweet, but avoid it at lunchtimes, when it draws a huge office crowd and gets too busy. 63-97 Kensington High St., W8. ℂ **020/7368-4500.** www.wholefoods market.com. Tube: High St. Kensington.

HOME DESIGN, FURNISHINGS & HOUSEWARES
See also "Art & Crafts," earlier in this section.

Caravan ★★★   In the mood for a white rabbit lamp, or an owl money box? Then head for the showroom of interior stylist Emily Chalmers, who oversees this beautiful collection in flea market-style chic in Shoreditch. It has a vintage vibe to it, but everything is newly made. Perfect for dipping your toe into the vintage shopping scene. Chalmers is also the author of three books on interiors. 3 Redchurch St., E2. ℂ **020/7033-3532.** www.caravanstyle.com. Tube: Liverpool St./Train: Shoreditch High St.

Designers Guild   After more than 3 decades in business, creative director Tricia Guild and her young designers still lead the pack in all that's bright and whimsical. They are often copied but never outdone. There's an exclusive line of handmade furniture and accessories at the no. 267–271 location, and wallpaper and more than 2,000 fabrics at the neighboring no. 275–277 shop. The colors remain vivid forever, and the designs are always irreverent. Also available are children's accessories, toys, crockery, and cutlery. 267-271 and 275-277 King's Rd., SW3. ℂ **020/7351-5775.** www.designers guild.com. Tube: Sloane Sq.

MUSIC
Collectors should browse **Notting Hill,** because the handful of record shops near Notting Hill Gate Tube station are excellent. Also browse **Soho** around Wardour Street and near the Tottenham Court Road Tube stop. Sometimes dealers show up at Covent Garden on the weekends.

Dress Circle ★   This store is unique in London in that it's devoted to musical theatre and standard vocalists such as Frank Sinatra and Judy Garland. After half a century, recordings in the U.K. enter the public domain—hence the lower prices on re-released CDs of West End and Broadway musicals from the 1950s. New releases, of course, cost at least three times more. Karaoke recordings and even theatrical souvenirs are sold—perhaps a Bette Davis doll as Margo Channing in *All About Eve*. 57-59 Monmouth St., WC2. ℂ **020/7240-2227.** www.dresscircle.co.uk. Tube: Covent Garden.

Duke of Uke ★★   This fabulously named shop sells all things ukulele. It sells banjos and standard guitars as well, but really it's all about the Uke. There's great events here as well, so keep your eyes (and ears) open. 22 Hanbury St., E1. ℂ **020/ 7247-7924.** www.dukeofuke.co.uk. Tube: Whitechapel or Aldgate East.

TECHNOLOGY
Camera Café ★   The Camera Cafe is a cute little place just by the British Museum where they'll sell you a coffee, and let you play about with their secondhand

cameras. There's free Wi-Fi, too. If you're a photography fanatic, seek this place out. 44 Museum St., WC1. *07887/930-826.* www.cameracafe.co.uk. Tube: Holborn.

Lomography ★★ Lomo photography is big in the U.K. Highly saturated color images and funky replica vintage cameras make this a cool and fairly simple hobby to pick up: You can buy a camera for £50 and start shooting straight away. The Lomo shop has the biggest selection in London and some excellent examples of lomography to inspire you. 3 Newburgh St., W1. *020/7434-1466.* www.lomography.com. Tube: Oxford Circus.

TOYS & GAMES

Hamleys ☺ Possibly the finest toy shop in the world—more than 35,000 toys and games on seven floors of fun and magic. The huge selection includes soft, cuddly stuffed animals as well as dolls, radio-controlled cars, train sets, model kits, board games, outdoor toys, computer games, and more. 188-196 Regent St., W1. *0844/855-2424.* www.hamleys.com. Tube: Oxford Circus or Piccadilly Circus. Also at St. Pancras International Station, NW1 (*020/7479-7366).

Play Lounge ★ ☺ There's nothing dull about this toy shop aimed at young adults and big kids. If you like your Japanese figurines and interesting comics, you'll find something to keep you occupied. The shop is tiny, but it's packed from floor to ceiling with goodies. If you want a pop-up book and a scary Tim Burton-inspired collectable, you'll find it here. It's pricey sometimes, but they stock small toys and games on the counter that are perfect for pocket money. 19 Beak St., W1. *020/7287-7073.* www.play lounge.co.uk. Tube: Oxford Circus.

Pollock's Toy Museum ★★ ☺ The key part to this traditional toy shop is that it's attached to its own museum, so you can buy cute presents and toys (including magic sets) and then have a wander around the exhibition, which costs around £5. It's a lovely, old-fashioned shop—and you won't find a single video game. 25 Scala St., W1. *020/7636-3452.* www.pollockstoymuseum.com. Tube: Goodge St. Also at 44 The Market, WC2 (*020/7379-7866).

ENTERTAINMENT & NIGHTLIFE

Weekly publications such as *Time Out* carry full entertainment listings, including information on restaurants, nightclubs, and bars. You'll also find listings in all the daily newspapers, and the *Guide* distributed every Saturday inside the *Guardian* newspaper is an invaluable source of up-to-date information.

The Performing Arts

The theatrical capital of the world, London is home to some of the most famous companies on the planet, often housed in glorious buildings. Few things here are as entertaining and rewarding as a visit to the theatre.

The number and variety of productions, and the standards of acting and directing, are unrivaled, and a London stage has also become the first port of call for many a Hollywood star looking to show off their thespian skills. The London stage accommodates both the traditional and the avant-garde and is, for the most part, accessible and reasonably affordable.

GETTING TICKETS

To see specific shows, especially hits, purchase your tickets in advance. Founded in 2000, **London Theatre Direct** (*0845/505-8500;* www.londontheatredirect.com) represents a majority of the major theatres in the city and tickets for all productions can be purchased in advance, either over the phone or via their website. Alternatively, try the **Society of London Theatre** (© **020/7557-6700;** www.officiallondontheatre. co.uk), which has a ticket booth ("tkts") on the southwest corner of Leicester Square, open Monday to Saturday 10am to 7pm and Sunday 11am to 4pm. You can purchase all tickets here, although the booth specializes in half-price sales for shows that are undersold. These tickets must be purchased in person—not over the phone. A £2 service fee is charged. For phone orders, you should call **Ticketmaster** (© **0870/060-2340;** www.ticketmaster.co.uk).

Visitors from North America can try **Keith Prowse,** 234 W. 44th St., Ste. 1000, New York, NY 10036 (© **212/398-4175** in the U.S.; www.keithprowse.com) to arrange tickets and seek information before they leave home. Their London office is at 39 Moreland St., EC1 (© **0844/209-0382;** Tube: Angel). They'll mail your tickets, fax a confirmation, or leave your tickets at the appropriate production's box office. Instant confirmations are available for most shows. A booking and handling fee of up to 20% is added to the price of the ticket. **Applause Theatre and Entertainment Service,** 311 W. 43rd St., Ste. 601, New York, NY 10036 (© **800/451-9930** or 212/307-7050 in the U.S.; www.applause-tickets.com), can sometimes get you tickets when Prowse can't. In business for some 2 decades, it is a reliable and efficient company.

Ticket prices vary greatly depending on the seat and venue—from £25 to £85 is typical. Occasionally gallery seats (the cheapest) are sold only on the day of the performance, so you'll have to head to the box office early in the day and return an hour before the performance to get in line, because they're not reserved seats.

Many of the major theatres, such as the **National** (see below), offer reduced-price tickets to students and those under 18 on a standby basis, but not to the general public. When available, these tickets are sold 30 minutes prior to curtain. Line up early for popular shows, as standby tickets go fast. Of course, you must show a valid student ID.

TheatreFix (www.theatrefix.co.uk) is a website set up to help and encourage those aged 16 to 26 to attend London theatres. Sign up to the service and you can get cheap entry to many productions, as well as valuable advice if you are making your first trip to the city.

Finally, if you decide to check out the theatre on a whim—and you're not too fussy about what you see—**Lastminute.com** is a safe bet to pick up late tickets, often at discounted rates.

Warning: Beware of scalpers who hang out in front of theatres staging hit shows. Many report that scalpers sell forged tickets, and their prices can be outrageous.

MAJOR THEATRES

Donmar Warehouse ★★ Although its auditorium only seats 250 people, the Donmar Warehouse is still one of London's most important and acclaimed theatres. For the past 2 decades—first under the artistic directorship of Sam Mendes and, since 2002, Michael Grandage—the Donmar has staged some of London's most memorable productions with several, such as *Frost/Nixon* going on to tour internationally. It's renowned for an emphasis on performing new works and contemporary reworkings of the classics, so catching a performance here should be high on the priority list of any visiting theatre lover. 41 Earlham St., WC2. © **020/7240-4882.** www.donmar warehouse.com. Tube: Covent Garden.

National Theatre ★ Home to one of the world's greatest stage companies, the Royal National Theatre is not one but three theatres—the Olivier, reminiscent of a

Greek amphitheatre with its open stage; the more traditional Lyttelton; and the Cottesloe, with its flexible stage and seating. The National presents the finest in world theatre, from classic drama to award-winning new plays, including comedies, musicals, and shows for young people. A choice of at least six plays is offered at any one time. Box-office hours are Monday to Saturday 10am to 8pm. South Bank, SE1. © **020/7452-3000.** www.nationaltheatre.org.uk. Tube: Waterloo, Embankment, or Charing Cross.

Old Vic ★★   The Old Vic has stood on its site near Waterloo Station for more than 190 years, and since 2004 has been under the stewardship of actor Kevin Spacey. His tenure and aim to "inject new life" into London theatre has generally been regarded as a success. Spacey's star power has enabled him to attract Hollywood names such as Richard Dreyfuss and Jeff Goldblum, alongside powerhouse directors of the caliber of Trevor Nunn. Productions range from modern classics through to Shakespearean tragedies and modern farces. In 2010 the Old Vic also opened a new performance space in tunnels that run beneath Waterloo Station, with productions and musical events staged specifically to make the most of the atmospheric subterranean space. 103 The Cut, SE1. © **020/7928-2651.** www.oldvictheatre.co.uk. Tube: Waterloo.

Shakespeare's Globe   In May 1997, the new Globe Theatre—a replica of the Elizabethan original, thatched roof and all—staged its first slate of plays (*Henry V* and *A Winter's Tale*) yards away from the site of the 16th-century theatre where the Bard originally staged his works.

Productions vary in style and setting; not all are performed in Elizabethan costume. In keeping with the historic setting, no lighting is focused just on the stage, but floodlighting is used during evening performances to replicate daylight in the theatre (Elizabethan performances took place in the afternoon). Theatregoers sit on wooden benches of yore—in thatch-roofed galleries—but these days you can rent a cushion to make yourself more comfortable. About 500 "groundlings" can stand in the uncovered yard around the stage, just as they did when the Bard was here.

Due to the Globe's open-air nature there is a limited winter schedule, so check the website beforehand to see what's on; in any season the schedule can be affected by weather. New Globe Walk, Bankside, SE1. © **020/7902-1400**. www.shakespeares-globe.org. Tube: Mansion House or Southwark.

Theatre Royal Drury Lane   Drury Lane is one of London's oldest and most prestigious theatres, crammed with tradition—not all of it respectable. Nearly every star of London theatre has taken the stage here at some time. It has a wide-open repertoire but leans toward musicals, especially long-running hits. Guided tours (£11.50 adults, £9 children and seniors) of the backstage area and front of house are given Monday, Tuesday, Thursday, and Friday at 2:15 and 4:15pm, plus 10:15 and 11:45am Wednesday and Saturday. The box office is open Monday to Saturday from 10am to 8pm. Catherine St., WC2. © **0844/412-2955.** www.reallyuseful.com. Tickets £15–£45. Tube: Covent Garden.

FRINGE THEATRE

Some of the best theatre in London is performed on the "fringe"—at the dozens of venues devoted to alternative plays, revivals, contemporary drama, and musicals. These shows are usually more adventurous than established West End productions, and they're cheaper. Most offer discounted seats (often as much as 50% off) to students and seniors. Fringe theatres are scattered around London, so check listings in *Time Out* or websites such as **Kulturefalsh.net** or **LeCool.com**, both of which cover leftfield theatre.

Almeida ★★   The Almeida is known for its adventurous stagings of new and classic plays. The theatre's legendary status is validated by consistently good productions at lower-than-average prices. Performances are usually held Monday to Saturday. The Almeida is also home to the **Festival of Contemporary Music** (also called the Almeida Opera) from mid-June to mid-July, which showcases everything from atonal jazz to 12-tone chamber orchestra pieces. The box office is open Monday through Saturday 10am to 6pm. Almeida St., N1. ✆ **020/7359-4404.** www.almeida.co.uk. Tickets £6–£30. Tube: Angel or Highbury and Islington.

Young Vic ★★   Long known for presenting both classical and modern plays, the Young Vic tends to nurture younger talent than its sister theatre, the **Old Vic** (see above), and places a greater emphasis on working with young and emerging directors. Productions at the Young Vic could be almost anything, and are priced depending on the show—discounted tickets are available for students and anyone aged 26 or under. The box office is open Monday to Saturday 10am to 7pm. 66 The Cut, SE1. ✆ **020/7922-2922.** www.youngvic.org. Tube: Waterloo or Southwark.

4   CLASSICAL MUSIC, OPERA & DANCE

Currently, London supports a sometimes unwieldy yet impressive five major orchestras—the **London Symphony,** the **Royal Philharmonic,** the **Philharmonia Orchestra,** the **BBC Symphony,** and the **BBC Philharmonic**—as well as several choirs, and many smaller chamber groups and historic instrument ensembles. Look for the **London Sinfonietta,** the **English Chamber Orchestra,** and the **Academy of St. Martin in the Fields.**

Barbican Centre ★★   Standing fortress-like on the fringe of the City of London, the Barbican is the largest art and exhibition complex in Western Europe. Roomy and comfortable, it's the perfect setting for enjoying music and theatre, and is the permanent home address of the London Symphony Orchestra, as well as host to visiting orchestras and performers of all styles, from classical to jazz, folk, and world music.

   In addition to its hall and two theatres, the Barbican Centre encompasses the Barbican Art Gallery, the Curve Gallery, and foyer exhibition spaces; Cinemas One and Two, which show recently released mainstream films and film series; the Barbican Library, a general lending library that places a strong emphasis on the arts; the rooftop Conservatory, one of London's largest greenhouses; and restaurants, cafes, and bars. The box office is open Monday to Saturday from 9am to 8pm. Silk St., EC2. ✆ **020/7638-8891.** www.barbican.org.uk. Tube: Barbican or Moorgate.

Royal Albert Hall ★   Opened in 1871 and dedicated to the memory of Queen Victoria's consort, Prince Albert, this circular building is one of the world's most famous auditoriums. With a seating capacity of 5,200, it's a popular place to hear music by major world-class performers from both the classical and the pop worlds.

   Since 1941, the hall has hosted the **BBC Henry Wood Promenade Concerts,** known as "the Proms," an annual series that lasts for 8 weeks between mid-July and mid-September. The Proms incorporate a medley of mostly British orchestral music, and have been a national favorite since 1895. The final evening (the "Last Night of the Proms") is the most famous, when rousing favorites "Jerusalem" and "Land of Hope and Glory" echo through the hall. After its 8-year restoration, the Albert Hall now allows tours both front of house (£8.50) and backstage (£12). The box office is open daily 9am to 9pm. Kensington Gore, SW7. ✆ **0845/401-5045.** www.royalalberthall.com. Tube: S. Kensington.

Royal Opera House ★★ The Royal Ballet and the Royal Opera are at home again in this magnificently restored theatre. The entire northeast corner of one of London's most famous public squares has been transformed, finally realizing Inigo Jones's original vision for his colonnaded Covent Garden.

Performances at the Royal Opera are usually sung in the original language, but supertitles are projected. The Royal Ballet, which ranks with top companies such as the Kirov and the Paris Opera Ballet, performs a repertory with a tilt toward the classics, including works by earlier choreographer-directors Sir Frederick Ashton and Sir Kenneth MacMillan. The box office is open Monday to Saturday from 10am to 8pm. Bow St., WC2. ☎ **020/7304-4000.** www.roh.org.uk. Tube: Covent Garden.

Sadler's Wells ★ One of London's premier venues for dance and opera, Sadler's Wells occupies the site of a series of theatres, the first built in 1683. The original facade has been retained, but the interior was completely revamped in 1998 with a stylish, cutting-edge design. The new space offers classical ballet, modern dance of all degrees of "avant-garde-ness," and children's theatrical productions, usually including a Christmas ballet. Performances are generally at 7:30pm. The box office is open Monday to Saturday from 10am to 8pm. Rosebery Ave., EC1. ☎ **0844/412-4300.** www.sadlers-wells.com. Tube: Angel.

Southbank Centre ★★ Its brutalist concrete exterior may not be to everyone's taste, but there's no denying that the Southbank Centre contains three of the most acoustically perfect concert halls in the world, the Royal Festival Hall, the Queen Elizabeth Hall, and the Purcell Room. Together, the halls present more than 1,200 performances a year, including classical music, ballet, jazz, popular music, and contemporary dance. Also here is the **Hayward Gallery** (p. 106). The box office opens daily 9am to 8pm.

The Centre itself usually opens daily at 10am, and offers an extensive array of things to eat, see, and do, including free exhibitions and musical performances in the foyers. South Bank, SE1. ☎ **0844/875-0073.** www.southbankcentre.co.uk. Tube: Waterloo or Embankment.

Wigmore Hall An intimate auditorium, Wigmore Hall offers an excellent series of voice recitals, piano and chamber music, early and Baroque music, and jazz. With over 400 performances a year, plus workshops and community projects, Wigmore Hall is a vitally important venue, ensuring new generations are introduced to the joys of classical music. The box office is open Monday to Saturday 10am to 7pm and Sunday from 10:30am to 5pm. 36 Wigmore St., W1. ☎ **020/7935-2141.** www.wigmore-hall.org. uk. Tickets £10–£35. Tube: Bond St. or Oxford Circus.

The Bar & Pub Scene
BARS & COCKTAIL LOUNGES

Alibi As Shoreditch has become ever more popular over the last decade, many of those originally drawn to this arty enclave of East London have been pushed out. Dalston and Bethnal Green have mopped up the overspill, and now hold the title of London's hippest areas. The Alibi is the best among a number of bars to open in Dalston in 2010, and implements a policy of giving interesting record labels and promoters a small space in which to throw big parties. 91 Kingsland High St., E8. ☎ **020/7249-2733.** www.thealibilondon.co.uk. Tube: Old St. then bus 243/Train: Dalston Kingsland or Dalston Junction.

Book Club   The Book Club offers up a lively mix of art exhibitions, club nights, poetry slams, thinking, and drinking. It's a different yet winning combination, and judging by the crowds that spill out into the street most nights, one that the locals have taken to with open arms. 100 Leonard St., EC2. ℰ **020/7684-8618.** www.wearetbc.com. Tube: Old St./Train: Shoreditch High St.

Bourne & Hollingsworth   Blink and you could easily miss this cupboard-sized space hidden under a Fitzrovia newsagent. If you do manage to find the entrance, you could be forgiven for thinking you're the first to have managed the feat since the 1940s—you're greeted by a scene reminiscent of black-and-white movies. From the floral wallpaper to the china teacups for your cocktail, this is quite unlike any other bar in London. 28 Rathbone Place, W1. ℰ **020/7636-8228.** www.bourneandhollingsworth.com. Tube: Tottenham Court Rd.

Cottons   As you'd expect in any Caribbean bar worth its salt, rum is the order of the day at Cottons. With over 100 different varieties, from all over the world, it might take several attempts to make a dent in their selection—but luckily this welcoming and lively basement bar is well worth repeat visits. The associated restaurant also provides a fresh and modern take on Jamaican cuisine, and is the perfect accompaniment to the signature Cottons Punch. Open every day noon until 2am. 70 Exmouth Market, EC1. ℰ **020/7833-3332.** www.cottons-restaurant.co.uk. Tube: Farringdon.

Dream Bags Jaguar Shoes   What to do with the commercial signs from two long-gone shops? If you're in Shoreditch then the best bet is just to turn it into the name of your cool new bar-club, which also doubles as a cafe and "gallery" filled with Shoreditch hipsters. Dreambags has been packing them in for over 5 years now, and has recently been joined by a sister bar the **Old Shoreditch Station,** directly across the road. Open every day from noon to 1am. 32-36 Kingsland Rd., E2. ℰ **020/7729-5830.** www.jaguarshoes.com. Tube: Old St./Train: Hoxton.

Gordon's Wine Bar 🍴   Gordon's can lay claim to being one of London's oldest and, in the eyes of those who have fallen for its charms, most unique wine bars. Descend the stairs into the bar's grotto-like basement and if you're lucky enough to find yourself a table, settle in for an evening of wine, sherry, and cheese. The service isn't always impeccable, but you can't fault the atmosphere, hence the eclectic mix of office workers, students, and artistic sorts who pack it out most nights. 47 Villiers St., WC2. ℰ **020/7930-1408.** www.gordonswinebar.com. Tube: Charing Cross or Embankment.

Ice Bar   A novelty, yes, but London's only bar constructed entirely from imported Swedish ice is still worth checking out. For obvious reasons the temperature is always kept at a chilly 5°F (−15°C) year-round, so you'll want to make sure you wrap up tight in the silver cape and hood they provide. It's open Monday to Wednesday 3:30 to 11:45pm, Thursday 3:30pm to 12:30am, Friday 1:15pm to 1:15am, Saturday 11am to 1:15am, and Sunday 2 to 11:45pm. 31-33 Heddon St., W1. ℰ **020/7478-8910.** www.below zerolondon.com. Admission Mon–Wed and Sun £12; Thurs–Sat £15. Tube: Oxford Circus.

Loungelover   Expensive, garish, but also ever popular, Loungelover is adjacent to and run by the same people as the equally colorful restaurant **Les Trois Garcons** (p. 143). It's a warren of rooms, each with its own identity; the effect has been compared to a walk through a film set. The elegant cocktails are among the most original creations in London, often with quirky names. Food is available on tapas-like platters. Even if you're only stopping in for a drink, make a reservation because space is limited. It's open Monday to Thursday and Sunday 6pm to midnight, Friday 5:30pm to 1am, and Saturday 6pm to 1am. 1 Whitby St., E1. ℰ **020/7012-1234.** Tube: Old St./Train: Shoreditch High St.

Mark's Bar ★★ Attached to noted restaurant Hix, this dark and stylish bar offers up a slice of Manhattan deep in the heart of Soho. Its imaginative drinks menu, devised by Nick Strangeway, is packed full of historical curiosities that "hark back to another era before the Temperance Movement had reared its ugly head." Leave your mojitos at the door and instead try something a little different, such as the 19th-century inspired "Punch à la Regent." Open noon to 12:30am Monday through Saturday; 11am until 11pm Sunday. 66-70 Brewer St., W1. ℂ **020/7292-3518.** www.hixsoho.co.uk. Tube: Piccadilly Circus.

Phoenix Artist Club The favored watering hole of many a London actor, this basement bar has seen plenty of decadent sights over the years. This is where Laurence Olivier made his stage debut in 1930, although he couldn't stop giggling even though the play was a drama. Live music is occasionally featured, but it's the hearty welcome, good beer, and friendly patrons from ages 20 to 50 who make this theatre bar a worthwhile detour. It's "members only" after 8pm, but arrive early, find yourself a secluded spot, and you'll be able to drink long into the night. 1 Phoenix St., WC2. ℂ **020/7836-1077.** www.phoenixartistclub.com. Tube: Tottenham Court Rd.

69 Colebrooke Row ★★ Showing that size certainly isn't everything, 69 Colebrooke Row is one of London's smallest bars but also a must-visit for a true cocktail aficionado. Serving up a range of exquisite bespoke beverages, Tony Conigliaro is widely regarded as one of the U.K.'s finest drinks' creators, and applies the same sense of experimentation and scientific play to the bar that chefs like Heston Blumenthal have brought to the kitchen. It's open 5pm until midnight Sunday to Wednesday, 5pm to 1am Thursday, and 5pm to 2am Friday and Saturday. 69 Colebrooke Row, N1. ℂ **07540/528-593.** www.69colebrookerow.com. Tube: Angel.

The Social While most bars in the West End exist solely to speed the separation of your money from your wallet, this curiously thin bar has much nobler aims. Founded by the team behind the Heavenly record label, The Social offers up great new bands, surprise big-name DJs, a decent selection of beers, and the guarantee that come 10pm on a Friday night the place will be jumping. Now entering its second decade, The Social shows no sign of slowing down, which is just how we like it. 5 Little Portland St., W1. ℂ **020/7636-4992.** www.thesocial.com. Tube: Oxford Circus.

Vertigo 42 ★ 📷 For a truly unique London experience head to Vertigo 42, the champagne bar at the top of Tower 42 (until 1990 the tallest building in London). At 183 m (600 ft.), the bar offers panoramic views across all of London. Although the price of drinks may match the bar's own vertiginous heights, for special occasions few spots can match it. Tower 42, 25 Old Broad St, EC2. ℂ **020/7877-7842.** www.vertigo42.co.uk. Tube: Bank or Liverpool St.

PUBS

The quintessential British experience of dropping into the "local" for a pint of real ale is a great way to soak up the character of the different villages that form London. Note, websites such as **Beerintheevening.com** and **Fancyapint.com** host user reviews of nearly every London pub. Pub opening hours are flexible but fairly standard: In general you'll find them open from 11am or noon until at least 11pm daily (sometimes 10:30pm Sun). Many also open later on Friday and Saturday, and most can stay open if they like when things are still buzzing on any night of the week.

West End

French House A remnant from Soho's louche past, the French House is a curious creature. No pint glasses and no mobile phones are the rules of this house, and woe betide anyone who tries to flout either. A favorite of writers, poets, and actors over the years, the French House makes few concessions to modernity—and that's just the way its bohemian patrons like it. 49 Dean St., W1. ℂ **020/7437-2477.** www.frenchhousesoho. com. Tube: Leicester Sq.

Harp ★   Wedged between Covent Garden and Trafalgar Square, the Harp is a much loved traditional pub offering an authentic experience, and just as importantly, a refuge from the hustle and bustle outside. Break up the shopping trip with a leisurely pint (or two) from their interesting range of ales and lagers. 47 Chandos Place, WC2. ℂ **020/7836-0291.** www.harpcoventgarden.com. Tube: Leicester Sq. or Charing Cross.

Punchbowl   London's pubs are many things, but rarely would you use the word "glamorous" to describe one. Still, if you do want to combine star-spotting with your ale supping, then you could do a lot worse than check out the Punchbowl. Famous for being owned by the film director and former Mr. Madonna, Guy Ritchie, the Punchbowl has more to offer than just the occasional passing Hollywood star. Head chef Chris Molloy has built up a solid reputation for serving up original modern British cuisine alongside the ale. 41 Farm St., W1. ℂ **020/7493-6841.** www.punchbowllondon.com. Tube: Green Park.

The City & Clerkenwell

Counting House   Located bang in the heart of the City, London's financial district, the Counting House is, suitably enough, housed in a former bank. As watering holes go this is a rather impressive one and its size, imposing architecture and great glass domed ceiling offer a drinking experience unlike most other London pubs. 50 Cornhill, EC3. ℂ **020/7283-7123.** Tube: Bank.

Wilmington Arms   Located just a short hop from bustling Exmouth Market, the Wilmington is a quality pub serving Clerkenwell locals a fine selection of seasonal ales, lagers, and decent, unfussy pub food in comfortable surroundings. Settle into the comfy sofas, and work your way through the day's newspapers, while the pub's well-stocked jukebox provides the soundtrack. If that all sounds a little too sedate then head out back where you can also catch up-and-coming indie bands and comedians on most nights. 69 Rosebery Ave., EC1. ℂ **020/7837-1384.** www.thewilmingtonarms.co.uk. Tube: Farringdon.

Ye Olde Mitre Tavern 📖   Ye Olde Mitre is the name of a working-class inn built here in 1547, when the Bishops of Ely controlled the district. Despite being slap bang in the heart of London, one of those historical anomalies that are so prevalent in Britain meant that until the 1930s it was considered part of Cambridgeshire. Hidden away and hard to find, it's a rough gem of a pub well worth searching out. 1 Ely Court, EC1. ℂ **020/7405-4751.** Tube: Chancery Lane.

West London

Churchill Arms   Stop here for a nod to the Empire's end. Loaded with Churchill memorabilia, the pub hosts a week of celebration leading up to Churchill's birthday on November 30. Decorations and festivities are also featured for Halloween, Christmas, and St. Paddy's Day, helping to create the homiest village pub atmosphere you're likely to find in London. 119 Kensington Church St., W8. ℂ **020/7727-4242.** Tube: Notting Hill Gate or High St. Kensington.

Ladbroke Arms   Previously honored as London's "Dining Pub of the Year," the Ladbroke Arms is still highly regarded for its food. An ever-changing menu includes roast cod filet with lentils and salsa verde; and aged bone-in rib steak with mustard, peppercorn, and herb and garlic butter. With background jazz and rotating art prints, the place strays from the traditional pub environment. The excellent Eldridge Pope Royal is usually on tap. 54 Ladbroke Rd., W11. © **020/7727-6648.** www.capitalpubcompany.com. Tube: Notting Hill Gate.

North London

Holly Bush ★★ The Holly Bush is the real thing: authentic Edwardian gas lamps, open fires, private booths, and a tap selection of Fuller's London Pride, Adnams, and Harveys. Hidden away in a quiet area of Hampstead, the Holly Bush provides a warm welcome to those who can find it. After a hard day's shopping or walking on the heath, settle into one of its many snugs and revive yourself with a quality pint and traditional pub food from its well-regarded kitchen. 22 Holly Mount, NW3. © **020/7435-2892.** www. hollybushpub.com. Tube: Hampstead.

Lock Tavern You're lucky if you can find a space inside the Lock Tavern: The garden and roof terrace fill up within seconds when the sun shines, and the place is home to some of the most painfully trendy people ever to have spent hours perfecting a nonchalant, messed-up look. Despite this if you're young (or just young at heart) the Lock Tavern remains one of the best pubs in North London, and well worth a visit after an expedition to **Camden Market** (p. 152). The pub's association with some of the best promoters in London—and the annual Field Day Festival, held every August in Victoria Park and featuring some of the biggest leftfield and indie bands around—ensure that you'll often find some of the coolest DJs from around the world slumming it behind the decks upstairs. 35 Chalk Farm Rd., NW1. © **020/7482-7163.** www.lock-tavern.co.uk. Tube: Chalk Farm.

East London

Camel 🎁 The pie's the thing at the Camel, a small but friendly backstreet hostelry that has made a name for itself serving up some of the best pub grub in the East End. On winter weekends few places can match this cozy, intimate space for a warm welcome, and some justly famous home-cooked pies draw in those in the know from across the city. 277 Globe Rd., E2. © **020/8983-9888.** Tube: Bethnal Green.

Griffin One of the last remaining bastions of old Shoreditch, the Griffin comes complete with a cast of almost Dickensian characters. There's hardly anywhere to sit, the place is a bit (well, very) run down, and the less said about the toilets the better. But like an old dog the Griffin has its own peculiar charm, and many of those who can be found propping up the bar wouldn't have it any other way. 93 Leonard St., EC2. © **020/7739-6719.** www.regent-inns.co.uk. Tube: Old St.

Prospect of Whitby One of London's most historic pubs, the Prospect was founded in the days of the Tudors, taking its name from a coal barge that made trips between Yorkshire and London. Come here for a tot, a noggin, or whatever it is you drink, and soak up the atmosphere. The pub has got quite a pedigree. Dickens and diarist Samuel Pepys used to drop in, and painter Turner came here for weeks at a time studying views of the Thames. In the 17th century, the notorious Hanging Judge Jeffreys used to get drunk here while overseeing hangings at the adjoining Execution Dock. Tables in the courtyard overlook the river. 57 Wapping Wall, E1. © **020/7481-1095.** DLR: Shadwell/Train: Wapping.

Southeast London

Gipsy Moth The food is variable and space inside is at a premium, but on a hot summer day you'll find few nicer spaces to take the weight off your feet than the Gipsy Moth's sizable garden. Parked up right next to the Cutty Sark—and within a stone's throw of the Old Royal Naval College—it provides a welcome rest after a day spent taking in Greenwich's sights. 60 Greenwich Church St., SE10. ℭ **020/8858-0786.** www. thegipsymothgreenwich.co.uk. DLR: Cutty Sark.

South Bank

George Inn With its historic courtyard, wooden beams, and associated trappings, the George is many tourists' idea of an authentic English pub—indeed, it's even run by the National Trust. For that very reason it's often busy, and many locals give it a clear steer. Worth popping in for one, but not the best for an evening's drinking. 77 Borough High St., SE1. ℭ **020/7407-2056.** Tube: Borough or London Bridge.

Royal Oak A real ale fan's delight, the Royal Oak often stocks several draught beers you won't find anywhere else in London—and for that reason is always busy. It's not exclusively for beer buffs though, and the pub itself is a remarkably pleasant inn with tasty, simple food and a friendly crowd. 44 Tabard St., SE1. ℭ **020/7357-7173.** Tube: Borough.

Southwest London

Cask & Glass Tucked away just around the corner from Victoria rail station, the Cask and Glass is a popular spot with office staff requiring a post-work refresher before braving the journey home. Friendly and full of character, it's a touch on the small side, but there's plenty of space out front, and a healthy selection of Shepherd Neame ales to keep you entertained. 39-41 Palace St., SW1. ℭ **020/7834-7630.** Tube: Victoria.

Draft House Northcote ★★ For anyone serious about their ales, a visit to the Draft House is a must. Set up by the visionary Charlie McVeigh, it is an attempt to recapture all the best qualities of a British pub, and thereby create the perfect example. At any one time you'll find dozens of lagers, ales, and beers from all over the world on offer—and to help you in your quest to try them all, the Draft House is one of the only pubs in London to serve ⅓-pint measures. 94 Northcote Rd., SW11. ℭ **020/7924-1814.** www.drafthouse.co.uk. Train: Clapham Junction.

The Club & Music Scene

LIVE MUSIC

Every night in hundreds of venues across London, you'll find live music being played, from international superstars to those taking their first hesitant steps. Online guides such as **Spoonfed** (www.spoonfed.com) are often a good place to find more leftfield events. Most small venues will allow you to purchase tickets on the night, but for larger and more popular events you may have to buy way in advance. Most venues have ticketing information on their own websites; failing that, check **SEEtickets. com**, **WeGotTickets.com**, or **Ticketweb.co.uk**.

Rock & Pop

Bush Music Hall ★★ One of London's more beautiful venues, this former Victorian music hall was renovated and reopened in 2001; despite its fairly small capacity, bands and punters alike love its unique ambience. In recent years it's become a favored venue for larger acts to perform one-off, often secret shows with the likes of Suede performing here in 2010 before their headline dates at the larger O2 Arena. 310 Uxbridge Rd., W12. ℭ **020/8222-6955.** www.bushhallmusic.co.uk. Tube: Shepherd's Bush.

CAMP Set up by James Priestly, the man behind the legendary Secret Sundaze parties, the CAMP (City & Arts Music Project) may lack the niceties of other venues, but already in its short life this rough-and-ready basement has hosted some of the most anticipated gigs of recent times. Expect to hear all manner of edgy, underground music—from visiting American indie bands to homegrown dubstep and techno DJs. 70–74 City Rd., EC1. © **020/7253-2443.** www.thecamplondon.com. Tube: Old St.

O2 Academy Brixton ★ For many indie and rock bands a night at Brixton Academy represents a true measure of success. With a capacity of just under 5,000 it's one of London's most impressive venues, and that is reflected by the high caliber of artists that occupy its stage most nights. Voted best London venue by the readers of indie bible *NME* 12 times, this former Art Deco cinema is now a rock institution. Shows at the Academy tend to sell out well in advance and ticket touts outside the venue can charge a hefty premium, but shows tend to be announced well in advance so look ahead and book through the venue's website if you'd like to experience one of London's premier live music venues. 211 Stockwell Rd., SW9. © **020/7771-3000.** www.o2academy brixton.co.uk. Tube: Brixton.

Roundhouse ★★ Housed in a Victorian steam engine-repair shed, the Roadhouse in Camden is once again a cultural venue, presenting live music from emerging young talent, and even theatre and dance. Famous for all-night psychedelic raves in the 1960s, it reopened in 2006 attracting a young, new London crowd. At its peak it can house 3,300 patrons standing. In days of yore, Jimi Hendrix, Paul McCartney, and The Who performed here. Chalk Farm Rd., NW1. © **0844/482-8008.** www.roundhouse.org. uk. Tube: Chalk Farm.

Union Chapel ★★★ 📷 You'd be hard pressed to find a more beautiful setting for a concert than this 19th-century Islington church. Settle in on one of the venue's wooden pews and let yourself be awestruck by the surroundings. To suit the venue's natural ambience, music here tends toward the more reflective end of the spectrum with folk, ambient electronica, and acoustic pop and rock particularly suited. Compton Ave., N1. © **020/7359-4019.** www.unionchapel.org.uk. Tube: Highbury and Islington.

Jazz & Blues

Blues Kitchen One of London's only dedicated blues bars, Camden's Blues Kitchen is the place to listen to stripped-down music from the Mississippi Delta while enjoying a plate loaded with authentic Cajun cooking. Hosting DJ nights, real Blues legends from the States, and the occasional indie star looking to reconnect with their roots, a night at the Blues Kitchen is a lively alternative to the identikit indie nights that inhabit most Camden venues. 111–113 Camden High St., NW1. © **020/7387-5277.** www.theblueskitchen.com. Admission from free to £3. Tube: Camden Town.

Café Oto 💼 Experimental is the watchword at Café Oto—on some nights the casual visitor might be forgiven for wondering if the sound coming out of the speakers is music at all, let alone jazz. For anyone open to some leftfield sonic experiences, however, Café Oto is a delight, and one of the few venues in London where acclaimed musicians can be sure to find an appreciative audience for even their most challenging works. 18–22 Ashwin St., E8. © **020/7923-1231.** www.cafeoto.co.uk. Admission £5–£10. Train: Dalston Kingsland or Dalston Junction.

Pizza Express Don't let the chain name fool you: This restaurant/bar serves some of the best jazz in London by mainstream artists along with its thin-crust pizza. You'll generally encounter local bands or visiting groups, often from the United States. The place draws an equal mix of Londoners and visitors in the 20-to-40 age bracket. Although the club has been enlarged, it's still important to reserve ahead of time. The restaurant is open daily from 11:30am to midnight; jazz plays from 7:30 to 11pm. 10 Dean St., W1. ℂ **020/7734-3220.** www.pizzaexpresslive.com. Admission £15–£35. Tube: Tottenham Court Rd.

Ronnie Scott's Jazz Club   Inquire about jazz in London, and people immediately think of Ronnie Scott's, the European vanguard for modern jazz. Only the best English and American combos, often fronted by top-notch vocalists, are booked here. In the Main Room, you can watch the show from the bar or sit at a table, at which you can order dinner. The Downstairs Bar is more intimate. The Soho club is open Monday to Saturday 6pm to 3am, Sunday 6pm to midnight. Reservations are recommended. 47 Frith St., W1. ℂ **020/7439-0747.** www.ronniescotts.co.uk. Admission £10–£50. Tube: Leicester Sq. or Tottenham Court Rd.

Vortex ★   If Ronnie Scott's is the sanitized, tourist-friendly face of London's jazz scene, then Vortex in Dalston is the real deal, and the place where you're as likely to find yourself seated next to a jazz musician as watching them on stage. The club offers up an exciting mix of established players and up-and-coming talent and caters for jazz fans of all persuasions, from the traditional to the more leftfield. Open 7 nights a week, the venue plays host to internationally acclaimed names, and purchasing advance tickets is always recommended. 11 Gillett Sq., N16. ℂ **020/7254-4097.** www.vortexjazz.co.uk. Admission £8–£15. Train: Dalston Kingsland or Dalston Junction.

NIGHTCLUBS

Cable   With its warren-like maze of tunnels and railway arches, the area around London Bridge has long been home to some of London's best clubs. This current king of SE1 is also one of its newest arrivals: Launched in 2009 by the team who previously ran much missed End, Cable has quickly become a byword for quality underground dance music, from house, disco, and techno through to dubstep and drum and bass. 33 Bermondsey St., SE1. ℂ **020/7403-7730.** www.cable-london.com. Admission £5–£15. Tube: London Bridge.

Corsica Studios ★★ 🎒   Housed under the railway arches behind the Coronet, Corsica Studios harks back to the days before clubbing became corporate and safe. While on first impressions the club may seem rather spartan, that's because those involved know that a good PA, a dark space, and a few lights are all the best DJs need to work their magic. From techno and electronica, through to leftfield disco and experimental rock, Corsica Studios provides a haven for those seeking underground sounds. For this reason, it is regularly voted among the U.K.'s best small clubs. 5 Elephant Rd., SE17. ℂ **020/7703-4760.** www.corsicastudios.com. Admission £5–£15. Tube: Elephant & Castle.

Fabric ★   While other competitors have come and gone, Fabric continues to draw in the big crowds. Consistently ranked as one of the best clubs on the planet, every weekend Fabric plays host to the biggest DJs in town. On some crazed nights, at least 2,500 members of young London, plus a large percentage of international visitors, crowd into this mammoth place. It has a trio of dance floors, bars wherever you look, unisex toilets, and a sound system that you feel as much as hear. Friday nights tend to veer toward more live performances, dubstep, drum and bass, and electro music, while Saturday nights present the best techno and house DJs around. Open Friday 9:30pm to 5am, Saturday 10pm to 7am. 77a Charterhouse St., EC1. ℂ **020/7336-8898.** www.fabriclondon.com. Admission £10–£20. Tube: Farringdon.

The Nest ★   Opened in 2010, the Nest (formerly the basement of a furniture warehouse) is the most serious venue yet to appear in buzzing Dalston. Live events during the week usually feature bands at the cutting edge of whatever scene is current, and weekends are given over to respected techno, house, and disco DJs. The club is usually full to capacity by midnight. 36 Stoke Newington Rd., N16. © **020/7354-9993.** www.ilovethenest. com. Admission £5–£10. Train: Dalston Kingsland or Dalston Junction.

Notting Hill Arts Club   West London has been left behind in the cool stakes in recent years, but this remains one of the hippest nighttime venues in London. Located close to the HQs of many big record labels, you can often find a very music industry crowd here checking out the latest buzz bands, and Thursday night's YoYo party can see the likes of Mark Ronson take to the decks. The music is eclectic, varying from night to night—from jazz and world music through to electro, hip-hop, and indie. It's open Monday to Friday from 6pm to 2am, Saturday 4pm to 2am, and Sunday 4pm to 1am, and bands perform Monday to Thursday, Saturday, and Sunday. 21 Notting Hill Gate, W11. © **020/7460-4459.** www.nottinghillartsclub.com. Admission £5–£15. Tube: Notting Hill Gate.

Plastic People ★★ 🎞   For much of London's clubbing cognoscenti, this 200-capacity basement in Shoreditch is simply the best this city has to offer—and it's easy to see why. With probably the sharpest sound system in town and a crowd who know their music, Plastic People manages to attract DJs more used to playing to parties numbered in the thousands. For dubstep, techno, or house, few other venues can compare to a night at Plastic People. 149 Curtain Rd., EC2. © **020/7739-6471.** www.plastic people.co.uk. Admission £5–£15. Tube: Old St./Train: Shoreditch High St.

XOYO   XOYO (pronounced "X-O-Y-O") launched in 2010 to much fanfare and no little disaster, but despite an opening week that saw power cuts, closures, and general chaos, the venue has established itself as a valuable addition to London clubland. Thanks to the involvement of some top-rank promoters—such as Eat Your Own Ears and Bugged Out!—XOYO has become the place to check out exciting new bands from around the world and dance til the morning in the company of big-name DJs. 32-37 Cowper St., EC2. © **020/7490-1198.** www.xoyo.co.uk. Admission £5–£15. Tube: Old St.

COMEDY CLUBS

Comedy Store   This is London's showcase for established and rising comic talent. Inspired by comedy clubs in the U.S., the venue has given many comics their start, and today a number of them are mainstream TV personalities. Visitors must be 18 and older; dress is casual. Reserve through **Ticketmaster** (© **0844/847-1637**); the club opens 1½ hours before each show. Tuesday to Sunday, doors open at 6:30pm and the show starts at 8pm; on Friday and Saturday, an extra show starts at midnight (doors open at 11pm). *Insider tip:* On Tuesday the humor is more cutting edge. 1a Oxendon St., off Piccadilly Circus, SW1. © **0844/847-1728.** www.thecomedystore.co.uk. Admission £13–£20. Tube: Leicester Sq. or Piccadilly Circus.

99 Club   With shows running 7 nights a week, 52 weeks a year, you know the people behind the 99 Club are serious about their comedy. It's regularly voted one of the best places in London for alternative stand-up, and those on stage range from award-winning TV regulars through to emerging talent. A safe bet any night of the week. 28a Leicester Sq., WC2. © **07760/488-119.** www.99clubcomedy.com. Admission £8–£16. Tube: Leicester Sq.

DANCE CLUBS & CABARET

Bathhouse 👣   Unless you happen to work in the City, the Bathhouse isn't the easiest place to find—but trust us, it's worth the effort. This former Victorian opium den reopened in 2010 after an extensive renovation had brought it back to its decadent best. Now home to some of London's best cabaret nights—including wildly popular burlesque and rock 'n' roll sensation, the Boom Boom Club—you'll find a mixed crowd of openminded office workers and dressed-up burlesque scenesters taking in the live shows, or dancing through the night as DJs play from inside a giant golden birdcage. Nights change fairly regularly at the Bathhouse, so check the website for listings. 8 Bishopsgate Churchyard, EC2. ✆ **020/7920-9207.** www.thebathhousevenue.com. Admission £9–£45. Tube: Liverpool St.

Last Days of Decadence Shoreditch has seen some curious trends over the past decade, but even seasoned East Enders are surprised to wander past Last Days of Decadence and find themselves immersed in a scene straight from the "Roaring Twenties." Every weekend this Art Deco-stylized bar is commandeered by legions of flappers and dapper gents, who dance the night away to the hits of pre-Depression America. You'll need to make an effort to fit in, but once inside you'll be sipping Prohibition cocktails and dancing the Charleston in no time. 144-145 Shoreditch High St., E1. ✆ **020/7033-0085.** www.thelastdaysofdecadence.com. Admission from free to £10. Tube: Old St./Train: Shoreditch High St.

The Gay & Lesbian Nightlife Scene

Admiral Duncan A popular, fun and above all lively pub in the center of Soho, the Admiral Duncan has long been one of London's most popular gay bars, and most nights you'll find the pub packed with shot-downing regulars. Despite the fun within, the Admiral Duncan also occupies a sadder place in the history of Gay London, as the site of a bombing in 1999 that claimed the lives of three people. It's open daily from noon. 54 Old Compton St., W1. ✆ **020/7437-5300.** Tube: Piccadilly Circus or Leicester Sq.

Candy Bar ★ This is the most popular lesbian bar-club in London at the moment. It has an extremely mixed clientele, ranging from butch to femme, and young to old. The design is simple, with bright colors and lots of mirrors upstairs and darker, more flirtatious decor downstairs. It's open Monday to Thursday 5 to 11:30pm, Friday and Saturday 5pm to 2am, and Sunday 5 to 11pm. Men are welcome as long as a woman escorts them. 4 Carlisle St., W1. ✆ **020/7494-4041.** www.candybarsoho.com. Admission £5–£6. Tube: Tottenham Court Rd.

Dalston Superstore ★★ Cafe by day, disco bar by night, this Superstore is a welcome addition to trendy Dalston, providing a space for gays, lesbians, and their straight friends to party away from the mainstream scene. It's packed most nights with a friendly, arty, and openminded crowd, and the music is much the same as at any cutting-edge bar in this part of town, with disco, electro, and underground house normally on the playlist. 117 Kingsland High St., E8. ✆ **020/7254-2273.** Train: Dalston Kingsland or Dalston Junction.

Fire One of the biggest gay clubs in London, Fire goes all night throughout the weekend, from Friday night right through to Monday morning, pumping out house and electro of various flavors to a devoted, full-on crowd. It's hot and sweaty, but not to worry… shirts soon come off at this hedonist's playground. The contrast between those staggering out of Fire on a Monday morning and commuters heading to work is one of the more surreal London sights. 34-41 Parry St., SW8. ✆ **020/3242-0040.** www.fireclub.co.uk. Tube: Vauxhall.

George & Dragon A great deal of "Queer as Folk" life is shifting from Vauxhall and Soho to increasingly fashionable Shoreditch. Its epicenter is this pub where the late Alexander McQueen used to show up; Boy George still drops in. London's *Evening Standard* raved, "it's possibly the best pub in the world . . . ever." It's also been accused of "attracting flotsam," of being "grotty," and of looking "green and slimy."

Regardless of the spin, the place is a subcultural phenomenon. Expect a kitsch decor of pink walls, a talking horse head on the wall, cowboy hats, and a sequined guitar worthy of Elvis. 2-4 Hackney Rd., E2. © **020/7012-1100.**

Heaven This club, housed in the vaulted cellars of Charing Cross railway station, is a long-running London landmark, and one of the biggest and best-established gay venues in Britain. Painted black and reminiscent of an air-raid shelter, the club is divided into different areas, connected by a labyrinth of catwalk stairs and hallways. With the closing of the iconic Astoria, Heaven now hosts G-A-Y, on Thursdays, Fridays, and Saturdays. The biggest gay and lesbian party in the U.K. if not Europe, G-A-Y has featured performances from big name pop acts from Madonna to the Spice Girls. The Arches, Villiers St., WC2. © **020/7930-2020.** www.heaven-london.com. Admission £12–£20. Tube: Charing Cross or Embankment.

Royal Vauxhall Tavern ★ The Royal Vauxhall Tavern was here long before Vauxhall became London's gay village, but even back in the late 1890s it was home to some of London's most colorful cabaret, so in some respects not too much has changed. London's oldest-surviving gay venue, the Royal Vauxhall is a much-loved institution and an essential stop-off before hitting one of the local clubs. Today it's open 7 nights a week and you're likely to find all manner of fun inside from camp burlesque and cabaret to bingo, comedy nights, and plain old-fashioned discos. 372 Kennington Lane, SE11. © **020/7820-1222.** www.theroyalvauxhalltavern.co.uk. Tube: Vauxhall.

Alternative Entertainment

ALT-CINEMA

Visiting the cinema—in central London at least—can be an expensive experience. Plus, given that mainstream Hollywood films are shown at most theatres, you could be in any city in the English-speaking world. Scratch beneath the surface, however, and you'll find alternative cinematic experiences. The **Curzon in Mayfair,** 38 Curzon St., W1 (© **0871/703-3989;** www.curzoncinemas.com; Tube: Green Park) caters for true cineastes with screenings of foreign and art-house films, Q&A sessions with directors, and one-off screenings of classics from the archive. Tickets usually cost around £10.

LITERARY EVENTS

A growing number of literary events have brought books out of silent libraries and into London's noisy nightclubs. The capital's premier regular event is **Book Slam** (www.bookslam.com), which takes place on the last Thursday of every month at the **Clapham Grand,** 21–25 St. John's Hill, SW11 (© **020/7223-6523;** Train: Clapham Junction); tickets are usually £10. Heavyweight authors such as Hanif Kureishi, Dave Eggers, and Nick Hornby have all guested alongside a variety of book-loving pop- and rock-stars. Expect everything from poetry and book readings to live music and DJs.

Websites such as **Flavorpill** (www.flavorpill.com/london) and **Londonist** (www.londonist.com) carry information on forthcoming literary events.

COOL KARAOKE

There are plenty of places where enthusiastic amateurs can do terrible things to popular songs. Despite the British reputation for reserve, you'll find karaoke nights in pubs and bars all over the city, not to mention dedicated karaoke bars such as **Lucky Voice,** 52 Poland St., W1 (© **020/7439-3660;** www.luckyvoice.co.uk; Tube: Oxford Circus).

Alternatively, head east to **Hot Breath ★** (www.thehouseofhotbreath.com) at the Bethnal Green Working Men's Club, 44 Pollard Row, E2 (© **020/7739-2727;**

LONDON'S olympic & PARALYMPIC GAMES

Returning to London for the first time in over 60 years, this pageant of sporting excellence will transform the city. Most of the action will take place in and around **Stratford** (Tube/Train: Stratford), and it is here that you will find the new Olympic Stadium, Velodrome, Aquatics Centre, Basketball Arena, and Hockey Centre. Away from the East End there will be equestrian events in **Greenwich Park** (Train: Greenwich), beach volleyball at **Horse Guards Parade** (Tube: Charing Cross), and everything from boxing to table tennis at **ExCel,** Royal Victoria Dock, 1 Western Gateway, E16 (✆ **020/7069-5000;** DLR: Custom House).

For up-to-date information on what's on, where, and when—plus details of the associated non-sporting events that will accompany the Olympiad—check www.london2012.com. Applications for tickets closed in April 2011, but if you missed out there may still be a chance to see some of the action. London 2012 will be releasing tickets for a select few events closer to the games and those who have bought tickets they can no longer use will be able to re-sell them through the official London 2012 site. Finally, there are always the men's and women's marathons and road cycling events, which will be run through the streets of central London and start and finish on The Mall.

For **hotels** situated handily for the Olympic Park, and recommended nearby **restaurants,** see p. 116.

www.workersplaytime.net. Tube: Bethnal Green), one of the funniest karaoke nights in town, running approximately monthly. Out-of-tune singing is just half the fun, so leave your inhibitions at the door and prepare to get involved in everything from synchronized dancing, through to hot dog eating competitions, while making liberal use of the dressing-up box. Tickets usually cost £5–£10.

WHERE TO STAY

Recession? When it comes to hotel openings and revamps, the question appears to be, "What recession?" Barely a month goes by without a new boutique hotel or a multimillion-pound refurbishment being announced—London is a boomtown for accommodations.

At the cheapest and most expensive ends of the spectrum, the city's offering is hard to beat. The grand hotels of Mayfair still offer the kind of gracious service and country-house ambience that are copied around the world. The more recent rise of the no-frills crashpad has been a welcome development in a city where rooms remain among the most expensive on the planet.

There are surprises in store for anyone not used to London's idiosyncratic ways, however: Air-conditioning is far from standard; the venerable age of many of London's best hotels means that rooms are smaller, and more variable, than in most modern cities; and hidden charges—especially for international phone calls and Wi-Fi access—are regrettably still common.

A recent boom in London hotel building, combined with the demands of an international clientele, means that the standard of rooms across the city is better than it has ever been. Unfortunately, it hasn't made prices any easier to swallow. An ever-increasing number of travelers coming to the city each year has left some hoteliers unembarrassed about over-charging and poor service.

London boasts some of the most famous hotels in the world—temples of luxury like **Claridge's** and the **Savoy**—but there's still a dearth of the kind of mid-range, family-run hotels that make staying in Paris or Rome such a pleasure. Even at the luxury level, you may be surprised at what you don't get. Many of the grand gems are so steeped in tradition that they lack modern conveniences standard in luxury hotels worldwide. The best have modernized with a vengeance, but others retain distinctly Edwardian amenities. While London has an increasing number of sleek, high-tech palaces—complete with high-end sound systems and gadget-filled marble bathrooms—these hotels frequently lack the personal service and spaciousness that characterize the grand old favorites.

The biggest change to the London hotel landscape this century has been the rise of the **boutique hotel.** The best of them offer the charm of a B&B with the facilities of much larger hotels, but sufficient numbers of very ordinary small hotels have rebranded themselves "boutique" as to make travelers wary. We've sorted the wheat from the chaff, concentrating on reasonably priced choices with the best that category has to offer.

If you are on a tighter budget, there are options other than hotels. London has a tradition of families turning their homes into B&Bs, and the best of them offer a much more friendly welcome than you'll find at a budget hotel. Just don't expect all of the hotelier's bells and whistles. If this appeals to you, your first stop should be the **London Bed and Breakfast Agency** (© **020/7586-2768;** www.londonbb.com), a long-running agency for inexpensive accommodations in private homes for around £30 to £100 per person per night, based on double occupancy (although some rooms will cost a lot more). **London B&B** (© **800/872-2632** in the U.S.; www.londonbandb.com) offers B&B accommodations in private family residences or unhosted apartments. Homes are inspected for quality and comfort, amenities, and convenience.

Plenty of travelers have found apartments and rooms to rent through **Craigslist. org** over the last years, but an increasing number of scam artists have made it impossible to recommend. A much better bet is **AirBnB.com**, where owners rent out everything from single rooms to whole houses, but with a user-rating and verification system that discourages scammers. **Crashpadder.com** is more focused on the single-room booking, but has some real bargains. **Onefinestay.com** is another great bet for finding characterful homes to stay in—they offer space in private homes (or even whole houses) while the owners are away, but back it up with add-on hotel-style services like chefs and maids.

Low-cost airlines and higher standards in London hostels have led to the rise of "flashpacking"—ultra-cheap, no-luggage short breaks in hostels and the cheapest of hotels. **Hostelbookers.com** is consistently good for finding these bargain accommodations, but be ready to share facilities.

West End
BLOOMSBURY
Very Expensive

Renaissance Chancery Court ★★ This opulent landmark 1914 building opened as a hotel in 2003, and it's retained some of the best architectural features of its Edwardian heyday while adopting cutting-edge comforts. The glamorous and exceedingly comfortable rooms are all furnished with fine linens and decorated in hues of cream, red, and blue. Some of the best are on the sixth floor, opening onto a cozy interior courtyard hidden from the world outside. The building has been used as a backdrop for such films as *Howard's End* and *The Saint* because filmmakers were drawn to its soaring archways and classical central courtyard.

252 High Holborn, London WC1V 7EN. www.marriott.com. ✆ **020/7829-9888** or 800/468-3571 in the U.S. and Canada. Fax 020/7829-9889. 358 units. £169–£374 double. Rates include English breakfast. AE, DC, MC, V. Tube: Holborn. Parking £35. **Amenities:** 2 restaurants; 2 bars; babysitting; concierge; health club & spa; room service. *In room:* A/C, TV, hair dryer, Internet (£15 per day), minibar.

Expensive

Montague on the Gardens ★★   English country-house style within sight of the British Museum makes the Montague a winning combination for traveling culture buffs. It's a little way back from the busy West End streets but still just a short walk from the theatres and the shopping of Oxford Street and Covent Garden. Guest rooms are individually sized and decorated; most aren't huge, but all are cozy and spotless. Some beds are four-posters, and most sport half-canopies. Bi-level deluxe king rooms feature pullout couches and would be classified as suites in many other hotels.

15 Montague St., London WC1B 5BJ. www.montaguehotel.com. ✆ **020/7637-1001** or 877/955-1515 in the U.S. and Canada. Fax 020/7637-2516. 100 units. £135–£175 double. AE, DC, MC, V. Tube: Russell Sq. **Amenities:** 2 restaurants; bar; concierge; health club; room service. *In room:* A/C, TV, fax (in some rooms), hair dryer, Wi-Fi (free).

Moderate

Arosfa ★ 🎁   Tiny but very well appointed, this refurbished Georgian townhouse is a cut above the usual Gower Street hotels. It's in a prime location, within walking distance of the British Museum, the British Library, and Theatreland with neat but unspectacular rooms and a popular lounge—a great place for finding out what's going on locally. Summer visitors should ask for a room at the front of the hotel; they're air-conditioned. We also like the triple in the basement, easily the roomiest on offer.

83 Gower St., London WC1E 6HJ. www.arosfalondon.com. ✆ **020/7636-2115.** Fax 020/7323-5141. 17 units. £65–£160 double. Rates include English breakfast. MC, V. Tube: Goodge St. *In room:* TV, hair dryer, Wi-Fi (free).

Inexpensive

Harlingford Hotel 🗝   Made up of three 19th-century townhouses, the Harlingford is an eccentric array of staircases and meandering hallways set in the heart of Bloomsbury. It's run by a management team that seems genuinely concerned about the welfare of its guests, unlike some of its close neighbors. Double-glazed windows cut down on the street noise, and all the bedrooms are inviting. The most comfortable rooms are on the second and third levels, but there are some steep stairs and no elevator. Avoid the rooms on ground level, as they are darker and have less security.

61-63 Cartwright Gardens, London WC1H 9EL. www.harlingfordhotel.com. ✆ **020/7387-1551.** Fax 020/7387-4616. 43 units. £112 double. Rates include English breakfast. AE, MC, V. Tube: Russell Sq., King's Cross, or Euston. **Amenities:** Tennis courts (in Cartwright Gardens). *In room:* TV, hair dryer, Wi-Fi (free).

Thanet Hotel   The Thanet stands out among the swathe of similar hotels in this area: The place is always packed, so it must be doing something right. It no longer charges the same rates it did when it appeared in *England on $5 a Day*, but it's still an affordable option on a quiet Georgian terrace between Russell and Bloomsbury squares, and close to the British Museum, the theatre district, and Covent Garden. For the most part, rooms are small and adequately furnished. However, standards vary considerably within the hotel in size, amenities, and Wi-Fi access—so ask to see your room first.

8 Bedford Place, London WC1B 5JA. www.thanethotel.co.uk. ✆ **020/7636-2869.** Fax 020/7323-6676. 16 units. £110–£115 double. Rates include English breakfast. AE, MC, V. Tube: Holborn or Russell Sq. **Amenities:** Breakfast room. *In room:* TV, hair dryer, Wi-Fi (free in lower-floor rooms and public areas).

KING'S CROSS
Expensive

Rough Luxe ★ 📷 Just minutes from St. Pancras International Station, this small boutique hotel was salvaged from the remains of one of the area's many nondescript guesthouses. Despite the setting in a row of Georgian townhouses, the decor is almost industrial, resembling the interior of a warehouse art gallery. No two rooms are alike. Three units come with private bathroom, with glass-enclosed showers and "rainfall" shower heads. Decades of wallpaper and paint were peeled away, leaving distressed walls of hand-painted mosaic wallpaper and plaster. Many of the antiques found throughout were purchased at an auction of the Savoy Hotel's throwaways.

1 Birkenhead St., London WC1H 8BA. www.roughluxe.co.uk. ⓒ **020/7837-5338.** Fax: 020/7837-1615. 9 units (3 with bathroom). £155–£210 double. Rates include continental breakfast. AE, MC, V. Tube: King's Cross. **Amenities:** Breakfast room. *In room:* TV, hair dryer.

Inexpensive

Jesmond Dene Hotel The King's Cross area is a bit of a curate's egg; unparalleled travel links—you can be in Paris or the Lake District within 3 hours—but at the cost of a scruffy, noisy district. So, hurray for the Jesmond Dene. This small but neat B&B is great value, surprisingly quiet, and renowned for friendly, helpful service. Not a place for a 2-week holiday but if you're looking for a base to explore London, that's also handy for day-trips, you could do a lot worse.

27 Argyle St., London WC1H 8EP. www.jesmonddenehotel.co.uk. ⓒ **020/7837-4654.** Fax 020/7833-1633. 20 rooms, some with private bathroom. £70 double without bathroom, £100 double with bathroom. AE, DC, MC, V. Tube: King's Cross. *In room:* TV, Wi-Fi (free).

COVENT GARDEN
Very Expensive

Covent Garden Hotel ★★★ The phrase we hear most often from guests who've stayed here is "expensive, but worth it." The former hospital building lay neglected for years until it was reconfigured in 1996 by hoteliers Tim and Kit Kemp—whose flair for interior design is legendary—into one of London's most charming boutique hotels. Upstairs, accessible via a dramatic stone staircase, soundproof bedrooms are furnished in English style with Asian fabrics, many adorned with hand-embroidered designs. The staff is among the friendliest and most knowledgable in London—always useful in an area thronged with theatres, galleries, and rare bookstores.

10 Monmouth St., London WC2H 9HB. www.firmdale.com. ⓒ **020/7806-1000** or 800/553-6674 in the U.S. Fax 020/7806-1100. 58 units. £290–£335 double. AE, DC, MC, V. Tube: Covent Garden or Leicester Sq. **Amenities:** Restaurant; bar; babysitting; concierge; exercise room; room service. *In room:* A/C, TV/DVD, movie library, CD player, hair dryer, minibar, Wi-Fi (£20 per day).

One Aldwych ★★★ Hoteliers take note—One Aldwych is an object lesson in how to combine old-school London elegance with state-of-the-art facilities. Guests bask in an artfully simple layout that includes stylish minimalist furniture, big bay windows, masses of flowers, and lashings of contemporary art. The bedrooms are sumptuous, decorated with elegant linens and rich colors, and accessorized with raw-silk curtains and deluxe furnishings. On Friday and Saturday evenings, and at Sunday brunch, movies are shown in the screening room. And, unusually for such a smart hotel, sustainability is taken seriously; the glorious swimming pool is chlorine-free, toilets and showers use significantly less water than in most hotels, and the inhouse Axis restaurant uses local produce when possible.

1 Aldwych, London WC2B 4RH. www.campbellgrayhotels.com. ☎ **020/7300-1000** or 800/745-8883 in the U.S. Fax 020/7300-1001. 105 units. £390–£470 double. AE, DC, MC, V. Parking £37. Tube: Temple or Covent Garden. **Amenities:** 2 restaurants; 3 bars; babysitting; concierge; health club; pool (indoor); room service. *In room:* A/C, TV/DVD, CD player, CD library, hair dryer, minibar, Wi-Fi (free).

The Savoy ★★ After a 3-year, £200 million restoration, the Savoy is back in glitzy, high-octane business. Updating such an iconic hotel—at various times home to Coco Chanel, Humphrey Bogart, Marlene Dietrich, Oscar Wilde, and Churchill's war cabinet—can be tricky but initial signs are that it has been a success. It's lost none of its turn-of-the-century appeal with rich fabrics and acres of gold leaf on display but there's been a subtle updating to draw the 21st-century *belle monde* back to their spiritual home. The restoration has left no two rooms the same, despite their mix of Art Deco and Edwardian palettes, so ask to see your room before you move in. Us? We'll take one of the Edwardian rooms near the rear—the combination of Thames views and a real fireplace is London at its finest.

Strand, London WC2R 0EU. www.fairmont.com/savoy. ☎ **020/7836-4343.** Fax 020/7420-6040. 268 units. £325–£995 double. AE, DC, MC, V. Tube: Embankment or Charing Cross. **Amenities:** 3 restaurants, including Savoy Grill (see review, p. 130); 2 bars; babysitting; concierge; exercise room; room service. *In room:* A/C, TV/DVD, movie library, CD player, hair dryer, minibar, Wi-Fi (£10 per day).

Moderate

The Fielding ★ 📋 A firm favorite among theatre-goers, The Fielding is a little slice of Dickensian London in the heart of Covent Garden. Named after local novelist Henry Fielding of *Tom Jones* fame, it lies on a pedestrian street still lined with 19th-century gas lamps. Rooms are, according to your taste, either quirky and cozy, or old-fashioned and claustrophobic, and the furnishings and fabrics, although clean, have known better times. With a location like this the Fielding keeps guests coming back.

4 Broad Court, Bow St., London WC2B 5QZ. www.thefieldinghotel.co.uk. ☎ **020/7836-8305.** Fax 020/7497-0064. 24 units. £115–£170 double. AE, DC, MC, V. No children under 13. Tube: Covent Garden. *In room:* TV, Wi-Fi (free).

SOHO
Very Expensive

St. John Hotel ★★ 📋 The rise of the "restaurant with rooms" continues, and this offering from much lauded caterers **St. John** (p. 143) was the most anticipated opening of 2011. Right on Leicester Square, the former post-theatre eatery Manzi's has been converted into a shrine to Modern British cooking, with some cozy—and for the area, reasonably priced—rooms. Bedrooms are simple in white wood with turquoise floors, but this is a hotel for exploring—an elegant cocktail bar and great pre- and post-theatre dining should keep you from your room for a night or two at least.

1 Leicester St., London WC2H 7BL. www.stjohnhotellondon.com. ☎ **020/7251-0848.** 15 units. £276–£380 double. AE, DC, MC, V. Tube: Leicester Sq. **Amenities:** Restaurant; bar, room service. *In room:* Wi-Fi (£15 per day).

Soho Hotel ★★★ Entering the Soho Hotel always gets our hearts racing. The fans waiting for whichever Hollywood star is staying this week; the sleek lobby with its giant cat sculpture and hip staff; the buzz from the bar and the restaurant. *Tatler* called it "the most glamorous hotel in the world," which might be pushing it, but there's no denying it's a magnet for the glitterati. And behind the glitz it's a well-run, deceptively spacious hotel. The rooms are huge for Soho, and individually designed in granite and oak. All the famous Kemp (see Covent Garden Hotel, above) touches can be found, from boldly striped furnishings to deep bathtubs for a late-night soak.

4 Richmond Mews, London W1D 3DH. www.firmdale.com. ℭ **020/7559-3000.** Fax 020/7559-3003. 91 units. £290–£360 double. AE, MC, V. Tube: Oxford Circus or Piccadilly Circus. **Amenities:** Restaurant; bar; concierge; exercise room; room service. *In room:* A/C, TV/DVD, CD player, hair dryer, Wi-Fi (£20 per day).

Expensive

Dean Street Townhouse ★★★ 🛍

Deep in the heart of town, this boutique hotel in a restored four-story Georgian townhouse is a chic base for exploring Theatreland and the nightlife of Soho. Formerly the home of the Gargoyle Club, it has been converted to receive paying guests, and its Georgian architecture has been more or less preserved. Atmosphere and location are the draw here—the price is that rooms are small even for central London. Units have four-poster beds, hand-painted wallpaper, and other retro-chic touches. The innovative all-day dining room with a weekly, changing menu of seasonal British food is a magnet for the post-theatre crowd, and lends evenings at the Townhouse a buzzy, cosmopolitan feel. Book your stay well in advance—this isn't the place for a last-minute bargain.

69–71 Dean St., London W1D 3SE. www.deanstreettownhouse.com. ℭ **020/7434-1775.** 39 units. £90–£270 double. AE, MC, V. Tube: Oxford Circus or Tottenham Court Rd. **Amenities:** Restaurant (see review, p. 132); bar. *In room:* TV/DVD, hair dryer, minibar, Wi-Fi (free).

Hazlitt's Hotel 1718 ★ 🛍

Character, character, character. Some hotels don't have it, however hard they try, but Hazlitt's has it in spades. You step from the heart of buzzing Soho into what feels like an untouched Georgian literary salon. Public areas are bookish and calm, decorated in a lived-in, 18th-century style, while the rooms mix up antiques, ancient portraits, glorious free-standing baths, and fireplaces. Soho's a 24-hour kind of area, so unless you're a very heavy sleeper, opt for a room facing the back.

6 Frith St., London W1D 3JA. www.hazlittshotel.com. ℭ **020/7434-1771.** Fax 020/7439-1524. 23 units. £159–£295 double. AE, DC, MC, V. Tube: Leicester Sq. or Tottenham Court Rd. **Amenities:** Babysitting; concierge; room service. *In room:* A/C, TV, hair dryer, minibar, Wi-Fi (free).

MAYFAIR

Very Expensive

Claridge's ★★★

No hotel epitomizes the rebirth of London's grand old hotels quite like Claridge's. Sure, it still boasts the Art Deco finery and a history stretching back to 1812, but Gordon Ramsay's flagship restaurant and two hip bars have made it a favorite with the fashion and media sets. Much of its '30s style remains, and the hotel's strong sense of tradition and old-fashioned "Britishness" are also intact; in spite of the gloss and the hip clientele, afternoon tea here remains a quintessentially English experience. The rooms are the most varied in London, ranging from the costly and stunning Brook Penthouse—complete with a personal butler—to the less expensive, so-called superior queen rooms with queen-sized beds.

Brook St., London W1A 2JQ. www.claridges.co.uk. ℭ **020/7629-8860.** Fax 020/7499-2210. 203 units. £339–£659 double. AE, DC, MC, V. Parking £50. Tube: Bond St. **Amenities:** 3 restaurants; 2 bars; babysitting; concierge; health club & spa; room service. *In room:* A/C, TV/DVD/VCR, hair dryer, minibar, Wi-Fi (free).

The Connaught ★★★

Built as a home-away-from-home for the denizens of Britain's toniest country houses, no hotel has updated the classic British style with quite as much élan as The Connaught. Leaded skylights, liveried doormen who seem to know every guest's name, and shady, masculine bars and restaurants are the picture of restrained 21st-century glamor, while the rooms are spacious Edwardian gems. Traditionalists opt for the Old Wing but we prefer the New Wing—it's where The Connaught's mix of the old and new is most successful.

Carlos Place, London W1K 2AL. www.the-connaught.co.uk. ℂ **020/7499-7070** or 800/63-SAVOY (637-2869) in the U.S. Fax 020/7495-3262. 122 units. £339–£369 double. AE, DC, MC, V. Parking £48. Tube: Green Park. **Amenities:** 2 restaurants; 2 bars; babysitting; concierge; health club & spa; room service. *In room:* A/C, TV/DVD, hair dryer, minibar, MP3 docking station, Wi-Fi (free).

The Dorchester ★★★   Few hotels have the time-honored experience of "the Dorch," which has maintained a tradition of fine comfort and cuisine since it opened in 1931. Breaking from the neoclassical tradition, the most ambitious architects of the era designed a building of reinforced concrete clothed in terrazzo slabs. The Dorchester boasts guest rooms outfitted with Irish linen sheets on comfortable beds, plus all the electronic gadgetry you'd expect, and double- and triple-glazed windows to keep out noise, along with plump armchairs, cherry wood furnishings, and, in many cases, four-poster beds piled high with pillows.

53 Park Lane, London W1A 2HJ. www.thedorchester.com. ℂ **020/7629-8888** or 800/727-9820 in the U.S. Fax 020/9629-8080. 244 units. £295–£565 double. AE, DC, MC, V. Parking £45. Tube: Hyde Park Corner or Marble Arch. **Amenities:** 3 restaurants, including Alain Ducasse (see review, p. 126); bar; babysitting; concierge; health club & spa; room service. *In room:* A/C, TV/DVD, CD player, fax, hair dryer, minibar, Internet (£20 per day).

Expensive

The Chesterfield Mayfair ★★   Only in super-expensive Mayfair could the Chesterfield be considered a bargain, but it serves up that ritzy grand hotel feeling at a better price than The Connaught or The Dorchester (see above). The hotel, once home to the Earl of Chesterfield, still sports venerable features that evoke an air of nobility, including richly decorated public rooms featuring woods, antiques, fabrics, and marble. The secluded Library Lounge is a great place to relax, and the glassed-in conservatory is a good spot for tea. The guest rooms are dramatically decorated and make excellent use of space—there's a ton of closet and counter space.

35 Charles St., London W1J 5EB. www.chesterfieldmayfair.com. ℂ **020/7491-2622** or 877/955-1515 in the U.S. and Canada. Fax 020/7491-4793. 107 units. £155–£215 double. AE, DC, MC, V. Tube: Green Park. **Amenities:** 2 restaurants; bar; babysitting; concierge; use of nearby health club; room service. *In room:* A/C, TV/DVD, hair dryer, minibar, Wi-Fi (free).

ST. JAMES'S
Very Expensive

Haymarket Hotel ★★★   The understated Georgian entrance, right by the Haymarket Theatre, hides a surprisingly bold and colorful hotel. Public areas are a riot of turquoise, fuchsia, mango, and even acid green while rooms are classy in black and white. Although completely modernized and perhaps the most sophisticated small hotel in the city, many satisfying proportions of the original 19th-century John Nash architecture remains. Bedrooms are sumptuously elegant with fine linens and the latest amenities. There's even an indoor pool lounge.

1 Suffolk Place, London SW1Y 4BP. www.firmdale.com. ℂ **020/7470-4000.** Fax 020/7470-4004. 50 units. £250–£330 double. AE, DC, MC, V. Tube: Charing Cross or Piccadilly Circus. **Amenities:** Restaurant; bar; concierge; exercise room; pool (indoor); room service. *In room:* A/C, TV/DVD, CD player, hair dryer, Wi-Fi (£20).

The Stafford ★★★   Famous for its American Bar, its St. James's address, and the warmth of its Edwardian decor, the century-old Stafford attracts a tasteful, discerning clientele. All the guest rooms are individually decorated, reflecting the hotel's origins as a private home. Many singles contain queen-sized beds. Some of the deluxe units offer four-posters that will make you feel like Henry VIII. Much has been done to preserve the original style of these rooms, including preservation of the original A-beams on the upper floors, but you can bet that no 18th-century visitor ever slept with the electronic safes, stereo systems, and quality furnishings that these rooms feature.

16–18 St. James's Place, London SW1A 1NJ. www.kempinski.com/london. © **020/7493-0111.** Fax 020/7493-7121. 107 units. £290–£740 double. AE, DC, MC, V. No parking. Tube: Green Park. **Amenities:** Restaurant; bar; babysitting; concierge; exercise room; room service. *In room:* A/C, TV/DVD, CD player, hair dryer, Wi-Fi (free).

MARYLEBONE
Very Expensive

The Langham ★★★   Halfway between the high-end shopping of Bond Street and the calm and beauty of Regent's Park, The Langham is an opulent and practical choice in central London. Guest rooms are attractively furnished and comfortable, featuring French provincial furniture and red oak trim. The bathrooms, and the English breakfast, are bigger and better than most. The hotel is within easy reach of Mayfair as well as Soho's restaurants and theatres. Sure, it's expensive; but we love The Langham for its beguiling mix of old and new: Any place that's home to the Art Deco elegance of afternoon tea's birthplace, the Palm Room, *and* a spa as sleek as the Chuan Spa water spa added in 2011, is always going to win hearts.

1C Portland Place, London W1B 1JA. http://london.langhamhotels.co.uk. © **020/7636-1000** or 800/223-6800 in the U.S. Fax 020/7323-2340. 425 units. £255–£335 double. AE, DC, MC, V. Tube: Oxford Circus. **Amenities:** 2 restaurants; bar; concierge; health club & spa; pool (indoor); room service. *In room:* A/C, TV/DVD, hair dryer, minibar, Wi-Fi (£20 per day).

Expensive

Durrant's Hotel ★   For quintessential English charm in the "fairly sensible" price range, Durrant's is our choice. This historic hotel with its Georgian-detailed facade is snug, cozy, and traditional—you could invite the Queen here for tea. Over the 100 years that they have owned the hotel, the Miller family has incorporated several neighboring houses into the original structure. A walk through the pine-and-mahogany-paneled public rooms is like stepping back in time: You'll even find an 18th-century letter-writing room. The rooms are rather bland except for elaborate cove moldings and comfortable furnishings, including good beds. Some are air-conditioned, and some are, alas, small.

26–32 George St., London W1H 5BJ. www.durrantshotel.co.uk. © **020/7935-8131.** Fax 020/7487-3510. 92 units. £250 double; £265 family room for 3. AE, MC, V. Tube: Bond St. or Baker St. **Amenities:** Restaurant; bar; babysitting; concierge; room service. *In room:* A/C (in most), TV, hair dryer, Wi-Fi (£10 per day).

Mandeville Hotel ★★   Marylebone Village is one of London's best-kept secrets—a charming warren of independent shops, neighborhood restaurants, and busy bars within walking distance of high-end Bond Street shopping and the calm of Regent's Park. The jewel in its crown is the refurbished Mandeville. This once-staid property is now a hot address—one of London's leading interior designers, Stephen Ryan, was brought in to restyle the lobby, restaurant, and bar. Bedrooms too have had a makeover and are thankfully free of the chintz of some Marylebone hotels—rich autumnal tones and masculine furnishings are the order of the day here.

Mandeville Place, London W1U 2BE. www.mandeville.co.uk. © **020/7935-5599.** Fax 020/7935-9588. 142 units. £127–£246 double. AE, DC, MC, V. Tube: Bond St. **Amenities:** Restaurant; bar; concierge; exercise room; room service. *In room:* A/C, TV, hair dryer, minibar (in some), Wi-Fi (£13 per day).

Moderate

Hart House Hotel ★ ☺ Hart House is a long-standing favorite of Frommer's readers. In the heart of the West End, this well-preserved Georgian mansion lies within walking distance of West End shopping and dining. The rooms—furnished in a combination of styles, ranging from antique to modern—are spick-and-span, each one with its own character. Favorites include no. 7, a triple with a big bathroom and shower. Or ask for no. 11 if you'd like a brightly lit aerie. Hart House has long been known as a good, safe place for traveling families, with many triple rooms and special interconnecting family units.

51 Gloucester Place, London W1U 8JF. www.harthouse.co.uk. ✆ **020/7935-2288.** Fax 020/7935-8516. 15 units. £110–£150 double. Rates include English breakfast. MC, V. Tube: Marble Arch or Baker St. **Amenities:** Babysitting. *In room:* TV, hair dryer, Wi-Fi (£5).

The Sumner ★ 👜 It's no wonder this Georgian townhouse hotel is so popular—boutique hotels on quiet streets just minutes from Hyde Park and Oxford Street are as rare as hen's teeth. It retains much of its original architectural allure: The standard rooms are midsize and attractively furnished, but you can also choose deluxe rooms with artwork and better furnishings. All the guest rooms are designer-decorated and luxuriously appointed, and there is also an elegant sitting room with a working fireplace and timber flooring.

54 Upper Berkeley St., London W1H 7QR. www.thesumner.com. ✆ **020/7723-2244.** Fax 087/0705-8767. 20 units. £135–£170 double. Rates include buffet breakfast. AE, MC, V. Tube: Marble Arch. *In room:* A/C, TV, fridge, hair dryer, Wi-Fi (free).

Inexpensive

Lincoln House Hotel ★ The rooms may be small, but Lincoln House makes up for it with bags of character and a central location. Built in the late 18th century, during the reign of King George III, this refurbished and tastefully decorated hotel is a converted townhouse with a traditional charm—and it's just a 5-minute walk to Marble Arch Tube and Hyde Park. Midsize bedrooms are completely modernized but decorated in a traditional fashion. You have a choice of enjoying an English breakfast downstairs or a continental breakfast served in your room.

33 Gloucester Place, London W1U 8HY. www.lincoln-house-hotel.co.uk. ✆ **020/7486-7630.** Fax 020/7486-0166. 24 units. £95–£125 double. AE, DC, MC, V. Tube: Marble Arch. *In room:* TV, fridge (in some rooms), hair dryer, Wi-Fi (free).

Wigmore Court Hotel 🏃 A convenient family hotel, this inn lies near the street made famous as the fictional address of Sherlock Holmes—Baker Street. It's also close to Marble Arch, Oxford Street, and Madame Tussaud's. A somber Georgian structure, it has been converted into a fine B&B suitable only for serious stair climbers, as there is no elevator. There's traffic noise outside, so request a room at the rear. Bedrooms, many quite spacious, are comfortably furnished. Most units contain double or twin beds, plus a small bathroom.

23 Gloucester Place, London W1U 8HS. www.wigmore-hotel.co.uk. ✆ **020/7935-0928.** Fax 020/7487-4254. 19 units. £70–£89 double. MC, V. Tube: Marble Arch. **Amenities:** Guest kitchen. *In room:* TV, Wi-Fi (free).

South Bank
EXPENSIVE

London Bridge Hotel ★★ There's no doubt the London Bridge Hotel puts you right in the thick of things—the river, Borough Market, London's newest and tallest skyscraper, and the South Bank are all just seconds away, and efficient Tube and train links put the rest of London within easy reach too. A former telephone exchange building, this 1915 structure was successfully recycled into a bastion of comfort and charm. Bedrooms are completely up to date and offer homelike comfort and plenty of amenities. Rooms in the front have double-glazed windows to cut down on noise.

8–18 London Bridge St., London SE1 9SG. www.londonbridgehotel.com. ℭ **020/7855-2200.** Fax 020/7855-2233. 140 units. £125–£286 double. Children 11 and under stay free in parent's room. AE, DC, MC, V. Tube: London Bridge. **Amenities:** 2 restaurants; bar; babysitting; access to nearby health club. *In room:* A/C, TV/DVD, hair dryer, minibar, Wi-Fi (free).

West London

PADDINGTON & BAYSWATER
Moderate

Mornington Hotel ★ There's nothing flashy about the Mornington, but a 2010 refurbishment, easy access to London's parks, and staff who win plaudits from guests over and over again make it the best bet in the area. Just north of Hyde Park and Kensington Gardens, the hotel has a Victorian exterior and Scandinavian-inspired decor. The area isn't London's most fashionable, but it's close to Hyde Park and convenient to Marble Arch, Oxford Street shopping, and the ethnic restaurants of Queensway. Renovated guest rooms are tasteful and comfortable.

12 Lancaster Gate, London W2 3LG. www.morningtonhotel.co.uk. ℭ **020/7262-7361** or 800/633-6548 in the U.S. Fax 020/7706-1028. 66 units. £89–£145 double. Rates include breakfast. AE, DC, MC, V. Parking £25. Tube: Lancaster Gate. **Amenities:** Bar. *In room:* TV, Wi-Fi (free).

Inexpensive

Garden Court Hotel We wish there were more hotels like this in London. Family-run for more than 50 years, meticulously managed, and set on a tranquil Victorian garden, it's a great bet for visitors to Hyde Park or Portobello. Most accommodations are spacious, with good lighting, generous shelf and closet space, and comfortable furnishings. If you're in a room without a bathroom, you'll generally have to share with the occupants of only one other room. There are many homelike touches throughout the hotel, including ancestral portraits and silk flowers. Rooms open onto the square in front or the gardens at the rear.

30–31 Kensington Gardens Sq., London W2 4BG. www.gardencourthotel.co.uk. ℭ **020/7229-2553.** Fax 020/7727-2749. 32 units, 24 with bathrooms. £79–£120 double. Rates include English breakfast. MC, V. Tube: Bayswater. *In room:* TV, hair dryer, Wi-Fi (£2.50 per day or £5 for whole stay).

Norfolk Court & St. David's Hotel Another very reasonable garden square B&B, run by hosts George and Foula Neokleous, in a friendly, if sometimes ramshackle, style. Only a 2-minute walk from Paddington Station, the hotel was built when Norfolk Square knew a grander age. The bluebloods are long gone, but the area is still safe and to be recommended. The refurbished bedrooms are well maintained and furnished comfortably, and you can't beat the price. Make sure you try the cooked breakfast—it always wins plaudits.

14–20 Norfolk Sq., London W2 1RS. www.stdavidshotels.com. ℭ **020/7723-4963.** Fax 020/7402-9061. 75 units, 70 with bathrooms. £65 double without bathroom, £80 double with bathroom. Rates include English breakfast. AE, MC, V. Tube: Paddington. *In room:* TV, Wi-Fi (free).

Tudor Court Hotel Originally built in the 1850s and much restored and altered, this Victorian structure is now a small hotel of tranquility and comfort, lying only a

3-minute walk from Paddington Station. It is a standout in a section of less desirable hotels. Bedrooms are midsize, completely restored, and comfortably furnished, with a choice of single, double (or twin), triple, and family rooms available. Rooms without bathrooms have a washbasin, with facilities right outside the door. The hotel's maintenance and affordable price make this one a winner—that, plus helpful staff.

10–12 Norfolk Sq., London W2 1RS. www.tudorcourtpaddington.co.uk. 📞 **020/7723-6553/5157.** Fax 020/7723-0727. 38 units. £96 double w/bathroom. Rates include English breakfast. AE, DC, MC, V. Limited street parking. Tube: Paddington. *In room:* TV, Wi-Fi (in rooms w/bathroom; free).

NOTTING HILL
Moderate
The Main House ★★ 🏆 The term home-from-home is bandied around all too frequently when hotels are discussed, but The Main House deserves the tag. Each guest gets a high-ceilinged floor of this Notting Hill townhouse to themselves, decorated in rare style from on-the-doorstep Portobello Road market—expect gilded mirrors, watercolors of elegantly dressed 1930s' women, and similar antiques. Some extra little touches make this place unique: A wonderfully cheap deal on the chauffeur service, mobile phones to keep your call costs down, and gleaming wood floors swathed in animal skins (reflecting owner Caroline Main's time as an explorer).

6 Colville Rd., London W11 2BP. www.themainhouse.co.uk. 📞 **020/7221-9691.** 4 suites. £110–£140 suite. MC, V. Parking £2.50 per hour. Tube: Notting Hill Gate. **Amenities:** Bikes; access to health club & spa; Internet (free); room service. *In room:* TV, hair dryer.

Umi Hotel ★ ☺ Location, location, location. This charming little hotel would be a steal in most of London, but given its proximity to Hyde Park, Portobello Road, and hip (and very pricey) Notting Hill's browsing and dining, it's a true find. Located in side-by-side row houses on a quiet square, Umi offers a bit of character that is often missing in budget hotels. Still, don't expect luxury—although the decor is modern and inviting, it's pretty basic. But that's just fine, given that the basics are done so well. Rooms are small (this is London after all) but spotless. Added bonus: The hotel offers both single and family rooms that can sleep four. Ask for one of the rooms at the front, as the view of the square's garden is gorgeous.

16 Leinster Sq., London W2 4PR. www.umihotellondon.co.uk. 📞 **020/7221-9131.** Fax 020/7221-4073. 117 units. £150–£165 double. AE, DISC, MC, V. Tube: Bayswater or Queensway. **Amenities:** Restaurant; cafe; bar; concierge. *In room:* TV, Wi-Fi (£3 per hour).

Inexpensive
Gate Hotel This antiques-hunters' favorite is the only hotel along the length of Portobello Road—and because of rigid zoning restrictions, it will probably remain the only one for many years to come. It has seven cramped but cozy bedrooms over its three floors, and be prepared for some very steep stairs. Rooms are color coordinated, with a hint of style, and have such extras as full-length mirrors and built-in wardrobes. Especially intriguing are the wall paintings that show the original Portobello Market: Every character looks plucked straight from a Dickens novel.

6 Portobello Rd., London W11 3DG. www.gatehotel.co.uk. 📞 **020/7221-0707.** Fax 020/7221-9128. 7 units. £80–£100 double. Rates include continental breakfast (served in room). AE, MC, V. Tube: Notting Hill Gate or Holland Park. **Amenities:** Room service. *In room:* TV, minibar, hair dryer, Wi-Fi (£5 per day).

Southwest London
WESTMINSTER
Very Expensive

Royal Horseguards Hotel ★★ 📷 We've awoken to the sound of the Queen's Household cavalry trotting past, looked out of our window to see the Thames and the London Eye, and thought to ourselves, "Is this the best located hotel in London?" It's certainly hard to beat. Set in the grandeur of the one-time National Liberal Club, with sweeping views all along the Thames, the Royal Horseguards is fairytale London. The rooms are clean and masculine, the restaurant—a converted library—harks back to the hotel's illustrious past and the whole thing adds up to a very special London experience.

2 Whitehall Court, London SW1A 2EJ. www.guoman.com/theroyalhorseguards. ℂ **0871/376-9033** or 0845/305-8332. Fax 0871/376-9133 or 0845/305-8371. 281 units. £365–£800 double. AE, DC, MC, V. Tube: Embankment. **Amenities:** Bar; restaurant, gym; concierge; room service. *In room:* A/C, TV/DVD, Internet (free).

Moderate

Mint Hotel ★ Next to Tate Britain and Parliament, this purpose-built inn formerly known as the City Inn Westminster has a vast array of rooms at the heart of tourist London. The best units are the 67 City Club rooms or the 16 suites, but all are comfortable, with a fresh, light, and contemporary design. Business clients predominate during the week, but on weekends rates are often slashed to bargain prices. Ask when booking, and try for a guest room opening onto the Thames or Parliament.

30 John Islip St., London SW1P 4DD. www.cityinn.com. ℂ **020/7630-1000.** Fax 020/7233-7575. 460 units. £119–£159 double. AE, DC, MC, V. Tube: Pimlico or Westminster. **Amenities:** Restaurant; 2 bars; concierge; exercise room; room service. *In room:* A/C, TV/DVD, CD player, hair dryer, minibar, Wi-Fi (free).

VICTORIA, BELGRAVIA & PIMLICO
Very Expensive

41 Hotel ★★★ 🛎 This is the very antidote to chain hotels—30 individually designed rooms, packed with romantic touches like open fireplaces and scented candles, all within walking distance of Hyde Park and Buckingham Palace. 41 Hotel is best suited to couples or those traveling alone—especially women. Public areas feature an abundance of mahogany, antiques, fresh flowers, and rich fabrics. Read, relax, or watch TV in the library-style lounge, where a complimentary continental breakfast and afternoon snacks are served each day. Guest rooms are individually sized, but all feature elegant black-and-white color schemes and magnificent beds with Egyptian-cotton linens.

41 Buckingham Palace Rd., London SW1W 0PS. www.41hotel.com. ℂ **020/7300-0041** or 877/955-1515 in the U.S. and Canada. Fax 020/7300-0141. 30 units. £275–£295 double. Rates include continental breakfast, afternoon snacks, and evening canapés. AE, DC, MC, V. Tube: Victoria. **Amenities:** Bar; babysitting; concierge; room service. *In room:* A/C, TV/DVD, CD player, hair dryer, MP3 docking station, Internet (free).

The Goring ★★★ This place is the very best of London's family-run hotels. In truth it has everything going for it; a location in the heart of royal London, close to Buckingham Palace, the royal parks, and Westminster Abbey, a staff that knows its stuff, and an air of regal splendor. Guest rooms offer all the comforts, including luxurious bathrooms with extra-long tubs and red marble walls, and the beds are among the most comfortable in town. Queen Anne and Chippendale are the decor styles, and the maintenance is of the highest order. The rooms overlooking the garden are best. Business travelers may baulk (though many of us will cheer) at a ban on mobile phones and laptops in public areas, where you can take afternoon tea (see review, p. 147).

15 Beeston Place, London SW1W 0JW. www.thegoringhotel.com. ⓒ **020/7396-9000.** Fax 020/7834-4393. 71 units. £410–£960 double. AE, DC, MC, V. Parking £30. Tube: Victoria. **Amenities:** Restaurant; bar; babysitting; concierge; access to nearby health club. *In room:* A/C, TV/DVD, movie library, CD player, CD library, hair dryer, Wi-Fi (£15 per day).

Moderate

B&B Belgravia ★   In its first year of operation (2005), this elegant townhouse won a Gold Award as "the best B&B in London." It richly deserved it. Design, service, quality, and comfort paid off. The prices are also reasonable, the atmosphere in this massively renovated building is stylish, and the location is grand: Just a 5-minute walk from Victoria Station. The good-size bedrooms are luxuriously furnished. There is also a DVD library, and tea and coffee are served 24 hours a day. Late risers may want to avoid Room 1—it's above the breakfast room and isn't the quietest.

64–66 Ebury St., London SW1W 9QD. www.bb-belgravia.com. ⓒ **020/7259-8570.** Fax 020/7259-8591. 17 units. £120–£130 double; £150–£160 family room. Rates include English breakfast. AE, MC, V. Tube: Victoria.. *In room:* TV, Wi-Fi (free).

Diplomat Hotel ★ 💼   Part of the Diplomat's charm is that it is a small and reasonably priced hotel located in an otherwise prohibitively expensive neighborhood. Only 15 minutes' walk from Harrods, it was built in 1882 as a private residence by noted architect Thomas Cubitt. The high-ceilinged guest rooms are tastefully done in Victorian style. You get good—not grand—comfort here. Rooms are a bit small and usually furnished with twin beds.

2 Chesham St., London SW1X 8DT. www.thediplomathotel.co.uk. ⓒ **020/7235-1544.** Fax 020/7259-6153. 26 units. £130–£170 double. Rates include English breakfast. AE, MC, V. Tube: Victoria. *In room:* TV, hair dryer, Wi-Fi (free).

Inexpensive

Morgan House Hotel   This Georgian house has a convenient address, and its rooms are often fully booked all summer. Guest rooms are individually decorated and have orthopedic mattresses. Many are small to midsize, while others are large enough to house up to four people. Hallway bathrooms are well maintained and adequate for guests who don't have their own private facilities. A hearty English breakfast is served in a bright, cheerful room, and there's a small courtyard open to guests.

120 Ebury St., London SW1W 9QQ. www.morganhouse.co.uk. ⓒ **020/7730-2384.** Fax 020/7730-8442. 11 units, 4 with private bathroom. £78 double without bathroom, £98 double with bathroom. Rates include English breakfast. MC, V. Tube: Victoria. **Amenities:** Breakfast room. *In room:* TV, hair dryer, Wi-Fi (free).

KNIGHTSBRIDGE
Very Expensive

The Capital ★★★   A luxury shopper's and gourmet's delight, The Capital manages, year after year, to combine boutique hotel charm with the amenities you'd expect in a far larger establishment. Only 45m (148 ft.) from Harrods department store, this family-run townhouse hotel is also at the doorstep of London's "green lung," Hyde Park. Famed designer Nina Campbell furnished the spacious bedrooms with sumptuous fabrics, art, and antiques. David Linley, nephew of the Queen, also assisted in the design. The liveried doorman standing outside has welcomed royalty, heads of state, and international celebrities.

22 Basil St., London SW3 1AT. www.capitalhotel.co.uk. © **020/7589-5171.** Fax 020/7225-0011. 49 units. £305–£365 double. AE, DC, MC, V. Parking £30 per night. Tube: Knightsbridge. **Amenities:** Restaurant; bar; babysitting; access to nearby health club. *In room:* A/C, TV, hair dryer, minibar, Wi-Fi (£15 per day).

Knightsbridge Hotel ★★ ✦   A berth on a quiet, traffic-free, tree-lined street sets the Knightsbridge apart from its more prosaic neighbors: Repeat visitors from all over the world have succumbed to the charms of a small, comfortable hotel in this high-rent district. Built in the early 1800s as a private townhouse, the Knightsbridge has been updated with such *luxe* touches as granite-and-oak bathrooms, an honor bar, and Frette linens. Most bedrooms are spacious and furnished with traditional English fabrics. The best rooms are nos. 311 and 312 at the rear, each with a pitched ceiling and a small sitting area. The hotel is fabulously located, sandwiched between fashionable Beauchamp Place and Harrods, with many of the city's top museums close at hand.

10 Beaufort Gardens, London SW3 1PT. www.firmdale.com. © **020/7584-6300.** Fax 020/7584-6355. 44 units. £230–£320 double. AE, DC, MC, V. Tube: Knightsbridge. **Amenities:** Self-service bar; babysitting; room service. *In room:* TV/DVD, CD player, hair dryer, minibar, Wi-Fi (£20).

Expensive

30 Pavilion Road ★★ ⬛   A leafy rooftop restaurant, understated country-house ambience, and the most British of personal service—it's no surprise that many of the guests of this converted pumping station are repeat visitors. At this Knightsbridge oasis, you press a buzzer and are admitted to a freight elevator that carries you to the 3rd floor. Upstairs, you'll encounter handsomely furnished rooms with antiques, tasteful fabrics, comfortable beds (some with canopies), and often a sitting alcove. Some of the tubs are placed right in the room instead of in a separate unit.

30 Pavilion Rd., London SW1X 0HJ. www.30pavilionroad.co.uk. © **020/7584-4921.** Fax 020/7823-8694. 10 units. £180 double; £200 suite. Rates include continental breakfast. AE, DC, MC, V. Tube: Knightsbridge. **Amenities:** Babysitting; room service. *In room:* A/C, TV, Wi-Fi (free).

KENSINGTON
Very Expensive

Baglioni Hotel ★★★   Arguably West London's chicest address, Baglioni, part of the Italian hotel chain, is the personification of *la dolce vita* in London. This pricey citadel attracts those who were born to shop (Harrods is a 10-min. walk away, Kensington High St. only 5). Of the 67 stunning and luxuriously furnished bedrooms, 49 are suites. The best and most elegant bedrooms open onto Kensington Gardens. What an enclave: Ebonized wood floors and deluxe furnishings in mocha, taupe, and black are just part of the allure. Suites come with their own espresso machine, and the 24-hour room service is the most skilled and smoothly functioning in London.

60 Hyde Park Gate, London SW7 5BB. www.baglionihotels.com. © **020/7368-5700.** Fax 020/7368-5701. 67 units. £279–£329 double. AE, MC, V. Parking £38. Tube: High St. Kensington. **Amenities:** Restaurant; bar; babysitting; concierge; room service. *In room:* A/C, TV/DVD, movie library, CD player, CD library, hair dryer, minibar, Internet (free).

The Milestone ★★★ A firm favorite with Frommer's readers, The Milestone epitomizes everything good about the classic London hotel—understated elegance, service that regularly goes that extra mile, cozy public rooms awash with fresh flowers, dark woods, antique furnishings, and fabric wallcoverings, and a location close to some genuine London icons. Guest rooms and suites are spread over six floors and vary in size, decor, and shape (a few rooms are a bit small). For an iconic view, request a room overlooking Kensington Palace and Kensington Gardens.

1 Kensington Court, London W8 5DL. www.milestonehotel.com. © **020/7917-1000** or 877/955-1515 in the U.S. and Canada. Fax 020/7917-1010. 63 units. £250–£400 double. AE, DC, MC, V. Tube: High St. Kensington. **Amenities:** Restaurant; bar; babysitting; concierge; health club; room service. *In room:* A/C, TV/DVD/VCR, CD player, fax, hair dryer, minibar, MP3 docking station, Wi-Fi (free).

Expensive

Parkcity Hotel ★★★ Entering the Parkcity is always a surprise—it's a modern, sleek-lined wolf in historical sheep's clothing. The staid Victorian frontage gives way to a thoroughly up-to-date hotel. Much better equipped than many of the hotels in the area (it has a business center and a gym), and boasting a staff that always seems to go an extra mile for guests, the hotel is building quite a repeat customer base. All rooms are bright and airy with a pleasingly modern sheen, but in the summer avoid the rooms overlooking the patio if you want peace and privacy.

18–30 Lexham Gardens, London W8 5JE. www.theparkcity.com. © **020/7341-7090.** Fax 020/7835-0189. 62 units. £150–£190 double. AE, MC, V. Tube: Gloucester Rd. **Amenities:** Restaurant; bar; concierge; exercise room; room service, Wi-Fi (free in ground floor public areas). *In room:* AC, TV/DVD player, minibar, Internet (£6.50).

Inexpensive

Easyhotel ✦ This is the hotel that brought budget airline thinking to London's accommodation scene. Rooms are tiny (if spotlessly clean) at 6 to 7 sq. m (65–75 sq. ft.), with most of the space taken up by standard double beds. Ask for a room with a window to lessen the claustrophobia. There are flatscreen TVs in every unit, but it costs an extra £5 fee to use the set. Still if all you're looking for in a hotel is somewhere to rest your head it's hard to argue with the price. Housekeeping service costs an optional £10 per day, there is no elevator, and checkout time is 10am. You must book by credit card through the hotel website.

14 Lexham Gardens, London W8 5JE. www.easyhotel.com. © **020/7706-9911.** 34 units. £30–£50 double. MC, V. Tube: High St. Kensington or Earl's Court. *In room:* A/C, TV, Wi-Fi (£10).

CHELSEA
Very Expensive

Draycott Hotel ★★★ Everything about the Draycott reeks of British gentility, style, and charm. Guests are greeted like old friends when they enter by a staff that manages to be both hip and cordial. The hotel took its present-day form when a third brick-fronted townhouse was added to a pair of interconnected townhouses that had been functioning as a five-star hotel since the 1980s. That, coupled with tons of money spent on English antiques, rich draperies, and an upgrade of those expensive infrastructures you'll never see, including security, has transformed this place into a gem. Bedrooms are outfitted differently, each with haute English style and plenty of fashion chic. As a special feature, the hotel serves complimentary drinks—tea at 4pm daily, champagne at 6pm, and hot chocolate at 9:30pm.

26 Cadogan Gardens, London SW3 2RP. www.draycotthotel.com. ℭ **800/747-4942** in the U.S. or 020/7730-6466. Fax 020/7730-0236. 35 units. £312–£430 double. AE, DC, MC, V. Tube: Sloane Sq. **Amenities:** Bar; access to nearby health club & spa; room service. *In room:* A/C, TV/DVD, CD player, minibar, Wi-Fi (free).

San Domenico House ★★ Reclining in a four-poster bed, antiques scattered around the room, it's hard to believe that you're technically in a B&B. A redbrick Victorian townhouse that has been tastefully renovated in recent years, San Domenico House is in the heart of Chelsea near the shops of Sloane Square and the King's Road. Bedrooms come in varying sizes, ranging from small to spacious, but all are opulently furnished with flouncy draperies, tasteful fabrics, and sumptuous beds. Our favorite spot is the rooftop terrace; with views opening onto Chelsea, it's ideal for a relaxing breakfast or drink.

29 Draycott Place, London SW3 2SH. www.sandomenicohouse.com. ℭ **020/7581-5757** or 800/324-9960 in the U.S. Fax 020/7584-1348. 15 units. £235–£255 double. AE, DC, MC, V. Tube: Sloane Sq. **Amenities:** Babysitting; room service; Wi-Fi (free in lobby). *In room:* A/C, TV, hair dryer, minibar, Internet (£9 per day).

SOUTH KENSINGTON & EARL'S COURT
Expensive

The Rockwell ★★ 👔 Proof that London high style doesn't always come with a high price tag. This independently owned bastion of deluxe comfort occupies a converted Georgian manse in South Kensington. Its bedrooms are tricked out with oak furnishings and Neisha Crosland wallpaper, each crafted to combine traditional English aesthetics with modern design. The bedrooms themselves are large and inviting and dressed with the finest of Egyptian cotton, feather pillows, and merino wool blankets. All are bright and airy with large windows and simple lines, but we prefer the garden units with their own private patios.

181 Cromwell Rd., London SW5 0SF. www.therockwell.com. ℭ **020/7244-2000.** Fax 020/7244-2001. 40 units. £160–£180 double. AE, DC, MC, V. Tube: Earl's Court or Gloucester Rd. **Amenities:** Restaurant; bar; access to nearby gym; room service. *In room:* A/C, TV, minibar, Internet (free).

Moderate

Base2Stay 🍃 Visitors who value their independence, and bang for their buck, welcomed the opening of Base2Stay—no-frills apartment accommodation with no hidden extras. What you get are stylish, comfortably furnished rooms with small kitchenettes. The cheapest rooms contain bunkbeds for two, and suites can be made by way of interconnecting rooms. Living may be stripped to the basics, but this is no hostel, as there is a 24-hour reception as well as daily maid service. Its green credentials are impeccable too.

25 Courtfield Gardens, London SW5 0PG. www.base2stay.com. ℭ **020/7244-2255** or 800/511-9821 in the U.S. Fax: 020/7244-2256. 67 units. £122 bunk beds for 2; £135–£190 double. AE, MC, V. Tube: Earl's Court. **Amenities:** Wi-Fi (free). *In room:* A/C, TV, kitchenette.

Inexpensive

Henley House ★ 🍃 This B&B stands out from the pack around Earl's Court— and it's better value than most. The redbrick Victorian row house is on a communal fenced-in garden that you can enter by borrowing a key from the reception desk. The decor is bright and contemporary; a typical room has warmly patterned wallpaper, chintz fabrics, and solid-brass lighting fixtures. The staff members take a keen interest in the welfare of their guests and are happy to take bewildered newcomers under their wing, so this is an ideal place for London first-timers.

30 Barkston Gardens, London SW5 0EN. www.henleyhousehotel.com. ✆ **020/7370-4111.** Fax 020/7370-0026. 21 units. £75–£125 double. Rates include continental breakfast. AE, DC, MC, V. Tube: Earl's Court. *In room:* TV, hair dryer, Wi-Fi (free).

The City, Shoreditch & Clerkenwell

VERY EXPENSIVE

Andaz Liverpool Street Hotel ★★ The Andaz really has the best of both worlds—tradition and modernity coming together beautifully under its elegant Victorian roof. The original hotel, designed in 1884 by Charles Barry, known for his work on the Houses of Parliament, is an opulent gem with grand public areas featuring a stained-glass dome, and a 2007 refit brought it bang up to date without losing the period charm. The hotel's exterior is abloom in all its Victorian glory, complete with a stained-glass dome. Bedrooms are contemporary and comfortable, with state-of-the-art bathrooms and color schemes of dark red and white.

40 Liverpool St., London EC2M 7QN. www.andaz.com. ✆ **020/7961-1234** or 800/228-9000 in the U.S. Fax 020/7961-1235. 267 units. £150–£410 double. AE, DC, MC, V. Tube: Liverpool St. **Amenities:** 5 restaurants; 5 bars; health club; room service. *In room:* A/C, TV/DVD, hair dryer, minibar, MP3 docking station, Wi-Fi (free).

Mint Hotel ★★ Mint's Westminster sister hotel (p. 187) has long been a favorite of Frommer's readers, so we were expecting something special from their Tower Bridge 2011 opening. Initial reports say it doesn't disappoint. Views from the rooftop bar (and many of the rooms) are like an I-Spy of London sights: Tower Bridge, the City, and the Tower are all laid out before you. Rooms are similarly top-notch, with a clean-lined, Modernist feel and iMac TV/entertainment centers. Although it's early days, we've also heard good things about the friendly and knowledgable staff.

7 Pepys St., London EC3N 4AF. www.minthotel.com. ✆ **020/7709-1000.** Fax 020/7709-1001. 583 units. £144–£438 double. AE, DC, MC, V. Tube: Tower Hill. **Amenities:** Restaurant; 2 bars; concierge; room service. *In room:* A/C, TV/DVD, CD player, Internet (free).

The Zetter ★★★ It was only a matter of time before a hotel blended the edgy Shoreditch scene with the creature comforts demanded by City types. This converted Victorian warehouse features seven rooftop studios with patios and panoramic views of the London skyline, among other lures, including a sky-lit atrium flooding its core with natural light. Many of the features of the original structure were retained, as tradition was blended with a chic, urban modernity. Bedrooms, ranging from small to midsize, are spread across five floors, and open onto balconies that circle the atrium. The whole refurbishment was done with real concern for the environment—recycled timber and bricks in the construction, high-efficiency heating and cooling systems, and "smart" rooms that turn off heating and lighting when not in use, all contribute to the Zetter's low carbon footprint. Ask for a room at the back of the hotel—they back onto a quiet square.

St. John's Sq., 86–88 Clerkenwell Rd., London EC1M 5RJ. www.thezetter.com. ✆ **020/7324-4444.** Fax 020/7324-4445. 59 units. Mon–Thurs £180–£360 double; Fri–Sun £153–£360 double. AE, DC, MC, V. Tube: Farringdon. **Amenities:** Restaurant (see review, p. 142); bar; concierge; room service. *In room:* A/C, TV/DVD, CD player, MP3 docking station, Internet (free).

EXPENSIVE

The Rookery ★ 🎁 Quirky, eccentric, and laden with a sense of the antique, The Rookery is a great choice for travelers who want a hotel with the atmosphere of Dickens' or Dr. Johnson's London. Opening in the late 1990s, it salvaged three of the few remaining then-derelict antique houses in Clerkenwell, a neighborhood midway between the West End and the City. The result is an oasis of crooked floors, labyrinthine hallways, and antique accessories and furnishings that manage to mix the fun with the functional. Bedrooms are charming and quirky, furnished with carved 18th- and 19th-century bed frames, and lace or silk draperies.

Peter's Lane, Cowcross St., London EC1M 6DS. www.rookeryhotel.com. ☎ **020/7336-0931.** Fax 020/7336-0932. 33 units. £126–£185 double. AE, DC, MC, V. Tube: Farringdon. **Amenities:** Concierge; room service. *In room:* A/C, TV, minibar, Wi-Fi (free).

MODERATE

The Fox & Anchor ★ 🛏 The traditional English pub just got hip. Entering from the Smithfield meat market, you'd be forgiven for thinking this was just a great little inn—brass fitting, etched glass, and acres of mahogany—but upstairs houses six classy rooms. Wood-floored and modern, and kitted out with high-end flatscreen TVs, sound systems, and huge free-standing baths, they're more glamorous than your usual room above a pub. The meat market location has its pros and cons. Con: it can get a little noisy. Pro: the breakfast is a carnivore's dream.

115 Charterhouse St., London EC1M 6AA. www.foxandanchor.com. ☎ **020/7550-1000.** Fax 020/7250-1300. 6 units. £112–£280 double. Rates include breakfast. AE, DC, MC, V. Tube: Barbican or Farringdon. **Amenities:** Restaurant; bar. *In room:* TV, minibar, Wi-Fi (free).

INEXPENSIVE

The Hoxton ★ 🎁 The appeal of The Hoxton is straightforward—reasonable prices and quality service in a district best known for hotels with prices out of the range of those of us without an expense account. It's not just room rates that are competitive: 5p-a-minute calls to North America and supermarket prices for the minibar food are proof that budget airline tactics can work in a hotel. Of course there are downsides; the price means bedrooms are utilitarian and none too roomy, and booking in advance is vital. The Hoxton's popularity as a Shoreditch post-club crash-pad also means it can be noisy at the weekends; but for a reasonably priced stay at the heart of the Shoreditch scene, there's no better option.

81 Great Eastern St., London EC2A 3HU. www.hoxtonhotels.com. ☎ **020/7550-1000.** Fax 020/7550-1090. 205 units. £49–£199 double. Rates include light breakfast. AE, DC, MC, V. Tube: Old St. **Amenities:** Grill; bar; access to nearby gym (£7). *In room:* TV, fridge, hair dryer, Wi-Fi (free).

East London

EXPENSIVE

The Boundary ★ 🛏 With Terence Conran—founder of interior design store Habitat—at the helm you'd expect something rather special from this converted East End warehouse, and you wouldn't be disappointed. The 17 rooms are a design junkie's dream, many boasting pieces specially created for the hotel, alongside chunky, reclaimed bathroom suites. And we were pleasantly surprised to see that, unlike in many new boutique hotels, rooms are spacious and airy. Plus there's enough going on downstairs (and up) to make this somewhere you won't want to leave. There's a rococo French restaurant in the basement, a roof terrace for barbecues and East London views in the summer, and a wonderful little bakery/cafe for lazy weekend breakfasts.

2–4 Boundary St., London E2 7DD. www.theboundary.co.uk. ☎ **020/7729-1051.** Fax 020/7729-3061. 17 units. £140–£280 double. AE, DC, MC, V. Tube: Liverpool St. or Old St. **Amenities:** 3 restaurants, including Albion (see review, p. 144); bar; room service. *In room:* TV, iPad, minibar, Wi-Fi (free).

Town Hall Hotel ★★   There were sharp intakes of breath when this grand hotel opened in 2010 on an ordinary Bethnal Green side-street. An imposing design hotel, with one of the hippest young chefs doing the food, this far east? The gamble has paid off, and London's East End finally has the luxury accommodation it needed. The former Bethnal Green Town Hall has been converted into a palace of design and taste. Rooms are somber and clean-lined with beautiful mid-century design pieces, the Viajante restaurant is the hottest ticket in town, and the bar has some of the friendliest and most creative staff this side of Manhattan. The smart pool and spa are a rare treat for East London, too.

8 Patriot Sq., London E2 9NF. www.townhallhotel.com. ℂ **020/7871-0460.** Fax 020/7160-5214. 98 units. £174–£201 double. AE, DC, MC, V. Tube: Bethnal Green. **Amenities:** 2 restaurants, including Viajante (p. 144); bar; exercise room; indoor pool; spa. *In room:* A/C, TV/DVD, Wi-Fi (free).

THE THAMES VALLEY & THE CHILTERNS

by Stephen Keeling

T he rich landscapes of the Chilterns and Thames Valley are rooted in 1,000 years of English tradition. Much of the tourist buzz comes from the region's connections with English high society: Royal castles, racecourses, rowing galas, and Britain's poshest university town. Yet it's also the home of innovative restaurants, dynamic local theatre, and a network of cycle paths and hiking trails rooted firmly in the 21st century.

5

SIGHTSEEING   **Windsor Castle** is still home to the Royal Family, a place to enjoy the pageantry of the daily Guard Mounting ceremony (or to even see the Queen herself). Upriver, the ancient university town of **Oxford** is dripping with history, elaborate medieval architecture, and a vibrant student population that gives it a surprisingly cosmopolitan atmosphere. Touring the nearby **Chilterns,** you can visit the cottage where John Milton composed poetry, or the village where Roald Dahl created his most beloved characters.

EATING & DRINKING   In a region with such a storied past, ancient pubs and fine English ales take center stage. Grab a pint at Oxford's **White Horse,** or sample craft beers in St. Albans, the home of the Campaign for Real Ale. The region's more creative, contemporary side is on show in a host of Michelin-starred institutions; dine on snail porridge at Heston Blumenthal's **Fat Duck,** or modern French cuisine at **Raymond Blanc's** exalted restaurants.

HISTORY   The area has a rich history. Travel back to Roman times at **St. Albans,** or take a peek into the lives of the English nobility at **Blenheim** and **Woburn.** You can meditate on the roots of freedom at **Runnymede,** where King John signed the Magna Carta, and wander the corridors of **Eton,** England's oldest school.

ARTS & CULTURE   Fuelled by its famous university, Oxford is also the cultural capital of the region, with a range of plays, performances, and concerts almost every night. Take in some Shakespeare at the **Oxford Playhouse,** or a high-quality classical recital at the **Sheldonian,** before wandering over to the **Jericho Tavern** for a late-night folk concert. Art lovers can linger over the Old Masters at the **Christ Church Picture Gallery,** or head south to the thoughtful showcase for modern painter Stanley Spencer.

THE best TRAVEL EXPERIENCES IN THE THAMES VALLEY & THE CHILTERNS

- **Taking a ghostly tour in Oxford:** Oxford isn't just dreaming spires, old libraries, and colleges; it's got ghosts too. Bill Spectre's Oxford Ghost Trails is an entertaining introduction to the creepy side of the city, a walking tour that takes in plenty of supernatural stories and sights. See p. 213.
- **Cruising on the Thames:** England's most-celebrated river is best experienced from the water. Jump on a boat trip at Windsor, Oxford, or Henley, or take the plunge and charter your own vessel; in a week you can cruise from the outskirts of London all the way to the City of Dreaming Spires. See p. 209.
- **Hiking the Ridgeway:** The Ridgeway National Trail runs for 87 miles from the Wiltshire Downs to the top of the Chilterns at Ivinghoe Beacon. The trail follows a prehistoric track through a bucolic landscape of rolling hills and beech forests, perfect for a day or more of easy hiking. See p. 230.
- **Punting the River Cherwell:** An hour or two of punting on a lazy summer's day in Oxford is as English as taking afternoon tea, though admittedly not as easy. Experts glide through the water like Venetian gondoliers, but be warned—it's lots of fun but harder than it looks. See p. 217.
- **Dining Tudor style at Hatfield House:** It is a touch touristy, but the Hatfield Banquets are tasty, entertaining, and a genuine attempt to open a window into the world of Elizabethan dining. See p. 237.

WINDSOR ★ & ETON

21 miles W of London

Windsor is a charming, largely Victorian town, with lots of brick buildings and a few remnants of Georgian architecture. All this is completely overshadowed of course by its great castle, which dominates the area like a giant crown of stone. **Windsor Castle** has been the home of the royal family since the reign of Henry I some 900 years ago, a pedigree that makes it an enticing target for day-trippers from London. Despite the inevitable crowds this is a sight you should not miss; the State Apartments are especially lavish, adorned with some exceptional paintings from the royal collection.

Essentials

GETTING THERE   Trains make the 35-minute trip from Paddington Station in London (First Great Western) to Windsor & Eton Central (opposite the castle entrance) every 20 to 30 minutes or so from around 5am to 11pm, with one change at Slough. Trains run at similar intervals for the 1-hour trip from Waterloo Station direct to Windsor & Eton Riverside Station (a short walk from the castle). The off-peak round-trip cost is £8.50 from Paddington and £9.30 from Waterloo.

The Thames Valley

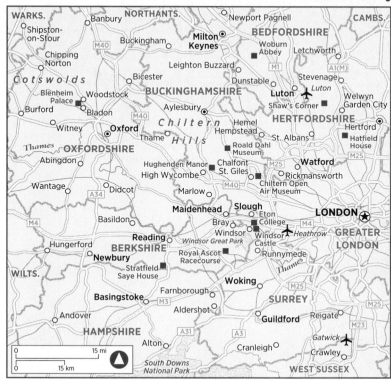

VISITOR INFORMATION The **Royal Windsor Information Centre** is at the Old Booking Hall, Windsor Royal Shopping Center on Thames Street, in the center of town (✆ **01753/743900;** www.windsor.gov.uk). It is open May through August, Monday to Friday 9:30am to 5:30pm, Saturday 9:30am to 5pm, and Sunday 10am to 4pm; and September through April, Monday to Saturday 10am to 5pm and Sunday 10am to 4pm. It can also help with last-minute ticket offers for the Theatre Royal Windsor.

ORGANIZED TOURS The tourist office can put you in touch with a **Blue Badge** guide (✆ **01628/82827;** www.rendezvousguides.co.uk) to lead you on a **walking tour** of town. The cost depends on the number of people and the length of the tour, but is usually £6 per person. Advance booking is essential.

City Sightseeing Open Top Bus Tours (✆ **01708/866000;** www.city-sightseeing. com) make 45-minute loops of Windsor and Eton with 11 hop-on, hop-off stops (mid-Mar–mid-Nov daily 10am–5pm). Tickets, valid for 24 hours, are £8 for adults, £4 for children 5 to 15, and free for children 4 and under.

Touring this historic waterway is still possible on foot or by boat. Stretching for 184 miles, the **Thames Path ★★** is a national trail that follows the river from its source, in the Cotswolds, through Oxford, Henley, and Windsor all the way to London's Docklands. It usually takes a minimum of 10 days (with plenty of pubs and B&Bs along the way), but you can also tackle smaller sections. For the less-energetic, boats glide along the river, offering a languid alternative to the road. **Salter's Steamers** (© **01865/ 243421; www.salterssteamers.co.uk)** runs services in segments between Staines and Oxford, via Abingdon, Reading, Henley, Marlow, Windsor, and Maidenhead. Most segments cost around £10 one-way. If you fancy the role of captain yourself, contact **Kris Cruisers,** in Datchet (© **01753/543930; www. kriscruisers.co.uk).** The outfitter rents the largest fleet of fully equipped boats on the Thames, containing between two and eight berths. From Datchet, you can travel upstream to Windsor and Eton and on to Henley and Oxford. Prices start at £660 per week.

Exploring the Area

Eton College ★★ HISTORIC SITE   Eton is home of what is arguably the most famous public school in the world (non-Brits would call it a private school). The school was founded by 18-year-old Henry VI in 1440, and since then 20 prime ministers have been educated here, as have such literary figures as George Orwell, Aldous Huxley, Ian Fleming, and Percy Bysshe Shelley. Other notable students include Prince William, second in line to the throne, and David Cameron, elected prime minister in 2010. The real highlight inside is the Perpendicular **College Chapel,** completed in 1482, with its 15th-century paintings and reconstructed fan vaulting.

The history of Eton College is depicted in the **Museum of Eton Life,** located in vaulted wine cellars under College Hall (originally used as a storehouse by the college's masters). The displays include a turn-of-the-20th-century boy's room, schoolbooks, and canes used by senior boys to apply punishment—the brutal flogging that characterized much of the school's history. Note that admission to the school and museum is by **guided tour only.**

Keats Lane, Eton. © **01753/671000.** www.etoncollege.com. Admission £6.50 adults, £5.50 seniors and children 8–14. Mar 25–Apr 20 and early July–early Sept daily 10:30am–4:30pm; late Apr–June and early Sept–early Oct Wed and Fri–Sun 1:30–4:30pm. Dates vary every year, and Eton may close for special occasions; call ahead. Take a train from Paddington Station to Windsor (see "Getting There," above). If you go by train, you can walk from the station to the campus. By car, take the M4 to exit 5 to go straight to Eton. **Insider tip:** Parking is difficult, so we advise turning off the M4 at exit 6 to Windsor; you can park here and take an easy stroll past Windsor Castle and across the Thames Bridge. Follow Eton High Street to the college.

Queen Mary's Dolls' House ☺ ARCHITECTURE   A palace in perfect miniature, the Dolls' House was given to Queen Mary in 1923. It was a gift of members of the royal family, including the king, along with contributions made by some 1,500 tradesmen, artists, and authors. The house, designed by Sir Edwin Lutyens, was created on a scale of 1 to 12. It took 3 years to complete. It is a miniature masterpiece; each room is exquisitely furnished, and every item is made exactly to scale. Working elevators stop on every floor, and there is running water in all five bathrooms.

Castle Hill, Windsor. ℭ **01753/831118** for recorded information. Admission is included in the entrance fee to Windsor Castle (see below). Mar–Oct daily 9:45am–5:15pm; Nov–Feb daily 9:45am–4:15pm. As with Windsor Castle, it's best to call ahead to confirm opening times.

St. George's Chapel ★★★ CHURCH A perfect expression of the Medieval Perpendicular style, this chapel contains the tombs of 10 sovereigns. The present St. George's was founded in the late 15th century by Edward IV, on the site of the original Chapel of the Order of the Garter. You first enter the nave, which contains the tomb of George V (1936) and Queen Mary (1953). Off the nave in the Urswick Chapel, the Princess Charlotte memorial provides an ironic touch; if she had survived childbirth in 1817, she, and not her cousin Victoria, would have ruled the British Empire. In the north nave aisle is the tomb of George VI (1952), the speech-impaired monarch featured in the movie *The King's Speech,* while the altar contains the remains of Edward IV (1483) and Edward VII (1910). The Edward IV "Quire," with its imaginatively carved 15th-century choir stalls, evokes the pomp and pageantry of medieval days. In the center is a flat tomb, containing the vault of the beheaded Charles I (1649), along with Henry VIII (1547) and his third wife, Jane Seymour (1537; she provided him a son). The latest royal burials here (in the King George VI Memorial Chapel) were Queen Elizabeth the Queen Mother and Princess Margaret in 2002.

Castle Hill, Windsor. ℭ **01753/848885.** www.stgeorges-windsor.org. Admission is included in the entrance fee to Windsor Castle (see below). Mon–Sat 10am–4pm (last admission 4pm). Closed for a few days in June and Dec.

Windsor Castle ★★★ CASTLE Looming high above the town on a chalk ridge, Windsor Castle is an awe-inspiring site, an enormous hulk of stone dating back to the days of William the Conqueror. The history and art here are undeniably impressive, but what really draws the crowds is the association with the royal family; this is no ruin or museum, but one of the three homes of Queen Elizabeth II. Indeed, Windsor is the world's largest inhabited castle and the Queen is often in residence, especially at weekends (when the royal standard flies). Getting a glimpse is not that hard, as the town's hoteliers often have advance warning of when Her Majesty comes and goes. Even if you don't see the Queen, the Windsor **Changing of the Guard ★** offers more pageantry than the London version. The guard marches through the town, stopping traffic as it wheels into the castle to the tunes of a full regimental band; when the Queen is not here, a drum-and-pipe band is mustered. From April to July, the ceremony takes place Monday to Saturday at 11am. The rest of the year, the guard is changed every 48 hours Monday to Saturday. It's best to call ℭ **020/7766-7304** for a schedule.

The castle was originally constructed in wood in the 1080s; Henry II started to rebuild it in stone in the 12th century and was the first monarch to live at Windsor. Today many parts of the castle are open to the public, including the precincts and the **State Apartments.** On display in the latter are many works of art, armor, three Verrio ceilings, and several 17th-century Gibbons carvings. Several works by Rubens adorn the King's Drawing Room. In the relatively small King's Dressing Room is a Dürer, along with Rembrandt's portrait of his mother and Van Dyck's triple portrait of Charles I. Of the apartments, the grand reception room, with its Gobelin tapestries, is the most spectacular.

The elegant **Semi-State Rooms ★★** are open only from the end of September until the end of March. They were created by George IV in the 1820s as part of a series of royal apartments designed for his personal use. Seriously damaged by fire in 1992, they have been returned to their former glory, with lovely antiques, paintings,

The most appealing way to see the area around Windsor is from the water. Informative **boat tours** depart from Windsor Promenade, Barry Avenue, for a 40-minute round-trip to Boveney Lock. The cost is £5.40 for adults, £2.70 for children 5 to 15. You can also take a 2-hour tour through Boveney Lock and up past lavish private riverside homes, the Bray Film Studios, Queens Eyot, and Monkey Island for £8.60 for adults, £4.30 for children. In addition, there's a 45-minute tour from Runnymede on board the *Lucy Fisher,* a replica of a Victorian paddle steamer. It passes Magna Carta Island, among other sights, and costs £5.40 for adults, £2.70 for children. The boats offer light refreshments and have a well-stocked bar; the decks are covered in case of an unexpected shower. Tours are operated by **French Brothers, Ltd.,** Clewer Boathouse, Clewer Court Road, Windsor (✆ **01753/851900; www. boat-trips.co.uk).**

and decorative objects. The Crimson Drawing Room is evocative of the king's flamboyant taste, with its crimson silk damask hangings and sumptuous art. The **Drawings Gallery** shows revolving exhibitions of material from the royal library.

We recommend that you take a free guided tour of the castle precincts (30 min.). Guides are very well informed and recapture the rich historical background of the castle. With more time, consider the enlightening behind-the-scenes tours of the **Great Kitchen** (30 min; selected dates in Aug and Sept).

Castle Hill, Windsor. ✆ **01753/831118** (information line); ✆ **020/7766-7300** (for tickets). www.royal collection.org.uk. Admission £16.50 adults, £15 students and seniors, £9.90 children 5–17, free for children 4 and under, £43.50 family of 5 (2 adults and 3 children 16 and under). Mar–Oct daily 9:45am–5:15pm; Nov–Feb daily 9:45am–4:15pm. Last admission 1 hr. before closing. Closed for periods in Apr, June, and Dec, when the royal family is in residence.

Windsor Farm Shop ★ 🍴 SHOP   Had any of the Queen's jars of jam lately, or maybe her homemade pork pie, or a bottle of her special brew? If not, head for this outlet, which sells produce from her estates outside Windsor, including pheasants and partridges bagged at royal shoots. The cream, yogurt, ice cream, and milk come from the two royal dairy farms. The meat counter is especially awesome, with its cooked hams and massive ribs of beef. The steak-and-ale pies are quite tasty. You can also purchase 15-year-old whisky from Balmoral Castle in Scotland. Stock up on the Queen's vittles and head for a picnic in the area.

Datchet Rd., Old Windsor. ✆ **01753/623800.** www.windsorfarmshop.co.uk. Mon–Sat 9am–5pm; Sun 10am–5pm.

Where to Eat

Cornucopia Bistro ★★ FRENCH   Justly regarded as the best deal in town, this French restaurant is usually full, so book ahead if you can. The dining room is simple and perennially under-staffed (though service is always friendly), but this is all about the exquisite food: Think perfectly steamed mussels, venison and red-wine pâté, buttery lamb shank, and top-notch wine. Set menus (which change weekly) are a real bargain at £13 to £14 for three courses.

6 High St., Windsor. ✆ **01753/833009.** www.cornucopia-bistro.co.uk. Reservations recommended. Main courses £13–£20. AE, MC, V. Mon–Thurs noon–2:30pm and 6–9:30pm; Fri–Sat noon–2:30pm and 6–10pm; Sun noon–2:30pm.

Strok's CONTEMPORARY ENGLISH/CONTINENTAL This pricey restaurant, located near the castle, is Windsor's most elegant, possessing garden terraces, a conservatory, and a dining room designed a bit like a greenhouse. For starters, try the tongue-tingling foie gras parfait. The main courses are all good, but stand-outs include the goat's cheese tortellini, and wild seabass risotto with roasted peppers, tiger prawns, and confit of cherry tomato.

Sir Christopher Wren's House Hotel, Thames St., Windsor. ✆ **01753/442422.** www.sirchristopherwren. co.uk. Main courses £15–£27. AE, DC, MC, V. Daily 12:30–2:15pm and 6:30–9:45pm.

Watermans Arms PUB FARE Just over the bridge to Eton, this Tudor pub, built in 1542, is a firm student favorite. In addition to the real ales from the local Windsor & Eton Brewery, there's classic pub food: Traditional fish and chips; sausage, onion gravy, and mash; and traditional English ploughman's. Best of all is the beef and Guinness pie. Special English roast dinners, including beef and lamb, are offered on Sunday, costing £8.95.

Brocas St., Eton. ✆ **01753/861001.** www.watermans-eton.com. Main courses £6.50–£12. MC, V. Daily 11:30am–11:30pm.

IN BRAY

The Fat Duck ★★★ CONTEMPORARY ENGLISH The buzz continues at the home of master chef Heston Blumenthal, and for once the hype really is justified (three Michelin stars and voted Best Restaurant in the World in 2005!). Who said that ice cream can't be made of crab, or that mashed potatoes can't be mixed with lime jelly? The snail porridge is a tasty sensation, equaled by the salmon poached in licorice and powdered Anjou pigeon. It's all quite simply astounding. Finish your meal with whiskey wine gums and feel good that the huge wad of cash you've just blown was well worth it (the tasting menu is your only option).

1 High St., Bray. ✆ **01628/580333.** www.thefatduck.co.uk. Reservations required. £160 tasting menu. AE, DC, DISC, MC, V. Tues–Sat noon–2pm and 7–9:30pm, Sun noon–2pm. Leave the motorway at exit 4. On the roundabout, take the exit to Maidenhead (A404M/M4) and follow the dual carriageway to the roundabout at the M4. Take the 1st left exit to Maidenhead Central. At the 2nd roundabout, take the exit to Bray and Windsor (A308). Continue a half-mile and turn left at the sign to Bray Village (B3028). After entering the village, continue past the bottleneck; the Fat Duck is on the right adjacent to the Hinds Head Hotel.

Waterside Inn ★★ CONTEMPORARY FRENCH Yet another Michelin three-star winner in this tiny village, helmed by the indomitable Roux brothers and Belgian head chef Fabrice Uhryn. The beautifully crafted food will blow you away: Fillets of sole are filled with a soft scallop and herb mousse wrapped in a spinach leaf, Dieppe-style sauce with mussels and brown shrimps; while grilled rabbit fillets are served on a celeriac fondant, with glazed chestnuts and Armagnac sauce. The set menus (from £42) are the best value, but if you want to splurge it doesn't get much better than the tasting menu (£140), an epic six-course culinary adventure.

Ferry Rd., Bray. ✆ **01628/620691.** www.waterside-inn.co.uk. Reservations recommended. Main courses £49–£58; set menu £42 for 2 courses (Wed–Fri), £57 for 3 courses (Wed–Sat), £72 for 3 courses (Sun). AE, DC, MC, V. Wed–Sun noon–2pm and 7–10pm. Follow directions to Fat Duck, above, and turn right along Ferry Rd.

Shopping

Windsor Royal Shopping, the shopping center at the main railway station (✆ **01753/797070;** www.windsorroyalshopping.co.uk), has a concentration of shops, mostly the usual chains but also locally owned **Simply Windsor Gifts** (𝄪 **07799/622649;** www.simplywindsorgifts.co.uk) and **Essentially Soap** (𝄪 **07711/182363;** www.essentiallysoap.co.uk).

A colorful traditional English perfumery, **Woods of Windsor,** 50 High St. (𝄪 **01753/868125;** www.woodsofwindsor.co.uk), dates from 1770. It offers soaps, shampoos, scented drawer liners, and hand and body lotions, all prettily packaged in pastel-floral and bright old-fashioned wraps.

At **Billings & Edmonds,** 132 High St., Eton (𝄪 **01753/861348;** www.billings andedmonds.co.uk), you may think you've blundered into a time warp. This distinctive clothing store supplies school wear, suits made to order, and a complete line of cufflinks, shirts, ties, and accessories.

Entertainment & Nightlife

Except for pub life, Windsor is fairly quiet at night. The major cultural venue is **Theatre Royal,** Thames Street (𝄪 **01753/853888;** www.theatreroyalwindsor.co.uk), with a tradition of putting on plays that goes back 2 centuries. This is one of the finest regional theatres in England, often drawing first-rate actors from London's West End. The box office is open Monday to Saturday from 10am to 8pm (call the phone number above for bookings). Performances are Monday to Saturday at 8pm, with matinees on Thursday at 2:30pm and Saturday at 4:45pm. Most tickets cost between £11 and £30.

Where to Stay
EXPENSIVE

Macdonald Windsor Hotel ★★   Opening in 2010 in the heart of Windsor, the Macdonald is currently the top choice in town, with plush, comfy rooms, hearty breakfasts, and even under-floor heating in the bathrooms for those chilly English winters. The Georgian townhouse was given an artful makeover by award-winning interior designer Amanda Rosa, blending contemporary style with original Georgian fittings.

23 High St., Windsor, Berkshire SL4 1LH. www.macdonaldhotels.co.uk/windsor. 𝄪 **0844/8799101.** 120 units. £145–£180 double. AE, DC, MC, V. Parking £18–£22. Children 12 and under stay free in parent's room. **Amenities:** Restaurant; bar; room service. *In room:* A/C, TV, minibar, Wi-Fi (free).

The Oakley Court ★★   Built beside the Thames by a Victorian industrialist, the castle-like Oakley Court is hard to match for historic ambience and classical English country style. Today it's affiliated with the Principal Hayley hotel chain. The building's jutting Gothic gables and bristling turrets have appeared in several classic Hammer horror movies, as well as *The Rocky Horror Picture Show.* Although the grandest public areas are in the main house, most rooms are in a trio of well-accessorized modern wings that ramble through the estate's 15 hectares (37 acres) of parks and gardens. Most suites offer four-poster beds and views of the River Thames.

Windsor Rd., Water Oakley, Windsor, Berkshire SL4 5UR. www.principal-hayley.com. 𝄪 **01753/609988.** Fax: 01628/637011. 118 units. £125–£250 double; £225–£310 suite. AE, DC, MC, V. Take the river road, A308, 3 miles from Windsor toward Maidenhead. Free parking. **Amenities:** Restaurant; bar; babysitting; health club; Jacuzzi; indoor heated pool; room service; sauna; 2 outdoor tennis courts. *In room:* A/C, TV, hair dryer, minibar, Wi-Fi (£6.50 per hr. or £15 per 24 hr.).

The Runnymede-On-Thames ★★   Because of the dearth of top-of-the-line hotels within Windsor itself, more and more guests are seeking out this hotel and spa on the shady banks of the Thames between Windsor and Staines. Rooms are smart, spacious, and stylish, with plenty of extras (free Wi-Fi, bathrobes, and so forth), and the on-site spa is one of the finest in the greater London area, offering exercise programs and healthful treatments, plus a splendid outdoor pool. The contemporary buffet-style **Leftbank** restaurant is perfect for drinks and dinner, opening onto a tranquil section of the Thames.

Windsor Rd., Egham, Surrey TW20 0AG. www.runnymedehotel.com. © **01784/220960.** Fax: 01784/ 436340. 180 units. Mon–Thurs £175–£215 double; Fri–Sun £130–£230 double. Rates include English breakfast. AE, MC, V. Take the A308 out of Windsor, a 15-min. drive. **Amenities:** 2 restaurants; bar; babysitting; exercise room; outdoor pool (summer only); room service; spa; 3 outdoor tennis courts. *In room:* A/C, TV, hair dryer, Wi-Fi (free).

MODERATE

Langton House 🏆 This homey B&B near the castle is run by welcoming hosts Paul and Sonja Fogg, who have converted a Victorian townhouse that dates from 1890, when it housed Queen Victoria's minor government officials. The large, double-fronted facade is built of dark red brick. It served as a nursing home before being turned into a B&B that offers comfortably furnished, midsize bedrooms, each with a private bathroom equipped with a shower stall. It's only 5 minutes from the castle.

46 Alma Rd., Windsor, Berkshire S14 3HA. www.langtonhouse.co.uk. © **01753/858299.** Fax: 01753/ 858299. 4 units. £93 double. Rates include English breakfast. AE, MC, V. Free parking. **Amenities:** Bicycle storage, Wi-Fi (free). *In room:* TV, hair dryer.

Park Farm B&B Located just a mile and half south of Windsor Castle (on the B3022), this family-owned B&B feels like a manor in the middle of the country. Hospitable hosts Caroline and Drew run the vast country house. Rooms are compact but modern and extremely cozy, with spotlessly clean bathrooms (showers only). The full English breakfasts won't disappoint (you can also order bacon sandwiches to go).

St. Leonards Rd., Windsor, Berkshire SL4 3EA. www.parkfarm.com. © **01753/866823.** 5 units. £85 double. Rates include English breakfast. AE, MC, V. Free parking. **Amenities:** Common-use fridge and microwave. *In room:* TV, hair dryer, Wi-Fi (free).

Rainworth House 🏆 This gem of a B&B is justly popular (advance bookings are essential), and only a short drive or taxi ride from central Windsor. The house is a handsome red-brick property set within 1.2 hectares (3 acres) of gardens and fields, 2 miles from the town. Host Doreen Barclay maintains beautiful en-suite rooms with four-poster beds and wood beams; some have views of the surrounding countryside. Doreen's sumptuous gut-busting English breakfasts are worthy of a Michelin star.

Oakley Green Rd., Oakley Green, Windsor, Berkshire SL4 5UL. www.rainworthhouse.com. © **01753/ 856749.** 5 units. £78–£90 double. Rates include English breakfast. AE, MC, V. Free parking. Take the A308, 2½ miles from Windsor toward Maidenhead. *In room:* TV, Wi-Fi (free).

Side Trips from Windsor

Windsor Great Park ★ PARK Just to the south of Windsor sprawls this 2,023-hectare (5,000-acre) park, once the private hunting ground of Windsor Castle but mostly open to the public today. It's best known for the enclosed **Deer Park** at the northern end, where red deer are often grazing in open view; look out also for several hundred green parakeets fluttering around, descendents of escaped pets living in the park since the late 1990s.

There is no admission charge, except for the **Savill Garden,** part of the Royal Landscape section at the southern end. Created in the 1930s, the 14-hectare (35-acre) garden is one of the finest in England. The display starts in spring with rhododendrons, camellias, and daffodils beneath the trees; then, throughout the summer, spectacular displays of flowers and shrubs are presented in a natural and wild state. The garden is 4 miles from Windsor along the A30; turn off at Wick Road and follow the signs. The nearest rail station is at Egham; you'll need to take a taxi a distance of 3 miles. A self-service restaurant and gift shop are on site.

Adjoining Savill Garden are the **Valley Gardens,** full of shrubs and trees in a series of wooded natural valleys running to **Virginia Water,** an ornamental lake created in 1753. Both are open daily year-round. There is no admission charge to enter the Valley Gardens, but parking is a flat £6, or £1.50 for the first hour at Virginia Water.

Windsor Great Park. ✆ **01753/860222.** www.thecrownestate.co.uk. Admission to park free; admission to Savill Garden (✆ **01784/435544;** www.theroyallandscape.co.uk). Mar–Oct £8.50 adults, £7.95 seniors, £3.75 children 6–16; Nov–Feb £6.25 adults, £5.75 seniors, £2.25 children; £16–£21 family ticket, children 5 and under free. Daily 10am–6pm (4:30pm in winter).

Legoland Windsor ☺ THEME PARK   Just outside Windsor, Legoland is a 60-hectare (150-acre) children's theme park, based on the Lego toy system, that opened in 1996. Although a bit corny, it's a favorite for kids. Attractions, spread across several activity centers, include Duplo Land, offering a boat ride, puppet theatre, and waterworks, plus Miniland, showing European cities and villages recreated in minute detail from millions of Lego bricks. Knight's Kingdom takes you back to the days of knights and dragons and includes a blazing dragon roller coaster. The Land of the Vikings features a river-rapids ride, while Adventure Land is a collection of more conventional rides.

Winkfield Rd. (B3022), 2 miles south of Windsor. ✆ **0870/504-0404.** www.legoland.co.uk. Admission varies through the season, starting with cheaper online tickets from £37 for adults, £27 for seniors and children 3–15. Mid-Mar–mid-Nov daily 10am–5pm (until 7pm on school holidays). Closed late Nov–early Mar.

Runnymede HISTORIC SITE   Three miles southeast of Windsor is Runnymede, a 76-hectare (188-acre) water meadow on the south side of the Thames, in Surrey. This is where it's believed that King John put his seal on the Great Charter in 1215, after intense pressure from his feudal barons and lords. The charter forced the king to accept a long list of individual liberties and is regarded as the founding document of English constitutional law, as well as inspiration for the U.S. Constitution (a copy of the Magna Carta is displayed in Washington D.C.'s National Archives). The **Magna Carta Memorial,** a large pillar of engraved English granite, is clearly sign-posted and reached after a short walk. The domed pavilion that shelters it was placed here by the American Bar Association in 1957, to acknowledge the fact that American law stems from the English system. Runnymede is also the site of the moving **John F. Kennedy Memorial,** an acre of ground given to the United States by the people of Britain in 1965.

Runnymede, ½ mile west of the hamlet of Old Windsor on the south side of the A308. ✆ **01784/432891.** www.nationaltrust.org.uk. Free admission. Daily dawn to dusk. If you're driving on the M25, exit at Junction 13. The nearest rail connection is at Egham, ½ mile away. The train ride from London's Waterloo Station takes about 25 minutes.

Ascot Racecourse RACECOURSE   The first race meeting at Ascot, which is directly south of Windsor at the southern end of Windsor Great Park, was held way back in 1711. Ascot Racecourse has been a symbol of high society (and ludicrously extravagant hats), ever since, as pictures of the royal family enjoying the races there have been flashed around the world.

Ascot only hosts 27 days of racing yearly; the town itself isn't worth visiting otherwise. The highlight of the Ascot social season is the **Royal Meeting** (or **Royal Week**), just

5 days in June. To attend you must buy tickets for one of three distinctly different observation areas. These include the Royal Enclosure (members only); the Grandstand, largest of the three; and the Silver Ring, which does not enjoy direct access to the paddocks and has traditionally been the site of most of Ascot's budget seating. At other times you can buy cheaper tickets in all areas (when the Royal Enclosure is known simply as "Premier Admission"). Book online at www.ascot.co.uk from early November.

Ascot, 28 miles west of London. (C) **0870/722-7227.** www.ascot.co.uk. Admission £17–£29 for Silver Ring, £49–£69 for the Grandstand; free for children 15 and under (except to the Royal Enclosure). Car parking £17. Trains make the 50-minute trip between London's Waterloo and Ascot Station every 20–40 minutes during the day (£11.70 off-peak round-trip). Ascot Station is about 10 minutes from the racecourse.

Cliveden ★★ GARDEN   Once the home of the formidable Astor family, the lavish Italianate mansion of Cliveden stands on a constructed terrace of mature gardens high above the Thames. The estate's original house and sweeping lawns were created by William Winde in 1666 for the second duke of Buckingham. After a fire destroyed the old house, Sir Charles Barry, the architect of the Houses of Parliament, built the current gracefully symmetrical structure in the 1850s. In 1893 the American billionaire William Waldorf Astor purchased the estate. After William's son Waldorf (the second Viscount Astor) and wife Nancy (who became the first female English MP) took over in 1906, the mansion became the center of an extravagant, if somewhat right-wing, social scene; in the 1930s the "Cliveden Set" were heavily criticized for supporting appeasement vis-à-vis Germany. The house remained part of the Astor legacy, a repository of a notable collection of paintings and antiques, until 1968, shortly after the Profumo affair had implicated the third Viscount Astor. The National Trust now owns Cliveden, but leases the property as a private hotel. Non-guests are permitted only limited access to the house.

The surrounding **gardens** are open to the public year-round, and are far more enjoyable for casual visitors. They feature a distinguished variety of plantings, ranging from Renaissance-style topiary to meandering forest paths, and vistas of statuary and flowering shrubs. Highlights include a glade garden, a magnificent parterre, and an amphitheatre where "Rule Britannia" was played for the first time.

Cliveden Rd., Taplow, 10 miles northwest of Windsor. (C) **01628/605069.** www.nationaltrust.org.uk. Admission to grounds Feb–Oct £8.15 adults, £4.50 children 5–15, free for children 4 and under, family ticket £20; Nov–Dec £5.45 adults, £2.70 children, family ticket £14. Admission to house (extra £1.50 adults, 75p children) is limited and by timed ticket only from the information kiosk: Apr–Oct Thurs and Sun 3–5:30pm (3 rooms of the mansion are open to the public, as is the Octagon Temple, with its rich mosaic interior). Grounds open mid-Feb–Mar daily 11am–5pm, Apr–Oct daily 11am–5:30pm, Nov–Dec daily 11am–4pm. From Windsor, follow the M4 toward Reading to Junction 7 (in the direction of Slough West). At the roundabout, turn left onto the A4, signposted MAIDENHEAD. At the next roundabout, turn right, signposted BURNHAM. Follow the road for 2½ miles to a T-junction with the B476. The main gates to Cliveden are directly opposite.

WHERE TO EAT & STAY

Cliveden House ★★★   The Astor's former estate is one of the most beautiful and luxurious hotels in England. Rooms—named after famous guests who've stayed here, including T. E. Lawrence and Charlie Chaplin—are sumptuous, each furnished in impeccable taste. The bathrooms with deep marble tubs are among the country's finest. Less preferred rooms are those recently added in the Clutton Wing. Nothing (except perhaps renting Lady Astor's bedroom itself) is more elegant here than walking down to the river and boarding a hotel boat for a champagne cruise before dinner. In the morning, you can go horseback riding on the 152-hectare (376-acre) estate along the riverbank.

Cliveden, Taplow, Maidenhead, Berkshire SL6 0JF. www.clivedenhouse.co.uk. 🕾 **01628/668561.** Fax: 01628/661837. 39 units. £210–£400 double; £540–£725 suite. There is a National Trust charge of £9 per person per stay. AE, DC, MC, V. **Amenities:** 3 restaurants; bar; babysitting; health club & spa; 2 pools (1 heated indoor, 1 outdoor); room service; outdoor tennis court (lit). *In room:* A/C (in some), TV, hair dryer, Wi-Fi (free).

HENLEY-ON-THAMES

35 miles W of London

Henley-on-Thames, a small, affluent town on the river, is the location of the **Royal Regatta,** one of England's most vaunted high-society events held annually in early July. Lying on a stretch of the Thames that's known for its calm waters, unobstructed bottom, and predictable currents, Henley is a rower's dream. The regatta, which started in 1839, is the major annual competition among international oarsmen and oarswomen, who find it both challenging and entertaining—though the real action takes place on the riverbanks, where the great and the good mix over Pimm's Cup and champagne.

If you visit at other times, Henley's Elizabethan buildings, tearooms, and inns can make for an appealing stopover en route to Oxford.

Essentials

GETTING THERE   Trains depart from London's Paddington Station every hour during the day, but require a change at the junction in Twyford (some also require an additional change at Reading). The trip takes 40 minutes to 1 hour. Off-peak round-trip tickets are £15.50.

If you're driving from London, take the M4 toward Reading to Junction 8/9, and then head northwest on the A404 (M) and A4130. From Windsor you can take the A308 to the same M4 junction.

The Henley Royal Regatta ★★

The Henley Royal Regatta, held the first week in July, is the country's premier rowing event. For a close-up view from the Stewards' Enclosure, you'll need a guest badge, obtainable only through a member—in other words, you have to know someone in order to get special privileges. Admission to the Regatta Enclosure, however, is open to all. Entry fees are £55 to £65. For information, contact the Secretary, Henley Royal Regatta, Henley-on-Thames, Oxfordshire RG9 2LY (🕾 **01491/572153;** www.hrr.co.uk). During the annual 5-day event, up to 100 races are organized each day, with starts scheduled as frequently as every 5 minutes. This event is open only to all-male crews of up to nine at a time.

In late June, rowing events for women are held at the 3-day Henley Women's Regatta. If you want to float on the waters of the Thames yourself, stop by the town's largest and oldest outfitter, **Hobbs & Sons, Ltd.,** Station Road Boathouse (🕾 **01491/572035;** www.hobbs-of-henley.com), established in 1870. Open April through October daily from 8:30am to 5:30pm, Hobbs has an armada of watercraft, including rowboats that rent for £15 to £20 per hour. Motorboats go for £26 to £58 per hour. Prices include fuel. An on-premises chandlery shop sells virtually anything a boat crew could need, as well as T-shirts and boaters' hats.

Exploring the Area

River & Rowing Museum MUSEUM   This museum celebrates the Thames and those oarsmen and oarswomen who row upon it. A short walk south of Henley Bridge, the **Rowing Gallery** follows the history of rowing from the days of the Greeks. It's all here: Models of arctic whaleboats in the 1700s, elaborate Venetian gondolas fit for a Doge, and coastal lifeboats that pulled many a victim from the cold waters of the North Sea. In a more modern exhibit, you'll find the boat in which British oarsmen captured the gold medal at the 1996 Olympic Games in Atlanta. The **Thames Gallery** reaches out to embrace the saga of the river itself, while the **Henley Gallery** tells the story of the town. The showstopper here is an Iron Age hoard found in Henley in 2003, made up of 32 cold coins dating from around A.D. 50. The **Wind in the Willows Gallery** celebrates Mr. Toad, Ratty, Badger, and Mole, E. H. Shepard's whimsical creations largely inspired by his time at Pangbourne, a short paddle down the Thames from here.

Mill Meadows. 📞 **01491/415600.** www.rrm.co.uk. Admission £8 adults; £6 children 4–16; £22 family ticket for 4, £26 for 5, and £28 for 6. May–Aug daily 10am–5:30pm; Sept–Apr daily 10am–5pm.

Where to Eat

Argyll 🍴 PUB FARE   This is a traditional pub, with plenty of cozy nooks, wood fires in winter, and a beer garden for sunny days. Suffolk's Greene King cask ales dominate (IPA and Abbot Ale), but it's also a popular lunch spot with locals. The doorstep sandwiches (with fresh crusty bread and salad) are a good deal (from £4.50), and most of the main courses—Cumberland sausages and mash, beer-battered haddock—come in at under £10.

15 Market Place. 📞 **01491/573400.** www.theargyllhenley.co.uk. Main courses and platters £8.50–£19. AE, MC, V. Sun–Thurs 10am–midnight; Fri–Sat 10am–1am.

Crooked Billet GASTROPUB   This venerable old pub, a few miles northwest of Henley, is well worth an excursion. The cask ales (Brakspears Best Bitter) are superb, but most people come to eat from the menu of contemporary Italian, French provincial, and popular bistro dishes that changes seasonally. Expect delights such as smoked eel, slow roast Barbary duck, and spinach and ricotta filo strudel. Simple classics like the Welsh rarebit and a glass of stout, or warm treacle (sugar syrup) sponge with custard sauce are equally satisfying. The inn dates back to around 1642, and highwayman Dick Turpin supposedly hid out here in the 1730s, on account of his romantic attachment to the landlord's daughter.

Newlands Lane. 📞 **01491/681048.** www.thecrookedbillet.co.uk. Main courses £13–£25. AE, MC, V. Daily noon–2:15pm and 7–10pm.

Hotel du Vin Bistro ★ BISTRO   Henley's top hotel also contains the best restaurant, a stylish bistro serving the best of modern British cooking, local ingredients fused with French techniques and a few outright French classics: The moules marinière makes a piquant starter. The core of the menu is all about fusion, though: Try the roast Yorkshire grouse with fondant potato, crisp ham, and orange jus, or just the delicately baked fish pie.

New St. ✆ **01491/848400.** www.hotelduvin.co.uk. Main courses and platters £14–£22. AE, MC, V. Daily noon–2pm and 6–11pm.

Where to Stay

Falaise House ★　This is a first-class B&B in a Georgian townhouse built in 1755, with immaculate en-suite rooms (standard, deluxe, and superior); all are equally well equipped, with the main difference being that standard rooms are smaller. The owners, Jane and Richard, are gracious hosts, the location is perfect, and the finishing touch is the breakfasts: a vast choice of fresh fruit and cooked meals, including Scottish smoked salmon and scrambled eggs.

37 Market Place, Henley-on-Thames, Oxfordshire RG9 2AA. www.falaisehouse.com. ✆ **01491/573388.** 6 units. £85–£175 double. AE, MC, V. Public parking nearby (free overnight and Sun only). *In room:* TV, hair dryer, Wi-Fi (free).

Hotel du Vin ★★　The Hotel du Vin chain took the former Georgian Brakspears Brewery and imaginatively converted it into a fine example of industrial recycling. What has emerged is the poshest hotel in the area. Each of the beautifully furnished rooms, with solid oak pieces, is named after a vineyard. The decorator ordered that all walls be painted a "toast color," and installed thick wall-to-wall carpeting and "dreamboat beds." Fine Egyptian linens and spectacular power showers in the bathrooms are additional enticements.

New St., Henley-on-Thames, Oxfordshire RG9 2BP. www.hotelduvin.co.uk. ✆ **01491/848400.** 43 units. £145–£195 double; £210–£425 suite. AE, DC, MC, V. Parking £15. **Amenities:** Restaurant; bar; room service. *In room:* TV, hair dryer, minibar, Wi-Fi (£10 per 24 hr.).

Lenwade Bed & Breakfast ♦　Built in the early 1900s, this welcoming Victorian guesthouse is owned and operated by Jacquie and John Williams. Entering from a small courtyard filled with flowering vines and lush foliage, you'll see a 1.5-m (6-ft.) stained-glass window thought to depict Joan of Arc. Another memorable detail is the winding staircase with its original handrails. The small to midsize bedrooms are individually decorated and comfortably furnished, while breakfast (a huge spread of juices and hot and cold dishes) is served at a congenial communal table.

3 Western Rd., Henley-on-Thames, Oxfordshire RG9 1JL. www.lenwade.com. ✆ **01491/573468.** 4 units. From £75 double (£55 single). Rates include English breakfast. No credit cards. Free parking. **Amenities:** Free bicycle storage. *In room:* TV, hair dryer, Wi-Fi (free).

Side Trips from Henley

Mapledurham House ★ HISTORIC SITE　The stately Blount family mansion lies beside the Thames in the unspoiled village of Mapledurham, just outside Reading. The aristocratic Blount family has lived here since 1490—the current mansion was completed in 1612 and is currently owned by John Eyston, a Blount descendant. Inside, you'll see Elizabethan ceilings and a great oak staircase, as well as portraits of the two beautiful sisters with whom the poet Alexander Pope, a frequent visitor here (1707–15), fell in love. The family chapel, built in 1789, is a fine example of modern Gothic architecture. On the grounds, the last working **water mill** on the Thames still produces flour. Film buffs note that the 1976 Michael Caine movie *The Eagle Has Landed* was filmed at Mapledurham (standing in for a Norfolk village), and is supposed to have inspired the fictional Toad Hall (from *The Wind in the Willows*).

　The most romantic way to reach this gorgeous old house is to take the boat that leaves the promenade next to Caversham Bridge in Reading at 2pm on Saturday,

Sunday, and bank holidays, from Easter to September. The journey upstream takes between 30 and 80 minutes, and the boat leaves Mapledurham again at 5pm for the return trip to Caversham, giving you plenty of time to explore. The round-trip boat ride from Caversham costs £7 for adults and £5.50 for children 5 to 15. (An additional landing fee of £2 for adults and £1 for children is charged, but this is deducted from the cost of house entry.) You can get more details about the boat from **Thames Rivercruise Ltd.,** Pipers Island, Bridge Street, Caversham Bridge, Reading RG4 8AH (℃ **0118/9481088;** www.thamesrivercruise.co.uk).

Mapledurham, Reading. ℃ **01189/723350.** www.mapledurham.co.uk. Admission to house and mill £7 adults, £3 children 5–16, free for children 4 and under; house only £4.50 adults, £2 children; mill only £3.50 adults, £1.50 children. Sat–Sun and bank holidays 2–5:30pm. Closed Oct–Easter. From Henley-on-Thames, head south along the A4155 to Reading; follow signs to the A329 through town. Mapledurham is signposted off this road, 3 miles west of the center. Or take the boat trip described above.

Stratfield Saye House & Estate ★ HISTORIC HOME   This combined house and country park provides tangible evidence of the fortune of one of England's greatest heroes, the Duke of Wellington. His descendants have lived here since he bought the estate in 1817 to celebrate trouncing Napoleon at the Battle of Waterloo (a grateful Parliament granted a large sum of money for its purchase). The park's centerpiece is Stratfield Saye House itself, built around 1630 by Sir William Pitt, Comptroller of the Household to James I; the original red brick was covered in stucco in the 18th century. Wellington added the conservatory in 1838 and the outer wings in 1846. Many memories of the Iron Duke remain in the house, including his billiard table, battle spoils, and pictures. The funeral carriage that once rested in St. Paul's Cathedral crypt is also on display as part of the Wellington Exhibition in the old stables. In the gardens is the grave of Copenhagen, the charger ridden at Waterloo by the duke. There are also extensive landscaped grounds, together with a tearoom and a gift shop. Access to the house is by guided tour only.

Stratfield Saye, 6 miles south of Reading, off the A33 to Basingstoke. ℃ **01256/882882.** www.stratfield-saye.co.uk. Admission Mon–Fri £7 adults, £6 students and seniors, £4 children 3–15, free for children 2 and under; Sat–Sun £9.50 adults, £8.50 students, £5 children; garden only Mon–Fri £3, Sat–Sun £3.50 (all cash only). Easter weekend (Thurs–Mon) and mid-July–early Aug Mon–Fri 11:30am–3:30pm, Sat–Sun 10:30am–3:30pm; grounds close at 5pm. From Henley, head south along the A4155 to Reading, then the A33 toward Basingstoke.

MARLOW

This Thames-side town, 35 miles northwest of London and 8 miles east of Henley-on-Thames, is best known for its **fishing** associations, though many also prefer its more pastoral look to the larger Henley. Its most famous feature is the **suspension bridge,** completed in 1832 according to the design of William Tierney Clark, who went on to build the far larger bridge linking Buda and Pest in Hungary. Local son and Olympic hero **Sir Steve Redgrave**—born in Marlow in 1962—is honored with a statue in pleasant Higginson Park (between the river and the town center).

Beehive Treats, 18 Spittal Street (℃ **01628/475154;** www.beehivetreats.com), is a handsome old-fashioned candy shop in the center, specializing in traditional candies and real licorice.

To reach Marlow from Henley, take the A4155 and follow the signs. Along this middle stretch of the Thames is some of the most beautiful rural scenery in England. It was in these surroundings that **Izaak Walton** wrote his immortal work on fishing, *The Compleat Angler,* published in 1653.

Stanley Spencer Gallery ★ GALLERY Just 3 miles downriver from Marlow (and some 11 miles from Henley), **Cookham** is another affluent river town notable chiefly as the former home of **Stanley Spencer** (1891–1959), one of Britain's greatest artists. If you've never heard of him, check out the Stanley Spencer Gallery, housed in a former Methodist chapel, and be prepared to be enlightened; the gallery owns more than 100 of his early Modernist paintings and drawings, many of them a curious but powerful fusion of Biblical scenes and everyday life in Cookham in the 1920s and 1930s. Perhaps the most intriguing exhibit is the battered old pram Spencer used to carry his easel and canvas while rambling around the village.

The Kings Hall, High St., Cookham. ℂ **01628/471885.** www.stanleyspencer.org.uk. Admission £5 adults, £4 students and seniors, free for children under 18. Apr–Oct daily 10:30am–5:30pm; Nov–Mar Thurs–Sun 11am–4:30pm. From Marlow, continue southeast along the A4155.

Where to Eat & Stay

Macdonald Compleat Angler Hotel ★★ Marlow attracts many well-heeled fishermen who like to stay at this pricey hotel because of its associations with Izaak Walton. The hotel certainly has plenty of charm and character, though most of it was built long after the venerable Walton passed this way. Nevertheless, it occupies an emerald swath of lawns stretching down to the banks of the Thames, and is a well-organized and impeccably polite center of English chintz, predictably elegant bars, and very fine dining. Each room is outfitted like a private country home, with antiques or reproductions and plush, comfortable beds. The more expensive rooms look out on the Thames. The finest accommodations are in a modern wing with balconies overlooking the rushing weir.

Marlow Bridge, Bisham Rd., Marlow, Buckinghamshire SL7 1RG. www.macdonaldhotels.co.uk/compleatangler. ℂ **0844/879-9128.** Fax: 01628/486388. 64 units. £120–£220 double; £250–£370 suite. AE, DC, MC, V. Free parking. **Amenities:** 2 restaurants; bar; babysitting; room service; Wi-Fi in public areas (£10 per day). In room: A/C, TV, hair dryer, minibar.

The Vanilla Pod ★★ FRENCH/ENGLISH Housed in an elegant property that was once home to T. S. Eliot, this restaurant offers truly excellent cuisine and a menu that changes weekly to take advantage of the best produce in any season. Starters are memorable, especially the quail terrine with foie gras and vanilla carrot purée, or the butternut squash risotto with chorizo sausage. Delectable main dishes are likely to include roasted gilt head sea bream with curried cauliflower, currants, and pine nuts; and roasted duck breast paired with cherries.

31 West St. ℂ **01628/898101.** www.thevanillapod.co.uk. Reservations required (as far in advance as possible). Set-price lunch £16 (2 courses), £20 (3 courses); 3-course dinner £40; 7-course gourmand dinner £50. AE, MC, V. Tues–Sat noon–2pm and 7–10pm. Closed 2 weeks around Easter.

OXFORD ★★★

54 miles NW of London

The city of Oxford, dominated by **Britain's oldest university,** is a bastion of English tradition, history, and eccentricity. Here students still get selected to join the archaic Bullingdon Club, rowing competitions attract a larger audience than football, and students still take exams dressed in black gowns (seriously). The creator of *Inspector Morse*, Colin Dexter, lives in town, and where else would you film the Harry Potter series?

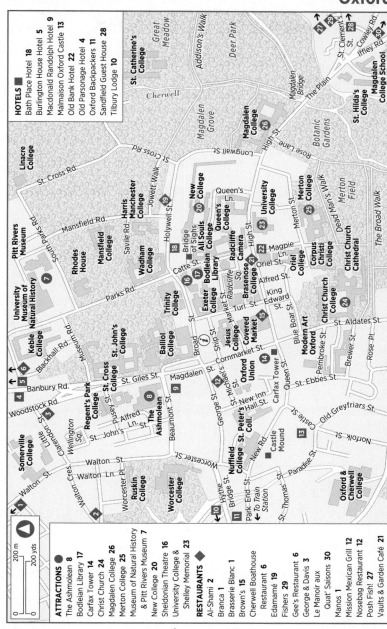

Oxford

St. Catherine's College

Great Meadow

Addison's Walk

Deer Park

Cherwell

Magdalen Bridge

The Plain

St. Clement's St.

Cowley Rd.

Iffley Rd.

St. Hilda's College

Magdalen College School

Linacre College

St. Cross Rd.

St. Cross Rd.

Jowett Walk

Magdalen Grove

Magdalen St.

Longwall St.

High St.

Rose Lane

Botanic Gardens

Magdalen College **26**

Merton Field

Dead Man's Walk

The Broad Walk

Pitt Rivers Museum

Mansfield Rd.

South Parks Rd.

Savile Rd.

Harris Manchester College

Holywell St.

New College

Queen's Ln.

University College **23**

Merton College **25**

Merton St.

Rhodes House

Mansfield College

Wadham College

Bridge of Sighs

All Souls College

Queen's College

University Museum of Natural History **7**

Keble College **6**

Blackhall Rd.

Museum Rd.

Parks Rd.

Catte St.

Radcliffe Library

Radcliffe Sq.

Radcliffe Camera

High St.

Magpie Ln.

Oriel St.

Corpus Christi College

Christ Church Cathedral

Bodleian Library

Exeter College

Brasenose College

Oriel College

Alfred St.

King Edward St.

Christ Church College **24**

Trinity College

Turl St.

St. John's College

Balliol College

Broad St.

Ship St.

Jesus College

Market St.

Cornmarket St.

Covered Market

Blue Boar St.

Modern Art Oxford

St. Aldates St.

Brewer St.

Rose Pl.

St. Cross College

St. Giles St.

Magdalen St.

George St.

St. Michael's St.

Oxford Union **14**

Carfax Tower

Queen St.

St. Ebbes St.

Pembroke St.

Regent's Park College

Banbury Rd.

Woodstock Rd.

St. John's St.

Alfred St.

Beaumont St.

New Inn Hall St.

Castle St.

Old Greyfriars St.

Somerville College

Walton Cres.

Little Clarendon St.

Clarendon St.

Wellington Sq.

Pusey St.

The Ashmolean **8**

St. Peter's Coll.

Nuffield College

New Rd.

Castle Mound

Norfolk St.

Ruskin College

Walton St.

Walton Ln.

Worcester St.

Hythe Bridge St.

Park End St.

To Train Station

St. Thomas'

Paradise St.

Oxford & Cherwell College

Worcester College

0 — 200 m
0 — 200 yds

5

THE THAMES VALLEY & THE CHILTERNS | Oxford

211

Oxford certainly retains a special sort of magic. The hallowed halls and gardens of ancient colleges such as Magdalen and Christ Church are architectural gems, but not museums—students live and work here year-round. The High hasn't changed much since Oscar Wilde skipped along it, and the water meadows and spires that inspired John Donne, Christopher Wren, C. S. Lewis, Iris Murdoch, and J. R. R. Tolkien are still there.

When it comes to food, Oxford doesn't disappoint. The city is the base of French-born celebrity chef Raymond Blanc, who masterminds a creative roster of dishes at **Brasserie Blanc** and the super exclusive **Le Manoir aux Quat' Saisons.** With a huge population of students there's also plenty of cheap eats in town, with the **Covered Market** a good place to start.

Pubs in Oxford have a fittingly rich heritage, and you'll be drinking in the same oak-paneled rooms once frequented by Samuel Johnson, Lawrence of Arabia, Graham Greene, Bill Clinton, and Margaret Thatcher; even *The Hobbit* was first read in the **Eagle and Child.** The city does have a life beyond the university: Radiohead played their first gig at Oxford's **Jericho Tavern** in 1986, an alternative venue that still hosts live bands.

Essentials

GETTING THERE Trains from London's Paddington Station reach Oxford in around 1 hour (direct trains run every 30 minutes). A cheap (off-peak) round-trip ticket costs £22.

If you're driving, take the M40 west from London and follow the signs. **Parking** is a nightmare in Oxford; if you find parking in town it will cost you around £30 per day (cars are banned from much of the center anyway). However, there are five large **park-and-ride** lots (www.parkandride.net) around the city's ring road, all well sign-posted. After 9:30am Monday to Friday, and all day Saturday and Sunday, you pay £2.20 for a round-trip ticket for a bus ride into the city. The bus drops you off at St. Aldate's/Cornmarket or Queen Street in the city center. The buses run every 8 to 10 minutes in each direction until 11:30pm Monday to Saturday and between 11am and 5pm on Sundays.

VISITOR INFORMATION The **Oxford Tourist Information Centre** is at 15–16 Broad St. (✆ **01865/252200;** www.visitoxford.org). It sells a comprehensive range of maps, brochures, and souvenir items, as well as those Oxford University T-shirts that only tourists wear (students advertise their college, not the university). Guided walking tours leave from the center daily (see "Exploring the City," below). Hours are Monday to Saturday 9:30am to 5pm (5:30pm in summer), Sunday, and bank holidays 10am to 4pm.

GETTING AROUND Central Oxford, which includes all the most interesting colleges and sights, is very compact and easily explored on foot, but there are plenty of local buses for those traveling farther afield. Local reliable taxi operators are ABC (✆ **01865/775577**) and Radio Taxis (✆ **01865/242424**).

Exploring the City

Most first-time visitors to Oxford have trouble determining exactly where the university is. Indeed, the quickest way to sound like an ill-informed tourist in Oxford is to ask, "Where's the university?" This is because Oxford University is in fact made up of 39 autonomous, self-governing colleges sprinkled throughout the center of town;

Oxford University has a complex history and a confusing structure, so it makes sense to take one of the many available **tours** to get a more detailed understanding.

For an easy orientation, take a 1-hour, open-top bus tour with **City Sightseeing Oxford** (✆ **01865/790522; www.city sightseeingoxford.com**). Tours start from the railway station; other pickup points are the Sheldonian Theatre, Gloucester Green Bus Station, and Pembroke College. Buses leave daily at 9:30am and then every 10 to 15 minutes in the summer and every 30 minutes in winter. The last bus departs at 4pm November to February, at 5pm March and October, and at 6pm April to September. The cost is £13 for adults, £11 for students, £10 for seniors, and £6 for children 5 to 14 years old; a family ticket for two adults and three children is £32. Tickets can be purchased from the driver and are valid for 24 hours.

If you have more energy, take the entertaining 2-hour **walking tour** through the city and the major colleges from the Oxford Tourist Information Centre, 15–16 Broad St. (✆ **01865/ 252200; www.visitoxfordandoxford shire.com**), daily at 11am, 1, and 2pm. These cost £8 to £8.50 for adults and £4.50 to £5 for children 16 and under, but they only include entry to colleges that don't charge admission fees; you can arrange a private tour (from £89)

of other colleges such as Christ Church with the tourist center, but you must pay extra for college entry. The Tourist Information Centre also offers a long list of excellent **theme tours,** everything from "Magic, Murder & Mayhem" and "Pottering in Harry's Footsteps" to "Jewish Heritage" and "Stained Glass." Our favorites include the 2-hour **"Inspector Morse Tour"** (Sat and Mon at 1:30pm, Mar–Sept; £8), where enthusiastic guides enliven a tour of all the locations associated with the city's celebrated TV detective (and his local pubs), created by Oxford author Colin Dexter.

For something spooky, try **Bill Spectre's Oxford Ghost Trails** (✆ **07941/ 041811; www.ghosttrail.org**), on Friday and Saturday at 6:30pm. Dressed as a Victorian undertaker, Bill illustrates his ghoulish walks with props and tricks, taking in all the most famous and gruesome Oxford ghost stories. He charges £7 for adults and £4 for children.

Alternatively, contact Felicity Tholstrup at **Hidden Oxford** (✆ **01865/ 512650; www.hiddenoxford.co.uk**), who specializes in critically acclaimed tailormade tours of the city. Finally, **Oxford River Cruises** (✆ **0845/2269396; www. oxfordrivercruises.com**) runs several boat tours along the River Thames, from the tranquil 1-hour "River Experience" (Apr–Oct; £9 adults, £6 children 15 and under) to a sunset picnic cruise (May–Sept) for £45 adults and £30 children.

5

THE THAMES VALLEY & THE CHILTERNS

Oxford

there is no campus as such and no central university building. Rarely will you see signs for "Oxford University." Students apply to specific colleges within the university umbrella, and apart from a handful of lectures (and final exams), it is the colleges that organize tuition and most activities; the majority of students experience sports, social events, and clubs at a college level and mixing between colleges is rare.

Touring every college would be a formidable task, so it's best to focus on just a handful of the most intriguing and famous ones described below. Note that most of the free colleges are open only in the afternoon. Whichever college you visit, be prepared to share the hallowed lawns and lanes with crowds of tourists. You may also be surprised by the neverending stream of polluting buses and fast-flowing pedestrian traffic in central Oxford.

The Ashmolean ★★ MUSEUM   This oft-overlooked history museum contains some real gems, not least the **Alfred Jewel,** a rare Anglo-Saxon gold ornament, dating from the late 9th century, adorned with the words "Alfred ordered me made" (in Old English). There's also some high-quality paintings from the Italian Renaissance (Raphael and Michelangelo among them), a large ancient-Egypt section, and some rare Asian ceramics and sculptures. An extensive renovation was completed in 2009, providing five floors and 39 new galleries. The museum was formally created in 1908, but traces its roots back to a collection that was started in the 1620s. The rooftop restaurant, the Ashmolean Dining Room, is a great place for a bite after a visit.

Beaumont St. at St. Giles. ✆ **01865/278002.** www.ashmolean.org. Free admission. Tues–Sun 10am–6pm. Closed Dec 24–26.

Bodleian Library ★★ LIBRARY   This famed library was established in 1602, initially funded by Sir Thomas Bodley, and today is a complex of several buildings in the heart of Oxford. Over the years, it has expanded from the Old Library on Catte Street and now includes the iconic Radcliffe Camera next door. The Bodleian is home to an astonishing 50,000 manuscripts and more than 11 million books (including a rare Gutenberg Bible). You can enter the Exhibition Room and wander the quadrangles of these handsome structures for free, but to get a better understanding of their history take a tour of the interior. Standard tours (1 hr.) start with the University's oldest teaching and examination room, the Divinity School (completed in 1488), and include Duke Humfrey's medieval library. Purchase tickets in the lodge on the right-hand side of the Great Gate on Catte Street. The highly recommended extended tours also include the Old Library and Radcliffe Camera (90 min.). These tours normally run every Sunday at 11:15am and 1:15pm, most Saturdays at 10am, and most Wednesdays at 9:30am.

Catte St. ✆ **01865/277182.** www.bodleian.ox.ac.uk. Admission £1 Divinity School only; £6.50 (standard tour) or £4.50 for mini-tour (30 min.); £13 (extended tour). Mon–Fri 9am–5pm; Sat 9am–4:30pm; Sun 11am–5pm. Closed Dec 24–Jan 3. Call to confirm specific tour times.

Carfax Tower ★ CHURCH   For a bird's-eye view of the city and colleges, climb the 99 steps up this 23-m (75-ft.) Gothic church tower in the center of town. This structure is distinguished by its clock and figures that strike on the quarter-hour. Carfax Tower is all that remains of St. Martin's Church, which stood on this site from 1032 until 1896, when most of it was demolished to accommodate a wider road. The tower used to be higher, but after 1340 it was lowered, following complaints from the university to Edward III that townspeople threw stones and fired arrows at students during town-and-gown disputes. Look for the church clock, adorned by two "quarter boys" who hit the bells at every quarter of the hour.

Carfax, Queen St., at the end of High St. ✆ **01865/790522.** www.citysightseeingoxford.com. Admission £2.20 adults, £1.10 children 15 and under. Children 4 and under are not admitted. Daily 10am–5:30pm. Closed Dec 24–Jan 1.

Christ Church ★★ CHURCH   Nothing quite matches the beauty and grandeur of Christ Church, one of the most prestigious and the largest of Oxford colleges. Christ Church has a well-deserved reputation for exclusivity, wealth, and power: It has produced 13 British prime ministers, including William Gladstone, with other alumni including John Locke, John Wesley, William Penn, W. H. Auden, and Lewis Carroll. Even today it's unofficially known by the rather supercilious nickname "the House"; the college chapel, which dates from the 12th century, also serves as Oxford

A Secret Home for Old Masters

Often overlooked by the average visitor is an unheralded little gem known as **Christ Church Picture Gallery** (ⓒ **01865/ 276172; www.chch.ox.ac.uk**), entered through the Canterbury Quad of Christ Church. (*Insider Tip:* To visit the gallery without paying for entrance to the rest of the college, enter through Canterbury Gate off Oriel Square, from King Edward St.) Here you'll come across a stunning collection of Old Masters, mainly from the Dutch, Flemish, and especially the Italian schools, including works by Michelangelo and Leonardo da Vinci. The gallery is open May through September, Monday to Saturday from 10:30am to 5pm, Sunday 2 to 5pm; October through April, Monday to Saturday from 10:30am to 1pm and daily 2 to 4:30pm. Admission is £3 for adults, £2 for students and seniors. If you've already paid to visit the college, you get a 50% discount.

Cathedral; and bowler-hatted "custodians" still patrol the pristine lawns. No surprise that Evelyn Waugh, in his novel *Brideshead Revisited,* had effete snob Sebastian Flyte attend Christ Church. More recently, many scenes from the *Harry Potter* films have been shot here, with the cloisters, quads, and staircases standing in for Hogwarts.

The college was established by Cardinal Wolsey as Cardinal College in 1525, and refounded as Christ Church by Henry VIII in 1546. It boasts the most distinctive main entrance in Oxford, Christopher Wren's **Tom Tower,** completed in 1682. The tower houses Great Tom, an 18,000-lb bell. It rings at 9:05pm nightly, which used to be closing time for all colleges (no longer—students have keys). The 101 times it peals originally signified the number of students in residence when the college was founded. Walk through the gate and you'll immediately face the largest quadrangle of any college in Oxford ("Tom Quad"), with a small ornamental pond and a statue of Mercury in the center. The two main highlights inside the college are the 16th-century Great Hall, where there are some portraits by Gainsborough and Reynolds, and the cathedral, with its delicate vaulting dating from the 15th century.

St. Aldates. ⓒ **01865/276150.** www.chch.ox.ac.uk. Admission £7.50 adults, £6 students, free for seniors, and children 17 and under. Mon–Sat 9am–5pm; Sun 1–5pm. Last admission 4:30pm. Closed Dec 25.

Magdalen College ★★ HISTORIC SITE   Pronounced *Maud*-lin, this is the most beautiful college in Oxford, thanks to its bucolic location on the banks of the River Cherwell and some dazzling Gothic architecture, notably the elegant Magdalen Tower. There's even a deer park in the grounds and tranquil Addison's Walk, a picturesque footpath along the river.

The college was founded in 1458 by William of Waynflete, bishop of Winchester and later chancellor of England. It's another influential college with an alumni ranging from Thomas Wolsey to Oscar Wilde; prominent ex-students in the current Conservative Party include William Hague and George Osborne.

Soaring above the tranquil Botanic Garden (the oldest in Britain), Magdalen Tower is the tallest building in Oxford (44m/144 ft.), completed in 1509 and where the choristers sing in Latin at dawn on May Day. You can also visit the 15th-century chapel, where the same choir sings Evensong Tuesday to Sunday at 6pm.

High St. ⓒ **01865/276000.** www.magd.ox.ac.uk. Admission £4.50 adults, £3.50 seniors and students, free for children 15 and under. July–Sept daily noon–7pm; Oct–June daily 1–6pm or dusk (whichever is earlier). Closed Dec 23–Jan 3.

5

THE THAMES VALLEY & THE CHILTERNS

Oxford

A Quiet Oasis

The oldest in Great Britain, the **Botanic Garden**, opposite Magdalen (📞 **01865/286690; www.botanic-garden.ox.ac.uk**), was first planted in 1621 on the site of a Jewish graveyard from the early Middle Ages. Bounded by a curve of the Cherwell, it still stands today and is the best place in Oxford to escape the tourist hordes. The Botanic Garden is open March through October, daily from 9am to 5pm (until 6pm May–Aug); November through February, daily from 9am to 4:30pm (last admission 45 min. before closing). Admission is £3.80 for adults, £3 for university students, and free for school-age children in full-time education.

Merton College ★ HISTORIC SITE   Founded in 1264, Merton College is among the three oldest colleges at the university (along with University College and Balliol), and the most academically successful college in the last 20 years. Merton's eclectic alumni list includes T. S Eliot, J. R. R. Tolkien, unlikely Rhodes Scholar Kris Kristofferson, and even Naruhito, Crown Prince of Japan. The college is especially noted for its library, built between 1371 and 1379, and said to be the oldest college library in England. Though a tradition once kept some of its most valuable books chained, now only one book is secured in that manner, to illustrate that historical custom. One of the library's treasures is an astrolabe (an astronomical instrument used for measuring the altitude of the sun and stars) thought to have belonged to Chaucer.

14 Merton St. 📞 **01865/276310.** www.merton.ox.ac.uk. Admission £2. Mon–Fri 2–4pm; Sat–Sun 10am–4pm. Closed for 1 week at Easter and Christmas.

Museum of Natural History & Pitt Rivers Museum ★ ☺ MUSEUM   These two enlightening museums lie a short walk northeast of the center, well off the beaten path for most tourists but worthy diversions. The Museum of Natural History houses the university's extensive collections of zoological, entomological, and geological specimens—everything from stuffed crocodiles and a giant open-jaw of a sperm whale to the fossil tooth of a prehistoric megalodon and tsetse fly collected by the explorer David Livingstone.

The Pitt Rivers Museum was founded in 1884 and displays over half a million archeological and ethnographic objects from all over the world. Highlights include a precious Tahitian mourner's costume, collected by Captain Cook in 1773–74, ghostly Japanese Noh masks, and thick Inuit fur coats. The Pitt Rivers' entrance is at the far wall of the Natural History Museum.

Parks Rd. and S Parks Rd. Museum of Natural History: 📞 **01865/272950.** www.oum.ox.ac.uk. Free admission. Daily 10am–5pm. Pitt Rivers Museum: 📞 **01865/270927.** www.prm.ox.ac.uk. Free admission. Mon noon–4:30pm, Tues–Sun 10am–4:30pm.

New College HISTORIC SITE   New College is another must-see, primarily for its exceptional architecture and spacious grounds; it's a favorite *Harry Potter* location and has seen Kate Beckinsale, Hugh Grant, Naomi Wolf, and even Louisiana Governor Bobby Jindal pass through its pristine grounds. The college was founded in 1379 by William of Wykeham, Bishop of Winchester, but the real masterpiece here is the chapel, with its handsome interior, stained glass (some designed by Joshua Reynolds), Jacob Epstein's remarkable modern sculpture of Lazarus, and a fine El Greco painting of St. James. Another treasure of the college is a crozier (pastoral staff of a bishop) belonging to the founding father. Don't miss the beautiful garden outside the college, where you can stroll among the remains of the old city wall.

Holywell St., at New College Lane. ✆ **01865/279500.** www.new.ox.ac.uk. Admission £2 adults, £1.50 seniors and students, free for children 16 and under Easter–Oct; free Nov–Easter. Easter–Oct daily 11am–5pm; Nov–Easter daily 2–4pm.

Sheldonian Theatre THEATRE This ravishing piece of Palladian architecture stands next to the Bodleian, completed in 1668 according to a design by Sir Christopher Wren. As well as admiring the immaculate interior and ceiling frescos, you can climb up to the cupola and enjoy fine views over Oxford. University ceremonies (including graduation) are regularly held here, but it also hosts a varied program of classical recitals and concerts; contact the Oxford Playhouse (✆ 01865/305305; www.oxfordplayhouse.com) for tickets.

Broad St. ✆ **01865/277299.** www.ox.ac.uk/sheldonian. Admission £2.50. Mar–Oct Mon–Sat 10am–12:30pm and 2–4:30pm; Nov–Feb Mon–Sat 10am–12:30pm and 2–3:30pm. Closed when used for events.

University College & Shelley Memorial ★ HISTORIC SITE This modest and forward-looking college is one of the oldest in the university, founded in the 1240s by William of Durham. It's best known for the monument to Romantic poet Percy Bysshe Shelley, who came here in 1810 but was expelled the following year (for writing a pamphlet, *The Necessity of Atheism*). The memorial, solemnly displayed in a special hall, is an elegant white-marble sculpture of a reclining nude and a drowned Shelley, as he washed up on the shore at Viareggio in Italy. Less romantic but equally influential alumni include Bill Clinton and Stephen Hawking.

High St. ✆ **01865/276602.** www.univ.ox.ac.uk. Free admission. Daily 9am–4pm; ask first at the porter's lodge at the entrance about visiting the Shelley Memorial (small groups only).

Where to Eat
VERY EXPENSIVE

Le Manoir aux Quat' Saisons ★★★ CONTEMPORARY FRENCH This elegant showcase for celebrity Gallic owner and chef Raymond Blanc offers the finest cuisine in the region. Some 12 miles southeast of Oxford, the gray-and-honey-colored stone manor house, originally built by a Norman nobleman in the early 1300s, provides a wonderful backdrop to Blanc's seasonal menu. (He's known for using local and sustainable produce.) Perennial favorites include the smoked haddock soup with sea bass tartare and caviar as a starter, as well as the slow-roasted aromatic Cornish turbot and utterly irresistible raspberry soufflé. Everything is artfully prepared and presented.

 Punting the River Cherwell

Punting on the River Cherwell is an essential, if slightly eccentric, Oxford pastime. At the **Cherwell Boathouse,** Bardwell Road (✆ 01865/515978; www.cherwellboathouse.co.uk), you can rent a punt (a flat-bottomed boat maneuvered by a long pole and a small oar) for the hourly rate of £14 (weekdays) or £16 (weekends), plus a £70 to £80 deposit. **Magdalen Bridge Boathouse,** the Old Horse Ford, High Street (✆ 01865/202643; www.oxfordpunting.co.uk), has an hourly charge of £16 (weekdays) or £20 (weekends). Punts are available from mid-March to mid-October, daily from 10am until dusk.

Church Rd., Great Milton. ℭ **800/237-1236** in the U.S., or 01844/278881. Fax 01844/278847. www.
manoir.com. Reservations required. Main courses £41 lunch or dinner; lunch *menu du jour* £63; 5-course
lunch or dinner £110; dinner or Sat–Sun lunch *menu découverte* £135. AE, DC, MC, V. Daily noon–2:30pm
and 7–10pm. Take exit 7 off M40 and head along the A329 toward Wallingford; after about 1 mile, look
for signs for Great American Milton Manor.

EXPENSIVE

Cherwell Boathouse Restaurant ★ FRENCH/CONTEMPORARY ENGLISH

This Oxford landmark on the River Cherwell has an intriguing menu that changes every
2 weeks, to take advantage of the freshest vegetables, fish, and meat. The success of
the main dishes is founded on savory treats such as pork belly with a foie gras terrine,
crispy pork cutlets with a Provençal sauce, and confit of duck in a port sauce. Save
room for the traditional English puddings, which are justly celebrated.

Bardwell Rd. ℭ **01865/552746.** www.cherwellboathouse.co.uk. Reservations recommended. Main
courses £15–£22; fixed-price dinner from £21; Mon–Fri set lunch £19. AE, MC, V. Daily noon–2:30pm and
6–9:30pm. Closed Dec 24–30. Bus: Banbury Rd.

Fishers SEAFOOD   Oxford's best seafood restaurant. Predictably, the interior is
decorated with a nautical theme, with porthole windows and red sails fluttering in the
breeze. The fish always tastes remarkably fresh, and the long list of starters includes
everything from beer-battered tiger prawns to deep-fried whitebait. Irish rock oysters
are served over crushed ice, and you can also order sensational hot and cold shellfish
platters. Canadian lobster is flown in, but the traditional favorite of students is haddock and chips. Black mussels from the Scottish Highlands, succulent turbot from
Wales, and red mullet caught by Cornish fishermen round out the menu. The light
set lunch is a bargain at just £5.

36-37 St. Clement's St. ℭ **01865/242003.** www.fishers-restaurant.com. Reservations required. Main
courses £9.95–£23; light set lunch £5 (2 courses). MC, V. Mon–Sat noon–2:30pm and 6–10:30pm; Sun
12:30–3pm and 6–10pm.

MODERATE

Brasserie Blanc ★ BRASSERIE   Master restaurateur Raymond Blanc took a former piano shop and converted it into this stylish eatery. The menu is a tribute to the
food his mother once cooked him in Besançon, France. The informal brasserie, with its
striking modern interior, offers a taste of this famous chef's creations without the high
prices of the swanky Le Manoir aux Quat' Saisons (see above). Options are more
straightforward here, featuring highly praised dishes such as slow-cooked beef and
onions with a parsnip purée or gnocchi with braised chestnuts and Roquefort sauce.

71-72 Walton St. ℭ **01865/510999.** www.brasserieblanc.com. Reservations recommended. Main courses
£8.25–£16. AE, MC, V. Mon–Fri noon–2:45pm and 5:30–10pm; Sat noon–10:30pm; Sun noon–9pm.

Gee's Restaurant ★ CONTEMPORARY ENGLISH   This restaurant, in a spacious Victorian glass conservatory dating from 1898, was converted from what was once
the leading florist of Oxford. Its original features were retained by the owners, who have
turned it into one of the most nostalgic and delightful establishments in the city. Classic English dishes are likely to include confit of pig cheeks with dandelion, exquisite
pheasant and ham terrine, and roast partridge with bread sauce and game chips. Finish
with a British classic: steamed treacle (sugar syrup) sponge pudding. It's worth staying
for the live jazz every Sunday evening (8–9:45pm), even if you're just having drinks.

61 Banbury Rd. ℭ **01865/553540.** www.gees-restaurant.co.uk. Reservations recommended. Main courses
£14–£23; fixed-price 2-course menu £24, fixed-price 3-course menu £27; set lunch and pre-theatre menu
£14–£17. AE, MC, V. Mon–Sat noon–2:30pm, Sun noon–3:30pm; daily 6–10:30pm. Bus: Banbury Rd.

Prices tend to be high at Oxford restaurants, but there are a few bargains to be had in the **Covered Market** (between the High Street and Cornmarket; www.oxford-covered-market.co.uk). Outpost of Bristol's gourmet pie company, **Pieminister** (*©* 01865/241613; www.pieminister.co.uk) sells savory meat pies from £5. The original **Ben's Cookies** (*©* 01865/247407; www.benscookies.com) bakes up delicious cookies for around £1.20, and **Fasta Pasta** (*©* 01865/241973) is a great place to pick up sandwiches that start at £2. You can get fine British and European cheeses at the **Oxford Cheese Shop** (*©* 01865/721420; www.oxfordfinefood.com) or home-baked breads and cakes from **Nash's Bakery** (*©* 01865/242695), which was established in nearby Bicester in 1930. And there's always **Brown's** (see below) for a hearty English fry-up.

INEXPENSIVE

Al-Shami LEBANESE   Bearing the archaic name for the city of Damascus, this enticing Lebanese restaurant knocks out superb Middle Eastern cuisine. Many diners don't go beyond the appetizers, which include more than 40 delectable hot and cold *meze*—everything from falafel and hummus to Armenian sausages and fried chicken livers. They may be described as "small dishes," but six-to-eight plates between two diners makes for a filling meal. Chargrilled chopped lamb, chicken, or fish constitute most of the main-dish selections. Desserts are chosen from the cart, and vegetarian meals are also available.

25 Walton Crescent. *©* **01865/310066.** www.al-shami.co.uk. Reservations recommended. Main courses £5.75–£12. MC, V. Cover charge £1 per person, plus 10% service charge. Daily noon–midnight.

Branca ★ ITALIAN   This quality Italian bistro in the trendy enclave of Jericho, a short stroll north of the center, cooks up perfectly seasoned fish and al dente pasta, and a decent house Chianti is offered as well. The seafood risottos are a light and creamy delight, topped with just enough chopped parsley and lemon zest, but don't ignore the main dishes. Pork is masterfully done here: The pan-fried pork cutlet with Parmesan herb breadcrumbs and tomato-chili salsa is exceptional. Meat and vegetables are sourced locally.

111 Walton St. *©* **01865/556111.** www.branca-restaurants.com. Reservations recommended. Main courses £9.95–£16, pasta from £6.75, pizza from £8.45. MC, V. Daily noon–11pm.

Brown's (Covered Market) ★★ TRADITIONAL ENGLISH   Don't confuse this no-frills diner, deep inside the Covered Market, with the posh (and overrated) *Brown's* on Woodstock Road. If you're curious about traditional Brit cafes, or just crave a "greasy spoon," you're in for a treat. Think sausage sandwiches, proper fish and chips, hearty fry-ups (fried bacon, mushrooms, eggs, and toast), apple pie and custard, and mugs of tea guaranteed to cure the deepest hangovers. They even have cereals if you're feeling guilty. Customers range from Oxford professors to locals on their lunch break.

Ave. 4, Covered Market (Market St. entrance). *©* **01865/243436.** Main courses £3.50–£8. No credit cards. Mon–Sat 8:30am–5:30pm.

Edamamé JAPANESE   Oxford's best Asian restaurant serves authentic Japanese home-cooked food at reasonable prices. The *ramen* (noodles) in particular attract a steady stream of local foodies and Japanese expats. Lunch offers are an especially good deal, with breaded pork cutlet with rice and miso soup costing under £10. Thursday is sushi night; expect a long wait at this and other peak times (weekend evenings).

15 Holywell St. (opposite New College) Ⓒ **01865/246916.** www.edamame.co.uk. Reservations not accepted. Main courses £6–£8; sushi sets from £8. MC, V. Wed 11:30am–2:30pm; Thurs–Sat 11:30am–2:30pm and 5–8:30pm; Sun noon–3:30pm.

George & Davis DESSERT/CAFE   This is Oxford's ice-cream headquarters, a brightly painted cafe serving artisanal homemade ice cream, as well as decent bagels, with plenty of *schmears* (cream cheese spreads), cookies, ethically sourced coffees and teas, and scrumptious cakes. Expect indulgent flavors such as Dime bar crunch, super chocolate, and golden secret (honeycomb and chocolate in a cream base), topped with gummy bears, M&Ms, nuts, or chocolate sprinkles.

55 Little Clarendon St. Ⓒ **01865/516652.** www.gdcafe.com. One ice-cream scoop £2.05, bagels from £2.60. MC, V. Daily 8am–midnight.

Manos ★★ GREEK   Even Greek expats end up at this cozy *taverna*, a sunny place with great food enhanced by traditional Greek folk songs wafting through the air. Portions are big, and salads are heavy on the feta cheese, which is always a good sign; the indomitable Manos himself cooks up a wicked chicken souvlaki (flatbread filled with marinated grilled chicken or falafel, hummus, tzatziki, and salad), and a mouthwatering moussaka.

105 Walton St. Ⓒ **01865/311782.** www.manosfoodbar.com. Reservations recommended. Main courses £5.95–£7.95. MC, V. Mon–Wed 9am–9pm; Thurs–Sat 9am–10pm; Sun 11:30am–8pm.

Mission Mexican Grill ★ MEXICAN   This place isn't quite on the level of the *taquerías* in San Francisco's Mission District (this is England after all), but it's a worthy tribute to Cal-Mex food nonetheless. The burritos here—a specialty—are some of the best on the island, with high-quality and flavorful meat, beans, sour cream, and flour tortillas. The *carnitas* burrito (pork roasted slowly with herbs and orange zest) is spot on, and makes a tasty meal. The veggie options are also good (it's hard to beat grilled vegetables, guacamole, and black beans).

8 St. Michael's St. Ⓒ **01865/202016.** www.missionburritos.co.uk. Burritos £5.45–£5.95. MC, V. Sun–Wed 11am–10pm; Thurs–Sat 11am–11pm. There's another location at 2 King Edward St. Ⓒ **01865/722020.**

Nosebag Restaurant CAFE/HEALTH FOOD   Yes, it sometimes is mobbed with tourists and students, but there's a good reason this is a long-standing local favorite. It's the most conveniently located cafe in town and serves solid homemade quiches, curries, casseroles, and lasagnas, all paired with a choice of three salads. Vegetarians are well catered for here (think sweet-pepper-and-lentil lasagna, and coconut root vegetable curry). The evening menu is a bit more expensive.

6–8 St. Michael's St. Ⓒ **01865/721033.** www.nosebagoxford.co.uk. Main courses £8.35–£11.50. MC, V. Mon–Thurs 9:30am–9:30pm; Fri–Sat 9:30am–10pm; Sun 9:30am–8:30pm.

Posh Fish! ★ FISH & CHIPS   It's worth taking a bus or taxi around 2 miles out of the center for this classic Brit treat to take-out or eat in (there's plenty of space). Huge portions of crispy battered haddock or plaice can be ordered with curry sauce, beans, mushy peas, and real, thick English chips. Aficionados can also enjoy battered sausage, kebabs, fish cakes, pies, and a full fry-up (any time of day). There are jacket potatoes for the (relatively) healthy.

150 London Rd., Headington. Ⓒ **01865/765894.** Main courses £3.50–£6. Daily 11:30am–midnight. Bus 8 or 9: Headington.

Vaults & Garden Café ★ CAFE/HEALTH FOOD   This cozy English cafe serves tasty soups in cups (try the leek and potato), artisan bread, and organic vegetables from nearby Worton Organic Garden. It's another of Oxford's good choices for vegetarians, with dishes such as roast-vegetable Spanish tortilla, roasted butternut squash, and tofu-and-brown-rice vegetable stir-fry gracing the menu, and organic beef lasagna for meat-eaters. All main courses are served with salad, brown rice, or potatoes. The cafe occupies a gorgeous 14th-century hall on the grounds of the University Church of St. Mary the Virgin.

University Church of St. Mary the Virgin, Radcliffe Square. (℗ **01865/279112.** www.vaultsandgarden.com. Main courses £6–£8. MC, V. Mon–Thurs 9:30am–9:30pm; Fri–Sat 9:30am–10pm; Sun 9:30am–8:30pm.

Shopping

Golden Cross, an arcade of first-class shops and boutiques, lies between Cornmarket Street and the Covered Market. Parts of the colorful gallery date from the 12th century; many buildings remain from the medieval era, along with some 15th- and 17th-century structures. The market has a reputation as the Covent Garden of Oxford, with live entertainment on Saturday mornings in summer. In the arcade shops is a diverse selection of merchandise, including handmade Belgian chocolates, clothing for women and men, and luxury leather goods.

Alice's Shop, 83 St. Aldate's (℗ **01865/723793;** www.aliceinwonderlandshop. co.uk), is set within a 15th-century building that has housed some kind of shop since 1820, mostly a general store (selling brooms, hardware, and the like). Alice Liddell, thought to have been the model for *Alice in Wonderland,* used to buy her barley sugar sweets here when Lewis Carroll was a professor of mathematics at Christ Church. Today, the place is a favorite stopover of Lewis Carroll fans from as far off as Japan, who gobble up commemorative pencils, chess sets, bookmarks, and, in rare cases, original editions of some of Carroll's works. Open daily 10:30am to 5pm (July–Aug 9:30am–6:30pm).

The **Bodleian Library Shop,** Old School's Quadrangle, Radcliffe Square, Broad Street (℗ **01865/277091;** www.shop.bodley.ox.ac.uk), specializes in Oxford souvenirs, from books and paperweights to Oxford banners and coffee mugs. It's open Monday to Friday 9am to 5pm, Saturday 9am to 4:30pm, and Sunday 11am to 5pm.

Castell & Son (The Varsity Shop), 13 Broad St. (℗ **01865/244000;** www. varsityshop.co.uk), is the best outlet in Oxford for clothing emblazoned with the Oxford logo or heraldic symbol. Choices include both whimsical and dead-on-serious neckties, hats, T-shirts, pens, beer and coffee mugs, and cufflinks. It's commercialized Oxford, but has got a sense of relative dignity and style. It's open Monday to Saturday 9am to 5:30pm, and Sunday 10am to 5pm. A second location is at 109–114 High Street (℗ **01865/249491**).

The best bookstore in Oxford is venerable **Blackwells,** at 48–51 Broad St. (℗ **01865/333536;** www.bookshop.blackwell.co.uk), open Monday to Saturday 9am to 6:30pm, Sunday 11am to 5pm.

Entertainment & Nightlife

Students tend to unwind in pubs, private college bars (which have "bops" or discos), and private student apartments in Oxford, so the nightlife can seem relatively tame to outsiders. There is, however, a steady supply of high-quality classical and choir music on offer, and a few places offer more energetic live music. In any case, the pubs are some of the most historic and atmospheric in the country (and London is only an hour away if you crave clubs).

THE PERFORMING ARTS

Highly acclaimed orchestras playing in truly lovely settings mark the **Music at Oxford** series (www.musicatoxford.com), based at the **Oxford Playhouse Theatre,** Beaumont Street (✆ **01865/244806;** www.oxfordplayhouse.com). The season runs from October to early July. Tickets range from £10 to £40. Many performances are held in the Sheldonian Theatre and Christ Church Cathedral, particularly attractive locations (p. 217 and p. 214). The box office is open Monday to Saturday from 9:30am to 6pm (or until half an hour after the start of an evening performance) and on Sunday starting at least 2 hours before a performance.

New Theatre (formerly the Apollo), George Street (✆ **01865/320760;** www. newtheatreoxford.org.uk; or Ticketmaster ✆ **0844/8471585;** www.ticketmaster. co.uk for tickets), is Oxford's primary theater. Tickets range from £10 to £50. A continuous run of comedy, ballet, drama, opera, and even rock contributes to the variety. Both the Welsh National Opera and the Glyndebourne Touring Opera appear here regularly. We highly recommend that you purchase tickets in advance, though some shows may have tickets available the week of the performance. The box office is open Monday to Saturday from 10am to 8pm (to 6pm if there is no evening performance).

THE PUB SCENE

Pubs lie at the heart of Oxford social life. Almost every pub in the center has a long (and notorious) history, usually linked to the university or a specific college (see "Pubs with a Pedigree", below).

At the **Eagle and Child,** 49 St. Giles St. (✆ **01865/302925**), literary history suffuses the dim, paneled alcoves and promotes a sedate atmosphere. In the 1930s and 1940s it was frequented by the "Inklings," a writer's group that included the likes of C. S. Lewis and J. R. R. Tolkien. In fact, *The Chronicles of Narnia* and *The Hobbit* were first read aloud at this pub. Known as the "Bird and Baby," this hallowed ground still welcomes the local dons (it's actually owned by St. John's College). It's a must-see for Tolkien fans; the rooms are daubed with extracts from his work (some original), but remember that you won't be the only tourist here, and it's otherwise a fairly quiet, ordinary pub. In contrast, the **Head of the River,** Abingdon Road at Folly Bridge, near the Westgate Centre Mall (✆ **01865/721600**), is a lively place offering traditional ales and lagers, along with good sturdy bar food. In summer, guests can sit by the river and rent a punt or a boat with an engine. The congenial **King's Arms,** 40 Holywell St. (✆ **01865/242369**), hosts a mix of students, tourists, and professors. One of the best places in town to strike up a conversation, the pub, owned by Young's Brewery, features several of the company's ales on tap, along with visiting lagers and bitters that change periodically. The tiny **White Horse ★**, 52 Broad St. (✆ **01865/ 204801,** www.whitehorseoxford.co.uk), squeezed between Blackwell's bookstores, is always a good place to soak up the collegiate atmosphere. It's one of Oxford's oldest pubs, dating from the 16th century, a popular feature in the *Inspector Morse* series and renowned for its real ales (try the Wychwood Hobgoblin). Most Oxford pubs open from around 11am to midnight.

THE CLUB & MUSIC SCENE

In the 1980s, **Freud Café,** 119 Walton St. (✆ **01865/311171;** www.freud.eu), turned an 18th-century Greek Revival church, stained-glass windows and all, into a

PUBS WITH A pedigree

Every college town the world over has a fair number of bars, but few can boast local watering holes with such atmosphere and history as Oxford.

A short block from the High, overlooking the north side of Christ Church, the **Bear Inn** ★, 6 Alfred Street (© **01865/ 728164**), is an Oxford landmark, built in the 13th century and mentioned time and again in English literature. The Bear brings together a wide variety of people in a relaxed way. You might talk with a rajah from India, a university don, or a titled gentleman who's the latest in a line of owners that goes back more than 700 years. Former owners of the Bear developed an astonishing habit: Clipping neckties. Around the lounge bar you'll see the remains of thousands of ties, which have been labeled with their owners' names.

Even older than the Bear is the **Turf Tavern** ★★, 7 Bath Place (off Holywell St.; © **01865/243235;** www.theturf tavern.co.uk), on a very narrow passageway near the Bodleian Library. The pub is reached via St. Helen's Passage, which stretches between Holywell Street and New College Lane. (You'll probably get lost, but any student worth his or her beer can direct you.) Thomas Hardy used the place as the setting for *Jude the Obscure*, and it was "the local" of the future U.S. president Bill Clinton during his student days at Oxford. In warm weather, you can choose a table in any of the three

separate gardens that radiate outward from the pub's central core. For wintertime warmth, braziers are lighted in the courtyard, and a potent mulled wine is served. The pub is owned by Suffolk's Greene King, which means meaty Abbot Ales, IPA, and Speckled Hen, as well as a range of wines.

Just outside town, hidden away some 2½ miles north of Oxford, the **Trout Inn** ★★★, 195 Godstow Rd., Wolvercote (© **01865/510930;** www. thetroutoxford.co.uk), is a private world where you can get ale and beer and excellent pub fare. Have your drink in one of the historic rooms, with their settles (wooden benches), brass, and old prints, or go outside in sunny weather to sit on a stone wall. On the grounds are peacocks, ducks, swans, and herons that live in and around the river and an adjacent weir pool; they'll join you if you're handing out crumbs. The Smoking Room, the original 12th-century part, complements the inn's relatively "new" 16th-century bars. Hot meals are served all day in the restaurant, with daily specials including salads in summer and grills in winter. On your way there and back, look for the view of Oxford from the bridge. To get here, take bus no. 6A, 6B, or 6C to Wolvercote, and then walk southwest along Godstow Road (toward Wytham) a half-mile. Hours are Monday to Saturday 11am to 11pm, Sunday 11am to 10:30pm.

bar, jazz and folk venue with an expansive array of cocktail choices (the food is rather mediocre). There is no cover. Hours are Sunday to Thursday 11am to midnight, Friday and Saturday 11am to 2am.

O2 Academy Oxford, 190 Cowley Rd. (© **0844/4772000;** www.o2academy oxford.co.uk), is the best live indie-music venue in the city; tickets range from £5 to £25 (cash only on the door). Shows usually start at 6pm Tuesday to Saturday, and also at 2:30pm on Saturday.

The **Jericho Tavern,** 56 Walton St. (© **01865/311775;** tickets at www.wegot tickets.com), comprises two levels. Downstairs, patrons consume the suds inside, where there's a modern decor, or outside in the beer garden. Upstairs is another area for drinking. Live music (mostly alternative rock or folk) is featured Friday and Saturday, when a £5 to £9 cover is charged. Open Monday through Friday noon to midnight, Saturday and Sunday 10am to midnight.

Thirst, 7–8 Park End St. (✆ **01865/242044;** www.thirstbar.com), is a popular student hangout with a lounge bar and a small garden. Resident DJs rule the night. Open Friday through Wednesday 6:30pm to 2am, Thursday 8pm to 2am.

Where to Stay
EXPENSIVE

Macdonald Randolph Hotel ★   Open since 1864, the venerable Randolph is an Oxford landmark with elegant guest rooms furnished in a conservative English style. Fans of Inspector Morse should check out the Morse Bar (the hotel makes a lot of the associations), while the lounges, though modernized, are cavernous enough for dozens of separate and intimate conversational groupings. Some rooms are quite large; others are a bit cramped, and overall the hotel is a little overpriced: You are paying primarily for the location and the rich history.

Beaumont St., Oxford OX1 2LN. www.macdonaldhotels.co.uk/Randolph. ✆ **0844/879-9132.** Fax: 01865/791678. 151 units. £230–£280 double; £528–£607 suite. AE, DC, MC, V. Limited parking £27 or public parking £30 for 24 hr. **Amenities:** Restaurant; 2 bars; babysitting; concierge; room service; spa. *In room:* TV, CD player, hair dryer, Wi-Fi (£9.99 per day).

Malmaison Oxford Castle ★★ 🛏   This place was formerly for inmates detained at Her Majesty's pleasure, and many aspects of prison life, including barred windows, have been retained. Guest rooms, in a converted Victorian building, are actually remodeled "cells" that flank two sides of a large central atrium, a space that rises three stories and is crisscrossed by narrow walkways. The former inmates never had it so good—great beds, mood lighting, power showers, satellite TV, and serious wines. In spite of its origins, this is a stylish and comfortable place to stay.

3 Oxford Castle, Oxford OX1 1AY. www.malmaison.com. ✆ **01865/268400.** 94 units. £185–£245 double; £275–£345 suite. AE, DC, MC, V. Parking (pre-booking required) £20. **Amenities:** Restaurant; bar; exercise room; room service. *In room:* TV/DVD, CD player, minibar, Wi-Fi (free).

Old Bank Hotel ★★   The first hotel created in the center of Oxford in 135 years, the Old Bank opened in 1999 and immediately surpassed the traditional favorite, the Randolph (see above), in both style and amenities. Located on Oxford's main street and surrounded by some of its oldest colleges and sights, the building dates back to the 18th century and was indeed once a bank. The hotel currently features a collection of 20th-century British art handpicked by the owners. Bedrooms are comfortably and elegantly appointed, many opening onto views. A combination of velvet and shantung silk-trimmed linen bedcovers gives the guest rooms added style.

92-94 High St., Oxford OX1 4BN. www.oldbank-hotel.co.uk. ✆ **01865/799599.** Fax 01865/799598. 42 units. £230–£350 double. AE, DC, MC, V. Free parking. Bus: 7. **Amenities:** Restaurant; bar; babysitting; room service. *In room:* A/C, TV, CD player, hair dryer, Internet (free).

Old Parsonage Hotel ★★   This extensively renovated hotel, near St. Giles Church and Keble College, looks like an extension of one of the ancient colleges. Originally a 13th-century hospital, it was restored in the 1660s. In 1991, it was completely renovated and made into a first-rate hotel. This intimate old property is filled with hidden charms, such as tiny gardens in the courtyard and on the roof terrace. In this tranquil area of Oxford, you'll feel like you're living at one of the colleges yourself. The rooms are individually designed but not large; each opens onto the private gardens.

1 Banbury Rd., Oxford OX2 6NN. www.oldparsonage-hotel.co.uk. ℂ **01865/310210.** Fax 01865/311262. 30 units. £131–£152 double. AE, DC, MC, V. Free parking. **Amenities:** Restaurant; bar; room service. *In room:* A/C, TV, hair dryer, Internet (free).

MODERATE

Bath Place Hotel ★ 🏨 The Bath Place Hotel comprises 17th-century weavers' cottages converted into a small inn of charm and grace, one of the "secret addresses" of Oxford. It lies on a cobbled alleyway off Holywell Street in the center of Oxford, between New College and Hertford College. Flemish weavers built the cottages around a tiny flagstone courtyard. Completely refurbished to a high standard, the inn today offers comfortable and well-appointed bedrooms.

4–5 Bath Place, Oxford OX1 3SU. www.bathplace.co.uk. ℂ **01865/791812.** 15 units. £110–£140 double; £115–£140 family room. Rates include continental buffet or room-service breakfast. DC, MC, V. Parking £10; free parking 6 min. walk from hotel. **Amenities:** Bar and lounge; room service. *In room:* TV, minibar, Wi-Fi (free).

Burlington House Hotel ★★ 🍴 This top choice on the edge of town makes up for the slightly inconvenient location with fabulous service, bargain prices, and immaculate, boutique-like rooms. Inside, old fittings and fireplaces blend with modern beds and flat-screen TVs; the power showers are especially welcome. Breakfasts are another highlight, with high-quality continental and hot items to try (marmalade omelet anyone?). The hotel sits on Banbury Road near a bus stop with frequent buses into the center (10- or 20-min. walk), and there are plenty of bars and restaurants nearby, too.

374 Banbury Rd., Oxford OX2 7PP. www.burlington-hotel-oxford.co.uk. ℂ **01865/513513.** 12 units. £84–£160 double. AE, DC, MC, V. Rates include breakfast. Free parking (weekends only). Bus: 2 or 7. **Amenities:** Lounge; dining room. *In room:* A/C, TV, hair dryer, Wi-Fi (free).

INEXPENSIVE

Oxford Backpackers 🍴 Oxford has three dorm-style hostels, and this one just about tops the others, though they all offer a fairly typical backpacker experience: Lots of young people, basic bathrooms (with hot showers), lockers, aging bunks and mattresses, and noise from the nearby clubs (especially weekends). Breakfast is basic but filling, with plenty of coffee, juice, bread, and spreads. And the location is handy, between the bus and the train station. Note that guests must be 18 or older to stay here.

9a Hythe Bridge St., Oxford OX1 2EW. www.hostels.co.uk. ℂ **01865/721761.** 68 beds (7 dorms). £12–£19 dorm beds. MC, V. Rates include continental breakfast. Reception open daily 8–10am and 5–7pm. **Amenities:** Bar with satellite TV, pool table, Internet (£1 for 30 min.); Wi-Fi (free).

Sandfield Guest House ★ Just off the main road to the M40 and London (A420) in the student suburb of Headington, friendly hosts Paul and Natália Anderson have created a welcoming B&B. It's 10 minutes by bus from central Oxford. Rooms are well equipped and very comfy—everything is new and spotlessly clean. (Room no. 3 has a slightly larger bathroom.) The full, cooked English breakfasts are high quality, very filling, and accompanied by yogurt, cereal, and fresh fruit. Headington is a pleasant neighborhood in its own right, with shops and a few restaurants within walking distance.

19 London Rd., Headington, Oxford OX3 7RE. www.sandfieldguesthouse.net76.net. ℂ **01865/767767.** 4 units. £80–£100 double; £45 single. Rates include English breakfast. MC, V. Free parking. Bus: U1. *In room:* TV, hair dryer, Wi-Fi (free).

Tilbury Lodge ★★ 🏚 This unassuming red-brick home on the outskirts holds one of Oxford's secret gems, a B&B with fresh, modern decor, new bathrooms, and spacious rooms. It's the extras that make this special: Bathrobes, foot-massage machines, and a bevy of sweet treats baked by the affable owners, Stephan and Melanie. Expect homemade fudge, cookies, tea and coffee, and warm scones on arrival. The breakfasts are hard to beat, a wonderful spread of fresh fruits, yogurts, homemade breads, muffins, and tasty cooked plates. The city center is just 10 minutes by bus (the bus stop is on the corner).

5 Tilbury Lane, Oxford OX2 9NB. www.tilburylodge.com. ℂ **01865/862138.** 9 units. £85–£100 double. Rates include English breakfast. MC, V. Bus: 4C, S1. Free parking. **Amenities:** Conservatory lounge. *In room:* TV, CD player, hair dryer, Wi-Fi (free). From Oxford, take the A420 then Westway to Botley, turn right onto Eynsham Rd. (B4044) and look for Tilbury Lane (first right). Closed Dec–Jan.

Side Trips from Oxford
WOODSTOCK

The small country town of **Woodstock,** 8 miles northwest of Oxford, was the birthplace in 1330 of the Black Prince, ill-fated son of King Edward III. Today it's a picturesque collection of 18th-century stone houses and the gateway to **Blenheim Palace** (see below), home of the dukes of Marlborough since the early 1700s. There's little of interest in the town itself, though the **Oxfordshire Museum,** Fletcher's House, Park Street (ℂ **01993/811456;** www.tomocc.org.uk), is worth a quick look; it chronicles the history, culture, and crafts of Oxfordshire and has an attractive garden with a full-size replica of a megalosaurus—kids will love this. The museum is open Tuesday to Saturday 10am to 5pm and Sunday 2 to 5pm; admission is free.

Bus S3, operated by **Stagecoach** (ℂ **01865/772250;** www.stagecoachbus.com), leaves Oxford about every 10 to 15 minutes during the day. The trip to Woodstock takes a little more than 30 minutes. If you're driving, take the A44 from Oxford. The **Tourist Information Centre,** located inside the Oxfordshire Museum (ℂ **01993/ 813276;** www.oxfordshirecotswolds.org), is open Monday to Saturday 10am to 5pm year-round.

Blenheim Palace ★★★ HISTORIC SITE The extravagantly baroque Blenheim Palace is England's answer to Versailles. Blenheim is still the home of the Dukes of Marlborough, descendants of the first duke John Churchill, an on-again, off-again favorite of Queen Anne, and victor of the Battle of Blenheim (1704), a crushing defeat of Britain's archenemy Louis XIV. The lavish palace of Blenheim was built for him as a gift from the queen in the 1720s. The family, virtually bankrupt, hung on to the palace thanks to the brutally commercial marriage of Charles, 9th Duke of Marlborough (1871–1934) to Consuelo Vanderbilt, heiress to the wealthy American railroad dynasty. Blenheim was also the birthplace of the 9th duke's first cousin, Sir Winston Churchill. The room in which he was born in 1874 is included in the palace tour, as is the Churchill exhibition: four rooms of letters, books, photographs, and other relics.

The palace was designed by Sir John Vanbrugh, who was also the architect of Castle Howard; the landscaping was created by Capability Brown. The interior is loaded with riches: antiques, porcelain, oil paintings, tapestries, and chinoiserie. The present owner is the 11th Duke of Marlborough (b. 1926), whom you may see wandering around. The duke had a small cameo in Kenneth Branagh's movie *Hamlet* (1996), which was filmed at Blenheim.

Insider tip: **Marlborough Maze,** 540m (1,800 ft.) from the palace, is the largest symbolic hedge maze on earth, with an herb and lavender garden, a butterfly house,

The small village of Bladon, about 6½ miles northwest of Oxford and a short drive from Blenheim Palace, is the final resting place of Sir Winston Churchill. Following his state funeral in St. Paul's Cathedral, Churchill was buried in Bladon in January 1965. His relatively modest grave lies at the **Church of St. Martin,** a simple Gothic structure rebuilt in the 1890s. Churchill's white tomb also contains the remains of his wife, Clementine, who was buried here in 1977. Other members of the family are buried nearby, and there is a small exhibition of photos on Churchill and the funeral inside the church. To reach St. Martin's Church (© **01993/880546)** from Oxford, take the A44 toward Woodstock, and then go on the A4095 toward Whitney.

and inflatable castles for children. Also, be sure to look for the castle's gift shops, tucked away in an old palace dairy. Here you can purchase a wide range of souvenirs, handicrafts, and even locally made preserves.

Brighton Rd., Woodstock. © **08700/602080.** www.blenheimpalace.com. Admission £19 adults (parks and gardens £11), £15 students and seniors (parks and gardens £8), £11 children 5–15 (parks and gardens £5.50), and £50 family ticket (parks and gardens £28); free for children 4 and under. Daily 10:30am–5:30pm. Last admission 4:45pm. Closed mid-Dec–mid-Feb (except for park).

THE CHILTERNS

North of the Thames Valley, the Chiltern Hills form a rolling green barrier between Oxford and the outer suburbs of London. While the hills are not dramatic or especially big (the highest point is just 267m/876 ft. at Haddington Hill, near Wendover), it is a protected area harboring **pretty villages,** ancient **beech woodlands,** handsome **stately homes,** and **intriguing museums.** The hills are actually part of a chalk escarpment stretching some 50 miles from Goring-on-Thames in Oxfordshire, through Buckinghamshire, to Bedfordshire and the edge of East Anglia, but everything is an easy drive or bus ride from London or Oxford.

Essentials

GETTING THERE   To make the most out of this region, you'll need a car, though all the main towns are connected to London by frequent buses and trains. The Chilterns' largest towns are Aylesbury in the north and High Wycombe in the south. **Aylesbury** is 1 hour by train from London's Marylebone Station (£13), or 25 minutes off the M25 via the A41. Trains to High Wycombe (£11) from London Marylebone take just 30 minutes.

VISITOR INFORMATION   The **Aylesbury Tourist Information Centre,** Kings Head Passage, off Market Square (© **01296/330559;** www.visitbuckinghamshire. org), is open April through October, Monday to Saturday 9:30am to 5pm, and November through March, Monday to Saturday 10am to 4:30pm. The High Wycombe **Tourist Information Centre** (© **01494/421892;** www.visitbuckinghamshire.org) is located inside High Wycombe Library at the Eden Shopping Centre, 5 Eden Place (near the bus station). It's open Tuesday to Friday 9:30am to 5:30pm, Saturday 9:30am to 4pm. You should also check out www.chilternsaonb.org and www.chilternsociety.org.uk for more information.

Exploring the Area

AYLESBURY

The biggest town at the northern end of the Chilterns, Aylesbury has retained much of its 18th-century provincial charm and character, despite rapid expansion in recent years. The most historic streets surround **St. Mary's Church,** in the center, which dates from the 13th century and features an unusual spire from the reign of Charles II. The 15th-century **King's Head Public House** (℘ **01296/381501;** daily 11:30am–midnight), one of the few working pubs owned by the National Trust, at King's Head Passage, Market Square, has seen many famous faces in its time, including Henry VIII, who was a frequent guest while he was courting Anne Boleyn. The thriving town **market** is definitely worth a look, held on Wednesday, Friday, and Saturday (with a flea market on Tues). Aylesbury also hosts the **Roald Dahl Festival,** a procession of giant puppets based on the author's characters, every July 2. Dahl was a long-time resident of the Chiltern area (see "Great Missenden," below).

Buckinghamshire County Museum ☺ MUSEUM   This museum is located in two buildings, a house and a grammar school, both dating from the 18th century. The complex also includes the **Roald Dahl Children's Gallery,** where the author's children's books, especially *Charlie and the Chocolate Factory* and *James and the Giant Peach,* come to life as visitors ride in the Great Glass Elevator and crawl inside the Giant Peach. Even in the main museum, innovative displays, focusing on the cultural heritage of Buckinghamshire, are interactive and touchable. Entry to the Children's Gallery is through a timed ticket system; visits last an hour and entry is on the hour, but there are a limited number of tickets so booking ahead is advised.

Church St. ℘ **01296/331441.** www.buckscc.gov.uk/museum. Free admission to main museum. Children's Gallery £6 adults, £4 children 3–18, free for children 2 and under, family ticket £18. Mon–Sat 10am–5pm; call ahead to confirm times to Children's Gallery.

Tiggywinkles ★★ ☺ SANCTUARY   This earnest animal hospital and hedgehog center is guaranteed to get kids and animal lovers swooning with excitement. Tiggywinkles treats over 10,000 animal casualties every year (mostly from road accidents); be prepared to get weepy as baby deer limp around on crutches and tiny hedgehogs shuffle mournfully along trails of leaves. The visitor center uses interpretation boards and videos to describe the history of the hospital, the type of animals treated, and some of the techniques employed; in the spring and summer visitors can also see the nursery areas where the animals are treated.

Aston Rd., Haddenham. ℘ **01844/292292.** www.sttiggywinkles.org.uk. Admission £4.90 adults, £3.20 children 5–18, free for seniors, children 4 and under, £14 family ticket. Easter–Sept Mon–Sun 10am–4pm; Oct–Easter Mon–Fri 10am–4pm. Haddenham is 5 miles southwest of Aylesbury via the A418. Trains run about every half-hour to Haddenham from London Marylebone. Arriva bus no. 110 from Aylesbury gets you within walking distance.

Waddesdon Manor ★★ ARCHITECTURE   Built in the 1870s by Baron Ferdinand de Rothschild (who was a member of the Austrian branch of the Rothschild banking dynasty), this château-like monument to the Gilded Age features whimsical French neo-Renaissance architecture and a priceless collection of elegant French furniture, carpets, and Sèvres porcelain. The place is so ornate it doubled for Buckingham Palace in the movie *The Queen* (2006). Eighteenth-century artwork by several famous English painters (Gainsborough and Reynolds among them) is exhibited, and you can also view a writing desk owned by Marie-Antoinette. Don't miss the wine cellar, crammed with the finest bottles from Château Lafite Rothschild. An aviary in the surrounding gardens houses exotic birds. On the premises are a restaurant and a gift shop, both featuring a vast assortment of Rothschild wines.

High St. (A41), Waddesdon. ✆ **01296/653226.** www.waddesdon.org.uk. Admission to house and grounds £14–£15 adults, £10–£12 children 5–16, free for children 4 and under; grounds only £6–£7 adults, £3–£4 children 5–16, £15–£19 family ticket, free for children 4 and younger. House Apr–Oct Wed–Fri noon–4pm, Sat–Sun 11am–4pm, closed Nov–Mar; grounds and aviary Jan–mid-Mar Sat–Sun 10am–5pm, mid-Mar–Dec Wed–Sun 10am–5pm. Audio guide can be rented at the entrance for £2 (free for children). Waddesdon is 12 miles from Aylesbury via the A41. Take Arriva bus no. 16 or 17.

CHALFONT ST. GILES

Just 25 miles from London, perched on the eastern edge of the Chilterns, Chalfont St. Giles has been relatively successful in preserving its traditional center despite the rapid urbanization all around, with local shops, pubs, and cafes clustered around the rustic green and village pond. It's best known as the place where poet **John Milton** lived during the Great Plague in 1665. To reach the village, take the A355 north from the M40 (junction 2), until you come to the signposted turn for Chalfont St. Giles to the east. Carousel bus A30 runs to the village from Heathrow Airport and from Amersham (London Tube station).

Chiltern Open Air Museum ★ MUSEUM   This absorbing 18-hectare (45-acre) museum has been restoring aging Chiltern buildings and relocating them here since the 1970s, and now more than 30 are on view (you can go inside most of them). Among the rustic wooden barns and farm buildings are a reconstruction of an Iron Age round-house, a Victorian prefab chapel, an 1860 forge, and an 18th-century thatched barn converted into two simple cottages. In between is parkland grazed by sheep and rolling woods.

Newland Park, Gorelands Lane. ✆ **01494/872163.** www.coam.org.uk. Admission £8 adults, £5 children 5–16, £23 family ticket. Daily 10am–5pm. The museum is signposted from the A413 at Chalfont St. Giles. Walking from the village should take around 30 min.

John Milton's Cottage ★ HISTORIC HOME   John Milton finished off his epic poem *Paradise Lost* in this humble 16th-century cottage in 1665, during his refuge from the plague. It's the only one of his homes still standing, evocative of his generally frugal, hardworking life. The great poet had been working on the poem for 7 years and was already blind by the time he stayed here. Its four rooms contain many relics and exhibits devoted to Milton, including a precious collection of 17th-century first editions.

21 Deanway, at School Lane. ✆ **01494/872313.** www.miltonscottage.org. Admission £5 adults, £3 children 14 and under. Mar–Oct, Tues–Sun 10am–1pm and 2–6pm.

GREAT MISSENDEN

Tucked away in the heart of the Chilterns, the large village of Great Missenden is best known for the former **home of Roald Dahl,** the internationally famous children's author. Though the village center retains some Victorian row (terraced) houses, it's not especially attractive and it is the Dahl connection that provides the real allure. His home, **Gipsy House** (on Whitefield Lane, just outside the village), is still privately owned by his widow, Felicity, but you can visit the garden on select open days throughout the year (entry £4). See www.ngs.org.uk for details. You can also view Dahl's simple tomb at St. Peter and St. Paul's Church (often strewn with toys and flowers), and visit his excellent museum.

Roald Dahl Museum & Story Centre ★★ ☺ MUSEUM   This fabulous tribute to Roald Dahl chronicles the life of the beloved author and includes a replica of the hut where he created his most popular characters. Kids will love the hands-on **Story**

The **Ridgeway National Trail** (www.nationaltrail.co.uk) links the downs of Wiltshire with the Chilterns via a well-marked and wonderfully scenic 87-mile path from Overton Hill, near Avebury (p. 333) to Ivinghoe Beacon in Buckinghamshire. The path follows an ancient track used since prehistoric times, and is by far the most enticing way to experience the woods and lanes of the Chilterns. You'll probably take 6 full days to walk the whole thing, an average of 14 miles a day. The trail website has lodging and transport details, as well as specialist tour companies that can arrange the whole trip. There's also the **Chiltern Way,** a circular trail of around 125 miles; see www.chilternsociety.org.uk for more information.

The **Chilterns Cycleway** is a 170-mile cycle loop through the Chilterns, taking in the best of its scenery and villages. The route is mainly on-road and is signposted throughout. You'll find several bike-rental shops along the way, including Dees Cycles at 39 Hill Ave., Amersham (✆ **01494/727165**), and Henley Cycles at 69 Reading Rd., Henley-on-Thames (✆ **01491/578984**).

5

Centre, which allows fans to dress up as Dahl characters, make up stories and poems, or get creative in the craft room. The on-site **Café Twit** serves Puro fair-trade coffee, organic juices, Bogtrotter chocolate cake, giant cookies, and sweet chili jam.

81-83 High St. ✆ **01494/8921922.** www.roalddahlmuseum.org. Admission £6 adults, £4 children 5–18, £19 family tickets. Tues–Fri 10am–5pm, Sat and Sun 11am–5pm. Closed Dec 24–25. Great Missenden is 40 min. by train from London Marylebone; the museum is a 5-min. walk from the station. Driving from London, take the A413; from High Wycombe it's a short ride along the A4128.

HIGH WYCOMBE

High Wycombe, 30 miles west of London, mostly serves as a commuter suburb of the capital today, and there's little to see in the center. Focus instead on the far more appealing village of West Wycombe, and the great stately home on the outskirts, Hughenden. **Turville,** 5 miles west of High Wycombe, is as gorgeous a traditional English village you're likely to find, serving as a backdrop for the British hit TV series *The Vicar of Dibley.*

Hughenden Manor ★★ HISTORIC HOME   This handsome red-brick Victorian mansion gives insight into the remarkable Benjamin Disraeli, one of the most enigmatic figures of 19th-century England and still the only prime minister of Britain to hail from a Jewish family. He wrote several popular political novels (including *Sybil*) and served briefly as prime minister in 1868, but his fame rests on his stewardship as Conservative prime minister from 1874 to 1880. He fashioned a close working relationship with Queen Victoria (who made him Earl of Beaconsfield in 1876), and engineered the British purchase of shares in the Suez Canal. He died in 1881 and was buried in the graveyard of Hughenden Church.

Disraeli acquired Hughenden Manor in 1848, a country house that befitted his fast-rising political and social position. Today, it contains an odd assortment of memorabilia, including a lock of Disraeli's hair, letters from Victoria, and a portrait of Lord Byron.

High Wycombe. ✆ **01494/755565.** www.nationaltrust.org.uk. Admission £7.25 adults, £3.70 children 5–15, free for children 4 and under, £18 family ticket; garden only £2.90 adults, £2 children. Mar–Oct daily noon–5pm; Nov, Dec, and Feb daily 11am–3pm. The manor is 1½ miles north of High Wycombe on the A4128. From High Wycombe, take Arriva bus 300 (High Wycombe–Aylesbury).

WEST WYCOMBE ★

The ravishing village of West Wycombe is one of the most atmospheric in the Chilterns, with rows of neat Georgian and Victorian cottages enhanced by the **Church of St. Lawrence,** perched on West Wycombe Hill and topped by a huge golden ball. Parts of the church date from the 13th century; its interior was copied from a 3rd-century Syrian sun temple. The view from the hill is worth the trek up alone. Near the church stands the **Dashwood Mausoleum,** built in 1765 in a style derived from Constantine's Arch in Rome, but the main attraction here is **West Wycombe Park** (see below for admission information), seat of the Dashwood family. Now owned by the National Trust, the mansion is one of the best examples of Palladian-style architecture in England thanks to infamous libertine Sir Francis Dashwood who began to overhaul the property in exuberant Italianate style in the 1740s. The interior is lavishly decorated with paintings and antiques from the 18th century, with ceiling frescos copied from Italian *palazzi*. The rococo-style gardens are also well worth exploring, littered with ornamental buildings and statuary.

Sir Francis also commissioned the excavation of the **Hell-Fire Caves** (see below for admission information) on the estate to serve as a meeting place for the notorious **Hellfire Club,** which spent its time partying and drinking. The cave is about a half-mile long, filled with stalactites and stalagmites, and dotted with statues.

West Wycombe Park: High St. ✆ **01494/755571.** www.nationaltrust.org.uk. Admission £7.25 adults, £3.60 children 5–15, free for children 4 and under, £18 family ticket; grounds only £3.60 adults, £2.10 children. June–Aug Sun–Thurs 2–6pm; grounds only Apr–May Sun–Thurs 2–6pm. Located 2 miles west of High Wycombe at the west end of West Wycombe, south of A40; take Arriva bus 40 (from High Wycombe to Thame).

Hell-Fire Caves: Church Lane, West Wycombe. ✆ **01494/533739.** www.hellfirecaves.co.uk. Admission £5 adults, £4 seniors and children 3–16, £15 family ticket. Apr–Oct daily 11am–5:30pm; Nov–Mar 11am–dusk.

WOBURN

On the southern border of Bedfordshire, at the very northern edge of the Chilterns (some 44 miles north of London) lies the village of Woburn and its justly celebrated abbey (actually a mansion). The great 18th-century Georgian home has been the traditional seat of the dukes of Bedford for more than 3 centuries.

Woburn Abbey ★★★ ABBEY   You'll need the best part of a day to do this spectacular Georgian country house justice. The history of the abbey dates back to 1145, when it really was a religious house for Cistercian monks, but it did not become the family home of the Russell family until 1619 (William Russell became the first Duke of Bedford in 1694). Most of what you see today dates from building programs in the 1740s and 1802.

Its three floors are crammed with 18th-century French and English furniture, lavish silver and gold collections, and a wide range of porcelain. Paintings by Gainsborough, Reynolds, Van Dyck, and Canaletto are on display (including the latter's 21 views of Venice, in the dining room), while the Blue Drawing Room is supposedly where the tradition of afternoon tea was "invented" in 1840. Look out also for George Gower's *Armada Portrait* of Elizabeth I. Her hand rests on the globe, as Philip's invincible armada perishes in the background.

Today, Woburn Abbey is surrounded by a 1,214-hectare (3,000-acre) deer park, home to 10 species of deer, including native Red Deer and Fallow Deer, and the largest herd of Pere David Deer in the U.K.

Woburn Safari Park (£19 adults, £14 children 3–15, £60 family ticket) was added to the grounds in 1970, and today is a thriving business with a separate entrance. It boasts lions, tigers, giraffes, camels, monkeys, and other animals. Kids will enjoy this and it can be fun, but it's a little incongruous considering the surroundings; skip it unless you crave the novelty of seeing exotic animals in the English countryside.

Woburn Park, Bedfordshire, a half-mile southeast of the village of Woburn, 13 miles southwest of Bedford. ℭ **01525/290333.** www.woburn.co.uk/abbey. Admission £13 adults, £11 seniors, £6.25 children 3–15; park only £3 adults, £2 seniors, £1 children. House mid-Apr– Oct daily 11am–5pm (last entry 4pm); park daily 10am–4pm. If driving from London, take the M1 north to junction 12 or 13, where directions are signposted. House closed Nov–early Apr. There is no public transportation directly to Woburn Abbey, but the house is only a 15-minute taxi ride from Flitwick train station.

Where to Eat & Stay

The Black Horse ★ GASTROPUB   Our favorite pub in Woburn opened in 1824 as a coaching inn, and it retains a dark, woodsy interior evocative of that era. It sits behind a stucco-sheathed Georgian facade on the town's main street. Accompanying the ales and a simple but selective wine list are cold cuts and cheese, with main courses ranging from chargrilled steaks and sweet potato and roast vegetable croquettes, to Woburn venison hotpot and a hearty sausage and mash. Most ingredients are seasonal, and locally and ethically produced. Afternoon tea comes with fruit scones, clotted cream, and homemade jam. Suffolk's Greene King IPA and Abbot Ale are served on tap.

1 Bedford St., Woburn. ℭ **01525/290210.** www.blackhorsewoburn.co.uk. Main courses £11–£15. AE, MC, V. Daily 11am–midnight.

Bugle Horn PUB FARE   This traditional country pub serves great homemade food at reasonable prices. The Bugle began as a Georgian farmhouse, but became a wine store for Hartwell House (see below) in the early 1800s and a pub soon afterward. The menu features all the classics: Lancashire hotpot; chicken, leek, and ham pie; scampi and chips; and beer-battered fish and chips. Seasonal and organic ingredients are used where possible. It has an enticing garden for those warm summer afternoons, and superb cask ales—Charles Wells Bombardier and Wadworth 6X among them.

Oxford Rd., Hartwell, Aylesbury. ℭ **01296/747594.** www.vintageinn.co.uk/thebuglehornhartwell. Main courses £11–£15. Fixed-price menu £8. AE, MC, V. Daily 11am–midnight.

Hartwell House ★★   This is one of England's great showcase country estates, just 2 miles southwest of Aylesbury on the A418. The mansion was built in landscaped parkland in the 17th century for the Hampden and Lee families, ancestors of Robert E. Lee, the Confederate general in the U.S. Civil War. Wander from the morning room to the oak-paneled bar, pausing in the library where a former tenant, the exiled Louis XVIII, signed the document returning him to the throne of France. Bedrooms are as regal as the prices. The stellar guest rooms ooze with comfort, charm, and character, and the **dining room,** which is equally pricey, features seasonal local farm produce and exceptional traditional and contemporary English cuisine (main courses £22–£30).

Oxford Rd., Aylesbury, Buckinghamshire HP17 8NR. www.hartwell-house.com. ℭ **01296/747444.** 33 units. £215–£500 double; £500–£700 suite. AE, MC, V. Free parking. **Amenities:** 2 restaurants; bar; exercise room; indoor heated pool; room service; spa; 2 outdoor tennis courts; laptop rental £20 for 24 hr. *In room:* A/C, TV, hair dryer, Wi-Fi (free).

Inn at Woburn   After visiting Woburn Abbey (see above), head to this Georgian coaching inn for food and accommodation at the gates of the estate. Guests are housed in one of several well-furnished and beautifully maintained rooms, while a more modern block provides "executive bedrooms," which don't have the charm of the older units but are more up to date and comfortable. If you fancy a break from pub fare, **Olivier's Restaurant** serves imaginative contemporary English and continental cuisine such as baby monkfish tail with a crab ravioli (main courses £13–£18), while afternoon tea is served in the bar.

1 George St., Woburn, Bedfordshire MK17 9PX. www.woburn.co.uk/inn. © **01525/290441.** 57 units. £118–£169 double; £200–£235 suite. Children 15 and under stay free in parent's room. AE, DC, MC, V. **Amenities:** Restaurant; bar; concierge; room service. *In room:* TV, hair dryer, minibar.

Nag's Head Inn ★ GASTROPUB   Roald Dahl was a regular in this lovely old English pub (it's a short walk from the Roald Dahl Museum; p. 229), which also provides comfortable guest rooms. The food blends traditional English dishes with French flair—think puff pastry topped with mushrooms in a calvados sauce, lamb with butternut squash purée and red onion jus, and seafood gratin in a Chardonnay cream.

The seven **double bedrooms** come with flat-screen TVs (Wi-Fi in public areas), and are a good deal at £90 to £110.

London Rd., Great Missenden. © **01494/862200.** www.nagsheadbucks.com. Main courses £15–£24. AE, MC, V. Daily noon–midnight (Sun noon–10:30pm).

West Lodge Hotel ★ 🍴   Close to Aylesbury, this Victorian hotel (once a gardener's lodge on the adjacent Rothschild estate) outdoes all others in the area with its facilities and value for money. The comfortable bedrooms are furnished with nice extras (tea- and coffee-making facilities, trouser press, and so forth), and private shower-only bathrooms. The **restaurant** serves a huge breakfast (included) and dinner, and the village also has Thai and Indian restaurants.

45 London Rd. (A41), Aston Clinton, Aylesbury, Buckinghamshire HP22 5HL. www.westlodge.co.uk. © **01296/630362.** 9 units. £84–£94 double. AE, MC, V. **Amenities:** Restaurant; bar; Jacuzzi; room service; sauna. *In room:* TV/DVD, hair dryer, Wi-Fi (free).

ST. ALBANS ★

27 miles NW of London; 41 miles SW of Cambridge

Founded as the Roman city of Verulamium in the 1st century, the city of St. Albans grew up on the hill above the Roman site 500 years later. It's still home to some of the best **Roman ruins** in the country, and an inspiring **cathedral.** The city was named after a Roman soldier who became the first Christian martyr in England, around A.D. 250. A great **abbey** grew up to protect his shrine, becoming a major pilgrimage site in the Middle Ages, a role it has started to regain in recent decades. St. Albans flourished in later years as the first major stop on the coaching route north from London, which explains the large number of **historic pubs** in the center today.

Essentials

GETTING THERE   ThamesLink trains whisk you from London's King Cross Station to St. Albans in just 35 minutes (£10). If you're driving, take the M25 Junction 21A or 22; M1 Junctions 6, 7, or 9; and finally the A1 (M) Junction 3.

VISITOR INFORMATION   The **Tourist Information Centre** is at the Town Hall, Market Place (© **01727/864511;** www.stalbans.gov.uk). Hours are Monday to Friday 10am to 4:30pm, and Saturday 10am to 4pm. Check also www.allaboutstalbans.com.

ORGANIZED TOURS   The Tourist Information Centre (see above) provides entertaining themed **guided walks** (www.stalbanstourguides.co.uk) that generally cost £3 for adults and £1.50 for children 5 to 15 (children 4 and under are free). These include "The Ghost Walk" (£4 adults, £2 children), "The Wars of the Roses," "Monks, Mysteries & Mischief," and "Crime and Punishment."

Exploring the Area

Cathedral of St. Albans ★ CATHEDRAL   This majestic cathedral is the oldest site of continuous Christian worship in Britain. It contains the shrine of St. Alban, the first British martyr, who was buried here after being executed by the Roman authorities around A.D. 304. Construction of the cathedral began in 1077; it is one of England's earliest Norman churches, but displays a variety of architectural styles from Romanesque to Gothic. The bricks, especially visible in the tower, came from Verulamium, the old Roman city located at the foot of the hill. The nave and west front date from the 13th century.

The new chapter house, the first modern structure built beside a great medieval cathedral in the country, was opened by the Queen in 1982. The building houses an information desk, gift shop, and restaurant. There is also a video, detailing the history of the cathedral, that you can view for free (donations appreciated). In addition to church services, organ recitals are often open to the public. The church's choir can sometimes be heard rehearsing, if it's not on tour.

Sumpter Yard, Holywell Hill (on the High St.). ⓒ **01727/860780.** www.stalbanscathedral.org.uk. Free admission. Daily 8:30am–5:45pm.

Museum of St. Albans MUSEUM   This museum chronicles the history of St. Albans from the departure of the Romans to the present day; the life and subsequent cult of St. Alban is explained, and there's an especially detailed section on Victorian St. Albans. Look out for the startlingly well-preserved 15th-century leather shoe. Located in the city center, the museum is a 5-minute walk from St. Albans City Station.

Hatfield Rd. ⓒ **01727/819340.** www.stalbansmuseums.org.uk. Free admission. Mon–Sat 10am–5pm, Sun 2–5pm. Closed Dec 25–Jan 2.

Roman Theatre HISTORIC SITE   Built around A.D. 140, this is the only example of a Roman theatre in Britain, an evocative sight just a short distance from Verulamium (see below). Not much remains, of course, but the stage and banked stone-seating are clearly visible, and a stage column has been re-erected to give some sense of its former grandeur. Southeast in nearby Leavesden, experience a different kind of magic come 2012, when Warner Bros. Studios open its "The Making of Harry Potter" film tour, see p. 238.

Hemel Hempstead Rd., Bluehouse Hill ⓒ **01727/835035.** www.romantheatre.co.uk. Admission £2.50 adults, £2 students and seniors, £1.50 children 5–16, free for children 4 and under. Daily 10am–5pm. Located on the western outskirts of St. Albans, just off the A4147, in an area known as Bluehouse Hill.

Verulamium Museum ★★ MUSEUM   Roman Britain is brilliantly evoked at this enlightening museum, located on the site of the ancient Roman city of the same name. Here you'll view some of the finest Roman mosaics in Britain as well as recreated Roman rooms, rare bronze statues, and Celtic coins. Part of the Roman town hall and the outline of houses and shops are still visible in the park that surrounds the museum.

Check out also the new building housing the 1,800-year-old **Hypocaust** (underfloor heating system) and ornate mosaic floor in the park. The site has been left *in situ,* and is now protected by a modern shell. Opening times are April to September Monday to Saturday 10am to 4:30pm and Sunday 2 to 4:30pm; October to March the site closes at 3:45pm. Admission is free.

St. Michael's St. (C) **01727/751810.** www.stalbansmuseums.org.uk. Admission £3.80 adults, £2 seniors and children 5–16, free for children 4 and under, £10 family ticket. Mon–Sat 10am–5:30pm, Sun 2–5:30pm. Closed Dec 24–Jan 2. By car, Verulamium is 15–20 min. from junction 21A on the M25; it is also accessible from Junction 9 or 6 on the M1; follow the signs for St. Albans and the Roman Verulamium. St. Albans City Station is 2 miles from the museum.

Where to Eat

Freddie's ★ CONTINENTAL   This elegant, modern restaurant attracts a loyal clientele of locals and visitors. The menu is fun, eclectic, and sure to please everyone in your group. The seared monkfish fillet is always good, but there are also solid meat dishes to savor: English lamb shank with its own jus, herb mash potato and broccoli, and duck breast with banana chutney. Save room for the delectable dark rum crème brulée or baked-apple-and-blackberry crumble with hot custard.

52–56 Adelaide St. (C) **01727/811889.** www.freddies.org.uk. Reservations highly recommended. Main courses £11–£22; set lunch from £15. AE, DC, MC, V. Daily noon–2:30pm and 6–10pm.

La Costa Nostra ★ ITALIAN   This family-run trattoria, just a short walk from the center or train station, knocks out authentic Italian food,. It's especially good for two items: exquisite pizzas and freshly made calzones, stuffed with tomato, mozzarella, ham, mushrooms, and artichokes. Though it's essentially a pizza and pasta specialist, a seasonal menu of heavier steaks and fish is also offered, as is a range of *gelati* for dessert.

62 Lattimore Rd. (C) **01727/832658.** www.lacosanostraltd.co.uk. Reservations recommended. Main courses £8.95–£20; pasta from £6.90, pizza from £6.60. MC, V. Mon–Fri noon–2:30pm and 6–10:30pm, Sat 6–11pm.

Shopping

The twice-weekly **street market,** held every Wednesday and Saturday along St. Peters Street, features over 170 stalls, a mixture of discounted factory merchandise, fruit and vegetable sellers, and upmarket purveyors of everything from merino-wool blankets to artisan cheese. The excellent **Farmers' Market** runs on the second Sunday of each month, from 8am to 2pm, in tandem with a flea market inside the Old Town Hall (admission 20p). A better bet for genuine arts and crafts is the **St. Albans Artisans, Arts & Crafts Market,** held the second Saturday of every month (10am–4pm), also in the Old Town Hall.

You'll find a selection of intriguing shops amid the quieter streets and lanes clustered around the cathedral. For antiques and local crafts, visit **By George Craft Arcade,** 23 George St. ((C) **01727/853032**), St. Albans's largest antiques and craft center. The building also houses a tearoom and crafts arcade. It's open Monday to Saturday 9:30am to 5pm and Sunday 1 to 5pm.

Little Wonders, 10 Holywell Hill ((C) **01727/863800**), is an award-winning toy store guaranteed to astound little ones; it sells ethically made traditional wooden toys and games. Fans of the graphic novel should check out **Chaos City Comics** ((C) **01727/838719;** www.chaoscitycomics.com), at 20 Heritage Close. Check out www.shopstalbans.co.uk for more shopping ideas.

Entertainment & Nightlife

St. Albans's nightlife centers on a thriving pub scene and a small but healthy roster of provincial theatre. The Company of Ten, with its base at the **Abbey Theatre,** Westminster Lodge, Holywell Hill ((C) **01727/857861;** www.abbeytheatre2.org.uk), is one of the leading amateur dramatic companies in Britain. The troupe presents 10 productions each season in either the well-equipped main auditorium or a smaller studio. Performances begin at 8pm; tickets cost from £8 to £10. The box office is open Monday to Saturday 10:30am to 7pm.

Maltings Arts Theatre, in the Maltings Shopping Centre (☎ **01727/844222;** www.stalbans.gov.uk), presents performances ranging from Shakespeare plays to movies and live concerts. Performances are generally presented at 2 or 8pm Saturdays, with most tickets ranging from £4 to £12. Tickets can be purchased by telephone, in person when the theatre is open for performances, or at www.allaboutstalbans.com.

Bigger touring shows and concerts use the **Alban Arena,** Civic Centre (☎ **01727/ 844488;** www.alban-arena.co.uk).

THE PUB & BAR SCENE

As befits an ancient town (and the home of the Campaign for Real Ale, or CAMRA), St. Albans boasts some classic old pubs, notably **Ye Old Fighting Cocks,** 16 Abbey Mill Lane (☎ **01727/869152;** www.stufish.wordpress.com), one of the oldest watering holes in England. Named after the cockfights that once took place here, the pub allegedly dates back to A.D. 793, though the current site probably dates to the 11th century. The dark, timber-smothered interior is the perfect place to enjoy traditional cask ales.

Another atmospheric spot for a pint is **The Goat,** 37 Sopwell Lane (☎ **01727/ 833934;** www.goatinn.co.uk), with at least five real ales on tap such as St. Austell's Tribute and Eagle IPA. This Tudor inn has been serving drinks since the 1580s. **The Boot,** at 4 Market Place (☎ **01727/857533**), rounds out a history-laden pub crawl; this alehouse has been open since at least 1719 in a creaky timber building that dates back to the medieval period. It's also a decent venue for live bands, as is the **Farmer's Boy,** 134 London Rd. (☎ **01727/766702**), which serves brews from the town's only microbrewery.

Where to Stay

Black Lion Inn ✦   This is the most inviting pub-hotel in the area, as well as one of the best bargains. A former bakery, built in 1837, it lies in the most colorful part of town, St. Michael's Village, where bustling coaches from London once arrived. Bedrooms are simple and plain and, although a bit cramped, they're well maintained; some have original exposed brick and timber features.

198 Fishpool St., St. Albans, Hertfordshire AL3 4SB. www.theblacklioninn.com. ☎ **01727/848644.** Fax: 01727/891041. 16 units, 14 with bathroom. £65–£73 double; £87 family room. AE, MC, V. Free parking. **Amenities:** Bar; babysitting; Wi-Fi (free, in public areas). *In room:* TV, hair dryer, Wi-Fi (free, in some).

St. Michael's Manor ★★   Set on 2 hectares (5 acres) of beautifully maintained lakeside gardens, this handsome property dates from 1586. Rooms are individually decorated with fine antique pieces and come stocked with everything from mineral water to a teddy bear to sleep with. The manor also has a superb restaurant, the **Terrace Room,** with an ornate Victorian conservatory overlooking the floodlit lawns.

Fishpool St., St. Albans, Hertfordshire AL3 4RY. www.stmichaelsmanor.com. ☎ **01727/864444.** 30 units. £105–£260 double. Rates include breakfast. AE, MC, V. Free parking. **Amenities:** Restaurant; bar; room service. *In room:* A/C, TV/DVD, hair dryer.

Wren Lodge ★   This is the best B&B in St. Albans, with cozy rooms decked out in Edwardian style (the house dates from 1910), a lovely common lounge (with books and DVD library), and Victorian glass sun room. The filling breakfasts can be taken in the garden on sunny days; home-baked bread and homemade marmalade accompany great plates of fruits, cereals, eggs, and toast.

24 Beaconsfield Rd., St Albans, Hertfordshire AL1 3RB. www.wrenlodge.co.uk. ℘ **01727/855540.** 4 units, 2 with bathroom. £34 per person. AE, MC, V. Free parking. **Amenities:** Lounge. *In room:* TV/DVD, Wi-Fi (free). The lodge is a 15-min. walk from the cathedral and the town center.

Side Trips from St. Albans

The de Havilland Aircraft Heritage Centre MUSEUM The home of the vaunted Mosquito, known as the most versatile aircraft of World War II, is a must-see for aficionados and aspiring pilots. The museum has more than 25 vintage aircraft on view (the Mosquito among them), including modern military and civil jets such as the Comet, along with aircraft engines and other memorabilia.

On the grounds of Salisbury Hall (5 miles south of St. Albans), on the B556 to South Mimms, at M25 junction 22. ℘ **01727/822051.** www.dehavillandmuseum.co.uk. Admission £6 adults, £5 seniors, £4 children 5–16, £16 family ticket, free for children 4 and under. Mar–Oct Tues, Thurs, and Sat 2–5:30pm; Sun and bank holidays 10:30am–5:30pm. Closed Nov–Feb. Bus: 84.

Hatfield House ★★ HISTORIC SITE This stately Jacobean mansion and its beautifully manicured gardens make for an alluring day-trip from London or St. Albans. Built in 1611 by Robert Cecil, 1st Earl of Salisbury and Chief Minister to King James I, it has been the home of the Cecil family ever since (the current owner is the 7th Marquess of Salisbury). Yet Hatfield is more famous for the royal palace that previously occupied this spot, the childhood home of Elizabeth I. In 1558, Elizabeth learned of her succession to the throne of England while at Hatfield; the site of this famous moment is marked by the Queen Elizabeth Oak.

Indeed, though only the banqueting hall of the first palace remains, it is the Elizabeth association that gives the house much of its appeal. The queen's gloves and a pair of her silk stockings are on display, and the Marble Hall contains the celebrated "Rainbow Portrait" of Elizabeth. The **State Rooms** contain the most important paintings, furniture, and tapestries. More recently, the house served as Lara Croft's stately home in movies starring Angelina Jolie.

The **Hatfield Banquets** are staged with much gaiety and music in the banqueting hall of the Old Palace on Fridays from 7 to 11:30pm. Guests share long tables for a four-course feast with continuous entertainment from a group of players, minstrels, and jesters. Wine is included in the cost of the meal, but pre-dinner drinks are not. The menu isn't particularly medieval, and you're granted the (modern-day) luxury of knives and forks. The entertainment is a bit cheesy and the banquets are very touristy, but they are lots of fun and packed every night. The cost of the banquet starts at £50. Call ℘ **01707/262055** for details.

6 miles east of St. Albans on the A414. ℘ **01707/287010** for information. www.hatfield-house.co.uk. Admission house and park £9 adults and seniors, £5.50 children 5–15; park only £3 adults and seniors, £2 children 5–15. House Easter–Sept Wed–Sun and bank holidays noon–5pm (last admission 4pm); park and gardens 11am–5:30pm. Closed Oct–Good Friday. From St. Albans, take the A414 east and follow the brown signs that lead directly to the estate. Bus: Take the university bus from St. Albans City Station. Hatfield House is directly across from Hatfield Station.

Shaw's Corner ★ 🏠 HISTORIC HOME The great Irish playwright and socialist George Bernard Shaw lived in this peaceful ivy-smothered house from 1906 to 1950, knocking out all his best work in the small revolving shed in the garden (including

A new attraction in Leavesden, Hertfordshire promises to lift the lid on the magic of Harry Potter, offering visitors a unique behind-the-scenes tour for the first time. Guests at the **"Warner Bros. Studio Tour London—The Making of Harry Potter"** will be able to see firsthand the sheer scale and detail of the actual sets, costumes, animatronics, special effects and props used in all eight of the *Harry Potter* films. Following in the footsteps of Daniel Radcliffe, Emma Watson, and Rupert Grint, visitors will get to walk on to some of the most memorable, and most recognisable sets, such as the Great Hall, Dumbledore's office, the Gryffindor common room, and Hagrid's hut. Visitors will also have the opportunity to see the spectacular real life animatronics in a Creature Effects workshop, which will feature iconic *Harry Potter* film creatures including Buckbeak the Hippogriff, Aragog, the giant spider, Fawkes the phoenix and the enormous Basilisk head. For Harry Potter fans (sometimes known as *"Potterites"* or *"Potterheads") it's a chance to see the environment where all their favourite actors and characters have worked, and been created.* Tickets are priced at £28 for adults and £21 for children, and must be booked in advance via a dedicated website www.wbstudiotour.co.uk or through approved tour operators.

Pygmalion, on which the musical *My Fair Lady* was based). Once incredibly influential, Shaw is far less popular today and the house serves as something as a shrine to his memory. The interior remains practically as he left it at his death (which is what he intended). In the hall, for example, his hats are still hanging. Shaw wrote 6 to 8 hours a day, even when he'd reached his 90s, and evidence of his longtime relationship with the written word is obvious; one of his old typewriters is still in position, ready to go.

Off Hill Farm Lane, in the village of Ayot St. Lawrence. © **01438/829221.** www.nationaltrust.org.uk. Admission £5.80 adults, £2.90 children 5–15, free for children 4 and under. Mar–Oct Wed–Sun and bank holidays 1–5pm. Closed Nov–Feb. From St. Albans, take the B651 to Wheathampstead. Pass through the village, go right at the roundabout, and then take the 1st left turn; 1 mile up on the left is Brides Hall Lane, which leads to the house.

5

St. Albans

THE THAMES VALLEY & THE CHILTERNS

KENT, SURREY & SUSSEX

by Nick Dalton & Deborah Stone

The Southeast might at first seem like "England Lite"— perfectly pleasant but lacking the mountains and might, and missing the grandeur of many other areas. Look a bit deeper, however, and you find a world within a world, a place offering extraordinary experiences and extreme beauty. And, from London, it's a lot easier to get here than to the places with peaks and lakes.

CITIES & TOWNS This is not the region for big, industrial cities, but there are smaller, individual places that provide a contrast to the rest of England. **Canterbury,** in Kent, with its glorious cathedral is the seat of England's religion. Little **Rochester** nearby is full of history, a quaint riverside spot where Charles Dickens used to dream up his tales. **Brighton,** the Sussex seaside resort, is an unlikely city, a vibrant mix of arts and bawdy coastal fun. Little **Chichester** has the air of a country town, while in Guildford, **Surrey,** the 20th-century red-brick cathedral stands high on a hilltop, and presides over a city barely outside London.

COUNTRYSIDE Kent is called the **Garden of England,** a lush place dotted with stately homes and gardens (such as Winston Churchill's Chartwell). Move into Sussex and there are the **South Downs,** a chain of hills (the heart of Britain's newest National Park) that stretch for 100 miles and provide walks with views of country and coast. It is an ancient landscape, where forests mix with wild heathland, and it continues into the **Surrey Hills** where **Leith Hill** is a lofty viewpoint (294m/965 ft.), the highest spot in the Southeast.

EATING & DRINKING The bounty of the sea is here, and brings simple pleasures. Sampling the oysters of **Whitstable** from quayside stalls or fresh fish at Brighton's unpretentious Regency seafront restaurant are experiences second to none—although there are also Michelin-starred restaurants for a real treat. The produce from Kent's market gardens provides a delectable garnish, and the county grows copious amounts of hops that are turned into real ales by brewers big and small.

COAST This is a land that sent Nelson off to sea (from Chatham dockyards), where J. M. W. Turner painted his evocative seascapes (on show at Margate's new **Turner Contemporary** museum), and where the mighty **White Cliffs** delineate Dover and beyond. But more than anything, this is a region of beaches, resort towns, and coastal strolls, much of it possible to enjoy on day-long jaunts from London.

THE best TRAVEL EXPERIENCES IN KENT, SURREY & SUSSEX

o **Walking the Thames:** Only a few miles from London the river turns into a rural delight, with grassy footpaths along the banks, the sound of oars breaking the water, little boats putt-putting by, and relaxed riverside pubs to pop into. See p. 286.

o **Hiking the South Downs:** Stand on these chalk hills, gazing at the sea and undulating countryside; the hills follow the south coast and are an inspiring walk with almost constant sea views. Go for an afternoon's stroll, or throw yourself into a week-long hike. See p. 276.

o **Eating seafood at Whitstable:** This fishing town's quay on a warm Sunday afternoon is the place to be, snacking on a single oyster or sitting down to a full seafood lunch after browsing stalls selling everything from fish to antiques. See p. 250.

o **Experiencing Leeds Castle:** Britain's most gorgeous castle sits in the middle of a lake surrounded by landscaped parkland. Picnic, walk, and marvel at the serene sight that has survived for centuries. See p. 259.

o **Seeing the sea as Turner did:** The new seafront Turner Contemporary art museum in Margate not only has a collection of the artist's wonderful seascapes, it sits on the site of the boarding house he used to stay in and has windows recreating the view and the light that so entranced him. See p. 251.

CANTERBURY ★★

56 miles SE of London

This medieval city appeared in *The Canterbury Tales,* Chaucer's story of pilgrims telling tales as they journeyed from London to the shrine of Thomas Becket, Archbishop of Canterbury, who was murdered by four knights of Henry II in 1170. The shrine was finally torn down in 1538 by Henry VIII, as part of the Reformation, but Canterbury was already a tourist attraction.

The city, on the River Stour, is the **ecclesiastical capital of England** and still gives its name to the Archbishop of Canterbury, leader of the Church of England. The slaying of Thomas Becket was its most famous incident, but it witnessed other major events, too. Richard the Lionheart popped in on his way back from the Crusades, Henry VIII's Catholic daughter Bloody Mary ordered 41 Protestants to be burned at the stake between 1555 and 1558, and Charles II passed through on the way to claim his crown in 1642. There are still plenty of traces of the old city walls, but the city suffered badly during the Blitz of 1941, when much of its medieval feel was destroyed. Today it's a busy (very busy) mix of day-trippers and students from the University of Kent. And there's still plenty to see, not least the **cathedral:** one of the great religious monuments. The city is also a good place to use as a base for exploring the coast and countryside.

Essentials

GETTING THERE   There are trains to Canterbury from London's Victoria, St. Pancras, and Charing Cross stations (calling at Waterloo East and London Bridge).

All take about 1½ hours and cost about £30 one-way. The National Express bus from London's Victoria Coach Station takes 1½ to 2 hours and leaves every hour, costing from about £7.

If you're driving from London, take the A2, and then the M2. Canterbury is signposted all the way. The heart of the city is traffic-free, but it's only a short walk from several parking areas to the cathedral.

VISITOR INFORMATION A few doors from St. Margaret's Church, the **Canterbury Tourist Information Centre,** 12–13 Sun St. (© **01227/378100;** www. canterbury.co.uk), is generally open Monday to Saturday 9:30am to 5pm (to 4pm off-season). Only from here can you buy the **Canterbury Attractions Passport**

(£20 adults; £17 seniors; £15.50 children 5–15), which gives entrance to the cathedral, St. Augustine's Abbey, The Canterbury Tales, and a city museum).

GETTING AROUND   You may want to bicycle around Canterbury. **Downland Cycles,** St. Stephens Road (*(C* **01227/479643;** www.downlandcycles.co.uk), rents out bikes for £15 a day (tandems £35, to be paid for in advance). A credit card is needed as deposit.

An interesting and easy family ride is the Crab & Winkle route to the coast at Whitstable. It follows the route of the world's first passenger railway line of the same name, built by George Stephenson in 1830 and torn up by British railways in 1953. It's about 7½ miles round-trip. For more information, see www.crabandwinkle.org.

ORGANIZED TOURS   Canterbury Tourist Guides (*(C* **01227/459779;** www.canterbury-walks.co.uk) have daily walking tours costing £6 for adults, £5.50 for students and seniors, £4.25 for children 11 and under, and £16 for a family ticket. Meet at the Tourist Information Centre (see above). Tours tend to leave year-round daily at 11am, with an additional 2pm tour July to September and bank holidays.

Canterbury Historic River Tours (*(C* **07790/534744;** www.canterburyriver tours.co.uk) operates 40-minute boat trips with commentary that lets you see Canterbury from a different perspective. Prices are £7.50 for adults, £6.50 for seniors and students, £5 for children 12 to 16, and £4.50 for children 11 and under. March to October, tours leave daily every 15 to 20 minutes between 10am and 5pm. Tours begin just below the Weavers House restaurant, at 3 St. Peters Street.

Exploring the Area

Canterbury Cathedral ★★★ CATHEDRAL   This is one of the most visited sites in Britain, and still one of the leading places of pilgrimage in Europe. St Augustine, sent by Pope Gregory the Great, arrived in A.D. 597 as a missionary and became the first archbishop, establishing his seat ("Cathedra"). It was here in 1170, that Thomas Becket was murdered on a dark December evening in the northwest transept. The quire (which housed Becket's shrine until it was demolished during the Reformation) is one of England's earliest examples of Gothic architectural style.

The cathedral, along with St. Augustine's Abbey and St. Martin's Church, forms a World Heritage Site. Its foundations date from the time of Augustine, but the earliest part of the building is the great Romanesque crypt from around A.D. 1100, which still contains traces of wall painting.

The 72-m (235-ft.) **Bell Harry Tower ★★**, completed in 1505, is the most distinctive feature of the cathedral. You enter through the ornate **Christ Church Gate ★** (from the early 16th century). The fan-vaulted colonnades of the **Great Cloister ★** on the northern flank of the building never fail to impress. From the cloister you can enter the **Chapter House,** with its magnificent web of intricate tracery from the 1300s. This architectural ensemble supports the roof and a wall of stained glass, depicting scenes from Becket's life.

There are medieval tombs of the likes of King Henry IV and Edward the Black Prince. The later Middle Ages are represented by the great 14th-century nave as well as by the Bell Harry Tower. Sitting amid walled precincts, the cathedral is surrounded by medieval buildings and ruins. The wonderful Romanesque water tower once supplied the bakery and brewery.

Becket's tomb is in Trinity Chapel, near the high altar. The saint is said to have worked miracles, and the cathedral has some rare stained glass depicting those feats.

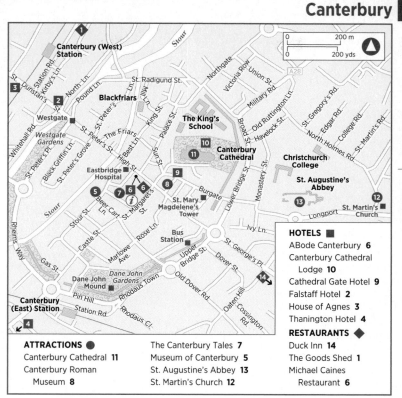

The glass, regarded as the country's finest, was removed at the start of World War II and therefore survived Hitler's bombs.

The Precincts. ✆ **01227/762862.** www.canterbury-cathedral.org. Admission £9 adults, £8 seniors, £6 children 17 and under. Easter–Sept Mon–Sat 9am–5:30pm; Oct–Easter Mon–Sat 9am–5pm; year-round Sun 12:30–2:30pm. Guided tours (daily except Sun) £5 adults, £4 students and children.

Canterbury Roman Museum MUSEUM   This museum provides a subterranean experience—it's built around archeological excavations of a house site containing mosaics unearthed by a wartime bomb. Interactive exhibits and Roman artifacts that can be handled bring the past to life for all ages. The Roman town of Durovernum Cantiacorum (Canterbury) was established after Emperor Claudius's invasion in A.D. 43, and it flourished for nearly 400 years. Other exhibits include the reconstruction of a Roman market.

Butchery Lane. ✆ **01227/785575.** www.canterbury.gov.uk. Admission £6 adults; £5 students and seniors, up to 4 children 5–16 free per family; £8 family ticket. Daily 10am–5pm; last admission 4pm.

The Canterbury Tales ☺ MUSEUM   Ah, classic Middle Ages literature turned into a sideshow! But it does it in such a fun way that it's hard to object. Indeed,

Chaucer was a populist author of his day. Here, inside the ancient setting of St. Margaret's church, which gets a splendid makeover as a scene from 14th-century England, Chaucer's stories (and the murder of Thomas Becket) come to life for all the family. Headsets, tableaux, and life-size figures enhance the experience.

23 St. Margaret's St. (off High St., near the cathedral). ℂ **01227/479227.** www.canterburytales.org.uk. Admission £7.95 adults, £6.95 students and seniors, £5.90 children 5–15, free for children 4 and under. Mar–June and Sept–Oct daily 10am–5pm; July–Aug daily 9:30am–5pm; Nov–Feb daily 10am–4:30pm.

Museum of Canterbury ★ ☺ MUSEUM   Here you'll find the city's history, from the Romans to Nazi bombs, Viking raids to religion, told with an impressive array of interactive, family-friendly video, computer, and hologram effects. Also celebrated are the children's animated TV series *Bagpuss* and *The Clangers,* which were created nearby, and author Joseph Conrad—he lived nearby and his study is here. The setting is the ancient Poor Priests' Hospital with its medieval interiors and soaring oak roofs. Within it is the Rupert Bear Museum, a homage to the oh-so-English cartoon bear, which is as appealing to grandparents who remember the pioneering strips in the *Daily Express* as to youngsters who can play with giant toys.

Stour St. ℂ **01227/475202.** www.canterbury.gov.uk Admission £8 adults; £6 students and seniors; up to 4 children 5–16 free per family. Daily 10am–5pm (last admission 4pm). Closed Christmas week, Boxing Day, New Year's Day, and Good Friday.

St. Augustine's Abbey ★★ ABBEY   This is where the cathedral's founder was buried; only ruins remain, but it is still a major religious site. After Augustine was sent by Pope Gregory to convert the Saxons, Ethelbert, the Saxon king, allowed Augustine and his followers to build a church outside the city walls, and it endured until Henry VIII tore it down. The abbey church rivaled the cathedral in size, and the ruins are still cathedral-like in their proportions. Nearby are the abbey buildings that were converted into a royal palace by Henry VIII and used briefly by several monarchs, including Elizabeth I and Charles I. Entry includes an audio tour and the small museum.

Corner of Lower Chantry Lane and Longport Rd. ℂ **01227/767345.** www.english-heritage.org.uk. Admission £4.50 adults, £3.80 students and seniors, £2.30 children 5–15. Mar 21–June 30 Wed–Sun 10am–5pm; July–Aug daily 10am–6pm; Sept–Mar 20 Sat–Sun 11am–5pm.

St. Martin's Church CHURCH   The oldest church in the English-speaking world still used for worship, this was Augustine's first project when he arrived in A.D. 597. However, it was built on the site of a Roman building, and it's possible that some of the walls are actually from the Roman period. The place is a jigsaw of time: The nave is mostly masonry but with occasional courses of Roman brick; the chancel is similar, but its east wall is flint, although one end, and part of the south wall, are wholly of Roman brick. As a whole, the church is distinctly of the 7th century.

Church St. ℂ **01227/768072.** www.martinpaul.org. Free admission. Open daily during daylight hours.

Where to Eat

ABode Canterbury ★★★ ENGLISH/CONTINENTAL   The beautifully designed restaurant, part of the Michelin-starred chef's empire, is in the ABode, the town's top hotel (see below). Local ingredients from Kent, the "garden of England," are used, and the cooking is simple and effective. One of the signature dishes is roast sirloin of Kentish beef with wild mushroom purée, roasted salsify, and Madeira jus. You might also find local rabbit, and seafood from Whitstable.

ABode Canterbury hotel, High St. ℭ **01277/826684.** www.abodehotels.co.uk or www.michaelcaines. com. Reservations required. Main courses £19–£25. AE, DC, MC, V. Mon–Sat noon–2:30pm and 6–10pm; Sun noon–2:30pm.

Duck Inn 🍴 ENGLISH   A historic country pub where the sign above the low door urges you to "Duck!" The 16th-century building once belonged to the grandmother of James Bond author Ian Fleming (he wrote the first draft of *You Only Live Twice* in its garden, and the place gets a mention). You can dine in the garden, surrounded by open fields in summer, while the quaint interior is perfect year-round. There's also simple bed-and-breakfast rooms (£65 double).

Pett Bottom, near Bridge. ℭ **01227/830354.** Reservations not necessary. Main courses £8.25–£13.95. AE, DC, MC, V. Tues–Fri noon–3pm and 6–11pm; Sat–Sun noon–11pm. Drive 5 miles outside Canterbury, near the village of Bridge on the road to Dover.

The Goods Shed ★★ ENGLISH   Everything that's good about well-sourced food you'll find at the Goodsshed, a barn of a market near the station (the restaurant is on a platform overlooking the action). Meat arrives as whole carcasses in the butchery, there's rustic bread from the bakery, and the daily menu reflects the other produce on offer. That might mean braised ox cheeks, creamed shallots, and bay leaf, or Kentish Ranger chicken, prunes, and cobnuts (like a local hazelnut). Breakfast, lunch, and dinner all adhere to the same high standard, and there are banquets, for 12 or more, for around £35.

Station Rd. West. ℭ **01227/459153.** www.thegoodsshed.net. Reservations not necessary. Main courses £11–£20. AE, MC, V. Tues–Fri 8–10:30am, noon–2:30pm, and 6–9:30pm; Sat 8–10:30am, noon–3pm, and 6–9:30pm; Sun 9–10:30am, noon–3pm.

Shopping

The Goods Shed, Station Road West (ℭ 01227/459153; www.thegoodsshed. net), is a massive, ethically sound food market, and while you might not be able to take home the delectable fresh produce, you'll also find lots of other souvenirs such as chutneys and mustards. See review above, under "Where to Eat."

The **Chaucer Bookshop,** 6–7 Beer Cart Lane (ℭ 01227/453912; www.chaucer-bookshop.co.uk), sells first editions (both old and modern), out-of-print books, leather-bound editions, and a large selection of local history books.

Entertainment & Nightlife

The **Old Brewery Tavern,** part of the ABode-hotel complex (ℭ 0871/402-3262; www.alberrys.co.uk), is an attraction in its own right, with an entrance on Stour Street. It's a modern take on a pub, all pale wood and white walls, and serves a gastropub innovative-but-casual menu (two courses £9.95). It's a good place for an early pint, with as much attention paid to the beer selection as the food, while most evenings it turns into a club with DJs (10pm–2am; free entry). The ABode's **Michael Caines Champagne and Cocktail Bar** (ℭ 01227/766266; www.michaelcaines. com) is sleek and modern, the city's most stylish bar, the place where you can get a simple glass of fizz or treat yourself to a magnum of the best. A favorite local pub, **Alberry's Wine Bar,** 38 St. Margaret's St. (ℭ 01227/452378; www.alberrys. co.uk), offers a clubby atmosphere every night with a DJ spinning hip-hop, drum and bass, or chart music. There's a cover of several pounds after 9pm Tuesday to Thursday, and after 10pm on Friday and Saturday.

The **Cherry Tree,** 10 White Horse Lane (📞 **01227/451266**), has a wide selection of beers, including Cherry Tree ale.

The **Gulbenkian Theatre,** University of Kent, Giles Lane (📞 **01227/769075;** www.kent.ac.uk/gulbenkian), features touring drama, comedy, and music, as well as regular movies, modern but pushing toward the artier side of things. It's on the edge of town, so you'll need to drive or get a cab. The **Marlowe Theatre,** The Friars (📞 **01227/787787;** www.marlowetheatre.com), features drama, jazz, and classical concerts, along with dance and ballet. Tickets cost £10 to £40. The box office at the Marlowe is open Monday to Saturday 10am to 9pm (Tues from 10:30am, closing 7pm on non-performance nights). Most shows begin at 7:30pm.

Where to Stay
EXPENSIVE
ABode Canterbury ★★ This is the place to stay, a hotel with a history dating back to 1588, but now part of the luxurious ABode chain, closely associated with chef Michael Caines (described by *The Sunday Times* as Britain's number 1 restaurateur). The location is perfect (inside the ancient city walls and within minutes of the cathedral), and the rooms are even more so. They're ranked "comfortable" (an understatement), "desirable," "enviable," and "fabulous"—and they all live up to their publicity, with hand-crafted beds, minimalist chic, and stylish wet rooms. The **Michael Caines Restaurant** is Canterbury's best (p. 244).

High St., Canterbury, Kent CT1 2RX. www.abodehotels.co.uk. 📞 **01227/766266.** Fax 01227/784874. 72 units. £99–£185 double; from £295 suite. AE, DC, MC, V. Parking £5. **Amenities:** Restaurant; bar; babysitting; exercise room; room service. *In room:* TV/DVD, hair dryer, Wi-Fi (free).

MODERATE
Canterbury Cathedral Lodge Within the cathedral precincts, this modernistic building with its castlelike walls and mini-turrets is a luxury hotel and conference center. Most of the simple-but-elegant rooms have cathedral views, which can also be enjoyed from the private Campanile Garden; there is also the Library to relax in. Guests get breakfast (served in the **Refectory restaurant,** with terrace seating in the summer) and free cathedral entry.

The Precincts, Canterbury, Kent CT1 2EH. www.canterburycathedrallodge.org. 📞 **01227/865350.** Fax 01227/8653885. 29 units. £75–£119 double. Rates include English breakfast. AE, DC, MC, V. Free parking (booking required). **Amenities:** Restaurant (breakfast only, except for groups). *In room:* TV, hair dryer, Wi-Fi (free).

Falstaff Hotel The Falstaff radiates history. Sitting next to the Westgate Tower was a 15th-century coaching inn, which has spread organically into an old wood mill and a pub. Rooms, unsurprisingly, aren't large and the furniture might be more modern than you'd expect, but you can live with that as you gaze up at the original ceiling beams in the original inn. Rooms in the annexes tend to be more modern. The public areas make you feel as though you're an extra in a costume drama. There's a flagstone terrace opening out from the bar.

8–10 St. Dunstan's St., Canterbury, Kent CT2 8AF. www.thefalstaffincanterbury.com. 📞 **01227/462138.** Fax 01227/463525. 46 units. £80–£100 double. Rates include English breakfast. AE, DC, MC, V. Free parking. **Amenities:** Restaurant; bar; room service. *In room:* TV, hair dryer, Wi-Fi (£5 per 24 hr.).

House of Agnes ★★★ 🏚 This quirky, luxurious B&B in a timbered building was an inn back in the 14th century. It's so named because it was the fictional home of Agnes Wickfield in Charles Dickens's *David Copperfield.* In the house are eight rooms themed on world cities, from the flamboyantly medieval Canterbury to the pale New England feel of the Boston. The Stables Rooms, opened in late 2010, are an additional eight rooms opening onto their own terrace. Some can be linked for families, one has a spa bath and shower, and the others have smart shower cubicles. And then there's the walled garden: huge, with a centuries-old ash, and yews that date back to the spot's time as a Roman cemetery.

71 St. Dunstans St., Canterbury, Kent CT2 8BN. www.houseofagnes.co.uk. *©* **01227/472185.** Fax 01227/470478. 16 units. £75–£130 double. Rates include English breakfast. AE, MC, V. Free parking. **Amenities:** Lounge. *In room:* TV/DVD, MP3 docking station, hair dryer, Wi-Fi (free).

INEXPENSIVE

Cathedral Gate Hotel The name says it all: This is right next to the Christchurch Gate and overlooks the Buttermarket. Built in 1438, it's packed with original details, such as twisting corridors, and beams in the odd-shaped rooms in the roof. It's impossible to give some of them en suite facilities, so the hotel remains a good-value option at the city's heart. The restaurant offers cheap tourist fare (fish and chips, chili, lasagna). There's also a small reception bar, and you can take your drink to the lounge with its cathedral view, or to the roof terrace.

36 Burgate, Canterbury, Kent CT1 2HA. www.cathgate.co.uk. *©* **01227/464381.** Fax 01227/462800. 25 units, 12 with bathroom (shower only). £62–£75 double without bathroom, £105 with bathroom. Rates include continental breakfast; English breakfast for £7.50. AE, DC, MC, V. Parking nearby £5. **Amenities:** Restaurant; bar; room service. *In room:* TV, hair dryer.

Thanington Hotel ★ ♦ This small, luxury, family-run hotel in a late 18th-century building is a stone's throw from the cathedral. It may have only 15 rooms, but it has a decent pool in an outbuilding with glass doors opening onto the pretty garden with a fish pond, and a private bar (with an impressive collection of malt whiskies). The rooms are understated, and superior rooms have four-poster beds.

140 Wincheap, Canterbury, Kent CT1 3RY. www.thanington-hotel.co.uk. *©* **01227/453227.** 15 units. £60–£140 double. Rates include English breakfast. AE, MC, V. Free parking. **Amenities:** Bar; 2 breakfast rooms; TV lounge; indoor pool. *In room:* TV, hair dryer, Wi-Fi (free).

ROCHESTER ★ & CHATHAM ★

Rochester and Chatham are 30 miles SE of London

The north Kent coast is an area that pays tribute to a pair of historic figures: Charles Dickens and Admiral Nelson. The twin towns of Rochester and Chatham are less than a mile apart, on either side of the meandering River Medway. The river proved such a safe, deep spot that it was where England's warships were built for hundreds of years, from wooden galleons to submarines. And it was the dockyards that, curiously, were responsible for much that we remember of Dickens's work. He came here as a youngster when his father started work at the Navy yard, fell in love with the area, and featured its locales in his novels. Nowadays it's a place where history rules, and you get a feel for the past in its museums and festivals.

Essentials

GETTING THERE Southeastern trains (about £16) run from London's St. Pancras to Chatham every half an hour (40-min. trip), and hourly from Victoria (1-hr. trip), and from Cannon Street (1hr. 15 min.) at rush hours; they call at Rochester several minutes earlier.

If you're driving from London, once you're on the M25 heading east, you simply follow the M20, then turn left at junction 4 onto the A228 for Rochester, junction 6 onto the A229 for Chatham.

VISITOR INFORMATION The Medway **Visitor Information Centre** is at 95 High St., Rochester (📞 **01634/843666;** www.medway.gov.uk). Open hours vary but are mostly Monday to Friday 9am to 5pm, Saturday 10am to 1pm.

Exploring the Area

ROCHESTER Charles Dickens, having found literary fame, bought Gad's Hill Place in Higham, just outside Rochester, in 1856 and lived there until his death in 1870. The author was regularly seen wandering around this and other towns (such as Gravesend). The house (where Hans Christian Anderson came to visit and stayed 5 weeks) is now Gad's Hill School and not open to the public. The Rochester area was the inspiration for many of Dickens's greatest works. Restoration House in Rochester was the fictional Satis House, Miss Havisham's home in *Great Expectations*. In *The Pickwick Papers* Mr. Pickwick stays in the Bull Hotel (now the Royal Victoria and Bull), and walks on the now-gone Rochester Bridge. Rochester, renamed Cloisterham, is also the setting for his unfinished novel, *The Mystery of Edwin Drood*. The town loves its famous son: **The Dickens Festival** (www.rochesterdickensfestival.org.uk) in early June has been running for more than 30 years and is a boisterous mix of music, dance, drama, and street theatre celebrating Victorian times. There's also a **Dickensian Christmas** with a parade in early December, and a Christmas market at Rochester Castle. Rochester's Sweeps Festival celebrates the traditional May Day annual holiday of chimney sweeps with a parade, top folk musicians, and Morris dancers.

Rochester has England's second oldest **cathedral,** founded in A.D. 604, although the present building is from 1080. Admire one of the country's finest Romanesque facades, the nave's Norman architecture, some fine Gothic styling, and an inspiring 14th-century Chapter Library door. The cathedral is open daily from 7:30am to 6pm (Sat to 5pm). Admission is free; audio guides £3. Rochester Castle is one of the best preserved and finest examples of Norman architecture in England. The grounds are good for a picnic stop.

Restoration House, 17 Crow Lane (📞 **01634/848520;** www.restorationhouse. co.uk), is an exquisite Elizabethan city-mansion and inspiration for part of Dickens's novel *Great Expectations*. In 1668 it was used as a stopover for soon-to-be King Charles II as he returned from exile following Oliver Cromwell's death. Much original decor has been exposed in continuing renovation. It has a large walled garden, part formal, part productive. The house is open only Thursdays and Fridays, June to September (£6.50 for adults, £5.50 for seniors, and £3 for children 6–16; garden only £3).

CHATHAM Charles Dickens, born in Portsmouth, came to Chatham as a child in 1817, when his father took a job at the dockyard. The family lived here until 1822 when they moved to London but Dickens never lost his affection for the area. In 1856 he bought Gad's Hill Place, near Rochester (see above). Given his imagination, it's likely he would have appreciated **Dickens World** on Leviathan Way (📞 **01634/890421;** www. dickensworld.co.uk). It's an indoor theme park where you can take a Great Expectations boat ride, visit Scrooge's haunted house, see a 4-D cinema show at Peggotty's Boathouse or an animatronic version of Dickens's life, and come face to face with the author's literary creations in a Victorian setting. It's open Tuesday to Friday 10am to 4:30pm, weekends and holidays until 5:30pm (£13 adults, £11 seniors, and £8 children 5–15).

Upnor Castle (☎ **01634/847747;** www.english-heritage.org.uk), off the A228 in the village of Upnor, is an Elizabethan fortification to protect warships moored at Chatham (but it failed to do so in 1667, when the Dutch sailed past it to attack the English fleet). Open daily April to October, 10am to 6pm; closed November to March (£5 adults, £3.50 seniors and children 5–15).

Historic Dockyard Chatham ★★★ ☺ HISTORIC SITE   From the Spanish Armada to the Falklands Crisis, ships were built and repaired here. By the mid-18th century it was the largest industrial set-up in the world, with thousands of skilled workers. Records date back to 1547 and within a few years most of the English fleet wintered on the Medway. Nelson's flagship, HMS *Victory,* was built here and launched in 1765. Today it exudes history, and has featured in many movies such as *Sherlock Holmes,* with Robert Downey, Jr., and *The Golden Compass.*

In addition to beautifully preserved buildings, you can visit the Victorian Navy sloop HMS *Gannet,* the submarine HMS *Ocelot,* which served until 1991, and the World War II destroyer HMS *Cavalier.* There's also a huge covered slipway from 1838 with a display of a midget sub, tank, and other vehicles; an exhibition of Nelson and the Battle of Trafalgar, and the Royal Navy Lifeboat Institute's national lifeboat collection. Even the restaurant, Wheelwrights, is part of history, housed in a 1738 building forged from old warship timbers. Its menus are full of Kent produce.

Nearby is **Fort Amherst** (☎ **01634/847747;** www.fortamherst.com), a fort from the times of the Napoleonic war with a large network of tunnels. It was part of original fortifications that extended 4 miles and enclosed the Royal Dockyard. Entry varies, but the grounds are open Monday to Friday 10am to 3:30pm.

The Historic Dockyard. ☎ **01634/823800.** www.thedockyard.co.uk. Admission £16 adults, £13 seniors and ex-service members, £11 children 5–16, £42 family ticket. Daily Feb–Nov 10am–6pm (4pm in Nov); closed Dec–Jan. From junctiont 1 of the M2, follow the brown tourist signs.

Where to Eat & Stay

Ship and Trades   This former quayside engineering shop from 1875, overlooking one of the yacht basins at the dockyard, has been converted into a smart pub-cum-hotel by local brewer Shepherd Neame. The result is excellent beer (try the Spitfire) in a relaxed, modern setting with ropes, maps, and other nautical memorabilia on the walls. Waterfront seating looks across the Medway. The bar has decent pub fare while the upstairs restaurant serves modern and traditional meals. Main courses (£7.25–£17) include liver and bacon in gravy, and a 16-oz. T-bone steak.

Ship and Trades offers 11 guest rooms, smartly modern (one especially designed for disabled access) and available on a bed-and-breakfast basis.

Maritime Way, Chatham Maritime, Kent ME4 3ER. www.shipandtradeschatham.co.uk. ☎ **01634/895200.** 11 units. £70 double. Rates include English breakfast. AE, MC, V. **Amenities:** Breakfast room. *In room:* TV, hair dryer. Wi-Fi (about £10 per 24 hr., access from www.btopenzone.com).

WHITSTABLE ★ & MARGATE ★★

Whitstable is 50 miles SE of London; Margate is 65 miles SE of London

This is one of Britain's few areas of north-facing coast, and has a very different light to other regions—which is why the painter J. M. W. Turner was attracted to it. It is an area devoted to the pleasures of the sea, whether the charms of seafood (**Whitstable**) or the fun of the seaside (**Margate**). But it is also a place to get away from it all on the **unspoiled beaches** between the towns of Herne Bay and Margate. Across the headland (the Isle of Thanet) looking out to the east, you'll find **Broadstairs** (with the seafront Charles Dickens pub, housed in the old assembly rooms where Dickens himself was a visitor) and **Ramsgate,** which sits on Pegwell Bay, a sandy beach protected by cliffs, and a National Nature Reserve.

Essentials

GETTING THERE   Trains (Southeastern) run from London's St. Pancras Station twice an hour (with a change at Rochester), and hourly from Victoria, each taking about 90 minutes to Whitstable, a little longer to Margate. A one-way journey costs about £25. There are two trains an hour from Canterbury West to Margate (30 min. trip), and four trains an hour from Canterbury East to Whitstable, changing at Ramsgate or Faversham and taking up to 1 hour. There are two trains an hour between Whitstable and Margate, taking around 20 minutes.

By car from London head south on the M25 east, then the M20. At junction 7 head east on the A249 and then join the M2, also east. When the motorway ends, take the A299.

VISITOR INFORMATION   Whitstable has a touch-screen **Tourist Information Point** at the harbor office (✆ **01227/378100;** www.canterbury.co.uk). Margate's **Tourist Information Centre,** 12–13 The Parade (✆ **01843/577577;** www. visitthanet.co.uk), is open Easter to September, daily 10am to 5pm; the rest of the year, Tuesday to Saturday 10am to 5pm.

Exploring the Area

WHITSTABLE   Whitstable is an oyster-fishing port that has reinvented itself as the home of oyster feasts, and lots more fish too. It all started a few years ago with the **Whitstable Oyster Company,** a pleasingly informal restaurant. Others followed and now the quayside is awash with stalls selling oysters (half a dozen shucked for £4.40 from **Wheelers Oyster Bar**), crab, cooked fish, and lots of chips. At weekends you'll also find a market atmosphere with stalls selling all manner of crafts and bric-a-brac. There are seafront pubs, notably the **Old Neptune** (✆ **01227/272262**), right on the beach.

As befits a reborn seaside town, there are galleries, coffee bars, and individual shops. But this is a place to wander. Lots of tiny alleys connect the streets to the sea, and there's a seafront path that's busy with families, jolly groups, and couples holding hands. Turn left on the path and you pass wonderful little cottages (including one with a blue plaque proclaiming it to be the former home of horror film actor Peter Cushing), then beach huts and, as the seafront curls around, the village of Seasalter. Go the other way and you find the quayside and its black-painted wooden sheds, which includes delights such as the **Fish Market,** selling the day's catch (whitebait, for instance), as well as cooking it to eat on paper plates outside and the **Crab and Winkle** restaurant upstairs, with its range of fish products for souvenirs. Walk around the quay to East Quay, where you can find a quieter stretch of pebble beach, just before the **Hotel Continental,** to sit on and eat your chips. Round the headland and you come to the village of Tankerton. There are plenty of parking lots near the seafront.

MARGATE   This was one of England's earliest seaside resorts, where 18th-century tourists came to enjoy the newly fashionable, health-giving properties of sea bathing. Margate has been through some hard times, but, located on beautiful beaches at one of England's easternmost tips, it was always going to re-emerge. Its renaissance is led

by **Turner Contemporary** ★★, an art gallery (© **01843/233000;** www.turner
contemporary.org), which opened in April 2011, to celebrate the artist J. M. W.
Turner. He first came here to go to school at age 11, he returned to sketch here at age
21, and from the 1820s until his death in 1851, he was a regular visitor. He told writer
and art critic John Ruskin that "…the skies over Thanet are the loveliest in all
Europe," and more than 100 of his works, including his famous seascapes, were
inspired by the East Kent coast.

The modernist building is on the site of the Cold Harbour guesthouse, where
Turner regularly stayed. It recreates the sea and quayside views that the artist saw.
The gallery, the biggest exhibition space in the Southeast outside London, features
changing exhibitions of Turner's work, along with that of other artists.

Alongside the gallery, the **Harbour Arm,** a concrete pier that protects the seafront, has been revamped into a happening place. There's also the **Lighthouse Bar**
(© **07980/727668**), smart and modern with a wood-burning stove; **BeBeached**
(© **07961/402612;** www.bebeached.co.uk), a "real food cafe" with veggie tenden-
cies; a gallery used by local artists, and **Caitlin's Beach Cruisers** (© **07956/395896;**
www.caitlinsbeachcruisers.com), which rents out restored and retro bicycles.

The seafront **Dreamland** amusement park (www.dreamlandmargate.com) is
being reborn as a "heritage" amusement park in a multimillion-pound project; its
Scenic Railway wooden rollercoaster (which was here when the park opened in 1921)
is being refurbished and joined by historic rides rescued from around the U.K. The
listed Art Deco cinema is being restored, too, and will open as a concert venue, the
grounds are being restored to their former glory, and the place will be full of the
sights, sounds, and smells of a classic amusement park. Completion is tentatively
scheduled for sometime in 2012.

All these are within a few yards of each other, and facing the sea. In one direction
are **Margate Main Sands,** a long stretch of golden sand that still has charms from
past times such as donkey rides and deckchairs. On the promenade (The Parade), you
can gorge on fish and chips, candy floss (cotton candy), and cockles and whelks, but
you'll also come across trendy cafes, such as the Harbour Cafe Bar. On the other side
of the Harbour Arm a narrower, but far longer, beach stretches up to the grander
Cliftonville area. Dip into Margate's old town and you'll find the Creative Quarter,
with a growing number of individual shops and galleries.

One other quirky attraction is the **Shell Grotto** (© **01843/220008;** www.shell
grotto.co.uk). Below ground, 4.6 million sea shells cover 20m (70 ft.) of tunnels leading to an oblong chamber. The result is beautiful, Roman-like in execution (cockles,
whelks, and oysters create trees of life, gods, and even an altar), but it's a mystery. It
was discovered when the ground fell while a farmer dug a duck pond in 1835, and no
one has any idea who built it. There's some suggestion that it was a sun temple, with
rays entering through a hole in a small dome at summer solstice. Whatever the
answer, it really is somewhere that will leave you speechless. There's also a small
museum, Eighth Wonder Cafe and, of course, a shop. It's open daily from Good
Friday to Halloween, 10am to 5pm; in winter, it's open weekends only, 11am to 4pm.
Admission for adults is £3, £1.50 children 4 to 16.

Where to Eat

The Sportsman ★★ ENGLISH At this gastropub *par excellence*, chef/owner
Stephen Harris has a Michelin star for his modern take on country food. Here they
even make their own salt from buckets of seawater (the pub is just off the beach at

Seasalter, a coastal stroll from Whitstable). There's a daily menu on the chalkboard, with dishes such as seared thornback ray, brown butter, cockles, and sherry vinegar dressing, and the famed Monkshill Farm pork belly and apple sauce, slow cooked with the world's best crackling. There's also a tasting menu, available Tuesday to Saturday, pre-ordered and for a maximum of six people.

Faversham Rd., Seasalter, Whitstable. © **01227/273370.** www.sportsmanseasalter.co.uk. Reservations recommended. Main courses £15–£22; tasting menu (Tues–Sat) £55. AE, DC, MC, V. Tues–Sat noon–2pm and 7–9pm; Sun noon–2:30pm; bar open daily.

Tartar Frigate ★★ SEAFOOD   One of Kent's leading fish restaurants, the Frigate is in an 18th-century flint building looking over Viking Bay. The restaurant is upstairs, with glorious views; the pub below. The ultimate dish is the Grand Seafood platter (£55 for two), heaped with two crabs, half a lobster, cockles, mussels, shrimp, oysters, and more. The lively bar has live music and is a focal point of Broadstairs Folk Week each August; you can also take your beer onto the beach.

37 Harbour St., Broadstairs. © **01843/862013.** www.tartarfrigate.co.uk. Reservations recommended. Main courses £15–£18; set menu (Mon–Fri), £14 for 2 courses, £17 for 3 courses. AE, MC, V. Pub open 11am–11pm (closes 10:30pm Sun).

Whitstable Oyster Company ★★ SEAFOOD   This still leads the pack in the converted seafront Royal Native Oyster Stores warehouse, with piles of oyster shells outside and oyster beds off the beach. A half-dozen oysters start at £9, and dishes include whole local lobster served simply with potato salad. The place opened in 1978 when the oyster company was near closing; the family-run business now includes the Whitstable Brewery, with ales such as Harbour Light, Hotel Continental, Whitstable Brewery Bar, and the East Quay bar and Lobster Shack restaurant.

The Horsebridge, Whitstable. © **01227/276856.** www.whitstableoystercompany.com. Reservations recommended. Main courses £13–£23. AE, MC, V. Mon noon–2:30pm; Tues–Thurs noon–2:30pm and 6:30–9pm; Fri noon–2:30pm and 6:30–9:30pm; Sat noon–9:45pm; Sun noon–8:30pm.

Entertainment & Nightlife

Whitstable is an unlikely place for nightlife, but the **Whitstable Brewery Bar** (© **01227/772157;** www.facebook.com/whitstablebrewerybar) is bringing the clubbing scene to this little town. It's on East Quay, on the far side of the quay from most of the seafront attractions, and looks like a shed from the outside but is smart and modern with a big DJ booth, lighting rig, and sound system inside. It's open every Friday and Saturday night until 3am for soul, funk, drum 'n' bass, and house, often featuring well-known DJs. The bar is also open Saturday and Sunday during the day for a more laid-back experience, and has tables out on the pebble beach. The nearby sister East Quay Venue is open for special events, including live music of the caliber of the Blockheads and comedian Adrian Edmondson's band the Bad Shepherds.

Margate has **Rokka** (© **01843/230183;** www.rokka.com), at the bottom of the High Street, facing the sea. By day it's a swish coffee bar, by night the chic red-and-white decor is enveloped in a rosy glow and it becomes a hip bar with guest DJs, even bongo players. It's open Friday and Saturday evenings until 2am (no cover). There is also a branch in Ramsgate. In Margate on a summer's night the Harbour Arm is a good place to hang out, having a drink outside The Lighthouse Bar, maybe a bite to eat in BeBeached (see above); it all turns into a bit of a party atmosphere.

Where to Stay

Hotel Continental This neat, rather French-style hotel is part of the growing Oyster Company empire and sits alone on the seafront. There are 23 rooms, some with iron balconies overlooking the sea. There are also eight converted fishermen's huts on the beach; they are on two floors, done in dark wood with green painted shutters. The Anderson Hut is perfect for families, sleeping four adults and two children. The airy bistro serves a decent menu, and the bar is big and sunny.

29 Beach Walk, Whitstable, Kent CT5 2BP. www.hotelcontinental.co.uk. (🕾) **01227/280280.** Fax 01227/284114. 31 units. £70–£145 double; £100–£175 huts. Rates include English breakfast. MC, V. Free parking. **Amenities:** Restaurant; bar. *In room:* TV, hair dryer, free Wi-Fi.

The Reading Rooms This Georgian townhouse is divided into three large rooms, each occupying an entire floor and overlooking a tree-lined square. The feel is aerie, fairytale luxury with oak floors, candelabra, hand-carved super-king beds, and lots of white, from original plasterwork to linens. It's a B&B, although breakfast arrives as room service. The sea is a stroll away.

31 Hawley Square, Margate, Kent CT9 1PH. www.thereadingroomsmargate.co.uk. (🕾) **01843/225166.** Fax 01304/206705. 3 units. £135–£180 double. Rates include English breakfast. AE, MC, V. Free overnight parking; £2 daily. **Amenities:** Room service. *In room:* TV/DVD, hair dryer, Wi-Fi (free).

Walpole Bay Hotel This Margate institution that was opened in 1914, extended in 1927, and is now being brought back to its old grandeur. The entire hotel is a living museum; it was owned by the same family until 1995 when the present owners took over. It sits above the sea in the Cliftonville area of Margate. There's a flower-bedecked covered veranda, a snooker room, a 1920s' ballroom with its original sprung maple dance floor… and the original Otis elevators. The restaurant (with terrace) has splendid local plaice and sea bass (main courses £8.95–£17) as well as Sunday luncheons, accompanied by a pianist on a 1908 pianola. There are also cream teas. Oh, and the rooms are neatly Edwardian in feel.

Fifth Ave., Cliftonville, Margate, Kent CT9 2JJ. www.walpolebayhotel.co.uk. (🕾) **01843/221703.** Fax 01843/297399. 3 units. £65–£125 double. Rates include English Breakfast. AE, MC, V. Free parking. **Amenities:** Restaurant; 2 bars, snooker room. *In room:* TV/DVD, hair dryer, Wi-Fi (free).

DOVER'S WHITE CLIFFS & MORE

76 miles SE of London; 84 miles NE of Brighton

The White Cliffs of Dover, captured in the World War II song by Dame Vera Lynn, are truly one of Britain's iconic images. Unfortunately, you have to be at sea (probably on a ferry heading from France) to appreciate them. Dover was a seaside resort back in Victorian times but today is mostly known as a port. It's on (and in) the cliffs that you'll find the town's main attraction, **Dover Castle.** Beneath its medieval might is a warren of wartime tunnels. Five miles to the north is the fishing port of Deal, and 8 miles south is Folkestone, another port but also a traditional beach resort.

Essentials

GETTING THERE Trains run about every 30 minutes from London's St. Pancras Station (Southeastern, costing about £35 one-way), and there are two trains an hour from Canterbury East (Southeastern, about £7). Because of its importance as a ferry port, there are regular National Express buses from London's Victoria Coach Station until late (from about £7). If you're driving from London, once you're on the M25 heading east, you simply follow the M20.

VISITOR INFORMATION Dover's **Tourist Information Centre** on Old Town Gaol Street (℃ **01304/205108;** www.whitecliffscountry.org.uk) is open June to August, daily 9am to 5:30pm; the rest of the year, Monday to Friday 9am to 5:30pm, Saturday and Sunday 10am to 4pm. **Discover Folkestone** (℃ **01303/258594;** www.discoverfolkestone.co.uk), in Folkstone's Bouverie Place shopping center, is open Monday to Friday 9am to 5pm.

Exploring the Area

The best view of the **white cliffs** ★★★ is on board a ferry from France. Otherwise, walk to the end of the Prince of Wales pier, the largest of the town's western docks. From here, the cliffs loom above you. While you go to Dover for specific sights, **Folkestone** is a much more attractive prospect as a town. It features winding streets (including arty shops in the Creative Quarter), a grassy, cliff-top promenade, and a pretty little quayside (with views of the white cliffs). The beach, a short walk down the hill, stretches away into the distance. Just south of Folkestone is Hythe, from where the **Romney, Hythe, & Dymchurch railway** (℃ **01797/362353;** www. rhdr.org.uk) runs along the coast to wild and windy Dungeness. The fishermen's cottages made from old railway carriages provide stark contrast to the modern power station. Here you'll find an **RSPB reserve** (℃ **01797/320588;** www.rspb.org.uk), a flat expanse of pebble beach and marsh that is home to seabirds and a stop-off for migrant birds. It is open daily 9am to 9pm (or to sunset if that's earlier), and has a visitor center (10am–5pm; until 4pm Nov–Mar); admission is £3 adults, £1 children 15 and under. Allow time for the locally caught fish and chips at the station's **Light Railway Cafe** on the way back.

Deal Castle ★ CASTLE   Deal Castle is one of the finest surviving Tudor artillery castles and can be explored from top to bottom, including its dank passages. The seafront fort, built around 1540, is the most spectacular example of the low, squat forts constructed by Henry VIII; its 119 gun positions also made it the most powerful. The circular keep was protected by an outer moat, the entrance approached by a drawbridge with an iron gate. The admission price includes an audio tour.

On the seafront. ℃ **01304/372762.** www.english-heritage.co.uk. Admission £4.50 adults, £3.80 seniors, £2.30 children 5-16. Daily 10am–6pm.

Dover Castle ★★★ CASTLE   Rising nearly 120m (400 ft.) above the port is one of the oldest and best-known castles in England. Its keep was built at the command of Henry II, in the 12th century, but the castle was returned to active duty as late as World War II. Over the past several years the castle has been undergoing a multimillion-pound makeover. Plenty has gone into the Great Tower, the interior of which is a multimedia experience of the royal court of Henry II. It is considered the most ambitious attempt to recreate a medieval palace in more than a century, with hangings, furnishings, and other objects created by craftsmen. You can walk the battlements, laze on the lawns, and see the Pharos, one of Europe's best-preserved Roman lighthouses. The castle also houses the **Secret Wartime Tunnels,** 60m (200 ft.) below ground, which actually date back to medieval times. They were first adapted during the Napoleonic Wars to house cannons in case the French invaded. They were turned into a secret World War II bolthole, the headquarters of Operation Dynamo, when 300,000 troops were evacuated from Dunkirk. Touring them (including an operating theatre and hospital), you can feel the weight of the white cliffs above you, and can hardly imagine what it must have been like during the war's darkest days. Don't miss the hidden cliff-top balcony, where Churchill stood during the Battle of Britain. This can be a full day out for the entire family.

Castle Hill. ✆ **01304/211067.** www.english-heritage.co.uk. Admission £13 adults, £11 students and seniors, £6.70 children 5–15. Price includes castle audio tour and tunnels tour. Daily Apr–Sept 10am–6pm (Aug 9:30am); Oct 10am–5pm, Nov–Mar daily 10am–4pm.

Roman Painted House ★★ HISTORIC SITE   Britain's "buried Pompeii," a Roman building 1,800 years old, has exceptionally well-preserved walls and an under-floor heating system. It's famous for its unique Bacchic murals. Brass-rubbing is also offered. You'll find it in the town center near Market Square.

New St. ✆ **01304/203279.** www.theromanpaintedhouse.co.uk. Admission £3 adults, £2 seniors and children 16 and under. Open 10am–5pm, variable dates but generally late Apr–May Tues and Sat only; Easter and June–mid-Sept Tues–Sun; Oct–Mar by prior arrangement.

Where to Eat

The Allotment ★★ ENGLISH   The name says it all: The owner/chef is an allotment holder and most of the produce used comes from his and friends' vegetable patches. The result is an urban bistro praised, rightly, by Britain's Good Food Guide as being at Dover's culinary forefront. The food is straightforward but inventive (maybe roasted Dungeness mackerel followed by slow-roasted "crying" shoulder of Canterbury lamb). The place also serves breakfast (sourdough pancakes, eggs Benedict, and the like) as well as lunch.

9 High St., Dover. ✆ **01304/214467.** www.theallotmentdover.co.uk. Reservations recommended. Main courses £7.50–£16. AE, DC, MC, V. Tues–Sat 8:30am–11pm.

Wallett's Court ★ MODERN ENGLISH   This restaurant is at a country-house hotel, with refreshing English cuisine, a rich, traditional setting, and a countryside backdrop. And the menu, well… the Kentish venison three ways (roast loin, pan-fried liver, and suet pudding) with celeriac fondue, red-onion marmalade, and truffled pomme purée sets the standard. Or you might find goose breast, guinea fowl, or fish such as turbot. The menu changes with the seasons. There is also a good-value 2-course set lunch (£15).

Wallett's Court, West Cliffe, St. Margaret's-at-Cliffe, Dover. ✆ **01304/852424.** www.wallettscourthotel spa.com. Reservations recommended. 3-course dinner menu £40, 4 courses £45; set-menu lunch £15 for 2 courses. AE, DC, MC, V. Daily 7:30–9:30am, noon–2pm, and 7–9pm.

Where to Stay

East Lee Guest House   This former home of local artist William Henry East is smartly furnished to keep the feel of its Victorian origins. Run by the same couple for more than 30 years, it's a welcoming B&B, an easy stroll from the heart of town. Bedrooms have the feel of a bygone age (although with all modern conveniences), and breakfast is served in the elegant dining room.

108 Maison Dieu Rd., Dover, Kent CT16 1RT. www.eastlee.co.uk. ✆ **01304/210176.** Fax 01304/206705. 4 units. £65–£70 double. Rates include English breakfast. Free parking in street. MC, V. *In room:* TV, hair dryer. Wi-Fi (£3 unlimited).

The Relish   A pastel-hued Victorian mansion in the heart of Folkestone, The Relish combines boutique flair and personal care. There's a complimentary glass of wine or beer each day, as well as unlimited coffee, tea, and homemade cakes. Rooms are richly modern, and have rainforest showers and organic toiletries. There's a terrace that looks over Augusta Gardens, a park accessible only to residents of The Relish and to the spiffy Radnor Estate, which backs on to it.

Augusta Gardens, Folkestone, Kent CT20 2RR. www.hotelrelish.co.uk. ⒸＴ **01303/850952.** Fax 01303/850958. 10 units. £95–£145 double. Rates include English breakfast. MC, V. Unrestricted street parking. **Amenities:** Breakfast room. *In room:* TV/DVD/CD, hair dryer, Wi-Fi (free).

Wallett's Court ★ 🏨   A Norman conquest-era manor house (mentioned in *The Domesday Book*), Wallett's Court is set in a wide-open landscape not far from the cliff-tops. It was rebuilt in Tudor style in the 1400s, and boasts a beautiful Jacobean stair-case, which takes you up to three bedrooms with four-posters. The rest of the rooms are in converted Kentish hay barns, stables, and cow sheds. All are individually deco-rated with notable Edwardian country-house chic. There's a neat old bar with open fire for winter, a terrace for summer. The smart spa has a splendid pool, and the restaurant is terrific (see Where to Eat). There are walks along the cliff-tops, and a path leads down to pretty St. Margaret's Bay with its sandy beach and white cliff backdrop.

West Cliffe, St. Margaret's-at-Cliffe, Dover, Kent CT15 6EW. www.wallettscourthotelspa.com. ⒸＴ **01304/852424.** Fax 01304/853430. 17 units. £140–£210 double; £210–£250 suite. Rates include English break-fast. AE, DC, MC, V. Closed Dec 24–27. Off the A258 just east of Dover. **Amenities:** Restaurant; bar; babysitting; health club and spa; indoor heated pool; room service. *In room:* TV/DVD, CD player, hair dryer, Wi-Fi (free).

KENT'S CASTLES & GARDENS

Kent is home to a wealth of country houses, castles, and gardens, many of them the finest in England. **Leeds Castle** is perhaps the finest castle anywhere, but there's so much more to see around the county. Names like Anne Boleyn, Winston Churchill, Charles Darwin, and William Waldorf Astor crop up as you tour the area. You could spend all your time here, but will probably want to explore farther afield too. If you're going to whittle things down, go for Knole, Hever, Leeds, Penshurst, and Chartwell. You'll need a car to be able to get around, as most are, in the way of country houses, in the countryside. If you're starting from London, it's an easy drive (there are many routes heading southeast, which all reach the M25 ring road, Kent's unofficial north-ern boundary) with many of the places do-able as a day-trip. You could also head for Canterbury (see "Essentials," in the "Canterbury" section, p. 240). Guided tours of homes and castles are generally on offer, but even the most ardent historical buffs can find themselves with information overload, so often it's best to simply wander around and soak up the atmosphere.

Exploring the Area

Chartwell ★ HISTORIC HOME   This was the home of Sir Winston Churchill, from 1922 until his death in 1965. It's not as grand as his birthplace (Blenheim Pal-ace; p. 226), but it has wonderful views over the Weald of Kent. And the rooms are as if the politician had just stepped out into the garden: maps, documents, photo-graphs, pictures, mementos, and so forth. There are displays of his trademark suits and hats, as well as gifts from people around the world in thanks for leading the Allies to wartime victory. Churchill was an accomplished artist, and many of his paintings

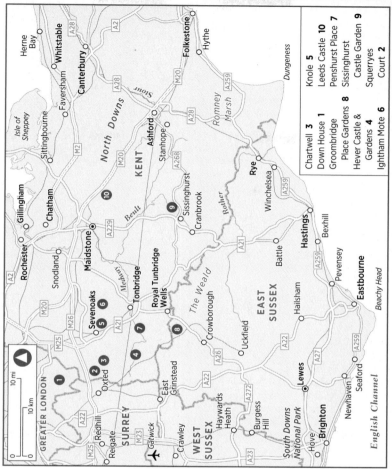

Chartwell **3**
Down House **1**
Groombridge
Place Gardens **8**
Hever Castle &
Gardens **4**
Ightham Mote **6**

Knole **5**
Leeds Castle **10**
Penshurst Place **7**
Sissinghurst
Castle Garden **9**
Squerryes
Court **2**

are displayed in a garden studio. The garden walls that he built with his own hands are still standing strong, and the kitchen gardens they contain are undergoing restoration to be more in keeping with how he tended them (produce is now used in the on-site restaurant). **_Insider tip:_** The house can get busy, and entry is on a timed ticket so it pays to get there early.

Mapleton Rd., Westerham. ⓒ **01732/868381.** www.nationaltrust.org.uk. Admission to house, garden, and studio £12 adults, £5.90 children 5–16, £30 family ticket (garden only £5.90/£2.95/£15. In winter garden only £3/£1.50). House mid-Mar–early July and late Aug–Oct Wed–Sun 11am–5pm; early July–mid-Aug Tues–Sun 11am–5pm; closed Nov–mid-Mar. Garden, exhibition, and restaurant open only Nov–mid-Dec Tues–Sun 11am–4pm, mid-end Dec daily 11am–4pm. M25 junction 5, then follow signs.

Down House HISTORIC HOME   Naturalist Charles Darwin lived here for 40 years until his death in 1882. When he moved in he wrote "House ugly, looks neither old nor new." Nevertheless, he lived there "in happy contentment" for 4 decades. The drawing room, dining room, billiard room, and old study have been restored to the way they were when Darwin was working on his famous, and still controversial, book *On the Origin of Species,* published in 1859. The original landscaping remains, along with the Sand Walk, the "Thinking Path," where Darwin took his daily solitary walk.

Luxted Rd., Downe. © **01689/859119.** www.english-heritage.org.uk. Admission £9.30 adults, £7.90 students and seniors, £4.70 children 5–16, £23 family ticket. Apr–June and Sept–Oct Wed–Sun 11am–5pm; Nov–Dec 20, Feb and Mar Wed–Sun 11am–4pm; July–Aug daily 11am–5pm. Closed Dec 21–Jan 31. From Westerham, take the A233 several miles north and follow signs for Downe.

Groombridge Place Gardens ☺ GARDEN   These formal gardens, dating from the 17th century but with modern additions, are divided into walks, gardens, and other experiences. The White Rose Garden is compared to that at fabled Sissing-hurst, the English Knot Garden is based on panels in the drawing room of an English country house, and Fern Valley is a forest of huge tree ferns. Children are well catered for with the Enchanted Forest, full of playgrounds, flowers, swings, and deer, Cru-soe's World, and Dinosaur and Dragon Valley.

At the heart is a beautiful 17th-century moated manor house. Sir Christopher Wren is believed to have been involved in its design. Sir Arthur Conan Doyle was a regular visitor to take part in séances, and the manor was the setting for the Sherlock Holmes mystery *The Valley of Fear.* The gardens are often visited after an exploration of Knole, near Sevenoaks.

Groombridge. © **08192/861444.** www.groombridge.co.uk. Admission £8.95 adults, £7.45 seniors and children 3–12, £30 family ticket. (Extra £1 mid-July–early Sept and some peak days). Mid- March–Oct, 10am–5:30pm.

Hever Castle & Gardens ★★ CASTLE   Hever Castle dates from 1270, when the massive gatehouse, outer walls, and moat were built. Some 200 years later, the Bullen (or Boleyn) family added a comfortable Tudor house. Hever was the childhood home of Anne Boleyn, second wife of Henry VIII and mother of Queen Elizabeth I.

In 1903, William Waldorf Astor bought the estate and restored the castle, building the Tudor Village and creating the gardens and lakes. The Astor family's contribution to Hever's rich history can be appreciated through the castle's collections of furniture, paintings, and art, as well as the workmanship in the woodcarving and plasterwork.

The gardens are ablaze with vibrant shades throughout most of the year. The spec-tacular Italian Garden contains statuary and sculpture dating from Roman to Renais-sance times. The formal gardens include a walled Rose Garden, fine topiary work, and a maze. There's also a large lake and many streams, cascades, and fountains.

Hever, near Edenbridge. © **01732/865224.** www.hevercastle.co.uk. Admission to castle and gardens £14 adults, £12 students and seniors, £8 children 5–15, £36 family ticket. Audio tour £3. Daily mid-Feb–Christmas: Gardens 10:30am–5pm; castle noon–5pm (closes at 4pm Feb, Mar, Nov, Dec). Follow the signs northwest of Royal Tunbridge Wells; it's 3 miles southeast of Edenbridge, and 30 min. from junc-tion 6 of the M25.

Ightham Mote ★ HISTORIC SITE   Ightham Mote, dating from 1320, is a gor-geous moated manor house with lots of Tudor touches such as the chapel with its painted ceiling, timbered outer wall, and ornate chimneys. You'll cross a stone bridge over a moat to its central courtyard. From the Great Hall, with its magnificent win-dows, a Jacobean staircase leads to the old chapel on the first floor, where you go through the solarium to the Tudor chapel. Other highlights include the crypt and a dog kennel that is a Grade I listed building. Ightham Mote passed from one medieval knight to another, to Henry VIII's courtiers. and to high-society Victorians. Each left his mark: When the last owner died (an American responsible for much of the restoration) he left the house to the National Trust, which chose to keep the Robinson Library laid out as it was in a 1960 edition of *Homes & Gardens*.

Mote Rd., Ivy Hatch. (C) **01732/810378.** www.nationaltrust.org.uk. Admission £11 adults, £5.50 children 5-15, £28 family ticket. Mar-Oct Thurs-Mon, June-Aug Wed-Mon 11am-5pm; Nov-mid-Dec Thurs-Sun 11am-3pm. Garden also open Feb weekends. Drive 6 miles east of Sevenoaks on the A25 to the village of Ivy Hatch; the estate is 2½ miles south of Ightham; signposted from the A227.

Knole ★★ ARCHITECTURE   Begun in the mid-15th century by Thomas Bourchier, Archbishop of Canterbury, and set in a 404-hectare (1,000-acre) deer park, Knole is one of the largest private houses in England and is one of the finest examples of pure English Tudor-style architecture.

Henry VIII liberated the former archbishop's palace from the church in 1537. He spent considerable sums of money on Knole, but history records only one visit (in 1541) after extracting the place from the reluctant Archbishop Cranmer. It was a royal palace until Queen Elizabeth I granted it to Thomas Sackville, 1st Earl of Dorset, whose descendants have lived here ever since. (Virginia Woolf, often a guest of the Sackvilles, used Knole as the setting for her novel *Orlando*.)

The house covers 2.8 hectares (7 acres) and has 365 rooms, 52 staircases, and 7 courts. The elaborate paneling and plasterwork provide a background for the 17th- and 18th-century tapestries and rugs, Elizabethan and Jacobean furniture, and collection of family portraits. If you want to see a bed that's to die for, check out the state bed of James II in the King's Bedroom.

5 miles north of Tunbridge, at the Tunbridge end of the town of Sevenoaks. (C) **01732/462100.** www. nationaltrust.org.uk. Admission to house £9.50 adults, £4.75 children 5-15, £24 family ticket; gardens £5 adults, £2.50 children. House mid-Mar-Oct Wed-Sun noon-4pm, gardens every Wed of the month late Mar-late Oct 11am-4pm (last admission 3:30pm); park open daily to pedestrians and to cars only during house hours. To reach Knole from Chartwell, drive north to Westerham, pick up the A25, and head east for 8 miles. Frequent train service is available from London (about every 30 min.) to Sevenoaks; then take the connecting hourly bus service or a taxi, or walk the remaining 1½ miles to Knole.

Leeds Castle ★★★ CASTLE   Once described by Lord Conway as the loveliest castle in the world, Leeds Castle dates from A.D. 857. First constructed of wood, it was rebuilt in 1119 in stone on two small islands in the lake, making it an almost impregnable fortress. Henry VIII took to it and converted it into a royal palace.

There are strong ties to America through the 6th Lord Fairfax, who, as well as owning the castle, owned 2 million hectares (5 million acres) in Virginia and was a close friend and mentor of the young George Washington. The last private owner, the Hon. Lady Baillie, who restored the castle with a superb collection of fine art, furniture, and tapestries, bequeathed it to the Leeds Castle Foundation. Since then the royal apartments, known as Les Chambres de la Reine (the Queen's Chambers), in the Gloriette, the oldest part of the castle, have been open to the public. The Gloriette, the last stronghold against attack, dates from Norman and Plantagenet times with later additions by Henry VIII.

Within the surrounding parkland, a lovely place to walk, is a wildwood garden and a collection of rare swans, geese, and ducks. The **Aviary** collection includes parakeets and cockatoos, the **Culpepper Garden** is an English-country flower garden, while the **Dog Collar Museum** speaks for itself, with a collection dating back to the Middle Ages.

Beyond are greenhouses, a maze, underground grotto, and a vineyard that was recorded in *The Domesday Book* (1086) and is once again producing white wine. There is also a 9-hole **golf course,** which is open to the public. You won't go hungry: There are various cafes including **Fairfax Hall,** a restored 17th-century tithe barn.

7 miles east of Maidstone, off junction 8 of the M20. Trains on the London Victoria–Maidstone/Ashford International line call at Bearsted, from where there are bus transfers (see Castle website, below). ℂ **01732/868381.** www.leeds-castle.com. £18 adults, £10 children 4–15. Daily Apr–Sept 10am–5pm; Oct–Mar until 4pm.

Penshurst Place ★★ ☺ HISTORIC SITE   Penshurst is one of Britain's outstanding country houses, as well as one of England's greatest defended manor houses, standing in a peaceful rural setting that has changed little over the centuries. In 1338, Sir John de Pulteney, four times lord mayor of London, built the manor house whose Great Hall still forms the heart of Penshurst. Henry VIII's son, the boy king Edward VI, presented the house to Sir William Sidney and it has remained in that family ever since. The Nether Gallery, below the Long Gallery with its suite of ebony-and-ivory furniture from Goa, houses the Sidney family collection of armor. You can also see the splendid state dining room. In the Stable Wing is a toy museum, with playthings from past generations. On the grounds are nature and farm trails plus an adventure playground for children.

6 miles west of Royal Tunbridge Wells. ℂ **01892/870307.** www.penshurstplace.co.uk. Admission to house and grounds £9.80 adults, £6.20 children 5–16, £26 family ticket; grounds only £7.80 adults, £5.80 children 5–16, £23 family ticket. Daily Apr–Oct, house noon–4pm, grounds 10:30am–6pm (weekends only in Mar). From M25 junction follow the A21 to Tunbridge, leaving at the Tunbridge (north) exit; then follow the brown tourist signs.

Sissinghurst Castle Garden ★★ GARDEN   In 1930 Bloomsbury set writer and noted gardener Vita Sackville-West and her diplomat husband Harold Nicolson moved into the property. The grounds had fallen into sorry disrepair but in the years that followed Vita turned them around, using the ruins of an Elizabethan manor to which they belong as a focal point. Today they are truly spectacular. In spring, the gardens are awash with flowering bulbs and daffodils fill the orchard. The white garden reaches its peak in June. The large herb garden, a skillful montage that reflects Sackville-West's profound plant knowledge, has something to show all summer long. The cottage garden, with its flowering bulbs, is at its finest as summer fades, while an on-site restaurant uses fruit and vegetables from the gardens and meat from the tenant farmer.

Sissinghurst, near Cranbrook. ℂ **01580/710700.** www.nationaltrust.org.uk. Admission £9.50 adults, £4.70 children 5–15, £24 family ticket. Mid-Mar–Oct Fri–Tues 10:30am–5pm. Estate daily dawn–dusk, free. 53 miles southeast of London. It's often approached from Leeds Castle, which is 4 miles east of Maidstone at the junction of the A20 and M20. From this junction, head south on the B2163 and A274 through Headcorn. Follow the signposts to Sissinghurst.

Squerryes Court HISTORIC SITE   This manor house, built in 1861, has been owned by the Warde family for 250 years. British General James Wolfe, who commanded forces in the bombardment of Quebec, lived here. There are still pictures and relics of his family on display. The Wardes have restored the formal gardens using an 18th-century plan, with avenues, parterres, and hedges, as well as adding borders, spring bulbs, and old roses for year-round tones. There is a fine collection of Old Master paintings from the Italian, 17th-century Dutch, and 18th-century English schools, along with antiques, porcelain, and tapestries, but if time is limited the gardens are what you should see. General Wolfe received his commission on the grounds—the spot is marked by a cenotaph.

A half-mile west of Westerham (10 min. from M25 junction 5 or 6). © **01959/562345.** www.squerryes. co.uk. Admission to house and garden £7.50 adults, £7 students and seniors, £4 children 15 and under, £16 family ticket; garden only £5 adults, £4.50 seniors, £2.50 children 15 and under, £9.50 family ticket. Apr 1–Sept 30 Wed, Sun, and bank holidays, house 12:30–5pm, grounds 11:30am–5pm. House and grounds closed Oct–Mar. Take the A25 just west of Westerham and follow the signs.

RYE & HASTINGS

Rye: 62 miles SE of London; Hastings: 63 miles SE of London

Rye was once an important port and a smugglers' haunt, but the sea receded and it was left high and dry 2 miles inland. It was occupied by the French after the Norman invasion of 1066, but reclaimed for England in 1247 by Henry III. It was all but leveled in 1377, only to be rebuilt in Elizabethan style. Today you come here to wander narrow, twisting cobblestone streets and admire the ancient buildings, which prop each other up like a house of cards.

Just along the coast is **Hastings,** the site (roughly) of the Battle of Hastings in 1066 where King Harold was defeated by the invading troops of William, Duke of Normandy. From this point England's history became entwined with that of France and nothing was the same again. The battle actually occurred at what is now **Battle Abbey** (8 miles away), but William used Hastings as his base. The town itself is a rather faded seaside resort, a pale shadow of Brighton, 35 miles to the west.

Essentials

GETTING THERE   From London, there are hourly Southeastern trains to Rye and Hastings from Charing Cross Station, changing at St. Leonards. The trip to either takes just over 2 hours and costs about £28. Battle is a stop on the line. The Southeastern journey from St. Pancras takes about 1¼ hours, with a change at Ashford International; the trip costs about £33.

If you're driving to Rye from London, take the M25, M26, and M20 east to Maidstone, going southeast along the A20 to Ashford. At Ashford, continue south on the A2070. To Hastings, head south on the A21. To Battle, cut south to Sevenoaks and continue along the A21 to Battle via the A2100.

Hastings is linked by bus to Maidstone, Folkestone, and Eastbourne. If you're in Rye or Hastings in summer, several frequent buses run to Battle.

VISITOR INFORMATION   **Rye Tourist Information Centre** is at 4–5 Lion Street (© **01797/226696;** www.visitrye.co.uk), open daily April to September 10am to 5pm, October to March 10am to 4pm. **Rye Heritage Centre,** on Strand Quay (© **01797/226696;** www.ryeheritage.co.uk), houses a sound-and-light show of 700 years of history (£3.50 adults, £2.50 students/seniors, £1.50 children 15 and under). **Hastings Tourist Information Centre,** Queen's Square, Priory Meadow (© **01424/451111;** www.visit1066country.com), is open Monday to Friday 8:30am to 6:15pm, Saturday 9am to 5pm, and Sunday 10:30am to 4pm. **Battle Tourist Information Centre,** at Battle Abbey Gatehouse (© **01424/776789;** www.visit1066country. com), is open daily April to September 10am to 6pm, October to March 10am to 4pm.

Exploring the Area

In **Rye,** the old town's entrance is **Land Gate,** where a single lane of traffic passes between massive, 12m-high (40-ft.) stone towers. The top of the gate has holes through which boiling oil used to be poured on unwelcome visitors, such as French raiding parties. Rye's pottery, white glazed and hand-painted, has been made for centuries. **Rye Pottery,** Wishward Street (*©* **01797/223038;** www.ryepottery.co.uk), keeps the tradition going; forget mugs and trinkets—here are statues depicting characters from *The Canterbury Tales* and the Bayeaux Tapestry. The little streets are also full of antiques and bookstores. The town is limited in attractions but has some lovely old inns, so it's a good place to stay to explore the county's houses and gardens.

Battle Abbey & Battlefield ★★★ ☺ RUINS   Stand on the grassy swath where King Harold, last of the Saxon kings, fought to the death on October 14, 1066, and you can feel history come alive. Harold, as legend has it, was killed by an arrow through the eye. It was the end of Anglo-Saxon England, and you can learn all about it here at one of the south's brightest attractions. The modern visitor center features sword-rattling, computer-animated film of the battle, while interactive displays portray England at the time of the conquest. There's an audio tour of the battlefield itself, which takes you to the very spot where Harold is said to have died. The abbey was founded by William the Conqueror to celebrate his victory, but most of what's left is in ruins, destroyed during the Dissolution of the Monasteries from 1538 to 1539 by Henry VIII. Abbot's House, the main building, is now a private school.

This is a great place for children, with a themed play area, activity sheet, and places to run around with a sword (available in the gift shop). It's also the place for a picnic in the parkland that was the monastery grounds, before having a quick look around the medieval town of Battle, which sprung up around the abbey.

Battle High St., Battle *©* **01424/773792.** www.english-heritage.org.uk. £7.30 adults, £6.60 students and seniors, £4.40 children 5–15, £18 family ticket. Apr–Sept daily 10am–6pm; Oct–Mar daily 10am–4pm.

Hastings Castle ★★ CASTLE   This was the first Norman castle in England, built immediately after the Norman conquest. Now only ruins remain on the hilltop site overlooking the sea. The fortress was unfortified by King John in 1216, and was later used as a church. There is an audiovisual presentation of the castle's history, as well as the battle of 1066. It's a nice walk, or you can take the funicular, which connects with town.

Castle Hill Rd., West Hill, Hastings *©* **01424/444412.** www.smugglersadventure.co.uk. Admission £4.25 adults, £3.95 seniors and students, £3.50 children 5–15, £13 family ticket. Easter–Sept daily 10am–5pm. West Hill Cliff Railway from George St. to the castle £1.60 adults, £1 children.

Lamb House HISTORIC HOME   Author Henry James lived here from 1898 to 1916. Many of his mementos are scattered throughout the big, brick house, which is set in a large walled garden with lawns and mature trees. Its previous owner joined the gold rush in North America but perished in the Klondike, and James bought it for a modest £2,000. Some of his well-known books were written here.

West St. (at the top of Mermaid St.), Rye. *©* **01580/762334.** www.nationaltrust.org.uk. Admission £4 adults, £2.10 children 5–15. Mid-Mar–mid-Oct Tues and Sat 2–6pm. Closed late Oct–early Mar.

Rye Castle Museum MUSEUM   The museum is actually in an old brewery and documents the town's history, notably boat building, and how Rye was England's seventh-biggest port in the 16th century. The castle is the nearby Ypres Tower, built around 1250 by King Henry III, to defend the coast against attack by the French. It's been a private home, mortuary, and prison, but now continues the coastal-history theme and has views across farmland once covered by the sea.

3 East St., Rye 🎧 **01797/226728.** www.ryemuseum.co.uk. Museum £2.50 adults, £2 students and seniors, free for children 15 and under; Ypres Tower £3 adults, £2.50 students and seniors, free for children 15 and under; combined ticket £5/£4. Museum Apr-Oct Sat-Sun and holidays 10:30am-5pm; Ypres Tower Apr-Oct daily 10:30am-5pm, Nov-Mar 10:30am-3:30pm.

St. Mary's Parish Church CHURCH   The 12th-century church has a 16th-century clock flanked by gilded cherubs (known as Quarter Boys because of their striking of the bells on the quarter-hour). The church is often called the "Cathedral of East Sussex," owing to its size and ornate beauty. If you're energetic you can climb the wooden stairs and ladders up the bell tower for an impressive view.

Church Square, Rye. 🎧 **01797/224935.** www.ryeparishchurch.org.uk. Tower £2 adults, £1 children 7-16 (1 free child per adult). Church free admission (contributions appreciated). June-Aug daily 9:15am-5:15pm; until 4:15pm rest of the year.

Smallhythe Place 🏛 HISTORIC HOME   This was for 30 years the country house of Dame Ellen Terry, the English actress acclaimed for her Shakespearean roles, who had a long theatrical association with Sir Henry Irving. She died in the house, on the outskirts of Winchelsea, in 1928. Its timber-framed structure, known as a "continuous-jetty house," was built in the early 16th century and is filled with Terry memorabilia—playbills, props, makeup, and a striking display of costumes. An Elizabethan barn, adapted as a theatre in 1929, is open most days.

Smallhythe (on the B2082 near Tenterden, about 6 miles north of Rye). 🎧 **01580/762334.** www. nationaltrust.org.uk. Admission £5.80 adults, £3.15 children 5-15, £15 family ticket. Late-Feb-Oct Sat-Wed 11am-5pm, Dec Sat-Sun noon-3pm. Closed Nov and Jan-mid-Feb. Take bus no. 312 from Tenterden or Rye.

Where to Eat

Landgate Bistro MODERN ENGLISH   A very modern restaurant sits inside a pair of Georgian cottages. This is a haven of local produce and everything is homemade, from the soda and sourdough bread to the ice cream. Seasonal starters include fresh local crab and gruyere tart, or turbot and Rye Bay scallops with back bacon and sherry and shallot sauce. There's always a selection of fresh fish (Dover sole, sea bass, gurnard, turbot) plus local meat dishes such as Romney Marsh lamb with French beans and gratin potatoes. There is also a set lunch (£13 for 2 courses, £16 for three courses).

5-6 Landgate, Rye. 🎧 **01797/222829.** www.landgatebistro.co.uk. Reservations required on Sat-Sun. Main courses £10-£15 lunch, £13-£19 dinner. AE, DC, MC, V. Wed-Fri 7-10pm, Sat noon-3pm and 7-10pm, Sun noon-3pm.

Where to Stay

Bannatyne Spa Hotel ★   It might sound big and modern, but this is a small country-house hotel between the seaside towns of Hastings and Battle with their 1066 attractions. Originally the private estate of General Murray, former governor of Quebec, the building was destroyed by fire in 1923 but rebuilt so that you wouldn't know the difference. Many of the rooms (most smartly modern, but some with four-posters) have views of the beautiful gardens. There's free use of the spa with its outdoor hot tubs. The **Conservatory restaurant** (main courses £11–£24) is good for steaks from local farms.

Battle Rd. (A2100), Hastings, East Sussex TN38 8EA. www.bannatyne.co.uk. 🎧 **01424/851222.** Fax 01424/852465. 41 units. £95-£130 double; £150-£170 suite. Rates include English breakfast. AE, DC, MC,

V. Free parking. Head 3½ miles northwest of Hastings, to the junction of the A2100 and B2159. **Amenities:** Restaurant; bar; golf course (9 holes); health club & spa; room service; outdoor tennis court (lit). *In room:* TV, hair dryer, Wi-Fi (free).

The George ★   This boutique hotel snuggles inside a coaching inn dating back to 1575. The half-timbered architecture is charming (some of the timbers may be from the wreck of an English ship broken up at Rye after the defeat of the Spanish Armada), and inside it's simply gorgeous, a heady mix of fabrics and good design. Rooms are pale and inviting: rich linens, marble-top baths and, in some, a four-poster bed. The **restaurant** has a local and seasonal menu (main courses £14–£18), which features Mediterranean-inspired dishes (and has courtyard tables), while the bar, **George's Tap,** promises to stay open until the last guest has given in.

High St., Rye, East Sussex TN31 7JT. www.thegeorgeinrye.com. ⓒ **01797/222114.** Fax 01797/224065. 24 units. £135–£195 double; £245 suite. Rates include English breakfast. AE, DC, MC, V. Free overnight parking on street; parking lot nearby, £2 per 24 hr. **Amenities:** Restaurant; bar; babysitting; room service. *In room:* TV/DVD, hair dryer, Wi-Fi (free).

Hope Anchor Hotel   At the end of a cobbled street on a hill dominating the town stands this 17th-century building, once home to a gang of smugglers. It enjoys panoramic views of the surrounding countryside and sea. There are oak beams, open fires, and a **modern restaurant** that is somehow timeless, serving local food. Bedrooms are individually furnished, many with historic features, and some with four-poster beds. The adjoining fisherman's cottage has a double room, but can sleep four more on sofabeds, so is ideal for families.

Watchbell St., Rye, East Sussex TN31 7HA. www.thehopeanchor.co.uk. ⓒ **01797/222216.** Fax 01797/223796. 15 units. £90–£150 double; £160–£210 family room. Rates include English breakfast. AE, MC, V. Free parking. **Amenities:** Restaurant; bar; babysitting; room service. *In room:* TV, hair dryer, Wi-Fi (in most; free).

Mermaid Inn ★★   The Mermaid is one of the most romantic inns in Sussex. It was the haunt of the cutthroat Hawkhurst Gang of smugglers, and of author Russell Thorndike's fictional smuggler Dr. Syn (one room is called Dr. Syn's Bedchamber, connected to the bar by a secret staircase). Rooms are wonderful, with beams everywhere, and the Elizabethan Chamber, with a four-poster bed, is like something out of a Hollywood version of a stately home.

Mermaid Street, Rye, East Sussex TN31 7EY. www.mermaidinn.com. ⓒ **01797/223065.** Fax 01797/225069. 31 units. £90–£220 double. Rates include English breakfast. AE, DC, MC, V. Free parking. **Amenities:** Restaurant; bar; babysitting; room service. *In room:* TV, hair dryer, Wi-Fi (in some; free).

BRIGHTON

52 miles S of London

Brighton is a party place. It's where Londoners flee for a day out, or a fun weekend. It's now officially a city, and it is packed with bars, clubs, restaurants, and hotels. It was one of England's first great seaside resorts, and then went through a bad time as its clientele started holidaying abroad. Now it's back, bigger and brighter than ever. It has taken on the ambience of London, which is only an hour away, with boutique lodgings, hip nightspots, and trendy shops. It's not for everyone, though: Once you're here, you'll find little respite from the crowds, and the beaches are pebble. Yet many visitors can't help loving Brighton.

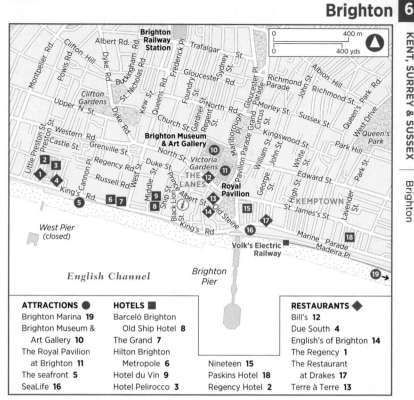

ATTRACTIONS ●	HOTELS ■		RESTAURANTS ◆
Brighton Marina **19**	Barceló Brighton		Bill's **12**
Brighton Museum &	Old Ship Hotel **8**		Due South **4**
Art Gallery **10**	The Grand **7**		English's of Brighton **14**
The Royal Pavilion	Hilton Brighton		The Regency **1**
at Brighton **11**	Metropole **6**	Nineteen **15**	The Restaurant
The seafront **5**	Hotel du Vin **9**	Paskins Hotel **18**	at Drakes **17**
SeaLife **16**	Hotel Pelirocco **3**	Regency Hotel **2**	Terre à Terre **13**

It was the fun-loving Prince of Wales (later George IV) who helped Brighton to its lofty position when he arrived in 1783. The town blossomed with attractive town-houses and smart squares and crescents. From the Prince Regent's title came the word *Regency*, which sums up an era, but more specifically refers to the period between 1811 and 1820. George IV's successor, Queen Victoria, found the place a bit too much. The **Prince Regent's Royal Pavilion** summer home is still here. Despite its being surrounded by old-time fun—the beachfront lined with bars, fish-and-chips shops, and cheap souvenir stalls; the pier with its amusements—Brighton is indeed fashionable once again.

Essentials

GETTING THERE Fast trains leave London Victoria (Southern) and London Bridge (First Capital Connect) stations roughly every 15 minutes; the journey is less than an hour. A ticket starts at about £15. National Express buses from London's Victoria Coach Station take around 2 hours; tickets are about £12.

If you're driving, the M23 (signposted from central London) leads to the A23, which takes you straight into Brighton.

VISITOR INFORMATION The **Tourist Information Centre,** 4–5 Pavilion Buildings (📞 **01273/290337;** www.visitbrighton.com), is next to the Royal Pavilion shop. It's open Monday to Saturday 10am to 5pm (until 4pm summer Sun and bank holidays).

GETTING AROUND You really don't want to drive around Brighton—parking is difficult and expensive, and the seafront gets clogged with traffic. There are plenty of local buses (📞 **01273/886200;** www.buses.co.uk), and you can get a Saver ticket (£3 for 1 day, £14 for a week) for unlimited travel on daytime buses. It's available in shops, at newsagents, and online. Free route maps are available at the Tourist Information Centre (see above).

SPECIAL EVENTS In May, the **Brighton Festival** (📞 **01273/709709;** www. brightonfestival.org) is the largest arts festival in England. It features drama, literature, visual art, dance, and concerts ranging from classical to rock.

Exploring the Area

Brighton Marina MARINA A mile or so east of the city, tucked beneath the chalky cliffs, is the modern marina. It's Britain's biggest, with 1,600 moorings, and there are plenty of sea-view houses and flats too. But this is also a massive entertainment complex with more than 20 restaurants (mostly chains, including Marco Pierre White's and Frankie & Benny's), bars, a modest outlet mall, a 26-lane bowling alley, a cinema, a health club, children's playgrounds, and bicycle rental. You can even stay here, at the **Hotel Seattle** (**www.aliashotels.com**; 📞 01273/679799) or in a luxury pad that's available for rental. There's also the **Walk of Fame** (www.walkoffame. co.uk), a Hollywood-style tribute to those with Brighton connections: from The Who (their mod movie *Quadrophenia* was set here) to *Brighton Rock* author Graham Greene. It's an easy walk from town, there's a 24-hour bus, plenty of free parking, or you can take the miniature **Volks Electric Railway** (📞 **01273/292718,** www. volkselectricrailway.co.uk), Britain's first electric train, which started running in 1873.

Brighton Marina, Waterfront. 📞 **01273/628627.** www.brightonmarina.co.uk. Bus: no. 7.

Brighton Museum & Art Gallery ★★ MUSEUM Once the Royal Pavilion's magnificent stable block, this is now a treasure-trove of beautiful and curious things. The museum is in the park adjoining the Pavilion (see below), and a recent £10 million redevelopment has created a bright, white environment to showcase one of the most important collections of decorative arts in England outside London. And it's free. First thing you come to is the 20th-century Decorative Art and Design gallery, where Salvador Dalí's Marilyn Monroe Lips sofa rubs shoulders, as it were, with some exquisite pieces by Charles Rennie Mackintosh. There are modernistic bentwood chairs and the original ornate copper elevator interior from London's Selfridge's department store. Farther on you find the history of Brighton, from its discovery by the bright young things to the dark days of World War II bombings, plus exhibitions of stage costumes and fashion, while upstairs are modernist paintings including works by Walter Sickert, as well as special exhibitions and a cafe.

Royal Pavilion Gardens. 📞 **03000/290900.** www.brighton-hove-rpml.org.uk. Free admission. Tues-Sun 10am–5pm.

The Royal Pavilion at Brighton ★★★ HISTORIC SITE From the outside, the Pavilion appears a bit seaside-resort garish, a melee of vaguely eastern-looking domes, painted an unattractive beige, that you suspect might house an entertainment

HITTING THE heights

The **360 Tower,** a new Brighton landmark being built on the seafront, just opposite the Hilton Metropole, is due to open in the summer of 2012. It's on the site of the entrance to the now-derelict West Pier. The slim tower's circular, spaceship-like, viewing deck is also its elevator, carrying crowds up to the 150-m (492-ft.) summit. It will be Britain's highest viewing tower, and is by the same team that created the London Eye (p. 107), the iconic big wheel by the Thames in London. The website (www.westpier.co.uk) has the latest information.

complex. Yet the place is a pleasure palace of another kind. This was the royals' idea of a seaside hideaway. It's a phantasmagoric collection of Oriental architecture, furniture, and fittings; a playful place that fitted in with the resort's somewhat wild reputation even when it was built. Everywhere you look, mythical creatures roar and writhe on ceilings, walls, and artwork. It was created for the Prince Regent, later King George IV, between 1787 and 1823. Queen Victoria later stayed here, but both it and Brighton were a little too much for her prim and proper tastes.

The dining room is simply superb, the 24-seat table under a domed roof (painted to resemble a palm canopy) from which hangs the most amazing chandelier you'll ever see: a huge dragon breathing fire over floral lights and shards of mirror. The music room is hardly less breathtaking: eight chandeliers, and a fireplace from which another dragon emerges.

The Pavilion is also an example of the Industrial Revolution that was starting to sweep Britain at the time; the original wooden farmhouse construction was surrounded by an innovative iron framework on which the rest was built (part is visible through holes where restoration work takes place). The Pavilion was a hospital for maimed Indian soldiers after World War I (there's a fascinating exhibition), and narrowly escaped being demolished after World War II. A cafe upstairs allows you to rest amid the Regency wonders. The Pavilion is at the city's heart, surrounded by protected gardens, in which there's a skating rink at Christmas. Entry includes a free audio guide.

© **01273/290900.** www.royalpavilion.org.uk. Admission £9.80 adults, £7.80 students and seniors, £5.60 children 5–15, £25 family ticket, free for children 4 and under. Apr–Sept daily 9:30am–5:45pm; Oct–Mar daily 10am–5:15pm.

The seafront ★★ WALKWAY Brighton's promenade exists on two levels: There's the wide path and cycleway that runs along King's Road, above the level of the beach; and there's the beachfront path, down some steps, which is awash in candy sellers and mini-carousels, bars, and shellfish stalls. It runs from Brighton Pier (a Victorian structure now featuring a fun fair with roller-coaster and other hair-raising, over-water rides, bars, and restaurants) to the entrance of the old West Pier (where the I360 is being built), with businesses occupying arches under the road. Star attractions are the **Brighton Smokehouse,** where fish are smoked in a beach hut, and you can buy a hot kipper sandwich for £2.80; the free **Brighton Fishing Museum** (© 01273/723064; www.brightonfishingmuseum.org.uk), with fishing boat and lots of memorabilia and old photos; the **Fortune of War** (© 01273/205065), a run-down pub

LITERARY lights: KIPLING & WOOLF

This part of the country was home to various artistic and literary figures. **Charleston ★★★** (✆ **01323/811265;** www.charleston.org.uk), on the A27 at Charleston, was the country residence of artists Vanessa Bell and Duncan Grant, the glittering faces of the artistically influential Bloomsbury Group early in the 20th century. The house is a work of art in itself, with the group's decorative style covering walls, doors, and furniture. There are other Bloomsbury works, plus pieces by Picasso, Renoir, and more. The house was also sometime home to economist Maynard Keynes, while Virginia and Leonard Woolf, novelist E. M. Forster, and biographer Lytton Strachey visited often. Virginia was Vanessa's sister. The walled garden has a Mediterranean theme, with some enigmatic sculptures. It is open April until October, Wednesday to Saturday 1 to 6pm (July–Aug from noon) and Sunday 1 to 5:30pm. Admission is £9 for adults, £8 for seniors, £5 for children 6 to 16, and £23 for a family ticket. You can see the house only with a tour, included in the price, except Sundays when it is open access. The annual literary and arts festival (late May) is a regular sell-out.

Just east of Brighton, near Lewes, is Rodmell, where Virginia Woolf lived until her death in 1941. **Monk's House** (✆ **01323/870001;** www.nationaltrust. org.uk), bought by Virginia and Leonard Woolf in 1919, and Leonard remained there until his death in 1969. Much of it was furnished and decorated by Vanessa Bell and Duncan Grant. The house, where Woolf did much of her writing, has a tenant, and so has limited visiting hours: April to October, Wednesday and Saturday, 2 to 5:30pm (£4.20 adults, £2.10 children 5 to 15, £11 family ticket).

In the village of Burwash, on the A265, 27 miles northeast of Brighton, is **Bateman's ★** (✆ **01435/882302;** www. nationaltrust.org.uk), the 17th-century house in which author Rudyard Kipling lived from 1902 until his death in 1936. "Heaven looked after it in the dissolute times of mid-Victorian restoration and caused the vicar to send his bailiff to live in it for 40 years, and he lived in peaceful filth and left everything as he found it," wrote the creator of *The Jungle Book* about the place.

Bombay-born Kipling loved Sussex, a love expressed in *Puck of Pook's Hill,* written in 1906. The following year he won the Nobel Prize for literature. Kipling lived in the U.S. after his marriage to Caroline Balestier in 1892. They moved to England in 1896, to a house at Rottingdean on the Sussex Downs, where he wrote the line: "What should they know of England who only England know?" The couple set out to explore Sussex in a steam-driven car, and one day spotted Bateman's. "It is a good and peaceable place standing in terraced lawns nigh to a walled garden of old red brick, and two fat-headed oasthouses with redbrick stomachs, and an aged silver-grey dovecot on top," Kipling wrote.

A World War I memorial, unveiled by Kipling, is in Burwash church. The church and an inn opposite appear in *Puck of Pook's Hill* under "Hal o' the Draft." Bateman's is filled with rugs, bronzes, and other mementos collected in India and elsewhere. The house and gardens are open mid-March to October, Saturday to Wednesday 10am to 5pm. Admission is £7.45 for adults, £3.70 for children 5 to 15, and £19 for a family ticket. Gardens only are also open November to Christmas, 11am to 4pm, with free admission.

that still keeps going; and the **Ohso Social** (© 01273/46067; www.ohsosocial. co.uk), a cafe/bar/restaurant with a terrace that has a driftwood feel and views over the pier (great in the evening as all the lights go on). You'll find music pouring out of bars, bands playing on the beach, rollerbladers whizzing by, and people just out for a stroll.

SeaLife ★★ AQUARIUM   This was the world's first aquarium, opening as the Royal Aquarium in 1872. It retains a *Twenty Thousand Leagues Under The Seas* feel, thanks to its subterranean setting. Many of the tanks are under low, vaulted ceilings, but the days of dolphin tanks are long gone, and it's now part of a major set-up. There is plenty to see here: Rays, crabs, and other local sealife as well as exotic fish. That's just the opener before you walk into a darkened Amazonia Jungle zone and eventually emerge into a glass tunnel snaking through a massive tank alive with fish, sharks, and a pair of magnificent turtles. (Lulu is 70-plus years old and weighs 152 kg/335 lb.) You can then pop upstairs to see it all from above in a glass-bottom boat.

Marine Parade. © **0871/4232110.** www.visitsealife.com/Brighton. Admission £16 adults, £11 children 3-14, £45 family ticket. Daily 10am–5pm.

Where to Eat

EXPENSIVE

The Restaurant at Drakes ★ MODERN BRITISH/FRENCH   This is the smartest and perhaps best restaurant in Brighton, combining contemporary British style with French twists. The atmosphere in this basement is intimate and soothing. Food is inventive (a starter of local scallops and black pudding purée with roasted apples and beurre blanc, perhaps, followed by poached and roasted breast of Sussex White chicken with pithivier of braised leg meat, cep mushroom purée, thyme croquettes, and truffle sauce). Drakes may be best but you could be anywhere; if you want true Brighton, go to the Regency (see below).

Drakes Hotel, 44 Marine Parade. © **01273/696934.** www.therestaurantatdrakes.co.uk. Reservations recommended. Set menu £30 for 2 courses; £40 3-course dinner. AE, MC, V. Daily 12:30–2pm and 7–9:45pm.

MODERATE

Due South ★★ MODERN BRITISH   Due South is under the arches, all woody and warm and right by the sea. It's the perfect place for a perfect restaurant. Due South boasts "organic, free-range, and biodynamic" ingredients. Most come from within a 35-mile radius of Brighton beach. There is great seafood (sea bass, scallops, a selection of oysters) but also dishes you wouldn't expect in a little seafront eatery (South Brockwells Farm pheasant stuffed with wild mushroom, with game liver parfait, game spiced brioche, potted leg, and warm consommé jelly).

139 King's Rd. Arches. © **01273/821218.** www.duesouth.co.uk. Reservations recommended. Main courses £12–£18 (seafood is market price). AE, MC, V. Daily noon–3:30pm and 6–10pm.

English's of Brighton SEAFOOD   This is a seafood tradition, run by the same family for more than 60 years, amid Edwardian style in the heart of town. You can drop in for a glass of champers and a snack at the marble-topped oyster bar, or head to the richly decorated Red Room for a full meal (in summer the terrace is very pleasant). It's good English fare with starters such as potted shrimp or dressed crab. The likes of Dover sole and lobster dominate the main courses, although you'll also find tuna, and they do a good local steak. There are also interesting and good-value set menus, and a seven-course tasting menu (£40).

28 East St. ℂ **01273/327980.** www.englishs.co.uk. Reservations recommended. Main courses £12–£23. AE, DC, MC, V. Mon–Sat noon–10pm; Sun 12:30–9:30pm.

INEXPENSIVE

Bill's ★ 📷 MODERN BRITISH   Once the maverick Bill's Produce Store, selling and serving local produce in a fresh, cheery way, it's now Bill's with the concept expanded into a chain (even in London's Covent Garden). The original, in an old bus depot in the heart of town, is still excellent. There are big breakfasts (plenty of bubble and squeak: Mashed potato fried with cooked cabbage), then lunch, snacky things, and early dinner… lots of hummus, Thai green prawn curry, and the like, along with burgers and steaks.

The Depot, 100 North St. ℂ **01273/692894.** www.billsproducestore.co.uk. Reservations not necessary. Main courses £7.50–£16. AE, MC, V. Mon–Sat 8am–8pm; Sun 10am–4pm.

The Regency ★★★ ENGLISH   If you're only going to eat in one Brighton restaurant, it should be this one. A fish restaurant that starts at the cod and chips end and effortlessly takes in fabulous Dover sole (grilled or meunière), vast crab salads, and delectable sardines, right up to the Shellfish Extravaganza (£40) yet doesn't glorify the product or the prices. It's a happy family place with views over the sea, and some outside tables. And if you need history, it's been serving since the 1930s, and was previously the seaside getaway of Harriott Mellon, widow of banker Thomas Coutts, wife of the 9th Duke of St. Albans, and the richest woman in Europe.

131 King's Rd. ℂ **01273/325014.** www.theregencyrestaurant.co.uk. Reservations not necessary. Main courses £6.75–£17. AE, MC, V. Daily 8am–10:30pm.

Terre à Terre ★★ 📷 VEGETARIAN/VEGAN   This is a vegetarian restaurant, sure, but it's also a place for people who like eating dishes made out of vegetables rather than wanting something coyly pretending to be meat. Dishes come from around the continents (curries, stir-fries, rosti, souffles) and are embellished with a touch of Brighton charm. The restaurant is a jolly brasserie and does a sort of global tapas (a selection menu is £21 for two), and serves organic wines.

71 East St. ℂ **01273/729051.** www.terreaterre.co.uk. Reservations recommended. Main courses £13–£15. AE, DC, MC, V. Tues–Fri noon–10:30pm; Sat noon–11pm; Sun noon–10pm.

Shopping

For shopping, head to the **Lanes,** a collection of alleyways and small streets behind North Street and its big-name shops. The area is full of boutiques, cafes, and arty stores of all kinds. Those in the know slide along to **North Laine**—between the Lanes and the train station—which is seen as the area for up-and-coming talent. Innumerable shops in the Lanes carry old books and jewelry, and many boutiques are found in converted backyards on Duke Lane just off Ship Street. At the heart of the Lanes is Brighton Square, which is ideal for relaxing or people-watching near the fountain on one of the benches or from a cafe-bar.

Brighton has plenty of big-name shops too. Try **Churchill Square,** which is home to major chain stores.

Regent Arcade, which is located between East Street, Bartholomew Square, and Market Street, sells artwork, jewelry, and other gift items, as well as high-fashion clothing. Bargain hunters head for the **Kemptown Flea Market,** Upper James

Street, held Monday to Saturday 9:30am to 5:30pm and Sunday 10:30am to 5pm. A more famous **flea market** is held in the parking lot of the train station, but only on Sunday from 6am to 2pm.

Entertainment & Nightlife

Offering drama year-round is the **Theatre Royal,** New Road (℡ **08700/606650**), with pre-London shows. Bigger concerts are held at **Brighton Centre,** King's Road (℡ **01273/290131;** www.brightoncentre.co.uk), a 5,000-seat facility featuring mainly pop-music shows.

Komedia, 44 Gardner St. (℡ **01273/687171;** www.komedia.co.uk), is a venue that hosts everything from top indie bands (British Sea Power) to the Banff Film Festival tour, and from top comedy to Brighton Jazz Club. **The Latest Music Bar,** 14 Manchester St. (℡ **01273/687171;** www.thelatest.co.uk), combines the latest in live music with party-style club nights. Pubs all over the city regularly have live music, often free.

There are plenty of nightclubs in Brighton; some have been around for a while, others come and go. Check **www.visitbrighton** or **www.brightonlife.com** for up-to-date info. There's often free admission early on or midweek rising to £10, but times and prices often vary from week to week or season to season.

Honeyclub (℡ **01273/202807;** www.thehoneyclub.co.uk), 214 King's Rd. Arches, is a bar by day and a lively club at night, with downstairs dance floor. **Audio,** 10 Marine Parade (℡ **01273/606906;** www.audiobrighton.com), is another of the places that continues to buzz, with a clutch of different, hard-hitting club nights. **Casablanca,** Middle Street (℡ **01273/321817;** www.casablancajazzclub.com), is still clubbing but with a funk-latin-jazz feel.

brighton's GAY SCENE

Brighton has long been regarded as Britain's gay capital. It has the country's biggest gay festival (Pride, in early Aug), and a thriving scene of bars, clubs, and hotels. Most of the action is in the Gay Quarter in Kemp Town, a compact strip just off the seafront. **Dr Brighton,** 16 King's Rd. (℡ **01273/328765;** www. doctorbrightons.co.uk), opposite the pier is one of the mainstays, and has a street party during Pride. **Legends,** 31 Marine Parade (℡ **01273/624462;** www.legends brighton.com), is one of the country's leading gay hotels and has two venues, **Legends** cafe-bar and **The Basement** nightclub. **The Marlborough,** 4 Princes St. (℡ **01273/570028**), is a richly traditional pub opposite the Royal Pavilion with a cabaret theatre. Of the clubs, **Revenge,** 32–34 Old Steine (℡ **01273/606064;** www.revenge.co.uk), is the biggest, with lots of gay-friendly live acts from reality TV shows such as *X Factor.* **The Charles Street Bar & Club,** 8 Marine Parade (℡ **01273/624091;** www.charles-street. com), combines a downstairs bar, which spills onto the street, with a popular club above. Of the hotels, **Colson House,** 17 Upper Rock Gardens (www.colsonhouse. co.uk; ℡ **01273/694922**), features eight rooms themed after stars such as Marilyn Monroe; while the **Amsterdam,** 11 Marine Parade (www.amsterdam.co.uk; ℡ **01273/68825**), combines a men-only sauna, chill-out bar with sun terrace, and decent restaurant. The official tourist office site, www.visitbrighton.com, has a sizable gay section while www.gscene. com is a local site devoted to gay and lesbian matters.

Oceana, West Street (☎ **0845/2968590**), is a massive place, with five themed bars (e.g. Aspen ski lodge, Tahiti), and two nightclubs. The main one has Europe's largest illuminated dance floor, and the retro New York disco.

Pubs are a good place to kick off an evening, especially the **Colonnade Bar,** New Road (☎ **01273/328728**), serving drinks for over 100 years. It gets a lot of theatre business because of its proximity to the Theatre Royal. **Cricketers,** Black Lion Street (☎ **01273/329472;** www.goldenliongroup.co.uk), is worth a stop because it's Brighton's oldest pub, parts of which date from 1549. Or just walk along the beach and see what takes your fancy.

Where to Stay
EXPENSIVE

The Grand ★★ Brighton's leading hotel opened in 1864 and entertained some of the most eminent Victorians and Edwardians; today it still lords it over the seafront. Inside is as grand as out, with a plush lobby and sweeping staircase. Rooms are big and airy, with huge windows—many overlooking the sea. The **King's restaurant** is suitably grandiose and serves English classics with a modern edge, while the Victoria lounge and bar opens into a huge sea-view conservatory and is the place for everything from morning coffee to a classy cream tea to a relaxing evening cocktail.

97–99 King's Rd., Brighton, East Sussex BN1 2FW. www.devere.co.uk. ☎ **01273/224300.** Fax 01273/ 224321. 201 units. £110–£390 double; from £310 suite. Rates include English breakfast. AE, DC, MC, V. Parking £25. **Amenities:** Restaurant; bar; babysitting; concierge; exercise room; indoor heated pool; room service; spa. *In room:* TV, hair dryer, minibar, Internet (free).

Hilton Brighton Metropole ★★ Sitting alongside The Grand, this is the other big hotel on the seafront, a giant (Brighton's biggest hotel) of red brick and iron balconies. The lobby is unassuming, but the rooms are big and high-ceilinged, so much so that even the king-size beds in many are dwarfed by their surroundings. The decor is simple and modern. There's a decent pool, along with a spa. Breakfast is a joy in the lofty, white, Windsor restaurant (like a cross between an orangerie and a ballroom) with its huge sea-view windows, ornate plasterwork, and giant chandeliers. The room, which is part of the hotel's Victorian heritage is, by evening, a rather nice **restaurant** offering a set menu (£25 for 3 courses). The hotel's position means that it will look out onto the i360 Tower.

106 King's Rd., Brighton, East Sussex BN1 2FU. www.hilton.co.uk/brightonmet. ☎ **01273/775432.** Fax 01273/207764. 334 units. £80–£160 double; £229–£244 suite. Rates include English breakfast. AE, DC, MC, V. Parking £16. **Amenities:** Restaurant; 2 bars; babysitting; concierge; exercise room; indoor heated pool; room service; spa. *In room:* TV, hair dryer, Internet (£15 for 24 hr.).

Hotel du Vin Down a little street just off the seafront, this member of a small, upmarket chain looks delicious in a jumble of Gothic and Tudor-revival buildings. Its entrance is beneath a stone arch, and neat window frames are painted a pale green. Inside it's dark and cool in a mod-ish sort of way, with a double-height lounge and bar beneath a high-beamed ceiling. There's also a discreet, woody **bistro** and trendy **Pub du Vin.** Rooms are light and modern. Top choice is the One-of-a-kind room, massive with wooden floors, a four-poster bed, and two free-standing baths in the middle of the room.

Ship St., Brighton, East Sussex BN1 1AD. www.hotelduvin.com.uk. ☎ **01273/718588.** 49 units. £125–£355 double. AE, DC, MC, V. Parking £15 (£19 weekends). **Amenities:** Restaurant; bar; room service. *In room:* TV/DVD, hair dryer, Internet (free).

MODERATE

Barceló Brighton Old Ship Hotel ★   An inn in 1559, this seafront hotel has its place in history: It hosted the Prince Regent's Ball in 1819, a Paganini violin recital in 1831, and the banquet celebrating the opening of the London to Brighton Railway in 1841. The largely Victorian rebuild is now a boutique affair and the rooms are pleasing in a contemporary-traditional way. A limited number have sea views. The **Location 3 restaurant,** with its continental feel, attracts far more than hotel guests, while the woody bar spills out onto a promenade seating area.

31 King's Rd., Brighton, East Sussex BN1 1NR. www.barcelo-hotels.co.uk. ℂ **01273/329001.** Fax 01273/ 820718. 154 units. £98–£165 double. Children under 12 stay free in parent's room. AE, DC, MC, V. Parking £20. **Amenities:** Restaurant; bar; concierge; room service. *In room:* TV, hair dryer, Wi-Fi (free).

Hotel Pelirocco ★★★ 🎁   Take your sunglasses with you when you check into this seafront townhouse, the arty rock 'n' roll face of Brighton. The Pelirocco is a riot of color, with rooms all themed around pop culture or personalities: Soul Supreme (Motown), Ali (Muhammad Ali), Pretty Vacant (Sex Pistols). The **PlayStation bar,** open until 1am Sunday to Thursday, and until 4am at weekends, is a place of brightly hued cocktails and a clientele to match. The food is just as fun, all cupcakes and samosa-style nibbles (continental breakfast is an extra charge). It's the ultimate kitsch weekend break.

10 Regency Square, Brighton, East Sussex BN1 2FG. www.hotelpelirocco.co.uk. ℂ **01273/327055.** 19 units. £90–£115 double. Rates include English breakfast. AE, DC, MC, V. Parking £10. **Amenities:** Bar. *In room:* TV/DVD, hair dryer. ·

Nineteen ★ 🎁   One road back from the beach, near the pier, Nineteen is an oasis of white, punctuated by works from local artists. King rooms have glass-brick platform beds illuminated by subtle blue lighting. The Courtyard room has a private courtyard that's a fern jungle with a chemical-free hot tub filled anew for every guest. The classy continental breakfast (with champagne, buck's fizz, or bloody Mary at weekends) is served in-room, and there's a kitchen where you can help yourself to coffee and cakes.

19 Broad St., Brighton, East Sussex BN2 1TJ. www.hotelnineteen.co.uk. ℂ **01273/675529.** Fax 01273/ 675531. 8 units. £85–£250 double. Rates include continental breakfast. 2-night minimum Sat–Sun. AE, DC, MC, V. Parking £8. **Amenities:** Bar; concierge; room service. *In room:* TV/DVD, CD player, hair dryer, Wi-Fi (free).

Paskins Hotel   This has been an eco-friendly hotel since before that was trendy, with organic breakfasts, washing towels with soap nut shells and such. The Paskins is a Victorian townhouse, a couple of streets back from the seafront near the pier. Inside, Edwardian, Art Nouveau, and Art Deco touches create a rich, arty feel. The rooms are individually furnished (you can get a four-poster). The full-English breakfast is a treat, with locally cured bacon and small-batch sausages (they try up to 50 varieties a year), and homemade veggie sausages made from sun-dried tomatoes and tarragon.

18 Charlotte St., Brighton, East Sussex BN2 1AG. www.paskins.co.uk. ℂ **01273/601203.** Fax 01273/ 621973. 19 units. £90–£150 double. Rates include English breakfast. AE, MC, V. Parking £5. **Amenities:** Room service. *In room:* TV, hair dryer, Wi-Fi (free).

INEXPENSIVE

Regency Hotel   Just back from the sea, this Regency townhouse, once the home of Jane, dowager duchess of Marlborough and great-grandmother of Sir Winston Churchill, is a skillfully converted family-managed hotel with a bar and modern comforts. Most rooms enjoy views across the square and out to the sea. Some have a historic feel (with four-posters); others (including several family rooms) are simple and modern. The Regency Suite has antique furniture, and a balcony facing the sea.

28 Regency Square, Brighton, East Sussex BN1 2FH. www.regencyhotelbrighton.com. ✆ **01273/ 202690.** Fax 01273/220438. 14 units (shower only). £60–£155 double. Rates include English breakfast. AE, DC, MC, V. Parking £13. **Amenities:** Breakfast room; bar; room service. *In room:* TV, hair dryer, Wi-Fi (free).

CHICHESTER & ARUNDEL

Chichester: 31 miles W of Brighton; 69 miles SW of London. Arundel: 21 miles W of Brighton; 58 miles SW of London

Chichester has it all. On one side there's the sea, a natural harbor with 48 miles of coastline, where you'll see plenty of yachts. On the other side is the undulating countryside of the **South Downs,** Britain's newest National Park. And Chichester itself? It has all the charms of a smart market town yet is actually a city, courtesy of its **cathedral.** It can also boast being the former Roman city of Noviomagus. The streets are neat and historic, no more so than at the Tudor Market Cross, a stone structure at the centre of East, West, North, and South streets near the cathedral. And there are many upmarket shops (there aren't many places in England where you'll find an Orvis store). It's an arty place and home to the **Chichester Festival,** one of the country's leading arts festivals, which takes place each July in the 1950s-era Festival Theatre in Oaklands Park. At other times of the year the building also hosts everything from orchestras to the likes of folk-rock veterans Fairport Convention.

Arundel is a small town a short drive from Chichester. It is dominated by the might of **Arundel Castle,** yet there is more to it than that: The River Arun crosses it, serene and regal (this was once a river port), then meanders, like a scene from the Middle Ages, through water meadows that make for lovely walks.

Essentials

GETTING THERE Trains depart from London's Victoria Station every 30 minutes during the day. The trip takes 1½ hours to Arundel, another few minutes to Chichester. The Southern service costs about £25 to either. However, if you visit Chichester for the theatre, you'll need to stay over—the last train back is mid-evening.

If you're driving, take the A3 from London, turning onto the A286 for Chichester. From Chichester take the A27 east to Arundel.

VISITOR INFORMATION Chichester Tourist Information Centre, 29A South St. (✆ **01243/775888;** www.visitchichester.org), is open October to March, Monday 10:15am to 5:15pm and Tuesday to Saturday 9:15am to 5:15pm; April to September it's open Monday to Saturday 9:15am to 5:15pm and Sunday 10:30am to 3pm. **Arundel Tourist Information Centre,** 1–3 Crown Yard Mews, River Road (✆ **01903/882268;** www.sussexbythesea.com), is open April to October, Monday to Saturday 10am to 5pm (to 6pm July–Aug), Sunday 10am to 4pm; off-season hours are daily 10am to 3pm.

Exploring the Area

Arundel Castle ★★ CASTLE The ancestral home of the dukes of Norfolk, Arundel Castle is a much-restored mansion of considerable importance. Its legend is associated with some of the great families of England—the Fitzalans and the powerful Howards of Norfolk. This castle received worldwide exposure when it was chosen as the backdrop for *The Madness of King George* (it was "pretending" to be Windsor Castle in the film). Arundel Castle suffered badly during the Civil Wars when it was stormed by Cromwell's troops, in likely retaliation for the sizable contribution to Charles I made by the 14th Earl of Arundel. In the early 18th century the castle had to be virtually rebuilt, and in late Victorian times it was remodeled and extensively restored again. Today it's filled with works by Old Masters such as Van Dyck and Gainsborough, and with antiques. The Civil War story is brought to life by mannequins and an audio presentation. The castle sits on 16 hectares (40 acres) of grounds, including a walled kitchen and formal gardens reclaimed from car parking several years ago. It is all circled by a 445-hectare (1,100-acre) park containing Swanbourne Lake.

Mill Rd., Arundel ✆ **01903/882173.** www.arundelcastle.org. Admission £7.50–£16 adults, £7.50–£13 students and seniors, £7.50 children 5–16, £39 family ticket, free for children 4 and under. April–Oct Tues–Sun, grounds 10am–5pm, castle keep 11am–4:30pm, rooms noon–5pm (last admission 4pm). Closed Nov–Mar.

Arundel Cathedral CATHEDRAL   The Roman Catholic Cathedral of Our Lady and St. Philip Howard stands at the highest point in Arundel. A. J. Hansom, inventor of the Hansom cab, built it for the 15th Duke of Norfolk. However, it was not consecrated as a cathedral until 1965. The interior includes the shrine of St. Philip Howard, featuring Sussex wrought-iron work.

London Rd., Arundel. ✆ **01903/882297.** www.arundelcathedral.org. Free admission; donations appreciated. Daily 9:30am–dusk. From the middle of town, continue west from High St.

Chichester Cathedral CATHEDRAL   Completed in 1123, the cathedral is light and airy and topped by a sharp, narrow spire. This spire was completed in 1867 after the earlier one fell in 1860. As well as being architecturally stunning, the cathedral is accumulating a growing collection of modern art. Look for the abstract stained-glass window by Marc Chagall; the painting, *Noli Me Tangere*, of Christ appearing to Mary at Easter by Graham Sutherland; and the mural, *The Baptism of Christ,* by German artist Hans Feibusch. There is also a 3m-high (10-ft.) stainless-steel hand of Christ floating high in the Nave, the work of Jaume Plensa, the internationally renowned sculptor whose Crown Fountain graces Chicago's Millennium Park.

Cathedral Cloisters, South St., Chichester. ✆ **01243/782595.** www.chichestercathedral.org.uk. Free admission. Daily 7am–6pm (from 7:15am in winter). Guided tours Mon–Sat 11:15am and 2:30pm.

Fishbourne Roman Palace HISTORIC SITE   This is what remains of the largest Roman residence discovered in Britain. Built around A.D. 75, it has many mosaic-floored rooms and even an under-floor heating system. The gardens have been restored to their 1st-century plan. There is also a state-of-the-art computer graphic reconstruction of the palace. Roman artifacts are on display in the Discovery Centre. There are guided tours twice a day.

North of the A259, off Salthill Rd. (signposted from Fishbourne; 1½ miles from Chichester). ✆ **01243/785859.** www.sussexpast.co.uk. Admission £7.60 adults, £6.80 students and seniors, £4 children 5–15, £21 family ticket. Jan Sat–Sun 10am–4pm; Feb daily 10am–4pm; Mar–July and Sept–Oct daily 10am–5pm; Aug daily 10am–6pm; Nov–Dec 10am–4pm (not always open during this time; call first).

Goodwood RACECOURSE   This stately home, in the hills of the South Downs, is best known as one of the world's most famous motor-racing circuits, which is now restored to its look of 50 years ago. The course is too small for modern racers, but there are historic car events here such as the Festival of Speed (July) and Goodwood Revival (Sept). The track offers bring-your-own-car driving experiences. Goodwood House is a Jacobean mansion that was extended into the palace of today in the following centuries. It contains a superlative art collection (Van Dyck, Canaletto, Stubbs, Reynolds) and plenty of Regency furniture. The 4,856-hectare (12,000-acre) estate also features the Goodwood horse-racing circuit, notable for the Glorious Goodwood event (end of July), two golf courses, and clay and game shooting.

Take the A3 to Milford, the A283 to Petworth, then the A285 to Halnaker, and follow the signposts to Goodwood. *C* **01243/755000.** www.goodwood.co.uk. House mid-March–late Sept Sun–Mon 1–5pm; Aug Sun–Thurs 1–5pm. Admission £9.40 adults, £4 children 12–18, free children 11 and under.

Pallant House Art Gallery GALLERY This is a gallery of modern art, set up in 1982 following the gift of a collection featuring Henry Moore and Graham Sutherland; it has since attracted many important bequests. There's *The Beatles 1962* by Peter Blake, which preceded his design of their Sgt. Pepper album cover; the studio and archive of German artist Hans Feibusch (who fled from Nazi persecution and has a mural in Chichester Cathedral), plus works by Duncan Grant, Picasso, and more. Its Field & Fork restaurant serves sophisticated food into the evening, including the likes of game pie, truffled Savoy cabbage, and peppered jus (£20 for two courses, £27 for three courses).

9 North Pallant, Chichester. *C* **01243/774557.** www.pallant.org.uk. Admission £9 adults, £2.30, children 5–15, £17 family ticket. Tues half-price, Thurs free from 5pm.

Weald & Downland Open Air Museum MUSEUM In the beautiful Sussex countryside, historic buildings saved from destruction are reconstructed on a large downland site. They show the development of local traditional building, from medieval times to the 19th century. Exhibits include a Tudor market hall, a working water mill producing stone-ground flour, a blacksmith's forge, plumbers' and carpenters' workshops, a toll cottage, a charcoal burner's camp, and a 19th-century school. A reception area with shops is set in Longport House, and there's a 16th-century building rescued from the site of the Channel Tunnel.

At Singleton, 6 miles north of Chichester on the A286 (the London Rd.). *C* **01243/811363.** www.weald down.co.uk. Admission £9.50 adults, £8.50 seniors, £5 students and children 5–15, £26 family ticket. Apr–Oct daily 10:30am–6pm; Nov–Dec 22 daily 10:30am–4pm; Jan 3–Feb 18 Wed and Sat–Sun 10:30am–4pm; Feb 19–Mar daily 10:30am–4pm. Bus no. 60 from Chichester.

SOUTH downs WAY

The South Downs Way runs for 100 miles, from the promenade at Eastbourne, all the way to Winchester in Hampshire. It climbs the chalk cliffs of Beachy Head, passes by the giant chalk figure of the Long Man of Wilmington, skirts Charleston Farmhouse (where the Bloomsbury set of artists lived), takes an undulating, breathtaking path to the north of Brighton, and forges onward. It follows chalk ridges, dips into river valleys, and crosses bare hillsides feeling as remote as anything you'll find in more far-flung parts of the country. It would take an average walker 8 days to complete (and there are plenty of pubs and hotels on or near the route), but it's as easy to enjoy an afternoon stroll on any of the sections. Stop at one of the parking lots at Beachy Head, for instance, and start walking. Visit **www.national trail.co.uk** for full information and maps.

West Wittering Beach ★★ BEACH   West Wittering, a short drive from Chichester, is one of southern England's best beaches, a natural, unspoiled south-facing sweep of sand a mile or more long and backed by dunes. It's on private land, the West Wittering Estate, hidden away down a narrow lane, so you have to pay to park, but it's free for pedestrians. The parking lot is next to a big field behind the dunes, a place for kicking a ball about and barbecues when the sea breeze is too strong. There's also a cafe, a bucket and spade shop, and toilets. At one end is the National Trust's East head, a sand dune spit where you can take salt-splashed strolls for free.

Off the A27 (from the middle of Chichester, follow signs to Wittering). © **01243/514143.** www.west witteringbeach.co.uk. Parking lot April–June and mid-Sept–mid-Oct £3 weekday, £5 weekend; July–mid-Sept £5 weekday, £7 weekend; £2 rest of year. British Summer Time (late Mar–late Oct) 6:30am–8:30pm; rest of year 7am–6pm.

Where to Eat

Comme Ça ★ FRENCH   This restaurant celebrated its 25th anniversary in 2011, and it's easy to see why, with its French dishes combined with local ingredients. The decor is more English country than faux French, although the beautiful patio, draped in greenery with wrought ironwork and canopy, does make you feel as if you should be in Provence. There are two set menus, available for lunch or dinner, which include dishes such as hare roulade with forest mushrooms and game farce (stuffing) served with a port and lavender jus, or puff pastry feuilleté of mixed fish and seafood with parsley and chive white-wine sauce. The bar, with log fire, has its own hearty menu, which includes a smoked haddock tartiflette, mussels in wine, and charcuterie.

67 Broyle Rd., Chichester (a 10-min. walk from the middle of town). © **01243/788724.** www.commeca. co.uk. Reservations required. Fixed-price menu 2 courses lunch/dinner £22/£30, 3 courses £25/£35. Bar menu main courses £16–£17. AE, DC, MC, V. Wed–Sun 11:30am–2pm; Tues–Sat 6–10pm.

Queen's Room Restaurant ★★★ ENGLISH   This wonderful restaurant is in a small upstairs hall in Amberley Castle. You sit among suits of armor, medieval weapons, historic paintings, an open fire and candles, and under a barrel-vaulted 12th-century ceiling. A pair of cannons are outside the door, and there really is a feeling of being part of history. And the food is as good as you'd hope: roast loin of rabbit, polenta, black pudding, spinach, and root vegetable purée, for instance; or roast partridge, confit leg, sweet corn purée, and partridge reduction. And starters include fois gras and Jerusalem artichoke risotto. There are wines from around £30, or you can treat yourself to a Chateau Petrus 2002 for £4,450. It's a fabulous experience, in a fabulous setting. The fairytale Mistletoe Lodge treehouse in the grounds is also available as a private dining room for two, and the chef will create a personal menu.

Amberley Castle hotel (see below), Amberley, near Arundel. © **01798/831992.** www.amberleycastle. co.uk. Reservations required. Set lunch £28 for 2 courses, £33 for 3 courses; set dinner £53 for 2 courses, £63 for 3 courses. Tasting menu £85. AE, DC, MC, V. Daily noon–2pm and 7–9pm.

Entertainment & Nightlife

Chichester Festival Theatre ★★   A 5-minute walk from the Chichester Cathedral, this 1,400-seat theatre sits on the edge of Oaklands Park. It opened in 1962, and its first director was Lord Laurence Olivier. The theatre features plays and musicals, likely to star top names, plus orchestras, jazz, opera, theatre, ballet, and a Christmas show. The Minerva Studio Theatre, from the late 1980s, features more experimental performances. The famed Chichester Festival is actually a season of performances that runs from April to September and includes plays both classic and contemporary, along with musicals and associated events. Always special, the festival's 50th anniversary in 2012 is set to be particularly so (© **01243/781312** for the box office, or 01243/784437 for general info; www.cft.org.uk).

Where to Stay

Amberley Castle ★★★ 🏨 Yes, it is a real castle. And, yes, it is everything you might expect. Suits of armor, muskets, and swords everywhere, a library full of interesting old books, and even a working portcullis, which is dropped each evening from the tower over the gateway arch. The Amberley goes back 900 years and has seen its share of celebs—Elizabeth I stayed awhile, and Oliver Cromwell did his best to stop anyone from leaving during a siege when it was a royal stronghold. Now you'll find dark, warm, medieval-tinged rooms mostly with four-poster beds, all with spa baths and flat-screen TVs, and some with signs asking you to shut the door to keep the peacocks out. Two rooms even have private access to a tower leading to the battlements and views across the South Downs. The gardens are full of yew topiary, the grounds are dotted with ponds, and there's a professional 18-hole putting course. **The Queen's Room** restaurant (see Where to Eat) is a destination in itself; this is also where you enjoy your breakfast: a choice of continental or splendid full English.

Amberley, nr. Arundel, West Sussex BN18 9LT. www.amberleycastle.co.uk. © **01798/831992.** Fax 01798/831998. 19 units. £230–£520 double. Rates include English breakfast. AE, DC, MC, V. Free parking. Take the B2139 north of Arundel; the hotel is 1½ miles southwest of Amberley. **Amenities:** Restaurant; putting course; room service; outdoor tennis court. *In room:* TV, hair dryer, minibar, Wi-Fi (variable but free).

Norfolk Arms ☺ This is an old coaching inn, right on the main street. The two bars and Arun restaurant are in the typical English country-inn style. Bedrooms are simple but classic, some of them in a separate modern wing overlooking the courtyard. Four bedrooms are large enough for families.

22 High St., Arundel, West Sussex BN18 9AD. www.norfolkarmshotel.com. © **01903/882101.** Fax 01903/884275. 34 units. £70–£90 double. Children 13 and under stay free in parent's room. Rates include English breakfast. AE, DC, MC, V. Free parking. **Amenities:** Restaurant; 2 bars; room service. *In room:* TV, hair dryer, Wi-Fi (£10 per 24 hr.).

Ship Hotel A classic Georgian building, the Ship is only a few minutes' walk from Chichester Cathedral. Built as a private house in 1790 for Admiral Sir George Murray, it retains an air of elegance and comfort but with a modern touch. A grand staircase leads from the entrance to the bedrooms, which are named after historic ships. Some have four-poster beds; others are specially for families (£135 plus £25 per child). The revamped restaurant is a brasserie affair, all white walls and wooden floors and tables, serving smart fish, burgers, pasta, and such (main courses £10–£16).

57 North St., Chichester, West Sussex PO19 1NH. www.theshiphotel.net. © **01243/778000.** Fax 01243/788000. 36 units. £110–£185 double. Rates include English breakfast. AE, DC, MC, V. Free parking. **Amenities:** Restaurant; bar; room service. *In room:* TV, hair dryer, Wi-Fi (free).

GUILDFORD

30 miles S of London; 45 miles NE of Brighton

This is Surrey's picturesque county town (actually city); quaint streets, timbered buildings, the River Wey running through it, and lots of history, including a castle. Charles Dickens claimed that the High Street, which slopes to the river, was one of the most beautiful in England. And the Guildhall has a clock dating from 1683. It is a lovely place to stay and wander, but it is also an excellent base for exploring farther afield, such as the Surrey Hills (p. 281), or the banks of the river.

Essentials

GETTING THERE   Trains depart London's Waterloo Station and take 35 minutes; the South West Trains cost about £11. Guildford is an easy drive from London, on the A3, several miles outside the M25.

VISITOR INFORMATION   **Guildford Tourist Information Centre** is at Guildford House, 155 High St. (_C_ **01483/444333;** www.visitguildford.com/www. visitsurrey.com). It's open May to September, Monday to Saturday 9am to 5pm and Sunday 10am to 4:30pm; October to April, Monday to Saturday 9:30am to 5pm.

Exploring the Area

The streets and the river walk are all there to be enjoyed. **Guildford Castle** dates from shortly after the Norman Conquest of 1066, and although only the tower remains, sitting atop its man-made mound, it has been well renovated this century and contains exhibits on its history. It's open May to September, daily 10am to 5pm; October and March 11am to 4pm. Adults £2.60, children 5 to 15 £1.30. The grounds (free entry, daily 8am–dusk) were turned into gardens to celebrate Queen Victoria's Golden Jubilee in 1888. The ornamental bedding displays are renowned; you'll also find plenty of places to stop and relax, as well as an open-air theatre.

Guildford Museum in Castle Arch, Castle Hill, just off the High Street (_C_ **01483/444751;** www.visitguildford.com; Mon–Sat 11am–5pm; free admission), dates back to 1898 and features a collection of old Surrey items donated by famed garden designer Gertrude Jekyll in 1907.

Stoke Park is a huge area comprising woodland and formal gardens, plus a boating pond, paddling pool, children's play area, tennis courts, putting green, all-weather sports pitches, indoor and outdoor bowls, a trim trail, and a skateboard park. It's also where the Surrey County Show and GuilFest are held (see "Entertainment & Nightlife," below).

Dapdune Wharf ★ HISTORIC SITE   The Wey was one of Britain's first waterways to be made navigable, opening to barge traffic in 1653 and linking with the Thames. The Godalming Navigations, opened in 1764, allowed barges to go an additional 4 miles upstream. The visitor center has interactive exhibits and displays telling the story of the work, and of those who sailed the barges. There's the site where huge Wey barges were built, and you can climb aboard the _Reliance,_ one of three surviving barges. There are also short boat trips on an electric boat. The 19-mile towpath is open to walkers.

Wharf Rd. (just off the A322 in Guildford). _C_ **01483/561389.** www.nationaltrust.org.uk. Admission to wharf £3 adults, £2 children 5-15. Boat rides £3.50 adults, £2 children 5-15. Open late Mar-Oct Thurs-Mon (daily during school holidays) 11am-5pm. Closed Nov-Mar.

Guildford Cathedral ★ CATHEDRAL   Different from most cathedrals, this modern, red-brick affair sits on an open hilltop and is visible from much of the city and far beyond. Work was started in 1936 and, after a halt during World War II, was consecrated in the presence of the Queen in 1961. It's still a work in progress, with statues at the West Front completed in 2005, and work now focusing on landscaping of the grounds. The result is a stirring 1930s' architectural masterpiece, with an interior of grand simplicity.

Stag Hill. ✆ **01483/547860.** www.guildford-cathedral.org. Free admission; guided tours £3. Open daily.

Loseley House ★ HISTORIC SITE   The Loseley estate has been in the same family since the early 16th century, and they had this gorgeous Elizabethan mansion built in the 1560s. It's been visited by Queen Elizabeth I, James I (the Drawing Room has a gilded ceiling created especially for his visit), and Queen Mary. It's full of works of art that include paneling from Henry VIII's Nonsuch Palace and a unique carved chalk chimney piece. There is a superb walled garden, divided into flowers, herbs, and roses, the latter featuring more than 1,000 historic bushes. The Courtyard Tearoom, in the old kitchen and scullery, serves cakes from its own bakery, as well as lunches.

Loseley Park (2½ miles southwest of Guildford). ✆ **01483/304440.** www.loseley-park.com. Admission to house and gardens £8 adults, £7 students and seniors, £4 children 5-15; gardens only £4.50 adults, £4 students and seniors, £2.25 children. House May–Aug Tues–Thurs and Sun 1-5pm; gardens May–Sept Tues-Sun 11am-5pm.

RHS Garden Wisley ★★★ GARDEN   Possibly Britain's most important garden and the home of the Royal Horticulture Society. It's actually a whole world of gardens, from the herbaceous borders that line Battleston Hill to the wild, rhododendron woods at the summit; from the clipped show gardens to the wildflower heaven, which rolls down to the little stream. This isn't just a pretty garden, it's a scientific project, where seeds and plants are in trials so at the right time you might find a profusion of runner beans or chrysanthemums down in the trial beds. It is a good place to spend the day—and not just for garden-lovers and families with tots who run around the landscaped grassland and through the trees. The huge Glasshouse, on a man-made lake, opened in 2007 and displays delicate plants from several climatic zones in a theme park-like faux rock setting. In the early part of each year it's also turned into a butterfly house. Wherever you walk, and no matter what season, you'll find something different. There's also the good Conservatory cafe and restaurant, and various coffee bars, but it's a joy to bring a picnic and sit under the towering trees outside the gate. Large plant and gift shops mean there's no shortage of souvenirs.

Wisley (just off the M25, junction 10, on the A3 London–Portsmouth Rd.). ✆ **01483/224234.** www.rhs. org.uk. Admission £9.90 adults, £3.60 children 6-16, free for children 5 and under. Mar-Oct Mon-Fri 10am-6pm, Sat-Sun 9am-6pm; Nov-Feb Mon-Fri 10am-4:30pm, Sat-Sun 9am-4:30pm (last admission 1 hr. before closing).

Entertainment & Nightlife

The **White House,** 8 High St. (✆ **01483/302006**), is a riverside pub with a conservatory overlooking a lovely waterside garden. It is a great place to wind down on a summer's evening. **The Electric Theatre,** Onslow Street (✆ **01483/444789;** www.visitguildford.com), is a modern riverside venue that features music, drama, film, and other shows. **The Boiler Room,** 13 Stokefields (✆ **01483/440022;** www.theboilerroom.net), is a hip live music venue featuring emerging acts (Sun–Thurs 7pm–midnight, Fri–Sat to 1am; tickets £4–£7).

In mid-July Guildford's Stoke Park is home to **Guilfest** (✆ **0871/230-1106;** www.guilfest.co.uk), one of the country's most relaxed music festivals. From Friday evening to Sunday a vast collection of acts, from modern-day stars such as James Blunt to the likes of 70s' space rockers Hawkwind play on seven stages in an atmosphere that is more garden party than rock-fest; it's regularly voted one of Britain's top family festivals. It's an easy walk from the station, and there's plenty of free parking nearby so you can pop in for a day. Unlike some festivals, it is usually possible to get tickets at the gate.

Guildford Lido, also in Stoke Park, is a classic 1930s' outdoor swimming pool. The 50-m (164-ft.) pool is heated and surrounded by landscaped gardens. It is open May 1 to mid-September daily 10:30am to 6:30pm, with several early-morning sessions from 6:30am. The lawns make a wonderful spot for picnics, and there is a cafe. Also in the park is **Guildford Spectrum** (✆ **01483/443355**) one of Britain's leading leisure complexes, including a pool with slides, a 25-m (82-ft.) swimming pool, teaching pool, and diving pool, as well as bowling, ice-skating, and other sports. Times and prices vary.

Where to Eat & Stay

Asperion   This boutique guesthouse, which aims to be socially responsible, is within walking distance of town. There are sustainable practices, green energy, ethical and social banking. Organic breakfasts are sourced from local suppliers, and there are fair-trade tea and coffee, organic chocolate and toiletries in the rooms, and organic wine from the bar. The rooms are crisp and white, with Egyptian cotton sheets and down duvets.

73 Farnham Rd., Guildford, Surrey GU2 7PF. www.asperion.co.uk. ✆ **01483/579299.** Fax 01483/457977. 15 units. £85–£105 double. Rates include English breakfast. AE, MC, V. *In room:* TV, hair dryer, Internet (free).

Holiday Inn Guildford   Albeit on the wrong side of the A3 from the city, this modern hotel amid trees nevertheless makes a good stab at sophistication, with dark wood finishes in the lobby and bar. Most of the guests are on business, but it's a good place for those heading off exploring. The rooms are big and stylishly simple, and a pool and restaurant add to the attraction.

Egerton Rd., Guildford, Surrey GU2 7XZ. www.ichotelsgroup.com. ✆ **0870/400-9036.** Fax 01483/457256. 168 units. £114–£265 double. AE, DC, MC, V. Free parking. Off the A3, about 2 miles southwest of the heart of Guildford. **Amenities:** Restaurant; bar; babysitting; exercise room; indoor pool; room service; Wi-Fi (£15 per day). *In room:* TV, hair dryer.

Mandolay ★   Mandolay comprises four 19th-century townhouses converted into a luxury hotel that sits at the end of the High Street. There's been plenty of expansion and grooming over the past decade, and the place now has a seriously swish atmosphere with a sleek modern touch. The **m.Brasserie and Grill** is open 7 days a week for smart, locally sourced lunches and dinners, often with imaginative combinations such as lamb rump with artichoke, or the crispy filet of sea bass with chili, crab, mussels, pappardelle pasta, and saffron sauce (main courses £10–£17). The m.Bar is also one of Guildford's most sophisticated bars.

36–40 London Rd., Guildford, Surrey GU1 2AE. www.guildford.com. ✆ **01483/303030.** Fax 01483/534669. 72 units. £120–£175 double. AE, DC, MC, V. Free parking. **Amenities:** Restaurant; bar. *In room:* TV, hair dryer, Wi-Fi (free).

THE SURREY HILLS

30 miles from London

The Surrey Hills were designated an Area of Outstanding Natural Beauty in 1958, and offer some of the Southeast's most beautiful and accessible countryside There's the highest point in the region at **Leith Hill,** while the commons and heathland are remarkably dramatic, with yews and pines in natural formation and studded with gorse bushes (their bright yellow flowers are extravagant in spring). The ancient woodlands (home to many deciduous trees) are also full of rhododendrons, adding powerful shades in late spring (although these foreign invaders, introduced by the Victorians, strangle other undergrowth and are slowly being eradicated). Among the hills and trees are an almost unending web of paths as well as narrow, winding lanes often cut between chalky embankments. They're the perfect setting for a fantasy movie. The hills stretch across the chalk North Downs that run from Farnham in the west—above Guildford, Dorking, and Reigate—to Oxted in the east. To the south you'll find the Greensand Hills, which take in the Devil's Punch Bowl (see below). In between are the river valleys of the Wey, Tillingbourne, and Mole, and heaths of Frensham, Thursley, and Blackheath.

Essentials

GETTING THERE   There are regular South West trains to Dorking (45 min. from London Victoria or Waterloo, about £10) and Guildford (35 min. from Waterloo, about £11). However, you really need a car to explore the byroads among the hills. The A3 from London is the main artery, with many small routes running south, just south of the M25.

VISITOR INFORMATION   The **Surrey Hills Partnership,** Warren Farm Barns, Headley Lane, Mickleham, Dorking (✆ **01372/220653;** www.surreyhills. org), has information on its website that features a downloadable information pack with maps. The office is not for personal callers, but does take phone calls during office hours. Also see the "Guildford" section, above.

Exploring the Area

Box Hill ★ ☺ NATURE RESERVE   This is an iconic destination for walking, for children to run free, and for appreciating the countryside safely south of London (but not too far away). It's an area of woodland and open chalk downland, with views across the edge of the South Downs. There are walks in the woods and on open paths, a hilltop Discovery Zone for youngsters to play in, and a cafe that is usually busy with red-cheeked hikers.

Box Hill Rd., Tadworth (just off the A24, a half-mile north of Dorking). ✆ **01306/885502.** www.national trust.org.uk. Free access, but National Trust pay parking lot.

Devil's Punchbowl ★★ NATURE RESERVE   This is a remarkable piece of countryside, like something one might expect to find in America's northwest: A natural basin, heavily forested and with a real wilderness feel, even though it's right by the London–Portsmouth road. It's thought to get its name from the way mist gathers in the bowl and pours over the rim. The fact that it's surrounded by an expanse of lowland heath and Hindhead Commons makes it even more fascinating. The Punchbowl is Europe's largest spring-eroded valley, and its beauty can be appreciated from the viewpoint 50 yards from the cafe at the parking lot, although a circular walk deep inside is recommended. Its setting will become even more natural following the opening of the £371-million Hindhead A3 tunnel in 2011.

On the A3, 10 miles southwest of Guildford. ✆ **01428/608771.** www.nationaltrust.org.uk. Free access, but National Trust pay parking lot.

Leith Hill ★ NATURE RESERVE   This is the highest point in southeast England, topping 304m (1,000ft). You can walk up the hill and find all manner of woodland paths (full of rhododendrons in early summer) marked on a free map. It is topped by an 18th-century Gothic tower with a spiral staircase, and 360-degree views (try the telescope) as far as London in one direction and across rolling countryside almost to the English Channel in the other. There's the chance of a cup of tea from the cafe and, in late spring, you can cross the road at the bottom and delve into the bluebell woods and a magical circular walk.

Leith Hill, near Coldharbour village (4 miles southwest of Dorking); A25 Guildford–Dorking Rd. runs nearby. ✆ **01306/712711.** www.nationaltrust.org.uk. Hill has free access. Admission to Tower £1.30 adults, 70p children 5–15. Times vary, from Tues–Sun in Aug to weekends in winter; Apr–Oct 10am–5pm, then to 3pm. Free parking on roads, and National Trust pay parking lot.

Polesden Lacey GARDEN   This Regency villa is set among the hills, with gardens dropping down (and with views over) a farming valley. The house is full of antiques, paintings, and tapestries. But many people come here simply to enjoy the countryside. There are marked walks in the gardens, the wooded grounds, and around the 567-hectare (1,400-acre) estate. The 18th-century gardens, with sweeping lawn, and other areas divided into rooms with roses and herbaceous borders, are a treat.

Signposted from Great Bookham, off the A246 Leatherhead-Guildford Rd. ✆ **01372/452048.** www.nationaltrust.org.uk. Admission to grounds £7.40 adults, £3.70 children 5–15, £19 family ticket; house and grounds £12 adults, £6 children, £30 family ticket. Grounds daily Feb–Oct 10am–5pm, Nov–Jan 10am–4pm; house Mar–Oct Wed–Sun and bank holidays 11am–5pm, weekends 11am–4pm rest of the year (closed some weekends and Jan, Feb, Nov by guided tour only).

Where to Eat & Stay

Devil's Punch Bowl Hotel ★   Right alongside the Punchbowl and Hindhead Commons, this is a warm and pleasing place that's good for a drink (in the traditional, richly decorated bar with a selection of real ales), a decent dinner, or a night's rest. Some of the rooms are simple, others are sizable with four-poster beds. The **restaurant** offers few surprises but covers the bases (wild boar sausages, steak, lamb shank) with mostly local ingredients at a good price (main courses £6.95–£13), and there is also a bar menu and Sunday carvery.

52 London Rd., Hindhead, Surrey GU26 6AG. www.devilspunchbowlhotel.co.uk. ✆ **01428/606565.** Fax 01428/605713. 32 units. £55–£80 double. Rates include English breakfast. AE, MC, V. On the A3, just north of Hindhead. **Amenities:** Restaurant; bar, Wi-Fi (free). *In room:* TV, hair dryer.

Mercure Burford Bridge Hotel ★   At the foot of beautiful Box Hill, and near the Mole River, this is a four-star place with many historical associations. Keats, Wordsworth, and Robert Louis Stevenson all stayed here. Some rooms are in the original buildings, some in more modern (but still reasonably old) additions, and all are classically furnished. Breakfast is not included. The gardens have lovely views, and the **Emlyn restaurant** is elegantly modern.

Box Hill, Dorking, Surrey RH5 6BX. www.mercure.com. ✆ **01306/884561.** Fax 01306/887821. 57 units. £130–£171 double. AE, DC, MC, V. Free parking. Take the A24 1½ miles north of Dorking. **Amenities:** Restaurant; bar; concierge; outdoor pool; room service. *In room:* TV, hair dryer, Wi-Fi (£4 per hr., £12 for 10 hr.).

Mercure White Horse Hotel   Charles Dickens was known to have popped into the bar here, and the White Horse was the fictional home of the Marquis of Granby in *The Pickwick Papers*. This timbered inn, in the middle of the upmarket town of

Dorking, has four-poster beds in some rooms, which are smart and comfortable if not all striking. The **Coach House restaurant** offers a moderately priced table d'hôte dinner, as well as an a la carte menu. The bar, with its log fire, fills with locals from the town.

High St., Dorking, Surrey RH4 1BE. www.mercure.com. ✆ **01306/887241.** Fax 01306/880386. 78 units. £62–£132 double. AE, DC, MC, V. Free parking. **Amenities:** Restaurant; bar; room service. *In room:* TV, hair dryer, Wi-Fi (£4 per hr., £9 for 3 hr.).

THE THAMES NEAR LONDON

You don't have to go far from London to find the beauty of the countryside and the attractions of the River Thames. **Richmond-upon-Thames** is actually so close it's even on the Tube. And **Kingston-upon-Thames** is only a swift train ride. Both are attractive towns that make the most of their riverside, but they're also bustling places with plenty of shops, as well as good restaurants.

Essentials

GETTING THERE   Richmond is at the end of one of the branches of the Tube's District Line; a journey from the Earls Court interchange takes around 20 minutes. It is also on a fast South West train line from London Waterloo, a journey of around 15 minutes, costing about £4. Slower local trains makes a loop from Waterloo, via Richmond and Kingston, in both directions, before arriving back at Waterloo.

VISITOR INFORMATION   Richmond **Visitor Information Centre,** in the Old Town Hall, Whitaker Avenue (✆ **020/8734-3363;** www.visitrichmond.co.uk), is open Monday to Saturday 9am to 5pm. For Kingston, see www.kingston.gov.uk.

Exploring the Area

Kingston ★ is an ancient market town, and today it's still very much in the business of selling things. The **market,** a mass of vegetable, fruit, fish, and meat stalls, sells good coffee and snacks and operates in the Market Place Monday to Saturday, 9am to 5pm. Each Monday (8am–2pm), in the Cattle Market parking lot there's a market selling everything from fashions to tools to plants. Kingston is also a major shopping destination, with **Bentalls** department store the hub of the three-floor indoor Bentall Centre. There's a large branch of Britain's leading department store, John Lewis, across the street. The Rotunda entertainment complex features a four-screen Odeon cinema, plus seven restaurants including a branch of Marco Pierre White's Frankie & Benny's American/Italian chain. **Kingston Museum** in Wheatfield Way (✆ **020/ 8547-5006;** www.kingston.gov.uk; Mon–Wed and Fri–Sat, 10am–5pm; free admission) has a gallery devoted to pioneer photographer and movie-maker Eadweard Muybridge, who was born here. There are also good history displays. The coronation of several Anglo-Saxon kings took place here, and an ancient **Coronation Stone** is outside the Guildhall near historic Clattern Bridge, and the excellent Rose Theatre.

While Kingston is the shopping and entertainment hub, **Richmond** ★ is its arty cousin with more individual shops and restaurants. It's somehow summed up by the river's lazy curve through the town, rather than its straight rush through in Kingston. There are cafes and restaurants dotted along the riverside walk, and more cafes plus lovely antiques shops, galleries, and clothes boutiques up Richmond Hill. At the top of the hill is a breathtaking view of the river, the only view in England to be protected by an Act of Parliament. From here you can see down to the National Trust's

fascinating **Ham House and Gardens,** close to Petersham Meadows, which has
cows grazing in summer and was painted by J. M. W. Turner, among others. This is
where you'll find the glorious **Petersham Nurseries** (✆ **0208/940-5230;** www.
petershamnurseries.co.uk), which, in addition to selling plants, has a bohemian cafe
that's earned a Michelin star.

Chessington World of Adventures ★★★ THEME PARK   One of Britain's
leading theme parks, Chessington offers a full-blown mix of white-knuckle rides: the
revolving, head-dunking Ramases revenge; the feet-swinging roller-coaster Vampire;
and the spinning coaster Dragon's Fury. There are attractions for all ages, including
the zoo on which the park was based with tigers, lions, gorillas, seals, penguins, and
more, plus a SeaLife hall. It's an exceptional place for families and the young-at-heart
alike, with plenty of restaurants, coffee shops, and bars. The Holiday Inn Chessington, a modern safari-themed hotel outside the park, has views from the bedrooms,
restaurant, and terrace over to the African-themed Wanyama Reserve with its zebras.
There are special park/hotel packages, but the hotel is also a good place from which
to explore the area.

On the A243, 3 miles south of Kingston. ✆ **0871-663-4477.** www.chessington.com. Admission £37
adults, £27 children 11 and under (free for children under 1m/3 ft., 4 in. tall), £102 family ticket. Zoo days:
£ 12 children 12 and over, £7.80 children 11 and under (free for children under 1m/3 ft., 4 in tall). Around
25% discount for online purchases. Parking £2. Theme park open daily, school holidays, and weekends
10am–6pm; otherwise until 5pm. Zoo only Jan–Mar weekends 10am–3pm.

Hampton Court Palace ★ HISTORIC SITE   Henry VIII's Lord Chancellor,
Cardinal Wolsey, began building this magnificent palace with its glorious gardens in
1515, but the king liked it so much he claimed it for himself and made it even
grander. Highlights include the Tudor Great Hall with its richly ornamented ceiling,
and the Chapel Royal with a fan-vaulted wooden ceiling. The 16th-century kitchens
are fantastic—the largest to survive from Tudor times—and you can still visit the
courts Henry had built for real tennis. ***Insider tip:*** Hampton Court Palace is featured
on the London Pass (see "A Money-Saving Pass," p. 110), which gives entry to many
attractions in the city but also features a number of places in the surrounding areas.

Hampton Court (a 1-mile walk from Kingston, slightly farther along the Thames Path). ✆ **0844/482-
7777.** www.hrp.org.uk. Admission £14 adults, £12 seniors and students, £7 children 5–15, £38 family
ticket. Apr–Sept daily 10am–6pm; Oct–Mar 10am–4:30pm. Closed Dec 24–26. Short walk from Hampton Court rail station (around 35 min. from London Waterloo, but 35–50 min. from Kingston or Richmond as it sits at the end of a branch line).

Richmond Park ★ PARK   This is the king of royal parks: 1,012 hectares (12,500
acres) of hills, woods, and grassland with views as far as St. Paul's Cathedral in one
direction and Windsor Castle in the other. The circular road is a wonderful drive, past
herds of red and fallow deer. Attractions include the Isabella Plantation, beautiful in
late spring with its azaleas and rhododendrons. The park is also home to tawny owls
and sparrow hawks, and there are swans and waterfowl on Pen Ponds. The gardens
at Pembroke Lodge are pretty in summer, and the Georgian mansion is a cafe with
indoor and outdoor seating.

Richmond Park is between Richmond and Kingston and has gates at Richmond, Petersham (pedestrian), Ham and Kingston as well as at Sheen and Roehampton. ✆ **020/8948-3209.** www.royalparks.
org.uk. Free admission. Daily 7am to dusk (opens at 7:30am mid-Sept–Feb). There are several free
parking lots, Pembroke Lodge restaurant, a cafe, and various official refreshment vans.

The Thames Path runs 184 miles from the sea to the river's source in the Cotswolds. Having passed through London, and skirted Kew Gardens and the huge Old Deer Park, it instantly takes on a more rural feel, like something out of a 19th-century canvas once you get to Richmond. From Richmond you pass through Petersham Meadows, where you still expect to see someone cutting hay, past Marble Hill House and Marble Hill Park (on the other side, but here you'll find a foot ferry plying the placid waters between tree-lined banks) and arrive at the grandeur that is Ham House—well worth a visit (see above). Continuing on, you walk alongside fields and a nature reserve, with views across to Eel Pie Island and the town of Twickenham behind. Soon you come to Teddington Lock and Weir. It's here that the first Thames lock was built in 1810. Barge Lock, the river's largest, is here.

This is the point at which the Thames is no longer tidal. It's a good place for a break: Cross the Victorian footbridge and drop in at **The Anglers** (© **020/8977-7475;** www.theanglersteddington.co.uk), a pub/restaurant with a riverside garden that can hold 600 people in summer. The modern British food is good anytime, but weekend barbecues and hog roasts are exceptional, washed down with Fuller's beer, brewed by the river in Chiswick. From Teddington it's a swift walk to Kingston, where you cross Kingston Bridge to continue along the edge of Hampton Court Park to Hampton Court Palace itself. For official information, visit **www.nationaltrail.co.uk/ThamesPath**, but **www.thames-path.org.uk** gives an enthusiastic section-by-section commentary.

River cruises ★ CRUISE **Turk Launches,** Town End Pier, 68 High Street, Kingston (© **020/8546-2434;** www.turks.co.uk), a family company with a 300-year history of boat building and operating, runs a Richmond–Kingston–Hampton Court service from April to October. The stretch of river includes Twickenham, little Eel Pie Island, and Teddington Lock. The latter, between Richmond and Kingston, dates back more than a century, and is the point where the tidal Thames ends. It is spanned by a Victorian footbridge. There are also specials such as a Sunday jazz cruise, dinner and dance cruises, and disco cruises. The fleet of five boats ranges from a Mississippi-style sternwheeler to the elegant 1892 side-wheeler Yarmouth Belle to little Jeff, which was one of the Dunkirk ships, rescuing troops during the war. **Parr Boats,** Queen's Promenade, Portsmouth Road, Kingston (© **020/8546-2434;** www.parr boats.co.uk), operates during the same season, with Kingston to Hampton Court trips, and a circular trip from Richmond to Teddington. Fares start from £3.50 for a Kingston–Hampton Court trip.

Entertainment & Nightlife

Kingston's riverfront options are somewhat limited. The brash, modern **Bishop out of Residence** pub is an option on a summer's evening, and sells good Young's beer, and there are several bars and restaurants with outdoor seating overlooking the river at Charter Quay near the Rose Theatre. In Richmond the **White Cross** (© **020/8940-6844**), at the end of Water Lane is a classy old pub, where drinkers perch outside by the slipway. The chain bar/restaurant **Pitcher & Piano** (© **020/ 8940-3062;** www.pitcherandpiano.com), 11 Bridge St., has cast-iron balconies overlooking the river, while the **Cricketers** (☎ 020/8940-4372) and **Prince's Head** (☎ 0208/940-1572) are classic British pubs on Richmond Green. The **Roebuck** (☎ 020/8948-2329) on Richmond Hill is a neat, dark, pub where you can stand outside and enjoy sunsets over the river below, and the **Marlborough** (☎ 0208/940-8513), around the corner at 46 Friars Stile Rd., is a decent gastropub (with excellent Young's beer) that looks unassuming from its small entrance but spreads out into a huge, parklike garden.

Where to Eat & Stay

The Bingham ★ A delicious, heady combination of restaurant and hotel in two Georgian townhouses by the river. The former, a vision in opulent white, has a Michelin star, courtesy of chef Shay Cooper. It features striking dinners, with delights such as roast halibut with parsnip remoulade, walnut gnocchi, lemon purée, and black trompettes (set menu £45 for three courses; seven-course tasting menu £65); set lunches (£23 for three courses); breakfasts; and afternoon tea with cucumber sandwiches (£21).

Individually decorated rooms, some with river views, are cool and modern yet with a hint of the 1930s about them. The private terrace and landscaped gardens add a finishing touch of discreet luxury.

61–63 Petersham Rd., Richmond, Surrey TW10 6UT. www.thebingham.co.uk. ☎ 020/8940-0902. 15 units. £190–£265 double. AE, DC, MC, V. Free parking (limited); otherwise £10. **Amenities:** Restaurant; bar. *In room:* TV/DVD, hair dryer, Wi-Fi (free).

Richmond Hill Hotel This is a boutique hotel, albeit with loads of rooms, with views down across the meadows and the Thames winding away into the distance, in one direction, and Richmond Park in the other. Rooms are in both a Georgian building and a modern wing (the former tend to be slightly larger), but all have a modern touch. Suites have a mix of king-sized bed, balconies, and dressing rooms. The Cedars health club is in the grounds and free for guests. The **Pembroke restaurant** (main courses £10–£20; set menu £19 for 2 courses) does sprightly, brasserie-style versions of never-fail dishes (Thai chicken curry, fish and chips, grilled salmon).

144 Richmond Hill, Richmond, Surrey TW10 6RW. www.richmondhill-hotel.co.uk. ☎ 020/8940-2247. Fax 020/8940-5424. 149 units. £101–£159 double. AE, DC, MC, V. Free parking. **Amenities:** Restaurant; bar; health club; room service. *In room:* TV, hair dryer, Wi-Fi (free for 20 min. per day, then £4.95 for 1 hr.).

river ROCKS

The area of southwest London and Surrey was at the forefront of British rock music, where London's response to the Beatles was fermenting in the early 1960s. The Rolling Stones, The Yardbirds, Downliners Sect, and other cult names played here regularly. The old clubs have gone but newer places fly the flag. The **Eel Pie Club** (www.eel pieclub.com) is a successor to the place that existed on Eel Pie Island; it's at the Cabbage Patch pub, 67 London Rd., Twickenham, across from the station, and has shows by the Downliners and other survivors. The **Boom Boom Club** (**020/8761-9078;** www.feenstra.co.uk), a short drive from Kingston, in Sutton, attracts the likes of the Zombies, Yardbirds, and even Jefferson Starship to its small, friendly home at Sutton United Football Club, Gander Green Lane.

White Hart   A striking timbered building just across Kingston Bridge, and an easy walk from Hampton Court Palace, the White Hart is part of the brewer Fuller's chain. It has a lively public outdoor area at the front, and a private one at the back. Rooms are a decent size, smartly furnished in comfy country style, and one has a four-poster. Food is posh pub fare (main courses £8.50–£16) such as Fuller's beer-battered hake with hand-cut chips (fries). There's a Virgin Active Health Club, across the bridge.

1 High St., Hampton Wick, Surrey KT1 4DA. www.fullershotels.com. © **020/8977-1786.** 37 units. £120–£170 double. AE, DC, MC, V. Free parking. **Amenities:** Restaurant; bar; access to nearby health club. *In room:* TV, hair dryer, Wi-Fi (£4.95 for 1 hr.).

HAMPSHIRE & DORSET

by Donald Strachan

Hampshire and Dorset are where England began. They formed the core of Alfred's 10th-century kingdom of Wessex, the capital of which was Winchester. They became Wessex once again—this time fictional—in the 19th-century Dorchester tales of writer Thomas Hardy. A tour of these southern English counties leads you gently from London's coattails to the rural peace of tiny villages, coastal walks, and serene, idyllic isolation.

SIGHTSEEING Jane Austen wrote about the middle-class inhabitants of Hampshire in her six novels, including *Pride and Prejudice* and *Sense and Sensibility.* Fans can visit her memorial in **Winchester Cathedral** and the house where she lived, **Chawton Cottage.** The Gothic fan vaults at **Sherborne Abbey** showcase medieval ingenuity, and the nearby **Jurassic Coast** is home to more natural wonders.

EATING & DRINKING Both Hampshire and Dorset look seaward for culinary inspiration—seafood here is much more than fish and chips wrapped in yesterday's newspaper. Restaurants including Weymouth's **Crab House Café** and Portsmouth's **Restaurant 27** offer contrasting visions of contemporary coastal dining. The country pubs of the **New Forest** are places to eat gastropub food and drink local ales.

OUTDOOR ACTIVITIES Besides the twin (and rival) cities of **Southampton** and **Portsmouth,** these are almost entirely rural counties. Keen walkers will find empty tracts, out of season, on the **Isle of Wight** and the **New Forest National Park.** For livelier sands and surfing, it has to be the Victorian resort of **Bournemouth** and its trendy neighbor, **Boscombe.**

HISTORY Like the food, the history of these coastal counties is forever tied to the English Channel. Portsmouth has long been England's naval capital, and the **Historic Dockyard** is where Nelson's HMS *Victory* and the remains of Henry VIII's flagship, the *Mary Rose,* are berthed. Across the Solent, on the Isle of Wight, **Osborne House,** where Queen Victoria lived and died, is a preserved time capsule.

THE best TRAVEL EXPERIENCES IN HAMPSHIRE & DORSET

o **Cycling or hiking to a New Forest pub (or two):** The National Park is criss-crossed by a network of bike and walking trails, and dotted with some of southern England's best country pubs. Arm yourself with a good map, and work up an appetite for hearty Hampshire produce washed down with a Ringwood ale. See p. 302.

o **Exploring below-decks on Nelson's flagship:** HMS *Victory* is the centerpiece of Portsmouth's Historic Dockyard. A 45-minute guided tour, which covers everything from the ballast to the mainsail, is packed with enough living history and grizzly anecdotes to please everyone. See p. 298.

o **Admiring Lyme Regis from the tip of the Cobb:** This 18th-century sea defense snakes out to sea from Lyme's sandy beach, wrapping the pretty little harbor in a protective embrace. Afterward, browse a quirky resort high street that's almost unchanged since Jane Austen visited. See p. 319.

o **Enjoying fresh air and fine food in the West Wight:** The tiny yachtie port of Yarmouth makes a quaint jumping-off point for the best of the Isle of Wight. A brisk half-day walk takes in the Needles and Freshwater Bay, and leaves time for refined dining in a formal restaurant or gastropub. See p. 308 and 309.

o **Acquainting yourself with architectural genius in Sherborne:** The fan vault was the peculiarly English Gothic solution to supporting a huge ceiling with grace and elegance. Sherborne Abbey showcases one of Britain's most impressive examples—pack your binoculars to view it up close. See p. 321.

WINCHESTER ★★

72 miles SW of London; 12 miles N of Southampton

Hampshire's history hotspot, and the capital of the ancient kingdom of Wessex, **Winchester** has long been linked with King Alfred, who is honored today by a statue on the High Street. Alfred the Great, born in 849, was crowned king in 871, ruling until his death in 899. He is known as "the Great," because he defended Anglo-Saxon England against Viking raids, formulated a code of laws, and fostered a rebirth of religious and scholarly activity.

Its past glory but a memory, Winchester is today a well-kept market town on the water meadows along the Itchen River, with a well curated (and free) **City Museum** and an interesting array of **independent shops.** Of course, Hampshire is also a draw for Jane Austen fans. You can visit her grave in **Winchester Cathedral,** as well as **Chawton Cottage,** where she lived during her most productive years.

Essentials

GETTING THERE Frequent daily trains run from London's Waterloo Station to Winchester. The trip takes around 1 hour from around £30 for a round-trip. Arrivals are at Winchester Station, Station Hill, a 10-minute walk northwest of the center.

If you're driving from Southampton, head north on the A335 until it joins the northbound M3; from London, take the M3 motorway southwest.

VISITOR INFORMATION The **Tourist Information Centre,** Broadway (✆ **01962/840500;** www.visitwinchester.co.uk), is open Monday to Saturday 10am

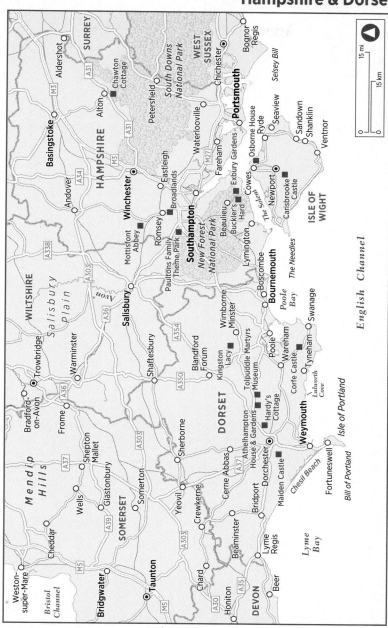

SURREY

Aldershot

WEST
SUSSEX

Bognor
Regis

Selsey Bill

Chawton
Cottage

Alton

South Downs
National Park

Petersfield

Chichester

Portsmouth

HAMPSHIRE

Basingstoke

Waterlooville

Osborne House

Seaview

Sandown

Andover

Eastleigh

Fareham

Exbury Gardens

Ryde

Shanklin

Winchester

Broadlands

Cowes

Newport

Ventnor

Romsey

Southampton

Beaulieu

Buckler's
Hard

Carisbrooke
Castle

ISLE OF
WIGHT

Mottisfont
Abbey

New Forest
National Park

Lymington

The Solent

Paultons Family
Theme Park

The Needles

WILTSHIRE

Salisbury
Plain

Avon

Salisbury

Boscombe

English Channel

Warminster

Shaftesbury

Wimborne
Minster

Bournemouth

Poole
Bay

Trowbridge

Blandford
Forum

Bradford-
on-Avon

Poole

Swanage

Frome

Kingston
Lacy

Wareham

Tolpuddle Martyrs
Museum

Corfe Castle

Tyneham

Lulworth
Cove

Isle of Portland

Shepton
Mallet

DORSET

Sherborne

Athelhampton
House & Gardens

Wells

Glastonbury

Somerton

Yeovil

Dorchester

Weymouth

Mendip
Hills

Cerne Abbas

Hardy's
Cottage

Cheddar

Crewkerne

Bridport

Maiden Castle

Chesil Beach

Fortuneswell

Bill of Portland

SOMERSET

Beaminster

Lyme
Regis

Lyme
Bay

Weston-
super-Mare

Chard

Bristol
Channel

Beer

Bridgwater

Taunton

Honiton

DEVON

to 5pm (May–Sept also Sun 11am–4pm). Keep up with the latest local happenings at **twitter.com/King_Alf**.

ORGANIZED TOURS   The Tourist Information Centre (see above) has a helpful free pamphlet, *The Winchester Walk*, that details a self-guided circuit round the town and environs. Guided **walking tours,** which depart from the tourist office and last 1½ hours, cost £4 per person. Departure times vary by season; check once you're in town.

Exploring Winchester

The interactive, hands-on displays at the historic **City Mill,** Bridge Street (© **01962/870057;** www.nationaltrust.org.uk), are especially suited to school-age kids. Visitors can access the bowels of a working corn mill, and view displays on the history and processes involved in flour-making. Admission costs £3.60 adults, £2 children. Hours are 10:30am to 5pm daily between mid-March and Christmas, plus February school vacation week (usually the third week of the month). The excellent little **City Museum ★**, The Square (© **01962/863064**), traces the history of Winchester from its establishment as Roman Venta Belgarum in A.D. 70 to the present day. Admission is free. It's open April to October Monday to Saturday 10am to 5pm, Sunday noon to 5pm; off-season it closes an hour earlier and all-day Monday.

Castle Great Hall ★ HISTORIC SITE   This is the only remaining part of the castle first erected in Winchester by William the Conqueror and rebuilt by Henry III. Dating from the 1200s, it is one of the finest examples of a medieval hall in England, with its timber roof supported on columns of Purbeck marble. The English Parliament met here for the first time in 1246; a Victorian mural lists every Hampshire Member of Parliament between 1283 and 1868. The castle also hosted the trial of Sir Walter Raleigh, who was condemned to death in 1603 for conspiring against James I. The giant painted oak Round Table hanging on the west wall doesn't in fact stretch back to the time of King Arthur—it's been carbon dated to around 1280, and was probably the property of Edward I.

Castle Ave. © **01962/846476.** www.hants.gov.uk/greathall. Free admission. Daily 10am–5pm.

Hospital of St. Cross ★★ HISTORIC SITE   Founded in 1132, the Hospital (for hospitality, not medicine) is the oldest charitable institution in England. It was established by Henri du Blois, grandson of William the Conqueror, as a link for social care and to supply life's necessities to the local poor and famished travelers. It continues the tradition of providing refreshments to visitors today: Simply stop at the Porter's Lodge for a Wayfarer's Dole, and you'll receive some bread and ale. In the inner courtyard of the hospital, you can see the Brethren's houses from 1450, the refectory, and a church, which is a fine example of Norman architecture (ca. 1250).

St. Cross Rd. © **01962/851375.** www.stcross.f2s.com. Admission £3.50 adults, £3 students and seniors, £1.50 children under 13. Apr-Oct Mon-Sat 9:30am–5pm, Sun 1-5pm; off season Mon-Sat 10:30am-3:30pm.

Winchester Cathedral ★★★ CATHEDRAL   The longest medieval cathedral in Britain dates from 1079, and its Norman heritage is still in evidence. When a Saxon church stood on this spot, St. Swithun, Bishop of Winchester and tutor to young King Alfred, suggested modestly that he be buried outside. Following his subsequent indoor burial, it rained for 40 days. The legend lives on: If it rains on St. Swithun's Day, July 15, you'll get a prediction of rain for 40 days.

ATTRACTIONS ●	HOTELS ■	RESTAURANTS ◆
Castle Great Hall **2**	Hotel du Vin **3**	Black Rat **9**
Hospital of St. Cross **6**	Lainston House **1**	Chesil Rectory **8**
Winchester Cathedral **4**	Wykeham	Hotel du Vin **3**
Winchester College **7**	Arms **5**	Wykeham Arms **5**

The Perpendicular Gothic nave, with its two aisles, is the architectural highlight. The elaborately carved choir stalls from 1308 are England's oldest, as is the retro-choir's medieval tiled floor. The astonishing Great Screen was carved between 1470 and 1490, although the original statues fell victim to the iconoclasm of the Reformation years. Those in place today are Victorian replacements.

Jane Austen is buried in the north aisle; note how her original gravestone makes no mention of her writing. The son of William the Conqueror, William Rufus (who reigned as William II), is also buried at the cathedral, as are the bones of Danish King of England, Cnut (985–1035).

The Close. ✆ **01962/857200.** www.winchester-cathedral.org.uk. Admission £6 adults, £4.80 seniors, £3.50 students, free for children 15 and under. Free guided tours hourly 10am–3pm; Mon–Sat 9am–5pm; Sun 12:30–3pm.

Winchester College ★ HISTORIC SITE   Winchester College was founded by William of Wykeham, Bishop of Winchester and chancellor to Richard II, who also founded New College, Oxford. Its buildings have been in use since 1393, making it the oldest continuously open school in England. Exploration is possible only by guided tour, lasting an hour and covering the Chamber Court, the 14th-century

Gothic chapel, and the College Hall, among other sights. *Insider tip:* During term time, you can attend Evensong for free on a Tuesday. Arrive by 5:30pm.

73 Kingsgate St. ℂ **01962/621209.** www.winchestercollege.org. Admission £6 adults, £5 students and seniors. Guided tours Tues and Thurs 10:45am and noon; Mon, Wed, and Fri–Sat 10:45am, noon, 2:15, and 3:30pm; Sun 2:15 and 3:30pm.

BEYOND THE CITY

Chawton Cottage ★ HISTORIC HOME   This cottage is where Jane Austen spent the last 7½ years of her life, her most productive period. In unpretentious but pleasant surroundings, she penned new versions of three of her books and wrote three more, including Emma. You can also see examples of Austen's needlework and jewelry, the rector's George III mahogany bookcase, and a silhouette likeness of the Reverend Austen presenting his son to the Knights. Jane Austen became ill here in 1816 with what would have been diagnosed by the middle of the 19th century as Addison's disease. She died in College Street, Winchester, in July 1817.

Chawton (1 mile southwest of Alton off the A31, 15 miles east of Winchester). ℂ **01420/83262.** www. jane-austens-house-museum.org.uk. Admission £7 adults, £6 students and seniors, £2 children 6–16. June–Aug daily 10am–5pm; Sept–Dec and Mar–May daily 10:30am–4:30pm; Jan–Feb Sat–Sun 10:30am–4:30pm.

Shopping

Fill up your suitcases at **Cadogan,** 30–31 The Square (ℂ **01962/877399;** www. cadoganandcompany.co.uk), which carries an upscale selection of traditional woolens, shirts, and accessories for men and women. For a unique piece of jewelry or a handmade hat, stop by designer Carol Darby's **Free Spirit** ★, 6 Little Minster St. (ℂ **01962/867671**). The oldest book dealer in town is **P&G Wells,** 11 College St. (ℂ **01962/852016;** www.bookwells.co.uk), offering both new releases and local interest titles. For window-browsers, the artisan stores along **Parchment Street** and **Great Minster Street** provide plenty of interest.

The city's farmers' market, on the second and final Sunday mornings of every month, is among the best in England. See **www.hampshirefarmersmarkets.co.uk.**

Entertainment & Nightlife

Your best spots for a decent pint are the tiny, traditional bar at the **Eclipse,** 25 The Square (ℂ **01962/865676;** www.eclipseinn.co.uk); or, if you don't mind a gentle 10-minute walk from the center, the **Black Boy** ★, 1 Wharf Hill (ℂ **01962/861754;** www.theblackboypub.com). The latter is a freehouse specializing in locally brewed ales. To keep partying until late, the place to go is the **Porthouse,** Upper Brook Street (ℂ **01962/869397;** www.porthousenightclub.com), a nightclub sprawling across three floors. Different nights have different themes, from urban music to pop. Doors open at 9pm, and you'll pay £3 to £5 admission, depending on the night.

For a dose of culture, try the **Theatre Royal Winchester,** Jewry Street (ℂ **01962/840440;** www.theatreroyalwinchester.co.uk). The eclectic program might include anything from mainstream comedy to touring opera or a kids' show.

Where to Eat & Stay

Black Rat ★★   MODERN ENGLISH   If you like your food with an adventurous edge, this fine-dining spinoff from the Black Boy pub (see above) is the best choice in town. The dining room is decked with mighty oak tables and the decor is simple— although the kitchen is anything but, having been awarded its first Michelin star in

2011. Dishes always use ingredients from reputable local suppliers; main courses might include cider-braised pig cheeks with chorizo and truffled butter beans or saddle of royal venison with spiced red cabbage.

88 Chesil St. $\mathcal{C}$ **01962/844465.** www.theblackrat.co.uk. Reservations recommended. Main courses £18–£20. MC, V. Mon–Sun 7–9:30pm; Sat–Sun noon–2:30pm.

Chesil Rectory ★★ ENGLISH There's a buzz again about this eatery housed in Winchester's oldest building, thanks largely to a revamped menu and some exceptional fixed-price meal deals. The food is adjusted seasonally to take advantage of regional produce. In a dining room aglow with half-timbered architecture and whitewashed panels, expect dishes full of brawny flavor and heady perfumes, such as steamed filet of brill with sautéed girolles or wild mushroom Wellington with seasonal greens.

1 Chesil St. $\mathcal{C}$ **01962/851555.** www.chesilrectory.co.uk. Reservations recommended. Main courses £13–£18; Mon–Sat lunch and 6–7pm fixed-price 2 courses £15, 3 courses £20. DC, MC, V. Mon–Sun noon–2:30pm; Mon–Sat 6–10pm.

Hotel du Vin ★★ Everything's cozy at this wine-themed boutique inn built into a townhouse that dates from 1715. It brings a touch of urban chic to Winchester, with rooms that are intimate and contemporary without being aggressively overdesigned. Superior units are larger, with handsprung, king-size beds and views over the hotel's quiet, walled garden. *Insider tip:* Stay-and-eat packages tend to be priced the best on Sunday nights.

The modern English take on French fare in the **Bistro ★** is good value, with a menu that always features regional ingredients: Try the pan-fried halibut with Jerusalem artichoke purée, golden beetroot, and girolles; or the roast saddle of venison with a polenta croquette—and choose your bottle from the finest wine list in the county. Main courses range between £14 and £21. It's open daily for lunch and dinner.

14 Southgate St., Winchester, Hampshire SO23 9EF. www.hotelduvin.com. $\mathcal{C}$ **01962/841414.** Fax 01962/842458. 24 units. £145–£230 double. AE, DC, MC, V. Free parking. **Amenities:** Restaurant; bar. *In room:* A/C, TV/DVD, hair dryer, Wi-Fi (free).

Lainston House ★★ The beauty of this restored William and Mary redbrick manor house strikes visitors as they approach via a long, curving, tree-lined drive. It's situated on 25 hectares (63 acres) of rolling land and linked with the name Lainston in *The Domesday Book.* Elegance is key inside the stately main house, where panoramically big suites are located. Double rooms are less spacious but also comfortable and harmoniously furnished—and all come with a choice of pillows from a menu of options.

Sparsholt, Winchester, Hampshire SO21 2LT. www.lainstonhouse.com. $\mathcal{C}$ **01962/776088.** Fax 01962/776672. 50 units. £245–£360 double; £485–£525 suite. MC, V. Free parking. Off the B3420, 1½ miles northwest of Winchester. **Amenities:** Restaurant; bar; babysitting; exercise room; room service; 2 outdoor tennis courts. *In room:* TV, hair dryer, Jacuzzi (in some), Wi-Fi (free).

Wykeham Arms A long-time favorite in central Winchester, the Wykeham lies behind a 200-year-old brick facade near the cathedral and school. Rooms are furnished in a period style, with antiques or reproductions. Most are a bit small but attractively appointed; ask for one that's been recently refurbished. The annex has the most luxurious and spacious rooms.

The downstairs **dining room** is equally atmospheric, with a roaring log fire, chunky inn-style furniture, and a parquet floor. Food ranges from simple, hearty

DAY-TRIPPING IN THE test VALLEY

Join the dots in the gentle countryside around **Romsey,** along the banks of the River Test, to create a day-trip with something for the entire family. **Mottisfont Abbey** ★, near Romsey (✆ **01794/340757;** www.nationaltrust.org.uk/mottisfont), began as a 13th-century Augustinian priory before being transformed (thanks to the Reformation) into a grand, riverside private home. The gardens are radiant in the height of summer, especially the **walled rose garden** ★★, home to Britain's national collection of old-fashioned roses. Perfumes and colors are in full effect during June, when the garden gets very busy on weekends. Admission costs £7.60 adults, £3.80 children 5 to 16. Hours are 10am to 5pm daily from late February through October; a winter garden was inaugurated in 2011, and that's open November through January Friday to Monday 10am to 5pm. Nearby **Broadlands** ★ (✆ **01794/505010;**

www.broadlands.net), one of the most stately examples of Palladian architecture in rural England, was landscaped by Capability Brown in the 18th century. It was the family home of Earl Mountbatten until he was assassinated by the Provisional IRA in 1979. The estate is closed for major restoration work until mid-2012. The excellent 2011 addition to **Paultons Family Theme Park,** Ower, near Romsey (✆ **023/8081-4442;** www.paultonspark.co.uk), is Peppa Pig World, aimed at under-5s, which joins fairly gentle roller-coasters, a fun log ride, and several other theme-park favorites ideal for children 7 to 12. Admission costs £21 per person (seniors pay £19), with children under 1m (3 ft., 4 in.) entering free. You can save a couple of pounds each by pre-booking family tickets online. Paultons is open daily between April and August, Thursday to Monday in September and October, Friday to Monday in March, and weekends only in November and December.

dishes like Wyk Pie (minced beef topped with potato and cheese) to contemporary flourishes such as seared scallops served with cauliflower purée and fried seaweed. Main courses range from £8 to £16; reservations are recommended at weekends.

75 Kingsgate St., Winchester, Hampshire SO23 9PE. www.fullershotels.com. ✆ **01962/853834.** Fax 01962/854411. 14 units. £139–£164 double. Rates include English breakfast. AE, MC, V. Free parking. No children 13 and under. **Amenities:** Restaurant; bar. *In room:* TV, hair dryer, minibar, MP3 docking station, Wi-Fi (free).

PORTSMOUTH ★ & SOUTHSEA

75 miles SW of London; 19 miles SE of Southampton

There are at least 10 places in the world called **Portsmouth,** but the forerunner is this old port city on the Hampshire coast, seat of the British Navy for 500 years. The seaport was rebuilt admirably after World War II devastation, and its **Historic Dockyard** is an essential stop for visitors interested in the nautical history of England. From Sally Port, in **Old Portsmouth,** countless naval heroes have embarked to fight England's battles, including on June 6, 1944, when Allied troops set sail to invade occupied France.

Genteel **Southsea,** adjoining Portsmouth, is a popular seaside resort with a pebble beach, lush gardens, and a small **D-Day Museum** displaying the Overlord Embroidery, England's postwar answer to the Bayeux Tapestry. Ascend the harborfront **Spinnaker Tower** to see the twin city laid out below you.

Historic Dockyard & Old Portsmouth

ATTRACTIONS ●
Charles Dickens'
  Birthplace **1**
D-Day Museum **8**
HMS *Victory* **2**
Mary Rose Museum **4**
National Museum of
  the Royal Navy **3**
Portchester Castle **1**
Royal Navy Submarine
  Museum **5**
Southsea Castle **8**
Spinnaker Tower **6**

RESTAURANTS ◆
Montparnasse **9**
Restaurant 27 **9**

HOTELS ■
The Clarence **7**
Westfield Hall **7**

Essentials

GETTING THERE Trains from London's Waterloo Station stop at both local stations, Portsmouth & Southsea (for the center) and Portsmouth Harbour (for the Historic Dockyard). There's a frequent service throughout the day, and the trip takes between 1½ and 2 hours from around £34 for a round-trip.

By car from London and points north, head south on the M3 then turn east on the M27 and follow signs.

VISITOR INFORMATION The **Visitor Information Service,** The Hard, Portsmouth (✆ **023/9282-6722;** www.visitportsmouth.co.uk), is open daily 9:30am to 5:15pm. There's also a **Southsea** information office, on Clarence Esplanade, open March to October daily during the same hours; between November and February, hours are Wednesday to Sunday 9:30am to 4:30pm. You can pick up event news and the odd deal by following them at **twitter.com/visitportsmouth**.

Exploring Portsmouth Harbour

You can buy a combination ticket that includes admission to several attractions on the **Portsmouth Historic Dockyard,** the highlight of any visit to the city: HMS *Victory,*

HMS *Warrior 1860,* the Mary Rose Museum, and the National Museum of the Royal Navy are linked on a single admission that costs £20 for adults, £17 for seniors, £14 for children 5 to 15 and students, and £56 for a family. The ticket also includes a boat trip around the harbor (summer months only). Stop by the visitor center at the **Historic Dockyard,** Victory Gate, The Hard (© **023/9283-9766**), or buy tickets online at **www.historicdockyard.co.uk**. The center is open April through October, daily 10am to 6pm; and November through March, daily 10am to 5:30pm. Last ticket sales are 1½ hours before closing. There's also plenty going on at **twitter.com/PompeyDockyard.**

HMS *Victory* ★★★ HISTORIC SITE   The highlight of any visit to the Historic Dockyard is the engaging 45-minute guided tour of Admiral Lord Nelson's flagship, a 104-gun, first-rate ship that is the oldest commissioned warship in the world, built from over 3,000 trees and launched May 7, 1765. It earned its fame on October 21, 1805, in the Battle of Trafalgar, when the English scored a victory over the combined Spanish and French fleets. The spot on the upper deck where Nelson was shot by a French sniper is marked with a plaque, as is the area below-decks where he lived the final minutes of his illustrious life. His flagship, after being taken to Gibraltar for repairs, returned to Portsmouth with Nelson's body pickled in one of the ship's brandy barrels. Tall visitors should be prepared for lots of ducking while below-decks.

See above for address and admission prices. Apr–Oct daily 10am–4:30pm; Nov–Mar daily 10am–3:45pm. Closed Dec 24–26.

***Mary Rose* Museum ★** MUSEUM   The *Mary Rose,* flagship of the fleet of King Henry VIII's wooden men-of-war, sank in the Solent Channel in 1545 in full view of the king. In 1982, the *Mary Rose* once again broke the water's surface after more than 4 centuries on the ocean floor, not exactly in shipshape condition, but surprisingly well preserved. The hull and more than 20,000 items brought up by divers constitute England's most significant aquatic archeological discovery. On display are the equipment of the ship's barber-surgeon, with cabin saws, knives, ointments, and plaster all ready for use; longbows and arrows, some still in shooting order; carpenters' tools; leather jackets; and some fine lace and silk.

    Note: The hull of the *Mary Rose* is closed to the public until late 2012 while a new £35-million museum is constructed over the remains of the vessel. The current Mary Rose Museum remains open throughout.

See above for address and admission prices. Apr–Oct daily 10am–5:30pm; Nov–Mar daily 10am–4:45pm. Closed Dec 24–26.

National Museum of the Royal Navy MUSEUM   Twin sites on the Dockyard make up the only museum in Britain devoted exclusively to the history of the Royal Navy. The best of the multimedia displays focuses on the "real" Horatio Nelson, the revered Admiral and naval hero who lost an eye at the Siege of Calvi in 1794, lost an arm at the Battle of Tenerife in 1797, and was killed aboard HMS *Victory* at Trafalgar in 1805. Additionally, there are unique collections of ship models, naval ceramics, figureheads, medals, uniforms, weapons, and other naval memorabilia.

See above for address and admission prices. www.royalnavalmuseum.org. Apr–Oct daily 10am–5pm; Nov–Mar daily 10am–4:15pm. Closed Dec 24–26.

Royal Navy Submarine Museum MUSEUM   Across Portsmouth Harbour in Gosport lies HMS *Alliance,* now part of the Submarine Museum, which traces the history of underwater warfare and life from the earliest days to the present. Alongside the refurbished historical galleries, the highlight is the 45-minute tour of HMS *Alliance* itself; after a brief audiovisual presentation, visitors are guided through the boat by ex-submariners.

To reach Gosport, take one of the ferries that depart from behind Portsmouth Harbour rail station; between four and eight depart every hour, taking 4 minutes, with a round-trip price of £2.50 adults, £1.60 children.

Haslar Jetty Rd., Gosport. © **023/9251-0354.** www.submarine-museum.co.uk. Admission £10 adults, £7 children 5–15 and students, £8 seniors, £28 family ticket. Apr–Oct daily 10am–5:30pm; Nov–Mar daily 10am–4:30pm. Last tour 1 hr. before closing. Closed Dec 24–27 and Dec 31–Jan 1. Bus: 29, 30.

Spinnaker Tower ★ OBSERVATION POINT   Towering over Portsmouth Harbour, this 170-m (558-ft.) sail-shaped edifice has become (quite literally) one of the biggest attractions along the south coast. On a clear day, you can see for up to 23 miles in all directions—including across the Solent to the Isle of Wight. Glide to the top in a panoramic lift (90 sec.), take a high-speed internal lift (30 sec.), or attempt the 570 steps from the base to the crow's-nest. From up there, you can experience the thrill of "walking on air," by daring to traverse the largest glass floor in Europe. At the top-floor Tower Café & Bar, order and enjoy sandwiches or afternoon tea (weekdays only) while drinking in the panorama.

Gunwharf Quays. © **023/9285-7520.** www.spinnakertower.co.uk. Admission £7.55 adults, £6.75 students and seniors, £5.95 children 3–15, free for children 2 and under. Children 15 and under must be accompanied by an adult. Daily 10am–6pm (Aug Sun–Thurs until 7:30pm).

Exploring the Rest of Portsmouth & Southsea

Ask in Portsmouth's visitor center (see above) about the **Millennium Promenade Walk,** a marked waterfront walking route linking The Hard, by Portsmouth Harbour, with atmospheric **Old Portsmouth,** where you'll find the few remaining streets of the original maritime city. The walk should take under 1 hour at a leisurely pace. Finish with a pint of real ale at the **Still & West** ★, Bath Square (© **023/9282-1567**), Portsmouth's best quay-side pub, and admire the harbor views.

Charles Dickens' Birthplace HISTORIC HOME   This 1804 small terrace house, in which the Victorian novelist was born in 1812, has been restored and furnished to illustrate the middle-class tastes of the early 19th century. The first Sunday of the month sees readings of the author's work at 11am and 3pm. A series of special events are planned to celebrate the bicentenary of Dickens's birth in 2012.

393 Old Commercial Rd. (off Mile End Rd./M275 and off Kingston Rd.), Portsmouth. © **023/9282-7261.** www.charlesdickensbirthplace.co.uk. Admission £3.50 adults, £3 seniors, £2.50 children 6–17, £9.50 family ticket, free for accompanied children 13 and under. Daily 10am–5pm. Closed Oct–Mar.

D-Day Museum ★ MUSEUM   The highlight of this museum, devoted to the Normandy landings, is the Overlord Embroidery, is a modern-day Bayeux Tapestry that creatively illustrates the background to and story of Operation Overlord, the D-Day landings of June 6, 1944. The giant appliquéd embroidery, believed to be the largest of its kind (82m/272 ft. long and 1m/3 ft. high), was commissioned in 1968, designed by Sandra Lawrence, and took 20 women of the Royal School of Needlework 5 years to complete. An audiovisual program includes displays such as reconstructions of various stages of the mission, and there's a comprehensive collection of memorabilia about the landings.

Clarence Esplanade, Southsea. ☏ **023/9282-7261.** www.ddaymuseum.co.uk. Admission £6 adults, £5 seniors, £4.20 students and children 6–17, £16 family ticket, free for accompanied children 13 and under. Apr–Sept daily 10am–5:30pm; Oct–Mar daily 10am–5pm. Closed Dec 24–26.

Portchester Castle ★ CASTLE   On a spit of land on the northern edge of the Solent are the remains of this castle, plus a Norman church. Built in the late 12th century by King Henry II, the castle is set inside the Roman walls of a 3rd-century fort built as a defense against Saxon pirates, when this was the northwestern frontier of the declining Roman Empire. Though the original castle itself is long gone, the keep remains (and was used as a prison during the Napoleonic Wars), and from it you can take in a panoramic view of the harbor and coast. The free historical audioguide is excellent.

Church Rd., Portchester (off the A27 btw. Portsmouth and Southampton, near Fareham). ☏ **023/9237-8291.** www.english-heritage.org.uk. Admission £4.50 adults, £3.80 seniors, £2.30 children 5–15, free for children 4 and under. Apr–Sept daily 10am–6pm; Oct–Mar daily 10am–4pm.

Southsea Castle CASTLE   A fortress built of stones from Beaulieu Abbey in 1544 as part of King Henry VIII's coastal defense plan, the castle has been much altered since. It's now a museum, with exhibits that trace the development of Portsmouth as a military stronghold, as well as the naval history and the archeology of the area. It was from here that Henry VIII watched his flagship, the *Mary Rose,* sink in the Solent.

Clarence Esplanade, Southsea. ☏ **023/9282-7261.** www.southseacastle.co.uk. Admission £3.50 adults, £3 seniors, £2.50 students and children ages 6–17, £9.50 family ticket, free for accompanied children 13 and under. Daily 10am–5:30pm. Closed Oct–Mar.

Where to Eat

Finding great food close to the main sights of the Historic Dockyard isn't easy. The outlet retail mecca that is **Gunwarf Quays,** Portsmouth Harbour (☏ **023/9283-6700;** www.gunwharf-quays.com), is home to a number of quality, if unadventurous, chain restaurants such as Japanese-style noodle bar Wagamama, pizzeria Zizzi, and eclectic, family-friendly Giraffe. Alternatively, the **Old Customs House,** Gunwharf Quays (☏ **023/9283-2333;** www.theoldcustomshouse.com), serves hearty pies and a menu of pub classics in the atmospheric former revenue-men's headquarters, built in 1811. Main courses range between £9 and £11. There's a selection of Fuller's ales on tap—it's a good place for a pint even if you don't want to dine.

Montparnasse ★ ENGLISH/FRENCH   With a long-established reputation for serving the best food in the city, Montparnasse offers a welcoming atmosphere and bijou bistro surrounds. The cooking is a now-familiar but superbly executed fusion of English and French flavors, with an emphasis on locally reared meat and locally caught fish. Expect to be bowled over by such dishes as roast breast of grouse served with chicory and orange, or filet of sea bream with potato dumplings.

103 Palmerston Rd., Southsea. ☏ **023/9281-6754.** www.bistromontparnasse.co.uk. Reservations recommended. Main courses £14–£20; fixed-price 2-course dinner £32, fixed-price 3-course dinner £37. AE, MC, V. Tues–Sat noon–2pm and 7–9:30pm.

Restaurant 27 ★★ 🍴 CONTEMPORARY BRITISH   An unassuming side-street off Southsea's fading esplanade is the unlikely home for one of Hampshire's genuine destination restaurants. Behind a whitewashed exterior, the contemporary dining room offers creative, modern cooking to match. Menus change with the seasons, but you can expect the likes of 30-hour belly of pork with chervil root, prune, and licorice, or Hampshire lamb with black pudding and bubble and squeak.

27a South Parade, Southsea. ℂ **023/9287-6272.** www.restaurant27.com. Reservations recommended. Fixed-price dinner (3 courses) £40; fixed-price lunch (Sun) £27. AE, MC, V. Wed–Sat 7–9pm, Sun noon–2:30pm.

Where to Stay

IN SOUTHSEA

The Clarence ★★ This large Edwardian villa has been given a chic makeover, making it the ideal choice in town for a romantic weekend. Rooms are decorated in

📎 A FLYING visit TO SOUTHAMPTON

The south coast's main city and passenger terminus isn't really a place to linger. Its supremacy as a port dates from Saxon times, when the Danish conqueror Cnut was proclaimed king here in 1017. Southampton was especially important to the Normans and helped them keep in touch with their homeland. During World War II, some 31 million men set out from here (in World War I, more than twice that number), and Southampton was repeatedly bombed, destroying much of its old character. On the Western Esplanade is a memorial tower to the Pilgrims, who set out on their voyage to the New World from Southampton on August 15, 1620.

The city's main cultural draw is the **Maritime Museum,** Wool House, Town Quay (ℂ **023/8022-3941**), housed in an impressive 14th-century stone warehouse. Its exhibits, which trace the history of Southampton, include a model of the docks as they looked at their peak in the 1930s. Also displayed are artifacts from some of the great ocean liners whose home port was Southampton, including the *Titanic,* which was partially built in Southampton and sailed from here on its fateful, fatal voyage. Admission to the museum costs £2.50 for adults, £1.50 students; free for children 6 and under. Hours are Monday to Friday 10am to 4pm, Saturday and Sunday 11am to 4pm.

The modest but still interesting **Southampton City Art Gallery,** Civic Centre, Commercial Road (ℂ **023/8083-3007**),

houses an eclectic collection that includes everything from altarpieces to abstracts, and spans almost 700 years of painting. Among mostly minor works, the highlight is Pre-Raphaelite Edward Burne-Jones's series of 10 gouache studies for the *Perseus Story* (1878). Admission is free, and opening hours are the same as those of the Maritime Museum.

If you have an early ferry to catch, the best place both to eat and to overnight is the **White Star ★**, 28 Oxford St. (www.whitestartavern.co.uk; ℂ **023/8082-1990**). Stripped wood floors and bookish decor in the bar-style dining room complement a gently fashionable atmosphere and clientele. Full meals on the changing menu might include such classics-with-a-twist as haunch of local venison with celeriac vanilla mash, and red cabbage, and there's a selection of creative lunchtime "small plates" such as devilled squid with red-pepper ketchup. Main courses range from £14 to £18 at dinner. Upstairs, midsize rooms are decorated in muted, modern tones with walk-in showers and Egyptian cotton fabrics. As you climb the price grades, rooms get bigger and add roll-top baths. Doubles cost £99 to £149.

The city's **Tourist Information Centre,** 9 Civic Centre Rd. (ℂ **023/8083-3333;** www.visit-southampton.co.uk), is open Monday to Saturday 9:30am to 5pm, Sunday and bank holidays 10am to 3:30pm.

modern tones with dazzling feature walls, and all include king-size beds and sharp, contemporary embellishments. Executive rooms are worth the £10 to £20 extra, for much more space: Our favorite is room no. 1, which comes with a sunken bath that has its own TV. All that's missing from an almost perfect boutique package is a good view. Children under 18 are not permitted.

Clarence Rd., Southsea, Hampshire PO5 2LQ. www.theclarencehotel.co.uk. © **023/9287-6348.** Fax 023/9229-6346. 8 units. £95–£199 double. Rates include English breakfast. AE, MC, V. Free parking. **Amenities:** Bar; room service. *In room:* A/C, TV, movie library, hair dryer, Jacuzzi (in some), Wi-Fi (free).

Westfield Hall   Close to the pebble beach at Southsea, two adjacent early-20th-century homes with large bay windows have been turned into a hotel with a certain friendly charm and some character. One of the most inviting and most comfortable of the little family-run hotels in the area, this establishment offers beautifully maintained, comfortably furnished bedrooms—including new superior doubles with king-size beds. Contact the hotel directly for the best rate.

65 Festing Rd., Southsea, Hampshire PO4 0NQ. www.whhotel.info. © **023/9282-6971.** Fax 023/9287-0200. 26 units. £64–£125 double. Rates include English breakfast. AE, DC, MC, V. Free parking. **Amenities:** Restaurant; bar; room service. *In room:* TV, hair dryer, Wi-Fi (free).

IN NEARBY WICKHAM

Old House Hotel ★ 📖   This handsome early Georgian (1715) structure set in a pleasant village has undergone a classic refurbishment, giving it the feel of an English country-house hotel. The paneled rooms on the hotel's ground and first floors contrast with the beamed bedrooms on the upper floors, which were once the servants' quarters. All bedrooms have period furniture—many are original antiques—and warm, comfortable beds. Four contemporary "Garden Suites" (they are actually rooms, not suites), located in an annex, are more spacious but less characterful than rooms in the main building.

The Square, Wickham, Fareham, Hampshire PO17 5JG. www.oldhousehotel.co.uk. © **01329/833049.** Fax 01329/833672. 16 units. £95–£170 double. Rates include English breakfast. AE, MC, V. Free parking. **Amenities:** Restaurant; bar. *In room:* TV, hair dryer, Wi-Fi (free). Bus: 69 from Fareham. Exit M27 at junction 10. The village is 2 miles north of the junction of the B2177 and A32.

THE NEW FOREST ★

95 miles SW of London; 10 miles W of Southampton

Covering 56,658 hectares (140,000 acres), the **New Forest National Park** is a tract of serene, rolling—and not entirely wooded—terrain largely demarcated by William the Conqueror as a private hunting preserve. Henry VIII loved to hunt deer here, but he also saw an opportunity to build up the British naval fleet by supplying oak and other hard timbers to the boatyards at **Buckler's Hard** on the Beaulieu River, the remains of which survive. It was Henry, too, who oversaw the 16th-century Dissolution of **Beaulieu Abbey,** the grounds of which are now home to the **National Motor Museum.**

Away from the main roads, where signs warn drivers of wild New Forest dwarf ponies and deer, you'll find a private world of pasture, heath, and mixed woodland. The smallest National Park in the U.K. is a haven of peace and quiet, ideal for walking and **cycling**—and for sampling some of southern England's best country **pubs.** Fall is the best time to visit, when summer crowds have thinned, the winding roads have emptied, and the woodland colors are in full effect.

Essentials

GETTING THERE   Direct trains leave London Waterloo half-hourly during the day for Brockenhurst, the main station in the heart of the New Forest. Journey time is around 1½ hours and around £40 for a round-trip. Minor New Forest stops like Sway, New Milton, and Ashurst are mostly served by local trains. Either change at Brockenhurst or connect from Southampton or Bournemouth.

If you're driving from Southampton, head west on the A35. From farther east and north, enter the New Forest from junction 1 or 2 of the M27, if possible, to avoid the traffic bottleneck at Lyndhurst. Traffic queues in high season and on good-weather weekends can be alarmingly long.

GETTING AROUND   The relatively gentle contours of the New Forest are ideal for **cycle** touring. Either bring your own in the car—Lyndhurst is a natural start-point for a pedal-powered adventure—or rent. If you're arriving by train, try ideally located **New Forest Cycle Hire,** Brockenhurst Train Station (*©* **01590/623407;** www. newforestcyclehire.co.uk). Mountain bikes cost £14 per day, kids' bikes £6 to £7. Their website suggests excellent cycle routes for first-timers.

VISITOR INFORMATION   The **New Forest Visitor Information Centre,** Main Parking Lot, Lyndhurst (*©* **023/8028-2269;** www.thenewforest.co.uk), is open daily from 10am to 5pm. The Centre is the best place to pick up maps and advice on walking trails suited to your group.

Exploring the New Forest

Cocoa lovers should stop at **Beaulieu Chocolate Studio ★**, High Street, Beaulieu (*©* **01590/612279;** www.beaulieuchocolatestudio.co.uk). The shop's selection includes bars of artisan chocolate and individual chocolates with fillings ranging from the adventurous (chili and lime) to the everyday (runny orange and strawberry creams). It's all handmade on the tiny premises. Nearby **Exbury Gardens ★**, Exbury (*©* **023/8089-1203;** www.exbury.co.uk), is known for its Rothschild Collection of rhododendrons, azaleas, and camellias. The magical 81-hectare (200-acre) site is at its blooming best in spring, but there's something here for every season. Admission costs £9 for adults, £8.50 seniors, and £2 children 3 to 15. The gardens are open mid-March through October daily from 10am to 5pm. The attractive Georgian High Street at **Lymington ★** is the best spot for window browsing—and it's also a staging post for a ferry to the **Isle of Wight** (p. 306).

Beaulieu ★ HISTORIC SITE   The Palace House, surrounded by gardens, was the gatehouse of an abbey before it was converted into a private residence in 1538—and it has remained in the family of resident Lord Montagu ever since. The original Cistercian Beaulieu Abbey ★ was founded in 1204, and although much was destroyed during the Reformation overseen by Henry VIII, you can still enjoy the tranquil cloisters and herb garden, and see the lay brothers' refectory.

The 2011-renovated **National Motor Museum ★★**, one of the most comprehensive automotive museums in the world, displays more than 250 vehicles. Famous autos include four land-speed record holders, among them Donald Campbell's *Bluebird*. Some of the vehicles used in James Bond movies are on display, as well as those once used by everybody from Eric Clapton to Marlene Dietrich. Themed tours of the collection run daily at noon and 2pm.

Beaulieu (5 miles southeast of Lyndhurst and 14 miles southwest of Southampton). (C) **01590/612345.** www.beaulieu.co.uk. Admission £17 adults, £15 seniors and students, £9.75 children 13–17, £8.75 children 5–12, £45 family ticket. June–Sept daily 10am–6pm; Oct–May daily 10am–5pm. Closed Dec 25. Bus: 112 from Lymington or Hythe (Mon–Sat only).

Buckler's Hard ★ HISTORIC SITE   Two parallel, unassuming rows of 18th-century shipwrights' cottages, tumbling down to the banks of the tidal River Beaulieu, are all that's left of one of the most significant shipyards in British history. It was here that much of Nelson's fleet was built, including the admiral's favorite ship, *Agamemnon,* as well as *Eurylus* and *Swiftsure.* The Maritime Museum exhibits focus on the village's shipbuilding history; on Henry Adams, master shipbuilder, who lived in the cottage closest to the dock (now the Master Builder's House Hotel; see below); and on models of Sir Francis Chichester's yachts.

The walk back to Beaulieu, 2½ miles through the woodland along the riverbank, is well marked.

Buckler's Hard. (C) **01590/616203.** www.bucklershard.co.uk. Admission £5.95 adults, £5.60 seniors, £4.30 children 5–17, £18 family ticket. River cruise (Easter–Oct only) £4.50 adults, £4 seniors, £2.50 children, £11 family ticket. Nov–Feb daily 10am–4:30pm; Mar–June and Sept–Oct daily 10am–5pm; July–Aug daily 10am–5:30pm.

IN NEARBY CHRISTCHURCH

Christchurch Priory ★ 📷 CHURCH   The founding stones of this imposing, yet intimate sacred space were laid in the first decades after the Norman conquest of England. The rounded arches of the nave arcades are typical of an Augustinian priory church dating to the 1090s, but the Great Quire and Lady Chapel, separated by a magnificent stone **Quire Screen** ★ dating to 1320, are products of the later Gothic style. Protruding from the wall above the ambulatory is the priory's so-called "Miraculous Beam," placed there by a mysterious carpenter said to be the resurrected Jesus Christ himself—hence the church's (and town's) re-christening in the 12th century.

Quay Rd., Christchurch. (C) **01202/485804.** www.christchurchpriory.org. Free admission (£3 donation appreciated). Mon–Sat 9:30am–5pm, Sun 2:15–5:30pm; closes 1 hr. earlier in winter months.

Where to Eat

The Pig ★ MODERN BRITISH   There's a distinctive food philosophy at this innovative restaurant with rooms that opened in mid-2011. It's one based firmly on New Forest produce, vegetables from their own garden, home-cured meats, and foraged ingredients where available—all sourced from within 15 miles, prepared with minimum fuss by head chef James Golding, and served in a Victorian greenhouse. Menus change daily, but expect the likes of Beaulieu pheasant with thyme roasted root vegetables and sloe sauce, or filet of Lymington plaice with Dorset clams and pink fur potatoes.

Beaulieu Rd., Brockenhurst. (C) **01590/622354.** www.limewoodgroup.co.uk. Reservations required. Main courses £13–£20; fixed-price 2-course lunch (Mon–Sat) £13. MC, V. Daily noon–2pm and 7:30–9:30pm.

Where to Stay

Chewton Glen Hotel & Spa ★★★   A gracious country house on the fringe of the New Forest National Park, Chewton Glen is among the finest places to stay in southwest England (with princely rates to match). Accommodations vary widely and come in different shapes, sizes, and period styles, but all are luxurious. In the old house, a magnificent staircase leads to well-furnished double rooms opening onto

Drinking & Dining Pubs in the New Forest

The New Forest is blessed with an array of good country pubs—dining destinations in themselves as much as places to just enjoy a pint of local ale. The unremarkable exterior of the **Ship in Distress** ★, 66 Stanpit, Christchurch (✆ **01202/485123; www.theshipindistress.com**), hides a fine place for not only liquid sustenance but also some of the best-prepared seafood in the county. Dishes change with the catch: Expect the likes of roast filet of cod with black pudding and celeriac mille feuille. Most main courses cost around £16, rising to £28 for a mixed shellfish platter. Lunch and dinner is served daily; book ahead at weekends.

The tranquil **Mill at Gordleton** ★★, Silver Street, Hordle, near Lymington (✆ **01590/682219; www.themillat gordleton.co.uk**), is a refined take on a riverside inn, complete with babbling brook and weeping willows in the garden. The management has a firm commitment to locally sourced, organic produce, which is prepared with skill in such dishes as English wild duck with thyme braised potatoes, and red cabbage. Main courses range from £17 to £27. There's also a bar menu with simpler, cheaper lunches and snacks. The Mill is open daily for lunch and dinner; children are welcome at lunch only. Reservations are recommended for the restaurant.

The **Red Lion** ★, Rope Hill, Boldre, near Lymington (✆ **01590/673177; www.theredlionboldre.co.uk**), is a cozy, mazelike inn with roots in the 15th century. The menu is in the "traditional pub grub" mold, but dishes like ham and chips with a free-range egg, or slow roasted Hampshire pork belly are well executed. Main courses cost between £9 and £17. In summer, the garden is one of the best spots in the New Forest for sitting in the sun with a pint of ale from nearby Ringwood brewery.

The bar at the **Master Builder's House Hotel** (see below) also serves tasty, affordable fare to non-guests.

views of the spacious grounds. The best units are the Croquet Lawn Rooms, which open onto the greens and have big private balconies or terraces.

Christchurch Rd., New Milton, Hampshire BH25 6QS. www.chewtonglen.com. ✆ **01425/275341,** or 800/398-4534 in the U.S. Fax 01425/272310. 58 units. £299–£595 double; from £535 suite. 2-night minimum stay most weekends. AE, DC, MC, V. Free parking. After leaving the village of Walkford, follow signs off the A35 (New Milton–Christchurch Rd.). **Amenities:** Restaurant; bars; bikes; golf course (9 holes); health club & spa; 2 heated pools (1 indoor, 1 outdoor); room service; tennis courts (2 indoor, 2 outdoor). *In room:* A/C, TV/DVD, CD player, hair dryer, minibar, MP3 docking station (in most), Wi-Fi (free).

Master Builder's House Hotel ★ The phrase "snug and secluded" could have been invented for the remote former house of Admiral Nelson's "master builder," Henry Adams (1744–1805). The decor throughout is appropriately nautical in feel, but never completely abandons its contemporary edge. Superior rooms (all in the wonderfully labyrinthine original building) have an estuary and garden view, and are worth the extra money over standard rooms in the new wing.

A **cozy, wood-beamed bar** serves tasty dishes like dressed Lymington crab or a daily pie served with mash and seasonal vegetables, with main courses ranging between £8.50 and £19. There's also a more **formal restaurant** for evening dinners (guests add £30 per person to room rate for dinner).

Buckler's Hard, Hampshire SO42 7XB. www.themasterbuilders.co.uk. ✆ **01590/616253.** 25 units, 8 in historic building. £105–£180 double. Rates include English breakfast. AE, MC, V. Free parking. **Amenities:** Restaurant; bar; bike rental (1 wk. notice required); Wi-Fi (free). *In room:* TV, hair dryer.

Montagu Arms Hotel ★★ The gnarled old ivy clinging to the brick walls of this roadside inn tells you right away what to expect inside. In the heart of Beaulieu village, this hotel has an interesting history: The garden walls were constructed with stones salvaged from Beaulieu Abbey after it was demolished by Henry VIII. The hexagonal column supporting a fountain in the hotel's central courtyard is one of six salvaged, according to legend, from the ruined abbey's nave. Bedrooms—individually decorated in the lavish, English-country-house tradition—come in a range of shapes and sizes, and some contain a traditional four-poster bed.

Palace Lane, Beaulieu, Hampshire SO42 7ZL. www.montaguarmshotel.co.uk. ℂ **01590/624467.** Fax 01590/612188. 22 units. £148–£238 double; £208–£348 suite. Extra person £35. Rates include English breakfast. AE, DC, MC, V. Free parking. **Amenities:** 2 restaurants; 2 bars; use of nearby health club & spa; room service. *In room:* TV, hair dryer.

THE ISLE OF WIGHT ★

91 miles SW of London; 4 miles S of Southampton

A trip to the Isle of Wight is like stepping back in time. This diamond-shaped island at the mouth of the Solent measures just 13 miles from Cowes in the north to St. Catherine's Point in the south, and 23 miles from Alum Bay in the west to the easternmost point, near Bembridge. It is known for its family-friendly, sandy **beaches** and its ports, long favored by the yachting set.

The island has attracted such literary figures as Alfred, Lord Tennyson, and Charles Dickens. Tennyson wrote his poem "Crossing the Bar" en route across the Solent from Lymington to **Yarmouth.** Queen Victoria lived (and died) on the island, making her home at **Osborne House.** More recently, Jimi Hendrix headlined the iconic 1970 Isle of Wight Festival, just 3 weeks before his death.

GETTING THERE Efficient car and passenger ferries link the Isle of Wight with Portsmouth, Southampton, and Lymington, on the edge of the New Forest.

Red Funnel (ℂ **0844/844-9988;** www.redfunnel.co.uk) operates between 12 and 18 daily vehicle ferry services from Southampton to East Cowes; the trip takes around 1 hour. Car fares include up to six passengers, and are priced according to season and demand. Off season, look for deals that might go as low as £50 for the round-trip; in summer, fares of £150-plus aren't unusual. A quicker option is the Red Jet, a high-speed, passenger-only catamaran operating from Southampton's Town Quay and going to West Cowes; the trip takes 25 minutes. Fares vary slightly by season, but expect a round-trip fare to cost around £23 for adults, £15 for seniors, and £11 for children 5 to 15. Off-peak fares are a little lower.

Wightlink (ℂ **0871/376-1000;** www.wightlink.co.uk) operates three routes. A passenger-only catamaran connects Portsmouth Harbour and Ryde, taking 20 minutes and costing £21 for adults, £16 seniors, and £11 for children, round-trip standard return. Daytime departures are every 30 minutes in summer and every hour in winter. Ferries also connect Portsmouth with Fishbourne (40 min.), and Lymington with Yarmouth (35 min.), in West Wight. The latter two routes can accommodate cars, too. You might be able to secure a winter Super Saver fare for under £40 for a car and four passengers; in high summer, fares can cost quadruple that or more.

Hovertravel (ℂ **01983/811000;** www.hovertravel.co.uk) provides the quickest route across the Solent, connecting Southsea with Ryde by hovercraft (for foot passengers only) in around 10 minutes. Standard adult round-trip tickets cost £20, £11 for seniors, and £10 for children 5 to 15. "Flights" depart hourly for much of the day.

VISITOR INFORMATION The island's tourism services are undergoing major changes, but for now the main **Tourist Information Centre** is at 81 Union St., Ryde (✆ **01983/813813;** www.islandbreaks.co.uk). It's open daily from 10am to 3pm. Additional information centers are at Fountain Quay, Cowes (open Tues and Fri–Sat); the Guildhall, High Street, Newport (open daily); 67 High St., Shanklin (open Mon–Tues and Fri–Sat); High Street, Sandown (open Mon, Wed–Thurs, and Sat); and the Quay, Yarmouth (open Wed and Fri–Sat). Hours are usually 10am to 3pm.

GETTING AROUND A Rover ticket allows you unlimited travel on the island's bus network. A 24-hour Rover costs £10 for adults and £5 for children 5 to 18; 48-hour Rover tickets cost an extra 50%. A 1-week Freedom ticket costs £22, £11 for children. For further information, contact **Southern Vectis** (✆ **0871/200-2233;** www.islandbuses.info).

Roads are winding and scenic, so if you don't have a car, consider renting a bike or moped. Rentals are available at **Top Gear,** 1 Terminus Rd., Cowes (✆ **01983/299056;** www.islecycle.co.uk), and cost £15 per day for a bike (£12 if you pre-book). In Ryde, try **TAV Cycles,** 140 High St. (✆ **01983/812989;** www.tavcycles.co.uk), where cycles rent for £12 a day.

SPECIAL EVENTS **Cowes Week** is the world's oldest sailing regatta, filling a week in early August each year with nautical high-jinks. The final Friday sees a major firework display. See **www.cowesweek.co.uk.** Set up in 2004 as "boutique" alternative to Glastonbury, **Bestival ★** (www.bestival.net) occupies Robin Hill Country Park for a long weekend in September. Expect the very best in electronica, indie rock, folk, and urban music. Book tickets well ahead of your arrival.

Exploring the Isle of Wight

Cowes is probably the island's most famous town, and the premier port for yachting in Britain. Henry VIII ordered the castle built here, now the headquarters of the Royal Yacht Squadron. In West Wight, **Yarmouth ★** is prettier, a tiny port frequented all summer by yachties from the mainland. Yarmouth is also the jumping-off point for walking the most scenic stretch of the Isle of Wight's 65-mile **Coastal Path ★**. Strike west from Yarmouth's main parking lot toward the sand cliffs of **Alum Bay** and onto the three chalk pinnacles known as the **Needles,** at the island's westernmost point. Once you've conquered the lighthouse, head east as far as **Freshwater Bay,** along a stretch well known to poet Tennyson, who lived for 40 years at nearby Faringford House (now a hotel). The sheltered pebble cove here is popular with local families. Return to Yarmouth via the gently gladed cycleway that follows the Yar Estuary north. The whole circuit should take around 6 hours at a gentle pace.

The best sands for children are to be found at **Sandown** (also home to **Dinosaur Isle Museum;** ✆ **01983/404344;** www.dinosaurisle.com). Nearby **Shanklin** also has a decent beach and a more characterful, if slightly faded, Victorian esplanade. **Shanklin Old Village ★**, dates from a time long before the arrival of the Victorian holidaymakers. Farther along the coast, **Ventnor ★** is sometimes called the "Madeira of England" because it rises from the sea in a series of steep hills. It's resolutely Victorian in feel, packed with smart villas visibly influenced by the then-fashionable Gothic Revival architectural style.

Carisbrooke Castle ★ CASTLE The chief claim to fame of this fine medieval castle is the fact that King Charles I was imprisoned (and tried to escape from) here prior to his execution in London in 1649. Within a largely intact ring of walls (climb

7

The Isle of Wight

HAMPSHIRE & DORSET

The Isle of Wight is home to a small but reputable wine industry. At the island's biggest producer, **Rosemary Vineyards**, Smallbrook Lane, Ryde (*C* **01983/ 811084; www.rosemaryvineyard.co.uk),** you can taste a range of regular and fruit wines. Whites are generally made from flowery German varietals; the rosé (£7) is lively and fruity. Tasting is free. The island is also famous for the quality of its garlic, and you'll find all things for alliophiles at the **Garlic Farm,** Mersley Lane, Newchurch (*C* **01983/867333; www.thegarlicfarm.co.uk).** On sale are pickles, garlic grappes grown on the farm, cookbooks, and more—even garlic beer. Isle of Wight seafood is excellent, and you'll find a fresh supply at **Ventnor Haven Fishery,** Esplanade, Ventnor (*C* **01983/852176).** They also sell fish and chips.

up for classic Wight countryside views), you'll also find the 16th-century Well House, where, during periods of siege, donkeys took turns treading a large wheel connected to a rope that hauled up water from a well. Also inside the courtyard is a museum with exhibits on the social history of the Isle of Wight, the recreated bedroom used by Charles I during his imprisonment, and displays on the later, tragic death here of Charles's daughter, Princess Elizabeth.

Castle Hill, Carisbrooke (1¼ miles southwest of Newport). *C* **01983/522107.** www.english-heritage.org. uk. Admission £7 adults, £6 seniors and students, £5 children 5–15. Apr–Sept daily 10am–5pm; Oct–Mar daily 10am–4pm. Bus: 7, 12, or 38.

Osborne House ★★ HISTORIC HOME   Queen Victoria's most cherished residence owes much to the characteristic thoroughness of her beloved husband, Prince Albert, who contributed to the design of their honey-colored Italianate mansion. The rooms remain as Victoria knew them, down to the French piano she used to play and the cozy clutter of her sitting room. Grief-stricken at the death of Albert in 1861, she asked that Osborne House be kept as it was, and so it has been. The house is surrounded by lush, tranquil gardens, with a panoramic terrace that looks right across the Solent to Portsmouth's 21st-century Spinnaker Tower (p. 299). Victoria died on January 22, 1901, in her bedroom at Osborne House.

The Avenue, East Cowes (1 mile southeast of the town center). *C* **01983/200022.** www.english-heritage. org.uk. House and grounds £11 adults, £9.30 seniors, £5.50 children 5–15, family ticket £27. Apr–Sept daily 10am–5pm; Oct daily 10am–4pm; Nov–Mar (inside of house by 1-hr. pre-booked guided tour only) Wed–Sun 10am–2:30pm. Bus: 4 or 5.

Where to Eat

For flavors from beyond these shores, stop in for tapas and a glass of Tempranillo at **El Toro Contento** ★, 2 Pier St., Ventnor (*C* **01983/857600;** www.eltorocontento. co.uk). The long menu of authentic Spanish dishes includes the likes of shrimp cooked with garlic and sherry, and simple plates of Serrano ham and chorizo. Platters range from £3 to £7.50; in the evenings, there's also paella.

Brasserie at the George ★ MODERN ENGLISH/FRENCH   This exquisite hotel restaurant decorated with modern painted panels, has the best view of Yarmouth pier and the Solent through floor-to-ceiling glass windows. The place is known for its quality ingredients, deftly handled and beautifully presented in showcase fixed-price dinners. Start with a ballotine of pheasant with raisins, carrot, and hazelnuts;

follow that with filet of Solent cod with braised baby fennel and a Pernod cream sauce; and round things out with the George's exceptional English cheese board.

In the George Hotel (see below), Quay St., Yarmouth. © **01983/760331.** www.thegeorge.co.uk. Main courses £15–£28; set lunch 2 courses £16, 3 courses £20; dinner tasting menu £65. AE, MC, V. Daily noon–3pm and 7–10pm. Bus: 7.

New Inn ★ 🍴 GASTROPUB   This dining pub has earned its reputation over more than a decade. Fish is a specialty here, and the menu features favorites as well as sustainable alternatives like hake and megrim sole, alongside shellfish platters loaded with local crab and lobster. Meat eaters are catered for with the likes of breast of local pheasant with wild mushrooms, redcurrants, and rosemary sauce. If you prefer pub classics, try a doorstep sandwich, the ploughman's platter, or the fish pie. The wine list is way above the pub average and includes local bottles.

Mill Rd., Shalfleet. © **01983/531314.** www.thenew-inn.co.uk. Reservations recommended at weekends. Main courses £10–£15. AE, MC, V. Daily noon–2:30pm and 6–9:30pm. Bus: 7.

Robert Thompson at the Hambrough ★★★ CONTEMPORARY ENGLISH   Inside a stylish boutique hotel, this Michelin-starred restaurant is the finest on the island—and, indeed, among the best in Britain. Trained in some of the leading kitchens in England, titular chef Robert Thompson makes clever use of the countryside's bounty in such dishes as sautéed mallard duck breast with foie gras and veal sweetbreads. However, his best dishes have a seafood accent. Details depend on the catch, but expect the likes of butter poached Ventnor lobster served with a lasagna of baby gem lettuce and salsify. Fixed-price menus are offered at both lunch and dinner, with the latter offering more choice and more elaboration in cooking and preparation.

Inside Hambrough Hotel, Hambrough Rd., Ventnor. © **01983/856333.** www.thehambrough.com. Reservations required. 3-course set lunch £26; 3-course set dinner £55. DC, MC, V. Tues–Sat noon–1:30pm and 7–9:30pm. Bus: 3 or 6.

Where to Stay

An excellent alternative to the recommendations below—and suited to families seeking hotel accommodations—is the cheerful **Wight Mouse Inn,** Newport Road, Chale (**www.innforanight.co.uk**; © 01983/730431). This remote old coaching inn close to the southern tip of the island has 10 small to midsize bedrooms prettily decorated in a "modern-country" style. Children are welcome and can burn off energy in Popzone, an indoor play area. Doubles range from £50 to £65, with family rooms generally £5 to £10 more. Breakfast is £8 extra.

For self-catering cottages or apartment rentals, try local specialists **Wight Locations** (**www.wightlocations.co.uk**; © 01983/811418) or **Island Cottage Holidays** (**www.islandcottageholidays.co.uk**; © 01929/481555).

If there's a festival on—particularly a major one like Cowes Week (see above)—book ahead of your arrival. ***Insider tip:*** Ask your hotel about special prices on ferry crossings; they may be able to save you up to £50 per car if you're coming in peak season.

George Hotel ★★   The island's most elegant lodgings are at this former governor's residence dating from the 17th century. Between the quay and the castle, overlooking the Solent, this is a tranquil, wood-paneled oasis in the port beloved by yachties. The good-size bedrooms are individually decorated, each with style and an eye for comfort, tradition, and refinement. Even if you aren't a guest, reserve a table at the **Brasserie** (see above). *Insider tip:* The hotel website occasionally advertises low-season doubles at £99 for direct bookings.

Quay St., Yarmouth, Isle of Wight PO41 0PE. www.thegeorge.co.uk. © **01983/760331.** Fax 01983/760425. 17 units. £190–£287 double. Rates include English breakfast. 2-night minimum Sat. AE, MC, V. Parking £6. **Amenities:** Restaurant (see above); bar; room service. *In room:* A/C, TV, hair dryer. Bus: 7

Seaview Hotel Old-fashioned seaside charm is what the Isle of Wight is all about—and few places capture that mood as well as the Seaview. There's been a hotel here since 1898, and rooms in the original building retain a traditional feel (but no shortage of modern comforts). Go for a Gold room at the front for giant bay windows and Solent views. Newer "Seaview Modern" rooms are larger and pleasantly contemporary, but lack the character of the nautically themed main building. Hotel staff is as welcoming as anywhere on this friendly island.

High St., Seaview, Isle of Wight PO34 5EX. www.seaviewhotel.co.uk. © **01983/612711.** Fax 01983/613729. 28 units. £125–£220 double; from £210 suite. Rates include English breakfast. MC, V. Free street parking. **Amenities:** Restaurant; bar. *In room:* TV/DVD, CD player, Internet (free). Bus: 8.

BOURNEMOUTH ★

104 miles SW of London; 31 miles SW of Southampton

This south-coast resort at the doorstep of the New Forest didn't just happen: **Bournemouth** was carefully planned and executed—a true city in a garden, with Dorset's best **sandy beach**—and it's filled with an abundance of Victorian and Edwardian architecture. (The resort was discovered back in Queen Victoria's day, when sea bathing became an institution, and the beach hut was "invented" here in 1908.)

Bournemouth's most distinguished feature is its chines—narrow, shrub-filled, steep-sided ravines along the coastline. For the best view of them, walk along the waterfront promenade, appropriately called the **Undercliff.** These days, the artificial reef off adjacent **Boscombe** attracts a surfing crowd, who pack the sands alongside the traditional bucket-and-spade family visitors.

Essentials

GETTING THERE A train from London's Waterloo Station to Bournemouth takes 2 hours, with frequent service throughout the day, with round-trips from around £49. Bournemouth also has direct rail links with the New Forest (including Brockenhurst), Birmingham, and Manchester.

If you're driving, take the M3 southwest from London then the M27 westbound, followed by the A31, and then the A338 south to Bournemouth. *Insider tip:* In summer months, the A31 and A338 can get very busy. Leave early, or bring plenty of patience.

VISITOR INFORMATION The **Tourist Information Centre** is at Westover Road (© **08450/511701;** www.bournemouth.co.uk). From June through August, it's open daily from 9:30am to 5pm. Between February and May, and during October and November, it's open Monday to Saturday 10am to 4:30pm. In December and January, hours are Monday to Friday 10:30am to 4pm. For more on local beaches and watersports, see **www.coastwiththemost.com.**

Exploring Bournemouth & Boscombe

It's probably only worth a special journey here if you (or the children) like a **beach ★**. This seaside resort has 7 miles of uninterrupted sands stretching from Hengistbury Head to Alum Chine, 1½ miles of it sandwiched between the twin piers at Bournemouth and Boscombe. However, you should choose your spot carefully. Sands are quieter away from the piers, and families will enjoy the stretches around Westbourne or Southbourne, beyond Boscombe. Surfers, on the other hand, should make right for the artificial **Urban Reef,** 200m (656 ft.) offshore and just east of Boscombe Pier. Arrange lessons or hire equipment through **Sorted Surf Shop,** 42 Sea Road, Boscombe (𝄢 **01202/399099;** www.sortedsurfshop.co.uk). Beach access everywhere is free, and swimming is lifeguard-patroled in season. If you want to do Boscombe in style, rent a designer **beach pod,** complete with kitchenette, at the contemporary Overstrand development (𝄢 **0845/055-0968;** www.bournemouthbeachhuts.co.uk). A pod costs between £85 and £250 per week, depending on season.

Museum fans will find an intriguing, slightly bizarre collection of Victoriana in the time-capsule that is the **Russel-Cotes Art Gallery & Museum,** East Cliff Promenade (𝄢 **01202/451858;** www.russel-cotes.bournemouth.gov.uk). The former owners were avid traveler-collectors of international objets d'art, with an evident penchant for the Pre-Raphaelite. Admission is free, and hours are 10am to 5pm Tuesday through Sunday.

Where to Eat

The **Green Room,** inside the Green House (see "Where to Stay," below) is another place to consider for fans of contemporary creative British cooking.

The Crab at Bournemouth ★★ 🍴 SEAFOOD   This glass-fronted restaurant almost opposite Bournemouth Pier is the best place in town to enjoy seafood in a contemporary, refined setting. (Not surprisingly, it's packed most weekends.) Dishes take their culinary influences from near and far, so expect to see the likes of Dorset coast crab bisque alongside tagine of local monkfish with couscous, or tandoori whole sea bream. There are good choices for meat lovers and vegetarians, too, but the seafood is the reason to come.

Exeter Rd. 𝄢 **01202/203601.** www.crabatbournemouth.com. Reservations recommended. Main courses £13–£25; fixed-price lunch 2 courses £15, 3 courses £20. AE, DC, MC, V. Daily noon–2:30pm and 5:30–9:30pm.

Highcliff Grill ★ SEAFOOD/GRILL   The chargrill is the star at this smart brasserie-style restaurant, a long-time recommendation in West Cliff. A short, focused menu includes American-style beef steaks, salmon, chicken, and pork filet on the grill. There's also a limited but tempting seafood selection, likely to include mussels in Gewürztraminer wine or an open ravioli of crab and prawn served with a shellfish foam. Dress is "smart-casual," and the ambience is businesslike.

Inside Marriott Highcliff (see below), St. Michael's Rd. 𝄢 **01202/200800.** Reservations recommended. Main courses £14–£29; 3-course set lunch (Sun) £22. AE, MC, V. Mon–Sat 6–9:30pm; Sun 1–3pm and 6–9pm.

Urban Beach Café ★ INTERNATIONAL   This laid-back two-floor boardwalk bar-eatery brings a slice of Pacific style to beachfront Boscombe. The menu is appropriately informal, mixing local classics, like a sustainable fish pie, with the likes of rope-grown mussels in a Thai broth. At night, the dining moves upstairs, and adds more formal dishes like braised English lamb shank with colcannon, and local seabream filet with chorizo and mussel chowder. You can also come here for breakfast (until 11:30am) or just stop by for a coffee or a glass of their homemade cola.

Overstrand, Undercliff Dr., Boscombe. ✆ **01202/443960.** www.urbanreef.com. Reservations recommended. Main courses £7.50–£19. MC, V. Daily 9am–10:30pm (dinner menu available 6:30–10:30pm); closes 6pm Sun–Mon Nov–Mar.

Entertainment & Nightlife

THE ARTS & MUSIC

Bournemouth is an essential stop for most shows touring the U.K.—the **Bournemouth International Centre** ("the BIC") and **Pavilion** dominate the center of town, and both have a program that includes everything from children's spectaculars, to bands, comedians, and musicals. Look for performances by the world-famous **Bournemouth Symphony Orchestra ★**, which offers regular local concerts. The venues have joined forces: Ticket information for either is available by calling ✆ **0844/576-3000,** or see **www.bic.co.uk**. If niche indie-rock is more your thing, check what's on at the **O2 Academy,** 576 Christchurch Rd. (✆ **0844/477-2000** for tickets; www.o2academybournemouth.co.uk). Friday is jazz night at the **Cottonwood Hotel,** East Overcliff Drive (✆ **01202/553183;** www.cottonwood.uk.com). The music usually kicks off at 8:30pm.

THE PUB & BAR SCENE

You'll find Bournemouth's alt-cool bar crowd keeping much later hours on the squashy sofas and stripped-wood floors inside **Sixty Million Postcards ★**, 19–21 Exeter St. (✆ **01202/292697;** www.sixtymillionpostcards.com). It's lively till late. Ale fans are in for a treat at the **Goat and Tricycle ★**, 27–29 West Hill Rd (✆ **01202/314220;** www.goatandtricycle.co.uk). This traditional pub has an ever-changing range of 11 cask ales on tap. Hours are noon to 11pm daily; it's in West Cliff, a 10-minute walk from the center. Downstairs at the **Urban Beach Café** (see above) is all about the bar after 6pm.

Where to Stay

Opened in 2010, the **Park Central Hotel,** Exeter Road, Bournemouth, Dorset BH2 5AJ (**www.parkcentralhotel.co.uk**; ✆ 01202/203600), provides an excellent alternative to our favorites below. Airy, spacious rooms (though with small bathrooms) are simply decorated in a modern style, and have an enviable central Bournemouth location, almost opposite the pier. Rates range widely depending on the season, from £56 to £168 for a double room. In-house restaurant the **Crab at Bournemouth** (see above) is the town's best seafood eatery.

The Green House ★★ Boutique-chic has arrived in Bournemouth in the shape of this luxurious—and eco-friendly—hotel in East Cliff. Opened in 2010, The Green House has good-size, crisply designed rooms: All units in the Large and Master categories add rolltop baths to a spec that includes designer decor and walk-in rainfall showers throughout. Sustainability is more than just a marketing gimmick here: The wallpaper was all printed with vegetable ink, flat-panel TVs are low-energy certified, and even the pillows are stuffed with organic down. Check the website for low-season special deals.

The on-site **Green Room** restaurant is rapidly establishing a reputation for outstanding creative British cuisine using local, ethically reared ingredients. A 3-course set menu is good value at £25.

4 Grove Rd., Bournemouth, Dorset BH1 3AX. www.thegreenhousehotel.com. ✆ **01202/498900.** Fax 01202/551559. £100–£240 double. Rates include English breakfast. AE, MC, V. Free parking. **Amenities:** Restaurant; bar; bike rental. *In room:* TV/DVD, hair dryer, MP3 docking station, Internet (free).

Langtry Manor ★   The Red House, as this hotel was originally called, was built in 1877 for Lillie Langtry, a gift from Edward VII to his favorite mistress. The house has all sorts of reminders of its illustrious inhabitants, including initials scratched on a windowpane. Bedrooms vary a great deal, from ordinary twins to the romantic Lillie Langtry Suite, Lillie's own room, with a four-poster bed and a double heart-shaped bathtub. If you really want to splurge, rent the Edward VII Suite, furnished as it was when His Royal Highness lodged here, complete with an impressive fireplace.

26 Derby Rd. (north of Christchurch Rd., A35), East Cliff, Bournemouth, Dorset BH1 3QB. www.langtry manor.co.uk. ✆ **01202/553887.** Fax 01202/290115. 27 units. £95–£235 double; from £225 suite. Rates include English breakfast. Closed 2 weeks in Jan. AE, MC, V. Free parking. **Amenities:** Restaurant; bar; access to nearby health club; room service. *In room:* TV, hair dryer, Jacuzzi (in some), minibar, Wi-Fi (free).

Marriott Highcliff   Although perhaps not as grand as in its heyday, this landmark 1888 hotel has the best perch on West Cliff, and has recently undergone a £4.5-million refurbishment. Many rooms have views that stretch almost the full length of Bournemouth's glorious 7 miles of beach. The high-ceilinged interior has been tastefully decorated, and each bedroom is traditionally furnished in elegant English style. Rooms are generally spacious, and service is attentive.

St. Michael's Rd., West Cliff, Bournemouth, Dorset BH2 5DU. www.marriott.co.uk. ✆ **01202/557702,** or 800/228-9290 in the U.S. Fax 01202/293155. 160 units. £160–£240 double; from £220 suite. AE, DC, MC, V. Parking £10. **Amenities:** Restaurant (Highcliff Grill; see review, above); babysitting; bar; concierge; health club & spa; 2 pools (1 indoor, 1 outdoor); room service; tennis court. *In room:* A/C, TV/DVD, hair dryer, minibar, Wi-Fi (£15 per 24 hr.).

Wood Lodge Hotel 💣   Lying a short walk from the ocean, in a quiet part of East Cliff, this hotel dates from the early 20th century and has been beautifully restored and modernized. An Edwardian presence still permeates, and there are four rooms on the bottom for those who don't like stairs. It makes an ideal budget choice close to the beach.

10 Manor Rd., East Cliff, Bournemouth, Dorset BH1 3EY. www.woodlodgehotel.co.uk. ✆ **01202/290891.** Fax 01202/290892. 15 units. £36–£45 per person double (children 13 and under half-price). Rates include English breakfast. MC, V. Free parking. **Amenities:** Restaurant; bar. *In room:* TV, hair dryer, Wi-Fi (free).

En Route to Dorchester: A 17th-Century Mansion

Kingston Lacy ★ HISTORIC SITE   An imposing 17th-century mansion set on 101 hectares (250 acres) of gentle wooded parkland, Kingston Lacy was the family home of the Bankes family for more than 300 years. They entertained such distinguished guests as King Edward VII, Kaiser Wilhelm, Thomas Hardy, and George V. The house has one of England's finest provincial art collections, including works by Rubens, Titian, and Van Dyck, as well as an important collection of Egyptian artifacts. Allow at least 1½ hours to see it.

The present structure replaced **Corfe Castle** (see box "The Island That Isn't: Purbeck"), the Bankes' family home that was destroyed in the English Civil Wars. During her husband's absence, while performing duties as chief justice to King Charles I, Lady Bankes led the defense of the castle, withstanding two sieges before being forced to surrender to Cromwell's forces in 1646, because of the actions of a treacherous follower. The keys to Corfe Castle still hang in the library at Kingston Lacy.

At Wimborne Minster, on B3082 (Wimborne–Blandford Rd.),1½ miles west of Wimborne. ✆ **01202/ 883402.** www.nationaltrust.org.uk. Admission to the house, garden, and park £11 adults, £5.25 children

THE island THAT ISN'T: PURBECK

The so-called "Isle" of Purbeck is a peninsula dangling off the Dorset coast south of Poole Harbour. It's best reached by taking the A351 from Poole to Wareham and beyond, or catching the 5-minute **Sandbanks Chain Ferry** (© **01929/450203;** www.sandbanksferry.co.uk) that connects the millionaires' mansions of Sandbanks with Shell Bay, in the National Trust's Studland Nature Reserve. Foot passengers pay £1; it's £3.20 for a car and occupants (cash only).

The man-made highlight of Purbeck is the romantic ruin of **Corfe Castle** ★ (© **01929/481294;** www.nationaltrust. org.uk/corfecastle), silhouetted on the hill above the quaint but well-touristed village of the same name. The castle was the ancestral home of the Bankes family (see Kingston Lacy, above), and was sacked and destroyed by Parliamentary forces in 1646 during the English Civil Wars. It's open daily all year, and admission costs £6.50 for adults, £3.25 for children 5 to 16. If you want to arrive at Corfe in style, ride the **Swanage Railway** (© **01929/425800;** www. swanagerailway.co.uk), where traditional steam trains with old-fashioned carriages ply a 6-mile track. The timetable is complex (see the website), but there's a good service most days between April and October. A standard round-trip costs £9 for adults, £7 for children.

The natural highlights of Purbeck lie along its English Channel coast (an extension of the **Jurassic Coast;** see p. 317). **Durdle Door** ★, a mighty rock arch formed by millennia of sea erosion, is linked by coastal path with **Lulworth Cove** ★★, a photogenic, horseshoe-shaped bay half a mile to the east. Six miles west of Corfe Castle, off the B3070, the "ghost village" of **Tyneham** ★ was requisitioned in 1943 by the War Office for use as a tank range—with a promise it would be returned to its occupants after World War II. It never was. You can look inside the tiny, preserved Victorian schoolhouse and parish church, both frozen in the 1940s. From Tyneham, a 20-minute walk brings you to **Worbarrow Bay,** where there's a small pebble beach and fewer crowds than at nearby Lulworth. The tank range is still live, but is now open most weekends and all summer; see **www.tyneham.org.uk** for opening times.

The finest local lodging option is the riverside **Priory** ★★, Church Green, Wareham (www.theprioryhotel.co.uk; © **01929/551666**). Rooms are individually and luxuriously decorated, many with original antiques. Romantic Boathouse Suites come with whirlpool tubs. Prices range from £205 to £350 for a double; suites cost £330 to £415. At weekends, there's a 2-night minimum stay and dinner is included in the rate.

For more on Purbeck, see **www. visitswanageandpurbeck.co.uk.**

5–16, £30 family ticket; garden only £5.25 adults, £2.70 children, £15 family ticket. House mid-Mar–Oct Wed–Sun 11am–5pm; garden and park mid-Mar–Oct daily 10:30am–6pm, Nov–mid-Dec and Jan–mid-Mar daily 10:30am–4pm.

DORCHESTER ★

120 miles SW of London; 27 miles W of Bournemouth

In his 1886 novel, *The Mayor of Casterbridge,* Thomas Hardy bestowed upon **Dorchester** literary immortality. Differences between his fictional Casterbridge and the town of Dorchester were thinly veiled on purpose, and visits to **Hardy's Cottage** are as popular as ever. Actually, Dorchester was notable even in Roman times, when Maumbury Rings were filled with the sounds of 12,000 spectators screaming for the blood of the gladiators. You can get a sense of how wealthy locals lived at England's best-preserved **Roman Townhouse.**

Dorchester remained important enough to warrant a 1669 visit from Cosimo III, Grand Duke of Tuscany, but was soon notorious for the Bloody Assizes of "Hanging Judge" Jeffreys—over 300 local men were executed or transported for involvement in the Duke of Monmouth's unsuccessful 1685 rebellion against King James II. Today Dorchester is a thriving market town with an excellent **County Museum,** but it also seems to go to bed right after dinner. It's a great base for exploring the countryside and coast of southern and western Dorset.

Essentials

GETTING THERE   Direct trains run from London's Waterloo Station to Dorchester South at least hourly during the day, stopping en route at Winchester, Southampton, and Bournemouth. The trip takes around 2½ hours, costing around £55 for a round-trip. Dorchester has two train stations: Dorchester South at Station Approach and Dorchester West on Great Western Road.

If you're driving from London, take the M3 then M27 southwest to its end, and continue westward on the A31, following signs to Dorchester. Expect the journey to take around 3 hours, more during peak holiday periods.

VISITOR INFORMATION   The **Tourist Information Centre** is on Antelope Walk (© **01305/267992;** www.westdorset.com). It's open April through October, Monday to Saturday 9am to 5pm, and November through March, Monday to Saturday 9am to 4pm.

ORGANIZED TOURS   To learn more about author and Dorchester's favorite son Thomas Hardy (1840–1928), you can join organized walks that follow in the footsteps of his novels in and around the area. They are conducted occasionally April through October by the **Thomas Hardy Society** (© **01305/251501**). Visit **www. hardysociety.org** and click "Events."

Exploring Dorchester & Environs

Dorchester's **Roman Townhouse,** Colliton Park (entrance in Northernhay; © **01305/221000;** www.romantownhouse.org), is the best preserved of its kind in Britain. Many of the original intricate mosaics from this once grand residence in Roman "Durnovaria" have been left *in situ.* Admission is free. About 2 miles southwest of the center are the remains of the vast Iron Age fort known as **Maiden Castle ★.** The site was occupied for around 4,000 years, and its dramatic hillside concentric fortifications date to the period just before the Romans arrived. The site is well signposted and open to walk round.

Ten miles northeast of Dorchester, the one-room **Tolpuddle Martyrs Museum,** Memorial Cottages, Tolpuddle (© **01305/848237;** www.tolpuddlemartyrs.org.uk) tells the story of six local farm workers who in 1834 successfully fought brutal odds, a rigged trial, and a sentence of 7 years exile to Australia to form a labor union. Admission is free, and April through October hours are Tuesday to Saturday 10am to 5pm, Sunday 11am to 5pm; November to March hours are Thursday to Saturday 10am to 4pm, Sunday 11am to 4pm.

Athelhampton House & Gardens ★ HISTORIC SITE   This is one of southern England's great medieval houses, a manor whose earliest rooms date from the reign of King Edward IV, and whose site matches one of King Athelstan's 10th-century palaces. The wood-paneled Great Hall is particularly resonant of Athelhampton's Tudor provenance. The rest is packed with furniture from just about every period since: It feels like a lived-in film set, and indeed served that role for the 2009 movie *From Time to Time*. Thomas Hardy was a frequent visitor, and set his short story "The Waiting Supper" here.

The gardens are even more inspiring. Laid out in 1891, they are full of vistas, and their beauty is enhanced by the River Piddle flowing alongside. You'll see tulips and magnolias, roses, and lilies, the famous topiary pyramids, and also a 15th-century dovecote.

Athelhampton, nr. Puddletown. ✆ **01305/848363.** www.athelhampton.co.uk. Admission £9.25 adults, £8.75 seniors, free for children 15 and under. Mar–Oct Sun–Thurs 10:30am–4:30pm; Nov–Feb Sun 11am–dusk. Take the Dorchester-Bournemouth Rd. (A35) east of Dorchester for 5 miles then follow signs.

Dorset County Museum ★ MUSEUM   Dorchester's skillfully curated museum is the place to aquaint yourself with Dorset history and archeology, as well as the lives and works of notable local writers like J. Meade Falkner, author of smuggling tale *Moonfleet* (1898), and poet William Barnes (1801–86). There's also a gallery devoted to memorabilia from Thomas Hardy's life, including a re-creation of the study at his Dorchester home, and an archeological gallery with displays and finds from Maiden Castle (see above). The major news of 2011 was the arrival of a fossilized giant pliosaur skull, found in Weymouth Bay.

High West St. (next to St. Peter's Church). ✆ **01305/262735.** www.dorsetcountymuseum.org. Admission £6.50 adults, £5 seniors and students, free for 2 accompanied children 5–15, additional children £2, free for children 4 and under. Apr–Oct Mon–Sat 10am–5pm; Nov–Mar Mon–Sat 10am–4pm.

Hardy's Cottage ✋ HISTORIC HOME   Thomas Hardy was born in this thatched cottage on the fringe of Thorncombe Wood, Higher Bockhampton, in 1840. The home where he later wrote *Far from the Madding Crowd* (1874), and its lovely cottage garden are a National Trust property, and they're open to the public. Unless you're a real Hardy geek, there's not a great deal to see, but the pleasant setting and adjacent woodland offer a chance to take a stroll and perhaps spot badgers, deer, and species of indigenous birds. Approach the cottage on foot—it's a 10-minute walk after parking your vehicle in the space provided in the woods. Alternatively, ask at Dorchester's tourist office (see above) for a free self-guided 3-mile walk from the town to Hardy's Cottage, via water meadows and ancient woodland.

Higher Bockhampton (3 miles northeast of Dorchester and ½ mile south of Blandford Rd./A35). ✆ **01305/262366.** www.nationaltrust.org.uk. Admission £4. Mar 14–Oct Thurs–Mon 11am–5pm. Closed Nov–Mar 13.

Where to Eat & Stay

The best spot in the town itself for afternoon tea, a lunchtime light bite, or a selection of changing daily hot specials is the **Horse with the Red Umbrella,** 10 High West St. (✆ **01305/262019**). For a good pint of Dorset ale, stop in at the **Blue Raddle,** 9 Church St. (✆ **01305/267762;** www.theblueraddle.co.uk). Children 13 and under are not admitted.

Summer Lodge ★★★   This sophisticated Relais & Châteaux country-house hotel, located 15 miles north of Dorchester in the midst of rural Dorset, prides itself on providing care, courtesy, and comfort for discerning guests. Once home to heirs of the earls of Ilchester, the house, which boasts a wing designed by Thomas Hardy, now stands on 1.6 hectares (4 acres) of secluded gardens and sports a cozy Georgian-style drawing room. The atmosphere remains relaxed and informal, however, and lavish bedrooms have views either of the garden or over village rooftops to fields beyond.

The celebrated **restaurant** sports a menu that successfully combines classic English and modern influences, and is a favorite haunt of foodies from across the county. Dinner main courses range from £22 to £28; set lunch is £24.

Summer Lane, Evershot, Dorset DT2 0JR. www.summerlodgehotel.co.uk. © **01935/482000.** Fax 01935/482040. 24 units. £225–£360 double; £325–£445 suite. AE, DC, MC, V. Free parking. Head north from Dorchester on the A37. **Amenities:** Restaurant; bar; bike rental; concierge; exercise room & spa; indoor heated pool; room service; tennis court. *In room:* A/C, TV/DVD, CD player/library, hair dryer, MP3 docking station, Wi-Fi (free).

Yalbury Cottage ★★ 🛏️   This thatched-roofed cottage with chimney corners and beamed ceilings is in a small country village within walking distance of Hardy's birthplace. The cottage is some 350 years old and was once home to the keeper of the local water meadows. Midsize rooms are simply decorated with new beds and plain cream walls, plus individual design touches like elm headboards crafted by local woodcarvers. Room no. 4 has the best view, over empty pastures and right at the sunrise.

The outstanding **restaurant**—also open to non-guests Tuesday to Saturday evening and Sunday for lunch—serves French-influenced cuisine that pushes the local/seasonal mantra to the limit: No meat on the menu is sourced from farther than 9 miles away, for example. Dinner costs £29 for 2 courses, £34 for 3 courses.

Lower Bockhampton, Dorchester, Dorset DT2 8PZ. www.yalburycottage.com. © **01305/262382.** Fax 01305/266412. 8 units. £95–£115 double. Rates include English breakfast. MC, V. Free parking. Head 2 miles east of Dorchester on the A35 and follow signs to Lower Bockhampton. **Amenities:** Restaurant; lounge; bar. *In room:* TV/DVD, hair dryer, Wi-Fi (free).

DORSET'S JURASSIC COAST: WEYMOUTH TO LYME REGIS ★★

Weymouth: 137 miles SW of London, 8 miles S of Dorchester; Lyme Regis: 155 miles SW of London, 63 miles S of Bristol

Stretching from Swanage, in Purbeck, to Exmouth, in East Devon, the 95-mile **Jurassic Coast** is a UNESCO World Heritage site named after the rock strata laid down between 135 and 190 million years ago along its length. (The beaches they shelter have been a favorite haunt of fossil hunters for 2 centuries.) The most appealing base here is **Lyme Regis,** a quirky resort with steep and winding streets that are barely unchanged since Jane Austen visited in 1803 and 1804.

At **Weymouth,** you'll find a sandy strand, one of Dorset's best seafood **restaurants,** and lots of traditional English seaside fun. The town also claims a tragic place in English history: It was at Weymouth that the Black Death first arrived on English soil in 1348, on its way to killing half the country's population.

Essentials

GETTING THERE   The easiest train connection for this stretch of coastline is Weymouth, served via an approximately half-hourly direct train from London's Waterloo Station, calling at Southampton and Bournemouth en route. Journey time is just under 3 hours, costing around £59 for a round-trip.

To get to Lyme Regis direct from London Waterloo, take the hourly London–Exeter train and disembark at Axminster (2¾ hr. away). From there, catch bus no. 31 from Axminster Station to Lyme Regis (20 min.; hourly service during the day).

If you're driving to the Jurassic Coast from the east, head west along the A35 as far as Dorchester. To get to Lyme Regis, continue farther along the A35 beyond Bridport, cutting south to the coast at the junction with the A3070. For Weymouth, head immediately south from Dorchester for 9 miles on the A354.

VISITOR INFORMATION In Lyme Regis, the **Tourist Information Centre,** Guildhall Cottage, Church Street (② **01297/442138;** www.westdorset.com), is open November through March, Monday to Saturday 10am to 3pm, and April through October, Monday to Saturday 10am to 5pm and Sunday 10am to 4pm. The **Weymouth Tourist Information Centre,** The Esplanade (② **01305/785747;** www.visitweymouth.co.uk), is open daily 9:30am to 5pm between Easter and October, closing an hour earlier the rest of the year. For more on the World Heritage Coast, see **www.jurassiccoast.com**, follow **twitter.com/jurassic_coast**, or download the Jurassic iPhone and iPad app from the iTunes Store.

Exploring the Jurassic Coast

The highlight of the Jurassic Coast is wandering the steep, winding streets and unique harbor at **Lyme Regis ★** (see "Shopping in Lyme Regis", below). Completed in its current form in 1756 as a breakwater, the handsome **Cobb ★** has protected Lyme's thriving little seaport for 2½ centuries. Along with providing the iconic image from the 1981 movie *The French Lieutenant's Woman* (written by local John Fowles), the Cobb is the place to head if you fancy trying scenic **mackerel fishing.** In good weather, boats depart the harbor regularly on trips lasting 1 hour and costing £8. The surrounding coast is a fascinating place for botanists and zoologists thanks to the predominance of blue Lias, a sedimentary rock well suited to the formation of fossils (especially ammonites), and of landslips from cliffs weakened by 19th-century quarrying. Each landslide reveals new finds. In 1810, Mary Anning (at the age of 11) discovered one of the first articulated ichthyosaur skeletons nearby. She went on to become one of the world's first professional fossilists (a fascinating tale told in *The Dinosaur Hunters,* by Deborah Cadbury). She's buried in the churchyard of Lyme's Parish Church, **St. Michael Archangel,** on Church Street.

Just east of Lyme, the seaside village of **Charmouth** is the best jumping-off point for beachfront walks at the foot of **Golden Cap.** At 191m (627 ft.), they're the tallest seacliffs along the southern coast and in times past they served as a fine brandy smugglers' lookout. The best spot here for a coastal pint is the **Anchor Inn,** Seatown, Chideock (② **01297/489215**). Suitably refreshed in this former smugglers' tavern, you can strike out for a clifftop walk or stroll along the adjacent pebble beach.

Dorset's best produce fills the shelves at **Washingpool Farm Shop ★**, North Allington, Bridport (② **01308/459549;** www.washingpool.co.uk). The offerings change with the seasons but always include local organic meats and vegetables, imaginative chutneys, cakes baked in the farm kitchen, and even Dorset wines.

Starting just east of Bridport, at West Bay, the pebble bank known as **Chesil Beach ★** begins its 18-mile sweep to Portland. It's said that an experienced Dorset seaman can tell exactly where he is along the beach just from the size of the pebbles underfoot—an anecdote that plays a role in J. Meade Falkner's fictional children's smuggling tale, *Moonfleet.* Drive parallel to the Chesil, along the B3157, for spectacular coastal views, especially around the village of **Abbotsbury.** *Warning:* Don't be tempted to swim off the Chesil: Currents here are extremely dangerous, and at least 50 major shipwrecks have occurred just offshore, with many thousands of souls drowned.

Adjacent to the Chesil's eastern end lies **Weymouth,** a busy resort first popularized by King George III and home to this coast's best sandy beach, with a shallow shelf ideal for young bathers. Weymouth will host sailing events for the **2012 Olympic and Paralympic Games,** with the action taking place off Portland Harbour, in Weymouth Bay; see **www.london2012.com**. If you're arriving around the period July 28 to August 11, 2012, book your hotel well ahead of time.

Where to Eat

NEAR LYME REGIS

Wild Garlic ★★   Exposed brick, chunky wooden tables, and a daily menu on the chalkboard give this eatery owned by TV *Masterchef* winner Mat Follas a studied "refined rustic" look. Food is heavily influenced by the tastes and aromas of West Dorset, by Follas's love of foraging, and by the proximity to the sea—there's a fish of the day on every menu. Dishes are generally simple, and rely on the finest, freshest ingredients producing big flavors—think brill ceviche for starters, followed by Barnsley (lamb) chops served with coarse pesto and crushed new potatoes, and rounded off with an Eton mess.

4 The Square, Beaminster. ✆ **01308/861446.** www.thewildgarlic.co.uk. MC, V. Reservations recommended. Main courses £16–£22. Wed–Sat 9:30am–3pm and 7–11pm.

NEAR WEYMOUTH

Crab House Café ★★   Seafood shacks don't come any tastier, any fresher, or any more ethical than this oyster farm turned eatery on the eastern edge of Chesil Beach. The menu makes extensive use of their own shellfish, and brought-in fish is sourced from three fleets within 40 miles of the restaurant. House specialties include whole crab however you like it—brought to the table with tools and a bucket—and whatever's landed today, which may include unusual (and sustainable) species like gurnard or flounder. Sides and garnishes are organic or biodynamically farmed, and

---

📎 Shopping in Lyme Regis

Lyme's tumbledown Broad Street is little changed since Jane Austen set *Persuasion* here in 1816. (The book was posthumously published.) You'll doubtless find a thumbed copy at **Sanctuary,** 65 Broad St. (✆ **01297/445815**), an eccentric but superb secondhand bookstore with a warrenlike basement and stock that ranges from 1931 *Kelly's Directory of Dorsetshire* to used pulp fiction, and everything in-between. Almost opposite, **Lucy Ann ★,** 4a Broad St. (✆ **01297/443968;** www. lucyann.co.uk), sells funky, handmade jewelry at reasonable prices, made onsite using semiprecious stones. Lyme's former mill now hosts interesting independent shops, among them the **Town Mill Brewery,** Mill Lane (✆ **01297/ 444354; www.townmillbrewery.com),** a modern microbrewery that brews and sells on the premises. The **Town Mill Cheesemonger ★,** Mill Lane (✆ **01297/442626; www.townmill cheese.co.uk),** one of the Southwest's best cheese vendors, is the place to pick up the local specialty, Dorset Blue Vinney.

from the property's own garden where possible. Reservations are essential on weekends or during holiday periods.

Ferrymans Way, Portland Rd., Wyke Regis. © **01305/788867.** www.crabhousecafe.co.uk. MC, V. Reservations highly recommended. Main courses £13–£26. Wed–Thurs noon–2pm and 6–8:30pm; Fri–Sat noon–2:30pm and 6–9pm; Sun noon–3:30pm. Closed mid-Dec–mid-Feb. From Weymouth, follow signs toward Portland; restaurant is on the right before the causeway.

Where to Stay

For a refined take on the English seaside experience, **B+B Weymouth** ★, 68 The Esplanade, Weymouth DT4 7AA (**www.bb-weymouth.com**; © 01305/761190), offers simple, contemporary, Scandinavian-inspired rooms opposite the beach. Doubles range from £70 to £100 depending on the season; there's a £10 supplement for a Saturday stay or for a sea view.

IN LYME REGIS

Alexandra Hotel ★★ A major 2008 revamp gave this hotel, built in 1753, a chic, contemporary edge to lift its classy Georgian styling to the next level. Perched on a hill about 5 minutes from both the center and the harbor beach, it has the best bedrooms and amenities in town. In rooms once occupied by such "blue-bloods" as Dowager Countess Poulett and Duc du Stacpoole, you'll sleep in grand comfort in the Alex's handsome beds. Most rooms command superb sea views over Lyme Bay, but paying a little extra for one of the two Gould Rooms guarantees the best full-length bay window panorama in Dorset.

Pound St., Lyme Regis, Dorset DT7 3HZ. www.hotelalexandra.co.uk. © **01297/442010.** Fax 01297/443229. 26 units. £125–£215 double. Rates include English breakfast. MC, V. Free parking. **Amenities:** Restaurant; bar; babysitting; room service; Wi-Fi (free). *In room:* TV, hair dryer, MP3 docking station (in some).

Kersbrook Built of stone in 1789 and crowned by a thatched roof, the Kersbrook sits on a ledge above Lyme, on small, quaint gardens landscaped according to original 18th-century plans. All the comfortable, small to medium-size bedrooms have a traditional charm, but those up in the eaves have the most character and the best views.

Pound Rd., Lyme Regis, Dorset DT7 3HX. www.kersbrook.co.uk. © **fax 01297/442596.** 10 units. £85–£95 double. Rates include English breakfast. AE, MC, V. **Amenities:** Bar. *In room:* TV, hair dryer, no phone.

SHERBORNE ★

128 miles SW of London; 19 miles NW of Dorchester

A little gem of a town with well-preserved medieval, Tudor, Stuart, and Georgian buildings, Sherborne is in the northwestern corner of Dorset, surrounded by gentle hills, wooded glades, and chalk downs. It was here that Sir Walter Raleigh lived before his fall from fortune, in **Sherborne Castle.** There are 13 centuries of local Christian history, much of it encapsulated in the stones of Gothic **Sherborne Abbey.**

Essentials

GETTING THERE Frequent direct trains depart from London's Waterloo Station through the day, stopping at Salisbury en route. The trip takes 2¼ hours and costs around £51 for a round-trip.

If you're driving from London, take the M3 west, continuing southwest on the A303 and then joining the southbound B3145 beyond Wincanton. Plan for a journey time of around 3 hours.

VISITOR INFORMATION The **Tourist Information Centre,** Digby Road (*©* **01935/815341;** www.westdorset.com), is open April to October Monday to Saturday 9am to 5pm, and November to March Monday to Saturday 10am to 3pm.

Exploring Sherborne

Provincial Sherborne's compact center is a delightful place to stroll for an hour, and the tiny cluster of surviving medieval buildings around the abbey (see below) are especially atmospheric. **Church Lane,** leading from the Conduit (a hexagonal building where the monks washed their clothes), seems transplanted from another era. **St. Johns' Almshouses,** Half Moon Street, were built in 1438 to house 12 poor men and 4 women, although the cloister is a later neo-Gothic addition. You can see inside from May through September between 2 and 4pm.

Sherborne Abbey ★★ ABBEY This monumental abbey church, founded in A.D. 705 as the Cathedral of the Saxon Bishops of Wessex, dominates the 21st-century town. In the late 10th century, it became a Benedictine monastery, and since the Dissolution it has been Sherborne's rather grand parish church. Look immediately up to see the soaring, intricate **fan-vaulted ceiling** ★★ stretching the full length of the nave. Fan vaults were peculiarly English, and a particularly graceful solution to spreading the weight of a large ceiling, originating in the West Country in the early 15th century. Sherborne's was added by Abbot Ramsam around 1485. In addition to being staggeringly beautiful, it's notable for the intricate carved bosses and corbels that were so high up that they escaped the destructive iconoclasts of the English Reformation. Pack binoculars to appreciate them fully. There are more fine monuments at ground level, including Purbeck marble effigies of medieval abbots, as well as Elizabethan "four-poster" and canopied tombs. In the south transept, a 1698 baroque statue of the Earl of Bristol stands between his two wives.

Abbey Close. *©* **01935/812452.** www.sherborneabbey.com. Free admission (donations for upkeep welcomed). Apr–Sept daily 8am–6pm; Oct–Mar daily 8am–4pm.

Sherborne Castle ★ HISTORIC SITE "Castle" is in fact a misnomer for this Elizabethan residence, built for Sir Walter Raleigh after he decided that it wouldn't be feasible to restore the Old Castle (see below) to suit his stately needs. The original 1594 residence was a square mansion; later owners added four Jacobean wings to make it more palatial. After King James I had Raleigh imprisoned in the Tower of London, the monarch gave the castle to a favorite Scot, Robert Carr, banishing the Raleighs from their home. In 1617, it was bought by Sir John Digby, and has been the Digby family home ever since. The mansion was enlarged by Sir John in 1625, and in the 1750s, the formal Elizabethan gardens and fountains of the Raleighs were altered by Capability Brown, who created a serpentine lake between Sherborne's two castles. The 8 hectares (20 acres) of lawns and pleasure gardens around the lake are a delightful spot to stroll. Highlights of the house's interior include paintings by Gainsborough, Lely, and Kneller; an intact basement kitchen dating from 1595; and a portrait of Raleigh said to be an accurate likeness.

Off New Rd. (1 mile east of center). *©* **01935/813182.** www.sherbornecastle.com. Castle and gardens £9.50 adults, £9 seniors, free for children 15 and under; £5 grounds only. Apr 1–Oct 31 Tues–Thurs, Sat–Sun, and bank holidays 11am–4:30pm. Closed Nov–Mar.

Sherborne Old Castle ★ ☺ CASTLE The town's original castle was built by the powerful Bishop Roger de Caen in the early 12th century, but was seized by the

WILTSHIRE & SOMERSET

by Stephen Keeling & Donald Strachan

8

The Regency charms of Bath, the prehistoric mysteries of Stonehenge, and the monumental architecture of New Sarum: Wiltshire and Somerset, two of England's most ancient counties, practcially define the best of the West Country. Wiltshire, the closer of the two to London, is a largely rural idyll and home to the compact, medieval city of Salisbury. In Somerset, you'll discover everything from the regenerated harborfront in Victorian Bristol to the Gothic glory of Wells Cathedral.

SIGHTSEEING Regal Bath achieved fame and fortune twice in its history, first as a spa in Roman times, then thanks to the Georgian builders of the elegant **Royal Crescent.** Salisbury and **Wells** have retained much of the architecture and atmosphere of cities that reached their powerful peaks in medieval times. The counties also contain some of the finest stately homes in southern England, notably at **Wilton House,** near Salisbury, and **Montacute,** in south Somerset.

EATING & DRINKING Somerset and Wiltshire are also known for their produce. **Cheddar** cheese, named after a small Somerset village, is still aged in limestone caves there. **Scrumpy** cider hails from Somerset. Wiltshire is hunting country, and the county's best gastropubs usually feature game on the menu. That most English of traditions, **afternoon tea** has been big in Bath for centuries, and is paired here with a Sally Lunn or Bath bun.

HISTORY The history of Britain is written in the buildings of Wiltshire and Somerset. **Avebury** and Stonehenge date back to prehistoric times, way before the Romans first popularized their spa at Bath. Cathedrals in the small cities of Salisbury and Wells are as close to the ideal Gothic as you'll find in England. Regency architecture is rarely as beautiful as it is at Bath's Royal Crescent, and **Bristol,** a powerhouse port of the Victorian Industrial Revolution, is forever linked with Isambard Kingdom Brunel.

NATURE The west Somerset coast is hiking country, with the wilderness of the **Exmoor National Park** home to some fine long-distance trails—the Two Moors Way and the Southwest Coast Path—that can be tackled in bits or all at once. The **Mendips** offer serene, rolling vistas above ground, but they're much more spectacular below ground, with limestone caves shaped over millennia at Cheddar and **Wookey Hole.** In the magnificent, year-round garden at Stourhead, nature had a helping hand from the 18th-century's most skilled landscapers.

THE best TRAVEL EXPERIENCES IN WILTSHIRE & SOMERSET

o **Soaking in the Thermae Bath Spa:** Nothing beats watching the sunset over the enchanting rooftops of Georgian Bath, as you slowly simmer in the outdoor hot-spring pool at Thermae. The waters are the same as those enjoyed by the Romans, but the facilities are definitely 21st-century England. See p. 339.

o **Ballooning over Bristol:** Float over southwest England's largest city, taking in the historic docks, River Avon, and Brunel's Clifton Suspension Bridge. Bristol is a lot more scintillating by air—and surprisingly affordable. See p. 348.

o **Meeting the English Gothic at Salisbury:** Britain isn't short of pointed arches and flying buttresses, but rarely has Gothic been expressed so harmoniously as at Salisbury Cathedral. It was built in under 40 years, leaving it unpolluted by later styles. Climb the bell tower for views that stretch far beyond the water meadows so loved by Constable. See p. 327.

o **Exploring the Mendip Caves:** Under the southern lip of Somerset's Mendip Hills, water and limestone have mixed over millennia to create cave formations of great beauty. Wookey Hole and Cheddar Gorge may be well touristed, but they'll fill little minds with natural wonder. See p. 356.

o **Tasting scrumpy in rural Somerset:** West Country apples and a brewing tradition stretching back longer than anyone can record make Somerset the home of the traditional, alcoholic cider known as scrumpy. Tour the county's best niche producers, then visit one of the oldest Christian sites in Britain, Glastonbury Abbey, to taste their award-winning version. See p. 362 and 358.

SALISBURY ★★, STONEHENGE ★★ & SOUTH WILTSHIRE

90 miles SW of London; 53 miles SE of Bristol

Long before you enter the city, the spire of **Salisbury Cathedral** comes into view—just as John Constable and J. M. W. Turner captured it on canvas. The 121-m (404-ft.) pinnacle of the Early English Gothic cathedral is the tallest in England, but is just one among many historical points of interest in this thriving county city.

Salisbury, once known as "New Sarum," lies in the valley of South Wiltshire's River Avon. Filled with Tudor inns and tearooms, it is also an excellent base for visitors keen to explore nearby **Stonehenge** or even **Avebury.** The old market town also has a lively arts scene, and is an interesting destination on its own. If you choose to linger for a day or two, you find an added bonus: Salisbury's pub-to-citizen ratio is among the highest in England.

Essentials

GETTING THERE   Trains for Salisbury depart half-hourly from Waterloo Station in London; the trip takes under 1½ hours and costs around £39 for a round-trip. The city also has fast, regular connections with Portsmouth, Bristol, Cardiff, and Southampton.

If you're driving from London, head west on the M3 and then M27 to junction 2, continuing the rest of the way on the A36.

VISITOR INFORMATION   Salisbury's friendly **Tourist Information Centre** is on Fish Row (© **01722/334956;** www.visitsalisbury.com). It's open Monday to Saturday 9:30am to 5:30pm; between June and August, it's also open Sunday 11am to 3pm. For information on the wider south Wiltshire area, you should also consult **www.visitwiltshire.co.uk.**

SPECIAL EVENTS   The **St. George's Day Celebrations** in April is a traditional medieval celebration of the city's patron saint. You can witness St. George slaying the dragon in the Wiltshire mummers' play and enjoy the acrobats and fireworks. *Note:* The festival isn't always on St. George's Day itself (April 23); check ahead of time with the Tourist Information Centre (see above).

During the annual **Salisbury International Arts Festival** (© **01722/332977;** www.salisburyfestival.co.uk) the city drapes itself in banners, and street theatre—traditional and unusual—is offered everywhere. There are also symphony and chamber-music concerts in Salisbury Cathedral, children's events, and much more. It takes place from mid-May to the beginning of June.

Exploring Salisbury

You can easily see Salisbury on foot, either on your own or by taking a guided daytime or evening walk with **Salisbury City Guides** (© **07873/212941;** www.salisbury cityguides.co.uk). Tickets are £4 for adults and £2 for children 4 to 15. Check with the Tourist Information Centre (see above) about themed walks, including the ever-popular ghost walk, and walks for children.

The slightly haphazard collection at the **Salisbury & South Wiltshire Museum ★**, King's House, 65 The Close (© **01722/332151;** www.salisburymuseum.org.uk), includes displays that place nearby Stonehenge and Wiltshire's other prehistoric sites in context. The "History of Salisbury" gallery houses a small collection of Turner's Salisbury watercolors. The museum is open Monday to Saturday 10am to 5pm, and between June and September also Sunday noon to 5pm. Admission is a little steep at £6 for adults, £2 children under 16.

The medieval **Church of St. Thomas & St. Edmund,** St. Thomas's Square (© **01722/322537;** www.stthomassalisbury.co.uk), is notable for a 1475 **Doom painting ★★**, above the chancel arch. Once common in English churches, such depictions of the Last Judgment were largely whitewashed or erased during the Reformation. Salisbury's survived—by chance—and is notable in particular for a clothed female figure among the naked souls being dispatched to Hell. She was reputedly a local brothel keeper who later repented and gave all her "ill-gotten gains" to charity—still damned, but allowed to retain her modesty. Admission is free, and the church is open daily 8:30am to 6pm.

Mompesson House ARCHITECTURE   Built in 1701 by Charles Mompesson, while he was a Member of Parliament for Old Sarum (see below), Mompesson House is an archetypal example of the Queen Anne style, and is well known for its fine plasterwork ceilings and paneling. Also used as a location for the 1995 Oscar-winning movie *Sense and Sensibility,* it houses an important collection of 18th-century drinking glasses. Visitors can wander through the garden and order a snack in the tearoom.

The Close. © **01722/420980.** www.nationaltrust.org.uk/mompessonhouse. Admission £5.20 adults, £2.60 children 17 and under, £13 family ticket. Mid-Mar–Oct Sat–Wed 11am–5pm. Closed Nov–early Mar.

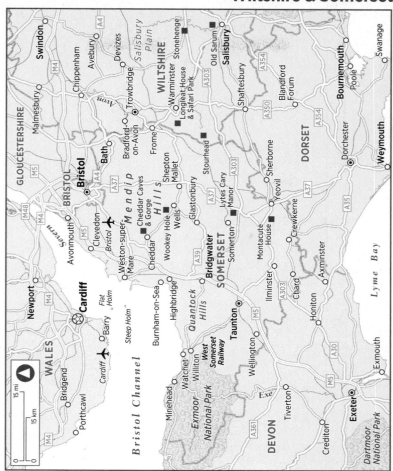

Salisbury Cathedral ★★★ CATHEDRAL   You'll find no better example of the Early English Gothic architectural style than Salisbury Cathedral. Construction on this magnificent building began as early as 1220 and took only 38 years to complete. (By contrast, many of Europe's grandest cathedrals took up to 300 years to build.) As a result, Salisbury Cathedral is one of the most homogenous and harmonious of all the great cathedrals.

The cathedral's 13th-century octagonal Chapter House possesses one of the four surviving original texts of the **Magna Carta**—one of the founding documents of democracy and justice, signed by King John in 1215—along with treasures, manuscripts, and artifacts from the diocese of Salisbury. Britain's largest cloisters and adjacent close further enhance the cathedral's beauty. At least 75 buildings are in the compound, some from the early 18th century and others from much earlier.

Insider tip: The 123-m (404-ft.) spire is the tallest in Britain, and was one of the tallest structures in the world when completed in 1315. In its day, this was seriously advanced technology. Amazingly, the spire was not part of the original design, and the name of the master mason is lost to history. In 1668, Sir Christopher Wren expressed alarm at the tilt of the spire, but no further shift has since been measured. The entire ensemble is still standing; if you trust towering architecture from 700 years ago, you can now explore the heights on a 1½-hour **Tower Tour ★★** costing £8.50 for adults, £6.50 for seniors and children 5 to 17, £25 for a family of five (fee includes cathedral donation). Between April and September, there are five tours a day Monday to Saturday (hourly from 11:15am), and two on Sunday (1 and 2:30pm). From October to March, there are usually one or two daily, depending on weather, but no tour on Sunday. Children must be 5 and over, and everyone will need an affinity for heights.

The Close. ℂ **01722/555156.** www.salisburycathedral.org.uk. Suggested donation £5.50 adults, £4.50 students and seniors, £3 children 5–17, £13 family ticket. Daily 7:15am–6:15pm; Chapter House closes 4:30pm (Apr–Oct 5:30pm) and all morning Sun.

Exploring Stonehenge & South Wiltshire

Old Sarum ★ RUINS   Believed to have been an Iron Age fortification, Old Sarum was used again by the Saxons and flourished as a walled town into the Middle Ages. The Normans built a cathedral and a castle here; parts of this old cathedral were taken down to build the city of "New Sarum," later known as Salisbury, leaving behind the dramatic remains you see today. In the early 19th century Old Sarum was one of the English Parliament's most notorious "Rotten Boroughs," constituencies that were allowed to send a Member of Parliament to Westminster despite having few—in Old Sarum's case, no—residents. The Rotten Boroughs were finally disbanded in 1832.

2 miles north of Salisbury off the A345 Castle Rd. ℂ **01722/335398.** www.english-heritage.org.uk/oldsarum. Admission £3.50 adults, £3 seniors, £1.80 children 5–15. Apr–June and Sept daily 10am–5pm; July–Aug daily 9am–6pm; Mar and Oct daily 10am–4pm; Nov–Jan daily 11am–3pm; Feb daily 11am–4pm. Bus: 5, 6, 7, 8, or 9, every 30 min. during the day, from Salisbury bus station.

Stonehenge ★★ 📷 HISTORIC SITE   This iconic circle of lintels and megalithic pillars is perhaps the most important prehistoric monument in Britain. The concentric rings of standing stones represent an amazing feat of late Neolithic engineering because many of the boulders were moved many miles to this site: the bluestones from Pembrokeshire in southwest Wales, the massive sarsens from the local Marlborough Downs. If you're a romantic, come see the ruins in the early glow of dawn or else when shadows fall at sunset. The light is most dramatic at these times, the shadows longer, and the effect is often far more mesmerizing than in the glaring light of midday. The mystical experience is marred only slightly by an ugly (but necessary) perimeter fence protecting the stones from vandals and souvenir hunters. Your admission ticket gets you inside the fence, but no longer all the way up to the stones.

The widely held view of 18th- and 19th-century Romantics, who believed Stonehenge was the work of the Druids, is without foundation. The boulders, many weighing several tons, are believed to have pre-dated the arrival in Britain of the Celtic culture. Controversy surrounds the prehistoric site, especially since the publication of *Stonehenge Decoded,* by Gerald S. Hawkins and John B. White, which maintains that Stonehenge was an astronomical observatory—that is, a

Neolithic "computing machine" capable of predicting eclipses. In truth, its purpose remains a mystery. However, it appears from the beginning to have been a monument to the dead, as revealed by radiocarbon dating from human cremation burials around the brooding stones. The site was used as a cemetery from 3000 B.C. until after the first of the giant stones was erected around 2500 B.C. It was used for about 1,500 years then abandoned.

Archeologists have also uncovered hearths, timbers, and other remains of what was probably the village of workers who erected these monoliths on Salisbury Plain. These ancient ruins appear to form the largest Neolithic village ever found in Britain. The trenches of this discovery, Durrington Walls, lie 2 miles from Stonehenge.

Insider tip: From the road, if you don't mind the noise from traffic, you can get a good view of Stonehenge without paying the admission charge for a close-up encounter. Alternatively, climb **Amesbury Hill,** clearly visible 1½ miles up the A303. From here, you'll get a free panoramic view.

Wilts & Dorset (*©* **01722/336855;** www.wdbus.co.uk) runs several buses daily between Salisbury and Amesbury (25 min. away), which is as close as you can get by public transportation. It's a half-hour walk to Stonehenge from there. There is also the hop-on, hop-off **Stonehenge Tour** bus (*©* **01983/827005;** www.stonehengetour.info), which runs several times an hour from Salisbury railway and bus stations, passing via Old Sarum (see above) all the way to the stones, taking 35 minutes each way. A round-trip ticket costs £11 for adults, £5 for children; including entrance to Stonehenge and Old Sarum, prices are £18 adults, £15 students, and £9 children. The fate of the planned Stonehenge visitor center remains unclear, after government spending cuts in 2010 canceled £10 million of funding.

At the junction of the A303 and A344. © **01980/623108.** www.english-heritage.org.uk/stonehenge. Admission £6.90 adults, £5.90 students and seniors, £3.50 children 5–15, £17 family ticket. June–Aug daily 9am–7pm; Mar 16–May and Sept–Oct 15 daily 9:30am–6pm; Oct 16–Mar 15 daily 9:30am–4pm. If you're driving, head north on Castle Rd. from the center of Salisbury. At the first roundabout (traffic circle), take the exit toward Amesbury (A345) and Old Sarum. Continue along this road for 8 miles, and then turn left onto the A303 in the direction of Exeter. You'll see signs for Stonehenge, leading you up the A344 to the right. It's 2 miles west of Amesbury.

Wilton House ★★ ☺ HISTORIC SITE   This grand Palladian home of the earls of Pembroke dates from 1551 but has undergone numerous alterations after successive fires, most recently in the early 19th century, and is especially noted for its exquisite 17th-century staterooms, designed by architect Inigo Jones (1573–1652). Shakespeare's troupe is said to have entertained at Wilton—although this is as yet unproven—and Eisenhower and his advisers prepared here for the D-Day Normandy landings, with only the Van Dyck paintings as silent witnesses. The house is stocked with beautifully maintained furnishings by the likes of Chippendale and world-class art, including paintings by Rubens, Bruegel, Rembrandt, and Reynolds. You can also visit a reconstructed Tudor kitchen and Victorian laundry.

On the 8.4-hectare (21-acre) estate are giant cedars of Lebanon trees, the oldest of which were planted in 1630, as well as rose and water gardens, riverside and woodland walks, and an adventure playground for children.

Wilton, 3 miles west of Salisbury on the A36. © **01722/746714.** www.wiltonhouse.co.uk. Admission to house and grounds £14 adults, £5 seniors, £4 children 5–15, £34 family ticket; grounds only £5.50 adults, £4 children 5–15, £17 family ticket. Easter–Aug Sun–Thurs 11:30am–4:30pm (last admission 3:45pm); grounds also open weekends in Sept.

Where to Eat
IN THE CENTER
Anokaa ★ MODERN INDIAN   Through the length and breadth of the country, creative chefs continue to give the traditional Indian-British "curry" a 21st-century makeover. This relaxed and colorful dining room serves up contemporary cuisine from a variety of Indian regions, from Punjab in the north to Kerala in the south. *Anokaa* means "different," and when you taste the chicken lababdar, flavored with coconut, ginger, and sweet chili, or the tandoori seared lamb rack, you'll understand why. At lunchtime, it's buffet service only: Although the choice is limited, the cooking is well executed, and at £9 offers excellent value.

60 Fisherton St., Salisbury. © **01722/414142.** www.anokaa.com. Reservations recommended. Main courses £10–£16. MC, V. Daily noon–2pm and 5:30–10:30pm.

Charter 1227 ★ FRENCH/ENGLISH   A 2011 menu relaunch has set this pleasantly decorated restaurant, on the second floor of a red-brick building in Salisbury's marketplace, buzzing again. The accessible offering mixes British bistro classics with some refined French-influenced cooking. Expect to choose between the likes of pan-roasted filet of beef with potato terrine and a horseradish velouté, and fish served with double-cooked chunky chips and homemade tartare sauce. And yes, the chef still makes the customer favorite, sticky toffee "pud" with butterscotch sauce.

6–7 Ox Row, Market Square, Salisbury. ✆ **01722/333118.** www.charter1227.co.uk. Reservations recommended. Main courses £12–£19; set lunch £13 for 2 courses, £16 for 3 courses. AE, DC, MC, V. Tues–Sat noon–2:30pm and 6–9:30pm.

WEST OF THE CITY

Compasses Inn ★★ GASTROPUB   Behind the whitewashed walls and latched wooden door of this remote thatched inn lies one of the finest pub kitchens in Wiltshire. The chalkboard menu covers country gastro classics like pork and leek sausages with mash or local game pie, but also lets fly with some exceptionally creative combinations served in hearty portions. Expect the likes of slow-cooked veal brisket with parsley mash and a wild mushroom sauce, or poached breast and roast leg of guinea fowl served in a haricot bean and lentil broth with a shallot and bacon rosti. Real ales on tap include local brews.

Lower Chicksgrove, Tisbury, nr. Salisbury. ✆ **01722/714318.** www.thecompassesinn.com. Reservations recommended. Main courses £8.50–£16. MC, V. Daily midday–2pm and 6:30–9pm. Take the westbound A30 from Salisbury to Shaftesbury, turning off 1½ miles west of Fovant toward Chicksgrove, from where you should follow signs down a single-track road.

Howard's House ★ INTERNATIONAL   This elegant hotel-restaurant in one of Wiltshire's most beautiful villages showcases finely honed cooking that makes use of first-class ingredients. The menu changes daily, but is likely to include such starters as lasagna of wild rabbit, tarragon, and whole-grain mustard. Main courses feature expertly balanced combinations of flavors, as exemplified by a filet of wild turbot with thyme ravioli, fondant potato, and oyster beinget. An alternative, informal seasonal "terrace menu" might include tian of Devon crab with watercress or a selection of warm filled ciabattas.

Teffont Evias, nr. Salisbury. ✆ **01722/716392.** www.howardshousehotel.co.uk. Reservations required. Fixed-price 3-course lunch £20, or a la carte £23 for 2 courses, £28 for 3 courses; dinner £36 for 2 courses, £45 for 3 courses. Terrace menu main courses £8.95–£11. AE, MC, V. Daily 12:30–2pm and 7–9pm. For directions, see the Howard's House Hotel listing, below.

Entertainment & Nightlife

THE PERFORMING ARTS

The Salisbury arts scene is thriving and varied. The **Salisbury Playhouse,** Malthouse Lane (✆ 01722/320333; www.salisburyplayhouse.com), produces some of the finest theatre in southwest England—their program could feature anything from Shakespeare to a touring contemporary drama, and always includes productions aimed at youngsters. At the **City Hall,** Malthouse Lane (✆ 01722/434434; www.cityhallsalisbury.co.uk), next door, you're more likely to encounter a big-name comedian or tribute band. It has an accessible program of events to suit most tastes and ages. The **Salisbury Arts Centre,** Bedwin Street (✆ 01722/321744; www.salisburyartscentre.co.uk), housed within the former St. Edmund's Church, features a wide range of performing and visual arts. Offerings include a broad, occasionally edgy mix of music, contemporary and classic theatre, and dance performances, plus cabaret, comedy, and family shows. Regular workshops are available for all ages in arts, crafts, theatre, and dance. The lively cafe/bar is a pleasant meeting place.

THE PUB SCENE

Hopback is the local brewer to look out for, and the best of Salisbury's many pubs usually have at least one of their fine beers on tap. Standing just outside the center, **Deacons ★**, 118 Fisherton St. (✆ **01722/504723**), has a local reputation for keeping and serving ale the way it should be. The tiny, characterful bar is worth the short walk. Even in a city full of ancient, half-timbered inns, there's nowhere quite like the **Haunch of Venison ★**, 1 Minster St. (✆ **01722/411313;** www.haunchofvenison. uk.com). The haphazard interior layout and wood-paneled rooms of this former chophouse ooze medieval charm—and are reputedly haunted. **Rai d'Or,** 69 Brown St. (✆ **01722/327137;** www.raidor.co.uk), may look rather nondescript in comparison, but the bar usually sells a range of interesting local microbrews.

Where to Stay

IN SALISBURY

Salisbury and its environs are blessed with lots of good-quality hotels and guesthouses. Opened in late 2010, **Peartree Serviced Apartments ★**, Mill Road (www. peartreeapartments.co.uk; ✆ **01722/322055**), adds more space and the convenience of a kitchen to a basic hotel set-up. Apartments are well-designed, modern, and comfortable, and come in a range of sizes, from studios to two-bedroom units. They are also bookable by the night; prices range from £75 to £160.

Best Western Red Lion Hotel ★   Cross under the Red Lion's arch into a courtyard with an ancient Virginia creeper, a red lion, and a half-timbered facade, and you're transported right back to the 1300s. Each small to medium-size bedroom is individually furnished and tastefully decorated. For families, there's one spacious room, or if that's booked, a pair of interconnecting units. The antiques-filled hotel is noted for its unique clock collection, which includes an extraordinary Skeleton and Organ clock in the reception hall.

4 Milford St., Salisbury, Wiltshire SP1 2AN. www.the-redlion.co.uk. ✆ **01722/323334,** or 800/528-1234 in the U.S. Fax 01722/325756. 51 units. £70–£90 double. Rates include English breakfast. AE, DC, MC, V. **Amenities:** Restaurant; bar; room service; Wi-Fi (free). *In room:* TV, hair dryer.

Legacy Rose & Crown Hotel ★★   Owing to its tranquil location, this is our top choice in the city, an easy 10-minute walk over a stone bridge to the center of Salisbury. It's a half-timbered 13th-century gem that stands with its feet almost in the River Avon; from the hotel terrace, you can admire the cathedral spire beyond the water. The inn has both new and old wings: Room nos. 1 through 5 have original beamed ceilings and antique decor, but look out over a (generally quiet) road. Newer units are bigger with less character, but they have a view over the water meadows to Salisbury Cathedral. Take your pick.

Harnham Rd., Salisbury, Wiltshire SP2 8JQ. www.legacy-hotels.co.uk. ✆ **01722/399955.** Fax 08444/119-046. 29 units. £105–£160 double. Rates include continental breakfast. Free parking. AE, DC, MC, V. Take the A3094 1½ miles south from the center. **Amenities:** Restaurant; 2 bars; room service; Wi-Fi (free). *In room:* TV, hair dryer.

Mercure White Hart Hotel ★   Combining the best of old and new, the White Hart is a Salisbury landmark from Georgian times. Its classic facade is intact, with tall columns crowning a life-size hart (stag), but inside there's a contemporary flavor to the rooms and public spaces. First-floor Privilege rooms are worth the small additional premium: For around £20 extra, you can expect air-conditioning as standard, king-size beds, and recently renewed decor. *Insider tip:* Special online rates direct from the website include savings of £20 or more on no-cancel-ation or no-breakfast bookings.

1 St. John St., Salisbury, Wiltshire SP1 2SD. www.mercure.com. © **01722/327476,** or 800/221-4542 in U.S. Fax 01722/412761. 68 units. £114–£180 double. Rates include English breakfast. AE, DC, MC, V. **Amenities:** Restaurant; bar; room service. *In room:* A/C (in Privilege rooms), TV, hair dryer, minibar (in some), Wi-Fi (£5 per hr.).

Wyndham Park Lodge This appealing Victorian corner villa in a residential neighborhood offers great-value guest rooms and a friendly welcome just 10 minutes' walk from the center of Salisbury. The small to midsize rooms are comfortably furnished with Victorian and Edwardian antiques, and have either one double or two twin beds.

51 Wyndham Rd., Salisbury SP1 3AB. www.wyndhamparklodge.co.uk. © **01722/416517.** Fax 01722/328851. 4 units. £50–£75 double; £65–£85 family room for 3. Rates include English breakfast. Free parking. MC, V. *In room:* TV/DVD, hair dryer, Wi-Fi (free).

OUTSIDE THE CITY

Howard's House ★ This 17th-century dower house, which has been added to over the years, is the most appealing small hotel and restaurant in the idyllic rural terrain west of the city; it's popular with shooting and fishing enthusiasts. Much care is lavished on the decor, with fresh flowers in every bedroom and public room, including a cozy, new snug area added in 2010. Set in a tranquil medieval hamlet, the hotel

---

More Prehistoric Standing Stones: Avebury

Many visitors say a visit to **Avebury ★★** (© **01672/539250**), one of the most expansive prehistoric sites in Europe, is a more organic experience than a trip to Stonehenge—you can walk right up and around the stones, as no fence keeps you away. Also, the site isn't mobbed with tour buses year-round. Avebury is spread over an 11-hectare (28-acre) site, winding in and out of the circle of more than 100 stones around a village. The stones are made of sarsen, a sandstone local to Wiltshire, and some weigh up to 50 tons. Inside this large circle are two smaller ones, each with about 30 stones standing upright. Native Neolithic tribes are believed to have built these circles.

Avebury is on the A4361, between Swindon and Devizes, 1 mile off the A4. The closest rail station is at Swindon, 11 miles away, which is served by quarter- or half-hourly trains from London Paddington Station. Journey time is 55 minutes. An hourly bus service (no. 49)

runs from Swindon Station to Avebury, taking 40 minutes. See **www.stagecoachbus.com** for timetables. From Salisbury, take bus no. 5 or 6 to Pewsey, then change to bus no. 95 or 96. Total journey time is about 1½ hours. See **www.wdbus.co.uk** for timetables. Admission to the site is free, except June 20 to 22, around the summer solstice, when it's usually closed.

Also in Avebury is the **Alexander Keiller Museum** (© **01672/539250**), which houses one of Britain's most important archeological collections, including material from excavations at Windmill Hill and Avebury, plus artifacts from other prehistoric digs at West Kennet, Long Barrow, Silbury Hill, and the Sanctuary. Admission costs £4.40 for adults, £2.20 children 5–14, and £12 for a family ticket. It's open daily, 10am–4:30pm November through March, 10am–6pm otherwise.

has attractive gardens, and on chilly nights, log fires burn. Most rooms are spacious, with one room large enough for a family and another with a four-poster bed.

Teffont Evias, near Salisbury, Wiltshire SP3 5RJ. www.howardshousehotel.co.uk. © **01722/716392.** Fax 01722/716820. 9 units. £175–£195 double. Rates include English breakfast. Free parking. AE, MC, V. From Salisbury, head east on the A36 until you reach a roundabout (traffic circle). Take the 1st left leading to the A30. On the A30, continue for 3 miles to the turnoff (B3089) for Barford Saint-Martin. Continue for 4 miles to the village of Teffont Evias. **Amenities:** Restaurant (see above); bar. *In room:* TV, hair dryer, Wi-Fi (free).

Newton Farmhouse ★★ ☺ This restored 16th-century farm-guesthouse makes a perfect informal touring base for visiting Salisbury, the New Forest, and the best of Hampshire (see chapter 7). Rooms conform to the charming, haphazard layout of the original buildings, but are comfortable and full of character, with all bathrooms renovated in 2010. Interconnecting units are well suited to families, as is the tranquil garden. The only downside is the adjacent road, but you'll hardly hear a sound at night.

Southampton Rd., near Salisbury, Wiltshire SP5 2QL. www.newtonfarmhouse.com. © **01794/884416.** 9 units. £55–£150 double. Rates include English breakfast. Free parking. MC, V. On the A36, 7 miles southeast of Salisbury. **Amenities:** Pool (outdoor). *In room:* TV/DVD, hair dryer, Wi-Fi (free).

LONGLEAT & STOURHEAD ★★

Longleat: 108 miles SW of London, 28 miles SE of Bristol; Stourhead: 6 miles SW of Longleat

Two very different interpretations on what a country house and gardens should be in the 21st century grace the southwest corner of Wiltshire, adjoining the Somerset and Dorset borders. The **Stourhead** estate is home to one of Britain's magical formal gardens, a landscape crafted during the 18th century where architecture and nature combine amid exquisite beauty and harmony.

Rather than surrender his inheritance, the 6th Marquess of Bath took the unusual decision in the 1940s to open his country seat, **Longleat,** to visitors. The range of attractions surrounding this grandiose Elizabethan mansion has been expanding ever since, with 2011 seeing the Jungle Kingdom joining Longleat Safari Park, the railway, the hedge maze, and much more; it's all aimed squarely at the family day-tripper market. Stately it isn't, perhaps, but it's lots of fun with little ones in tow.

If you're driving, you can visit both Longleat and Stourhead in one busy day. Follow the directions to Longleat given below, and then drive 6 miles down the B3092 to Stourton, 3 miles northwest of Mere, to reach Stourhead.

Longleat House & Safari Park ☺ ZOO On first glimpse, this magnificent Elizabethan stately home built in the early Renaissance style is romantic enough, and once you're inside, it's hard not to be dazzled by the lofty rooms and their exquisite paintings (including a Titian) and furnishings. From the surviving Elizabethan Great Hall, which Elizabeth I visited in 1574, to the State Rooms and late Georgian Grand Staircase, Longleat is filled with all manner of gorgeous things. Its library holds the finest private book collection in the country.

Surrounding the house, the number of attractions aimed squarely at kids has continued to expand. Around Longleat House is **Longleat Safari Park,** which opened in 1966 as Britain's first drive-through animal park. It hosts several species of endangered wild animals, including white rhinos and Rothschilds giraffes, that are free to roam the Capability Brown-landscaped parkland. You can also see a pack of Canadian timber wolves, two separate prides of lion, and endangered Siberian tigers, all from the comfort and safety of your car. Alternatively, see the animals by train, for a railway adventure, or ride on a safari boat around the park's lake to view hippos and feed sea lions. The park provides some low-key theme-park amusements as well, including an Adventure Castle and a Hedge Maze. *Insider tip:* Beware summer weekends, which can get very busy.

Warminster, Wiltshire. © **01985/844400.** www.longleat.co.uk. Admission to Longleat House £12 adults, £8 seniors, £6 children 3–14; Safari Park £12 adults, £9 seniors, £8 children; special exhibitions and rides require separate admission tickets; passport ticket for all attractions £24 adults, £19 seniors, £17 children 3–14. Feb 11–Feb 18 & Apr–Oct Mon–Fri 10am–5pm, Sat–Sun 10am–5:30pm; Mar weekends only 10am–5pm. Closed Nov–mid-Feb. From Bath or Salisbury, take the train to Warminster; then take a taxi to Longleat (about 10 min.). Driving from Bath, take the A36 south to Warminster; then follow the signs. From Salisbury, take the A36 north to Warminster, following signs to Longleat.

Stourhead ★★ GARDEN In a county (and country) of superlative gardens, Stourhead stands out as perhaps the most celebrated example of 18th-century English landscape gardening. More than that, it's a delightful place to wander—among its trees, flowers, and colorful shrubs are tucked bridges, grottoes, and temples.

The house at Stourhead, designed by Colen Campbell, a leader in the Georgian neoclassical revival, was built for Henry Hoare I between 1721 and 1725. The Hoare banking family subsequently oversaw the creation of 33 hectares (100 acres) of landscaped gardens to complement it. Henry Hoare II (1705–85), known rather immodestly as "Henry the Magnificent," contributed greatly to the development of the landscape of his estate.

The **Temple of Flora** was the first building in the garden, designed by the architect Henry Flitcroft in 1744. The **Grotto,** constructed in 1748, is lined with tufa, a water-worn limestone deposit. The springs of the Stour flow through the cold bath, where a lead copy of the sleeping Ariadne lies. The **Pantheon** was built in 1753 to house Rysbrack's statues of Hercules and Flora and other classical figures. In 1765, Flitcroft added the **Temple of Apollo** to the route that leads you over the public road via a rock-work bridge constructed in the 1760s. Every corner you roam to brings a new angle on this magical creation. Although Stourhead is a garden for all seasons, it is at its most idyllic in summer, when the rhododendrons are in bloom.

Stourton. © **01747/841152.** www.nationaltrust.org.uk/stourhead. Admission to house and gardens £12 adults, £6 children 5–16, £29 family ticket; gardens only £7.30 adults, £4 children, £17 family ticket. House: mid-Mar–mid-July and Sept–mid-Oct Fri–Tues 11am–4:30pm; mid-Jul–Aug and mid-Oct–Nov 6 daily 11am–5pm; also decorated for Christmas and open Dec Fri–Sun 11am–3pm. Garden: daily 9am–6pm. Getting to Stourhead by public transportation is difficult; you can take the train from Bath to Frome, or from Salisbury to Gillingham (both 30-min. trips). From the former it's a 10-mile taxi ride, from the latter 7 miles.

BATH ★★★

115 miles W of London; 13 miles SE of Bristol

Few cities in England are as elegant as Bath. Set in the leafy Avon Valley, the town boomed in the 18th century, when England's high society flocked here to "take the waters." The spa town's ravishing Georgian architecture, Palladian mansions, and aged pubs have been virtually untouched by modern development, making this one of the most enticing destinations in the country; it's also one of the most popular.

Bath's historical roots are commemorated at the **Roman Baths and Pump Room,** sensitively restored and now an illuminating window into the lives of Roman Britons. **Majestic Bath Abbey** is the other major draw, but the city's

Georgian splendor is best absorbed by wandering down handsome terraces such as the Royal Crescent.

Bath was established by the Romans as a hot-spring spa in A.D. 43—the curative waters were thought to ease rheumatism. Today those same waters provide the best cure for a hard day of sightseeing, with Thermae Bath Spa providing modern, sophisticated facilities and an open-air pool in which to soak.

Bath also boasts a surprisingly eclectic dining scene, but afternoon tea is a particular art form here, taken in wonderfully atmospheric rooms with Sally Lunn's famous buns, sweet "Bath buns" at the Pump Rooms, or "with Mr. Darcy" at the Jane Austen Centre—the beloved author set much of *Persuasion* and *Northanger Abbey* in the city.

Nightlife in Bath revolves around its collection of venerable pubs, fine Georgian watering holes such as the Raven of Bath, and the Bell Inn in the artsy Walcot district. Expect real ales, meaty pies, and inviting log fires in the winter.

Essentials

GETTING THERE   Trains leave London's Paddington Station bound for Bath once every half-hour during the day; the trip takes about 1½ hours (£20–£28). The train ride from Bristol to Bath takes 11 to 15 minutes (£6.30); if you're arriving at Bristol Airport, catch the airport bus to Bristol's Temple Meads Station, where you can get the train to Bath.

If you're driving from London, head west on the M4 to junctions 17 (A350) or 18 (A46) and continue south to Bath.

VISITOR INFORMATION   The **Bath Tourist Information Centre** is at Abbey Chambers, Abbey Church Yard (✆ **09067/112000** toll call, 50p per minute; www.visitbath.co.uk), next to Bath Abbey. It's open June through September, Monday to Saturday 9:30am to 6pm and Sunday 10am to 4pm; October to May, Monday to Saturday 9:30am to 5pm and Sunday 10am to 4pm. Closed December 25 and January 1.

TOURS   To get a unique perspective of Bath, you may want to take the **Bizarre Bath Walking Tour** (✆ **01225/335124;** www.bizarrebath.co.uk), a 1½-hour tour of Bath's lesser-known sights during which the guides pull pranks and tell jokes. It runs nightly at 8pm from Easter to October (no reservations necessary; just show up at the Huntsman Inn at North Parade Passage). Cost is £8 for adults, £5 for students and children. Conventional **open-top bus tours** (50 min.) are operated by **Bath Bus Company** (✆ **01225/330444;** www.bathbuscompany.com) and cost £12 for adults, £9.50 for seniors and students, £6 for children 5 to 15.

Exploring Bath

Begin your tour of Bath at the River Avon and the shop-lined **Pulteney Bridge,** designed by Robert Adam in 1778 and often compared to the Ponte Vecchio in Florence. John Wood the Elder (1704–54) designed much of Georgian Bath; his masterpiece is the elegant **Circus ★★★** of 1768, a series of three Palladian crescents arranged in a circle, at the northern end of Gay Street. His son, the younger John Wood (1727–81) designed the nearby **Royal Crescent ★★★,** a gorgeous half-moon row of townhouses completed in 1774.

Bath Abbey ★★ ABBEY   Completed in 1611, Bath Abbey is the last of the great medieval churches of England, a fine example of the late Perpendicular style. The stupendous West Front is the sculptural embodiment of a dream that inspired the

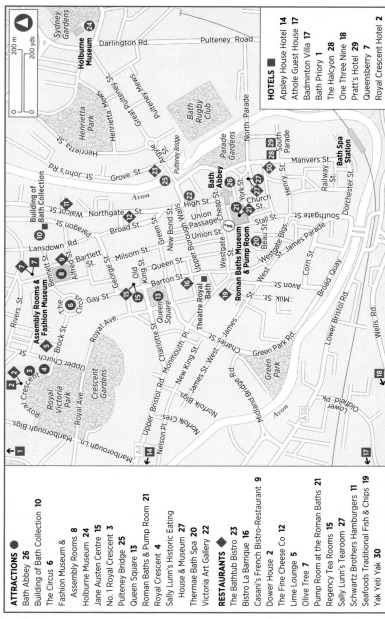

Bath

HOTELS

Apsley House Hotel **14**
Athole Guest House **17**
Badminton Villa **17**
Bath Priory **1**
The Halcyon **28**
One Three Nine **18**
Pratt's Hotel **29**
Queensberry **7**
Royal Crescent Hotel **2**

ATTRACTIONS ●

Bath Abbey **26**
Building of Bath Collection **10**
The Circus **6**
Fashion Museum &
 Assembly Rooms **8**
Holburne Museum **24**
Jane Austen Centre **15**
No. 1 Royal Crescent **3**
Pulteney Bridge **25**
Queen Square **13**
Roman Baths & Pump Room **21**
Royal Crescent **4**
Sally Lunn's Historic Eating
 House & Museum **27**
Thermae Bath Spa **20**
Victoria Art Gallery **22**

RESTAURANTS ◆

The Bathtub Bistro **23**
Bistro La Barrique **16**
Casani's French Bistro-Restaurant **9**
Dower House **2**
The Fine Cheese Co **12**
Lime Lounge **5**
Olive Tree **7**
Pump Room at the Roman Baths **21**
Regency Tea Rooms **15**
Sally Lunn's Tearoom **27**
Schwartz Brothers Hamburgers **11**
Seafoods Traditional Fish & Chips **19**
Yak Yeti Yak **30**

Abbey's founder, Bishop Oliver King, to pull down an older Norman cathedral on this site and build the one you see today. When you go inside and see its many ornate windows, you'll understand why the abbey is called the "Lantern of the West." For a bird's-eye view of the city, take the Abbey Tower Tour (45–50 min.), climbing 212 steps to the top of the abbey's vaulted ceiling, the clock face, and belfry (tours usually run Apr–Oct Mon–Sat 10am–4pm on the hour; Nov–Mar at 11am, noon, and 2pm).

Orange Grove. ✆ **01225/422462.** www.bathabbey.org. Free admission (suggested donation £2.50). Tower tours £6 adults, £3 children 5-14. Abbey Apr-Oct Mon-Sat 9am-6pm; Nov-Mar Mon-Sat 9am-4:30pm; year-round Sun 1-2:30pm and 4:30-5:30pm. Heritage Vaults Mon-Sat 10am-3:30pm (last admission).

Building of Bath Collection ★ MUSEUM   This is an ideal first stop for any tour of Bath, providing a deeper understanding of the architecture and construction of the city. A huge scale model of the city will help you get oriented, and there are special displays on everything from door and window styles to ancient tools and Georgian interior design.

The Countess of Huntingdon's Chapel, The Vineyards, The Paragon. ✆ **01225/333895.** www.bath-preservation-trust.org.uk. Admission £4 adults, £3.50 students and seniors, £2 children 6-16, £10 family ticket. Mid-Feb-Nov Sat-Mon 10:30am-5pm. Closed Dec-md-Feb.

Fashion Museum & Assembly Rooms ★ MUSEUM   The grand Assembly Rooms, designed by the younger John Wood and completed in 1771, once played host to dances, recitals, and tea parties. Damaged in World War II, the elegant rooms have been gloriously restored and look much as they did when Jane Austen and Thomas Gainsborough attended society events here.

Housed in the same building, the **Fashion Museum** offers audiotours through the history of fashion from the 16th century to the present day. Highlights include a 17th-century "silver tissue" dress, a whalebone corset, and an original suit from Christian Dior's legendary "New Look" collection. There's also a special "Corsets and Crinolines" display, where enthusiastic visitors can try on reproduction period garments.

Bennett St. ✆ **01225/477789.** www.fashionmuseum.co.uk. Admission (includes audiotour) £7.25 adults, £6.50 students and seniors, £5.25 children 6-16, £20 family ticket, free for children 5 and younger. Admission to the Assembly Rooms is an additional £2, free for children 16 and under. Nov-Feb daily 10:30am-4pm; Mar-Oct daily 10:30am-5pm. Last admission 1 hr. before closing. Closed Dec 25-26.

Holburne Museum MUSEUM   This once stuffy art museum has been utterly transformed by a stunning redevelopment by top Brit architect Eric Parry. The original classical facade has been enhanced by a ceramic and glass extension, with an interior of bright stylish galleries of decorative and fine arts, including paintings from Turner and Stubbs, and Gainsborough's famous *Byam Family*.

Great Pulteney St, at Sydney Place. ✆ **01225/428126.** www.holburne.org. Free admission; temporary exhibitions £6.50 adults, £5.50 seniors, £3 students and children 6-16, £12 family ticket. Mon-Sat 10am-5pm, Sun 11am-5pm.

Jane Austen Centre HISTORIC HOME   This small homage to Britain's favorite 19th-century writer occupies a graceful Georgian townhouse on a street where Ms. Austen once lived (at no. 25). Exhibits and a video convey a sense of what life was like when Austen lived here, between 1801 and 1806, though there are only a handful of artifacts on display directly connected to the author. Ladies can also learn the esoteric skill of using a fan to attract an admirer. The tearoom is also worth a visit (p. 340).

40 Gay St. ☎ **01225/443000.** www.janeausten.co.uk. Admission £7.45 adults, £5.95 students and seniors, £4.25 children 6-15, £20 family ticket. Apr-Oct daily 9:45am-5:30pm; Nov-Mar Sun-Fri 11am-4:30pm, Sat 9:45am-5:30pm. Closed Dec 24-26 and Jan 1.

No. 1 Royal Crescent MUSEUM This small but edifying museum provides a sense of what it was like to live at Bath's most sought-after address. The Georgian interior has been redecorated and furnished in late 18th-century style, replete with period furniture and authentic flowery wallpaper.

1 Royal Crescent. ☎ **01225/428126.** www.bath-preservation-trust.org.uk. Admission £6.50 adults, £5 students and seniors, £2.50 children 5-16, £13 family ticket. Mid-Feb-Oct Tues-Sun 10:30am-5pm; Nov-mid-Dec Tues-Sun 10:30am-4pm (last admission 30 min. before closing).

Roman Baths ★★★ & Pump Room ★ MUSEUM Blending Roman ingenuity and Georgian style, Bath's premier sight reopened after a magnificent renovation in 2010. Original stonework has been scraped and cleaned, and the steaming Great Bath now looks more like the Roman original. Comprehensive free audioguides, displays, and models help interpret the site as you wander past the Sacred Spring, remains of a Roman Temple, plunge pools, and the Great Bath itself, where actors dressed as various Roman characters mingle with visitors.

Most of what you see above ground was actually designed by the ubiquitous John Wood and Victorian architects in the 1890s, and only the stonework below the pillars is original Roman. Museum galleries house an intriguing array of artifacts thrown into the springs as offerings to the goddess Sulis Minerva, including thousands of Roman coins.

Coffee, lunch, and tea, usually with classical music from the Pump Room Trio, can be enjoyed in the 18th-century **Pump Room** (☎ **01225/444477;** daily 9:30am-5pm), overlooking the hot springs.

Bath Abbey Church Yard, Stall St. ☎ **01225/477785.** www.romanbaths.co.uk. Admission £12 adults (£13 July-Aug), £10 seniors, £7.80 children 6-16, £34 family ticket. Nov-Feb daily 9:30am-4:30pm; Mar-June and Sept-Oct daily 9am-5pm; July-Aug daily 9am-9pm.

Sally Lunn's Historic Eating House & Museum MUSEUM The oldest house in Bath (built around 1483), is an unashamedly touristy but fun monument to the Sally Lunn Bun (a light, semisweet bread, like a big brioche). Sally Lunn—the erstwhile creator of the bun—was a French Huguenot refugee who came to Bath in 1680. The tasty bun she created is eagerly wolfed down by hordes of tourists in the tearooms here, which also open for more formal dinners. You can skip the snacks and see displays on the house itself in the tiny museum, as well as Sally's original kitchen.

4 North Parade Passage. ☎ **01225/461634.** www.sallylunns.co.uk. Admission 30p adults; free for children, seniors, and cafe customers. Museum and cafe Mon-Sat 10am-6pm, Sun 11am-6pm; restaurant Mon-Thurs 5-9:30pm, Fri-Sat 5-10pm, Sun 5-9pm.

Thermae Bath Spa ★★ BATHS The waters at the old Roman baths are unfit for bathing, so if you want to sample the city's celebrated hot springs make for this plush, modern spa—the water might be Roman but the facilities are pure 21st-century. From the outdoor pool in the New Royal Bath complex you can watch the sun setting over the rooftops while you soak.

Hot Bath St. ☎ **0844/888-0844.** www.thermaebathspa.com. Admission New Royal Bath £25 for 2 hr., £35 for 4 hr. New Royal Bath daily 9am-10pm; Spa Visitor Centre Apr-Oct Mon-Sat 10am-5pm, Sun 10am-4pm. Closed Dec 24-25 and Dec 31-Jan 7. Closed Nov-Mar.

Taking Tea in Bath

Bath is the ideal place to indulge in that quintessentially English tradition of afternoon tea, served with jam, clotted cream, and scones. Try the **Pump Room ★★** at the **Roman Baths** (p. 339), which serves "Bath buns" (sweet buns sprinkled with sugar), or **Sally Lunn's ★** (p. 339). For £6.18 to £12, you can get a range of fabulous

Sally Lunn cream teas, which include toasted and buttered Sally Lunn buns served with strawberry jam and clotted cream, along with your choice of tea or coffee. The **Regency Tea Rooms ★**, at the Jane Austen Centre (p. 340), even offers "Tea with Mr. Darcy" sets for £12 to £21 for two, and basic cream tea sets from £5.50.

Victoria Art Gallery GALLERY   This relatively unknown gallery showcases a fine collection of British and European art, including paintings by artists who lived and worked in the Bath area such as Gainsborough. Singled out for special attention is the art of Walter Richard Sickert (1860–1942), now that he has been named as the "real" Jack the Ripper in Patricia Cornwell's 2002 bestseller, *Portrait of a Killer: Jack the Ripper—Case Closed*. Special exhibitions are shown in the two large modern galleries downstairs; these change every 6 to 8 weeks and are likely to feature anything from cartoons to boat sculpture.

Bridge St. ⓒ **01225/477233.** www.victoriagal.org.uk. Free admission. Tues–Sat 10am–5pm; Sun 1:30–5pm.

Where to Eat
VERY EXPENSIVE

Dower House ★ ENGLISH   This is one of the West Country's finest dining choices, and the best place to splurge on a classic high-class English eating experience. The setting is romantic, with hand-painted wall coverings and alfresco dining on the sunny terrace in the summer. The contemporary British menu is seasonal, featuring everything from Wiltshire Downlands lamb with vegetable gratin, goats curd, and caramelized sweetbread, to a summery wild sea bass with a smoked eel tortellini. You might finish with one of the lush desserts, such as a hazelnut chocolate teardrop autumn truffle ice cream with Marsala syrup.

Royal Crescent Hotel (see below), 16 Royal Crescent. ⓒ **01225/823333.** www.royalcrescent.co.uk. Reservations required. Fixed-price lunch £23 for 2 courses, £28 for 3 courses; fixed-price dinner £55 for 2 courses, £65 for 3 courses. AE, DC, MC, V. Daily noon–2pm and 7–9:30pm (until 10:30pm Sat).

Olive Tree ★★ MODERN ENGLISH/MEDITERRANEAN   A highly rated alternative to the Dower House (above), the Olive Tree offers a posh English dining experience. It's also another restaurant that emphasizes fresh, local produce and a seasonal menu, though the dishes have a more playful, creative quality here; think pressing of Somerset game and roasted duck foie gras to start, and tempting main courses such as hay roast roe venison with potato rosti, Savoy cabbage, and roasted roots, or filet of Stokes Marsh beef with horseradish mashed potato and crisp onion bhaji.

Queensberry hotel (see below), Russell St. ⓒ **01225/447928.** www.thequeensberry.co.uk. Reservations highly recommended. Main courses £17–£29. AE, MC, V. Mon–Sat noon–2pm and 7–10pm; Sun noon–2pm and 7–9:30pm.

EXPENSIVE

Casani's French Bistro-Restaurant FRENCH   For authentic French food in Bath, visit this beautiful Georgian building, where simple but stylish dishes are mostly inspired by Provence. The chef's signature dishes are snails-and-garlic ravioli and confit leg of duck with fondant potatoes. Other main specialties include roasted breast of pigeon with crushed potatoes; and slow cooked lamb shank with pea and baby onion ragout, creamy mash potatoes, and black olive and rosemary jus.

4 Saville Row. ⓒ **01225/780055.** www.casanis.co.uk. Reservations required. Main courses £14–£19; set lunch Tues–Sat £15 for 2 courses, £19 for 3 courses; set dinner (6–7pm) £18 for 2 courses, £22 for 3 courses. MC, V. Tues–Sat noon–2pm and 6–10pm.

MODERATE

The Bathtub Bistro ★ MODERN ENGLISH   This fashionable, cozy restaurant features home-style British cooking: Cheaper, hearty plates for lunch, such as ham hock, split pea and mint stew; and, for dinner, the exceptional crispy pork belly with bacon, red-pepper cabbage, black pudding, and rich cider sauce. There's also a reasonably priced steak, served with roasted tomatoes, mushrooms, and watercress.

2 Grove St. ⓒ **01225/460593.** www.thebathtubbistro.co.uk. Reservations recommended. Main courses £12–£15. MC, V. Mon–Sat noon–3pm and 6pm–late, Sun noon–3pm.

Bistro La Barrique ★★ FRENCH   Renowned chef Michel Lemoine created quite a buzz when he opened this branch of his popular Bristol-based restaurant in Bath, with his justly lauded *"petits plats"* (French tapas) concept. Order several dishes to share with some crusty French bread; the sea bass, creamed salted cod, and roast chicken with spinach and honey are solid choices, but the bourguignonstyle braised ox cheek with mash is truly exquisite. The relaxed atmosphere makes this a great place to just grab a glass of wine and small snack if you're not in the mood for a full meal.

31 Barton St. ⓒ **01225/463861.** www.bistrolabarrique.co.uk. Small plates £5.50–£5.95. MC, V. Mon–Fri noon–2:30pm and 5:30–10:30pm, Sat noon–10:30pm.

Lime Lounge ★★ MODERN ENGLISH/CONTINENTAL   Some of the best and friendliest service in the region separates this cozy bistro from the competition, though the food is also top-notch. The daytime menu features homemade soups and cakes, salads, burgers, and a range of sandwiches on specialty breads. Evenings are characterized by more substantial dishes such as pork with creamed apple and a cider and stilton sauce. But there are also riffs on old Brit classics: Think "posh" fish and chips (monkfish with Cajun and lime-dusted fat chips). Hot chocolate fans are also in for a treat.

11 Margarets Buildings, off Brock St. ⓒ **01225/421251.** www.limeloungebath.co.uk. Reservations recommended. Lunch from £7.95; dinner main courses £11–£15. MC, V. Mon–Sat 8am–late, Sun 10am–late.

INEXPENSIVE

The Fine Cheese Co. ★ ✦ DELI/CAFE   One of the country's finest artisan cheesemongers has a cafe next door serving cheese sandwiches, savory tarts, and cakes (think flaky pastry sausage rolls and chewy pistachio macaroons). They also knock out superb bowls of soups such as celery, new potato, and scallions, served with rye sourdough bread, and plates of cheese with fruit and crackers. Outdoor seating is available in the summer.

29 & 31 Walcot St. ⓒ **01225/483407.** www.finecheese.co.uk. Main courses from £6.95, sandwiches from £3.75. MC, V. Mon–Fri 9:30am–5:30pm, Sat 9am–5:30pm.

Schwartz Brothers Hamburgers ★ FAST FOOD   This gourmet-burger bar has been cooking up the region's finest hamburgers since 1977. Prime cuts of beef are chargrilled and served with fresh salad in a tempting range of varieties. Favorites include the garlic mayoburger and an irresistible Danish blue-cheese burger. They also do a large selection of decent veggie burgers. It tends to get busy after the pubs shut. Take-out only.

102 Walcott St. ✆ **01225/463613.** (There's a second location at 4 Saw Close. ✆ **01225/461726.**) www.schwartzbros.co.uk. Burgers from £3.80. Sun–Fri noon–late, Sat 11:30am–late.

Seafoods Traditional Fish & Chips ★ FISH & CHIPS   This family-owned shop has been serving this English fast-food staple for over 50 years, with cod, haddock, and plaice fried in a traditional, crispy batter and served with real thick-cut chips. They also do battered sausages, pies, mushy peas, fishcakes (cod, potatoes, and parsley), scampi, and even an extremely rich "posh" fish and chips (salmon). Take-out or grab a small table inside.

38 Kingsmead St. ✆ **01225/465190.** www.fishandchipsbath.co.uk. Main courses £5.35–£7.20. MC, V. Mon–Sat 11:30am–11pm.

Yak Yeti Yak ★ 🍴 NEPALESE   At this enticing Nepali basement restaurant you can eat exceedingly well for under £12, from a menu that includes subtly spiced dishes such as lamb slow-cooked with bamboo shoots, black-eyed peas and potato, or marinated chicken stir-fried with peppers and fresh chili. It's especially interesting for vegetarians, with superb Aloo Channa (potato and chickpeas stir-fried with cumin) and some of the best black dhal in the region.

12 Pierrepont St. ✆ **01225/442299.** www.yakyetiyak.co.uk. Main meat courses £6.95–£8.70, main vegetable dishes £4.70–£5.80. MC, V. Mon–Sat noon–2:30pm and 5–10:30pm; Sun noon–2:30pm and 5–10pm.

Shopping

Bath is crammed with markets, antiques centers, and shops. Prices here, however, are comparable to London's. Head to **Milsom Street** for old-fashioned department store **Jolly's** (✆ **0844/800-3704;** www.houseoffraser.co.uk; Mon–Thurs 9:30am–5:30pm; Fri 9:30am–6pm; Sat 9am–6pm; Sun 10:30am–5pm;), now part of the House of Fraser chain. Or go along the Corridor and North and South Passages, where you can pick up **Walcot Street,** home of arty, independent stores, including **The Fine Cheese Co.** (see above, under "Where to Eat"), which sells a vast array of artisan British cheeses.

The **Bartlett Street Antiques Centre,** 5 Bartlett St. (✆ **01225/466689;** Mon–Tues and Thurs–Sat 9:30am–5pm, Wed 8am–5pm), comprises 60 stands displaying furniture, silver, antique jewelry, paintings, toys, military items, and collectibles.

Near Bath Abbey, the **Beaux Arts Gallery,** 12–13 York St. (✆ **01225/464850;** www.beauxartsbath.co.uk; Mon–Sat 10am–5pm), is the largest and most important gallery of contemporary art in Bath, specializing in well-known British artists such as Ray Richardson, John Bellany, and Nicola Bealing.

The very upscale **Rossiters,** 38–41 Broad St. (✆ **01225/462227;** www.rossiters ofbath.com; daily 9:30am–5:30pm), sells very traditional English tableware and home-decor items. It'll ship anywhere in the world. **The Sausage Shop,** 7 Green St. (✆ **01225/318300;** www.sausage-shop.co.uk; Mon–Sat 8:30am–5:30pm), sells an equally varied selection of natural, homemade bangers in over 30 varieties, from Bath

Sausages (mild savory pork sausage with smoked ham, spinach, and Dijon mustard) to the more radical Somerset Scrumpy (pork with scrumpy, strong apple cider).

Entertainment & Nightlife

As befits one of Britain's oldest cities, there are plenty of characterful pubs in Bath, and nightlife tends to revolve around them (for nightclubs, Bristol is much better). Look for beers by **Abbey Ales,** Bath's only microbrewery. You'll find them among nine cask ales served at the **Bell,** 103 Walcot St. (✆ **01225/460426;** www.walcotstreet.com), which also features live music ranging from jazz and country to reggae and blues on Monday and Wednesday nights and Sunday. **The Raven of Bath,** 6–7 Queen St. (✆ **01225/425045;** www.theravenofbath.co.uk), also offers a range of excellent ales and wines, but is best known for its tasty pies.

Vegetarians and students love the **Porter,** 15 George St. (✆ **01225/424104;** www.theporter.co.uk), a grungier option specializing in vegetarian food and live music, open-mic nights, ambient DJs, and comedy. Next door is the **Moles Club** (✆ **01225/404445;** www.moles.co.uk), Bath's premier dance club and live music venue.

Where to Stay

VERY EXPENSIVE

Bath Priory ★★　Bath's most historic and luxurious hotel stands on .81 hectares (2½ acres) of award-winning gardens with manicured lawns and flower beds. The rooms are furnished with lavish antiques; our favorites are Heather and Lilac, on the top floor, with wonderful balconies overlooking the gardens (all rooms are named after flowers or shrubs). Rooms range from medium in size to spacious deluxe units, the latter with views, sitting areas, and generous dressing areas. Each has a lovely antique bed (two have four-posters).

Weston Rd., Bath, Somerset BA1 2XT. www.thebathpriory.co.uk. ✆ **01225/331922.** Fax 01225/448276. 27 units. £195–£400 double. Rates include breakfast. AE, DC, MC, V. Free parking. **Amenities:** Restaurant; bar; babysitting; exercise room; 2 pools (1 heated indoor, 1 outdoor); room service; spa. *In room:* A/C, TV, hair dryer, minibar, Wi-Fi (free).

Royal Crescent Hotel ★　Rates at this venerable hotel reflect the stunning location, in the center of the famed Royal Crescent. Guest rooms, including the Jane Austen Suite (a converted coach house), are luxuriously furnished with four-poster beds and marble tubs. Generally quite spacious, the bedrooms are also decked out with thick wool carpeting, silk wall coverings, and antiques. Each room is individually designed and offers such comforts as bottled mineral water and fruit plates.

16 Royal Crescent, Bath, Somerset BA1 2LS. www.royalcrescent.co.uk. ✆ **01225/823333.** Fax 01225/339401. 45 units. £195–£445 double; £440–£920 suite. Rates include English breakfast. AE, DC, MC, V. Parking £5. **Amenities:** Restaurant (Dower House, p. 340); bar; babysitting; exercise room; indoor heated pool; room service; sauna. *In room:* TV/DVD, hair dryer, minibar (in some), Wi-Fi (free).

EXPENSIVE

Apsley House Hotel ★★　This charming hotel, only about a mile west of the center of Bath, is one of the best deals in the city. It dates from 1830 and was built for the Duke of Wellington (you can stay in his room). Style and comfort are the keynotes here, and all the relatively spacious bedrooms are invitingly appointed with plush beds (some four-posters), country-house chintzes, antiques, and oil paintings.

141 Newbridge Hill, Bath, Somerset BA1 3PT. www.apsley-house.co.uk. ✆ **01225/336966.** Fax 01225/425462. 12 units. £70–£200 double. Rates include English breakfast. AE, MC, V. Free parking. Take the

A4 to Upper Bristol Rd., fork right at the traffic signals into Newbridge Hill, and turn left at Apsley Rd. **Amenities:** Bar; room service; Wi-Fi (free). *In room:* TV, hair dryer; Wi-Fi (free).

Queensberry A gem of a hotel, this early Georgian-era townhouse isn't your average homage to Jane Austen, with rooms that are more contemporary chic than Louis XIV. The Marquis of Queensberry commissioned John Wood the Younger to build this house in 1772, and though the rooms maintain their antique fittings and fireplaces, the furniture, rugs, and bright colors are all 21st century.

Russell St., Bath, Somerset BA1 2QF. www.thequeensberry.co.uk. ℃ **01225/447928.** Fax 01225/446065. 29 units. £155–£290 double; £230–£350 suite. AE, MC, V. Free parking. **Amenities:** Restaurant (see Olive Tree review, p. 340); bar; babysitting; room service; Wi-Fi (free, in lobby). *In room:* TV, CD player, hair dryer.

MODERATE

Athole Guest House ★★ 🔥 Spacious, luxurious rooms and a personal touch from the friendly owners make this one of the best deals of the city. The key is value for money; rooms cost less than £100 most of the year, yet you get the amenities associated with a four-star hotel, as well as free transfers from the train station. The house is Victorian, but the rooms are bright and contemporary. And the breakfasts are magical; from full English (with everything) to kippers, Welsh rarebit, and pancakes.

33 Upper Oldfield Park, Bath, Somerset BA2 3JX. www.atholehouse.co.uk. ℃ **01225/320000.** 4 units. £65–£130 double. Rates include English breakfast. 2-night minimum stay Sat–Sun. AE, MC, V. Free parking. **Amenities:** Free transfer from/to the railway or bus station. *In room:* A/C, TV, hair dryer, fridge, Wi-Fi (free).

The Halcyon ★ This is a true boutique hotel amid all the Georgian chintz, with a crisp contemporary theme; it's a hip place to stay, but, like most boutiques, it's not big on amenities. The property is a 1743 Georgian townhouse, but the compact rooms feature large, springy beds, bright colors (yellow, scarlet, or mauve), big plasma TVs, and the obligatory Philippe Starck fittings in the bathroom. Fun extras include jars filled with colored candy and gummy bears. Rooms on the first floor are biggest, and the ones at the front have the best views.

2/3 South Parade, Bath, Somerset BA2 4AA. www.thehalcyon.com. ℃ **01225/444100.** Fax: 01225/331200. 21 units. £99–£125 double. Breakfast extra £10. AE, MC, V. **Amenities:** Bar. *In room:* A/C, TV, Wi-Fi (free).

One Three Nine 🔥 This is another inviting alternative to Bath's numerous Georgian-theme hotels, a stylish contemporary B&B with nary an antique in sight. The house is a Victorian residence from the 1870s, but rooms feature modern English design, power showers, flat-screen TVs, and Molton Brown products. It's on the southern side of the city, on the A367 road to Exeter, just a 10-minute walk from the center of Bath, with minibuses passing by frequently.

139 Wells Rd., Bath, Somerset BA2 3AL. www.139bath.co.uk. ℃ **01225/314769.** Fax 01225/443079. 8 units. £60–£110 double. Rates include English breakfast. 2-night minimum stay Sat–Sun. AE, MC, V. Free parking. *In room:* A/C, TV/DVD, CD player, hair dryer, Wi-Fi (free).

INEXPENSIVE

Badminton Villa Located about a half-mile south of the city center, this is an atmospheric B&B that dates not from the Georgian era but the Victorian, constructed in 1883. Built of honey-colored blocks of Bath stone, it lies on a hillside with sweeping views over the city. Rooms are relatively free of the antiques that grace most historic hotels, but the wood and rattan furniture is tasteful nonetheless, and the breakfast and free Internet make this good value.

10 Upper Oldfield Park, Bath, Somerset BA2 3JZ. www.badmintonvilla.co.uk. © **01225/426347.** Fax 01225/420393. 4 units. £75–£80 double; £100 family room. No children 7 and under. Rates include English breakfast. MC, V. Free parking. Bus: 14. *In room:* TV, DVD, hair dryer, Wi-Fi (free).

Pratt's Hotel ★   Another historic choice, Pratt's is a relatively cheap way to get the classic Bath experience. Several elegant terraced Georgian townhouses—some of which have been taking guests since 1791 (Sir Walter Scott was a boarder)—were joined together to form this complex. Pratt's successfully milks this heritage with period decor, spacious rooms, and genteel afternoon tea in the hotel lounge. The bedrooms are nothing special, furnished in a comfortable though utilitarian style.

South Parade, Bath, Somerset BA2 4AB. www.prattshotel.com. © **01225/460441.** Fax 01225/448807. 46 units. £57–£67 double. Children 13 and under stay free if sharing a room with 2 adults. Rates include English breakfast. AE, DC, MC, V. Parking £12. **Amenities:** Restaurant; bar; room service; Wi-Fi (£6 per 90 min., £10 per day). *In room:* TV, hair dryer.

Side Trips from Bath
LACOCK ★
Tiny Lacock is one of the best-preserved villages in England. Turned over to the National Trust in 1944, it's crammed with enchanting medieval and 16th-century homes, gardens, and churches.

   Lacock Abbey, High Street (© **01249/730459;** www.nationaltrust.org.uk/ lacock), is actually a whimsical country house, built upon the foundations of a nunnery dating from 1232. The first-floor rooms and the Great Hall are open to visitors. While on the grounds, stop by the medieval barn, home to the **Fox Talbot Museum** (© **01249/730459**). This is where William Henry Fox Talbot carried out his early experiments with photography, making the first known photographic prints in 1833. The galleries here tell the story of the pioneer and display temporary photography exhibitions.

   The abbey grounds, cloisters, and museum are open November to February daily 11am to 4pm, and March to October daily 10:30am to 5:30pm. The abbey rooms are open November to February Saturday and Sunday noon to 4pm, and March to October Wednesday to Monday 11am to 5pm. Admission is £10 for adults and £5.10 for children 5 to 13; a family ticket costs £27. Admission to the grounds and museum only is £7.70 for adults, £3.80 for children, and £20 for a family ticket.

   Housed in a building that has been used as a pub since 1361, the **George Inn,** 4 West St. (© **01249/730263**), is the most atmospheric place to eat. Daily specials include classics like faggots (meatballs usually made with pork offal) with chips and peas, and steak and Wadworth Ale pie (main courses £8.95–£9.95). It's open Monday to Thursday 9am to 2:30pm and 5 to 11pm; Friday and Saturday 9am to 11pm; and Sunday 9am to 10:30pm.

   From Bath, take the A4 for about 12 miles to the A350, and then head south to Lacock.

CASTLE COMBE ★★
The village of Castle Combe is another gorgeous old village, comprising one street lined with aging stone cottages and easily explored during a morning or afternoon. It's especially popular with filmmakers: The financially disastrous *Dr. Doolittle* was

filmed here in 1966, and the 15th-century **Dower House,** used as Rex Harrison's residence in the movie, is one of Castle Combe's most attractive buildings. In 2009 the village provided the creepy backdrop for Benicio del Toro and Anthony Hopkins in *Wolfman,* while Steven Spielberg shot most of *War Horse* here in 2010.

Located 12 miles northeast of Bath, Castle Combe is reached by taking the A46 north 6 miles to the A420, then heading east to Ford and following the signs north to Castle Combe. From Lacock, take the A350 north to Chippenham; then get on the A420 west and follow the signs.

BRISTOL ★★

120 miles W of London; 13 miles NW of Bath

Bristol, the West Country's largest city (pop. 433,000), is a medieval port that has reinvented itself as a dynamic cultural center in the last few decades, home not just to a reinvigorated downtown but a host of pop icons, from 1990s "trip-hop" bands such as Tricky, Massive Attack, and Portishead, to irreverent graffiti artist Banksy and the risqué teenage UK TV series *Skins.*

Linked to the sea by 7 miles of the navigable River Avon, Bristol has long been rich in seafaring traditions. In 1497, Venetian John Cabot sailed from Bristol and was the first European to "discover" North America (at Newfoundland) since the Vikings. The city's most celebrated sights were built by Isambard Kingdom Brunel in the Victorian era: the Clifton Suspension Bridge and the SS *Great Britain.*

Essentials

GETTING THERE   Bristol Airport (✆ 0871/334-4444; www.bristolairport. co.uk) is conveniently situated beside the A38, a little more than 7 miles from the city center. The **Bristol Airport Flyer** bus (flyer.bristolairport.co.uk; £7 adults, £6 children) runs to the city bus station and the Temple Meads station (30 min.) every 10 minutes.

Frequent train services from London's Paddington Station run to Temple Meads, in the center of Bristol, and to Parkway, on the city's northern outskirts. The trip takes 1¾ hours and costs £13 to £28.

If you're driving, head west from London on the M4. The Park and Ride scheme is the hassle-free way to visit for the day; parking is free (follow the signs from the motorway) and buses into the center cost £2.50 to £3.50 round-trip.

VISITOR INFORMATION   Bristol's **Tourist Information Centre** is at E Shed, 1 Canon's Rd. (✆ 0906/711-2191; www.visitbristol.co.uk). It's next to the Watershed Media Centre on Harbourside. Hours are daily from 10am to 5pm (10am–6pm Apr–Sept).

ORGANIZED TOURS   Guided 2-hour **walking tours** are conducted on Saturdays at 11am from April to September. They cost £3.50 per person and depart from the Beetle sculpture at Anchor Square. Consult the Tourist Information Centre (see above) for more information. Or you can don an eye patch and join a 2-hour walking tour led by **Pirate Pete** (✆ 07950/566483; www.piratewalks.co.uk; £6 adults, £3.50 children), Saturday and Sunday at 2pm starting at the Beetle sculpture; Pete will tell you all about notorious Bristol residents like Blackbeard. **City Sightseeing** (✆ 0906/711-2191; www.citysightseeingbristol.co.uk) runs open-top bus tours of the city mid-March to October (£10 adults plus one free child).

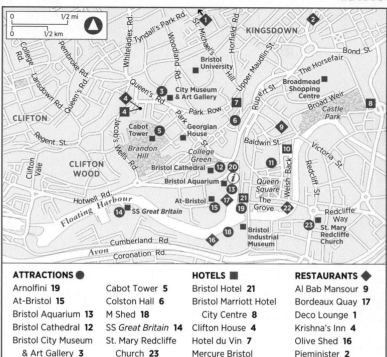

ATTRACTIONS ●

Arnolfini **19**
At-Bristol **15**
Bristol Aquarium **13**
Bristol Cathedral **12**
Bristol City Museum
   & Art Gallery **3**
Bristol Old Vic **11**

Cabot Tower **5**
Colston Hall **6**
M Shed **18**
SS *Great Britain* **14**
St. Mary Redcliffe
   Church **23**
Watershed **20**

HOTELS ■

Bristol Hotel **21**
Bristol Marriott Hotel
   City Centre **8**
Clifton House **4**
Hotel du Vin **7**
Mercure Bristol
   Brigstow Hotel **10**

RESTAURANTS ◆

Al Bab Mansour **9**
Bordeaux Quay **17**
Deco Lounge **1**
Krishna's Inn **4**
Olive Shed **16**
Pieminister **2**
Severnshed **22**

Exploring Bristol

The **Bristol Harbourside ★**, the city's rough-and-ready docks in the 19th century, is now the heart of the modern city, converted into wonderful hotels, excellent restaurants, shops, and art centers.

The other area of interest lies 2 miles to the west in the leafy Georgian neighborhood of **Clifton ★**, best known for the graceful **Clifton Suspension Bridge,** spanning the precipitous Avon Gorge. The architect, Isambard Kingdom Brunel, died 5 years before its completion in 1864.

At-Bristol ☺ PLANETARIUM   This entertaining, interactive science center is targeted primarily at kids and families, with special exhibits on animation, flight, human inventions, and a stunning planetarium. Kids will love the "walk-in tornado," "leaning lounge," and "play TV," where they get to direct or present their own shows.

Anchor Rd. 🕐 **0845/345-1235.** www.at-bristol.org.uk. Admission £12.50 adults, £8 children 3–15, £35.50 family ticket. Mon–Fri 10am–5pm; Sat–Sun and school holidays 10am–6pm. Bus: 8 or 9.

Bristol Aquarium ★ ☺ AQUARIUM   This absorbing showcase of British and tropical marine life boasts a life-size recreation of a sunken ship, a walk-in seahorse

Soak up Bristol's seafaring roots by jumping on board a **Bristol Ferry Boat Company** ferry ★★ (*℡* **0117/927-3416; www.bristolferry.com**). Boats run throughout the day along the River Avon, enabling you to hop-on and hop-off for £1.90 per trip or £4.90 for a circular tour of the entire route. For a more exhilarating view of the city, take to the skies with **Bristol Balloons** ★★ (*℡* **0117/947-1050; www.bristolballoons.co.uk**), which runs a variety of mesmerizing "flights" from just £90.

display, and an open-top giant coral installation, and is home to sharks and stringrays. As part of the admission price, visitors can also watch a selection of dazzling marine-themed 3D films on a four-story IMAX screen.

Anchor Rd. *℡* **0117/929-8929.** www.bristolaquarium.co.uk. Admission £14 adults, £12.50 seniors, £9.20 children 3–14, £43 family ticket. Daily 10am–5pm (to 6pm Sat–Sun and holidays). Closed Christmas Day. Bus: 8 or 9.

Bristol Cathedral ★ CATHEDRAL This handsome example of monumental Gothic architecture, originally an Augustinian abbey, dates back to the 12th century; the central tower was added in 1466. In 1539, the abbey was dissolved by Henry VIII, and it became a cathedral church soon after. The eastern end of the cathedral, especially the choir, is one of Britain's most brilliant examples of early Decorated Gothic style, while the Eastern Lady Chapel (1220) has exquisite heraldic stained glass. The finest late Norman architecture can be found off the south transept, amid the rich carvings of the Chapter House.

College Green, West End. *℡* **0117/926-4879.** www.bristol-cathedral.co.uk. Free admission; £2.50 donation requested. Mon–Sat 8am–6pm; Sun 7:20am–5pm. Bus: 8 or 9.

Cabot Tower ★ OBSERVATION POINT This 32-m (105-ft.) sandstone tower was built in 1897 to commemorate John Cabot's voyage from Bristol to Newfoundland 400 years earlier. Today climbing to the top provides the best views of the city.

Brandon Hill Park, just off Park St., West End. *℡* **0117/922-3719.** www.bristol-cathedral.co.uk. Free admission. Daily 8am to 30 minutes before dusk.

M Shed ★★ ☺ MUSEUM This absorbing museum opened in 2011, with three main galleries exploring the history and culture of the city through interactive displays and exhibits: Bristol People, Bristol Places, and Bristol Life. Everything from Bristol's musical traditions to the slave trade is covered—there's even remains of Bristol's very own dinosaur, Thecodontosaurus, discovered locally in the 19th century.

Wapping Rd, Princes Wharf. *℡* **0117-925-1470** or 0117-922-3143. mshed.org. Free admission. Tues–Fri 10am–5pm; Sat–Sun and bank holidays 10am–6pm.

SS *Great Britain* ★★★ HISTORIC SITE Bristol's pride and joy, the SS *Great Britain* was the world's first iron steamship when it was launched here in 1843. Two years later it crossed the Atlantic in 14 days—a record at the time. Thanks to a remarkable salvage project in 1970 and subsequent restoration, you can now roam the ship's Victorian interior, pondering the skill and vision of designer Isambard Kingdom Brunel. Admission includes the adjacent Dockyard Museum, which provides background and history on the ship, and entry to the replica of John Cabot's ship, *The Matthew* (www.matthew.co.uk), whenever she is in Bristol.

Great Western Dockyard, Gas Ferry Rd. ✆ **0117/926-0680.** www.ssgreatbritain.org. Admission £12 adults, £9.95 seniors, £6.25 children 5–16, £33.50 family ticket. Apr–Oct daily 10am–5:30pm; Nov–Mar daily 10am–4:30pm. Last admission 1 hr. before closing. Bus: 500 (from city center).

St. Mary Redcliffe Church CHURCH   The parish church of St. Mary Redcliffe is one of the finest examples of Gothic architecture in the region. Queen Elizabeth I, on her visit in 1574, is said to have described it as "the fairest, goodliest, and most famous parish church in England." The American Chapel (St. John's Chapel) houses the tomb and armor of Admiral Sir William Penn, father of Pennsylvania's founder, along with a whalebone donated by John Cabot after he sailed to America in 1497.

12 Colston Parade. ✆ **0117/929-1487.** www.stmaryredcliffe.co.uk. Free admission; donations welcome. Mon–Sat 9am–5pm; Sun 8am–7:30pm.

Where to Eat
EXPENSIVE

Bordeaux Quay CONTINENTAL/BRASSERIE   This solid harborside choice is convenient for the center of town and offers a range of dining options under the same roof. The **first-floor restaurant** offers fine dining—think Cornish sea bass with coco beans, butternut squash, curry spices, and spinach—while the ground floor **brasserie** (✆ **0117/943-1200**) offers cheaper fare in the form of burgers, goat's cheese tart, and mussels. For snacks and take-out there's the **Delicatessen** (✆ **0117/906-5563**), or you can just grab a drink at the wine bar.

V-Shed, Canon's Way (Harbourside). ✆ **0117/943-1200.** www.bordeaux-quay.co.uk. Reservations recommended for restaurant/brasserie. Main courses £14–£22 in the restaurant; £9.50–£13 in the brasserie. AE, MC, V. Restaurant Tues–Fri 6–10pm; Sat 5:30–10pm; Sun noon–3pm. Brasserie Mon–Fri 9–11:15am and noon–10:30pm; Sat 9–11am and noon–10:30pm; Sun 9–11:15am and noon–4pm. Deli Mon–Sat 9am–6pm, Sun 9am–4pm.

MODERATE

Olive Shed ★ 🍴 SPANISH/MODERN ENGLISH   This restaurant, with a riverside location in the heart of the city, uses fair-trade and organic produce for most food and drink items, including, unusually, all its wine. Menus are seasonal and change weekly, but expect vibrant combinations: rack of Somerset lamb with beetroot, watercress, and pumpkin-seed cake, or beetroot and chickpea fritters with peach and orange salsa. The tapas menu is just as inspiring, with feta-stuffed mini peppers complimenting classics such as anchovies, Spanish tortilla, and squid.

The Floating Harbour, Princes Wharf. © **0117/929-1960.** www.theoliveshed.com. Reservations recommended. Main courses £9.95–£18; tapas £2.95–£8.95. AE, MC, V. Daily noon–3pm and 6–11pm (winter hours Thurs–Sat noon–10pm, Sun 11am–4pm). Closed Dec–Jan.

Severnshed ENGLISH/MEDITERRANEAN   The best choice for reasonably priced waterfront dining in the heart of the city, this restaurant is said to be the former boathouse of Isambard Kingdom Brunel. The decor is very contemporary, however, with a menu that combines fresh, seasonal British produce with the flair of the Portuguese chef. The lobster risotto is superb, but all the main courses are excellent—from the beer-battered cod and chips to the pan-seared tuna with crab and lime butter and green beans. The tapas-like small plates (think whitebait and garlic lemon mayonnaise) are perfect for a lighter meal.

The Grove, Harbourside. © **0117/925-1212.** www.severnshedrestaurant.co.uk. Main courses £9.65–£18. AE, MC, V. Sun–Thurs 10am–11pm, Fri–Sat 10am–midnight.

INEXPENSIVE

Al Bab Mansour ★ MOROCCAN   Bringing a tiny piece of North Africa to Bristol, this budget Moroccan restaurant knocks out mouth-watering chicken marinated in lemon and spices, couscous, succulent lamb tagine, and falafel. It's located in St. Nicholas Market, a Georgian arcade crammed with several cheap food stalls. You can eat at tables in the covered arcade or inside the textiles-draped dining room.

St. Nicholas Market, Corn St. © **0797/997-6113.** www.albabmansour.co.uk. Main dishes £5.95–£6.95. Mon–Sat noon–4pm.

Deco Lounge ★ BISTRO/CAFE   This local chain of cafe/bars is a big hit in Bristol, with four branches in the city. This is one of the closest to the center, with a wide range of main meals (from burgers to jambalaya), sandwiches, cakes, tapas, coffee, beer, and cocktails. At night the wooden tables are lit with candles, making the trademark rustic chic interiors with cozy sofas even more inviting, and a touch romantic.

50 Cotham Hill, Cotham. © **0797/373-2688.** www.thelounges.co.uk. Main courses £7.25–£15; tapas £2.95. Daily 9am–11pm.

Krishna's Inn ★ *🐟* INDIAN   Bristol boasts several highly rated curry houses, but this no-frills, authentic south Indian restaurant is the best value. Classics such as chicken Malabar, Kerala fish curry, and green-banana curry are fragrant delights,

---

Bristol's Inner City Farm

The Cafe at St. Werburghs City Farm ★★, Watercress Road, St. Werburghs (© 0117/942-8241; www.sw cityfarm.org.uk), sources most of its food from surrounding allotments (the inner-city "farm") and numerous animals on-site. It's a brilliant idea; meals are cheap, wholesome, organic, and fresh. Expect a creative roster of dishes, from butter bean hummus and bubble and squeak with black pudding (blood sausage), to roast pumpkin and goat's cheese burrito (main courses from £5.95). Open Wednesday to Monday 10am to 4pm (5pm in summer). The farm is on the northwest edge of the city; take the A4032 out of the center, and turn north along Mina Road before it becomes the M32 (no direct buses; take a taxi or drive).

while the masala dosa (rice-flour pancake stuffed with potato curry), at just £2.50, makes a meal in itself.

4 Byron Place, Clifton. ℂ **0117/927-6864.** www.keralagroup.co.uk. Main courses £2.95–£6.95. AE, MC, V. Daily noon–3pm and 6–11:30pm (10:30pm Sun).

Pieminister ★★ TRADITIONAL ENGLISH   Bristol's very own pie shop sells scrumptious savory pies to eat in or take out. The menu offers nine pies, including minty lamb (lamb, carrot, swede, mint, and rose wine), the moo & blue (British beef steak with red-wine gravy and stilton), and the veggie Heidi pie (goat's cheese, sweet potato, spinach, red onion, and roast garlic). All are made from fresh produce and free-range meat, and crammed inside a thick crust of butter-rich pastry. There's a smaller branch at the Glass Arcade, Corn Street (Mon–Sat 10am–5pm).

24 Stokes Croft. ℂ **0117/942-9372.** www.pieminister.co.uk. Pies from £3.75; pie, mash, and gravy from £5.75. AE, MC, V. Mon–Sat 11am–7pm; Sun 11am–5pm.

Shopping

The biggest shopping area in Bristol is **Broadmead** (www.bristolbroadmead.co.uk), mainly pedestrianized with branches of all high-street stores, plus cafes, restaurants, and the **Galleries** (www.galleriesbristol.co.uk) shopping center at its heart. **Cabot Circus** (www.cabotcircus.com) is another huge shopping center with a similar range of tenants and the Showcase Cinema de Lux (www.cinemadelux.co.uk). In the adjacent **Quakers Friars** open-air piazza, you'll find smaller and more exclusive designers. For more cutting-edge fashion try **Park Street.**

In **Clifton,** the Georgian suburb where houses are interspaced with parks and gardens, you'll find a wide array of shops selling antiques, arts and crafts, and designer clothing.

Closer to the center is **St. Nicholas Market** (www.stnicholasmarketbristol.co.uk), which opened in 1745. It's still going strong, crammed with independent sellers of antiques, memorabilia, handcrafted gifts, jewelry, and second-hand clothes.

The **Bristol Blue Glass Factory & Shop** (ℂ **0117/972-0818;** www.bristol-glass.co.uk), at Unit 7, Whitby Road, Brislington, has been creating high-quality glass products for 400 years. Factory tours and glass-blowing demonstrations (free) take place daily.

Guilbert's Chocolates (**0117/926-8102;** www.guilberts.com), 16–17 Small St., has been hand-crafting luxury chocolates since 1910.

Entertainment & Nightlife
THE PERFORMING ARTS

The **Bristol Old Vic,** King Street (ℂ **0117/987-7877;** www.bristololdvic.org.uk), is the oldest working theatre company in the country, known for its musicals, traveling shows, and plays. The largest concert venue is **Colston Hall,** Colston Street (ℂ **0117/922-3686;** www.colstonhall.org), which hosts everything from touring rock bands to alternative comedy and classical music.

The **Tobacco Factory** ★ Raleigh Road, Southville (ℂ **0117/902-0060;** www.tobaccofactory.com), is a more dynamic studio theatre (it also hosts a cafe/bar, a Sunday market, and live music on Sun evenings). Tickets are cheaper than at the Old Vic, typically less than £10.

On Harbourside, **Arnolfini** ★★, 16 Narrow Quay (ℂ **0117/917-2300;** www.arnolfini.org.uk), is one of Europe's leading centers for the contemporary arts, with exhibitions and film screenings, in addition to live performance, dance, talks, a bookstore, and a decent cafe (Mon–Tues 10am–6:30pm; Wed–Thurs 10am–10:30pm; Fri–Sat 10am–11pm; Sun 10am–7pm).

For a lively program of independent film, digital media, and other live events, check out the **Watershed,** 1 Canons Rd., Harbourside (© **0117/927-6444;** www.watershed.co.uk).

THE PUB & BAR SCENE

Bristol has a buzzing nightlife, with most of the action in the city center area, on Harbourside, and along Park Street and Whiteladies Road. One of Bristol's oldest and most atmospheric pubs is the **Llandoger Trow,** King Street (© **0117/926-0783;** Mon–Sat 11am–midnight, Sun noon–11pm), established in 1664. Legend has it that this is where Daniel Defoe met Alexander Selkirk, Defoe's inspiration for *Robinson Crusoe* and also the man behind the Benn Gunn character in Robert Louis Stevenson's *Treasure Island*.

A funkier, more contemporary option is **Start The Bus ★★**, 7–9 Baldwin St. (© **0117/930-4370;** www.startthebus.tv; Sun 11am–1am, Mon–Wed 10am–1am, Thurs–Sat 10am–3am), a bar with comfy leather sofas, local art smothered on the walls, and everything from a weekly pub quiz to live gigs from the coolest bands in Bristol (Wilder was a major player here in 2010).

The **Mud Dock Café,** 40 The Grove (© **0117/934-9734;** www.mud-dock. co.uk; Sun–Mon 10am–5pm, Tues–Thurs 10am–11pm, Fri 10am–11pm, Sat 9am–11pm), is conveniently located on the harborside in the center of town. In addition to serving fine coffee, sandwiches, and beer, it doubles as a bike shop.

Real-ale lovers should try the tasty brews made by the **Bristol Beer Factory,** Durnford Street (© **0117/902-6317;** Mon–Fri 9am–5pm), an independent brewery in Southville. You can usually buy beers directly from the on-site shop, but the best place to drink them is the **Grain Barge ★**, Mardyke Wharf, Hotwells Road (© **0117/929-9347;** www.grainbarge.com; Tues–Thurs noon–11pm, Fri–Sat noon–11:30pm, Sun noon–11pm), a converted barge on the water, within sight of SS *Great Britain*.

If you prefer cider (the alcoholic kind, not the North American juice version), the **Apple,** Welsh Back (© **0117/925-3500;** www.applecider.co.uk; daily noon–midnight), occupies a smaller barge and quayside terrace farther along the river, with a fine selection of ciders and beers. Real aficionados make for the **Bristol Cider House ★**, 8–9 Surrey St. (© **0117/9420-8196;** www.bristolciderhouse. co.uk; daily noon–midnight), where more than 20 types of strong ciders and perries (from pears) are served.

THE CLUB & MUSIC SCENE

Music lovers gravitate to the performances at **St. George's,** Great George Street, off Park Street (© **0117/929-4929;** www.stgeorgesbristol.co.uk), a converted church from the 1700s. You will hear everything from jazz concerts to classical music performances.

Weekly club nights, acid jazz, and other types of live music rain down in **Thekla,** East Mud Dock (© **0117/929-3301;** www.theklabristol.co.uk), a converted freight steamer moored on the Grove. The **Old Duke,** 45 King St. (© **0117/927-7137;** www.theoldduke.co.uk), is popular for blues and traditional jazz. Another leading jazz venue is the **Bebop Club** at the Bear, Hotwell Road (© **0117/987-7796;** www.thebebopclub.co.uk). Shows take place on Fridays at 9pm, with most tickets less than £8.

Bristol's club scene is constantly evolving, but current major clubs include **Panache,** All Saints Street (✆ **0845/241-7185;** www.panachebars.com), which hosts the biggest student nights in the city (Phat Nights on Fri, cover £5; and Paparazzi on Sat £6); and **The Syndicate,** 15 Nelson St. (✆ **0117/945-0325;** bristol.thesyndicate.com; cover £2–£5), the biggest arena-like "superclub" in town. **Oceana,** South Building, Canons Road (✆ **0845/293-2860;** www.oceanaclubs. com/bristol; cover £5.50–£8), rounds out the top three with a little more glamor, housing five glitzy themed bars and two club floors (one for R&B, the other for 1980s' music). Clubs tend to open Thursday to Saturday from 9pm to 3am. Check **Bristol-nightlife.com** for the latest.

Where to Stay
EXPENSIVE

Bristol Hotel ★★   Luxury in a top location right on the harbor sets this place apart. Although rooms are small, they are beautifully decked out with sleek, modern lines, soothing colors, and stylish, contemporary furniture. The views over the city are a bonus, and the power showers, iPod docks, and Nespresso coffee machines are thoughtful extras.

Prince St., Bristol BS1 4QF. www.doylecollection.com. ✆ **0117/923-0333.** Fax 0117/923-0300. 187 units. £99–£120 double. AE, DC, MC, V. Free parking 5:30pm–9:30am. **Amenities:** 2 restaurants; bar; concierge; gym; 24-hr. room service, Wi-Fi (free). *In room:* A/C, TV, Internet (free).

Bristol Marriott Hotel City Centre   In the heart of town, at the edge of Castle Park, this modern 11-story hotel is one of Bristol's tallest buildings, and far superior to other chains in amenities, style, and comfort. Many improvements have been undertaken, and the hotel now attracts business travelers as well as foreign tourists. The comfortable guest rooms are conservatively modern.

2 Lower Castle St., Bristol BS1 3AD. www.marriott.co.uk. ✆ **0117/929-4281.** Fax 0117/927-6377. 300 units. £122–£135 double. AE, DC, MC, V. Parking £13. **Amenities:** 2 restaurants; bar; babysitting; concierge; exercise room; indoor heated pool; room service; spa. *In room:* A/C, TV, hair dryer, minibar, Wi-Fi (£6 per hr; £15 per day).

Hotel du Vin ★   This stylish boutique hotel is one of Bristol's best examples of recycling. Six 18th-century sugar-refining warehouses, lying in the vicinity of the docklands, were taken over and sensitively restored. Today, you'll find a series of "loft-style" bedrooms with the original industrial features of the warehouses retained for dramatic effect. Even if you're not a guest, you may want to stop for a drink in the **Sugar House Bar** or a first-class meal in the contemporary **French restaurant.**

Narrow Lewins Mead, Bristol BS1 2NU. www.hotelduvin.com. ✆ **0117/925-5577.** Fax 0117/925-1199. 40 units. £120–£165 double; £190–£245 suite. AE, DC, MC, V. Parking £13. **Amenities:** Restaurant; 2 bars; room service. *In room:* A/C, TV, DVD, hair dryer, minibar, Wi-Fi (free).

Mercure Bristol Brigstow Hotel ★   In a prime position on the water, this modern hotel opens onto panoramic riverside frontage in the heart of the city. The bedrooms are spacious and stylish, with muted colors and contemporary design; most rooms have ceiling-to-floor windows with views of the river or the city. Breakfast is an additional £17. **Ellipse,** the on-site restaurant, serves fresh and well-prepared food in light and airy surroundings, with views of the river.

5-7 Welsh Back, Bristol BS1 4SF. www.mercure.com. ✆ **0117/929-1030.** Fax 0117/929-2030. 116 units. £131–£155 double. AE, DC, MC, V. Parking £13. **Amenities:** Restaurant; bar; use of nearby gym; room service. *In room:* A/C, TV, hair dryer, minibar, Internet (£11 per day).

There's nothing quite like **Steep Holm** ★★ (📞 **01934/522125;** www.steepholm.org), a tiny, rugged island in the middle of the Bristol Channel. Once a military installation, today this rocky hump of limestone covering just 20 hectares (50 acres) and around 78-m (255-ft.) high, is a wild, uninhabited nature reserve owned by the Kenneth Allsop Memorial Trust. In May, the island is smothered in dazzling wild peonies in bloom, and at any time you can see the ruins of a 12th-century Augustinian priory, Victorian gun batteries, World War II remains, and sensational views of the Bristol Channel across to Wales. The former Barracks has been restored as a visitor center.

Boats to the island depart the seaside resort of Weston-super-Mare, 5 miles away in Somerset (Knightstone Harbour). Trips usually run May to October (call or e-mail for times), and cost £25 for adults and £15 for children 5 to 16. You can also visit **Flat Holm** (www.flatholm.co.uk) from the Welsh side of the channel.

INEXPENSIVE

Clifton House ★   Following a comprehensive renovation in 2010, this elegant early Victorian house blends contemporary style with many of its original features; marble fireplaces, vintage mirrors and ornate plasterwork in the rooms are offset with chic, modern furniture and comfy beds. Rates are very reasonable, it's an excellent option in the Clifton neighborhood, and the free parking is a real bonus.

4 Tyndall's Park Rd., Clifton, Bristol BS8 1PG. www.cliftonhousebristol.com. 📞 **0117/973-5407.** Fax 0117/923-7965. 15 units. £65–£85 double. Rates include English breakfast. MC, V. Free parking. Bus: 8 or 9. *In room:* TV, hair dryer, Wi-Fi (free).

Rookery Guest House 🦴   Don't be fooled by the plain exterior; this is one of the most welcoming B&Bs in the city, with clean, comfortable, and quiet rooms enhanced by a homey atmosphere and perfect hosts. Guests really are treated like family; there is a large rack of DVDs available in the lounge, and breakfasts are always hot, fresh, and cooked to order (with veggie options). Note that this is a convenient option for drivers, close to the M5, but not for the city center (25-min. drive). No children or pets.

227 Gloucester Rd. (A38), Patchway, Bristol BS34 6ND. www.therookery-guest-house-bristol.co.uk. 📞 **01454/850088.** 8 units £58–£60 double. Rates include English breakfast. AE, MC, V (with 3% surcharge). Free parking. *In room:* TV, DVD, Wi-Fi (free).

WELLS ★★ & THE MENDIP CAVES ★

123 miles SW of London; 21 miles SW of Bath

The tiny cathedral city of **Wells** is a little slice of medieval England sitting under the southern lip of the Mendip Hills, which divide southern Somerset from the more visited north of the county. Wells was a vital link in the Saxon kingdom of Wessex—important long before the arrival of William the Conqueror. Once the seat of a bishopric, it was eventually toppled from its ecclesiastical hegemony by the rival city of Bath. But the subsequent loss of prestige has paid off handsomely for 21st-century

Wells: After the pinnacle of prestige, it fell into a slumber—and much of its old look has been preserved, none better than **Wells Cathedral.**

At the point where the limestone Mendips dive into the flatter terrain known as the Somerset Levels, millions of years of erosion have created a vast underground network of caves. There's no need to be a serious spelunker to enjoy the family-oriented fun at either **Wookey Hole** or **Cheddar Caves and Gorge.**

Essentials

GETTING THERE Wells has no railway station, but does have good bus connections with surrounding towns and cities. One option is to take the train to Bath (see the section on Bath earlier in this chapter) and continue the rest of the way via bus no. 173 (1¼ hr.). Departures are generally every hour Monday through Saturday, and every 2 hours on Sunday. An alternative is to take the train to Bristol and then bus no. 376, which takes just over 1 hour. Call © **0117/955-3231** or 0845/606-4446 for schedules and information, or see **www.firstgroup.com/ukbus** for timetables.

If you're driving from London, take the M4 west, cutting south on the A4 toward Bath and continuing along the A39 into Wells.

VISITOR INFORMATION The **Visitor Information Service** is at the Town Hall, Market Place (© **01749/671770;** www.wellstourism.com). It's open November through March, Monday to Saturday 11am to 4pm, and April through October, Monday to Saturday 10am to 5pm and Sunday 10am to 4pm.

Exploring Wells

Besides the famous cathedral, the center's other highlight is the moat-surrounded **Bishop's Palace and Gardens** (© **01749/988111;** www.bishopspalace.org.uk). The Great Hall, built in the 13th century, is in ruins, and the tranquil grounds house the well springs which gave the city its name. The palace is still used by the Bishop of Bath and Wells. Admission costs £6 adults, £2.50 children 5 to 18, which includes a guided tour at 11:30am daily. The palace is open April to October 10:30am to 6pm. The cobbled lane known as the **Vicars' Close,** north of the cathedral, has some of the best preserved ecclesiastical terrace dwellings in Britain.

Wells Cathedral ★★★ CATHEDRAL   Begun in the 12th century, this magnificent edifice is among England's best-preserved examples of early Gothic architecture. The medieval sculpture (six tiers of statues) of its West Front is without equal in a country where so much religious statuary fell prey to iconoclastic zeal during the Reformation. This western facade was completed around 1230, the central tower coming later in the 14th century, with the internal fan vaulting erected later still. The most striking feature of the cathedral interior is the so-called **Scissor Arches ★★** at the crossing, an amazing feat of engineering; they were built between 1338 and 1348, when the west piers of the crossing tower began to sink. The inverted arches strengthened the top-heavy structure and prevented the tower from collapsing. It was the master mason, William Joy, who devised this ingenious solution, which has done the job nicely for 6½ centuries.

Much of the cathedral's stained glass dates from the 14th century, as does the **Lady Chapel,** constructed in the Decorated style. Up steps to the north of the crossing is the octagonal **Chapter House,** completed in 1306 but since restored. Young visitors might be more enchanted by the **Wells Clock,** which dates from 1390. Every quarter-hour, it chimes, and jousting knights gallop around a platform above its face.

Chain Gate, Cathedral Green. ℭ **01749/674483.** www.wellscathedral.org.uk. Free admission, but donations appreciated: £5.50 adults, £4 seniors, £2.50 students and children. Apr–Sept daily 7am–7pm; Oct–Mar daily 7am–6pm. Guided tours hourly 10am–3pm Mon–Sat.

Where to Eat

The best central spot for a casual pint and a meal that's a notch above typical pub grub is Wells's former jail, now the **City Arms,** 69 High St (ℭ **01749/673916;** www.thecityarmsatwells.com). Main courses range from £8 to £14.

Goodfellows FRENCH/SEAFOOD   Take your pick between fine fish dining or an eclectic lunchtime cafe menu at this central restaurant with a split-personality. The short, French-influenced seafood menu is the better choice; it changes according to the freshest catch, but might include the likes of gray mullet with cucumber spaghetti, fried garlic, and a dill butter sauce, and always offers meat options such as confit of duck with roasted autumn vegetables. The decor isn't noteworthy, but small details like attentive service and a bread basket baked inhouse each morning ensure a consistently excellent dining experience.

5 Sadler St. ℭ **01749/673866.** www.goodfellowswells.co.uk. Reservations recommended. Main courses £11–£22; cafe set-menus £10 and £15 including a glass of wine. MC, V. Tues–Sat midday–2pm, Wed–Sat 6:30–9:30pm.

Where to Stay

The Crown at Wells ★   This landmark building lies right on the Market Place in the heart of Wells, and has been used for overnighting since medieval times. The building retains most of its 15th-century character, although the bedrooms are completely up to date—in fact, many are furnished in a vaguely Nordic contemporary style with chunky light-oak furniture. For a more traditional feel, ask for one of a quartet of "suites" graced with four-posters. Rooms at the front of the building overlook the atmospheric, but occasionally noisy, Market Place.

Market Place, Wells, Somerset BA5 2RP. www.crownatwells.co.uk. ℭ **01749/673457.** Fax 01749/679792. 15 units. £95 double; £115 suite. AE, MC, V. **Amenities:** Restaurant; 2 bars. *In room:* TV/DVD, CD player, hair dryer, no phone, Wi-Fi (free).

Swan Hotel ★   Set behind a mustard-colored facade, this place was originally built in the 1400s as a coaching inn. Rooms vary in style and size, and have been undergoing a rolling process of conversion from traditional to contemporary-edged decor; some have four-poster beds, and the luxurious Cathedral Suite with its panoramic windows facing Wells Cathedral might just be the best hotel room in Somerset. The spacious and elegant public areas, renovated in 2010, have blazing, baronial fireplaces and beamed ceilings. *Insider tip:* The front terrace smack in front of the cathedral is the best-located place in town for a morning coffee.

11 Sadler St., Wells, Somerset BA5 2RX. www.bestwestern.co.uk. ℭ **01749/836300,** or 800/528-1234 in the U.S. and Canada. Fax 01749/836301. 48 units. £140–£188 double; £300 Cathedral Suite. Rates include English breakfast. AE, DC, MC, V. Free parking. **Amenities:** Restaurant; bar; room service. *In room:* TV, hair dryer, Wi-Fi (free).

Side Trips to the Mendip Caves

Cheddar Caves & Gorge ★ ☺ HISTORIC SITE   The town that gave its name to a cheese, Cheddar lies at the foot of Cheddar Gorge, under which lie the Cheddar Caves, underground caverns with impressive formations and plenty of fun, educational commentary. The caves were inhabited by Stone Age tribes, but the miles of tunnels lay undiscovered until workmen of George Cox found them in 1837. The most spectacular, **Gough's Cave,** is named after Cox's nephew (who discovered it in 1890), and has walls that shimmer with colors reflected from iron oxide, copper carbonate, and lead deposits in the limestone. The outstanding feature is the calcite waterfall in the chamber that Gough christened King Solomon's Temple. Adjacent **Cox's Cave** is also famed for its brilliant colors. You can also climb Jacob's Ladder for Gorge-top walks, and the Lookout Tower for views beyond the 137-m (450-ft.) cliffs of the Gorge and across Somerset. You can also book an "Adventure Caving" expedition for £18 adults (£15 children 12–17), which includes use of overalls, helmets, and lamps. Other attractions (all on the same ticket) include the **Crystal Quest,** an underground "fantasy adventure walk," and a Museum of Prehistory that contains the 9,000-year-old skeleton of "Cheddar Man."

Cheddar. ℂ **01934/742343.** www.cheddarcaves.co.uk. Admission £17 adults, £11 children 5-15, £45 family ticket, free for children 4 and under. July-Aug daily 10am-5:30pm; Sept-June daily 10:30am-5pm. Closed Dec 24-25. From the A38 or M5, cut onto the A371 to Cheddar.

Wookey Hole ★ ☺ HISTORIC SITE   Legend has it that in the first chamber of these slightly cheesy but fun caves, the Witch of Wookey was turned to stone by a Saxon abbot—along with her cat. The rest of the labyrinthine complex consists of a series of chambers hewn by groundwater and the subterranean River Axe over millennia into creepy caverns and deep, crystal-clear lakes. Parts of the complex were probably inhabited by prehistoric people at least 60,000 years ago, and in 1935 Wookey was the site of the world's first ever cave dive. The caves are still used to age Cheddar cheese in the traditional way.

Paper has been made here since the 17th century. The preserved **mill** hosts regular demonstrations of the ancient art as well as hands-on vats, where visitors can try making a sheet of paper; there's also an Edwardian Penny Arcade, where you can exchange new pennies for old ones to play the original machines, and a mirror maze.

Wookey Hole, Wells. ℂ **01749/672343.** www.wookey.co.uk. Tours (allow 2 hr.) £16 adults; £11 seniors, students, and children 3-14; £45 family ticket. Apr-Oct daily 10am-5pm; Nov-Mar daily 10am-4pm. Closed Dec 25-26 and weekdays in Dec and Jan. Follow the signs from the center of Wells for 2 miles. Bus: 172 from Wells.

GLASTONBURY & SOUTH SOMERSET ★

136 miles SW of London; 26 miles S of Bristol; 6 miles SW of Wells

Mystical **Glastonbury**—in the heart of the flattish terrain between the Mendip and the Quantock hills known as the Somerset Levels—may be one of the oldest inhabited sites in Britain. Excavations have revealed Iron Age lakeside villages on its periphery. It's an ancient Christian center too: Joseph of Arimathea, a biblical (and perhaps mythical) figure, is said to have journeyed to what was then the "Isle of Avalon" with the Holy Grail in his possession. According to one tradition, he buried the chalice at the foot of **Glastonbury Tor** (a conical hill), and a stream of blood burst forth. Scale the hill today for stunning views across the Levels.

Later in history, Arthurian myth held sway, and Glastonbury now harbors a subculture of mystics and hippies. It is England's New Age center, where Christian spirituality blends with druidic beliefs. It's also a good jumping-off point for Elizabethan **Montacute House,** in rural south Somerset.

Essentials

GETTING THERE   Connections to Glastonbury are awkward using public transportation. No direct train service runs to Glastonbury. You can, however, take a train to Bristol Temple Meads (trip time is 1¾ hr. from London Paddington, costing around £59 for a round-trip), where you can catch bus no. 376 to Glastonbury. Buses run twice an hour from this station, half of them direct and half requiring a change in Wells; journey time to Glastonbury is around 1¼ hours. See **www.firstgroup.com/ukbus** for timetables.

If you're driving from London, take the M4 west, and then cut south on the A4, via Bath, to Glastonbury.

VISITOR INFORMATION   The **Tourist Information Centre** is at the Tribunal, 9 High Street (© **01458/832954;** www.glastonburytic.co.uk). It's open October through March, Sunday to Thursday 10am to 4pm, Friday and Saturday 10am to 4:30pm; and April through September, Sunday to Thursday 10am to 5pm, Friday and Saturday till 5:30pm.

SPECIAL EVENTS   Every June the place really comes alive for Europe's most feted outdoor music event, the iconic **Glastonbury Festival ★★★**. It's been running since 1970, and always attracts the leading names from the rock and indie music scene, with occasional surprise guests. If you want tickets, you'll need to plan early: Register for festival information at **www.glastonburyregistration.co.uk** about a year ahead of time. There is no festival in 2012.

Exploring Glastonbury

In recent decades, this ancient Christian town has had its spirituality spiced up with some New Age ingredients: The High Street is lined with psychic readers, hippie bookstores, street flautists, tarot parlors, and all things hemp. The best views across the Somerset Levels are to be had after a short, sharp climb up 155-m (509-ft.) **Glastonbury Tor ★**. Topped by 15th-century **St. Michael's Tower,** the Tor (meaning "hill") is visible for miles around, looming above the town. In the same building as the Tourist Information Centre (see above) is the **Lake Village Museum** (© **01458/832954**). A small collection attempts to recreate the life of the Iron Age settlers in the surrounding Somerset Levels—at the time mostly marshy flatlands. Admission is £2.50 adults, £1 seniors and children. The museum opens April to September daily 10am to 5pm, and October to March Monday to Saturday 10am to 4pm.

Glastonbury Abbey ★ ABBEY   Though no more than a handsome ruined sanctuary today, Glastonbury Abbey was once one of the wealthiest and most prestigious monasteries in England. It provides Glastonbury's claim to historical greatness, an assertion augmented by legendary links to such figures as Joseph of Arimathea, King Arthur, and Queen Guinevere. It's also the reason there's a town here at all: Glastonbury largely grew up to service its abbey.

Joseph, so it goes, erected a church of wattle and daub in Glastonbury. (The town, in fact, may have had the oldest Christian church in England, as excavations have shown.) At one point, the saint is said to have leaned against his staff, which was immediately transformed into a fully blossoming tree; a cutting alleged to have survived from the Holy Thorn still blooms each Christmas and Easter. Some historians trace this particular story back to Tudor times. A large Benedictine Abbey of St. Mary grew out of that early wattle church. St. Dunstan, who was born in nearby

Baltonsborough, was the abbot in the 10th century and later became Archbishop of Canterbury. Edmund, Edgar, and Edmund "Ironside," three early English kings, were buried here.

Another famous chapter in the story, popularized by Tennyson in the Victorian era, holds that King Arthur and Queen Guinevere were buried on the abbey grounds. In 1191, monks supposedly dug up the skeletons of two bodies on the south side of the Lady Chapel, said to be those of the king and queen. In 1278, in the presence of Edward I, the bodies were removed and transferred to a black marble tomb in the choir. Both the burial spot and the shrine are marked.

In 1184, a fire destroyed most of the abbey and its vast treasures. It was eventually rebuilt, after much difficulty, only to be dissolved by Henry VIII in 1539. Its last abbot, Richard Whiting, was hanged at Glastonbury Tor. The best-preserved building on the lovely 15-hectare (36-acre) grounds is a 14th-century octagonal Abbot's Kitchen, where oxen were once roasted whole to feed the wealthier pilgrims.

The on-site shop sells award-winning **Glastonbury Abbey Cider ★**, made using apples from the abbey's orchards.

Magdalene St., Glastonbury. (✆ **01458/832267.** www.glastonburyabbey.com. Admission £5.50 adults, £5 students and seniors, £3.50 children 5–15, £16 family ticket. Dec–Jan daily 10am–4:30pm; Feb daily 10am–5pm; Mar daily 9:30am–5:30pm; Apr–May and Sept daily 9:30am–6pm; June–Aug daily 9am–6pm; Oct daily 9:30am–5pm; Nov daily 9:30am–4:30pm.

Somerset Rural Life Museum MUSEUM   The centerpiece of this museum chronicling the working history of the Somerset countryside is the Abbey Barn, built around 1370—a magnificent timbered room with stone tiles and sculptural details including the head of King Edward III. Exhibits in the Victorian farmhouse illustrate farming in Somerset during the "horse age," as well as rural domestic and social life in Victorian times. In summer, the museum stages demonstrations of butter-making, weaving, basketwork, and other traditional craft activities that are rapidly disappearing.

Abbey Farm, Chilkwell St., Glastonbury. (✆ **01458/831197.** Free admission. Tues–Sat 10am–5pm. Closed Jan 1, Good Friday, and Dec 25–28.

Where to Eat

The best place in Glastonbury itself for top-quality pub grub is the **Who'd A Thought It Inn,** 17 Northload St. (✆ **01458/834460;** www.whodathoughtit. co.uk). Classic dishes such as local pork sausages with mustard mash or steak-and-ale pie are faultlessly executed in pleasant, traditional surroundings. Main courses range from £8 to £11. The ales are supplied by Palmer's, a traditional brewer based on the Dorset coast.

Hundred Monkeys ★ INTERNATIONAL/VEGETARIAN   This friendly, vaguely hippie cafe-restaurant serves up everything from organic brunch to North African-flavored vegetarian dinners. The daily chalkboard dining menu is especially well suited to vegetarians—this is Glastonbury, after all—but always includes meat dishes, too. Expect the likes of winter vegetable ragout with goat's cheese and polenta, or a "Bolognese" of local beef with spaghetti. Outside of mealtimes, the range of specialty teas and homebaked cakes is superb, and the understated jazz soundtrack gives the place an unintrusive, slightly funky feel.

52 High St., Glastonbury. (✆ **01458/833386.** Reservations recommended at weekend evenings and Sun lunch. Main courses £8–£11. MC, V. Mon–Tues 10am–8pm; Wed–Thurs 10am–4pm, Fri–Sat 10am–9pm; Sun 11am–4pm.

Shopping

Bargain-hunters should head 2 miles south of town to **Clark's Village,** Farm Road, Street (© **01458/840064;** www.clarksvillage.co.uk). Over 90 familiar high-street and luxury-brand outlets, including Barbour and Whistles, offer genuine discounts on their end-of-line ranges. Opening hours are 9am to 6pm Monday through Saturday (Thurs until 8pm), and 11am to 5pm Sunday.

Where to Stay

Chalice Hill House ★★ 🏠 Glastonbury's lack of quality hotels is compensated for by a plethora of B&Bs—and this is the most seductive of the lot. The archetypal elegant Georgian interior has been decorated with a fusion of traditional 1830s' heritage and design influences from Glastonbury's New Age present. The recently redecorated Sun and Moon Room offers the best combination of space and aspect. Luxuriously tucked away in private grounds above a quiet cul-de-sac, the guest house is also just a short walk from the center.

Dod Lane, Glastonbury, Somerset BA6 8BZ. www.chalicehill.co.uk. © **01458/830828.** Fax 01458/835233. 3 units. £100 double. Rates include English breakfast. Free parking. AE, MC, V. *In room:* TV/DVD, hair dryer, Wi-Fi (free).

Side Trips in South Somerset

Lytes Cary Manor HISTORIC HOME This compact Elizabethan manor house was home to the Lyte family for 5 centuries, and it was here that 16th-century herbalist Henry Lyte wrote his famous plant directory, *Lytes Herbal.* The architectural highlights are the original Great Hall decorated with 16th-century stained glass showing family coats of arms, and a small family chantry chapel that dates to the 14th century. The manicured Arts and Crafts-inspired formal gardens are famed for their 1½ miles of topiary yews.

Nr. Charlton Mackerell, Somerton (11 miles south of Glastonbury). © **01458/224471.** www.national trust.org.uk. Admission £7 adults, £3.50 children 5–16, £17 family ticket. Mar 13–Oct 31 Fri–Wed 11am–5pm. Closed Nov–Mar 12. From Glastonbury follow the A39 south, turning onto the southbound B3151 at Street. Leave the B3151 at Somerton, following signs to Lytes Cary.

Montacute House ★★ HISTORIC SITE Begin your visit to this 16th-century rural country seat by circumnavigating the magnificent building—it's the best way to appreciate the glorious symmetry of its Elizabethan architecture. Upstairs, rooms off the Long Gallery ★—the longest of its kind in Britain—display a unique collection, belonging to London's National Portrait Gallery, that's a virtual *Who's Who* of royal Tudor and Elizabethan England. You can picnic outside in the substantial shadow of giant sequoia trees.

Montacute. © **01935/823289.** www.nationaltrust.org.uk. Admission £9.30 adults, £4.40 children 5–16, £22 family ticket. House: Mar 12–Oct Wed–Mon 11am–5pm (closed Nov–Mar 11). Gardens: Mar 12–Oct Wed–Mon 11am–5pm; rest of year Wed–Sun 11am–4pm. Signposted off the A3088, 4 miles west of Yeovil.

WEST SOMERSET & EXMOOR ★★

West Somerset stretches from the low-lying Quantock Hills to Exmoor on the Devon border, a captivating region of moorland and rolling hills that plunge into the Bristol Channel. The most precious sections are protected within the **Exmoor National Park,** best explored on foot or by car, but there are several enticing targets on the fringes.

Essentials

GETTING THERE The main train station in the region is Taunton, easily reached from London's Paddington Station every 30 minutes (trip time is around 2 hr; £26–£40). From Bristol, Bridgwater (trip time 1 hr; £8.10–£13) is more convenient.

At Taunton, you can take a bus to Minehead via Dunster operated by **First Somerset** (📞 **0845/6064446;** www.firstgroup.com), leaving hourly. Trip time is around 90 minutes.

If you're driving from London, head west along the M4, cutting south at junction 20 with the M5 until you reach junction 23 with the A39, going west to Minehead. The A39 passes Coleridge Cottage and Dunster before reaching Minehead and Exmoor.

VISITOR INFORMATION The **Exmoor National Park Centre** is at Dunster Steep (📞 **01643/821835;** www.exmoor-nationalpark.gov.uk), 2 miles east of Minehead. It's open from Easter to October, daily 10am to 5pm, plus limited hours the rest of the year (call ahead). **Taunton Tourist Information Centre,** Paul Street (📞 **01823/336344;** www.visitsomerset.co.uk), is open Monday to Saturday 9:30am to 4:30pm year-round and can help with transport and lodging.

GETTING AROUND The best way to see the region is by car—public transport is very limited, other than between Taunton and Minehead.

Exploring the Area

Coleridge Cottage HISTORIC HOME   The great Romantic poet Samuel Taylor Coleridge lived in this humble 17th-century cottage from 1797 to 1798, an incredibly productive period during which he penned *The Rime of the Ancient Mariner, Kubla Khan,* and *Christabel.* Today the parlor, reading room, and bed chambers above have been restored to look much as they were when Coleridge and his friends William and Dorothy Wordsworth (who lived nearby) explored the Quantock Hills together.

35 Lime St., Nether Stowey (just off the A39, 8 miles west of Bridgwater). 📞 **01278/732662.** www.nationaltrust.org.uk. Admission £4 adults, £2 children. Apr–Sept Thurs–Sun 2–5pm. Closed Oct–Mar. From Minehead, follow the A39 east about 30 miles, following signs to Bridgwater.

Dunster Castle ★★ CASTLE   Dunster Castle is one of the most picturesque stately homes in the West Country, located on a high, craggy hill overlooking the Bristol Channel. All that remains of the original Norman castle is the 13th-century gateway, and what you see today dates mainly from the faux-Gothic renovation of

Somerset Steam

The **West Somerset Railway** ★★ (📞 **01643/704996;** www.west-somerset-railway.co.uk) is one of Britain's longest and most alluring heritage railways, where vintage steam trains puff through the lush Somerset countryside between Bishop's Lydeard (4 miles west of Taunton on the A358), and Minehead on the coast. Trains run daily May to October (4–8 trains in each direction), and to limited schedules the rest of the year (check the website for details). Day Rover tickets give unlimited travel for the day (£16 adults, £7.80 children 5–15, £43 family ticket), but you can also buy one-way tickets: Bishop's Lydeard to Minehead is £10 one-way or £16 round-trip for adults.

8

WILTSHIRE & SOMERSET | West Somerset & Exmoor

Scrumpy Country

The West Country, and especially Somerset, is celebrated for its **strong apple ciders,** known locally as "scrumpy," best sampled at smaller producers that use traditional methods. Note that unlike North American ciders, British cider is alcoholic (scrumpy tends to be 7–8% alcohol).

○ **Hecks Traditional Farmhouse Cider,** 9–11 Middle Leigh, Street (*✆ 01458/442367;* www.hecksfarm housecider.co.uk), has been making cider since 1840 in the middle of the town of Street. In summer it's open Monday to Saturday 9am to 5:30pm and Sunday 10am to 12:30pm. In winter it's open Monday to Saturday 9am to 5pm and Sunday 10am to noon.

○ **Perry's Cider** (*✆ 01460/55195;* www. perryscider.co.uk), Dowlish Wake, south of Ilminster (see website for directions), is a rustic farm and cider

shop. It's open Monday to Friday 9am to 5:30pm, Saturday 9:30am to 4:30pm, and Sunday 10am to 1pm.

○ **Sheppy's Cider** (*✆ 01823/461848;* www.sheppyscider.com), just off the A38, 3 miles south of Taunton at Three Bridges, Bradford-on-Tone (M5 junction 26), has been making fine cider here since 1917. In addition to their farm shop, you'll find a small **rural life museum** (£2 adults, £1.50 children). It's open Monday to Saturday 8:30am to 6pm (tearoom 10am–4pm); also Sunday 11am to 4pm in July and August.

○ **Somerset Brandy Co.,** Pass Vale Farm, Burrow Hill, Kingsbury Episcopi (01460/240782; www.ciderbrandy.co. uk), is a 150-year-old family cider farm specializing in **cider brandy.** It's open Monday to Saturday 9am to 5:30pm.

○ **Glastonbury Abbey** also makes cider (p. 358).

1868–72. The Luttrell family owned the castle between 1376 and 1976, when it was given to the National Trust together with 12 hectares (30 acres) of surrounding parkland. The wonderfully preserved rooms inside blend Jacobean and Victorian features, including elaborate plasterwork ceilings, wood paneling, and paintings in the entrance halls. The King Charles Bedroom is said to be the most haunted room in the castle (future Charles II slept here in 1645). Save time for the gardens and their lemon trees and unusual "strawberry trees."

The village of **Dunster** itself has an ancient priory church and dovecote, a 17th-century gabled yarn market, water mill, and little cobbled streets dotted with whitewashed cottages.

Dunster, on the A396 (just off the A39). *✆* **01643/823-0004.** www.nationaltrust.org.uk. Admission to castle and grounds £8.50 adults, £4.10 children 5–13, £20 family ticket; grounds only £4.70 adults, £2.10 children, £12 family ticket. Castle Mar–Oct Fri–Wed 11am–5pm; closed Nov–Feb. Grounds Jan–early Mar and Nov–Dec daily 11am–4pm; mid-Mar–Oct daily 10am–5pm; closed Jan–Feb. Bus: 398 Minehead to Tiverton.

EXMOOR NATIONAL PARK ★★

Some of the most witheringly beautiful landscapes in western England lie within **Exmoor National Park** (*✆ 01398/323665;* www.exmoor-nationalpark.gov.uk), an unspoiled plateau of misty moors, wild ponies and herds of red deer on the Somerset and Devon borders. One of the smallest but most cherished National Parks in Britain, it includes the wooded valleys of the rivers Exe and Barle, the Brendon Hills, a sweeping stretch of rocky coastline, and such sleepy but charming villages as

Culbone, Selworthy, Parracombe, and **Allerford.** The moors reach their highest point at Dunkery Beacon, 512m (1,707 ft.) above sea level.

The best way to see Exmoor is on foot (see "Hiking Exmoor," below), but there is a handful of enticing sights to seek out by car if you don't have time to hike. In the Exe Valley lies **Winsford ★★** (just off the A396), one of the prettiest villages on the moor, a jumble of thatched cottages on a green surrounded by streams and seven tiny bridges. The **Tarr Steps ★**, 4 miles northwest of Dulverton via the B3223, is an astonishing prehistoric clapper bridge across the River Barle. The bridge is 55-m (180-ft.) long and was built of stone around 1000 B.C. The main parking lot is around 400m (1,312 ft.) from the bridge via a footpath, but there are plenty of longer walking options in the area. At the eastern Devon end of Exmoor lie the gorgeous waterside twins of **Lynton** and **Lynmouth** (p. 366).

Where to Eat & Stay

Luttrell Arms ★★   The best choice in Dunster, this modern hotel is the outgrowth of a guesthouse from the 14th century. Bedrooms range in size and are attractively decorated in keeping with the hotel's long history; five units have four-poster beds. Rooms in a section called the "Latches" are cottagelike in style, with tight stairways and narrow corridors. It's also the best eating option, with a **formal restaurant** serving modern British food and a **traditional pub** with log fires and garden in the summer.

32–36 High St., Dunster, Somerset TA24 6SG. www.luttrellarms.co.uk. ℂ **01643/821555.** Fax 01643/821567. 28 units. £97–£126 double. Rates include English breakfast. AE, MC, V. Free parking. **Amenities:** Restaurant; bar; babysitting; room service. *In room:* TV, hair dryer.

Three Acres Country House ★★   This enchanting country house on the edge of Exmoor offers luxury and scintillating views over the moors. With only six rooms, it retains a tranquil, exclusive feel; the three superior rooms are larger and face south. All rooms are furnished in a warm, modern style, with cozy armchairs. Breakfast includes seasonal fruit salads, organic yogurt, and daily specials that might include Exe Valley cold smoked trout.

Hiking Exmoor

Hiking is the best way to soak up the subtle charms of Exmoor. Serious walkers should tackle the **South West Coast Path ★** that begins in the resort of Minehead in the east and goes along the coast all the way to Poole Harbour in Dorset (630 miles). Few visitors have time to walk the entire trail, but if you leave Minehead in the morning, you will have seen the path's most beautiful scenery and reach Porlock (10 miles), or even Lynmouth (21 miles) by nightfall. For more information, contact the **South West Coast Path Association** (ℂ 01752/896237; www.southwestcoastpath.com). Another enticing option is the 102-mile **Two Moors' Way ★★** (www.devon.gov.uk/walking/two_moors_way.html), linking Lynmouth and Exmoor with Dartmoor in Devon (p. 365). The trail is hard to follow in parts, but crosses some mesmerizing country.

At the **Dulverton National Park Centre,** 7–9 Fore St., Dulverton (ℂ 01398/323841), you can pick up a brochure that lists events, guided walks, and visitor information.

Brushford, Dulverton, Somerset TA22 9AR. www.threeacrescountryhouse.co.uk. ☏ **01398/323730.** 6 units. £45–£60 double. Rates include English breakfast. AE, MC, V. Free parking. **Amenities:** Restaurant; bar. *In room:* TV, hair dryer, Wi-Fi (free).

Town Mills ★★★ This gorgeous converted millhouse in the center of Dulverton (the old mill stream runs underneath the building) is perfect for exploring Exmoor and the surrounding area. Rooms are boutique-like, with mostly all-white and timber furnishings and plenty of thoughtful touches; there is white port in the room on arrival, and chocolates on the pillows. The owners are friendly and generous, and the breakfasts are first-class; the on-site tearoom is open 10am to 5pm every day for lunch, tea, and cakes.

Dulverton, Somerset TA22 9HB. www.townmillsdulverton.co.uk. ☏ **01398/323124.** 6 units. £85 double. Rates include English breakfast. MC, V. Free parking. **Amenities:** Restaurant. *In room:* TV, hair dryer, Wi-Fi (free).

DEVON

by Christi Daugherty

With its spectacular coast, pastoral scenery, and dramatic red cliffs, Devon is endlessly rewarding to explore. You can get lost on foreboding Dartmoor, spend whole days exploring historic hillside villages like Clovelly, or lounge on the (sometimes) sunny beaches around Torquay. Whether you're into surfing, hiking, or sipping tea, Devon will have something that appeals to you.

9

CITIES   Devon is largely rural, but **Exeter** is a bustling, workaday city that still retains bits and pieces of its historic past in the form of a gorgeous cathedral and ancient guildhall. There's even a Norman gatehouse that once opened the way to William the Conqueror's castle. **Plymouth** was the last bit of England the Pilgrims visited before setting off for the New World, and tiny fragments of its largely lost history can be found in its medieval **Barbican.**

COUNTRYSIDE   From green **pastures** to dark, gloomy **moors** to breathtaking **cliffs** plunging down to the blue sea, Devon changes constantly as you move through it. Dartmoor's brooding hills, topped with rugged, bare stones worn down by centuries of wind and rain, are surrounded by fields of soft pink heather—the scent of it is everywhere in the summer. Thatch-roofed cottages and ancient pubs complete the picture of rural idyll.

EATING & DRINKING   Devon is famed for its **scones** and **clotted cream,** and for the afternoon tea at which those are traditionally consumed. But there's much more to the local cuisine than tea and cake. In fishing villages along the coast, restaurants serve **seafood** fresh off the boats, and use only the lightest of sauces so that the briny taste comes to the fore. In Dartmoor and Exmoor, **venison** and local **lamb** predominate, along with **pheasant** in season.

COAST   With towering red cliffs overlooking ivory crescent beaches and the midnight-blue sea, Devon's coastline is dramatic. Historic villages like **Clovelly** in the south and **Lynmouth** and **Lynton** in the north, cling to the edges of land, the sea held just at bay. By contrast, **Torquay** is a modern resort town, packed with beach lovers, surfers, and snorkelers.

THE best TRAVEL EXPERIENCES IN DEVON

○ **Getting lost on Dartmoor:** The narrow, winding roads traversing this vast and hilly wilderness are notoriously un-numbered and unmarked. To find your way around, you follow signs indicating the names of villages ahead. Inevitably you lose your way, which is when you'll discover all the most beautiful places. See p. 376.

○ **Spending a day at the beach near Torquay:** With 20 sandy beaches within a few miles of one another, Torquay is perfect for sun-worshippers. Surfers can catch a wave, and even on the hottest summer day, the water is bracingly cold. Whether you prefer busy beaches with paddling pools or private sandy spots surrounded by cliffs, you'll find your space here. See p. 383.

○ **Climbing the streets of Clovelly:** This protected, historic town has cobbled streets so steep and narrow that donkeys still haul goods from the top of the hill to the bottom. For walkers, the precipitous stroll down to the seafront is simply beautiful, as the streets are lined with flower-bedecked cottages. See p. 370.

○ **Taking the cliff train from Lynmouth:** This century-old, water-powered train climbs 183m (600 ft.) from the fishing village of Lynmouth at the foot of the cliff to the little town of Lynton at the top. The views along the way are sweeping. The entire experience is both exhilarating and, frankly, terrifying. See p. 368.

○ **Traveling by boat from Dartmouth to Totnes:** A winding journey through some of Devon's greenest and peaceful countryside, this river-boat journey is a relaxing way to spend an afternoon. The fields and pastures pass by, dotted with sheep and ponies, and you'll see jagged hills off in the distance. On a sunny day, it's heavenly. See p. 390.

LYNTON-LYNMOUTH & THE NORTH DEVON COAST ★★

206 miles W of London; 59 miles NW of Exeter

For centuries, Lynton and Lynmouth have attracted artists drawn by the twin **Victorian villages**' beauty and picturesque setting at the edge of Exmoor National Park. The harbor town is Lynmouth, while Lynton is on the cliff 183m (600 ft.) above it; the two are linked by a cliff railway. Thomas Gainsborough called Lynmouth "the most delightful place for a landscape painter this country can boast." Another notable visitor was poet Percey Bysshe Shelley, who honeymooned here with his 16-year-old bride, Harriet Westbrook, and on a later visit wrote *Queen Mab*. From the clifftop, you can look across the Bristol Channel to the Welsh coast.

Exmoor National Park straddles the border between Devon and Somerset. Less distinctive than its gloomier sibling, Dartmoor, it nonetheless provides miles of captivating countryside to hike across, and is home to an astonishingly beautiful stretch of coastline.

Essentials

GETTING THERE These villages are rather remote, and we recommend that you rent a car to get here. Another option is to take one of the First Great Western trains

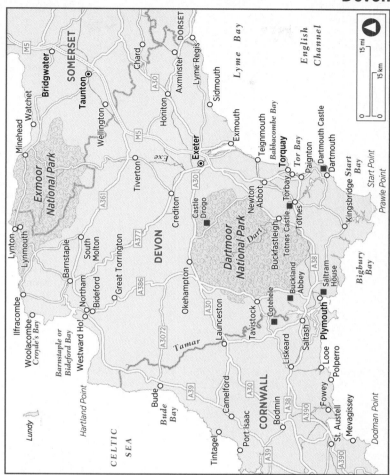

from Exeter to Barnstaple; buses travel from there to Lynton about once an hour. Call ✆ **01598/752225** for bus schedules.

If you're driving, take the A39 to the Lynton-Lynmouth exit and follow the signs.

VISITOR INFORMATION The **Tourist Information Centre** is at the Town Hall, Lee Road, Lynton (✆ **0845/660-3232;** www.lynton-lynmouth-tourism.co.uk). It's open Easter to October, Monday to Saturday 9:30am to 5pm and Sunday 10am to 4pm; and November to Easter, Monday to Saturday 10am to 4pm and Sunday 10am to 2pm.

Exploring the Area

The main attractions of Lynton and Lynmouth are the towns themselves. Seemingly hewn from the cliffside in stone and slate, they have, over time, become part of the topography. On rainy days, Lynmouth, at the top of the cliff, seems to disappear in mist. The two are linked by an extraordinary water-powered train system, the **Lynton & Lynmouth Cliff Railway** (© **01598/753486;** www.cliffrailwaylynton.co.uk). The century-old train uses no electricity. Instead, the railway employs a complicated network of cables and pulleys, and the water tanks pull the train cars up approximately 150m (500 ft.). The train carries about 40 passengers at a time for £2.85 adults, £1.85 children 4–13. Trains depart daily from March to October, at 2- to 5-minute intervals.

If you'd prefer, you can hike between the two towns, although be aware the climb is steep.

This area is popular with hikers—or "ramblers"—drawn by the numerous trails and the striking countryside. A popular short walk is known as the North Walk, a 1-mile trail leading to the **Valley of the Rocks ★**. This grouping of rugged rock formations rises from a grass-covered valley to peaks of bare sandstone and shale, believed to have been carved during the Ice Age. The centerpiece of the formation is Castle Rock, known for its resident herd of wild goats.

To learn more about the best hikes in the area, go to the tourist office (see above), where you can pick up maps, guides, and other information. A good option is the book *Walking in North Devon,* which contains numerous tried and tested walks in the region.

From Lynton it's a 12-mile drive north on the A39 to another historic coastal town—the village of **Porlock**—composed of a tiny cluster of thatched cottages in a peaceful estuary that seems straight out of Middle Earth. The poet Coleridge lived here while writing *Kubla Khan.*

About a 20-minute drive south of Lynton is the faded Edwardian town of **Ilfracombe,** a traditional English seaside village that's virtually preserved in aspic. Its rock candy shops, seaside promenade, and fish-and-chips eateries are straight out of a film. Sea-battered but not uncharming, Ilfracombe is well located for walks around the headland and for days spent at its beaches, which are reached through tunnels carved through the rock (follow signs).

A 10-minute drive south down the coast from Ilfracombe brings you to the small village of **Croyde,** and the surfing mecca of **Croyde's Bay.** This isolated area of rugged coastline has miles of sandy beach, much of it pounded by thunderous surf—perfect for surfers, but not so great for swimmers. However, about a mile away, around the rocky headland of **Baggy Point,** are the beaches of **Saunton Sands** and **Braunton Burrows,** which provide expansive stretches of sand dunes to explore, and quieter water can be found in sheltered coves on either side of Croyde.

South of Croyde is the quixotically named **Westward Ho!,** named after the book by the author Charles Kingsley, who lived in nearby Bideford. When Kingsley's novel became a huge hit in 1855, a local developer smelled opportunity and came up with the idea of building a planned holiday village with the same name. The town is charming enough, but the main draw is its **Blue Flag Beach,** which stretches for miles of flat, soft sand and rolling surf.

Where to Eat & Stay

Bonnicott House ★   Spacious and welcoming, Bonnicott House sits on the crest of the cliff with sweeping views of the town and surrounding countryside. Bedrooms are done in shades of light blue, cream, or pale green, and most have a mix of well-chosen antiques and more modern furniture. Beds are comfortable and big, while bathrooms are small but have all the necessities. The gardens here are beautifully cultivated and pleasant to wander through. The guest lounge has a fireplace crackling on cold days; when the sun is out, the light pours in. Breakfasts are good and hearty, and the owners know everything about the area.

10 Watersmeet Rd., Lynmouth, Devon EX35 6EP. www.bonnicott.com. ⓒ **fax 01598/753346.** 8 units. £60–£100 double. Rates include English breakfast. MC, V. Free street parking. **Amenities:** Lounge; bar. *In room:* TV, hair dryer, no phone.

Hewitt's at the Hoe ★   This exquisite mansion hotel, surrounded by lush gardens and thick forests, clings to the edge of the cliff near Lynmouth. Once the home of the man who built the cliff railway, the building has been sympathetically restored over the years—the polished oak paneling gleams—and filled with quality antiques. Most rooms have sweeping views of the sea, and all have big, comfortable beds and sizable bathrooms. The owners cultivate a country-house atmosphere, so you feel like a welcome guest in a gracious home. Breakfasts are pleasingly ample, tea and scones are served each afternoon in the lounge, and the dinners (£35 per person; hotel guests only), served in the elegant dining hall, are worth staying in for.

The Hoe, North Walk, Lynton, Devon EX35 6HJ. www.hewittshotel.co.uk. ⓒ **01598/752293.** Fax 01598/752489. 5 units. £120–£160 double; from £370 self-catering apt (per week). AE, MC, V. Free parking. **Amenities:** Restaurant; bar; Jacuzzi; room service. *In room:* TV, hair dryer, minibar.

Life's a Beach

Devon is famed for its beaches, and for good reason: Golden crescents of sand or stone at the feet of soaring red cliffs—beaches here are dramatic settings for an afternoon of sunbathing or surfing. Here's a list of some of the best:

- **Blackpool Sands** (signposted from Dartmouth on the A379): This peaceful cove lies at the foot of a steep, forested cliff. Nearly a mile long and almost perfectly crescent shaped, it's popular for windsurfing, sailing, and sunbathing.
- **Croyde Bay** (10 miles south of Ilfracombe on the coastal road): Said to have the best surfing in Devon, with hollow barrel waves at low tide, Croyde Bay has miles of beaches, long stretches of sand dunes, and sheltered bays.
- **Ilfracombe Tunnels** (follow signs for Ilfracombe, and then tourist signs in town for seafront and tunnels): These secluded beaches are accessed by four tunnels from the town of Ilfracombe. The beaches have wonderful views of Lundy Island and South Wales. A tidal swimming pool is popular with children.
- **Oddicombe Beach** (at the edge of Torquay, accessed by a steep footpath): A small, isolated sandy beach at the foot of enormous cliffs, Oddicombe is popular but not overcrowded.
- **Westward Ho!** (from Clovelly, take the B3236, follow signs): With 2 miles of flat, golden sand and plenty of space for sunbathing, Westward Ho! is handy for those staying in Clovelly, and popular with surfers drawn by its low-tide waves.

St. Vincent House ★ This charming house was built by a master mariner in 1834 and has since been sensitively converted. Guest rooms are small but sunny, with tiny bathrooms and comfortable beds. The house itself is lovely. Many of the original features of the seaman's home, including a beautiful Regency spiral staircase, have been retained. The Belgian owner, Jean-Paul Saltpetier, is a gourmet chef, and breakfasts are wonderfully varied (for England) with options like Belgian waffles, vegetarian cooked breakfast, and smoked salmon, alongside the inevitable English breakfast. New guests are welcomed with a glass of sherry to help them settle in.

Castle Hill, Lynton, Devon EX35 6JA. www.st-vincent-hotel.co.uk. ℂ **01598/752244.** Fax 01598/752244. 7 units. £74–£80 double. No credit cards. Free parking. Closed Nov–Easter. **Amenities:** Restaurant; lounge. *In room:* TV, hair dryer, Wi-Fi (free).

Vanilla Pod BRITISH This relaxed and friendly eatery is a great option in Lynton. During the day it's a coffee bar, where you can linger over a pastry or a sandwich and latte. At night it's a candle-lit restaurant with a simple menu that emphasizes fresh local meats, fish, and produce. The menu changes regularly but can include pan-fried sea bass, caught that morning, Bray Valley trout, or Exmoor venison. There are plenty of options for vegetarians as well, and the desserts are irresistible.

10-12 Queen St. ℂ **01598/753706.** Sandwiches and light lunches £3.50–£5; main courses (dinner) £7–£12. MC, V. Daily 10am–9pm (often later in summer).

CLOVELLY ★★

240 miles SW of London; 11 miles SW of Bideford

The lovely village of Clovelly, a short drive south along the coastal road from Westward Ho!, spreads across one side of a steep hill in a way that all but forbids you to pass without stopping. This is a **no-car zone,** as the precipitous and narrow cobblestone High Street makes driving virtually impossible. Instead, you park at the top and make the trip down on foot; everybody does the same—even supplies for the village stores are still carried down on sleds pulled by donkeys. It's worth the effort because every step provides views of tiny cottages, with their terraces of flowers lining the main street.

Somewhat controversially, you have to pay an admission charge just to enter the village. It's not particularly expensive, and certainly worth the price considering it also covers parking and entry to two (tiny) **museums** (see below), but there is some dispute about the legality of charging visitors this fee. Still, given that the money goes toward the upkeep of this historic village, few people object.

Once you've paid the toll, you won't find many sights within town, but that's really not the point: The major attraction of Clovelly, you might say, is Clovelly itself. Victorian author Charles Kingsley (who lived here) once said, "It is as if the place had stood still while all the world had been rushing and rumbling past it."

After you've worked your way all the way down to the quayside, the climb back to the top can look intimidating. If it's too much for you, do what many other visitors do and, behind the Red Lion Inn, catch a Land Rover. For £2 per person, it will take you up via a back road. In summer, the wait for the ride can get rather long, though.

Insider tip: To avoid the tourist crowds in the summer, stay out of Clovelly from around 11am until 4pm. When the midday crowds are filling the town, visit nearby villages such as Bucks Mills (3 miles to the east) and Hartland Quay (4 miles to the west).

Essentials

GETTING THERE   It's not easy to get to Clovelly by public transportation. From London's Paddington Station, you have to catch a train to Exeter (around £69 for a round-trip), and then from there you take a local train to Barnstaple. Travel time from Exeter to Barnstaple is 1¼ hours on First Great Western trains. From Barnstaple there are relatively frequent buses to Clovelly (though sometimes you need to change at Bideford). Check at the station for details. The entire journey essentially takes all day.

If you're driving from London, head west on the M4, cutting south at the junction with the M5. At the junction near Bridgwater, continue west along the A39 toward Lynton. The A39 runs all the way to the signposted turnoff for Clovelly.

VISITOR INFORMATION   To gain entry to the village, you're required to buy a ticket from the **Clovelly Visitor Centre** (✆ **01237/431781;** www.clovelly.co.uk). The cost is £6 for adults, £3.65 for children 7–16, and £16 for a family ticket. This also covers parking for the day; a tour of a fisherman's cottage; and admission to the Kingsley Exhibition, a tiny museum devoted to (former resident) Charles Kingsley, author of *The Water Babies*. The center is open July through September, daily 10am to 4pm; April through June and October, Monday to Saturday 9am to 5:30pm; and November through March, daily 9am to 4:30pm. If you arrive outside of these times, you don't have to pay the entrance fee, nor do you pay if you're staying overnight in the village (in which case the Land Rover service is also free).

Where to Eat & Stay

East Dyke Farmhouse ★   Set above Clovelly village itself, with gorgeous views over field and sea, this working farmhouse is a lovely place to stay. Named after the Iron Age hill fort that backs onto the garden (yes, really), the house has three comfortable and reasonably sized bedrooms. One room is a twin; the others are doubles. Breakfasts are filling and delicious (and more varied than just the usual "full English" once common in places like this). The owners do their utmost to make you feel at home, and provide a wealth of information about the local area.

Higher Clovelly, Devon EX39 5RU. ✆ **01237/431-216.** 3 units. £55–£60. Rates include breakfast. No credit cards. **Amenities:** Restaurant; bar. *In room:* TV, hair dryer, Wi-Fi (free).

New Inn Hotel   About halfway down High Street is the village pub, a good meeting place at sundown. The small restaurant here uses fresh local produce to make French-influenced British cuisine—it's a good option for dinner in a town with very few restaurants. Guest rooms here are actually based in two buildings on opposite sides of the steep street (with only a 3.5-m/12-ft. leap between balconies—not that you should even think about doing that). Each room is relatively small but comfortable, although the decor could use a facelift in places. Two rooms are large enough for families. If you're driving, you can park in the lot at the entrance to the town. It's advisable to pack a smaller overnight bag because your luggage will have to be carried down (but it's returned to the top by donkey).

High St., Clovelly, Devon EX39 5TQ. ✆ **01237/431303.** Fax 01237/431636. 19 units. £103–£119. Rates include English breakfast. MC, V. **Amenities:** Restaurant; bar. *In room:* TV, Wi-Fi (free).

EXETER

201 miles SW of London; 46 miles NE of Plymouth

Exeter was a Roman city founded in the 1st century A.D. on the banks of the River Exe. Two centuries later it was encircled by a mighty **stone wall,** traces of which remain today. Over the subsequent centuries, numerous invaders—including Saxons, Vikings, and Normans—stormed the fortress. None was more thorough than William the Conqueror, who brought Exeter to its knees in 1067.

As time passed, the city grew and prospered. By the 17th century, it was an economic powerhouse, and a leading trading place for wool. But in the 19th century, as wool became less profitable and industrialization powered other cities forward, its importance waned.

In the 20th century, the city became a favorite target of the German Luftwaffe, which flew 18 raids over Exeter between 1940 and 1942, flattening much of the city's historic architecture and killing many of its inhabitants. In May 1942, in response to the British bombing of Lubeck, 16 hectares (40 acres) of the city were leveled in a devastating attack. The town was rebuilt in the 1950s, but its grand Georgian crescents and priceless timbered Tudor buildings were replaced by utilitarian, modern shops and office towers. Fortunately, some of the city's historic structures were spared, and Exeter still has a **Gothic cathedral,** a renowned university, and several **historic houses.**

Its location makes Exeter a good base for exploring Dartmoor and Exmoor National Parks (see "Dartmoor National Park," later in this chapter).

Essentials

GETTING THERE   First Great Western trains travel from London's Paddington Station to Exeter St. David Station every hour; the trip takes 2½ hours. One-way fares cost £40 to £50. Trains also run every 20 minutes between Exeter and Plymouth; that trip takes 1 hour.

A **National Express** bus departs from London's Victoria Coach Station every 2 hours during the day; the trip takes 4½ hours. One-way fares cost £28. For information and schedules, call ✆ **0871/781-8181** or visit **www.nationalexpress.com**. You can also take **Stagecoach** bus no. X38 or X39 between Plymouth and Exeter. During the day, two buses depart per hour for the 1-hour trip.

If you're driving from London, take the M4 west, cutting south to Exeter on the M5.

VISITOR INFORMATION   The **Tourist Information Centre** is at the Civic Centre, Paris Street (✆ **01392/665700**). It's open from September to June, Monday to Saturday 9am to 5pm, and in July and August, Monday to Saturday 9am to 5pm and Sunday 10am to 4pm.

SPECIAL EVENTS   The **Exeter Summer Festival,** held over 2 weeks in June or July, includes more than 150 classical music performances and events—from concerts and operas to lectures. The schedule varies from year to year. Information about this year's event is posted on the town's website by April or May (✆ **01392/265200;** www.exeter.gov.uk).

Exploring Exeter

Exeter Cathedral ★★ CATHEDRAL   The Anglican cathedral at Exeter can trace its history to 1050, when the Bishop of Devon and Cornwall was transferred north to escape Viking sea raids. Only temporary church buildings stood on the site until 1112, when William Warelwast, a nephew of William the Conqueror, was given the district and began building a church in the Norman style. The twin Norman towers he designed still stand, but the building was not completed until 1400, when styles had changed, so most of the building is a spectacular concoction of Gothic architecture, with a remarkable vaulted ceiling that's 20m (66 ft.) tall and 90m (300 ft.) long. The structure is not complete—sadly, the cloisters were destroyed by Oliver Cromwell's forces, and a German bomb finished off the twin chapels of St. James and St. Thomas in 1942. Its sheer size is moving, and the early carving work is delightful. Its famous choir sings Evensong Monday to Friday at 5:30pm and again at 3pm on Saturday and Sunday.

1 The Cloisters. ℂ **01392/285983.** www.exeter-cathedral.org.uk. Admission £5 adults, £3 children 15 and under. Open Mon–Sat 9am–4:45pm.

Exeter Guildhall ARCHITECTURE   This grand old building on Exeter's main shopping street has been at the center of life here for more than 600 years. Outside, the architecture is a mishmash of Tudor and faux Tudor. The elaborate frontage is faux—it was added in the 1590s (and was described by a wit at the time as "just as picturesque as it is barbarous"). The interior was similarly "restored" by the Victorians. But much did survive their well-intended meddling, including the medieval oak-paneled hall and the original beamed ceilings.

High St. ℂ **01392/665500.** Free admission. Mon and Wed–Fri 10:30am–1pm. Hours change frequently; call before visiting.

Powderham Castle ★ CASTLE   Originally built in the late 14th century (but much altered in the 19th century), this is a grand, Gothic-influenced structure with sprawling grounds. Today it's still in the hands of the descendants of its original owners, the Countess and Earl of Devon. Inside, the decor is traditional, with family portraits and fine furniture, some 17th-century tapestries, and a chair used by William III for his first council of state at Newton Abbot. The chapel dates from the 15th century, with hand-hewn roof timbers and carved pew ends. If the castle looks strangely familiar, it might be because it featured in the film *The Remains of the Day.*

Powderham, Kenton. ℂ **01626/890243.** www.powderham.co.uk. Admission £9.80 adults, £8.80 seniors, £7.80 children 5–14, £28 family ticket, free for children 4 and under. Sun–Fri 11am–4:30pm. Closed Nov–Mar. Take the A379 Dawlish Rd. 8 miles south of Exeter; the castle is signposted.

Where to Eat

Michael Caines Restaurant at ABode Exeter ★★ FRENCH   This swanky restaurant in the ABode Hotel (see below), at the edge of Cathedral Green, is where Exeter goes for important business lunches, celebratory family dinners, and critical first dates. Executive Chef Michael Caines is double Michelin starred, and one meal

---

 A Relic from William the Conqueror

At the top of Castle Street, the impressive **Norman Gatehouse** is actually one of the few surviving fragments of William the Conqueror's castle. The gatehouse and walls are all that survive, but you can enjoy the panoramic view and gardens while contemplating the longevity of the stone around you.

---

will explain why—he uses the freshest local produce, and he has a fine touch with French cuisine. The dining room is comfortably stylish with white table linens and cream walls. The menu changes constantly, but starters could include a delicate tartlet of Devon quail or pan-fried Brixham scallops with roasted parsnips. Main courses might feature roasted partridge with braised chicory, slow-roasted pheasant with pumpkin and lentils, or loin of local venison. Desserts are decadent, and service is outstanding. This place is popular, so make reservations at least a day in advance.

In the ABode Exeter at the Royal Clarence Hotel, Cathedral Yard. 📞 **01392/223638.** www.michael caines.com. Reservations required. Main courses £22–£25; fixed-price 2-course lunch £17, 3-course lunch £24; 7-course table d'hôte menu £68. AE, DC, MC, V. Mon–Sat noon–2pm and 7–10pm.

Ship Inn ★ 🍴 ENGLISH   In a lovely historic building that dates back to the 16th century, this inn was, in its day, visited by Sir Francis Drake, Sir Walter Raleigh, and Sir John Hawkins. Today it's a busy pub restaurant where you can have a drink or two, or stay for a full meal. A selection of snacks is available in the bar; full meals are served in the restaurant upstairs. The menu offers fairly good pub options, including steak, fried and grilled fish, and sandwiches and hamburgers at lunchtime. Prices are reasonable.

St. Martin's Lane. 📞 **01392/272040.** Reservations recommended. Restaurant main courses £6–£13. MC, V. Daily noon–9pm.

Treasury Restaurant ★ CONTINENTAL   A small but classy eatery in St. Olaves Hotel in the center of town, the Treasury is a good option for those who like the personal touch. The dining room is beautifully decorated with white linens and dark, polished wood floors—the tables are gathered loosely around a fireplace. The menu reflects the sophisticated palate of the congenial owners. The food is French-influenced local cuisine, so starters could include farmhouse-style ham hock terrine with brioche, or pan-fried local scallops with apple and cider sauce. Main courses include roasted local lamb with wild mushroom gateau, or whole lemon sole served on the bone with capers. The cheese plate is worth trying for its rich local creations.

In the St. Olaves Hotel, Mary Arches St. 📞 **01392/217736.** Reservations recommended. Main courses £16–£25. MC, V. Daily noon–2pm and 7–9:30pm.

Shopping

If you're looking for arts and crafts or antiques, head to the historic Quay off Western Way. The **Quay Gallery Antiques Emporium** (📞 **01392/213283;** www.exeter quayantiques.co.uk) houses 10 dealers who sell furniture, porcelain, metalware, and other collectibles. The **Antique Centre,** on the Quay (📞 **01392/493501**), has 20 dealers, each with its own specialty era. The **South Gate Gallery,** 64 South Street (📞 **01392/435-8000**), sells original local art and prints.

The High Street, which runs through the town's center, is the primary shopping street in Exeter for clothing, books, food, and other day-to-day goods. The modern **Princesshay** shopping center (on Princesshay Street, signposted off the High Street; 📞 **01392/459838**) also has plenty of useful shops and restaurants including Accessorize (for inexpensive jewelry), an Apple Store, Dorothy Perkins, Topshop, and Debenhams (for clothing).

Entertainment & Nightlife

Exeter is a lively university town offering an abundance of classical music concerts and theatre productions, as well as clubs and pubs.

Concerts, opera, dance, and film can be found year-round at the **Exeter Phoenix,** Bradninch Place, Gandy Street (✆ **01392/667080;** www.exeterphoenix.org.uk), and Exeter University's **Northcott Theatre,** Stocker Road (✆ **01392/493493;** www.exeternorthcott.co.uk), which is also home to a professional theatre company.

The **Well House Tavern,** Cathedral Close (✆ **01392/223611**), is a friendly, historic place to stop for a pint or a pub meal. The building dates to the 14th century, and the atmosphere is laid-back and welcoming.

Perched at the edge of the canal, **Double Locks,** Canal Banks (✆ **01392/256947;** www.doublelocks.co.uk), welcomes a lively crowd. It features live music (jazz, rock, and blues) with no cover charge, and you can get traditional pub grub to go with your pint. In the summer, you can sit outside and watch the boats go by.

Where to Stay
EXPENSIVE
ABode Exeter at the Royal Clarence Hotel ★
A short walk from the rail station and just steps from the cathedral, the ABode Exeter is one of the city's most talked about hotels, with a cutting-edge restaurant, a gorgeous tavern, and coolly modern rooms. The hotel building dates to the 18th century, but inside, clever design has combined history with modernity and comfort. Rooms have a contemporary feel, with handmade, Vi-Spring beds, monsoon showers, and personal DVD players. Michelin-starred chef **Michael Caines** runs the hotel's acclaimed restaurant (p. 373), and the Well House Tavern, a historic pub, offers more casual dining.

Cathedral Yard, Exeter, Devon EX1 1HD. www.abodehotels.co.uk/exeter. ✆ **01392/319955.** Fax 01392/439423. 53 units. £120–£175 double; £230–£330 suite. AE, DC, MC, V. Parking £9. **Amenities:** Restaurant (Michael Caines, p. 373); cafe; 2 bars (including Well House Tavern; see above); babysitting; exercise room; room service; spa. *In room:* A/C, TV, hair dryer, Wi-Fi (free).

Buckerell Lodge Hotel ★
Resembling a gracious country manor house, this picture-perfect hotel, set amid sprawling grounds and gardens, is a popular wedding location. The building may be Victorian, but bedrooms are contemporary and spacious, done up in neutral tones of taupe with splashes of bright color. The best (most-expensive) rooms are in the main house; the others, though cheaper, are in a more sterile modern addition. The hotel restaurant, Veitch's, is formal and a little old-fashioned, serving French-influenced cuisine. There's also a more relaxed bar where you can order light meals.

Topsham Rd., Exeter, Devon EX2 4SQ. www.akkeronhotels.com. ✆ **0844/855-9112.** Fax 01392/424333. 54 units. £115–£130 double. AE, DC, MC, V. Free parking. Take the B3182 1 mile southeast, off junction 30 of the M5. **Amenities:** Restaurant; bar; room service. *In room:* TV, hair dryer, Wi-Fi (free).

MODERATE
Gipsy Hill Hotel
This late-Victorian country estate surrounded by gorgeous gardens is on the eastern fringe of the city—just far enough away to feel bucolic. Rooms are comfortable, although not at all fancy. One has a (slightly creaky) four-poster bed squeezed into a space so small you can barely get around it, which is odd given that some other rooms are much larger. Like the rooms, the restaurant is a bit old-fashioned, but it's handy if you don't feel like going into town, and in the summer you can dine outside. Generally, the place could use some updating (carpets are thin, curtains are fussy, walls are oddly unadorned), but the grounds are delightful, the staff is helpful, and the price is reasonable. They'll even let you bring your dog.

9

DEVON | Exeter

Gipsy Hill Lane (via Pinn Lane), Monkerton, Exeter, Devon EX1 3RN. www.gipsyhillhotel.co.uk. ☏ **01392/465252.** Fax 01392/464302. 37 units. £60–£100 double. AE, DC, MC, V. Free parking. **Amenities:** Restaurant; bar; babysitting; room service. *In room:* TV, hair dryer, Wi-Fi (free).

St. Olaves Hotel ★★   In a creamy white Georgian townhouse with a secluded walled garden, St. Olaves is a special place to stay. The location is ideal, within a short walk of Exeter's sights, especially the cathedral, which is so close that you can hear its bells. Outside, it's pristine, while inside it's been tastefully furnished with a mix of antiques and modern furniture. Guest rooms are spacious and comfortable, done in tones of ivory and blue. Bathrooms are not huge, but they have power showers. The **Treasury Restaurant** has an interesting, French-influenced menu and a refined ambience.

Mary Arches St. (off High St.), Exeter, Devon EX4 3AZ. www.olaves.co.uk. ☏ **800/544-9993** in the U.S., or 01392/217736. Fax 01392/413054. 14 units. £100–£125 double; £165 family room; £155 suite. Rates include English breakfast. MC, V. Free parking. **Amenities:** Restaurant (Treasury Restaurant, p. 374); bar; room service. *In room:* TV, hair dryer.

INEXPENSIVE

Park View Hotel   This hotel, near the heart of town and the train station, offers cheap and cheerful rooms with no frills. The tall Georgian townhouse has comfortable but plainly furnished rooms in varying sizes (the layout of the old house means that some are bigger than others). Some have teeny tiny private bathrooms, but cheaper rooms use shared bathrooms. The usual fried English breakfast is served in a slightly crowded dining room that looks out over the hotel's pleasant garden.

8 Howell Rd., Exeter, Devon EX4 4LG. www.parkviewexeter.co.uk. ☏ **01392/271772.** Fax 01392/253047. 13 units, 10 with bathroom. £60 double without bathroom; £72 double with bathroom. Rates include English breakfast. MC, V. Free parking. **Amenities:** TV lounge. *In room:* TV.

Woodbine Guesthouse   This centrally located B&B has sunny small rooms at a reasonable price. In a Victorian house near the town's landmark clock tower and park (some guest rooms look out over the park's green fields), the Woodbine is certainly convenient. Its rooms are small (you won't be able to swing a cat here), but they have all you need, including Lilliputian en suite bathrooms. Fried English breakfast is served in the cozy dining room.

1 Woodbine Terrace, Exeter, Devon EX4 4LJ. www.woodbineguesthouse.co.uk. ☏ **01392/203302.** Fax 01392/254162. 5 units. £66 double. Rates include English breakfast. MC, V. Free parking. *In room:* TV, free Wi-Fi.

DARTMOOR NATIONAL PARK ★★★

213 miles SW of London; 13 miles W of Exeter

Ominous and brooding, this vast, sprawling moorland park undulates and curves for miles, stretching across the county from Exeter in the east to Tavistock and Okehampton in the west. As you travel across it, the landscape constantly changes, rising to steep hills (as high as 621m/2,037 ft.), and then plunging into deep gorges with rushing water. It is distinguished by its flora of spiny **moor shrubs,** and the **scented heather** that rouges the hillsides in the summer and turns black in the winter. Famously, Dartmoor is home to herds of **wild ponies** that nibble peacefully on the heather and occasionally block traffic on the tiny, winding roads. The area's wild look led Arthur Conan Doyle to set his spookiest tale, *The Hound of the Baskervilles,* here.

Essentials

GETTING THERE   You really need a car to get around the moors, particularly in the winter. In the summer, the **Transmoor Link** bus service runs between the villages on the moor and surrounding towns. For timetables, contact **Travel Line** (**℡ 0871/200-2233;** www.traveline.info).

Inspiring Sherlock Holmes

The High Moorland Visitors Centre sits inside an impressive 19th-century building. Two centuries ago, the building was The Old Duchy Hotel. Arthur Conan Doyle stayed there while researching *The Hound of the Baskervilles*. So the view from the center, down the wind-swept hill, is the view that inspired his descriptions of the desolate moor.

If you're driving from Exeter, head west on the B3212 to such centers as Dartmoor, Chagford, Moretonhampstead, and North Bovey. From these smaller towns, tiny roads—often not really big enough for two cars—cut deeper into the moor. Old signposts list the names of towns on these roads, which are too small to be numbered. Prepare to pull over if traffic comes the other way.

VISITOR INFORMATION   The **Tourist Information Centre,** Town Hall, Bedford Square, Tavistock (☎ **01822/612938**), is in the bustling town of Tavistock just outside the park. It has brochures and information about nearby towns. From April to October, it's open daily from 9:30am to 5pm. From November to March, it's open on Monday, Tuesday, Friday, and Saturday from 10am to 4:30pm. The **High Moorland Visitors Centre** (Old Duchy Hotel, Princetown; ☎ **01822/890414**) is an essential stopping point for a thorough exploration of the park. It stocks maps for hiking and biking across the moors, as well as guides and brochures. Its staff can answer any questions you might have. It's open daily 10am to 5pm in the summer, and 10am to 4pm the rest of the year.

CHAGFORD

218 miles SW of London; 13 miles W of Exeter; 20 miles NW of Torquay

Chagford is a charming ancient village in north Dartmoor overlooking the River Teign and surrounded by high granite tors (rocky hilltop outcrops). Its High Street and picturesque town square still have some original store fronts, giving it a lovely lost-in-time look, and its plentiful pubs and tea shops make it a good place to stop for lunch.

The village has many historic buildings, including the 16th-century **Endecott House** in the town square, named after John Endecott, a Pilgrim and governor of the Massachusetts Bay colony, who lived in Chagford before striking out for America. The house is now used as the town's meeting hall.

The village hall **(Jubilee Hall)** near the public parking lot is another local gathering place, which holds Friday markets and the local library.

The 13th-century **Three Crowns Hotel** is another building worth exploring for its sheer longevity. Not far away, the **Church of St. Michael** dates to the 15th century, and retains many of its original features. It was the scene of a tragic murder hundreds of years ago (see "The Real Lorna Doone," below).

To get here, catch Stagecoach bus no. 173. If you're driving from Exeter, drive west on the A30, and then south on the A382 following signs to Chagford.

Exploring the Area

Buckland Abbey ABBEY   Built in the 13th century by Cistercian monks who created a vast estate around it, the abbey was later converted into a home by Sir Richard Grenville, which was then purchased by Sir Francis Drake. Over the years,

9

Chagford

DEVON

The Real Lorna Doone

In Chagford, the Church of St. Michael was the scene of a famous tragedy in which a beautiful local girl was killed on her wedding day. According to legend, on October 11, 1641, young Mary Whiddon was married in the church. As her guests gathered in front of the building to cheer the new bride and groom, she was gunned down when she walked out the door. The killer was a jealous suitor whose proposals she had refused. The event was fictionalized in R. D. Blackmore's classic *Lorna Doone.* Poor Mary is buried in the church's graveyard. The inscription on her gravestone reads BEHOLD A MATRON, YET A MAID. By tradition, every bride married in the church leaves a flower on her tombstone.

the shape of the building was changed, but it's still an extraordinary structure, and the grounds are lovely and peaceful, with orchards and, in the spring, bluebell forests. The house has a mixture of rooms furnished in period style and interactive galleries telling the tale of the building and of the men who lived there.

Buckland Abbey, Yelverton. ☎ **01822/853607.** www.nationaltrust.org.uk. Admission £9 adults, £5 children 16 and under, £23 family ticket. Mid-Mar–Oct daily 10:30am–5:30pm; Nov Fri–Sun 11am–4:30pm; Dec–early Mar 11am–4:30pm. Last admission 45 min. before closing. The house is 3 miles west of Yelverton off the A386; follow signs.

Castle Drogo ★ ☺ CASTLE   This massive granite castle, in the hamlet of Drew-steignton, 17 miles west of Exeter, might look medieval, but it was really a flight of fancy, designed and built between 1910 and 1930. Constructed of granite, and castel-lated and turreted like a fortress, the castle occupies a bleak but dramatic position high above the River Teign, with views sweeping out over the gloomy moors.

The castle has always been—and is still—a family home, but it's open to guided tours, which include a series of formal rooms done up in Edwardian style. In many ways, the secluded gardens are more strikingly beautiful than the house. They include a sunken lawn enclosed by raised walkways, a circular croquet lawn (you can rent a croquet set to play here), shaped yew hedges, and a children's playroom.

Drewsteignton, 4 miles northeast of Chagford and 6 miles south of the Exeter-Okehampton Rd. (A30). ☎ **01647/433306.** www.nationaltrust.org.uk. Admission to castle and grounds £8.80 adults, £4 children 16 and under, £22 families; grounds only £5 adults, £3 children. House: Mar–Oct daily 11am–5pm; Nov Sat–Sun 11am–4:30pm; Dec 1–23 daily 11am–4pm; closed Dec 24–Feb 28. Grounds: Mar–Oct daily 9am–5:30pm; Nov–Dec 23 daily 11am–5pm; Jan–Feb daily 11am–4pm; closed Dec 24–31. Take the A30 and follow the signs.

Where to Eat & Stay
VERY EXPENSIVE

Bovey Castle ★★★ ☺   Less a castle than a country manor house, Bovey is a grand old pile. Built in 1907, it sprawls across 162 hectares (400 acres) of rolling fields, waterland, and pasture. Guests can amuse themselves with trout fishing and archery, as well as the usual golf (there's an 18-hole, championship course). You can learn to be a country lord here (they offer classes in the making of cider and sloe gin) or lady of leisure (there's an elegant spa). There is even a falconry display after break-fast. The spacious bedrooms are tastefully decorated with country prints, traditional furniture, and comfortable beds. There are 14 self-catering lodges on the grounds, which offer more space and privacy. You can choose from three restaurants and a bar, which is just as well as the town of North Bovey is a 20-minute walk away, through meadows and across streams.

North Bovey, Devon TQ13 8RE. www.boveycastle.com. ☎ **01647/445000.** Fax 01647/445020. 63 units. £220–£345 double; £515–£615 suite. AE, MC, V. Rates include English breakfast. **Amenities:** Restaurant; bar; archery center; children's farm; equestrian center; exercise room; falconry; fly-fishing; 18-hole golf course; movie theatre; 2 pools (1 indoor, 1 outdoor); room service; spa; 2 outdoor tennis courts. *In room:* A/C, TV, hair dryer, minibar, Wi-Fi (free).

Gidleigh Park Hotel ★★★   This gorgeous hotel, surrounded by impeccable gardens and run with grace and style, has been lavished with awards over the years, and for good reason—it's simply extraordinary. Amid 22 hectares (54 acres) of private forest and flowers, the sprawling Arts and Crafts mansion has panoramic vistas of the surrounding hills. Guest rooms are spacious and tastefully decorated in tones of cream and ivory; much of the furniture was handmade. Bathrooms are big, modern, and elegant; beds are orthopedic and comfortable. The hotel restaurant—headed by double-Michelin-starred chef Michael Caines—is revered by food critics throughout the nation. In fact, many people stay here primarily for the food. The spa treatments, the tennis courts, and the miles of grounds on which to wander make this a perfect country retreat.

Gidleigh Park (2 miles outside town), Chagford, Devon TQ13 8HH. www.gidleigh.com. ℂ **01647/432367.** Fax 01647/432574. 24 units, 1 cottage. £320–£530 double; £1,175 suite. Rates include English breakfast, morning tea, and dinner. AE, MC, V. **Amenities:** Restaurant; bar; babysitting; bowling green; croquet lawn; golf course; putting green; spa treatments; tennis court. *In room:* TV, hair dryer, Wi-Fi (free).

INEXPENSIVE

Easton Court Bed & Breakfast ★   Just outside Chagford, this pleasant guesthouse amid lush gardens and paddocks is a favorite of the literati and theatre folk. Evelyn Waugh lived here while writing *Brideshead Revisited,* and the atmosphere is still that of a relaxed English country cottage. Guest rooms are snug and comfortable, decorated in subtle shades of cream and white; many have brass beds and William Morris prints. All have peaceful countryside views. The owners are friendly, and breakfast is hearty.

Easton Cross, Chagford, Devon TQ13 8JL. www.easton.co.uk. ℂ **01647/433469.** 5 units. £70–£75 double. Rates include English breakfast. MC, V. No children 10 and under. Take the A382 1½ miles northeast of Chagford. **Amenities:** Guest lounge. *In room:* TV, CD player, hair dryer.

Globe Inn   This friendly pub restaurant on Chagford's main street has looked out for wayfarers since the 16th century. The pub is traditional, with dark wood paneling and floors and big fireplaces. Locals and visitors meet here for drinks and traditional English cuisine. The guestrooms upstairs are comfortable and modern, with plenty of space.

High Street, Chagford, Devon TQ13 8AJ. www.globeinnchagford.co.uk. ℂ **01647/433-485.** 7 units. £70–£90 double. Rates include English breakfast. MC, V. **Amenities:** Pub/restaurant. *In room:* TV, hair dryer, free Wi-Fi.

Whiddons ENGLISH TEA   At teatime, drop in at Whiddons, a tea shop in a 16th-century thatched cottage. You can sip your Earl Grey or English Breakfast tea while nibbling freshly baked scones and delicate cucumber sandwiches. It makes a great break from sightseeing.

On the High St., Chagford. ℂ **01647/433-406.** Sandwiches/scones £4–£8. MC. V. Mon–Sat 9am–4pm.

OTHER TOWNS IN DARTMOOR

Most travelers enter the moors through **Oakehampton,** a pleasant enough workaday town right at the edge of Dartmoor. It has a handful of restaurants and a gas/petrol station (rare in the moors—fuel up first), so you're likely to run into other visitors if you stop in.

A few miles inside the moor on the A382, the peaceful market town of **Moreton-hampstead** is perched on a hillside, surrounded by moorland. Along with little tea shops and pubs, it contains rare 17th-century colonnaded almshouses and an old Market Cross, which for hundreds of years has marked the site of the local market, still held here on Fridays and Saturdays.

From Moretonhampstead, you can head 6 miles down the winding narrow B3212 to the little village of **Postbridge,** which has a rare, ancient "clapper" bridge. Clapper bridges were made by supporting large flat slabs of granite (some weighing several tons) on sturdy stone piers. (The word "clapper" is believed to be a corruption of the

"My Dear Mother"

Down a winding country road near Widecombe-in-the-Moor, the tiny village of Buckland-in-the-Moor, with its chocolate-box thatched-roof cottages and fluffy Dartmoor ponies, has a unique church. Built in the 13th century of locally quarried stone, **St. Peter's Church** has a distinctively modern clock on its tower, which denotes the hours with letters instead of numbers. The letters, which may at first seem to be in no particular order, actually spell out My Dear Mother. The clock was donated in 1931 by a parishioner whose mother had recently died, and he had it made to memorialize her.

Inside, the ancient church has wonderfully preserved carving work and an extraordinarily rare medieval rood screen with much of its original painting. The screen shows a variety of religious figures believed to include the Archangel Gabriel, the Virgin Mary, and St. Anne, among others. Most such screens were destroyed when the Catholic church was suppressed in England, and some of the paintings here have been defaced. But what survives gives you a wonderful view of how medieval English churches might have once looked.

Anglo-Saxon word *cleaca,* which meant "stepping stones.") Historians believe this particular bridge was built in early medieval times to speed the movement of tin across the moor by pack horse.

The much-visited Dartmoor village of **Widecombe-in-the-Moor,** 7 miles northeast of Moretonhampstead, is worth visiting for both its overall prettiness and its 14th-century church (the church of St. Pancras). You can have a drink in one of its tea shops. On a sunny day, it's a good spot for a picnic.

The highest town in all the moors is **Princetown** (435m/1,427 ft.; it's on the B3212). It's a favorite starting point for hill walkers striking out across the moors, but it's a gloomy old place. The looming form of Dartmoor Prison dominates it, and the weather seems always to be gray. The prison was built in 1809 to house American and French prisoners of war. For the curious, there's a **prison museum** (www.dartmoor. pison.co.uk) that tells the tale of the place and sells crafts made by the inmates.

Exploring the Moors on Foot & Horseback

Dartmoor is notoriously wild and challenging for hikers and cyclists, but thousands of hardy folk traverse it every year. It is crisscrossed with about 500 miles of trails covering sometimes rough terrain. Its bogs pose a challenge for those who off-road, and the weather here can be downright dangerous, with sudden thick fogs and high winds. In short, feel free to explore, but be prepared with good hiking boots, a compass, plenty of water, and proper maps. Or, in the interest of safety, take a guided walk.

The **Dartmoor National Park Authority (DNPA)** runs **guided walks** of varying difficulty, ranging from 1½ to 6 hours and treks of some 9 to 12 miles. Details are available from the **High Moorland Visitor Centre,** Tavistock Road, Princetown (✆ **01822/890414;** www.dartmoor-npa.gov.uk). Guided tours cost £3 for a 2-hour walk, £5 for a 3-hour walk, £6.50 for a 4-hour walk, and £8 for a 6-hour walk. These prices are subsidized by the National Park services.

Local stables offer day treks on horseback across the moors at the cost of around £25 per hour with an experienced guide. Try **Skaigh Stables,** at Belstone (✆ **01837/840917;** www.skaighstables.co.uk), just off the A30 Exeter-Okehampton road. Their treks traverse dramatic moorland and take in amazing views. Morning and afternoon rides are offered from mid-April until the end of September, with 2-hour rides from £36 per person. Another option is the **Doone Valley Stables,** Hallslake, Lynton (✆ **01598/741234;** www.doonevalleytrekking.co.uk), which offers guided treks through breathtaking countryside.

Where to Eat & Stay

Castle Inn   A good stopover on the road between Okehampton and Tavistock, this inn dates from the 12th century. With its pink facade and row of rose trellises, it is the hub of the village. The owners have maintained the character of the roomy old rustic lounge. The menu is stocked with quality pub food—grilled fish, sausages and mash, meat pies, and steaks—and it's well priced. Bedrooms are attractively furnished, some with mahogany and Victorian pieces. It's a friendly, peaceful place to spend the night or stop for dinner.

Lydford, near Okehampton (1 mile off the A386), Devon EX20 4BH. www.castleinndartmoor.co.uk. ✆ **01822/820241.** Fax 01822/820454. 8 units. £65–£90 double. MC, V. **Amenities:** Restaurant; bar. *In room:* TV, Wi-Fi (free).

Cherrybrook Hotel   This family-run guesthouse in the center of the Dartmoor National Park sits inside a rugged 200-year-old farmhouse perched high on a hill overlooking the moors. The guest lounge and bar, with their beamed ceilings and slate floors, are meeting places where travelers share their adventures. The rooms were renovated in 2009, and are pleasantly done up in neutral tones with pine furniture and colorful throw pillows. Bathrooms contain power showers providing plentiful hot water. The hotel's perch on a high moor makes it popular with hikers and cyclists. This is a dog-friendly hotel, and because the owners have dogs too, it's best for dog-friendly guests.

On the B3212, between Postbridge and Two Bridges, Yelverton, Devon PL20 6SP. www.thecherrybrook. co.uk. ✆/fax **01822/880260.** 7 units. £79–£90 double. Rates include English breakfast. MC, V. Closed Dec 22–Jan 2. **Amenities:** Restaurant; bar; lounge. *In room:* TV, hair dryer, Wi-Fi (free).

Horn of Plenty Hotel ★   In a gracious, vine-covered Regency house set amid acres of lush gardens, this elegant hotel and restaurant is popular with travelers and food critics alike. The decor is tasteful and romantic, with chenille-covered sofas and peaceful views of green heather-covered hills. Guest rooms are done up in soothing tones of cream or mauve, with polished wood floors, big comfortable beds, and thick curtains. Lunch and dinner in the sunny dining room are events: The cooking is inventive, with an emphasis on fresh, local meats and produce. Later, you can have a drink on the terrace before wandering up to your welcoming room.

Gulworthy, Tavistock, Devon PL19 8JD. www.thehornofplenty.co.uk. ✆ **01822/832528.** 10 units. £160–£250 double. Rates include English breakfast. Fixed-price 3-course lunch £25; fixed-price 3-course dinner £48. AE, MC, V. **Amenities:** Restaurant; bar. *In room:* TV/DVD, hair dryer.

Lewtrenchard Manor   This 17th-century Jacobean house on the northwest edge of Dartmoor sits almost completely alone in a valley. The craggy stone building has many original features, including oak paneling, leaded windows, and beamed ceilings. Its extensive grounds wander through gardens, and across streams and ponds. The walled garden was recently restored, and the hotel's vegetables are grown there. The rooms in the oldest part of the building are the most interesting, with paneled walls and antiques. Those in the newer parts of the building are just as pleasant, though they're more contemporary in feel.

Lewdown, Devon EX20 4PN. www.lewtrenchard.co.uk. (C) **01566/783222.** Fax 01566/783332. 14 units. £135–£340 double; £280–£365 suite. Rates include English breakfast. 2-night minimum stay on weekends. AE, DC, MC, V. **Amenities:** Restaurant; bar; room service. *In room:* TV, hair dryer.

TORQUAY & PAIGNTON ★

223 miles SW of London; 23 miles S of Exeter

Hugely popular with British families escaping to the seaside during school breaks, the town of **Torquay** is a rambling **Victorian relic,** with its tall, 19th-century villas perched regally at the edge of the sea. The area around Torquay is known as Torbay, and includes the charming seaside community of **Paignton** and the small fishing port of Brixham. Their location smack dab in the middle of 22 miles of dramatic coastline with miles of good **beaches** within easy reach makes this a handy place to base yourself while you're exploring coastal Devon. Surfers bob on the waves at all times of the year, and the restaurants, bars, and pubs are packed with the young, sand-covered set. In some ways, it's a traditional seaside town with game arcades, fish-and-chips stands, and candy stalls, but its increasing wealth also means that there's a hip undercurrent as well, bringing in better restaurants and shops.

Essentials

GETTING THERE   First Great Western trains run throughout the day from London's Paddington Station to Torquay's station in the town center on the seafront, costing around £74 for a round-trip. The trip takes 2½ hours. For rail information, call (C) **0845/7484950** or visit **www.nationalrail.co.uk**.

Buses from London's Victoria Coach Station leave every 2 hours during the day for the 5-hour trip to Torquay.

If you're driving from Exeter, head west on the A38, veering south at the junction with the A380.

VISITOR INFORMATION   The **Tourist Information Centre** is at Vaughan Parade ((C) **01803/211-2111;** www.englishriviera.co.uk). It's open June through September, Monday to Saturday 9:30am to 5:30pm and Sunday 10am to 4pm, and October through May, Monday to Saturday 9:30am to 5pm.

> ### Pretty Paignton
>
> On the western side of Torquay, the seaside community of Paignton is a great place to spend a sunny afternoon. It still retains much of its original Victorian seafront, including a promenade and pier, and the beach is brightened by traditional English painted beach huts, like rows of little houses in miniature.

Exploring the Area

For most visitors, Torquay's main draw can be summed up in one word: Beaches. Within a few miles of the town center there are 20 beaches upon which you can lounge. Inspired by this, the local tourism board dubbed the area the "English Riviera," and you'll see those optimistic words everywhere you go. "Riviera" is certainly a stretch, but some of the beaches are very good: Some are sandy while others are pebble-covered, and many are at the base of dramatic cliffs.

Babbacombe Beach BEACH   Arguably the locals' favorite beach, Babbacombe stretches out toward the sea beneath red cliffs that soar 75m (240 ft.) above it. You can rent a beach lounger, or just stretch out on the sand, taking in the view. A funicular chugs up the steep cliffs—the view from the top is endless.

Seafront, Babbacombe, Torquay. Free admission.

Babbacombe Model Village ☺ OFFBEAT SITE   This knee-high world recreates much of England in miniature—towns, countryside, farms, parts of London, and the rail system are all recreated across 1,6 hectares (4 acres) of charming weirdness. Children adore it, the lights work (the mini-Piccadilly Circus is particularly amazing), the trains chug by and, frankly, it is all just rather strange.

Hampton Ave., Babbacombe, Torquay. ✆ **01803/315315.** www.babbacombemodelvillage.co.uk. Admission £8 adults; £5.50 children 3-14. Year-round daily 10am-dusk.

Kents Cavern ☺ HISTORIC SITE   A fun place to take the kids and an archeological site of genuine scientific interest, this cave system was created around 2 million years ago and was occupied for hundreds of years by early species. In 2009, teeth and bones from Ice Age animals including hyenas, wooly rhinos, and deer were discovered during a dig in the cave. Tours wander through caverns and caves where the early creatures lived; guides are great with children.

89 Ilsham Rd, Torquay. ✆ **01803/215135.** www.kentscavern.co.uk. Admission £9 adults; £8 children 3-15. Tours hourly in the summer 11am-4:30pm, 4 times daily in the winter.

Oldway Mansion ARCHITECTURE   This lavish, Palladian mansion offers a window into the glory of England's Gilded Age. Built in 1874 by Isaac Merritt Singer, founder of the sewing-machine empire, the building is a symphony of excess. The grand staircase is made of marble, and the balusters are made of bronze. The ceiling is covered in an ornate painting based on a design from the Palace of Versailles. A first-floor gallery, a reproduction of the Hall of Mirrors in Versailles, leads into a gilded ballroom. The house is surrounded by 7 hectares (17 acres) of Italian gardens. Singer's son, Paris, famously had a love affair with the dancer Isadora Duncan, who used Oldway as both rehearsal space and performance venue.

Torbay Rd., Preston, near Paignton. ✆ **01803/207933.** Free admission. Year-round Mon-Fri 9am-5:30pm.

Where to Eat

The Boathouse Bar & Grill STEAKS & SEAFOOD   It's worth coming to this seafront restaurant in the Paignton area of Torquay for the view alone. From your table on the terrace you can see clearly across the bay to the neighboring town of Brixham. This is a relaxed place, popular with surfers and locals, and the menu has a something-for-everyone approach with pizzas, burgers, steaks, and fresh local fish. You can feast on the Boathouse surf 'n'turf (steak and shrimp), or try a local rib-eye steak with grilled tomatoes, mushrooms, and french fries. Start with nachos or dough balls while you sip a cocktail from the busy bar and enjoy the view.

Marine Drive, Paignton. ✆ **01803/665066.** www.boathousebar.co.uk. Reservations recommended. Main courses £8-£12. MC, V. Daily noon-2pm and 6:30-11pm.

The Elephant ★★ MODERN BRITISH   With a perfect location on Torquay's seafront, this Michelin-starred restaurant is considered by many foodies to be Torquay's best gourmet eatery. The restaurant is essentially divided into two: Upstairs is a formal fine-dining option dubbed The Room, while downstairs is a more laid-back

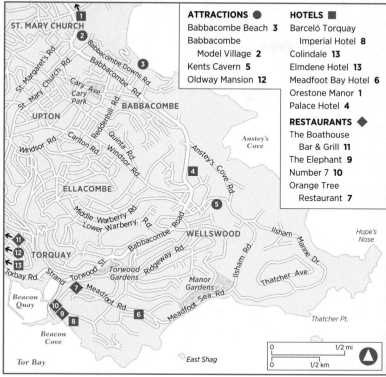

Torquay

ATTRACTIONS ●
Babbacombe Beach **3**
Babbacombe
  Model Village **2**
Kents Cavern **5**
Oldway Mansion **12**

HOTELS ■
Barceló Torquay
  Imperial Hotel **8**
Colindale **13**
Elmdene Hotel **13**
Meadfoot Bay Hotel **6**
Orestone Manor **1**
Palace Hotel **4**

RESTAURANTS ◆
The Boathouse
  Bar & Grill **11**
The Elephant **9**
Number 7 **10**
Orange Tree
  Restaurant **7**

(cheaper) brasserie. Both specialize in using the local seafood, fresh off the docks, along with local meats and produce grown in the area, and both have a French-influenced cooking style. In the brasserie, dishes include options like squid with chorizo and chili marmalade, and breast of local duck with chervil root and wild mushrooms. In The Room, you could start with local scallops on cabbage and lemon risotto, and then move on to roasted halibut with lobster royal and celeriac turnovers.

3–4 Beacon Terrace, Torquay. ℂ **01803/200044.** www.elephantrestaurant.co.uk. Reservations required. Brasserie: Main courses £14–£19. The Room: Set menu £55. AE, MC, V. Brasserie: Tues–Sat noon–2pm and 6:30–9pm. The Room: Tues–Sat 7–9:30pm.

Number 7 SEAFOOD   This bustling seafood bistro in the harbor is packed every night, and the main draw is the kitchen's talent for cooking fresh local fish. In a small, crowded dining room you can try fish fresh off the boat, including lemon sole, stuffed with prawns and baked in cheese and wine. Or try scallops simmered with mushrooms, vermouth, and lemon. Eating here can be a bit hectic, but the food makes it worth it—and the prices are reasonable.

Beacon Terrace, Torquay. ℂ **01803/295055.** www.no7-fish.com. Reservations necessary. Main courses £11–£20. MC, V. Lunch Wed–Sat noon–2pm, dinner daily 6:30–11pm.

Orange Tree Restaurant ★ MODERN BRITISH   Set back from the seafront near Torquay Harbour, this restaurant has character, atmosphere, and good food. The chefs create innovative, French-influenced dishes and change the menus seasonally. Starters can include options like pan-fried red mullet with black-olive salsa, or Brixham crab bisque with scallops. Main courses might feature pan-seared sea bass with toasted almonds and capers, or local lamb marinated in garden herbs and served with rosemary *jus*. The atmosphere here is friendly and relaxed, and the food can be exceptional.

14–16 Parkhill Rd., Torquay. ✆ **01803/213936.** www.orangetreerestaurant.co.uk. Reservations required. Main courses £15–£22. MC, V. Mon–Sat 7–9:30pm.

Entertainment & Nightlife

Torquay's nightlife is geared rather strongly at the young and pretty, and many of the bars and clubs are clustered around Babbacombe Road near the seafront. Among these are **Barcode,** Palk Street, Torquay (✆ **01803/200110**), a trendy place with big, comfortable chairs and even bigger cocktails. The food on offer isn't bad either—the music is turned up later in the evening, but early on you can just about hold a conversation. **Bohemia,** 39–41 Torwood Street, Torquay (✆ **01803/292079;** www.clairesnightclub.co.uk), packs out with 20-somethings for Thursday-to-Sunday house music. The cover varies from £3 to £20. If you prefer a relaxing pub, try **Hole in the Wall,** 6 Park Lane, Torquay (✆ **01803/200755**), an ancient inn, with beamed ceilings and cobbled floors, that claims to be the oldest in town. They pour a mean pint.

Torquay is very popular with young people on holiday, so after about 10:30pm in the summer, and on weekend nights the rest of the year, the town can seem overrun by drunken young people. It can be genuinely unpleasant to walk down Babbacombe Road at that time, and can even feel threatening. At that time of day, you may want to avoid the areas where most bars are located, or take a taxi.

Where to Stay
EXPENSIVE

Barceló Torquay Imperial Hotel ☺   A faded local grande dame, this big Victorian hotel was all the rage in 1866 when it first opened. It's still one of the city's best-known hotels, sitting amid acres of flourishing gardens and looking out over rocky cliffs to the Channel. The lobby area is extraordinary, with soaring ceilings and marble floors. The swimming pools and "kids club" mean it's good for families traveling with children. Guest rooms are hit or miss, though. Standard rooms are plain and a bit disappointing, with cream walls and cheap-looking furniture, while deluxe rooms have an old-fashioned elegance, with flowered curtains and bedspreads. Some rooms have balconies and sweeping sea views. Many rooms have been renovated, and are somewhat more contemporary, while others haven't been so fortunate. The Regatta restaurant has views of the waterfront, and makes a great spot for lunch.

Park Hill Rd., Torquay, Devon TQ1 2DG. www.barcelo-hotels.co.uk. ✆ **01803/294301.** Fax 01803/298293. 169 units. £223–£273 double. Rates include English breakfast. AE, MC, V.

A Hotel by Any Other Name

Agatha Christie frequently used Torquay's Imperial Hotel as a setting in her books, but she never identified it by its real name. She called it the Esplanade in *The Rajah's Emerald,* the Castle in *Partners in Crime,* and the Majestic in *Peril at End House.*

Parking £15. **Amenities:** Restaurant; bar; health club; 2 heated pools (indoor, outdoor); room service; sauna; solarium; spa; squash courts; steam room; tennis courts. *In room:* TV, hair dryer, minibar, Wi-Fi (£14 per day).

Orestone Manor ★   A few miles outside Torquay in the village of Madencombe, Orestone Manor is in a gabled Victorian house surrounded by colorful gardens. The lounge exudes old-fashioned grandeur, but many of the guest rooms have been decorated in contemporary style. The best are spacious and sunny with waxed wood floors, and have a sitting area with sofas and chairs. Rooms in the gables are quite small and a bit of a climb, but these have the best views. The restaurant is highly rated for its use of fresh local produce and seafood, and on sunny days you can breakfast on the terrace. The only drawback is that prices are rather high for what's on offer.

Rockhouse Lane, Maidencombe, Torquay, Devon TQ1 4SX. www.orestonemanor.com. © **01803/328098.** Fax 01803/328316. 12 units. £150–£225 double. Rates include English breakfast. AE, MC, V. Free parking. Closed 2 weeks in Jan. Drive 3½ miles north of Torquay on the A379. **Amenities:** Restaurant; bar; babysitting; outdoor pool; room service. *In room:* TV, hair dryer, Wi-Fi (free).

Palace Hotel   From the outside, this elegant hotel (built in the 1920s) is wedding cake pretty in creamy white and sky blue. It stands poised amid glorious terraced gardens, as if F. Scott Fitzgerald were going to walk by at any moment in search of a cocktail. Unfortunately, the illusion ends when you walk in the door. Like so many of these grand old hotels, this one feels tattered around the edges. Guest rooms are old fashioned, with dark wood furniture and tired carpets. Mattresses can be lumpy and tabletops water-marked. The lounges and restaurants are better maintained, but staff seem hapless, and you may wait some time for that cup of tea. Unless you get a steep discount or somebody else is paying, it's not really worth the high price charged.

Babbacombe Rd., Babbacombe, Torquay, Devon TQ1 3TG. www.palacetorquay.com. © **01803/200200.** Fax 01803/299899. 141 units. £140–£230 double; £270–£310 suite. Rates include English breakfast. AE, DC, MC, V. Free parking. Bus: 32. Driving from the town center, take the B3199 east. **Amenities:** Restaurant; 2 bars; babysitting; croquet; exercise room; 9-hole golf course & putting green; 2 pools (1 indoor, 1 outdoor); room service; sauna; 2 squash courts; 6 tennis courts. *In room:* TV, hair dryer, minibar.

MODERATE

Meadfoot Bay Hotel   This immaculate guesthouse was created from a Victorian family residence, just 5 minutes' walk uphill from the seafront. Guest rooms are decorated in contemporary style, with off-white walls and white comforters, and beds are wrapped in Frette linens. Bright throws, cushions, and art provide splashes of color. Bathrooms are small but modern. Some rooms have direct access to the sunny garden, while others have a balcony. When they arrive, guests are welcomed with a drink from the bar, or a cup of tea, but prices are still a little high for what's offered here.

Meadfoot Sea Rd., Torquay, Devon TQ1 2LQ. www.meadfoot.com. © **01803/294722.** 19 units. £90–£150 double. Rates include breakfast. MC, V. No children under 14. **Amenities:** Bar. *In room:* TV/DVD, hair dryer, Wi-Fi (free).

INEXPENSIVE

Colindale ★ 🏃   This rambling Victorian guesthouse has a welcoming, lived-in look—the lounge has soft sofas you can sink into, and a fire crackles comfortingly in the old stone fireplace on cold days. Its location is handy: It's a 5-minute walk from Corbyn Beach and even closer to the railway station. Rooms are attractive, with good fabrics, comfortable beds, and cheerful decor—colors vary from room to room. In a lovely touch, guests can borrow "honesty books" from the hotel's well-stocked shelves. Breakfasts—hot or continental—are excellent. Colindale offers good value for the price.

20 Rathmore Rd., Chelston, Torquay, Devon TQ2 6NY. www.colindalehotel.co.uk. ✆ **01803/293947.** 8 units. £60–£75 double. Rates include English breakfast. MC, V. Free parking. No children 10 and under. **Amenities:** Bar; breakfast room; TV lounge. *In room:* TV, hair dryer, Wi-Fi (free).

Elmdene Hotel ★ 🛍 This well-run B&B near the seafront has legions of fans who visit it over and over for the good service, quiet, attractive guest rooms, and friendly vibe. A short walk from shops, sights, and the train station, it sits on a leafy street just far enough away from the hustle and bustle to ensure peace. Rooms are spacious and decorated with a masculine touch, in tones of maroon and white or cream and taupe. Bathrooms are tiny but have all you need. There's a small bar downstairs where you can have an evening cocktail—in the summer you can drink it in the garden. If you don't feel like going out to eat, light meals are also available. Breakfasts include healthful yogurts and cereals as well as eggs and bacon. The owners know everything about the town and will happily point you in the right direction.

Rathmore Rd., Torquay, Devon TQ2 6NZ. www.elmdenehotel.co.uk. ✆/fax **01803/294940.** 8 units. £56–£74 double. Rates include breakfast. MC, V. Free parking. **Amenities:** Bar. *In room:* TV, hair dryer, no phone, Wi-Fi (free).

TOTNES ★

224 miles SW of London; 12 miles NW of Dartmouth

A hilly castle town on the banks of the River Dart, Totnes rests quietly in the past. This is a charming place where you always seem to be walking either up or down a steep hill. Its cobbled streets are lined with **Elizabethan** and **Tudor buildings,** as well as one of the original city gates through which visitors have passed since the Middle Ages. The town centers on the dramatic ruins of a **Norman castle,** an ancient guildhall, and the 15th-century **Church of St. Mary.**

Essentials

GETTING THERE   First Great Western trains travel hourly to Totnes from London's Paddington Station; the trip takes 2¾ hours, costing around £74 for a round-trip.

If you're driving from Torquay, head west on the A385.

Between Easter and October, you can travel between Totnes and Dartmouth by boat. Contact **Dartmouth River Boats,** 5 Lower Street, Dartmouth (✆ **01803/555872;** www.dartmouthrailriver.co.uk). Round-trip tickets cost £14.

VISITOR INFORMATION   The **Tourist Information Centre** is at the Town Mill, Coronation Road (✆ **01803/863168;** www.totnesinformation.co.uk). It's open April through October, Monday to Friday 9:30am to 5pm, Saturday 10am to 4pm; November through March it's open Monday to Friday 10am to 4pm and Saturday 10am to 1pm.

Exploring the Area

Elizabethan Museum MUSEUM   In a 16th-century house so authentic it's a wee bit crooked, this museum demonstrates what the life of a wealthy merchant was like in those times. There's a display of furniture, costumes, documents, and farm implements.

70 Fore St. ✆ **01803/863821.** www.devonmuseums.net. Admission £2 adults, £1.50 seniors, £.75 children 3–13. Mon–Fri 10:30am–5pm. Closed Nov–mid-Mar.

Totnes Castle CASTLE   Crowning the hilltop at the northern end of High Street, this well-preserved castle keep is all that's left of a castle built by the Normans, shortly after the conquest of England in 1066, to subdue and dominate what was, until then, a Saxon town. It's a fine example of motte-and-bailey construction (in which the central castle was built on a steep, man-made hill surrounded by a high stone wall). Climb to the top of the castle's hill for sweeping views of the town and surrounding countryside.

Castle St. ✆ **01803/864406.** www.englishheritage.org.uk. Admission £3.40 adults, £3.10 students and seniors, £2 children 3–13. Apr–June and Sept daily 10am–5pm; July–Aug daily 10am–6pm; Oct daily 10am–4pm. Closed Nov–Mar.

Totnes Guildhall MUSEUM   In many ways the symbol of Totnes, this admirable old building was originally constructed as a priory (monastery) in 1553. Today it's a museum with an old gaol (jail) and the table Oliver Cromwell used to sign documents during his visit to Totnes in 1646.

Ramparts Walk. ✆ **01803/862147.** www.totnestowncouncil.gov.uk. Admission £1.35 adults, £.30 children 3–13. Mon–Fri 10:30am–4:30pm.

Where to Eat & Stay

Greys Dining Room ★★ BRITISH/ENGLISH TEA   A Devon institution, Greys is beloved for its reverence for teatime, and rightly so. It serves fine breakfasts and lunches as well, but each afternoon it comes into its own, setting out the silver and china to welcome you into another era, where dining rooms are paneled in oak and filled with antiques. You can choose from 40 different teas, as well as from a dazzling selection of freshly made cakes and scones with decadent clotted cream.

96 High St., Totnes. ✆ **01803/866369.** Main courses £5–£10. MC, V. Wed–Sat 10am–5pm.

Orchard House ★ 🍴   This B&B in an old stone farmhouse a few miles outside Totnes is a real find for those who want to spend some time in the peaceful countryside. Set amid an apple cider orchard, it's a relaxing place and the owners do all they can to ensure that you feel at home. Guest rooms have brass or pine beds, creamy walls, and dark wood wardrobes, and each unit has a sweeping view of green lawns, pastures, and gardens. The well-equipped rooms include little refrigerators stocked with fresh milk and water. Breakfasts are made with local eggs and meats.

Horner, Halwell (near Totnes), Devon TQ9 7LB. www.orchard-house-halwell.co.uk. ✆ **01548/821448.** 3 units. £55–£60 double. Rates include breakfast. No credit cards. Closed Nov–Feb. *In room:* TV/DVD, hair dryer, MP3 docking station, no phone, Wi-Fi (free).

Royal Seven Stars Hotel   A former coaching inn in the center of Totnes, this hotel dates from 1660 and overlooks a square in the town center, near the banks of the River Dart. The interior courtyard, once used for horses and carriages, is now enclosed in glass and decorated with antiques and paintings, making an inviting entrance to the inn. Guest rooms are modern and spacious, nicely decorated with white walls and red accents (throws, cushions, splashes of wallpaper). Downstairs, the handy restaurant and pub mean you don't have to go out if you don't want to; this is a good place for dinner whether or not you're spending the night here.

The Plains, Totnes, Devon TQ9 5DD. www.royalsevenstars.co.uk. ✆ **01803/862125.** Fax 01803/867925. 16 units. £119–£159 double. Rates include English breakfast. AE, MC, V. **Amenities:** Restaurant; bar; room service. *In room:* TV, hair dryer, Wi-Fi (free).

9

DEVON | Totnes

Butterflies, exotic birds, and adorable otters all frolic happily in the Disney-like environment of the **Buckfast Butterflies & Dartmoor Otter Sanctuary** at the edge of Dartmoor. The sanctuary not only provides safe haven for all its creatures, but also nurses wounded otters back to health. Human guests are welcome but dogs are forbidden (otters hate them). The sanctuary is in the town of Buckfastleigh (© **01364/642916;** www.ottersandbutterflies.co. uk), and is open from April to October daily 10am to 5:30pm. Admission is £5 for adults, £2.50 for children 3 to 15.

DARTMOUTH ★

236 miles SW of London; 35 miles S of Exeter

With its houses stacked on the side of a steep hill like toy pieces in some bizarre game of balance, Dartmouth is an alluring, historic seaside town. This ancient seaport at the mouth of the River Dart has an esteemed maritime history. This was where knights set out for the Crusades in the 12th century, and it was the home of the Royal Navy for so long that Warfleet Creek at the edge of town is believed to have been so named in honor of the many fleets that gathered in the harbor nearby before setting off for battle. Given that military history, it's no surprise that the river is flanked by two once-heavily fortified castles—**Dartmouth Castle** and **Kingswear Castle.** Wonderfully, much survives of this town's long history—streets are lined with houses dating to Tudor and Elizabethan times, and even more from the 18th and 19th centuries.

Essentials

GETTING THERE   Dartmouth is not easily reached by public transportation. Cross-Country trains run to Totnes and Paignton where you can catch buses that run about once an hour to Dartmouth. Call © **0870/6082608** or visit **www.stagecoachbus. com** for schedules.

If you're driving, at Totnes turn onto the A381 and follow signs for Dartmouth. There's only one parking lot in town, and it can get full in the summer. If that happens, park at the edge of town by the leisure center, in the park-and-ride lot on the A3122—signs will direct you there.

You can also travel between Totnes and Dartmouth by boat from Easter to October on **Dartmouth River Boats,** 5 Lower Street, Dartmouth (© **01803/555872;** www.dartmouthrailriver.co.uk). A round-trip journey costs £14.

VISITOR INFORMATION   The **Tourist Information Centre** is at the Engine House, Mayors Avenue (© **01803/834224;** www.discoverdartmouth.com). It's open April through October, Monday to Saturday 9:30am to 5:30pm and Sunday 10am to 2pm; in the off season, hours are Monday to Saturday 9:30am to 4:30pm.

Exploring the Area

Dartmouth is a gorgeous town just to wander in. It does have sights worth seeing, but the main attraction is the town itself, with its watercolor Victorian houses stacked above one another on the steep hill. While you're wandering, pop into the local church, **St. Petrox,** on Castle Road, a 17th-century stone structure with an ivy-draped graveyard where the tombstones evoke the sorrows of Dartmouth's maritime past. The church is open daily from 7am to dusk.

It's also worth walking along the waterfront to **Bayard's Cove,** near the end of Lower Street. One of Dartmouth's oldest surviving neighborhoods, its cobbled streets and half-timbered buildings are wonderfully complete. It prospered in the 1600s thanks to its ship-repair services. In 1620, this is where the Pilgrims' historic ships, the *Speedwell* and the *Mayflower,* were repaired.

You can explore the area by boat as well. **Dartmouth River Boats,** 5 Lower Street, Dartmouth (⟨ **01803/555872;** www.dartmouthrailriver.co.uk), ply the waters around the town. Schedules vary according to the seasons. For tickets and information, go to the kiosk at the Dartmouth Embankment, or check the website. Prices range from £10 to £20 for adults.

Dartmouth Castle CASTLE   Standing ruggedly on the shore at the edge of Dartmouth, this castle looks no worse for wear after 600 years. Originally built during the 15th century as fortified defense against French invasion, it was later outfitted with artillery and employed by the Victorians as a coastal defense station. A tour of its bulky ramparts and somber interiors provides insight into the changing nature of warfare through the centuries, and offers sweeping views of the surrounding coast and flatlands.

Castle Rd. (½ mile south of the town center). ⟨ **01803/833588.** www.english-heritage.org.uk. Admission £4.70 adults, £4.20 seniors, £2.80 children 5-15. Apr-June and Sept daily 10am-5pm; July-Aug daily 10am-6pm; Oct daily 10am-4pm; Nov-Mar Sat-Sun 10am-4pm.

Dartmouth Museum MUSEUM   This small, quirky museum is located in a marvelous historic building—a merchant's house built between 1635 and 1640, and set amid an interconnected row of 17th-century buildings known as the Butter Walk. The overhanging, stilt-supported facade was originally designed to provide shade for the butter, milk, and cream sold there. The museum's displays are quite limited— some old photographs, rather a lot of ships in bottles, and so forth. Some of the rooms are quite charming, however.

The Butterwalk. ⟨ **01803/832923.** Admission £1.50 adults, £1 seniors, £.50 children 5-15. Apr-Oct Mon-Sat 10am-4pm. Closed Nov-Mar.

Where to Eat

Angelique ★★ CONTINENTAL   This inventive restaurant with a Michelin-starred chef strives to offer something for everyone. The ground-floor restaurant is lively and casual, with an open kitchen where you can watch the staff work. The upstairs dining room is more elegant and romantic, perfect for a quiet meal. The top floor is a cocktail bar, ideal for a drink before or after dinner. The menu changes daily but always uses fresh local ingredients. Dishes could include Devon crab salad with pickled fennel and lemongrass, or pan-fried local fish with oxtail ravioli.

If you like the place, you can spend the night. There are six attractive, **comfortable bedrooms** (£85–£95 double).

2 South Embankment. ⟨ **01803/839425.** www.thenewangel.co.uk. Reservations required. Main courses £19–£31; fixed-price 2-course menu £22, 3-course menu £26. AE, MC, V. Wed-Sun noon-2:30pm; Tues-Sat 6:30-9:30pm.

The Cherub Inn PUB FARE   First built in 1380 as the harbormaster's house, this historic pub still retains many of its early features, including leaded windows and timbered walls. With its fireplaces and drinking nooks, this is a fine place to stop for a pint or a steak and kidney pie. Drinking and casual dining takes place downstairs in the beamed main pub; upstairs, there's a more formal restaurant.

13 Higher St., Dartmouth. ℭ **01803/832571.** Main courses £6–£11. MC, V. daily noon–11pm.

Kendricks Restaurant INTERNATIONAL   This restaurant in the heart of the historic port district is a laid-back place to have dinner or a cocktail. The menu is wide-ranging, featuring everything from grilled ribs and steaks to sizzling fajitas. There are salads, fresh-made soups with homemade bread, and enormous hamburgers. Prices are reasonable and the mood is lively.

29 Fairfax Place. ℭ **01803/832328.** www.kendricksrestaurant.co.uk. Reservations recommended. Main courses £8–£20. MC, V. Daily 6:30–10pm.

Where to Stay

Cladda ★   This lemon-colored Victorian gingerbread house is a 5-minute walk uphill from the seafront. Guest rooms are sunny and a good size, with fresh cream-and-white color schemes and comfortable beds. There are suites if you want more space and a sitting area and kitchen of your own, and self-catering apartments that are significantly cheaper if you intend to stay for a week (£295–£545 per week).

88–90 Victoria Rd, Dartmouth, Devon TQ6 9EF. www.cladda-dartmouth.co.uk. ℭ **01803/835957.** 6 units. £80 double; £125 suite. Rates include English breakfast. DC, MC, V. *In room:* TV, fridge, hair dryer, Wi-Fi (free).

Hill View House ★   This B&B in a typical Dartmouth five-story Victorian house is perched—as the name implies—up the hill from the harbor, with sweeping views of the town and the sea. Its five guest rooms are tastefully furnished in shades of cream and white, and they range in size from pretty spacious to rather tiny. Bathrooms are very small, but have all that you need. The owners are welcoming and helpful, and the price is reasonable.

76 Victoria Rd, Dartmouth, Devon TQ6 9DZ. www.hillviewdartmouth.co.uk. ℭ **01803/839372.** 5 units. £70 double. Rates include English breakfast. DC, MC, V. *In room:* TV, hair dryer, Wi-Fi (free).

Royal Castle Hotel ★   A sympathetically restored, grand old inn on the waterfront, the Royal Castle has been welcoming guests—including Queen Victoria, Charles II, and Edward VII—for hundreds of years. The glassed-in courtyard, with its winding wooden staircase, displays the service bells once connected to the guest rooms. Rooms are spacious and decorated in pale, soothing colors, with big comfortable beds—many units have sweeping views of the marina, though these cost more. Bathrooms have been renovated. Breakfasts are so filling you may not need to eat again until dinner, and staff are consistently polite. The hotel pub—with its thick wood beams—is in the oldest part of the building, and is a great place for an evening drink.

11 The Quay, Dartmouth, Devon TQ6 9PS. www.royalcastle.co.uk. ℭ **01803/833033.** Fax 01803/835445. 25 units. £126–£166 double. Rates include English breakfast. AE, MC, V. Free parking. **Amenities:** Restaurant; 2 bars; babysitting; room service. *In room:* A/C (in some), TV, hair dryer, Wi-Fi (surcharge).

PLYMOUTH

242 miles SW of London; 161 miles SW of Southampton

"It's seen better days"—if ever a town fit that cliché, it's Plymouth. Historic and once-beautiful, Plymouth was founded in the 11th century and grew to become the principal seaport of Tudor England. All the known world sailed here and walked its narrow medieval streets. Few places in the south of England are as rich in romantic lore.

Sadly, most of that old Plymouth has gone. German bombing raids during World War II all but devastated the city; as many as 75,000 buildings were destroyed. Whatever the Nazis didn't destroy, spectacularly bad development in the 1950s and '60s did. Huge swathes of the city were replaced with oppressive, brutalist concrete buildings. Today, Plymouth is the kind of city that one passes through and winces at the thought of how good it must once have looked.

However, not all the historic old town was lost. The Elizabethan section, known as the **Barbican,** contains many original buildings, and a few good sights relating to the first Pilgrim Fathers who colonized America. The *Mayflower* and *Speedwell,* which sailed from Southampton in August 1620, docked into Plymouth after suffering storm damage. The *Speedwell* was abandoned; the *Mayflower* made the trip alone. The next stop from here was the New World.

In Britain, Plymouth is more associated with its most famous son, Sir Francis Drake—the swashbuckling admiral and one-time favorite of Queen Elizabeth I, who fought off the Spanish Armada in 1588. Legend has it that he was playing bowls up on Plymouth Hoe (a stretch of cliff overlooking the bay) when a messenger galloped over to tell him of the impending invasion. "There is plenty of time," he is said to have replied, "to finish this game and beat the Spaniards."

Unless you're a Tudor history buff, there is little to detain you in this workaday town. The Barbican is interesting, and its historic sights impressive—but not impressive or plentiful enough to warrant more than an afternoon's detour.

Essentials

GETTING THERE   First Great Western trains run frequently throughout the day from London's Paddington Station to Plymouth; the trip takes 3¼ to 4 hours, costing around £75 for a round-trip. For rail information, call © **08457/484950** or 000-125; or visit **www.firstgreatwestern.co.uk**. In Plymouth, the rail station is on North Road, north of the center. Several buses run from the rail station to the heart of Plymouth.

Buses run daily from London's Victoria Coach Station to Plymouth. The trip takes about 5½ hours. Fares cost around £33.

If you're driving from London, take the M4 west to the junction with the M5 going south to Exeter. From Exeter, head southwest on the A38 to Plymouth.

VISITOR INFORMATION   The **Tourist Information Centre** is at the Mayflower, in the Barbican (© **01752/306330;** www.visitplymouth.co.uk). It's open April through October, Monday to Saturday 9am to 5pm and Sunday 10am to 4pm; November to March, Monday to Friday 9am to 5pm and Saturday 10am to 4pm.

Exploring the Area

To commemorate the spot from which the *Mayflower* sailed for the New World, a white archway, erected in 1934 and capped with the flags of Britain and the United States, stands at the base of Plymouth's West Pier, on the Barbican. Incorporating a granite monument that was erected in 1891, the site is referred to as both the ***Mayflower* Steps** and the **Memorial Gateway.**

The **Barbican** is a mass of narrow streets, old houses, and quay-side shops selling antiques, brass work, old prints, and books. Fishing boats still unload their catches at the wharves, and passenger-carrying ferryboats run short harbor cruises.

Merchant's House MUSEUM   Arguably the most complete Tudor building in Plymouth, Merchant's House now contains a museum of local history. Its higgledy-piggledy collection includes an old ducking stool (devices that were used to punish women for crimes and minor infractions by strapping them to a chair and plunging them into a river). There's also a replica Victorian schoolroom.

33 St. Andrew's St. ℂ **01752/304774.** Admission £2 adults, £1 children 5-16, £4.80 families. Apr-Oct Tues-Sat 10am-5pm. Closed Nov-Mar. Any city center bus.

Plymouth Gin Distillery DISTILLERY   One of Plymouth's oldest-surviving buildings, this is where the Pilgrims spent their last night before sailing for the New World. Plymouth Gin has been produced here for 200 years on a historic site that dates back to a Dominican monastery built in 1425. Public guided tours (including a tasting) are offered, and a Plymouth Gin Shop is on the premises.

Black Friars Distillery, 60 Southside St. ℂ **01752/665292.** www.plymouthgin.com. Admission £6 adults, children free (with adult only). Daily 10:30am-4:30pm, Sun 11:30am-3:30pm. Bus: 54.

Smeaton's Tower OBSERVATION POINT   Built in 1759, this strikingly pictur-esque, candy-striped lighthouse was moved to its current location atop Plymouth Hoe in the late 1800s, when it was found to be in danger of collapsing the cliff on which it once stood. Today it's no longer in use, but has been fully restored to its original condition. At a little over 21m (70 ft.) tall, the views of Plymouth and the English Channel from the top are spectacular.

The Hoe. ℂ **01752/603300.** Admission £2 adults, £1 children 5-16, £4.80 families. Apr-Oct Tues-Sat 10am-5pm. Closed Nov-Mar. Any city center bus.

Where to Eat

Tanners Restaurant ★★ INTERNATIONAL   This restaurant has a very good reputation among local diners. It's certainly one of the most handsome places to eat around here; the converted 15th-century house has mullioned windows, exposed stone, antique tapestries, and even an illuminated water well. Locally caught seafood is a specialty, although meat lovers are equally well catered for. Typical dishes include filet of John Dory with crab butter sauce, and roast duck breast with squash and balsamic figs. For dessert you may find vanilla crème brûlée or a traditional carrot cake with cinnamon ice cream. The £20 set menu (available Tues–Thurs) is excellent value.

Prysten House, Finewell St. ℂ **01752/252001.** www.tannersrestaurant.com. Reservations required. Fixed-price 3-course dinner (Tues-Thurs) £20; main courses £14-£28. AE, DC, MC, V. Tues-Fri noon-2:30pm; Sat noon-2pm; Tues-Sat 7-9:30pm.

Tudor Rose Tea Rooms BRITISH   This ultra-traditional restaurant in an old Tudor pub dates from 1640—when, according to a sign on the wall, "New Street was new." The menu is neither innovative nor particularly varied, but it's good, no-nonsense fare. Lunch dishes include fish and chips, steak and kidney pudding, and sausage and mash; or you could just come for a traditional afternoon tea, complete with dainty sandwiches and cakes. Best of all, prices are very reasonable.

36 New St. ℂ **01752/255502.** www.tudorrosetearoom.co.uk. Sandwiches and light lunches £3.50-£5; lunch main courses £4-£11; afternoon tea £5-£7. MC, V. Daily 10am-5pm (often later in summer).

Where to Stay

Athenaeum Lodge   This bijou guesthouse is located about 10 minutes' walk from the Barbican district. Jane and David Kewell are the kind of owners who really seem to enjoy what they do, and their knowledge of the local area is second to none. The decor may be a little traditional for some tastes, but bedrooms are comfortable and spotlessly clean. Breakfasts are well done (though don't expect much variety). A few extras, such as free Wi-Fi and a computer for guests' use, put this place above the norm for B&Bs of this size and price range.

4 Athenaeum St., The Hoe, Plymouth, Devon PL1 2RQ. www.athenaeumlodge.com. ℭ **01752/665005.** 8 units. £30–£60 double; £50–£70 family room. Rates include English breakfast. DC, MC, V. Limited free parking overnight; £2 permit parking nearby. **Amenities:** Guest computer. *In room:* TV, Wi-Fi (free).

Caledonia Guest House 🏷   A 2-minute walk from the beautiful sea views of Plymouth Hoe, this B&B in a converted Victorian townhouse offers exceptional value for money. Bedrooms are clean and cozy, although not all have private bathrooms (make sure you ask for an en suite unit if this matters). It won't win any design awards, but it's comfortable and well equipped. Disabled visitors and those with mobility problems are particularly well catered for here; despite its age, the building has been fairly well adapted for wheelchair users. There are also thoughtful touches such as guide rails and Braille menus available.

27 Athenaeum St., The Hoe, Plymouth, Devon PL1 2RQ. www.thecaledonia.co.uk. ℭ **01752/229052**. 7 units (6 with bathroom). £50 double without bathroom; £55–£65 double with bathroom. Rates include English breakfast. MC, V. **Amenities:** Breakfast room. *In room:* TV, hair dryer, Wi-Fi (free).

CORNWALL

by Rebecca Ford

With its distinctive blend of dramatic cliffs, soft sandy beaches and picturesque fishing villages, Cornwall's stunning coastline attracts thrill-seeking surfers as well as families and couples seeking a romantic hideaway.

Add to that its mild climate, its rich history—this was once a separate Celtic nation—and its celebrated attractions, like the eco-friendly Eden Project and Tate St. Ives, and it's easy to see why this is England's top holiday playground. It's no wonder that writers such as Daphne du Maurier and artists like Barbara Hepworth found it so inspiring.

10

SIGHTSEEING   You can walk through a tropical rainforest when you step inside one of the **Eden Project's** futuristic biomes, or go deep underground on a tour of a **tin mine**—Cornwall's unique mining landscapes have been recognized as a UNESCO World Heritage site. Stately homes such as **Lanhydrock House** offer the whole family a fascinating glimpse into the past, while the **National Maritime Museum** in **Falmouth** gives visitors a chance to learn about the realities of life at sea.

EATING & DRINKING   Cornwall is noted for the quality of its seafood, with visitors flocking to celebrity-chef Rick Stein's restaurant in **Padstow**—or just enjoying fish and chips eaten beside the sea. The county is also known for its eponymous pasties (a traditional Cornish meat pie)—locals all have their favorite pasty shops—rich clotted cream (delicious eaten for tea with jam and scones), and strong cider.

OUTDOOR ACTIVITIES   Cornwall's extensive coastline and inland waters offer endless opportunities for **sailing, surfing,** and **canoeing,** while many of its disused railway lines have been turned into safe **cycle** routes, like the popular **Camel Trail** that runs for 18 miles along the tranquil Camel estuary. **Walkers** have a maze of quiet footpaths, historic trails, and exhilarating cliff walks to choose from.

RELAXATION   The Cornish love the sea, so you'll be in good company if you want to spend your holiday relaxing on one of the county's glorious **beaches,** such as Porthminster at St. Ives or Porthcressa on the Isles of Scilly. The mild south coast is studded with glorious **gardens,** including Trengwainton where lush banana plants and giant tree ferns mingle with fragrant flowers.

THE best TRAVEL EXPERIENCES IN CORNWALL

- **Seeing exotic gardens:** Thanks to its mild climate, Cornwall is home to some of England's finest gardens, and exploring them is a delight. Wander through the magical Lost Gardens of Heligan (p. 406); or sniff lush blooms in the subtropical Abbey Gardens on the island of Tresco (p. 414).

- **Learning about Cornwall's mining heritage:** For centuries Cornwall was known for its tin, which has been mined here since the Iron Age. The picturesque remains of the industry have now been designated a UNESCO World Heritage site, so don't miss the chance to discover the mysterious subterranean world of the miners. See p. 417.

- **Getting a glimpse of artistic St. Ives:** Its exceptional light and inspirational coastal scenery have made this fishing village a haven for artists since the 19th century. You can see the work of Cornish artists at Tate St. Ives, and the studio and former home of sculptor Barbara Hepworth, one of the 20th-century's foremost artists. See p. 415.

- **Just "being" in the Isles of Scilly:** Yes, just "being" on Scilly is a treat. This unspoiled archipelago off the Cornish coast is a paradise of pristine powdery beaches, sparkling seas, and rich birdlife. It almost feels as if the modern world never touched these tranquil jewels. See p. 412.

- **Exploring the coast:** Cornwall's glorious coastline offers something for everyone—from energetic surfers and swimmers to photographers who just want to capture its beauty. There are dramatic cliffs, endless sands, and crashing waves on the north coast, and secluded coves and sleepy estuaries on the south.

THE SOUTHEAST CORNER ★

Looe: 264 miles SW of London, 20 miles W of Plymouth; Polperro: 271 miles SW of London, 26 miles W of Plymouth, 6 miles SW of Looe

Tucked away between the River Tamar and the River Fowey, this attractive corner of Cornwall is home to delightful fishing villages, sleepy churches, and fine historic sights. With its secret creeks and country lanes, it seems a world away from the lively surf scene around Newquay on the north coast: This is a region best explored slowly.

Looe is a charming little port divided by the River Looe, which is spanned by a handsome, arched stone bridge. While West Looe is mainly residential, East Looe is a popular seaside center. Nearby **Polperro** is one of Cornwall's prettiest villages, with a clutch of 16th- and 17th-century fishing cottages clustered around a little harbor.

Fowey, farther to the west, is another pretty port with steep streets stretching down to the waterfront. Novelist Daphne du Maurier lived close by, and if you're a fan it's well worth coming to Fowey's annual literary festival, which celebrates her work. These tiny villages can all be extremely busy in high season.

Sitting sedately on the upper reaches of the River Fowey is the ancient market town of **Lostwithiel,** once the capital of Cornwall. A busy port until the river silted up in medieval times, and a wealthy administrative center until the 18th century, the town has several historic buildings worth exploring, including its church. Just a short drive away you'll find some great attractions that will suit the whole family: Lanhydrock House and Restormel Castle.

Essentials

GETTING THERE   The nearest mainline station is at Liskeard, 3½ hours by **First Great Western** train (✆ **08457/000125;** www.firstgreatwestern.co.uk) from London's Paddington Station, with a delightful branch line to Looe. It costs from £41 per person one-way.

If you're **driving** to Looe, take the A38 west once you've crossed the Tamar into Cornwall, and then the B3253. To get to Polperro, follow the A387 southwest from Looe. For Lostwithiel, take the A38 west, then the A390. Continue on this southwest to branch off for Fowey.

VISITOR INFORMATION   **Looe Tourist Information Centre,** Guildhall, Fore Street (✆ **01503/262072;** www.visit-southeastcornwall.co.uk), is open Easter to September, daily 10am to 5pm; October, daily 10am to 2pm; and November to Easter, Monday to Friday 10am to 1pm. **Fowey Tourist Information Centre,** 5 South St. (✆ **01726/833616;** www.fowey.co.uk), is open daily 10am to 4:30pm. **Lostwithiel Tourist Information** is at Lostwithiel Community Centre on Liddicoat Road just off the A390 (✆ **01208/872207;** www.lostwithieltouristinformation. webs.com). It's open Easter to November Monday to Friday 10am to 5pm, Saturday 10am to 1pm; November to Easter Monday to Friday 10am to 1pm.

Exploring the Area

If you love beer and trains then a trip on the **Looe Valley Line's** Rail Ale Trail is a must. Running from Liskeard to Looe, along the river valley, it stops close to four historic pubs along the way. Ranger tickets give you the freedom to travel the line for a full day, visiting pubs and maybe enjoying country walks too. Visit www.railaletrail. com for more information.

LOOE

Looe Island NATURE RESERVE   Nature lovers can take the 20-minute boat trip out to this small island, which is home to nesting seabirds, seals, and wild flowers. A Benedictine chapel was built here in the 12th century, but by the 1700s it was the haunt of smugglers.

The *Islander* boat leaves from the lifeboat station slipway in East Looe. ✆ **01873/273939.** www.cornwall wildlifetrust.org.uk. Return boat trips £6 adults, £4 children, landing fee £2.50 adults, £1 children. Trips run Easter–Sept, are tide dependent, and last around 2 hours.

Old Guildhall Museum & Gaol MUSEUM   Dating back to the 16th century, Looe's former courthouse is the oldest building in the town. It has been converted into a small museum tracing the town's history, with model ships, photos, and domestic artifacts.

Higher Market St., East Looe. ✆ **01503/263709.** Admission £1.80 adults, 80p children 16 and under, £4.50 family ticket. Easter, then late May–late Sept daily 11:30am–4:30pm. Closed Oct–mid-May.

FOWEY

When the river silted up and Lostwithiel could no longer function as a port, Fowey (pronounced *Foy*) took its place. Raided by a Spanish fleet in 1380, its strategic importance was endorsed when an artillery fort, **St. Catherine's Castle** (www. english-heritage.co.uk; free admission; daily) was built here in the 16th century by Henry VIII. Reached by a winding footpath from Ready Money Cove, it offers great views of the harbor. A ship sailed from here to fight with Drake against the Spanish Armada, and Fowey was later a departure point for forces massing for the D-Day

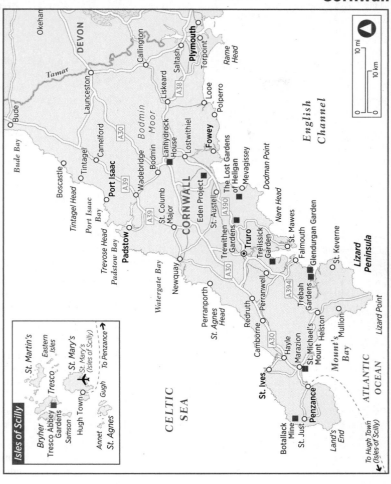

landings of World War II. In addition to dropping into the small **Fowey museum** in the Town Hall (Trafalgar Square; **01726/833513;** admission £1; Easter–mid-Oct Mon–Fri 10:30am–4:30pm), you should also visit **St. Fimbarrus' Church** (free admission) down by the quay. It was founded in the 7th century and is the southern point of the Saints' Way walking trail (see "Stepping Out in Cornwall," p. 420).

LOSTWITHIEL

Tin was for centuries the lifeblood of Cornwall, and the industry was regulated from the Stannary Parliament, which sat in Lostwithiel from the 14th to 17th centuries. Sittings for the parliament took place in the old **Duchy Palace,** erected in 1292 by Edmund, King John's grandson. The Duchy (or dukedom) of Cornwall was created to provide the heir to the throne with an income—and it still exists today. Appropriately, then, the palace is being restored by Prince Charles's Prince's Regeneration Trust (www.princes-regeneration.org).

The parish church **St. Bartholomew's** is even older, dating back to the 12th century; it's much larger than you might expect—a reminder of Lostwithiel's former prominence.

Lanhydrock ★★ ☺ HISTORIC SITE   This magnificent Victorian country house was rebuilt on the site of an earlier building. You can explore 50 rooms, from the grand Long Gallery to the servants' quarters "below stairs." There are extensive grounds, too, with footpaths leading to Restormel Castle.

Between Lostwithiel and Bodmin, off the A390. ℂ **01208/265950.** www.nationaltrust.org.uk. Admission: House and garden £10 adults, £5.10 children, £26 family ticket; garden only £5.80 adults, £3.10 children. Free to National Trust members. House: Late Feb–late Oct Tues–Sun 11am–5pm (closed 5:30pm Apr–Sept); gardens: Year-round daily 10am–6pm.

Restormel Castle RUINS   Just a short drive from Lostwithiel, this striking ruined castle stands on a defensive mound made by the Normans around 1100, though the stone walls you see today are from the 13th century. It was last used during the English Civil War. Stroll around the ramparts for great views or just have a relaxing picnic beneath the ancient stones.

Nr. Restormel Rd. (1½ miles north of Lostwithiel off the A390). www.english-heritage.co.uk. Admission £3.20 adults, £1.60 children 5–15, free for English Heritage members. Apr–late June and Sept 10am–5pm; July–late Aug 10am–6pm; Oct 10am–4pm. Note that hours are variable.

Where to Eat
FOWEY

Boat House ITALIAN   If you'd like an alternative to seafood, this Italian restaurant down by Fowey town square offers stone-baked pizzas and a selection of pasta dishes. The interior is contemporary with maritime prints on the walls and dark wooden floors. Given the location, you won't be surprised that fish features in some dishes, such as the Boat House Special (roast salmon with asparagus and ribbon pasta), or the mussels cooked with olives and chili.

Town Quay. ℂ **01726/832221.** www.boathouse.fowey.com. Main courses £8–£13. MC, V. Daily 11am–9pm. Closed Jan & Feb.

Food for Thought ★ BRITISH   This historic building, probably once a merchant's house, dates back to the 14th century and its charming waterside setting makes it a great choice for dining in Fowey. Local mussels with garlic and Cornish cider are a popular starter, while main courses range from "posh" fish and chips (think sea bass in a real ale batter) to rack of lamb with rosemary sauce and a filet of local beef served with béarnaise sauce. A fixed-price menu is a more inexpensive option. The lunchtime menu includes salmon fishcakes and crab sandwiches.

4 Town Quay. ℂ **01726/832221.** www.foodforthought.fowey.com. Main courses £9.95–£25. AE MC, V. Daily 11am–2:30pm and 7–9:30pm, but closed Sun evenings Mar–Apr. Closed Nov–mid-Mar.

The Galleon Inn BRITISH   The riverside location makes this busy pub, which started as a warehouse around 400 years ago, a popular choice. You can dine outside on fine days, on a menu that features old favorites like fish pie, vegetarian lasagna, and sausage and mash, as well as steaks and grills. A range of real ales are served, and there's live music on Friday nights in winter and Sunday lunchtimes.

12 Fore St. ☎ **01726/833014.** www.galleon-inn.co.uk. Main courses £6.25–£14. V. Daily noon–2:30pm, Mon–Sat 6–9pm, Sun 6–8:30pm.

LOOE

The Old Sail Loft ★ SEAFOOD   This 16th-century smugglers' haunt has been transformed into a cozy restaurant, with original oak beams and maritime relics adding atmosphere to the interior. The extensive menu features a popular Cornish seafood chowder as a starter, with main courses including salmon filet in a beer batter served with chunky chips, and John Dory on a garlic and chive mash. A steak and game suet pudding with onion gravy would keep the carnivores happy.

Quay St. East Looe. ☎ **01503/262131.** www.theoldsailloftrestaurant.com. Main courses £13–£20. AE, MC, V. Jan–Apr and Nov–Dec Mon and Wed–Sat noon–2pm and 6–9pm; Easter–Oct Mon–Sat noon–2pm and 6–9pm.

Squid Ink Restaurant ★★ SEAFOOD   Just off the quay-side in East Looe, this chef-owned restaurant has a contemporary feel with an unfussy interior and a menu that features fresh local fish cooked with Asian and Mediterranean flavors. Dishes vary depending on what has been caught that day but might include pan-fried gurnard filet with pumpkin purée, or catch of the day with mussels cooked in paper with white-wine and saffron. They also feature a meat and a vegetarian dish each day.

Lower Chapel St. ☎ **01503/262674.** www.squid-ink.biz. Reservations required for lunch. Main courses £17–£19. MC, V. Oct–Jan Wed–Sat noon–4pm and 6–9pm; Easter–Sept Tues–Sat noon–4pm and 6–9pm. Hours may vary so call ahead to verify.

Trawlers on the Quay ★★ SEAFOOD   This award-winning seafood restaurant comes under the Barclay House umbrella and offers consistently high-quality food. The focus is on imaginatively cooked seafood with fusion flavors, with the menu changing regularly. Chargrilled cuttlefish with wasabi dressing is a typical starter, with pan-fried brill or sea bass served with a green peppercorn sauce for a main course. Meat lovers and vegetarians are also catered for, and the restaurant serves cream teas in the afternoons.

Quay St., East Looe. ☎ **01503/263593.** www.trawlers-restaurant.co.uk. Reservations recommended. Main courses £9.95–£16. AE, MC, V. Easter–Oct daily noon–2pm and 6–9pm.

LOSTWITHIEL

Trewithen ★★ BRITISH   In the heart of historic Lostwithiel, close to the Duchy Palace, is this lovely little restaurant set in an 18th-century building. The cuisine is modern British, and the style of dining is relaxed. Dishes include sirloin steak sandwiches, chicken-and-mushroom pie, as well as homemade soups and salads. Indulgent desserts include warm treacle tart and a flourless chocolate cake. Scrambled egg with smoked salmon is one of several options for brunch. Dine in the courtyard garden on fine days.

Fore St. ☎ **01208/872373.** www.trewithenrestaurant.com. Main courses £8.50–£13. MC, V. Tues–Sat 11am–2pm, 6:30–9pm.

PELYNT

Jubilee Inn BRITISH   Built in the 16th century, this inn takes its name from Queen Victoria's jubilee celebration, when it underwent restoration. In winter there's a real fire in the bar and it's a popular spot for Sunday roasts and traditional pub food like local sausages with mash and gravy, fish and chips, and steaks. Vegetarians have several dishes to choose from as well. Freshly made sandwiches and jacket potatoes are available at lunchtime. **Rooms** are available, too.

Jubilee Hill (4 miles from Looe, 3 miles from Polperro). ✆ **01503/220312.** www.jubilee-inn.co.uk. Main courses £8.95–£14. MC, V. Mon–Fri noon–2:30pm and 6–9pm; Sat–Sun noon–3pm and 6–9pm.

POLPERRO

The Blue Peter Inn ★★ 🍴 BRITISH/SEAFOOD   This lovely, friendly pub, perched beside the harbor in Polperro, was once two fishermen's cottages. The atmospheric interior reflects its 600-year history, and there's a real fire in the bar on chilly winter days. The menu changes daily and features fresh-caught fish such as sardines, mackerel, or scallops. However, some dishes are suitable for vegetarians and there's a good selection of soups and sandwiches, too. There's often live music on Friday and Saturday evenings.

Quay Rd. ✆ **01503/272743.** www.thebluepeter.co.uk. Main courses £8.95–£11. V. Daily 11am–8:30pm (9pm in summer).

The Kitchen BRITISH   This pink cottage, halfway to the harbor from the parking area, was once a wagon-builder's shop. It's now a tearoom/restaurant offering good English cooking, all homemade from fresh ingredients. The menu features local, seasonal produce and on Sunday a traditional roast is served. Typical dishes include smoked fish platter or steak with salad. Breakfast is served until 11:30am, and there are cream teas and cakes in the afternoon.

The Combes. ✆ **01503/272780.** Reservations required for Sun lunch. Main courses £4.50–£8.95. MC, V. Tues–Sat 10am–5pm, Sun noon–4pm.

Nelson's Restaurant SEAFOOD   Nelson's features succulent preparations of regional fish and shellfish that arrive fresh from local fishing boats. The menu changes daily but usually includes fresh crab, Dover sole, lobster, and many other exotic fish. Fresh meat, poultry, and game, all from local suppliers, are also available and beautifully prepared. A lower deck features a cafe/bar and bistro.

Saxon Bridge. ✆ **01503/272366.** www.polperro.co.uk. Reservations recommended. Main courses £8–£24. MC, V. Tues–Sat noon–2pm and 6:30–10pm; Sun noon–4pm. Closed mid-Jan–mid-Feb.

Shopping

Polperro is good for works by Cornish artists (the **Polperro Gallery** especially; ✆ **01503/272577;** www.polperrogallery.co.uk) as well as antiques, while East Looe has plenty of individual shops. Check out **Purely Cornish,** Fore Street (✆ **01503/262680;** www.purelycornish.co.uk) for local food, drink, and hampers, and the **Pasty Shop,** on Buller Street, for freshly made pasties. Fowey has a couple of good bookstores, with plenty of Daphne du Maurier titles. **Watts Trading,** Fore Street (✆ **01208/872304;** www.wattstrading.co.uk) in Lostwithiel, is devoted to organic items with everything from woolens to wooden toys. Lostwithiel is a good center for antiques, too. Cider lovers should call into **Cornish Orchards** (✆ **01503/269007;** www.cornishorchards.co.uk), Westnorth Manor Farm, Duloe, near Looe, to visit the farm shop and purchase fresh cider and apple juice.

Entertainment & Nightlife

The **Daphne du Maurier Festival** (www.dumaurierfestival.co.uk) takes place for one week each May in Fowey. The program usually features a mix of talks and readings by authors, as well as musical performances. Fowey pubs to check out include the **Galleon Inn,** 12 Fore St. (✆ **01726/833014;** www.galleon-inn.com), which often has live music on Friday nights, and **Safe Harbour** on Lostwithiel Street (✆ **01726/833379;** www.cornwall-safeharbour.co.uk), which serves local ales.

Where to Stay

LOOE

Barclay House ★★★ 🔔 ☺ This excellent family-operated country-house hotel stands on a wooded hillside surrounded by more than 2.4 hectares (6 acres) of private woodlands overlooking the Looe River Valley. But it's also just on the edge of town at the entrance to Looe, and about a 5-minute walk from the harbor and railway station. You can have breakfast outside on the terrace in summer. Units are stylish and spacious and fitted with soft twins or a king-size bed, and there are self-catering cottages, too.

The **restaurant,** open to non-guests, serves delicious and imaginative dishes featuring seasonal local produce: shallot tart with goat's cheese, for instance, followed by Cornish rib-eye beef with tomato and chili jam. Vegetarians are well catered for, and after dinner you can relax in the lounge on a squishy sofa.

St. Martins Rd. (the main Plymouth–Looe Rd., B3253), East Looe, Cornwall PL13 1LP. www.barclayhouse. co.uk. ℭ **01503/262929.** Fax: 01503/262632. 20 units, including 8 cottages. £120–£190 double with breakfast, £170–£240 for double with breakfast and dinner; £299–£1,499 cottage per week. A 5% discount is available for guests arriving by train (the railway station is under 5 minutes' walk away). AE, MC, V. **Amenities:** Restaurant; bar; outdoor heated pool, gym with sauna. *In room:* TV, hair dryer.

Talland Bay Hotel ★ A country house dating from the 16th century, situated on 1 hectare (2½ acres), this hotel has recently been refurbished in a contemporary style, and many of its individually furnished bedrooms have sea views. The subtropical garden is an enchanting place in which to relax, while the hotel is only a few minutes' walk from the long distance coastal path. Some rooms are in a comfortable annex and the hotel accepts pets. There's a **brasserie** for relaxed meals as well as a fine-dining **restaurant.**

Talland-by-Looe, Porthallow, Cornwall PL13 2JB. www.tallandbayhotel.co.uk. ℭ **01503/272667.** Fax 01503/272940. 21 units. Oct–late Mar £100–£175 double; Apr–Sept £130–£225 double; cottage (sleeps 4) £130–£160. Half-board options also available. MC, V. Take the A387 4 miles SW of Looe. **Amenities:** Restaurant; bar; room service; Wi-Fi (free). *In room:* TV, hair dryer.

Well House ★ The Well House prides itself on its fine food. Located 3 miles from Liskeard, it has 2 hectares (5 acres) of gardens opening onto vistas of the Looe Valley. It offers beautifully furnished bedrooms, some contemporary and others in traditional country-house style, with many thoughtful extras such as fresh flowers. Two attractive terrace rooms are at the garden level. Most rooms have a twin bed or else a large double. The award-winning **restaurant** is a draw in itself; it offers both lunch and dinner tasting menus—including one designed specifically for vegetarians.

St. Keyne, Liskeard, Cornwall PL14 4RN. www.wellhouse.co.uk. ℭ **01579/342001.** Fax 01579/343891. 9 units. £155–£215 double; £255 family suite. Half-board options also available. MC, V. From Liskeard, take the B3254 to St. Keyne, 3 miles away. **Amenities:** Restaurant; bar; heated outdoor pool; croquet lawn, tennis court. *In room:* TV, hair dryer, Internet (free).

FOWEY

Fowey Hall Hotel ★★ ☺ This handsome late-Victorian house perched just above the little town of Fowey, is just a short walk from the town's center and local beaches. Some of the bedrooms are in the original house, thought by many to have been the inspiration for Toad Hall in Kenneth Grahame's *The Wind in the Willows*; other rooms are in a newer garden wing. It's a particularly good place to come for families as there's a government-registered nursery, outdoor play area, and a family dining area—while adults can eat later in the lovely oak-paneled **restaurant.** The spa has a 12-m (40-ft.) indoor heated pool and offers a wide range of treatments.

Hanson Dr., Fowey, Cornwall PL23 1ET. www.foweyhallhotel.co.uk. ☎ **01726/833866.** Fax 01726/834100. 36 units, including 12 family suites. £170–245 double; £260–£420 large suite. Dinner, B&B option also available. MC, V. **Amenities:** Restaurant, babysitting; spa with indoor pool; billiard room; crèche. *In room:* TV/DVD, hair dryer.

POLPERRO

Trenderway Farm ★ 🎒   For a quiet, romantic adult hideaway, the B&B rooms on this working farm are a perfect option. Rooms are either in the 16th-century farmhouse or converted outbuildings, and are pretty and well kept. A hearty traditional breakfast can be taken in the conservatory or outdoors on the terrace. Two of the suites have mini kitchens, in case you wish to cater for yourself. No children accepted.

Pelynt, nr. Polperro, Cornwall PL13 2LY (between Looe and Polperro, off the B3359). www.trenderway farmholidays.co.uk. ☎ **01503/272214.** Fax: 01503/272991. 6 units. £90–£155 double; barn conversion (with log-burning stove and washing machine) £595–£895 per week. MC, V. *In room:* TV (some also have DVD), hair dryer, fridge.

ST. AUSTELL TO THE LIZARD ★★★

St. Mawes: 300 miles SW of London, 2 miles E of Falmouth, 18 miles S of Truro

This sheltered stretch of coastline is characterized by its sleepy, wooded estuaries; subtropical plants; and secret, sandy coves—no wonder it was once prime smuggling country. It's a great area for sailing, boating, and walking. Overlooking the mouth of the Fal River, at the tip of the Roseland Peninsula, **St. Mawes** is one of Cornwall's prettiest villages. **The Lizard Peninsula** is the U.K. mainland's most southerly point and home to Frenchman's Creek, inspiration for Daphne du Maurier's novel. Cornwall's best-known attractions are here, too, such as the futuristic **Eden Project** near St. Austell, the glorious **Lost Gardens of Heligan,** and the **National Maritime Museum** in Falmouth. And then there's **Truro,** the county town of Cornwall and its best shopping center.

Essentials

GETTING THERE **Trains** leave London's Paddington Station for St. Austell and Truro several times a day. The trip takes 4½–5 hours. At Truro you can connect with trains for the 25-minute journey to Falmouth. Buses run from Truro to St. Mawes and Falmouth or you can take a taxi from Truro or St. Austell. You can book the bus as a through journey to Falmouth when you book the train with **First Great Western** (© **08457/000125;** www.firstgreatwestern.co.uk). One-way tickets from London start from £45.

National Express buses (© **0871/781-8181;** www.nationalexpress.com) leave London's Victoria Coach Station three times a day for Truro. The trip takes 7–8 hours. If you're **driving**, the A391 branches off the A30 to St. Austell, farther along the A30 the A39 branches off for Truro and then Falmouth.

VISITOR INFORMATION Truro's **Tourist Information Center,** Municipal Buildings, Boscawen Street (© **01872/274555;** www.tourism.truro.gov.uk), is open Easter to late October, Monday to Friday 9am to 5:30pm, Saturday 9am to 4pm; rest of year Monday to Friday 9am to 5pm.

Exploring the Area

The glorious **Roseland Peninsula** ★★ is an easy drive from Truro and dotted with sleepy little settlements (**Veryan** has some fascinating 19th-century roundhouses, built to prevent the Devil from hiding in corners), country churches, and tranquil creeks. At the very tip is the relaxed waterfront village of **St. Mawes,** a favorite place for sailing and boating, and a good base for exploring the rest of the Roseland. Its former importance as a port is evident when you visit its **castle,** built by Henry VIII to protect the coast. The castle is open April to June and September Sunday to Friday 10am to 5pm; July to August daily 10am to 6pm; October daily 10am to 4pm; and November to late March Friday to Monday 10am to 4pm. Admission is £4.20 adults, £3.60 seniors, £2.10 children 5–15, and free for children 4 and under. (Also free to English Heritage members.) **Passenger ferries** leave St. Mawes hourly (every 30 min. Mon–Fri in summer) each day for the 20-minute trip to Falmouth.

The Roseland Peninsula's most famous church is **St.-Just-in-Roseland,** a glorious little 13th-century church on a tidal creek, with a much-photographed churchyard that contains many subtropical plants. It was built on the site of a 5th-century Celtic church. It's a short drive from here to the **King Harry Ferry,** a chain-link car ferry that connects the Roseland with the west bank of the Fal and cuts almost 30 minutes off the journey to Truro and/or Falmouth. It runs daily all year (expect long waits in summer).

The **Lizard Peninsula** is larger and even quieter than the Roseland. **Helston** (famed for its annual May Flora Festival at which you'll see the Furry Dance) is the largest town, and other settlements, such as **Porthleven,** are scattered around the gloriously romantic coast—a mix of dramatic cliff stacks, crashing seas, and secret sandy coves. The treacherous waters have long proved hazardous to sailors, and at **Lizard Point**—the mainland's most southerly spot, reached off the A3083 from Helston—you can visit the **Lighthouse Heritage Centre** (www.lizardlighthouse. co.uk) and go into the famous twin-towered lighthouse, which was commissioned in 1752. Originally lit by coal fires, it was not automated until 1998. A couple of miles away is **Kynance Cove,** a beautiful beach owned by the National Trust. The northeast corner of the Lizard is characterized by the sleepy waters of the **Helford**

River, its creeks and woods seemingly unchanged since the days when it was the haunt of smugglers.

Truro is a lively city with a long history. Fine Georgian and Victorian buildings, built by wealthy mine owners and merchants, give its streets an elegant air. The most striking building is the magnificent **Truro Cathedral,** St. Mary's Street (*©* **01872/ 276782;** www.trurocathedral.org.uk; Mon–Sat 7:30am–6pm, Sun 9am–7pm; free admission), built in soaring Gothic style in late Victorian times and finally completed in 1910. There is some fine stained glass, and organ recitals are frequently held here. The **Royal Cornwall Museum,** River Street (*©* **01872/272205;** www.royal cornwallmuseum.org.uk; Mon–Sat 10am–4:45pm; free admission), is also worth a visit with its displays of both Cornish and non-Cornish fine art, photographs, archeology, and minerals.

FALMOUTH

National Maritime Museum ★★ ☺ MUSEUM The busy port of Falmouth has been much redeveloped in recent years. The excellent National Maritime Museum is set in a striking contemporary building on the quay-side, with a Lookout Tower that makes the most of the sea views. Boats hang suspended above the main atrium, and there are displays on everything from shipbuilding to great survival stories. Sir Ernest Shackleton's string vest, interactive displays on the weather, and a pool where you can try your hand at "sailing" a remote controlled craft make this a great place for the entire family.

Discovery Quay. *©* **01326/313388.** www.nmmc.co.uk. Admission £9.50 adults, £7.75 seniors, £6.50 full-time students and children 6–15, free for children 5 and under, £27 family ticket. Daily 10am–5pm.

ST. AUSTELL AREA

The Eden Project ★★★ ☺ GARDEN Looking rather like giant spaceships, the vast "greenhouses," or geodesic domes of the Eden Project—set in a former china clay quarry—reproduce climates from different parts of the world, allowing you to wander through a "rainforest" and see how chocolate grows; or see cork trees in the Mediterranean biome. You'll learn about conservation, as well as have a chance to see thousands of different plants and learn about their importance as medicine, food, and fuel. There are outdoor gardens, too, plus trails and play areas for the kids—it's easy to spend a full day here. Go early to avoid waiting to enter.

Bodelva, St. Austell. *©* **01726/811911.** www.edenproject.com. Admission £18 adults, £6 children 5–16, free children 4 and under; reductions available if buying online, or if arriving by public transport (show ticket). Late Mar–late Oct daily 9:30am–6pm (last admission 4:30pm); Nov–mid Mar daily 9:30am–4:30pm (last entry 3pm). Note: Winter hours can vary, so check website before visiting. The project lies 6 miles from the St. Austell train station, to which it is linked by bus.

Lost Gardens of Heligan ★★★ ☺ GARDEN It was in 1990 that these extraordinary gardens at Heligan, once the seat of the Tremayne family, were discovered, slumbering and overgrown, having fallen into neglect after World War I. Visiting them is rather like traveling back in time to Queen Victoria's day. Europe's largest garden restoration project sprawls over 81 hectares (200 acres) of pure enchantment. There are wild areas, a subtropical "jungle," and, most moving of all, the Victorian kitchen garden where gardeners scrawled their names in August 1914—almost all of them were soon to die in the war. Heligan is close to the fishing village of **Mevagissey,** which is worth a visit too—but allow the best part of a day to explore the gardens.

Pentewan, 6 miles south of St. Austell. ℭ **01726/845100.** www.heligan.com. Admission £10 adults, £9 seniors, £6 children 5-16, free for children 4 and under, £27 family ticket. Apr-Sept daily 10am-6pm (last admission 4:30pm), Oct-Mar daily 10am-5pm (last admission 3:30pm). Closed Dec 24-25. From St. Austell, take the B3273 to Mevagissey, then follow signs to Heligan.

Wheal Martyn China Clay Country Park ★ ☺ MUSEUM   Since the mid-18th century, the St. Austell area has been noted for its china clay, which is used in porcelain production. China clay quarries sprang up all over this corner of Cornwall, their deep pits and mountains of waste creating a distinctive industrial landscape once termed the "Cornish Alps." Here two former clay works have been turned into a fascinating museum, giving an insight into the lives of the men and women who worked here. Outside, there's an original water wheel, as well as a nature trail and a walk to a viewing point where you can see two working clay pits.

Wheal Martyn, Carthew, 2 miles north of St. Austell. ℭ **01726/850362.** www.wheal-martyn.com. Admission £8.50 adults, £4.75 children 6-16, £22 family ticket. Daily 10am-4pm in winter, 10am-6pm in summer.

Where to Eat
FALMOUTH
Gylly Beach Café ★ BRITISH   Perched on one of Cornwall's finest blue-flag beaches, and overlooking Falmouth Bay, this award-winning cafe serves upmarket versions of seaside favorites, like fish and chips. It's a great place for families to come for a hearty breakfast or a light lunch, while in the evenings the menu takes on a more sophisticated flavor. In addition to steaks, you might find lamb ragout with garlic and rosemary mash, as well as a vegetarian dish such as paprika and bean cassoulet.

Gyllyngvase Beach, Cliff Rd. ℭ **01326/312884.** www.gyllybeach.com. Main courses £11-£17. MC, V. Daily 9am-9pm (closing time varies).

ROSELAND PENINSULA
Smugglers at Tolverne ★ ⛨ BRITISH   You need to make an effort to find this former smugglers' inn, which is tucked away down a winding lane overlooking the Fal estuary. It's worth it, though. Owned since 2010 by the Tregothnan estate, this cozy restaurant has rapidly built up a local following. Fresh, local ingredients are combined in dishes such as Cornish sea bass with saffron potatoes and marsh samphire, while dessert choices could well include ginger cake with toffee sauce and ice cream.

Tolverne, Philleigh. ℭ **01872/580309** or 01872/580000. www.tregothnan.com. Main courses £14- £18. MC, V. Mar-Sept daily noon-3pm and 6-9pm. From the A3078 follow signs to the King Harry Ferry, then turn off for Tolverne.

TRURO
Charlottes Tea House ★ BRITISH   Hidden away on the first floor of the former Coinage Hall in the heart of Truro, this traditional tearoom offers great views of the town while you enjoy tea and cakes, or light snacks and soups. The afternoon cream tea is a feast of scones, Cornish clotted cream, and jam. Waiting staff wear Victorian-style dress, and the dark-wood furnishings add to the "olde-worlde" atmosphere.

Coinage Hall, 1 Boscawen St. ℭ **01872/263706.** Main courses under £15. V. Mon-Sat 10am-5pm.

Saffron ★★ BRITISH   This established restaurant in the heart of Truro excels at taking local, seasonal produce and turning it into imaginative dishes. The cuisine draws on influences from around the world, so you could find Cornish duck and apricot tagine with couscous on the menu, alongside local skate served with tagliatelle. Vegetarians are also catered for—perhaps a starter of twice-baked cheese soufflé. Their "Cornish Ten Deadly Sins" brunch would set anyone up for a day's exploring, with organic eggs, bacon, sausages, and black pudding (blood sausage).

5 Quay St. ✆ **01872/263771.** www.saffronrestauranttruro.co.uk. Main courses £10–£17; £20 for 3-course meal. MC, V. May–Oct daily 10am–10pm; winter Mon 10am–3pm, Tues–Sat 10am–10pm.

Shopping

Truro city center has plenty of high-street shops from M&S to surfwear chains, as well as independent stores. **Lemon Street Market** (www.lemonstreetmarket.co.uk) is an attractive indoor center with lots of small shops and the great Lander gallery. Here you can buy plenty of locally made artworks, from paintings to jewelry. There's a couple of good cafes, too.

St. Mawes has a couple of galleries and good places for stocking up on souvenirs. The **Waterside Gallery** on Marine Parade (✆ **01326/270136;** www.waterside gallery.co.uk) stocks beautiful works by Cornish artists. Falmouth has a good selection of shops, with a mix of clothes shops, art galleries, food stores, and souvenir shops. As well as the High Street area, there are also shops at Discovery Quay, by the Maritime Museum.

Where to Stay

ROSELAND PENINSULA–ST. MAWES

Hotel Tresanton ★★★ ☺   Olga Polizzi's sleek seaside retreat casts an aura of a chic house party, 1930s' style, and even includes a cinema where screenings are held. This glamorous hotel offers a combination of beautiful old and new furnishings in its spacious, airy bedrooms, and makes a point of being family friendly, with a kids' playroom and garden. All rooms have a sea view, while nos. 22 to 27 have their own balconies. The elegant **restaurant** has a gratifying terrace and serves a daily changing menu, which features seafood such as oysters and lobster.

St. Mawes, Cornwall TR2 5DR. www.tresanton.com. ✆ **01326/270055.** Fax 01326/270053. 29 units. £190–£340 double; £320–£500 suite. 2-night minimum stay Sat–Sun. MC, V. Free parking. **Amenities:** Restaurant; bar; babysitting; children's playroom; massage room; room service. *In room:* TV, hair dryer.

Idle Rocks Hotel ★★★   Perched right on the seawall, the Idle Rocks hotel has a wonderfully relaxing atmosphere, friendly staff, and an excellent restaurant. Water laps at the wall, and you could sit for hours on the terrace enjoying the views of the harbor and the constant traffic of sailboats and dinghies. Rooms are spacious and comfortable, and most have sea or river views: It is well worth paying the extra for the view. Four cottage rooms in the annex are so close to the water that the waves can splash against the windows. The **waterfront restaurant** serves imaginative dishes using excellent local produce. Cream teas, served on the terrace on fine days, are popular, too.

Harbourside, St. Mawes, Cornwall TR2 5AN. www.idlerocks.co.uk. ✆ **01326/270771.** Fax 01326/270062. 27 units. £109–£209 double. AE, MC, V. Parking £5. **Amenities:** Restaurant; bar; Wi-Fi (free). *In room:* TV, hair dryer.

THE HELSTON PENINSULA

The Hen House ★★ 🎁   Genuinely eco-friendly and comfortable, this little B&B is tucked away among a maze of country lanes on the Helston peninsula. Two farm outbuildings have been converted into good-size en suite bedrooms, and there is also a self-catering barn. Good local food is served at breakfast, pets are welcome, and complimentary tai-chi sessions are available for guests. The rooms are set in tranquil gardens, with a wildflower meadow.

Manaccan, Helston, Cornwall TR12 6EW. www.thehenhouse-cornwall.co.uk. © **01326/280236.** 3 units (1 self-catering unit). £90 double (including breakfast); self-catering barn £200–£500 per week. MC, V. No children 11 and under. Free parking. Discounts on B&B bookings of more than 4 nights. *In room:* TV/ DVD, hair dryer, fridge, Wi-Fi (free).

THE REMOTE WEST PENZANCE

280 miles SW of London; 77 miles SW of Plymouth

With its Iron Age settlements, beguiling beaches, and working fishing ports, this is where you'll feel the heart of Celtic Cornwall beating. It is the western-most corner of England, the delicious air of remoteness enhanced by the fact that the railway line terminates at the Penzance, the largest town in this area. Artists and sculptors have long been attracted to this region and you'll have plenty of opportunities to purchase works in local galleries.

Penzance has a rich history—not surprising given that its name means "Holy Headland" in Cornish. It was raided and burned by Spanish pirates in the 16th century, but rose from the ashes to become an important "coinage" town where tin was assayed. When the railway arrived in Victorian times it became a popular seaside resort and still makes a good base for exploring Cornwall's western tip. Land's End, St. Michael's Mount, and the old fishing ports of Newlyn and Mousehole are all close by, and regular ferries leave for the Isles of Scilly. Popular white sandy beaches are at Sennen Cove and Porthcurno.

Essentials

GETTING THERE There are daily trains and buses to Penzance from London. The train takes around 5½ hours from Paddington Station (costing around £65 for a round-trip), the bus 8½–9 hours from Victoria Coach Station. The A30 runs through the heart of Cornwall down to Penzance, where an unclassified road leads into the town itself.

VISITOR INFORMATION **Penzance Tourist Office,** at Station Approach, Penzance (© **01736/362207;** www.purelypenzance.co.uk), is open Easter to September, Monday to Friday 9am to 5pm, Saturday 10am to 4pm; rest of year Monday to Friday 9am to 5pm.

Exploring the Area

Botallack Mine ★★ HISTORIC SITE On the western tip of Cornwall, the remains of the Crowns engine houses at Botallack are one of the county's most romantic sights. This former metal mine had shafts that stretched 800m (2,625 ft.) under the seabed and was so famous that Queen Victoria paid a visit. It closed in 1914, but the remains of the buildings still cling to the cliffs, and there are some great walks in the area.

Short drive from Botallack, nr. St. Just in Penwith. © **01736/788588.**

Minack Theatre ★★ THEATRE One of the most unusual theatres in Britain, this open-air amphitheatre was cut from the side of a rocky Cornish hill near the village of Porthcurno, 9 miles southwest of Penzance. Its legendary creator was Rowena

From Penzance, a 2-mile promenade leads to the fishing village of **Newlyn ★**. Stanhope and Elizabeth Forbes founded an art school here in 1899, and the village has been an artists' colony ever since. **Newlyn Art Gallery** (✆ **01736/363715; www.newlynart gallery.co.uk**) displays the works of contemporary artists. There are two spaces: One at New Road, Newlyn, and the other at The Exchange, Princes Street. Penzance is also home to

Penlee House Gallery and Museum (✆ **01736/363625; www.penleehouse. org.uk**), which displays works by Newlyn artists. There are also several galleries in Mousehole and at St. Just in Penwith. An **Art Pass** (available from Newlyn Art Gallery, Penlee House, Tate St. Ives, Barbara Hepworth Museum, and Leach Pottery) allows unlimited access to these galleries for 7 days for £15.

Cade, an arts enthusiast who began creating the theatre in 1931. An exhibition hall on the premises showcases her life and accomplishments.

Up to 750 visitors at a time can sit directly on grass- or rock-covered ledges, watching performances with sweeping views of the sea as a backdrop. Performances are likely to include everything from Shakespeare (the Minack's first production was *The Tempest*) to Gilbert and Sullivan, from opera to ballet. *Insider tip:* Make sure you bring a raincoat with a hood, in case it rains.

Porthcurno. ✆ **01736/810181.** www.minack.com. Theatre tickets £8–£9.50 adults, £4–£5 children 15 and under; tour tickets £4 adults, £3 seniors, £2 children 12–15, free children 11 and under. Day visits Apr–late Sept daily 9:30am–5pm; Oct daily 10am–4:30pm; Nov–late Mar daily 10am–3:30pm. Performances late Apr–late Sept. From Penzance, take the A30 heading toward Land's End; after 3 miles, bear left onto the B3283 and follow the signs to Porthcurno.

St. Michael's Mount ★★ CASTLE   Two thousand years ago, the rocky islet of St. Michael's Mount was an important tin trading post. It became a place of pilgrimage in the 6th century, and a Benedictine monastery was built here in the 12th century. Its strategic position became evident in 1588, when beacons were lit to warn of the advancing Spanish Armada, and during the Civil War, the islet was heavily fortified by Royalist forces. Today you can visit the castle, home to the St. Aubyn family since the 17th century, and explore the terraced gardens where exotic plants thrive. If the tide is out, you can walk across the causeway from Marazion in a few minutes; if the tide's in then boats run regularly from Marazion (weather allowing). The steps up to the castle are steep and rough, so wear sturdy shoes. To avoid disappointment, call the number listed below to check on the tides—and never try to beat the tide. Allow 3 hours for a visit.

St. Michael's Mount, Mount's Bay. ✆ **01736/710507.** www.stmichaelsmount.co.uk. Admission castle £7 adults, £3.50 children 5–15, free children 4 and under, £18 family ticket; admission gardens £3.50 adults, £1.50 children 5–15, free children 4 and under; combined tickets £8.75 adults, £4.25 children 5–15, free children 4 and under, £22 family ticket. Free to National Trust members. Castle late Mar–Oct Sun–Fri 10:30am–5pm, Nov–late Mar guided tours Tues and Fri 11am and 2pm. Gardens mid Apr–late Jun Mon–Fri 10:30am–5pm; July–Aug Thurs–Fri 10:30am–5:30pm; Sept Thurs–Fri 10:30am–5pm; closed Oct–mid Apr.

Trengwainton Garden ★ GARDEN   First laid out in the 19th century, these sheltered gardens display a fine collection of camellias, magnolias, and rhododendrons, as well as banana palms and a stream lined with feathery bamboos and

Australian tree ferns. The walled kitchen garden has been restored and is filled with contemporary varieties of fruit and vegetables.

West of Heamoor, off the Penzance–Morvah Rd. ℂ **01736/363148.** www.nationaltrust.org.uk. Admission £5.90 adults, £2.90 children 11 and under, £15 family ticket. Free to National Trust members. Mid-Feb–late Oct Sun–Thurs 10:30am–5pm.

Shopping

This area is a great place for arts-and-crafts purchases, with galleries of various sizes in Penzance, Mousehole, Newlyn, and St. Just in Penwith selling watercolors, drawings, prints, jewelry, and craftworks. **Lamorna Pottery** (ℂ **01736/810330;** www.lamornapottery.co.uk), in the village of Lamorna near Penzance, has a good reputation for glazed ceramic ware.

Entertainment & Nightlife

The main performance venue is the **Minack Theatre** (see review, above). There is an independent cinema on Causewayhead in Penzance (www.merlincinemas.co.uk). The **Ship Inn,** South Cliff (ℂ 01736/731234; www.shipmousehole.co.uk), is in the heart of Mousehole and a great place to soak up the village atmosphere—it serves food, too. **The Pirate Inn,** Alverton Road (ℂ **01736/366094;** www.thepirateinn penzance.com), is a family-friendly pub on the outskirts of Penzance. It has a beer garden and restaurant and puts on live folk music on Tuesday evenings.

Where to Eat & Stay

Camilla House ★   This comfortable guesthouse is located near the promenade, within walking distance of shops and restaurants. A local mariner built this house for his family in 1836. The small to midsize bedrooms give you the feeling of being "at home," and the owners are helpful in providing information on local attractions. Rooms are individually decorated, and there are good views from the top floor. A delicious English breakfast is served in a charming dining room.

12 Regent Terrace, Penzance, TR18 4DW. www.camillahouse.co.uk. ℂ/fax **01736/363771.** 8 units. £73–£89 double. Rates include breakfast. MC, V. Free parking. Closed Jan 9–29. *In room:* TV, hair dryer, Wi-Fi (free)

The Coldstreamer Inn ★ BRITISH   This traditional pub just outside Penzance has gained a reputation for serving great modern British food, with a daily changing menu that features local fish, meat, and vegetables. Dishes might include wild bream

---

Mousehole

A short drive west, along the coast from Penzance, is the picturesque fishing village of **Mousehole** (pronounced *Mou*-zel) one of the loveliest in Cornwall; people come for miles to see its annual display of Christmas lights (www.mouseholelights.org.uk). On December 23, Stargazy Pie, a fish pie in which the fish heads stick up through the top—"gazing" at the stars—is eaten here. Still a working port today, the village was almost completely destroyed by Spanish pirates in the 16th century. A sign on a house commemorates Dolly Pentreath 1777, said to be the last known monoglot speaker of Cornish, while there is a Wild Bird Sanctuary (Raginnis Hill) that has been caring for sick and injured birds since 1928.

and pea risotto, and lamb chops served with pearl barley and caramelized shallots. Save room for desserts such as chocolate torte with clotted cream. There are three **double rooms** (£70–£80 with TV and Wi-Fi), recently refurbished in unfussy, contemporary style.

Guval, nr. Penzance, TR18 3BB. ℂ **01736/362072.** www.coldstreamer-penzance.co.uk. Main courses £9.50–£11. MC, V. Food served daily noon–3pm and 6–9pm.

Cornish Range ★ SEAFOOD This former pilchard factory in Mousehole has plenty of character and makes a great base for exploring the area. Even if you're not staying here, its popular restaurant, which focuses on seafood, is one of the best in the area. Dishes that feature locally caught fish might include mussels with white wine as a starter, then saffron roasted hake or Goan seafood curry as a main course. Vegetarians aren't neglected, with choices such as wild mushroom risotto. There are also three comfortable **bedrooms** (£80–£110 double with TV), each attractively furnished with a private bathroom and king-size bed.

6 Chapel St., Mousehole, TR19 6SB. ℂ **01736/731488.** www.cornishrange.co.uk. Reservations recommended for dinner in summer. Main courses £13–£18. MC, V. Easter–late Sept daily 10:30am–2:30pm and 5:30–9pm; winter open most evenings, but only weekends Jan–Feb (call ahead to check hours).

Ennys ★ 👔 Run by the amiable and welcoming Gill Charlton, Ennys is a luxury guesthouse set in peaceful surroundings, a mile from any road down a long private drive. This historic Georgian estate boasts landscaped gardens in a bucolic setting and inside has well-appointed rooms with original works of art on the walls, and furnishings from local craftsmen. For a birthday, honeymoon or special occasion this guesthouse is ideal, but what really marks it apart is its concierge service that means your every whim (be it theatre tickets and restaurant reservations to yoga, surfing or wild swimming) is taken care of while you relax.

St. Hilary, Penzance, Cornwall TR20 9BZ. www.ennys.co.uk. ℂ **01736 740262.** Fax 01736 740055. 6 units. 3 cottages.£105–£165 double; £155–£195 suite. Rates include breakfast and afternoon tea. MC, V. Free parking. No children 16 and under. **Amenities:** Dining room; outdoor heated pool; tennis court. *In room:* TV/DVD, hair dryer, MP3 Docking Station, no phone, Wi-Fi (free).

2 Fore Street ★★★ 👔 BRITISH Sitting close to Mousehole harbor, this lovely, relaxed bistro is justifiably acclaimed for its modern British cuisine and pleasant staff. The daily changing menu features fresh local produce, and dishes range from Cornish steak with hand-cut chips to pan-fried mackerel with beetroot. Imaginative vegetarian dishes are always available. It's great for lunch and for dinner, and the neat little courtyard garden is a delight on fine days. There's a stylish **self-catering apartment,** "The Boat Watch," upstairs, with two double bedrooms, furnished in contemporary style (£80 per night or £275–£675 per week).

2 Fore St., Mousehole, Cornwall TR19 6QU. ℂ **01736/731164.** www.2forestreet.co.uk. Reservations recommended. Main courses £10–£16. MC, V. Food served daily from 10am for coffee and cakes; regular menu daily noon–3pm and 6–9:30pm. Closed Jan–mid Feb.

THE ISLES OF SCILLY ★

27 miles SW of Land's End

Off the Cornish coast, the Isles of Scilly (or just "Scilly"—but never the "Scilly Isles"), a cluster of small granite masses in the Atlantic, are one of the mildest and most unspoiled places in the U.K. The archipelago comprises five inhabited and around 140 uninhabited islands. St. Mary's is the largest island with a population of around

1,500 people, while the other inhabited islands are Tresco, St. Agnes, St. Martin's, and Bryher. The Isles of Scilly figured prominently in the myths and legends of ancient Greece and Rome; in Celtic legend, they were inhabited by holy men.

The islands are studded with burial chambers, standing stones, and smugglers' hide-outs. Because visitors can't drive here, the islands are beautifully quiet and great locations for **walking** and **cycling,** as well as for **bird-watching.**

Essentials

GETTING THERE Isles of Scilly Skybus Ltd. (ℭ 0845/7105555; www.ios-travel.co.uk) operates 2 to 10 flights per day, depending on the season, between Land's End Airport and Hugh Town on St. Mary's Island. Flight time is 15 minutes.

Weather permitting, **British International Helicopters,** Penzance Heliport Eastern Green (ℭ **01736/363871** for recorded information; www.islesofscilly helicopter.com), operates up to 26 helicopter flights Monday to Saturday between Penzance, St. Mary's, and Tresco. Flight time is 20 minutes.

Slower going is a ship that leaves from the **Isles of Scilly Travel Centre,** on Quay Street in Penzance (ℭ **0845/710-5555;** www.ios-travel.co.uk). It departs up to 6 days a week between April and October, with a journey time of about 2¾ hours.

VISITOR INFORMATION The **Tourist Information Centre,** Hugh Street, St. Mary's (ℭ **01720/424031;** www.simplyscilly.co.uk), is open summer (usually Apr–Oct) Monday to Saturday 8:30am to 5:30pm, Sunday 9am to 2pm; winter (usually Nov–Mar), Monday to Friday 9am to 5pm, Saturday 9am to noon.

Exploring the Area

Each island has its own character, and you can travel between them by boat. **St. Mary's** boasts Scilly's only town, **Hugh Town.** It was constructed on a sandbar that lies between the principal part of St. Mary's and a hill in the west, called the **Garrison.**

From Hugh Town, you can see the island's highest point, **Telegraph Tower,** rising 48m (158 ft.). This is a memorable walk, and you can also pass on the way a stone burial chamber, **Bants Carn,** dating from the 3rd century B.C.

Other attractions include the **Isles of Scilly Museum,** on Church Street (ℭ **01720/422337;** www.iosmuseum.org; Easter–Sept Mon–Sat 10am–4:30pm, Sat 10am–noon; winter hours vary), which illustrates the history of the islands from 2500 B.C., with assorted relics discovered here; and **Longstone Heritage Centre,**

OUTDOOR activities IN SCILLY

The Isles of Scilly offer plenty of opportunities for walking, and if you are on St. Mary's you can rent bikes from **St. Mary's Bicycle Hire,** The Strand (ℭ **07796/638506).** A variety of boat trips, including bird-watching specials, are available from the **St. Mary's Boatmen Association,** The Strand (ℭ **01720/423999;** www.scillyboating.co.uk).

There is a **Diving School** on St. Martin's, which offers BSAC diving courses, dive charters, and even snorkeling safaris (ℭ **01720/422848;** www.scillydiving.com).

Holy Vale (daily 10am–3pm; usually closed Oct–late Mar), where you can learn about island life.

Tresco, which has the most luxurious hotel on Scilly, has an exceptionally mild climate and its famous **Abbey Garden** attracts large numbers of visitors.

St. Martin's has a rugged northern coast and a glorious beach, Great Bay, in the northeast. It's a good place for diving as well as for walking. **St. Agnes** is perhaps the most laid-back of the inhabited islands, and the most southerly, too. It doesn't have a hotel and is extremely popular with bird-watchers.

Abbey Garden ★★ 🎁 GARDEN   Started by Augustus Smith in the mid-1830s, this area was once a barren hillside. Today, the gardens are a nature lover's dream, with thousands of exotic plants from 80 different countries. The ruined priory was allegedly founded by Benedictine monks in the 11th century, though some historians date it from A.D. 964. Of special interest is the Valhalla Museum, a collection of 30 figureheads from ships wrecked around the islands.

Tresco. 🕐 **01720/424108.** www.tresco.co.uk. Admission £10 adults, free for children 15 and under. Daily 10am–4pm.

Shopping

St. Mary's has plenty of good arts-and-crafts shops, including **Phoenix Stained Glass Studio,** Portmellon Industrial Estate (🕐 **01720/422900;** www.phoenix stainedglass.co.uk), where you can watch stained-glass items being made.

Where to Eat & Stay

ST. MARY'S

Star Castle Hotel ★ 😊   This hotel, built as a castle in 1593 to defend the Isles of Scilly against Spanish attacks, offers views out to sea and over the town. A young Prince of Wales (later King Charles II) took shelter here, in 1643, when he was being hunted by parliamentary forces. Eight rooms are in the castle and three on the ramparts. The 27 rooms in the annex open directly onto the gardens. The rooms in the castle are more characterful, with four-poster beds and beamed ceilings, but the garden apartments are more spacious. The **Conservatory restaurant** specializes in fish, and both the hotel's restaurants are open to non-guests in the evening.

The Garrison, St. Mary's, Isles of Scilly TR21 0TA. www.star-castle.co.uk. 🕐 **01720/422317.** Fax 01720/ 422343. 38 units. £170–£286 double; £258–£378 luxury garden suite. Rates include half-board. AE, MC, V. Closed Jan. A 4-course meal in the restaurants is £35. **Amenities:** 2 restaurants; bar; indoor pool; room service; Wi-Fi (free). *In room:* TV, hair dryer.

TRESCO

New Inn   An interconnected row of 19th-century fishermen's cottages and shops, the New Inn is situated at the center of the island. The bedrooms are tastefully decorated in a modern style in blue and creamy yellow shades; each features matching twin or double beds. The more expensive units offer sea views.

The New Inn has a good **restaurant** as well as a **bar.** The menu features plenty of seafood, such as crayfish and crab linguine, and baked sea bream with fennel and a white-wine sauce. Burgers with chips are also on offer, as are vegetarian dishes. In summer, drinks and food can be enjoyed in the patio garden.

Tresco, Isles of Scilly TR24 0QQ. www.tresco.co.uk. 🕐 **01720/422844.** Fax 01720/423200. 15 units. £150–£240 double. MC, V. **Amenities:** Restaurant; 2 bars; beer garden; outdoor pool. *In room:* TV, hair dryer.

ST. IVES ★★

319 miles SW of London; 21 miles NE of Land's End; 10 miles NE of Penzance

This north-coast fishing village, with its sandy beaches, narrow streets, and well-kept cottages, is England's most famous artists' colony. The incredible light on this small peninsula has attracted artists and visitors alike since the 19th century, but it was after the arrival of sculptor Barbara Hepworth in the 20th century that St. Ives really gained prominence. The town is charming, with a bustling harbor, good shops, plenty of places to eat and drink, and some fine beaches—**Porthmeor Beach** for sand and surf and **Porthminster beach,** a splendid sandy stretch that is ideal for families. There's a traditional seamen's chapel on the promontory known as **The Island,** which also has great views of the bay. The town is extremely busy in summer.

Essentials

GETTING THERE   There are no direct trains to St. Ives, so it's necessary to change at St. Erth, on the main line from London Paddington Station, which is just a short—and very scenic—ride to St. Ives. **National Express buses (℃ 0871/781-8181;** www.nationalexpress.com) run to the town from London Victoria.

During the summer, many streets in the center of town are closed to vehicles, so it's best to leave your car in the public parking lot just outside the town. From May to the end of September, there is a train park-and-ride service between St. Erth/Lelant Saltings to St. Ives.

Exploring the Area

Barbara Hepworth Museum & Sculpture Garden ★★ MUSEUM   Dame Barbara Hepworth lived at Trewyn from 1949 until her death in 1975, at the age of 72. In her will, she asked that her working studio be turned into a museum where future visitors could see where she lived and created her world-famous sculptures. Today, the museum and sumptuous garden, now an extension of London's Tate, are virtually just as she left them. On display are sculptures and drawings, covering the period from 1928 to 1974, as well as photographs, documents, and other Hepworth memorabilia. You can also visit her workshops, housing a selection of tools and some unfinished carvings.

Barnoon Hill. ℃ **01736/796226.** www.tate.org.uk/stives/hepworth. Admission £5.25 adults, free for children 18 and under. Mar–Oct daily 10am–5:20pm (last admission 5pm). Nov–Feb Tues–Sun 10am–4:20pm (last admission 4pm), with garden closing at 4:20pm or dusk, whichever is earlier.

Tate St. Ives ★★★ ☺ GALLERY   This branch of London's famous Tate Gallery exhibits changing groups of work from the Tate's pre-eminent collection of St. Ives painting and sculpture, dating from about 1925 to the present day. The gallery is administered jointly with the Barbara Hepworth Museum (see above). There are three changing exhibitions a year, and you might see works by artists such as Barbara Hepworth, Alfred Wallis, Ben Nicholson, Naum Gabo, Peter Lanyon, Terry Frost, Patrick Heron, Simon Starling, and Roger Hilton. Children will love their own inter-active room, the trails, and the activities available. If you're feeling full of energy still you can hire bodyboards just opposite and enjoy the surf.

Porthmeor Beach. ℃ **01736/796226.** www.tate.org.uk/stives. Admission £6.25 adults, free for children 18 and under; £9.75 joint ticket for Tate St. Ives and the Barbara Hepworth Museum. Mar–Oct daily 10am–5:20pm (last admission 5pm); Nov–Feb Tues–Sun 10am–4:20pm (last admission 4pm). Closes occasionally to change displays; call for dates.

Where to Eat

Alba Restaurant ★★ ☺ BRITISH   Situated in the former lifeboat building on the wharf, Alba has quickly established a reputation for fine modern British food. It's set over two floors, the upper of which has fine sea views, while the lower gives you the opportunity to watch the chefs at work. Local produce such as Cornish beef is served with roast shallots and a red-wine jus, while Cornish crab is served with linguine with chili and basil. There are separate menus for vegetarians and for children, and set lunches offer good value.

Old Lifeboat House, The Wharf. ⓒ **01736/797222.** www.thealbarestaurant.com. AE, MC, V. Main courses £12–£19. Daily noon–2:30pm and 5:30–9:30pm.

Porthminster Beach Café ★ SEAFOOD   This upmarket beachside cafe specializes in local seafood and stunning sea views. The daily changing menu has Asian and Mediterranean influences, and dishes might include line-caught sea bass, fried cuttlefish with black spices and citrus miso, or Parmesan baked sardines. Desserts range from caramel bananas to rich chocolate--and-orange crème brûlée served with marmalade ice cream. It's also open for coffee in the mornings.

Porthminster Beach. ⓒ **01736/795352.** www.porthminstercafe.co.uk. Reservations recommended. Main courses £8.75–£19. MC, V. Daily from 9am for coffee, then food served noon–4pm and 6–10pm.

Shopping

St. Ives has some of the best shopping in Cornwall, with plenty of good-quality beach and outdoor wear stores as well as galleries and shops selling local arts, crafts, gifts, and food. The main shopping street is cobblestoned Fore Street, with plenty of quaint shops hiding in little streets at the bottom of the hill. Along The Wharf by the harbor is the **Fishermen's Co-operative** store (ⓒ **01736/796276;** www.fishermens co-op.co.uk), selling all sorts of outdoor and waterproof clothing for the changeable weather. A **Farmers' Market** is held every Thursday on The Stennack.

Entertainment & Nightlife

St. Ives is full of pubs and bars, with a couple of small nightclubs. For more relaxed entertainment, head to **St. Ives Jazz Club** at The Western Hotel, Royal Square (ⓒ 01736/798061; www.stivesjazzclub.com) on Tuesday evenings, where you can enjoy modern jazz. **The Royal Cinema** (ⓒ **01736/796843;** www. stives.merlin cinemas.co.uk), a small cinema on The Stannack, Royal Square, shows latest releases.

   The best pubs around this area include the **Gurnard's Head** between St. Ives and St. Just (ⓒ **01736 796 928;** www.gurnardshead.co.uk) and **Tinners Arms** in Zennor (ⓒ **01736 796 927;** www.tinnersarms.co.uk). Another suggestion for a good meal, and day out further afield is **The Victoria Inn** (ⓒ **01736 710309;** www. victoriainn-penzance.co.uk).

Where to Stay

Primrose Valley Hotel ★★ 📱   This Edwardian villa has been stylishly converted to receive guests from its position in a residential cul-de-sac across the railway tracks from Porthminster Beach. The furnishings are contemporary, from the soft Italian leather chairs to the oak tables. As befits a house of its age, the bedrooms vary in size, and four of them open onto views of the sea. Although there's no formal reception desk, there is a beauty therapy room where you can relax and enjoy some pampering. Breakfast is a treat, with high-quality local produce a feature.

Porthminster Beach, St. Ives, Cornwall TR26 2ED. www.primroseonline.co.uk. ☎ **01736/794939.** 9 units. £105–£170 double; £199–£240 suite. Rates include breakfast. AE, MC, V. Limited free parking. No children 8 and under. **Amenities:** Bar serving snacks; beauty room. *In room:* TV/DVD, hair dryer, Wi-Fi (free).

ST. AGNES TO PADSTOW ★★

Padstow: 211 miles SW of London, 59 miles NE of Lands End, 50 miles NE of Penzance

The coast from St. Ives to Port Isaac has a drama all its own, encompassing wild and windy cliff-tops, golden stretches of sand, and fascinating relics of the county's mining heritage. It's a holiday hotspot, and some areas, such as the resort of **Newquay,** get extremely busy in high season. However, there are some fine walks and charming villages to explore.

Essentials

GETTING THERE   The nearest mainline railway station to Padstow is Bodmin Parkway, where trains stop on their way from London Paddington down to Penzance. Sometimes buses connect with train services, but you might need to get a taxi. If you're driving, the A389 runs from Bodmin to Wadebridge, where you join the A39 going west, then branch off onto the A389 again to reach Padstow.

Newquay airport (☎ **01637/860600;** www.newquaycornwallairport.com) is just 3 miles outside Newquay, and receives flights from London Gatwick, the Isles of Scilly, and other airports in the U.K. Car rental is available here.

VISITOR INFORMATION   **Padstow Tourist Information Office,** North Quay (☎ **01841/533449;** www.padstowlive.com), is open summer Monday to Friday 9am to 5pm, Saturday and Sunday 10am to 4pm. Winter hours are Monday to Friday 10am to 4pm, Saturday 10am to 2pm. The **Newquay Tourist Information Office,** Marcus Hill (☎ **01637/854020;** www.visitnewquay.org), is open April to

A Heritage of Tin	

Cornwall is rich in metals, particularly tin, which has been extracted here since Roman times. Although South Crofty, the last working tin mine in Europe, closed in 1998, in 2011 indium, a metal used in iPhones, was discovered there, leading to speculation that it might re-open. The county's unique mining landscapes, dotted with the picturesque ruins of engine houses, have been declared a UNESCO World Heritage site (www.cornish-mining.org.uk). Among the sites to visit are **Cornish Mines and Engines,** a National Trust site near Redruth, with the last steam-powered beam engine made in Cornwall; **Poldark Mine,** Wendron, near Helston

(☎ 01326/573173; www.poldark-mine. co.uk; Apr–Oct Sun–Fri 10am–5:30pm; June–July also Sat 10am–5:30pm; admission/guided tour £22 adults, £9.50 children 16 and under, £24 family ticket; admission/site only £2.50 adults, free for children 16 and under), an 18th-century mine that has a superb underground tour (not for the faint-hearted); and **Geevor** (☎ 01736/788662; www. geevor.com; Apr–Oct Sun–Fri 9am–5pm and Nov–Mar 9am–4pm, admission £9.50 adults, £5 seniors and children 5–16, free children 4 and under, £29 family ticket), a mine that shut in 1990 and reopened as a "time warp" museum.

10

CORNWALL | St. Agnes to Padstow

417

September Monday to Friday 9:15am to 5:30pm, Saturday and Sunday 10am to 4pm. From September to March it's open Monday to Friday 10am to 4pm, Saturday to Sunday 10am to 3pm.

Exploring the Area

The area around St. Agnes is carpeted with gorse-covered heathland that surrounds the ruined engine houses of the Wheal Coates mine: The National Trust parking lot (free for members) is a good starting point for walks (from the outskirts of St. Agnes, follow signs to the Beacon). **St. Agnes Beacon,** a prominent hilltop, offers excellent views over the surrounding countryside. Fires were lit here to warn villagers of impending attack from the Spanish Armada.

The village itself is a charming jumble of cottages, with several galleries and crafts shops. **Trevaunance Cove** is a lovely sandy beach that's popular with families and surfers. Just outside the village, set in a steep-sided valley is **Blue Hill Tin Streams ★** (✆ **01872/553341;** www.bluehillstin.com), the last place in Cornwall where tin is being produced—using the ancient method of "streaming." You can tour the works from April to late October Monday to Saturday 10am to 2pm, July and August 10am to 4pm; admission is £6 adults, £3 children. Take the B3285 to Perranporth from St. Agnes, turn left to Wheal Kitty, then right at the grass triangle.

Newquay, a resort with sandy beaches at the foot of the cliffs, is the surfing capital of Britain and attracts a party-loving crowd—particularly in high season. **Fistral Beach** and **Watergate Bay** are its best-known beaches, and although the town itself lacks charm, the coastline is stunning.

Picturesque **Padstow** is a gem, a bustling fishing village on the Camel estuary that still has a small working fleet. With a history stretching back to the 6th century, it became an important trading port and customs post (Sir Walter Raleigh lived here when he was Warden of Cornwall). **St. Petroc's Church** is a medieval structure with a fine 15th-century font. Padstow makes a good base for exploring this part of Cornwall. Large numbers of visitors come to sample the food of local celebrity chef Rick Stein, whose empire has expanded to cover much of the town (hence the nickname "Padstein") and includes a cookery school (Riverside; ✆ **01841/532700;** www.rickstein.com). Sit by the quayside and enjoy some fish and chips or an ice-cream cone, and pop into the lovely **London Inn** at 6/8 Lanadawell Street (✆ **01841/532554;** www.staustellbrewery.co.uk), the local pub, for a drink or a bar meal.

On the other side of the Camel, just beyond the busy family beach at **Polzeath,** is the medieval **Church of St. Enodoc,** where the poet Sir John Betjeman is buried. It almost disappeared under encroaching sands in the 18th and 19th centuries, to the extent that access was only possible through the roof. The church today is surrounded by the fairways of the St. Enodoc Golf Club.

Outdoor Activities

Newquay's **Surf Academy,** Holywell Bay (✆ **01637/831369;** www.cornwallsurfacademy.com), offers surf lessons and courses lasting from 1 to 5 days. Surf rental is also available. Padstow is the finish point for the **Camel Trail,** a cycle/walking route that runs for 18 miles along a disused railway line by the River Camel from Wadebridge. Bike rental is available from **Trail Bike Hire,** South Quay, Padstow (✆ **01841/532594;** www.trailbikehire.co.uk).

The quaint fishing village and popular film location of **Port Isaac** is a short drive to the north, its tightly packed cottages and narrow lanes attract large numbers of summer visitors. Its most famous residents, the sea-shanty singing *Fishermen's Friends*, still perform on many summer Friday nights at The Platt (www.portisaacs fishermansfriends.com).

Prideaux Place ★★ ☺ HISTORIC SITE   Overlooking Padstow, this handsome Elizabethan house has for centuries been the home of the Prideaux family. Remodeled in the 18th and 19th centuries, its interiors boast fine plasterwork, paintings, and furniture. The historic gardens are being restored, while the surrounding deer park is thought to be the oldest in the country—legend has it that should the deer die out, the Prideaux family will disappear with them.

Padstow. ⓒ **01841/532411.** www.prideauxplace.co.uk. Admission £8 adults, £2 children 6–16, free for children 5 and under. Easter–late Apr and mid-May–early Oct house Sun–Thurs 1:30–4pm, grounds and tea room 12:30–5pm. Closed mid-Oct–Easter and early May.

Where to Eat
PADSTOW
Pescadou ★ ☺ SEAFOOD   Pescadou is the harbor-side restaurant of the Old Custom House hotel, and has a good reputation for its fish and seafood dishes. The atmosphere is unstuffy and informal. The menu varies depending on what has been caught locally, but is likely to include moules marinières, filets of turbot and red mullet served with a garlic mash, and a Padstow lobster served with salad. Meat and vegetarian dishes feature, too, and there are some dishes for children.

South Quay. ⓒ **01841/532354.** www.oldcustomhousepadstow.co.uk. Main courses £8.50–£18. MC. Daily noon–3pm and 7–9pm.

Rick Stein's Café ★★ BRITISH   Located in the heart of Padstow, this lovely cafe offers relaxed dining in a cozy setting: Wooden floors, comfy seats, and the option to call in for breakfast, for coffee and cake, or for a more substantial meal. Main courses tend to have an Asian influence, so look out for chicken satay with lime leaves, or lamb and spinach karahi curry offered alongside Cornish steak with chips. It is the least expensive of the restaurants owned by Rick Stein in Padstow—and it has **guestrooms** available (£97–£145 double including breakfast). At weekends a minimum of 2 nights, including a Saturday must be booked. Other fine-dining establishments include his **Seafood Restaurant** (Riverside) and **St. Petroc's Bistro** (New Street).

10 Middle St. ⓒ **01841/532700.** www.rickstein.com. Main courses £11–£17. MC, V. Daily 8am–9:30pm (lunches noon–3pm; dinner 6:30–9:30pm).

SUMMERSCOURT
Viners ★★ 🍴 BRITISH   Tucked away in the Cornish countryside, this friendly stone-built pub is run by the first chef to win a Michelin star in Cornwall. With gardens and a children's play area, it's popular with families for Sunday lunch, while the menu features dishes such as a pot-roast lamb, or chicken breast stuffed with cream cheese. There are daily specials, as well as lighter snacks available, and Sunday lunch includes a vegetarian choice.

Carvynic, Summerscourt (7 miles inland from Newquay, off the A3058). ⓒ **01872/510544.** www. vinersrestaurant.co.uk. Reservations recommended. Main courses £9.95–£23. AE, MC, V. Tues–Sat 6:30–9pm, Sun noon–mid-afternoon.

The **South West Coast Path** (www.south westcoastpath.com), Britain's longest national marked trail, runs for 630 miles, from Minehead in Somerset to Poole in Dorset. It encompasses the length of the Cornish coast and is challenging in places but also offers easier exhilarating walks. The **Saints' Way** runs 30 miles from coast to coast, from Padstow in the north to Fowey in the south. Route cards are available from Boscastle Visitor Centre (𝄞 **01840/250010**). A circular walk, the **Copper Trail** (www.ldwa.org.uk), runs for 60 miles along footpaths and tracks around the Moor, past many ancient sites.

NEWQUAY

Fifteen Cornwall ★★★ ☺ ITALIAN   Part of Jamie Oliver's stable, Fifteen Cornwall is the perfect place to dine while watching the sun setting over the sea. The ethos of Fifteen is to offer disadvantaged young people the chance to train in the catering industry, while offering guests good food from local suppliers. The cuisine is Italian with a Cornish twist, and dishes might include pasta with cavalo nero pesto, or filet of beef in lardo di Colonnata with borlotti beans. In the evening there is a six-course tasting menu, while they also serve breakfasts—very popular with families.

On the Beach, Watergate Bay. 𝄞 **01637/861000.** www.fifteencornwall.co.uk. Reservations recommended. Main courses £17–£23. AE, MC, V. Daily 8:30–10am (Sun 10–11:30am), noon–4:30pm, and 6:15pm–midnight. All children welcome at breakfast and lunch, and those aged 7–12 at dinner before 7pm (over 12 can dine at any time).

Shopping

Newquay is a great place for surfing shops, with **The Shop on the Beach** at Watergate Bay (𝄞 **01637/860051;** www.shoponthebeach.com) one of the more popular spots for surfwear, wetsuits, books, boards, and kites, but centers such as St. Agnes and Padstow are good places for browsing. Both have a number of arts-and-crafts galleries, such as **Jo Downs'** (𝄞 **01841/533854;** www.jodowns.com) handmade glass shop at 24 Middle Street in Padstow. Padstow also has branches of some high-street stores, such as **White Stuff** and an excellent baker, the **Chough Bakery,** 3 The Strand (𝄞 **01841/533361;** www.thechoughbakery.co.uk), where you can buy fresh-made Cornish pasties.

Where to Stay

Cyntwell B&B ★ 🎁   This sweet little cottage in the heart of Padstow dates back to the 18th century. Steep narrow steps lead to the en suite bedrooms, all of which have been sympathetically refurbished. They are all light and bright and vary in size, reflecting the age of the property. All but one has a bath as well as a shower. No children 6 and under.

4 Cross St., Padstow PL28 8AT. www.cyntwell.co.uk. 𝄞 **01841/533447.** 4 units. £65–£88. Rates include breakfast. MC, V. *In room:* TV, hair dryer.

The Scarlet ★★★ 🎁   The Scarlet must surely be the coolest hotel in Cornwall. It only opened in 2010 and has been built to be as stylish and as eco-friendly as possible. Making the most of its expansive sea views, the contemporary rooms all have some outside space and funky furnishings. There's an excellent spa with a stunning indoor pool, as well as a natural outdoor pool that's cleansed by a reed bed. Local produce takes pride of place in the **restaurant** (three-course meal £40), which might feature dishes such as roast halibut with a pine nut and chervil crust. The hotel is aimed at adults, while its nearby sister hotel, the **Bedruthan Steps,** is very family friendly.

Tredragon Rd., Mawgan Porth TR8 4DQ (around 6 miles north of Newquay). www.scarlethotel.co.uk. ℂ **01637/861800.** Fax 01637/861225. 37 units. £190–£350 smallest rooms, £320–£480 largest rooms. 2-night minimum stay at weekends. MC, V. **Amenities:** Restaurant; spa; 2 swimming pools; library; pool table; hot tub. *In room:* TV, some rooms have large freestanding bathtubs as well as showers, hair dryer.

TINTAGEL, BUDE & BODMIN MOOR

264 miles SW of London; 49 miles NW of Plymouth; 6 miles NW of Camelford

Divided in two by the A30, **Bodmin Moor** is a windswept upland that has been designated an Area of Outstanding Natural Beauty (AONB). Wild and bleak, it is sparsely populated but dotted with prehistoric remains such as Trethevy Quoit, a neolithic burial chamber near St. Cleer. The Moor's highest point is **Brown Willy** (419m/1,375ft).

The north coast is typified by dramatic cliffs and foaming seas. **Bude,** the largest town in this rugged corner of Cornwall, is just a few miles from the Devon border and a popular beach resort—**Widemouth Bay** is a favorite with surfers. The village of **Boscastle,** farther south, has an unspoiled beauty with picturesque cottages huddled along steep, narrow streets. The main visitor attraction, however, is **Tintagel Castle,** the legendary birthplace of King Arthur.

Essentials

GETTING THERE   By **train,** Bodmin Parkway Station is on the main railway line from London Paddington to Penzance. By **car,** Bodmin is close to the junction of the A30 and A38. Tintagel is about a 30-minute drive away.

VISITOR INFORMATION   Bodmin's **Tourist Information Office,** Shire Hall, Mount Folly Square (ℂ **01208/76616;** www.bodminlive.com), is open Easter to late October Monday to Saturday 10am to 5pm; October to Easter Monday to Friday 10am to 5pm, not open Saturday.

Exploring the Area

Families and steam-train fans can take a trip on the **Bodmin and Wenford Railway** (ℂ **0845/125-9678;** www.bodminandwenfordrailway.co.uk), a scenic railway running between Bodmin Parkway and Boscarne Junction. Bike rental, if you want to cycle the Camel Trail, is available from **Bodmin Bikes,** Dennison Road, Bodmin (ℂ **01208/73192;** www.bodminbikes.co.uk).

Tintagel Castle ★★★ CASTLE   Since medieval times this romantic castle has been associated with the legends of King Arthur. Whether or not the tales of Arthurian chivalry and the famous Round Table are true, it's worth coming here just for the views, which encompass some of the most dramatic coastal scenery in the West Country. Steep cliffs and a rugged sea combine to paint a powerful portrait.

Once a Roman settlement, the site was a trading post of Celtic kings in the 6th century, while the ruins of the castle that you see today date back to 1233. Essentially built in two sections, they stand high above the sea on a rocky promontory; to get to them you must take a steep walk from the parking area and ascend 100 rock-cut steps. You can also visit Merlin's Cave at low tide. The Arthurian legend continues to fascinate—in 1998, excavations uncovered a 1,500-year-old inscribed slate saying that "Artognau" had this made.

Bossiney Rd. (½ mile northwest of Tintagel). 𝄞 **01840/770328.** www.english-heritage.org.uk. Admission £5.50 adults, £5 students and seniors, £3.30 children 5–15, £14.30 family ticket. English Heritage members free. Daily Apr–Sept 10am–6pm, Oct 10am–5pm, and Nov–Mar 10am–4pm.

Shopping

You can stock up on Cornish wine and champagne at **Camel Valley Vineyards,** Nanstallon, Bodmin (𝄞 **01208/77959;** www.camelvalley.com), which offers tours (Apr–Sept Mon–Fri 2:30pm), tastings, and also has a shop.

Where to Stay

South Tregleath Farm ★ 👜　Staying on this working dairy farm gives you a taste of the "real" rural Cornwall with plenty of contemporary comforts. Guests have their own sitting room, which has stunning views of the surrounding countryside, and the rooms are individually furnished. Well-behaved dogs are welcome, and children can help to collect eggs from the farm's free-range hens.

Washaway, Bodmin, Cornwall PL30 3AA. www.south-tregleath.co.uk. 𝄞 **01208/72692.** 3 units. £65–£80 per room. Rates include breakfast. No credit cards. Free parking. **Amenities:** Fridge in guest lounge; evening meals available by arrangement. *In room:* TV, Wi-Fi (free).

THE COTSWOLDS

by Stephen Keeling

Between Oxford and the River Severn, the pastoral Cotswolds comprise a stretch of rolling limestone hills, steep escarpments, and meandering streams. Some of England's most ravishing villages dot this bucolic region, made rich from the medieval wool trade and distinctively built of honey-brown Cotswold stone.

SIGHTSEEING   Witheringly beautiful villages such as **Bibury, Painswick, Broadway,** and **Chipping Campden** are likely to be your most endearing memories of the region. Eating at medieval inns, soaking up the picture-perfect scenery, and wandering the narrow lanes—before the crowds arrive—is at the heart of the Cotswold experience. There are plenty of traditional sights, of course: **Gloucester** is home to a handsome cathedral; Cheltenham is a sophisticated spa town; and **Sudeley Castle** provides some historical glamor.

EATING & DRINKING   When it comes to food, the Cotswolds is all about fresh, locally grown produce. You'll find **farmers' markets** and organic farm shops, like the one near **Cirencester,** throughout the region, and organic meat and vegetables are served at numerous restaurants. You can buy **fresh fish** at trout farms, like those at Bibury and Donnington. **Cheltenham** is the gastronomic capital of the region, with a host of stylish and acclaimed restaurants led by **Le Champignon Sauvage.**

OUTDOOR ACTIVITIES   The lesser-traveled roads of the Cotswolds make tempting targets for **cyclists,** and there are plenty of rental shops and specialist cycle tour companies to help. Another enticing outlet for healthy activity is the **Cotswold Way,** a 100-mile trail that cuts across the most seductive of the region's landscapes, towns, and mercifully, historic pubs.

ARTS & CULTURE   Cheltenham is also the region's art and culture hub, celebrated for its roster of **festivals** that cover everything from folk, jazz, and classical music to literature. Elsewhere, the 19th-century Arts and Crafts Movement has a shrine in the form of **Kelmscott Manor,** the home of William Morris, while the **New Brewery Arts center** in Cirencester harbors 12 contemporary artists who craft all manner of goods for sale.

THE best TRAVEL EXPERIENCES IN THE COTSWOLDS

o **Hiking the Cotswold Way:** This rustic hiking trail is one of the most popular in England, for good reason—it winds its way through 100 miles of lush Cotswold countryside, taking in some of the region's most awe-inspiring towns and villages: Chipping Camden, Painswick, and Bath. See p. 427.

o **Shopping for English antiques:** The Cotswolds is a major center for high-quality antiques, and you could spend several weeks digging around for bargains in its numerous antique stores; expect anything from Georgian furniture to Victorian dolls. Stow-on-the-Wold is the best place to begin. See p. 442.

o **Climbing Broadway Tower:** Make your way up this 17-m (55-ft.) folly designed by Capability Brown—the second highest point in the Cotswolds—for gasp-inducing views across the entire region. See p. 444.

o **Going to the races:** Every year in March, Cheltenham hosts the Gold Cup, the most prestigious horse-jump race in the U.K. Races are often dramatic, raucous affairs, and a unique slice of English life. See p. 432.

o **Sleeping in a four-poster bed:** The Cotswolds are littered with old country houses, pubs, and inns that have been converted into plush hotels, unashamedly cashing in on the region's historic appeal with a liberal sprinkling of four-poster beds—the Swan Hotel in Bibury is a good example. See p. 431.

BURFORD ★

176 miles NW of London; 20 miles W of Oxford

Built of classic honey-gold Cotswold stone, the unspoiled medieval town of **Burford** serves as the best gateway to the region coming from London or Oxford. The town was one of the last of the great wool centers, the industry bleating out its last breath during Queen Victoria's reign. Today it's best known for its Norman church and its High Street lined with old coaching inns and antique shops.

On Your Bike

Biking the country roads of the Cotswolds is one of the best ways to experience the quiet beauty of the area. For a self-guided tour (but with a lot of help), you can hook up with **Cotswold Country Cycles** (✆ 01386/438706; www.cotswoldcountrycycles.com), whose tours are designed to take you off the beaten track. Lodging is arranged in advance, often at manor houses or historic homes. A typical offering is the 3-day, 2-night adventure called "Simply Cotswolds," based in Chipping Campden (p. 447) and starting at £225 per person. A simpler option is offered by **Hartwells Cycle-Hire** (✆ 01451/820405; www.hartwells.supanet.com), which rents bikes (£12 a day, £7 children 15 and under) from its base on Bourton-on-the-Water (p. 437).

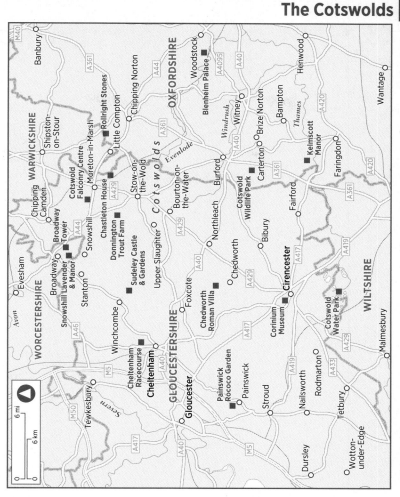

The River Windrush, which toward Burford is flanked by willows and meadows, passes beneath a packhorse bridge and goes around the church and away through more meadows toward **Widford.** Strolling along its banks is a delightful experience and a fitting introduction to the Cotswolds.

Essentials

GETTING THERE If you're driving, Burford is easy to reach from Oxford via the A40. Otherwise, you'll have to take the bus; the best option is the **Swanbrook** (*©* **01452/712386;** www.swanbrook.co.uk) Oxford to Gloucester service that passes through Burford (the Oxford stop is at the Taylorian Institute on St. Giles

Street). Three buses per day (just one on Sun) make the 45-minute run to Burford (£3.40 one-way).

VISITOR INFORMATION The **Tourist Information Centre** is at the Old Brewery, Sheep Street (② **01993/823558;** www.cotswold.info/places/burford. shtml). It's open November through February, Monday to Saturday 9:30am to 4pm, and March through October, Monday to Saturday 9:30am to 5:30pm.

Exploring the Area

Though the wool trade has long since vanished, most of Burford remains unchanged in appearance, with medieval stone houses in the High Street, which sweeps down to the River Windrush, covered with roofs of Stonesfield slate. Burford's magnificent **Church of St. John the Baptist** (www.burfordchurch.org), dating from 1175, is almost cathedral-like in size, while the **Tolsey,** 126 High St., is where, from the 12th century, wool merchants paid their tolls and taxes. On the upper floor is the tiny **Tolsey Museum** (② **01993/823236;** Apr–Oct Tues–Sun 2–5pm; free), where you can see a medieval seal bearing Burford's insignia, the "rampant cat."

Before you leave Burford, we suggest a slight detour to **Swinbrook,** a pretty village by the River Windrush immediately to the east. It's best known as the one-time home of the fabled Mitford sisters. Visit the local parish church to see the grave of writer Nancy Mitford (1904–73) and the impressive tiered monuments to the Fettiplace family, once the landed gentry of the region.

Cotswold Wildlife Park ☺ ZOO Two miles south of Burford on the A361 lies the incongruous but entertaining Cotswold Wildlife Park, a guaranteed hit with children. The 65 hectares (160 acres) of gardens and forests around this Victorian manor house have been transformed into a jungle of sorts, with a Noah's Ark consortium of animals ranging from voracious ants to rare Asiatic lions, rhinos, and a Madagascar exhibit for fans of the DreamWorks movie. Children can also romp around the farmyard and the adventure playground. A narrow-gauge railway runs from April to October, and there are extensive picnic areas as well as a cafeteria.

A361, south of Burford. ② **01993/823006.** www.cotswoldwildlifepark.co.uk. Admission £13 adults, £8.50 seniors and children 3–16, free for children 2 and under. Apr–Oct daily 10am–4:30pm; Nov–Mar daily 10am–3:30pm (last entry 1 hr. before closing).

Kelmscott Manor ★★ HISTORIC HOME This handsome Elizabethan mansion was the home of William Morris (1834–96), artist, craftsman, socialist, and founder of the influential Arts and Crafts Movement. The manor was built around 1600, from local limestone, and leased by Morris and the Pre-Raphaelite painter Dante Gabriel Rossetti in 1871. Inside you'll find a fine collection of Morris's work and personal possessions, from handcrafted furniture to original textiles, paintings, carpets, ceramics, and metalwork. Morris is buried in the grounds of nearby St. George's Church. Admission to the house is by timed ticket (last entry 4:30pm).

Kelmscott, Lechlade, Gloucestershire (off the A417), 10 miles south of Burford. ② **01993/823006.** www.kelmscottmanor.org.uk. Admission £9 adults, £4.50 students and children 8–16, free for children 7 and under. Apr–Oct Wed and Sat 11am–5pm. Closed Nov–Mar.

Where to Eat & Stay

Bay Tree Hotel ★★ This atmospheric old inn was built for Sir Lawrence Tanfield, the unpopular lord chief baron of the exchequer to Elizabeth I. Modern comforts have been discreetly installed in the English country-style accommodations, some of which have four-poster beds. Try to get a room overlooking the terraced gardens at the rear of the house. The house has oak-paneled rooms with stone fireplaces throughout, and a high-beamed hall with a minstrel's gallery. The elegant **restaurant** is open daily for modern English food, while lighter meals and drinks can be enjoyed in the Woolsack Bar.

12–14 Sheep St., Burford, Oxfordshire OX18 4LW. www.cotswold-inns-hotels.co.uk. © **01993/822791.** Fax 01993/823008. 21 units. £170–£180 double; £220–£255 suite. Rates include English breakfast. AE, DC, MC, V. Free parking. **Amenities:** Restaurant; bar; babysitting; room service. *In room:* TV, hair dryer, Wi-Fi (£9.99 for 24 hr.).

Burford House ★★★ Just eight immaculate and beautifully furnished rooms occupy this gorgeous 17th-century inn. Each comes adorned with antiques, spacious bathrooms, and huge tubs. Fresh cookies, water, tea, and coffee are supplied daily. Even if you don't stay here, come to eat. **Lunch** (Mon–Sat) and **dinner** (Thurs–Sat) feature the best of contemporary English cooking, with fresh organic vegetables, meats, and poultry sourced as locally as possible. Failing that, stop by for morning coffee with toasted crumpets (savory griddle cakes made from flour and yeast, a bit like a thick pancake), or the decadent afternoon teas with homemade scones, cakes, and pastries.

99 High St., Burford, Oxfordshire OX18 4QA. www.burford-house.co.uk. © **01993/823151.** Fax 01993/823240. 8 units. £179 double; £279 suite. Rates include English breakfast. Free street parking available nearby. AE, DC, MC, V. **Amenities:** Restaurant; bar. *In room:* TV, DVD, CD, hair dryer, Wi-Fi (free).

Lamb Inn ★ A meal in this pretty wisteria-clad restaurant and hotel is the perfect way to cap off a visit to Burford. Good set pub lunches dominate the restaurant at midday; set dinners are more formal, candlelit affairs. Expect dishes such as filet of Cotswold beef with horseradish mash, grilled trout with almond and vanilla sauce and roasted hake with saffron (two-course lunch £20, three-course lunch £25; two-course dinner £30; three-course dinner £35). The pub has a mellow atmosphere with cheaper meals and a carefully chosen selection of ales on tap. Built in 1420 as weavers' cottages and littered with fine antique furnishings, the Lamb is also an enticing place to spend the night, with bedrooms blending modern comforts and original fittings.

Sheep St., Burford, Oxfordshire OX18 4LR. www.cotswold-inns-hotels.co.uk. © **01993/823155.** Fax 01993/822228. 15 units. £155–£180 double. Rates include English breakfast. MC, V. Free parking at the nearby Bay Tree Hotel (see above). **Amenities:** Restaurant; bar; room service. *In room:* TV, hair dryer, Wi-Fi (£6 per 90 min.; £10 per 24 hr.).

The Cotswold Way

The **Cotswold Way** (www.nationaltrail.co.uk/cotswold) meanders for just over 100 miles from Chipping Campden to Bath (p. 335), taking in the best of the area's landscapes and traditional villages. You can hike the trail easily in a week or so, staying in country pubs or cozy B&Bs along the way. Several companies can arrange all the details. **Cotswold Walking Holidays** (© 01242/518888; www.cotswoldwalks.com) is a dependable choice, offering 7-night self-guided tours (including B&B, route instructions/map, and luggage transportation) for £395 per person. They also offer 3-night tours from £190 per person. Alternatively, the **Sherpa Van Project** (© 0871/5200124; www.sherpavan.com) will just transfer your luggage between accommodations from £7 per bag per day. Check also www.cotswold-way.co.uk.

CIRENCESTER ★

20 miles SW of Burford; 89 miles W of London; 16 miles S of Cheltenham; 36 miles W of Oxford

Cirencester is the unofficial "capital of the Cotswolds." Founded by the Romans as Corinium and then destroyed by the Saxons 300 years later, it boomed again in the Middle Ages thanks to the great Cotswold wool trade. Little remains from the medieval period, but plenty of well-preserved stone houses from the 17th and 18th centuries are still intact.

Today, Cirencester is chiefly a market town that makes a good base for touring. Visit the **Market Place** in the center on Monday or Friday 9am to 3pm, when it's packed with local traders.

Essentials

GETTING THERE   Cirencester has no railway station, but Cheltenham-bound Great Western trains depart every hour from London's Paddington Station for the 80-minute trip to Kemble (£23–£29), which is 4 miles southwest of Cirencester. You may have to transfer trains at Swindon. From Kemble station, buses travel to Cirencester (20–25 min.) but don't always meet the trains; **Stagecoach** (www.stagecoach bus.com) has seven departures (Mon–Sat only).

If you're driving from London, take the M4 west to junction 15, then the A419 north to Cirencester.

VISITOR INFORMATION   The **Cirencester Visitor Information Centre** is located in the Corinium Museum, Park Street (✆ **01285/654180;** www.cirencester. gov.uk). Hours are Monday to Saturday from 10am to 5pm, Sunday from 2 to 5pm (Nov–Mar closes at 4pm).

Exploring the Area

Church of St. John the Baptist CHURCH   A church may have stood here in Saxon times, but the present building overlooking the Market Place in the town center dates from the 15th and 16th centuries. In size, it appears more like a cathedral than a mere parish church, with a variety of styles, largely Perpendicular, as in the early 15th-century tower. Among the treasures inside are a 15th-century "wineglass" pulpit and a silver-gilt cup given to Anne Boleyn 2 years before her execution.

Market Place. ✆ **01285/659317.** www.cirenparish.co.uk. Free admission; donations welcomed. Mon–Sat 9:30am–5pm; Sun 2:15–5pm.

Corinium Museum ★★ MUSEUM   The Roman town of Corinium was the second largest in Roman Britain, and this museum houses a fine collection of archeological remains from that period, found locally in and around Cirencester. Highlights include intricate mosaic pavements, excavated on Dyer Street in 1849, and rare provincial Roman sculpture, including such figures as Minerva and Mercury. The museum has been completely modernized to include full-scale reconstructions and special exhibitions on local history from the Iron Age through the English Civil War.

Park St. ✆ **01285/655611.** www.cotswold.gov.uk. Admission £4.50 adults, £3.75 seniors, £3 students, £2.25 children 5–16. Mon–Sat 10am–5pm; Sun 2–5pm (closes at 4pm Nov–Mar).

Cotswold Water Park ★ WATER PARK   For fresh air and easy walks, head south from the Market Place for 3 miles on the A419 to this 40-square-mile reserve of parkland and woodland trails. Britain's largest water park contains more than 140 lakes surrounded by picnic tables, barbecue sites, and a network of footpaths.

Concessions here will hook you up for sailing, fishing, canoeing, cycling, kayaking, horseback riding, and water-skiing (but no jet-skiing and no waterslides). All equipment needed is available for rent on-site. Swimming is possible June through September at Lake 32 (www.ukwatersports.co.uk) and Lake 16 (www.southcerneyoutdoor.co.uk).

Gateway Centre, Spine Rd., South Cerney (B4696). ✆ **01285/861459.** www.waterpark.org. Basic admission free, otherwise varies according to activity and location; see website for details. Gateway Information Centre open daily 9am–5pm.

New Brewery Arts ARTS & CRAFTS The heart of this arts complex is the workshop area of 12 resident crafts workers who produce everything from baskets to chandeliers. Other components of the center include three galleries, featuring crafts and fine-art exhibitions alike, a theatre, education classes, a shop selling the best in British crafts, and a coffeehouse.

Brewery Court. ✆ **01285/657181.** www.breweryarts.org.uk. Free admission. Mon–Sat 9am–5pm; Sun 10am–4pm.

Shopping

For antiques in Cirencester, try **William H. Stokes,** the Cloisters, 6–8 Dollar St. (✆ **01285/653907;** www.williamhstokes.co.uk), which specializes in oak furniture, tapestries, and other items from the 16th and 17th centuries.

The **Organic Farm Shop ★★** just 2 miles outside Cirencester at Abbey Home Farm, Burford Road (B4425; ✆ **01285/640441;** www.theorganicfarmshop.co.uk), sells over 100 varieties of fresh, home-produced organic vegetables and herbs. It's open Tuesday to Thursday (and Sat) 9am to 5pm, Friday 9am to 6:30pm and Sunday 11am to 4pm. Even if you're not buying it's a great place to visit, and also has a cafe that serves up the produce.

Entertainment & Nightlife

For a pint, head for the town favorite, the **Crown,** 17 W. Market Place (✆ **01285/653206;** www.crownciren.com), a friendly pub enjoyed by locals and students alike, with out-of-towners predominating in summer. The place boasts a 400-year-old tradition of serving ale and victuals on this site, and it has the most convivial nightlife in town. The **Waggon & Horses ★★**, 11 London Rd. (✆ **01285/652022;** www.thewaggonandhorses.co.uk), is an 18th-century coaching inn that not only serves at least six real ales on tap, but also surprisingly good Thai food (cooked up by a real Thai chef).

Where to Eat & Stay

Barnsley House ★★ The Cotswolds is studded with expensive country-house resorts, but few are as chic, glamorous, and trendy as the former home of garden designer Rosemary Verey. On any weekday, this country house might be visited by regulars Kate Moss, Kate Winslet, Elizabeth Hurley, or Damien Hirst. The 17th-century mansion is surrounded by the best-landscaped gardens in the Cotswolds, and the soothing Garden Spa is spell-binding. The rooms blend stone fireplaces, wooden floors, and beams with contemporary furnishings and the latest technology—you can even take a bath while watching a DVD. The on-site **Potager Restaurant** uses local and fresh produce from the gardens to conjour up English dishes with an Italian influence, such as pumpkin cappelletti, and smoked haddock and pea risotto (main courses £12–£27).

Barnsley (4 miles NE of Cirencester), B4425, Gloucestershire GL7 5EE. www.barnsleyhouse.com. ✆ **01285/740000.** Fax 01285/740925. 11 units. £275 double; £295–£495 suite. Rates include continental breakfast. AE, MC, V. Free parking. **Amenities:** Restaurant; bar; room service; spa; private cinema. *In room:* TV/DVD, CD player, CD & DVD library, hair dryer, minibar, MP3 docking station, Wi-Fi (free).

Best Western Stratton House Hotel ★ Now part of the Best Western stable, this inviting country house is especially well priced, despite looking a bit tired and old-fashioned in places. Built in several stages throughout the 18th century, with a modern wing added in the 1990s, it has large, well-furnished rooms (the "cozy" rooms being the smallest of the lot); some have four-poster beds. It's 1¼ miles (20-min. walk) northwest of Cirencester town center.

Gloucester Rd. (A417), Cirencester, Gloucestershire GL7 2LE. www.strattonhousehotel.co.uk. ✆ **01285/651761.** Fax 01285/640024. 40 units. £40–£77 double. Rates include English breakfast. AE, DC, MC, V. Free parking. **Amenities:** Restaurant; bar; room service. *In room:* TV, hair dryer, Wi-Fi (£9.99 per 24 hr.).

Fleece Hotel For a historic choice in the center of town, it's hard to beat this half-timbered Elizabethan coaching inn. Charles II hid out on this site, posing as a servant to the house mistress, Jane Lane, in 1651, with Cromwell's troops in hot pursuit. The inn was enlarged in the Georgian period and today offers comfortable, small-to-mid-size rooms decorated in an old-fashioned English country style. Two rooms are large enough for families, and two have four-poster beds. The on-site **1651 restaurant and bar** serves reasonable English and Continental cuisine.

Market Place, Cirencester, Gloucestershire GL7 2NZ. www.fleecehotel.co.uk. ✆ **01285/658507.** Fax 01285/651017. 28 units. £86 double. Rates include English breakfast. Children 15 and under stay free in room with up to 2 paying adults. AE, MC, V. Free parking. **Amenities:** Restaurant; bar; room service. *In room:* TV, hair dryer.

Ivy House ★★ Just 3 minutes' walk from the town center, this congenial B&B gets high marks for location and comfy, no-nonsense rooms. The attractive ivy-smothered Victorian was built in 1870, and features compact but spotless rooms supplied with bottled water, tea, coffee, hot chocolate, and cookies. Breakfast is a real treat—try the home-baked granola.

2 Victoria Rd., Cirencester, Gloucestershire GL7 1EN. www.ivyhousecotswolds.com. ✆ **01285/656626.** 4 units. £65–£75 double. Rates include English breakfast. MC, V. Free parking. *In room:* TV, hair dryer, Wi-Fi (free).

Old Bungalow Guest House ★ If you like cozy, friendly B&Bs you'll love this unassuming place, but book well ahead—it has a loyal clientele of regulars. The rooms are simple but homey and feature all the usual amenities; three rooms come with a double and single bed, while the rest just have double beds. Gary and Hannah are gracious and informative hosts, and their breakfasts are always beautifully prepared. They also have a modern self-catering one-bedroom bungalow in the gardens (full kitchen) from £75.

93 Victoria Rd., Cirencester, Gloucestershire GL7 1ES. www.bandbcirencester.co.uk. ✆ **01285/654179.** 6 units. £65–£83 double. Rates include English breakfast. AE, DC, MC, V. Free parking. No children 9 and under. **Amenities:** Bar. *In room:* TV, hair dryer, Wi-Fi (free).

A Side Trip from Cirencester
BIBURY ★★

Bibury is one of the loveliest spots in the Cotswolds. In fact, William Morris called it England's most beautiful village.

On the banks of the tiny River Coln, 7 miles northeast of Cirencester on the B4425, Bibury is especially noted for **Arlington Row.** Built in 1380 as a monastic wool store, it was converted into a row of weavers' cottages in the 17th century. Today these houses are Bibury's biggest and most photographed attraction, but it's rude to peer into the windows, as many do, because people still live here.

To get a view of something a bit out of the ordinary for the Cotswolds, check out **St. Mary's Parish Church.** Much of its original Romanesque architecture has been left intact, as well as the 14th-century Decorated-style windows. The so-called "Decorated" style was the second period of English Gothic architecture, mainly from the late 13th to the mid-14th centuries, when adornments became more elaborate and stone construction lighter and more spacious.

It's also worth visiting the **Bibury Trout Farm** (© **01285/740215;** www.bibury troutfarm.co.uk), in the heart of the village, where visitors can stroll around the fish ponds as rainbow trout are fed. You can buy fresh or smoked trout at the farm shop. Admission is £3.95 for adults, £3.50 for seniors, and £2.95 for children 5 to 15 (free for children 4 and under). The farm is open Monday to Saturday 9am to 6pm, and Sunday 10am to 6pm (it closes at 4pm Nov–Feb).

The **Swan Hotel ★★** (**www.cotswold-inns-hotels.co.uk;** © 01285/740695; £160–£280 double; £250–£325 suite) offers the finest accommodation, tearoom, and restaurant in the village. It originated as a riverside cottage in the 1300s, but most of what you see today dates from the 17th century. Rooms are outfitted in a traditional, warm-toned design evocative of a discreetly upscale stately home, with tartan and flowered fabrics and fall-inspired colors. A three-course dinner in the **Gallery Restaurant** is normally £33 per person; full afternoon tea set is £18.

With no connecting buses into Bibury, you'll need to drive or take a taxi from Cirencester. For more information visit www.bibury.com.

CHELTENHAM ★

99 miles NW of London; 43 miles W of Oxford; 9 miles NE of Gloucester

Once the spa capital of England, Cheltenham boasts some of the nation's best examples of Regency architecture, excellent restaurants, and extensive 19th-century gardens. Cheltenham owes its size and position to the discovery of a mineral spring in 1716. King George III arrived in 1788 to take the waters (thought to have curative powers), launching a boom that lasted well into the 1800s. The spa is still here, but these days more people visit for the **Gold Cup,** the premier meet of British steeple-chase horse racing.

Cheltenham is also a major cultural center, with a decent roster of museums, live music venues, and numerous festivals in addition to its lauded architecture. Indeed, the main street, the Promenade, is one of the most beautiful thoroughfares in the Cotswolds.

Essentials

GETTING THERE   Great Western trains depart twice an hour from London's Paddington Station for the 2½-hour trip (£38–£84). You may have to change trains at Swindon. Trains between Cheltenham and Bristol take an hour, with continuing service to Bath.

If you're driving from London, head northwest on the M40 to Oxford, and continue along the A40 to Cheltenham.

Organized horse racing came to Cheltenham in 1815, with the location of **Cheltenham Racecourse** (*(℃)* **0844/ 5793003; www.cheltenham.co.uk**), in the nearby village of Prestbury (just a few minutes from the town center), dating from 1831. Since 1898 it's been the home of National Hunt (steeplechase) horse racing in the U.K. Meetings are hosted from October to April, but the highlight of the season is the **Cheltenham Gold Cup,** which is normally held in the middle of March, during what's dubbed the "Cheltenham Festival." The cheapest tickets ("Best Mate Enclosure") range from £12 to £15 (£35–£40 for the actual Gold Cup). Race day buses link Cheltenham railway station to the racecourse. See the website for more details.

VISITOR INFORMATION   The **Tourist Information Centre,** 77 Promenade (*(℃)* **01242/522878;** www.visitcheltenham.com), is open Monday to Saturday from 9:30am to 5:15pm. On Wednesday mornings, it opens at 10am.

To explore on your own, you can also get info from the **Cheltenham Tourist Information Centre,** 77 The Promenade (*(℃)* **01242/522878;** www.visitcheltenham. gov.uk).

Exploring the Town

Cheltenham Art Gallery & Museum ★ MUSEUM   This absorbing museum chronicles the town's rise to fame in the Regency period; it also houses one of the foremost collections of the Arts and Crafts Movement, notably the fine furniture of William Morris and his followers. Another gallery is devoted to Edward Wilson, Cheltenham's native son, who died with Captain Scott in the Antarctic in 1912. Note that some galleries will be closed while the museum undergoes an ambitious redesign in 2011 to 2012.

Clarence St. *(℃)* **01242/237431.** www.cheltenhammuseum.org.uk. Free admission. Daily 10am–5pm (Nov–Mar 4pm). Closed bank holidays.

Holst Birthplace Museum MUSEUM   This is a small but enlightening tribute to Gustav Holst, composer of *The Planets,* who was born in this Regency house in 1874. The rooms inside have been faithfully restored in Victorian and Edwardian style, with displays and personal items, including his piano, telling the story of Holst and his music.

4 Clarence Rd. *(℃)* **01242/524846.** www.holstmuseum.org.uk. Admission £4.50 adults, £4 seniors and children 5–16, £10 family ticket. Feb–mid-Dec Tues–Sat 10am–4pm. Closed late Dec–Jan.

Pittville Pump Room HISTORIC SITE   Cheltenham spring water is the only natural, consumable alkaline water in Great Britain and can still be drunk at one of the town's finest Regency buildings, built in the 1820s. The Greek Revival Pittville Pump Room is now used primarily as a concert and private-function venue, but you can still sample the pungent spring water from the original pump (free).

East Approach Dr., Pittville Park (2 miles north of the center). *(℃)* **0844/521621.** www.cheltenhamtown hall.org.uk. Free admission. Wed–Mon 10am–4pm. From the town center, take Portland St. and Evesham Rd.

Where to Eat

Brasserie Blanc ★ FRENCH/CONTEMPORARY ENGLISH   Already a bit of a dining legend in Oxford, Master Chef Raymond Blanc's *brasserie de luxe* has decor inspired by turn-of-the-20th-century Paris, a row of unusual sculptures that runs up the middle, and a hip and knowledgeable staff. Cuisine is beautifully presented and prepared with the freshest available ingredients. Mouth-watering examples include Raymond's hot smoked salmon and haddock fishcake; Loch Fyne mussels in white wine and cream; and pork and leek sausages, with chive and mustard butter sauce and mash.

Queen's Hotel, the Promenade. © **01242/266801.** www.brasserieblanc.com. Reservations recommended. Main courses £7.25–£15 lunch, £8.25–£16 dinner; fixed-price 2-course lunch £13, 3-course lunch £15; fixed-price 2-course dinner £16, 3-course dinner £18. AE, DC, MC, V. Daily noon–2:45pm and 5:30–10:30pm.

Daffodil ★ CONTEMPORARY ENGLISH   It's hard to top this magnificent setting in the auditorium of a former 1920s' Art Deco cinema, where the old movie screen has been replaced with the kitchen. The food is top-notch—check out the homemade salmon fishcakes or roast venison—and the service is usually friendly and attentive, but it can be hit and miss when it gets busy. It is best to avoid the restaurant altogether during the Christmas office-party season.

18-20 Suffolk Parade. © **01242/700055.** www.thedaffodil.com. Reservations recommended. Main courses £14–£21. Fixed-price lunch £14 for 2 courses, £16 for 3 courses. AE, DC, MC, V. Mon–Fri noon–2pm and 6:30–10pm, Sat noon–2pm and 6–10:30pm.

Le Champignon Sauvage ★★ FRENCH   This Michelin-star winner is among the culinary highlights of the Cotswolds, with top-notch French cuisine and especially scrumptious desserts. Main courses can include such artfully crafted dishes as wood pigeon with a carrot tagine; lamb with pea purée, pistachio and wilted lettuce; and hake poached with artichokes. Dessert choices include a sensational bitter

Festival Town

Cheltenham has a well-deserved reputation as a cultural center, with an especially rich line-up of annual festivals. The **Folk Festival** (tickets from £25) kicks things off in February, while the **Jazz Festival** (end Apr–early May) features a roster of international artists and the **Science Festival** (June) boasts lectures from a who's who of British and international science. Also in June, the alternative **Wychwood Music Festival** (www.wychwoodfestival.com) at Cheltenham Racecourse offers 3 days of music, comedy, cabaret, workshops, and film from £100. The **Music Festival** (July) showcases classical music, while the **Literature Festival** (Oct) offers an eclectic schedule of events, talks, and readings. See www.cheltenhamfestivals.co.uk for more details. For something a bit more offbeat, try the annual **Cheese Rolling Festival** (www.cheese-rolling.co.uk), at Cooper's Hill, 6 miles south of town on the A46. Usually held at the end of May, huge rounds of Double Gloucester cheese are rolled down the hill to wild (and boozy) applause—check the website first, as the authorities often try to ban or limit attendance. Note that the "Cheltenham Festival" actually refers to horse racing (p. 432).

chocolate and olive tart with fennel ice cream; and a tongue-tingling salted chicory iced mousse. The downside? It's expensive (of course), and the decor is a bit dull considering the quality of the food.

24–26 Suffolk Rd. ✆ **01242/573449.** www.lechampignonsauvage.co.uk. Reservations required. Fixed-price 2-course meal £48, 3-course meal £59, 4-course meal £68. AE, DC, MC, V. Tues–Sat 12:30–1:30pm and 7:30–8:45pm. Closed 2 weeks in June, 1 week in Dec.

Shopping

Start in the **Montpellier quarter** for individual boutiques, crafts, and specialty shops. The **Courtyard,** on Montpellier Street in the heart of the quarter, is an award-winning shopping mall that offers a blend of shops specializing in fashion, furniture, and gift items. A good mix of restaurants, cafes, and wine bars rounds out the mall.

From Montpellier, continue to the nearby **Suffolk quarter** to find most of Cheltenham's antiques stores, as well as a growing number of artisan jewelers, clothes and accessories, rugs, and prints shops.

An enjoyable short stroll to the **Promenade** takes you by stores featuring clothing and shoes, as well as several bookstores. **Cavendish House,** on the Promenade (✆ **01242/521300**), has been a department store since 1823, and is now part of the House of Fraser group.

From the Promenade, take Regent Street to **High Street,** which is mostly pedestrian-only, and you'll find several brand-name department stores in the **Beechwood Shopping Centre.**

The **weekly market** is in the Henrietta Street parking lot on Thursday (9am–2pm), while a **Farmers' Market** is held on the second and last Friday of the month on the Promenade (9am–3pm).

Entertainment & Nightlife

The major venue for entertainment is the **Everyman Theatre,** Regent Street (✆ **01242/572573;** www.everymantheatre.org.uk). Designed in the 1890s, the theatre attracts some of England's top dramatic companies with a program of Shakespeare, musicals, comedies, and other genres. Tickets range from £7.50 to £55, depending on the event.

You'll find more theatre at the **Playhouse,** Bath Road (✆ **01242/522852;** www.playhousecheltenham.org), which often presents new local, amateur productions of drama, comedy, dance, and opera staged every 2 weeks. Tickets usually run from £12 to £35.

THE PUB & BAR SCENE

The Beehive, 1–3 Montpellier Villas (✆ **01242/702270;** www.thebeehivemontpellier.com), is an award-winning pub known for its fine local ales (including Battledown Brewery), Thatchers ciders, board games, a superb upstairs restaurant, and courtyard garden. The pub is open daily noon to midnight.

For something a little more sophisticated, the **Montpellier Wine Bar,** Bayshill Lodge, Montpellier Street (✆ **01242/527774;** www.montpellierwinebar.com), offers alfresco dining and a decent selection of wines by the glass (open daily 10am–11pm).

Subtone, 117 Promenade (✆ **01242/575925;** www.subtone.co.uk), is Cheltenham's most popular nightclub and live music venue, with a host of visiting DJs and bands from around the globe (open Thurs–Sat 9pm–3 or 5am; cover £2–£7).

Where to Stay

Beaumont House One of the best-rated B&Bs in the area, this house is set in a lovely garden a short walk from the town center. Its luxurious bedrooms are among the best in the area—indeed, they've won awards. No guest rooms are alike, ranging from small singles to spacious rooms suitable for families. Comfort and style combine with a warm welcome to make this a desirable choice—and the price is right, too.

56 Shurdington Rd., Cheltenham, Gloucestershire GL53 0JE. www.bhhotel.co.uk. ✆ **01242/223311.** Fax 01242/520044. 16 units. £89–£165 double; £249 suite. AE, MC, V. Free parking. **Amenities:** Bar. *In room:* TV, hair dryer, Wi-Fi (free).

Big Sleep This local chain has revolutionized budget accommodations in the region, offering fresh, modern but cheap bedrooms near the center of town. Occupying the big, white cube that used to house the Inland Revenue, the interior features a crisp all-white color scheme and compact rooms with big beds, molded plastic chairs, and exuberant art on the walls. Breakfast comprises a buffet of fruit, cheese, toast, and eggs.

Wellington St., Cheltenham, Gloucestershire GL50 1XZ. www.thebigsleephotel.com. ✆ **01242/696999.** Fax 01242/520044. 60 units. £55–£160 double; £90–£300 family studio. Rates include breakfast. AE, MC, V. Parking £5 per stay (3pm–10:30am; £1 per hr. thereafter). **Amenities:** Bar; free use of nearby Fitness First gym. *In room:* TV, hair dryer, Wi-Fi (£1.99 per hr; £7.50 per day).

George Hotel ★ This elegant hotel, set in a Regency-period building from the 1840s, is the top choice in town, perfectly located 2 minutes from the Promenade. The interior is chic and contemporary; small and standard doubles are modern and comfy but nothing special, with the superior and deluxe doubles considerably more stylish.

St George's Rd., Cheltenham, Gloucestershire GL50 3DZ. www.stayatthegeorge.co.uk. ✆ **01242/235751.** Fax 01242/224359. 21 units. £120–£165 double; £185 suite. AE, DC, MC, V. Free parking. **Amenities:** Restaurant; bar; room service; free membership at CLC Sports Centre. *In room:* TV, hair dryer, Internet (free).

The Greenway ★★ An elegant and beautifully furnished former Elizabethan manor house from the 1580s, this is an ivy-clad Cotswold showpiece. Restored with sensitivity, the Greenway rents rooms in both its main house and its converted coach house. Bedrooms, midsize to spacious, are sumptuously outfitted, with a blend of high-tech amenities and Tudor-inspired style.

Shurdington, near Cheltenham, Gloucestershire GL51 4UG. www.thegreenway.co.uk. ✆ **01242/862352.** Fax 01242/862780. 21 units. £150–£245 double; £245–£410 suite. Rates include English breakfast and early-morning tea and coffee. AE, DC, MC, V. Free parking. Take the A46 less than 4 miles southwest of Cheltenham. **Amenities:** Restaurant; bar; room service. *In room:* TV, hair dryer, Internet (free).

Lypiatt House ★ 🦶 Offering the best-value accommodations in town, this beautifully restored Victorian home stands in the Montpellier area, the most fashionable part of Cheltenham. Bedrooms are spacious and beautifully furnished with a mix of modern and original Victorian fittings, the friendly owners are incredibly helpful, and there's an elegant drawing room with a colonial-style conservatory and "honesty bar."

Lypiatt Rd., Cheltenham, Gloucestershire GL50 2QW. www.lypiatt.co.uk. ✆ **01242/224994.** Fax 01242/224996. 10 units. £90–£120 double. Rates include English breakfast. AE, MC, V. Free parking. **Amenities:** Bar. *In room:* TV, Wi-Fi (free).

Side Trips from Cheltenham

Sudeley Castle & Gardens ★ CASTLE   This 15th-century mansion is one of England's finer stately homes. It has a rich history that began in 1442, when it was built by Baron Ralph Boteler, passing to the royal family just 25 years later. In 1548, Catherine Parr, the sixth wife of Henry VIII, lived and died here. Her marble tomb is in St. Mary's chapel on the grounds.

After the English Civil War the castle was virtually abandoned, and only restored in the Victorian period. For the past 40 years, Lady Ashcombe, an American by birth, has owned the castle with her children, often struggling to keep it open. The castle houses many works of art by Constable, Turner, Rubens, and Van Dyck, among others, and has several permanent exhibitions of magnificent furniture and glass, and many artifacts from the castle's past. To tour the private apartments, there is an additional cost of £12 per person. These highly recommended "connoisseur tours" are available Tuesday to Thursday at 11am, 1, and 3pm and include the stone-built drawing room, the library, and the billiard room.

Winchcombe, 6 miles northeast of Cheltenham. ⓒ **01242/602308.** www.sudeleycastle.co.uk. Admission £7.20 adults, £6.20 seniors, £4.20 children 5–15, £21 family ticket. Castle Apr–Oct daily 10:30am–5pm (last admission 4:30pm); closed Nov–Mar. From Cheltenham, take the regular bus to Winchcombe and get off at Abbey Terrace. Then walk the short distance along the road to the castle. If you're driving, take the B4632 north out of Cheltenham, through Prestbury, and up Cleve Hill to Abbey Terrace, where you can drive right up to the castle.

GLOUCESTER

Cheltenham's thriving neighbor, just 10 miles west, gets far fewer visitors, despite being the county town of Gloucestershire. The main attraction is **Gloucester Cathedral ★★** (daily 7:30am–6pm; www.gloucestercathedral.org.uk) off Westgate Street, burial place of King Edward II and the greatest example of grandiose Perpendicular style in the country. Note in particular the **East Window ★**, completed in the 1350s and the largest medieval window in Britain; and the graceful **Cloisters,** completed in 1367 with the first fan vaulting in the country (you might recognize this area from the *Harry Potter* movies). You can also clamber up the 269 steps of the 69-m (225-ft.) **Tower ★** for mesmerizing views of the surrounding countryside (Apr–Oct afternoons only; £3 adults, £1 children). Admission to the cathedral is free, but adults are asked for a donation of £5.

If you have more time, stroll over to the revitalized Gloucester Docks and the illuminating **Gloucester Waterways Museum** (ⓒ **01452/318200;** www.gloucester waterwaysmuseum.org.uk), which covers just about everything associated with Britain's extensive canal network through historic boats, hands-on displays, and archive films. The museum opens daily 11am to 4pm (July–Aug 10:30am–5pm). Admission is £4.75 for adults, £3.75 for over 60s, £ 3.25 for children 4 to 16, and free for children 3 and under. Trains and buses regularly connect Gloucester and Cheltenham.

PAINSWICK ★

This sleepy stone-built Cotswold wool town, 10 miles southwest of Cheltenham, vies with Bibury for the title of the most beautiful in the region. Its mellow gray stone houses and inns date from as early as the 14th century. It's best admired by strolling down ironically named **New Street** in the center of the village, which dates from 1450.

St. Mary's Church, the centerpiece of the village, was originally built between 1377 and 1399, and was reconstructed into its present form in 1480. Its churchyard contains 99 massive yew trees, each of which is at least 200 years old. Local legend states that no matter how hard well-meaning gardeners have tried, they've never been able to grow more than 99 of them.

Painswick Rococo Garden ★, on the B4073, a half-mile north of Painswick (*℗* **01452/813204;** www.rococogarden.co.uk), is a rare English garden from the flamboyant rococo period, which dominated art and design in England from 1720 to 1760. Today, the garden is best known for its spectacular display of snowdrops that appear in the early spring, sometimes when snow is still on the ground. Admission is £6 for adults, £5 for seniors, £3 for children 5 to 16, and £16 for a family ticket (two adults, two children); visits are possible from mid-January to October, daily 11am to 5pm.

Bus no. 46 links Cheltenham Promenade and Painswick every hour (reduced service Sun), taking around 30 minutes.

Where to Eat & Stay

By far the hippest place to stay around here is **Cotswold 88** ★★, Kemps Lane (www.cotswolds88hotel.com; *℗* **01452/813688**), a former vicarage turned stylish boutique with rooms decorated with works by photo artists David Hiscock and Leigh Bowery. Its similarly fashionable restaurant and bar serve afternoon tea, modern English cuisine, and snappy cocktails with a view.

If you're looking for something simpler (and cheaper), opt for the **Royal Oak** ★, St. Mary's Street (*℗* **01452/813129;** www.theroyaloakpainswick.co.uk), which serves excellent pub food, real ales (including local organic ale from Stroud Brewery), and Thatcher's Heritage and Black Rat farmhouse ciders.

BOURTON-ON-THE-WATER ★

85 miles NW of London; 36 miles NW of Oxford

The quintessential Cotswold village, Bourton-on-the-Water, tends to be overrun with tourists and bus tours all year, especially in summer. Get up early enough and you'll still experience the magic that attracted them in the first place; a dream-like collection of 15th- and 16th-century stone cottages, willow trees, and five romantic stone bridges over the River Windrush.

Essentials

Hereford-bound First Great Western trains run hourly from London's Paddington Station to nearby Moreton-in-Marsh, a trip of 1½ hours (£29). From here, bus no. 801, operated by **Pulham's Bus Company** (*℗* **01451/820369;** www.pulhams coaches.com), travels the 6 miles to Bourton-on-the-Water (40 min.) around nine times daily. The same bus stops at Stow-on-the-Wold and terminates at Cheltenham Royal Wells Bus Station (35 min. from Bourton).

If you're driving from Oxford, head west on the A40 to the junction with the A429 (Fosse Way). Take it northeast to Bourton-on-the-Water.

Exploring the Area

Once you've soaked up the bucolic charms of the village (preferably at the crack of dawn), make time for attractions in the surrounding area, best explored by car. Within the town itself is a handful of mildly interesting museums, each of which was established from idiosyncratic collections amassed over the years by local residents. Kids might enjoy the **Bourton Model Railway Exhibition & Toy Shop,** High Street (*℗* **01451/820686;** www.bourtonmodelrailway.co.uk; £2.50 adults, £2 seniors and children 5–15; June–Aug daily 11am–5pm, Sept–May Sat–Sun 11am–5pm; closed Jan), and the **Model Village at the Old New Inn,** High Street (✆ **01451/820467;** www.theoldnewinn.co.uk/village.htm), a scale model (1:9) of Bourton-on-the-Water completed in 1937. Though it's realistic and big enough that you can walk through it, the models haven't been touched up in years and it's rather pricey considering you'll be finished in 15 minutes. Admission is £3.60 adults, £3.20 for seniors, £2.80 for children 4 to 13, and free for children 3 and under. It's open daily 10am to 5:45pm (winter daily 10am–3:45pm).

Birdland ☺ ZOO   This handsomely designed attraction sits on 3.4 hectares (8½ acres) of field and forests on the banks of the River Windrush, about 1 mile east of Bourton-on-the-Water. It houses about 500 birds, including three species of penguins, guaranteed to amuse even the most jaded of children. Other feathered friends include pelicans, storks, flamingos, cranes, parrots, toucans, kookaburras, and pheasants. Birdland also has a picnic area and a children's playground.

Rissington Rd. ✆ **01451/820480.** www.birdland.co.uk. Admission £7.25 adults, £6.25 seniors, £5 children 3–15, £23 family ticket, free for children 2 and under. Apr–Oct daily 10am–6pm; Nov–Mar daily 10am–4pm (last admission 1 hr. before closing).

Cotswold Motoring Museum & Toy Collection ☺ MUSEUM   Children and adults will love this collection of vintage cars, motorcycles, caravans, and associated bric-a-brac. The exhibits include everything from London taxis and Morris Minors to Brough Superior bikes and a plush Jaguar XK140. Some kids might especially enjoy seeing the little car from the BBC TV show *Brum,* which was filmed here.

Sherborne St. ✆ **01451/821255.** www.csmaclubretreats.co.uk. Admission £4.35 adults, £2.90 children 4–16, £13 family ticket, free for children 3 and under. Mid-Feb–mid-Dec daily 10am–6pm. Closed late Dec–early Feb.

Cotswold Perfumery ★ FACTORY TOUR   This perfume maker has been in business since 1965, one of only a handful in Europe that make and sell their products on-site. Perfumes are sold in the shop, ranging from £2 to £35 each, depending on their size. To get a greater understanding of what goes into them, take the 45-minute factory tour, which also chronicles the history of the perfume industry and its production (tours must be pre-booked).

Victoria St. ✆ **01451/820698.** www.cotswold-perfumery.co.uk. Factory tours £5 adults, £3.50 children 4–16. Mon–Sat 9:30am–5pm; Sun 10:30am–5pm. Closed Dec 25–26.

Cotswold Pottery ★ ARTS & CRAFTS   Tucked away at the back of the village, this delightful ceramics workshop is the home and studio of artists John and Jude Jelfs (John is a wheel-thrown pot specialist, while Jude focuses on hand-built sculpture). You'll often be able to see them working inside, where examples of their exceptional pieces are on sale, from mugs and teapots to larger ornamental pots and sculpture.

Clapton Row. ✆ **01451/820173.** www.cotswoldpottery.co.uk. Free admission. Mon–Sat 9:30am–5pm, Sun 10:30am–5pm.

Where to Eat & Stay

Chester House Hotel ★   This Victorian house, built on the banks of the Windrush River, offers immaculate rooms that mix a fresh contemporary style with antique beds and fittings (some with four-posters). The **Chester House bar and lounge** is a great place to eat, open from 9am for morning coffee and serving contemporary French and English food and snacks until 5pm. The bar is open for drinks until 11pm.

THE GREAT COTSWOLD ramble

One of southern England's most inspiring walks, the well-worn footpath known as **Warden's Way** meanders for 13 miles beside the edge of the swift-moving River Eye, between Winchcombe and Bourton-on-the-Water. If you're short of time, try the section between the villages of Upper and Lower Slaughter (1 mile each way), with an optional extension to Bourton-on-the-Water (2½ miles). From its well-marked beginning in Upper Slaughter's central parking lot, the path passes sheep grazing in meadows, elegantly weathered houses crafted from local honey-colored stone, stately trees arching over ancient millponds, and footbridges that have endured centuries of pedestrian traffic and rain.

Most visitors turn around at Lower Slaughter, but Warden's Way continues another 1½ miles to Bourton-on-the-Water by following the dead-straight Fosse Way, route of an ancient Roman road. Most of it, from Lower Slaughter to Bourton-on-the-Water, is covered by tarmac; it's closed to cars and therefore ideal for walking or biking. *Note:* You're legally required to close each of the several gates that stretch across the footpath.

You can follow this route in reverse, but parking is more plentiful in Upper Slaughter than in Lower Slaughter.

Victoria St., Bourton-on-the-Water, Cheltenham, Gloucestershire GL54 2BU. www.chesterhousehotel. com. ℭ **01451/820286.** Fax 01451/820471. 22 units. £90–£125 double; £125–£155 family room. Rates include continental or English breakfast. AE, MC, V. Closed Jan. Free parking. **Amenities:** Restaurant; bar; babysitting. *In room:* TV, hair dryer, Wi-Fi (free).

Cranbourne House ★★   This is the best B&B in town, a short walk from the center. Rooms are richly equipped and decorated, mainly with adorable French period furnishings dating from the 1890s. Breakfasts here are particularly good and worth lingering over; expect locally sourced full English fry-ups, oatmeal, fresh fruit, jams, smoked trout, and black pudding (blood sausage). Homemade cakes, tea, coffee, and hot chocolate are laid on in the afternoon.

Moore Rd., Bourton-on-the-Water, Cheltenham, Gloucestershire GL54 2AZ. www.cranbournehouse bandb.co.uk. ℭ **01451/821883.** Fax 01451/821883. 6 units. £130 double. Rate includes English breakfast. MC, V. Free parking. **Amenities:** Wi-Fi in public areas (free). *In room:* TV, hair dryer.

Dial House Hotel ★   The top hotel in town is also the oldest structure and the best place to eat. The house dates back to 1698 and is set in .6 hectares (1½ acres) of manicured gardens, overlooking the River Windrush. Each room has individual character, and some boast four-poster beds. Two of the rooms, as charming as those in the main building, are in a converted coach house. Log fires burn on chilly nights, and there are two small dining rooms, one with an inglenook fireplace. The **restaurant** features artfully crafted seasonal dinner menus, playful twists on English, French, and continental classics.

The Chestnuts, High St., Bourton-on-the-Water, Gloucestershire GL54 2AN. www.dialhousehotel.com. ℭ **01451/822244.** Fax 01451/810126. 14 units. £135–£225 double; £205–£245 suite. Rates include English breakfast. MC, V. Free parking. **Amenities:** Restaurant; bar; room service. *In room:* TV, hair dryer, Wi-Fi (free).

Old Manse Hotel ★ 👜   An architectural gem, the Old Manse sits in the center of town by the river. Built of Cotswold stone in 1748, with chimneys, dormers, and small-paned windows, it has been frequently modernized. Rooms are midsize and cozy, much like something you'd find in the home of your favorite great-aunt.

Victoria St., Bourton-on-the-Water, Cheltenham, Gloucestershire GL54 2BX. www.oldenglishinns.co.uk/bourton-water. ✆ **01451/820082.** Fax 01451/810381. 15 units. £90–£110 double. Rates include English breakfast. AE, DC, MC, V. Free parking. **Amenities:** Restaurant; bar. *In room:* TV, hair dryer, Wi-Fi (free).

Side Trips from Bourton-on-the-Water
UPPER & LOWER SLAUGHTER ★★

Nestled between Bourton-on-the-Water (2 miles) and Stow-on-the-Wold (4 miles) are two of the prettiest villages in the Cotswolds: Upper and Lower Slaughter. Don't be put off by the name—"Slaughter" is actually a corruption of *de Sclotre,* the name of the original Norman landowner. Houses here are constructed of the usual russet-colored Cotswold stone, and a stream meanders right through the center of Lower Slaughter, providing a home for free-wandering ducks, which beg scraps from kindly passersby.

The only conventional "sight" here is the **Old Mill** in Lower Slaughter (✆ **01451/820052;** www.oldmill-lowerslaughter.com), a sturdy 19th-century stone structure built on the River Eye with the sole purpose of grinding out flour. Entrance to the mill costs £1.25 for adults, and 50p for children 5 to 15, which also includes an ice-cream parlor and tearoom (daily 10am–6pm).

To reach Lower Slaughter from Bourton-on-the-Water, head west along Lansdowne Road, turning right (north) onto the A436; after a short distance, you'll see a signpost pointing left into Lower Slaughter along an unmarked road. The walk along the river to Upper Slaughter takes around 1 hour (see "The Great Cotswold ramble", above).

Where to Eat & Stay

Lords of the Manor Hotel ★★★ A 17th-century manor house set on several acres of rolling fields, the Lords of the Manor successfully maintains the quiet country-house atmosphere of 300 years ago. Set within gardens with a stream featuring brown trout, it offers luxurious, modern rooms and exceptional service. Half the rooms are in a converted old barn and granary, and many have heart-melting views.

Upper Slaughter, Gloucestershire GL54 2JD. www.lordsofthemanor.com. ✆ **01451/820243.** Fax 01451/820696. 27 units. £195–£320 double; £380 suite. Rates include half-board. AE, DC, MC, V. **Amenities:** Restaurant; bar; room service. *In room:* TV/DVD, hair dryer, minibar, MP3 docking station.

Lower Slaughter Manor ★★ This is another atmospheric country inn with spacious and sumptuously furnished rooms, some with four-poster beds. Bedrooms in the main building have more old English character, although those in the annex are equally comfortable and include the same luxuries. The hotel dates from 1658, when it was owned by Sir George Whitmore, high sheriff of Gloucestershire.

Lower Slaughter, Gloucestershire GL54 2HP. www.lowerslaughter.co.uk. ✆ **01451/820456.** Fax 01451/822150. 19 units. £230–£310 double; £370–£450 suite. Rates include English breakfast. AE, DC, MC, V. No children 11 and under. **Amenities:** Restaurant; lounge; room service; tennis court. *In room:* TV, hair dryer, Internet (free).

STOW-ON-THE-WOLD ★

21 miles S of Stratford-upon-Avon; 9 miles SE of Broadway; 10 miles S of Chipping Campden; 4 miles S of Moreton-in-Marsh

Straggling along the top of a 240-m (800-ft.) escarpment, the old wool town of Stow-on-the-Wold makes an enticing base for exploring the northern Cotswolds. Stow lies smack in the middle of the Fosse Way (A429), one of the Roman trunk roads that cut a swath through Britain, and roads fan out from here all over the region.

The town grew to prominence as a major sheep market, with alleyways known as "tures" running between the buildings once used to herd flocks into the square to be sold. The handsome market square is still there, but the sheep have gone, replaced by cafes, pubs, and antique shops. These days the town's market roots are maintained by the **Stow Fair,** a traditional bi-annual horse market attended by Romani people (or "Travelers") from all over the country. It's a colorful but controversial event, with thousands descending on the area (many in traditional horse-drawn caravans), on the nearest Thursdays to May 12 and October 24. Locals are divided about the disruption it often causes, but the market can be fun to visit, with horse trading enlivened by young Romani woman parading the town in their finest (and brightest) threads.

Essentials

GETTING THERE   Several First Great Western trains run daily from London's Paddington Station to Moreton-in-Marsh, a trip of 1½ hours (£29). From Moreton-in-Marsh, **Pulham's** (© **01451/820369;** www.pulhamscoaches.com) runs frequent buses to Stow-on-the-Wold (20 min; £1.40.) and on to Bourton-on-the-Water (10 min; £1.40.) and Cheltenham (50 min.).

If you're driving from Oxford, take the A40 west to the junction with the A424, near Burford. Head northwest along the A424 to Stow-on-the-Wold.

VISITOR INFORMATION   The privately run **Tourist Information Centre** (Go-Stow) is at 12 Talbot Court and Sheep Street (© **01451/870150;** www.go-stow.co.uk). It's usually open Monday to Saturday 10am to 5pm, and Sunday 11am to 4pm, with reduced hours in winter (Nov–Easter); it tends to opens at 11am and closes between 3 and 5pm most days, but call ahead to confirm.

Exploring the Area

Other than browsing the shops and pubs, there's not a lot to see in the town itself beyond the 15th-century **Market Cross** in the Market Square, the old wooden **stocks** on the green (where offenders would be pelted with eggs), and the stately **Church of St. Edward,** built between the 11th and the 15th centuries. The **Royalist Hotel,** at the end of Digbeth Street, is said to be the oldest inn in England, with parts of it dating back to the first incarnation of A.D. 947.

Chastleton House ★★ HISTORIC SITE   Make time for this captivating Jacobean country house, built between 1607 and 1612 by a prosperous Welsh wool merchant. What makes this place different is the state of the interior; the Jones family owned the property, little-changed until 1991. The National Trust has since preserved the time-warped flavor of the rooms, with no ropes or barriers, and the kitchen ceiling is still blackened by soot—it's like stepping back into the 17th century. The extensive gardens also include England's first ever croquet lawn (the laws of the game were codified here in 1865).

Chastleton, Oxfordshire, 5 miles east of Stow-on-the-Wold via the A436. © **01494/755560.** www. nationaltrust.org.uk/main/w-chastleton. Admission £8.25 adults, £3.85 children 5–15, free for children 4 and under, £20 family ticket. Apr–Sept Wed–Sat 1–5pm; Mar and Oct Wed–Sat 1–4pm. Admission by timed ticket (180 available each day). Last admission 1 hr. before closing.

Cotswold Falconry Centre ☺ ZOO   For a fascinating lesson on birds of prey, stop by this family-friendly bird center, housing between 80 to 100 eagles, hawks, and

Don't be fooled by the village's sleepy, country setting: Stow-on-the-Wold has developed over the last 20 years into the antiques buyer's highlight of Britain, boasting at least 60 merchandisers scattered throughout the village and its environs.

Set within four showrooms inside an 18th-century building on the town's main square, **Antony Preston Antiques Ltd.** (✆ 01451/831586; www.antony preston.com), specializes in English and French furniture, including some large pieces such as bookcases, and decorative objects that include paperweights, lamps, and paintings on silk.

Baggott Church Street Ltd., Church Street (✆ 01451/830370; www. baggottantiques.com), is the smaller, and perhaps more intricately decorated, of two shops founded and maintained by a local antiques merchant, Duncan ("Jack") Baggott, a frequent denizen at estate sales of country houses throughout Britain. The shop contains four showrooms loaded with furniture and paintings from the 17th to the 19th centuries.

Covering about half a block in the heart of town, **Huntington's Antiques Ltd.,** Church Street (✆ 01451/830842; www.huntington-antiques.com), contains one of the largest stocks of quality antiques in England. Wander at will through 10 ground-floor rooms, and then climb to the second floor where a long gallery and a quartet of additional showrooms bulge with refectory tables, unusual cupboards, and all kinds of finds. Shops tend to open Monday to Saturday 10am to 5pm, with limited hours in winter and on Sundays.

falcons. You'll also see over 40 owls, mean-looking vultures, and rare caracara, many of which are bred at the center.

Batsford Park (just north of Moreton-in-Marsh, off the A429). ✆ **01386/701043.** www.cotswold-falconry. co.uk. Admission £7 adults, £6 seniors and students, £3 children 4–14, free for children 3 and under, £17 family ticket. Mid-Feb–mid-Nov daily 10:30am–5:30pm. Flying displays daily at 11:30am, 1:30, and 3pm.

Donnington Trout Farm FARM   This small family farm raises both brown and rainbow trout in spring-fed tanks and ponds. The shop sells smoked trout, eel, and salmon from the on-site smokery, as well as their justly celebrated smoked trout pâté. They also offer fly-fishing on the farm (call for more details).

Upper Swell, Gloucestershire (from Stow-on-the-Wold, take the B4077 1 mile west to Upper Swell). ✆ **01451/830873.** www.donningtontrout.co.uk. Free admission. Tues–Sat 10am–5:30pm.

Rollright Stones ★ HISTORIC SITE   Some 6 miles east of Stow-on-the-Wold, these enigmatic Stone Age monuments date back an astounding 4,000 years, though their purpose remains a mystery. Not as dramatic as Stonehenge, the weathered circle of 77 megalithic oolitic limestone blocks known as the King's Men is just as intriguing. The complex also includes the Bronze Age King Stone, and the much older Whispering Knights, four standing stones thought to be part of a Neolithic tomb. Souvenirs and a booklet about the site can be purchased at Wyatts Farm Shop, 1 mile east of the Stones (across the crossroads on the way to Great Rollright), where there is also a cafe and restrooms.

Little Rollright, Oxfordshire. No phone. www.rollrightstones.co.uk. Admission £1 adults, 50p children 7–16. Daily sunrise to sunset. From Stow-on-the-Wold, take the A436 toward Chipping Norton, then the road to Little Rollright at the junction with the A44.

Where to Eat & Stay

VERY EXPENSIVE

Wyck Hill House ★   This is sleepy old Stow's pocket of posh. Parts of this otherwise Victorian country house, set on 40 hectares (100 acres) of grounds and gardens, date from 1720. The interior adheres to 18th-century authenticity, with room after room leading to paneled libraries and Adam sitting rooms. The well-furnished guest rooms are in the main hotel, in the coach-house annex, or in the Orangery, a building erected in the 1980s with larger-than-usual bedrooms outfitted in a vaguely Mediterranean theme. Some rooms offer four-poster beds and views of the surrounding countryside.

A424 Burford Rd., Stow-on-the-Wold, Cheltenham, Gloucestershire GL54 1HY. www.wyckhillhouse hotel.co.uk. © **01451/831936.** Fax 01451/832243. 60 units. £115–£250 double; £300–£425 suite. Rates include English breakfast. AE, MC, V. Free parking. Drive 2½ miles south of Stow-on-the-Wold on the A424. **Amenities:** Restaurant; bar; room service; spa. *In room:* TV, hair dryer, Wi-Fi (free).

EXPENSIVE

Fosse Manor Hotel ★   Fosse Manor offers great value for an English country-house experience. Built in a neo-Gothic style in 1901 by the Lord of Maugersbury Manor, it's been a hotel since the 1950s. Inside, the interior is conservatively modern, with compact but homey principal and superior bedrooms, and far more luxurious deluxe rooms. All rooms include DVD players or a Sony PlayStation (which can also play DVDs). The **restaurant** is top-notch, featuring modern British cooking with a rich array of locally sourced produce.

Fosseway, Stow-on-the-Wold, Cheltenham, Gloucestershire GL54 1JX. www.fossemanor.co.uk. © **01451/830354.** Fax 01451/832486. 22 units. £74–£155 double. Rates include English breakfast. Children 9 and under stay free in parent's room. AE, DC, MC, V. Free parking. Take the A429 1¼ miles south of Stow-on-the-Wold. **Amenities:** Restaurant; bar; lounge; room service; Wi-Fi in public areas (free); DVD library. *In room:* TV/DVD, hair dryer.

Kings Arms ★★   The Kings Arms is a fine choice for real ale and pub food (think tankers of prawns and warm salt beef sandwiches), right in the center of town, but it's also an excellent B&B. Rooms are decorated in a contemporary Cotswold country style, with exposed stone walls and roof beams contrasting with the modern beds, drapes, and furnishings. The upscale **Chophouse** ★★ restaurant cooks up some of the finest steaks, fish, and game in the region.

Market Square, Stow-on-the-Wold, Gloucestershire GL54 1AF. www.kingsarmsstow.co.uk. © **01451/ 830364.** 11 units. £74–£155 double. Rates include English breakfast. AE, DC, MC, V. Free parking. **Amenities:** Restaurant; bar. *In room:* TV, Wi-Fi (free).

Number Four at Stow ★★★   Stow's best hotel is a stylish boutique that also operates one of the best restaurants in town, showcasing a seasonal menu of locally sourced produce. **Cutler's Restaurant** offers the finest of modern British cooking, from its cream-of-parsnip soup to roast Cotswold partridge; Sunday lunches are a real treat (main courses £13–£19). The hotel rooms are chic and contemporary with king-size beds and flat-screen TVs—no period decor and no antiques.

Fosseway, Stow-on-the-Wold, Cheltenham, Gloucestershire GL54 1JX. www.hotelnumberfour.co.uk. © **01451/830297.** Fax 01451/831768. 18 units. £110–£125 double. AE, DC, MC, V. Free parking. **Amenities:** Restaurant; bar; lounge; room service. *In room:* A/C, TV, hair dryer, Wi-Fi (free).

Stow Lodge Hotel   Venerable Stow Lodge was built as a Rectory in the mid-1700s, and is ideally located on the market square. Rooms are ample and well furnished in classic English country style, with plenty of flowery bedspreads and curtains, red carpets, and cozy armchairs; one has a four-poster bed. Rooms 17 and 18—the smallest in the hotel—share a private bathroom.

The Square, Stow-on-the-Wold, Cheltenham, Gloucestershire GL54 1AB. www.stowlodge.co.uk. **01451/830485.** Fax 01451/831671. 20 units. £85–£137 double. Rates include English breakfast. MC, V. Free parking. Closed Dec 16–Jan 25. No children 4 and under. **Amenities:** Restaurant; bar; room service, Wi-Fi (free in lounge). In room: TV, hair dryer.

MODERATE

Mole End ★★ This is consistently rated Stow's top B&B, with spacious, luxurious rooms decked out like a Victorian dolls house. Owners Trevor and Jane are incredibly thoughtful hosts, and the breakfasts will have you feeling warm and happy the entire day. Mole End is about a 10-minute walk from the market square on the edge of town, with open views of the surrounding country.

Moreton Rd., Stow-on-the-Wold, Gloucestershire GL54 1EG. www.moleendstow.co.uk. **01451/870348.** 3 units. £80–£105 double. Rates include English breakfast. MC, V. Free parking. In room: TV, hair dryer, Wi-Fi (free).

BROADWAY ★

15 miles SW of Stratford-upon-Avon; 93 miles NW of London; 15 miles NE of Cheltenham

The Cotswolds is blessed with many beautiful villages, but Broadway is especially charming. Flanked by stone cottages and chestnut trees overlooking the Vale of Evesham, its **High Street** is a real gem, remarkable for its harmonious style and design. It tends to get swamped by coach tours in the summer, of course, and once you've walked up and down the main street, you've done Broadway. Yet most of the tourists are gone by evening and many prime attractions of the Cotswolds, and Shakespeare Country (p. 453), are nearby, making this an appealing alternative to Stow as a base for exploring the region.

Essentials

GETTING THERE The nearest train stations are at Moreton-in-Marsh (7 miles away) or at Evesham (5 miles away). Buses to Broadway are infrequent, however, so it's best to take a taxi from either place (try Cotswold Horizons; **01386/858599**).

If you're driving from Oxford, head west on the A40, and then take the A44 to Woodstock, Chipping Norton, and Moreton-in-Marsh.

VISITOR INFORMATION The **Tourist Information Centre** is at Unit 14, Russell Square (**01386/852937;** www.beautifulbroadway.com). The office is open year-round Monday to Friday 10am to 5pm, and Sunday 2 to 5pm.

Exploring the Area

Broadway's **High Street ★★** is one of the most beautiful in England. Many of its striking facades date from 1620 or a century or two later. The most famous is that of the **Lygon Arms** (see below), a venerable inn that has been serving wayfarers since 1532. Even if you're not staying here, you may want to visit for a meal or a drink.

Broadway Tower OBSERVATION POINT On the outskirts of Broadway stands this whimsical folly, created by Capability Brown for the 6th Earl of Coventry in 1798. You can climb the 17-m (55-ft.) tower on a clear day for a panoramic vista of 12 shires. It's the second highest point (312m/1,024 ft.), and the most awe-inspiring view in the Cotswolds. You can also bring a picnic here and eat lunch in the surrounding grounds.

Middle Hill, A44 (1 mile SE of Broadway). ✆ **01386/852390.** www.broadwaytower.co.uk. Admission £4.50 adults, £2.50 children 4–14, £12 family ticket. Daily 10:30am–5pm.

Snowshill Lavender ★ FARM   Visit this fragrant lavender farm in high summer, when an ocean of lilacs, purples, and blues seems to stretch to the horizon. You can stroll into the middle of the fields, breathing in the aromas, buy the product in the shop, or munch lavender scones, cakes, and shortbread in the Lavender Tea Room. Lavender planting started here in 2000, and today there are some 21 hectares (53 acres) of lavender under cultivation.

Hill Barn Farm, Snowshill. ✆ **01386/854821.** www.snowshill-lavender.co.uk. Admission to shop free; admission to lavender fields during flowering £2.50 adults, £1.50 children 15 and under. Apr–May and Sept–Oct Wed–Sun 10am–5pm, June–Aug daily 10am–5pm.

Snowshill Manor OFFBEAT SITE   This pleasant Cotswold manor house owes its appeal to the bizarre collection of curios that lies within its honey-stone walls. Parts of the house date from around 1500, but most of what you see today was built in the 17th century. In 1919, the then-dilapidated house was purchased by Charles Paget Wade, a craftsman and eccentric who collected over 22,000 unusual handicrafts up to his death in 1951. You'll find a little bit of everything here: Flemish tapestries, toys, lacquer cabinets, narwhal tusks, mousetraps, and cuckoo clocks—a glorious mess, like a giant attic of the 20th century. The highlight is the collection of 26 suits of Samurai armor in the Green Room.

Snowshill, 3 miles south of Broadway. ✆ **01386/852410.** www.nationaltrust.org.uk/main/w-snowshillmanor. Admission £8.50 adults, £4.30 children 5–15, free for children 4 and under, £22 family ticket. Apr–June and Sept–Oct Wed–Sun noon–5pm; July–Aug Mon and Wed–Sun 11:30am–4:30pm. Admission by timed ticket. Last admission 4pm. Closed Nov–Mar.

Where to Eat & Stay

The best place in Broadway for a cup of tea is **Tisanes Tea Rooms,** 21 The Green (✆ **01386/853296;** www.tisanes-tearooms.co.uk), offering perfectly blended teas with a variety of sandwiches and salads (daily 10am–5pm).

VERY EXPENSIVE

Buckland Manor Hotel ★   Broadway's posh country-manor option just about lives up to expectation, with elegant gardens, an imposing slate-roofed 13th-century manor house, and luxurious rooms enhanced with antiques and mullioned windows. Some of the large bedrooms have four-poster beds and fireplaces. The hushed wood-paneled public spaces are pure old-fashioned aristocratic England, littered with rugs, antiques, and comfy armchairs.

Buckland, Gloucestershire WR12 7LY. www.bucklandmanor.co.uk. ✆ **01386/852626.** Fax 01386/853557. 13 units. £235–£290 double. Rates include early-morning tea and English breakfast. AE, MC, V. Free parking. Take the B4632 about 2 miles south of Broadway. No children 11 and under. **Amenities:** Restaurant; bar; room service; tennis court. *In room:* TV, hair dryer, Internet (free).

Dormy House Hotel ★★   Dormy House is pricey but exceptional, featuring rooms that blend the core of this 17th-century farmhouse with lavish, contemporary furnishings. The owners have also brought glamor to an old adjoining timbered barn, converted into two executive suites and eight deluxe doubles, a real step up in comfort from the standard doubles. The **Dining Room ★★★** and **Barn Owl Brasserie**

are both charming and well-managed restaurants; the former is open for dinner and a popular Sunday lunch (£22.50), turning out high-quality classics such as Gressingham duck, local partridge, and Hereford beef, while the brasserie offers slightly cheaper but just as creative fare for lunch and dinner.

Willersey Hill, Broadway, Worcestershire WR12 7LF (take the A44 2 miles southeast of Broadway). www.dormyhouse.co.uk. © **01386/852711.** Fax 01386/858636. 48 units. £173–£213 double; £213 four-poster room; £238 suite. Rates include English breakfast. AE, DC, MC, V. Free parking. Closed Dec 24–29.**Amenities:** Restaurant; bar; babysitting; gym; room service. *In room:* TV, hair dryer, Internet (free).

The Lygon Arms ★   It's not as good as it once was, but this many-gabled structure still basks in its reputation as one of the great old English inns. The oldest rooms date from 1532 or earlier, and the timber and flagstone floors, wood paneling, doors, and stone mullions have been retained. Standard doubles are comfy enough, with modern amenities, but the premium and deluxe doubles are worth the extra; you get a choice of swish, contemporary rooms with Bang & Olufsen sound system and flat-screen TV, or traditional rooms in the main house with beamed ceilings, antiques, and open fires.

High St., Broadway, Worcestershire WR12 7DU. www.barcelo-hotels.co.uk. © **01386/852255.** Fax 01386/854470. 78 units. £119–£330 double. Breakfast £30. AE, DC, MC, V. Free parking. **Amenities:** 2 restaurants; cafe; bar; health club; pool (indoor); room service; spa. *In room:* TV, hair dryer, Internet (£15 for 24 hr.).

EXPENSIVE

Russell's ★★   Ths chic boutique hotel is also one of the best places to eat in the region. If you've had enough of heritage hotels look no further; everything about the rooms is modern and stylish, from the art on the walls to the fixtures and flat-screen TVs. The food in the **restaurant** is high-quality bistro; bread is made here each morning while the menu features filo-baked goat's cheese, fresh fish, sticky toffee pudding, and British cheeses. Expect sexy main courses (£11–£23) like pumpkin risotto and confit belly of lamb with white pudding (a traditional sausage made with pork and outmeal). The same crew owns highly rated **Broadway Brasserie ★** (© **01386/858435;** www.broadwaybrasserie.co.uk), at 20a High St., next door.

20 High St., Broadway, Worcestershire WR12 7DT. www.russellsofbroadway.co.uk. © **01386/853555.** 7 units. £98–£170 double. Rates include English breakfast. AE, DC, MC, V. Free parking. **Amenities:** Restaurant; bar. *In room:* TV, hair dryer, Internet (free).

MODERATE

The Olive Branch ★   In the heart of an expensive village, this is a terrific bargain. The old coaching house, dating from 1592, retains its traditional Cotswold architectural features, as well as a large-walled English garden. Most rooms are decked out in white and light pinks, a simple but less chintzy interpretation of the usual country-house theme. One family room can accommodate up to four people, and one room has a four-poster bed.

78 High St., Broadway, Worcestershire WR12 7AJ. www.theolivebranch-broadway.com. © **01386/853440.** Fax 01386/859070. 8 units. £82–£110 double. Rates include English breakfast. AE, DC, MC, V. Free parking. **Amenities:** Lounge; Wi-Fi (free). *In room:* TV, hair dryer; minibar.

Windrush House ★★   In high-priced Broadway, Evan and Judith Anderson run a congenial and affordable B&B. It's not your average guesthouse; bedrooms have been refurbished in a chic contemporary style more akin to a boutique, with individual color schemes, opulent fabrics, and flat-screen TVs. All rooms toy with traditional English design, but our favorite is the Bourton Room, which sports a hip

Victorian neo-Gothic vibe. Breakfasts feature local produce and eggs laid by the owner's chickens.

Station Rd., Broadway, Worcestershire WR12 7DE. www.broadway-windrush.co.uk. ℂ **01386/853577.** Fax 01386/852850. 4 units. £90 double. Rates include breakfast. AE, DC, MC, V. Free parking. *In room:* TV, hair dryer, Wi-Fi (free).

A Side Trip from Broadway: Chipping Campden ★★

Chipping Campden epitomizes the dreamy English village that you've seen depicted in a thousand postcards. Except for the heavy traffic in summer, the long **High Street** still looks as it did centuries ago and it's lined with stone houses dating from the 16th century. One of the most arresting buildings along here is the arched **Market Hall,** erected in 1627 to provide shelter for the local produce market.

The village landmark is the soaring tower of the **Church of St. James** (ℂ 01386/841927; www.stjameschurchcampden.co.uk; free admission, suggested donation £1). You'll see it for miles around. Constructed mostly in the Perpendicular style over 250 years from 1260, it is one of the finest churches in the Cotswolds. The church is open March to October Monday to Saturday 10am to 5pm, and Sundays 2 to 6pm (Nov and Feb Mon–Sat 11am–4pm, Sun 2–4pm; Dec–Jan Mon–Sat 11am–3pm, Sun 2–3pm).

The **Court Barn Museum** (ℂ 01386/841951; www.courtbarn.org.uk), next to the church, celebrates the rich Arts and Crafts heritage of the area. C. R. Ashbee brought the Guild of Handicraft to Chipping Campden in 1902, and though it closed 6 years later, a tradition of craftsmanship remained in the village. The museum opens April to September Tuesday to Sunday 10am to 5pm (Oct–Mar 10am–4pm). Admission is £4 for adults and £3.25 for students and seniors (free for children 15 and under).

The **Old Silk Mill,** Sheep Street (Mon–Fri 9am–5pm, Sat 9am–noon), is where the Guild of Handicraft was actually established in 1902. Today it has been revived with a series of craft workshops. One of them is **Hart Gold & Silversmiths** (ℂ 01386/841100; www.hartsilversmiths.co.uk), where silver and gold is expertly smithed by descendants of George Hart (born in the 1890s), an original member of the Guild of Handicraft.

Elsewhere, the **Robert Welch Studio Shop,** Lower High Street (ℂ 01386/840522; www.welch.co.uk), is where the Welch family has been crafting silverware, stainless steel, and cutlery for more than 50 years. The shop is open Monday to Saturday 9:30am to 5:30pm and Sunday 10am to 4pm.

If antiques and antiques-hunting are your passion, visit **School House Antiques,** High Street (ℂ 01386/841474; www.schoolhouseantiques.co.uk). For new, secondhand, and antiquarian books, look up **Draycott Books,** 2 Sheep St. (ℂ 01386/841392).

The **Tourist Information Centre** is at the Old Police Station, High Street (ℂ 01386/841206; www.chippingcampdenonline.org). It's open daily 10am to 5:30pm in summer, and 10am to 1pm in the off season.

WHERE TO EAT & STAY

The Cotswold House Hotel ★★ This stately, formal Regency house, dating from 1800 and situated opposite the old wool market, is the best place to stay in the village. The four cottage bedrooms tucked away in the garden are more secluded and beautifully furnished; the Montrose Rooms include trendy touches such as color-changing shower lights, and sand and light sculptures. The inn-house restaurant **Hick's** ★ and their garden terrace is the most romantic place to take **afternoon tea** in the village.

The Square, Chipping Campden, Gloucestershire GL55 6AN. www.cotswoldhouse.com. ℂ **01386/840330.** Fax 01386/840310. 30 units. £150–£295 double; £620–£800 cottage or suite. Rates include English breakfast. AE, MC, V. Free parking. **Amenities:** 2 restaurants; 2 bars; spa (indoor pool); babysitting; room service. *In room:* A/C (in suites), TV/DVD, hair dryer, minibar, Internet (free).

Ebrington Arms ★★ GASTROPUB   One of the best pubs in the Cotswolds, Ebrington Arms is 2 miles from Chipping Campden and best known for exceptional English food. The menu includes twists on traditional classics—ploughman's platter and a fine fish and chips—but also roasted guinea fowl, Cornish plaice, and Gloucestershire Old Spot pork. Save room for the glazed rice pudding, or addictive marmalade bread and butter pudding. They also offer three cozy rooms (£110–£130) upstairs, including breakfast.

Ebrington, Chipping Campden. ℂ **01386/593223.** www.theebringtonarms.co.uk. Reservations recommended. Main courses £9–£18. AE, MC, V. Free parking. Restaurant daily noon–2:30pm and 6:30–9pm (8:30pm Sun). Pub daily noon–midnight.

The Kings Hotel ★   The Kings is a solid 18th-century pub and restaurant choice in the heart of Chipping Campden. It's also another pub that doubles as a wonderfully atmospheric hotel, with 14 stylish rooms in the main house, and five cottage rooms that offer a little more space and luxury. When it comes to eating, the Kings boasts the best bar snacks in town, as well as real ales including local Hook Norton. Artfully prepared modern British food features at the main **restaurant** and the more informal **brasserie.** Expect dishes such as monkfish, saffron, razor clam, and shrimp chowder, with violet gnocchi; and duo of mallard and partridge breasts, with pommes fondant.

The Square, Chipping Campden, Gloucestershire GL55 6AW. www.kingscampden.co.uk. ℂ **01386/840256.** Fax 01386/841598. 19 units. £115–£195 double. Rates include English breakfast. AE, MC, V. Free parking. **Amenities:** 2 restaurants; bar; *In room:* TV, hair dryer, minibar, Wi-Fi (free).

Kissing Gate Bed & Breakfast ★★★ ✦   Fans of B&Bs will adore this mellow place in the quaint village of Ebrington, just 2 miles east of Chipping Campden. Welcoming hosts Anne and Dougal run an informal, friendly home with just three bright and airy rooms for a bargain price. You'll be treated to homemade cookies, fresh milk, and plenty of tea or coffee on arrival, and there's a common-use fridge, books, and board games to enjoy. Bacon, eggs, sausages, and fresh produce are all locally sourced.

Coldicott Leys, Ebrington, Chipping Campden, Gloucestershire GL55 6NZ. www.kissinggate.net. ℂ **01386/593934.** 3 units. £75 double; £130 family room. Rates include English breakfast. AE, MC, V. Free parking. *In room:* TV, hair dryer, Wi-Fi (free).

Seagrave Arms ★★   The Seagrave is an inviting country inn and restaurant with six en-suite guest rooms. The sensitively restored Georgian house features open log fires in winter and a sheltered courtyard for alfresco dining in the summer. Rooms are simple but comfy, and the contemporary English food is the real star: Locally sourced produce accompanies award-winning real ales from local breweries Hook Norton, Cotswold, and Purity, and even a Gloucestershire wine. Expect dishes such as roasted wild mallard with marrow, pear, and vanilla purée, and lemon curd cheesecake (main courses £11–£17).

Friday St., Weston Subedge, Chipping Campden, Gloucestershire GL55 6QH. www.seagravearms.co.uk. ✆ **01386/840192.** 6 units. £90–£110 double. Rates include English breakfast. AE, MC, V. Free parking. Take Dyers Lane 1 mile north of Chipping Campden High St. **Amenities:** Restaurant; bar. *In room:* TV.

Staddlestones B&B ★ 🔖 This enticing family-run B&B is just a few minutes' walk from the center of Chipping Campden. Originally a war veteran's cottage, it is a massive bargain. Guests are treated like family, and rooms are spotless and equipped with everything you need for a comfortable stay. The Garden Room is a like a small suite, with a separate sitting room, and ideal for families.

7 Aston Rd., Chipping Campden, Gloucestershire GL55 6HR (take the B4081 signposted to Mickleton from the High St). www.staddle-stones.com. ✆ **01386/849288.** 3 units. £65 double. Rates include English breakfast. No credit cards. Free parking. No children 11 and under. *In room:* TV, DVD/CD player, hair dryer, Wi-Fi (free).

THE HEART OF ENGLAND

by Stephen Keeling

12

The West Midlands occupies the heart of England, an incredibly dynamic region that contains the finest Shakespearean theatre in the world, the grandest medieval castle in the country, and is the birthplace of the Industrial Revolution. The clubs, pubs, and galleries of England's second city provide the contemporary allure, while the Welsh border country offers a pastoral and far less touristy contrast of small market towns and hiking trails.

SIGHTSEEING   Everyone makes a pilgrimage to Shakespeare's **Stratford,** of course, but don't skip **Warwick Castle,** an awe-inspiring example of medieval craftsmanship and power. Nearby **Coventry Cathedral** is a poignant reminder of the destructiveness of war, while cathedrals at Worcester and Hereford provide more conventional but equally jaw-dropping architecture. Even choco-skeptics should visit the spiritual home of British chocolate, **Cadbury World,** on the edge of Birmingham, where the aromas of melting cacao will have you converted before you can say "Fruit and Nut."

EATING & DRINKING   **Birmingham** is the culinary heart of the region, with all three of its top-rated restaurants—Purnell's, Simpsons, and Turners—more than a match for anything in London. Make time, though, for the real star of the city, the Pakistani-inspired Balti curry houses. South Asian food is especially good throughout the West Midlands, but you'll also find Michelin-rated gems in the most unlikely of places; many people journey to the small town of **Ludlow** just to eat.

HISTORY   **Stratford** is the most obvious historical target in the heart of England, but not just because of Shakespeare; its wonderfully preserved halls and houses offer an unusually authentic window into life in Tudor England. Georgian elegance is on full display in nearby **Leamington Spa,** while the grit, grime, and boundless invention that characterized the Industrial Revolution are commemorated at the enlightening museums of **Ironbridge** and the **Potteries.**

ARTS & CULTURE   Unsurprisingly, Birmingham is also the cultural capital of the West Midlands, with a rich spread of world-class performance spaces for theatre, ballet, and popular music. The **National**

Exhibition Centre is based here, and the city has also developed an exciting contemporary arts scene. Established venues such as the **Ikon Gallery** compliment spaces for emerging artists in the Digbeth and Eastside areas.

THE best TRAVEL EXPERIENCES IN THE HEART OF ENGLAND

○ **Seeing the Royal Shakespeare Company perform in Stratford:** The Royal Shakespeare Company is the world's premier ensemble when it comes to performing the Bard's full repertoire, and few experiences match seeing them perform in Stratford on a warm summer evening. The RSC Theatre by the river was recently given a gorgeous renovation. See p. 452.

○ **Dining on a Balti:** If you like South Asian food you're in for a treat. Birmingham's Balti Triangle is crammed with cheap Indian and Pakistani restaurants touting a dish concocted by Kashmiri chefs right here. Seasoned and spicy meats are cooked fresh over a hot flame, and served in the pan with vegetables. See p. 472.

○ **Cruising the canals of Birmingham:** It's not Venice, but Birmingham is laced with canals that offer a unique perspective of the city—its grim industrial past and its brighter present of renovated wharves, cafes, and shopping malls. Rides by barge are affordable and fun, and you can even rent your own boat. See p. 466.

○ **Hiking the Malvern Hills:** Fine views and fresh walks are rarely so easily accessible, but the wonderfully rustic Malvern Hills lie just a short walk from Great Malvern station. Stroll the paths that inspired Edward Elgar, and rehydrate with the Queen's favorite mineral water. See p. 476.

○ **Shopping for secondhand books at Hay-on-Wye:** An unlikely location for a book pilgrimage perhaps, but this tiny town on the Welsh border is crammed with bookstores—selling everything from rare tomes to dog-eared paperbacks for a pound. See p. 693.

STRATFORD-UPON-AVON ★★

91 miles NW of London; 40 miles NW of Oxford; 8 miles S of Warwick

The birthplace of **William Shakespeare,** England's greatest playwright, Stratford commemorates the Bard with a spread of beautifully maintained historic sights from the Tudor period. The other major draw for visitors is the **Royal Shakespeare Theatre,** where Britain's foremost actors perform during a long season that lasts from April to November.

Shakespeare was born here in 1564, and though he spent most of his career in London, this otherwise plain-looking town has been cashing in on the connection ever since. Crowds, bus tours, and unashamed tourism now dominates the center, but visiting the sights themselves, and especially taking in a play or two, transports you right back to the 16th century.

Essentials

GETTING THERE The Chiltern Railways train service from London Marylebone to Stratford-upon-Avon takes about 2¼ hours, with a round-trip ticket starting at £40.

The Royal Shakespeare Theatre

In Shakespeare's day, Stratford didn't have a theatre—all the Bard's plays were performed in London. The current red-brick **Royal Shakespeare Theatre** (© 01789/403444; www.rsc.org.uk) was completed in 1932 on the banks of the Avon, and reopened in 2010 after an ambitious renovation. It remains a major showcase for the acclaimed **Royal Shakespeare Company (RSC),** with a season that runs from April to November and typically features five Shakespearean plays. The RSC also stages productions in the smaller **Swan Theatre,** an intimate 430-seat space next to the Royal Shakespeare Theatre.

For **ticket reservations** book online or call © **0844/8001110.** A small number of tickets is always held for sale on the day of a performance, but it may be too late to get a good seat if you wait until you arrive in Stratford. The box office is open Monday to Saturday 9am to 8pm, although it closes at 6pm on days when there are no performances. Seats range in price from £5 to £35.

Even if you're not seeing a performance, you can take a guided **Theatre Tour,** which lasts an hour and runs every 2 hours from 9:15am (Mon–Sat) and from 10:15am (Sun and bank holidays). Tickets cost £6.50 for adults and £3 for children 17 and under. Advance booking is recommended.

You can also take an elevator up the newly constructed 36-m (118-ft.) **Tower** (Mon–Sat 9am–5pm; Sun 10am–5pm) for a unique bird's-eye view of the town. Tickets cost £2.50 for adults and £1.25 for children 17 and under.

If you're driving from London, take the M40 to junction 15 and continue to Stratford-upon-Avon on the A46/A439.

VISITOR INFORMATION The **Tourist Information Centre,** Bridgefoot (© **0870/160-7930;** www.shakespeare-country.co.uk), provides any details you may wish to know about the Shakespeare houses and properties; it will also assist in booking rooms (see "Where to Stay," below). The center is open April through September, Monday to Saturday 9am to 5:30pm and Sunday 10am to 4pm; October through March, Monday to Saturday 9am to 5pm and Sunday 10am to 3pm.

ORGANIZED TOURS Guided bus tours of Stratford-upon-Avon are conducted by **City Sightseeing,** Civic Hall, Rother Street (© **01789/412680;** www.city sightseeing-stratford.com). In summer, open-top double-decker buses depart daily every 15 minutes from 9:30am to 6pm. You can take a 1-hour ride without stops, or you can get off at any or all of the town's five Shakespeare properties. Though the bus stops are clearly marked along the historic route, the most logical starting point is the sidewalk in front of the Pen & Parchment Pub, at the bottom of Bridge Street. Tour tickets are valid all day, so you can hop on and off the buses as many times as you want. The tours cost £12 for adults, £9.50 for seniors and students, and £6 for children 5 to 15 (children 4 and under ride free). A family ticket goes for £25. Tour frequency depends on the time of year; call for information.

Exploring the Area

Most of Stratford's historic attractions are administrated by the **Shakespeare Birthplace Trust** (© **01789/204016;** www.shakespeare.org.uk). One combination ticket (£20 for adults, £18 for seniors and students, and £12 for children 5–15 and

Warwickshire: Shakespeare Country

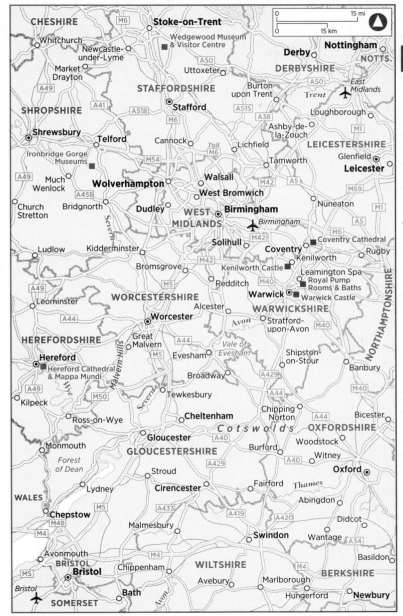

CHESHIRE

Whitchurch

Newcastle-under-Lyme

Stoke-on-Trent

Wedgewood Museum & Visitor Centre

Derby

Nottingham

NOTTS.

M6

A50

A50

Market Drayton

Uttoxeter

DERBYSHIRE

East Midlands

A49

STAFFORDSHIRE

Burton upon Trent

Trent

SHROPSHIRE

A41

A518

Stafford

A515

A38

Loughborough

M1

Shrewsbury

Telford

M6

Cannock

Toll M6

Lichfield

Ashby-de-la-Zouch

LEICESTERSHIRE

Ironbridge Gorge Museums

M54

Tamworth

Glenfield

M69

Much Wenlock

A49

Walsall

Leicester

Church Stretton

Bridgnorth

Wolverhampton

West Bromwich

M42

A5

Nuneaton

M1

Dudley

WEST MIDLANDS

Birmingham

A5

Ludlow

Kidderminster

Solihull

M42

Coventry Cathedral

Birmingham

Coventry

Rugby

Bromsgrove

M42

Kenilworth

A458

Severn

A49

Leominster

M5

Redditch

M40

Kenilworth Castle

Leamington Spa

Royal Pump Rooms & Baths

A44

WORCESTERSHIRE

Alcester

Warwick

Warwick Castle

WARWICKSHIRE

Worcester

Avon

Stratford-upon-Avon

M40

A49

Great Malvern

A44

Vale of Evesham

NORTHAMPTONSHIRE

HEREFORDSHIRE

Hereford

M5

Evesham

Shipston-on-Stour

Hereford Cathedral & Mappa Mundi

Malvern Hills

Broadway

A429

Banbury

A49

Wye

M50

Tewkesbury

A44

M40

Kilpeck

Severn

Chipping Norton

Bicester

Ross-on-Wye

Cheltenham

_C o t s w o l d s_

OXFORDSHIRE

Monmouth

Gloucester

A40

Woodstock

Forest of Dean

GLOUCESTERSHIRE

Burford

A429

Witney

A40

WALES

Stroud

Fairford

Thames

Oxford

Lydney

Cirencester

A433

A419

Abingdon

A420

Chepstow

M5

Malmesbury

Didcot

M48

M4

Swindon

Wantage

A34

Avonmouth

M4

Chippenham

WILTSHIRE

M4

Basildon

BRISTOL

Bristol

Avebury

Marlborough

BERKSHIRE

M5

Bristol

Bath

Avon

Hungerford

Newbury

SOMERSET

0   15 mi

0   15 km

16–17 in full-time education) lets you visit the five most important sights, described below. You can also buy a family ticket, £50 for two adults and three children—a good deal. Buy the ticket at your first stop at any one of the Trust properties. Free admission for children 4 and under.

Anne Hathaway's Cottage ★ HISTORIC HOME   The childhood home of Anne Hathaway, Shakespeare's long-suffering wife, is the Trust property most evocative of the Tudor period—a pretty thatched wattle-and-daub cottage in the hamlet of Shottery, 1 mile from the center of Stratford. The Hathaways were yeoman farmers, and their descendants lived in the cottage until 1892. As a result, it was never renovated and provides a rare insight into the life of a family in Shakespearean times. Many original furnishings, including various kitchen utensils and the courting settle (the bench on which Shakespeare is said to have wooed Anne), are preserved inside the house. Will was only 18 when he married Anne Hathaway in 1582; she was 8 years older.

Cottage Lane, Shottery (take the City Sightseeing bus (p. 452) from Bridge St., or walk via a marked pathway from Evesham Place in Stratford across the meadow to Shottery). ℭ **01789/292100.** www.shakespeare.org.uk. Admission £7.50 adults, £6.50 seniors and students, £4.50 children 5–15 and 16–17 in full-time education, £20 family ticket. Combination tickets available (see above). Apr–Oct daily 9am–5pm; Nov–Mar 10am–4pm. Closed Dec 23–26.

Hall's Croft HISTORIC HOME   Hall's Croft is an outstanding Tudor home with a walled garden, furnished in the style of a middle-class home of the time. It was in this 16th-century house that Shakespeare's eldest daughter Susanna probably lived with her husband, Dr. John Hall, who was widely respected and built up a large medical practice in the area. Fascinating exhibits illustrate the theory and practice of medicine in Dr. Hall's time.

Old Town St. (near Holy Trinity Church). To reach Hall's Croft, walk west from High St., which becomes Chapel St. and Church St. At the intersection with Old Town St., go left. ℭ **01789/292107.** www.shakespeare.org.uk. Admission includes Shakespeare's Birthplace and Nash's House & New Place; £13 adults, £12 seniors and students, £8 children 5–15 and 16–17 in full-time education, £34 family ticket. Combination tickets available (see above). Apr–Oct daily 9am–5pm; Nov–Mar 10am–4pm. Closed Dec 23–26.

Holy Trinity Church (Shakespeare's Tomb) CHURCH   In a bucolic setting near the River Avon is the Norman parish church where Shakespeare is buried ("and curst be he who moves my bones"). The Parish Register records his baptism in 1564 and burial in 1616; copies of the original documents are on display. Shakespeare's tomb lies in the chancel, a privilege bestowed upon him when he became a lay rector in 1605. Alongside his grave are those of his widow, Anne, and other members of his family. Nearby on the north wall is a bust of Shakespeare that was erected approximately 7 years after his death—within the lifetime of his widow and many of his friends.

Old Town St. (walk 4 min. past the Royal Shakespeare Theatre, with the river on your left). ℭ **01789/290128.** www.stratford-upon-avon.org. Free admission to church; Shakespeare's tomb £2 adults, £1 students. Apr–Sept Mon–Sat 8:30am–6pm, Sun 12:30–5pm; Mar and Oct Mon–Sat 9am–5pm, Sun 12:30–5pm; Nov–Feb Mon–Sat 9am–4pm, Sun 12:30–5pm. Closed to visitors Good Friday, Christmas Day, Boxing Day (St. Stephen's Day), and New Year's Day.

Mary Arden's Farm & Palmer's Farm ★ FARM   So what if millions of visitors have been tricked into thinking this timber-framed farmhouse, with its old stone dovecote and various outbuildings, was the girlhood home of Shakespeare's mother, Mary Arden? It's still one of the most intriguing sights outside Stratford, even if local

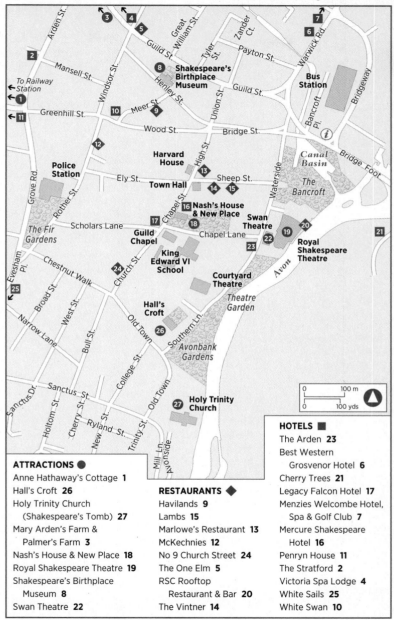

ATTRACTIONS ●

Anne Hathaway's Cottage **1**
Hall's Croft **26**
Holy Trinity Church
  (Shakespeare's Tomb) **27**
Mary Arden's Farm &
  Palmer's Farm **3**
Nash's House & New Place **18**
Royal Shakespeare Theatre **19**
Shakespeare's Birthplace
  Museum **8**
Swan Theatre **22**

RESTAURANTS ◆

Havilands **9**
Lambs **15**
Marlowe's Restaurant **13**
McKechnies **12**
No 9 Church Street **24**
The One Elm **5**
RSC Rooftop
  Restaurant & Bar **20**
The Vintner **14**

HOTELS ■

The Arden **23**
Best Western
  Grosvenor Hotel **6**
Cherry Trees **21**
Legacy Falcon Hotel **17**
Menzies Welcombe Hotel,
  Spa & Golf Club **7**
Mercure Shakespeare
  Hotel **16**
Penryn House **11**
The Stratford **2**
Victoria Spa Lodge **4**
White Sails **25**
White Swan **10**

historian Dr. Nat Alcock discovered in 2000 that the actual childhood home of Arden was the less-romantic red-brick farmhouse, Glebe Farm, next door, built around 1514. Glebe Farm has now been properly renamed, and what was known for years as "Mary Arden's House" has been dubbed Palmer's Farm. The outhouses of both properties have been converted into a working farm. Visitors can tour the property and see firsthand how a farming household functioned in the 1570s—yes, cows to be milked, bread to be baked, and vegetables cultivated in an authentic 16th-century manner. In the barns, stable, cowshed, and farmyard is an extensive collection of farming implements illustrating life and work in the local countryside from Shakespeare's time to the present.

Station Rd., Wilmcote (take the A3400 (Birmingham) for 3½ miles). ℰ **01789/293455.** www. shakespeare.org.uk. Admission £9.50 adults, £8.50 students and seniors, £5.50 children 5–15 and 16–17 in full-time education, £23 family ticket. Combination tickets available (see above). Nov–Mar daily 10am–4pm; Apr–Oct daily 10am–5pm. Closed Dec 23–26.

Nash's House & New Place HISTORIC HOME   Shakespeare retired to New Place in 1610 (a prosperous man by the standards of his day) and died here 6 years later. Regrettably, the house was torn down, so only the garden remains. A mulberry tree planted by the Bard was so popular with latter-day visitors to Stratford that the garden's owner chopped it down. It is said that the mulberry tree that grows here today was planted from a cutting of the original tree. You enter the gardens through Nash's House (Thomas Nash married Elizabeth Hall, a granddaughter of the poet). Nash's House has 16th-century period rooms and an exhibition illustrating the history of Stratford.

Chapel St. ℰ **01789/292325.** www.shakespeare.org.uk. Admission includes Shakespeare's Birthplace and Hall's Croft; £13 adults, £12 seniors and students, £8 children 5–15 and 16–17 in full-time education, £34 family ticket. Combination tickets available (see above). Nov–Mar daily 11am–4pm; Apr–June and Sept–Oct daily 10am–5pm; July–Aug daily 10am–6pm. Closed Dec 23–26. Walk west down High St.; Chapel St. is a continuation of High St.

Shakespeare's Birthplace Museum ★★ MUSEUM   The son of a glover and whittawer (leather worker), Will Shakespeare was born in this house in 1564. Filled with Shakespeare memorabilia, including a portrait and furnishings of the writer's time, this Trust property is a half-timbered structure, dating from the early 16th century. The house was bought by public donors in 1847 and has been preserved as a national shrine ever since. You can visit the living room, the bedroom where Shakespeare was probably born, a fully equipped kitchen of the period (look for the "baby-minder"), and a Shakespeare museum, illustrating his life and times.

Built next door to commemorate the 400th anniversary of the Bard's birth, the modern **Shakespeare Centre** serves both as the administrative headquarters of the Birthplace Trust and as a library and study center. An extension houses the birthplace visitor center.

Henley St. (in the town center near the post office, close to Union St.). ℰ **01789/204016.** www. shakespeare.org.uk. Admission includes free entry to Hall's Croft and Nash's House & New Place; £13 adults, £12 seniors and students, £8 children 5–15 and 16–17 in full-time education, £34 family ticket. Combination tickets available (see above). Nov–Mar daily 10am–4pm; Apr–Jun and Sept–Oct daily 10am–5pm; July–Aug daily 9am–6pm. Closed Dec 23–26.

Where to Eat
MODERATE
Lambs ★ CONTEMPORARY ENGLISH   Near the Royal Shakespeare Theatre, this stylish cafe/bistro is housed in a building dating from 1547. It's ideal for a quick light meal or pre-theatre dinner. The menu changes monthly, but expect finely executed

English classics such as slow-roasted lamb shank with creamed potato and glazed carrots, as well as more exotic creations such as sweet potato, peas, and coconut curry with basmati rice. And it's hard to beat the addictive sticky toffee pudding for dessert.

12 Sheep St. ℂ **01789/292554.** www.lambsrestaurant.co.uk. Reservations required for dinner Fri–Sat. Main courses £9.25–£16; fixed-price lunch menu £12 for 2 courses, £15 for 3 courses. MC, V. Mon 5:30–10pm; Tues–Sat noon–2pm and 5–10pm; Sun noon–2:30pm.

Marlowe's Restaurant CONTEMPORARY ENGLISH The place to come for olde English atmosphere—the large bar, with a fireplace blazing with logs in winter, opens onto a splendid oak-paneled room, and in summer there is a spacious courtyard for alfresco dining. The food is also pretty good; start with seared scallops or chicken livers flambéed in masala cream, and continue with one of the chargrilled dishes such as a filet steak with pan-fried mushrooms and grilled tomatoes. Drunken duck has been a long-time specialty here: It's marinated in gin, red wine, and juniper berries before it's roasted in the oven.

18 High St. ℂ **01789/204999.** www.marlowes.biz. Reservations recommended. Main courses £10–£43. AE, MC, V. Elizabethan Room Mon–Thurs 5:30–10pm; Fri 5:30–10:30pm; Sat 5:30–11pm. Bistro daily noon–2:15pm; Mon–Sat 5:30–11pm.

No 9 Church Street ★★ CONTEMPORARY ENGLISH This is one of Stratford's finest and most stylish restaurants, with a creative seasonal menu by talented chefs Wayne Thomson and Dan Robinson. Starters include piquant delights such as Warwickshire rarebit, marinated mushrooms, artichokes, and crispy pancetta, with main courses such as the elaborate Tusmore Estate pheasant with red cabbage, Braeburn apple purée, glazed carrot, bacon, and chestnuts. Leave room for the Bramley apple and sultana tipsy cake with cinnamon palmiers.

9 Church St. ℂ **01789/415522.** www.no9churchst.com. Reservations recommended. Main courses £12–£17. MC, V. Tues–Sat noon–2:30pm, 5:30–9:30pm; Sun noon–4pm.

The One Elm ENGLISH The One Elm is a convenient option thanks to its long hours of food service. Guests can enjoy its pub atmosphere, ground-floor restaurant, or its tranquil courtyard for dining and drinking (try the real ale from Warwickshire brewery Purity). Dishes utilize fresh produce, including ethically sourced Guatemalan coffee, and free-range pork, chicken, eggs, and high-quality beef, sourced from Leamington Spa butcher Aubrey Allen. Grab a sandwich; a classic bar meal such as ham, egg and chips; or the Deli Board, featuring all sorts of antipasti and charcuterie such as mustard sausages and marinated anchovies. Among the most enticing main dishes are the smoked salmon fishcakes.

1 Guild St. ℂ **01789/404919.** www.oneelmstratford.co.uk. Main courses £10–£17; Deli Board £11. MC, V. Mon–Sat 11am–10pm; Sun noon–3pm and 6:30–9:30pm.

RSC Rooftop Restaurant & Bar ENGLISH/CONTINENTAL This restaurant enjoys the best location in town—it's wrapped around the top of the Royal Shakespeare Theatre itself—with floor-to-ceiling windows providing an unobstructed view of the swans on the Avon. Consider the cafe a venue for lunch, preshow dining, or a supper of freshly prepared and simply cooked modern English food. Main courses might include John Dory with mussel and parsley, or lip-smacking roast partridge with rosti potato, Brussel tops, and crisp bacon.

In the Royal Shakespeare Theatre, Waterside. ℂ **01789/403449.** www.rsc.org.uk. Reservations recommended. Main courses £13–£19; fixed-price menu £11 for 1 course, £15 for 2 courses, or £18 for 3 courses. AE, MC, V. Mon–Sat 11:30am–11pm; Sun noon–2:30pm.

INEXPENSIVE

Havilands ENGLISH TEA/CAFE   This well-respected caterer opened a charming tearoom and take-out in 2009, serving fresh, locally sourced food. Grab a stilton and grape sandwich; turkey, cranberry, and stuffing quiche; or spicy teacake, and relax on the sunny terrace. They also serve high-quality pies, soups, and salads.

4-5 Meer St. ✆ **01789/415477.** www.havilandscatering.com. Cakes from £1.20, sandwiches from £1.95. MC, V. Daily 9am–4:30pm.

McKechnies CAFE/COFFEEHOUSE   This cozy cafe serves the best coffee in Stratford. It's another independent place that sources its food and milk from local suppliers; tasty all-day Warwickshire breakfasts (dry cured bacon, Hatton sausage, field mushrooms, fresh beef, tomatoes, and free-range eggs), toasted ciabattas, chunky farmhouse sandwiches, zesty soups, and cupcakes from locally based Tea Cake Company. The cappuccino is justly celebrated (beans sourced from James' Gourmet Coffee Company), and they also serve 17 types of tea.

37 Rother St. ✆ **01789/299575.** www.mckechniescafe.talktalk.net. Soups/sandwiches from £3.50. MC, V. Mon–Sat 8am–5:30pm, Sun 9:30am–4:30pm.

The Vintner ENGLISH/CONTINENTAL   In a timber-framed structure little altered since its construction in the late 15th century, the Vintner may very well be the place where William Shakespeare went to purchase his wine. The Vintner is both a cafe/bar and a restaurant owned by the same family for 5 centuries; its location makes it ideal for a pre-theatre lunch or supper. When possible, fresh local produce is used. Good-tasting main courses include salmon fishcakes with wilted spinach and sorrel sauce, and well-priced steaks. For dessert, try that British favorite, sticky toffee pudding with vanilla ice cream.

4-5 Sheep St. ✆ **01789/297259.** www.the-vintner.co.uk. Reservations not necessary. Main courses £7.75–£15. DC, MC, V. Mon–Sat 9:30am–10pm; Sun 9:30am–9pm.

Shopping

Set within an antique house with ceiling beams, the **Shakespeare Bookshop,** 39 Henley St. (✆ **01789/292176;** www.shakespeare.org.uk; Wed–Sat 9:30am–5:30pm, Sun noon–5pm), across from the Shakespeare Birthplace Centre, is the region's premier source for textbooks and academic treatises on the Bard and his works. It specializes in books for every level of expertise on Shakespearean studies, from picture books for junior-high students to weighty tomes geared to those pursuing a Ph.D. in literature.

Entertainment & Nightlife

THE PUB & BAR SCENE

Despite the millions of tourists passing through, Stratford is essentially a small town where nightlife revolves around the RSC Theatre and local pubs. Everyone who visits Stratford grabs at least one drink at the **Dirty Duck ★★** (✆ **01789/297312;** www.dirtyduck-pub-stratford-upon-avon.co.uk; restaurant daily noon–10pm, bar daily 11am–11pm), close to the RSC Theatre on Waterside. The creaky old pub has been a popular hangout for Stratford players since the 18th century, its walls lined with autographed photos of its many famous patrons. Real ales include Old Speckled Hen and Greene King IPA, while typical English pub food is featured in the Conservatory Restaurant.

Also part of the Greene King stable, the **Garrick Inn ★**, at 25 High St. (✆ **01789/ 292186;** www.garrick-inn-stratford-upon-avon.co.uk; daily 11am–11pm), is the oldest pub in Stratford, a handsome black-and-white timbered structure that dates back to the 14th century. The open fireplace and curry nights (Wed) attract plenty of locals in addition to tourists.

Stratford's oldest structure (not its oldest pub) is reputed to be the **White Swan** on Rother Street (✆ **01789/297022;** www.pebblehotels.com; daily noon–9pm). It's a hotel today, but the lounge and bar is an atmospheric place for a drink, with cushioned leather armchairs, oak paneling, and fireplaces.

Where to Stay

EXPENSIVE

The Arden ★★★ Stratford's best hotel and the most convenient for the RSC Theatre reopened in 2010 after a comprehensive refurbishment. All the rooms have been decked out in an elegant, contemporary English style with the latest amenities, some with views of the river; the main difference between the Deluxe, Superior, and Classic rooms is size. The excellent location and on-site dining choices—the **Waterside Brasserie and Champagne Bar**—means you won't need to stray far from the hotel.

Waterside, Stratford-upon-Avon, Warwickshire CV37 6BA. www.theardenhotelstratford.com. ✆ **01789/ 298682.** Fax 01789/206989. 45 units. £125–£185. Basic package rates include English breakfast. AE, MC, V. Free parking. **Amenities:** 3 restaurants; 2 bars; room service. *In room:* TV/DVD, hair dryer, Wi-Fi (free).

Best Western Grosvenor Hotel A pair of Georgian townhouses, built in 1832 and 1843, join to form this hotel, one of the top choices in Stratford. In the center of town, with lawns and gardens to the rear, it's a short stroll from the Avon River, Bancroft Gardens, and the Royal Shakespeare Theatre. Bedrooms are midsize to spacious, each personally designed with a high standard of tasteful modern furnishings, a cut above usual chain-hotel fare.

12–14 Warwick Rd., Stratford-upon-Avon, Warwickshire CV37 6YT. www.bwgh.co.uk. ✆ **01789/269213.** Fax 01789/266087. 73 units. £109–£124 double. Breakfast £10 extra. AE, MC, V. Free parking. **Amenities:** Restaurant; bar; babysitting; room service. *In room:* TV, hair dryer, Wi-Fi (free).

Menzies Welcombe Hotel, Spa & Golf Club ★★ For a formal, historic country house near Stratford, there's nothing better than the Welcombe. Built in 1866 in a grand Jacobean style, this property is a 10-minute ride from the heart of town. Its key feature is an 18-hole golf course, but the spa is equally appealing and it makes for a romantic stay whatever you aim to do in Stratford. Bedrooms are luxuriously outfitted in traditional Jacobean style, with fine antiques and elegant fabrics. Most rooms are seemingly big enough for tennis matches, but those in the garden wing, although comfortable, are small.

Warwick Rd., Stratford-upon-Avon, Warwickshire CV37 0NR. www.menzies-hotels.co.uk. ✆ **01789/ 295252.** Fax 01789/414666. 78 units. £78–£142 double. AE, DC, MC, V. Free parking. Take the A439 1¼ miles northeast of the town center. **Amenities:** 2 restaurants; bar; golf course; gym w/aerobics studio; indoor pool; room service; spa; tennis court. *In room:* TV, hair dryer, Wi-Fi (free).

Mercure Shakespeare Hotel ★ Filled with historical associations, the original core of this hotel dates from the 1400s. Quieter and plusher than the Falcon (see below), it is equaled in the center of Stratford only by the Arden (see above).

Bedrooms are named in honor of noteworthy actors, Shakespeare's plays, or Shakespearean characters. The oldest are capped with hewn timbers, and all have modern comforts. Even the newer accommodations are at least 40 to 50 years old and have rose-and-thistle patterns carved into many of their exposed timbers.

Chapel St., Stratford-upon-Avon, Warwickshire CV37 6ER. www.mercure.com. ✆ **01789/294997.** Fax 01789/415411. 74 units. £142–£173 double. Children 12 and under stay free in parent's room. AE, DC, MC, V. Parking £10 per day. **Amenities:** Restaurant; bar; room service, Wi-Fi (free, in public areas). *In room:* A/C, TV, hair dryer, minibar (in some), Wi-Fi (£4.90 per hr.).

MODERATE

Cherry Trees ★★ 🎁   This small B&B has a fabulous location, a short walk across the bridge to the RSC Theatre and the center of Stratford. The Garden Room features a king-size four poster, there's a modern leather king-size bed in the Terrace Room (both have large conservatories and access to the garden), and the gorgeous Tiffany Suite offers a king-size bed and separate sitting room. Whichever room you choose, you'll be welcomed with tea and scones on arrival, get a huge cooked breakfast, and have access to a well-stocked fridge and selection of teas.

Swans Nest Lane, Stratford-upon-Avon, Warwickshire CV37 7LS. cherrytrees-stratford.co.uk. ✆ **01789/292989.** 3 units. £95–£120 double. Rates include breakfast. MC, V. Free parking. *In room:* TV, hair dryer, Wi-Fi (free).

Legacy Falcon Hotel   The Falcon blends the very old and the very new, with parts of the hotel dating back to the 16th century; connected to its rear by a glass passageway is a more sterile extension added in 1970. The rooms in the older section have oak beams, diamond leaded-glass windows, antiques, and good reproductions. In the inn's intimate Merlin Lounge, you'll find an open copper-hooded fireplace where fires are stoked under beams salvaged from old ships.

Chapel St., Stratford-upon-Avon, Warwickshire CV37 6HA. www.legacy-hotels.co.uk. ✆ **0844/411-9005.** Fax 0844/411-9006. 83 units. £87–£130 double. AE, DC, MC, V. Free parking. **Amenities:** 2 restaurants; 2 bars; room service. *In room:* TV, hair dryer, Wi-Fi (free).

The Stratford ★   This is definitely not one of the historic inns of Stratford-upon-Avon, but a plush, modern hotel with up-to-date conveniences. A member of the QHotels group, its location is only a short walk from the banks of the River Avon. The bedrooms are spaciously and elegantly appointed, some with four-poster beds and Tudor-style, but others are more geared to commercial travelers seeking streamlined conveniences—not romance. Deftly prepared market-fresh dishes change with the seasons in the on-site **Quills Restaurant.**

Arden St., Stratford-upon-Avon, Warwickshire CV37 6QQ. www.qhotels.co.uk. ✆/fax **01789/271-000.** 102 units. £80–£105 double. AE, DC, MC, V. Free parking. **Amenities:** Restaurant; bar; small exercise room; room service; Wi-Fi (free, in public areas). *In room:* TV, hair dryer, Internet (free for 2 hr. per day, then £7 per 24 hr.).

White Sails ★★   This luxurious B&B is just a 15-minute walk from the town center. The four spacious rooms sport a crisp, contemporary design, enhanced with modern art, sculptures, and huge beds (the Warwick room has a four-poster). Thoughtful extras include chocolates by the bed and a tea tray stocked with treats. There's a huge choice at breakfast, from full English to cinnamon toast, cereals, and fruit, and the hosts are a mine of local information.

85 Evesham Rd., Stratford-upon-Avon, Warwickshire CV37 9BE. www.white-sails.co.uk. ✆ **01789/264326.** 4 units. £97–£122 double. Rates include English breakfast. MC, V (1.5% surcharge). Free

parking. **Amenities:** Guest lounge with complimentary sherry; ironing facilities. *In room:* TV, hair dryer, minibar, fridge, Wi-Fi (free).

White Swan This cozy, intimate hotel, housed in Stratford's oldest building, is one of the most atmospheric in Stratford. The rooms are clean and perfectly adequate, although some could do with a renovation, but this hotel is all about location and history over luxury. Many of the original bedrooms have been well preserved, despite the addition of modern conveniences. Paintings dating from 1550 hang on the lounge walls.

Rother St., Stratford-upon-Avon, Warwickshire CV37 6NH. www.pebblehotels.com. ✆ **01789/297022.** Fax 01789/268773. 41 units. £75–£95 double. Breakfast from £5.50. AE, DC, MC, V. Parking £5 for 24 hr. **Amenities:** Restaurant; bar; room service, Wi-Fi (free). *In room:* TV, hair dryer.

INEXPENSIVE

Penryn House ★ 🍴 The location is convenient and the price is right at this B&B, where hosts Anne and Robert Dawkes are among the most welcoming in town. They justifiably take special pride in their breakfasts, right down to their superb "Harvest of Arden" English apple juice. Free-range Worcestershire eggs are served along with fresh seasonal fruit and locally produced bacon and sausage. They even prepare a vegetarian breakfast if requested. The bedrooms are a bit small, but well furnished and comfortable. The location is close to the train station, Anne Hathaway's Cottage, and the heart of town.

126 Alcester Rd., Stratford-upon-Avon, Warwickshire CV37 9DP. www.penrynguesthouse.co.uk. ✆ **01789/293718.** Fax 01789/266077. 7 units. £60–£70 double. Rates include breakfast. MC, V. Free parking. *In room:* TV, hair dryer, Wi-Fi (free).

Victoria Spa Lodge🍴 This B&B is old-fashioned, atmospheric, and a great deal. Opened in 1837, the year Queen Victoria ascended the throne, this was the first establishment to be given her name, and it is still going strong. The lodge was originally a spa frequented by the Queen's eldest daughter, Princess Vicky. Rooms are clean and comfy, decked out in a variety of classic English styles, from period Victorian and floral country inn, to a more contemporary look.

Bishopton Lane (1½ miles north of the town center, where the A3400 intersects the A46), Stratford-upon-Avon, Warwickshire CV37 9QY. www.victoriaspa.co.uk. ✆ **01789/267985.** Fax 01789/204728. 7 units. £65 double. Rates include breakfast. MC, V. Free parking. *In room:* TV, hair dryer, Wi-Fi (£10 per day).

WARWICK

94 miles NW of London; 9 miles NE of Stratford-upon-Avon

This small Midland town is best known for **Warwick Castle,** one of the finest medieval fortresses in England. The castle reflects the town's importance in the Middle Ages, when it was the base of the **earls of Warwick,** initially of the Norman Beauchamp family. The Great Fire of 1694 destroyed most of the medieval town, and though it was rebuilt, Warwick declined in influence thereafter, despite remaining the county town.

Today the historic center is charming but easily explored on a day-trip from Stratford. Nearby lie the romantic ruins of Kenilworth Castle, the elegant town of Leamington Spa, and Coventry, a much larger industrial city celebrated for its modern cathedral.

Essentials

GETTING THERE Chiltern Railways trains run frequently between Stratford-upon-Avon and Warwick (22 min.). A one-way ticket costs around £4.70.

Stagecoach bus no. 16 departs Stratford-upon-Avon every hour during the day. The trip takes roughly half an hour. Go to **www.stagecoachbus.com** for schedules. Take the A46 if you're driving from Stratford-upon-Avon.

VISITOR INFORMATION The **Tourist Information Centre** is at the Court House, Jury Street (*(C)* **01926/492212;** www.visitwarwick.co.uk), and is open Monday to Friday from 9:30am to 4:30pm, Saturday 10am to 4:30pm, and Sunday 10am to 3:30pm (closes 30 min. later in summer; closed Dec 24–26 and Jan 1).

Exploring the Area

Lord Leycester Hospital HISTORIC SITE This attractive group of 14th-century timber-framed buildings is the most enticing sight in the old heart of Warwick. It was never a hospital in the modern sense, but rather a charitable institution "for the housing and maintenance of the needy, infirm or aged." Originally built to house local guilds, the hospital was founded in 1571 by Robert Dudley, Earl of Leicester, as a home for old soldiers. It's still used by ex-service personnel and their spouses. On top of the West Gate is the attractive little chapel of St. James, dating from the 12th century but renovated many times since. American writer Nathaniel Hawthorne wrote of his visits to Master's Garden in 1855 and 1857; the gardens were later restored based on the observations he made in his writings.

60 High St. *(C)* **01926/491422.** www.lordleycester.com. Admission £4.90 adults, £4.40 seniors, £3.90 children 5–15, free for children 4 and under. Easter–Oct Tues–Sun 10am–5pm; Nov–Easter Tues–Sun 10am–4:30pm.

St. Mary's Church CHURCH Destroyed in part by the fire of 1694, this church is among the finest examples of late-17th- and early-18th-century architecture. The Beauchamp Chapel, spared from the flames, encases the Purbeck marble tomb of Richard Beauchamp, a well-known earl of Warwick who died in 1439 and is commemorated by a gilded bronze effigy. Even more powerful than King Henry V, Beauchamp has a tomb that's one of the finest remaining examples of the Perpendicular Gothic style from the mid-15th century. The tomb of Robert Dudley, Earl of Leicester, a favorite of Elizabeth I, is against the north wall. The Perpendicular Gothic choir dates from the 14th century; the Norman crypt and chapter house are from the 11th century. It's also worth climbing the 134 steps to the top of the tower, for scintillating views of the town and surrounding countryside.

21 Church St. *(C)* **01926/403940.** www.saintmaryschurch.co.uk. Free admission (£2 donation recommended); tower £2.50 adults, £1 children 5–15. Apr–Oct daily 10am–6pm; Nov–Mar daily 10am–4:30pm. All buses to Warwick stop at Old Sq., 2 blocks from the church.

Warwick Castle ★★★ CASTLE Perched on a rocky cliff above the River Avon close to the town center, this magnificent 14th-century fortress looms over the town like a giant fist. It's the definitive medieval castle, with chunky towers, crenellated battlements, and a moat surrounded by gardens, lawns, and woodland where peacocks roam freely. You'll need the best part of a day to do it justice.

Ethelfleda, daughter of Alfred the Great, built the first significant fortifications here in 914, while William the Conqueror ordered the construction of a motte-and-bailey castle in 1068. The mound is all that remains today of the Norman castle, which Simon de Montfort sacked in the Barons' War of 1264.

The Beauchamp family, which controlled the medieval earldom of Warwick during its most illustrious period, is responsible for the appearance of the castle today; much of the external structure remains unchanged from the mid-14th century. When the castle was granted to Sir Fulke Greville by James I in 1604, he spent £20,000 (an enormous sum in those days) converting the existing castle buildings into a luxurious mansion. The Grevilles have held the Earl of Warwick title since 1759, but sold the castle to Tussaud's in 1978. As a result, the ornate interiors have been embellished with exhibitions and waxwork displays to create a vivid picture of the castle's turbulent past and its important role in the history of England.

The Kingmaker exhibit features Richard Neville, Earl of Warwick, as he prepares his household for the Battle of Barnet in 1471, while the former private apartments house a display of a carefully reconstructed Royal Weekend House Party in 1898 (featuring wax models of a young Winston Churchill, the Prince of Wales, later King Edward VII, and the Duchess of Marlborough). The Great Hall at the heart of the castle contains the impressive Kenilworth buffet, a table made in oak by local craftsmen for the Great Exhibition of 1851. The lavish State Rooms, built to entertain noble guests and loaded with treasures, are also open to visitors during an ongoing restoration program.

Finally, the Castle Dungeon is a ghoulish memorial to the dark side of the castle's history (unsuitable for children under 10). Kids will prefer the Pageant Playground, and the slightly kitsch Princess Tower, which tells the story of a fairytale princess preparing for a castle wedding.

Warwick. (©) **0870/442-2000.** www.warwick-castle.co.uk. Admission £21 adults, £15 children 4-16, £16.20 seniors, £72 family ticket, free for children 3 and under; 15% discount for tickets purchased online; Castle dungeon extra £7.80. Daily 10am–5pm. Closed Dec 25.

Where to Eat

Brethren's Kitchen ENGLISH TEA   For a break from sightseeing, it's hard to beat the Tudor ambience at this tearoom, part of the historic Lord Leycester Hospital (p. 462) with cool stone floors and wonderful exposed oak beams. Order the full cream tea with scones and fresh cream, or a variety of tempting homemade cakes. They also do cheap but tasty lunches of home-cooked soup or sandwiches—try the Warwickshire pork sausages.

Lord Leycester Hospital, 60 High St. (©) **07733/550497.** www.brethrenskitchen.co.uk. Main courses £6–£12. AE, MC, V. Feb-Dec Tues-Sat 10am–5pm, Sun 11am–5pm. Open bank holiday Mondays. Closed Jan.

Catalan ★ 🍴 MEDITERRANEAN   It's the castle, not the cuisine, that draws you to Warwick, but this bistro is notable for serving affordable food that tastes good and is prepared with fresh ingredients. If you come for lunch, you'll be greeted with a Spanish tapas menu that is experimental and tasteful. There's also lighter fare such as sandwiches, panini, and salads. Dinner is more elaborate, with dishes such as steamed fresh mussels in white wine or grilled lamb cutlets with garlic mash.

6 Jury St. (©) **01926/498930.** www.cafecatalan.com. Reservations recommended. Main courses £12–£20; Mon–Fri 2-course fixed-price lunch £12. AE, MC, V. Mon-Sat noon–3pm and 6-9:30pm.

Tailors ★★★ 🍴 CONTEMPORARY ENGLISH   Tailors serves incredibly creative food from two of the regions up and coming young chefs. The seasonal menus are a masterpiece; expect exquisite combinations such as braised shoulder and filet of Lincolnshire pork with black pudding (blood sausage), white beans, smoked almonds, and caramelized sprouts, or filet of scotch beef and poached lobster with caramelized potatoes, young spinach, and a thermidor foam. Everything is artfully presented and tastes sensational.

22 Market Place. 🕐 **01926/410590.** www.tailorsrestaurant.co.uk. Reservations recommended. Lunch £9.95 for 2 courses; dinner £30 for 2 courses, £35 for 3 courses. AE, MC, V. Tues–Sat noon–2pm and 6:30–9:30pm.

Entertainment & Nightlife

Real ale drinkers should make for the **Old Fourpenny Shop Hotel** (🕐 **01926/ 491360;** www.4pennyhotel.com), 27–29 Crompton St., which offers a changing selection of traditional cask beers from all over the country and a selection of quality wines. The **Rose & Crown,** at 30 Market Place (🕐 **01926/411117;** www.roseand crownwarwick.co.uk), is another inn and restaurant that's a great place for a drink, with beers such as Black Sheep, Warwickshire Purity Gold, and a weekly guest ale on tap.

Where to Stay

Glebe Hotel ★ 🎁 This 1820s' rectory to the Church of St. Peter has been welcoming wayfarers to Warwick since it was successfully converted into a small country-house hotel in 1948. Each of the compact bedrooms has been individually designed with a tented ceiling and a four-poster or coronet-style bed. The **Cedars Conservatory Restaurant** looks out onto the gardens, and there's even a small swimming pool with hydrojets. The hotel is a 10-minute drive from the center of Warwick.

Church St., Barford, Warwickshire CV35 8BS. www.glebehotel.co.uk. 🕐 **01926/624218.** Fax 01926/ 624625. 39 units. £140–£150 double. AE, DC, MC, V. Free parking. **Amenities:** Restaurant; bar; exercise room; hot tub; indoor pool; sauna; solarium; spa. *In room:* TV, hair dryer, Wi-Fi (free).

Hilton Warwick ★ Though it's outside of town, the Hilton is the best choice if you're using Warwick as a base to explore the area. Rooms are standard chain fare, but comfortable enough and come with flat-screen TVs and all the usual amenities. Lying at the junction of a network of highways, it's popular with business travelers, but tourists also find that its comfort and easy-to-find location make it a good base for touring. The hotel sports a low-rise modern design with a series of interconnected bars, lounges, and public areas.

Warwick Bypass (A429 Stratford Rd.), Warwick, Warwickshire CV34 6RE. www.hilton.co.uk/warwick. 🕐 **800/445-8667** in the U.S. and Canada, or 01926/499555. Fax 01926/410020. 181 units. £71–£150 double. AE, DC, MC, V. Parking £5 per day. Take the A429 2 miles south of Warwick or 7 miles north of Stratford-upon-Avon to junction 15 of the M40. **Amenities:** Restaurant; cafe; bar; babysitting; health club; indoor pool; room service; sauna; steam room; Wi-Fi (in public areas, £3 for 15 min.; £8.50 per hr.). *In room:* A/C (in deluxe rooms), TV, hair dryer, Internet (£15 per day).

Park Cottage ★★ This gorgeous B&B set in a 15th-century timber-frame cottage once was owned by the earls of Warwick. It's justly popular in large part thanks to thoughtful hosts Janet and Stuart Baldry and their exceptional rooms. All feature wood or parquet floors, oak beams, and antique furniture; the Elizabeth Room has a beautifully carved four-poster. The cottage is literally opposite the castle entrance, and is adorned with hanging baskets overflowing with blossoms.

113 West St., Warwick, Warwickshire CV34 6AH. www.parkcottagewarwick.co.uk. 🕐 **01926/410319.** Fax 01926/497994. 7 units. £68–£85 double. Rates include breakfast. DC, MC, V. Free parking. **Amenities:** Bar. *In room:* TV, hair dryer, Wi-Fi (free).

Side Trips from Warwick
ROYAL LEAMINGTON SPA★

Like other English spa towns, Leamington Spa boomed in the 18th century when taking spring water was popularized for its medicinal qualities. In 1814 the handsome **Royal Pump Rooms & Baths** were opened on The Parade, close to the River Leam, and a plethora of fine Georgian buildings followed in subsequent years. Today the town makes an inviting day-trip, with the pump rooms now containing the absorbing **Leamington Spa Art Gallery & Museum** (www.warwickdc.gov.uk; Tues, Wed, Fri, and Sat 10:30am–5pm, Thurs 1:30–8pm, Sun 11am–4pm; free), a visitor information center (✆ **01926/742762;** Mon–Fri 10am–4:30pm, Sat 10am–3pm, Sun 10am–2pm), and a cafe where you can take afternoon tea. You can also stop by **Aubrey Allen ★★** at 108 Warwick St. (✆ **01926/311208;** www.aubreyallen. co.uk), one of Britain's most respected butchers. The shop's deli section is a great place to load up for a picnic (cheeses, quiches, cured meats) or light meals (think curries or breakfast sausage baps).

Stagecoach (www.stagecoachbus.com) runs regular bus services between Leamington and Warwick, just 3 miles west.

KENILWORTH CASTLE ★★

The big attraction in Kenilworth, an otherwise dull English market town 5 miles north of Warwick, is enigmatic **Kenilworth Castle** (✆ **01926/852078;** www. english-heritage.org.uk), founded in the 1120s by Geoffrey de Clinton, a lieutenant of Henry I. At one time, its walls enclosed an area of 2.8 hectares (7 acres), but it is now in majestic ruins. Caesar's Tower, with its 5m-thick (16-ft.) walls, is all that remains of the original structure.

The castle is open daily, March to August from 10am to 6pm, September and October from 10am to 5pm, and November to February from 10am to 4pm. It's closed January 1 and December 24 to December 26. Admission is £8 for adults, £7.20 for seniors, £4.80 for children 5 to 16, and free for children 4 and under; a family ticket goes for £21. Entry includes the excellent audioguides.

Stagecoach buses X17 and 16 (www.stagecoachbus.com) connect Kenilworth with Warwick, Leamington Spa, and Coventry.

COVENTRY CATHEDRAL ★

Thirteen miles northeast of Warwick is Coventry, the second largest city in the Midlands, and an industrial center with few tourist attractions save one—it's remarkable cathedral. Coventry's fine medieval center was totally destroyed by German bombers during the Coventry Blitz in 1940, and postwar planners replaced it with brutalist shopping malls and concrete buildings. Coventry's 14th-century St. Michael's Cathedral was also destroyed by the bombs; only the tower, spire, outer wall, and the bronze effigy and tomb of its first bishop survived. In 1962, Sir Basil Spence's controversial replacement was consecrated. Today **Coventry Cathedral,** 7 Priory Row (✆ **024/ 7652-1200;** www.coventrycathedral.org.uk), is considered one of the most poignant and religiously evocative modern churches in the world.

Outside is Sir Jacob Epstein's bronze masterpiece, *St. Michael Slaying the Devil.* Inside, the outstanding feature is the 21m-high (70-ft.) altar tapestry by Graham Sutherland, said to be the largest in the world. The floor-to-ceiling abstract stained-glass windows are the work of the Royal College of Art. The West Screen (an entire wall of stained glass installed during the 1950s) depicts rows of stylized saints and prophets with angels flying among them.

In the undercroft of the cathedral is a visitor center, the Walkway of Holograms, where the otherwise plain walls are accented with 3-D images of the Stations of the Cross, created with reflective light. One of the most evocative objects here is a charred cross wired together by local workmen from burning timbers that crashed to the cathedral's floor during the Nazi bombing. Located in the ruins next door, the Blitz Experience Museum contains five 1940s' room reconstructions commemorating the destruction of the city (additional £2.50).

The cathedral is open Monday to Saturday from 9am to 5pm, and Sunday noon to 3:45pm; the tower is open during summer months when staff availability permits. Admission to the cathedral is £7 for adults; £5 for seniors, students, and children 12 to 18; free for children 11 and under; and £20 for a family ticket. Tower admission is £2.50 adults, £1 children. Sundays are free.

Stagecoach buses X17 and 16 connect Warwick, Leamington Spa, and Coventry. Virgin Trains runs every half-hour from London's Euston Station to Coventry (trip time: 1¼ hr.). From Stratford-upon-Avon, four **National Express** buses, with a trip time of 45 minutes, travel to Pool Meadow bus station, at Fairfax Street in Coventry. A single-day round-trip ticket costs £5.20.

BIRMINGHAM ★

120 miles NW of London; 25 miles N of Stratford-upon-Avon

England's second-largest city, **Birmingham** has undergone something of a renaissance in recent decades, transforming itself from a dreary industrial conurbation to a vibrant cultural and education center. While it still bears some of the scars of industrial excess, an energetic building boom, revitalized canals, new areas of green space, and the cultivation of a first-rate symphony and ballet company, as well as art galleries and museums, have all made Birmingham far more appealing.

Birmingham city center is a rich trove of grand Victorian buildings, including the **Museum and Art Gallery** and its precious collection of pre-Raphaelite paintings. The city's other showstoppers lie on the outskirts: The **Black Country Living Museum** commemorates the region's industrial heritage while **Cadbury World** celebrates Britain's favorite chocolate.

Shopping in Birmingham doesn't quite match London, but there are some real highlights. The iconic **Selfridges** building is worth visiting as much for the architecture as for the plush department store inside, while the **Jewellery Quarter** is home to numerous artisan jewelry makers.

Birmingham's **culinary scene** is led by a trio of acclaimed restaurants famous throughout the country—at Purnell's, Simpsons, and Turners expect the very best of English contemporary cuisine. In stark contrast, the **Balti Triangle** is one of the top places in the country to try Indian and Pakistani food.

As befits the home of Ozzy Osbourne, UB40, '80s pop idols Duran Duran, and, more recently, The Streets (aka local boy Mike Skinner), Birmingham nightlife is eclectic and extremely lively. Choose from ancient pubs like the **Old Crown,** hip bars such as **Revolution,** live music venues such as **02 Academy,** megaclubs like **Gatecrasher Birmingham,** and stand-up comedy joints like **Glee Club.**

Essentials

GETTING THERE   Major international carriers operate transatlantic flights with direct service to **Birmingham International Airport** (BHX; ℂ **0844/576-6000;**

ATTRACTIONS ●	RESTAURANTS ◆	HOTELS ■
Aston Hall **18**	Asha's **12**	Mint Hotel **4**
Barber Institute of Fine Arts **10**	Bank **3**	Nite Nite **9**
Birmingham Museum &	Canalside Café **8**	Novotel Birmingham
Art Gallery **11**	Great British Eatery **7**	Centre **6**
Ikon Gallery **5**	Purnell's **16**	Premier Inn Birmingham
Museum of the Jewellery Quarter **17**	Simpsons **7**	Central (East) **19**
National Sea Life Centre **2**	Turners of Harborne **7**	Staying Cool at
Sherborne Wharf Heritage	The Warehouse Café **14**	the Rotunda **13**
Narrow Boats **1**		
Thinktank at Millennium Point **15**		

www.birminghamairport.co.uk). Birmingham's airport lies about 8 miles southeast of the city center and is easily accessible by public transportation. The AirRail Link monorail (free) connects the terminals with the Birmingham International Rail Station and National Exhibition Centre (NEC) every 10 minutes (daily 5:15am–2am). Rail services operate regularly from Birmingham International to Birmingham city center (New Street) every 10 minutes (the journey takes 10 min. and costs £3.10 one-way).

Virgin Trains connect London Euston and Birmingham New Street every 15 to 30 minutes and take 1 hour 25 minutes (tickets from £43). CrossCountry trains leave Manchester's Piccadilly Station nearly every hour for Birmingham New Street. The trip takes 1½ hours (tickets from £16). Chiltern Railways trains from Stratford-upon-Avon arrive at Birmingham Moor Street every hour (£6.40).

From London, the best route driving is via the M40, which leads onto the M42, the motorway that circles south and east of Birmingham. Once on the M42, any of the roads from junctions 4 to 6 will lead into the center of Birmingham. The drive takes about 2 to 2½ hours, depending on traffic conditions. Parking is available at locations throughout Birmingham.

VISITOR INFORMATION   The Birmingham Visitor Centre, at the Rotunda, 150 New St., in the city center (✆ **0870/2250127**; www.visitbirmingham.com), is open Monday to Saturday 9:30am to 5:30pm, Sunday 10:30am to 4:30pm. It will assist travelers in arranging accommodations, obtaining theatre or concert tickets, and planning itineraries.

GETTING AROUND   Birmingham's city center hosts a number of attractions within easy walking distance, but if you opt to stay on the outskirts you'll likely use either the city's buses or trains of Midland Metro system. **Centro** (✆ **0121/200-2787**; www.centro.org.uk) provides information on all local bus and rail services within Birmingham and the West Midlands area. Bus routes are mainly operated by National Express West Midlands; Day-Saver tickets are £3.60, while single journeys are £1.60–£1.80 (no change given). Midland Metro is a 13-mile tram system connecting Birmingham Snow Hill train station with Wolverhampton (£3.20), but there are plans to extend the line into the city center.

Taxis line up at various spots in the city center, at rail stations, and at the National Exhibition Centre. Travelers can also ring up a radio-cab operator such as **TOA Taxis** (✆ **0121/427-8888**; www.toataxis.net).

Exploring the Area

Stephenson Place, at the intersection of New and Corporation streets, is a good starting point for touring the city center. A short walk east along New Street leads to the new Bull Ring shopping center, where the real star is the distinctive bubble-wrap exterior of **Selfridges** (www.selfridges.com). Opened in 2003 and designed by architects Future Systems, the famous department store is smothered in 15,000 aluminum discs. It's open 10am to 8pm Monday to Saturday and 11am to 5:30pm on Sundays.

A 5-minute stroll in the other direction along New Street leads to Victoria Square, where **Council House** (✆ **0121/303-2438**; www.birmingham.gov.uk), the city's most impressive Victorian building, anchors the piazza. Built in 1879, it is still the meeting place for the Birmingham City Council and an impressive example of the Italian Renaissance style.

Continuing west along Broad Street is the **Gas Street Basin** (✆ **0121/236-9811**), dotted with canal boats and waterside pubs. From the Basin, you can take a cruise along the canals via **Second City Boats** (✆ **0121/236-9811**; www.secondcityboats.co.uk) or just walk by the towpaths to the **Mailbox** (✆ **0121/632-1000**; www.mailboxlife.com) on Wharfside Street, a fashionable shopping and entertainment center.

Another up-and-coming area to check out is **Digbeth** on the east side of the center. Once the city's industrial heartland, it is now the home of dilapidated warehouses being converted into cutting-edge art galleries. For more information about the Eastside area, visit www.weareeastside.org.

Aston Hall ★ MUSEUM   This stunning Jacobean mansion reopened in 2009 following a £13 million development project. Completed for the Holte family in 1631, it became, in 1864, the first stately home to be owned by a municipality. Inside, display rooms chronicle the history of the mansion, including its role in the English Civil War, while the Astonish Gallery describes the history of Aston itself, through historic bric-a-brac and hands-on displays. The artfully renovated interior of the mansion is the real highlight, however, especially the magnificent Long Gallery.

Trinity Rd., Aston (10- to 15-min. walk from Aston or Witton train stations). © **0121/675-4722.** www.bmag.org.uk/aston-hall. Free admission. Apr–Oct Tues–Sun noon–4pm. Bus: 65, 104, and 105 stop nearby in Lichfield Rd.

Barber Institute of Fine Arts ★★ MUSEUM   Don't be put off by the stark, stone-and-brick building that houses the Barber Institute collection: It is one of the finest small art museums in England. The choice selection of paintings includes works by Bellini, Botticelli, Bruegel, Canaletto, Delacroix, Gainsborough, Gauguin, Murillo, Renoir, Rubens, Turner, Van Gogh, and Whistler.

University of Birmingham (just off Edgbaston Park Rd., near the University's East Gate, 2½ miles south of the city center). © **0121/414-7333.** www.barber.org.uk. Free admission. Mon–Sat 10am–5pm; Sun noon–5pm. Bus: 61, 62, or 63 from the city center.

Birmingham Museum & Art Gallery ★ MUSEUM   Known chiefly for its collection of pre-Raphaelite paintings (including works by Ford Maddox Brown, Dante Gabriel Rossetti, Edward Burne-Jones, and Holman Hunt), the gallery also houses exceptional paintings by English watercolor masters from the 18th century. In addition, there is a museum section with an Egyptian mummy, plus tools and artifacts that are 400,000 years old. Completed in 1885, the elegant Victorian building that houses the museum is almost as interesting as the collections inside it. The museum is instantly recognized by its "Big Brum" clock tower.

Chamberlain Square. © **0121/303-1966.** www.bmag.org.uk. Free admission; varying charges for special exhibitions. Mon–Thurs and Sat 10am–5pm; Fri 10:30am–5pm; Sun 12:30–5pm.

Black Country Living Museum MUSEUM   Much of the area immediately surrounding Birmingham is called the Black Country (after the black smoke that billowed over the area during the iron-working era). That period is commemorated at the Black Country Living Museum in Dudley, a suburban town about 10 miles northwest of central Birmingham. The museum occupies a sprawling landscape in the South Staffordshire coal fields, an early forge of the Industrial Revolution, and recreates what it was like to work and live in the Black Country of the 1850s. An electric tramway takes visitors to a thick underground coal seam, and trolleys move through a reconstructed industrial village with a schoolhouse, anchor forge, working replica of a 1712 steam engine, and trade shops.

Tipton Rd., Dudley (3 miles north of junction 2 exit on the M5; parking £2). Tipton train station, on the Birmingham to Wolverhampton line, is 1 mile from the museum. © **0121/557-9643.** www.bclm.co.uk. Admission £14 adults, £11 seniors, £7.10 children 5–16, £36 family ticket. Mar–Oct daily 10am–5pm; Nov–Dec daily 10am–4pm; Jan–Feb Wed–Sun 10am–4pm.

Cadbury World ★ FACTORY TOUR   Chocoholics beware—this is the British home of all things cocoa. It's not quite Willie Wonka's Chocolate Factory, but it comes pretty close. The exhibition inside contains 14 themed zones, starting with the origins of chocolate in Aztec Mexico, and ending, unsurprisingly, with a vast store so crammed with rare and special-edition chocolate you'll be tempted to take out a small loan. The only part of the actual factory you get to see is the packaging plant, where chocolate is wrapped and put into boxes for distribution.

Linden Rd., Bournville (follow the signs from M5 junctions 2 and 4, or M42 junction 2). © **0844/880-7667.** www.cadburyworld.co.uk. Tickets £14 adults, £11 seniors and students, £10 children 4–15, £43 family ticket. Feb–Dec Mon–Fri 10am–3pm, Sat–Sun 10am–4pm. Closed Jan; call ahead to confirm seasonal changes. 15-min. walk from Bournville train station (Cross-City Line from Birmingham New Street station).

Ikon Gallery GALLERY   This internationally respected contemporary art gallery occupies a renovated neo-Gothic building in the regenerated canal district of the city center (just up from Gas Street Basin, p. 468). The gallery features high-quality temporary exhibitions over a variety of forms, including sound, film, mixed media, photography, painting, sculpture, and installation.

1 Oozells Square, Brindleyplace. ✆ **0121/248-0708.** www.ikon-gallery.co.uk. Free admission. Tues–Sun 11am–6pm.

Museum of the Jewellery Quarter MUSEUM   Just a 10-minute walk from the city center is the Jewellery Quarter (www.the-quarter.com) encompassing more than 100 jewelry shops. A unique time capsule of the ancient craft of jewelry, the quarter also offers bargain hunters the opportunity to arrange repairs, design a custom piece, or just browse. The museum itself occupies the old Smith and Pepper factory, where guided tours include a demonstration of jewelry-making techniques at a jeweler's bench.

75–79 Vyse St. ✆ **0121/554-3598.** www.bmag.org.uk/museum-of-the-jewellery-quarter. Admission £4 adults, free for children 15 and under. Tues–Sat 10:30am–4pm.

National Sea Life Centre AQUARIUM   This is one of England's best aquariums, and a must-see if you're traveling with children. Best known for its seahorse breeding program, its one-million-liter ocean tank also houses giant green sea turtles, hammerhead sharks, and thousands of tropical reef fish, with a fully transparent underwater tunnel you can walk through. The latest attraction is the Sensorama 4-D Cinema, where 3-D glasses are enhanced by sensations such as wind, salt spray, and real oceanic smells depending on the film.

The Waters Edge, Brindleyplace (from New Street station follow signs for the ICC and the NIA). ✆ **0121/643-6777.** www.sealifeeurope.com. Admission £18 adults, £17 seniors and students, £14 children 3–14. Mon–Fri 10am–5pm, Sat–Sun 10am–6pm.

Sherborne Wharf Heritage Narrow Boats CRUISE   One of the more intriguing ways to see Birmingham is by water, as the city is laced with canals created as the "motorways" of their day during the Industrial Revolution. Many of these canals have been cleaned and restored, and sightseeing boats depart from the International Convention Centre Quayside, taking you on 1-hour tours of Birmingham from the water. It's the best way to appreciate the renaissance of the city, as swathes of abandoned wharves and warehouses are gradually converted to offices, shops, and cafes.

Heritage Marina (near the junction of Macclesfield and Trent & Mersey Canals in Scholar Green). ✆ **0121/455-6163.** www.sherbornewharf.co.uk. Tickets £6.50 adults, £5.50 seniors, £5 children 5–16. Departures Easter–Oct daily at 11:30am, 1, 2:30, and 4pm. Call ahead in off season, when tours are conducted Sat–Sun at 1 and 2:30pm, only if weather permits.

Thinktank at Millennium Point ☺ MUSEUM   This science museum is both educational and fun, appealing to adults and kids alike. It examines the past, presents today's technology, and explores future scientific breakthroughs that may occur. Science and history meet in 10 different galleries across four floors, where children can have close encounters with the exhibits, doing everything from grabbing a handful of polar-bear blubber to taking control of a digger. An IMAX theatre plays educational movies.

Curzon St. ✆ **0121/202-2222.** www.thinktank.ac. Admission £12 adults, £8.40 seniors, students, and children 3–15; with IMAX £21 adults, £15 seniors, students, and children 3–15. Daily 10am–5pm. Call for IMAX schedule.

Where to Eat

EXPENSIVE

Purnell's ★★ CONTEMPORARY ENGLISH The cooking of Glyn Purnell is bold and innovative, but despite the Michelin star, his two-course lunch menu is Birmingham's best bargain. You dine in a room with arched floor-to-ceiling windows, a chic, contemporary setting with a bar and lounge area for diners only.

Purnell's dishes might include such main courses as pigeon rolled in licorice charcoal, tamarind, and roasted duck liver, served with coco and Savoy cabbage. The salad of Devonshire crab—with apple and celeriac mayonnaise and smoked paprika honeycomb—is a real delight, and the desserts are just as playful. Think burnt English custard egg surprise with a warm autumn fruit crumble, hazelnuts, and quince sorbet.

55 Cornwall St. ✆ **0121/212-9799.** www.purnellsrestaurant.com. Reservations required. 2-course lunch £22; 3-course lunch £26; 2-course dinner £38; 3-course dinner £46; 8-course tasting menu £68. AE, MC, V. Tues–Fri noon–4:30pm; Tues–Sat 7–9:30pm. Closed 1 week at Easter, last week in July, 1st week in Aug, and 1 week at Christmas.

Simpsons ★★★ CONTEMPORARY ENGLISH/FRENCH The grandest and best dining in Birmingham, set in an impressive Georgian mansion. Michelin-starred chef Andreas Antona purchases his ingredients fresh every day, using only the finest of seasonal produce. Specialties are forever changing, but main courses might include a magnificent home-salted cod, with crispy-fried whitebait; or a more elaborate cutlet of suckling pig, with roasted parsnip purée, Savoy cabbage, apple fondant, crispy black pudding, and sage-and-onion sauce.

20 Highfield Rd., Edgbaston. ✆ **0121/454-3434.** Fax 0121/454-3399. www.simpsonsrestaurant.co.uk. Reservations recommended (required Fri–Sat). Main courses £25–£29; 3-course lunch £35, 3-course dinner £38. AE, DC, MC, V. Daily noon–2pm (to 2:30pm Sat–Sun); Mon–Thurs 7–9:30pm; Fri–Sat 7–10pm. Closed Dec 24–27 and Dec 31–Jan 1.

Turners of Harborne ★★ FRENCH/CONTEMPORARY ENGLISH Birmingham's third Michelin-starred restaurant offers a subtle contrast to the other two, with chef Richard Turner conjuring up a menu that is contemporary and cutting-edge but inspired by classical French cooking. Rabbit is served with croustillant of confit leg, Puy lentils, carrots, tarragon sauce, and mustard foam, while the filet of halibut comes with pearl barley, garlic, snails, and parsley. Don't miss the soufflé served with prune and Armagnac ice cream for dessert.

69 High St. ✆ **0121/426-4440.** www.turnersofharborne.com. Reservations recommended. 2-course lunch £22, 3-course lunch £26; 3-course dinner £50. AE, DC, MC, V. Tues–Fri noon–2pm and 6:45–9:30pm; Sat 6:45–9:30pm.

MODERATE

Asha's ★★ INDIAN High-quality meals and low prices make this one of the best Indian restaurants in the city. It's named after singing legend Asha Bhosle, who came up with the concept and remains associated with the chain. The menu features all the usual Indian regional classics, but with a contemporary twist: The peppered garlic prawns come with salad drizzled in raspberry citrus dressing, and the sensitively spiced curries are served with mounds of white rice and thick sour cream. The house specialty is Tandoori kebabs, perfect for sharing—try the fiery Jaipur chicken tikka.

Edmund House, 12–22 Newhall St. ✆ **0121/200-2767.** www.ashasuk.co.uk. Reservations recommended. Main courses £13–£24. AE, DC, MC, V. Mon–Wed noon–2:30pm and 5:30–10:30pm; Thurs–Fri noon–2:30pm and 5:30–11pm; Sat 5–11pm; Sun 5–10pm.

Birmingham's best-known culinary experience was actually created by Pakistani Kashmiri chefs in the Sparkhill area of the city in the late 1970s. *Balti* literally means bucket, but it refers to a Kashmiri style of cooking meat and vegetables very fast over a hot flame. A good balti-style curry should be flavorful but not necessarily spicy, and is traditionally served with naan bread, not rice. With the city's large Pakistani Kashmiri population, there are now over 50 *balti houses* in Birmingham's Balti Triangle (roughly within Ladypool Road, Stoney Lane, and Stratford Road, south of the city center), most of which are bare-bones, BYOB affairs. One of the better ones is **Adil**, 353–355 Ladypool Rd. (✆ **0121/449-0335; www.adilbalti.co.uk**), which claims to be the original Birmingham balti house, open Sunday to Thursday noon to midnight, Friday 4pm to midnight, and Saturday noon to 1am.

Bank BRASSERIE   The Birmingham outpost of this chic brasserie consistently delivers, with chefs working feverishly in the open-plan kitchen. For a main dish, you can sample superb choices such as roast chicken, potato gnocchi, mushrooms, and garlic butter, or the smoked haddock and leek risotto with poached egg. Desserts include a classic English chocolate fudge pudding with vanilla ice cream.

4 Brindleyplace. ✆ **0121/633-4466.** www.bankrestaurants.com. Reservations recommended. Main courses £15–£23. AE, DC, MC, V. Mon–Fri noon–11pm; Sat 11:30am–11:30pm; Sun 11:30am–10pm.

INEXPENSIVE

Canalside Café CAFE/COFFEEHOUSE   This old waterside lock-keeper's cottage is a laid-back cafe during the day and a decent pub by night, with a range of real ales on tap. The food is solid, home-cooked stuff: Vegetable soups, sandwiches, and a selection of organic and vegan choices. Sit outside in sunny weather and watch the barges glide past, or enjoy the cluttered, antique-strewn interior.

Canalside Cottage, 35 Worcester Bar, Gas St. ✆ **0121/248-7979.** Main courses from £3.95. MC, V. Daily 11am–11pm.

Great British Eatery ★ FISH & CHIPS   This is a super-modern fish-and-chips shop, serving traditional fried treats with a focus on British produce and simple but clean presentation. Everything is cooked to order here, in beef dripping at very high temperatures; as a result, the fish itself is not fried as you might expect, but beautifully steamed within its crispy batter casing. The thick-cut chips (fries) are given the same treatment, and they also serve savory pies. Take out or eat in, and enjoy a local beer from Holden's or Warwickshire brewery Purity.

13 Broadway Plaza, Francis Rd. ✆ **0121/456-5955.** www.greatbritisheatery.co.uk. Main courses £3–6. MC, V. Mon–Tues noon–9pm; Wed–Sat noon–10pm.

The Warehouse Café ★ VEGAN CAFE   Located in the Birmingham headquarters of Friends of the Earth, this hippie, chic cafe offers fresh, organic vegetarian and vegan dishes at budget prices. It even uses solar power. Feast on pearl barley risotto of wild mushrooms and leeks served with cauliflower cheese beignets; sage and walnut cream with rocket and Parmesan salad; or a more exotic Malaysian laksa (coconut noodle broth).

54-57 Allison St. ✆ **0121/633-0261.** www.thewarehousecafe.com. Main courses £8.25–£9.45. Mon–Sat 11am–10pm; Sun 11am–6pm.

Shopping

In addition to the **Jewellery Quarter** (see above), Birmingham is a great town for shopping. There are hundreds of retail stores, and many people in the Midlands come here just to shop, especially along **Cannon Street** and **New Street,** with numerous top-brand designer stores.

The city's **Mailbox** complex, at Wharfside Street (✆ **0121/632-1000;** www.mailboxlife.com), is a gargantuan shopping center, with such stores as Harvey Nichols, Emporio Armani, Fat Face, Hugo Boss, Jaeger, and Crabtree & Evelyn, along with restaurants and a spa. For a touch of Victorian elegance, head to the **Great Western Arcade** (www.greatwesternarcade.co.uk), just opposite Snow Hill railway station, which houses smaller, independent stores. And in addition to fine Indian food, the **Balti Triangle** (see above and www.balti-birmingham.co.uk) is crammed with stores selling all manner of textiles, food, and jewelry from the Indian subcontinent.

In the heart of town, the shiny new **Bullring,** near St. Martin's Square (✆ **0121/632-1500;** www.bullring.co.uk), has been developed into Europe's largest city-center retail area. It's more affordable and less classy than the Mailbox, with such mainstays as H&M, Gap, FCUK, and Skechers. Here also is the iconic **Selfridges** building (see above). A short walk from the Bullring is the **Custard Factory** (✆ **0121/224-7777;** www.custardfactory.co.uk), built 100 years ago and now home to galleries, artists, independent shops, and restaurants.

Art lovers should head farther into the **Eastside** district, where galleries such as **VIVID,** 140 Heath Mill Lane (✆ **0121/766-7876;** www.vivid.org.uk; Thurs–Sat noon–5pm), and **Eastside Projects,** 86 Heath Mill Lane (✆ **0121/771-1778;** www.eastsideprojects.org; usually Thurs noon–6:30pm, Fri–Sat noon–5pm), organize a variety of mixed-media contemporary art exhibitions.

Entertainment & Nightlife

THE PERFORMING ARTS

Connected to the Convention Centre, **Symphony Hall,** Broad Street (✆ **0121/780-3333;** www.thsh.co.uk.), has been hailed as an acoustical gem since its completion in 1990. Home to the **City of Birmingham Symphony Orchestra,** it also hosts special classical music events.

The restored **Birmingham Hippodrome,** Hurst Street (✆ **0844/338-5000;** www.birminghamhippodrome.com), is home to the **Birmingham Royal Ballet** and visiting companies from around the world. It hosts a variety of events, from the Welsh National Opera to musicals to dance. The box office is open Monday to Saturday 9:30am to 8:30pm.

The **National Indoor Arena (NIA),** King Edward's Road (✆ **0844/338-8000;** www.necgroup.co.uk), seats 13,000 and is a favorite site for jazz, pop, and rock concerts, as well as sporting events and conventions. The same group manages the **LG Arena** (✆ **0121/780-4141;** www.lgarena.co.uk) at the National Exhibition Centre, the venue for the biggest concerts and events.

The **Birmingham Repertory Theatre,** Broad Street, at Centenary Square (✆ **0121/236-4455;** www.birmingham-rep.co.uk), houses one of the top companies in England. The widely known "Rep" comprises the Main House, which seats 800 theatregoers, and the Door, a more intimate 120-seat venue that often stages new and innovative works. The box office is open Monday through Saturday 10am to 8pm on performance days, 10am to 6pm on nonperformance days. Tickets usually range from £11 to £20.

The **Midlands Arts Centre,** in Cannon Hill Park (✆ **0121/446-3200;** www.macarts.co.uk), is close to the Edgbaston Cricket Ground and reached by bus numbers 1, 45, or 47. The MAC houses three performance areas and stages a lively range of drama, dance, and musical performances, as well as films. The box office is open daily from 9am to 8:45pm.

The **New Alexandra Theatre,** Station Street (✆ **0121/643-5536;** www.alexandratheatre.org.uk), hosts national touring companies, including productions from London's West End. Contact the box office for show details.

Note: Tickets for all Birmingham theatres are available through Birmingham visitor offices.

THE PUB & BAR SCENE

As befits England's second city, Birmingham boasts a varied and energy-charged nightlife with clusters of bars and venues in a wide range of neighborhoods. Most visitors are content with the traditional nightlife hub concentrated along Broad Street and Brindleyplace in the city center, but you should also check out the clubs and bars in the flourishing Eastside and Digbeth districts. It's here you'll also find Birmingham's oldest pub, the **Old Crown,** 188 High St., Deritend (✆ **0121/248-1368;** www.theoldcrown.com). The pub has roots back in 1368, and is open daily noon to 11pm. The Jewellery Quarter is also home to some atmospheric pubs, notably **The Lord Clifden ★**, 34 Great Hampton St., Hockley (✆ **0121/523-7515;** www.thelordclifden.com), celebrated for its collection of street art, including pieces by Banksy. It's open daily 10am to 2am. Farther out in Moseley (south of the center), the **Prince of Wales ★★**, at 118 Alcester Rd. (✆ **0121/449-4198;** www.theprincemoseley.co.uk), is a congenial local watering-hole with an inviting beer garden (Lady Gaga popped in for a drink in 2010). It's open Monday to Thursday noon to 11pm, Friday and Saturday noon to midnight, and Sunday noon to 10:30pm.

If pubs are not your thing, **Revolution,** back on Broad Street (✆ **0121/665-6508;** www.revolution-bars.co.uk), is a vodka bar drawing a hip under-40 crowd (Mon–Wed 11:30am–midnight, Thurs–Sat 11:30am–3am, Sun noon–2am). Cocktail lovers should check out **Island Bar ★**, 14–16 Suffolk St., (✆ **0121/632-5296;** www.bar-island.co.uk), with live music and club nights at the weekend, and a Tiki Bar every Thursday.

THE CLUB & MUSIC SCENE

The live music scene is especially strong in Birmingham, with alternative venues such as the **Hare and Hounds** pub, 106 High St. (✆ **0121/444-2081;** hareandhoundskingsheath.co.uk), in Kings Heath featuring a healthy roster of everything from hip-hop DJs to protest folk rock and poetry nights. The **02 Academy,** 16–18 Horsefair, Bristol St. (✆ **0121/622-8247;** www.o2academybirmingham.co.uk), also hosts a wide range of live acts as well as club nights like **Propaganda** every Friday, the U.K.'s biggest indie dance night.

Live music and especially stand-up **comedy** dominates at the **Glee Club** in the Arcadian on Hurst Street. (✆ **0871/472-0400;** www.glee.co.uk/birmingham). The **Jam House,** 3–5 St. Paul's Square (✆ **0121/200-3030;** www.thejamhouse.com), is a popular live music bar directed by Jools Holland with an emphasis on blues, soul, and boogie-woogie. Jazz also has a following in the city, with **Jazz Club** (www.birminghamjazz.co.uk) at **The Rainbow,** 160 High St., in Digbeth, a key gig to showcase new and established British musicians. Visit the website for dates.

The Gay Scene

Birmingham has a thriving gay and lesbian community, with more than a dozen gay venues in the "gay village" in and around **Hurst Street,** just south of the city center. One of the most popular venues is **Nightingale,** 18 Kent St.

(📞 0121/6226-1718; www.nightingale club.co.uk), with five bars and two frenzied dance floors. The cover varies but is often around £5. Open Monday and Thursday to Saturday 9pm to 4am. Good resources include www.gaybrum.com.

Digbeth also contains some of the city's best nightclubs, including the **Factory Club** (📞 0121/772-2094; www.factoryclub.co.uk) and **The Medicine Bar** at the Custard Factory on Gibb Street; and the hangar-like **Air Nightclub** on Heath Mill Lane (www.airbirmingham.com), the current home of dance institution **Godskitchen** (📞 01789/739-989; www.godskitchen.com) on Saturday nights. One of the newest additions to the scene is megaclub **Gatecrasher Birmingham,** at 182 Broad St. (📞 0121/633-1520; www.gatecrasher.co.uk).

Finally, the **Oceana** complex in Hurst Street (📞 0845/402-5390; www.oceana clubs.com/birmingham) is like an entertainment resort with seven themed rooms (2 clubs and 5 bars) from the futuristic Icehouse to the Aspen Ski Lodge and a 1970s' New York disco. Usually open Thursday to Saturday 9:30pm to 3:30am (and sometimes Mon for student nights).

Where to Stay

EXPENSIVE

Mint Hotel ★ 🍴 A favorite of business travelers, the former City Inn has been given a comprehensive makeover. Rooms are now stylish and very sleek with a whole roster of high-tech amenities, floor-to-ceiling windows, power showers, and a library of CDs and DVDs; they can be a bit like peas-in-a-pod, but are always well kept and comfortable. The on-site **City Café** is one of the best in the city for hotel dining.

1 Brunswick Sq., Brindleyplace, Birmingham B1 2HW. www.minthotel.com. 📞 **0121/643-1003.** Fax 0121/643-1005. 238 units. £99–£145 double. AE, DC, MC, V. Parking £13. **Amenities:** Restaurant; bar; gym; 24-hr. room service. *In room:* A/C, TV, hair dryer, iMac multimedia entertainment system, Wi-Fi (free).

Novotel Birmingham Centre In the city center, this is a well-run chain hotel that offers good, comfortable rooms that have a bit of style. Bedrooms, midsize for the most part, are in the motel style. The on-site brasserie serves affordable food made with fresh ingredients, and the bar is a popular rendezvous. All in all, especially considering the reasonable prices, this isn't a bad choice.

70 Broad St., Birmingham B1 2HT. www.novotel.com. 📞 **0121/643-2000.** Fax 0121/643-9786. 148 units. £109–£143 double. Children stay free in parent's room. AE, MC, V. Free parking. **Amenities:** Restaurant; bar; exercise room; Jacuzzi; room service; sauna. *In room:* A/C, TV, hair dryer, minibar, Wi-Fi (free).

Staying Cool at the Rotunda ★★★ These chic serviced apartments occupy the restored and iconic 1960s' Rotunda in the city center, with suitably awe-inspiring views from the top three floors it occupies. Each apartment has floor-to-ceiling windows, Apple Mac computers, and an iPod player, and a full kitchen. The apartments combine contemporary design with a cool Brit 1960s' style, and come in four sizes—small, medium, large, and extra large. Amenities are the same in all guest rooms, but the small rooms really are tiny. The location is perfect for exploring the city and enjoying the nightlife.

150 New St., Birmingham B2 4PA. www.stayingcool.com. ✆ **0121/643-0815.** 15 units. £99–£200 double. AE, MC, V. Parking £18. *In room:* A/C, TV, hair dryer, kitchen, Wi-Fi (free).

INEXPENSIVE

Elmdon Lodge ★★ 🥄 One of the most comfortable—and affordable—guesthouses lies in south Birmingham, in the suburb of Acocks Green, which is linked by public transportation to the center of the city. The guesthouse is only a 5-minute walk from the Acocks Green rail station. A welcoming family-run hotel, Elmdon is filled with bedrooms that are comfortably furnished in a homelike style. Rooms come in various sizes and configurations, from single to family rooms and triples, each with a small private bathroom with shower. Guests meet fellow guests in the breakfast lounge. The hotel stands in a landscaped garden, which also has a private parking lot.

20–24 Elmdon Rd., Acocks Green, Birmingham B27 6LH. www.elmdonlodge.co.uk. ✆ **0121/706-6968.** Fax 0121/628-5566. 18 units. £59–£90 double. Rates include English breakfast. AE, MC, V. Free parking. *In room:* TV, Wi-Fi (free, in some).

Nite Nite ★★ This novel hotel certainly wins the prize for most original accommodation, perfect for short stays and for guests who spend most of their time out on the town. Rooms are tiny cubes, a bit like a luxury cabin on a yacht, dominated by a huge TV and a bed that takes up most of the space. There are no windows; this is a Japanese-style "capsule hotel" experience, though the bathrooms are great and everything is spotlessly clean.

18 Holliday St., Birmingham B1 1T. www.nitenite.com. ✆ **08458/909099.** Fax 0121/634-3236. 104 units. £56–£72 double. AE, DC, MC, V. Parking £14 per 24 hr. **Amenities:** Restaurant; bar; ironing rooms located on each floor. *In room:* A/C, TV, hair dryer, Wi-Fi (free).

Premier Inn Birmingham Central (East) Lying between the M6 motorway and the city center, this is a modern, well-kept, and well-run chain hotel. It offers substantially comfortable, though rather standard, bedrooms. For the motorist just passing through Birmingham or spending only a night, it should be ideal. The hotel also has an affordable on-site restaurant, so you don't have to drive into the center of Birmingham at night.

Richard St., Waterlinks, Birmingham B7 4AA. www.premierinn.com. ✆ **0870/238-3312.** Fax 0121/333-6490. 60 units. £70 double. AE, MC, V. Free parking. **Amenities:** Restaurant; bar. *In room:* A/C, TV, hair dryer, Wi-Fi (free).

WORCESTER & THE MALVERNS

The ancient town of **Worcester** has been an important trading center since Neolithic times thanks to its strategic location on the River Severn. Royal Worcester Porcelain was established here in 1751, while the town's most celebrated product, Lea & Perrins Worcestershire Sauce, goes back to 1838. Royal Worcester closed in 2009, but the sauce factory is still there, and just as secretive as ever. The cathedral provides the obvious focus for most visitors, surrounded by a hodgepodge of Tudor, Georgian, and modern streets.

The beautiful and historic Malvern hills lie just west of Worcester, rising suddenly from the Severn Valley and stretching for 9 miles. The genteel Victorian spa town of **Great Malvern** itself is still the home of legendary Morgan Cars, though the town's other icon, Malvern Water, closed in 2010 (the local spring water has been a royal favorite for more than 400 years). Hiking the hills is the main pastime here, with an abundance of refreshing air and country vistas that inspired England's greatest composer, Sir Edward Elgar.

Essentials

GETTING THERE   From London's Paddington Station, First Great Western trains leave every 2 hours to Worcester (from £33) and Great Malvern (from £27). Trains run between Worcester and Great Malvern every 15 minutes or so (and take around 15 min.). Tickets are £4.30.

VISITOR INFORMATION   The **Worcester Tourist Information Centre** is located in the old Guildhall on the High Street (*C* **01905/726311;** www.visit worcester.com). It's open Monday to Saturday 9:30am to 5pm. The **Malvern Tourist Information Centre,** 21 Church St., Great Malvern (*C* **01684/892289;** www. malvernhills.gov.uk), is open daily 10am to 5pm. On Sundays from December to March, it closes at 4pm.

TOURS   One of the best ways to see Worcester is from the river aboard one of the 45-minute cruise trips (£5) offered by **Worcester River Cruises,** 22 Britannia Rd., (*C* **01905/611060;** www.worcesterrivercruises.co.uk). A cream tea cruise costs £14. Cruises operate from 10am to midnight daily April to October.

Exploring the Area

The Commandery MUSEUM   Originally the 11th-century Hospital of St. Wulstan, the Commandery serves as an absorbing museum today, with hand-held audioguides leading through six themed areas chronicling the history of Worcester and the building. Transformed over the years into a sprawling 15th-century, timber-framed building, the Commandery primarily served as the country home of the Wylde family. This was also the headquarters of King Charles II during the Battle of Worcester in 1651, the last engagement in the English Civil War. Beginning with the Monastic Hospital in 1480, displays cover the affluent Wylde family, the tumultuous events of 1651, the 19th century (when the Commandery served as a college for the blind), and the building's last role, as a printworks after World War II.

109 Sidbury St., Worcester. *C* **01905/361821.** www.worcestercitymuseums.org.uk. Admission £5.40 adults; £4.10 seniors, £2.30 children 5-16, free for children 4 and under. Mon–Sat 10am–5pm; Sun 1:30–5pm. The Commandery is a 3-min. walk from Worcester Cathedral.

Malvern Museum MUSEUM   This small but enlightening museum is just a 5-minute walk from Malvern Priory and the Tourist Information Centre in Great Malvern. Seven themed rooms tell the story of the town, from local prehistoric sites and the Benedictine monastery established in 1085, to Malvern's famous mineral water and the creation of the Morgan Motor Works in the 1890s.

Abbey Rd., Great Malvern. *C* **01684/567811.** www.malvernmuseum.co.uk. Admission £2 adults, 50p children 5-16, free for children 4 and under. Apr–Oct 10:30am–5pm. Closed Wed.

Morgan Motor Company ★★ FACTORY TOUR   Few vehicles have had such a cult following as Morgan sports cars, now one of only a handful of automobile brands to be made in the U.K. by an independent manufacturer. All Morgan cars are assembled by hand and the waiting list is around 1 to 2 years. You can observe Morgan craftsmen at work on guided tours of the factory, which also explain the history

Hiking in the Malverns

The **Malvern Hills** ★★ run north–south for about 9 miles between Great Malvern and the village of Colwall, offering fine views across the Severn Valley and some relatively easy and rewarding hikes. The entire length of the hills is open to the public and is criss-crossed with bridleways and footpaths. The quickest access point is **St. Ann's Well Café** ★★ (🕿 01684/560285; www.hillsarts.co.uk/stannswell), St. Ann's Road, a popular pit-stop where Malvern Spring water seeps from the ground, around 0.8 miles from Great Malvern train station. From here you can make a 3.5 miles (2-hr.) loop up to the highest point in the Malverns, Worcestershire Beacon at 425m (1,394 ft.), or an equally bracing stroll around North Hill and North Quarry (2¾ miles). Visit www.malvern hillsaonb.org.uk or www.malvernhills.org.uk for more information.

of the Morgan Motor Company, founded by Harry Morgan in 1909 (his grandson still runs the firm).

Spring Lane off Pickersleigh Rd. (B4208), Great Malvern. 🕿 **01684/584580.** www.morgan-motor.co.uk. Guided tours £10 per person. Mon–Thurs 8:30am–5pm, Fri 8:30am–3:30pm. Tours must be pre-booked.

Sir Edward Elgar's Birthplace Museum ★★ HISTORIC HOME This charming red-brick country cottage is where one of England's greatest composers was born on June 2, 1857. Serving as a memorial to Elgar, the cottage houses a unique collection of manuscripts and musical scores, photographs, and other personal memorabilia. Just yards from the cottage, a visitor center introduces you to the man and his music, even showing film clips of the composer with his beloved dogs. Sir Elgar wrote, among other pieces, *The Enigma Variations* and the *Dream of Gerontius*.

St. Wulstan's Church, 2 miles west of Great Malvern on the Ledbury Road, is where Elgar is buried with his wife and daughter.

Crown E. Lane, Lower Broadheath. 🕿 **01905/333224.** www.elgarfoundation.org. Admission £7 adults, £6 seniors, £4 students, £3 children 16 and under, £14 family ticket. Daily 11am–5pm. Closed Dec 24–Jan 31. Drive out of Worcester on the A44 toward Leominster. After 2 miles, turn off to the right at the sign. The house is a half-mile ahead on the right.

Worcester Cathedral ★★ CATHEDRAL Set majestically on the banks of the River Severn, Worcester Cathedral is most famous for its Norman crypt and unique chapter house, but its handsomely carved central tower is also one of the most striking in England. The crypt dates from 1084 and contains the tombs of King John, whose claim to fame is the Magna Carta, and Prince Arthur, the popular elder brother of Henry VIII. The 12th-century chapter house is one of the finest in England and, along with the cloisters, evokes the cathedral's rich monastic past. Climb the tower for stupendous views of the city. From Easter to October visitors can just "turn up for a tour" Monday to Saturday at 11am and 2:30pm (tours Sat only Nov–Easter).

College Yard, at High St. 🕿 **01905/732900.** www.worcestercathedral.co.uk. Free admission; adults asked for a £3 donation. Tower £4 adults, £2 children 15 and under, family ticket £8; tours £3 adults, free for children. Daily 7:30am–6pm; tower Easter–Sept Sat and school holidays 11am–5pm.

Worcester Porcelain Museum ★ MUSEUM See the world's largest collection of Worcester porcelain, displayed in various galleries evoking the Georgian, Victorian, and 20th-century periods. An entertaining audio tour tells the story of the Worcester porcelain since its founding in 1751. Look out for the ornate "Nelson Teapot," commissioned for the Lord Admiral himself in 1802, and the "Wigornia Creamboat," a delicately crafted 18th-century jug that is one of the rarest pieces in the collection. More-detailed, behind-the-scenes tours of the old factory (which closed in 2009) last about an hour, but they only run with groups of 12 or more (call ahead to confirm). Portmeirion Pottery now owns the Royal Worcester brand—the latter went bankrupt in 2008 after 258 years of trade.

Severn St, Worcester. ✆ **01905/746000.** www.worcesterporcelainmuseum.org.uk. Admission £6 adults; £5 seniors, students, and children under 18; £12 family ticket. Behind-the-scenes tours £6 for all visitors and include museum entry. Easter–Oct Mon–Sat 10am–5pm; Nov–Easter Tues–Sat 10:30am–4pm.

Where to Eat

The Fig Tree ★★ MEDITERRANEAN   This stylish contemporary restaurant is the best place to eat in Malvern, just a short walk from the train station. The menu takes inspiration from all over the Mediterranean. Feast on a sumptuous chargrilled lamb souvlaki, with minted yogurt, saffron rice, and salad, or some exquisite seafood ranging from chargrilled seabass and swordfish to squid served Spanish style with chorizo and seared salmon scallops. All meats are locally sourced.

99b Church St., Great Malvern. ✆ **01684/569909.** www.thefigtreemalvern.co.uk. Reservations recommended. Main courses £12–£17. AE, MC, V. Tues–Sat 12:30–2:30pm and 6–10pm.

Little Ginger Pig ★ ENGLISH/CONTINENTAL   This bright, healthful cafe and bistro strives to serve fresh ingredients, sourced as locally, seasonally, and as "free range" as possible. Grab a coffee and cake or a light lunch of salads and baguette sandwiches during the day, or enjoy the cozy candle-lit ambience at night. The same crew runs the Balcony Café in the City Art Gallery & Museum on Foregate Street, a good choice for a take-out sandwich.

9 Copenhagen St., Worcester. ✆ **01905/338913.** www.littlegingerpig.co.uk. Main courses £3.30–£6.50. AE, MC, V. Cafe Mon–Sat 9:30am–4:30pm; Bistro Mon–Wed 8:30am–3pm, Thurs–Sat 8:30am–11pm.

Mac & Jac Café Deli DELI/CAFE   This bright, modern deli and cafe in the heart of Worcester is perfect for a coffee, a take-out sandwich, homemade flatbreads with a variety of fillings, or a light lunch. There are also plenty of vegetarian options, such as a tasty leek, tarragon, and goat's cheese risotto. Peruse the deli for zesty fishcakes, Scotch eggs, and irresistible cakes. Mostly local produce is used here.

44 Friar St., Worcester. ✆ **01905/731331.** Main courses £3.50–£8.50. AE, MC, V. Tues–Thurs 10am–4pm; Fri 9am–5pm, Sat 9–6pm.

Pub at Ye Old Talbot Hotel PUB FARE   This venerable hotel, pub, and bistro contains heaps of Victorian nostalgia and old-fashioned wood paneling that has been darkened by generations of cigarette smoke and spilled beer. It offers predictable pub grub—cod and chips, beer and ale pie—that's a bit better than expected, especially when it's accompanied with a pint of the house's half-dozen ales on tap.

Friar St., Worcester. ✆ **01905/235730.** www.yeoldetalbot-worcester.co.uk. Main courses £6.99–£15. AE, MC, V. Bar daily 11am–11pm; Bistro Mon–Sat 7am–10pm, Sun 8am–10pm.

Puccini's ★★ ITALIAN   This excellent trattoria and cafe is a local favorite for good reason: The food is simple, freshly prepared, and tasty, with perfectly cooked pastas, pizzas, and fresh fish dishes. Highlights include a classic lasagna al forno and the wonderful Puccini pizza, topped with goat's cheese, caramelized red onion, pine nuts, and rocket. For something a little more complex, try the whole baked sea bass, in fennel, red onion, and lemon.

12 Friar St., Worcester. 𝒞 **01905/27770.** www.puccinisrestaurant.co.uk. Reservations recommended. Main courses £13–£15; pizza and pasta £6.25–£11. AE, MC, V. Mon noon–2:30pm, Tues–Fri noon–2:30pm and 5:30–10pm, Sat noon–10:30pm, Sun noon–4pm.

Where to Stay

VERY EXPENSIVE

The Elms Hotel ★ ☺ This is one of the most impressive hotels in the region, a Queen Anne mansion built in 1710 by Gilbert White, a disciple of Sir Christopher Wren. Like Bant's (see below), it lies on the outskirts of Worcester, is easy to get to, and offers a sort of fantasy version of olde England. The Elms, however, is far more upscale, complete with mahogany or walnut 18th- and 19th-century antiques, a lavish modern spa, and log-burning fireplaces. Bedrooms come in various shapes and sizes, and feature twin or double beds. The Elms welcomes families more than any other hotel in the area. *Insider tip:* If you notify the staff in advance, a member will round up all your baby needs in advance, from food to nappies (diapers to Americans).

On A443 (2 miles west of Abberley, near Worcester), Worcester WR6 6AT. www.theelmshotel.com. 𝒞 **01299/896666.** Fax 01299/896804. 21 units. £115–£345 double. Basic package rates include English breakfast. AE, DC, MC, V. Free parking. Take the A443 for 6 miles west of Worcester, following the signs to Tenbury Wells. **Amenities:** Restaurant; bar; babysitting; croquet lawn; room service; spa; tennis court. *In room:* TV, hair dryer, Wi-Fi (free, in some).

EXPENSIVE

The Abbey ★ This is Great Malvern's most romantic hotel, an ivy-smothered pile, dating back to the town's Victorian heyday, right next to the Benedictine priory. Standard rooms are simply but comfortably decorated in a classical English style, while superiors are a notch up in style and space, many with views of the Malvern Hills.

Abbey Rd., Great Malvern, Worcestershire WR14 3ET. www.sarova.com/abbey. 𝒞 **01684/892332.** Fax 01684/892662. 103 units. £64–£143 double. Rates include English breakfast. AE, DC, MC, V. Free parking. **Amenities:** 2 restaurants; bar; room service; Wi-Fi (free) in public areas. *In room:* TV, hair dryer, Internet (free).

Bant's Pub ★ This gorgeous 16th-century country inn lies a 10-minute drive outside Worcester in rolling countryside. It's not so convenient for exploring the center of the city, but perfect for driving around the area. The oak-beamed rooms are warmly decorated and extremely cozy. It's been owned and managed by the Bant family since 1985, and the pub downstairs serves local cider, beer, and solid bar food sourced from local suppliers.

Worcester Rd. (A422), Upton Snodsbury, Worcester WR7 4NN. www.bants.co.uk. 𝒞 **01905/381282.** Fax 01905/381173. 9 units. £70–£145 double. AE, DC, MC, V. Free parking. **Amenities:** Restaurant; bar. *In room:* TV, video/DVD player, hair dryer, Wi-Fi (free).

Cotford Hotel ☺ A 5-minute walk east of the town center, this stately Victorian home dates from 1851, when it was built as the local bishop's residence. Constructed of Cotswold stone and accented with lavish gingerbread, the main appeal derives from its monumental historic premises, the warm welcome, and such Victorian touches as the tile-floored wide entrance hallway. The bedrooms, mostly midsize, are brightly furnished in a fresh but classic English style, with wrought iron beds and drape curtains.

51 Graham Rd., Great Malvern, Worcestershire WR14 2HU. www.cotfordhotel.co.uk. ✆ **01684/572427.** Fax 01684/572952. 15 units. £110–£125 double. Rates include English breakfast. AE, DC, MC, V. Free parking. **Amenities:** Restaurant; bar; access to nearby pool and sauna; room service. *In room:* TV, hair dryer, Internet (£4.95 per 2 hr; £9.95 per day).

Cottage in the Wood ★   There is indeed a cottage in the woods associated with this hotel—it contains four cozy bedrooms and dates from the 17th century. But most of the inn occupies a nearby Georgian house from the late 1700s. Originally built for the semi-retired mother of the lord of a neighboring estate, it's referred to as the "Dower House" and is appropriately outfitted in an attractive Laura Ashley style. The bedrooms are small, but this place is so charming and offers such panoramic views that most visitors don't mind.

Holywell Rd., Malvern Wells, Worcestershire WR14 4LG. www.cottageinthewood.co.uk. ✆ **01684/588860.** Fax 01684/560662. 31 units. £84–£182 double. Rates include English breakfast. AE, MC, V. Free parking. After leaving Great Malvern on the A449, turn right just before the B4209 turnoff on the opposite side of the road. The inn is on the right. **Amenities:** Restaurant; bar; babysitting; room service; Wi-Fi (free). *In room:* TV/DVD/video player, hair dryer, Wi-Fi (free).

INEXPENSIVE

Manor Coach House ★★   This is the Worcester's best B&B, a series of modern red-brick apartments converted from the outbuildings adjacent to the main house. The simple but elegant and spotless rooms are well equipped and include a two-floor suite with kitchenette (ideal for families). Apartment no. 4 has access to an outdoor deck, perfect for lounging in the sun. Add in a huge home-cooked breakfast to start the day, and you have an excellent deal.

Hindlip Lane, Hindlip, Worcester WR3 8SJ (just off the A449). www.manorcoachhouse.co.uk. ✆ **01905/456-457.** Fax 01905/767772. 5 units. £70 double. AE, DC, MC, V. Rates include breakfast. Free parking. *In room:* TV/DVD, hair dryer, Wi-Fi (free).

THE WELSH MARCHES

The borderlands between England and Wales became known as the **Welsh Marches** in the Middle Ages, an alluring area of rolling hills and market towns encompassing the modern counties of Herefordshire and Shropshire.

Situated on the Wye River, 16 miles east of the Welsh border, the city of **Hereford** is a bustling market town today, known for its fine cathedral and world-famous cattle industry. Its white-faced Hereford breed has spread to nearly every continent.

Heading north, **Ludlow** is an essential stop; a mellow town on the tranquil Teme River lined with Georgian and Jacobean timbered buildings, and a handful of world-class restaurants and pubs.

One of the finest Tudor towns in England, **Shrewsbury** is noted for its black-and-white buildings of timber and plaster, including Abbot's House (dating from 1450), and the tall gabled Ireland's Mansion (ca. 1575) on High Street. These houses were built by the powerful and prosperous wool traders, or drapers, in the shadow of the town's once great castle.

With more time (and a car), you can explore the Wye Valley, with **Hay-on-Wye**, right on the Welsh border, the nucleus of Britain's secondhand book trade, and **Ross-on-Wye** downriver, a good base for the sylvan charms of the lower Wye valley.

Essentials

GETTING THERE By train from London's Paddington Station, Hereford is a 3-hour trip via First Great Western and Arriva, and involves changing at Newport in South Wales (£34 one-way). Shrewsbury is 2½ to 3 hours from London Euston via Virgin Trains and a change to London Midland at Birmingham (one-way from £42).

VISITOR INFORMATION Hereford's **Tourist Information Centre** (✆ **01432/ 268430;** www.visitherefordshire.co.uk) is located at 1 King St. and is open April to September daily 9:30am to 4:30pm, and October to March Monday to Friday 10am to 4:30pm.

The **Shrewsbury Tourist Information Centre,** in Rowley's House Museum on Barker Street (✆ **01743/281200;** www.visitshrewsbury.com), is open May to September Monday to Saturday from 10am to 5pm, Sunday 10am to 4pm. From October to April, its hours are Monday to Saturday from 10am to 4pm.

Exploring the Area

Hereford Cathedral & Mappa Mundi ★★ CATHEDRAL This is one of the oldest and most beguiling cathedrals in England (its cornerstone was laid in 1080). The cathedral is primarily Norman and includes a 13th-century Lady Chapel, as well as a majestic "Father" Willis organ, one of the finest in the world. Exhibited together in the new library building at the west end of the cathedral are two priceless historical treasures: the **Mappa Mundi** of 1300, which portrays the world oriented around Jerusalem, and a 229-book **Chained Library** of medieval manuscripts, with some dating from the 8th century. In the summer you can also climb the 218 steps to the top of the Tower for bird's-eye views of the town.

Cathedral Close, Hereford. ✆ **01432/374200.** www.herefordcathedral.org. Free admission and tours, donation of £5 suggested. Admission to Mappa Mundi and Chained Library £6 adults, £5 seniors and children 5–18, £14 family ticket, free for children 4 and under. Cathedral Mon–Sat 9:15am–5:30pm, Sun 9:15am–3:30pm; exhibits Mon–Sat 10am–4pm, Sun 11am–3:30pm (Apr 16–Oct 31 only).

Ludlow Castle ★ CASTLE This spell-binding Norman castle was built around 1094 as a frontier outpost to keep out the as-yet-unconquered Welsh. The original castle, or the inner bailey, was encircled in the early 14th century by a very large outer bailey and transformed into a medieval palace by Roger Mortimer, the most powerful man in England at the time. Since 1811 the castle has been owned by the earls of Powis. Many of the original buildings still stand, including the Chapel of St. Mary Magdalene, with one of England's last remaining circular naves.

Castle Square, Ludlow. ✆ **01584/873355.** www.ludlowcastle.com. Admission £5 adults, £4.50 seniors, £2.50 children 6–16, £14 family ticket, free for children 5 and under. Dec–Jan Sat–Sun 10am–4pm; Feb–Mar and Oct–Nov daily 10am–4pm; Apr–July and Sept daily 10am–5pm; Aug daily 10am–7pm. Last admission 30 min. before closing time.

Ludlow Museum ☺ MUSEUM This small museum was completely renovated in 2008, telling the story of Ludlow in four galleries: wildlife, archeology, history, and geology. There are several hands-on interactive displays, including a video microscope that lets you examine geological specimens. Visitors can also try on helmets used in England's Civil War. It's a great place for kids.

Castle Square, Ludlow. ✆ **01694/781306.** www.shropshire.gov.uk. Free admission. Apr–Oct Mon–Sat 10am–5pm; June–Aug also Sun 10am–5pm. Closed Nov–Mar.

Shrewsbury Abbey ★ ABBEY Founded in 1083, this small but handsome abbey church remains an active place of worship today. The church is the only surviving

WYE river VALLEY ★★

The **River Wye** snakes its way south from the Welsh mountains through some of the most scenic landscapes in the region, emptying into the Severn estuary at Chepstow on the Welsh border. The most enticing sections are the upper reaches around Hay-on-Wye, and the lower river, where it cuts through the magical woods of the **Forest of Dean.** You'll need a car to make the most of the area.

A good place to base yourself is **Ross-on-Wye,** a small town 16 miles southeast of Hereford. Perched above a loop on the river, Ross is a relaxed, arty place, with a handful of 17th-century buildings and plenty of cafes and B&Bs.

It's just 7 miles south along the river from Ross to **Symonds Yat Rock,** a stupendous viewpoint over the entire valley.

Some 20 miles west of Hereford, **Hay-on-Wye** straddles the Welsh–English border, a tiny but attractive riverside town celebrated the world over thanks to **books.** Hay's first secondhand bookstore opened in 1961, and now virtually the whole place is given over to the trade—it's the greatest market for used books in the world. The **Hay Festival** (www.hayfestival.com) takes place over 10 days in May and attracts major names in the world of literature and the arts.

portion of a once great Benedictine monastery, fictional setting of the Brother Cadfael tales by Ellis Peters. Visitors can see displays devoted to the abbey's history as well as the remains of the 14th-century shrine of St. Winefride. Look for Wilfred Owen's name on the war memorial inside—the poet was a parishioner here before his death in World War I.

Abbey Foregate, Shrewsbury. ⓒ **01743/232723.** www.shrewsburyabbey.com. Free admission; donations of £2 requested. Mon–Sat 10:30am–3pm, Sun 11:30am–2:30pm. Shrewsbury Abbey is just off Robertson Way and Monk Moor Rd., at Judith Butts Lane.

Shrewsbury Castle CASTLE   Built in 1083 by a Norman earl, Roger de Montgomery, this red sandstone castle was designed as a powerful fortress to secure the border with Wales. The Great Hall and walls were constructed during the reign of Edward I, but 200 years ago, Thomas Telford extensively remodeled the castle. Today, it houses the Shropshire Regimental Museum, which includes a rather dry collection of pictures, uniforms, medals, and weapons associated with various Shropshire regiments; it's enlivened by a lock of Napoleon's hair and an American flag captured during the seizure and burning of the White House during the War of 1812.

Castle St., Shrewsbury. ⓒ **01743/361196.** www.shrewsburymuseums.com/castle. Admission £2.50 adults, £1.50 seniors, free for students and children 18 and under. Sept 10–Dec 22 and Feb 13–May 26 Mon–Sat 10:30am–4pm; May 27–Sept 9 Mon–Sun 10:30am–5pm. Closed Thurs all year, and Dec 23–Feb 12. Call ahead, as hours may change.

Shropshire Hills Discovery Centre ★ MUSEUM   This center depicts the complex geology, ecology, history, and culture of Shropshire through the illuminating Secret Hills exhibition. Engulfed by meadows and topped off with a green grass roof, the center features an Iron Age roundhouse and a stunning life-size model of a mammoth, a replica of the actual mammoth skeleton found at Condover, near Shrewsbury, in 1986. You'll also learn about Shropshire's many medieval castles, and see a panoramic movie shot from a balloon floating over the surrounding hills.

School Rd., Craven Arms. © **0345/678-9024.** www.shropshire.gov.uk/shropshirehills.nsf. Admission £4.50 adults, £4 students and seniors, £3 children 5-16, £14 family ticket, free for children 4 and under. Apr-Oct Thurs-Mon 10am-5:30pm, Tues-Wed 10am-9pm; Nov-Mar Thurs-Mon 10am-4:30pm, Tues-Wed 10am-9pm. Last admission 1 hr. before closing. Lies beside the A49 on the southern outskirts of Craven Arms, 7 miles northwest of Ludlow.

Where to Eat

Café @ All Saints ★ CAFE/COFFEEHOUSE   This coffee bar and restaurant is Hereford's number-one spot for casual dining. It occupies the west end of a beautifully restored medieval church right in the center of town, still used for services. The simple, daily-changing menu features good coffee, homemade bread, cakes, and sandwiches stuffed with local Herefordshire produce. Light meals might include pan-fried sardines stuffed with harissa (spicy red-pepper paste), or roast courgette with Shropshire blue cheese. There's live music some evenings.

All Saints Church, High St., Hereford. © **01432/370415.** www.cafeatallsaints.co.uk. Reservations not necessary. Main courses £3.40-£8.95; sandwiches from £5.15. MC, V. Mon-Sat 8am-5pm.

Church Inn PUB FARE   Ludlow's most atmospheric and evocative pub, the Church is everybody's favorite source of beer, gossip, and good cheer. Drinks have flowed here since at least 1446—even earlier, according to some historians. Whether you eat informally in the bar or head for the more formal restaurant, the food and prices are exactly the same: Straightforward, British, and rib-sticking, with traditional pub grub such as beef pie, breaded scampi, and chicken breasts with Shropshire blue cheese and mushroom sauce. The owners only use fresh local produce.

Church St., Buttercross, Ludlow. © **01584/872174.** www.thechurchinn.com. Main courses £6.95-£15. MC, V. Mon-Sat 11am-11pm, Sun noon-10:30pm. Meals served daily noon-3:30pm and 6:30- 9pm.

Golden Cross ★★ CONTEMPORARY ENGLISH   This handsome medieval hotel is reputed to be the oldest inn and watering hole in Shrewsbury, dating from 1428. Today it's also a mouth-watering restaurant specializing in seasonal, local produce and twists on classic English and continental cuisine. Expect creations such as oxtail ravioli with horseradish cream, parsley salad, and parmesan, or an exceptional potato gnocchi served with roasted sweet English onions and goat's cheese fondue. Local cheese Shropshire Blue always features somewhere, along with utterly addictive puddings.

14 Princess St., Shrewsbury. © **01743/362507.** www.goldencrosshotel.co.uk. Reservations recommended. Main courses £11-£18. MC, V. Daily noon-2:30pm and 6-10pm.

Mr. Underhill's ★★★ CONTEMPORARY ENGLISH/MEDITERRANEAN   Serious foodies think nothing of journeying here from Oxford or Birmingham for dinner. Chris Bradley, the chef and owner, turned this threadbare inn into a charming Michelin-starred restaurant beneath the ruins of an 11th-century castle. The menu changes every night; you might start with a cone of pickled artichoke with crunchy sprinkles and follow with hake on fondant tomato with chorizo and orange. For dessert, think Yorkshire rhubarb sponge with custard ice cream.

Many diners choose to overnight here, and we recommend you follow their example. The **B&B** rate is £130 to £170 for a double.

Dinham Weir, Ludlow. © **01584/874431.** www.mr-underhills.co.uk. Reservations required. Fixed-price 9-course dinner plus coffee and petits fours £54-£63. MC, V. Wed-Sun 7-11pm.

The Peach Tree ★ 🍴 ENGLISH/CONTINENTAL   Parts of this oak-beamed restaurant and cafe, a solid choice for a cheap lunch, date from the 15th century. The food is based on solid, time-tested recipes made with fresh ingredients and loads of European savoir-faire. Dishes range from a satisfying Shropshire steak burger on ciabatta with fat chips to a more complex risotto of slow roasted tomatoes, spinach, sage, and melted goat's cheese.

21 Abbey Foregate, Shrewsbury. ℂ **01743/355055.** www.thepeachtree.co.uk. Reservations recommended Sat–Sun. Main courses £9.95–£20. AE, DC, MC, V. Daily 8am–10pm (last order).

Where to Stay

Castle House ★   This fine Georgian hotel occupies an ideal location in central Hereford. Each room features a unique style, but all with a classical English theme, elegant furniture, and a raft of extras and amenities. The bowl of fruit and decanter of sherry is a thoughtful touch. Rates include a gut-busting English breakfast, and there's a fabulous afternoon tea for £10.

Castle St., Hereford, Herefordshire HR1 2NW. www.castlehse.co.uk. ℂ **01432/356321.** Fax 01432/365909. 16 units. £190 double. AE, DC, MC, V. Free parking. **Amenities:** 2 restaurants; bar; babysitting; room service. *In room:* TV, Wi-Fi (free).

The Catherine of Aragon Suite ★★★   Always wanted to spend the night in a romantic 500-year-old house, but crave five-star luxury at the same time? This enchanting timber-framed B&B seamlessly blends the two, set in the oldest residential property in the heart of Shrewsbury (dating from the 1490s). The only catch is that for now, at least, there's literally just one suite, set in its own lavishly decorated wing of the house with living room, bathroom, and wood-paneled bedroom with two double beds. The breakfast is outstanding and Tony and Mary Walters are superb hosts.

The Old House, 20 Dogpole, Shrewsbury, Shropshire SY1 1ES. www.aragonsuite.co.uk. ℂ**01743/271092.** Fax 01743/465006. 1 unit. £125–£135 double. Rates include breakfast. AE, DC, MC, V. *In room:* TV, hair dryer, Internet (free).

De Grey's Townhouse ★★   Ludlow is blessed with an abundance of attractive accommodation options, but it's hard to beat this "tea shop with rooms" for atmosphere, comfort, and historic charm. Framed with oak beams and white-washed walls, the cozy rooms are enhanced with elegant period furniture and wonderfully spacious, modern bathrooms. Breakfast is served in the celebrated tearooms downstairs, accompanied by fresh bread and warm pastries cooked in the on-site bakery—you'll be hypnotized by the aromas long before you see them. Note that Internet should be available by the end of 2011.

Broad St., Ludlow, Shropshire SY8 1NG. www.degreys.co.uk. ℂ **01584/872764.** 9 units. £110–£145 double. Rates include English breakfast. AE, DC, MC, V. Free parking. **Amenities:** Tearoom. *In room:* TV, hair dryer.

Grove Farm House ★   Shrewsbury's best B&B is a ravishing Georgian farmhouse just 6 miles south of the town, ideally located for touring by car. Rooms are furnished in a bright, contemporary style, with thoughtful extras such as bathrobes and a hospitality tray loaded with homemade biscuits. In the morning, you'll have a veritable feast, beginning with a cold buffet and including a cooked full English breakfast. Afternoon tea with homemade cake is available by arrangement.

Condover, Shrewsbury, Shropshire SY5 7BH (drive south on the A49 and look for the left turn to Condover). www.grovefarmhouse.com. ℂ **01743/718544.** 4 units. £75–£85 double. Rates include English breakfast. AE, DC, MC, V. Free parking. *In room:* TV/DVD/CD, hair dryer, Wi-Fi (free

IRONBRIDGE

135 miles NW of London; 36 miles NW of Birmingham; 18 miles SE of Shrewsbury

Some 200 years ago, the small village of **Ironbridge** was humming with industrial activity. Today the factories and smelters are long gone, and tourists and tour buses come to soak up a heavy dose of Britain's industrial heritage. This stretch of the Severn Valley has been an important industrial area since the Middle Ages because of its iron and limestone deposits. But the event that clinched the area's importance came in 1709, when a Quaker ironmaster, Abraham Darby I, discovered a method for smelting iron by using coke as a fuel, rather than charcoal. This paved the way for the first iron rails, boats, wheels, aqueducts, and the first iron bridge itself, cast here by Darby's grandson in 1779. The village of Ironbridge grew up around the bridge in subsequent years, and since the late 1960s most of the gorge, including the adjacent settlement of Coalbrookdale, has formed a giant historical park, home to 10 absorbing museums.

Essentials

GETTING THERE . The nearest train and long-distance bus station is in **Telford,** 5 miles north of Ironbridge and well connected to London and Birmingham. The Gorge Connect bus service links Telford Central Station to Ironbridge, a 20-minute ride. Fares are 50p per ride or £2.50 for an unlimited Day-Rover pass, useful as the bus also connects all the major sights in Ironbridge. The catch is that the bus only runs on weekends and bank holiday Mondays April to October; buses run every 30 minutes or so between 9:30am and 3:54pm from Telford. Alternatively, Arriva runs regular buses Monday to Friday to Ironbridge from Telford and Shrewsbury. See www.arrivabus.co.uk for timetables.

VISITOR INFORMATION The **Ironbridge Tourist Information Centre,** the Tollhouse (𝄴 **01952/884391;** www.visitironbridge.co.uk), is open Monday to Friday 9am to 5pm, Saturday and Sunday 10am to 5pm.

Exploring the Area

The Ironbridge Valley plays host to several illuminating museums, collectively called the **Ironbridge Gorge Museums** ★★ (𝄴 **01952/433522** Mon–Fri, or 01952/432166 Sat–Sun; www.ironbridge.org.uk). These include the **Coalbrookdale Museum of Iron** with its Darby Furnace (£7.60 adults; £7.10 over 60; £5.10 full-time students and children 5–18); **Darby Houses,** the restored 19th-century homes of the Quaker ironmasters (£4.75 adults; £3.75 over 60; £3.25 full-time students and children 5–18); the remarkable **Iron Bridge** ★★, with its original tollhouse (free); the **Museum of the Gorge** (£3.75 adults; £3.10 over 60; £2.45 full-time students and children 5–18) with a scale model of the gorge in 1796; the **Jackfield Tile Museum** (£7.60 adults; £7.10 over 60; £5.10 full-time students and children 5–18), where you can see demonstrations of tile pressing, decorating, and firing; **Blists Hill Victorian Town** ★★, with its illuminating open-air recreation of a 19th-century village (£14.95 adults; £11.95 over 60; £9.95 full-time students and children 5–18); the absorbing **Coalport China Museum and Tar Tunnel** ★★, with ceramics displays (£7.60 adults; £7.10 over 60; £5.10 full-time students and children 5–18) and a tour of an underground mine (£2.60 adults; £2.25 over 60; £2 full-time students and children 5–18); **Broseley Pipeworks,** a 50-year-old abandoned tobacco pipe-making factory (£4.75 adults; £3.75 over 60; £3.10 full-time students and children 5–18); and **Enginiuty,** an interactive exhibit that allows kids to become engineers for a day (£7.85 adults; £6.75 over 60, full-time students, and children 5–18). *Insider tip:* If time is short, we recommend that you at least visit the Iron Bridge, Blists Hill Victorian Town, and the Coalport China Museum.

A passport ticket to all museums in Ironbridge Gorge is £23 for adults, £18 for seniors, £15 for students and children 5 to 18, £6.50 for families of two adults and up to three children, and free for children 4 and under. Between April and October the sites are open daily from 9am to 5pm with the exception of Broseley Pipeworks, which is open daily from the end of May to the end of September from 1 to 5pm. The Tar Tunnel, Darby Houses, and Broseley Pipeworks are closed from November to March, with the other sites open 10am to 5pm (Blists closes at 4pm).

Where to Eat & Stay

Best Western Valley Hotel   This riverside inn blends modern amenities and historic ambience—it was originally built as a private home around 1750, and was enlarged over the years into the sprawling, brick building you see today. Fifteen of the hotel's rooms lie within the original stable and are accessible via a glass-roofed courtyard. Although rooms in the main house usually have more panoramic views, many visitors prefer the coziness of the former stables. All units are well maintained and modern; some have four-poster beds.

Outfitted with crisp napery, Windsor-style chairs, and a high ceiling, the hotel's highly rated restaurant, **Chez Maw** (✆ **01952/432247;** www.chezmawrestaurant. co.uk), serves contemporary British food. Try the free-range Staffordshire chicken breast, with house smoked sausage, cannellini bean and root vegetable cassoulet, or the roasted filet of Loch Duarte salmon, with parsnip and potato mash, purple sprouting broccoli, and red wine and pancetta sauce.

Buildwas Rd., Ironbridge, Telford, Shropshire TF8 7DW. www.thevalleyhotel.co.uk. ✆ **01952/432247.** Fax 01952/432308. 44 units. £64–£87 double. Breakfast rates extra. AE, DC, MC, V. **Amenities:** Restaurant; 2 bars; room service. *In room:* TV, hair dryer, Wi-Fi (free).

Library House ★★ 🏨   This restored landmark, parts of which date from 1752, has been used for many purposes, including a doctor's surgery clinic and even the village library, from which the B&B takes its name. Today it's one of the finest hotels in the area, with a dazzling breakfast and delightful bedrooms, named after English writers George Eliot, Hardy, Milton, and Chaucer. Each one is individually designed and decorated, from Georgian to contemporary to Oriental styles. There is also a pretty terraced garden.

11 Severn Bank, Ironbridge, near Telford, Shropshire TF8 7AN. www.libraryhouse.com. ✆ **01952/432299.** Fax 01952/433967. 4 units. £80–£90 double. Rates include breakfast. No credit cards. *In room:* TV/DVD, hair dryer, no phone.

THE POTTERIES

162 miles NW of London; 59 miles NW of Leicester; 46 miles N of Birmingham; 41 miles S of Manchester

Anyone with an interest in pottery should make a pilgrimage to **Stoke-on-Trent,** one of author Arnold Bennett's famous *Five Towns.* Kilns were busy here in the 14th century, long before Josiah Wedgwood (1730–95), England's most distinguished potter, arrived. Most of the great kilns have disappeared, but shops such as Wedgwood,

Royal Doulton, Portmeirion, Moorcroft, and Aynsley are among the 30 pottery attractions still based in the city.

Today Stoke-on-Trent is a loose confederation of six towns (Tunstall, Burslem, Stoke, Fenton, Longton, and Hanley, the most important) with little else to detain you, though it's also famous for being one of the original 1960s' centers of what's dubbed **northern soul** (the focus being on lesser-known Motown-style soul groups). Northern soul has made a comeback in recent years; venues like King's Hall host "all-nighters" (9pm–7am) four times a year, though the dancers are likely to be in their 40s these days.

Essentials

GETTING THERE   From London's Euston Station, Virgin Trains take 1½ hours to Stoke-on-Trent. Trains make half-hourly departures daily (one-way from £28).

By car from London, drive along the M1 and then the M6 to the A500 at junction 15. It will take you 2 to 3 hours.

VISITOR INFORMATION   The **Stoke-on-Trent Tourist Information Centre,** Victoria Hall, Bagnall Street, Cultural Quarter (✆ **01782/236000;** www.visit stoke.co.uk), is open Monday to Friday 9am to 5pm, and Saturday 10am to 2pm.

Exploring the Area

Dudson Museum ★ MUSEUM   This is a fascinating showcase for the oldest-surviving family business in the local ceramics industry. You can explore the original Dudson factory courtyard and even step inside the cavernous bottle oven to view a collection of rare pieces. Exhibitions trace the history of the Dudson company from 1800 to the present day.

Hope St., Hanley, Stoke-on-Trent. ✆ **01782/285286.** www.dudson.com. Free admission. Mon–Fri 10am–3pm.

Gladstone Pottery Museum ★ MUSEUM   This is the only complete Victorian pottery factory that has been restored as a museum, with craftspeople providing daily demonstrations in the original workshops. Various galleries depict the rise of the Staffordshire pottery industry, tile history, and so on (check out the toilets of all shapes, sizes, colors, and decoration). There are great hands-on opportunities for plate painting, pot throwing, and ornamental-flower making.

Uttoxeter Rd., Longton. ✆ **01782/237777.** www.stokemuseums.org.uk/gpm. Admission £6.95 adults, £5.50 seniors and students, £4.75 children 4–16, £20 family ticket, free for children 3 and under. Daily 10am–5pm (last admission 4pm).

Moorcroft Museum & Factory Tour FACTORY TOUR   Moorcroft was founded in 1898 by William Moorcroft, who produced his own special brand of pottery and was his own exclusive designer until his death in 1945. The small museum highlights his decorative designs, but the main event is the factory tour. It's a bit like going back in time; things have changed little on the factory floor since Moorcroft's day. You'll observe all the handmade processes of mold-making, slip casting, hand turning, tube lining, hand painting, kiln firing, and finally glazing.

Sandbach Rd., Burslem. ✆ **01782/820500.** www.moorcroft.com. Factory tours £4.50 adults, £3.50 seniors, £2.50 children 11–16. Tours Mon and Wed–Thurs 11am and 2pm, Fri 11am only; all tours must be booked 2 weeks in advance. Museum and shop Mon–Fri 10am–5pm, Sat 9:30am–4:30pm. A taxi from the Stoke-on-Trent train station will run to about £10. If you're driving from London, follow the M1 north to the M6. Take it north to junction 15, which becomes the A500. Follow the signs.

The Great Potteries Outlet Tour

With around 25 high-quality factory shops and outlets spread around the Stoke area, your biggest headache is likely to be shipping all your purchases back home. **Wedgwood** (see below) is an obvious target, but there are plenty of other worthy choices:

- o **Aynsley China,** Sutherland Road, Longton, Stoke-on-Trent (© **01782/339420**), has a wide selection of the U.K.'s favorite best-quality fine bone china.
- o **Dudson Factory Outlet,** Nile Street, Burslem, Stoke-on-Trent

(© **01782/821075**). See review under "Exploring the Area," below.

- o **Moorcroft Factory Shop,** Phoenix Works, Nile Street, Cobridge, Stoke-on-Trent (© **01782/820505**). See review under "Exploring the Area," below.
- o **Portmeirion Factory Shop,** 473 King St., Longton, Stoke-on-Trent (© **01782/326661**), has tons of choices, with seconds (pieces that have minor flaws), and Spode and Royal Worcester ware, at least 30% off retail prices.

The Potteries Museum & Art Gallery ★★ MUSEUM   Stoke's premier museum is the best place to learn about the history of the Potteries, with the world's greatest collection of Staffordshire ceramics and even a World War II Spitfire on show. But the real star attraction is the Staffordshire Hoard, the most precious collection of Anglo-Saxon treasure and gold ever found (valued at over £3 million in 2011). Wonder at intricate filigree gold hilt collars from swords made 1,500 years ago, and ornate gold mounts in the shape of a bird's head.

Bethesda St., City Centre, Stoke-on-Trent. © **01782/232323.** www.stoke.gov.uk/museum. Free admission. Mon–Sat 10am–5pm, Sun 2–5pm. Bus: 23, 23A, and 25 from Stoke-on-Trent train station to Hanley bus station.

Wedgwood Museum & Visitor Centre ★ MUSEUM   Wedgwood is the most celebrated pottery brand in England, and these two related sites offer an enlightening introduction. The museum covers 3 centuries of design, beginning with the birth of Josiah Wedgwood in 1730, and including his Etruria factory and the company's Victorian showroom.

The nearby **Wedgwood Visitor Centre** (© **0870/606-1759;** www.thewedgwood visitorcentre.com) includes a demonstration hall where you can watch clay pots being formed on the potter's wheel, and witness plates being turned and fired, then painted. An art gallery and gift shop sell factory-made items (note that factory tours are no longer available).

Barlaston, Stoke-on-Trent. © **01782/371919.** www.wedgwoodmuseum.org.uk. Museum admission £6 adults, £5 seniors, students, and children 5–16, £18 family ticket. Visitor Centre and Museum £10 adults, £8 seniors, students, and children 5–16, £32 family ticket. Mon–Fri 9am–5pm, Sat–Sun 10am–5pm. Closed Dec 24–Jan 2. Take a taxi from Stoke-on-Trent train station, a 6-mile trip that will cost around £10. If you're driving from London, head north along the M1 until you reach the M6. Continue north to junction 14, which becomes the A34. Follow the A34 to Barlaston and follow the signs.

Where to Eat & Stay

The Old Plough ★ PUB FARE   This atmospheric old-fashioned pub is the best place to eat in Stoke, with a menu anchored by a choice of perfectly chargrilled, hearty steaks and homemade sauces. The dining room is decorated with all sorts of vintage bric-a-brac, old posters, pub signs, and the like, and the real ales, and friendly and attentive staff, round out the experience.

147 Etruria Rd., Etruria, Stoke-on-Trent. © **01782/269445.** Reservations recommended. Main courses £15–£38. MC, V. Daily 11:30am–11pm.

Premier Inn Stoke (Trentham Gardens) ★   It's hard to beat this chain hotel for convenience, style, and overall comfort. The property is a generic modern block, geared to business travelers and motorists, but it's got all the amenities, offers a filling breakfast (extra), and is easy to find, just off the M6 junction 15. Online deals make this a real bargain.

Stone Road, Stoke-on-Trent, Staffordshire ST4 8JG. www.premierinn.com. © **0871/5279050.** Fax 0871/5279051. 119 units. £57–£67 double. AE, DC, MC, V. Free parking. **Amenities:** Restaurant; bar. *In room:* A/C, TV, hair dryer, Wi-Fi (free).

The Upper House   If you are looking for something with a little more character, consider this inviting B&B, a grand country house built in 1845 for Josiah Wedgwood's grandson. Rooms are fittingly decked out in a clean period style, with frilly drapes and wooden beds. The **restaurant** serves an excellent afternoon tea daily 3 to 5pm (from £5.50), and Thai food on Wednesday nights. Lunch is served daily noon to 2pm, while dinner is served from Monday to Saturday from 6pm.

The Green, Barlaston, Stoke-on-Trent, Staffordshire ST12 9AE. www.theupperhouse.com. © **01782/373790.** Fax 01782/374027. 24 units. £110 double. Rates include breakfast. MC, V. Free parking. **Amenities:** Restaurant; bar and lounge. *In room:* TV, hair dryer, Wi-Fi (free).

CAMBRIDGE & EAST ANGLIA

by Nick Dalton & Deborah Stone

East Anglia—Essex, Cambridgeshire, Suffolk, and Norfolk—was a kingdom in itself in Anglo-Saxon times, and, as you head east from London, it's easy to see how. The farther east you go, the lower and flatter it becomes; swathes of open fields, crisscrossed by dykes and ditches, turn to forest and heath until you come to the watery haven of the Norfolk Broads, like America's bayous but with cream teas.

The coast is equally low and striking. And yet at the heart of all this is that seat of university learning, Cambridge, with its ornate colleges and chapels.

CITIES & TOWNS   Here are some of England's oldest cities. **Colchester** was England's Roman capital, **Norwich** is one of Britain's most perfect medieval cities, and **Ipswich** is a picturesque river port. **Bury St. Edmunds** is an ancient religious settlement, while the spire of **Ely's** cathedral rises starkly from the pancake-flat fens. And exquisite **Cambridge** has college buildings dating back to the 14th century, the grassy Backs dividing them from the River Cam, where students still punt, pushing along flat-bottomed boats with long poles.

COUNTRYSIDE   In some places you can see for miles across **fens, heath,** and **marshes,** but there are gentle **hills** too and acres of **farmland** punctuated by small villages of pastel-painted cottages. This is a landscape (captured in oils by John Constable) perfect for walking and cycling. And the **Norfolk Broads,** an expanse of waterways where you can sail and potter about in a cabin cruiser, offer scenery like nowhere else in the country.

EATING & DRINKING   **Crabs** from Cromer, **fish** from traditional smokehouses, **pork** from pigs that have grown up smelling the sea air in Suffolk, and even famed **sea salt** from Maldon in Essex: This is a place of good food, which can be found everywhere from traditional butcher's shops to fine restaurants. The region is also home to two of the country's most celebrated brewers, Greene King (Bury St. Edmunds) and Adnams (Southwold), whose beer dominates the many charming pubs.

COAST   Whether it's the boisterous, traditional resort towns such as **Clacton** in Essex or **Great Yarmouth** in Norfolk, or somewhere more refined, such as **Southwold** and **Aldeburgh** in Suffolk, or a remote boutique hotel on the north Norfolk coast, there's something here for all tastes. There are charming estuaries, long stretches of beach, bird sanctuaries in brackish, windblown spots, and even the option of a seal-spotting boat trip.

THE best TRAVEL EXPERIENCES IN CAMBRIDGE & EAST ANGLIA

o **Punting on the Cam:** Perched precariously on the back of a little boat and trying to propel (and steer) with a big pole is great fun as you pass by Cambridge's iconic colleges. Take a picnic and relax under a willow on a grassy bank, before heading back. See p. 497.

o **Spending a day in Southwold:** Walking across the common with views over the sea, strolling through the chain store-free streets, then heading down the steps onto the beach, and finishing with a walk along the river quayside, for some fish and chips. See p. 521.

o **Walking in north Norfolk:** The beaches are big and windswept, often backed by bird reserves and ponds. There's a real feel of being out on the edge and, indeed, this is as far as you can go before you hit the Continent. See p. 528.

o **Seeing Ely Cathedral:** This medieval masterpiece rises from the pancake-flat Fens, and can be seen from miles around; it's just as impressive when you actually get close up. See p. 504.

o **Exploring the Blackwater Estuary:** This is a hidden Essex delight, a waterway of times gone by, where Thames sailing barges still tie up at Hythe Quay. It's the place to sit with a beer at sunset. See p. 512.

CAMBRIDGE

55 miles N of London; 80 miles NE of Oxford

The university town of Cambridge is a city of contrasts: Its historic college buildings with their magnificent chapels, turrets, and spires provide a romantic backdrop to delight even the most traveled tourist, while its high-tech industries—dubbed "Silicon Fen"—lead the way in global technology. Of course these two aspects of Cambridge are connected—brilliant minds with brilliant ideas.

Visit Cambridge and it feels like a little of that fairy dust rubs off on you too, as you discover the **Bridge of Sighs** while punting on the River Cam; walk along **The Backs** of the colleges as the spring bulbs produce a carpet of flowers and explore the narrow streets in the footsteps of Sir Isaac Newton, John Milton, Charles Darwin, Virginia Woolf, and many more. But Cambridge is not just a collection of old colleges (as inspiring as they are). It's a living, working town with many non-university residents who bring additional atmosphere to the city.

At its heart is the vibrant market place, a cobbled square with stalls every day, and running through the city is the **River Cam,** which drifts past magical open spaces such as Midsummer Common, Jesus Green, The Backs, and Sheeps Green. Every visitor should spend a few hours punting on the river, floating past the riverside pubs and restaurants, or perhaps punting up to Grantchester Meadows (many people will know that name from the song on the Pink Floyd's *Ummagumma* album; band members Roger Waters, Syd Barrett, and Dave Gilmour grew up in the city) for afternoon

East Anglia

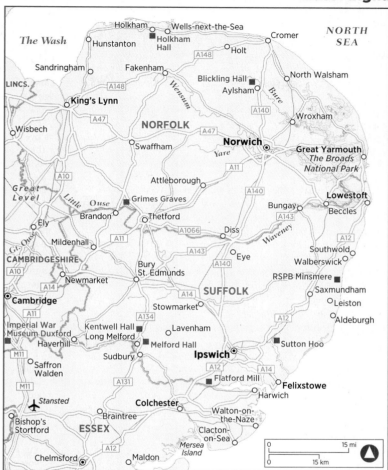

13

CAMBRIDGE & EAST ANGLIA | Cambridge

tea. Afterward you can relax in one of those pubs yourself—there are more than 100 in the city. The Mill and Fort St. George are two of the best riverside pubs.

Essentials

GETTING THERE First Capital Connect trains from London's Kings Cross take 45 minutes to an hour. A one-way ticket costs from £20. Trains from London's Liverpool Street with NXEA take 80 minutes and cost from £17.

If you're driving from London, head north on the M11. If you're driving from the northeast, use the A1 and from the Midlands take the M6 onto the A14.

VISITOR INFORMATION   For free information on attractions and public transport visit the **Cambridge Tourist Information Centre,** Peas Hill, CB2 3AD (✆ **0871/226-8006,** or 0044/122-346-4732 from overseas; www.visitcambridge. org). Staff can also book tours and lodging. The center is open year-round, Monday to Saturday 10am to 5pm (Apr–Nov also Sun and bank holidays 11am–3pm).

GETTING AROUND   City parking is expensive and the traffic can be unbearable. There are five Park and Ride sites, at Trumpington, Madingley Road, Milton, Newmarket Road, and Babraham Road. Park and Ride round-trip bus tickets cost £2.30 from machines (£2.60 from bus drivers); children ride free. Buses leave every 10 minutes (every 15 min. on Sun and bank holidays) and call at a number of stops around the city.

Cambridge is best seen on foot, or you can join the locals and cycle everywhere. **Station Cycles** (✆ **01223/307125;** www.stationcycles.co.uk) has bikes for rent for £8 for a half-day, £10 for a day, or £25 for a week. A £75 deposit is required. There's a shop in the railway station parking lot and at Grand Arcade in Corn Exchange Street near the market. Both are open Monday to Friday 8am to 6pm (7pm on Wed), Saturday 9am to 5pm, and Sunday 10am to 4pm, and they have left-luggage facilities. Park your bike for free at the Park Street or Grand Arcade car parks. A free pushchair loan is available to cycling parents with children on bicycle seats, from Park Street and Station Cycle's station car park shop. **City Cycle Hire** in Newnham Road (✆ **01223/365629;** www.citycyclehire.com) also has bikes for £6 per half-day, £9 per day, or £17 per week.

Stagecoach (✆ **01223/423578;** www.stagecoachbus.com) serves the area with a network of buses. A day pass costs from £3.40, or £5.70 for a family day pass. The tourist office has bus schedules.

SPECIAL EVENTS   Try to coincide your visit with one of the city's many festivals. **Cambridge Folk Festival** (www.cambridgefolkfestival.co.uk) in the last weekend of July is the best known, but sells out quickly. Full weekend tickets are about £110. Alternatively, try **Strawberry Fair** (www.strawberry-fair.org.uk) on Midsummer Common in June to see local bands, cabaret, dance, and family entertainment. The **Cambridge Shakespeare Festival** (✆ **07955/218824;** www.cambridgeshakespeare.com) in July and August has open-air Shakespeare performances in the grounds of several colleges.

ORGANIZED TOURS   The **Cambridge Tourist Information Centre** (see "Visitor Information," above) has several 2-hour walking tours of the city, from £8 to £15 for adults, and up to £7 for children under 12. Book tours by calling ✆ **01223/457574** or visit www.visitcambridge.org.

City Sightseeing (✆ **01223/423578;** www.city-sightseeing.com) uses open-top, double-decker buses from outside Cambridge railway station, and has 20 hop-on, hop-off stops. Daily tours with recorded commentary depart every 20 minutes from Silver Street near The Backs, between 9:30am and 4pm in summer and 10:20am to 3pm in winter. Tickets are valid for 24 hours, and the tour is a convenient way to get to out-of-town attractions such as the American Cemetery, and those on the outskirts (Cambridge Folk Museum and Cambridge University Botanic Gardens). The fare is £13 for adults, £9 for seniors and students, £7 for children 6 to 15, and free for children 5 and under. A family ticket for £32 covers two adults and up to three children.

City walking tours with **Cambridge Tailor-made Tours** (✆ **01223/561766;** www.cambridgetmtours.co.uk) are available for small or large groups and are led by Blue Badge guides. Prices depend on the size of the group.

Cambridge

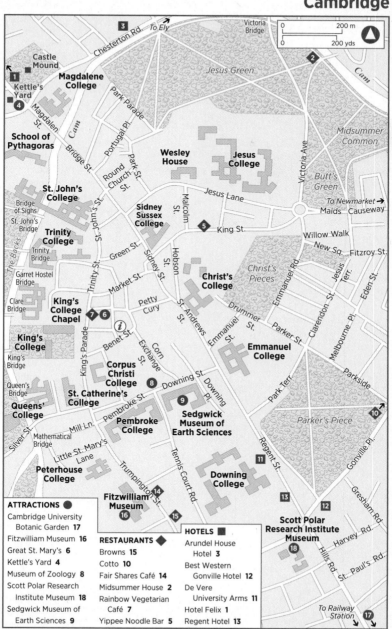

ATTRACTIONS ●

Cambridge University
Botanic Garden **17**
Fitzwilliam Museum **16**
Great St. Mary's **6**
Kettle's Yard **4**
Museum of Zoology **8**
Scott Polar Research
Institute Museum **18**
Sedgwick Museum of
Earth Sciences **9**

RESTAURANTS ◆

Browns **15**
Cotto **10**
Fair Shares Café **14**
Midsummer House **2**
Rainbow Vegetarian
Café **7**
Yippee Noodle Bar **5**

HOTELS ■

Arundel House
Hotel **3**
Best Western
Gonville Hotel **12**
De Vere
University Arms **11**
Hotel Felix **1**
Regent Hotel **13**

Exploring Cambridge University

Scholars have been studying at Cambridge since the early 13th century, with Henry III granting the students his protection in 1231. At this stage they were a loosely organized group, but during the medieval period the university was arranged in a similar style to Oxford, with a foundation course leading to graduation and degrees. It wasn't until the late 14th century that the university began acquiring its own premises, beginning with the site now known as Senate House Hill. Land and buildings were sometimes donated by wealthy people on condition that students, mostly studying to become clergymen, prayed for them. The university grew even more quickly in the 16th century, with Henry VIII founding Trinity College. Already established colleges, such as Emmanuel and Magdalene, took over larger premises, and the study of Greek, Latin, and classics (as well as divinity) indicated a move away from simply educating clerics. During the late 1600s and 1700s mathematics and science began to dominate the university. This was thanks largely to Sir Isaac Newton, who formulated the principles of gravity. During this period, the University Press, the Botanic Garden, and the University Library were established. Reforms during the 19th century rearranged the university into something like the institution we know today, and two colleges for women were established: Girton in 1869 and Newnham in 1872. However, women could not become full members of the university until 1947, and it wasn't until the 1960s that some of the older colleges began to admit female students. Cambridge University now consists of 31 colleges, all co-educational except three that remain female-only: Newnham, Murray Edwards College, and Lucy Cavendish. The colleges are all open to the public at certain times, but each has its own opening times and admission prices. The following are some of the most interesting colleges, and if you have time you could also visit **Magdalene College,** on Magdalene Street, founded in 1542; **Pembroke College,** on Trumpington Street, founded in 1347; **Christ's College,** on St. Andrew's Street, founded in 1505; and **Corpus Christi College,** on Trumpington Street, which dates from 1352.

Emmanuel College HISTORIC SITE   Emmanuel, on St. Andrew's Street, was founded in 1584 by Sir Walter Mildmay, Elizabeth I's chancellor of the exchequer. Mildmay was a Puritan and of the 100 Cambridge graduates who emigrated to New England before 1646, 35 were from Emmanuel. The college's gardens, designed by Sir Christopher Wren, are particularly attractive, as are the cloister and chapel, consecrated in 1677.

Insider tip: John Harvard, of the eponymous American university in Cambridge, Massachusetts, was among the Emmanuel graduates who immigrated to New England. There's a memorial to him in the chapel.

St. Andrew's St. ℂ **01223/334200.** www.emma.cam.ac.uk. Free entry to grounds and chapel.

King's College ★★ HISTORIC SITE   Henry VI founded King's College in 1441, and although most of its buildings date from the 18th century and later, the world-famous **King's College Chapel** ★★★ was started in the Middle Ages and is regarded as one of Europe's finest Gothic buildings. Rubens's *Adoration of the Magi,* painted in 1634, is a highlight, as are the striking stained-glass windows (most paid for by Henry VIII). An exhibition in the seven northern side chapels shows why and how the chapel was built. Carols are broadcast worldwide from the chapel every Christmas Eve, and there are concerts and organ recitals throughout the year, with tickets available from the Shop at King's, on King's Parade.

Insider tip: See the chapel as it should be enjoyed, by attending a service. Even-song on an early summer's evening is one of the most uplifting experiences you'll ever have in the city. And while the chapel is beautiful inside, it is best viewed from The Backs, where you can also take a picnic and have a break from sightseeing. E. M. Forster came here to contemplate scenes for his novel *Maurice.*

King's Parade. ℭ **01223/331100.** www.kings.cam.ac.uk. Admission £6.50 adults; £4.50 children 12–16, students, and seniors; free for children 11 and under.

Peterhouse College HISTORIC SITE   This is the oldest Cambridge college, founded in 1284 by Bishop of Ely Hugh de Balsham. The Hall was built in 1286 but only the hall remains of the original buildings, rebuilt in the 1860s in the Gothic Revival style by Sir George Gilbert Scott, who was responsible for the Parliament buildings in London. The stained-glass windows were designed by British Arts and

 punting ON THE CAM

You haven't really experienced Cambridge if you haven't been punting on the **River Cam.** There's nothing more enjoyable on a sunny day than sitting back in one of the flat-bottomed wooden boats and gliding elegantly past the ivy-covered colleges and their immaculate gardens along the mirror-like river. All you have to do is put the long pole, about 5m (16 ft.), straight down into the shallow water until it finds the riverbed, then gently push and retrieve the pole in one deft, simple movement. Actually, it's easy once you know how to do it, but watching inexperienced enthusiasts lose their pole or steer into the riverbed is a traditional form of entertainment in Cambridge. Rent a punt from **Scudamore's Punting Company** any time of the year to punt past The Backs from its Magdalene Bridge or Mill Lane stations, or you can punt up to Grantchester from its Mill Lane Boatyard in Granta Place, Mill Lane (ℭ **01223/359750;** www.scudamores. com). Punts cost £18 per hour (maximum of six people per punt). A credit card imprint is required as deposit. **Grantchester** is 2 miles upriver, and was immortalized by the World War I poet Rupert Brooke in "The Soldier": "Stands the Church clock at ten to three? And is there honey still for tea?" asks the poem, and in fact the church clock was left frozen in time at 10 minutes to three when it was stopped for repairs in 1985. If you walk the 1 mile from the river at **Grantchester Meadows** to the village you can see for yourself, and have tea at the **Orchard Tea Garden** (ℭ **01223/ 551125;** www.orchard-grantchester.com) near the church or have a drink at the 400-year-old pub **The Green Man,** in the High Street (ℭ **01223/844669;** www. thegreenmangrantchester.co.uk).

Crafts founder William Morris. The chapel, called Old Court, dates from 1632 and was renovated in 1754. Ask to enter at the porter's lodge at the gate.

Insider tip: Little St. Mary's, the church next door, was the college chapel until 1632 and has a memorial to Godfrey Washington, who died in 1729. The Washington family's coat of arms contains an eagle on top of stars and stripes, and is believed to be the inspiration for the United States flag.

Trumpington St. ✆ **01223/338200.** www.pet.cam.ac.uk. Free entry to grounds.

Queens' College ★★ HISTORIC SITE   Founded by English queens Margaret of Anjou, the wife of Henry VI, and Elizabeth Woodville, the wife of Edward IV, the college dates from 1448 and is regarded as the most beautiful of Cambridge's colleges. Entry and exit is by the old porter's lodge in Queens' Lane. Its second cloister is the most interesting, flanked by the 16th-century half-timbered President's Lodge. The old hall and chapel are usually open to the public when not in use.

Insider tip: The Mathematical Bridge, an arched, wooden, self-supporting bridge connecting the college's two parts, is best viewed from the Silver Street Bridge, dating from 1902.

Silver St. ✆ **01223/335511.** www.quns.cam.ac.uk. Late June–early Oct 10am–4:30pm admission £2.50 adults, free for children 11 and under (free admission other times). Oct daily 2–4pm (weekends 10am–4:30pm); Nov–late May daily 2–4pm (sometimes 4:30pm; also closed late May–late June and some other dates).

St. John's College ★★ HISTORIC SITE   St. John's was founded in 1511 by Lady Margaret Beaufort, mother of Henry VII, who established Christ's College a few years earlier. The impressive gateway has the Tudor coat of arms, and the Second Court is a fine example of late Tudor brickwork. The college's best-known feature is the Bridge of Sighs crossing the River Cam. It was built in the 19th century, inspired by the covered bridge at the Doge's Palace in Venice. It connects the older part of the college with New Court, a Gothic Revival folly with a main cupola and pinnacles that students nicknamed the wedding cake. Wordsworth was an alumnus of this college, and visitors are welcome to attend choral services in the chapel.

Insider tip: The Bridge of Sighs is closed to visitors but can be seen from Kitchen Bridge.

St. John's Street. ✆ **01223/338600.** www.joh.cam.ac.uk. Admission £3.20 adults, £2 seniors and children 12–17, free for children 11 and under. Mar–Oct 10am–5:30pm; Nov–Feb Sat 10am–3:30pm.

Trinity College ★★ HISTORIC SITE   This is Cambridge's largest college, not to be confused with Trinity Hall. It was founded in 1546 when Henry VIII consolidated a number of smaller colleges on the site. The courtyard is the most spacious in Cambridge, built when Thomas Neville was master. The Wren Library, from 1695, was designed by Sir Christopher Wren. It contains manuscripts and books that were in the college library by 1820, together with various special collections including 1,250 medieval manuscripts, early Shakespeare editions, many books from Sir Isaac Newton's own library, and A.A. Milne's Winnie-the-Pooh manuscripts.

Insider tip: Sir Isaac Newton first calculated the speed of sound here, at Neville's Court, and Lord Byron used to bathe naked in the Great Court's fountain with his pet bear. The university forbade students from having dogs, but there was no rule against bears. Years later, Vladimir Nabokov walked through that same courtyard dreaming of the young lady he would later write about as *Lolita.*

Trinity St. ✆ **01223/338400.** www.trin.cam.ac.uk. The Wren Library Mon–Fri noon–2pm, Sat 10:30am–12:30pm. Various other areas are open at different times; ask at the porter's lodge. Admission free.

Exploring the Rest of Cambridge

Cambridge University Botanic Garden ★★ GARDEN   The winter garden is noted for the extravagance of stems and bark while the woodland garden bursts into life with flowering spring bulbs. The garden opened in 1846 and much of the tree collection dates back to the original layout. The magnificent avenue of trees along Main Walk includes giant redwoods grown from seeds collected in California in 1851, the first ever brought to England.

1 Brookside, Bateman St. ✆ **01223/336265.** www.botanic.cam.ac.uk. Admission £4 adults, £3.50 students and seniors, children 15 and under free. Mar–Oct and all weekends and bank holidays. Daily Apr–Sept 10am–6pm; Feb, Mar, and Oct 10am–5pm; Jan, Nov, and Dec 10am–4pm.

Fitzwilliam Museum ★★ MUSEUM   Suits of armor, Greek and Roman pottery, Chinese jades, Japanese ceramics, and an art collection that includes Rubens, Van Dyck, Canaletto, Hogarth, Gainsborough, Constable, and the Impressionist painters: You'll find them all here in a first-class museum that isn't so large that fatigue sets in. There's also a good cafe and gift shop and regular lectures of a standard you would expect from this Cambridge University-owned institution.

Trumpington St., near Peterhouse. ✆ **01223/332900.** www.fitzmuseum.cam.ac.uk. Free admission; donations appreciated. Tues–Sat 10am–5pm, Sun noon–5pm; closed Mon, Good Friday, Dec 24–26 and 31, and Jan 1. Sat guided tours at 2:30pm (£4).

Great St. Mary's CHURCH   Closely associated with events of the Reformation because the leaders of the movement (Erasmus, Cranmer, Latimer, and Ridley) preached here, this university church was built mostly in 1478 on the site of an 11th-century church. The cloth that covered the hearse of King Henry VII is on display in the church. There is a fine view of Cambridge from the top of the tower.

Senate House Hill. ✆ **01223/741716.** www.gsm.cam.ac.uk. Admission to tower £3 adults, £1.50 children 5–16. Tower summer daily 10am–4:30pm, winter until 4pm; Sun year-round noon–4pm. Church daily 9am–6pm.

Kettle's Yard ★★ HISTORIC HOME   This oasis of calm and good taste was the home of Jim and Helen Ede during the 1950s to early 1970s. As curator of London's Tate Gallery in the 1920s and 1930s, Jim built up an enviable collection of paintings and sculptures, including work by Joan Miró, Henry Moore, and Barbara Hepworth, which are still on display more or less where the Edes left them. Around the corner is Kettle's Yard Gallery, with a respected collection of 20th-century and contemporary art, and ever-changing exhibitions.

Castle St. ✆ **01223/748100.** www.kettlesyard.co.uk. Free admission; donations appreciated. Tues–Sun and Mon bank holidays 1:30–4:30pm (late Sept–early Apr 2–4pm). Closed Mon, Good Friday, Dec 24–28, and Jan 1.

Museum of Zoology ★★ MUSEUM   You can see specimens collected by Cambridge graduate Charles Darwin during his voyage on the *Beagle* in the 1830s on display here, as well as rare examples of the dodo and great auk. Specimens from other historic collections gathered during the great expeditions of the 19th century are also here.

Downing St. ✆ **01223/336650.** www.museum.zoo.cam.ac.uk. Free admission; donations appreciated. Tues–Sun and Mon bank holidays 1:30–4:30pm (late Sept–early Apr 2–4pm). Closed Mon, Good Friday, Dec 24–28, and Jan 1.

Scott Polar Research Institute Museum ★★ MUSEUM   After a £1.75 million redesign and reopening in 2010, the only word to describe this unique museum is cool. Very cool. The history of polar exploration is here and includes the last letters of Captain Scott, the expedition diaries of Sir Ernest Shackleton, and artifacts from the British search for the Northwest Passage.

Lensfield Rd. ℭ **01223/336562.** www.spri.cam.ac.uk. Free admission; donations appreciated. Tues–Sat 10am–4pm. Closed Sun, Mon, and public holidays.

Sedgwick Museum of Earth Sciences ★★ MUSEUM   You have to get past the skeleton of an Iguanodon dinosaur to see the rest of this fabulous collection, which includes the remains of a 125,000-year-old hippopotamus found in Cambridgeshire. You'll see a treasure-trove of fossils, rocks, and minerals from around the world as you explore 550 million years of history.

Downing St. ℭ **01223/333456.** www.sedgwickmuseum.org. Free admission; donations appreciated. Mon–Fri 10am–1pm and 2–5pm, Sat 10am–4pm. Closed Sun and public holidays.

Where to Eat
EXPENSIVE

Midsummer House ★★ FRENCH   This has been the best dining in town for many years, and it's the only two-star Michelin restaurant in East Anglia. Its lovely riverside setting on Midsummer Common gives it an extra-special atmosphere. A two-course a la carte dinner menu costs £55, but on Fridays and Saturday, you must choose from two more expensive Tasting Menus at lunch and dinner.

Midsummer Common. ℭ **01223/369299.** www.midsummerhouse.co.uk. Reservations essential. Set lunch £30 for 2 courses, £35 for 3 courses; fixed-price 3-course dinner £73. AE, MC, V. Wed–Sat noon–2pm; Tues–Thurs 7–9:30pm; Fri–Sat 6:30–9:30pm.

MODERATE

Cotto ★ BRITISH/CONTINENTAL   Cotto offers quality food and on the pricey side of moderate, but the £40 three-course fixed-price dinners have seasonal menus and locally sourced ingredients. Main courses such as salt marsh lamb shank or slow roasted venison daube can't be hurried. Lunch dishes are individually priced and include the delightful grilled vegetable salad with Wobbly Bottom goat's cheese for £8.50. Cakes and pastries are also available.

183 East Rd. ℭ **01223/302010.** www.cottocambridge.co.uk. Reservations recommended for dinner. Fixed-price dinner £40; lunch main courses £7.50–£17. AE, MC, V. Tues–Sat 9am–3pm; Thurs–Sat 7–10pm.

INEXPENSIVE

Browns ★ ♣ BRITISH/CONTINENTAL   Browns is popular with students, locals, and visitors, and very welcome after a day of sightseeing. Once part of the famous old Addenbrookes Hospital, the wicker chairs, high ceilings, fans, and conservatory-style airiness create a convivial atmosphere for what is essentially a posh burger restaurant with classic British fare. Try the Suffolk pork belly, or steak, mushroom, and Guinness pie. If you're feeling continental, there are steak frites. It's also a good place for breakfast, brunch, and afternoon tea. Group deals attract students, so it can be noisy or lively depending on how you feel. Outdoor seating is available.

23 Trumpington St. (opposite the Fitzwilliam Museum). ℭ **01223/461655.** www.browns-restaurants. co.uk. Reservations accepted Sat–Sun. Main courses £9–£19. AE, MC, V. Mon–Thurs 10am–10:30pm; Fri–Sat 10am–11pm, Sun 10am–10pm.

Fair Shares Café 🎁 BRITISH   This cafe is highly recommended by locals for its wholesome homemade lunches. Fair-trade products are used wherever possible, and the cafe is run in a non-profit partnership of the church (where it's located) and Cambridgeshire Mencap volunteers, ensuring a friendly, communal atmosphere. Note that some of the volunteers have learning disabilities.

Emmanuel United Reformed Church, Trumpington St. ℂ **01223/351174.** Main courses £4.50–£8. AE, MC, V. Tues–Fri 10:30am–3pm.

Rainbow Vegetarian Café VEGETARIAN/VEGAN   This long-established pioneer of vegetarian eating now offers vegan and gluten-free food and organic wine and cider, as well as an extensive vegetarian menu. Spinach lasagna is the Rainbow's signature dish, but super specials include artichoke parcels and Jamaican patties. There is also a children's menu, and free organic jars of baby food. This award-winning Cambridge institution also serves fair-trade coffee and homemade cakes in its basement setting.

9A King's Parade (across from King's College). ℂ **01223/321551.** www.rainbowcafe.co.uk. Reservations not accepted. Main courses £8–£10. Tues–Sat 10am–10pm; Sun–Mon 10am–4pm.

Yippee Noodle Bar CHINESE   You'll find informal canteen dining here, but there's a sense of style, too. The food is fast and fresh, with a choice of noodles or rice dishes. The communal benches are typical of most noodle bars, and it's very popular with local young people. It is good for vegetarians.

7–9 King St. ℂ **01223/518111.** www.yippeenoodlebar.co.uk. Main courses £7.60–£9.50. Mon–Fri noon–10:30pm; Sat–Sun noon–3pm and 5–10:30pm.

Shopping

There are great shopping opportunities, starting in the central Market Square. Monday to Saturday is the **General Market** with fruit and vegetables, clothes, books, and jewelry, while on Sundays there's the **Arts and Crafts and Local Produce Market** selling crafts plus homemade cakes, fresh bread, and organic food. **All Saints Garden Art and Craft Market** off Trinity Street is also good for gifts and mementos on Saturdays, and there are gift shops galore in **King's Parade,** which runs into Trinity Street and then St. John's Street. There's been a bookstore since 1581 on the present site of the **Cambridge University Press bookshop,** 1–2 Trinity St. (ℂ **01223/333333;** www.cambridge.org), although the bookstore **Heffers,** 20 Trinity Street (ℂ **01223/568568;** www.heffers.co.uk), is a Cambridge institution.

   Rose Crescent, near the market, offers smart clothes and cosmetics shops, while the **Benet Street Area,** or Arts Quarter, off King's Parade, has fashion, ceramics, and jewelry shops. The newest shopping destination is **Grand Arcade,** in St. Andrews Street (ℂ **01223/568568;** www.grandarcade.co.uk), with many high-street shops including **John Lewis** (ℂ **08456/049049;** www.johnlewis.com). Meanwhile, the older **Lion Yard,** St. Tibbs Row (ℂ **01223/350608;** www.thelionyard.co.uk), is right at the heart of the city. But if you're looking for a more bohemian choice of shops, go to **Mill Road,** off Parker's Piece, for all kinds of secondhand shops including **Cambridge Antiques Centre,** at Gwydir Street off Mill Road (ℂ **01223/356391;** www.cambsantiques.com).

Entertainment & Nightlife

Cambridge Corn Exchange, 3 Parsons Court (ℂ **01223/357851;** www.cornex. co.uk), is your best bet for mainstream touring shows, bands, and comedians, and **Cambridge Arts Theatre,** 6 St. Edward's Passage (✆ **01223/503333;** www. cambridgeartstheatre.com), has some wonderful stage productions. It used to be the venue for **Cambridge Footlights,** the university theatre group that produced some of Britain's best-known actors, comedians, and satirists, such as John Cleese and Graham Chapman of the Monty Python team, and Emma Thompson, Hugh Laurie, and Stephen Fry. The Footlights Spring Revue now takes place at the **Amateur Dramatic Club,** in Park Street near Jesus Lane (✆ **01223/300085;** www.adctheatre.com), and it's the place to see other university or local drama productions. **The Junction,** Clifton Way (✆ **01223/511511;** www.junction.co.uk), has well-known bands, comedians, and contemporary stage and dance shows, plus club nights.

Cambridge also has some wonderful old pubs. The oldest is **The Pickerel Inn,** Magdalene Street (✆ **01223/355068**), dating from 1432. It has ceiling beams and little alcoves and is near the river. **The Eagle,** Benet Street, off King's Parade (✆ **01223/505020**), is where Nobel Laureates Watson and Crick first announced their discovery of the DNA double helix. It was also loved by American airmen during World War II. **The Anchor,** Silver Street (✆ **01223/353554**), and **The Mill (Tap & Spile),** 14 Mill Lane, off Silver Street Bridge (✆ **01223/357026**), are good for sitting out near the river. Alternately, escape other tourists at **The Free Press,** Prospect Row (✆ **01223/368337;** www.freepresspub.com), with its cozy bars and courtyard, or try **The Cambridge Blue,** 85–87 Gwydir St. (✆ **01223/471680;** www.the-cambridgeblue.co.uk), which serves good food and has a great beer garden.

Where to Stay

EXPENSIVE

De Vere University Arms ★ At first glance this 19th-century hotel looks as though it belongs to one of the colleges, particularly with its picturesque position on Parker's Piece a few minutes' walk from the heart of the city. Look beyond the modern extension and you'll find many original architectural features, an elegant bar that serves afternoon tea, and the highly regarded **Restaurant 17.** There are Classic and Executive rooms plus two suites, some with four-poster beds, some with Sony PlayStations. Family rooms are also available.

Regent St., Cambridge CB2 1AD. www.devere.co.uk. ✆ **01223/273000.** Fax 01223/315256. 119 units. £140–£200 double; £250 suite. Rates include English breakfast. AE, MC, V. Parking £16. **Amenities:** Restaurant; bar; babysitting; room service. *In room:* TV, hair dryer, Wi-Fi (free).

Hotel Felix ★★ Take a break from the city in this highly rated boutique hotel, a 15-minute walk from the middle of town and set in three acres of landscaped gardens. Both stylish and luxurious, the Victorian mansion is a blend of old and new with specially commissioned modern art and unfussy decor. It has an exceptional restaurant, **Graffiti** (main courses £13–£23), which offers dishes such as filet and braised blade of Tilbury Meadow beef, shallot tart tatin, crisp bone marrow, and cavolo nero. There's a large terrace for drinks, dining, and afternoon tea.

Whitehouse Lane, Huntingdon Rd., Cambridge CB3 OLX. www.hotelfelix.co.uk. ✆ **01223/277977.** Fax 01223/277973. 52 units. £198–£245 double; from £295 suite. Rates include English breakfast. AE, MC, V. Free parking. **Amenities:** Restaurant; bar; access to health club; room service. *In room:* TV, CD, hair dryer, Wi-Fi (£10 per day).

MODERATE

Arundel House Hotel Overlooking the River Cam and Jesus Green, this is one of the loveliest sites in Cambridge. The hotel consists of six connected Victorian houses—all fronted with dark-yellow local bricks. Though not as well appointed as the University Arms or the Felix (see above), it competes successfully with the Gonville (see below) and has very good food. Rooms overlooking the river and green cost more, as do those on lower floors (there's no elevator).

53 Chesterton Rd., Cambridge CB4 3AN. www.arundelhousehotels.co.uk. © **01223/367701.** Fax 01223/367721. 103 units. £95–£150 double; £135–£160 family room. Rates include continental breakfast. AE, MC, V. Free parking. **Amenities:** Restaurant; bar. *In room:* A/C, TV, hair dryer, Wi-Fi (free).

Best Western Gonville Hotel Just a few minutes' walk from town and with a view over Parker's Piece, the city's large expanse of open parkland, this modern hotel is a perfectly acceptable choice, if a little uninspiring. The hotel has a bar, **Chancellors** restaurant, and the Atrium brasserie. Prices are very competitive.

Gonville Place, Cambridge CB1 1LY. www.gonvillehotel.co.uk. © **800/780-7234** in the U.S. and Canada, or 01223/366611. Fax 01223/315470. 80 units. £95–£159 double. AE, MC, V. Free parking. **Amenities:** Restaurant; bar; room service. *In room:* TV, hair dryer, Wi-Fi (free).

INEXPENSIVE

Regent Hotel This is another hotel overlooking Parker's Piece, and very convenient for the sights. It's one of the most desirable of Cambridge's reasonably priced small hotels. The building, a lovely Regency mansion, dates from the 1840s and was Newnham College until it outgrew the site. Rooms are pale and comfortable, and there is a small bar.

41 Regent St., Cambridge CB2 1AB. www.regenthotel.co.uk. © **01223/351470.** Fax 01223/464937. 22 units. £114–£145 double. Rates include continental breakfast. AE, MC, V. **Amenities:** Bar. *In room:* A/C, TV, hair dryer, Wi-Fi (£2 per day).

ELY & THE FENS

70 miles NE of London; 16 miles N of Cambridge

You can see Ely's magnificent cathedral miles before you reach England's second smallest city. The ship of the Fens, as the cathedral is known, was built in the 11th century when Ely was an island surrounded by freshwater marshes. Pilgrims traveled to Ely for centuries to visit the shrine of Saint Etheldreda, until it was destroyed in the Reformation in the mid-1500s. Ten centuries after it was built, the cathedral is still attracting a quarter of a million visitors every year. Most people visit Ely to see the cathedral, and rightly so. It's an extraordinary building with a powerful history to match, and well worth the trip across the Fens, so once you're here this small place—more a market town in feel than a city—on the River Ouse is a lovely place to spend a few hours. Get to know the city properly by taking the **Eel Trail** from **Oliver Cromwell's House,** which now doubles as a tourist office, and follow it through the city and down to the river where **The Maltings** has a restaurant and bar overlooking the river. The circular walk then heads back to town through delightful **Cherry Hill** park up to **Ely Cathedral** and the rest of the city's tourist attractions, its independent shops, colorful pubs, and good range of cafes and restaurants.

Essentials

GETTING THERE There are First Capital Connect trains from London's Kings Cross (some direct, some involve a change at Cambridge onto an INEA service), costing about £24 one-way. If you're driving from Cambridge, take the A10 north.

The **Tourist Information Centre** is at Oliver Cromwell's House, 29 St. Mary's St. (© **01353/662062;** www.ely.org.uk). It's open April to October, daily 10am to 5:30pm, and November to March, Sunday to Friday 11am to 4pm, Saturday 10am to 5pm.

Exploring the Area

Ely Cathedral ★★ CATHEDRAL   The cathedral was built by a monastic community originally founded in the 7th century by Princess Etheldreda, who was declared a saint 17 years after her death in 680. For centuries pilgrims visited the cathedral to see the shrine of Saint Etheldreda, the daughter of the king of East Anglia and estranged wife of King Egfrith of Northumbria. Now the 11th-century cathedral, within the grounds of what is left of the monastery that replaced the one she founded, is regarded as one of England's most beautiful ecclesiastic buildings, as well as an inspirational place of worship. Three services are held every day, all visitors welcomed, and there are concerts and other cultural events throughout the year. However, most visitors are happy just to wander through the cathedral, starting at the Galilee Porch into the West Tower, where a 19th-century labyrinth is laid out on the floor. Ely is the fourth longest cathedral in England, and the massive Norman nave with its string of impressive columns leads to the Octagon Tower and its distinctive lantern roof, which was built in the 14th century when the Norman central tower collapsed. The Octagon is in the Gothic style, but incorporates medieval carvings that tell the story of Etheldreda. Free guided tours are included in the entrance fee from Monday to Saturday, with regular tours during the summer, fewer in the off season. For an extra charge there are guided Octagon Tower tours and West Tower tours. Both include climbing up the towers, which have magnificent views. The Refectory Café, accessed through the West Tower or Cathedral Bookshop, is open daily (afternoons only on Sun). The shop also sells gifts and souvenirs, and there is a Stained Glass Museum in the South Triforium. The **Almonry Tea Rooms and Restaurant** is on the grounds, in a vaulted undercroft, with garden seating in summer.

© **01353/667735.** www.elycathedral.org. Admission £6.50 adults, £5.50 students and seniors, free for children 11 and under. Apr–Oct daily 7am–7pm; Nov–Mar Mon–Sat 7:30am–6pm, Sun 7:30am–5pm.

Ely Museum MUSEUM   Just a few minutes from the cathedral and set in the city's former gaol, this lovely little museum recounts Ely's history from the days of dinosaurs to World War II. You can find out about the Iceni rebellion against the Romans led by Queen Boudica, the effect of the Norman invasion of 1066, and life among the waterways of the Fens from medieval times onward.

Old Gaol, Market St. © **01353/666655.** www.elymuseum.org.uk. Admission £3.50 adults, £2.50 students and seniors, free for children 16 and under. Summer Mon–Sat 10:30am–5pm, Sun 1–5pm; winter Mon–Sat 10:30am–4pm, Sun 1–4pm (closed Tues in winter). Check for Christmas opening.

Oliver Cromwell's House HISTORIC HOME   Oliver Cromwell was the Lord Protector of the Commonwealth after the Civil Wars between 1642 and 1651 left England a short-lived republic for the first and only time in its history. Charles I was executed and Cromwell became "king in all but name"—an extraordinary accomplishment for a gentleman farmer and MP for Cambridge. He lived in Ely for 10 years, and this restored Cromwell family home not only gives an insight into the man himself—a Puritan who "banned Christmas"—but also into 17th-century domestic life. The tourist information office is in part of the building.

29 St. Mary's St. (next to St. Mary's Church). ✆ **01353/662062.** www.visitely.eastcambs.gov.uk. Admission £4.50 adults, £4 seniors and students, £3.10 children 6–16, £13 family ticket, free for children 5 and under. Apr–Oct daily 10am–5pm; Nov–Mar Sun–Fri 11am–4pm, Sat 10am–5pm.

Where to Eat

Escape the crowds at **The Almonry Restaurant & Tea Rooms,** in The College, Ely Cathedral, High Street (✆ **01353/666360;** www.elycathedral.org). Not only is the setting peaceful (a 12th-century undercroft with a garden for summer dining) but the home-cooked lunches and afternoon teas are excellent. Lunch starts at around £11. It's open Monday to Saturday 9am to 5pm and Sunday 11am to 5pm.

Boathouse ★ BRITISH/CONTINENTAL This is the best gastropub-cum-restaurant in town, housed in a converted boathouse that opens onto the Great Ouse, 10 minutes' walk from the city's heart. The menu is seasonal and ingredients are locally sourced; for instance, co-owner Richard Bradley's home-produced sausages are made from Gloucestershire Old Spot pork. There's a set lunch on weekdays with starters including pigeon and black-pudding salad, and main courses such as steamed steak and kidney pudding. Evening meals and Sunday lunches are chosen from an individually priced menu.

5 Annesdale. ✆ **01353/664388.** www.theboathouseely.co.uk Reservations recommended. 2-course lunch £12; 3-course lunch £16; dinner main courses from £11–£16. AE, MC, V. Daily noon–2:30pm (Sun noon–2:45pm) and Mon–Thurs 6:30–9pm, Fri–Sat 6:30–9.30pm, Sun 6:30–8:30pm.

Old Fire Engine House ★ 🍴BRITISH This converted fire station with a walled garden and art gallery is near Oliver Cromwell's House. The menu is British farmhouse, with dishes such as seasonal soups served with crusty bread. Main dishes include rabbit with prunes and bacon, while afternoon tea (£16) is a selection of finger sandwiches, scones with clotted cream, and homemade jam followed by homemade cakes and pastries. In summer you can dine in the garden.

25 St. Mary's St. (opposite St. Mary's Church). ✆ **01353/662582.** www.theoldfireenginehouse.co.uk. Main courses £15–£16. MC, V. Daily noon–2pm, 3:30–5:15pm, and 7:15–9pm.

Where to Stay

Lamb Hotel This coaching inn was known as The Holy Lambe in the 1400s by pilgrims visiting the cathedral, across the street. Today the Lamb is beautifully decorated (rich-hued walls and wooden floors), with traditionally furnished rooms with modern comforts and big polished wood beds. The **restaurant** (main courses £7.50–£15) has a selection of steaks, including a 14-oz. bone-in rib, and there's lots of use of Colman's mustard, which is made in the region. The bar is warm and comfy.

2 Lynn Rd., Ely, Cambridgeshire CB7 4EJ. www.thelambhotel-ely.com. ✆ **01353/663574.** Fax 01353/662023. 31 units. £75–£110 double. Rates include English breakfast. AE, MC, V. Free parking. **Amenities:** Restaurant; bar; room service. *In room:* TV, hair dryer, Wi-Fi (free).

NEWMARKET

62 miles NE of London; 13 miles NE of Cambridge

This old market town on the Cambridgeshire–Suffolk border is the home of **Newmarket Racecourses** and the Jockey Club, and more thoroughbred horses are bred here than anywhere else on the planet. It's no surprise, then, that Newmarket is the headquarters of British horse racing. The town has been vital to the sport since the reign of James I, the Stewart king who first declared the chalky downs outside town perfect for horse racing. His great-grandson Charles II had a house built here so he could attend races, and frequently brought the royal court to Newmarket for weeks at a time. Part of the house survives, now known as **Palace House.** A house opposite is said to have been used by Charles II's mistress Nell Gwynn. **The National Stud** is the showcase for British thoroughbred breeding (tours are available), while the **National Horseracing Museum** is in the High Street. But probably the most exciting reason for visiting is to spend a day at the races. You'll find the Rowley Mile racecourse and July Course on Newmarket Heath. Spring and fall flat races take place at **Rowley Mile,** while summer flat races are at the gorgeous **July Course,** which also stages outdoor concerts and big-name events. The town itself is small with a mix of chain stores and independent shops. Look for **Powters the Pork Shop,** Wellington Street (*C* **01638/662418;** www.powters.co.uk), where you can buy authentic Newmarket sausages. The originals, made by Musks Ltd., are available online (www.musks.com).

Essentials

GETTING THERE   There are regular trains from London's Liverpool Street (change at Cambridge), costing about £28 one-way. If you're driving from Cambridge, head east on the A133.

VISITOR INFORMATION   The **Tourist Information Centre** (*C* **01638/ 719749;** www.visiteastofengland.com) is at the Guineas Shopping Centre. A self-guided walking leaflet, Newmarket Horseshoe Trail, is available there.

Exploring the Area

National Horseracing Museum MUSEUM   Discover the history of 300 years of horse racing in this unique museum housed in the old subscription rooms (early 19th-century betting room). See fine paintings of famous horses, statues, silverware, and royal memorabilia including the preserved head of Persimmon, the best horse bred by the royal family. There's also the skeleton of Hyperion who sired the winners of 748 British races. You can book an Equine Tour (by phone) to take you behind the scenes at stable yards and training grounds; there are various tours and prices start at about £25, including museum entrance. **Palace House** was built for Charles II for his visits to the races; this is all that survives of a much larger palace, but there are still fascinating historical details to see. It now comes under the administration of the National Horseracing Museum and tours are sometimes available. Call for details.

99 High St. *C* **01638/667333.** www.nhrm.co.uk. Admission £6.50 adults, £5.50 seniors, £3.50 children 15 and under, £15 family ticket. Mar–Oct daily 11am–4:30pm (opens 10am on race days); off season Mon–Sat 10am–4:30pm.

National Stud ENTERTAINMENT COMPLEX   See behind the scenes at the home to some of the world's finest horses and a renowned breeding stud operation. During the 75-minute tour you'll see mares, foals, and stallions. Booking is recommended.

Next to the July Course (see above) on the A1303. *C* **01638/663464.** www.nationalstud.co.uk. Admission £7 adults, £5 seniors and children 5–15, £20 family ticket, free for children 4 and under. Feb–Sept daily 11:15am and 2pm; Oct daily 11:15am. Closed Nov–Jan.

Newmarket Racecourses RACECOURSE   The **July Course** is known for its beech trees and thatched-roof buildings; it is one of the loveliest racecourses in the world and part of the English social calendar. Races take place in June, July, and August, highlighted by the July Cup. The **Rowley Mile,** the "Course of Champions," is the focus for spring and fall races with some of the highest-class races in the world. Prestige events include the Guineas Races, the Cesarewitch Handicap, and the Champion Stakes.

Newmarket Racecourses, Westfield House, The Links, Newmarket. ℂ **0844/579-3010.** www.new marketracecourses.co.uk. Ticket prices vary, but are around £10 to £40; online bookings receive a 20% discount. Free for children 17 and under.

Where to Eat & Stay

Best Western Heath Court Hotel   This hotel is close to the Gallops, the exercise area for stables at Newmarket Heath, and a short walk from town. It's very popular during the horse-racing season. The **Carvery** has a pub-like atmosphere and is open for lunch and dinner on weekdays, dinner on Saturday, and lunch on Sunday. **Bertie's Restaurant** has a wide choice of snacks and meals.

Moulton Rd., Newmarket, Suffolk CB8 8DY. www.heathcourthotel.com. ℂ **01638/667171** or 800/780-7234 in the U.S. and Canada. Fax 01638/666533. 43 units. £60–£172 double; £105–£172 studio; £65–£214 family room; £125–£269 suite. Extra bed £40. AE, DC, MC, V. Free parking. **Amenities:** Restaurant; bar; room service. *In room:* TV/DVD, hair dryer, Wi-Fi (free).

Rutland Arms Hotel   This old Georgian building, once a coaching inn and built around a cobbled courtyard, retains a lot of character and is in the heart of Newmarket. It has elegant en suite bedrooms, the reasonably priced **Carriages** restaurant, and the Nell Gwynn lounge bar with open fires in winter.

33 High St., Newmarket, Suffolk CB8 8NB. www.oxfordhotelsandinns.com. ℂ **01638/664251.** Fax 01638/666298. 46 units. £55–£68 double. Rates include English breakfast. MC, V. Free parking. **Amenities:** Restaurant; bar; room service. *In room:* TV, hair dryer, Wi-Fi (£3 per hr.).

Swynford Paddocks ★   This is a beautiful 17th-century country house where Lord Byron once lived and worked. The grounds overlook a stud farm and are idyllic, while the luxury hotel is known for its individually designed rooms, each named after a racing great and some with four-poster beds and claw-foot baths. **Silks Brasserie,** a conservatory with a wooden floor and a colonial touch, serves lunch and dinner. Children's meals are available. There is also outdoor dining and afternoon tea.

London Rd., Six Mile Bottom, Newmarket, Suffolk CB8 0UE. www.swynfordpaddocks.com. ℂ **01638/570234.** Fax 01638/570283. 15 units. £135–£175 double; prices rise during races. Rates include English breakfast. AE, DC, MC, V. Free parking. **Amenities:** 2 restaurants; bar; room service. *In room:* TV, hair dryer, Wi-Fi (free).

SAFFRON WALDEN

40 miles NE of London; 14 miles SE of Cambridge

The town is named after the saffron crocus, harvested here to make dye for East Anglia's pre-industrial textile-makers, and it is now one of the best-preserved medieval market towns in Britain. There is also Georgian architecture (and it's not totally free from modern additions), but concentrate on the half-timbered buildings, many filled with antiques shops and galleries. You'll want to see the spectacular **St. Mary the Virgin Church,** award-winning **Saffron Walden Museum,** the ruined mote-and-bailey castle, and the ancient turf maze on the common nearby. **Fry Public Art Gallery** is fascinating and **Bridge End Garden** a surprise treat, and there are colorful stalls on Tuesdays and Saturdays in the Market Place. A **Country Market** takes place on Friday mornings at the back of the town hall. The two nationally important attractions just outside town are **Audley End,** one of the grandest stately homes in England, and the **Imperial War Museum Duxford,** which has many vintage aircraft including World War II planes and a Concorde.

Many of Saffron Walden's old buildings are plastered with fine examples of pargeting, a decorative effect that is unique to parts of East Anglia. You'll see more at the nearby village of **Thaxted,** where **St. John the Baptist Church** is one of the most impressive in Essex. Gustav Holst lived in the village from 1914 to 1925 and worked on *The Planets* here. He also started a music festival that was resurrected in 1980 and takes place in the summer. **Finchingfield** is another pretty Essex village worth calling at for a stroll around the antiques shops or to feed the ducks on the village green.

Essentials

GETTING THERE   NXEA Trains take about an hour from London's Liverpool Street Station to Audley End (about £17), 2 miles away. If you're driving from London, it's just off the M11 at junction 8.

VISITOR INFORMATION   The **Tourist Information Centre,** 1 Market Place (✆ **01799/524002;** www.visitsaffronwalden.gov.uk), should have free copies of "The Saffron Walden Town Trail."

Exploring the Area

Audley End HISTORIC SITE   Charles II is one of the former owners of this house, originally built in 1538 on the grounds of Walden Abbey after the Reformation. Architects Sir Christopher Wren and Robert Adam were involved in redesigns through the centuries, and landscape legend Capability Brown remodeled the grounds. The highlights these days are the kitchen, dairy, larder, and laundry in the recently refurbished service wing, as well as the gardens and parkland and the restored stable block. The house is on the B1383.

Insider tip: Entrance is free to English Heritage members; 1-week or 2-week Overseas Visitors Passes are available from £20. Buy online for collection at any English Heritage property.

Audley End, Saffron Walden. ✆ **01638/667333.** www.english-heritage.org.uk. Admission £13 adults, £7.50 children 5–15, £33 family ticket. Wed–Sun Apr–Sept 11am–5pm (grounds until 6pm), Oct until 4pm (grounds 5pm); closed Nov–Mar. Grounds only weekends Nov–Christmas and early Feb, then Wed–Sun until end Mar mostly 10am–4pm. House sometimes open only for guided tours; see website for details.

Bridge End Garden GARDEN   This award-winning Victorian garden was voted East Anglia's best picnic spot. The grade II listed garden was laid out by the Gibson family in the 19th century as a series of garden rooms including a kitchen garden.

Bridge St. and Castle St. ✆ **01799/524002.** www.visitessex.com. Free admission anytime.

Imperial War Museum Duxford MUSEUM   This is Britain's leading air museum, vast hangars at a real airfield (it was a World War I airfield and one of the earliest Air Force stations). Arrive early because there's lots to see. Duxford Airfield played its part in both World Wars, as you'll see in the 1940s' Operations Room and the permanent Battle of Britain exhibition, which has a Spitfire and Hurricane on display. There are more than 30 historic aircraft in the AirSpace hangar, including a Concorde which you can tour, while the American Air

Museum houses a huge collection of U.S. warplanes. And there's much more, including some of the best air shows in Britain and other regular events.

Duxford Airfield, Duxford. ✆ **01223/835000.** www.iwm.org.uk. Admission £17 adults, £14 seniors, children 15 and under free. Mid-Mar-Oct daily 10am-6pm, Nov-Mar daily 10am-4pm (last admission 5pm in summer, 3pm in winter).

Saffron Walden Museum MUSEUM This very traditional but charming museum is award winning and family friendly, with displays of local history, archeology, furniture, ceramics, and natural history. The ruins of the town's 12th-century castle are on the grounds, which are perfect for picnics.

Museum St. ✆ **01799/510334.** www.visitsaffronwalden.gov.uk. Admission £1.50 adults, free for children under 18. Mar-Oct Mon-Sat 10am-5pm; Sun and bank holidays 2-5pm; Nov-Feb Mon-Sat 10am-4:30pm, Sun and bank holidays 2-4:30pm. Closed Dec 24-25.

St. Mary the Virgin Church CHURCH The largest church in Essex is, like many East Anglian churches, light and airy. It was built in 1430, under the watchful eye of John Wastell, who designed the Chapel at King's College, Cambridge.

Church Path. ✆ **01799/506024.** www.stmaryssaffronwalden.org. Admission £1.50, free for children under 18. Open daily.

Where to Eat & Stay

The Cricketers ★ There are no hotels in Saffron Walden, although the Tourist Information Office (see above) can help you find B&Bs. Alternatively, try The Cricketers in Clavering, just the other side of Newport, which has a mix of contemporary and four-poster bedrooms in a 16th-century inn. It's been owned and run by TV chef Jamie Oliver's parents, Trevor and Sally, since the 1970s, so the food is award winning and was well regarded even before Jamie became a catering superstar. Main meals are pricey—£15 for homemade steak-and-ale pie is the cheapest—but the food is good.

Wicken Rd., Clavering, Essex CB11 4QT. www.thecricketers.co.uk. ✆ **01799/550442.** Fax 01799/550882. 14 units. £95-£115 double. AE, MC, V. Free parking. **Amenities:** Restaurant; bar. *In room:* TV, hair dryer, Wi-Fi (free).

CONSTABLE COUNTRY

63 miles NE of London; 8 miles NE of Colchester

Dedham Vale was already known as Constable Country when the artist John Constable was still alive. Nearly 200 years later, this Area of Outstanding Natural Beauty on the Essex–Suffolk border is still a magnet for art lovers. Many are drawn to **East Bergholt,** the pretty village where Constable was born; to **Dedham,** the small market town where he went to school; and to **Flatford Mill,** which he immortalized in his paintings. There's a display dedicated to Constable at the National Trust's **Bridge Cottage** near Flatford Mill. Constable Country also takes in three long-distance footpaths: the **Essex Way,** the **Stour Valley Path,** and the **Suffolk Coast and Heaths Path.** It's also only an easy hour's walk through lovely countryside from **Manningtree** railway station.

In addition to the Constable connection, Dedham is home to the **Sir Alfred Munnings Art Museum,** which was created in the artist's own home after his death in 1959. His widow set up a trust fund to establish the museum, and it is filled with his work and personal possessions. Not far away, at **Sudbury,** is the former home of 18th-century artist Thomas Gainsborough. As founder of the English school of painting, he was much admired by Constable, who once said: "I fancy I see a Gainsborough in every hedge and hollow tree." Gainsborough's house contains more of his paintings, drawings, and prints than can be seen anywhere else. But the greatest glory of Constable Country is still what it was in Constable's time: A lazy river meandering through green fields past ancient trees and hedgerows under the huge East Anglian skies.

Essentials

GETTING THERE Trains (NXEA) leave hourly from London's Liverpool Street Station to Sudbury, an 80-minute journey (changing at Marks Tey), or several times an hour to Manningtree, around an hour's ride; both cost about £25 one-way. It's also possible to take the train to Colchester, 5 miles from Dedham. Taxis are available at the station, and there are buses from the bus station on **Queen Street** (*𝄞* **01206/ 282645;** www.firstgroup.com).

If you're driving from London, take the A12 past Colchester and turn off at East Bergholt, following signs for Dedham.

Exploring the Area

The focal point of Dedham is the Georgian high street with its small independent shops and cafes and the Dedham Grammar School on Royal Square, where Constable was once a pupil. The school had a Royal Charter from Elizabeth I in 1575 and attracted wealthy families to the town during Georgian times, hence the Georgian facades over medieval buildings and the Georgian Assembly Rooms, which are still used for social events. At Dedham's heart is St. Mary's Church, which featured in much of John Constable's work and where his painting *The Ascension* is on permanent display. Many people from this part of Essex were among the Pilgrims to America, and there are carvings in the church pews to commemorate *The Mayflower* and other U.S. connections.

Flatford Mill & Bridge Cottage HISTORIC SITE   There is no public access to Flatford Mill, which now runs art courses, but you can walk around the mill pond and along grassy footpaths by the river, providing ample opportunity to follow in Constable's footsteps or just have a picnic. Signposts direct drivers to the Flatford Mill parking lot, and there's a small Tourist Information Centre on the road down to the mill. Farther along the road is Bridge Cottage, owned by the National Trust, where there's a permanent exhibition about Constable and a cafe in the rest of the cottage. **River Stour Trust** boat trips leave from nearby (Sun and bank holidays; *𝄞* **01787/313199;** www.riverstourtrust.org), or you can walk along the riverbank.

Flatford, East Begholt. *𝄞* **01206/298260.** www.nationaltrust.org.uk. Free admission. Opening hours vary according to season.

Sir Alfred Munnings Art Museum MUSEUM   Munnings was born in 1878, and his early work captured the disappearing country people and scenes of East Anglia, but he is best known for his equestrian paintings; he was the official war artist to the Canadian Cavalry Brigade during World War I. His most famous paintings are of racehorses and courses, and many of these are displayed in the relaxing surroundings of his Dedham home. Munnings left his paintings to the nation, and his widow set up the trust that now runs the museum, which includes two galleries, beautiful gardens, and a cafe.

Castle House, East Lane, Dedham. *©* **01206/322127.** www.siralfredmunnings.co.uk. Admission £5 adults, £1 children 5–15. Apr–Oct Wed–Thurs and Sat–Sun 2–5pm.

Where to Eat & Stay

Maison Talbooth ★★★   This Victorian country house, which overlooks the Stour Valley, has been transformed into an award-winning designer hotel with 12 luxury suites, a day spa, and a modern outdoor pool with sun-lounge area and hot tub, plus a tennis court. Lunch and afternoon tea are available, and its sister hotel, **Milsoms,** on the same road (*©* **01206/322795**), has an informal all-day bistro as well as en suite rooms. The company also owns **Le Talbooth** restaurant (*©* **01206/322367**), a short drive away in Gun Hill, over the other side of the A12.

Stratford Rd., Dedham, Colchester CO7 6HN. www.milsomhotels.co.uk. *©* **01206/322367.** Fax 01206/ 322752. 12 units. £195–£405 double. Rates include continental breakfast. AE, MC, V. Take the Stratford Road ½ mile west of the town. **Amenities:** Bar; babysitting; outdoor heated pool; room service; spa; tennis court. *In room:* TV, hair dryer, Wi-Fi (free).

The Sun Inn ★   This old coaching inn has beautiful boutique hotel bedrooms, two with four-poster beds, a cozy bar with real ale and Suffolk cider, and a highly respected restaurant serving local produce with an Italian twist. There's a lunchtime bar menu and children's menu.

High St., Dedham, Colchester CO7 6DF. www.thesuninndedham.com. *©* **01206/323351.** 5 units. £105–£160 double (special offers available). Rates include English breakfast. AE, DC, MC, V. Free parking. **Amenities:** Restaurant; bar; room service. *In room:* TV, CD player, hair dryer.

SUDBURY

This busy little market town, at the heart of the pre-Industrial Revolution weaving industry, was one of the "wool towns" that created so much wealth in East Anglia, as you can see with one glance at the impressive **St. Peter's Church,** which dominates the market place where there are stalls on Thursdays and Saturdays. Although no longer used as a church, it is a focal point of community events with regular concerts and exhibitions. Outside is a statue of artist Thomas Gainsborough, who was born in a house down the hill. **Gainsborough's House** is now the main attraction in Sudbury, but there are also marvelous walks across the commons and meadow around the River Stour, which encloses the town on three sides. **Sudbury Heritage Centre & Museum** traces the town's history from before its mention in the 1086 *Domesday Book* through its woolen-cloth prosperity in the Middle Ages to the 19th-century silk mills, which ensured the town continued to be wealthy until the 20th century. Nearby is **Long Melford,** full of antiques shops, a beautiful "wool church," and the National Trust's **Melford Hall** (*©* **01787/376395;** www.nationaltrust.org.uk), where Beatrix Potter was a regular visitor.

Exploring the Area

Gainsborough's House HISTORIC HOME   Thomas Gainsborough was born here in 1727, and by the time he died in 1788 he had become one of Britain's greatest painters. The biggest collection of his paintings, drawings, and prints are exhibited here in this house, built in 1500, with its Georgian facade and later additions. The museum also holds exhibitions of other artists' work and runs art courses.

46 Gainsborough St. ℂ **01787/372958.** www.gainsborough.org. Admission £4.50 adults, £2 students and children 5–18. Mon–Sat 10am–5pm. Closed Sun, Dec 24–Jan 2, and Good Friday.

Sudbury Heritage Centre & Museum MUSEUM You'll find the town's Tourist Information Office here as well as the museum, which is in the old gaol. Pick up a leaflet for the Talbot Trail, which starts here and guides you to the town's places of interest.

Gaol Lane. ℂ **01787/881320.** www.sudburysuffolk.co.uk. Free admission. Mon–Sat 10am–4pm. Closed Sun, Dec 24–Jan 2, and Good Friday.

Where to Eat & Stay

The Mill ★★★ You can still see the working mill wheel behind a glass screen in the oak beam restaurant of this old world hotel. You can also see the mummified cat behind another glass screen, which the medieval builders bricked into the mill floor for good luck. This isn't a boutique hotel but it has a relaxing atmosphere with views over the commons to the river from the restaurant and bar. You can get snacks in the bar, which has an outdoor terrace, but booking is recommended for the restaurant in summer.

Walnut Tree Lane, Sudbury, Suffolk CO10 1BD. www.themillhotelsudbury.co.uk. ℂ **01787/375544.** Fax 01787/373027. 56 units. £51–£71 double. Rates include English breakfast. AE, DC, MC, V. **Amenities:** Bar; restaurant; room service; Wi-Fi (free, in public areas). *In room:* TV, hair dryer.

COLCHESTER & THE ESSEX COAST

62 miles NE of London; 48 miles E of Cambridge; 59 miles S of Norwich

Colchester is the U.K.'s oldest recorded town and was the Roman capital of Britain. It still has the remains of Roman walls, gates, and a temple to prove it, but unlike other cities steeped in history it has never made much of its cultural heritage. It was at Camulodnum, now Colchester, that the British kings of Gosbecks surrendered to Emperor Claudius in A.D. 43. The Romans took over the settlement, but 17 years later it was razed to the ground and every Roman executed by Queen Boudicca and the Iceni tribe of Suffolk and Norfolk.

The Norman invaders of 1066 built **Colchester Castle** over the Roman Temple of Claudius, and you can still spot the Roman tiles and bricks they used. During the English Civil War in 1648, the town was besieged by the Parliamentary army for nearly 3 months, which is when the Roman walls were breached (stretches of the wall are visible). Over the centuries, Colchester has thrived as a busy market town and is one of the most popular shopping destinations in Essex. However, as tourists finally begin to discover East Anglia, Colchester's hidden delights are getting more of the limelight. This includes the varied coastline 16 miles away, which has bucket-and-spade seaside resorts such as **Walton-on-the-Naze** and **Clacton-on-Sea** plus Walton's more upmarket relative **Frinton-on-Sea.** They may not compare with the dramatic coastline of the west, but the sand is good and you pass through some lovely villages to reach the sea. More unique is the **Blackwater Estuary,** where you'll find **Mersea Island** and **Maldon,** home of Maldon sea salt.

Essentials

GETTING THERE There are up to five Colchester-bound trains (NXEA) leaving London's Liverpool Street, most taking less than an hour and costing about £23 one-way. If you're driving from London, take the A12; from Cambridge take the A120 and join the A12 north.

VISITOR INFORMATION The **Tourist Information Centre** is opposite Castle Park at 1 Queen St. (*C* **01206/282920;** www.visitcolchester.com). April to June, it's open Monday to Saturday 9am to 5pm; July and August, Monday to Saturday 9:30am to 5:30pm and Sunday 11am to 4pm; and October to March Monday to Saturday 10am to 5pm and Sunday 11am to 4pm.

Exploring the Area

Beth Chatto Gardens ★ GARDEN Essex has the least rainfall in Britain, and these famous gardens pioneered the concept of drought-tolerant planting in the U.K. when they opened in 1960, before ecology was trendy. The result is a gravel garden that's at its best in spring and early summer. There's also a luscious water garden, which is every shade of green from early summer to fall. A little cafe sells locally made cakes and ice creams.

Elmstead Market. *C* **01206/331292.** www.bethchatto.co.uk. Admission £6, free for children 13 and under. Mon–Sat 9am–4pm, Sun 10am–4pm.

Colchester Castle ☺ CASTLE Just off the main shopping area and within the delightful Victorian Castle Park, you'll find Colchester's most important historical building: the castle. The Norman keep is said to be the biggest and best preserved in Europe, and inside you'll find hands-on displays that recount Britain's history over the last 2,000 years. There are plenty of child-friendly activities to make family visits even more enjoyable, regular exhibitions, and a good cafe. The park has riverside walks, a cafe, and children's play area and boating lake.

Castle Park. *C* **01206/282939.** www.colchestermuseums.org.uk Admission £6 adults, £3.80 children, £16 family ticket. Mon–Sat 10am–5pm, Sun 11am–5pm.

Colchester Zoo ☺ ZOO You can spend a full day at this award-winning zoo, which has one of the largest collection of animals in Europe. Highlights include seeing the elephants and giraffes, and walking through the underwater viewing tunnel to watch the sea lions. This is a big site, with some fairly steep paths in places.

Maldon Rd., Stanway. *C* **01206/331292.** www.colchester-zoo.com. Admission £16–£18 adults, £13–£15 seniors, £10–£11 children 5–15. Daily 9:30am to between 4:30 and 6.30pm depending on season.

Hollytrees Museum MUSEUM This is an award-winning social-history museum in an impressive Georgian mansion with collections of toys and decorative arts from the last 300 years, plus domestic items from the recent past which will take you for a walk down memory lane.

High St. *C* **01206/282940.** www.colchestermuseums.org.uk. Free admission. Mon–Sat 10am–5pm, Sun 11am–5pm.

Natural History Museum MUSEUM The decommissioned All Saints Church is the unusual setting for this natural heritage museum, which looks at the Essex countryside, coast, and urban environments.

Entertainment & Nightlife

The Mercury Theatre, Balkerne Gate (✆ **01206/573948;** www.mercurytheatre. co.uk), is a first-class rep theatre that produces serious drama but also features touring shows, bands, and comedians. Big name touring shows can be seen at **Charter Hall,** Cowdray Avenue (✆ **01206/282020;** www.charter-hall.co.uk). **Colchester Arts Centre,** Church Street (✆ **01206/500900;** www.colchesterartscentre.com), is also a good venue for live bands and comedy shows, while **Essex University,** Wivenhoe Park, has Comedy Central Live nights, plus music and films, at its **Lakeside Theatre** (✆ **01206/573948;** www.essex.ac.uk).

There are many traditional pubs in Colchester, and one of the oldest is **The Marquis,** 24–25 North Hill (✆ **01206/577630**), which has real ale and pub food, plus bands, karaoke, quiz nights, and televised sport. It's popular with students so expect it to be lively. More upmarket is **The King's Arms,** 63 Crouch St. (✆ **01206/572886;** www.gkpubs.co.uk), a stripped-wood contemporary-style pub that has a wine menu as well as local Greene King beers and serves food from 11am to 9pm. Farther along

WEST MERSEA & maldon

You don't need a ferry to get over to Mersea Island; the narrow causeway, which is flooded twice a day by the incoming tide, is exciting enough. This sparsely populated chunk of land in the Blackwater Estuary has fine walks in unspoiled countryside and one of the most popular fish restaurants in Essex. The best place to head for a walk is **Cudmore Grove Country Park,** East Mersea (✆ **01206/383868;** www.visitparks. co.uk), where there's a beach and paths for walkers and cyclists, while **The Company Shed,** 129 Coast Rd., West Mersea (✆ **01206/382700;** www.west-mersea. co.uk), is the place to eat. Once just a fish shack, it is now a fishmonger's where you can choose what you want from the catch of the day, and they'll cook it for you to eat at old retro Formica tables (bring your own drink and bread). In summer the place is packed and parking hard to find.

At the southern end of the Blackwater Estuary you'll find Maldon, a picturesque little seafaring town where distinctive Thames sailing barges are moored at Hythe Quay. The town is on a small hill winding down to the Hythe, the most popular area of town. Here you'll find riverside pubs **The Jolly Sailor** (✆ **01621/ 853463;** www.jollysailor.com), which offers meals and lodging, and **The Queens Head** (✆ **01621/854112;** www. thequeensheadmalson), which has seasonal menus. Next door is **Promenade Park,** with a riverside walk, great children's play areas, and good parking facilities. Maldon is the second oldest town in Essex after Colchester, with a rich history of Saxon, Danish, and Viking conflicts. Now it's just a lovely place to explore the mud flats and marshes, for instance at nearby **Heybridge Basin,** where you can walk along the sea wall with corn fields on one side and migrating seabirds on the other. Farther east around the coast is **Bradwell-on-Sea,** possibly the most remote corner of Essex, where you can walk to the remarkable, barn-like chapel of **St. Peter-on-the-Wall** (✆ **01621/ 776203;** www.bradwellchapel.org), built by St. Cedd in A.D. 645. The original building is still in use today.

is **The Bull,** 2–4 Crouch St. (℡ **01206/366647;** www.thebullcolchester.co.uk), regarded as the city's top music venue.

Where to Eat & Stay

North Hill Hotel ★ 🏨 A historic building with contemporary style is a winning combination in this simple but splendid hotel. It's on a quiet road close to the High Street and only a 10-minute walk from the main railway station. There's an NCP parking lot opposite where you can get discounted parking (£5 per visit). **The Green Room Restaurant** uses local produce such as Mersea Island oysters and Blythburgh pork for its seasonal menus. There are traditional British dishes such as steamed steak and kidney pudding, too. The lunch menu starts at £6.25 for salmon and herb fishcakes and rises to £7.95 for beer-battered fish and chips.

North Hill, Colchester CB2 1AD. www.northhillhotel.com. ℡ **01206/574001.** 13 units. £88 double; £98 family room. Rates include English breakfast. AE, MC, V. Parking £5. **Amenities:** Restaurant; bar; room service. *In room:* TV, hair dryer, Wi-Fi (free).

BURY ST. EDMUNDS

70 miles NE of London; 25 miles E of Cambridge; 9 miles N of Lavenham

This is a cathedral city and a classic old market town, still "a handsome little town, of thriving and cleanly appearance," as Charles Dickens described it in *The Pickwick Papers*. Bury St. Edmunds was founded thanks to its **Benedictine abbey** in 1020, and named after King Edmund of the East Angles, who was buried here in 903. According to legend, England's reformer barons met in the abbey in 1214 and agreed to force King John to sign the Charter of Liberties, which led to the Magna Carta of 1215—the most significant document in English history because it introduced the right of law. Of course Bury St. Edmunds now has many modern buildings, such as the smart, new **Arc shopping center,** but there are several lovely old corners with impressive echoes of its medieval past, too. The city was also prosperous during the 17th and 18th centuries thanks to East Anglia's textiles industry, as you can see from the number of fine buildings, such as the **Theatre Royal,** the only surviving Regency theatre in the U.K., and the **Athenaeum,** once the Assembly Rooms, where balls were held in Georgian times, 300 years ago. As an introduction to the town, you can book a **guided tour** at the Tourist Information Centre. Markets are held on Wednesdays and Saturdays.

Essentials

GETTING THERE Trains from London's Liverpool Street (change at Ipswich), or Kings Cross (change at Cambridge), take 1½ hours. Trains from Cambridge (£8.50) take 40 minutes and **Stagecoach** buses (℡ **01223/423578;** www.stagecoachbus. com) leave the city's Drummer Street Station.

By car from London take the M25 to the M11, and the A45 near Cambridge. It takes about 1½ hours. It's a 45-minute drive from Cambridge on the A45.

VISITOR INFORMATION The **Bury St. Edmunds Tourist Information Centre,** 6 Angel Hill (℡ **01284/764667;** www.stedmundsbury.gov.uk), is open Easter to October, Monday to Saturday 9:30am to 5pm. May to September it also opens Sunday 10am to 3pm. From November to Easter it's open Monday to Friday 10am to 4pm, Saturday 10am to 1pm; and bank holidays 10am to 3pm.

The 17-day **Bury St. Edmunds Festival** (© **01284/ 758000;** www.buryfestival.co.uk) is held every May and includes everything from classical to contemporary music, exhibitions, talks, walks, films, plays, and a fireworks display.

Exploring the Area

Abbey of Bury St. Edmunds ★★ ABBEY   The abbey was among the largest Norman buildings in Europe and there are still signs of its greatness, particularly the lofty **Abbey Gate** on Crown Street. The abbey fell into disrepair after Henry VIII's Dissolution of the monasteries, but the stone gate tower survived and is now the entrance to the formal garden set in the old abbey grounds. Just along the street is **St. Mary's Church** (© **01284/754680;** www.stmarystpeter.net), part of the original complex, the third largest parish church in the country, and burial place of Henry VIII's sister Mary, mother of Lady Jane Grey who briefly succeeded Henry VIII's son Edward VI. A team of stewards is on hand with information. Next door is the Norman tower, gateway to the abbey precincts, which houses the bells of the adjoining cathedral. **St. Edmundsbury Cathedral** was the parish church of St. James when it was built in the 12th century. A 16th-century nave was added, followed by a 19th-century chancel (by ecclesiastical architect Sir Gilbert Scott, designer of London's Albert Memorial), and it was declared a cathedral in 1914. It remained unfinished until 2005, when a tower was finally built, and 2010 saw the inauguration of a grandiose new organ and the unveiling of an arched, painted wooden ceiling in the tower. In the Cathedral Centre is a good Refectory, which serves lunch and snacks from Monday to Saturday, and a shop selling souvenirs such as CDs of the choir. You can still see a few abbey ruins, including Samson Tower, in the abbey grounds, now the **Abbey Gardens.** This was laid out as a botanic garden in 1831. It is now a public park, with colorful summer bedding displays, the Sensory Garden, and the Pilgrim's Herb Garden. There's also an aviary, play area, crazy golf, and other sports facilities, plus a cafe.

Angel Hill. © **01284/748720.** www.stedscathedral.co.uk. Free, but donations welcomed. Daily 8am–6pm. St. Mary's © **01284/754680.** www.stmarystpeter.net. Donations welcomed. Abbey Gardens and ruins open year-round Mon–Sat 7:30am to dusk, Sun 9am to dusk.

Greene King Brewery Visitor Centre BREWERY   Real ale fans will enjoy a pilgrimage to the home of Abbot Ale and Old Speckled Hen. The visitor center museum tells the story of how the Greene and King families founded the present company in 1887, and there are tours through the historic brewery with tastings at the Brewery Tap.

Westgate Street. © **01284/714297.** www.greeneking.co.uk. Tours £8, children 11 and under not admitted. Tours daily; contact center for times and advance booking.

Ickworth House HISTORIC SITE   The extraordinary home of the eccentric Hervey family is a central rotunda with two wings running east and west, set in formal gardens within a superb country estate. It's a fabulous place for walking, cycling, or just exploring. The house was built for the 4th Earl of Bristol, and the central rotunda contains many of the family's personal possessions, including an impressive collection of silver. One wing is now a lovely cafe and restaurant while the other is an extremely comfortable hotel, with a fine restaurant open to non-guests.

The Rotunda, Horringer. © **01284/735270.** www.nationaltrust.org. Admission to house, park, and gardens £8.30 adults, £3.65 children 5–15, £22 family ticket; park and gardens only £4.20 adults, £1 children, £12 family ticket. House open Mar–Oct 11am–5pm; closed Nov–Feb. Gardens open Mar–Oct daily 10am–5pm; Nov–Apr daily 11am–4pm; park open daily 8am–8pm.

Moyse's Hall Museum MUSEUM   The building dates back to 1180 and is one of the last Norman houses left in the U.K. It has had many uses, including the town gaol and a pub, and became the local museum in 1899. The Medieval Gallery focuses on the abbey and has a locket containing Mary Tudor's hair.

Cornhill. ✆ **01284/706183.** www.moyseshall.org. Admission £4 adults, £2 children 5–15, £9 family, free for children 4 and under. Daily 10am–5pm. Closed bank holidays.

Suffolk Regiment Museum MUSEUM   One of the finest regimental collections in the U.K., housed in the former officers' mess. The rhino-horn powder flask of Tippoo Sultan of Mysore is among the medals, badges, uniforms, flags, and more.

The Keep, Gibraltar Barracks, Newmarket Rd. ✆ **01284/769505.** www.suffolkregiment.org. Free admission. Open 1st and 3rd Wed of each month and 1st Sun of each month 9:30am–3:30pm.

Theatre Royal THEATRE   The best way to experience the intimacy of the only surviving Regency theatre in the U.K. is to see a show, but you can also tour the building, which opened for business in 1819. Tours vary, so contact the theatre for details.

5 Westgate St. ✆ **01284/769505.** www.theatreroyal.org.

West Stow Country Park & Anglo Saxon Village HISTORIC SITE   Six miles outside Bury St. Edmunds off the A1101 you'll find this reconstructed village on the site of an Anglo-Saxon settlement. There are historic re-enactments and guided walks. The village is set on 50.5 hectares (125 acres) of country park (free admission), which has nature trails, woods, a river and lake, play areas, a shop, and a cafe.

West Stow. ✆ **01284/728718.** www.stedmundsbury.gov.uk Admission village £6 adults, £4 children, £18 family ticket. Tickets allow 5 additional visits or entrance to Moyse's Hall (see above). Village daily 10am–5pm. Country park daily 9am–8pm (closes 5pm in winter).

Entertainment & Nightlife

The **Theatre Royal** (see above) has been entertaining the people of Bury St. Edmunds for several centuries, but now there's also **The Apex,** Charter Square (✆ **01284/758100;** www.theapex.co.uk), where you can see concerts and live bands. The modern entertainment venue is in the new Arc shopping center a few minutes from the center of town. There are plenty of traditional pubs in town, but one you should see is the **Nutshell,** at the Traverse and Abbeygate Street (✆ **01284/764867**), the smallest pub in England. If that's looking a bit full, try the 17th-century **Dog & Partridge,** 29 Crown St. (✆ **01284/764792**), where the bar scenes from the BBC detective series *Lovejoy* were filmed. The **Masons Arms,** 14 Whiting St. (✆ **01284/753955**), has a family atmosphere and welcomes children, with home-cooked food and a patio garden. The award-winning **One Bull** pub, Angel Hill (✆ **01284/848220;** www.theonebull.co.uk), serves superior pub grub in a relaxed but contemporary atmosphere, while its sister pub, **The Beerhouse,** 1 Tayfen Rd. (✆ **01284/766415;** www.burybeerhouse.co.uk), sells real ales and plans to open a micro-brewery.

Where to Eat & Stay

Angel Hotel ★   Ivy covers the grand Georgian facade of what was originally a smaller 15th-century coaching inn overlooking Abbey Gardens and the cathedral. It aims for an upmarket, home-away-from-home atmosphere with both contemporary and shabby-chic bedrooms, and the **Angel Eaterie** offers a good-value set-price lunch menu and a la carte menu at lunch and dinner. Keep an eye out for special offers.

3 Angel Hill, Bury St. Edmunds, Suffolk P33 1LT. www.theangel.co.uk. © **01284/714000.** Fax 01284/714001. 75 units. £125–£145 double; £205–£260 suite. Rates include English breakfast. AE, DC, MC, V. Free parking. **Amenities:** 2 restaurants; bar; babysitting; room service. *In room:* A/C (in some), TV, hair dryer, Wi-Fi (free).

Ickworth Hotel ★★★ ☺ Wellies (boots) at the grand front door of this stately home-turned-grand-family-hotel speak volumes. Borrow them for walks in 728 hectares (1,800 acres) of parkland, then just put them back. It's English country-house hospitality and part of the Luxury Family Hotels group. Half of this Palladian palace is National Trust (guests have free entry), but hotel guests get to stay in the high-ceilinged rooms and walk the echoing corridors. Rooms are big and comfy, with the personal feel of a house, and children can run free; there are also one- and two-bedroom apartments in the Dower House, in the grounds near the church, and the three-bedroom Butler's Lodge in a walled garden. There's a big swimming pool in a barn, a cellar games room with table tennis and PlayStation, and a tennis court and trampoline outside; adults get the spa. There are two excellent restaurants, **Frederick's** (adults only) and the **Conservatory,** the original orangery, for family meals and huge breakfasts.

Horringer, Bury St. Edmunds, Suffolk IP29 5QE. www.ickworthhotel.co.uk. © **01284/735350.** 38 units (inc. 11 apartments in Dower House, and Butler's Lodge). £405–£485 double; £305–£385 apartments. Rates include dinner and breakfast. AE, DC, MC, V. Free parking. **Amenities:** 2 restaurants; bar; bikes; room service, indoor pool; spa. *In room:* TV/DVD, hair dryer, Wi-Fi (free).

LAVENHAM ★

66 miles N of London; 35 miles S of Cambridge; 9 miles S of Bury St. Edmunds

This is a classic Suffolk "wool village" with some of the best surviving examples of medieval architecture in England. It's full of half-timbered houses with the traditional Suffolk pink wash, but the jewel in the crown is the **Guildhall** on the main square, now owned by the National Trust. The huge **Church of St. Peter and St. Paul** has wonderful carvings on the misericords and the chancel screen, as well as ornate tombs.

Essentials

GETTING THERE Trains go from London's Liverpool Street Station to Colchester with connections to Sudbury. For connecting buses, contact **Chambers & Son** (© **01787/227233;** www.chamberscoaches.co.uk). Trip time is up to 2½ hours.

If you're driving from Bury St. Edmunds, take the A134 south then follow signs to Lavenham on the A1141.

VISITOR INFORMATION The **Lavenham Tourist Information Centre,** Lady Street (© **01787/248207;** www.southandheartofsuffolk.org), is open from Easter to October, daily 10am to 4:45pm and weekends from November to March.

ORGANIZED TOURS The Tourist Information Centre (see above) offers guided walking tours of the village from Easter to October (Sat 2:30pm, Sun, and bank holiday Mon 11am). Cost is £3, free for children 13 and under. Booking ahead is recommended.

Exploring the Town

There are plenty of antiques shops and lovely cafes. **Timbers,** High Street (*© 01787/247218*), houses 24 antiques and collectibles stalls, selling books, toys, military artifacts, glass, porcelain, and more. It's open daily. One of the most interesting cafes is **Tickled Pink Tearooms,** 17 High St. (*© 01787/249517*), in a historic timber-framed house built in 1530.

Church of St. Peter and St. Paul CHURCH   This cathedral-sized church was finished just before the Reformation. Work started in the late 1400s, and among the architects who worked on it was John Wastell, who was involved with King's College Chapel and Great St. Mary's in Cambridge, as well as the church at Saffron Walden. Master mason Reginald Ely, who worked on King's College Chapel, was also involved. Some of the carvings inside depict half-human, half-animals, and the main porch is also richly decorated.

Church St. (A1141, the Hadleigh–Bury St. Edmunds Rd.) Admission free. Open daylight hours.

Lavenham Guildhall HISTORIC SITE   The exhibitions inside this marvelously creaky old building explain how the textile industry once brought wealth to the area, but in the 19th century mechanized mills in the north produced cloth more cheaply and, like most of Suffolk, Lavenham had to fall back on agriculture. It caused poverty for generations, but it did save Lavenham and other villages from redevelopment, and in the last quarter of the 20th century many of these villages were transformed into pretty tourist destinations. The Guildhall's walled garden still houses the tiny village gaol. There's also a half-timbered tearoom with outside seating in fine weather.

Market Place. *©* **01787/247646.** www.nationaltrust.org. Admission £4 adults, £1.70 children 5–15, £9.70 family ticket. Guildhall, shop, and tearoom late Mar–Oct daily 11am–5pm; early Mar Wed–Sun 11am–5pm; Nov Sat–Sun 11am–4pm. Shop also Nov–Dec Thurs–Sun and Jan–Feb Sat–Sun. Tearoom Dec Sat–Sun.

Where to Eat & Stay

Great House Hotel ★   This is a boutique hotel with an award-winning restaurant. Although there are oak beams and an inglenook fireplace inside, its Georgian facade distinguishes it from other buildings in the marketplace, and four of its five rooms are suites with separate lounges, all stylishly decorated. The **restaurant,** listed in Britain's top 100 by *The Sunday Times,* serves French cuisine using local produce, for instance belly of Suffolk pork confit. A two-course lunch is £18; dinner is a la carte.

Market Place, Lavenham, Suffolk CO10 9QZ. www.greathouse.co.uk. *©* **01787/247431.** Fax 01787/ 248007. 5 units. £115–£225. Breakfast £10–£15. AE, MC, V. Free parking on street. **Amenities:** Restaurant. *In room:* TV, Wi-Fi (free).

Swan Hotel ★★★   Just over the road from the Guildhall is this distinctive, half-timbered hotel, one of the oldest and best-preserved buildings in the village. The rooms are all charmingly unique, with a mix of contemporary and antique furniture. Some of the rooms have four-poster beds, others look out onto the cloistered courtyard and gardens. You can eat in the historic **Airmens Bar** (U.S. Air Force men were stationed at Lavenham Airfield during World War II), in the gardens, or in the **Swan Brasserie.** More formal meals are served in the **Gallery Restaurant,** where a two-course lunch costs £15.

High St., Lavenham, Suffolk CO10 9QA. www.swanatlavenham.co.uk. ✆ **01787/247477.** Fax 01787/ 248286. 45 units. £180–£280 double; £220–£300 suite. Rates include English breakfast. AE, MC, V. Free parking on street. **Amenities:** Restaurant; bar; lounge; room service. *In room:* TV, hair dryer, Wi-Fi (free).

THETFORD

80 miles N of London; 29 miles N of Cambridge; 11 miles N of Bury St. Edmunds

Thetford has been an area of human settlement since Neolithic times (about 2500 B.C.) The prehistoric flint mine **Grimes Graves** is nearby and the prehistoric path **Icknield Way,** which runs close to Thetford, is the oldest road in Britain. **The Thetford Treasure**—silver spoons, gold rings, pendants, and necklaces hidden in Roman times— were discovered in 1979 and are now at the British Museum, but you can find out all about them at Thetford's **Ancient House Museum.** However, Thetford is most famous for its forest, a great outdoor destination if you want to go walking through pines and heathland, use the cycling paths, or just stop off for a picnic as you cross the border from Suffolk into Norfolk. Most people go to **High Lodge,** Brandon (✆ **01842/ 815434**), a Forestry Commission-run center with good facilities such as an adventure playground, sculpture trail, cafe, and even barbecue rentals. Parking is relatively expensive at £1.90 an hour (maximum £10), so it's best to make a day of it.

Essentials

GETTING THERE   Trains (NXEA) from Cambridge to Thetford take about 40 minutes, and from Norwich to Thetford (NXEA) it's about 30 minutes. From London King's Cross, and you can go via Ely as well as Cambridge, takes 1¾ hours. For onward buses contact **Brecks Bus Service** (✆ **01638/608080;** www.brecks.org), a service that you have to book in advance and that takes up to five passengers. If you're driving from London, take the M25 to the M11, then the A11 and B1107.

VISITOR INFORMATION   The **Thetford Tourist Information Centre** is at 20 King St., IP24 2AH (✆ **01842/751975;** www.explorethetford.co.uk). It's open Monday to Friday 9am to 5pm, Saturdays until 4pm.

Exploring the Area

Ancient House Museum MUSEUM   This museum has displays that tell Thetford's story and introduces you to famous residents such as Thomas Paine, who had a hand in American independence and the French Revolution. The museum is in a beautiful medieval merchant's house.

White Hart St., Thetford. ✆ **01842/752599.** Admission £3.50 adults, £1.90 children 4–16; free Oct–Mar. Tues–Sat 10am–5pm (closes 4pm Oct–Mar).

Dad's Army Museum MUSEUM   The much-loved BBC comedy series was filmed in Thetford and its forest, but it is only recently that a Dad's Army Museum of memorabilia has opened. After you've visited, have your photo taken next to the Captain Mainwaring statue. There's a self-guided Dad's Army Trail, which you can download from www.explorethetford.co.uk.

Cage Lane, Thetford. ✆ **01842/751975.** www.dadsarmythetford.org.uk. Free admission. Sat 10am–2pm, also Tues in Aug, and occasional other days.

Go Ape SPORTING ACTIVITY   This is a giant obstacle course of zip wires, ladders, walkways, bridges, and tunnels in the trees. Safety equipment is provided and 30 minutes' training, with instructors patrolling the course. Minimum age 10. Booking recommended.

Church St. (A1141, btw. Hadleigh and Bury St. Edmunds). © **0845/6439215.** Admission £30 adults, £20 children 10–17 (£1.50 telephone booking charge). Feb–Nov daily during school holidays; but often closed on Tues, and only open at weekends in Feb and Nov.

Grimes Graves HISTORIC SITE These are the largest and best-preserved Neolithic flint mines in Britain, and the only ones open to the public. They produced heads for spears, arrows, and knives for prehistoric tribes, and they're now under the stewardship of English Heritage. There are 400 pits, but nobody knew this unnaturally undulating scrubland was a series of flint mines until 1870, when they were excavated. You can only see them by climbing down a 9-m (30-ft.) ladder with an English Heritage guide who will assess your fitness to descend (children 4 and under and those with disabilities are not allowed down). It's worth taking a flashlight for a better view, and flat shoes are essential. There's also a visitor center and shop.

Lyndford, Thetford (on the B1107, 2¾ miles northeast of Brandon). © **01842/810656.** www.english-heritage.org.uk. Admission £3.30 adults, £2.70 students and seniors, £1.60 children 5–15, £8 family ticket. Mar–Oct Thurs–Mon 10am–5pm; Apr–Sept daily 10am–5pm.

SOUTHWOLD & ALDEBURGH

Southwold: 94 miles NE of London, 26 miles S of Norwich; Aldeburgh: 97 miles NE of London, 41 miles SE of Norwich

Southwold is a breath of fresh air on Suffolk's North Sea coast, with a sandy beach perfect for family holidays and a stylish twist to a functional but pretty town that attracts weekend Londoners. Southwold has wonderful pubs, thanks in part to the town's Adnams brewery; a landmark lighthouse; an award-winning pier; lovely boutiques; outrageously expensive beach huts; and a happy, holiday atmosphere almost year-round. The town's famous Greens, created after the great fire of 1659, give it a leisurely feeling of space, as do the commons and marshes down to the river quayside. From here (where there are fish stalls, fish-and-chips restaurants, and a pub), you can walk over a footbridge and back up the river to **Walberswick,** home of the British Open Crabbing Championships every August and a sandy beach, which is fast becoming a kitesurfing hotspot thanks to the easterly winds. Walk along the beach and you'll get to **Dunwich,** now little more than a few cottages since the town fell into the sea several centuries ago. Here the beach is more pebbles than sand and you can walk the 19 miles to **Aldeburgh** along the coastal path (partly just the beach), passing Maggi Hambling's Scallop sculpture before you reach the town and its pebble beach.

Aldeburgh is a yachtie town, famous for its festival and a magnet for Londoners. It's a collection of boutique shops and eating places, including the excellent but pricey **Lighthouse Restaurant** in the High Street. Benjamin Britten, who established the Aldeburgh Festival, is buried at St. Peter and St. Paul Church here.

Essentials

GETTING THERE From London's Liverpool Street Station, take a train (NXEA) to Ipswich, then the Lowestoft line and get off at Saxmundham for Aldeburgh (6 miles away) or at Halesworth for Southwold 9 miles away. Both take around 2 hours and cost nearly £40 one-way. **Anglian Buses** (© **01502/711109;** www.anglianbus. co.uk) run from Halesworth to Southwold, and **First Eastern Counties Buses** (© **08456/020121;** www.firstgroup.com) run from Saxmundham to Aldeburgh. The Lowestoft train also stops at Woodbridge.

If you're driving from London take the M25 to the A12 and follow signs to any of the towns mentioned above, which are just off the A12.

VISITOR INFORMATION There are **Tourist Information Centres** at 152 High St., Aldeburgh (© **01728/453637**), at 69 High Street, Southwold (© **01502/724729**), and at Station Buildings, Woodbridge (© **01394/382240**). For more information on all these towns go to www.visit-suffolk.co.uk.

SPECIAL EVENTS Aldeburgh was the home of composer Benjamin Britten (1913–76), best known for the opera *Peter Grimes*. Many of his compositions were first performed at the **Aldeburgh Festival** (© **01728/687110;** www.aldeburgh. co.uk), which he founded in 1948 with Peter Pears. The 2-week festival every June features internationally known performers.

Exploring the Area

In Southwold, **The Sailor's Reading Room** on East Cliff (© **01502/724729**) is worth looking in, and the lovely little **Southwold Museum,** on Victoria Street (© **01502/726097;** www.southwoldmuseum.org) is extremely interesting. You might also want to check out the **Dunwich Museum** (© **01728/648796;** www. dunwichmuseum.org.uk) to learn about Dunwich's history.

This coastline, from Felixstowe to north of Southwold is an Area of Outstanding Natural Beauty, but inland there's also **Woodbridge** to explore, a market town on the River Deben with riverside walks, antiques, and local produce shops. From Woodbridge you can also explore Framlingham Castle and Sutton Hoo (see below).

Aldeburgh Museum MUSEUM   Housed in the Moot Hall is a timber-framed meeting house dating from the 16th century, and it's still where the town council meets today. It doubles as a fascinating little museum with old maps, prints, and Anglo-Saxon burial urns, as well as other items of historical interest.

Moot Hall, Market Cross Place, Aldeburgh. © **01728/453637.** www.aldeburghmuseum.org.uk. Admission £1 adults, free for children. June–Aug daily noon–5pm; Apr–May and Sept–Oct daily 2:30–5pm. Closed Nov–Mar.

Framlingham Castle CASTLE   Unusually attractive, this is one of the few 12th-century castles still standing in East Anglia. Henry VIII's eldest daughter, Mary Tudor, took refuge here before succeeding her brother to the throne in 1553. There's a big grassy area to sit on inside.

9 Church St., Framlingham. © **01728/724033.** www.english-heritage.org.uk. Admission £6.30 adults, £3.80 children 5–15, £16 family ticket. Apr–Oct daily 10:30am–5pm; Nov–Mar Sat–Sun 11am–4pm.

RSPB Minsmere NATURE RESERVE   Avocets, marsh harriers, and booming bitterns are regularly spotted on this bird reserve, along with visiting geese, ducks, swans, and wading birds. The reserve starts among the trees and visitor center, and comes all the way down to the beach. There are lovely walks, any time of the year.

Westleton (on the coast several miles south of Southwold). © **01728/648281.** www.rspb.org.uk. Admission £5 adults, £1.50 children 5–15. Daily 9am–5pm (to 4pm Nov–Jan).

Snape Maltings ENTERTAINMENT COMPLEX   This is where the acclaimed **Aldeburgh Festival** is held, in a concert hall among historic buildings. But the barns

FESTIVAL time

This region has two very good music festivals each year. The **Maverick Festival** (www.maverickfestival.co.uk) is the live face of *Maverick*, Europe's leading country and Americana magazine. It's held each July 4 weekend in the appropriately rural setting of Easton Farm Park (signposted off the A12, near Framlingham), with its horses, geese, and varied animal calls. One outdoor stage and one in an ancient barn play host to leading but often alternative U.S. and British artists such as members of alt-country heroes the Jayhawks, and a number of Texan and Nashville acts.

Latitude (www.latitudefestival.co.uk) is one of Britain's hippest festivals, featuring scores of the latest bands, including very big names (such as Florence and the Machine), and some older ones (Grace Jones). The site is just off the A12 near Southwold.

13

CAMBRIDGE & EAST ANGLIA | Southwold & Aldeburgh

have also been converted into upmarket (if somewhat twee) shops, along with a cafe, tea shop, and pub. There's a farmers' market on the first Saturday of every month and at the Aldeburgh Food and Drink Festival here every September. But on any day it's good to park (it's free), have a picnic, and take a long walk along rush-lined paths with sailing boats appearing to be gliding amid the fields as waterways meander down to the sea.

Snape Maltings (on the B1069). 🕿 **01728/688303.** www.snapemaltings.co.uk. Admission free.

Southwold Lighthouse HISTORIC SITE This working lighthouse is in the middle of town and has been used since 1890. It's not often that a lighthouse is so easily accessible, and the views are obviously splendid. It also houses other items of historical interest.

Moot Hall, Market Cross Place, Southwold. 🕿 **01728/453637.** www.southwoldmuseum.org. Admission £1 adults, free for children. June–Aug daily noon–5pm; Apr–May and Sept–Oct daily 2:30–5pm.

Sutton Hoo ★★ ☺ MUSEUM The most stunning Viking treasures ever found in England were dug up here in the 1930s from a burial mound, which even housed a longboat. The originals are now safe in the British Museum but, even so, the copies along with an award-winning exhibition are good enough. This is a fabulous museum, and the grounds are extraordinary with a path that takes you past several burial mounds. There's also a cafe and an adventure playground—good for families.

Sutton Hoo, Woodbridge. 🕿 **01394/389700.** www.nationaltrust.org.uk. Admission £6.20 adults, £3.55 children 5–15, £17 family ticket. Mar Wed–Sun 10:30am–5pm; Apr–Oct daily 10:30am–5pm; Nov–Feb Sat–Sun 11am–4pm. Additional opening during winter/spring school holidays.

Where to Eat & Stay

Brudenell Hotel Right on the famous beach at the southern end of Aldeburgh, the Brudenell was totally refurbished in 2010 and its rooms are decorated in cool, calm seaside shades. Many of the bedrooms face the sea and the **restaurant** is relaxed with fabulous sea views and a locally sourced, seasonal menu.

The Parade, Aldeburgh, Suffolk IP15 5BU. www.brudenellhotel.co.uk. 🕿 **01728/452071.** Fax 01728/454082. 44 units. £147–£314 double. Rates include English breakfast. AE, MC, V. Free parking. **Amenities:** Restaurant; bar; room service. *In room:* TV, hair dryer, Wi-Fi (free).

The Crown ★★★   This is a lovely old hotel with contemporary style: The bed-rooms range from attic rooms to suites big enough for families. The hotel is at the heart of this quiet seaside town, and its two **restaurants** are renowned for excellent, modern British food. If the Crown is full try its sister hotel, The Swan, a few doors up the High Street overlooking the tiny market place. It's a little more genteel and therefore more expensive, but with a perfect lounge for afternoon tea. See the Adnams website, below, for other stylish hotels in Suffolk and Norfolk.

90 High St., Southwold, Suffolk IP18 6DP. www.adnams.co.uk. (✆) **01502/722186.** 14 units. £154–£184 double; £216 suite. Rates include English breakfast. AE, MC, V. Free parking. **Amenities:** 2 restaurants; bar; room service, Wi-Fi in lounge and bar (free). *In room:* TV, hair dryer.

NORWICH ★★

109 miles NE of London; 20 miles W of the North Sea

Norwich is the very essence of East Anglia. Until the Industrial Revolution it was England's second city and, like much of the region, hugely wealthy. As a result its **Norman cathedral** is one of the finest examples of Romanesque architecture in Europe and has the largest cloisters in England and the second tallest spire. But with the end of the East Anglian textile trade, and the silting up of Norwich's river port, the city became little more than a backwater in the late 19th and early 20th centuries. Happily this meant the city retained many of its medieval streets—it has 31 medieval churches—and it is now regarded as one of the most complete medieval cities in England.

Essentials

GETTING THERE   Trains from London's Liverpool Street Station take just under 2 hours (NXEA; from £45). If you're driving from London, take the M25, M11, and A11.

VISITOR INFORMATION   The **Norwich Tourist Information Centre** is in the Forum, 2 Millennium Plain, Bethel Street, NR2 1TF (✆ **01603/213999;** www. visitnorwich.co.uk), open daily 9:30am to 5pm (except Sun in winter).

GETTING AROUND   For buses, contact **Norfolk Bus Station,** Surrey Street, (✆ **0871/002233**). The city is compact but the bus saves walking out to some of the farther points. Buses are operated by First (✆ **0871/2002233;** www.firstgroup.com).

ORGANIZED TOURS   Walking tours of the city can be booked at the Tourist Information Centre in the Forum (see above), or try the hop-on, hop-off **City Sight-seeing** bus (✆ **01708/866000;** www.city-sightseeing.com).

Exploring the Area

Norwich's history and relaxed atmosphere have attracted tourists for decades now, and as the only city for miles it has excellent shopping facilities—particularly its huge market, which is open every day. **Royal Arcade** is one of the city's most picturesque shopping areas, where you'll find the **Colman's Mustard Shop** (✆ **01603/627889;** www.colmansmustardshop.com), selling mustard products and displaying some fas-cinating memorabilia. Colman's Mustard is one of Norwich's most famous names, and another is **Norwich City Football Club,** which has better catering facilities than any other soccer club in England thanks to its patron Delia Smith, the television cook. **Delia's Restaurant & Bar** is open Friday and Saturday nights at the stadium in Carrow Road (✆ **01603/218704;** www.deliascanarycatering.com).

A visit to Norwich should also include a walk along the **River Wenson** to see the ancient **Norwich Bishop Bridge** and the 15th-century arch at **Pulls Ferry.** And don't miss **Tombland,** the Anglo-Saxon market square where there are now plenty of restaurants and bars, plus **Tombland Antiques Centre,** 14 Tombland (✆ **01603/ 619129**), a three-floor house opposite the cathedral with 60-plus dealers. Nearby is cobbled **Elm Hill** with more Tudor houses than the whole of the city of London, many now attractive little shops and restaurants.

Blickling Hall ★★ HISTORIC HOME   This was the home of the Boleyn family—Anne Boleyn was Henry VIII's second wife and the trigger for the Reformation of the Catholic Church in England. This version of the house was built in the early 17th century and is one of the best examples of such architecture in the country. The long gallery has an elaborate 17th-century ceiling, and the Peter the Great Room has a fine tapestry. The house is set in ornamental parkland with a formal garden and an orangery.

Blickling (off the A140 Norwich–Cromer Rd., near Aylsham). ✆**01263/738030.** www.nationaltrust.org. uk. House and gardens £9.75 adults, £4.75 children 5–15, £26 family ticket; gardens only £6.50 adults, £3.30 children, £13 family ticket. Late July–mid-Sept Wed–Mon 11am–5pm; mid-Sept–late July Wed–Sun 11am–5pm.

Norwich Castle ★★ CASTLE   This handsome Norman keep was once part of a larger castle. It was used as a gaol in the 14th century and turned into a museum in 1894. It now has a fascinating collection of paintings from the Norwich School of Artists as well as other fine art, natural history, and archeological exhibits.

Castle Meadow. ✆**01603/493625.** www.norwich12.co.uk. Admission £6.20 adults, £4.40 children 4–16. Late June–Oct Mon–Sat 10am–5pm, Sun 1–5pm; closes 4:30pm rest of year.

Norwich Cathedral ★★ CATHEDRAL   Dating from 1096, the Norman-designed cathedral is noted for its long nave and high columns and took more than 200 years to build. The impressive choir stalls have handsome 15th-century misericords, and the 13th-century quadrangular cloisters are the largest monastic cloisters in England.

62 The Close. ✆**01603/218300.** www.cathedral.org.uk. Free admission; £4 suggested donation. Open daily 7:30am–6:30pm.

Sainsbury Centre for Visual Arts GALLERY   The private art collection of Sir Robert and Lady Sainsbury is on display at the University of East Anglia, 3 miles west of Norwich on Earlham Road. The 1978 award-winning exhibition hall was designed by Sir Norman Foster and has large areas of glass, providing superb light to view the collection of modern, ancient, classical, and ethnographic art, including work by Francis Bacon, Alberto Giacometti, and Henry Moore.

University of East Anglia, Earlham Rd. ✆**01603/593199.** www.scva.org.uk. Free admission. Tues–Sun 10am–5pm. Bus: 22, 25, or 35 from the city.

Second Air Division Memorial Library LIBRARY   The Second Air Division of the 8th U.S. Army Air Force is remembered in the Millennium Library with a special room containing books and a living documentation devoted to the Second Air Division while it was based in East Anglia.

The Forum, Millennium Plain. ✆**01603/774747.** www.2ndair.org.uk. Free admission. Mon–Sat 9am–5pm.

Where to Eat

The Britons Arms 🎁 BRITISH This wonderful coffeehouse and restaurant is in a medieval thatched building that's the only surviving béguinage in England from the Middle Ages. A béguinage was a religious refuge for women (it's never been a pub), and it is now a friendly daytime spot run by two sisters producing home-cooked hearty meals, puddings, and cakes. There's an open fire in winter and small terraced garden with views over the rooftops of historic Elm Hill.

9 Elm Hill. ℂ **01603/623367.** Main courses £10–£14. AE, MC, V. Tues–Fri 9:30am–5pm.

Roger Hickman's Restaurant ★ BRITISH This talented chef presents market-fresh and imaginative cuisine in a stylish dining room with top-notch service. Starters include venison with beets or roast scallops with crispy pork belly. Choose from main courses such as braised beef cheek or roasted globe artichoke.

79 Upper St. Giles St. ℂ **01603/633522.** www.rogerhickmansrestaurant.com. Reservations recommended. Fixed-price lunch £16 for 2 courses, £19 for 3 courses; fixed-price dinner £30 for 2 courses, £38 for 3 courses. AE, MC, V. Tues–Sat noon–2:30pm and 7–10pm.

St. Benedict's Restaurant ENGLISH/FRENCH There's a warm welcome, along with well-prepared food, at this modern brasserie with a simple setting. The chef, Nigel Raffles, shops for some of the freshest market produce available. Expect menus that include crisp lamb parcels with Moroccan carrot salad, and roast butternut squash with Romano pepper and fragrant rice.

9 St. Benedict's St. ℂ **01603/765377.** www.stbenedictsrestaurant.co.uk. Reservations recommended. Fixed-price lunch £6.95–£12; fixed-price dinner £19 for 2 courses, £24–£32 for 3 courses. AE, DC, MC, V. Tues–Sat noon–2pm and 7–10pm.

Entertainment & Nightlife

You'll find touring companies performing drama, opera, and ballet at **Theatre Royal,** Theatre Street (ℂ **01603/630000;** www.theatreroyalnorwich.co.uk), with senior and student discounts available for selected performances. The box office is open Monday to Saturday 9:30am to 6pm, closing at 8pm on performance days.

The **Norwich Playhouse,** 42–58 St. George's St. (ℂ **01603/598598;** www.norwichplayhouse.org.uk), has well-known names from music, comedy, and touring drama. The box office is open Monday to Saturday 9:30am until 6pm.

Maddermarket Theatre, 1 St. John's Alley (ℂ **01603/620917;** www.maddermarket.co.uk), is a half-timbered playhouse and home to the amateur Norwich Players, who specialize in classical and contemporary drama. The box office is open Monday to Saturday 10am to 5pm, to 7:30pm on performance days.

Norwich Puppet Theatre, St. James, Whitefriars (ℂ **01603/629921;** www.puppettheatre.co.uk), offers original puppet shows in the converted medieval church of St. James, while the **Norwich Arts Centre,** 51 St. Benedict's St. (ℂ **01603/660352;** www.norwichartscentre.co.uk), is a versatile entertainment complex in another converted church (St. Swithins), which showcases up-and-coming bands and hosts ballet, comedy, poetry, and exhibitions.

The oldest pub in Norwich is the **Adam & Eve,** 17 Bishopgate (ℂ **01603/667423;** www.adamandevenorwich.co.uk), an alehouse since at least 1249 when it was owned by monks. It's a small, cozy pub but there is outside seating and a small selection of well-kept real ale. Alternatively, try the **Fat Cat** ★★, 49 West End St. (ℂ **01603/624364;** www.fatcatpub.co.uk). It's been *The Good Pub Guide*'s "Beer Pub of the Year" four times and has a wide range of real ales including its own Fat Cat beer.

Where to Stay

De Vere Dunston Hall ★★   It has all the style of an Elizabethan mansion with tall brick chimneys and red-brick gables, but this 19th-century mansion-turned-hotel is a 21st-century dream of elegant comfort. It even has its own golf course on the grounds. There are wonderful four-poster bedrooms, large family rooms, and attic hideaways plus a spa with nice pool and three restaurants.

Ipswich Rd., Norwich, Norfolk NR14 8PQ. www.devere.co.uk. ☎ **01508/470444.** Fax 01508/470689. 169 units. From £109 double. AE, MC, V. Free parking. **Amenities:** 3 restaurants; bar; bikes; 18-hole golf course; hot tub; indoor pool; sauna; steam room; spa; gym. *In room:* TV, hair dryer, Wi-Fi (free).

Maids Head Hotel   In business since 1272, the Maids Head may well be the oldest continuously operated hotel in the U.K.; certainly Elizabeth I is said to have stayed here, and the four-poster Queen Elizabeth I Suite is very popular. The hotel is a mix of Elizabethan and Georgian architectural styles, and many bedrooms have oak beams, but there's nothing old-fashioned about the decor. You'll find the hotel opposite the cathedral, and you don't have to stay the night to use the **Maids Head Bar,** where Norfolk hero Horatio Nelson once drank.

Tombland, Norwich, Norfolk NR3 1LB. www.maidsheadhotel.co.uk. ☎ **01603/209955.** Fax 01603/613688. 84 units. From £89 double. AE, MC, V. Free parking. **Amenities:** Restaurant; bar; room service. *In room:* TV, hair dryer, Wi-Fi (free).

THE NORFOLK BROADS ★★

Wroxham: 7 miles NE of Norwich

The Norfolk Broads were created by locals cutting peat for fuel between the 12th and 14th centuries. Whether you're messing about with boats, walking past the reed beds and cow fields, or just sitting at a waterside pub watching the world go by, the Norfolk Broads are a unique holiday destination. The Broads are Britain's largest protected wetlands, its third largest inland waterway, and in 1989 they became the **Broads National Park** (☎ **01603/610734;** www.broads-authority.gov.uk). The lake-like waterways linked by the rivers Bure, Waveney, and Yare are to the east of Norwich, and along the county's coastal border with Suffolk. The Broads cover 124 miles of navigable waterways, which you can explore with your own boat, by taking a day-trip or by hiring a boat for a day or more. As you sail lazily through the waterways you'll spot alder trees, willows, and birch along the riverbanks and marshes, which are home to rare plants and animals. **Wroxham,** on the River Bure, is regarded as the capital of the Broads and is a good base for exploring the area.

Essentials

GETTING THERE   Trains (NXEA) from London's Liverpool Street Station go to Norwich; trains from Norwich to Hoveton and Wroxham station take 15 minutes; the full journey takes 2½ hours and costs £45. **Traveline** buses (☎ **0871/2002233;** www.travelineeastanglia.org.uk) cover all of Norfolk. If you're driving from Norwich take the A1151 to Wroxham.

VISITOR INFORMATION   **Broads Information Centre** at Hoveton/Wroxham, Station Road (☎ **01603/7560970**), is open Easter to October, daily 9am to 1pm and 2 to 5pm. Other offices are at Potter Heigham, Ranworth, and Whitlingham.

Exploring the Area

Barnes Brinkcraft, Riverside Road, Wroxham (© **01603/782625**), has day boats from £14 an hour to £240 a week, with the prices rising in the high season. Alternatively, book a tour with **Broads Tours,** near Wroxham Bridge, or in Potter Heigham (© **01603/ 782207** or 01603/670722; www.broads.co.uk). Trips start at £7 for 1-hour trips.

Bewilderwood ★★ ☺ AMUSEMENT PARK   This is less a theme park than a magical forest, with family adventures in tree houses, along rope bridges, and zip wires, and with boat trips and walks in the marshes.

Horning Rd., Hoveton. © **01603/783900.** www.bewilderwood.co.uk. Admission £11 adults, £8.50- £12 children depending on height (free for children under 1 m/3 ft.); £8.50 seniors. Daily Apr–Nov 10am–5:30pm or dusk, plus Feb school holidays.

Fairhaven Woodland & Water Garden ★★ GARDEN   These wonderful gardens are hidden among the trees and crisscrossed by little streams. They have an amazing collection of spring-flowering candelabra primulas in late May and early June, plus rhododendrons, azaleas, bluebells, and summer wildflowers. There's lovely foliage later in the year.

School Rd., South Walsham. © **01603/270683.** www.fairhavengarden.co.uk. Admission £5.50 adults, £5 seniors, £3 children 5-15. Daily Mar–Nov 10am–5pm, Dec–Feb 10am–4pm.

The Museum of the Broads MUSEUM   Find out how the Broads have shaped Norfolk's landscape and affected the lives of locals at this award-winning museum, which has an exhibition of boats from the last 200 years, and boat trips on the Victorian steam launch *Falcon* on Tuesdays, Wednesdays, and Thursdays from 11am to 3pm.

The Staithe, Stalham. © **01692/581681.** www.museumofthebroads.org.uk. Admission £4 adults, £3.50 children 5-15, £10 family ticket. Boat trips £3.50 adults, £2.50 children. Daily Easter–Oct 10:30am–5pm. Closed in winter.

NORTH NORFOLK COAST ★★

Hunstanton is 105 miles NE of London, 53 miles N of Cambridge

This low, beautiful stretch of beach, dunes, and marshes, interspersed with the odd tourist town, is a world of its own. It's a place for walking and thinking, bird-watching (whether you're an expert or not), and relaxing any time of year—on the vast stretches of sands or in front of a log fire in one of the region's exceptional small hotels. It can be entrancingly bleak in winter here (the wind whipping across the north-facing sands), but there's a friendliness that goes with being in a far-flung outpost of the country.

Essentials

GETTING THERE   Trains leave London's Liverpool Street Station for Norwich, where you can catch the Bittern Line to Cromer and Sheringham. Trains leave London's Kings Cross for Kings Lynn (hourly), takes 1 hour and 35 minutes and costs £30. The **Coasthopper bus** (© **01553/776980;** www.coasthopper.co.uk) runs between Cromer and Hunstanton (and onto Kings Lynn) daily, half-hourly in summer, roughly hourly in winter. In addition to one-way and round-trip tickets, there are a variety of passes including other buses and trains, and the 1, 3, or 5-day Coasthopper Rover; see website for details.

halting IN HOLT

The small town of Holt comes as a surprise. A few miles in from the coast you find a discreet, upmarket place that seems to have dropped in from the Cotswolds. The idiosyncratic department store Bakers & Larners rambles through a line of neat high street shop fronts, with a food hall that's like a mini Harrods, as well as an enviable selection of Barbours, posh wellies (boots), and the like. The art galleries go for big names—Doric Arts regularly has a selling exhibition of David Hockney prints, and Baron Art is full of Clarice Cliff pieces. You can get here on the Poppy Line steam train from Sheringham (it's a mile walk or a bus ride from the station; see "Exploring the Area" for information), and there are plenty of places to rest; Bakers & Larners coffee shop, the Horatio Mugs tearoom (named after local boy Lord Nelson), and the Feathers hotel, established 1650, with its pleasing Plume restaurant.

If you're driving from Norwich, take the A140 to Cromer, then the A149 coast road to Sheringham, Blakeney, Wells-next-the-Sea, Holkham, or Hunstanton.

VISITOR INFORMATION   There are **Tourist Information Centres** at Sheringham, Railway Approach (📞 **01263/824329;** www.sheringhamtown.co.uk), Wells-next-the-Sea, Staithe Street (📞 **01328/710885;** www.wellsnextthesea.co.uk), and Hunstanton, 21 High Street (📞 **01485/532610;** www.visitwestnorfolk.com).

Exploring the Area

The boisterous seaside town of **Cromer** (with its century-old wooden pier and its end-of-the-pier Pavilion Theatre featuring leading British variety acts) is a good starting point. It's only a few miles from **Sheringham,** another old-fashioned seaside town where you can enjoy a short walk along the front and maybe a swift lunch such as local fish at the Caribbean-hued Funky Mackerel Cafe with its seafront terrace, or a £4 lobster sandwich at Joyful West's Shellfish Bar on the high street. There's also the **North Norfolk Steam Railway** (also known as the Poppy Line), Sheringham Station, Station Approach (📞 **01263/820800;** www.nnrailway.co.uk), which does a 30-minute run from the little town center station to the outskirts of Holt, with sea views, undulating fields, and woodland.

The main A149 road then passes through **Salthouse** (a bird reserve of lagoons and marsh protected from the sea by a shingle bank), and on to **Cley next the Sea** (pronounced Clee), noted for both the Cley Smokehouse, on the high street (📞 **01263/740282;** www.cleysmokehouse.com), which produces home-cured seafood and meat, and the eco-friendly **Cley Marshes Norfolk Wildlife Trust** viewing hall (📞 **01263/740008;** www.norfolkwildlifetrust.org.uk), a free site with interactive displays, as well as a shop, cafe, and parking. Access to the reserve, which runs down to the sea costs £4, but members and children go free.

Wells-next-the-Sea is a pleasing little town, with its busy quay-side. Parking at the main beach parking lot offers a walk along the water's edge (and view of the occasional seal) into town. The beach, backed by pine forest and with mountainous dunes, stretches all the way around to **Holkham** beach, near the **Holkham Hall** estate. A bit farther on, the unspoiled coast ends at the bucket-and-spade seaside resort of **Hunstanton** (the only coastal town in Norfolk to face west). Despite top-quality sands here and the famous striped cliffs, you might want to simply head south 10 miles to **Sandringham,** the Queen's holiday retreat (see review, below), and a little farther for **Castle Rising** (© **01553/631330;** www.castlerising.co.uk), unassuming yet one of the country's finest examples of a 12th-century stone keep.

Blakeney National Nature Reserve ★★ NATURE RESERVE   West from Cley Marshes Norfolk Wildlife Trust, take a right-hand turn to Cley lifeboat station where there's a cafe and walks to Blakeney Point. You can see common and gray seals and birds at this National Trust reserve. Morston Quay is the base for boat trips.

Cley Rd., Blakeney. © **01263/740241.** www.nationaltrust.org.uk. Free access daily, but National Trust pay parking lot.

Holkham Hall ★★ HISTORIC SITE   This is the magnificent family home of the earls of Leicester. You can visit the Palladian-style stately home, take one of the marked walks around the deer park, and visit the Bygones Museum in the stables to see vintage cars, steam engines, mechanical toys, and displays on life here over the centuries. Across the road (A149) is Holkham beach, wild and unspoiled and part of an Area of Outstanding Natural Beauty. There's a boardwalk along the edge of the beach, sand dunes, and a huge expanse of sand when the tide goes out (and out).

Holkham (on the A149). © **01328/710227.** www.holkham.co.uk. Hall and museum admission £11 adults, £5.50 children 5-15, £28 family ticket. Apr-Oct Sun-Mon and Thurs noon-4pm. Museum only Apr-Oct daily 10am-5pm. Admission £4 adults, £2 children. Closed Nov-Mar, but the park, with cafe and shop, is open year-round, free, to walkers.

Sandringham House & Gardens ★★ HISTORIC SITE   One of the Queen's preferred residences with some rooms open to the public, a separate museum, and extensive woodland gardens with flowering bulbs and rhododendrons in spring and stunning fall displays. The house retains its Edwardian style with gifts from Russian and German royal relatives on show, while the museum is a collection of personal items and gifts from state visits abroad. The house is usually closed for a week in July.

Sandringham (off the A149). © **01485/541571.** www.sandringhamestate.co.uk. House, museum, and gardens admission £11 adults, £5.50 children 5-15, £28 family ticket. Late Apr-late Oct daily 11am-5pm (9:30am for visitor center, café, and shop; 10:30am for gardens). Closed rest of year.

Titchwell Marsh RSPB Reserve ★★ NATURE RESERVE   One of the first places many geese, ducks, and wading birds land as they head south from the Arctic is this reserve with its salt and freshwater ponds, which you can see from the impressive new Parrinder Hide, a striking architectural retreat where visitors can sit out of

 NORFOLK coast **PATH**

You can get from Cromer to Hunstanton on foot, via the Norfolk Coast Path. It leaves the coast for a short stretch across the hills to Sheringham, but hugs the beach and sea all the way to Cley, then takes a straight line to Wells (to the rear of marshland but keeping to the sea-side of the A149), then through the beach-front pines at Holkham. It's 46 miles, but passes by or near many excellent hotels to make a comfortable multiday trip. Or you can just go for as long as you fancy, getting the Coasthopper bus back. (If you're really keen, the trail heads inland, the same distance again, as the Roman, rod-straight Peddar's Way to Thetford Forest.) Visit www.nationaltrail.co.uk for maps and more information.

the wind. A raised walkway takes you to the beach, where you'll see more birds and possibly seals. See if you can spot the rusting World War II tanks.

Titchwell (on the A149). ✆ **01485/210779.** www.resp.org. Free admission; parking £4. Shop daily 9:30am–5pm, cafe daily 9:30am–4.30pm.

Where to Eat & Stay

Montague House ★★ 👪 In the quiet backstreets of Sheringham, this boutique B&B occupies a smart Edwardian house, packed with the owners' collection of art and antiques (including many large oils, old and modern), with the steam engines of the Poppy Line passing by the bottom of the pretty garden. The three bedrooms are all furnished individually, right down to the varied organic toiletries and truffles from local producers. The Gold Suite has a four-poster bed and all have flat-screen TVs. The country house-style breakfast room spills out onto a terrace, and doubles as a lounge and games room. Breakfasts cooked on the Aga are sensational, ranging from organic bacon to locally smoked kippers and haddock to blueberry pancakes and French toast. Picnic baskets and packed lunches are made to order.

3 Montague Rd., Sheringham, Norfolk NR26 8LN. www.montague-house.co.uk. ✆ **01263/822510.** 3 units. £80–£110 double; £100–£130 suite. Rates include English breakfast. MC, V. Free parking. *In room:* TV/DVD, hair dryer, Wi-Fi (free).

Titchwell Manor ★★ This old farmhouse has expanded into various outbuildings and is now one of the region's leading small hotels, with views across the RSPB Titchwell Marsh bird sanctuary to the sea. Rooms are all unique, from sumptuous conventional hotel rooms to the flagstones and modish decor of the timbered Herb Garden lodges, or the Victorian fittings and wood-burning stove in The Lounge, a cottage-like original room. All have lavish bathrooms, and foldaway beds for children are available (£15). In the hotel's public rooms there's a lounge with an open fire, and the **Conservatory restaurant,** overlooking the walled garden, features a modern menu with local produce such as venison from the Houghton estate and Brancaster oysters. The more informal **Eating Rooms,** with sea-view terrace, has a brasserie menu. There's also a good, friendly bar.

Titchwell, Kings Lynn, Norfolk PE31 8BB (on the A149). www.titchwellmanor.com. ✆ **01485/210221.** 31 units. £90–£250 double. Rates include English breakfast. AE, MC, V. Free parking. **Amenities:** 2 restaurants; bar; lounge. *In room:* TV, hair dryer, Wi-Fi (free).

Victoria at Holkham ★ 👪 This former pub on the Holkham estate (still home to Viscount Coke and family) is now a country chic hotel where Range Rovers disgorge panting Labradors, and smartly casual families flop down for a weekend in the wilds. Yet the polished Victorian interior has a colonial feel, full of stirring rugs and furniture imported especially from India. All the rooms are different, united by their exotic fabrics, richly shaded walls, and elegant bathrooms (some with rolltop baths); the Attic suite is great for families. The **restaurant** offers a rich menu, with beef, venison, and game from the Holkham estate. Outside, a stroll in one direction gets you into the Holkham parkland and the stately home (open to the public), in the other to the pine-fringed beach.

Park Road, Holkham, Wells-next-the-Sea, Norfolk NR23 1RG . www.holkham.co.uk. ✆ **01328/711008.** 10 units. £90–£460 double; Attic suite £420–£530. AE, MC, V. Free parking. **Amenities:** Restaurant; bar. *In room:* TV, hair dryer, Wi-Fi (free).

EAST MIDLANDS

by Rhonda Carrier

With walking, cycling, fell-running, rock-climbing, caving, horseriding, watersports, and fishing in abundance, the upland but not mountainous Peak District in northern Derbyshire is this region's big draw. Most of it falls within the Peak District National Park, designated Britain's first national park in 1951. However, green spaces and rich historical sites abound in neighboring Nottinghamshire and Leicestershire—alongside thoroughly modern British cities.

CITIES & TOWNS **Nottingham** has reinvented itself for the 21st century as a shopping and nightlife destination, yet historical gems, including a honeycomb of man-made caves that served, over time, as medieval tanneries, factories, and air-raid shelters, underpin its flashy facade. Similarly, **Leicester**'s Roman past still reasserts itself within the context of a many-layered multicultural city studded with modern attractions such as the National Space Centre.

COUNTRYSIDE Plunging waterfalls, swooningly gorgeous moors and dales, rolling hills, and verdant valleys bring walkers and cyclists from far afield to the lovely **Peak District;** less well known are the lush country and forest parks within Nottinghamshire's **Sherwood Forest,** remnants of former royal hunting terrain, and craggy **Charnwood Forest** in Leicestershire, dotted with volcanic rocks and home to a medieval deer park concealing the ruined dwelling of a beheaded queen.

EATING & DRINKING Cheese is big and bold in the East Midlands—the world-renowned blue-veined Stilton can only be produced in Derbyshire, Nottinghamshire, and Leicestershire, while the latter county is also known for its crumbly, nutty, orange-hued Red Leicester. Sample and buy them, and other local produce and specialties, including Melton Mowbray **pork pies,** at farm shops and **farmers' markets** all over the region, not least the renowned **Chatsworth Farm Shop,** or enjoy them at a cozy country pub. But make sure to sample one of Leicester's famed **Indian restaurants,** too.

NATIONAL PARKS Quirky **Matlock Bath,** on the edge of the Peak District, was once described as "Little Switzerland" by Daniel Defoe for its riverside cliffs. It has something for everyone, from cable-car rides up to a hilltop park with walking trails, tours of an old mine, and a fossil

museum, to the aptly named Giddy Edge walk, canoeing on the river, and a museum of photography. It's also the start of the UNESCO-listed Derwent Valley Mills World Heritage Site, a stunning array of early cotton mills.

THE best TRAVEL EXPERIENCES IN THE EAST MIDLANDS

- o **Exploring the Peak District:** Britain's original National Park is a walkers' and cyclists' paradise, especially the Monsal Trail past the stunning Monsal Falls, while Chatsworth House is the region's unmissable "jewel in the crown." See p. 534.
- o **Following in the footsteps of Robin Hood:** The legendary outlaw, who left his mark all over Sherwood Forest, lives on in lively local pageants and festivals, as well as special trails and footpaths. See p. 544.
- o **Marveling at Lincoln Cathedral:** Rising majestically from the heart of a walkable city of medieval streets lined by Tudor houses, Lincoln's fine Gothic cathedral was described by critic John Ruskin as no less than "the most precious piece of architecture in the British Isles." See p. 551.

- **Charting the growth of the National Forest:** Though not yet a true forest, this area of southern Derbyshire and northern Leicestershire is packed with attractions, from a woodland adventure park and wildlife aplenty to some of Britain's best off-road cycling. See p. 553.
- **Getting outdoorsy at Rutland Water:** The biggest man-made reservoir in all Europe offers up activities from watersports and walking to wildlife encounters, plus a unique museum within a half-submerged church.

DERBYSHIRE & THE PEAK DISTRICT

Derby: 130 miles N of London, 41 miles NE of Birmingham

Most of the county of Derbyshire falls within the Peak District National Park, designated Britain's first National Park in 1951 and attracting about 10 million visitors a year for its gritstone edges, waterfalls, and moorlands (Dark Peak to the north), and its limestone dales, rolling hills, and green valleys divided by dry-stone walls (White Peak to the south). Its popularity is explained by the 980 square miles of public paths and 133 square miles of open-access land all within easy reach of several major British cities, including Manchester (p. 562). South and east Derbyshire are certainly less scenically dramatic but have plenty of diversions in the form of historic houses and buildings, industrial heritage, and family attractions.

Essentials

GETTING THERE Direct trains to Derby from London St. Pancras or Euston take between 1½ hours to 2 hours, costing around £56 for a round-trip. To reach Buxton by train from London, you have to go first to Stockport and then change to a train from **Manchester** (p. 562), taking about 1 hour. If you're flying into Manchester, bus no. 199 runs directly from the airport to Buxton. Also handy for the Peak District are **East Midlands Airport** (www.eastmidlandsairport.com) near Derby, with flights to Europe and North Africa, and the Doncaster-Sheffield Airport and Leeds-Bradford Airport in Yorkshire.

Derby is minutes from the M1 running north from London, just over 124 miles away. Mainly direct **National Express** buses (☎ **0871/781–8178;** www.nationalexpress.com) from London to Derby take about 3¾ hours. Buses from London to Buxton (most requiring a change at Derby) take about 6 hours.

Buxton is a 25-mile drive southeast of Manchester, but the most scenic routes take longer. **Transpeak** (☎ **01773/712265;** www.trent.netescape.co.uk) runs regular Manchester–Nottingham buses stopping at points in Derbyshire, including Buxton, Bakewell, Haddon Hall, Matlock Bath, and Derby.

VISITOR INFORMATION Note that some Derbyshire attractions and tourist information and visitor centers have restricted opening times or close altogether for all or most of the winter. Call ahead to confirm opening times of the visitor centers below. An invaluable resource for any visitor to the area is www.peakdistrict.gov.uk.

Bakewell Visitor Centre, Old Market Hall, Bridge Street (☎ **01629/816558**).

Buxton Tourist Information Centre, inside Pavilion Gardens gift boutique (☎ **01298/25106;** www.visitbuxton.co.uk).

Castleton Visitor Centre, Buxton Road (☎ **01629/816572**).

Of the countless wonderful walking and cycling routes in the Peak District, the most evocative is the **Monsal Trail,** running for about 8 miles (about half can be cycled) along the old Midland Railway Line and passing the gorgeous Monsal Falls. It starts at Blackwell Mill Junction at Wyedale, about 3 miles east of Buxton and ends at Coombs Viaduct just over a mile south of Bakewell. Then there's the linking **High Peak and Tissington trails,** which combined offer about 30 miles of walking, cycling, and horse-riding tracks along former train lines studded with relics of the railway's past and interpretation panels. For more on these and other Peak District routes, including downloadable maps, and details of bike-rental centers and refreshment stops en route, see www.peakdistrict.gov.uk.

The Peak District National Park is also the southern starting point for the **Pennine Way** (www.nationaltrail.co.uk), Britain's oldest long-distance national walking trail, which begins at Edale and takes you 268 miles up to the Cheviot Hills in Northumberland, via the Yorkshire Dales National Park.

14

EAST MIDLANDS | Derbyshire & the Peak District

Derby Tourist Information Centre, Assembly Rooms, Market Place (© **01332/ 255802;** www.visitderby.co.uk).

Matlock Tourist Information Centre, Crown Square (© **01629/583388;** www.visitpeakdistrict.com).

Upper Derwent Visitor Centre, Fairholmes, Bamford (© **01433/650953**).

GETTING AROUND   Getting around the National Park is for many people the point of visiting (see "Best Peak District Trails," below). The official **bike-rental** centers are at Ashbourne, Derwent, and Parsley Hay (see www.peakdistrict.gov.uk/cycle). If you're not so hearty, use **local buses** (more frequent on Sun, especially in summer); timetables are available at tourist information centers or from www.nationalparks.gov.uk.

SPECIAL EVENTS   The **Buxton Festival** (© **01298/70395;** www.buxtonfestival.co.uk), a world-renowned feast of opera, music, and literature, is held during about 2 weeks each July. **Chatsworth House's** (p. 537) large-scale seasonal events include an **International Horse Trials** in May and a **Country Fair** in September. Derby, England's real ale capital, hosts the **CAMRA Summer Beer Festival** each July.

Well-dressing (www.welldressing.com) involves decorating Derbyshire's freshwater springs with a mosaic of petals, berries, bark, leaves, and moss, with ceremonies held in different villages and towns May to September. In the fall, Matlock Bath hosts its Victorian-origin **Illuminations and Venetian Nights** event, with neon-lit boats on the river and fireworks over the floodlit cliffs.

Exploring Derbyshire

BUXTON: GATEWAY TO THE NATIONAL PARK ★★

This picturesque spa town, nestled between two areas of the National Park, merits exploration in its own right. It can make a good base for discovering Derbyshire, though its setting in a valley means it's often swathed in cloud for weeks at a time. Its thermal waters were known to the Romans, whose settlement here was called Aquae Arnemetiae, but afterward was largely forgotten until the reign of Elizabeth I, when the baths were reactivated. Mary, Queen of Scots took the waters here while being held captive by the Earl of Shrewsbury and his wife, Bess of Hardwick, at nearby Chatsworth House (p. 537). Bess's descendant, the 5th Duke of Devonshire, had plans to turn Buxton into another Bath; he failed, but what you see today is largely the legacy of his 18th-century development, including **The Crescent,** modeled on Bath's Royal Crescent and finally greenlighted in late 2010 for transformation into a five-star hotel, thermal spa, and natural mineral-water spa (the previous thermal baths closed in the 1970s).

Buxton's **Pavilion Gardens ★★**, St. John's Road (© **01298/23114;** www.pavilion gardens.co.uk), restored between 1998 and 2004 to their Victorian splendor, have lakes, a bandstand, a minitrain, a cafe, and an ice-cream parlor. Events here include farmers' markets, fine-food fairs, books and antiques fairs, and the **Great Peak District Fair** each October, which includes the Buxton Beer Festival, family activities, and music. Gardens are open daily 9:30am to 5pm; admission is free.

On Buxton's outskirts is **Poole's Cavern ★**, Green Lane (© **01298/26978;** www.poolescavern.co.uk), a limestone cave inhabited by Stone Age people, Romans, and finally medieval outlaws. The cavern's chambers are studded with stalactites and stalagmites. After a tour (call for times; £8 for adults, £4.75 children 5–16), stroll through the surrounding **Buxton Country Park** up to the leaning Victorian folly Solomon's Temple on Grin Low Hill, with views across High Peak. The Park is home to a **Go Ape!** forest adventure course (© **0845/643925;** www.goape.co.uk), with admission prices from £20; call for hours.

THE NATIONAL PARK ★★★

Dark Peak (or **High Peak**) is the highest, wildest section of the National Park, and though it's dramatically scenic, it's bleak in bad weather (an impression reinforced by the military aircraft wrecks). In summer, staff at the **Upper Derwent Visitor Centre** (p. 535) near the dam will advise you on getting the most of its moorlands, forests, and reservoirs (Howden, Derwent, and Ladybower). At the base of **Mam Tor** ("Heights of the Mother"), pretty **Castleton** attracts visitors with the imposing Norman ruins of **Peveril Castle** (© **0870/333-1181;** www.english-heritage.org.uk; daily 10am to 4 or 5pm; admission £4.30 adults, £2.60 for children aged 5–16). Castleton is also home to four underground show caves, including **Blue John Cavern ★** (© **01433/620642;** www.bluejohn-cavern.co.uk) and **Treak Cliff Cavern** (© **01433/620571;** www.bluejohnstone.com/pages/cave.htm), the only two places in the world where the blue-and-yellow semiprecious mineral Blue John is found. The first is the best for visitors; it's open daily 9:30am to 5:30pm (10am–dusk in winter) and costs £9 to enter (£4.50 for children up to 15).

East of Castleton, scenic **Hathersage** plays up its possible links with the Robin Hood legend but has a firmer claim to fame as the place where Charlotte Brontë wrote part of *Jane Eyre,* while staying at the vicarage to visit a friend. Walkers and rock-climbers flock here for its surrounding moorland, gritstone edges, and tors (high rocky hills). It's also home to the David Mellor museum (p. 542).

About 12 miles southeast of Buxton, **Bakewell** is another good base and indeed the only town within the National Park itself. (For the Monsal Trail between Buxton and Bakewell, see "Best Peak District Trails," p. 535). This pleasant market town is best known as home to the eponymous pudding (though not the Bakewell tart, which hails from elsewhere). It's available all over but best sampled at **The Old Original**

Bakewell Pudding Shop (© **01629/812193;** www.bakewellpuddingshop.co.uk). Most visitors time their trip to coincide with the traditional market each Monday.

Bakewell is minutes from one of the greatest of English country houses, **Chatsworth House,** which you may well recognize from the 2005 movie adaptation of *Pride and Prejudice* (see below), and from nearby **Haddon Hall** ★ (© **01629/ 812855;** www.haddonhall.co.uk), another location for the movie. Home to the Manners family since the 16th century, this atmospheric, fortified medieval manor can be visited April to October (see website for specific days and times) and then also at Christmas, for traditional decorations, Tudor music, carols, and candlelight tours. Entry is £9.50 for adults, £5.50 for children aged 5 to 16. For a review of Lord Manners' hotel, The Peacock at Rowsley, see p. 540.

Also at Rowsley, **Caudwell's Mill** ★★ (© **01629/734374;** www.caudwells mill.co.uk) is a 19th-century roller flour mill where you can watch the machinery in action; learn about the flour-making process; buy flour, oat products, and recipe books; and enjoy fresh breads, cakes, cream teas, and other home-cooked fare in the cafe. There are also crafts galleries in the yard. It's open daily 10am to 5:30pm; entry is £4.50 adults, £2 children aged 5 to 15.

The southern section of the National Park has no large attractions, but **Dovedale** ★★★—National Trust-owned farmland—is good walking territory: Highlights are the famous stepping stones across the River Dove, the Lion's Head Rock, and the Dove Holes caves. The village of **Hartington** to the north is home to a Stilton cheese factory and a famous little cheese shop, a real ale brewery, the tiny Bereford Tea Rooms (also comprising the village post office and shop), and one of Derbyshire's most famous youth hostels (p. 543). It's popular with walkers using local trails, including the Tissington.

Chatsworth House ★★★ ☺ HISTORIC SITE   The "jewel of the Peak District" is currently home to the 12th Duke of Devonshire, Peregrine Cavendish, but it was his mother, Deborah Mitford (of the famous sisters) who was the driving force behind transforming this once-ailing estate into the impressive visitor attraction and charitable trust it is today (she now lives on the edge of the estate). In addition to the lavish interiors and art treasures, visitors can explore its superb grounds with their fountains, modern sculptures, maze, excellent adventure playground, and a farmyard. From horse trials to Christmas markets, there are reasons to visit year-round. You can even stay on the vast estate (see "Manifold Farm" review, p. 542), and there are eateries at the house and around the estate (see "Devonshire Arms" review, p. 540), plus the famed Chatsworth Farm Shop at nearby Pilsley and the new Chatworth Butchers & Delicatessen in Bakewell.

Chatsworth, 4 miles east of Bakewell. © **01246/565300.** www.chatsworth.org. "Discovery" tickets to entire site £16–£18 adults, £10–£11 children 4–15, but tickets to separate attractions available. House Feb school break and mid-Mar–late Dec daily 11am–5:30pm; garden, farmyard, and playground have slightly different hours.

EASTERN DERBYSHIRE

The Chatsworth estate came into the hands of the Cavendish family when it was bought by royal courtier Sir William Cavendish, forebear of the current duke. You can see more of the family's legacy a few miles east, at **Hardwick Hall** ★★ (Doe Lea, © **01246/850430;** www.nationaltrust.org.uk), built by William's third wife, Elizabeth Talbot ("Bess of Hardwick") in the 1590s. Another splendid house—boasting six towers and an evocative Long Gallery—Hardwick contains a wonderful collection of tapestries and embroideries, while outside you can roam its herb gardens, orchards, and lawns. Beginning in 2012 there'll be heritage tours of the historic stableyard. Entry is £11 (£5.50 children 5–16; less for just the garden); see the website for days and times. You can also rent two cottages on the estate.

North of here lie more historic buildings. **Renishaw Hall** (© **01246/432310;** www.sitwell.co.uk), home to the famous Sitwell family for almost 400 years, opens its doors and Italianate gardens to the public April to September and at Christmas, Wednesday to Sunday and bank holidays from 10:30am to 4:30pm; entry is £6 (£5.20 children 10–16). To the southeast, the hilltop 17th-century **Bolsover Castle** ★ (© **0870/333-1181;** www.english-heritage.org.uk) has restored interiors, one of the U.K.'s finest surviving indoor riding schools, a Discovery Centre, and events such as falconry displays and "Knight Academy." Bring a picnic and enjoy the views over the Vale of Scarsdale. It's open daily 10am to 4 or 5pm; admission is £7.80 (£4.70 children 5–16).

SOUTHERN DERBYSHIRE ★★

Just outside the National Park, south of Chatsworth, lies Matlock, Derbyshire's county town. But what will detain you is the former spa-resort of **Matlock Bath** ★, south of Matlock and nicknamed (a touch hyperbolically) "Little Switzerland" by Daniel Defoe for the cliffs rising on either side of the River Derwent. Though its thermal baths are gone, there are attractions aplenty, including the **Heights of Abraham** (see below), **Mining Museum** (© **01629/583834;** www.peakmines.co.uk), a **Museum of Photography & Old Times** (© **01629/583325;** www.lifeinalens. com), a **theme park** (© **01925/444888;** www.gulliversfun.co.uk), and an **aquarium** (© **01629/583624;** www.matlockbathaquarium.co.uk) that also has a petrifying well, hologram gallery, and gemstone and fossil exhibition. The Derwent is popular for canoeing.

Matlock Bath is the start of the UNESCO-listed **Derwent Valley Mills World Heritage Site** ★★ (www.derwentvalleymills.org), an unparalleled collection of early cotton mills dotted along 15 miles of the river valley leading south to Derby, some of them the world's first "modern" factories. **Cromford Mill** (© **01629/823256;** www.arkwrightsociety.org.uk) is where the eponymous Sir Richard pioneered the water frame spinning machine that revolutionized textile manufacture. There are separate or combined tours of the mill and workers' village (£5, or £4 for village only), plus various high-quality shops, a wholefood cafe, and a canalside bookstore and restaurant. The complex is open daily 9am to 5pm. From here it's 5 miles southeast to **Crich Tramway Village & the National Tramway Museum** (see below).

Southwest of Matlock Bath lies **Carsington Water** ★ (© **0870/179-1111;** www.moretoexperience.co.uk), a reservoir with watersports and bike rentals, a visitor center, and playgrounds. Then due south lies **Derby** itself, which—though hardly the most scenic or culturally compelling of British cities—has a fine Cathedral Quarter (www.derbycathedralquarter.co.uk) with Victorian arcades, Georgian and Renaissance buildings, and independent shops and galleries. Close by, the **Silk Mill Museum of Industry and History** ★ (© **01332/255308;** www.derby.gov.uk), occupying the site of George Sorocold's 1702 and 1717 mills—some of the world's oldest factories, part of which are still visible—tells of the local industrial heritage and achievements, with a focus on the development of Rolls-Royce aero engines and the railway industry, as well as mining, porcelain production, and foundry work.

Admission is free, and it's open Monday 11am to 5pm, Tuesday to Saturday 10am to 5pm, and Sunday and bank holidays 1 to 4pm. There's more local porcelain and history in the **Derby Museum & Art Gallery** (✆ **01332/641901;** www.derby.gov.uk) on the Strand (same hours; also free).

Around Derby are three National Trust (www.nationaltrust.org.uk) properties. Just north, near Quarndon, is **Kedleston Hall,** while south of the city, at Ticknall, is **Calke Abbey,** and providing a worthy finale to Derbyshire 16 miles west of Derby is **Sudbury Hall and the National Trust Museum of Childhood.**

Note that some attractions in southern Derbyshire are within the **National Forest** (p. 553), while just over the border in Staffordshire, **Alton Towers** (✆ **0871/222-3330;** www.altontowers.com) is one of the U.K.'s best theme parks.

Calke Abbey ★ HISTORIC SITE   This country house fallen into disrepair is a charming place to ramble around, with its overgrown courtyards, faded walled gardens, and peeling paintwork. As you do, consider that the same fate almost befell Chatsworth House (p. 537). Take advantage of fine weather to explore the vast parkland with its red and fallow deer and deer shelter, and restored wetland area, a wildlife haven. Four on-site cottages include two former gatehouse lodges.

Ticknall, 14 miles south of Derby. ✆ **01332/863822.** www.nationaltrust.org.uk. Admission house and garden £8.80, £4.50 children 5–16; less for park and stables, or garden only. Park daily 7:30am–7:30pm; see website for house, gardens, and stables.

Crich Tramway Village & the National Tramway Museum ★★ ☺ MUSEUM/ PARK   This restored period village with its cobblestones and collection of original facades from buildings around the U.K. displays trams both horse-drawn and modern and also has a viewing gallery from which you can watch trams being restored. Other attractions making it a great family venue include a woodland walk, an adventure playground, a family-friendly pub that was saved from demolition in Stoke and rebuilt here, a tearoom, an ice-cream parlor, and an old-fashioned candy shop.

Crich, 6 miles southeast of Matlock Bath. ✆ **01773/854321.** www.tramway.co.uk. Admission £12 adults, £7 children 4–15. Open Feb school break and Mar weekends 10:30am–4:30pm; Apr–Oct daily 10am–5:30pm; and some weekends in Dec 10:30am–6:30pm.

Heights of Abraham ★★ ☺ PARK   This wooded hilltop park is another excellent bet for a family day out, with walking paths, tours of a former mine, a fossil museum, and play areas. Best of all, you get here by cable-car from the base of the opposite cliff, High Tor. The fit can also climb High Tor itself, along a narrow winding path dubbed Giddy Edge.

Matlock Baths. ✆ **01629/582365.** www.heightsofabraham.com. Admission £13 adults, £8.80 children 5–16. Open Feb school break and late Mar–Oct daily 10am–4:30pm, plus weekends early–mid Mar.

Kedleston Hall ★ HISTORIC SITE   Set in its own historic parkland, this handsome neoclassical mansion was built by Robert Adam in the 1760s on a site occupied by the Curzon family since the 12th century. They still reside here, but visitors can tour some of the stunning interiors as well as investigating the Eastern Museum with its colonial and Asian artifacts acquired at the turn of the 20th century by the then Lord Curzon, Viceroy of India.

Near Quarndon, 6 miles north of Derby. ✆ **01332/842191.** www.nationaltrust.org.uk. Admission house and grounds £9.90 adults, £4.90 children 5–16. House mid-Feb–Oct Sat–Wed noon–5pm; park year-round daily 10am to between 4 and 6pm.

Sudbury Hall & the National Trust Museum of Childhood ★★ ☺ HISTORIC SITE/MUSEUM   The impressive 17th-century country home of the Lords Vernon boasts gorgeous plasterwork, wood carvings, and classical story-based murals, with the Great Staircase and Long Gallery particularly worthy of admiration. But it's also well worth visiting for its museum on childhood in days gone by, featurng interactive displays and the chance for kids to play at being Victorian chimney sweeps, schoolchildren and the like, plus a woodland adventure play space.

Sudbury, 14 miles west of Derby. ✆ **01283/585305.** www.nationaltrust.org.uk. Admission hall £7.45 adults, £3.80 children 5–18. Hall open mid-Feb–Oct Wed–Sun 1–5pm. See website for times and prices for museum and grounds.

Where to Eat

Café @ The Green Pavilion ★ 🎁 INTERNATIONAL   Buxton's best cafe, adjunct to a florist's shop and winner of a regional "Food Heroes" award for its commitment to using top local produce, is a welcoming spot for English breakfast; morning coffee and cakes; light lunches including sandwiches, salads, Derbyshire oatcakes, homity (open vegetable) pie, falafel, and New York style meatballs; and afternoon tea. The oudoor tables are great for people-watching in warmer weather. The cafe is tiny, so you may have to wait for a table, but all food can be ordered to take out—perhaps to make up a picnic in the nearby Pavilion Gardens (p. 536). Both the cafe and the flower shop sell homemade jams, preserves, and chutneys.

4 Terrace Rd., Buxton. ✆ **01298/77480.** www.greenpavilion.co.uk. Reservations not accepted. MC, V. Main courses £4–£7.50. Mon–Sat 7:30am–5:30pm, Sun 9am–5pm.

Devonshire Arms at Beeley ★ 🗡 TRADITIONAL BRITISH/INTERNATIONAL Part of the Chatsworth Estate, this village inn combines historic charm in the original part of the building, with its open fire and low beams, with a contemporary brasserie area with floor-to-ceiling windows affording views over the brook and square. Local produce is the order of the day, whether you eat from the breakfast menu (try fried Derbyshire oatcakes with dry cured bacon and sage Derby cheese, or Bakewell Pudding Shop muffin with black pudding, sausage, and fried eggs); the snack menu (noon–6pm), of which the highlight is curried belly-pork burger with crispy bacon, Irish porters, and skinny chips; the afternoon tea menu; or the main lunch and dinner menu, which includes daily-changing "market dishes." Some dishes are highly ambitious in conception (sometimes too much so), with Asian flavors prominent—for example, Cornish squid and Scottish mussel sausage with smoked treacle bacon, red chili, apples, and lemongrass.

The eight **rooms** (£134–£197 double), designed by the Duchess of Devonshire, with fabrics prepared by the seamstresses at Chatsworth, were slated for a refurbish as we went to press.

Devonshire Square, Beeley. ✆ **01756/718111**. www.devonshirebeeley.co.uk. Reservations recommended (dinner). AE, MC, DC, V. Main courses £6.95–£18. Daily 7:30–10am (breakfast to non-guests by prior arrangement only) and noon–9:30pm.

The Peacock at Rowsley ★ 🎁 MODERN EUROPEAN   This little haven of country-house chic was recently bought and refurbished by Lord Manners of Haddon Hall (p. 537), who lured the head chef back from working with Tom Aikens in London to oversee the smart, award-winning restaurant with its focus on local produce. The evening fine-dining menu includes the likes of fried duck liver with Yorkshire rhubarb, ginger, and macadamia nuts; and roast rib-eye of Derbyshire beef with three-grain risotto and kohlrabi. The bar menu (available lunch and dinner) has more accessible comfort-food dishes such as beer-battered fish and chips, sausages with mash, kale, and sage and onion gravy, ploughman's lunch (cheese, ham and pickle sandwich or salad), sandwiches, and croques.

The **16 rooms** (£155–£258 double) unite antiques with chic contemporary furnishings, fine fabrics, and crisp white sheets.

Rowsley. ✆ **01629/733518.** www.thepeacockatrowsley.com. MC, V. Reservations advised (dinner). Main courses £15–£32. Mon-Sat noon–2pm and 6:30–9pm; Sun noon–2pm.

PeliDeli ☺ BREAKFAST/SNACKS/LUNCH   This true local shop and cafe in the center of Matlock—winner of the Derbyshire Food & Drink Café of the Year award in 2010—offers seasonal produce hand-selected by the owners from local providers. Breakfast might consist of crumpets (savory griddle cakes) or onion bagel with cream cheese, and a hot or cold smoothie; later in the day choose from paninis or other sandwiches (perhaps Derbyshire ham and Derby cheese with real-ale chutney), and daily-changing soups and salad platters. If it's winter, warm up with one of the incredible hot chocolates with hazelnut syrup or Cointreau. There's a second branch in Wirksworth, 5 miles south of Matlock.

1 Jubilee Buildings, Crown Square, Matlock. ✆ **07980/694841.** www.pelideli.com. MC, V. Main courses £2–£5. Mon-Fri 8am–5pm, Sat 8:45am–4pm.

Royal Oak at Hurdlow ★ 🍴 ☺ TRADITIONAL BRITISH   This pub in the midst of countryside just off the Tissington Trail (p. 535) attracts weary walkers and cyclists with its open fires, cosy nooks, beer garden, cask-conditioned ales, and hearty pub food based on produce sourced within a small distance. Relaxed and friendly, it's a good place for families, especially at Sunday lunch, when there are traditional roasts but also sandwiches and other main courses such as haddock and chips, or butternut squash, spinach, and walnut lasagna. Kids get their own menu all week (£4.95 for a main course). For those who'd like to linger or are walking in the area, there's a bunk-barn with **rooms** to accommodate four, six, or eight guests and a communal kitchen, plus a family-friendly campsite. The Bunk Barn is £12 pppn and the campsite is from £13 per night for camper vans and £7-13 for tents (minimum stay of 2 nights between Apr and Sept).

Hurdlow. ✆ **01298/83288.** www.peakpub.co.uk. Reservations recommended (dinner). MC, V. Main courses £5.75–£21. Daily noon–9pm.

Entertainment & Nightlife

Derbyshire won't ever set the world alight with its nightlife, but there is no end of cosy pubs around the county for sampling its famed real ales. In Derby, sample produce from the city's micro-breweries at the **Greyhound** (✆ **01332/344155**) on Friar Gate, dating back to 1734; the characterful (and allegedly haunted) **Ye Olde Dolphin Inn** (✆ **01332/267711**) near the cathedral, which runs its own beer festivals; or the Victorian **Brunswick** (✆ **01332/290677**) near the station.

Shopping

Local produce is one of the great assets of Derbyshire, so farmers' markets and farm shops—of which the Chatsworth Farm Shop (p. 533) is the most famous—are in abundance here. Look out for Hartington Stilton and other handmade cheeses, gingerbread, and local honey. The main markets are listed below (check with local tourist boards if you are making a special trip).

Bakewell	Agricultural Centre	last Saturday of month, starts 9am
Buxton	Market Place	first Thursday of month, 8:30am to 4:30pm
Castleton	Village Hall	first Sunday of month, 10am to 3pm
Derby	Market Place	third Thursday of month, 9am to 3pm
Hartington	Hartington Moor	Sundays June to mid-September, 10am to 5pm

In the northern Peak District, the walkers' paradise of Hathersage is home to the **David Mellor Cutlery Factory, Design Museum,** and **Country Shop** (✆ **01433/ 650220;** www.davidmellordesign.com) showcasing (and selling) the work of the iconic designer and his son Corin, plus other local crafts. Inside the Round Building, an award-winning factory, you can watch some of Mellor's cutlery being made, and there's a stunning on-site cafe serving local produce.

Where to Stay

For the **Peacock at Rowsley** and the **Devonshire Arms at Beeley,** see p. 540. For the bunk rooms and campsite at the **Royal Oak at Hurdlow,** see p. 541.

The Chateau & Wye House Suites ★ ☺   A flexible option for anyone looking for a base in lively Buxton, these one-, two-, and three-bedroomed apartments occupy an impressive historic building (The Chateau) and two modern outbuildings in woodland and grounds with fountains. The quite chic, modern decor rivals that of many a boutique hotel, and luxuries include underfloor heating and Jacuzzi-style baths. Some apartments have a balcony and/or a small garden area. A minimum 2-night stay applies at weekends. *Insider tip:* Guests get discounts on some shows at the Opera House, about a 10-minute walk away (downhill).

Corbar Rd., Buxton, Derbyshire SK17 6RU. www.wyehouse.com. ✆ **0845/164-8950.** 19 units. £99–£135 1-bedroom apartment. MC, V. Free parking. *In room:* TV/DVD, kitchen (w/dishwasher), Wi-Fi (free).

Manifold Farm ★★ ☺ 🎁   If Chatsworth House is the "jewel in the crown" of the Peak District, where better to holiday in the region than a traditional holiday cottage on one of its estates? All cottages are comfortable and cosy rather than luxurious— exactly right for walkers, dog-owners, and families. Of a total of 17 cottages, Manifold, a former dairy farm south of Matlock, accounts for five. An attractive complex of stone buildings set around a courtyard, they sleep 2 to 10 guests. All but one has a log-burning stove, and each has its own garden. There's also a shared games room. For those who wish to explore, there's a network of footpaths on the doorstep, Carsington Water only 4 miles away, and Chatsworth House, within a 20-minute drive (weekly guests get free tickets). A fresh-baked farmhouse Victoria spongecake and tea-tray greet your arrival at your cottage.

Other options on Chatsworth's estates include **Swiss Cottage,** on a hill behind Chatsworth House, overlooking its own lake (it sleeps up to six), and the 16th-century **Hunting Tower,** on an escarpment also just above the House, sleeping four plus two in a stone annex. There are also four **hotels/pubs with rooms** on the estate, including the **Devonshire Arms at Beeley** (p. 540).

Shottle, Derbyshire DE56 2DX. www.chatsworth.org. ✆ **01246/565379.** 5 units. £440–£586/week cottage for 2; £689–£876/week cottage for 4 (3-night bookings sometimes available). MC, V. Free parking. **Amenities:** Games room. *In room:* TV/DVD/VCR, CD player, kitchen (w/dishwasher and washer/dryer).

Rivendale Leisure Park ★ 🗡 ☺   In a disused quarry amid stunning countryside with easy access to the "Trails Triangle" formed by the Tissington Trail (p. 535), High Peak Trail, and the cycleway around Carsington Water, this is a good budget and eco-friendly base for cyclists and walkers, who can relieve muscle strain in the wood-fired hot tub (or rent a tub for their own campsite). Bring your own caravan, motor home, or tent, or there are yurts with a stove (accommodating three to eight), camping pods (insulated wooden mountain huts for four, with electricity), static caravans, and B&B rooms. Some pitches are in a wildflower meadow or on an isolated hillside, and all guests have access to much of the surrounding meadows and woodland with its dragonflies, woodpeckers, owls, falcons, and more. Bring flashlights—there's little lighting so that guests can view the night sky in all its glory. There's a kids' play area, plus a restaurant/pub with a family room.

Buxton Rd., Alsop-en-le-Dale, Derbyshire DE6 1QU. www.rivendalecaravanpark.co.uk. © **01335/310441.** £11–£23 campsite; £38 yurt for 3, £48 camping pod for 4. MC, V. Free parking. **Amenities:** Restaurant/pub and cafe with Internet access; shop; shower and toilet building; electrical hook-up (exc. in meadow); play area. *In room:* TV and CD player (static caravan), hot-tub rental, fire pit loan, BBQ equipment (some), kitchen (some).

YHA National Forest ☺   There are several youth hostels in Derbyshire so appealing that even those not on a tight budget will be tempted to stay. This newly built hostel in the Derbyshire section of the National Forest is an especially good (and very eco-friendly) base for families, handy for Conkers, Rosliston Forestry Centre, and Snibston (p. 553), and for walking and cycling routes for all ages and abilities. All rooms are en suite (accommodating two to five guests), and some have double beds. The well-priced restaurant offers local produce, ales, and organic wines, though you can cut costs by using the well-equipped communal kitchen (including at breakfast, which costs £4.50 in the restaurant).

Other good hostels in the area are **Hartington Hall,** a 17th-century manor near Buxton, and **Ilam Hall,** a National Trust-owned Victorian Gothic manor in Dovedale.

8 Bath Lane, Moira, Derbyshire DE12 6BD. www.yha.org.uk. © **0845/371-9672.** 23 units. 2-bed room £43–£53, plus £3pppn for non-YHA members. MC, V. Free parking. **Amenities:** Restaurant; kitchen; lounge; games room; Wi-Fi (£1 per 20 min.).

NOTTINGHAMSHIRE

Nottingham: 127 miles N of London; 81 miles SE of Manchester; 280 miles S of Edinburgh

Derbyshire's neighbor is largely taken up (in terms of historic boundaries if not tree coverage) by **Sherwood Forest,** remnant of a former royal hunting forest and legendary stamping ground of Robin Hood, but it also lures visitors with a city and a few towns rich in both folklore and shopping opportunities, whether your tastes run to designer clothes or antiques. Nottinghamshire is also a good base for exploring the cathedral city of **Lincoln** over in Lincolnshire.

Essentials

GETTING THERE   Direct trains from London's St. Pancras or King's Cross Stations to Nottingham take just under 2 hours, costing around £52 for a round-trip, direct buses (© **0871/781-8181;** www.nationalexpress.com) 3¼ hours. By car from London, it's a 127-mile journey of at least 2½ hours, almost all of it on the M1 motorway, which runs a few miles west of Nottingham. For those heading from the north, Nottingham is 280 miles south of Edinburgh, 81 miles southeast of Manchester. For Transpeak buses from Manchester to Nottingham via the Peak District, see p. 534.

For those coming from farther afield, Nottingham is 15 miles northeast of **East Midlands Airport** (p. 534). **Robin Hood Airport Doncaster Sheffield** is just

References to Robin Hood, the archer and swordsman who "robbed from the rich to feed the poor," go back as far as the 13th century, but nobody knows whether the heroic outlaw is invention or was based on real outlaws. Regardless, Robin and his Merry Men continue to exert a powerful hold on the public imagination—as the popularity of the 2006–09 BBC series and 2010 Russell Crowe movie attest.

The **Robin Hood Trail** (www.robinhoodbreaks.visitnottingham.com) takes you to 12 locations pertaining to the legend, including spots where Robin Hood lived, fought, hunted, or preyed on the wealthy, among them

Nottingham Castle, Thieves Wood, Rufford Abbey Country Park, Sherwood Forest Country Park, King John's Palace, Edwinstone, and Clumber Park. You can follow most of the route by bike or drive it (download a free satellite-navigation guide and podcast on the website). An "In the footsteps of Robin Hood" CD and interactive map/guide (£1.99), from the Nottingham Tourism Centre or online, is indispensable. Don't confuse the above-mentioned trail with **Robin Hood Way** (www.robinhoodway.com), a 107-mile footpath from Nottingham to Southwell via Edwinstone, also taking in areas linked with the outlaw.

outside the county border, in South Yorkshire, while **Birmingham International Airport** is also within easy reach.

VISITOR INFORMATION **Nottingham Tourism Centre,** 1–4 Smithy Row (✆ 08444/775678; www.visitnottingham.com) is open Monday to Friday 9am to 5:50pm, Saturday 9am to 5pm, Sunday 10am to 4pm.

Sherwood Forest Visitor Centre, Edwinstowe (✆ 01623/823202; www.newark-sherwooddc.gov.uk/), Information office is seasonal—call ahead.

SPECIAL EVENTS The Sherwood Forest Visitor Centre is the focus for the week-long **Robin Hood Festival** (www.nottinghamshire.gov.uk/robinhoodfestival) in July or August, celebrating the outlaw with medieval crafts, children's theatre and food stalls, and jugglers, jesters, and other costumed characters. Alternatively, October sees the **Robin Hood Pageant** at **Nottingham Castle** (p. 547), with the castle green alive with historical reconstructions between the outlaws and the sheriffs' men, some of them on horseback, artisan displays, performances by jesters, wandering minstrels and storytellers, and archery sessions. Nottingham is also known for its **Goose Fair** (www.nottinghamgoosefair.co.uk), a huge 5-day fun fair dating back more than 700 years. Held each October, it was named after the thousands of geese that used to be driven to Nottingham from Lincolnshire to be sold.

To the east of the country, Newark hosts the **International Antiques and Collectors Fair** (www.iacf.co.uk/newark), Europe's largest such event, held every other month and attracting dealers and buyers from around the globe.

Exploring the Area

SHERWOOD FOREST NATIONAL NATURE RESERVE

Not all of Sherwood Forest is wooded: **Sherwood Forest Country Park** ★★★ (✆ 01623/823202; www.nottinghamshire.gov.uk) at Edwinstowe, 18 miles north of Nottingham, is the place to head, with its visitor center (see above) and the

800-year-old Major Oak, in the trunk of which Robin Hood hid (at least according to local lore). The visitor center (with a restaurant) is the starting point for marked walks and footpaths through the woods; you can also buy self-guided family trails maps or sign up for guided walks and activities, from archery and birds-of-prey sessions to costumed re-enactments, woodland crafts, and puppetry. The park is open daily 10am to 5pm in summer; 10am to 4pm in winter (to 5pm on Sat–Sun), with parking £3; the visitor center shuts all winter.

Edwinstowe is also the entry point for the **Sherwood Pines Forest Park ★★★** (© **01623/822447;** www.forestry.gov.uk), run by the Forestry Commission and with a visitor center of its own running more activities and events, plus another Go Ape! treetop adventure course, woodland play areas, and bike-rental, and a Forest Holidays site with wooden lodges (p. 550). The park is open May to September daily 8am to 10pm, October to April 8am to 6pm; parking is £3.

Another option is to head for the northernmost part of the forest, to Worksop, where **Clumber Park ★★★** (© **0844/800-1895;** www.nationaltrust.org.uk) offers masses of green space and spectacular scenery (it's the grounds of the long-lost country house of Clumber Hall, destroyed by fire in the 1930s), best discovered on more than 22 miles of cycle routes, one of them around the lake. You can also roam the walled kitchen garden (which provides many ingredients for the restaurant), seek out a few moments of peace in the Victorian chapel, or stroll the elegant paths of the 18th-century pleasure ground, designed to give the dukes of Newcastle who lived here secluded walks. At press time, a state-of-the-art Discovery & Visitor Centre was scheduled to open in the former stableyard. The park is open (and free) to visitors all the time; see the website for opening times of park facilities. Not far away lies **Cresswell Crags,** "Britain's oldest art gallery."

There's another great green space within the forest confines, at Ollerton: **Rufford Abbey Country Park ★** (© **01623/821338;** www.nottinghamshire.gov.uk/ruffordcp), a swath of historic parkland and gardens including woodland and lakeside walks, a play village with a maze and a children's garden, a modern sculpture trail, a contemporary craft center, the ruins of a medieval monastery with an exhibition on the life of Rufford's monks, and a camera obscura. It's open daily 10am to 5pm in summer, 10:30am to 4:30pm in winter, with slight seasonal variations; entry is free, parking £3.

Literary associations abound south of Mansfield, at **Newstead Abbey** and the **DH Lawrence Birthplace Museum** (see below).

Cresswell Crags Museum & Heritage Centre ★★ ☺ MUSEUM

The U.K.'s only known Ice Age rock art was discovered on this site in 2003, and you can also view stone tools and animal remains that were found within this limestone gorge honeycombed with caves and smaller fissures. Depending on when you visit you can take a Rock Art or Ice Age tour or just learn more about the site—one of the most northerly on Earth to have been inhabited by ancient peoples—in the museum and visitor center. Walking trails take you around the surrounding country park and wildlife reserve.

Crags Rd., Welbeck. © **01909/720378.** www.creswell-crags.org.uk. Admission £3 adults, £1.50 children 5–16; for tour prices, see website. Exhibition daily Feb and Oct 10am–4:30pm, Mar–Sept daily 10am–5:30pm, Nov–Jan Sat–Sun 10am–4:30pm; for cave tours (weekends and school holidays except winter) see website.

DH Lawrence Birthplace Museum ★ HISTORIC HOME

This unassuming terraced miner's cottage has been restored inside, to the way it would have looked when the writer most famous for the scandal-raising *Lady Chatterley's Lover* spent part of his childhood here. Guides give the background to Lawrence's working-class mining heritage. The same ticket gives access to the nearby Durban House Heritage Centre, with additional displays on the town's famous son, who was born in 1885 and attended Nottingham University, and on mining.

8a Victoria St., Eastwood. ✆ **01773/717353.** www.broxtowe.gov.uk. Admission £2.50 adults, £1.75 children 5–16. Tues–Fri and Sun 10am–5pm (to 4pm in winter).

Newstead Abbey ★★ ☺ HISTORIC SITE   This partly ruined Augustinian priory was once home to Romantic poet Lord Byron, and visitors can tour his private apartments and see some of his possessions, in addition to exploring various Victorian rooms plus the medieval cloisters and chapterhouse, now a chapel. A dressing-up room and wildlife trail through the gardens and parkland with their lakes, ponds, and cascades keep kids engaged.

Ravenshead. ✆ **01623/455900.** www.newsteadabbey.org.uk. Admission £8 adults, £3.50 children 2–16. Grounds daily 9am–4:30pm, house Apr–Sept Fri–Mon noon–5pm.

14

NOTTINGHAM ★

Nottinghamshire's county town founded its wealth on lace-making as well as coal-mining, but these days it's the shops and nightlife that draw most visitors, especially since the 2006 redevelopment of the Old Market Square. At the **Museum of Nottingham Life at Brewhouse Yard** (✆ **0115/915-3600**), a few minutes away from Nottingham Castle (see below), you'll find displays on the social history of Nottingham within five 17th-century cottages, plus some more man-made caves. This museum is beside **Ye Olde Trip to Jerusalem** (✆ **01159/473171;** www.tripto jerusalem.com), built into the rockface and dating from 1189—which is said to make it the oldest inn in England. It's a good spot for real ales.

About 3 miles west of the center of Nottingham, **Wollaton Hall** (✆ **0115/9153900;** www.wollatonhall.org.uk) is a well-preserved Elizabethan mansion on a hill with gardens and deer-filled parkland, and also home to a natural history museum. Entry is free; the hall and museum are open daily April to October 11am to 5pm (4pm in winter), the park from 8 or 9am to dusk. Car parking is £2. Also on the city's western fringes, the **Attenborough Nature Centre** ★ (✆ **0115/972-1777;** www.attenboroughnaturecentre.co.uk) is an award-winning new visitor facility within the Attenborough Nature Reserve, opened by Sir David on former gravel pits in 1966. Within the ecologically friendly buildings are interactive displays, a nature shop, and an organic/fair-trade cafe; outside are a sensory nature trail, guided walks, and wildlife-viewing activities, and a bird hide. There's access to the reserve from 7am to dusk (nature center times vary); entry is free.

Just east of the city, the **National Water Sports Centre** (✆ **0115/9821212;** www.nwscnotts.com) offers whitewater rafting, sailing, canoeing and kayaking, water-skiing, and powerboating, plus a country park with lakes, lagoons, and nature trails, an assault (obstacle) course, and a hostel-style hotel and a campsite.

City of Caves ★ ☺ HISTORIC SITE   Nottingham's famed caves, carved out of the soft Sherwood limestone underlying the city, were probably inhabited as early as the 11th century, and some remained so until 1845. Over time they were used as store rooms, factories, pub cellars, medieval tanneries, and air-raid shelters. These slightly schlocky but informative tours take you on a journey through Nottingham's history and include a recreation of the Slums of Drury Hill.

Upper Level, Broadmarsh Shopping Centre. ✆ **0115/9881955.** www.cityofcaves.com. Admission £5.95 adults, £4.50 children. Mon–Fri 11:30am–4:30pm, Sat–Sun 10:30am–4:30pm.

Galleries of Justice Museum ★ ☺ MUSEUM

Set inside Nottingham's old courtyard and county jail, this museum expands the local outlaws theme into a general exploration of crime and punishment via audio tour (Mon–Fri 10:30am–5pm), or you can choose a performance tour with costumed actors leading you through the magistrate's court down into the cells and then out into the exercise yard, where hangings often took place.

Lace Market. ✆ **0115/9520555.** www.galleriesofjustice.org.uk. Admission for performance tours £8.95 adults, £6.95 children 4–14. Sat–Sun and bank and school holidays 10:30am–5pm.

Nottingham Castle ★★ ☺ MUSEUM

Not a castle at all but a ducal mansion erected on the site of the city's medieval castle, this is now a cutting-edge museum and art gallery with collections of silver, glass, decorative items, and visual arts (much of it contemporary and global in scope), as well as local archeology and history. If that makes it sound a bit heavy-going, know that there are interactive displays and activities aimed at families, a medieval-style playground, and a picnic area.

Off Friar Lane. ✆ **0115/9153700.** www.nottinghamcity.gov.uk. Admission £5.50 adults, £4 children 15 and under. Tues–Sun 10am–5pm (4pm in winter).

EASTERN NOTTINGHAMSHIRE ★

Beyond Sherwood Forest and Nottingham, the county is low-key, but there are a few gems. The town of Southwell, 15 miles northeast of Nottingham, has an interesting array of historic buildings, the highlight being **Southwell Minster ★** (✆ **01636/ 812649;** www.southwellminster.org), a splendid example of Norman and Early English architecture with pyramidal spires of lead unique in Britain. In addition to the stunning interior, you can admire part of a Roman mural from the remains of a large and opulent villa excavated beneath the minster and churchyard in the 1950s. The cathedral is open daily 7am to 7pm, with free entry.

Lord Byron stayed in Southwell in his mother's rented house during holidays from school and then Cambridge University—though he had by then inherited Newstead Abbey (p. 546), he couldn't afford to make it habitable. Earlier, during the English Civil War, King Charles I spent his last night as a free man in the King's Head (now the Saracen's Head pub), before capitulating to the Scottish army at nearby Kelham. Cromwell may also have stayed in the King's Arms; his troops sequestered the archbishop's palace as stables, contributing to its ruin, and ransacked much of the town. Southwell's main sight today is **The Workhouse ★** (✆ **01636/817260;** www. nationaltrust.org.uk), the most complete in existence, giving a powerful overview of how life was for the 19th-century poor through its segregated work yards, day rooms, dorms, master's quarters, cellars, and recreated 19th-century garden, which produces fruit and vegetables for the shop. Living History events bring the venue, which is open March to October daily noon to 5pm, most vividly to life. Admission is £6.75 for adults, £3.40 for children 5 to 16.

There's more highly impressive ecclesiastical architecture not far away, at **Hawton,** south of Newark-on-Trent near the border with Lincolnshire. Art and architecture scholar Nikolaus Pevsner described its medieval **All Saint's Church ★** (✆ **01636/704811;** www.farndon-hawton.org.uk) as one of the most exciting buildings in all Britain, by virtue of the outstanding carvings on its Easter Sepulchre and on its sedilia. No one has ever solved the mystery of why a small village church was endowed with such incredible carvings.

The market town of **Newark-on-Trent** ★ is good for a wander, with historic buildings lining its main square, a local-history museum, and a ruined castle holding scenic sway over the River Trent; a heritage center on the grounds of the latter traces this town's role in the English Civil War, when, a major supporter of the Royalist cause, it was besieged three times. But Newark's main draw is its antiques emporia and shops and famous bi-monthly antiques fairs (see "Shopping," below).

Where to Eat

VERY EXPENSIVE

Restaurant Sat Bains ★★★ MODERN EUROPEAN Nottingham's only Michelin-starred restaurant is named after its TV celebrity chef, born in Derby and with experience of working with Raymond Blanc and at L'Escargot in London. The location—southwest of the center, near an industrial estate and motorway flyover—is uninspiring, but once inside the low-slung building by the River Trent, with its dining room, conservatory, and handful of guest rooms set around a courtyard, you'll forget all that as you embark on a journey of culinary revelation. Dinners are tasting menus of 5 (Tues–Thurs only), 7, or 10 courses, or you can go for broke with a bespoke version. You can also book the Chef's Table in order to watch Bains at work. There's also a new development kitchen hosting lunches and demonstrations. Locally foraged wild foods are used in abundance here; the menu changes seasonally but might include braised mutton with pickled onions and elder capers, leeks with thyme cream and hazelnuts, and sea buckthorn tart with pistachio and marshmallow. The attractive **rooms and suites** start at £90 for a double; midweek packages include a room, 7-course tasting menu, and breakfast at £120 to £140.

Lenton Lane, Nottingham. ℂ **0115/986-6566.** www.restaurantsatbains.com. Reservations required. Fixed-price dinner £55–£150. AE, DC, MC, V. Tues–Sat 7–9:30pm, lunch by arrangement.

EXPENSIVE

Launay's ★★ ☺ ⛔ MODERN EUROPEAN/INTERNATIONAL A few minutes' walk from the Sherwood Forest Visitor Centre (p. 544) and also handy for Center Parcs (p. 550), this much-lauded restaurant and bar in a 16th-century building overlooks the church where Robin Hood is said to have married Maid Marian. It comes into its own in summer, when you can sit out on the terrace and play boules. Seasonal local ingredients go into the English and French dishes tinged with modern global influences—think oysters with cauliflower pannacotta, smoked Avruga caviar, and crispy kale, or roast salmon with scallops, scallion mash, minted pea purée, broccoli, and Sauvignon Blanc sauce, plus the odd north African or Asian dish. If you have a sweet tooth, leave room for the fun Assiette de Friandises of retro candy-store treats, including a white chocolate mouse, candy floss (cotton candy), and a gingerbread man. Lunch is more down-to-earth, with sandwiches, pasta, fish and chips, and the like, plus good kids' dishes (£4–£4.95).

Church St., Edwinstowe. ℂ **01623/822266.** www.launaysrestaurant.co.uk. Reservations recommended. Main courses £12–£25. MC, V. Mon–Sat noon–3pm and 6:30–10pm, Sun noon–4pm.

MODERATE

Nottingham can be a good place for Indian food; try **The Cumin** at 62–64 Maid Marian Way (ℂ **0115/941-9941;** www.thecumin.co.uk), where the dishes are often inflected by the Punjabi family's background in Kenya.

Iberico World Tapas ★★ SPANISH/INTERNATIONAL In a historic building in the heart of Nottingham's history-drenched Lace Market, Iberico takes you to another world with its Moorish tiles, frescoes, and wrought ironwork. As with all tapas joints, this is the place to share lots of little platters of enticing goodies, both Spanish and more exotic, including the incredible black cod with spicy miso, and the likes of lime, salt, and pepper squid; smoked eel; quail in red wine; or crispy zucchini flowers. You can also get charcuterie and cheese platters, the former including both Spanish ham from acorn-fed pigs and locally cured Sonka. Express lunch deals (Tues–Fri) give you two tapas dishes, Catalan bread, and a dessert for a bargain (£10). There are also plenty of bar stools for whoever just wants to graze while sampling from the interesting list of sherries, or enjoy a churro and hot chocolate.

The Shire Hall, High Pavement, Nottingham. ℂ **0115/941-0410.** www.ibericotapas.com. Reservations recommended (dinner). Tapas dishes £3.50–£8. MC, V. Mon–Fri noon–2pm and 6–10pm, Sat noon–2pm and 6–10:30pm.

The Wollaton Pub & Kitchen ★ ☺ TRADITIONAL BRITISH   A runner-up in the *Observer Monthly's* list of the best Sunday lunches in the U.K., this London-style gastro-pub in west Nottingham opens from mid-morning for brunch through lunch and afternoon tea to dinner, offering largely traditional cuisine plus the odd surprise dish based on mainly local produce. The famous Sunday lunches, served to 5pm, include traditional roasts but also the likes of homemade chorizo sausage with fried egg and toasted English muffin, butternut squash, and blue-cheese pancakes. There's also a very good kids' menu, available all week, featuring everything from baked beans and cheese on toast to roast chicken.

Lambourne Dr., Wollaton, Nottingham. ℂ **0115/928-8610.** www.thewollaton.co.uk. Reservations recommended. Main courses £5.95–£21. MC, V. Mon–Thurs 11am–9pm, Fri 11am–10pm, Sat 10am–10pm, Sun 10am–9pm.

INEXPENSIVE

Rushton's Next Door ★ 🛍 INTERNATIONAL   Adjoining a deli of the same name, this Newark bistro has loyal locals returning to sample from a wide-ranging menu that takes in everything from omelet with the deli's own roast ham and Lincolnshire Poacher cheddar, to classic beef bourguignon, to *moules marinières*, Thai vegetable curry, and Moroccan lamb tagine. A chalkboard lists daily set menus. Alternatively, you can just come for coffee and cakes, including a velvety chocolate marquise, any time of day. The chef happily caters to kids' requests.

41/42 Stodman St., Newark. ℂ **0845/8800859.** www.rushtonsdeli.co.uk. Reservations recommended. Main courses £6.50–£19. MC, V. Mon–Sat 11:30am–9pm.

Shopping ★★

Nottingham's long-standing popularity as a shopping destination was enhanced by the multimillion-pound redevelopment of the vast **Old Market Square** in 2007—it's from this huge social space that most of the city's prime shopping streets branch off. Fashion is a specialty—this *is* the hometown of Brit designer par excellence **Paul Smith,** whose original shop remains at 10 Byard Lane (ℂ **0115/950-6712;** www.paulsmith.co.uk). Those who love designer threads and shoes will lose endless hours browsing this area of historic cobbled streets around **Low Pavement** and **Bridlesmith Gate.** For more bohemian fashions, head east from the Square into **Hockley,** where you'll also find everything from contemporary furniture to hip dance-music stores in the shadow of Nottingham's grand former lace mills. There are more quirky independent stores on **Derby Road** and **Maid Marian Way,** also not far from the Square.

For foodie visitors, the **Nottingham Regional Food Market** brings the cream of local produce to Old Market Square on the third Friday and Saturday of the month. **Farmers' markets** take place across the county, including Mansfield (first Tues of month), Southwell (second Fri), and Newark (fourth Thurs). Mansfield also has a six-day-a-week open market dating back 700 years, while Newark holds a traditional street market (Wed, Fri, Sat) and antiques, craft, and bric-a-brac markets (Mon and Thurs), in addition to the famous **International Antiques and Collectors Fair** (p. 544).

In the heart of Sherwood Forest, at Ravenshead, **Longdale Craft Centre** (✆ 01623/794858; www.longdalecraftcentre.co.uk) specializes in sculptures and antiques restoration but also includes a recreated Victorian craft village where dealers sell collectibles dated from 1960 onward. Also in the Forest, near Clumber Park, Welbeck Abbey, home to the Duke and Duchess of Portland, is the site of the **Harley Gallery** (✆ 01909/501700; www.harleygallery.co.uk) of crafts workshops in a former kitchen garden, plus the **Notcutts Dukeries Garden Centre** (✆ 0844/879-4166; www.dukeries.co.uk) in the original glasshouses, and **Welbeck Farm Shop** (✆ 01909/478725; www.thewelbeckfarmshop.co.uk) and the **School of Artisan Food** (✆ 01909/532171; www.schoolofartisanfood.org) in the former estate gasworks. The Farm Shop sells Stichelton, the first organic raw-milk blue cheese produced in Britain since the late 1960s (Stilton is now required to be pasteurized).

Entertainment & Nightlife ★

Nottingham's large student population keeps it buzzing, with the Old Market Square the meeting place for revelers setting out to discover the city's famous nightlife, especially the hip **Lace Market and Hockley** neighborhood, where late-night bars line cobbled streets. The recently developed canalside **Castle Wharf** houses a Jongleurs comedy club as well as lots of bars and restaurants in its former warehouses. Gay residents and visitors are well catered for with gay and gay-friendly bars and clubs and other venues. For events listings, pick up a free copy of **Left Lion** magazine from selected venues, or see www.leftlion.co.uk.

Where to Stay

For rooms at **Restaurant Sat Bains** in Nottingham, see p. 548.

As we went to press, **Forest Holidays** was scheduled to open a new site in Sherwood Forest; some of its trademark Forest Cabins will include a bedroom in a treehouse extension. There's also a **Center Parcs** holiday village (www.centerparcs.co.uk) in Sherwood Forest, and the **Sherwood Forest Youth Hostel** (0845/371-9139; www.yha.org.uk) at Edwinstowe.

Willoughby House ★★ 🖋 By virtue of its antiques market, Newark and its surroundings are chockfull of delightful B&Bs of a standard you'd be very hard pressed to find elsewhere. This lovingly run little spot in a handsome Georgian village house 4 miles north of Newark mixes a certain modern boutique chic with quirky antique touches to give it a wholly individual feel. The wonderful breakfast of local fare is served on beautiful china in a cosy dining room with a roaring fire on chilly mornings. Little treats such as homemade flapjacks, bathrobes, and a complimentary DVD selection also set the place apart, although other excellent options in the vicinity include **Bridge House B&B** (www.arnoldsbandb.co.uk; ✆ 01636/674663, **The Hollies** (www.theholliesnewark.co.uk; ✆ 01636/676533).

This ancient city, 20 miles northeast of Newark, was the site of a Bronze Age settlement. Then, in the 3rd century, it was one of four provincial capitals of Roman Britain. In the Middle Ages, it was the center of Lindsey, a famous Anglo-Saxon kingdom. After the Norman conquest, it grew increasingly important, its merchants becoming rich by shipping wool directly to Flanders.

Much of the past lives on, in the form of medieval streets, half-timbered Tudor houses, the Norman **castle** (✆ 01522/511068; www.lincolnshire.gov.uk), and, best of all, magnificent **Lincoln Cathedral** ★★★ (✆ 01522/561600; www.lincolncathedral.com), which dominates its surroundings like no other English minster, with a central tower 81-m (271-ft.) high and visible from up to 30 miles away. Construction on the original Norman cathedral was begun in 1072, but the present cathedral is Gothic in style, particularly the Early English and Decorated periods. Virtually in its shadow, the ruined **Lincoln Medieval Bishops' Palace,** Minster Yard (✆ 01522/527468; www.english-heritage.org.uk) was the site of the biggest diocese in England in the Middle Ages. Also worth a wander are the **Museum of Lincolnshire Life,** Burton Road (✆ 01522/528448; www.

lincolnshire.gov.uk) and **The Collection and Usher Gallery,** Lindum Road (✆ 01522/550990; http://www.lincolnshire.gov.uk), with paintings, antique clocks, ceramics, and literary mementos, including portraits of Lincolnshire-born Alfred Lord Tennyson.

Lincoln lacks appealing stop-over options. If you come to sightsee, have brunch or lunch at **The Cheese Society** (✆ 01522/511003; www.thecheesesociety.co.uk), serving breakfasts from 10 to 11:30am and lunch until 4:30pm, and featuring the likes of Lincolnshire Poacher cheese and scallion pâté with homemade chutney. In the evening, **Jews House Restaurant,** 15 The Strait (✆ 01522/524851; www.jewshouserestaurant.co.uk), in one of the city's most historic buildings, is popular for its inventive Modern European cuisine (sample dish: roast pigeon, truffle custard, smoked bacon foam, and girolles). The **Wig and Mitre pub,** 30–32 Steep Hill (✆ 01522/535190; www.wigandmitre.com), is good for eating and drinking.

On the coast 35 miles southeast of Lincoln, **Boston** has a Pilgrim Fathers Memorial dedicated to those who emigrated from here, often to found other settlements of the same name, most notably in Massachusetts.

Main St., Norwell, Nottinghamshire NG23 6JN. www.willoughbyhousebandb.co.uk. ✆ **01636/636266.** 4 units. Free parking. AE, MC, V. £65–£105 double. **Amenities:** Lounge; evening meals by arrangement. *In room:* TV, hair dryer, free Wi-Fi.

LEICESTERSHIRE & RUTLAND

Leicester: 100 miles N of London

In the south of the East Midlands region, industrialized **Leicester** (pronounced *Lester*) combines a vibrant multi-ethnic cultural scene and modern museums with a rich history, while surrounding **Leicestershire** harbors more historic sites, including one of England's most important battlefields. At its north, Leicestershire links with Derbyshire and Staffordshire by means of the **National Forest,** which, though only a "forest in the making," conceals many attractions. Leicestershire once included adjoining **Rutland,** a great place for outdoors activities focused around its reservoir. A jaunt to the south, into Northamptonshire, takes you to **Althorp,** resting place of Princess Diana.

Essentials

GETTING THERE   Frequent trains from London's St. Pancras to Leicester take just over 1 hour, costing around £50 for a round-trip; there you can change to a train to Melton Mowbray (15 min.). From St. Pancras or King's Cross to Oakham takes a little under 2 hours, with a change at Leicester or Peterborough in Cambridgeshire.

Leicester is just off the M1, 100 miles (2 hr.) north of London, with Melton Mowbray 17 miles farther northeast on the A607. Oakham is 25 miles (45 min.) east of Leicester off the main A47. **National Express** buses (© **08717/818181;** www.nationalexpress.com) from London's Victoria Coach Station to Leicester take from 2¼ hours.

The M1 between junctions 21 and 23 crosses the eastern edge of the National Forest near Leicester. Train stations useful to access the National Forest are Leicester and Loughborough in Leicestershire; Derby and Willington in Derbyshire; and Tamworth, Burton on Trent, Lichfield, and Tutbury & Hatton in Staffordshire. For local buses, see www.traveline.org.uk.

VISITOR INFORMATION   Leicester Tourist Information Centre: 7–9 Every St., Town Hall Square (© **0844/888-5181;** www.goleicestershire.com).

Melton Mowbray Tourist Information Centre, 7 King St, © **01664/480992;** www.goleicestershire.com).

Oakham Tourist Information Centre: Rutland County Museum & Visitor Centre, Catmose Street (© **01572/758441;** www.discover-rutland.co.uk).

Rutland Water Tourist Information Centre, Sykes Lane, Empingham (© **01780 686800,** www.discover-rutland.co.uk).

SPECIAL EVENTS   The globally acclaimed **Leicester Early Music Festival** (www.earlymusicleicester.co.uk) has recently expanded into an all-year event, but music devotees should come in September, when the city also hosts the **Leicester International Music Festival** (www.musicfestival.co.uk) featuring some of the biggest names in classical music. There's south Asian music, plus dance, food, and more at the **Leicester Belgrave Mela** (www.leicester-mela.co.uk) each July, while Diwali celebrations here are among the largest outside India itself. October sees food-lovers converge on Brooksby Hall near Melton Mowbray for the **East Midlands Food & Drink Festival** (www.eastmidlandsfoodfestival.co.uk).

Exploring the Area

LEICESTER & LEICESTERSHIRE ★

Leicester may be off the tourist trail but it lays claim to being one of England's 10 biggest cities, one of its most ethnically diverse, and also one of its oldest, founded by the Romans as Ratae Coritanorum in A.D. 50. Roman ruins are now among its main draws, at the **Jewry Wall Museum** (see below), a 10-minute walk outside the center. Call ahead to visit the **Guru Nanak Sikh Museum** close by at 9 Holy Bones (© **0116/251-7460;** www.thesikhmuseum.com), where paintings, coins, manuscripts, and models of shrines trace the evolution of Sikh history and culture.

This "forest in the making" (www. nationalforest.org) was established in 1990 to convert a 200-square-mile area of Leicestershire, Derbyshire, and Staffordshire into woodland, and in doing so create forestry and tourism jobs. Linking the ancient forests of Needwood in Staffordshire and Charnwood in Leicestershire, it stretches west from the outskirts of Leicester to Burton upon Trent and beyond.

Though it's still far from a true forest, the 20 million trees slated to be planted over the next 30 to 40 years will cover a third of the area, with the rest given over to farmland, villages, and open land. But it's already a great place to visit, especially with kids. The focal point is **Conkers** ★ (near Swadlincote in south Derbyshire; (C) 01283/ 216633; www.visitconkers.com), where indoor and outdoor zones and activities include an adventure playground, woodland discovery center, and Enchanted Forest with a simulated treetop walk and rope walkways. It's open daily 10am to 6pm (5pm in winter), and admission is £8.50 for adults, £6.95 for children 3 to 15. Also near Swadlincote, the **Rosliston Forestry Centre** ★★ ((C) 01283/563483; www. roslistonforestrycentre.co.uk) is another hive of activity, including bike rental, birds-of-prey sessions, archery, laser games, astronomy walks, and woodland playgrounds. You can stay in lodges on-site or camp nearby at **Beehive Woodland Lakes** ((C) 01283/ 763981; www.beehivefarm-woodland-lakes.co.uk). Early summer 2011 also saw the opening of the National Forest Cycling Centre with its off-road trails.

To the east, in Coalville in Leicestershire, **Snibston** ★ ((C) 01530/278444; www.leicester.gov.uk) is a former mine with an interactive museum in the former colliery buildings, a historic mining railway, and a country park and nature reserve with trails and play areas. The park is open daily January 8:30am to 4pm, February 7:30am to 5pm, March to October 7:30am to 6pm, and November to December 8am to 4pm (museum Apr–Nov daily 10am–5pm, Dec–Mar Mon–Fri 10am–3pm, and Sat–Sun and school holidays 10am–5pm). Admission is £6.95, £4.75 children 3 to 15 (colliery tours and train rides extra).

The National Forest embraces the western part of **Charnwood Forest,** with its craggy landscape dotted with volcanic rocks. A popular walk is to the summit of **Bardon Hill**—at 278m (918 ft.) Leicestershire's highest point. But Charnwood's highlight is **Bradgate Park & Swithland Wood Country Park** ★, Newton Linford ((C) 0116/236-2713), a medieval deer park with the ruins of Bradgate House, home to Lady Jane Grey, queen for 9 days before being beheaded in 1554, and an 18th-century hilltop folly, Old John Tower. The park is free to enter, dawn to dusk.

Other attractions within or on the fringes of the Forest include **Twycross Zoo** ((C) 0844/474-1777; www.twycrosszoo.com), **Ashby Castle** ((C) 01530/ 413343; www.english-heritage.org.uk), the summer **Maize Maze** ((C) 01283/ 533933; www.nationalforestmaze.co. uk), and even **llama-trekking** at Burton-on-Trent in Staffordshire ((C) 01283/ 711702; www.nationalforestllamatreks. co.uk).

Walking back toward the center brings you to the timber-framed **Leicester Guildhall,** Guildhall Lane ((C) **0116/253-2569;** www.leicester.gov.uk), built in stages between the 14th and 16th centuries and the city's first town hall. Inside are one of the oldest public libraries in Britain and period rooms including original police cells with waxworks of notorious local pickpockets. Host to a busy program of music, theatre, comedy, and kids' events, the Guildhall is open Saturday to Wednesday 11am to 4:30pm, Sunday 1 to 4:30pm, plus some school-holiday Thursdays and Fridays; basic admission is free. Nearby **Leicester Cathedral,** 21 St. Martin's Lane (ⓒ **0116/248-7400;** www.cathedral.leicester.anglican.org), also free (Mon–Sat 8am–6pm and Sun 7am–5pm), has unusual oak vaulting beneath its north porch. From here it's a 10- to 15-minute walk south to the New Walk **Museum & Art Gallery (see below).**

A 15-minute walk north of the center brings you to **Abbey Park** ★ (ⓒ **0116/252-7000;** www.leicester.gov.uk) and the evocative remains of the richest Augustinian monastery in England, built in 1132. It was at this abbey that, in 1530, Cardinal Wolsey died, demoralized and broken after his conflicts with Henry VIII. The park, open dawn to dusk, has a minirailway, pets' corner, boating lake, lavender maze, and state-of-the-art playground, opened by local hero, soccer player Gary Lineker.

Next up (accessible by bus no. 54 from the center) is the **National Space Centre** (see below) and, continuing the scientific theme next door, the **Abbey Pumping Station**, **Leicester's Museum of Science and Technology** ★, Corporation Road (ⓒ **0116/299-5111;** www.leicester.gov.uk), is an imposing red-brick Victorian sewage pumping station with displays on light and optics, historic transport, and public health, plus restored pump engines in action on Steam Days. Admission is free, except for special events, and it's open daily February to October 11am to 4:30pm.

West Leicestershire is distinguished by its being home to the **Bosworth Battlefield Heritage Centre and Country Park** (see below), while north of Leicester, at Loughborough, the **Great Central Railway** ★★ (ⓒ **01509/230726;** www.gcrailway.co.uk) is not only the U.K.'s only double-track mainline heritage railway but the only place in the world where full-size steam engines can be seen passing each other. Trains run weekends and bank holidays, and daily in summer; special events includes a Drive a Train Experience for kids and Santa trains. You can also dine aboard (in First Class). Prices vary by event; an All Line Day Runabout on non-event days is £14 for adults, £9 children 5 to 15. East of Loughborough is **Melton Mowbray,** which has a reputation as a foodie hub (p. 558), plus a small theme-park, **Twin Lakes** (ⓒ **01664/567777;** www.twinlakespark.co.uk). Carry on 14 miles northeast to reach **Belvoir Castle** on Leicestershire's northern border with Lincolnshire.

Belvoir Castle ★★★ ☺ CASTLE   This seat of the dukes of Rutland since the time of Henry VII, rebuilt by Wyatt in 1816, contains paintings by Holbein, Reynolds, and Gainsborough, as well as tapestries in its staterooms. The location for the movies *Little Lord Fauntleroy* and *Young Sherlock Holmes,* it hosts medieval jousting tournaments in summer, plus, on selected weekends, "historical cameos" performed by its costumed guides about local events such as the trial of the Belvoir Witches. For kids there's a quiz and treasure trail, an Old Nursery and School Room where they can play as children did in Regency times, plus gardens and woodlands.

Belvoir, 36 miles northeast of Leicester. ⓒ **01476/871002.** www.belvoircastle.com. Admission castle and gardens £12, £7 children 5–16. May–Aug Mon and Sun; gardens open 11am–5pm, castle open for guided tours at 11:15am, 1:15, and 3:15pm.

Bosworth Battlefield Heritage Centre & Country Park ★★★ HISTORIC SITE   This site commemorates the 1485 battle that ended one of England's most important conflicts, the War of the Roses between the houses of York and Lancaster. When the fighting subsided, King Richard III, last of the Yorkists, lay dead, and

Henry Tudor, a Welsh nobleman banished to France to thwart his royal ambition, was proclaimed victor. Henry became King Henry VII, and the Tudor dynasty was born. The site has been newly improved by the addition of a gallery about how archeologists discovered the true location of the battle, with displays including bullets fired by early handguns, and an outdoor interpretation and trail. Events include guided walks, falconry displays, ferret racing, re-enactments, and a medieval camp.

Sutton Cheney, 13 miles west of Leicester. © **01455/290429.** www.bosworthbattlefield.com. Admission £7 adults, £4 children 3–16. Daily Apr–Nov 10am–5pm, Dec and Feb–Mar to 4pm.

Jewry Wall Museum ★ ☺ MUSEUM   Set beside an excavated Roman baths with a wall that, at 12m (40 ft.), is higher than any other piece of ancient Roman architecture in Britain, this museum offers up some fine Roman mosaics and rare wall plaster, intricately painted. Also tracing the city's history from prehistoric times to the Middle Ages, it has plenty of hands-on displays for younger visitors.

St. Nicholas Circle, Leicester. © **0116/225-4971.** www.leicester.gov.uk. Admission free exc. special events. Daily Feb–Oct 11am–4:30pm.

National Space Centre ★ ENTERTAINMENT COMPLEX   Rising incongruously out of the Midlands townscape, the futuristic rocket tower that comprises part of this modern attraction showcases a number of satellites, capsules, and so on, and also has several mezzanine galleries with displays, interactive and otherwise. The rest of the building includes a domed Space Theatre with changing surround-sound shows. You save money on entry if you visit as part of a **Stay Play Explore** (www.stayplayexplore.co.uk) package, which includes other local attractions and accommodations.

Exploration Drive, Leicester. © **0870/607-7223.** www.spacecentre.co.uk. Admission £13 adults, £11 children 5–16. Tues–Fri 10am–4pm, Sat–Sun 10am–5pm.

New Walk Museum & Art Gallery ★ MUSEUM   Displays on archeology, natural history, geology, and space coexist here with a collection of 18th–20th-century paintings by British and European artists including Gainsborough, Hogarth, and Francis Bacon. Highlights are the Egyptian mummies and artifacts brought back to the Midlands by Thomas Cook, the 19th-century travel mogul, and *Charnia masonia*, discovered in Charnwood Forest (p. 553) and, at about 560 million years of age, the U.K.'s oldest fossil.

A Side Trip from Leicestershire: Althorp ★

If you're in the East Midlands in high summer, you might make a foray into Northamptonshire, specifically **Althorp** (© **01604/770107; www.althorp.com**), 32 miles south of Leicester. After her death in 1997, Princess Diana was brought to this, her childhood home, to be buried on an island in an artificial lake, which visitors can glimpse but cannot access. What you can do is tour a museum, in former stables, celebrating Diana's life through displays including her bridal gown and items relating to her charity work, and also look around the house, with paintings by Van Dyck, Reynolds, Gainsborough, and Rubens. You'll also see rare French and English furniture and porcelain by Sèvres and others. Admission is £13 (£6 children 5–17), but you can also get tickets just to the exhibition and grounds, or the grounds alone. It's open only from July 1 (Diana's birthday) to August 30, daily from 11am to 5pm.

53 New Walk, Leicester. ℂ **0116/22-54900.** www.leicester.gov.uk. Free admission. Mon–Sat 10am–5pm, Sun 11am–5pm.

RUTLAND ★★

Due south of Belvoir lies the U.K.'s smallest historic county (briefly absorbed by Leicestershire from 1974 to 1994). Home to just two towns, the county town of Oakham and market town of Uppingham, it finds its focus at **Rutland Water ★★★** (ℂ **01780/686800;** www.anglianwater.co.uk/leisure), western Europe's largest man-made reservoir and a prime spot for watersports and cruising, biking (rentals available), walking, climbing, fishing, outdoor adventure (wall-climbing and high ropes), and getting up close and personal with wildlife on the nature reserve. The museum within the half-submerged **Normanton Church** (ℂ **01780/686800**), on the edge of the water, has prehistoric remains and a female skeleton as well as an exhibition on the development of the reservoir. Most attractions and activities are available Easter to October; there are four main parking lots, charging £4/day.

Affluent Oakham is home to a fair few antiques shops plus the **Rutland Country Museum & Visitor Centre** (www.rutland.gov.uk/museum), with displays on local history, archeology, and rural life, plus a new Dinosaur Discovery Activity area for kids. It's free to enter (Tues–Fri 10am–5pm, Sat 10am–4pm). **Oakham Castle** (ℂ **01572/722577;** www.rutland.gov.uk) survives solely in the form of its great hall of 1180–90, which contains a collection of ceremonial horseshoes, some of them outsize, that had to be left as forfeits, according to an old custom, by royalty and peers passing through. They're hung upside-down—in Rutland, this is said to stop the devil from sitting in the shoe's hollow (the motif also appears in the local coat of arms). The castle is free and has the same hours as the museum.

Just east, stake out a corner of unspoiled nature at the **Rutland Falconry & Owl Centre** (ℂ **07778/152814;** www.rutland-falconry.com), open daily in summer 10am to late, in winter 10am to 4pm. Witness birds of prey in flight, photograph them, or bring binoculars to catch a glimpse of fallow deer, muntjac, foxes, badgers, and other mammals. Entry is £5, £3.50 children 5 to 16.

Where to Eat

VERY EXPENSIVE

For Stapleford Park and Hambleton Hall, see below, under "Where to Stay."

The Grey Lady ★ MODERN EUROPEAN   Not everyone is won over by the modern decor at this restaurant in a beautiful setting close by Charnwood Forest, and with great views. Prices can be eye-opening, too, though lunch is a good deal (£13 for two courses, £17 for three courses), and might include pork, apricot, and pistachio terrine, or salmon with courgette fritters and sauté potatoes. You can also get nibbles and finger-food, and olive-wood platters including a Ploughman's with local Stilton, vintage Red Leicester, hand-raised pork pie, and homemade chutney. Dinner is a little more elaborate. Sunday lunches (with kids' portions and pricing) are popular with families enjoying the great outdoors nearby.

Sharpley Hill, Newtown Linford. ℂ **01530/243558.** www.the-grey-lady.co.uk. Reservations recommended. Main courses £12–£24. DC, V. Daily noon–3pm (3:30pm Sun) and 5:30–10:30pm.

EXPENSIVE

Maiyango ★★ INTERNATIONAL   Leicester's only boutique hotel is best visited for its restaurant, which will whisk you away with its exotic decor, soundtrack of world beats, "gastronomic" cocktails, and dishes influenced by the chef's travels (though most of the produce comes from community allotments, farms, and other ultralocal suppliers). Many dishes lean firmly toward the East: Seared king scallops and Thai spiced mussels with cauliflower purée and micro crisp cress, for instance, or soy-scented sea bass with lime and ginger-foam basil linguine and roasted and creamed vegetables. Lunch features a slightly reduced version of the same menu at about £10 less per head. Book one of the booths for a full-on romantic experience.

The 13 **guest rooms** and one suite (from £87, including breakfast) have Asian inflected decor and super-king beds (save one room).

13–21 St. Nicholas Place. ✆ **0116/251-8898.** www.maiyango.com. Reservations recommended. Dinner £27 for 2 courses, £29 for 3 courses. MC, V. Mon–Tues noon–11pm, Wed noon–11.30pm, Thurs noon–mid-night, Fri noon–1am, Sat noon–1:30am, and Sun 6:30–10:30pm.

MODERATE

Boboli ★★ ☺ ITALIAN   Though somewhat off the tourist trail, this casual all-day eatery in a large village in south Leicestershire is worth the detour for convivial family meals done Italian style—especially a Sunday lunch, when traditional English roasts feature alongside tempting Tuscan fare such as Parma ham with fennel and orange salad. Children 11 and under get Sunday lunch for half price, or they can choose from the Boboli Bambini menu (£7.50 for two courses, until 8pm) or even get smaller portions from the main menu. Outside of main mealtimes, there's a snack menu of *piadine* (flat pizza sandwiches), veal burgers, and pastries. The same owners run the more formal and pricier **Firenze** in the same village.

88 Main St., Kibworth. ✆ **0116/279-3303.** www.bobolirestaurant.co.uk. Reservations recommended (dinner). Main courses £4.50–£16. MC, V. Tues–Sat 10am–10pm, Sun 10am–4pm.

Lake Isle ★★ 🏠 ☺ MODERN EUROPEAN   Named after the Yeats' poem *Lake Isle of Innisfree*, the tranquility of which it aims to replicate, this award-winning restaurant and hotel, in a market town 6 miles from Rutland Water, is great for a family lunch—for its good prices and for the wide choice including toasted sandwiches, omelets, and interesting pasta dishes. At dinner the options are more limited, but you won't complain when you sample such seasonal dishes as an autumnal antipasti (wild boar chorizo, venison salami, quail eggs, preserved pears, roquefort, walnuts, and winter leaves), or steamed plaice with crab croquettes, pickled marsh samphire, and tomato and tarragon cream sauce. The chef happily caters to the requests of kids, who are welcome (but who must eat before 6pm Fri–Sat). If you stay in one of the 12 comfy **guest rooms** (from £80 for a double, breakfast included) or one- or two-bedroom "cottages," babysitting is available.

16 High St. East, Uppingham. ✆ **01572/822951.** www.lakeisle.co.uk. Reservations recommended (dinner). Main courses £13–£19. MC, V. Mon 7–9pm; Tues–Thurs noon–2:30pm, and 7–9pm; Fri–Sat noon–12:30pm and 7–9.30pm; Sun noon–2pm.

Olive Branch ★★ ☺ PUB FOOD/MODERN BRITISH   Rustic charm abounds at this traditional inn in a pretty Rutland village, newly renovated to its former glory with the aid of local restorers and cabinet makers. In winter you can sit around open fires (scented with roasting chestnuts) and drink sloe gin, damson vodka, and mulled wine made with berries from surrounding hedgerows. In summer, enjoy barbecues in the garden accompanied by homemade lemonade, Pimms, and strawberry vodka. Despite the informal vibe, the food has garnered the Olive Branch many awards and titles, including Michelin Pub of the Year in 2008. Local ingredients including game and orchard fruits star in salads, sandwiches, and soups, pub classics, and more formal dishes—everything from fish and chips to seared scallops with black-pudding fritter and poached rhubarb. Even at dinner, the menu is set up so that those dining together can eat as their appetite, mood, and budget dictates; kids get a well-priced menu, too (£6.95 for two courses).

You can stay over in one of six gorgeous **guest rooms and suites** (from £115 double) in **Beech House,** on the opposite side of the street; one room is set up for families. The same folks run the equally charming **Red Lion Inn** at Stathern near Belvoir Castle.

Main St., Clipsham. ℂ **01780/410355.** www.theolivebranchpub.com. Reservations recommended. Main courses £7.75–£23. MC, V. Mon–Fri noon–2pm and 7–9:30pm; Sat noon–2pm, 2:30–5:30pm, and 7–9:30pm; Sun noon–3pm and 7–9pm.

INEXPENSIVE

Leicester's hub for Indian restaurants is Belgrave Road; try longstanding vegetarian **Bobby's,** 154–156 Belgrave Rd. (ℂ **0116/266-0106;** www.eatatbobbys.com), or the award-winning **Curry Fever,** 139 Belgrave Rd., (ℂ **0116/266-2941;** www.thecurryfever.co.uk).

Shivalli ★ 🍽 INDIAN The "Village Vegetarian" is actually on a busy main road in the center of Leicester; the village in question is Karnataka in southern India, famous for its *idli* (savory cakes), *vada* (savory donuts), *dosa* (crispy pancakes), and *upma* (a semolina dish), served on plantain leaves and eaten by hand. Like most Indian restaurants, Shivalli has its occasional detractor, but most diners are more than satisfied by the likes of spicy *rasam* soup, *rava masala dosa* (with chilies, coconut, cumin, potato, onions, and peas), and fluffy, fried *bathura* breads, all served at prices that seem almost obscenely low (the lunchtime buffet at just £4.95 keeps local office workers well fed).

21 Welford Rd., Leicester. ℂ **0116/255-0137.** www.shivallirestaurant.com. Reservations recommended. Main courses with rice £5.75–£9.50. MC, V. Mon–Fri noon–3pm and 6–11pm; Sat noon–11pm; Sun noon–10pm.

Shopping

If not exactly a shopping mecca, Leicester has a respectable array of big-name department stores, mostly within **Highcross** (www.highcrossleicester.com), formerly known as The Shires. **St. Martins Square** (www.martinssquare.com) is a pleasant enclave of restored buildings housing interesting smaller shops including **Just… Fairtrade,** 36 Silver St. (ℂ **07888/717270;** www.justfairtrade.com). **Belgrave Road,** running north out of the center, is home to the **Golden Mile,** named for its jewelry shops but also rich in stores offering fine Indian fabrics and saris.

In Melton Mowbray, **Ye Olde Pork Pie Shoppe,** 10 Nottingham St. (ℂ **01664/482068;** www.porkpie.co.uk), sells the town's famous pork pies as well as local meats, cheeses, chutneys and preserves, and Melton Hunt (fruit) cake. Nearby, at 8 Windsor St., **The Melton Cheeseboard** (ℂ **01664/562257;** www.meltoncheeseboard.co.uk) can't be beat for its local Stilton (produced by only six dairies in Leicestershire, Nottinghamshire, and Derbyshire) and Red Leicester. At nearby Eastwell, **Crossroads Farm Shop** (ℂ **01949/860242**), housed in a 17th-century building with a museum of farm memorabilia, offers home-produced vegetables, meat, eggs, and cakes, and local jams and cordials.

In Rutland, Oakham is a hotspot for antiques; try **Swans,** 17 Mill St. (ℂ **01572/724364;** www.antiquefrenchbeds.co.uk), and **Chedwich Antiques,** 31a Pillings

Rd. (☎ **01572/722952;** www.chedwich.co.uk). On Wednesdays and Saturdays, Oakham also holds an open-air **market** in its main square.

Entertainment & Nightlife

Leicester's new **Cultural Quarter** (http://cqart.leicester.gov.uk) includes **Phoenix Square,** Midland Street (☎ **01162/422800;** www.phoenix.org.uk), showcasing film and digital media, and the new **Curve Theatre,** Rutland Street (☎ **0116/242-3595;** www. curveonline.co.uk), for plays, comedy, and family shows. Otherwise, Leicester is a lively enough city for nightlife, partly by virtue of its large student population. For events, see **http://whatson.oneleicester.com,** or pick up flyers in record stores and boutiques.

Where to Stay

For **Beech House** (part of the Olive Branch restaurants) in Rutland, see p. 557. For **Maiyango** in Leicester and **Lake Isle** in Rutland, see p. 557. For the **YHA National Forest,** just inside Derbyshire, see p. 543.

Champneys Springs ★ The biggest name in "health farms" in the U.K., Champneys with its four venues (the others are in Bedfordshire, Hampshire, and Hertfordshire) was around long before hotel spas became a global obsession. Though the venue is modern and standard-category rooms are on the functional side (albeit bright and clean), the expertise comes through in the facilities and treatments—there's a dizzying choice of more than 100 traditional, alternative, and advanced therapies using products by the likes of Clarins and Elemis. The beautiful country-side setting on the edge of the National Forest will aid in your relaxation—guests are free to stroll in the parkland with its four lakes. Overnight packages include use of all facilities and participation in most fitness classes, buffet breakfast (cooked breakfast is extra), lunch, and a three-course evening meal (drinks extra); day packages are also available for those staying nearby.

Gallows Lane, near Packington, Leicestershire LE12 7HD. www.champneys.com. ☎ **0843/316-2222.** 89 units. From £129pp double, including meals. MC, V. Free parking. **Amenities:** 2 restaurants; cafe; bike rental; gym; indoor pool; whirlpool; thalassotherapy pool; spa with sauna and steam rooms; classes; shops; hairdressers; tennis court; golf range. In room: TV.

The Dandelion Hideaway ★★ 📱😊 Since spring 2011, lovely Osbaston House Farm (mainly goat breeding) on the fringes of the National Forest less than 3 miles from Bosworth Battlefield has offered family fun with a vintage country-chic twist in five canvas "cottages," all with fabulous countryside views. Included in a break here are child-oriented tours of the premises by the farmer, and some guest families are designated as keepers of the hen coop for their stay (everyone can help themselves to freshly laid eggs). The electricity-free, tent-like structures have wood-burning stoves, old-fashioned "slipper" baths, and for entertainment an explorer's trunk with binoculars for spotting rabbits, hares, buzzards, badgers, and perhaps even barn owls (there's an on-site nature hide), I-spy books to help you identify insects, birds, and trees, a magnifying glass, and classic card and board games. Each sleeps up to six in two regular bedrooms and a secret wooden cabin within the cottage, much loved by children.

Lount Rd., Osbaston, Nuneaton, Warwickshire CV13 0HR. www.thedandelionhideaway.co.uk. ☎ **01455/ 291291.** 5 units. £296–£589 3-night weekend stay, £241–£539 4-night midweek stay, £436–£846 1-week stay. MC, V. **Amenities:** Honesty shop and library area; farm tours. In room: kitchen, BBQ, games and activities chest, baby equipment (some at extra charge).

Hambleton Hall ★ A member of the prestigious French Relais & Châteaux group, this is one of the finest country-house hotels in England, with spectacular views over Rutland Water and an intimate vibe, with the emphasis on comfort and good food. Some rooms may be a little chintzy for the modern-hotel lover's taste, so study the website for one to suit you (some are designed by Nina Campbell). For families, the Croquet Pavilion has a double and a twin on two levels, and sitting and breakfast rooms. The fine-dining **restaurant** offers the likes of assiette of rabbit with pearl barley risotto and licorice sauce, and Whissendine veal with sweetbread ravioli and morel mushrooms, (about £35 for a main course), though set menus at lunch and dinner make things considerably more affordable.

Hambleton, Rutland LE15 8TH. www.hambletonhall.com. ℂ **01572/756991.** 17 units. £235–£400 double. Rates include breakfast. AE, MC, DC, V. Free parking. Minimum 2-night stay at weekends. **Amenities:** Restaurant; lounge; heated outdoor pool; croquet; room service, Wi-Fi (free). *In room:* TV, hair dryer.

Stapleford Park ★★ ☺ Another stunning country-house hotel, this one close to Melton Mowbray, Stapleford is full-on where Hambleton (see above) is restrained. Though the decor remains traditional (think boars' heads, antlers, and oil paintings), this is a resort with amenities including a Clarins spa, indoor pool, golf course, tennis courts, kids' club, and country pursuits galore, including falconry. Summer also sees sports camps for kids, and bikes can be borrowed. Rooms are all unique; indeed many were created and/or sponsored by eminent designers such as Osborne & Little. There are also two stone cottages in the grounds. There's a formal **restaurant** but also a "casual dining" menu in the lounges. Highly civilized extras include a morning paper, hot-water bottles on winter nights, and a decanter of sloe gin in your room.

Stapleford, Rutland LE14 2EF. www.staplefordpark.com. ℂ **01572/787000.** 55 units. £288–£538 double; £685 suite. Rates include English breakfast. AE, MC, DC, V. Free parking. **Amenities:** Restaurant; bar and lounges; bikes; gym; indoor pool; room service; spa; sauna; kids' club; tennis and badminton; games on request; falconry center; archery; shooting; kids' activity packs and treasure hunts. *In room:* TV/DVD, hair dryer, Wi-Fi (free).

THE NORTHWEST

by Rhonda Carrier

World-class cities within easy reach of wonderful, unspoiled countryside make the often-neglected northwest of England a must-see for those who really want to get to know modern Britain. The star turns are Manchester and Liverpool, reasserting themselves after decades in the doldrums while remaining firmly rooted in their industrial heritage, but there's rich history elsewhere, including Chester with its Roman amphitheatre, Lancaster with its witchhunter's castle, and even tacky Blackpool. There's also wildlife in the open spaces of Cheshire and Lancashire, plus seaside fun, unexpectedly good beaches, and traditional resorts.

15

CITIES & TOWNS   It may not be Britain's prettiest landscape, but the 21st-century revival of **Manchester's Salford Quays,** new home to much of the BBC, makes for a fascinating case study in urban regeneration—especially when contrasted with historical depictions of the area in the world-famous paintings of L. S. Lowry, many of them displayed in the state-of-the-art cultural center named after him.

COUNTRYSIDE   The narrow, steep-sided valley of the **Trough of Bowland** remains a bit of a hidden gem for walkers and cyclists, compared with the more touristy Lake District and Yorkshire Dales, with winding paths, blissful picnic spots, and a wild boar park, where kids can enjoy animal encounters and woodland walks.

EATING & DRINKING   Eating out is a serious business all over the northwest, but **Lancashire's Inn at Whitewell** particularly stands out for having featured in the 2010 BBC comedy *The Trip,* about a restaurant critic taking a friend on a foodie road-trip around the north of England.

COAST   Antony Gormley's ***Another Place*** raises the status of **Crosby,** north of Liverpool, from unremarkable seaside town to globally significant art site, with its beach studded with 100 cast-iron casts of the sculptor's own body, faces turned to the horizon in silent expectation.

THE best TRAVEL EXPERIENCES IN THE NORTHWEST

○ **Discovering Manchester's industrial heritage:** In England's second most popular city, explore the outstanding Museum of Science and Industry but also the buildings and artifacts of industry in the very fabric of the city. See p. 566.

○ **Witnessing the lightning-paced transformation of Liverpool:** This once-great maritime city is rapidly shaking off the effects of its late 20th-century decline, not least in the new 2011 Museum of Liverpool. See p. 585.

○ **Walking Chester Walls:** Walking Britain's most complete city walls, inspecting the remains of its largest Roman amphitheatre, and visiting the world-famous collection of Roman tombstones in the Grosvenor Museum. See p. 574.

○ **Experiencing surreal Formby:** Crossing the otherworldly sand dunes and pine woods with their rare red squirrel and natterjack toad populations to reach the beach with its Neolithic/early Bronze Age footprints of humans and animals. See p. 585.

○ **Stepping into the Forest of Bowland:** Touring one of Britain's wildest landscapes, via the riverside Ribble Way, Ribble Valley Food Trail, or Pendle Witch Trail, the latter following in the footsteps of the local ladies taken for trial at Lancaster Castle. See p. 593.

MANCHESTER ★★

202 miles NW of London; 86 miles N of Birmingham; 35 miles E of Liverpool

Said by many to be Britain's "second city" in terms of its economic and cultural importance, **Manchester** has re-emerged, phoenix-like, from post-industrial neglect and an IRA bombing to become a major shopping and leisure destination; old red-brick warehouses and factories housing boutique hotels, loft apartments, and nightclubs; and sleek new architecture juxtaposed with impressive Victorian remnants, make for one of the U.K.'s most compelling cityscapes. Meanwhile, large student, gay, and ethnic populations (many descended from immigrant factory laborers, including Britain's biggest Chinese population outside London), and a continuing influence on the global music scene, ensure that Manchester remains at the forefront of modern British culture, even if it's still best known worldwide for football (soccer).

Manchester also is a great jumping-off point for exploring the Peak District (p. 534) as well as for discovering Chester and surrounding Cheshire.

Essentials

GETTING THERE   Frequent direct trains from London Euston to Manchester Piccadilly take just over 2 hours, costing around £70 for a round-trip. There are also direct trains from Birmingham (about 1½ hr.), Leeds (just under 1 hr.), York (about 1¼ hr.), and Edinburgh (about 3¼ hr.). Direct **National Express** (© **0871/781-8181;** www.nationalexpress.com) buses from London to Manchester take about 5 hours. There are also direct buses from Birmingham (2–3 hr.), Leeds (about 1 hr.), and Edinburgh (about 6½ hr.).

Manchester is about 3½ hours from London, although traffic can be heavy on the M1 and M6 (the Midland Expressway will allow you to move more quickly past Birmingham, at a cost of about £5 depending on the time of day). Direct **National**

Express (☏ **0871/781-8181;** www.nationalexpress.com) buses from **Manchester International Airport** (☏ **08712/710-711;** www.manchesterairport.co.uk), 15 miles south of the center, links with London and other U.K. cities, plus many European and global destinations. Its station has frequent direct rail links with the city (about 20 min. away) and other destinations including Liverpool (about 1¼ hr.) and Leeds (about 1¼ hr.).

VISITOR INFORMATION Manchester Visitor Information Centre, Piccadilly Plaza, Portland Street (☏ **0871/222-8223;** www.visitmanchester.com), is open Monday to Saturday 9:30am to 5:30pm, Sunday 10:30am to 4:30 pm.

SPECIAL EVENTS Manchester is busy all year, but events that may be worth timing your visit with are the biennial **Manchester International Festival** (www.mif.co.uk; next in summer 2013), and, in October, the **Manchester Science Festival** (www.manchestersciencefestival.com) and the **Manchester Literature Festival** (www.manchesterliteraturefestival.co.uk). Other great events are **Chinese New Year** (late Jan/mid-Feb); the **Manchester Mega Mela** (July), with Asian music, dance, food, and more; **Diwali,** the Hindu festival of lights (late Oct/early Nov); and **Christmas,** with markets, a snow-slide, an ice rink, and illuminations.

Exploring Manchester

Manchester's central sights are walkable, but there's a good bus, tram, and local train network: **www.gmpte.com** is your resource for planning all journeys.

CENTRAL MANCHESTER

Having begun life as the Roman settlement Mamucium ("camp by the breast-like hill"!), Manchester was catapulted to the forefront of the industrial movement by both its textile industry and its role as a hub in the development of the railway. So it's apt that its excellent **Museum of Science & Industry,** which brings the city's industrial heritage stunningly to life, occupies the site of the world's first passenger railway station and offers visitors a ride on a replica steam train. The museum lies in the Castlefield district, where Roman Mamucium took seed and also where canals were built to transport supplies during the city's late-19th-century heyday. A stroll in the **Castlefield Urban Heritage Park** (Britain's first) will take you along the canals to the remains of the Roman fort; boat trips are also available, and there are some good picnic spots.

It's about a 10-minute walk from here into the actual city center and the **Manchester Art Gallery** (p. 566). En route, call in at the Victorian Gothic Revival **Manchester Town Hall ★**, Albert Square (for information and tours, ask at Manchester Visitor Information Centre), home to several government departments but partially open to visitors in office hours. Its Sculpture Hall includes famous figures involved in the city's history, including Gnaeus Julius Agricola, founder of Mamucium, while the Great Hall holds 12 imposing murals by Ford Madox Brown, on events central to Manchester's history and themes dear to Victorian Mancunians: Christianity, commerce, and the textile industry.

Past the Town Hall and the Art Gallery, the 60-m (197-ft.) **Wheel of Manchester ★** in Exchange Square (✆ **0161/8310-9918;** www.worldtouristattractions.co.uk; Sun–Thurs 10am–9pm, Fri–Sat 10am–midnight; £7.50 adults, £5 children 3–16), offers panoramic views over the city, including nearby **Manchester Cathedral ★**, Victoria Street (✆ **0161/833-2220;** www.manchestercathedral.org), which, while not rivaling that of York (p. 644), has impressive late-medieval wooden furnishings, including some beautifully carved early-16th-century choir stalls. The Fire Window evokes the infernos of the Nazi Blitz, which destroyed the cathedral's Victorian stained glass. The cathedral can be visited Monday to Friday 8:30am to 6:30pm, Saturday 8:30am to 5pm, and Sunday 8:30am to 7pm; free admission but donations are welcome and visitors are advised to call beforehand to check if making a special journey.

Also near the Wheel lies Urbis, a shimmering glass structure built to house a museum about urban cultures but undergoing transformation into the **National Football Museum** (✆ **0161/870-9275;** www.nationalfootballmuseum.com) at the time of writing. Also nearby is the recently reopened (and rehoused) **People's History Museum ★**, Left Bank (✆ **0161/838-9190;** www.phm.org.uk), which tells the story of democracy and of the working class in the U.K. It won't be to everyone's taste, but for those interested in the role played by northwest England in the Industrial Revolution, and Manchester's importance in the political arena, it's a must-see. Entry is free, with the museum open daily 10am to 5pm.

Other sights in the center include **Chetham's Library,** distinguished not only as Britain's oldest free public reference library (in continuous use since 1653) but also as the meeting place of Marx and Engels when the former visited Manchester, and retaining displays of books that they consulted. Part of Chetham's School of Music, the library

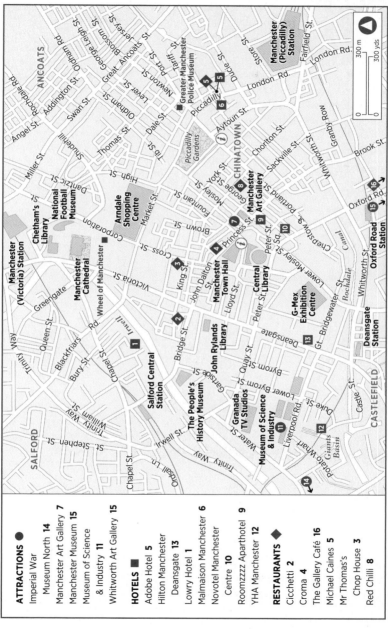

Manchester

ATTRACTIONS ●

Imperial War
Museum North **14**
Manchester Art Gallery **7**
Manchester Museum **15**
Museum of Science
& Industry **11**
Whitworth Art Gallery **15**

HOTELS ■

Adobe Hotel **5**
Hilton Manchester
Deansgate **13**
Lowry Hotel **1**
Malmaison Manchester **6**
Novotel Manchester
Centre **10**
Roomzzzz Aparthotel **9**
YHA Manchester **12**

RESTAURANTS ◆

Cicchetti **2**
Croma **4**
The Gallery Café **16**
Michael Caines **5**
Mr Thomas's
Chop House **3**
Red Chilli **8**

is open to the public Monday to Friday 9am to 12:30pm and 1:30–4:30pm; there are also guided tours/talks Wednesdays in term time (✆ **0161/838-7244**). There's more colorful local history on Newton Street on the edge of the Northern Quarter, where the **Greater Manchester Police Museum and Archives** ★ (✆ **0161/856-3287;** www.gmp.police.uk) offers up a fascinating survey of Manchester's hidden past within one of the city's earliest police stations, restored to its late 1800s and 1900s appearance, complete with cells with wooden pillows and an 1895 magistrates court, plus Crime Room with displays on forgery and forensic science. It's generally open to the public only on Tuesdays from 10:30am to 3:30pm, with free admission.

Manchester Art Gallery ★★★ ☺ GALLERY   Home to one of the best art collections in the north of England, this central venue—vastly expanded between 1998 and 2002 to include an airy modern glass and steel atrium—is best known for its Pre-Raphaelite paintings and its works by L. S. Lowry. It also houses British and European art from the 17th century to the present day, and a strong craft and design collection, from ceramics and dolls houses to contemporary furniture and lighting. Kids get their own gallery (Clore Interactive), free activity backpacks, and more.

The recently reopened **Gallery of Costume** ★, Platt Hall, Wilmslow Road (✆ **0161/245-7245;** Wed–Sat 1:30–4:30pm; free), located south of the center near the Whitworth Art Gallery, is part of the Manchester Art Gallery.

Mosley St. ✆ **0161/235-8888.** www.manchestergalleries.org. Free admission. Tues–Sun 10am–5pm.

Manchester Museum ★★ ☺ MUSEUM   This university-owned venue is both modern, with a focus on an interactive visitor experience, and old-fashioned, in that it's all-embracing: Within its walls you'll find everything from mummies, dinosaur skeletons, and stuffed animals to live amphibians and reptiles. The collections were being reshuffled at press time: After the opening of a new Living Worlds gallery in April 2011, new Ancient Worlds galleries will launch in 2012. Kids' amenities include a Play+Learn (and picnic) area and free backpacks.

Oxford Rd., near Booth St. ✆ **0161/275-2634.** www.museum.manchester.ac.uk. Free admission. Tues–Sat 10am–5pm, Sun–Mon 11am–4pm.

Museum of Science & Industry ★★★ ☺ MUSEUM   Another highly interactive modern museum, MOSI has a Victorian sewer to crawl through (with authentic smells and sounds), planetarium, 4-D theatre, and motion simulator ride, alongside one of the world's largest collections of working steam engines, plus fascinating displays on printing, electricity, textile manufacture, flight, and aerospace exploration. New in early 2011, the Revolution Manchester Gallery has sections on the city's role in developments in transport, computer technology, energy, and more.

Liverpool Rd. ✆ **0161/832-2244.** www.mosi.org.uk. Free admission (small charges for some elements). Daily 10am–5pm.

Whitworth Art Gallery ★★ ☺ GALLERY   Rounding off Manchester's fine array of free museums and galleries, the Whitworth, also south of the center, holds some of the U.K.'s finest art and design collections, including modern and historic fine art, prints, textiles, and rare wallpapers. There's also a busy program of activities, many for families, and an award-winning cafe (p. 570). At press time, the venue had just announced an upcoming £12-million redevelopment and expansion.

Whitworth Park. ✆ **0161/275-7450.** www.whitworth.manchester.ac.uk. Free admission. Mon–Sat 10am–5pm, Sun noon–4pm.

TRAFFORD & SALFORD QUAYS

A short hop west of the center, the metropolitan borough of Trafford—part of Greater Manchester—will be familiar to most visitors as home to the "Theatre of Dreams," Manchester United's home stadium of Old Trafford. Tickets to see the world's biggest team are notoriously scarce and expensive, but the **Manchester United Museum & Tour Centre ★★** (✆ **0161/868-8000;** www.manutd.com) offers displays on 130 years of football (soccer), plus the option to see the stadium through the eyes of its players on a tour. The center is open daily (except match days) 9am to 5pm, with tours running up to every 10 minutes (9:40am–6:30pm). Adults pay £14 for the museum and tour, children £10 age 5 to 15. Not far away lies the **Imperial War Museum North** and the Lowry (or Millennium) Bridge over the canal to the regenerated docklands area of **Salford Quays,** now home to The Lowry cultural center and MediaCityUK, site of several departments of the BBC (from 2011) and for ITV production, including the famous and long-running TV soap *Coronation Street* sets (from 2012).

Or stay in Trafford, where the **Trafford Centre** (✆ **0161/749-1717;** www.traffordcentre.co.uk) mall offers ample scope for retail therapy and dining but much more besides—there's also the **Legoland Discovery Centre ★★** (✆ **0871/222-2662;** www.legolanddiscoverycentre.co.uk) for ages 3 to 12 (including Miniland with Lego models of northern English attractions such as the Peak District and the Blackpool Illuminations), a high-ropes adventure course (✆ **0845/652-1736;** www.aerialextreme.co.uk), and the **Museum of Museums** (✆ **0844/478-0898;** www.museumofmuseums.org.uk), showcasing seemingly random items from various other museums and private collections, from vintage transport to Egyptology. Also by the mall is **Chill Factore** (✆ **0161/749-2222;** www.chillfactore.com), a year-round indoor real snow center.

Trafford is also home to the affluent market town of **Altrincham,** historically a part of Chester (p. 574), about 8 miles southwest of the center of Manchester. Home to many professional footballers (including Manchester United and Manchester City players), *Coronation Street* and other TV actors and music-industry celebrities, it's centered on its Old Market Place with part timber-framed buildings.

Dunham Massey Hall ★★ ☺ HISTORIC SITE Located within a vast deer park on the outskirts of Altrincham, this early Georgian house was home to the 7th Earl of Stamford, who caused a scandal by marrying a former bareback circus rider. Visitors get to learn about him and other inhabitants, explore the interiors, and stroll in Britain's biggest winter garden and around the estate (kids get free quizzes and trails).

Altrincham. ✆ **0161/941-1025.** www.nationaltrust.org.uk. Admission £10 adults, £5 children. Park daily 9am–5pm; garden 11am–5:30pm depending on time of year; house Mar–Oct Sat–Wed 11am–5pm.

Imperial War Museum North ★★ ☺ MUSEUM Like its counterpart in London (p. 107), the museum aims to show in a vivid fashion "how war shapes lives." Open since 2002 in an award-winning and symbolic building by Daniel Libeskind, it has both permanent displays and temporary exhibitions, some of them aimed at children, plus hourly audio-visual presentations projected onto the very walls of the galleries, to evoke in visitors the dread and panic experienced by those who lived through the Blitz. The museum overlooks an area of Manchester that was heavily bombed in 1940—the Manchester Ship Canal, then a key industrial zone.

The Quays, Trafford Wharf Rd. ✆ **0161/836-4000.** www.north.iwm.org.uk. Free admission. Daily 10am–5pm.

Where to Eat

VERY EXPENSIVE

For the **River Restaurant at The Lowry Hotel,** see p. 571. The **Second Floor at Harvey Nichols** (*C* **0161/828-8898;** www.harveynichols.com) is also highly regarded for its Modern European cookery; also on the second floor, there's the cheaper but still very good brasserie.

Michael Caines ★★ MODERN BRITISH/EUROPEAN   Widely held to be the best restaurant in town, this stylish and award-winning venue in the basement of the **ABode Hotel** near Piccadilly Station is named after one of Britain's most acclaimed chefs, who has other dining rooms in the same hotels in nearby Chester (p. 574), Glasgow, and, to the south, Exeter and Canterbury. Accessible fine dining, with the emphasis on regional produce, is the order of the day: Characteristic dishes are pan-fried scallops and belly pork with ginger and apple purée, pork scratching, and fennel cream sauce; and Yorkshire partridge with cumin and pumpkin purée, lentils, glazed onions, pickled pears and quince, and cumin-scented red-wine sauce. If you're not ravenously hungry or just wary of inflicting too much damage on your wallet, eat from the Grazing Menu in the Champagne Bar, order "grazing" portions of a la carte dishes at lunchtime (served within an hour if you're on a tight schedule), or dine early (6–7pm). Or there's the **MC Café Bar & Grill** and adjoining BarMC on the ground floor of the hotel, offering more casual eating and drinking from breakfast to late evening (including Sun brunches and roasts). Standard **doubles at the hotel** cost £160.

107 Piccadilly. *C* **0161/200-5678.** www.michaelcaines.com. Reservations recommended. AE, DC, MC, V. Main courses £21–£26. Mon–Sat noon–2:30pm and 6–10pm.

MODERATE

Central Manchester has the usual family-friendly chains, including **Carluccio's** and **Wagamama;** some of them also have branches in the Trafford Centre mall (p. 570).

Cicchetti ★★★ 🏠 ITALIAN   A wonderful newcomer to the Manchester eating scene, Cicchetti— the name for the tapas-style sharing dishes that are a specialty of Venice—is noisy, brash, and heaps of fun. In the rather incongruous setting of the ground floor of the House of Fraser department store, with views into the shop, it's perpetually crowded by Italian couples, families and groups of friends, and also attracts its fair share of famous northern footballers. Food could be an afterthought, but most dishes— the likes of tuna tartare, fried gnocchi with San Daniele ham, Italian sausage with spinach and chili, and arancini (Sicilian rice-balls)—is spot on, if not specifically Venetian. Cicchetti is an offshoot of the long-established San Carlo on the same street.

King Street West. *C* **0161/839-2233.** www.sancarlocicchetti.co.uk. Main courses £4–14. AE, DC, MC, V. Open Mon–Fri 8am–11pm, Sat and Sun 9am–11pm.

Mr Thomas's Chop House ★★ TRADITIONAL ENGLISH   Probably Manchester's best-preserved Victorian pub, "Tom's"—together with its nearby sister eatery, **Sam's Chop House**—offers a slice of vogueish tradition in the heart of the city. Named after 16th-century chophouses, where businessmen came to do their deals over hearty cuisine and fine wines or local ales, Tom's places the same emphasis on comforting, seasonal fare served in a convivial, informal atmosphere. Expect the likes of brown onion soup, lovingly cooked for 36 hours and served with a large Cheddar crouton, or homemade steak and kidney pie with chips, mushy peas, and a jug of

THE NORTHWEST | **Manchester**

Unsurprisingly, given that its name was shortened from "Ramson's Bottom," meaning "wild garlic valley," the market town of Ramsbottom, on the western slopes of the Pennines (14 miles north of Manchester), has become a bit of a pilgrimage site for foodies. In addition to a farmers' market (second Sun of each month), it hosts a 2-day **Chocolate Festival** (www.bury.gov.uk) in April, with family-friendly activities as well as chocolate, cocktail, wine, and beer sampling in venues such as **The Lounge** (℡ 01706/828392; www.theloungeramsbottom.co.uk) and **The First Chop** (℡ 01706/827722; www.thefirst chop.co.uk). But year-round, the town is worth visiting for its **Chocolate Café** (℡ 01706/822828; www.chocolate-cafe.co.uk), **Cultured Bean** (℡ 01706/825232; www.theculturedbean.com) coffee bar and chocolate shop (try the prize-winning chocolate torte), and **Ramsbottom Sweet Shop** (℡ 01706/822166; www.ramsbottomsweetshop.com). As if that weren't enough, it also has an award-winning Italian restaurant, **Ramsons** (℡ 01706/825070; www.ramsons-restaurant.com), a superb South Indian eatery, **Sanmini's** (℡ 01706/821831; www.sanminis.com), and other good restaurants and pubs.

gravy. The interior is almost unchanged since 1901, but do look closely at the "period" photos—they're actually of present-day regulars!

52 Cross St. ℡ **0161/832-2245.** www.thevictorianchophousecompany.com. Main courses £9.95–£25. AE, MC, V. Mon–Sat 11:30am–11pm; Sun noon–9pm.

Red Chilli ★ CHINESE   Reassuringly packed with Chinese diners, this is where those in the know come for serious Beijing and Sichuan cuisine. Concessions are made to western palates and notions about Chinese food, but look beyond the usual favorites on the menu for more authentic dishes (if in doubt, peek at what your Chinese neighbors are eating and ask for some of the same). We recommend the stir-fried sliced eel with chili sauce, and the spicy-hot poached mutton; or investigate the "Home Style" section of the menu with its frog's legs and whelk specialties. Despite a recent attempt to inject glamor into the decor, prices remain very fair, and portions are huge, so don't over order. There's a second branch in student territory, at 403–419 Oxford Rd. (℡ **0161/273-1288**).

70–72 Portland St. ℡ **0161/236-2888.** www.redchillirestaurant.co.uk. Reservations recommended for dinner. MC, V. Main courses £4.50–£18. Mon–Fri noon–11pm, Sat–Sun noon–midnight.

INEXPENSIVE

Like Bradford, Manchester is famous for its Indian restaurants, but even on the **"Curry Mile"** (Rusholme, south of the center), it's difficult to find one that is consistently good enough to recommend. On the other hand, there are some great Middle Eastern canteens here; try **Jazera,** 22 Wilmslow Rd. (℡ **0161/257-3337**), or **Sadaf,** 167 Wilmslow Rd. (℡ **0161/257-3557**).

Croma ★★ ☺ ITALIAN/PIZZA   Injecting a dose of minimalist chic into the budget Italian scene, Croma offers a winning formula with its gourmet salads, pizzas, and oven-baked pastas, all at very reasonable prices. Salads include the likes of tandoori chicken, or local Bury black pudding (blood sausage) and chorizo; for pizzas, think everything from margarita to peppered rump steak with field mushrooms, crème fraîche, mozzarella, and watercress. For parents, the excellent cocktails are also well

15

THE NORTHWEST

Manchester

priced, while the children's menu is a bargain at £4.95 for a drink, pizza, or pasta dish, small salad, ice cream, and baby-ccino (frothy milk). Young diners also get drawing materials and, at the second branch in the trendy suburb of Chorlton in south Manchester (500 Wilbraham Rd.; ℭ **0161/881-1117**), sometimes even the chance to make their own pizzas.

1-3 Clarence St. ℭ **0161/237-9799.** www.cromapizza.co.uk. Reservations accepted only for parties of 6 or more (none on Sat night). MC, V. Main courses £4.95–£7.95. Mon–Sat 11am–11pm, Sun 11am–10:30pm.

The Gallery Café ★★★ ☺ LUNCH/MODERN BRITISH   Though many of Manchester's museums and galleries have welcoming eateries, this homely café-restaurant within the Whitworth (p. 566), operated by award-winning local firm The Modern Caterer (who also run the café at Jodrell Bank), is worth the trip even if you're not on a cultural outing—it's been singled out by *The Good Food Guide* for its fresh, local, often organic produce prepared in an open kitchen. As befits the venue, you can get everything from sandwiches, soups, and cakes to hot main courses, though the emphasis is on the lighter end of the scale—think smoked mackerel wraps; broccoli and pine-nut bruschetta; pasta with zucchini, sweet peas, Parmesan. and lemon zest; and steak salad with endive, balsamic vinegar, and Pecorino. Fresh flowers on tables, changing artworks on the walls, and handwritten chalkboard menus complete the picture. Children are warmly welcomed with their own healthy dishes and free WAG BAG art packs.

Whitworth Art Gallery. ℭ **0161/275-7497.** www.themoderncaterer.co.uk. Mains around £4–£9. Open Mon–Sat 10am–4:30pm, Sun noon–3:30pm.

Shopping

Manchester is a shopping mecca, rivaling London in scope if not in size. Much of the center is made up of pedestrian-only shopping areas or streets full of designer shops, boutiques, and high-street stores, including **King Street** and **St. Ann's Square, Market Street,** the brand-new **Avenue** near Spinningfields, and the **Arndale Centre,** rebuilt as part of the remodeling of the center after the 1996 IRA bomb. Newcomers are chic department stores **Selfridges,** 1 Exchange Square (ℭ **0800/123400;** www.selfridges. com), and **Harvey Nichols,** 21 New Cathedral Street (ℭ **0161/828-8888**). Off Piccadilly Gardens, Oldham Street leads you into the hip **Northern Quarter,** best known for its indie fashion emporium **Afflecks** ★, 52 Church St. (ℭ **0161/839-0718;** www. afflecks.com), but home to plenty more retro boutiques, record stores, and so on, including kitsch gift store **Oklahoma,** 74–76 High St. (ℭ **0161/834-1136**). Also here is the excellent **Manchester Craft Centre,** 17 Oak St. (ℭ **0161/832-4274;** www.craftand design.com), within an atmospheric Victorian market building.

You'll find lots more shops—plus amenities, entertainment, and eateries galore—west of the center in the **Trafford Centre** (ℭ **0161/839-0718;** www.traffordcentre. co.uk), including a smaller branch of Selfridges.

Manchester's **Real Food Market** (ℭ **0161/234-7356**) takes place on the second and fourth weekend (Fri–Sat 10am–6pm) of the month in Piccadilly Gardens, offering products from local farms and producers, from Lake District reared meats and Lancashire cheeses to curries, plus handcrafted ethical gifts and jewelry. For other Manchester markets, see www.manchestermarkets.com.

Entertainment & Nightlife

Manchester is rich in the performing arts. Among the major venues is the **Lowry Theatre** ★★ (ℭ **0843/208-6000;** www.thelowry.com) at Salford Quays, with two main theatres, a studio space, and exhibition galleries with an emphasis on the work of L. S. Lowry (1887–1976), who documented England's bleak industrial north. In the center, the **Royal Exchange ★★** (© **0161/833-9833;** www.royalexchangetheatre.org.uk), Britain's largest theatre-in-the-round, stunningly housed in a glass-walled capsule suspended within the Great Hall of the Exchange on St. Ann's Square, offers a reliably exciting program. And **Bridgewater Hall,** Lower Mosley Street (© **0161/907-9000;** www.bridgewater-hall.co.uk), a state-of-the-art, 2,400-seat concert hall, is home to the renowned Hallé Orchestra, BBC Philharmonic, and Manchester Camerata, as well as hosting some pop and comedy. There are countless smaller venues, too; keep your finger on the pulse by consulting www.creativetourist.com.

The same website, as well as www.manchesterconfidential.co.uk, will help you when it comes to the exciting, ever-evolving **live music, nightlife,** and **bar scene** of the city that gave birth to The Smiths, New Order, Oasis, and The Stone Roses. If in doubt, head to the **Northern Quarter** for a reliably good night out, or even to the southern suburbs, to the fashionable student enclave **West Didsbury** with its good bars. Manchester's loud, proud, and straight-friendly **Gay Village** spreads across Canal Street in a once-seedy factory district of the center.

Where to Stay

Manchester's Malmaison, set in a handsome former warehouse, has two football-themed suites (Manchester United and Manchester City; doubles are about £129–£149). The city's **Hilton,** in a landmark modern tower, is best known for its **Cloud 23** bar offering stunning views from floor-to-ceiling windows; doubles cost about £169. The city's **ABode Hotel,** home to **Michael Caines** (p. 568), has doubles for about £160. **Staying Cool** has three stylish serviced apartments in the city, with prices from £145 for a double (less for longer stays).

There's a **Roomzzzz Aparthotel,** at 36 Princess St. (© **0161/236-2121**), plus a **Novotel,** at 21 Dickinson St. (© **0161/235-2200**). The latter has a hammam and sauna but no pool; doubles with an extra sofabed start at about £95.

Lowry Hotel ★★ ☺   Manchester's most expensive and best hotel is on the banks of the Irwell, with views over Santiago Calavatra's ultramodern Trinity Bridge. Though this makes it feel slightly apart and aloof, it's only a 5-minute walk from the center. The place to stay for just about every visiting celeb, it differs from most hotels in the global Rocco Forte group in that it's very modern, inside and out. But despite the minimalist esthetic, the level of comfort is the same, with all rooms and suites boasting marble bathrooms and walk-in wardrobes. The best have river views. Like most hotels in the group, it welcomes families, with complimentary connecting/adjoining rooms, a prize trail, a chest of games, toys, and DVDs, and free "mocktails." Children 9 and under eat free in the waterside **River Restaurant,** and there's an affordable menu for children 15 and under, plus kids' afternoon teas including a gingerbread matchstick man (L. S. Lowry style) to decorate. Slow-ish service is made up for by excellent food including, for adults, cured salmon, oyster, and citrus-marinated scallops, and Welsh saltmarsh lamb with rosti potato, eggplant flan, and sweetbreads.

50 Dearmans Place, Chapel Wharf, Manchester M3 5LH. www.thelowryhotel.com. © **0161/827-4000.** 165 units. £423–£453 double; from £970 suite. AE, DC, MC, V. Parking £12. **Amenities:** Restaurant; bar; gym; room service; spa, Wi-Fi. *In room:* TV, CD player (upon request), hair dryer, iPod docking station, minibar.

YHA Manchester   A good example of a modern youth hostel, this building is well located by the barge-filled canals of trendy Castlefield. It's a 10-minute walk from the bustle and chaos of the city center, right by the Museum of Science and Industry. The decor is bright, fresh, and fun, with an almost Pop Arty feel, and the staff is friendly. Rooms range from en suite private rooms for two- to five-bed dorms, and there's a dining room for cheap but decent meals, including optional breakfast costing around £5.

Potato Wharf, Manchester M3 4NB. www.yha.org.uk. *©* **0845/371-9647.** 35 units. From £15 per person, £11 children 17 and under. MC, V. Free parking. **Amenities:** Restaurant; games room; TV lounge; shop; communal kitchen; laundrette; discounted access to fitness center; Wi-Fi (free).

CHESHIRE ★★

Chester: 194 miles NW of London; 80 miles NW of Birmingham; 45 miles SW of Manchester; 28 miles S of Liverpool

With its magnificent country-house estates and other fine historic buildings set amidst pretty landscapes, Cheshire offers a green respite for those exploring the cities of the northwest. Of its cities and towns, **Chester,** full of Roman remnants, half-timbered houses and shops (some Tudor but others Georgian and Victorian) and good attractions for families, is well worth a day or two's exploration.

Essentials

GETTING THERE   Frequent direct trains from London's Euston Station to Chester take 2 hours, costing around £70 for a round-trip. There are also direct trains from Manchester (1½ hr.) and Liverpool (40 min.). Manchester and Liverpool airports are the handiest for Chester but you'll have to travel into the cities themselves for public transport links. For those exploring Cheshire, the train stations of Manchester (p. 562), Stockport, Macclesfield, Wilmslow, Crewe, and also Stoke on Trent (in Staffordshire) can all be handy.

There are a few direct **National Express** (*©* **0871/781-8181;** www.national express.com) buses between London and Chester, taking just over 6 hours, but most services require a change at Birmingham. There are also direct buses from Manchester (about 1 hr.) and Liverpool (50 min.).

If you are exploring the area without a car, consult www.traveline-northwest.co.uk.

Chester is about 3½ hours northwest of London, mainly via the M1 and M6. From Birmingham it's about 80 miles (1½ hr.), from Manchester about 45 miles (just under 1 hr.), and from Liverpool about 28 miles (40 min.).

VISITOR INFORMATION   **Chester Visitor Information Centre,** Town Hall Square (*©* **0845/647-7868;** www.visitchester.com), is open Monday to Saturday 9am–5:30pm, Sundays and bank holidays 10am–5pm.

SPECIAL EVENTS   Each April, the **Chester Food, Drink & Lifestyle Festival** (*©* **01244/355474;** www.chesterfoodanddrink.com) includes the Cheese Rolling Championships waged between Cheshire, Lancashire, and Stilton teams. It's followed by the classical **Summer Music Festival,** held over 2 weeks in July, and by the **October Shell Chester Literature Festival** (both *©* **01244/405637;** www.chesterfestivals.co.uk). Summer also sees the **Midsummer Watch Parades** (www.midsummerwatch.co.uk), one of Britain's oldest festivals, featuring medieval giants, devil and angel puppets, and flocks of geese, while Chester gets very festive at Christmas (www.chestermagic.co.uk), with a Victorian market, lantern parades, an ice rink, and a Big Wheel, all in Castle Square.

The season at **Chester Racecourse** (*©* **01244/304600;** www.chester-races. co.uk; May–Sept) includes a May Festival; a Roman day with races, displays, and

Chester

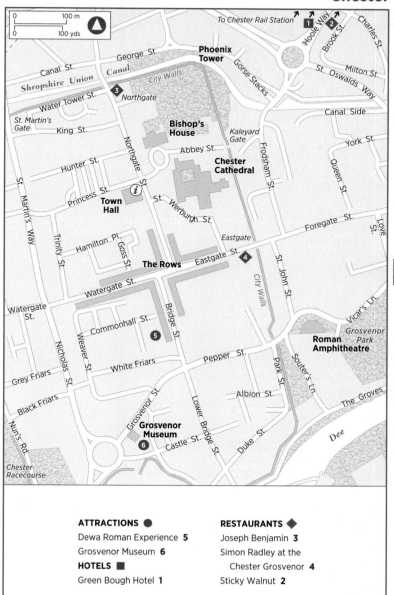

ATTRACTIONS ●
Dewa Roman Experience **5**
Grosvenor Museum **6**
HOTELS ■
Green Bough Hotel **1**

RESTAURANTS ◆
Joseph Benjamin **3**
Simon Radley at the
    Chester Grosvenor **4**
Sticky Walnut **2**

family entertainment; and an Autumn Festival. Also known as the Roodee, the early 16th-century course is the oldest still in use in Britain.

From May to August, Chester's costumed **town-crier** appears at the City Cross at noon (Tues–Sat), to shout news about exhibitions, attractions, and the like. Cheshire's great country houses run packed programs of events year-round; see individual reviews (below) and websites.

Exploring the Area

CHESTER ★★

The traditional county town of mainly rural Cheshire, Chester was founded by a Roman legion on the River Dee in the 1st century A.D. and reached its pinnacle as a bustling port in the 13th and 14th centuries. Though it declined as the river gradually silted up, its fortified **city walls ★★**, largely intact, are Britain's most complete. Climb the steps close to the much-photographed **Eastgate Clock** and walk along the top of the wall, past 18th-century buildings and some Roman ruins you can explore for free. The wall is walkable for almost all of its 2 miles; at its southwestern corner lie some fragments of medieval **Chester Castle** (✆ **01829/260464;** www. english-heritage.org.uk) plus, in old barracks within the castle confines, the **Cheshire Military Museum** (✆ **01244/327617;** www.cheshiremilitarymuseum. co.uk), open daily 10am to 5pm, with entry £3 for adults, £2 for children.

But the most interesting spot of this section of Chester is the remains of Britain's largest **Roman amphitheatre ★★**, which was used for military training and entertainment (cock-fighting, bull-baiting, classical boxing, gladiatorial combat, and more) by the 20th Legion. Half-exposed (the other half is covered by listed buildings), it only came to light in 1929 and further excavation took place in 2007–9, with a *trompe l'oeil* mural added in 2010 to give visitors at least the illusion of being surrounded by the entire structure. The site is free to access at any time. From here, you can take a pleasant stroll along the 18th-century riverside promenade, **The Groves**, newly refurbished in 2011.

Chester's rich heritage is proudly displayed at the **Grosvenor Museum,** and to more corny effect just around the corner at the **Dewa Roman Experience.** The other main sight in the center, **Chester Cathedral ★**, Abbey Square (✆ **01244/ 324756;** www.chestercathedral.com), was founded in 1092 as a Benedictine abbey and made an Anglican cathedral church in 1541. Notable features include the fine range of monastic buildings, particularly the cloisters and refectory, the chapterhouse, and the superb medieval woodcarving in the choir (stalls). Visiting times are Monday to Saturday 9am to 5pm, Sunday 1 to 4pm, but call ahead if making a special trip in case of services or events. Admission is £5 adults, £2.50 children, including a 45-minute audio-tour (of which there's a children's version).

Blue Planet Aquarium ★ ☺ AQUARIUM   Europe's biggest collection of sharks (and the opportunity to dive with some of them) and a new-in-2011 Coral Cave with state-of-the-art lighting effects are among the draws at this large aquarium, but try to avoid school holidays, when the place gets uncomfortably crowded.

Junction 10 of the M53, Ellesmere Port. ✆ **0151/357-8804.** www.blueplanetaquarium.com. Admission £15 adults, £11 for children 13 and under (taller than 95cm). Mon–Fri 10am–5pm, until 6pm Sat–Sun and school holidays.

Chester Zoo ★ ☺ ZOO   One of the best British zoos, this has a strong reputation for its conservation work and well-sized enclosures. The quirky 1970s-style monorail lets you peer down into many of the enclosures as you travel across the park, which is noted for its gardens replicating many of the animals' native environments. There are also play areas, a golf course, and a mini golf course.

Upton-by-Chester. ℂ **01244/380280.** www.chesterzoo.org. Admission varies by season; in school holidays, it's £15 adults, £12 children 3–15, with the monorail extra. Open from 10am daily, with closing times varying by season.

Dewa Roman Experience ☺ HISTORIC SITE   Primarily of interest to families, and best saved for a rainy day, this rather schlocky attraction features some recreated Roman streets and a studio where you can handle archeological remains and try on armor and so on. In school holidays it also runs tours of Chester led by Roman soldier patrols; note that these cost £2 but net you £1 off museum entry.

Pierpoint Lane, Chester. ℂ **01244/343407.** www.dewaromanexperience.co.uk. Admission £4.95 adults, £3.25 children 5–15. Feb–Nov Mon–Sat 9am–5pm, Dec–Jan daily 10am–4pm.

Grosvenor Museum ★ MUSEUM   This otherwise modest museum is home to a world-famous collection of Roman tombstones. You can also take in art, silver, and social and natural history collections, and if you're visiting with kids, join in on a rich program of family events.

27 Grosvenor St. ℂ **01244/402033.** www.cheshirewestandchester.gov.uk. Free admission. Mon–Sat 10:30am–5pm and Sun 1–4pm.

CHESHIRE COUNTRY HOUSES & GARDENS ★★

Though there is little to tempt visitors to the other major towns in Cheshire (including Warrington, Crewe, Widnes, and Macclesfield), this affluent county beloved by footballers and their wives and by soap-opera stars, and said to have more millionaires per square mile than anywhere else in the country (at least in the Alderley Edge area), has other attractions.

Just outside the pleasant market town of Knutsford, **Tatton Park** (p. 576) is one of the finest of all British country houses, while about 25 miles east, on the threshold of the Peak District (p. 534), lies another magnificent estate, **Lyme Park** (p. 576). Between the two, **Alderley Edge** ★★ (ℂ **01625/584412;** www.nationaltrust.org. uk), just outside the town of the same name—once home to the Beckhams and still Cheshire's "capital of bling"—is a dramatic red-sandstone escarpment dotted with ancient copper-mining relics. With free, open access (parking lot open daily 8am to 5–6pm), it offers woodland walks and lovely views over the Cheshire countryside, especially from Stormy Point, Castle Rock, and The Beacon, where fires were lit to warn of the imminent invasion by Spain in 1588. From the escarpment, there's a pathway to **Hare Hill** ★ (ℂ **01625/584412;** Apr and June–Oct Wed–Thurs and Sat–Sun 10am–5pm; daily in May; admission £3.40 adults, £1.70 children 5–15), a woodland garden with wire sculptures and exotic plants open daily. Refuel at the **Wizard Tearoom** (ℂ **07742/333463**) or **Wizard Pub** (ℂ **01625/584-000;** www.ainscoughs.co.uk), both on Macclesfield Road and named after the magician Merlin (King Arthur and his men are said to sleep beneath the sandstone cliffs here).

To the north, at Styal just past Wilmslow, **Quarry Bank Mill** ★★ (ℂ **01625/445896;** www.nationaltrust.org.uk) gives you the chance to find out all about the Industrial Revolution in the area, with hand-spinning demonstrations, working machinery, steam engines, a waterwheel, tours of the Apprentice House, which housed the pauper children who worked in the mill, and entry to the mill owners' gorgeous valley garden. There are also family trails and a play area. Styal village, built to house the mill workers, remains a vibrant community.

South of Wilmslow, near Goostrey, the **Jodrell Bank Centre for Astrophysics ★** (*✆* **01477/571339;** www.jb.man.ac.uk) saw the opening of a new Discovery Centre in April 2011, with a Space Pavilion for exhibitions and events and a glass-walled cafe with spectacular views of the iconic Lovell Telescope, one of the world's most powerful radio telescopes.

Lyme Park ★★ ☺ PARK   Set in gardens and its own huge deer park, this country house will be recognizable to many as Mr. Darcy's Pemberley in the BBC's 1995 *Pride and Prejudice*. For adults, a highlight is the liturgical Lyme Caxton Missal in the library, with a touch-screen facility so you can "turn" its pages and hear chants sung as they would have been 500 years ago; for kids, the Crow Wood Playscape, opened in 2011, is an innovative playground with a treehouse, rope, and timber walkways, tree-trunk climbing, and giant badger sets.

Disley. *✆* **01663/762023.** www.nationaltrust.org.uk. Admission £5 per vehicle, then house and garden £9.50, £4.75 children 5-16 (individual tickets also available). Park daily 8am–6pm, garden Mar–Oct daily 11am–5pm, house Mar–Oct Fri–Tues 11am–5pm.

Tatton Park ★★★ ☺ PARK   Also surrounded by a magnificent deer park, this superb mansion and estate is Cheshire's big-hitter, host to legions of prominent events throughout the year, including antiques fairs, classic car shows, flower shows, outdoor concerts and theatre, and Christmas events. As well as the mansion itself, visitors can access the lovely gardens and working rare-breeds farm, while kids love the adventure playground and seasonal fun-fair rides, and there's bike rental.

Knutsford. *✆* **01625/374400.** www.tattonpark.org.uk. Admission £5 per vehicle, then £8 adults, £4 children 5-15 (or £5/£3 per individual attraction). Apr–Oct daily park 10am–7pm, gardens 10am–6pm; Nov–Mar Tues–Sun and bank holiday Mon park 11am–5pm; for mansion and farm (closed Mon exc. bank holidays in high season) see website.

Where to Eat

As in Manchester, there's a **Michael Caines** restaurant at the ABode hotel, Grosvenor Road (*✆* **01244/347000**).

Dun Cow ★★ 🍴 MODERN BRITISH   This award-winning dining pub not far from Tatton Park was recently rescued from oblivion and stylishly revamped to become a hotspot for creative, beautifully executed cuisine based on top local produce. Menus change seasonally, but you might enjoy butter-roasted pigeon with liver parfait, black pudding (blood sausage), and blackberries, or rare-breed pork filet with wild-boar bacon, Koffman cabbage, dauphinoise potato, apple tart, sage, and cider jus. Desserts such as warm sugar-coated donuts with strawberry jelly, strawberry and tarragon milkshake, honey, and vanilla espuma are worth leaving room for. The bar, with its old beams and log fires, is a cozy spot for real ales.

Chelford Rd., Ollerton. *✆* **01565/633093.** http://chefmarcmattocks.co.uk. Reservations recommended. MC, V. Main courses £16–£20. Mon noon–3pm; Tues–Fri noon–3pm and 5–11pm; Sat noon–11pm; Sun noon–5pm.

Joseph Benjamin ★★★ 🍴 MODERN BRITISH/EUROPEAN   This award-winning restaurant, deli, and cookshop by Chester's city walls is a handy all-day spot for breakfast, lunch, and afternoon tea, plus a candlelit dinner and/or drinks in the latter part of the week. The compact menu of seasonal dishes based on local ingredients changes completely every few weeks but may include free-range chicken, shallot, and thyme terrine with plum chutney, or slow-roast shoulder of Welsh lamb with pepperonata, fried potatoes, and green-olive tapenade. It's invariably packed, but on a fine day a good alternative is to arm yourself with sandwiches from the deli counter and picnic in the cathedral gardens.

140 North Gate St., Chester. *©* **01244/344295.** www.josephbenjamin.co.uk. Reservations recommended. MC, V. Main courses £13–£18. Tues–Wed 9am–5pm, Thurs–Sat 9am–midnight, Sun 10am–5pm.

Simon Radley at the Chester Grosvenor ★★ MODERN FRENCH   Holder of a Michelin star, this fine-dining restaurant within the city's most revered hotel was revamped and renamed in 2008 (it used to be The Arkle). Resolutely formal (smart attire is requested, no children 11 and under, and cellphones have to be silenced), it may be a little stiff and rarefied for some. Dishes such as watercress whip with crayfish tails, garlic snails, and frog's-leg bonbon, and roast cushion of veal sweetbread, lobster knuckles, almond milk, and chickpea will be too far out for many non-foodies. For the latter, however, the eight-course tasting menu will be a slice of gourmet heaven. There's a similar vibe (and no children 11 and under rule) in the hotel's chic **Ark Bar and Lounge,** where you can enjoy morning coffee, light lunches, and afternoon tea—the latter with champagne if you wish, or in a "Gentleman's Indulgent" version accompanied by a gin and tonic or Eastgate ale. A more casual option is the Parisian-style **Brasserie,** open daily for breakfast, lunch, and dinner, which features lots of traditional English and Continental favorites with a twist, from steak and kidney with veal grenadin, veal kidney, and creamed spinach, to Parmesan gnocchi with wild mushrooms and pumpkin fritters. There's also a great children's menu.

The Chester Grosvenor & Spa itself—which belongs to the Duke of Westminster's family—is the *grande dame* of the city's hotel scene, although its rooms are lightened by boutique-hotel-style touches, and there's a super-modern spa with a steam room, herb sauna, ice fountain, themed shower, and salt grotto in addition to treatment rooms. The various packages include spa rituals and retreats, plus several family offers, some including tickets to local attractions such as Chester Zoo and one including a ghost tour of Chester followed by spooky movies and popcorn in your room. Doubles start at £220, suites at £425.

Eastgate, Chester. *©* **01244/895618.** www.chestergrosvenor.co.uk. Reservations required. A la carte menu £69; 8-course tasting menu £90. AE, DC, MC, V. Tues–Sat 6:30–9pm (last order), plus Sun preceding a bank holiday Mon (but closed Tues after that holiday).

Afternoon Tea, Cheshire-Style

Cheshire's many lovely tearooms are great for a decadent afternoon tea of traditional goodies plus sometimes local specialties such as spinach and Cheshire cheese tart. Most tearooms also serve morning coffee and cakes, hot and cold lunches, and children's meals, making them great all-day options for family eating that won't cost the earth. These are some of our favorite venues:

Restaurant at Lyme Park (p. 576).
Stables Restaurant, Tatton Park (p. 576).
Wizard Tearoom, Alderley Edge (p. 575).
Zugers Tea Rooms, St. John's Street, Chester (*©* **0151/334-1904;** www. zugerstearooms.co.uk).

Sticky Walnut ★★ 🍴 MODERN EUROPEAN Formerly the Village Bistro, this cozy restaurant has wowed customers under its new ownership, offering upscale, creative modern cooking at very good prices that make it well worth the slight schlepp from central Chester (it's a 10-min. walk outside the walls). This is hearty rather than fine dining, with a fashionable, rustic edge to it: According to the season, expect oven-roast beets with fresh ricotta, sticky walnuts, and spicy pumpkin seeds; rope-grown Shetland mussels, spicy sausage, onion, and white wine; and whole chargrilled mackerel with lemon marmalade and wild rocket.

11 Charles St., Hoole, Chester. ℂ **01244/400400.** www.stickywalnut.com/menu.html. Reservations recommended. Main courses £7–£13. MC, V. Tues–Sat noon–10pm, Sun noon–6pm.

Shopping ★★

Chester is a prime shopping destination, with the highlight being the unique **Rows,** with one tier of shops at street level, the others stacked on top along a sort of galleried balcony. Offerings on the Rows include both high-street stalwarts and quirkier one-offs, including tobacco shops, china shops, jewelers, and antiques dealers. Several Chester stores, including wine and spirits merchant **Corks Out,** 21 Watergate Street (ℂ **01244/310455**), are in atmospheric medieval crypts.

North of Chester, at Ellesmere Port, the **Cheshire Oaks (McArthur Glen) Designer Outlet** (ℂ **0151/348-5600;** www.cheshireoaksdesigneroutlet.com) has 145 designer and high-street stores offering reductions of up to 60%.

Where to Stay

For the **Chester Grosvenor and Spa,** see the "Simon Radley at the Chester Grosvenor" review, above, under "Where to Eat." There's an **ABode** (£89–£210 double, including breakfast) in a modern building in central Chester, with a **Michael Caines** restaurant. You'll find self-catering holiday cottages on the grounds of both **Tatton Park** (p. 576) and **Lyme Park** (p. 576).

Green Bough Hotel ★★★ Winner of countless awards, this luxurious haven, about a 10-minute walk from the center of Chester exudes the intimacy lacking at the Grosvenor, with just over a dozen individually designed rooms, a rooftop garden, a champagne bar, and a fine-dining restaurant, the **Olive Tree,** also award-winning for its imaginative cuisine using mainly local produce (think foragers' broth with pearl barley and Parmesan ice cream, crispy Gloucestershire Old Spot belly pork with cinnamon and apple compôte, and Madagascan vanilla soufflé with mango and lime coulis). The no-children-under-13 policy makes this a good contender for a romantic retreat, reinforced by the plush but understated decor, including cast-iron, half-tester, or carved wooden beds in many rooms.

60 Hoole Rd., Chester, Cheshire CH2 3NL. www.chestergreenboughhotel.com. ℂ **01244/326241.** 15 units. £175–£195 double; from £245 suite. Rates include full Cheshire breakfast. AE, DC, MC, V. Free parking. **Amenities:** Restaurant; bar; room service; free DVD library; treatments (at spa in center), free Wi-Fi. *In room:* TV, hair dryer, free Wi-Fi.

Kingsley Lodge ★★ 🛏 This is another intimate hideaway with a no-children-under-13 rule. It's a 1950s' Arts and Crafts-style villa in landscaped gardens in an exclusive residential neighborhood in Wilmslow, offering sumptuous boutique-style rooms and little else but peace and quiet. Since opening in 2002, it's been a bit of an insider secret among luxury hoteliers, style journalists, and discerning celebrities, who all fall for the timelessly chic decor with original works of art, handcrafted antique and modern furniture, and luxurious fabrics and wall coverings in neutral tones. Some rooms have picture windows looking over the gardens with their ponds and fountain; others have private terraces or balconies.

10 Hough Lane, Wilmslow, Cheshire SK9 2LQ. www.kingsleylodge.com. © **01625/441794.** 6 units. £199–£225 double, from £290 suite. MC, V. Rates include breakfast. Free parking. Amenities: Lounge. In room: TV/DVD, CD player, hair dryer, Wi-Fi (free).

Mickle Trafford Manor ★ 🍴 💼 This 16-century Tudor manor just northeast of Chester has great facilities for its price range: an outdoor hot tub, a sauna, and a small gym. The Master Bedroom boasts a vaulted beamed ceiling, vast bed, and double-ended bath, but all three guest rooms are very pleasant, and there's a sunny lounge with a conservatory plus a cosy hall with an open fire. Packed lunches can be ordered for days out.

Mickle Trafford, Cheshire CH2 4EA. www.mickletraffordmanor.co.uk. © **01244/300555.** 3 units. Free parking. Double £80–£95. Rates include English breakfast. MC, V. **Amenities:** Lounge and honesty bar; garden; hot tub; sauna; gym. In room: TV.

Wizard's Thatch ★★ 💼 Eccentric and not to everyone's taste, this cute-as-a-button ivy-covered thatched cottage, with its small-paned windows and beamed ceilings, houses three suites (one sleeping four) filled with antique knick-knacks and prints and four-poster beds draped with gold and red tapestries. It was named after the legendary magician of Alderley Edge (p. 575). Another place for a romantic break, it offers packages including champagne and chocolates on arrival, and boasts a pond where you can sit out by candlelight. Quirky decorative details include shelves lined by old ginger-beer bottles and framed *Punch* cartoons and ancient newspapers on the walls; the building's age means you have to contend with uneven floors, narrow stairs, and very low beams and doorways.

Summerhill Cottages, Macclesfield Rd., Alderley Edge, Cheshire SK9 7BG. www.wizardsthatch.co.uk. © **01625/599909.** 3 units. £185–£265 suite for 2. Free parking. **Amenities:** DVD and CD library; books and games. In room: TV/DVD, CD player, MP3 docking station (in 1 suite), kitchen facilities (fridge, toaster, and microwave), hair dryer, Wi-Fi (free).

LIVERPOOL ★★★ & MERSEYSIDE ★★★

Liverpool: 219 miles NW of London; 103 miles NW of Birmingham; 35 miles W of Manchester

Like Manchester, **Liverpool** has re-emerged from decline to become a world-class city, enjoying an unprecedented cultural and economic reawakening and proudly asserting its extraordinary maritime heritage. But the rest of heavily urbanized **Merseyside** bears some other gems, notably **Crosby** beach with its eerie Anthony Gormley art installation, **Formby** with its nature reserve and sand dunes studded with ancient footprints, and the thoroughly English traditional seaside resort of **Southport**.

Essentials

GETTING THERE Frequent trains from London's Euston Station to Liverpool take just over 2 hours direct but more usually 2½ hours, with a change at Crewe in Cheshire, costing £70 for a round-trip. There are also direct trains to Liverpool from Birmingham (about 1¾ hr.), Manchester (about 1 hr.), Chester (about 45 min.), Leeds (about 1¾ hr.), and York (about 2¼ hr.).

Direct Liverpool–Southport trains take about 45 minutes, and National Express buses cover the same route (26 miles) in about 55 minutes.

Direct **National Express** (📞 **0871/781-8181;** www.nationalexpress.com) buses from London's Victoria Coach Station take about 5¼ hours; there are also buses from Liverpool (about 2½ hr. or more), from Manchester (about 1¼ hr.), and from Leeds (about 2¼ hr.).

Liverpool is about 3¾ hours northwest of London by road, mainly on the M1 and M6, about 1¾ hours northwest of Birmingham, and about 45 minutes west of Manchester.

Liverpool **John Lennon Airport** (📞 **0871/521-8484;** www.liverpoolairport. com), serving mainly European and a few U.K. destinations, is linked by bus to central Liverpool and Manchester. There are also direct buses from **Manchester International Airport** to central Liverpool.

VISITOR INFORMATION **Liverpool Tourist Information Centre,** Whitechapel (📞 **0151/233-2008;** www.visitliverpool.com), is open Monday to Saturday 10am to 5pm, Sunday 11am to 4pm. There's also an information desk at the airport.

Albert Dock Visitor Centre, Anchor Courtyard (📞 **0151/233-2008;** www. visitliverpool.com), is open daily 10am to 5pm.

Southport Visitor Information Centre, 112 Lord St. (📞 **01704/533333;** www.visitsouthport.com), is open March to October Monday to Saturday 9am to 5:30pm, Sunday 10am to 4pm; November to February daily 10am–4pm.

SPECIAL EVENTS The Grand National at Sefton's **Aintree Racecourse** (📞 **0151/523-2600;** www.aintree.co.uk) in April is said to be the world's greatest steeplechase. Liverpool's **International Beatles Week** (www.beatlesfestival.co.uk) attracts about 100,000 fans and bands from more than 20 countries for a 7-day celebration in various venues each August. There's also a **Beatles Day** (www.beatlesday. tv) in July, with live music around town, Beatles buskers on the streets, a special concert at the Echo Arena, and people encouraged to wear moptop wigs, with all proceeds going to children's charities.

Southport's highlights are its seafront **Air Show** (www.militaryairshows.co.uk) in July and August **Flower Show** (www.southportflowershow.co.uk).

Exploring the Area
LIVERPOOL

The last decade or so has seen a significant transformation of this once-great merchant port, partly by virtue of its being awarded UNESCO World Heritage site status in 2004. Though generally best known for producing The Beatles, this 18th- and 19th-century industrial, maritime, and mercantile hothouse was a leader in both the expansion of the British Empire and the development of modern dock technology and maritime transport. The UNESCO listing applies to six areas—buildings at Pier Head, the Albert Dock and Stanley Dock Conservation Area, the Castle Street commercial center, the William Brown Conservation Area, and Duke Street ("Ropewalks"). But despite money being pumped into regeneration projects—the most obvious being Albert Dock and the new Liverpool One shopping center—much of Liverpool's appeal comes from its continued edginess, seediness, and dereliction coexisting with sparkling new shops, hotels, and attractions.

It's strange to think that Liverpool began as a 12th-century fishing village. Granted a charter as early as 1207 by King John, it grew to prominence in the 18th century

Liverpool

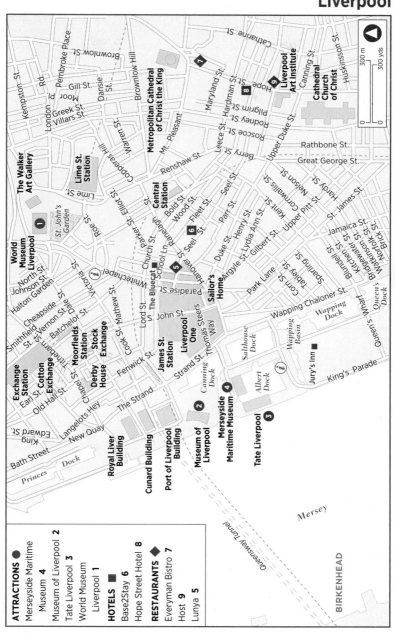

300 m
300 yds

Rathbone St.
Great George St.

ATTRACTIONS ●
Merseyside Maritime
Museum **4**
Museum of Liverpool **2**
Tate Liverpool **3**
World Museum
Liverpool **1**

HOTELS ■
Base2Stay **6**
Hope Street Hotel **8**

RESTAURANTS ◆
Everyman Bistro **7**
Host **9**
Lunya **5**

Mersey

BIRKENHEAD

15

THE NORTHWEST | Liverpool & Merseyside

through its sugar, spice, and tobacco trade with the Americas. Under Queen Victoria, it became Britain's biggest commercial seaport. Despite population hemorrhages over the past couple of decades, it retains a compelling ethnic mix, including Britain's oldest black community (descendants of 18th-century seamen, slaves, and traders' children) and Europe's oldest Chinese community (with 19th-century seamen forebears), plus many Welsh and Irish, the latter due to migration from the Great Famine.

It also continues its transformation into a major world city. Mid-2011 saw the partial opening of the **Museum of Liverpool** (p. 585) in a fabulous new landmark building on the Mann Island site at Pier Head, at the core of the waterfront World Heritage site. Pier Head is also home to the listed **Royal Liver Building ★**, one of the city's "Three Graces," along with the neighboring Cunard Building and Port of Liverpool Building. Home to the Royal Liver Assurance friendly society, the landmark Royal Liver Building stands out for the famous pair of metal-sculpture Liver Birds sitting on top of it—Liverpool's symbols, these mysterious cormorant-like birds are said to protect the city's people as well as sailors coming into its port, and if one were to fly away, the city would cease to be.

It's from Pier Head that you can catch a famous **Ferry 'Cross the Mersey ★★** (✆ **0151/639-0609;** www.merseyferries.co.uk), which serves as both a locals' shuttle service and a tour boat offering the best views of Liverpool's awesome skyline with its mixture of the historic and the ultra-modern. Round-trip River Explorer tickets are £11 adults, £6.50 children 5 to 15, and £4.50 children 3 to 4; you can also get joint tickets to stop off at attractions at terminals across the water: **Spaceport,** Seacombe Terminal (✆ **0151/330-1566;** www.spaceport.org.uk), with themed galleries and temporary exhibitions, and **U-Boat Story,** Woodside Terminal (✆ **0151/330-1000;** www.u-boatstory.co.uk), a real German submarine housing interactive displays and archive film footage. Seacombe Terminal is also home to a soft-play area and cafe. Alternatively, Mersey Ferries also runs **Manchester Ship Canal Cruises ★★** from Pier Head along the 35-mile waterway to Salford Quays (p. 567). In addition to giving you the chance to learn about the canal itself, which helped shape the history of Manchester and the northwest as a whole, the trip lets you take in Manchester sights such as the Imperial War Museum North (p. 567). Trips cost £37 for adults, £35 for kids, with return bus transfer.

Due south of Pier Head lies another hive of activity, the handsomely regenerated red-brick **Albert Dock complex** (www.albertdock.com), now home to shops, restaurants, hotels, and several attractions, including the **Merseyside Maritime Museum** (p. 584), the **Tate Liverpool** (p. 585), one of The Beatles Story sites (see below) and a new 60-m (197-ft.) **Echo Wheel** (✆ **0151/709-8651;** www.worldtouristattractions. co.uk), which may turn into a permanent fixture. The Dock is also the starting-point for tours of the city in the **Yellow Duckmarine,** a converted World War II DUKW amphibious landing craft, and the Yellow Boat Cruise, a water-based heritage tour (both ✆ **0151/708-7799;** www.theyellowduckmarine.co.uk).

There's plenty to lure you away from Liverpool's waterfront. At the city's heart is the **World Museum Liverpool** (see below). Close by, also on William Brown Street, the **Walker Art Gallery ★★** (✆ **0151/478-4199;** www.liverpoolmuseums.org.uk) has an outstanding collection of European art from the 1300s, but is especially rich in European Old Masters, Victorian, pre-Raphaelite, and contemporary British works, and also has an award-winning sculpture gallery and a kids' gallery. Another free venue, it's open daily 10am to 5pm.

In the new **Museum of Liverpool** (p. 585), you can learn much about local heroes The Beatles, a band that, hugely influenced by its place of birth, changed popular music and wider culture on a global scale. The Wondrous Place gallery displays unique band-related objects, including the original stage on which John Lennon's band The Quarrymen played in 1957 when he met Paul McCartney. But there are plenty more Liverpool sights and attractions for Beatles aficionados. Pier Head and Albert Dock are each home to a **Beatles Story "experience" ★**, (© 0151/709-1963; www.beatlesstory. com). The one at the Dock has band memorabilia including George Harrison's first guitar, a kids' discovery zone, a replica **Cavern Club** (where the band played in the early '60s), and even a Beatles-themed Starbucks; the smaller Pier Head site has special exhibitions and the Fab4D "multisensory" journey. They're open daily April to October, 9am to 7pm, 10am to 6pm the rest of the year; tickets (£13, £7 children 5–16) give access to both locations.

Of the many Beatles tours on offer, the best are **Cavern City Tours ★** (© 0151/236-9091; www.beatlestour. org), which end at and include a look around the legendary Cavern Club. Tickets for the 2-hour bus-and-club

tour cost £15. For truly ardent fans, **Pool of Life ★** (© 0151/283-4349; www.pooloflifetours.com) offers both full-day Beatles Extravaganza Tours (£95 per person) or custom tours lasting from 2 hours to 2 days. Alternatively, you can just drop into the **Cavern Club,** 10 Mathew St. (© 0151/236-9091; www.cavernclub.org), still an active bar and club hosting new and tribute bands, open daily from 10:30am.

To tour both **Mendips ★** and **20 Forthlin Road,** Lennon and McCartney's childhood homes, restored to how they would have looked in the 1950s, you need to book a place on a minibus from the city center (© 0151/427-7231; www.nationaltrust.org.uk/beatles); there's no independent access. Tickets cost £20 (£3.40 children 5–16). Tours run February to November and book up well in advance.

Finally, diehard fans may want to check into the **Hard Days Night Hotel,** North John Street (© 0151/236-1964; www.harddaysnighthotel.com), combining Beatles themes with boutique chic. Themed offers include an "All You Need Is Love" package at £384 for 2 people for 2 nights in a luxury room, with breakfast, Beatles Story entry, a Cavern City Tour, Cavern Club membership cards, and hotel T-shirts.

Heading south from here brings you to **The Bluecoat ★**, School Lane (© **0151/702-5324;** www.thebluecoat.org.uk), providing workspace for many of Liverpool's creative artists and showcasing visual art, live art, literature, music, and dance. The oldest building in the center (it was originally a school), this is where Yoko Oko gave her first paid performance, around the time she met Lennon. Family activities at weekends and a pretty courtyard make it kid-friendly.

South and uphill of the center lie Liverpool's two cathedrals. On St. James's Mount, the **Anglican Cathedral Church of Christ (Liverpool Cathedral) ★★** (© **0151/709-6271;** www.liverpoolcathedral.org.uk) was built between 1904 and 1978, making it the world's newest Gothic-style cathedral. It's also England's largest

15

THE NORTHWEST | Liverpool & Merseyside

church, with the world's highest vaulting under its tower, at 53m (175 ft.), and one of the world's longest cathedrals, at 186m (619 ft.). Its organ has nearly 10,000 pipes, the most found in any church, and its tower's bells are the highest (66m/219 ft.) and heaviest (31 tons) in the world! It's free to enter daily 8am to 6pm, but an Attractions Ticket (£5 adults, £3.50 children 5–16) gets you an audio-tour (kids' versions available) and buys you admission to the tower (two consecutive elevators, then 108 stairs) with its views as far as North Wales, as well as to the hidden gem of the Elizabeth Hoare Gallery with its ecclesiastical embroideries.

The tower's panoramic views take in the **Metropolitan Cathedral of Christ the King** (✆ **0151/709-9222;** www.liverpoolmetrocathedral.org.uk) about a half-mile northeast, along Hope Street. This circular Roman Catholic cathedral was started in 1930 to a design by Sir Edward Lutyens but ultimately scaled down and completed in 1967 to a Space Agey Modernist design by Sir Frederick Gibbert. Entry (daily 7:30am–6pm) is free, but you do pay £3 to visit the crypt, the only part that remains of Lutyens' design.

Several sights might tempt you to the city's outskirts. About 15 minutes' walk southeast of Liverpool Cathedral, along Princes Road, **Princes Park** and **Sefton Park** are English Heritage listed for their historic design and landscaping. Sefton, the largest, has a magnificent three-tier palm house bearing sculptures of Cook, Columbus, Darwin, Linnaeus, and other explorers, navigators, botanists, and so on, plus, in its grounds is a statue of Peter Pan that was unveiled in the presence of J. M. Barrie himself. The park's **Palm House** (✆ **0151/726-2415;** www.palmhouse.org.uk) hosts concerts, tea dances, and other events, while its Victorian bandstand is claimed to be the inspiration for The Beatles' *Sgt Pepper's Lonely Hearts Club Band.*

Sefton Park is handy for the bohemian shopping and eating street of **Lark Lane** (p. 588) and also for **Sudley House** ★, Mossley Hill Road (✆ **0151/724-3245;** www.liverpoolmuseums.org.uk), a unique and atmospheric instance of a Victorian merchant's residence that has retained its original pictures, including works by Millais, Rodin, Rossetti, Gainsborough, Reynolds, and Landseer, which you can view together with period furniture. It's free to visit daily from 10am to 5pm.

Farther south, down by the airport, is **Speke Hall, Garden & Estate** ★ (✆ **0844/800-4799;** www.nationaltrust.org.uk; mid-Mar–Oct Wed–Sun 11am–5pm, plus weekends late Feb–mid-Mar and Nov–mid-Dec 11am–4pm). It's a rare surviving Tudor manor with restored Victorian interiors including William Morris wallpaper, encircled by lovely gardens and woodland affording views of the Welsh hills. Events include Victorian-costumed guided tours, and the Home Farm Visitor Centre on the grounds has a play area and picnic tables. Entry to house, garden, and grounds is £8.40 adults, £4.20 children 5 to 16.

North of the center, **Anfield** ★★ (✆ **0151/260-6677;** www.liverpoolfc.tv), home to Liverpool Football Club, offers tours, some led by club "legends" and some for families, or you can just look round the museum. Those with kids might carry on about 10 minutes east along the A57 into Merseyside, to **Knowsley Safari Park** ★ (✆ **0151/430-9009;** www.knowsleysafariexperience.co.uk), with animals from African wild dogs to wildebeest, amusement rides, a woodland walk, and a treetop adventure course (www.aerialextreme.co.uk).

Merseyside Maritime Museum ★ MUSEUM Mass emigration via Liverpool, shipbuilding on Merseyside, Liverpool-linked sea tragedies including the *Titanic,* the Battle of the Atlantic, and transatlantic slavery are all examined at this museum, with the permanent displays backed up by floating exhibits, crafts demonstrations, and working displays. Some of the themes are reprised in the **International Slavery Museum,** currently within the Maritime Museum and sharing its contact details and opening times but slated to get its own entrance soon.

Albert Dock. ℂ **0151/478-4499.** www.liverpoolmuseums.org.uk. Free admission. Daily 10am–5pm.

Museum of Liverpool ★★★ MUSEUM   Only partly open at the time of writing, but already an impressive venue, this is yet another reason to linger in Liverpool. Its most compelling gallery, Wondrous Place, looks at how the city has produced such an amazing roll call of creative folk, from musicians to footballers, as well as examining the development of the Liverpudlian dialect, Scouse. Global City, meanwhile, is focused around a 180-seat theatre where work by local filmmakers, writers, and artists tells the story of how Liverpool came to be the commercial and mercantile equal of London and New York.

Pier Head. ℂ **0151/207-0001.** www.liverpoolmuseums.org.uk. Free admission. Daily 10am–5pm.

Tate Liverpool ★★★ ☺ GALLERY   A little sister to the Tate Britain and Tate Modern in London (p. 109), this bright and funky modern gallery is home to international modern and contemporary art collections and major changing exhibitions, some on artists as eminent as Picasso and Magritte. Like other Tates, it's strong on family activities and events, and has a great cafe (p. 587).

Albert Dock. ℂ **0151/207-0001.** www.liverpoolmuseums.org.uk. Free admission except special exhibitions. May–Sept Tues–Sun, June–Aug daily 10am–5:50pm.

World Museum Liverpool ★ ☺ MUSEUM   Since doubling in size in 2005, this museum has galleries devoted to dinosaurs, geology, "Space and Time" (with a planetarium), the natural world (including live bugs and an aquarium), world cultures, and the ancient world. Family activities and events are a forte, and the emphasis is very much on hands-on experiences, but try to avoid school holidays when the place gets uncomfortably busy.

William Brown St. ℂ **0151/478-4393.** www.liverpoolmuseums.org.uk. Free admission. Daily 10am–5pm.

THE REST OF MERSEYSIDE

Merseyside is highly urbanized even outside the confines of Liverpool, though the borough of Sefton north of Liverpool boasts some gems on its coast. The first stop north of the city is **Crosby,** where globally renowned sculptor Antony Gormley—also behind the Angel of the North (p. 664)—has sited his art installation ***Another Place ★★★*** (www.sefton.gov.uk). Along 2 miles of Crosby's beach and about a half-mile out to sea stand 100 cast-iron casts of Gormley's own body, sunk to various depths in the sand and appearing to stare out to the horizon in silent expectation. The work is generally read as a response to the ambivalence of emigration—sadness at leaving tempered by hope for a better future. The nearby **Crosby Lakeside Adventure Centre** (ℂ **0151/966-6868;** www.crosbylakeside.co.uk) offers watersports and other activities.

Next up as you follow the coast north is **Formby ★★,** an affluent town on the Irish Sea. In summer, its population—which includes (or has included) several famous local footballers—swells considerably as visitors flock to its beach, backed by sand dunes and pine woods that contain a National Trust reserve for some of Britain's dwindling red squirrels. Formby is also a rare breeding spot for natterjack toads, which can be heard "singing" in the late evening. On some parts of the beach, sand erosion has revealed Neolithic/early Bronze Age footprints of humans and animals, including red deer, while the sand dunes are famous for their asparagus, which used to be served on luxury liners setting out from Liverpool (there have been recent efforts to revive the crop and set up an "asparagus trail").

This stretch of coast as a whole is popular with kite-surfers and golfers alike; its several links golf courses include **Royal Birkdale** (© **01704/552020**; www.royal birkdale.com), sometimes host to The Open. Birkdale is on the outskirts of **Southport** ★★, a gloriously old-fashioned seaside resort in the proper English manner, with Britain's second longest **pleasure pier,** at more than half a mile, restored to its Victorian glory in the last decade and boasting an array of traditional seaside amusements including a carousel. Disconcertingly, the pier actually begins a long way inland, and you can catch a tram or a minitrain along its length; before reaching the sea, it crosses Marine Lake, where you can take out a minimotorboat or pedal-boat or ride the Mississippi-style paddlesteamer the **Southport Belle** (© **01704/539701**).

Next to the Marine Lake Bridge, in Kings Gardens, the **Model Railway Village** (© **01704/538001;** www.southportmodelrailwayvillage.co.uk) has miniature trains running through rural, village, and town scenes typical of Lancashire (of which Southport used to be a part). Weather permitting, it's open April to October, Saturday to Thursday 10am–5pm, plus Fridays during school holidays; tickets are £3.50 adults, £3 ages 1 to 15. Nearby, on Marine Drive, **New Pleasureland** (© **01704/532717;** www.southportfunfair.co.uk) is a recent (and lesser) reincarnation of the town's long-standing fun fair. Entry is free, with individual rides costing £1 to £3; it's open weekends (also bank/school holidays) April to October noon to late. A few steps away is the indoor **Dunes Splash World** (© **01704/537160;** www.splashworldsouthport. com), open Monday to Thursday 10am to 5:30pm (to 4pm Sat–Sun and bank holidays). Admission is £7.50 adults, £5.50 children 6 to 15, and £4.50 ages 3 to 5.

Away from the seaside tack, Southport can be surprisingly elegant, with fine examples of Victorian architecture and town planning. Indeed, it's been suggested that the years that Louis-Napoléon Bonaparte spent in exile on broad, tree-lined Lord Street, now famous for its shopping (see below), inspired his redevelopment of much of the medieval center of Paris when he eventually became emperor.

Southport is the starting point for the 215-mile **Trans Pennine Trail** (www. transpenninetrail.org.uk), linking the Irish Sea with the North Sea for walkers, cyclists, and horse-riders, via the Peak District (p. 534) and Yorkshire (p. 630).

Where to Eat

There are several quality chains in **Liverpool One** (p. 588), many of them good for kids, including **Wagamama,** a lively and open Asian fusion experience. For **The London Carriage Works,** see review for the Hope Street Hotel, below. At the Vincent Hotel in Southport (see review, below), you'll find the **V Café and Sushi Bar.**

The Dolphin ★ ☺ FISH & CHIPS A Southport institution just back from the Promenade, this huge, traditional "chippy" may lack glamor and a drinks license, but it can always be counted on for a warm welcome and great fish and chips, plus a huge selection of other fare including roasts, pies, sandwiches, beans on toast and the like, afternoon tea, and that seaside favorite the knickerbocker glory (ice-cream sundae). Kids' meals—fish fingers or fishcakes with chips and beans—will set you back a paltry £3 or so, while food to carry out is available if you fancy combining lunch or dinner with a stroll along the pier.

30–34 Scarisbrick Ave., Southport. © **01704/538251.** Main courses £3.45–£7.45. MC, V. Daily 11am–6pm.

Everyman Bistro ★ ❧ INTERNATIONAL Located beneath the Everyman Theatre, this is Liverpool's eating institution—a canteen-style affair attracting everyone from students and academics to local celebs with its fair prices and eclectic choice of dishes. The menu changes twice daily, but look out for the likes of "lamb scouse" with beetroot and red cabbage, or smoked haddock, horseradish, and pea fishcakes with citrus mayonnaise, and chocolate chip and whiskey pudding with bramble compôte. There are also pizzas, quiches, and salads.

5-9 Hope St., Liverpool. ℂ **0151/708-9545.** www.everyman.co.uk. Main courses £7.50–£8.95. MC, V. Mon–Thurs 11:45am–midnight, Fri 11:45am–2am, Sat 11am–2am.

Host ★★ 🎒 ASIAN FUSION Another thrilling addition to Liverpool's fast-changing eating scene, this 1950s-inspired dining room near Liverpool Cathedral offers Thai-, Chinese-, and Japanese-style nibbles, small plates and big plates, plus cocktails, making it a great place for a convivial meal with friends (the bench seating and some long communal tables militate against romance). Standout dishes include seared beef and curried pickled eggplant salad with chili and thai basil dressing, and hoi sin belly pork with peanut Asian slaw and coconut rice. The highly original desserts are almost scandalously good: Think chocolate and chili brownie, Ovaltine brûlée with chocolate and banana spring roll, and blossom berry tea jelly with plums, blueberries, and coconut sorbet.

31 Hope St., Liverpool. ℂ **0151/708-5831.** www.ho-st.co.uk. Reservations recommended. Main courses £8.25–£11. MC, V. Daily 11am–11pm.

Lunya ★★★ 🎒 ☺ SPANISH This Catalan fusion restaurant and deli in an 18th-century warehouse on the edge of the Liverpool One mall (p. 588) is a multiaward-winning addition to the city's eating scene. Recipes, ideas, and ingredients from Spain and the U.K. are brought together in exciting tapas dishes; it's hard to narrow down the field from the vast menu, but we can vouch for the pork belly in almond milk, and the Joselito Ibérico Bellota ham with baby figs. You can also get paella. This is a great place to bring kids, who get an excellent menu of child-friendly tapas including homemade meatballs, *patatas bravas*, *croquetas*, Spanish omelet, and, to round it off, homemade *churros* sprinkled with cinnamon and sugar, to dunk into extra-thick hot chocolate. Alternatively, the chefs will rustle up pretty much anything a fussy child might demand. Lunch (noon–5pm) is great value, with three tapas dishes with bread or a three-course set menu and drink for less than £10 or hot and cold sandwiches and a soup of the day. Lunya is also a great place to come for an unusual breakfast. The monthly Gourmet Night offers a six-course menu paired with top-notch wines, featuring the likes of pig's trotter escudella with lavender-syrup-coated Southport brown shrimp.

Eating in Liverpool's Museums & Galleries

Some of Liverpool's best eateries are set in its cultural venues: The World Museum's cafe is awful, but we do recommend the **Maritime Dining Rooms** (ℂ 0151/478-4056; www.liverpoolmuseums.org.uk) at the **Merseyside Maritime Museum,** as well as the **Tate Liverpool Café** (ℂ 0151/702-7400; www.tate.org.uk) and **Upstairs Bistro** (ℂ 0151/702-7783; www.thebluecoat.org.uk) at The Bluecoat. All have kids' menus.

18 College Lane, Liverpool. ☎ **0151/706-9770.** www.lunya.co.uk. Reservations recommended. Tapas dishes £3.45–£16. MC, V. Mon–Sat 9am–late, Sun 10am–11pm.

Shopping

Liverpool's rebirth has included the creation of the vast, retail-led **Liverpool One complex** ★★ (www.liverpool-one.com), which opened to widespread acclaim in 2008–9 on under-used land near the Albert Dock. Home to about 170 shops and services and divided into six districts, it's the U.K.'s 10th-largest shopping center, with its own terraced park. Forward-thinking in design, it's been criticized for drawing retailers away from the center proper (around Lime St. Station), but that area in turn is being transformed into Central Village, with completion scheduled for 2013. Where Liverpool One has mainly familiar high-street names such as John Lewis and Topshop, the nearby **Metquarter** (www.metquarter.com), opened on Whitechapel in 2006 and dubbed the "Bond Street of Liverpool," has mainly upmarket boutiques. For more bohemian shopping, head south to villagey **Lark Lane** (www.larklane.com) off Sefton Park.

In Southport, **Lord Street** attracts shoppers with its Victorian covered arcades full of high-street names as well as one-off boutiques.

Entertainment & Nightlife

European Capital of Culture in 2008, Liverpool is positively bursting with creative energies, whether it's in established venues or more underground spots. Among the former are the **Liverpool Philharmonic Hall** ★, Hope Street (☎ **0151/210-2895;** www.liverpoolphil.com), home to one of the best orchestras outside London and also hosting concerts by touring musicians.

The Liverpool rock, pop, and dance music scenes also continue to thrive, particularly in the Ropewalks district. **Nation,** Wolstenholme Square (☎ **0151/707-1309**), hosts the long-standing, world-famous **Cream** ★★ (www.cream.co.uk) dance night, typically held four times a year and attracting superstar DJs. For listings at Nation and elsewhere, see www.anightinliverpool.com, or pick up flyers in shops and cafes.

Liverpool is also very gay friendly, evidenced by plans announced in 2011 to revamp the newly pedestrianized Gay Quarter (focused on Stanley, Cumberland, Victoria, and Eberle streets) to make it one of the U.K.'s gay hubs. There's also a month-long festival of gay culture, **Homotopia** (www.homotopia.net; held Oct/Nov).

Where to Stay
VERY EXPENSIVE

Hope Street Hotel ★ Liverpool's first boutique hotel occupies a converted carriage house and retains its mid-19th-century exposed brickwork and beams, cast-iron columns, and waxed oak floors, which evoke Liverpool's shipbuilding past while exuding a warm, cozy atmosphere and modern vibe. The views are good, too, since it's up on a hill toward Liverpool Cathedral, and some rooms benefit from a private terrace. There are also some duplex suites, and one suite with an Italian wooden bathtub on a mezzanine. For a boutique hotel, it's surprisingly family-friendly, with extra beds provided for children 13 and under in the larger studio rooms, and toyboxes, coloring books, and DVDs available. The modern European **London Carriage Works** restaurant is generally good, although oversalted food and inadequate service can be issues.

40 Hope St., Liverpool L1 9DA. www.hopestreethotel.co.uk. ☎ **0151/709-3000.** 89 units. £180–£240 double; £255–£650 suite. AE, DC, MC, V. Parking £10. **Amenities:** Restaurant; bar; babysitting; gym; room service; in-room treatments; library; CD/DVD library. *In room:* TV/DVD, CD player, hair dryer, Wi-Fi (free).

EXPENSIVE

There's a **Malmaison** in Liverpool, at William Jessop Way (**www.malmaison.com**; ✆ 0151/229-5000), with views of the Mersey and Royal Liver Building from some rooms (£129–£186 doubles). Of its two suites themed for local football teams Liverpool and Everton, Kop has its own games room. For the **Hard Days Night Hotel,** see p. 583.

Vincent ★ An unexpected oasis of chic in kiss-me-quick Southport, the Vincent opened in a former cinema on elegant Lord Street in 2008 to largely positive reviews. Its boutique rooms are coolly contemporary, with vast beds, Japanese-style soaking tubs, and rainforest showers; the penthouse has a spa bath and outdoor Jacuzzi. Try to bag a higher room with better views and also less street noise. The glitzy, see-and-be seen **V-Café and Sushi Bar,** haunt of many a local footballer, serves an international menu and creative cocktails, including a mind-blowing chili martini.

98 Lord St., Southport PR8 1JR. www.thevincenthotel.com. ✆ **01704/883800.** 60 units. £93–£209 double. AE, MC, V. Parking £12. **Amenities:** Restaurant; bar; gym; room service; spa; golf simulator. *In room:* TV, Wi-Fi (free).

MODERATE

Formby Hall Golf Resort & Spa ★ 🎁 🏌 This modern hotel in parkland in the heart of the "Golf Coast" between Formby and Southport is a recent addition to an existing 18-hole championship golf course, 9-hole links course, and residential PGA academy. But even if you're not here to play golf, there's a highly regarded spa and health club. Rooms are fresh, attractive, and quite luxurious; under-12s stay for free in extra beds and a children's menu is available. The smart brasserie overlooks the golf course, or there's the 19th Hole Restaurant & Bar.

Southport Old Rd, Formby, Southport L37 0AB. www.formbyhallgolfresort.co.uk. ✆ **01704/875699.** 62 units. £60–£180 double; £120–£205 suite. Children 11 and under stay free in parent's room. Rates include English breakfast. AE, MC, V. Free parking. **Amenities:** 2 restaurants; 2 bars; gym; indoor pool; spa; room service; golf courses. *In room:* TV, hair dryer, minifridge, Wi-Fi (free).

Ramada Plaza Southport ★ 🏌 ☺ The best located of Southport's hotels for those who like to be reminded they're at the Great British seaside, this ocean-liner-like building has views over Marine Lake, the pier, and the sea. It's surprisingly stylish for a chain, with fresh contemporary decor in its light-flooded rooms (Marine Lake Executive rooms have 180-degree views of the coastline through picture windows) and a waterside **brasserie** with a pleasant terrace. Packages include theatre breaks (the hotel adjoins Southport Theatre), golf breaks, tickets to Aintree racecourse, and 2-night family breaks in rooms with two double beds. Guests get free access to the leisure center opposite, with an adults-only pool, family pool, learner pool, gym, sauna, and steam room. Rates include breakfast.

Marine Lake, Southport PR9 0DZ. www.ramadaplazasouthport.co.uk. ✆ **01704/516220.** 133 units. £89–£180 double; £124–£205 suite. MC, V. Free parking. **Amenities:** Restaurant; bar; free access to leisure club with indoor pool. *In room:* TV, fridge, Wi-Fi (free).

INEXPENSIVE

There's a **Staybridge Suites** in Liverpool (✆ 0151/703-9700; www.ichotelsgroup.com), at Keel Wharf just south of the Albert Dock, with self-catering studio and one-bedroom suites (with extra sofabeds) for about £89 to £109 (less with advance purchase). There's also a very good new **Novotel** just by Liverpool One, with a great basement pool and rooms for up to four guests from just £75.

Those visiting Liverpool on a budget are in luck: Its Albert Dock redevelopment, home to some outstanding cultural venues, houses two budget hotels that transcend the limits of their respective chains with guest rooms featuring some of the original warehouses' cast iron and red brick. **Express by Holiday Inn ★** (✆ www.exliverpool.com; ✆ **0151/702-6369**) offers doubles and family rooms with views over the Mersey or the dock itself for just £70 (or less with nonrefundable early booking). **Premier Inn** (www.premierinn. com; ✆ **0871/527-8622**), a similarly sympathetic conversion, has roughly the same rates on doubles and family rooms.

Base2Stay ★★★ 🏷 ☺ The second incarnation of a concept that has found great favour in London (p. 191), this innovative budget-meets-boutique hotel in the UNESCO-listed Ropewalks area offers visitors great value for money, as well as flexibility and a funky vibe. (Note that, at certain times, some rooms would fall in our "Expensive" category.) Opened in 2010 in a converted 1850s' engineering works, it offers in-room minikitchens instead of a restaurant or bar, the freedom to order in meals from local providers (some at a discount), and free coffee. The decor is muted, modern, and quite chic, but original architectural features in many rooms, including the original roof timbers, believed to have come from 18-century ships, bring dashes of character. Rooms include duplex Gallery Studios and the unique Secret Garden Suite with its own courtyard to sit out in. The latter, sleeping five, is the best option for families, although many rooms can sleep three or four, or some rooms can interconnect. The singles are very comfortable for solo travelers.

29 Seel St., Liverpool L1 4AU. www.base2stayliverpool.com. ✆ **0151/705-2626.** 106 units. £59–£155 double; £129–£225 suite. MC, V. **Amenities:** Lounge with free coffee machine; breakfast-box service (extra charge). *In room:* TV with free Internet, games, kitchenette, Wi-Fi (free).

Carleton House ★ 🏷 This charming, lovingly run little B&B within a handsome Victorian property a short walk east of Southport's Promenade offers singles, doubles/ twins, and family rooms stylishly decorated in creams and beiges, with flat-screen TVs. There's also a self-catering apartment in the garden. Breakfasts (including full English if desired) are excellent—the extremely friendly owners have a farming background and are passionate about local produce.

17 Alexandra Rd., Southport PR9 0NB. www.thecarletonhouse.co.uk. ✆ **01704/538035.** 12 units. £75–£95 double. Rates include English breakfast. MC, V. **Amenities:** Lounge. *In room:* TV, hair dryer, Wi-Fi (free).

LANCASHIRE ★★★

Blackpool: 246 miles NW of London; 51 miles NW of Manchester; 56 miles N of Liverpool; 88 miles W of Leeds

Often overlooked in favor of the more spectacular Lake District, Lancashire is best known as home to Britain's most-visited tourist attraction, **Blackpool's** Pleasure Beach. But while kitsch Blackpool, like Las Vegas, which it resembles in some respects, is an acquired taste, there are large swaths of this county with glorious wild landscapes perfect for lovers of the great outdoors, especially the scorchingly beautiful

Forest of Bowland. And Lancashire is also one of Britain's great foodie destinations, with many top-ranking chefs settling here to make the best of the superb local produce in their creative cuisine.

Essentials

GETTING THERE   Trains to Blackpool from London Euston require at least one change, at Preston (also in Lancashire) or Manchester, and take a little over 2¾ hours or more (around £74 for a round-trip). From Manchester, it's about a 1¼-hour trip. Direct trains from Liverpool take just under 1½ hours; from Leeds it's 2¼ hours. Direct **National Express** buses (© **0871/781-8181;** www.nationalexpress.com) from London take 7 hours or more, with some requiring a change at Manchester, about 1½ hours away. There are also direct buses from Leeds, taking about 3¼ hours.

Blackpool is just over 4 hours northwest of London by road, mainly via the M1 and M6, about 1 hour northwest of Manchester, 1¼ hours north of Liverpool, and about 1½ hours west of Leeds. **Blackpool International Airport** (www.blackpoolinternational. com), just south of the town, has links with a dozen or so other European destinations.

Trains from London Euston to Lancaster take just under 2½ hours; at Lancaster, you can change for Morecambe, about 10 minutes away. There are some direct trains from Leeds to Lancaster (about 2 hr.) and Manchester (just under 1 hr.). From Liverpool it's about 1¼ hours, with at least one change.

Lancaster is 1¼ hours north of Liverpool and about 1 hour northwest of Manchester, with direct National Express buses from the latter (1½ hr.). For public transport in the area, see www.lancashire.gov.uk.

VISITOR INFORMATION   **Blackpool Tourist Information Centre,** 1 Clifton St. (© **01253/478222;** www.visitblackpool.com), is open Monday to Saturday 9am to 5:30pm, Sunday 10am to 4pm.

Lytham St. Annes Tourist Information Centre, 67 St. Annes Rd. (© **01253/ 725610;** www.visitlythamstannes.co.uk), is open Monday to Saturday 10am to 5pm.

Morecambe Visitor Information Centre, Old Station Buildings, Marine Road Central (© **01524/582808;** www.citycoastcountryside.co.uk), is open April to October Monday to Saturday 9:30am to 5pm, Sunday 10am to 4pm; rest of year Monday to Saturday 9:30am to 5pm.

SPECIAL EVENTS   Lancashire's tacky take on the Northern Lights, the **Blackpool Illuminations** (www.visitblackpool.com/site/illuminations), bedeck the resort's promenade from late August or early September to November each year, featuring hundreds of neon figures (illuminated using green electricity, some from on-site wind turbines). Of course, this is a cynical ploy to extend the resort's season past summer.

Blackpool is a mecca for ballroom dancers and their fans, with five festivals a year (© **01253/625252;** www.blackpooldancefestival.com); the longest-running and most famous is the 8-day Blackpool Dance Festival each May, which featured in the Jennifer Lopez movie *Shall We Dance?*

Exploring the Area
BLACKPOOL ★

A bit like Las Vegas with a Victorian twist, this unremittingly tacky resort is centered on the U.K.'s biggest single tourist attraction, the theme park **Pleasure Beach** (see below). Beyond that, Blackpool has a promenade served by antique electric trams, 7 miles of rather insipid beaches (with donkeys to ride), three piers, and a surfeit of cheap restaurants, guesthouses, and amusement arcades. Blackpool is said to have more hotel and B&B rooms than all of Portugal.

The resort does have its charm, if you approach it in the right frame of mind. Depending on your tastes, central "attractions" are the landmark **Blackpool Tower** (see below), a **Madame Tussauds** waxworks museum (© **0871/282-9200;** www.madame tussauds.com/blackpool), the **Sea Life** aquarium (© **0871/423-2110;** www.visitsea life.com/Blackpool), and **Sandcastle Waterpark** (© **01253/343602**); www.sand castle-waterpark.co.uk), which includes some Aztec-themed slides. If it's culture you're after, don't despair—the **Great Promenade Show** (http://greatpromenadeshow.co.uk), an outdoor exhibition stretching just over a mile along New South Promenade, features artworks commissioned from established and emerging artists to celebrate the resort's natural and man-made attractions. One, *Desire,* is inspired by kiss-me-quick and holiday romances and casts a shadow of a broken heart on the ground; others come to life at night.

East of the promenade, you'll find another congenial spot in the form of historic **Stanley Park ★★**, with a golf course and crazy golf, a boating lake, tennis courts, bowling greens, a playground, and an Art Deco cafe hosting live jazz on Sundays. The park is also home to **Blackpool Zoo** (© **01253/830830;** www.blackpoolzoo.org.uk), with its new £1-million sea-lion pool, and **Blackpool Model Village & Gardens** (© **01253/763827;** www.blackpoolmodelvillage.com), with its miniature buildings.

Not far south of Blackpool, **Lytham St. Annes** is a genteel alternative to the larger resort, formed by the merging of two neighboring towns and globally famed for its golf. Of its four courses and links, the Royal Lytham & St. Annes (www.royallytham. org) is a host of the **British Open** (www.opengolf.com).

Blackpool Tower ★ ☺ ENTERTAINMENT COMPLEX   Built in 1894 as a half-size version of Paris's Eiffel Tower, this famous structure houses a Victorian ballroom, a circus, and an indoor adventure playground, but as the guide went to press they were scheduled to be joined by the **Blackpool Tower Eye,** a new observation experience on the uppermost level, with a 4-D Cinema Experience, and by the **Blackpool Tower Dungeon,** with live actors, a scary ride, shows, and special effects.

Promenade. © **0844/856-1000.** www.theblackpooltower.co.uk. Admission ballroom, circus, and playground £12 adults and children (individual tickets available). Opening times vary by attraction; see website.

Pleasure Beach ★★ ☺ THEME PARK   Dating back to 1896, this vast theme park is now home to 125-plus rides and attractions, from world-famous white-knuckle thrillers including the Pepsi Max Big One and Valhalla to gentler rides for young kids. New in spring 2011, the 12-ride Nickelodeonland includes the interactive SpongeBob's Splash Bash. There's a surprisingly chic in-park hotel (p. 598).

Ocean Boulevard. © **0871/222-1234.** www.pleasurebeachresort.com. Admission 2-day unlimited ride wristband £45 adults, £40 children 2–11, or various passes available. Easter–Nov, with hours varying by season; see website.

OTHER LANCASHIRE HOTSPOTS

Most of the rest of Lancashire couldn't be more different from Blackpool, although there is another theme park, the medieval-themed **Camelot ★** (© **01257/453044;** www.camelotthemepark.co.uk), at Chorley east of Southport, with rides for all ages, jousting tournaments, wizardry displays, a farm, and a new-in-2011 birds-of-prey and animal center. See the website for the complex opening days and times; entry costs £24 for anyone over 1m/3ft. 4in tall. There's more family fun of a very different nature a few miles west at Burscough (back toward Southport), at the **WWT Martin Mere**

Wetland Centre (p. 594) and also the north, just east of Preston, at Brockholes (p. 594). Preston itself, Lancashire's administrative center, is home to the Museum of Lancashire (📞 01772/534075; www.lancashire.gov.uk), closed for redevelopment as this guide went to press.

Northwest of here unfurls the Forest of Bowland ★★★ (www.forestofbowland. com), an Area of Outstanding Natural Beauty and vast outdoor playground popular with walkers and cyclists, dotted with pretty villages. Places of interest within its 312 sq. miles include the Bowland Wild Boar Park ★ (📞 01995/61554; www.wild boarpark.co.uk), with boar, longhorn cows, deer, llamas, and goats, feeding sessions, and pedal tractors and tractor rides for kids; the Roman Museum at Ribchester (📞 01254/878261; http://ribchesterromanmuseum.org), on the site of an old Roman fort, and Norman Clitheroe Castle ★ (📞 01772/534061; www. lancashire.gov.uk), with newly revamped galleries taking you on a journey through 350 million years of local history, heritage, and geology (with a rucksack, map, and magnifying glass for children).

Clitheroe stands at the heart of the Ribble Valley, where you can follow a sculpture trail from Brungerley Bridge to Crosshills Quarry. The trail forms part of the 73-mile Ribble Way ★, which follows the River Ribble from Longton west of Preston and goes through Ribchester and Clitheroe and then on into North Yorkshire (p. 641). Alternatively, you might discover the area via the award-winning Ribble Valley Food Trail ★★ (www.ribblevalleyfoodtrail.com), relaunched in 2011 to help locals and visitors discover shops and restaurants championing local produce, including meat from traditional Lancashire breeds, pies and pastries, ice cream, and handmade chocolate.

Just east of Clitheroe, Pendle Hill looms over "witch country." In the unspoiled village of Newchurch-in-Pendle at the foot of the hill, St. Mary's churchyard has a grave said to be that of local witch Alice Nutter, carved with a skull and crossbones, while the west side of the church tower bears a carving described as the "Eye of God," claimed to ward off evil. Learn all about the Pendle witches at the Pendle Heritage Centre ★★ (📞 01282/677150; www.htnw.co.uk/phc.html) at Barrowford to the east, which also has a recreated 18th-century walled garden, a woodland walk around the 15th-century cruck-framed barn with its farm animals, a tearoom, an art gallery, and a tourist information desk. It's open daily 10am to 5pm, and has free entry.

From the Centre, the 45-mile Pendle Witch Trail ★ follows the route taken by the "witches" through the Ribble Valley to stand trial in Lancaster ★, Lancashire's county town. By foot or by car, it takes you through the Trough of Bowland—a wild beauty spot—and into the historic city. The trial took place within medieval Lancaster Castle (see below), and you can also visit the Judges Lodgings ★ (📞 01524/32808; www.lancashire.gov.uk), the onetime townhouse residence of castle-keeper and notorious witchhunter Thomas Covell. Containing period furniture as well as a small museum of childhood, it costs £3 for adults (kids go free), with opening times varying by season (generally 10am, noon, or 1 to 4pm).

Like Durham (p. 655), Lancaster is a pleasant small city with one of the U.K.'s top universities and a handful of small-scale sights, including the City Museum and King's Own Royal Regiment Museum (📞 01524/64637; www.lancashire. gov.uk) and the Lancaster Maritime Museum (📞 01524/382264; same website). But one of the best things to do, especially on a fine day, is head up to Williamson Park with its Butterfly House for great views over Morecambe Bay to the Lake District (p. 601).

Lancaster flows seamlessly into **Morecambe ★**, a resort described in 1930s' ads as "the Sunset Coast" for its setting on a seemingly infinite bay to rival any seascape in the world. Between the days when it was known as the "Brighton of the North" or even the "Naples of the North," attracting the likes of Noel Coward, Wallace Simpson, and Coco Chanel, and its rating as number 3 in the 2003 book *Crap Towns: The 50 Worst Places to Live in the UK*, it underwent a slow but painful decline and lost both its piers and its pleasure beach. The reopening of its Art Deco Midland Hotel (p. 597) in 2008 seemed to bespeak great things to come, but change is still at snail's pace, and the future of the long-abandoned **Winter Gardens** (www.thewinter gardensmorecambe.co.uk), the magnificent red-brick pavilion that once housed a theatre, ballrooms, and baths—the setting for scenes in the 1960 Laurence Olivier movie *The Entertainer*– remains unsure.

If that all makes Morecambe sound unappealing, it's far from the truth: Despite the lack of a pier, the town offers a rare taste of the real, unreconstructed British seaside resort, with a pale-sand, kid-friendly beach, a handful of fun rides, a quirky outsize sculpture of Eric Morecambe—the much-loved comedian who changed his name from John Bartholomew in honor of his hometown—and little to do beyond slurp ice creams or buy a bag of fish and chips or some bay-caught cockles or potted shrimps, and sit on the seafront gazing out at the ocean on which Chanel is said to have landed her seaplane after flying up from Antibes.

Brockholes ★★ ☺ NATURE RESERVE   Open since spring 2011, this "unre-served reserve" features Britain's first floating visitor center, on a pontoon, together with wildlife hides, family nature activities, guided walks, open-air music and theatre, and even a Sunday cinema. Note that signing up for Wildlife Trust membership helps this free attraction to cover its costs.

Beside junction 31 of the M6. ℭ **01772/877140.** www.dev.brockholes.org. Free admission (car park charge £4 for up to 5 hr.). Apr–Oct daily 10am–6pm, rest of year daily 10am–5pm.

Lancaster Castle ★ CASTLE   Officially owned by the Duke of Lancaster (the Queen), this was where the Pendle witches (p. 593) brought to trial were imprisoned, and today's tours take you into the grand jury room, courts, and dungeons. Exhibits also touch the subject of convict transportation, as many hundreds of people were sentenced to deportation in these courts.

Castle Parade, Lancaster. ℭ **01524/64998.** www.lancastercastle.com. Admission £5 adults, £4 children 5–16. Daily 10am–5pm.

WWT Martin Mere Wetland Centre ★★ ☺ NATURE RESERVE   Great for a family outing, this reserve offers visitors the chance to stroll through waterfowl gardens and hand-feed their inhabitants, see aerial displays of wild ducks, geese, and swans, visit a beaver enclosure, attend otter and flamingo talks, follow the nature trail and/or reedbed walk, let off steam in the adventure play area, and even try a canoe safari.

Burscough. ℭ **01704/895181.** www.wwt.org.uk/visit-us/martin-mere. Admission £9.85 adults, £4.80 children 4–16. Daily Nov–Feb 9:30am–5pm, to 5:30pm rest of year.

Where to Eat
VERY EXPENSIVE

Longridge ★★ ▮ MODERN EUROPEAN   The finest produce from Lancashire, northern England, and the U.K. as a whole is used to admirable effect at the award-winning flagship restaurant of Paul Heathcote, a protégé of Raymond Blanc and Member of the British Empire since 2009 for his services to the northwest's hospitality industry. Set in a 19th-century cottage in a small town northeast of Preston, the chic dining room is a particularly good place to linger over a Sunday lunch comprising, perhaps, confit of duck leg from nearby Goosnargh with poached rhubarb and herb salad; roast rib of Bowland beef with all the trimmings; and Hawes fruit cake with Yarg cheese. Lunch is a good bargain (£15–£19 for 2 or 3 courses). There's also an on-site cookery school.

104-106 Higher Rd., Longridge. © **01772/784969.** www.heathcotes.co.uk. Reservations recommended. Main courses £18-£27. AE, DC, MC, V. Wed-Sat noon-2:30pm and 6-10pm, Sun noon-8:45pm.

Northcote ★★ ☺ MODERN BRITISH   Another top-notch place for Lancashire produce, this long-standing restaurant with guest rooms is beautifully situated on the edge of the Trough of Bowland. The food is as brave and beautiful as the landscape—think black pudding (blood sausage) and buttered pink trout with mustard and nettle sauce; Goosnargh duck with licorice, foie gras, cherry and peanut sandwich, and chicory; and apple crumble soufflé with Mrs. Kirkham's Lancashire cheese ice cream. If the prices are likely to curb your appetite, come at lunchtime and eat from the seasonal menu (£26 for three courses and coffee). Alternatively, there's an afternoon tea and lounge menu including cream teas, sandwiches, and salads, but at weekends it's only available to those staying in one of the 14 very comfortable **guest rooms** (£216–£267). The restaurant also warmly welcomes children and will happily provide smaller versions of dishes or simpler alternatives. There are also renowned Lancashire breakfasts open to all.

There are four other Ribble Valley Inns under the same ownership, two in Lancashire: The **Three Fishes** (© 01254/826888; www.thethreefishes.com) at Mitton, and **The Clog and Billycock** (© 01254/201163; www.theclogandbillycock.com) at Pleasington. Both are child-friendly and both focus on local seafood but also offer great "Length of Lancashire" cheeseboards.

Northcote Rd., Langho. © **01254/240555.** www.northcote.com. Reservations recommended (required for afternoon tea Mon-Fri). Main courses £23-£34. AE, DC, MC, V. Mon-Fri 7am-9:45am, noon-1:30pm, 3:30-5:30pm, and 7-9:30pm; Sat 7:45-9:45am, noon-1:30pm, 3:30-5:30pm (guests only), and 6:30-10pm; Sun 7:45-9:45am, noon-2pm, 3:30-5:30pm (guests only), and 7-9pm.

EXPENSIVE

Inn at Whitewell ★★ ☺ MODERN BRITISH   In the heart of the Forest of Bowland (Area of Outstanding Natural Beauty), this remote 14th-century coaching inn offers food in both its riverside dining room and garden and its several bar areas. The restaurant is more formal, though not off-puttingly so. The starter of crispy slow-roast belly pork with parched peas, parsnip purée, and apple sauce merits the journey here alone, while the filet of local beef served pink with a little cottage pie of braised oxtail and baby onions, celeriac purée, and red-wine jus is just one of several superb main courses. The livelier bar is the place to eat with kids, who get small portions from a menu that includes a famous fish pie and locally made Cumberland sausage with champ; prices here average about £10 for a main course, but you can also order starters as "light mains."

The 23 **guest rooms** (£120–£200 double) are cozy and a bit chintzy, with comfy traditional wool and horsehair mattresses; about half have open fires, while others have four-posters, rolltop baths, and eccentric Victorian bathing paraphernalia, and/or sofabeds. There's guests-only fishing on the river.

Whitewell. © **01200/448222.** www.innatwhitewell.com. Reservations recommended. Main courses £15-£26. MC, V. Daily noon-2pm, dinner 7:30-9:30pm.

MODERATE

Food by Breda Murphy ★★★ ☺ MODERN BRITISH A stop on the Ribble Valley Food Trail (p. 593), this is a little gem of a deli and daytime bistro offering creative modern fare based on local ingredients, devised by the eponymous Irish chef who often gives a modern twist to classic British dishes by incorporating influences gleaned from her travels in southeast Asia: Think slow-roast Bowland lamb shoulder with citrus-glazed carrots and coriander jus. There are also delicious open sandwiches, nibbles, and children's meals and portions. Just be careful not to overdo it if you want to indulge in a sensational dessert—perhaps a saffron-rice pudding with prune syrup, or a deep-filled rhubarb and apple pie with cinnamon custard. There are also luxurious afternoon teas.

Abbots Court, 41 Station Rd., Whalley. ⓒ **01254/823446.** www.foodbybredamurphy.com. Reservations recommended. Main courses £6–£16. MC, V. Tues–Sat 10am–6pm, plus occasional evenings.

Mandarin ★★ ☺ CHINESE In a town where terrible eating experiences await you on every corner, this Cantonese place, which celebrated its 50th birthday in 2011, is no insider secret—just ask any taxi driver or hotelier for their local eating recommendation to find out. A few blocks north of Blackpool Tower and in from its Promenade, this quite smart dining room offers few surprises to those familiar with British Chinese restaurants, although you'll find some daily specials chalked up on the board in Chinese (the highly obliging staff will translate). And you can't go wrong with tried-and-tested favorites including excellent dumplings and aromatic crispy duck. Younger diners are made to feel very welcome.

27 Clifton St., Blackpool. ⓒ **01253/622687.** http://mandaringroup.co.uk. Reservations recommended. Main courses £7–£13. MC, V. Mon 6–11:30pm, Tues–Sat noon–2pm and 6–11pm.

INEXPENSIVE

P Brucciani ★ 🍴 ☺ LUNCH/SNACKS This former milk bar retains its original "high-street Deco" styling of wood, chrome, Formica, and Bakelite, etched glass and mirrors, and penny-in-the-slot cubicles in the toilets. Opened in 1939, it was much frowned upon by some locals, who feared it would tarnish Morecambe's genteel Victorian image. Now almost a part of the resort's very fabric in its prime seafront promenade spot with killer views of the shimmering bay, it's a great place to step back in time, with old-fashioned knickerbocker glories and sundaes but also sandwiches, soups, and the likes of egg and chips or beans on toast, plus great coffee. There's also an ice-cream counter out front, selling Brucciani's own ice creams in traditional flavors.

217 Marine Parade, Morecambe. ⓒ **01524/421386.** Main courses £2.50–£5.50. MC, V. Daily 10am–5pm.

Yorkshire Fisheries ★ FISH & CHIPS The decor may be wanting in all respects—this is about as basic an eatery as you can imagine, with old wooden paneling and banquette seating—but Blackpool's oldest fish-and-chip shop is consistently rated its best by locals and visitors alike. Most of the former wouldn't go anywhere else for their haddock or cod and chips, to eat in or—for the full-on British seaside experience—to take to the beach a few minutes' walk away. The secret lies in the fresh, crispy batter, but the friendly staff and fair prices (£5 gets you fish, chips, mushy peas, bread and butter, and tea!) are big draws too.

16–18 Topping St., Blackpool. ⓒ **01253/627739.** Main courses about £5. No credit cards. Mon–Sat 11:30am–7pm.

Shopping

Farmers' markets, farm shops, and other local produce outlets are the shopping high-lights of Lancashire (for the Ribble Valley Food Trail, which includes shops, see p. 593). Of particular note is the **Bashall Barn Farm Food Visitor Centre ★★** near Clitheroe (✆ **01200/428964;** www.bashallbarn.co.uk), which brings together a farm shop, ice-cream parlour, coffee shop, and restaurant, and is home to the **Bow-land Beer Company Ltd.** (✆ **01200/428825;** www.bowlandbrewery.com), which runs tours and tastings. There's another local brewery you can tour at Burnley, **Moor-houses** (✆ **01282/422864;** www.moorhouses.co.uk), producer of Pendle Witches Brew and Black Cat.

Lancaster is also a good spot for food shopping, with a farmers' market on the second Saturday of each month plus the **Port of Lancaster Smokehouse** (✆ **01524/751493;** www.polsco.co.uk), offering smoked fish including salmon from the River Lune and Manx kippers, Morecambe Bay shrimps, fresh game in season, specialist cheeses, and more.

Entertainment & Nightlife

Blackpool is still alive and kicking as an entertainment hub, especially in summer, which sees a lot of traditional variety shows. Cultural venues include the **Grand Theatre** (✆ **01253/290190;** www.blackpoolgrand.co.uk) and the **Winter Gar-dens** (✆ **01253/625252;** www.wintergardensblackpool.co.uk), both impressive historic buildings with populist programming. The **Arena** at the Pleasure Beach hosts ice-skating spectaculars and other glitzy shows.

In terms of nightlife, the mood is boisterous—the resort is a popular hen- and stag-night choice, and the transvestite show bar **Funny Girls** (✆ **0844/247-2665;** www. funnygirlsonline.co.uk) a favorite venue. Blackpool also has the U.K.'s biggest night-club, **Syndicate** (✆ **01253/753222;** http://blackpool.thesyndicate.com), with a revolving dance floor. Since World War II, the resort has been known as a safe haven for gay communities, and since the 1990s it's been actively promoted as a gay tourist destination, so there are plenty of gay-friendly venues plus a dedicated radio station (www.gayradiouk.com).

For up-to-date listings, consult www.blackpoolevents.co.uk.

Where to Stay
VERY EXPENSIVE

For rooms at **Northcote** and the **Inn at Whitewell,** see p. 595.

Midland ★   It's all about the history at this newly revived Art Deco classic in the middle of Morecambe's promenade. That and the sea views, which are worth the extra money and are really the point of staying here. The reopening of the hotel led the *Guardian*, in 2008, to declare Morecambe the U.K.'s top coastal holiday destina-tion—a turnaround for the once-neglected resort. Seeing it now, you may be amazed that the cruiser-liner-like building was allowed to rot for decades. All praise to the developers for seamlessly incorporating iconic features such as the sweeping staircase and Eric Gill frescoes into the new venue. Rooms are spacious and stylish in a Pop Arty way, with ingenious bathrooms (it may take you a while to find the toilet). There's a slight starkness to them, as with many design hotels, but with nothing beyond your window but the sparkling water, you probably won't mind. The top floor is occupied by suites with private terraces, some with an open-air Jacuzzi. The light-flooded **restaurant** with its bay views offers a largely local menu including Morecambe Bay shrimps and scallops, but service isn't great. The spa treatments are wishy washy, too.

Marine Rd. West, Morecambe, Lancashire LA4 4BU. www.elh.co.uk. ⓒ **01524/424-000.** 44 units. £94–£276 double; £174–£348 suite. Rates include breakfast. MC, V. Free parking. **Amenities:** Restaurant; bar; treatment rooms; access to leisure club (at nearby sister hotel); room service. *In room:* TV, hair dryer, Wi-Fi (free).

EXPENSIVE

Big Blue Hotel ★ ☺   Situated at Blackpool Pleasure Beach itself, with some of the theme park's rides as a backdrop but mercifully effective soundproofing, this is a surprising boutique-style option behind a rather ugly facade Naturally, it's family-friendly, too, with reasonably priced rooms for up to four featuring a separate children's sleeping area complete with bunkbeds and an "entertainment area" with a TV and PlayStation connection (games and consoles can be rented from reception). Deluxe doubles have lounge areas with fireplaces and fabrics by Designers Guild; suites have separate lounges and coffee-makers. The hotel **brasserie,** serving European fare, has a fun children's menu that includes the option for younger diners to don chef's hats and aprons and make their own pizza. Some packages include Pleasure Beach wristbands; others include show tickets.

Pleasure Beach, Blackpool FY4 1ND. www.bigbluehotel.com. ⓒ **0871/222-4000.** 157 units. £91–£132 double; from £224 suites. Rates include breakfast (some promotional rates are room-only). AE, MC, DV, V. Free parking. **Amenities:** Restaurant; bar; gym with massage rooms; room service. *In room:* TV/DVD (some), hair dryer, kids' entertainment area (some), MP3 docking station (suites), Wi-Fi (free).

MODERATE

Red Pump Inn ★ **   For a warm welcome and peace and quiet, you could do little better than this superb, award-winning B&B deep in the Ribble Valley, with three comfortable rooms with great views of Pendle Hill or Longridge Fell, handmade wooden furniture, and flat-screen TVs. The emphasis is on taking it easy, so the full Lancashire breakfast is generally served between 9 and 9:45am, though you can take it earlier or later if you wish; choose from local bacon, eggs, and black pudding (blood sausage), with heart-shaped fried bread and homemade flat skinless sausages, smoked salmon and scrambled eggs on malted bloomer, or porridge with golden syrup. The feast will set you up beautifully for a walk in the surroundings, but packed lunches can also be ordered if you think you might get peckish. Fishing packages are available for the nearby River Hodder. The excellent food served in the **restaurant— the likes of slow-roasted Pendle pork belly—has also garnered awards, and result in the inn's inclusion on the Ribble Valley Food Trail (p. 593).

Blackpool on a Budget

Blackpool's best bargain for families is almost certainly the **Premier Inn East** (www.premierinn.com; ⓒ 0871/527-8110). Although it's 4 miles southeast of the resort's main attractions, it offers doubles and family rooms for around £50 to £60 (or an astonishing £29 with nonrefundable advance booking!). It's also beside the family-dining venue **Outside Inn** (ⓒ 01253/798477; www.outsideinnblackpool.co.uk), with indoor and outdoor play areas.

Clitheroe Rd., Bashall Eaves, Lancashire BB7 3DA. www.theredpumpinn.co.uk. ⓒ **01254/826-227.** 3 units. £70–£95 double. Rates include breakfast. MC, V. Free parking. **Amenities:** Restaurant; bar. *In room:* TV, free Wi-Fi.

INEXPENSIVE

Dolphinholme House Farm ★★★ 🎒😊   This family-run dairy farm, on the edge of the Trough of Bowland, offers a holiday where kids can run wild in nature. There's a river for paddling or swimming; woods for building dens; free-roaming roe deer and ducks; and the chance to help milk goats, collect eggs from the coop, and look after the rabbits. There's also a play barn, a swing, a sandpit, and a giant slide. The tents, which border the woods, are charmingly old-fashioned, with oil lamps and candles, a double bedroom, a bunkbed room for two, and a cupboard bed for two kids or one adult. The honesty larder stocks cheese from the goats, fresh bread, and other essentials and treats. You can also pre-order homemade Lancashire hotpot to cook on the tent's wood-fired stove, or over a campfire, or a smoke barrel with fish or chicken to smoke yourself. On some nights the communal bread oven is fired up to cook bread and pizza. The farm is well located for sightseeing, with the coast a 15-minute drive away.

Dolphinholme, Lancashire LA2 9DJ. www.featherdown.co.uk. ⓒ **01420/80804.** 10 units. Tent for up to 6 £295–£589 for 3-night weekend stay, £435–£845 for 4-night midweek stay, £595–£995 for 1 wk. MC, V. Free parking. **Amenities:** Bike rentals; hair dryer; shower block; washing machine; pre-order meals. *In room:* Baby equipment, board games, books, kitchen.

Ribby Hall ★ 😊   This five-star holiday village a 10-minute drive from the beaches of Blackpool and Lytham St. Annes, is a good base for families exploring the varied delights of Lancashire but keen to have the backup of on-site amenities and activities. In summer 2011, the family and adult swimming pools; equestrian center; boating lake; tennis, badminton, and squash courts; soccer school; exercise classes; kids' holiday club; and other offerings were joined by a spa and a hotel. In addition to the latter, there are self-catering cottages for up to six, two larger houses for up to 14, and Scandinavian-style pine lodges for up to six, with outdoor hot tubs. With its evening entertainment, Ribby Hall isn't the place for a low-key holiday, but there's nowhere better for those who want to get into the Blackpool spirit or for those holidaying with kids but keen to fit in a little "me" time.

Ribby Rd., Wrea Green, Lancashire PR4 2PR. www.ribbyhall.co.uk. ⓒ **0800/085-1717.** 182 units. Prices vary by type/size of accommodations and season; for a cottage sleeping 4 expect to pay £295–£950 per week. MC, V. Free parking. **Amenities:** 3 restaurants; 4 cafe/bars; babysitting; bike/boat rental; children's holiday club (ages 4–10); gym; 2 indoor swimming pools; games room; indoor play area; golf and mini-golf; equestrian center; fishing; sports facilities and classes; spa. *In room:* TV, hot tub (some), full kitchen (lodges, cottages, and houses).

Wyresdale Park ★★ 🎒😊   Great for lovers of unorthodox holidays, this estate minutes from the M6 on the edge of the Forest of Bowland is one of four U.K. sites (the others are in Essex, Shropshire, and Scotland) to offer a Country House Hideout camping experience inspired by great Victorian explorers. You camp by the lake, where you can boat, swim, and sail wooden boats. Each "colony" has a main tent with Raj-style furniture, a discovery tent with a microscope and telescope to help you learn about your surroundings, and a wind-up gramophone and library of suitably adventurous books, a shower tent, a wooden hot tub, and a cooking cart. If you run out of electricity, you generate some using the bicycle hooked up to a dynamo. Colonies accommodate up to two families (six in the main tent, plus two on campbeds in the discovery tent). The on-site honesty "bothy" stocks local produce including game from the estate, wine and beer, and firewood for the stove and hot tub. Guests get the run of the parkland with its woods, old fishing ponds, and free-roaming fallow deer.

Wyresdale Park Estate, Scorton, Lancashire PR3 1BA. www.countryhousehideout.co.uk. ℂ **01420/ 549150.** 5 units. Tent for up to 8 people (7 adults) £399–£715 for a 3-night weekend stay, £299–£715 for 4-night midweek stay, £595–£995 for 1 wk. MC, V. Free parking. **Amenities:** Bike rental. *In room:* Baby equipment, kitchen, library.

15

Lancashire

THE NORTHWEST

THE LAKE DISTRICT

by Louise McGrath

One of the most beautiful parts of Great Britain, the Lake District is characterized by its stunning mountain and lake scenery. Whether you come for hikes, camping, and watersports, or to follow the trail of Lake poets like William Wordsworth, there's a diverse range of activities. Some visitors come to delve into Beatrix Potter's world, others to enjoy lake cruises and first-class dinners at country hotels.

CITIES & TOWNS **Kendal's** former mill yards bustle with shops and its museums introduce Lakeland life. Boat trips from **Bowness** and **Windermere** ferry visitors around England's largest natural lake; at its northern end **Ambleside** is a popular base for walkers. Wordsworth fans visit his homes in **Rydal** and **Grasmere,** while flower-filled **Hawkshead** is in Beatrix Potter country. **Coniston,** dominated by the "Old Man" mountain, remembers Ruskin the writer, who lived nearby at Brantwood house. Lively **Keswick** presents year-round productions at its Theatre by the Lake.

COUNTRYSIDE Take a boat trip on **Windermere, Coniston, Derwentwater,** or **Ullswater** to explore the length and depth of the lakes, and see the granite fells rising up around you. Footpaths and cycle routes lead along the water's edge, through **Grizedale Forest,** and to the summit of England's highest peak, **Scafell Pike,** while roads snake across **Honister Pass,** offering dramatic valley vistas below. Venture to more isolated lakes like **Haweswater** to spot peregrine falcons and golden eagles.

EATING & DRINKING Herdwick lamb, Cumberland sausages, and **venison** are regularly on the menus, so the region might seem a meat-lover's paradise. But you'll find **fresh salmon, scallops** from Morecambe Bay, **artisan bread, chutneys,** and **vegetarian cafes** from Kendal to Keswick. Pick up Cumbrian produce at farm shops and Staveley Mill Yard, and sample local ales in pubs or direct from local **microbreweries** like Coniston and Keswick.

MOUNTAINS & LAKES With its miles of mountains, forest, and lakes, it's easy to see why **Lake District National Park** inspired the Lake poets. The park opens the way for windsurfing on the lakes, fell-walking on **England's highest peaks,** and technical climbing up sheer rock faces. But visitors should tread carefully across mountain, moor, lakeshore, and estuary, being mindful of the delicate **wildlife** habitats and important cultural sites, such as Hardknott **Roman** Fort.

THE best TRAVEL EXPERIENCES IN THE LAKE DISTRICT

- o **Taking a trip across the water:** A boat trip across Derwentwater to Hawes End, followed by an hour-long walk up Catbells fell for spectacular lake and fell views. See p. 623.
- o **Visiting Rydal Mount:** Go at lunchtime when it's quieter, then a tour of Dove Cottage near Grasmere, ending the afternoon with tea and gingerbread. See p. 615.
- o **Taking to the waters on Coniston:** A boat trip followed by a few hours in Ruskin's house and garden at Brantwood. See p. 618.
- o **Climbing Helvellyn:** It's only The Lake District's third-highest mountain but Striding Edge narrow ridge can be both tricky and exhilarating. See p. 614.
- o **Witnessing Borrowdale's breathtaking scenery:** Zigzag up to Honister Pass and stop at Honister Slate Mine to tackle the leg-wobbling Via Ferrata ladder system up the mountainside. See p. 622.

KENDAL

270 miles NW of London; 72 miles NW of Leeds; 64 miles NW of Bradford; 9 miles SE of Windermere

The River Kent winds through a rich valley of limestone hills, known as fells, and through Kendal, known as the "Gateway to the Lakes." Many visitors bypass Kendal on their way to the central Lakes, but this bustling town boasts some of the most intriguing museums in the region.

Visit the interactive **Kendal Museum** to learn about the town's past, especially its ruined **castle,** where Catherine Parr, the last wife of Henry VIII, was allegedly born. Other worthy visits include the Quaker Museum and Abbott Hall.

Kendal once relied on the woolen industry; today its mill yards are filled with shops, while a former brewery is a vibrant arts center. The town is also famous for its sweet mint cake, which hikers take on long walks through the surrounding limestone fells.

Essentials

GETTING THERE   Trains from London's Euston Station do not go directly to Kendal; Virgin Trains operate seven daily trains from London Euston to Oxenholme Lake District station about 1½ miles away. One-way tickets cost from £30. If you're planning on making several journeys by train, it is worth investing in a personal or family railcard. After a couple of journeys it pays for itself. From here, you'll be able to take a taxi or board one of the local trains that leave for Kendal approximately every hour and take just 4 minutes (total trip time from London to Kendal: 3½ hr.).

To get to Kendal from London by bus, take one of the daily **National Express** buses (trip time: 7½ hr.). Local buses are operated mainly by **Stagecoach** and travel to Bowness, Windermere, Ambleside, Penrith, Keswick and Ulverston. Megabus (www.megabus.com) offer some cheaper tickets but the buses might not be as

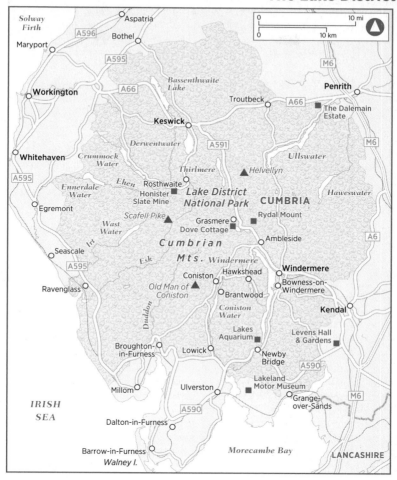

comfortable. If driving, take the M1 out of London, and then the M6 to Kendal (trip time: 5 hr.).

VISITOR INFORMATION **Kendal Tourist Information Centre,** Town Hall, Highgate (© **01539/797516;** www.golakes.co.uk), opens March through October, Monday to Saturday 10am to 5pm, and November through February, Monday to Saturday 10am to 4pm.

Exploring the Area

Abbot Hall Art Gallery GALLERY   Most visitors arrive at the gallery from Kirkland, first visiting the **Museum of Lakeland Life,** which gives an insight into bygone days. Opt instead for a riverside approach and you'll find the perfect place to pitch up and appreciate Abbott Hall's elegant Georgian facade. Its restored high-ceilinged rooms with ornate cornices and matching period antiques provide an ideal setting for paintings by local 18th-century portrait painter George Romney. The permanent collection also includes 20th-century British works, and there are regular temporary exhibitions by contemporary international artists.

Kirkland. ② **01539/722464.** www.abbothall.org.uk. Admission £5.75 adults; free for children and students 25 and under. Mon–Sat 10:30am–5pm (until 4pm Nov–Mar). Closed mid-Dec–mid-Jan.

Kendal Museum ☺ MUSEUM   Kendal Museum might be one of England's oldest museums, but it has refreshed its content with interactive exhibits that bring local history to life. Try on Roman shoes, explore local life 500 years ago via touch-screen computers, then make a medieval-style tiled floor. The natural history section travels from mountaintop to lakeside, and the World Wildlife Gallery displays a vast collection of exotic breeds. Don't miss the Alfred Wainwright exhibition; the fells' best-known visitor, he walked, talked, and wrote with a passion and flair about the Lakes until his death in 1991.

Station Rd. ② **01539/815597.** www.kendalmuseum.org.uk. Free admission (to end of 2011). Thurs–Fri noon–5pm; Sat 10:30am–5pm.

Levens Hall & Gardens HISTORIC SITE   Elizabethan pele towers are common in Cumbria, but few are in such a fine setting. Transformed into a mansion in the 1500s by James Bellingham, the house still has many original features, including the oak-paneled entrance hall and Elizabeth I's coat of arms above the drawing room fireplace. After strolling through the 17th-century **topiary garden,** orchard, and herb garden outside, enjoy hot food made from local produce in The Buttery.

8 Levens Park, Levens (4 miles south of Kendal). ② **01539/560321.** www.levenshall.co.uk. Admission house and gardens £12 adults, £5 children 5–16, £28 family ticket; gardens only £8.50 adults, £4 children, £21 family ticket. Apr–mid-Oct Sun–Thurs noon–5pm (gardens from 10am). Last admission 4:30pm.

The Quaker Tapestry ★ 👜 ARTS & CRAFTS   This isn't just any old display of needlework. The embroidered panels, which tell the history of the Quakers, were made by over 4,000 men, women, and children worldwide. They depict founding Quaker George Fox, Quaker preacher/missionary Mary Fisher (1623–98), and their role as stretcher bearers in World War I, among other charitable acts. Vegetarians will love the fresh, healthful options at their adjacent tearooms.

Friends Meeting House, Stramongate, Kendal. ② **01539/722975.** www.quaker-tapestry.co.uk. Admission £6.50 adults, £2 children 5–16, £2 adult with toddler, £14 family ticket (2 adults, 2 children). Late Mar–Oct Mon–Fri 10am–5pm (and some Sat in summer); Quaker Tapestry Tearooms close at 4:30pm.

Sizergh Castle & Garden ☺ CASTLE   A large courtyard leads to Sizergh Castle's entrance, where children can pick up quiz sheets that draw them into the castle's Elizabethan carvings and family portraits of the Strickland family, who have lived here for over 750 years. Chat with the guides to hear tales of priests who were disguised as artists but secretly said Mass during the Reformation. It's worth making time to sit beside the ponds and wildflowers in the rockery garden, and take in the 14th-century pele tower from the wide lawns. ***Insider tip:*** Come in the fall to see the show of fiery colors climbing the castle walls.

Sizergh, 3½ miles south of Kendal (northwest of interchange A590/591). ② **01539/560951.** www.nationaltrust.org.uk. Admission house and gardens (including gift aid) £8.45 adults, £4.30 children 5–16, £20 family ticket (2 adults, 2 children); gardens only £5.50 adults, £2.85 children. Mid-Mar–early Nov house Sun–Thurs 1–5pm; shop and gardens Sun–Thurs 11am–5pm.

Where to Eat

Bridge Street Restaurant ★ MODERN BRITISH   Kendal's most elegant restaurant, Bridge Street is located in a Georgian building. Its contemporary styling in soft, neutral hues creates a relaxed, intimate dining room, and the menu includes a mouth-watering selection. Try crispy aromatic duck parcels or seafood platter to share followed by rack of Kentmere lamb. Save some space for smooth chocolate torte and mouth-watering butterscotch ice cream.

1 Bridge St. Ⓒ **01539/738855.** www.bridgestreetkendal.co.uk. Reservations recommended at weekends. Main courses £13–£18. MC, V. Tues–Sat 6–9pm (last orders); Sun noon-2pm.

Wilf's Cafe ★ INTERNATIONAL   Set in Staveley Mill Yard, a few miles north of Kendal, walkers and foodies stop off at Wilf's for relaxing breakfasts, coffee, and a variety of homemade hot meals like veggie chili and Wilf's rarebits.

Mill Yard, Staveley. Ⓒ **01539/822329.** www.wilfs-cafe.co.uk. Main courses £6.25. MC, V. Daily 9am–5pm (summer weekends from 8:30am).

Shopping

Start out on **Stricklandgate** (home to the Westmoreland Shopping Centre; www.westmorelandshopping.com) and explore the **old yards** branching off it. Once the hub of spinning, dyeing, and weaving, today they are home to fashion, gifts, chocolate, and art shops. The liveliest are **Elephant Yard** (www.elephantyard.com), **Blackhall Yard** (www.blackhallyard.com), and **Wainwrights Yard** (www.wainwrightsyard.com).

Foodies shouldn't miss **Low Sizergh Barn** (Ⓒ **01539/560426;** www.lowsizerghbarn.co.uk;), south of Kendal on the A591, a farm shop with Lakes 'produce such as cheese, chutneys, and Cumberland sausage. North of Kendal, former sawmill **Staveley Mill Yard** (Ⓒ **01539/821234;** www.staveleymillyard.com) is now home to several food producers and Hawkshead Brewery.

Entertainment & Nightlife

The **Brewery Arts Centre,** Highgate (Ⓒ **01539/725133;** www.breweryarts.co.uk), is one of the best entertainment offerings in the Lake District. Located in a former brewery, there are two cinemas, a theatre, the Grain Store Restaurant, and two cafe/bars. The box office for all attractions is open Monday to Saturday 10am to 8:30pm and Sunday 11am to 8:30pm.

Where to Stay

Beech House ★   A steep walk up a hill leads to this pretty little townhouse B&B situated in a tranquil area. Behind its ivy-clad walls, the six rooms have been modernized with extras such as heated bathroom floors. Each of the boutique guest rooms is decorated differently, but in a warm and cozy style, some with rolltop tubs. The hearty breakfast is one reason to stay here, and can include Cumbrian sausages and pancakes drizzled with sugar and lemon.

40 Greenside, Kendal, Cumbria LA9 4LD. www.beechhouse-kendal.co.uk. Ⓒ **01539/720385.** Fax 01539/724082. 6 units. £80–£100 double. Rates include breakfast. 2-night minimum on weekends. MC, V. No children. *In room:* TV/DVD, hair dryer, Wi-Fi (free).

Best Western Castle Green Hotel in Kendal ★   Castle Green seems like a rambling country estate, but it once housed offices that have been cleverly converted into comfortable, contemporary bedrooms. All have modernized, tiled, en suite bathrooms, and some also boast garden views. The best guest rooms are the executive studio suites with extra space. Guests enjoy free membership in the hotel's health club, and can wine and dine in the popular on-site **Greenhouse restaurant** and Alexander's pub.

Castle Green Lane, Kendal, Cumbria LA9 6BH. www.castlegreen.co.uk. © **01539/734000.** Fax 01539/735522. 100 units. £102–£150 double; £142–£190 suite. Rates include English breakfast. AE, DC, MC, V. Signposted from the M6, junction 37. **Amenities:** Restaurant; pub; fitness center; indoor heated pool; room service; solarium; steam room. *In room:* TV, hair dryer.

WINDERMERE & BOWNESS ★★

274 miles NW of London; 10 miles NW of Kendal; 55 miles N of Liverpool

The largest lake in England is Windermere. Its eastern edge washes up on the town of Bowness (or Bowness-on-Windermere), with the town of Windermere 1½ miles away. From either town, you can climb **Orrest Head** in less than an hour for a panoramic view of the Lakeland. From that vantage point, you can even view **Scafell Pike,** rising to a height of 963m (3,210 ft.)—it's the tallest peak in all of England.

Directly south of Windermere, **Bowness** is an attractive lakeside town with lots of Victorian architecture. An important center for boating and fishing, Bowness has boat rentals of all descriptions to explore the lake.

The location of the towns keep the visitors flooding in, along with an abundance of accommodations, eateries, and pubs. The area is a particular favorite with families who come for the **World of Beatrix Potter, watersports,** and **boat trips** to **Lakeside Aquarium** and **Haverthwaite Steam Train.**

Essentials

GETTING THERE You can take a TransPennine Express (TPE) train to Windermere from Oxenholme, where Scotland and London trains arrive. One-way tickets from Oxenholme to Windermere cost about £10. To get to Bowness from Windermere, turn left from the rail terminal and cross the center of Windermere until you reach New Road, which eventually changes its name to Lake Road and leads into Bowness. It's about a 20-minute walk downhill. The Lakeland Experience bus also runs from the Windermere station to Bowness every 20 minutes.

The **National Express** bus link, originating at London's Victoria Coach Station, serves Windermere, with connections also to Preston, Manchester, and Birmingham. Local buses operated mainly by **Stagecoach** go to Kendal, Ambleside, Grasmere, and Keswick. If you're driving from London, head north on the M1 and the M6 past Liverpool until you reach the A685 junction heading west to Kendal. From Kendal, the A591 continues west to Windermere.

VISITOR INFORMATION **Windermere Tourist Information Centre** is on Victoria Street (© **01539/446499;** www.golakes.co.uk). It's open November through March, Monday to Saturday 9:30am to 4:30pm and Sunday 10am to 4pm, and April through October daily 9:30am to 5pm.

Exploring the Area

Blackwell ★★ 🎁 HISTORIC SITE Tucked away among trees overlooking Windermere, this Arts and Crafts house has been lovingly restored. Built in 1900 by Makay Hugh Baillie Scott (1865–1945) as a holiday home for wealthy industrialist

Sir Edward Holt, it slowly fell into disrepair as a post-World War I rental. The Lakeland Arts Trust stepped in to revive the early 20th-century architectural detail and furnish it with period pieces. Admire the contrasting Arts and Crafts style of the hall with its dark-wood paneling featuring intricate foliage carvings and showy peacock mosaic, and the stark, white drawing room, with cobalt blue fireplace and views over the lake.

Just off the A5074, 2 miles south of Bowness. © **01539/446139.** www.blackwell.org.uk. Admission £7 adults, £4 children 5–16 or if in full-time education with student card, £18 family ticket (2 adults, 4 children). Daily 10:30am–5pm (until 4pm Nov–Mar). Closed first 2 weeks in Jan.

Lake Cruises ★★★ CRUISE   England's largest lake (about 11 miles long), Windermere offers the archetypal day out (when the weather is agreeable). The best way to explore the lake is on cruises, which are operated by **Windermere Lake Cruises Ltd.** (© **01539/443360;** www.windermere-lakecruises.co.uk). There are round-trip services between Bowness, Ambleside, and Lakeside, and combined tickets can also include tickets for the **Lakes Aquarium** (see below) and steam train ride to Haverthwaite, or the bus to the **Lakeland Motor Museum** (see below). Freedom tickets allow you to use the boat as often as you like, and there are also relaxed cruises of the lake's islands. Seasonal car services operate to Ferry House across from Bowness, a route used regularly by visitors to **Hill Top Farm** (p. 619)

© **01539/443360.** www.windermere-lakecruises.co.uk. 24-hr. Freedom tickets £12.40 adults, £6.20 children 5–15, £34 family ticket (2 adults, 3 children); cruises from £9.15 adults, £5.30 children 5–15; boat and train £14 adults, £8.15 children, £40 family; boat and aquarium £16 adults, £8.95 children, £47 family ticket; boat, bus, motor museum £19.40 adults, £11 children, £54 family ticket. Timetable summer approx 9:15am–6:45pm, winter 10am–4pm.

Lakeland Motor Museum ★ MUSEUM   Opened in its new custom-made home in 2010, the museum has a vast collection of vintage bicycles, motorcycles, cars, and auto-memorabilia, but pride of place goes to the Campbell Bluebird Collection. Dedicated to the father-and-son team (Sir Malcolm and Donald Campbell) who between them held 21 land and water speed records, it features replicas of several of their vehicles, including the Bluebird K7 in which Donald was tragically killed on nearby Coniston Water during an attempt to break his own water speed record.

Lakes Aquarium ☺ AQUARIUM   Step into a watery world of red-bellied piranhas, grinning caiman, and leopard tortoises. The aquarium starts with local marine life and travels the world, with an underwater tunnel that brings you face to face with the big fish.

Lakeside. © **01539/530153.** www.lakesaquarium.co.uk. Admission £9.15 adults, £6.10 children 3–15, £7.75 seniors, £28 family ticket (2 adults, 2 children), £33 family ticket (2 adults, 3 children). Daily 9am–4pm (last entry).

World of Beatrix Potter ★★ ☺ ENTERTAINMENT COMPLEX   On arrival, you slip through a garden gate and watch a short film about Beatrix Potter, her stories and life as a Lakeland farmer and conservationist. Then you step *into* the tales, following a route past Jemima Puddle-Duck, the Peter Rabbit garden, and Mrs. Tiggy-Winkle's kitchen. There is also a shop with official Beatrix Potter merchandise. ***Insider tip:*** This place is mobbed on summer weekends, so try to come at any other time.

The Old Laundry, Bowness-on-Windermere. © **01539/488444.** www.hop-skip-jump.com. Admission £6.75 adults, £3.50 children 4–16. Easter–Oct daily 10am–5:30pm (to 4:30pm rest of year). Take the A591 to Lake Rd. and follow the signs.

Where to Eat

In addition to the restaurants reviewed here, see "Where to Stay," below, for dining options at hotels.

Francine's Coffee House & Restaurant 🍴 MODERN EUROPEAN The colorful array of hanging baskets provide a warm welcome. Inside, the compact eatery is clean and relaxed with white walls, flowers, and muted lighting. You can start the day with breakfast ciabattas, full English or vegetarian breakfast, or come later for the lunch and dinner set menu. There's also an a la carte menu. Savor dishes like game terrine, seared sea bream, or Lakeland lamb hotpot, rounded off with sticky-toffee pudding. Everything is meticulously presented.

27 Main Rd., Windermere. 📞 **01539/444088.** www.francinesrestaurantwindermere.co.uk. Main courses £9.95–£16. MC, V. Tues–Sun 10am–3pm and Wed–Sun 6:15–11pm.

Villa Positano ITALIAN Tucked away in the heart of Bowness, look out for the green canopy that marks the alley entrance to this long-running family favorite. Villa Positano is a lively restaurant, where the buzz of music and conversation is accompanied by classic Italian pasta, pizza, steak, and chicken dishes. In peak season, it gets crowded so book ahead or come early.

Ash St., Bowness. 📞 **01539/445663.** Reservations recommended. Main courses £5.95–£8.95. MC, V. Daily 5:30–10pm.

Shopping

Windermere is the place for sailing and watersports gear. **Windermere Canoe Kayak,** Ferry Nab Road, Bowness (📞 **01539/444451;** www.windermerecanoe kayak.com), sells and rents boats, or bikes if you want to cycle around the lake.

The busy town center of Bowness is packed full of gift, chocolate, jewelry, and swimwear stores. Head to the **World of Beatrix Potter** shop (see above) for toy Peter Rabbits and books, and the **Lakeland** kitchen gadget store in Alexandra Buildings next to the station (📞 **01539/488100;** www.lakeland.co.uk).

Entertainment & Nightlife

Bowness and Windermere are popular bases for gentle lake cruises (see above) as well as watersports. You can rent canoes from the waterfront at Bowness from **Windermere Canoe Kayak** (see above) or the **Low Wood Watersports & Activity Centre,** 3 miles north of Windermere on the A591 (📞 **01539/439441;** www. www. elh.co.uk), for sailing, kayaking, waterskiing, wakeboarding, and power-boating instruction and hire.

The oldest pub in Bowness is the **Hole in t' Wall,** Lowside (📞 **01539/443488**), dating back to 1612. The friendly bar room is decorated with a hodgepodge of antiquated farming tools, and a large slate fireplace lends warmth on winter days. There's a good selection of real ales on tap and an eclectic mix of vegetarian, seafood, and local game dishes.

Drive a short distance south of Windermere to Cartmel Fell, situated between the A592 and the A5074, for a pub-lover's dream. The **Mason Arms,** Strawberry Bank (📞 **01539/568486**), is a Jacobean pub with original oak paneling. The pretty garden offers a dramatic view of the Winster Valley beyond, while the pub offers so many beers that there's a 24-page catalog to help you order, and a reasonable menu with various tasty vegetarian options.

Southeast of Windermere, the **Punch Bowl,** off the A5074 in Crosthwaithe (© **01539/568234;** www.the-punchbowl.co.uk), is a 16th-century pub with a central room featuring a high-beamed ceiling with minstrel galleries. Outdoors, a stepped terrace on the hillside offers a tranquil retreat. Regional ales are available on tap.

Where to Stay

VERY EXPENSIVE

Cedar Manor Hotel ★   Cedar Manor might have been the 19th-century summer getaway for a wealthy industrialist, but today it is a luxury hotel. Each bedroom is spacious, well-furnished, and individually designed; some have canopied or four-poster beds. The award-winning **Cedar Manor Restaurant,** the perfect place for a candlelit dinner, caters to diners who like rib-eye steak and slow-cooked pork belly as well as for those with an acquired taste for game. Children aged 10 and younger are not allowed in the restaurant for dinner.

Ambleside Rd. (A591), Windermere, Cumbria LA23 1AX. www.cedarmanor.co.uk. © **01539/443192.** Fax 01539/445970. 11 units. £120–£210 double; £180–£250 suite. Rates include breakfast. 2-night minimum Sat–Sun. Restaurant £38 per person set menu. AE, MC, V. Free parking. **Amenities:** Restaurant; lounge. *In room:* TV/DVD (in some), fridge (in some), hair dryer, Wi-Fi (free).

Gilpin Lodge ★★★ 📷   Set in 40 hectares (100 acres) of grounds with a croquet lawn and llama paddock, this hotel exudes classical elegance, contemporary style, and an unimposing personal service. Whether you stay in the main house guest rooms or one of the suites, you'll find accommodations individually and tastefully styled. Some suites have private gardens with hot tubs, while the Lake House, opened in 2010, is an individually staffed boutique hotel with just six suites, an indoor pool, and a spa, providing the ultimate luxury retreat. And you don't need to stray far from the hotel as you can **dine** in style, too—after an aperitif in the champagne bar!

Crook Rd., B5284 nr. Windermere, Cumbria LA23 3NE. www.gilpinlodge.co.uk. © **01539/488818.** Main House, Orchard, and Garden wings 20 units; Lake House 6 units. Main House £190–£260 double; £280–£360 suite. Lake House £390–£410 per suite. Rates include English breakfast. Lake House also includes afternoon tea and chauffeur to/from Gilpin in the evening. Dinner £40 per person if booked with room. 2-night minimum on weekends. AE, MC, V. Free parking. **Amenities:** Restaurant; lounge, bar. *In room:* TV, hair dryer, spa tubs (some), Wi-Fi (free).

Holbeck Ghyll Country House Hotel ★★★   A tranquil oasis overlooking Lake Windermere, this 19th-century former hunting lodge has a high price tag but exudes luxury. Its **restaurant** serves some of the finest cuisine in the area, and rooms are individually designed, most with lake views. All have luxury beds, often crowned by a canopy, while the honeymoon room has a four-poster bed and a bathroom with a double spa tub. A separate lodge contains the hotel's six finest units, all with balcony or patio areas overlooking the lake. *Note:* Children 7 and under are prohibited in the restaurant.

Holbeck Lane (on the A591, 3½ miles northwest of town center), Windermere, Cumbria LA23 1LU. www. holbeckghyll.com. © **01539/432375.** Fax 01539/434743. 21 units. £250–£370 double; £315–£450 suite. Rates include English breakfast and dinner. Restaurant: Dinner £60 per person if not booked with room or for non-guests. Children 16 and under stay half-price in parent's room. AE, DC, MC, V. Free parking. **Amenities:** Restaurant; bar; gym; spa; tennis court, room service. *In room:* TV, hair dryer, kitchenette (in 4 units).

Linthwaite House Hotel ★   This hotel, built in 1900, is surrounded by woodlands and gardens, with a panoramic view of Lake Windermere. As befits its former role as an Edwardian gentleman's residence, it has individually decorated bedrooms, all refurbished with contemporary decor, many with lake views. All are fitted with sumptuous beds and come with tub/shower combinations. The many in-room amenities include bathrobes and satellite TVs. It's worth enjoying lunch or dinner in the hotel **restaurant,** which serves modern British cuisine such as rabbit confit or roast quail with English asparagus salad.

Crook Rd., Bowness-on-Windermere, Cumbria LA23 3JA. www.linthwaite.com. *C* **01539/488600.** Fax 01539/488601. 27 units. £189–£386 double; £347–£531 suite. Rates include English breakfast. Restaurant dinner and canapés £52; open daily noon–2pm lunch; 7–9pm dinner. AE, DC, MC, V. Free parking. **Amenities:** Restaurant; bar; room service; nearby spa. *In room:* TV, CD player, hair dryer, Wi-Fi (free).

The Samling ★★ 🏨 The Samling is set on substantial grounds offering panoramic lake views. It was fashioned from a late-18th-century stone-built manse where Wordsworth used to come to pay his rent on Dove Cottage in neighboring Grasmere. Of the 11 rooms, five are located in a converted stable block that's more akin to a ski lodge than a country house. The main-building rooms have more of a traditional British aura, but all are individually styled and spacious. Even if you're not a guest, consider an elegant **set-price dinner** here.

Ambleside Rd., Windermere, Cumbria LA23 1LR. www.thesamling.com. *C* **01539/431922.** 11 units. £190–£460 per double; £340–£560 suite. Rates include breakfast. Dinner: £45 for guests if booked with room; £68 non-guests. AE, DC, MC, V. Free parking. **Amenities:** Restaurant; bar. *In room:* TV, hair dryer, Wi-Fi (in some; free).

EXPENSIVE

The Belsfield ★ You can't fail to notice this hotel overlooking Windermere lake and Bowness Pier. A large, white Victorian mansion set in 2.4 hectares (6 acres) of gardens, it provides guests with a place they can sit in the summer sunshine and take in the vista. Rooms might not be as stylish as the pricier country houses nearby, but they are comfortable with antique-style furnishings that complement the architecture; several have lake views. What's more, the location is convenient, and facilities include a heated indoor pool, **Moonwaters restaurant,** and a bar and lounge.

Kendal Rd., Bowness, Cumbria LA23 3EL. www.corushotels.com/Belsfield-Windermere. *C* **01539/442448.** 64 units, 3 suites. £144–£180 double; £155–£205 suite. Rates include breakfast. AE, DC, MC, V. **Amenities:** Restaurant; bar; indoor pool and sauna. *In room:* TV, hair dryer, hospitality tray, Wi-Fi (free).

MODERATE

Beaumont House This stone-sided Lakeland villa is on a quiet residential street just off Windermere's commercial center. Each of the refurbished bedrooms is named after one of the characters in the Beatrix Potter books (our favorite is Jemima Puddle-Duck) and contains either an elaborate canopy bed or a four-poster, fitted with a quality mattress. No meals are served other than breakfast, so the owners keep local restaurant menus on hand for their guests to consult.

Holly Rd., Windermere, Cumbria LA23 2AF. www.lakesbeaumont.co.uk. *C* **01539/447075.** Fax 01539/488311. 10 units. £70–£140 double. Rates include English breakfast. MC, V. Free parking. **Amenities:** Free use of nearby health club. *In room:* TV/DVD (in some), hair dryer.

Fir Trees Guest House ★ One of Windermere's finest guesthouses, Fir Trees provides hotel-like standards at B&B prices. Opposite St. John's Church, halfway between Bowness and Windermere, it is a Victorian house redecorated with antique-style furnishings. Proprietors Bob and Bea Towers offer a warm welcome and beautifully maintained bedrooms, some large enough for families.

Lake Rd., Windermere, Cumbria LA23 2EQ. www.fir-trees.co.uk. © **01539/442272.** Fax 01539/442512. 9 units. £64–£96 double. Rates include English breakfast. MC, V. Free parking. **Amenities:** Beauty treatments available. *In room:* TV, hair dryer.

The Wild Boar Inn, Grill & Smokehouse★ Guests and diners come here for the comfortable and cozy atmosphere. Most guest rooms have been refurbished and individually styled, some with elaborate French-style beds or velvet headboards; a few have wood-burning stoves. The **restaurant** features an open kitchen where diners can see their wild boar sausages or house-smoked steaks sizzling on the grill. Afterward you can retreat to the quintessentially English bar and sit beside the open fire with one of the 50 whiskies or guest ales available.

Crook Rd., Windermere, Cumbria LA23 3NF. www.elh.co.uk. © **08458/504604.** 33 units. £80–£238 double. Rates include English breakfast. MC, V. Free parking. **Amenities:** Restaurant, bar. *In room:* TV, hair dryer.

AMBLESIDE

278 miles NW of London; 14 miles NW of Kendal; 4 miles N of Windermere

An idyllic retreat at the north end of Lake Windermere, Ambleside is just a small village, but it's one of the major places to stay in the Lake District, attracting hikers and rock climbers. It's wonderful in warm weather and even through late fall, when it's fashionable to sport a raincoat.

The town is most renowned for its **plethora of shops** selling outdoor gear, but it also has restaurants to suit all tastes, several lively pubs, and a jazz bar/cinema. But it's not all about eating, drinking, and shopping! There's a gentle walk up to **Stock Ghyll Force** (waterfall) and a steep drive across **Kirkstone Pass** toward Ullswater. Stop en route to take panoramic snapshots of Windermere.

Essentials

GETTING THERE Take a train to Windermere (see "Windermere & Bowness," earlier in this chapter), and then continue the rest of the way by bus.

Stagecoach has an hourly bus service from Grasmere and Keswick (see "Grasmere & Rydal," below, and "Keswick & Borrowdale," later in this chapter) and from Windermere. All these buses into Ambleside are labeled either no. 555 or 556.

If you're driving from Windermere, continue northwest on the A591.

VISITOR INFORMATION The **Ambleside Tourist Information Centre** is at Market Cross Central Buildings (© **01539/432582;** www.golakes.co.uk). It's open Monday to Saturday 9am to 5:30pm, Sunday 9am to 5pm.

Exploring the Area

The Homes of Football GALLERY This might seem a curious addition to a Lake District town, but this gallery draws in crowds of visitors intrigued by its extraordinary display of football photography from around the world. The work of photographer Stuart Roy Clarke, the gallery also presents nonfootball projects—but all display his knack for cultural perception and talent for capturing the moment. There are several signed prints and postcards for sale.

100 Lake Rd. © **01539/434440.** www.homesoffootball.com. Free admission. Daily 10am–5pm.

Stock Ghyll Force NATURAL ATTRACTION The 15-minute walk to this waterfall is suitable for those who can't manage the more strenuous fell walks. It's a little steep, but once at the top you'll find cascading waterfalls that powered local mills from the 14th century onward. The mills have long since gone, leaving visitors to enjoy the natural force of the water. Like many picturesque places in these parts, spring sees daffodils carpeting the route.

Stock Ghyll Lane.

Where to Eat

In addition to the restaurants reviewed here, see "Where to Stay," below, for other dining options.

Glass House Restaurant ★ MODERN BRITISH/MEDITERRANEAN A former saw mill dating back to the 15th century, this restaurant retained the working weir and some of the mill machinery when it was converted in the 1990s. Today, you'll find a split-level combination of medieval and contemporary architecture, with oak interior trim and large windows. The main courses include confit duck leg with Cumberland stuffing, and pan-fried sea bass with vegetable noodles.

Rydal Rd., Ambleside. ✆ **01539/432137.** www.theglasshouserestaurant.co.uk. Reservations recommended. Main courses £13–£19. MC, V. Wed–Mon noon–2:30pm and 6:30–10pm.

Lucy's on a Plate ★ 🍴 MODERN BRITISH A bustling cafe by day, this eatery becomes one of the best restaurants after dark, when the lights are dimmed for dinner. Local farm produce is used whenever possible to create well-crafted dishes like chargrilled rib-eye with matchstick potatoes and onion marmalade, or fresh mussels cooked in a coconut-milk sauce. The restaurant is famous for its hot puddings, especially its sublime sticky-toffee pudding or its "wicked" hot-chocolate sponge. During the day, drop by the adjoining delicatessen for enough delights to fill a picnic basket to enjoy in one lakeside setting.

Church St., Ambleside. ✆ **01539/432288.** www.lucysofambleside.co.uk. Reservations not needed. Main courses £14–£22. AE, DC, MC, V. Daily 10am–9pm.

Sheila's Cottage ★ ENGLISH/INTERNATIONAL Tucked down a quiet side street off the Lake Road, this pretty stone-fronted restaurant provides a homey retreat from the bustling town center. An open fire, beamed ceiling, and pine tables provide a rustic feel while the mixed menu can include Cumberland and Hawkshead Ale sausages, and creamy risotto with butternut squash and rosemary. You can also pop in for tea and cake. Homeyness at its best.

The Slack, Ambleside. ✆ **01539/433079.** Reservations not needed. Main courses £9.50–£20. MC, V. Daily 11am–9pm (last orders); can close earlier in winter; lunch noon–4:30pm; dinner from 5pm.

Shopping

You can often pick up a bargain on last season's breathable jackets or gortex boots in one of Ambleside's outdoor clothing and equipment shops. You'll also find maps, guidebooks, walking poles, camping equipment, and climbing gear. Try **Gaynor Sports,** Market Cross (✆ **01524/734938;** www.gaynors.co.uk), for discount wear; **Edge of the World,** Rydal Road (✆ **01539/433033;** www.edgeoftheworld.co.uk), for more fashion-conscious sweat tops and T-shirts, boots, and beanies; or **The Climbers Shop,** Compston Road (✆ **01539/432297;** www.climbers-shop.com), for crampons and other technical equipment.

Entertainment & Nightlife

Ambleside pubs spill onto the streets in the summer months, especially the **Royal Oak, Market Place** (✆ **01539/433382**), a popular bar with seating at the front entrance and a large umbrella for rainy evenings. The **Golden Rule,** Smithy Brow (✆ **01539/432257**), boasts a large selection of CAMRA (Campaign for Real Ale) beers. You can relax with a pint in one of the leather chairs or slip into another room for a game of darts. Behind the bar, a small garden provides a serene setting in warm weather.

If pints just aren't enough, then **Zefirelli's,** Compston Road (✆ **01539/433845;** www.zefirellis.com), might be just the ticket. It has a cinema showing Art House films, live music in the jazz bar, a cafe, a pizzeria, and a vegetarian restaurant all in one spot.

Where to Stay

The Best Western Ambleside Salutation In the heart of Ambleside, this large, white hotel is hard to miss. Its 47 spacious en suite rooms are decorated in soft, neutral colors. The hotel also has its own on-site health club that includes gym equipment with iPod docking stations and a heated indoor pool. After working out, you can enjoy bar snacks in the Bistro or more formal dining in the **Garden Restaurant.** The local menu can include warmed Morecambe Bay potted shrimp, Kescadale Farm sirloin steak, and English Lakes ice cream.

Lake Rd., Ambleside, Cumbria LA22 9BX. www.queenshotelambleside.com. ✆ **01539/432244.** Fax 01539/432721. 47 units. Sun–Thurs £109–£139 double; Fri–Sat £124–£149 double. Restaurant set menus 2 courses £23, 3 courses £28. Discounts available for early-bird room reservations. AE, MC, V. Free parking. **Amenities:** Restaurant; bistro/bar; health club. In room: TV, hair dryer.

The Log House ★ This genuine Norwegian log house was imported by local artist Heaton Cooper on his return from the country in the early 20th century. It has had many roles over the years, but today it has a restaurant, bar, and three guest rooms—all fresh, clean, and white and located in the cabin's roof space. The **restaurant**'s modern menu includes entrees such as chili-salt squid and chargrilled lamb salad, and main courses of hand-selected English beef or sea bass and chips, all made with seasonal, local produce.

Lake Rd., Ambleside, Cumbria LA22 0DN. www.loghouse.co.uk. ✆ **01539/431077.** 3 units. £82–£93 double. Rates include English breakfast. Weekends and public holidays 2-night minimum stay. MC, V. Free parking. On the left-hand side as you drive into Ambleside from Windermere. **Amenities:** Restaurant; bar. In room: TV, hair dryer, Wi-Fi (free).

Rothay Manor Hotel ★★ ☺ At this Regency manor house, the **restaurant** is the star, with ingredients sourced from the best regional suppliers. Savor baked halibut in rosemary butter or braised venison with wild mushrooms. Most bedrooms have shuttered French doors opening onto a balcony and a mountain view (two are wheelchair accessible). Classic Rooms have twin, double, or queen beds, while some suites can accommodate large families. There's even a children's "high tea" (6–6:30pm), which is really a dinner. There's a children's playground nearby, and croquet and boules on-site.

Rothay Bridge, Ambleside, Cumbria LA22 0EH. www.rothaymanor.co.uk. ✆ **01539/433605.** Fax 01539/433607. 19 units. £170–£200 double; £230–£280 suite. Rates include English breakfast. AE, DC, MC, V. Free parking. Take the A593 ½ mile south of Ambleside. **Amenities:** Restaurant; bar; babysitting; free use of nearby health club; Wi-Fi (free). In room: TV, hair dryer.

Waterhead Hotel ★   This townhouse hotel has a prized position beside Lake Windermere, and is a good base for exploring the lakes on foot or by car. The **restaurant,** bar, and guest rooms are contemporary and meticulously styled. Guest rooms are spacious, some with lake views. On sunny days you can relax outside on the waterfront lawns or sink into a sofa inside, beside the open fire. Guests can also use the watersports center and spa facilities at sister hotel Low Wood, just a mile along the lake.

Lake Rd., Waterhead, Ambleside, Cumbria LA22 0EP. www.elh.co.uk. ✆ **01539/432566.** Fax 01539/431255. 41 units. £113–£308 double. Rates include English breakfast. AE, MC, V. Free parking. **Amenities:** Restaurant; bar; nearby health club and watersports center. *In room:* TV, hair dryer.

GRASMERE & RYDAL ★★

282 miles NW of London; 18 miles NW of Kendal; 43 miles S of Carlisle

Rydal is just a hamlet, a few houses including Rydal Mount, home to the poet Wordsworth for several years. From the gardens you can spy the nearest lake, Rydal Water, where it is said that the poet used to sit and contemplate the view from a point on the western shore now called Wordsworth's Seat.

Farther along the A591 is **Grasmere,** a pretty village set beside a lake of the same name. Also home to Wordsworth, he called the area "the loveliest spot that man hath ever known." Today visitors pour into the village at any opportunity to visit locations associated with the poet—including his grave in the cemetery of St. Oswald's—and to buy bags of Grasmere gingerbread. The village is also a popular place for walks to the Langdale Pikes to the southwest and Helvellyn to the north. One of the most popular fells in the Lake District, the closest access route from here is straight up and down from the eastern shore of Thirlmere. For a longer, more spectacular hike, drive via Ambleside and Kirkstone Pass to Glenridding (a worthwhile drive in itself for its panoramic lake and fell views). From here you can hike across Striding Edge, a steep and dramatic ridge that leads westwards to the peak of Helvellyn. You can return to Thirlmere if you have transport from there or circle back round Red Tarn and back to Glenridding.

Essentials

GETTING THERE   Take a train to Windermere (see "Windermere & Bowness," earlier in this chapter) and continue the rest of the way by bus.

Stagecoach runs an hourly bus service to Grasmere from Keswick and Windermere. Buses in either direction are marked no. 555 or 556.

If you're driving from Windermere, continue northwest along the A591.

VISITOR INFORMATION   **Grasmere Tourist Information Centre,** Town Hall, Highgate (✆ **01539/797516;** www.golakes.co.uk), is open March through October, Monday to Saturday 10am to 5pm, and November through February, Monday to Saturday 10am to 4pm.

Exploring the Area

Dove Cottage, the Wordsworth Museum ★★ HISTORIC HOME   If you're on the Wordsworth "trail," then Dove Cottage is a good place to start. A small, white cottage with a tangle of pink roses clinging to the walls, it was the Dove and Olive pub years before it became Wordsworth's home in 1799. He spent a few happy years living here with his writer and diarist sister, Dorothy, and later his wife, Mary. A guided tour introduces visitors to the former drinking room downstairs and the study and compact bedrooms upstairs. After the tour, spend time in the garden where he composed "I Wandered Lonely as a Cloud." In the Wordsworth Museum behind the cottage, you can see manuscripts, paintings, and memorabilia, and maybe catch a special exhibition exploring the art and literature of English Romanticism.

On the A591, south of the village of Grasmere on the road to Kendal. *©* **01539/435544.** www. wordsworth.org.uk. Admission to Dove Cottage and the adjoining museum £7.50 adults, £4.50 children 5–16, £17 family ticket. Daily 9:30am–5:30pm. Closed Dec 24–26 and mid-Jan–early Feb.

Rydal Mount ★★ HISTORIC HOME   Delve into the world of William Wordsworth at this Lakeland house, where he lived from 1813 until his death in 1850. Many of the poet's belongings remain here, including his library and cutlass chair (a type of chair designed for men wearing swords), as well as his beloved daughter Dora's bedroom. Don't miss the attic study, which he added onto the original 16th-century farmer's lake cottage. A descendant of Wordsworth now owns the property, which also has a spectacular 1.8-hectare (4½-acre) garden, landscaped by Wordsworth. Walk among the rare trees and clamber up the terrace steps to the "summer house," where he would sit in contemplation while taking in views of Rydal Water.

Off the A591, 1½ miles north of Ambleside. *©* **01539/433002.** www.rydalmount.co.uk. Admission to house and gardens £6.50 adults, £5.50 seniors and students, £3 children 5–15, £16 family ticket, free for children 4 and under. Mar–Oct daily 9:30am–5pm; Nov–Dec and Feb Wed–Sun 11am–4pm; closed Jan.

Wordsworth Graves & St. Oswald's Church CHURCH   William Wordsworth died in the spring of 1850 and was buried in St. Oswald's Church graveyard. You can walk here from Dove Cottage, stopping in to see the resting place of the poet, his wife, Mary, and daughter, Dora, along with other family members. Take a peek in the church, where there's a memorial to Wordsworth in the 13th-century nave. Named after a 7th-century Christian king, the church comes to life during the Rushbearing Festival in July; a procession of parishioners re-enact an age-old custom of strewing rushes and flowers on what was once an earthen floor. Look out for the **Grasmere Gingerbread Shop** (*©* **01539/435428;** www.grasmeregingerbread.co.uk) by the church gate, famous for its fresh cookies.

Church Stile, Grasmere. Free admission. Daily 9am–5pm.

Where to Eat & Stay
VERY EXPENSIVE

Moss Grove Organic Hotel ★ 📖   This hotel in the heart of Grasmere focuses on organic produce (local when possible), sustainability, and being as environmentally friendly as possible. These days, this doesn't mean "living it rough." Instead you'll find spacious, individually furnished guest rooms, some with beds made from reclaimed wood, and fashionable wallpaper combined with neutral tones. All rooms provide a relaxing space to get away from it all. You can even arrange for organic chocolates and wine to be placed in your room.

Grasmere, Cumbria LA22 9RQ. www.mossgrove.com. *©* **01539/435619.** 11 units. £129–£265 double. £209–£325 suite. Rates include English breakfast. 2-night minimum stay at weekends. Dogs allowed in ground-floor superior room and suite for extra £20 per night. MC, V. Free parking. *In room:* TV, hair dryer; underfloor heating (executive rooms), spa bath, Wi-Fi (free).

Wordsworth Hotel & Spa ★★   Set next to the churchyard where Wordsworth is buried, this stone Lakeland house was once the Earl of Cadogan's hunting lodge. Today its refurbished bedrooms are luxurious, combining classical style with modern comforts. Expect Egyptian cotton sheets, bathrobes, flat-screen TVs, and Wi-Fi; some rooms have four-poster beds and village or mountain views. Families can book adjoining rooms with twin or single beds. Guests can enjoy cream tea in the lounge, casual eating by the fireside in the bistro, or Cumbrian classics in the **award-winning restaurant.**

Stock Lane, Grasmere, Cumbria LA22 9SW (turn left on the A591 at the GRASMERE VILLAGE sign, and follow the road over the bridge, past the church, and around an S-bend; the Wordsworth is on the right). www.grasmere-hotels.co.uk. ✆ **01539/435592.** Fax 01539/435765. 36 units. £118–£240 double; £238–£360 suite. Rates include English breakfast. Dinner £15 extra. AE, DC, MC, V. Free parking. **Amenities:** Restaurant; bar; exercise room; Jacuzzi; heated indoor pool; room service; sauna. *In room:* TV, hair dryer, Wi-Fi (free).

EXPENSIVE

Swan Hotel   Sir Walter Scott used to come here for a secret drink early in the morning, and Wordsworth mentioned the place in "The Waggoner." In fact, the poet's wooden chair is in one of the rooms. Many bedrooms are in a modern wing, added in 1975, which fits gracefully onto the building's older core (only the shell of the original 1650 building remains). Bedrooms are comfortably furnished, each with twin or double beds; the feature rooms have canopy or four-poster beds. The Walkers Bar is popular with hikers (and their dogs) after a day on the fells, then clean up for British roasts and steaks in the **Waggoner's restaurant.**

On the A591 (on the road to Keswick, ½ mile outside Grasmere), Grasmere, Cumbria LA22 9RF. www. macdonaldhotels.co.uk/swan. ✆ **0844/879-9120.** Fax 01539/435741. 38 units. £125–£179 double. Rates include breakfast. AE, DC, MC, V. Free parking. **Amenities:** Restaurant; bar; room service; spa. *In room:* TV, hair dryer, Wi-Fi (free).

MODERATE

Glen Rothay Hotel   Built in the 17th century as a wayfarer's inn, this hotel adjoins Dora's Field, immortalized by Wordsworth. Inside, the place has been modernized, but original details remain, including beamed ceilings and paneling. The comfortable bedrooms upstairs are tastefully furnished; three have four-poster beds and one a super-king bed and Jacuzzi bath. The remainder have double or twin beds, and compact tiled bathrooms, each with a shower.

On the A591 (1½ miles northwest of Ambleside), Rydal, Ambleside, Cumbria LA22 9LR. www.theglen rothay.co.uk. ✆ **01539/434500.** Fax 01539/34505. 8 units. £90 double; from £110 suite. Rates include English breakfast. MC, V. Free parking. **Amenities:** Restaurant; bar; room service. *In room:* TV, hair dryer.

Gold Rill Hotel ★★   This sprawling country-house hotel has the most prized location hotel in Grasmere, alongside the lake yet only a 2-minute walk to the center of the village. Surrounded by well-maintained gardens, the hotel has a heated outdoor pool and a private pier. Each midsize to spacious bedroom is individually furnished, some with king-size beds. For romantic breaks, you can arrange in advance for champagne, strawberries, and fresh flowers to be placed in the room. Guests can enjoy pub lunches or a fine evening dinner here, often prepared with local produce.

Red Bank Rd., Grasmere, Cumbria LA22 9PU. www.gold-rill.com. ✆ **01539/435486.** 31 units. £106–£128 double. Rates include English breakfast. MC, V. Free parking. **Amenities:** Restaurant; bar; heated outdoor pool; room service. *In room:* TV, hair dryer.

Lancrigg Vegetarian Country House Hotel ★★ 🛏   With an emphasis on vegetarian cooking, Lancrigg also caters to vegans and people with allergies. What's more, the hotel is set in a beautiful, secluded valley that used to attract the Lake poets to the area for inspiration. The spacious guest rooms are very English in style with floral prints and pastel shades; some have four-poster beds and ample seating areas. In addition to savoring the tasty and healthful culinary creations in the **restaurant,** you can pamper your body with a facial and massage in the spa.

Easedale, Grasmere, Cumbria LA22 9QN. www.lancrigg.com. ✆ **01539/435317.** Fax 01539/435058. 12 units. £110–£170 double. Rates include vegetarian breakfast. Dinner £24 extra per person. AE, MC, V. Free parking. Closed Dec–Jan. **Amenities:** Restaurant; spa and leisure club. *In room:* TV, hair dryer, Wi-Fi (free).

CONISTON & HAWKSHEAD

263 miles NW of London; 19 miles NW of Kendal; 52 miles S of Carlisle

Coniston Water lies in a tranquil wooded valley between Grizedale Forest and the high fells of Coniston Old Man and Wetherlam. Coniston village is famously associated with **John Ruskin;** visit the museum named after him, his grave in the cemetery, and his former house, **Brantwood,** across the lake. It's also a good place for hiking and rock climbing. The **Coniston Old Man** towers in the background at 790m (2,633 ft.), giving mountain climbers one of the finest views of the Lake District.

The pretty village of **Hawkshead** is just 4 miles east of Coniston, but to get there you have to drive around the north side of the lake along the B5285. Hawkshead is home to the 15th-century grammar school where Wordsworth studied for 8 years (it is said he carved his name on a desk that is still there). The main attraction here though is the **Beatrix Potter Gallery,** located in the former offices of her husband. Nearby, in Near Sawrey, is **Hill Top Farm,** former 17th-century home of the author.

Essentials

GETTING THERE   Take a train to Windermere and proceed the rest of the way by boat/bus. Local buses are operated mainly by **Stagecoach,** and for Hawkshead you'll need to catch a connecting bus in Ambleside.

Windermere Lake Cruises Ltd. (✆ **01539/443360;** www.windermere-lake-cruises.co.uk) operates a ferry service in summer from Bowness, directly south of Windermere, to Ferry House. From April to September, **Mountain Goat** (✆ **01539/445161;** www.mountain-goat.com) operates several shuttle buses per day from Ferry House to Hawkshead.

By car from Windermere, proceed north on the A591 to Ambleside, cutting southwest on the B5285 to Hawkshead.

VISITOR INFORMATION   **Coniston Tourist Information Centre,** Ruskin Avenue (✆ **01539/441533;** www.conistontic.org), is open from April (or Easter, whichever is earlier) to September, daily 9:30am to 5pm, and from October to March (Easter), daily 10am to 4pm.

Hawkshead Tourist Information Centre, Main Street (✆ **01539/436946;** www.hawksheadtouristinfo.org.uk), is open the same hours as Coniston Tourist Information Centre.

Exploring the Area

Beatrix Potter Gallery ★ GALLERY   This cream-colored cottage was once the office of Potter's husband, solicitor William Heelis. The interior remains largely unaltered since his day, but for the addition of Beatrix Potter's original illustrations, watercolors, and sketches. You can learn something of her role as a landowner and farmer.

She bought acres of land to protect it from development, much of which she donated to the National Trust in her will.

Main Street. © **01539/436355.** www.nationaltrust.org.uk/main/w-beatrixpottergallery. £4.60 adults, £2.30 children 5-17, £12 family ticket. Discount for Hill Top Farm with ticket. Mid-Feb–Mar Sat–Thurs 11am–3:30pm; Apr–end May and early Sept–Oct Sat–Thurs 11am–5pm; end May–early Sept Sat–Thurs 10:30am–5pm. Last admission 30 min. before closing. Take bus no. 505 from Ambleside and Coniston to the square in Hawkshead, or the boat from Bowness to Ferry House and the shuttle bus to Hawkshead.

Brantwood ★★ ☺ HISTORIC SITE With acres of garden and views across Coniston Water to the fells, Brantwood is the perfect place for a picnic lunch or coffee in the former stables, now converted into tearooms. The house was made famous by John Ruskin, poet, artist, and critic, and one of the great figures of the Victorian age, a prophet of social reform. He moved to Brantwood in 1872 and lived here until his death in 1900. Visitors today can see Ruskin's memorabilia, including some 200 of his pictures; the visit is made more fun for younger ones with quiz sheets.

Outside, part of the 101-hectare (250-acre) estate has nature trails. Look for the Coach House Gallery, which follows the Ruskin tradition of encouraging contemporary craftwork of the finest quality. You may want to visit the graveyard of Coniston's village church, where Ruskin was buried; his family turned down the invitation to have him interred at Westminster Abbey.

East shore of Coniston Water. © **01539/441369.** www.brantwood.org.uk. £6.30 adults, £5 students, £1.35 children 5-15, £13 family ticket. Mid-Mar–mid-Nov daily 11am–5:30pm; mid-Nov–mid-Mar Wed–Sun 11am–4:30pm; closed Dec 25–26.

Coniston Launch ★★ ☺ CRUISE These are traditional timber boats that operate a circular route calling at Coniston, Waterhead, Torver, and Brantwood. Discounts are offered in combination with admission to Brantwood house (see above) and you can hop on and hop off, or choose single fares if you're planning on walking back. Other cruises explore the more tranquil part of the lake to the south, again with cruise or single-fare options for walkers. In the summer they also run special "Swallows and Amazons" and "Campbells on Coniston" cruises.

Coniston Pier/Boat House. © **01768/775-753.** www.conistonlaunch.co.uk. Northern service £8.90 adults, £4.95 children 5-16, £22 family ticket (including Brantwood £15 round-trip for adults, £6.20 children, £34 family ticket). Southern service £13 round-trip for adults, £6.25 children, £28 family ticket (including Brantwood £18 adults, £7.50 children, £39 family ticket). Northern service mid-Mar–Oct daily 10:15am–5:40pm first/last boats from Coniston; round-trip approx. 50 min.; Nov–mid-Mar daily 10:30am–2:30pm first/last boats from Coniston (late Nov–Dec Sat–Sun only), no sailings Jan; Southern service mid-Mar–Sept 10:50am and 2:50pm from Coniston, round-trip approx. 1¾ hr.

Coniston Water NATURAL ATTRACTION This is one of the most beautiful lakes with the Old Man fell rising over it and the waters stretching south from Coniston for around 5½ miles. It's easy to drive along the western shore, with picnic places and lakeside paths dotted along the route, while roads on the eastern side are narrow, becoming clogged with tour buses in peak season. The more relaxing option is to travel by boat, taking in the fells from the water and imagining yourself a character in Arthur Ransome's *Swallows and Amazons,* inspired by Coniston Water.

Gondola HISTORICAL SITE/CRUISE The more romantic option is to cruise the lake in an original Victorian steam-powered yacht. The *Gondola,* launched in 1859 and in regular service until 1937, was rescued and completely restored with upholstered seating by the National Trust. Since 1980, it has become a familiar sight on

LAKE DISTRICT national park ★★★

Despite the reverence with which the English treat the Lake District, it required an act of Parliament in 1951 to protect its natural beauty. Spread over 885 sq. miles of hills, eroded mountains, forests, and lakes, the **Lake District National Park** is the largest and one of the most popular National Parks in the United Kingdom, receiving over 8 million day visitors a year. Lured by Romantic Lake poets' work, visitors arrive to take in the mountains, wildlife, flora, fauna, and secluded waterfalls. Much of the area is privately owned, but landowners work with National Park officers to preserve the landscape and its 1,800 miles of footpaths.

Alas, the park's popularity is now one of its major drawbacks. Hordes of weekend tourists descend, especially in summertime and on bank holiday weekends. Despite the crowds, great efforts are made to maintain the trails that radiate in a network throughout the district, preserving the purity of a landscape that includes more than 100 lakes and countless numbers of grazing sheep.

Before setting out to explore the lake, stop in at the **National Park Visitor Centre** (✆ **01539/446601;** www.lakedistrict. gov.uk), located on the lakeshore at Brockhole, on the A591 between Windermere and Ambleside. It can be reached by bus or by one of the lake launches from Windermere. Once here, you can pick up useful information and explore 12 hectares (30 acres) of landscaped gardens and parklands; lake cruises, exhibitions, and film shows are also offered. Lunches and teas are served in the tearooms.

Tourist information offices within the park are richly stocked with maps and suggestions for several dozen bracing rambles. Regardless of the itinerary you select, you'll spot frequent green-and-white signs, or their older equivalents in varnished pine with Adirondack-style routed letters, announcing FOOTPATH TO . . .

Coniston Water; sailings to Brantwood run throughout the summer. Service is subject to weather conditions, of course.

Coniston Pier/Boat House. ✆ **01539/432733.** www.nationaltrust.org.uk/main/w-gondola. £8.50 round-trip for adults, £4.50 children 5–16, £22 family ticket. Discount vouchers available for Brantwood and Ruskin Museum with ticket. Times vary according to capacity and weather conditions; bookings advisable.

Hill Top Farm ★★ HISTORIC HOME   It's a 2-mile walk from Hawkshead to Near Sawrey, a pretty country village where you can visit Beatrix Potter's former home. If driving, park your car beside the ticket office, but come first thing (before opening if you can), as entry is timed and waiting can be lengthy in peak season. The cottage is a few minutes' walk along the road. Enter through the gate beside the shop where a path leads past a tangle of wild flowers (in the summer) to the entrance. You might have time to explore the herb and vegetable garden before going inside, but don't miss your time slot! Inside, the world of Beatrix Potter comes alive. Almost unchanged, you'll see her paintings and personal items throughout, and guides are on hand to embellish them with a few tales.

Near Sawrey, Hawkshead. ✆ **01539/436269.** www.nationaltrust.org.uk/main/w-hilltop. £7 adults, £3.50 children 5–16, £18 family ticket. Discount at Beatrix Potter Gallery with Hill Top ticket. Mid-Feb–Mar Sat–Thurs 10:30am–3:30pm; Apr–end May and early Sept–Oct Sat–Thurs 10:30am–4:30pm; end May–early Sept 10am–5pm; last entry 30 min. before closing. Shuttle bus from Hawkshead/Ferry House.

Ruskin Museum MUSEUM   This museum, in the center of the village, is divided into the Coniston Gallery, the Ruskin Gallery, and the new Bluebird wing. The first gives an insight into Coniston's past, delving back thousands of years with displays and computer images of old Coniston. Among the artifacts you'll see a preserved hog, slate from the mines, lace and crafts from the local cottage industry, and Arthur Ransom's dinghy, *Mavis.* The Ruskin Gallery provides insight into John Ruskin through personal possessions and mementos, photographs, busts, letters, and his collection of mineral rocks. The Bluebird wing has numerous exhibits relating to Donald Campbell's *Bluebird,* and eventually it will hold a reconstruction of the fateful boat.

Off Yewdale Rd., Coniston. ℂ **01539/441164.** www.ruskinmuseum.com. £5.25 adults, £2.50 children 6–16, £14 family ticket. Early Mar–mid-Nov daily 10am–5:30pm; mid-Nov–early Mar Wed–Sun 10:30am–3:30pm. Closed Dec 24–26.

Entertainment & Nightlife

You can rent rowboats and sailing dinghies at **Coniston Boating Centre,** Lake Road, Coniston (ℂ **01539/441366;** www.lakedistrict.gov.uk). **Summitreks** also operates from the lakeside at Coniston Boating Centre, offering qualified instruction in canoeing and windsurfing. You can rent a wide range of equipment from the nearby office at Lake Road (ℂ **01539/441212;** www.summitreks.co.uk). A few miles south of Hawkshead, **Grizedale Forest** has nature and forest trails, mountain-bike cycling routes, and a cafe.

Where to Eat & Stay

Black Bull ENGLISH/INTERNATIONAL   A pub, inn, and brewery, the Black Bull dominates the main crossroads in Coniston. A former coaching inn dating back 400 years, it counts artists and poets among its former clients. It has a micro-brewery, the Coniston Brewing Company, which produces several types of ale, bitter, and stout. These make a good accompaniment to the beef chili, scampi, and roast chicken on the menu. There are also 15 en suite **guest rooms** (£90–£100 double, with English breakfast), all basic but clean and comfortable, two in small cottages.

Yewdale Rd., Coniston. ℂ **01539/441335.** Fax 01539/441168. www.blackbullconiston.co.uk. Reservations recommended. Main courses £9–£16. MC, V. Daily noon-2:30pm and 6:15-9:30pm.

Buckle Yeat Guest House   You'll pass this pretty 17th-century Lakeland house as you stroll to Hill Top Farm (see above). In the flower-filled front yard, you'll often see a stuffed mannequin of Mr. McGregor, feared by the rabbits in Beatrix Potter's *Tale of Peter Rabbit.* Inside, the decor is traditional, furnished with dark wood antiques and an open log fire where guests can warm themselves with Mr. McGregor, who is brought inside for the winter. Guest rooms are individually decorated but all are light and airy with a comfortable country feel.

Near Sawrey, Hawkshead, Cumbria LA22 0LF. www.buckle-yeat.co.uk. ℂ **01539/436446**. 6 units. £80–£90 per week. Rates include English breakfast. MC, V. Free parking. **Amenities:** Lounge; breakfast room. *In room:* TV, hair dryer.

The Drunken Duck Inn ★ MODERN BRITISH   People come to this out-of-the-way family-run inn to feast on its creative menu, which can include Cullen skink, roasted pumpkin risotto, or duck breast with bean cassoulet. Most of the 16 standard **guest rooms** are above the inn, but all are light and airy with quality furnishings (£95–£295 double, including breakfast). Superior and deluxe rooms have more space and king-size beds; some have courtyard and mountain views.

2½ miles north of Hawkshead, off the B5286, Barngates, Cumbria LA22 0NG. ☎ **01539/436347.** www. drunkenduckinn.co.uk. Reservations recommended. Main courses £11–£26. AE, MC, V. Restaurant daily noon–4pm and 6:30–9:30pm.

Queen's Head ENGLISH/INTERNATIONAL The Queen's Head is a 17th-century building that serves a special brew, Robinsons Stockport, from old-fashioned wooden kegs. Temptations on the menu can include a winter woodland venison casserole. The pub also rents **14 bedrooms** (£75–£90, including English breakfast); two rooms have four-poster beds, and all have a private bathroom, TV, and phone.

Main St., Hawkshead. ☎ **01539/436271.** www.queensheadhotel.co.uk. Reservations recommended. Main courses £12–£18. AE, MC, V. Daily noon–2:30pm and 6:15–9:30pm.

Sun Hotel ★ The most attractive pub, restaurant, and hotel in Coniston, this country-house hotel dates from 1902, and the attached inn from the 16th century. Situated on beautiful grounds above the village, 135m (450 ft.) from the town center, it lies at the foot of the Coniston Old Man (p. 617). Each bedroom, ranging in size from small to midsize, is decorated with flair; three are big enough for families. In the **restaurant,** main courses (£10–£14) include favorites like beef-and-ale pie and several vegetarian options.

Brow Hill (off the A593), Coniston, Cumbria LA21 8HQ. www.thesunconiston.com. ☎ **01539/441248.** Fax 01539/441219. 10 units. £95–£120 double. Rates include English breakfast. MC, V. Free parking. **Amenities:** Restaurant; bar. *In room:* TV, hair dryer.

Side Trips

The best places to visit in the South Lakes include the home of Lord and Lady Cavendish, **Holker Hall** (☎ 01539/558328; www.holker.co.uk); the **Laurel and Hardy Museum** in Ulverston (☎ 01229/582292; www.laurel-and-hardy.co.uk), and the **South Lakes Wild Animal Park** (☎ 01229/466086; www.wildanimal park.co.uk) in Dalton-on-Furness.

If you continue to the West Lakes, you can enjoy a coast-to-mountain ride on the **Ravenglass & Eskdale Railway** (☎ 01229/717171; www.ravenglass-railway. co.uk) and visit haunted **Muncaster Castle** (☎ 01229/717614; www.muncaster. co.uk), home to the World Owl Trust. Or you can head for Wasdale Head at the northern end of **Wast Water,** a popular starting point for the trek up **Scafell Pike.** Return to Coniston via the heady, winding roads of **Hardknott and Wrynose Passes.**

KESWICK & BORROWDALE ★★

294 miles NW of London; 31 miles NW of Kendal; 22 miles NW of Windermere

Keswick opens onto Derwentwater, one of the loveliest lakes in the region, and the town makes a good base for exploring the northern half of The Lake District National Park, particularly Borrowdale valley's spectacular mountain views and hiking routes.

Keswick is a busy town with a market charter dating back to the 13th century. The weekly **market** still takes place in the pedestrianized main street, which is dominated by the Moot Hall, a former assembly building now home to the tourist office. The town has several museums, including the Bond Museum and the Cumberland Pencil Museum. Above the small town is a historic stone circle thought to be some 4,000 years old.

From the town center, it's a short walk to **Friar's Crag,** the classic viewing point on Derwentwater. The walk will also take you past **Theatre by the Lake,** a professional repertory theatre, and the pier with launches that operate regular tours around the lake.

Essentials

GETTING THERE   Take a train to Windermere (see "Windermere & Bowness," earlier in this chapter) and proceed the rest of the way by bus. **Stagecoach** has a regular bus service from Windermere, Ambleside, and Grasmere (bus no. 555). If you're driving from Windermere, drive northwest on the A591.

VISITOR INFORMATION   **Keswick Tourist Information Centre,** at Moot Hall, Market Square (© **01768/772645;** www.golakes.co.uk and www.keswick. org), is open late March through late November, daily 9:30am to 5:30pm, and late November through late March, daily 9:30am to 4:30pm. The center is also the Adventure Hub of England and arranges bookings of outdoor activities for all levels of experience and ability.

Exploring the Area

From Keswick you have easy access to the pick of the peaks, including **Blencathra, Skiddaw, Helvellyn, Scafell,** and **Scafell Pike.** For something easier, try **Catbells,** on the west side of Derwentwater (see below). You can also enjoy the mountains by bicycle or car, heading through Borrowdale and stopping at **Honister Slate Mine** (see below), then down to **Buttermere** village and lake and **Crummock Water** for gentle waterfront strolls. You can return to Keswick via Whinlatter Pass (B292), which passes through **Whinlatter Forest Park.** Stop at the visitor center for gifts and lunch or cycling routes and horse riding. Kids will love the **Go Ape!** (© **0845/642215;** www.goape.co.uk) high-wire adventure that zips them from tree to tree.

One of the most scenic parts of the Lake District, the valley of **Borrowdale ★★** stretches south of Derwentwater to Seathwaite in the heart of the county. The valley is walled in by fell sides, and it's an excellent center for exploring, walking, and climbing. Many use it as a base for exploring Scafell, England's highest mountain, at 963m (3,210 ft.; see below). The southernmost village in the Borrowdale valley is Seatoller, the terminus for buses to and from Keswick. From here, head west along the B5289 through the Honister Pass and Buttermere Fell, one of the most dramatic drives in the Lake District. The road is lined with towering boulders. The lake village of Buttermere also merits a stopover for its lake-country scenery.

Bond Museum ★★ ☺ MUSEUM   This extraordinary collection of James Bond movie vehicles and memorabilia was opened by 007 aficionado Peter Nelson. He has spent years collecting movie and TV vehicles, many of which can be seen in the sister museum, **Cars of the Stars,** in the center of Keswick (© **01768/773757;** www. carsofthestars.com). The Bond collection became so vast, it required a dedicated space. Expect to see dozens of vehicles including the Aston Martin DB5 from *On Her Majesty's Secret Service* and the Russian T55 battle tank used in *Goldeneye.*

Southey Hill Trading Estate, Keswick. © **01768/775007.** www.thebondmuseum.com. Admission £6 adults, £4 children 4-16, £20 family ticket (includes brochure and photo pass). Mid–late Feb and early Apr–Oct daily 10am to 5pm.

Derwentwater ★★ ☺ CRUISE/NATURAL ATTRACTION   Just half a mile from Keswick's town center, Derwentwater is popular with walkers and other leisure seekers. The **Keswick Launch Company** operate a hop-on, hop-off circular service. You can board at Keswick and get off at Hawes End, then follow the paths leading to the summit of **Catbells,** a small fell suitable for younger and less-fit walkers. Your efforts will be rewarded with one of the most spectacular vistas in the Lake District. Either return by the same route or walk along the lake shore and then hop on boats from Low Brandlehow, High Brandlehow, Nichol End, Lodore, and Ashness. The circular route operates in both directions, but don't miss the last boat if you don't want a long hike back to town.

Keswick Launch Co., Lake Rd., Keswick. ☏ **01768/772263.** www.keswick-launch.co.uk. £9 adults, £4.50 children 5–16, £21 family ticket for hop-on, hop-off circular route (50 min.); single tickets also available. First/last boats from Keswick: Mid-late Mar and mid-late Nov clockwise daily 10am, 3pm (4pm late Mar–June and Sept–Oct; 5pm Easter holiday, July–Aug); counter-clockwise 9:45am, 3:30pm (4:30pm late Mar–June and Sept–Oct; 5:30pm July–Aug).

Honister Slate Mine ★★★ ☺ HISTORIC SITE   There are several reasons to stop at this slate mine on Honister Pass, not least being the dramatic views into the steep-sided valley below. Mine tours take visitors underground to hear about the centuries-old process of mining and splitting slate. If you're really brave, you can try the Via Ferrata, a system of cables and metal rails that allow nonclimbers a taste of traversing a rock face. The hardiest will want to opt for the zip wire, which whizzes you across a crevasse. Back at base, there's a cafe and a shop selling hand-crafted slate gifts.

Honister Pass, Borrowdale. ☏ **01768/777230.** www.honister-slate-mine.co.uk. Mine tours £9.95–£20 adults, £4.95–£20 children 15 and under, depending on tour; Via Ferrata Classic £30 adults, £20 children 10–15, £95 family ticket (2 adults and 2 children); Via Ferrata and zip wire £35 adults, £25 children 10–15, £115 family ticket; all-day pass packages available. Daily 9am–5pm; tours/Via Ferrata dependent on weather conditions.

Entertainment & Nightlife

Keswick's **Theatre by the Lake** (☏ **01768/774411;** www.theatrebythelake.co.uk) is a 400-seat theatre that produces a year-round program of drama productions. It is best to buy tickets in advance, particularly in the summer months when visitor numbers are high.

You'll find several pubs in the town center, including the **Oddfellows Arms** on Main Street (☏ **0871/2238000**) and **The Dog and Gun** on Lake Road (☏ **01768/773463**), both of which serve real ales such as Jennings and Coniston Bluebird. Farther out, try **Twa Dogs Inn** (☏ **01768/772599;** www.twadogs.co.uk), at the foot of Skiddaw mountain, a good place for a post-hike pint and a bite.

Where to Eat & Stay

At the Lakeland Pedlar ★, Bell Close, Keswick (☏ **01768/774492;** www.lake landpedlar), there's a bicycle shop (for rentals, parts, and repairs) upstairs and a veg-etarian, reasonably priced and very tasty cafe downstairs (main courses £5.50–£7.90). Options include breakfasts with vegan bacon-style rashers, homemade soups, Moroc-can chickpea tagine, Greek spinach pie, and a substantial children's menu with names they'll like ("pirate" and "musketeer"). There's a pay parking lot in front of the restaurant.

VERY EXPENSIVE

Armathwaite Hall Country House & Spa ★★ A country hotel with a rich history, it began as a house for Benedictine nuns in the 14th century, and was added to by a series of wealthy landowners until the mid-19th century. Today it is a luxury hotel surrounded by dense woodland bordering Bassenthwaite Lake. Guests arrive via a magnificent entrance hall lined with rich wood paneling. The bedrooms are handsomely furnished, with padded headboards crowning comfortable beds fitted with fine linen. Four-poster and family rooms are available. The **restaurant** serves flambéed signature dishes.

Bassenthwaite Lake (on the B5291, 7 miles northwest of Keswick, 1½ miles west of Bassenthwaite), Keswick, Cumbria CA12 4RE. www.armathwaite-hall.com. ✆ **01768/776551.** Fax 01768/776220. 43 units. £310–£330 double; £370–£420 suite. Rates include English breakfast. AE, DC, MC, V. Free parking. **Amenities:** Restaurant; bar; babysitting; health club; indoor heated pool; tennis court. *In room:* TV, hair dryer, Wi-Fi (free).

EXPENSIVE

Borrowdale Gates Hotel ★ This 1860 Victorian country house is set in one of the most favored spots of Alfred Wainwright (renowned writer of pictorial guides to the fells). Rooms range from medium to large and are decorated with rich Victorian colors and period reproductions. The cozy public areas, with their antiques and open-log fires, include four lounges, a bar, a restaurant, and dining area, all with garden views. The **restaurant** serves Cumbrian meats, but usually has a fish option too (£37 dinner for non-guests).

Grange-in-Borrowdale, Keswick, Cumbria CA12 5UQ (from Keswick, take the B5289 4 miles south to Grange; go over the bridge, and the inn sits on the right, just beyond the curve in the road). www.borrowdale-gates.com. ✆ **0845/833-2524.** Fax 01768/777254. 29 units. Sun–Thurs £120–£200 double. Rates include English breakfast. Dinner £30 extra per person. AE, MC, V. Free parking.. **Amenities:** Restaurant; bar. *In room:* TV, hair dryer.

Highfield Hotel ★ 🍴 Originally constructed in the late 1880s, two former private residences have been skillfully converted into an ample hotel with mountain and lake views. All rooms are a good size and handsomely outfitted, many with bay windows where you can soak up the view. The most magnificent is the spacious and elegant Woodford Room, with a four-poster bed and raised seating area. The elegant and award-winning **restaurant** has daily-changing menus that use the best local products, such as Cumbrian lamb.

The Heads, Keswick, Cumbria CA12 5ER. www.highfieldkeswick.co.uk. ✆ **01768/772508.** Fax 01768/780634. 19 units. £170–£220 double. Rates include breakfast and dinner. AE, MC, V. Free parking. Closed mid-Nov–mid-Feb. **Amenities:** Restaurant; bar. *In room:* TV.

Lodore Falls Hotel ★ This hotel overlooks Derwentwater and the nearby mountains. Built in traditional Lakeland slate over 200 years ago, its tradition of good rooms, food, and service continue today. The interior has been completely modernized, and the well-furnished bedrooms vary in size; it's worth opting for one of the larger ones. With a spa and beauty salon, lounge, cafe, and restaurant, the hotel is the perfect retreat after a day's walking.

Borrowdale Rd. (B5289), Borrowdale, Keswick, Cumbria CA12 5UX (on the B5289 3½ miles south of Keswick). www.lakedistricthotels.net/lodorefalls. ✆ **01768/777285.** Fax 01768/777343. 71 units. £172–£250 double; £362–£484 suite. 2-night minimum stay Sat–Sun. Rates include breakfast. MC, V. Free parking. **Amenities:** Restaurant; bar; children's playground; exercise room; 2 heated pools (1 indoor, 1 outdoor); room service; sauna; spa; tennis court. *In room:* TV, hair dryer.

Overwater Hall ★★★ 🏠 Built in the late 18th century, this is a Georgian mansion with a castellated roof added by the Victorians. All the bedrooms, though standard in size, are extremely ritzy, having been furnished with top-quality antiques. Surprisingly, this hotel permits dogs, but the hotel is so immaculate that you wouldn't know it. Guests can enjoy afternoon tea in the drawing room, and an exquisite set dinner in the **restaurant** each evening.

Overwater, Ireby (2 miles north of Bassenthwaite Lake), Cumbria CA5 1HH. www.overwaterhall.co.uk. ☎ **01768/776566.** Fax 01768/776921. 13 units. £170–£230 double. 2-night minimum stay Sat–Sun. Rates include English breakfast and dinner. MC, V. Free parking. **Amenities:** Restaurant; bar; lounge; room service. *In room:* TV, hair dryer.

MODERATE

The Pheasant ★ A former 17th-century coaching inn near the northwestern tip of Bassenthwaite Lake, this inn evokes old-fashioned English coziness. Fireplaces warm a moderately eccentric bar area, a fusion of antique and old-fashioned furniture, and individually decorated country-style bedrooms with windows overlooking forest and parkland. Two bedrooms offer sitting areas. The **restaurant** serves a fine daily menu, which can include turbot, mackerel, and sea bass.

Bassenthwaite Lake, Cockermouth, Cumbria CA13 9YE. www.the-pheasant.co.uk. ☎ **01768/776234.** Fax 01768/776002. 13 units. Mon–Fri £150–£166 double; £194 suite. Rates include breakfast. MC, V. Free parking. Located midway between Keswick and Cockermouth, signposted from the A66. **Amenities:** Restaurant; bar; room service. *In room:* TV (on request), hair dryer.

Skiddaw Hotel ☺ This hotel lies behind an impressive facade and entrance marquee built right onto the sidewalk in Keswick's market square. The owners have refurbished the interior, retaining the best features. Bedrooms are compact and eye-catching, with seven units large enough for families. The upgraded Summit rooms offer extras such as bathrobes and mineral water. Guests may use the pools and spa at Lodore Falls Hotel (see above), a 10-minute drive away, and golf at Keswick Golf Club during the week.

Main St., Market Sq., Keswick, Cumbria CA12 5BN. www.lakedistricthotels.net/skiddawhotel. ☎ **01768/772071.** Fax 01768/774850. 40 units. £154–£198 double. Rates include English breakfast. MC, V. 2-night minimum stay Sat–Sun. **Amenities:** Restaurant; bar; golf, pool, and spa nearby; room service; sauna, limited free on-site parking and free parking permits in adjacent public parking lot. *In room:* TV, hair dryer.

INEXPENSIVE

Edwardene Hotel This 1885 gray-slate house stands in a residential area, about a 3-minute walk from the town center. The three-story gabled house is well maintained with tasteful, comfortable accommodations. These rooms take their names from the Lakeland landscape—Myrtle, Bramble, Heather, Poppy, and so on. Attention to detail is paid by the hospitable owners, and guests assemble on chilly nights in the lounge by the fireplace. Cumberland sausages and free-range eggs are featured at breakfast.

26 Southey St., Keswick, Cumbria, CA12 4EF. www.edwardenehotel.com. ☎ **01768/773586.** Fax 01768/773824. 11 units. £86–£88 double; £124 family room. Rates include breakfast. MC, V. Free on-street parking. *In room:* TV, hair dryer.

Side Trips

Northwest of Keswick on the A591, **Bassenthwaite** is one of the most beautiful of Lakeland villages. It nestles on the edge of Bassenthwaite Lake, the northernmost and only true "lake" in the Lake District, visited yearly by many species of northern European migratory birds. You might also catch sight of **ospreys** at the viewpoint in **Dodd Woods,** at the eastern end of the lake. Many visitors stop at **Mirehouse** (© **01768/772287;** www.mirehouse.com), a historic house and estate with woodland playgrounds and tearooms.

You can also take the A66 from Keswick to the coastal town of **Maryport** in around 35 minutes, home to **Senhouse Roman Museum** (© **01900/816168;** www.senhousemuseum.co.uk). South along the A595 is Whitehaven, once an important port town. Follow its rise and fall at the intriguing **Beacon Museum** (© **01946/592302;** www.thebeacon-whitehaven.co.uk) in the renovated harbor and at the **Rum Story** museum on Lowther Street (© **01946/592933;** www.rumstory.co.uk).

PENRITH & ULLSWATER ★

296 miles NW of London; 26 miles E of Keswick

Set in a region of gently rolling fields and dramatic mountain rises, Ullswater is a favorite with those who enjoy spectacular natural beauty. A 9-mile expanse of water stretching from Pooley Bridge to Patterdale, **Ullswater** is the second-largest lake in the district and has always held a special attraction for artists and writers. It was on its shores that William Wordsworth saw his "host of golden daffodils." **Aira Force** waterfall, near the National Trust's Gowbarrow, inspired both Wordsworth and Coleridge with its beauty.

To the northeast of Ullswater is **Penrith.** Once capital of Cumbria, its name comes from the Celtic-derived language Cumbric and possibly means "Ford by the Hill." The namesake hill is marked today by a red-sandstone beacon and tower. Today, Penrith remains best known as a lively market town.

Essentials

GETTING THERE   Virgin Trains operates about three trains daily from London's Euston to Penrith Station, this region's main rail junction. A change of trains isn't usually necessary. One-way tickets cost from £21. Once in Penrith, passengers usually take a taxi to Ullswater.

National Express (© **0871/781-8181**) operates one daily bus that leaves from London's Victoria Coach Station at 11pm, arriving in Penrith at 5:30am. **Stagecoach** operates two buses per day that stop at Penrith on their way between Carlisle and Keswick. Passengers must take a taxi from Penrith to Ullswater.

By car, take the M1 out of London, getting on the M6 to Penrith. The trip should take no more than 6 hours.

VISITOR INFORMATION   **Penrith Tourist Information Centre,** Robinson's School, Middlegate (© **01768/867466;** www.golakes.co.uk and www.visiteden.co.uk), is open daily 10am to 4pm (closes Sun off season).

Exploring the Area

You can enjoy gentle walks to **Aira Force,** a spectacular waterfall set within National Trust-owned woodland on the edge of Ullswater (on the A592). There are also popular hikes from up to **Askham Fell and High Street,** once a Roman trade route, and to **Helvellyn** from Glenridding.

Ullswater watersports opportunities include the **Glenridding Sailing Centre** (*©* **01768/482541;** www.glenriddingsailingcentre.co.uk), which offers sailing, kayaking and canoeing tuition and boat hire. **Eden Adventure** (*©* **07525/653099;** www.edenoutdooradventures.com) also offers canoeing, along with organized hikes, rock climbing, and other outdoor activities. While using this area as a base for outdoor activities, you can also easily explore the many places of historic significance, from the times of the ancient Celts right through to modern day. One noteworthy site is **Long Meg and Her Daughters,** an ancient stone circle near Penrith.

Rheged is an all-weather entertainment venue, with a 3-D cinema, kids' craft centers, a soft play area, and an outdoor wooden "Roman" fort, as well as regular art exhibitions.

The Dalemain Estate ★ HISTORIC SITE

Despite the Georgian facade that greets visitors as they arrive at the estate, the first building here was a Saxon tower. This is long gone, but the 14th-century Old Hall and the Elizabethan wings remain, including the kitchen, which transformed it into a manor house. Tours pass through Tudor passages, Clifford family portraits and knick-knacks, and grand Georgian rooms. Set on a large estate, Dalemain has a deer park and extensive gardens that are most beautiful when the spring buds bloom.

On the A592, 2 miles north of Ullswater. *©* **01768/486450.** Admission house and garden £9 adults; £8.50 seniors; free for children 15 and under; garden only £6 adults and seniors. Late Mar–late Oct Sun–Thurs tearooms, garden, and gift shop 10:30am–5pm; house 11:30am–4pm. Late Oct–mid-Dec tearoom and gardens only Sun–Thurs 11am–4pm; house closed Nov–late Mar; gardens & tearooms closed mid-Dec–late Mar.

Penrith Castle CASTLE

The ruined castle dates back to 1399, its construction ordered by William Strickland, then Bishop of Canterbury. For the next 70 years, the castle continued to grow in size and strength until it finally became the royal castle and frequent residence for Richard, Duke of Gloucester.

Across from the train station along Ullswater Rd. www.culture24.org.uk or www.english-heritage.org.uk. Free admission. Daily 24 hr.

Penrith & Eden Museum MUSEUM

Originally constructed in the 1500s, the museum building was turned into a poor girls' school in 1670. Today, the museum surveys the history, archeology, and geology of Penrith and the Eden Valley, which was a desert millions of years ago. Recently refurbished, it now has the addition of a short film about prehistoric Lakeland stone.

Robinson's School, Middlegate. *©* **01768/212228.** Free admission. Mon–Sat 10am–5pm (also Sun Apr–Oct 1–4:45pm).

Ullswater Steamers ★★ ☺CRUISE

The best way to take in the mountain scenery around Ullswater is on the water. Steamers operate between Pooley Bridge in the north, Howtown on the east, and Glenridding in the south. You can take a 1-hour cruise, a round-trip, or buy a one-way ticket and walk back along the east side of the lake.

The Pier House, Glenridding and Pooley Bridge. *©* **01768/482229.** www.ullswater-steamers.co.uk. Round-trip tickets £9.30–£13 adults; £4.65–£6.35 children 5–15, £25–£31 family ticket. The lower prices are for trips to Howtown. Glenridding is on the A592 at the southern end of Ullswater. Pooley Bridge is 5 miles from the M6 junction 40 to Penrith.

Shopping

Major shopping areas include the covered **Devonshire Arcade,** with its name-brand stores and boutiques; the pedestrian-only **Angel Lane** and **Little Dockray,** with an abundance of family-run specialty shops; and **Angel Square,** just south of Angel Lane. And you can buy treats and sticky gifts at **The Toffee Shop** on Brunswick Road (☎ **01768/862008;** www.thetoffeeshop.co.uk), renowned for their handmade fudge and toffees.

Cranston's on Ullswater Road (☎ **01768/868680;** www.cranstons.net) specializes in the Cumberland sausage, and you can buy them family size. Head farther out of Penrith to the **Rheged Centre** (☎ **01768/868000;** www.rheged.com), at the junction of the A66/A592, a discovery center with stores selling educational children's toys, outdoor gear, farm produce, candy, books, and locally made paper.

Entertainment & Nightlife

In Penrith itself, the **Warehouse,** Burrowgate (☎ **01768/868984**), is popular with the younger crowd for drinks and dancing. The older crowd might prefer to explore some of the village pubs around Penrith and Ullswater where there's often food as well as local brews. The **Beehive Inn** (☎ **01768/862081;** www.thebeehivepenrith. co.uk) is one of the best pubs for families with children; it has a large garden with a play area for kids, and it has a good selection of real ales and pub grub. The renovated 18th-century former coaching house, the **George and Dragon** in Clifton (☎ **01768/865381;** www.georgeanddragonclifton.co.uk) is one for foodies, serving up a range of seasonal, local produce and an impressive array of wines.

In Askham, the **Queens Head,** Lower Green (☎ **01931/712225**), is a well-estsablished Lakeland pub where you can chat to locals over a pint, while the **Pooley Bridge Inn,** Pooley Bridge, Ullswater (☎ **01768/486215;** www.pooleybridgeinn. co.uk), is a rustic country inn, restaurant, and bar where you can eat or drink beside an open fire in the winter months or head outdoors in the summer months. It has the added bonus of being by Ullswater lake. At the south end of the lake, hikers make a beeline for the **Traveller's Rest** (☎ **01768/482298**) for a well-earned pint of Jennings Cumberland Ale after descending from Helvellyn.

Where to Eat & Stay

Brackenrigg Inn ★ 🌶   Since the prices at Sharrow Bay (see below) are a bit stunning, many discerning travelers instead book into this traditional inn and **restaurant** overlooking Ullswater. Accommodations range from smaller, standard doubles to more spacious superior rooms and premium ground-floor suites. There's also a convivial bar with an open fire. Chefs specialize in the market-fresh food of Cumbria, "but without all the fuss." The succulent lamb dishes are some of the best in the area.

Watermillock (on the A592), Cumbria CA11 OJN. www.brackenrigginn.co.uk. ☎ **01768/486206.** Fax 01768/486945. 17 units. £80–£140. Discount for children 3–16 staying in parent's room. Rates include breakfast. MC, V. Free parking. **Amenities:** Restaurant; bar. *In room:* TV.

George Hotel   A 300-year-old coaching inn built in the heart of town, this hotel welcomed Bonnie Prince Charlie in 1745. The front looks out onto Penrith's main street, full of small specialty shops. The guest rooms, spread over three floors, are individually decorated with light colors and up-to-date furnishings. The owners have upgraded all the bedrooms. The **Devonshire Restaurant** is a relaxed place to dine with a varied menu of fish, meat, and vegetarian options.

Devonshire St., Penrith, Cumbria CA11 7SU. www.lakedistricthotels.net/georgehotel. ✆ **01768/862696.** Fax 01768/868223. 34 units. £118–£152 double; £194 suite. Rates include Cumbrian breakfast. 2-night minimum stay Sat–Sun. MC, V. Free parking. Restaurant opens daily noon–2:30pm and 6–9pm. Reservations recommended. **Amenities:** Restaurant; bar; free use of nearby gym and indoor pool; room service. *In room:* TV, hair dryer.

North Lakes Hotel & Spas ★ ☺ The exterior of this hotel may lack character, but you'll find compensation inside. Rooms are bright and spacious, decorated with classic wood furniture, large couches, and soft pastel hues. Six rooms are large enough for families, and some have bunkbeds. Guests enjoy an inviting lobby sitting area with a huge stone fireplace and a grand barn-style, open ceiling with rustic beams.

Ullswater Rd., Penrith, Cumbria CA11 8QT. www.northlakeshotel.com. ✆ **01768/868111.** Fax 01768/868291. 84 units. £105–£132 double. Children 15 and under stay free in parent's room. English breakfast £12 per person; £4–£8 per child. AE, DC, MC, V. Free parking. **Amenities:** Restaurant; bar; babysitting; health club; 2 pools; room service; sauna; spa; 2 squash courts; steam room. *In room:* TV, hair dryer, Wi-Fi (free).

Sharrow Bay Country House Hotel ★★★ This was Britain's first country-house hotel, converted in the early 1950s into one of England's finest dining establishments. Sitting on 4.8 hectares (12 acres), the hotel offers 26 antiques-filled bedrooms, 17 of them in the gatehouse and cottages. Each is individually decorated and named after one or another of the glamorous (and often famous) women who have swept in and out of the lives of the articulate owners. Some of the rooms offer views of the lakes, trees, or Martindale Fells.

Howtown Rd., Ullswater, near Penrith (on Howtown Rd., 2 miles south of Pooley Bridge), Cumbria CA10 2LZ. www.sharrowbay.co.uk. ✆ **01768/486301.** Fax 01768/486349. 26 units. £280–£540 double; £430–£800 suite for 2. Rates include half-board. 2-night minimum stay Sat–Sun. AE, DC, MC, V. Free parking. **Amenities:** Restaurant; bar; 2 lounges; room service. *In room:* TV, hair dryer, minibar.

YORKSHIRE & THE NORTHEAST

by Rhonda Carrier

Roman relics, cathedrals, abbeys, castles, stately homes, museums, and literary shrines are just some of the attractions on offer in Yorkshire and the more northern regions of County Durham, Newcastle, and Gateshead (in the county of Tyne & Wear), and Northumberland. Leeds and Newcastle have embraced their industrial heritage while simultaneously transforming into cutting-edge modern cities. Together with richly historic York, they are also jumping-off points for those wanting to explore the wild and remote beauty that characterizes both the interior of the northeast of England and its incredible shoreline.

CITIES A thoroughly modern British city reawakening from a long slumber, **Newcastle** is as hip and happening a destination as you'll find anywhere in the U.K., with a reputation for its shopping and nightlife but also a whole array of cutting-edge museums such as Centre for Life and Discovery Museum, galleries, and other sights.

COUNTRYSIDE The **Yorkshire Dales** is justly revered by walkers. **Malhamdale**—praised by Wordsworth and painted by Turner—is a highpoint, especially its circular trail taking in Malham Cove, Malham Tarn (the lake—Britain's highest—that inspired Charles Kingsley's *The Water Babies*), and Gordale Scar. Or head for the **Aysgarth Falls,** where several waterfalls tumble in a scenic series.

EATING & DRINKING Foodies will find gastronomic contentment all over the Northeast, where many excellent restaurants and pubs use **local produce** to stunning effect. But don't miss the chance to try some of Britain's best Asian food, most notably in west Yorkshire, where Bradford and Leeds both offer **Indian restaurants** worth the trip in their own right.

COAST The double whammy of Northumberland's **Alnwick Castle,** which doubled as "Hogwarts" in two Harry Potter movies and hosts lots of medieval-themed events, and **The Alnwick Garden,** one of the world's most exciting contemporary (but also family-friendly) gardens, makes the town of Alnwick much more than just a base for those exploring the Northumberland coast a few minutes' drive away.

Yorkshire & Northumbria

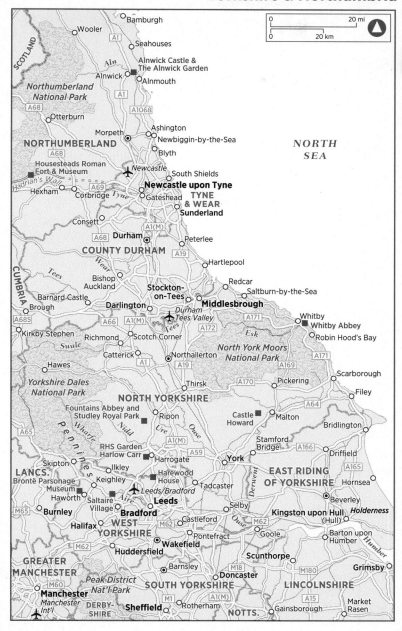

SCOTLAND

Bamburgh
Wooler
A1
Seahouses
Alnwick Castle &
The Alnwick Garden
Aln
Alnwick
Alnmouth

Northumberland
National Park
A1
A68
A1068
Otterburn
Ashington
Morpeth
Newbiggin-by-the-Sea
NORTHUMBERLAND
Blyth

A68
Housesteads Roman
Fort & Museum
Newcastle
South Shields
Hadrian's Wall
A69
Hexham
Corbridge
Tyne
Gateshead
Newcastle upon Tyne
TYNE
& WEAR
Sunderland

Consett
A1(M)
A68
Durham
Peterlee
COUNTY DURHAM
A19
Wear
Hartlepool

CUMBRIA
Tees
Bishop
Auckland
Redcar
Stockton-
on-Tees
Saltburn-by-the-Sea
Barnard Castle
Darlington
Middlesbrough
Brough
A685
A66
A1(M)
Durham
Tees Valley
A171
Whitby
Kirkby Stephen
Richmond
Scotch Corner
Tees
A172
Whitby Abbey
Swale
Catterick
Northallerton
Esk
Robin Hood's Bay
Hawes
A1
A19
North York Moors
National Park
A169
Scarborough
Yorkshire Dales
National Park
Thirsk
A170
Pickering
Filey

NORTH YORKSHIRE
Fountains Abbey and
Studley Royal Park
Ripon
Castle
Howard
Malton
A64
Bridlington
A65
Wharfe
Nidd
Ure
A1(M)
Stamford
Bridge
A166
Driffield
RHS Garden
Harlow Carr
Harrogate
A59
York
A165
Skipton
Ilkley
Harewood
House
EAST RIDING
OF YORKSHIRE
Brontë Parsonage
Museum
Keighley
Tadcaster
Hornsea
Haworth
Saltaire
Village
Leeds/Bradford
Aire
Derwent
Beverley
M65
Burnley
Bradford
Leeds
Selby
Holderness
Halifax
WEST
YORKSHIRE
Castleford
M62
M62
Kingston upon Hull
(Hull)
Barton upon
Humber
Wakefield
Pontefract
Goole
Humber
M62
Huddersfield
Scunthorpe
GREATER
MANCHESTER
Barnsley
M18
M180
Grimsby
M60
Peak District
Nat'l Park
SOUTH YORKSHIRE
Doncaster
LINCOLNSHIRE
Manchester
M1
A1(M)
A15
Market
Rasen
Manchester
Int'l
DERBY-
SHIRE
Sheffield
Rotherham
NOTTS.
Gainsborough

NORTH
SEA

LANCS.

0 ———— 20 mi
0 ———— 20 km

THE best TRAVEL EXPERIENCES IN YORKSHIRE & THE NORTHEAST

- o **Re-living horrible history:** One of the finest U.K. city-break destinations, York offers up many fascinating layers of a long history: Roman, Saxon, Danish, Norman, medieval, Georgian, and Victorian. The Jorvik Viking Centre takes visitors back to A.D. 975, while the mighty Minster melds architectural elements from different centuries as well as concealing Roman remnants in its Undercroft. See p. 642.

- o **Going all "Twilight" in Whitby:** Watched over by the ruins of its abbey, inspiration for Bram Stoker, the former whaling and smuggling port of Whitby is an atmospheric base for exploring a coastline along which wild, windswept bays rub shoulders with traditional family resorts. See p. 648.

- o **Pondering time at The Living Museum of the North:** The medieval cathedral city of Durham, a UNESCO World Heritage site with more than 600 listed buildings, is a delight to wander around as well as being ideally placed for exploring the glorious North Pennines and learning about local life at the re-created 19th-century pit village of Beamish. See p. 658.

- o **Walking Hadrian's Wall:** The most dramatic sections of one of the world's most famous Roman structures can be viewed by following parts of the Hadrian's Wall Path, while dramatic relics along its courses include the Housesteads Roman Fort and Roman Vindolanda. See p. 669.

- o **Being King of the Castle:** A contender for the title of Britain's most stupendous castle, Bamburgh Castle lords it over a wave-battered coastline rich in wildlife and dramatic history. See p. 670.

WEST YORKSHIRE

Leeds: 194 miles N of London; 218 miles S of Edinburgh

Long dismissed for its industrial blight, **Leeds,** Yorkshire's largest city, has moved forward dramatically over the past 2 decades, with many of its great Georgian and Victorian buildings renovated and complemented by attractive new architecture, and a growing reputation for shopping and nightlife. The large student population, multicultural communities, and gay-friendly vibe keep things fresh and continually evolving. In nearby **Bradford,** high-tech firms, art galleries, museums, and mill shops have displaced many of the textile factories that drew immigrants to work the mills from the mid-19th century, yet it's precisely these generations of Irish, German, Italian, eastern European, Asian, and African-Caribbean immigrants who give the city its distinctive flavor today. West of Bradford lies the literary pilgrimage site of Howarth, once home to the Brontë family, and lesser-known Heptonstall and Hardcastle Crags, the one-time home to poets Ted Hughes and Sylvia Plath.

Essentials

GETTING THERE Frequent **trains** from London's King's Cross to Leeds take about 2½ hours; most are direct (costing around £88 for a round-trip). You usually need to change at Leeds to reach Bradford—the onward journey takes about 20 minutes. Leeds is just 25 minutes from York (p. 642) by direct rail link; there are also direct trains to Leeds from Manchester (p. 562), taking a little under an hour, and from Birmingham (p. 466), taking about 2 hours.

National Express buses (✆ **0871/781-8181;** www.nationalexpress.com) from London to Leeds take about 4¼ hours.

Leeds is easily accessible by road from the rest of the country as it's at the cross-roads of the north–south M1 and the east–west M62. Leeds to Haworth by road is about 25 miles (45 min.), though Haworth is most idyllically accessed via the scenic **Keighley & Worth Valley Railway** (www.kwvr.co.uk), which runs steam and heritage diesel trains on weekends and some weekdays. The starting point, Keighley, is 25 minutes from Leeds by standard rail. There are also buses from Keighley to Haworth (www.keighleybus.co.uk).

VISITOR INFORMATION **Leeds Visitor Centre,** The Arcade, Leeds City Train Station (✆ **0113/242-5242;** www.visitleeds.co.uk), is open Monday 10am to 5:30pm; Tuesday to Saturday 9am to 5:30pm; and Sunday 10am to 4pm.

Bradford Visitor Information Centre, City Hall (✆ **01274/433-678;** www. visitbradford.com), is open Monday 10am to 5pm, and Tuesday to Saturday 9:30am to 5pm.

Haworth Visitor Information Centre, 2–4 West Lane (✆ **01535/647-721;** www.visitbradford.com/bronte-country), is open daily 10am–5pm.

Hebden Bridge Visitor and Canal Centre, Butlers Wharf, New Road (✆ **01422/ 843-831;** www.hebdenbridge.co.uk), is open Monday to Friday 9:30am to 5:30pm; Saturday 10:15am to 5pm; and Sunday 10:30am to 5pm.

SPECIAL EVENTS Leeds is a great place for big music events, with **Opera in the Park** followed by the poppy **Party in the Park** in the grounds of Temple Newsam each July, then the rock-heavy **Leeds Festival** in Branham Park in August. The **Leeds International Concert Season** comprises 200-plus concerts in and around the city year-round, some by national and international orchestras in the stunning Victorian Town Hall on Saturday nights. Film buffs flock to Bradford in March, when the National Media Museum hosts the annual **Bradford Film Festival,** attracting, to date, such big-screen luminaries as Lord Attenborough, Anthony Minghella, and Alan Parker.

Exploring the Area

LEEDS ★

The Romans set up a small camp called Cambodunum on this spot nearly 2,000 years ago, but the next step toward modern Leeds didn't come until the 7th century, when Northumbrian King Edwin established a residence here. In 1152, **Kirkstall Abbey** (✆ **0113/2305492;** www.leeds.gov.uk/kirkstallabbey)—now one of the best preserved Cistercian monasteries in the country—was formed, and in 1207 Leeds finally obtained its charter. Industrial advances played a great role in the city's growth, strengthening its position as the focus of the cloth trade in the region, and allowing for the development of the coalfields to the south with the introduction of steam power along with such upstart industries as printing, tailoring, and engineering. The Victorian era saw the glory days of Leeds, which has a surprisingly compact and walkable center. At its heart lie two free treats for art-lovers. The **Henry Moore Institute,** 74 The Headrow (✆ **0113/246-7467;** www.henry-moore.org/hmi), one of the largest sculpture galleries in Europe, was named after the greatest British sculptor of the 20th century, who was born in nearby Castleford and studied in Leeds. It hosts changing exhibitions on historical and contemporary sculpture; opening times are Thursday to Tuesday 10am to 5:30pm; Wednesday 10am to 9pm. Linked to it via a walkway, the **Leeds Art Gallery ★ (0113/247-8256;** www.leeds.gov.uk/artgallery) has one of the best 20th-century British sculpture and painting collections outside London, including more Moore, plus some Hepworth, Calder, and Bacon. Contemporary British art, including Anthony Gormley and Bridget Riley, is also a strong point. It's open Monday, Tuesday and Thursday to Saturday 10am to 5pm; Wednesday noon to 5pm; and Sunday 1 to 5pm.

Just east, on Millennium Square, the **Leeds City Museum ★ (℃ 0113/224-3732;** www.leeds.gov.uk/citymuseum), also free to visit, opened in 2008 with four floors of interactive galleries. Of most interest are the displays on the city itself: The Leeds Story, showing how it has been shaped by its landscape, people, fashion, housing, music, sport, and even shopping; and the Leeds Arena, with a giant map of the city you can walk on to discover its places of interest and different communities. There are also galleries on Ancient Worlds, Life on Earth, and the spread of African cultures across the globe. It's open Tuesday, Wednesday, and Friday 10am to 5pm; Thursday 11am to 5pm; Saturday and Sunday 11am to 5pm, plus bank holidays. A short walk away, the Clarence Dock is another 2008 development, this time of riverside cafes, restaurants, shops, apartments, and the **Royal Armouries Museum** (see below).

Another must-see with kids, 2 miles northeast of the center by St. James's Hospital (with direct buses), the **Thackray Museum (℃ 0113/244-4343;** www.thackray museum.org) tells the history of medicine from a child-friendly perspective: Galleries include Having a Baby, with an "empathy belly" to try on. Entry is £7 for adults, £5 for children 5 to 16; it's open daily 10am to 5pm.

Harewood House ★★ ☺ HISTORIC SITE Resplendent amid stunning Capability Brown gardens with terraces and lakeside and woodland walks, and with a famous Bird Garden with native and exotic species, this 18th-century residence, home to the 7th Earl and Countess of Harewood, boasts a fine Adam interior with superb ceilings and plasterwork, furniture by Thomas Chippendale, and works by Turner and other major British artists. A dressing-up box gets kids interested; also on-site is an adventure playground, an indoor play area, activity trails, planetarium star shows, a candy shop and ice-cream parlor, and a fish-and-chip shop.

Harewood, 8½ miles north of Leeds on the road to Harrogate. ℃ **0113/218-1010.** www.harewood.org. Admission varies by season and what you visit; standard high-season Freedom ticket giving access to everything £13 adults, £40 for a family of up to 5. Garden, grounds, and playground Apr–Oct daily 10am–6pm; see website for house, Bird Garden, and so on, and also for early-season (mid-Feb–Mar) and Christmas opening times.

Royal Armouries Museum ★★ ☺ MUSEUM The U.K.'s national museum of arms, armor, and artillery counts among its dastardly delights some of Henry VIII's armor, various experimental pistols, and weaponry from some of the world's biggest conflicts. It's best to time your visit to catch some of the thrilling activities and events: Drama and combat interpretations in the galleries or outside in the amphitheatre, horse shows with jousting, stable tours, falconry displays, and sword sessions (for ages 10–16). There's also a play area for those 10 and under and a History in Action family show in the cinema.

Armouries Dr., Leeds. ℃ **0113/220-1999.** www.armouries.org.uk. Free admission (charges for some shows and activities). Daily 10am–5pm.

Leeds

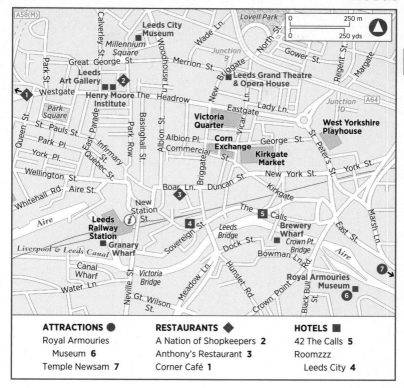

ATTRACTIONS ●
Royal Armouries
Museum **6**
Temple Newsam **7**

RESTAURANTS ◆
A Nation of Shopkeepers **2**
Anthony's Restaurant **3**
Corner Café **1**

HOTELS ■
42 The Calls **5**
Roomzzz
Leeds City **4**

Temple Newsam ★ ☺ HISTORIC SITE Birthplace, in 1545, of the ill-fated Lord Darnley, husband of Mary, Queen of Scots, this grand residence was begun in 1521 but largely remodeled in the 17th and 18th centuries. Nestled in vast woodland, farmland, and Capability Brown-designed parkland, it's another good spot for a family day out, with priceless works of art and period furniture within, plus Europe's largest working rare breeds farm, a tearoom, and an ice-cream shop on sunny days.

Off Selby Rd., Leeds. ℂ **0113/264-5535.** www.leeds.gov.uk/templenewsam. Admission house and farm £5.75, £3.50 children 5–16. House Tues–Sun 10:30am–5:30pm (to 4pm in winter); farm opens 30 min. earlier.

BRADFORD, BRONTË COUNTRY & AROUND ★

Demonized by Bill Bryson in his *Notes from a Small Island* ("Nowhere on my trip around Britain would I see a more depressing city"), Bradford, a Saxon settlement that grew into the world's wool capital, can be bleak but merits a day's attention if you're in the area. Aside its great multi-ethnic eating scene (see below)—Bryson concedes that the city has "a thousand excellent Indian restaurants"—Bradford's industrial heritage is the big draw, at the **Bradford Industrial Museum and Horses at Work** and at **Saltaire Village** (see below). Otherwise, in central Bradford, the

National Media Museum (© 0844/856-3797; www.nationalmediamuseum.org. uk) captures the history of photography, film, and TV over eight floors of interactive and traditional galleries and through activities including animation workshops, sleepovers, and IMAX screenings. Open Tuesday to Sunday 10am to 6pm, plus bank-holiday and school-holiday Mondays, it's free (but there are charges for the IMAX cinema and for most activities). The city also has a small but thought-provoking **Peace Museum,** 10 Piece Hall Yard (© **01274/434009;** www.peacemuseum.org.uk), and two modest art galleries, **Bradford 1,** Centenary Square (© **01274/437800**), and **Cartwright Hall,** Lister Park (© **01274/431212**). Since 2008 the latter has devoted its upper galleries to Connect, a permanent exhibition about the links between works of art from different cultures and times. Admission is free; opening hours are Tuesday to Saturday 10am to 5pm, Sunday 1 to 5pm, plus bank holidays.

Before venturing west into Brontë territory, families might want to hop 8½ miles southwest to **Halifax,** home to **Eureka! The National Children's Museum** (© **01422/330069;** www.eureka.org.uk), with six interactive galleries. Tickets (£9.95 adults, £3.45 children 1–2) give repeated access for a year; it's open 10am to 4pm Tuesday to Friday and 10am to 5pm Saturday and Sunday (daily in school holidays).

Just west of Halifax, **Hebden Bridge** has numerous claims to fame: It has the highest number of lesbians per head in the U.K., was awarded Fair Trade Zone status in 2003, and was named the world's fourth quirkiest place to live by the British Air-ways magazine in 2005, having built up a population of writers, musicians, artists, photographers, alternative practitioners, and green and New Age activists since the 1970s. American poet Sylvia Plath is buried in the adjoining hilltop village of **Hep-tonstall,** near the parents and uncle of her husband Ted Hughes, born in neighbor-ing Mytholmroyd. Hughes's former house in Hepstonstall is now a residential writing center (www.arvonfoundation.org).

Plath's collection *The Colossus* includes a poem about the beautiful valley of **Hard-castle Crags** (© **01422/844518;** www.nationaltrust.org.uk) to the north of Hed-ben Bridge. Described by the poet as "absolute as the ancient world," this landscape offers miles of woodland walks past streams and waterfalls (pick up trail maps in the new sustainably built visitor center in an old cotton mill).

Bradford Industrial Museum & Horses at Work ★ MUSEUM

Outside the city center at Eccleshill, this venue depicts how mill life was for local workers and owners in the 1870s, through permanent displays and daily demonstrations, includ-ing steam demonstrations on Wednesdays. Sometimes you'll also be able to watch displays by the museum's own horses, unless they're out working on the streets of Bradford or shooting for TV or a movie.

Moorside Mills, Moorside Rd. (9 miles west of Bradford), Eccleshill. © **01274/435900.** www.bradford museums.org. Free admission. Tues–Fri 10am–5pm, Sat–Sun 11am–4pm.

Brontë Parsonage Museum ★ MUSEUM

This stone-sided parsonage near the top of the village of Haworth west of Bradford contains the Brontë family's furniture, personal treasures, correspondence, pictures, books, and manuscripts, bearing testa-ment to their residence here from 1820 to 1861—during which time Charlotte wrote *Jane Eyre*, Emily wrote *Wuthering Heights*, and Anne wrote *The Tenant of Wildfell Hall*. The Brontës' father, Patrick, was perpetual curator of the Church of St. Michael, where Charlotte and Emily are now buried in the family vault. ***Insider tip:***

Avoid visiting in July and August, when the museum gets very crowded. For steam trains to Haworth station, see p. 633.

Church St., Haworth. 📞 **01535/642323.** www.bronte.org.uk. Admission £6.80, £3.60 children 5-15. Apr–Sept daily 10am–5:30pm, Dec, Feb–Mar 10am–5pm.

Saltaire Village ★★ HISTORIC SITE   Reprising the themes of the Bradford Industrial Museum, this UNESCO World Heritage site comprises a restored model factory-community that was developed in the mid-19th century by mill owner and philanthropist Sir Titus Salt. It remains a working village; besides simply strolling around to look at the well-preserved Victorian Italianate architecture, you can visit **Salts Mill** (www.saltsmill.org.uk), which has a local history exhibition and various galleries (one showcasing works by Bradford-born and educated painter and print-maker David Hockney), eateries, and shops.

About 4 miles northwest of Bradford (Salts Mill parking lot is on Victoria St.). 📞 **01274/531163.** www.saltairevillage.info. Free admission. Open all the time (Salts Mill Mon–Fri 10am–5:30pm, Sat–Sun 10am–6pm).

Where to Eat
VERY EXPENSIVE

Anthony's Restaurant ★★ MODERN BRITISH   Fans of Heston Blumenthal's experimental "molecular gastronomy" will want to make a beeline for Tony Flinn's Leeds eatery, where cutting-edge creations by the Brit chef who worked at Spain's legendary El Bulli include the likes of risotto of white onion with espresso and "Parmesan air," venison loin carpaccio with prawn and cocoa jelly, and a dessert of smoked chocolate with salted peanuts and milk jelly. It's not for the fainthearted, from a culinary or a financial standpoint, but three courses at lunch can be had for a bargain £24. Or head for the newer **Piazza by Anthony** in the Corn Exchange, incorporating a larger and less expensive all-day restaurant, an informal cantina, a champagne bar, a bakery, a patisserie, and a chocolaterie, as well as a cheese and artisan-food shop. There's also a second patisserie, serving lunches, at Queen Victoria Street in the Victoria Quarter.

19 Boar Lane, Leeds. 📞 **0113/245-5922.** www.anthonysrestaurant.co.uk. Reservations required. £36 a la carte 2 courses, £45 3 courses. AE, DC, MC, V. Tues–Thurs noon–2pm and 7–9pm, Fri–Sat 7–10pm.

EXPENSIVE

The **Fourth Floor Café** at Leeds department store Harvey Nichols (p. 638) makes good use of local meat, game, and vegetables in its modern British cooking; or try the **Brasserie** in Malmaison hotel (p. 665) for similar fare. For **Weaver's** in Howarth, see p. 640.

MODERATE

Leeds has branches of **Sam's Chop House,** and **Red Chilli** (p. 650). The latter is in the Electric Press building (www.electricpressuk.com) along with various other bars and eateries.

Corner Café ★ INDIAN   It's worth the 15-minute walk from the center of Leeds to sample the curries at this much-loved joint, one of the city's longest-standing Indian eateries. It attracts loyal locals with its fresh-tasting, generously proportioned curries, including excellent vegetarian options and weekend specials. Standouts are the fish pakora, king-prawn shimla, and eggplant and mushroom korma, but leave room for the homemade kulfis in weird but wonderful flavors including licorice and fennel. There's also a selection of beers from local micro-breweries. Takeout food is available at a 15% reduction.

104 Burley Rd., Leeds. ℂ **0113/234-6677.** www.wix.com/kateghaurimoore/cornercafe. Reservations recommended. Main courses £6.95–£9.95. DC, MC, V. Tues–Sat 6–10:30pm.

Fleece Inn & Restaurant ★ TRADITIONAL BRITISH   This super-cozy pub and B&B on the cobbled main street of Howarth counts Branwell Brontë—brother to the famous writers—among its former patrons. You can still rely on it for a true Yorkshire welcome in the company of locals supping award-winning regional cask ales in the stone-flagged bar with its open fire. The relaxed restaurant area is the place to enjoy simple, hearty dishes such as pan-fried bacon and black pudding with apple sauce, or giant Yorkshire pudding filled with sausage, creamy mash, and onion gravy, and splendidly calorific desserts including moist ginger pudding. There's a good-value kids' menu (£4.95 for a main course), a rooftop beer garden with scenic views, and live entertainment most weekends. **Bedrooms** (£65–£85), all en suite, are clean and handsomely furnished with local pine furniture.

7 Main St., Haworth. ℂ **01535/642-172.** www.fleece-inn.co.uk. Reservations recommended. Main courses £7.35–£12. MC, V. Mon–Fri noon–3pm and 5–9pm; Sat 10am–8pm; Sun 10–6pm.

INEXPENSIVE

A Nation of Shopkeepers ★ INTERNATIONAL   This bohemian bar/restaurant in central Leeds offers good-value eats amid thrift-store decor and twinkling fairylights. A wide range of tastes/moods are catered for on the menu with its traditional and veggie breakfast fry-ups, snacky sharing platters featuring the likes of shrimp popcorn and lemon-chicken skewers, globally inspired sandwiches and salads, and comfort-food classics (macaroni and cheese; local pies with mash, peas, and gravy; beer-battered fish and chips; and handmade "Boutique Burgers" in sourdough buns). Sundays see roasts, music, board games, and free newspapers. A courtyard with heaters lets you sit outside in most weather. Late evenings see DJs, while music quizzes, arts and crafts, and the like keep things lively.

27-37 Cookridge St., Leeds. ℂ **0113/2031-831.** www.anationofshopkeepers.com. Main courses £3.50–£9.50. MC, V. Sun–Thurs noon–10pm, Fri–Sat noon–9pm.

Karachi ★★ PAKISTANI   Selected by chef Rick Stein, in his "Food Heroes" TV series, as the best curry house in all Yorkshire, and held by some to be the best in the U.K., this Bradford canteen has for several decades been making up in flavor (and great value) what it lacks in chic. Pass over the gimmicky (meatball curry, kebab sandwiches) in favor of tried-and-tested classics including an incredible chicken jalfrezi, lamb karahi, and—Stein's favorite, now a signature dish—chicken-and-spinach karahi. Service is brusque, decor shabby, and the location unprepossessing, but with food like this (overseen by the same head chef for more than 35 years), you really won't care. Bring your own alcohol, and ask for cutlery if you need it—most customers scoop their curries with chapattis.

15-17 Neal St., Bradford. ℂ **01274/732015.** Main courses £2.90–£5.95. Mon–Thurs 11am–1am, Fri–Sat 11am–2am.

Shopping

Leeds is shopping central—many people head here to do nothing but that. On the central shopping street of **Briggate** you'll find several department and high-end fashion stores, including the first **Harvey Nichols** branch outside London

(© 0113/204-8888; www.harveynichols.com), and **Louis Vuitton** (© 0113/386-3120;** www.louisvuitton.com), plus high-street stalwarts such as **Zara** and **Topshop.** Fanning out from the top end of Briggate are the famous Victorian glass-roofed **arcades,** housing some of the city's most exclusive and quirky stores. For a full-on bohemian experience, head to **Exchange Quarter** with its cobbled streets lined with independent boutiques, trendy cafes, and piercing parlors. The Kirkgate end of **Call Lane,** a center for stylish nightlife, is fertile ground for vintage and alternative clothes. And on Vicar Lane, don't miss **Kirkgate Market** (www.leedsmarket.com), a vast traditional market held outdoors and within an imposing Edwardian building with ornamental dragons. Held daily except Sunday, it includes secondhand clothing on Mondays and a fleamarket on Thursdays. It's on this spot that Michael Marks opened his "penny bazaar" that eventually became the mighty Marks & Spencer empire.

In and around Bradford, look out for **mill shops** selling clothes made from mohair, pure wool, and other local textiles, furniture, and crafts. At Batley southeast of Bradford, Redbrick Mills houses the sole northern outpost of **Heal's** (© 01924/464918; www.heals.co.uk), selling furniture and homewares by Philippe Starck, Tom Dixon, and other design luminaries.

Offbeat Hebden Bridge is the place for arts-and-crafts galleries, secondhand bookstores, organic fair-trade delis, and the like. The **Innovation Shop and Café Bar** (© 01422/844160) offers interesting crafts and decorative items in a 17th-century mill, and the town's **farmers' market,** Lees Yard (© 01422/359034), on the first and third Sunday of the month, is great for local food and crafts.

Entertainment & Nightlife

Leeds is well known for its music and clubbing scene, whether you like rock, pop, dance, classical, opera, or jazz. The **Leeds Grand Theatre & Opera House,** New Briggate (© 0844/848-2706; www.leedsgrandtheatre.com), is an atmospheric venue with an 1878 Victorian facade; it hosts musicals and other shows in addition to performances by the highly regarded Opera North. At the other end of the spectrum, The Cockpit (www.thecockpit.co.uk) is an Indie institution with one of the best sweaty, alternative rock nights in the U.K. but also mixes up Metal, Punk, Emo, Pop, and Beats.

There's also a vast and endlessly evolving choice of bars and pubs all over the city, from high-concept to bohemian and more traditional, many of them tucked away in old railway arches. Call Lane in the Exchange Quarter is a good place to dip your toe in the water. Gay nightlife finds its focus at Lower Briggate.

Dance, theatre, and film lovers are also well catered for in Leeds. The **West Yorkshire Playhouse,** Quarry Hill (© 0113/213-7800; www.wyp.org.uk), dubbed "the national theatre of the north," has a wide repertoire, from Shakespeare to comedy and family shows. For up-to-date nightlife and cultural event listings in Leeds, see the fortnightly *Leeds Guide* (£1.50; www.leedsguide.co.uk).

Where to Stay

Leeds's **Malmaison** (p. 667; © 0113/398-1000; www.malmaison.com) occupies an old tram and bus depot on Sovereign Quay, with doubles for £109–£159. For the **Fleece Inn** in Haworth (£65–£85 double), see p. 638.

42 The Calls ★★★   On a cobbled canalside street in the heart of Leeds, this is the very essence of a great city-break hotel, with superb staff who greet guests with a complimentary glass of wine, an honesty bar, and fabulous beds. Some of the best breakfasts in the northeast (£15 English, £12 Continental) are served here, featuring local produce including a choice of 12 kinds of sausage, Whitby kippers, homemade jams and waffles, and toasted crumpets with Yorkshire ham, poached eggs, and mozzarella. The hotel occupies an 18th-century cornmill, so each room is unique: Exposed beams, brickwork, iron girders, and even former mill mechanisms all feature prominently. Some rooms have canal views. Families can make use of free cribs, extra beds (in Director's rooms), and interconnecting rooms.

42 The Calls, Leeds, West Yorkshire LS2 7EW. www.42thecalls.co.uk. ✆ **0113/244-0099.** 41 units. £150–£225 double; £285–£400 suite. AE, DC, MC, V. Parking (nearby) £15. **Amenities:** Bar; babysitting; concierge; room service (breakfast). *In room:* TV, hair dryer, Wi-Fi (free).

Rambles B&B ★★ 🎒 ☺ The most alluring option in the Hebden Bridge area, this converted stone barn 20 minutes' walk from the town itself has large grounds traversed by the Pennine Way (p. 535), making it the perfect spot for walkers. With such stunning countryside views, rooms could be an afterthought, but the hostess has created comfy, chintz-free rooms with excellent beds and bedding, flat-screen TVs, and thick fluffy towels. At press time, a King Room with an adjoining bunk room for kids was being set up, as was a stable-block for guests' horses. Scrumptious breakfasts include eggs from the hostess's own chickens and home-baked crumpets and muffins (for a £4 supplement you can get a cooked free-range breakfast, traditional or veggie). This place is a good option for those who don't have their own wheels—for a small fee you can get lifts to and from local transport hubs, restaurants, and so on.

Upper Blackshaw Royd, Blackshaw Head, Hebden Bridge, West Yorkshire HX7 7JU. www.rambles. me.uk. ✆ **07921/500-090.** 3 units. Double £50–£60. Rates include breakfast. No credit cards. Free parking. **Amenities:** Bicycle storage/washing; clothes- and boot-drying/warming facilities; honesty fridge/box; books, games, and DVDs. *In room:* TV/DVD, hair dryer, Wi-Fi (free).

Roomzzz Leeds City ★ 🍴 ☺ Claiming to combine the best features of boutique hotels and serviced apartments, this "apart-hotel" offers good facilities and high standards at an enticing price—especially for advanced purchase (rates rise as occupancy increases). There are three locations in Leeds, one in Manchester, and one in Cardiff. This, the most central one in Leeds, offers cleverly designed studios sleeping two guests, or one- or two-bedroom suites for four, all with compact kitchens with dishwashers and washer-driers. Furniture is multifunctional—in some units, desks become dining tables, for example—and some studios have little balconies. Ideal for short or longer stays, Roomzzz offers the flexibility for savvy families, for whom the Maxima Suites with their double bedroom and bunkbed room are perfect. Rates include a "Grab & Go" breakfast of fruit, fruit juice, pastries, and tea/coffee. There are other apart-hotels at **Leeds City West,** 15 minutes' walk from the center, handy for the airport, and in buzzy, student-enclave **Headingley.**

10 Swinegate, Leeds, West Yorkshire LS1 4AG. www.roomzzz.co.uk/leeds-city. ✆ **0844/499-4888.** 36 units. Standard midweek rate £88–£98 studio for 2; £106 1-bedroom suite; £118 2-bedroom suite. Rates include breakfast. AE, MC, V. Parking (nearby) £15. *In room:* Apple iMac or minicomputer/TV, hair dryer, kitchen (w/dishwasher and washer-drier), Wi-Fi (free).

Weaver's ★ This "restaurant and bar with rooms" on a cobbled street in Haworth is well worth checking into for the night—not least because staying over allows you to extend your gastronomic pleasure by partaking of a breakfast that might include a Virgin Bloody Mary; kedgeree frittatas; Pennine oatcake with melting Wensleydale cheese, mushroom, and tomato; or bangers (sausages) and onions in a bread cake.

The double, twin, and single rooms are eccentrically English in feel, with quirky wall-art and a certain junk-shop chic; the double offers views of the Brontë Parsonage Museum, village church, and moors. In the restaurant expect distinctive northern cooking featuring local ingredients: Perhaps carpaccio of seared Dales beef filet with pickled carrot, rocket, land cress, and horseradish ice cream, followed by slow-cooked shoulder of lamb, with fennel seed and coriander, masala crushed potatoes with lentils, and pan gravy.

15 West Lane, Haworth, West Yorkshire BD22 8DU. www.weaversmallhotel.co.uk. **(C)** **01535/643822.** 3 units. £90 twin; £110 double. AE, DC, MC, V. Rates include breakfast. **Amenities:** Restaurant. *In room:* TV, hair dryer.

NORTH YORKSHIRE

York: 212 miles N of London; 75 from York; 134 miles NE of Birmingham; 212 miles SE of Edinburgh

The landscape is the star of North Yorkshire, although history never takes a back seat—Romans, Anglo-Saxons, Vikings, medieval monks, kings, craftspeople, hill farmers, wool growers and mill founders all left their mark. You can see this in bewitching York, in the beguiling former spa-town of Harrogate and countryside north of it—rich in historical structures—and in the charming countryside of the Yorkshire Dales and Yorkshire Moors, both walkers' paradises studded with tranquil stone-built towns and villages. With such a stunning interior to explore, the North Yorkshire coast is often unjustly overlooked.

Essentials

GETTING THERE Frequent trains from London's King's Cross to York take just under 2 hours, costing around £88 for a round-trip. There are also direct trains to York from Manchester, Birmingham, and Edinburgh. Harrogate is just over half an hour from both York and Leeds (p. 632) by direct train.

Daily London–York **National Express** buses (**(C)** **0871/781-8181;** www.national express.com) take 5 hours and up; most require a change at Leeds (p. 633). London–Harrogate buses don't normally require a change.

York is 3½ hours north of London by road, not far off the main M1. From Manchester to York it's about 1½ hours, from Birmingham 2 hours. 20 minutes, and from Edinburgh 4 hours.

For **Leeds Bradford International Airport,** 31 miles west of York and 12 miles southwest of Harrogate (with buses to and from both). There are also direct trains to York from **Manchester International Airport** (p. 563).

By road, York–Harrogate is 22 miles (40 min.), York–Scarborough 40 miles (1 hr.). Cars are the most convenient option outside the cities, but **local buses** are better than in many areas of the U.K., especially in high season. For buses in the **Dales,** see www.dalesbus.org. The Moorsbus (www.northyorkmoors.org.uk/moorsbus) offers a similar network in the **North York Moors National Park;** there are buses into the park from York, Malton, Scarborough, Middlesbrough, Whitby, Northallerton, and Thirsk. The scenic **Esk Valley Railway** (www.eskvalleyrailway.co.uk) between Middlesbrough and Whitby also takes you into the heart of the park.

Scarborough and **Whitby** both have train stations. Scarborough is 3 to 3½ hours from London King's Cross with a change at York; Whitby is about 4¾ hours from London King's Cross with changes at both Darlington and Middlesbrough, so you're better off getting a bus from Scarborough. But the best way to arrive in Whitby is aboard the **North York Moors Railway** (www.nymr.co.uk) from Pickering, where you can relax in wood-paneled carriages pulled by historic steam engines across an otherworldly landscape.

VISITOR INFORMATION   For the many tourist information centers dotted around the Dales, see www.yorkshiredalesandharrogate.com/contactus.html. For the Moors, see www.northyorkmoors.org.uk/tourist-information-centres-290/.

York Visitor Information Centre, 1 Museum St. (✆ **01904/550099;** www.visityork.org), is open daily 9am to 5:30pm.

Harrogate Tourist Information Office, Royal Baths, Crescent Road (✆ **0845/389-3223;** www.harrogate.gov.uk), is open April to October Monday to Saturday 9am to 5:30pm, Sunday 10am to 1pm; and November to March Monday to Saturday 9am to 5pm.

Thirsk Tourist Information Centre, 49 Market Place (✆ **01845/522755;** www.yorkshire.com), is open Monday to Saturday 10am to 4pm (to 5pm in summer).

Scarborough Tourism Bureau, Town Hall, St. Nicholas Street (✆ **01723/383637;** www.yorkshire.com), is open daily 9am to 5pm.

The Moors National Park Centre, Lodge Lane, Danby, Whitby (✆ **01439/772737;** www.northyorkmoors.org.uk), is open April to October daily 10am to 5pm, mid-February to March and November and December daily 11am to 4pm, January to mid-February 11am to 4pm.

Whitby Moors and Coast Centre, Langborne Road (✆ **01723/383636,** www.yorkshire.com), is open Monday to Thursday 9am to 5pm, Friday 9am to 4:30pm.

SPECIAL EVENTS   The **Ebor Festival,** held over 4 days in August, is the highlight of the flat-racing season at the prestigious **York Racecourse** (www.yorkracecourse.co.uk). In 2012, York will host a large-scale production of the medieval **Mystery Plays** (www.yorkmysteryplays-2012.com) over 25 days in the Museum Gardens (the last full-scale production was in York Minster in 2000). In February, York also sees a 9-day **Viking Festival,** organized by Jorvik.

Harrogate's **Great Yorkshire Show** (www.greatyorkshireshow.co.uk), in early July, features cattle parades, sheep-shearing, pole-climbing, and more.

Exploring North Yorkshire

YORK ★★★

Still encircled by its 13th- and 14th-century walls, about 2½ miles long, with four gates, York is a many-layered and picturesque historical tapestry. There was a Roman York (Hadrian came this way), then a Saxon York, a Danish York, a Norman York (William the Conqueror slept here), a medieval York, a Georgian York, and a Victorian York, center of a flourishing rail empire. You can still walk the footpath of the medieval walls and explore much of the 18th-century city; the **Association of Voluntary Guides** (✆ 01904/550098; information desk in Visitor Centre; p. 633) runs free guided tours from Exchange Square (10:15am daily, plus 2:15pm and 6:45pm in summer).

Mighty **York Minster** (see below) makes the city an ecclesiastical powerhouse equaled only by Canterbury (p. 240). Steps away from it, **Treasurer's House ★,** Minster Yard (✆ 01904/624247; www.nationaltrust.org.uk), like the Minster, conceals Roman remains in its cellar—those of a road. You can also tour its 13 period rooms full of antiques, ceramics, textiles, and paintings, the Edwardian servants' attics, and the formal sunken garden. School-holiday activities and an interactive

York

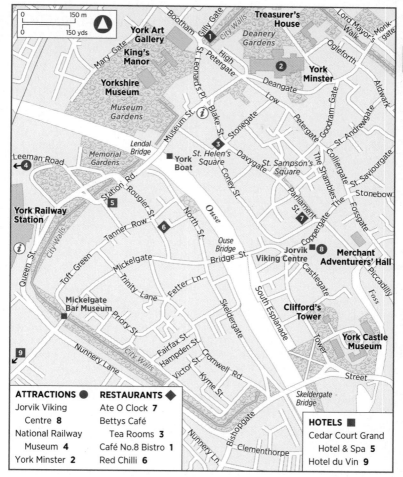

ATTRACTIONS ●
Jorvik Viking
Centre **8**
National Railway
Museum **4**
York Minster **2**

RESTAURANTS ◆
Ate O Clock **7**
Bettys Café
Tea Rooms **3**
Café No.8 Bistro **1**
Red Chilli **6**

HOTELS ■
Cedar Court Grand
Hotel & Spa **5**
Hotel du Vin **9**

exhibition and quiz make it child-friendly; there are also food events including Edwardian breakfasts. In February and November, visits are by guided tour (Sat–Thurs 11am–3pm); March to October you can explore at your own pace (Sat–Thurs 11am–4:30pm). Adults pay £6.30, children £3.10.

On Coppergate, the **Jorvik Viking Centre** (see below) offers up a reconstruction of the Viking city that once stood on the site; its nearby sister attraction, **Dig!,** gives you the chance to plunder excavation pits for clues as to how people lived in Roman, Victorian, medieval, and Victorian times, accompanied by an archeologist. There are further archeological treasures, plus rare animals, birds, and fossils, at the **Yorkshire Museum** ★ (✆ **01904/687687;** www.yorkshiremuseum.org.uk) within the city's free-to-visit botanical Museum Gardens. Opening times are generally 10am to 5pm daily; kids go free, adult tickets are £7, or £12 if you also visit the **York Castle Museum & Prison** ★, Eye of York (✆ **01904/687687;** www.yorkcastlemuseum. org.uk). Occupying the site of York Castle, this is best known for its re-creations of entire Victorian and Edwardian streets, but it also has period rooms, a collection of arms and armor, a Costume Gallery, and an exhibition on the building's former history as a gaol. It's normally open daily 9:30am to 5pm.

Over in Exhibition Square, the **York Art Gallery** (✆ **01904/687687;** www.york artgallery.org.uk) is a pleasant spot to while away an hour admiring fine paintings and ceramics, from 14th-century Italian panels and 17th-century Dutch masterpieces to 20th-century works by Yorkshire artist David Hockney. A short walk from it lies the **National Railway Museum.**

Jorvik Viking Centre ★★ ☺ ENTERTAINMENT COMPLEX   This attraction's "time capsule" takes visitors back to this spot as it would have looked in A.D. 97, warts and all: The pig sties, fishmarket, latrines, and other features, populated by animatronic figures, come complete with the requisite sounds and smells. An adjoining museum area has interactive displays, static exhibits, and costumed actors. Continual improvements—including a major refurbishment in 2010—keeps this among York's best attractions. Note that tickets allow unlimited entry for an entire year.

Coppergate, York. ✆ **01904/615505.** www.jorvik-viking-centre.co.uk. Admission £8.95 adults, £6 children 5-15; joint tickets with sister attraction Dig! (see above) £13 adults/£9.75 children 5-15. Apr-Nov daily 10am-5pm (to 4pm rest of year).

National Railway Museum ★★★ ☺ MUSEUM   The first national museum built outside London is an original steam-locomotive depot containing more than 100 locomotives, nearly 200 other items of rolling stock, and memorabilia galore that, together, trace the history of railways from the early 19th century. A simulator gives you the chance to experience the thrill of hurtling from London to Brighton at up to 765mph, while special events include the likes of a Wizard Week when you can take a steam ride pulled by "Hogwarts Castle," star of several Harry Potter films. There's also a miniature railway in the grounds.

Leeman Rd. ✆ **08448/153139.** www.nrm.org.uk. Free admission (small charges for some activities and events). Daily 10am-6pm.

York Minster ★★★ CATHEDRAL   York's superb Gothic cathedral traces its origins from the early 7th century but the present building is from the 13th century, with, like Lincoln's cathedral (p. 551), three 15th-century towers. The central tower is lantern shaped in the Perpendicular style; on a clear day the fit can climb its stone spiral staircase for panoramic views, at an extra charge. Don't miss the medieval stained glass, or, in the Undercroft beneath the central tower, the foundations of the Roman buildings where Emperor Constantine lived while he began his rise to greatness.

Chapter House St. ✆ **0844/939-0011.** www.yorkminster.org. Admission and guided tour £9 adults, free for children 15 and under; tower £5.50 adults, £3.50 children 8-16. Mon-Sat 9/9:30am-5:30pm, Sun noon-3:45pm; 60-90 min. guided tours Mon-Sat 9am-3pm.

HARROGATE & AROUND ★★★

About 22 miles west of York and 7½ miles north of Harewood House (p. 634), the enchanting Victorian spa town of **Harrogate** is most famous as home, since 1919, to the original **Bettys Café Tea Rooms** (p. 650). Prior to that, in Georgian times, it attracted European nobility and other wealthy visitors to its iron, sulfur, and common-salt rich waters, which continue to be bottled and commercially sold. Despite Dickens's damning description of it as "the queerest place with the strangest people in it leading the oddest lives!," the town continues to be considered one of the U.K.'s most desirable places to live, with for plant lovers the added bonus of the **RHS Garden Harlow Carr** (see below) on its outskirts.

Learn all about the history of the spa town in the **Royal Pump Room** (© **01423/556188;** www.harrogate.gov.uk), where you can still find Europe's strongest sulfur wells and taste their waters. Open Tuesday to Saturday 10am to 5pm, it costs £3.30 for adults, £1.90 for children. You might also visit the free **Mercer Art Gallery** (© **01423/556188;** www.harrogate.gov.uk), with mainly 19th- and 20th-century works; it's open Tuesday to Saturday 10am to 5pm, Sunday 2 to 5pm. The town's highlight, however, is its **Turkish Baths** ★★ (© **01423/556746;** www. harrogate.gov.uk), with Moorish arches and screens, glazed brickwork, arabesque painted ceilings, and terrazzo floors newly restored to their Victorian glory. Splurge on a treatment or just relax in the steam room. There are women's, men's, and mixed-session times (entry £13–£19).

Just 4 miles north of Harrogate, charming little **Ripley** ★★★ seems frozen in time. **Ripley Castle** (© **01423/770152;** www.ripleycastle.co.uk), focal point of the village, has been inhabited by the Ingilby family for 7 centuries, and Lady and St. Thomas Ingilby work hard to keep its history alive—kids' tours, for instance, bring the castle vividly to life for ages 5 to 13 through tales of Cromwell being kept at gunpoint here, wild boar hunts, and resident ghosts. Secret doors, spiral stairs up to a priest's hole, and lots of armor and weaponry add to the intrigue. Then there are the grounds, with a play trail, treasure hunt, tree-top rope course (www.logheights.co.uk), and deer park. The gardens are open daily 9am to 4:30 or 5pm, the castle for guided tours only—see the website for times and prices. The cozy **Boar's Head Hotel** (p. 654) is also owned by the Ingilbys.

Elsewhere in the village, the **Old Farmyard,** Orchard Lane (© **01423/772962;** www.theoldfarmyard.co.uk; Easter–Aug Sun and bank-holiday Mon noon–5pm), has displays of old farm machinery, animals, displays on the likes of butter- and rope-making, and horse-drawn trap rides. Adults pay £3.50, children £3. Around the corner, **Ripley Store** (© **01423/770044**), looking like something out of a movie set, stocks homemade ice cream, old-fashioned candy, and other local goodies.

Carry on up the road north from Ripley to the cathedral city of Ripon to reach Britain's largest monastic ruin, **Fountains Abbey within Studley Royal.**

Also off this main A61, this time to the east, **Newby Hall** ★ (© **0845/450-4068;** www.newbyhall.com) is an impressive 17th–18th-century house with fine Robert Adam interiors, often used as a movie location. Its fantastic Adventure Gardens were designed to include something for all ages; there's also a miniature railway through the lovely gardens, a sculpture park, a woodland discovery walk, and a farm shop. The Hall is open April to September Tuesday to Sunday (plus bank-holiday and July Mon); tickets to the hall and gardens are £12 for adults, £43 for a family of five.

Carry on to Ripon if you have a passion for ecclesiastical architecture: **Ripon Cathedral** (© **01765/603462;** www.riponcathedral.info) has one of the country's oldest Saxon crypts, sole survivor of a church founded on the site by St. Wilfrid in the 7th century, plus medieval wood-carvings thought to have inspired *Alice in Wonderland* author Lewis Carroll. Free to visit, it's open daily 8:30am to 6pm.

Fountains Abbey & Studley Royal Park ★★★ ☺ HISTORIC SITE   Founded on the banks of the Silver Skell by Cistercian monks in 1132, the dramatic ruins of Fountains Abbey now form the breathtaking focal point of the Georgian water gardens of Studeley Royal, created around the ruins in the 18th century and dotted with neoclassical statuary and follies. Together they're designated a UNESCO World Heritage site. The site also comprises a Cistercian corn mill—the last to stand in the U.K.—a medieval deer park populated by three breeds of wild deer, an exhibition on the abbey's history, and a play area and holiday activities for kids.

Ripon. ✆ **01765/608888.** www.fountainsabbey.org.uk. Admission £9 adults, £4.85 children 5-16. Abbey and water gardens daily Apr–Sept 10am–5pm, rest of year (except Fri Nov–Jan) 10am–5pm; deer park daily during daylight.

RHS Garden Harlow Carr ★★ ☺ GARDEN   This Royal Horticultural Society garden was created to complement the Yorkshire landscape of which it is a part, with the emphasis on water, stone, and woodland. Seasonal trails, a log maze, woodland dens, and observation beehives make it an unexpectedly fun place to bring kids. There's a branch of Bettys Café Tea Rooms (p. 650) on site.

Crag Lane, Harrogate. ✆ **01423/565418.** www.rhs.org.uk. Admission £8.25 adults, £3.30 children 6-16. Apr–Oct daily 9:30am–6pm (until 5pm in winter).

YORKSHIRE DALES NATIONAL PARK ★★

This National Park occupying the western half of North Yorkshire consists of some 700 sq. miles of hills and water-carved valleys filled with dramatic white-limestone crags, fields bordered by dry-stone walls, fast-flowing rivers, isolated sheep farms, and clusters of sandstone cottages. The main Dales are, in the south, **Ribblesdale, Malhamdale, Airedale, Wharfedale,** and **Nidderdale,** and in the north, **Wensleydale, Swaledale,** and **Teesdale.** Harrogate can make for a good base for exploring the park, as can **Grassington,** 26 miles northwest of Harrogate. This pretty stone-built village with its cobbled marketplace is ideal for those who wish to tour **Upper Wharfedale,** one of the most scenic parts of the Dales—the **Dales Way** footpath actually passes through the heart of the village. The **Grassington National Park Centre,** Hebden Road (✆ **01756/751690;** www.yorkshiredales.org.uk), has information and maps. Just south, **Bolton Abbey** (✆ **01756/718009;** www.boltonabbey.com) is worth a detour, with the ruined priory set in beautiful grounds with riverside, woodland, and moorland paths.

There are more National Park centers in the north near Richmond, at **Aysgarth Falls** (another scenic highlight of the Dales, with a series of waterfalls) and at **Reeth,** and then also at Malham and Hawes. **Malham,** 12 miles west of Grassington, is good for summer hiking amid some of Britain's most remarkable limestone formations. (**Insider tip:** avoid busy Jun–Aug in favor of May or Sept.) Malhamdale's scenery was extolled by no less an authority than Wordsworth, and rendered in paint by Turner. Its best walk is a circular 8-mile trail taking in scenic **Malham Cove** (a large rock amphitheatre), **Malham Tarn** (Britain's highest lake, which inspired Charles Kingsley's *The Water Babies*), and **Gordale Scar** (a deep chasm between overhanging limestone cliffs). If that's too strenuous, at least walk the 1 mile north of the village to the cove. The **Park Centre** (✆ **01969/652-380**) has maps and advice.

About 25 miles north of Malham, on the **Pennine Way National Trail** (p. 535), **Hawes** is capital of Wensleydale (of the famed cheese) and England's highest market town. In addition to a **Park Centre** (✆ **01969/666210;** www.yorkshiredales.org.uk), its old train station houses the **Dales Countryside Museum,** with displays on the local landscape and people. It's generally open daily 10am to 5pm, but call for January variations; adult tickets are £3, children go free.

NORTH YORK MOORS NATIONAL PARK ★★

To the east, the Moors, on the other side of the Vale of York from the Dales, have a wild beauty all their own, especially in summer when purple heather blooms. England's largest expanse of moorland, this is a deeply spiritual landscape dotted with early burial grounds, ancient stone crosses, and ruined abbeys. A 554-sq.-mile section of it has been preserved as a National Park popular among walkers and other lovers of the great outdoors.

If you're heading up from York, don't miss, en route to the Moors, **Castle Howard** (see below). North of it, the market town of **Pickering** is one of the gateways to the Moors, which are crisscrossed by an extensive network of public bridle and footpaths. Two noteworthy trails are **Lyke Wake Walk** (www.lykewake.org), a 40-mile east-to-west trek right across the Moors, linking the hamlets of Osmotherly and Ravenscar via the rugged path established by 18th-century coffin bearers. The more challenging **Cleveland Way** (www.nationaltrail.co.uk/ClevelandWay) follows a horseshoe-shaped line along the park's perimeter for 109 miles from Helmsley to Saltburn-by-the-Sea. Local tourist information centers have maps (see above, under "Essentials").

The delightful market town of **Helmsley** serves as a great base for exploring the Moors, with superb accommodations (see "Feversham Arms & Verbena Spa," p. 652), a ruined medieval **castle,** and easy access to the atmospheric nearby ruins of **Rievaulx Abbey** and **Byland Abbey.** See www.english-heritage.org.uk, or call ✆ **0870/333-1181** for all three sites. For local history of a different kind, head 14 miles west to the market town of **Thirsk,** famous as home to Alf Wight, vet and author (under the pseudonym James Herriot) of *All Creatures Great and Small.* His old surgery is now **The World of James Herriot,** Kirkgate (✆ **01845/524234;** www.worldofjamesherriot.org), a museum on Wight's life and on veterinary science as a whole, with an interactive gallery for kids. It's open daily April to October 10am to 5pm (11am–4pm the rest of the year); entry is £6 for adults, £4.20 children 5 to 15.

The National Park also embraces a large portion of the North Yorkshire coast, from just north of Scarborough to just past Boulby but circumventing Whitby.

Castle Howard ★★★ ☺ HISTORIC SITE This 18th-century palace designed by Sir John Vanbrugh, of Blenheim Palace (p. 226) fame, occupies dramatic grounds with lakes, fountains, gardens, and an adventure playground. Boat trips on the lake and kids' trails and quiz sheets make it a great family bet. Begun in 1699 for the 3rd Earl of Carlisle, Castle Howard has a striking facade topped by a painted and gilded dome, and, inside, a chapel with stunning 19th-century stained-glass windows by Sir Edward Burne-Jones. The many important paintings on display include a portrait of Henry VIII by Holbein and works by Rubens, Reynolds, and Gainsborough. On the grounds, the family mausoleum is by Hawksmoor.

Castle Howard. ✆ **01653/648333.** www.castlehoward.co.uk. Admission house and gardens £13 adults, £7.50 children 5–15, £34 family ticket. Apr–Oct daily 10am–5pm, plus at Christmas.

THE NORTH YORKSHIRE COAST ★★★

North Yorkshire's 45-mile coastline has an active if waning fishing industry, with some ports doubling as traditional seaside resorts. **Bridlington** and **Filey** in the south are low key, with wide, child-friendly beaches. On the chalk promontory of **Flamborough Head** between the two resorts, you can take bracing cliff-top walks to see some of the 200,000 seabirds, including puffins, that reside at the **RSPB Bempton Cliffs**

Reserve (📞 **01262/851179;** www.rspb.org.uk) from April to August. The site is open at all times; entry is £3.50 per car.

About 19 miles north of Bridlington, **Scarborough** claims to be the oldest seaside spa in Britain—supposedly located on the site of a Roman signaling station, its mineral springs with medicinal properties were discovered in 1622. Teetering on its headland are the remains of **Scarborough Castle** (see below), and south of that stretches the beach and esplanade, with souvenir stalls, amusement arcades, and fun rides set incongruously against a background of magnificent Victorian facades, some housing hotels that have sadly gone to seed. Other points of interest here are the medieval **Church of St. Mary,** final resting place of Anne Brontë, who died here after being brought from her home in Haworth in the hope that the sea air would revive her health, and, in an Italianate villa in the Crescent, **Scarborough Art Gallery** (📞 **01723/374753;** www.scarboroughartgallery.co.uk), with many works relating to this area of coastline. Costing £2 (free to children), it's open Tuesday to Sunday 10am to 5pm.

Of perhaps greatest appeal is the **Rotunda, the William Smith Museum of Geology** (📞 **01723/353665;** www.rotundamuseum.co.uk), overlooking South Bay and including a Dino Club for kids. It's £4.50 for adults (free to children 17 and under), and is open Tuesday to Sunday 10am to 5pm plus bank holidays. With kids, make sure to also ride the historic **North Bay Miniature Railway** (📞 **01723/368791;** www.nbr.org.uk), although outside high season it only runs at weekends (see the website for schedules). Single tickets are £2.40 for adults, £1.90 children 4–15.

About 19 miles up the coast, the village of **Robin Hood's Bay** was once a notorious smugglers' port (it has no link with the eponymous Nottinghamshire outlaw). Tucked into a deep ravine (don't take wheelchairs or buggies), its Lower Bay is a mix of quirky, old-fashioned shops and inns bordering a huge wild beach abounding in rock-pools. Buy fish and chips to eat on the beach or alfresco treats from Picnics on New Road, or a van parks up on the beach to sell farm ice cream, tea and coffee, and rental deckchairs.

Robin Hood's Bay is just shy of this coast's true star, the charming harbor town of **Whitby ★★★**, which began as a religious center in the 7th century, with the original Saxon monastery replaced in the 12th century by **Whitby Abbey** (see below). The town subsequently became a prominent whaling port and eventually an active smugglers' port. Among famous explorers to push off from its beaches were Captain James Cook, who as the king's surveyor circumnavigated the globe twice in ships made by local craftsmen; learn about him in the **Captain Cook Memorial Museum,** Grape Lane (📞 **01947/601900;** www.cookmuseumwhitby.co.uk), and ask at the tourist office (p. 642) about the **Captain James Cook Heritage Trail** taking in other North Yorkshire sites, including the **Captain Cook School Room Museum** (📞 **01642/724296;** www.captaincookschoolroommuseum.co.uk) inland at Great Ayton and the **Captain Cook & Staithes Heritage Centre** (📞 **01947/841454;** www.captaincookatstaithes.co.uk) up the coast from Whitby.

Scarborough Castle ★ ☺ RUINS   This impressive ruin began life as an Iron Age fort before being occupied by the Romans, the Vikings, and finally Henry II. The best time to visit is the summer holidays, when you might catch live-action events, but the awesome coast views from the expansive grounds can be appreciated year-round.

Castle Rd., Scarborough. 📞 **0870/333-1181.** www.english-heritage.org.uk. Admission £4.80 adults, £2.90 children 5-16. Apr–Sept daily 10am–6pm, Oct Mon and Thurs–Sun 10am–5pm; Nov–Mar Mon and Thurs–Sun 10am–4pm.

Whitby Abbey ★★★ ☺ RUINS   Looming ominously over the historic port from the East Cliff, this breathtaking ruin replaced a Saxon monastery that occupied the same site. Caedmon, the first identifiable English-language poet, was a monk here, and Bram Stoker was inspired by it in the writing of his *Dracula*. The excellent visitor center, which has great features for children, fills you in on this and more.

Abbey Lane, Whitby. ☎ **0870/333-1181.** www.english-heritage.org.uk. Admission £6 adults, £3.60 children 5–16. Apr–Sept daily 10am–6pm, Oct–Mar Thurs–Mon 10am–4pm.

Where to Eat
VERY EXPENSIVE

The bistros at the **Hotel du Vin** (p. 653) in both York and Harrogate are good spots for regional food with a French slant, such as roast beetroot with Yorkshire blue cheese risotto, or Pickering trout with saffron potato broth and rouille.

Café No.8 Bistro ★★ INTERNATIONAL   Ultra-handy for York Minster (p. 644), this calm little spot serves seasonal menus championing local ingredients, including Masham sausages and Ryedale ice cream, but dishes are often given an exotic twist. Chargrilled matured Wolds pave-steak with wild mushroom, fondant potato, and slow-roasted tomatoes will appeal to the traditionalist; the more adventurous may be tempted by the likes of beer-battered coconut prawns with sweet chili mayo. There's a great-value two-course weekday lunch deal, or come earlier and fill up on a breakfast or brunch that might include bubble and squeak with dry-cured bacon, poached egg, and roast cherry tomatoes, or that same bacon with Yorkshire blue cheese with sweet chili jam. In good weather, bag a table in the walled garden backing onto the city, and eat to the chime of the cathedral's bells.

8 Gillygate, York. ☎ **01904/653074.** www.cafeno8.co.uk. Reservations recommended. Main courses £9.95–£17. MC, V. Mon–Fri noon–10pm, Sat–Sun 10am–10pm.

Lanterna Ristorante ★★★ ITALIAN   Bringing together Yorkshire ingredients—black pudding and winkles, cuttlefish and other seafood gleaned during the owner's daily bike-trips to the fishmarket, vegetables from the restaurant's own allotments, and foraged items—with traditional recipes and treats from northern Italy (including white truffles and prosciutto), the Lanterna is Scarborough's culinary highlight. Amid dated but homey Piedmont decor, lucky locals including celebrities Alan Ayckbourn and David Hockney feast on the likes of homemade spaghetti with velvet crab, fillet of sea bass on a bed of sage, rosemary, and thyme, venison ravioli, and chickpea and oxtail stew, and sweet wild-nettle pudding or more familiar desserts including zabaglione made to order at the table.

33 Queen St, Scarborough. ☎ **01723/363616.** www.lanterna-ristorante.co.uk. Reservations recommended. Main courses £13–£37. MC, V. Mon–Sat 7–9:30pm. Closed 2 weeks in Oct (dates vary).

Yorke Arms ★★ MODERN BRITISH   Presided over by one of only six female Michelin-starred chefs in the U.K., this restaurant in an 18th-century coaching house and shooting lodge offers sensual cooking concocted from seasonal local produce, much of it organic. The unique dishes include Wensleydale soufflé with sea scallops, vanilla, and tomato; Whitby crab with potage of shellfish, salt cod, and tomato; Nidderdale lamb pie; beetroot sorbet and a beignet of Yorkshire blue cheese; and gooseberry peanut parfait with lemon and mint. If you struggle to choose, give yourself over to the surprise tasting menu, with eight courses paired with recommended wines. Sunday lunches are also unforgettable. On Saturdays, packages combine dinner for two with a night in one of the coolly chic **guest rooms** (rest of the week £158–£252 double). There's also a new two-bedroom cottage sleeping four. The Yorke Arms is located in a village tucked into the Nidderdale valley, 19 miles northwest of Harrogate.

Ramsgill-in-Nidderdale. ✆ **01423/755243.** www.yorke-arms.co.uk. Reservations recommended. Main courses £23–£32. AE, DC, MC, V. Mon–Sat noon–2pm and 7–9pm, Sun noon–2pm.

EXPENSIVE

York has a branch of **Red Chilli,** George Hudson Street (see p. 569 for review of Red Chilli in Manchester; ✆ **01904/733-668**).

Ate O Clock ★ INTERNATIONAL   As quirky as its name suggests, with a decor including clocks set to 8 o'clock, this laid-back restaurant on an alley in central York claims to offer Mediterrean-style dishes "with a twist of Scouse," but its influences are more international in scope. The wide-ranging menu embraces everything from sandwiches (from Yorkshire rump steak to hot smoked duck with mango chutney), omelets, risottos, burgers, and steaks, to the likes of terrine of smoked salmon with a rye bread and wasabi peanut-butter sandwich, or pork filet filled with black pudding and apple, cider-braised red cabbage, and celeriac purée. You can have lunch or pre- or post-dinner drinks or coffee on the heated patio.

13a High Ousegate, York. ✆ **01904/644080.** www.ateoclock.co.uk. Reservations recommended. Main courses £6.50–£23. MC, V. Tues–Fri noon–3pm and 6–9:30pm, Sat noon–2:30pm and 5:30–9:30pm.

Bettys Café Tea Rooms ★ ☺ ENGLISH TEA/CONTINENTAL   Don't come to Harrogate without paying at least one visit to the institution that is Bettys (if it's good enough for the Queen…). You can pre-book afternoon tea in the Imperial Room at weekends, served on silver cakestands and accompanied by a classical pianist; otherwise, you have to get in line for the pleasure of choosing from more than 300 breads, cakes, and chocolates, and about 50 teas and coffees, in the more informal cafe. Part of this, the Montpellier Café Bar, also offers all-day dining, including lunch-time open sandwiches and filled rolls, and dinner sharing plates, light meals, and main courses such as oak-smoked salmon rösti. The kids' menu bears such treats as macaroni, toasted sandwiches, and ice-cream shakes.

There are additional Tea Rooms at Harlow Carr Gardens (p. 646) and in York (two branches), Ilkley (west of Harrogate), and Northallerton (north of Thirsk).

1 Parliament St., Harrogate. ✆ **01423/814070.** www.bettys.co.uk. Reservations required (afternoon tea Sat–Sun). Main courses £8.80–£12. AE, DC, MC, V. Daily 9am–9pm.

The Magpie Café ★ ☺ SEAFOOD   Folks flock from far and wide for the tradi-tional fish and chips served in this old-fashioned restaurant on Whitby's harbor, with unforgettable views up to the famous abbey. The rest of the menu is almost a distrac-tion, but repeated visits may tempt you to investigate the offerings more fully— Whitby crab and kipper starters, sautéed local squid, seafood chowder, oysters from Lindisfarne (p. 671), or any of the daily fish specials are good starting points. Kids get a separate and almost equally vast menu. Fish and chips and many other dishes come in two sizes; order the smallest if you want any chance of tackling a dessert. Limited bookings are taken and you may have to wait for a table—if it's good weather, get a takeout and eat on the quay-side instead.

14 Pier Rd., Whitby. ✆ **01947/602058.** www.magpiecafe.co.uk. Reservations recommended. Main courses £5.95–£19. MC, V. Daily 11:30am–9pm.

MODERATE

Chaste ✦ MODERN BRITISH/INTERNATIONAL   Serving locally sourced seasonal produce in a congenial setting (think flag-stone floors, original beams, and a wood-burning stove), this is an appealing all-day option in the hiking center of Hawes, serving breakfast and morning coffee and cake through to afternoon tea and dinner. As popular with locals as with visitors for its fair prices, it's great for warming soups and tasty sharing platters for two—try The Big Cheeses, featuring four Dales cheeses served with chips and pickles. Main courses might include a pie of the day, black pudding topped with Ribblesdale goat's cheese with red-onion marmalade and raspberry dressing; or slow-roast pork belly with a creamy apple, butterbean, and thyme sauce, but vegetarians are always well catered for, and there's snackier fare including burgers, "butties" (sandwiches), and salads.

Market Place, Hawes. © **01969/667145.** www.chastehawes.co.uk. Reservations recommended (evening). Main courses £6.95–£9.50. MC, V. Tues–Sat 10am–9pm, Sun 11am–5pm.

Falling Foss Tea Garden ★★ 📷 ☺ ENGLISH TEA/SNACKS   Five miles outside Whitby, this magical venue is on the woodland grounds of a former gamekeeper's cottage and is a lovely stop-off for walkers doing the coast to coast trail. It's a great spot to bring kids, who will love exploring the ancient forest before or after a light lunch, cream tea, or ice cream. They can also paddle in the beck, play Pooh sticks on the footbridge (sticks provided), or use the wooden play area while you relax over a pot of tea. The Hermitage, a hermit's cave carved from stone, is a 5-minute walk through the trees. The homemade cakes and scones, sandwiches, and light snacks are made from mainly local ingredients. This is a garden, not a tearoom, so opening is subject to the weather, though amid the gnarled apple trees there is a yurt with a log burner.

Midge Hall, Sneaton Forest. © **07723/477929.** www.fallingfossteagarden.co.uk. Main courses £2.50–£4. No credit cards. Usually Apr–Oct daily 10:30am–5pm, but call to confirm, especially if raining.

Humble Pie and Mash ★ 📷 🍴 TRADITIONAL BRITISH   It's not all about fish and chips in Whitby—pies freshly made using free-range meat and organic pastry bring lovers of hearty old-fashioned English grub to this restored 16th-century shop with its open fire, 1940s' chintz, and soundtrack of wartime hits. Best eaten with mash, peas (garden or mushy), and liquor or gravy, the pies include slow-braised stout and leek, or Yorkshire sausage and black pudding, but also come in vegetarian incarnations, the most popular of which is Romany hommity pie with potatoes, garlic, onions, and cheese. With pie meals costing less than £5 and kids' prices for pies, sausage and mash, or sausage sandwiches, this is a great place for a budget-conscious but filling family lunch or supper. Take it easy if you're hoping to fit in one of the scrumptious desserts; jam roly poly (suet pudding with jam) is the star. Note that there's no drinks license. Takeout is available.

163 Church St., Whitby. © **07919/074954.** www.humblepienmash.com. Main courses £4.99. MC, V. Mon–Sat 12:30–8:30pm, Sun 12:30–5pm.

Shopping

York is the region's shopping highlight. Don't miss the cobbled **Shambles;** voted Britain's most picturesque street in the Google Street View awards, it's lined by wooden-framed buildings that lean so far across the narrow alley that some of their roofs almost touch. Once the city's meat-butchering center, it's now home to shops and cafes, many selling jewelry (a highlight of York shopping). York's antiques dealers tend to congregate on or around Gillygate; for independent one-off stores, try Stonegate. On the city outskirts, the **York Designer Outlet** (© **01904/682720;** www.yorkdesigneroutlet.com) has more than 100 upper-end brands under one roof, sold tax free and at up to 60% discounts.

York is also a great place to shop for food, with lots of delis and local food stores: Try **Demijohn,** 11 Museum St., (✆ **01904/637-487**), for handmade British wines, spirits, oils, and vinegars bottled to order; **Henshelwoods,** 10 Newgate (✆ **01904/673877**), for award-winning cheese; **Olio and Farina,** 3 Blake Street (✆ **01904/670885**), for Italian specialties; **The Hairy Fig,** 38–39 Fossgate (✆ **01904/677074**), for "on tap" vinegars, oils, fig vodka, and more; **The Yorkshire Food Company,** 130–134 Micklegate (✆ **01904/630497**), for local food and drink, much of it organic and fair-trade; and **The Yorkshire Pantry,** 18 High Petergate (✆ **01904/675100**), for much of the same. York also has a daily open-air **market** with more than 100 stalls.

For more foodie treats try the **Balloon Tree Farmshop and Café,** at Gate Helmsley between York and Bridlington (✆ **01759/373023;** www.theballoontree.co.uk), and, in Harrogate, the award-winning **Weeton's Farm Shop,** 23/24 West Park (✆ **01423/ 507100;** www.weetons.com) and **Fodder** (✆ **01423/546111;** www.fodderweb.co. uk), the latter based at the Great Yorkshire Showground a couple of miles from the center and unique both in that it ploughs profits back into the community and has its own 80-seat cafe. **Harrogate** is also good for boutiques and designer shops (Parliament Street and Montpellier Quarter) and independent stores (Commercial Street and around).

Entertainment & Nightlife

York is said to have a pub for every day of the year—more per square mile, some claim, than any city in the country—but unlike Leeds it's lively rather than rowdy, except around the Micklegate area (including Rougier Street). Stick to laid-back Goodramgate and the Swinegate area, where you'll find a good mix of traditional pubs and swanky bars appealing to all ages. The Coney Street area is the most upmarket. The oldest pub in town, **Ye Olde Starre Inne,** on Stonegate (✆ **01904/623063**), has a beer garden with Minster views.

Outside York, North Yorkshire tends to be quiet on the nightlife front, although there are many convivial country pubs offering folk and other live music. For culture vultures, Scarborough's **Stephen Joseph Theatre** (✆ **01723/370540;** www.sjt. uk.com) has hosted the premieres of most of the plays of award-winning playwright Alan Ayckbourn, who lives in the town.

Where to Stay
VERY EXPENSIVE

The **Yorke Arms** (p. 649), in the Nidderdale valley, has chic rooms.

Feversham Arms & Verbena Spa ★★★   This haven of luxury in a Moors market town has some suites suitable for families, but it's not the kind of place to bring energetic toddlers, for fear of disturbing the contented guests enjoying cream teas in their bathrobes by the outdoor pool (heated year-round). In any case, you'll want to install yourself in the spa—one of the U.K.'s very best, with a large chill-out area (low-lit by scented candles) and a bar and light-meals menu. The "Petite Double" rooms in the older part of the building are cozy, but once you've clocked the poolside or spa suites, you'll sell your soul to upgrade. The **restaurant** is overseen by a Michelin-starred chef, so think about a half-board option. Rievaulx Abbey is a pleasant walk away (3 miles), but you'll be loathe to leave the premises.

Helmsley, North Yorkshire YO62 5AG. www.fevershamarmshotel.com. ✆ **01439/770766.** 33 units. £180–£270 double; £340–£460 suite. Rates include Yorkshire breakfast (half-board option available). AE, DC, MC, V. Free parking. **Amenities:** Restaurant; bar; babysitting; outdoor heated pool (year-round); spa. *In room:* TV with DVD/CD player, hair dryer, Wi-Fi (free).

Swinton Park ★★★ ☺   Just 22 miles northwest of Harrogate in the heart of the Dales, this family-run home is a great base for exploring the National Park and North Yorkshire, as well as a luxurious destination in its own right. Set in a vast parkland with lakes, gardens, and deer, it offers a spa, a plush **restaurant** offering estate produce (including venison, grouse, trout, and vegetables and herbs from the walled garden), country pursuits galore (fishing, golf, and off-road driving), and a cookery school. Rooms and suites are individually designed and traditional in feel. Families are warmly welcomed, with a games/playroom, outdoor play area and games equipment (bikes, kites, and so on), kids' cookery lessons, and an on-site birds-of-prey center with daily flying displays. Family events include Easter-egg hunts and activity days. There's an excellent all-day kids' menu, and various suites with sofabeds, including the Turret Suite with circular rooms on three levels.

Masham, North Yorkshire HG4 4JH. www.swintonpark.com. ✆ **01765/680900.** 30 units. £180–£295 double; £305–£375 suite. Rates include breakfast (except for Fri–Sat night stays). AE, DC, MC, V. Free parking. **Amenities:** Restaurant; bar; babysitting; exercise room; outdoor activities; room service; spa; Wi-Fi (free, in lobby). *In room:* TV, CD player.

EXPENSIVE

Best Western Dean Court Hotel ★ ☺   Though part of a chain, this York stalwart derives some historical ambience from its occupation of a 19th-century building and its enviable location by the Minster. It's a good option for families: In addition to family rooms, it offers babysitting, toys, games, and PlayStations, a DVD library, practical items such as changing mats, and chefs who "will cook almost anything for youngsters and babies on request!" The most expensive rooms have four-poster beds, but all are comfortable, and staff are very attentive.

Duncombe Place, York, North Yorkshire YO1 7EF. www.deancourt-york.co.uk. ✆ **01904/625082.** 37 units. £140–£235 double. Rates include Yorkshire breakfast. AE, DC, MC, V. Parking £13. **Amenities:** 2 restaurants; bar; babysitting; DVD library; room service. *In room:* TV/DVD, hair dryer, Wi-Fi (free).

Cedar Court Grand Hotel & Spa ★★★   This newcomer to central York has already garnered legions of fans with its understated luxury and successful melding of historical detail (sweeping staircases, mosaic-tiled corridors) with a subtly contemporary feel. Occupying a former railway offices, it evokes, albeit obliquely, the Golden Age of travel, with the emphasis firmly on the leisure life: The **restaurant** serving classic British fare, whisky and cocktail lounge, and roof terrace for afternoon teas have lately been joined by a luscious spa and pool in the building's vaults. For the full-on sybaritic experience, check into the Penthouse Suite, which comes complete with butler service.

Station Rise, York, North Yorkshire YO1 6GD. www.cedarcourtgrand.co.uk. ✆ **01904/380038.** 107 units. £129–£399 double; £249–£1,530 suite. AE, DC, MC, V. Parking £15. **Amenities:** Restaurant; bar; babysitting; gym; indoor swimming pool; room service; spa. *In room:* TV, fridge (some), hair dryer, Wi-Fi (free).

MODERATE

In York, there's a well-reputed **Hotel du Vin,** The Mount (✆ **01904/557350**), and another (attracting more critical feedback) in Harrogate, 1 Prospect Place (✆ **01423/856800**); most rooms at both are in the moderate-to-expensive range, but some are very expensive. Both have good bistros.

There are three atmospheric stone holiday cottages, plus two luxury apartments, at **Fountains Abbey & Studley Gardens** (p. 646); cottages cost £596–£1,178 for a week's stay

Harrogate's boutique hotel eschews minimalism in favor of a more old-fashioned decadent feel, with opulent designer wallaper, French armoires, and indulgent bathrooms, in keeping with the Victorian details of the building itself. Though families are genuinely welcomed (there are two family suites and games to borrow), this is more the place to hole up with a partner, with a **restaurant** equally dedicated to hedonistic pleasures (check out the range of Valrhona chocolate desserts). You also get free entry to a nearby health spa, although the equally close Turkish baths (p. 645) offer the real deal. Rates vary widely by the day of the week/season/ local conference schedule.

Franklin Mount, North Yorkshire HG1 5EJ. www.balmoralhotel.co.uk. ✆ **01423/508208.** 23 units. £70–£170 double; £109–£190 suite. Rates include Yorkshire breakfast. **Amenities:** Restaurant; bar; free use of nearby spa; Wi-Fi (free). *In room:* TV, Wi-Fi (free, in some).

Boar's Head ★★ ☺ A cozier, more welcoming hostelry than this former coaching inn in the idyllic, film-set-like village of Ripley is hard to imagine. The decanter of sherry in your room on arrival and the vintage radios reinforce the feeling that you've stepped back in time. Divided between the main building on the village square and an annex across the road (best suited to families), rooms are old-fashioned and homey, with quirky touches such as wooden boats for the bath. Owned by the same family as the village castle (p. 645), the inn has a **formal restaurant** and a more relaxed **candlelit bistro** best suited to families; ingredients from the castle's kitchen garden are used to full effect in both.

Ripley, North Yorkshire HG3 3AY. www.boarsheadripley.co.uk. ✆ **01423/771888.** 25 units. £125–£150 double. AE, DC, MC, V. Free parking. **Amenities:** 2 restaurants; bar; DVD library, games. *In room:* TV/DVD, Wi-Fi (free).

Cropton & Keldy Forest Cabins ★★ ☺ These woodland sites in the Moors National Park are great for family breaks or holidays, with rangers' activities for a variety of ages—the likes of Forest Survival and Dusk Watch—plus forest cycle, walking, and pony-trekking trails. Accommodations are in quite plush log cabins of various sizes, some with outdoor hot tubs; the Keldy site has several with treehouse extensions housing an extra bedroom. You may have squirrels and other forest critters coming up to your terrace to say "Hi" as you relax in your hot tub. Though remote in feel, both sites are handy for day-trips to Whitby (p. 648), Scarborough (p. 648), and farther afield. Of the two, Cropton is the newest, smallest, and most peaceful site, but most rangers' activities depart from Keldy, 2 miles away, and it has better facilities, including a games room and a larger grocery. Cabin prices vary widely by time of year and length of stay (starting at 3-night weekend or 4-night weekday stays).

Near Pickering, North Yorkshire YO18 8HW. www.forestholidays.co.uk. ✆ **0845/130-8225.** 80 units. 3-night weekend stay from £192 1-bedroom cottage (Keldy Forest only); from £146 2-bedroom cabin. MC, V. Free parking. **Amenities:** Activities; bike rental; laundry facilities; forest trails; outdoor play area; shop. *In room:* TV/DVD, full kitchen, games, outdoor hot tub (some), BBQ equipment.

La Rosa Hotel ★ Super-kitsch seaside fun is offered in this Victorian building in Whitby, with to-die-for sea and abbey views and an enviable history as the place where Lewis Carroll stayed while in town (as a plaque outside attests). Decorated with fleamarket finds and vintage wallpapers, it has an *Alice in Wonderland* vibe, with Carroll's study re-imagined in the Lewis room but also nods to Bram Stoker, Angela Carter, J. M. Barrie, and everyone from cowgirls to pirates. All rooms are doubles save the attic Crow's Nest, which sleeps six and has a dressing-up box. Continental breakfast comes in a hamper delivered to your room; there's also a retro tearoom, offering free tea and coffee to guests, and a basement tapas and cocktail bar. There's no parking, so you'll have to take a chance on finding a paying spot on the street.

The owners extend their green ethos to their **campsite** 7 miles away, created using recycled, reclaimed, and found objects, with showers in a converted byre, a compost loo in a shepherds' hut, an open-air rolltop bath in the orchard, and accommodations in vintage caravans.

5 East Terrace, Whitby, North Yorkshire YO21 3HB. www.larosa.co.uk. ℰ **01947/606981.** 8 units. £86–£139 double. Rates include breakfast. MC, V. **Amenities:** Bar; tearoom. *In room:* TV, DVD (in Crow's Nest).

The Lawrance ★★ ◢   These newly opened, stylish serviced apartments in three period buildings in central Harrogate are a boon to everyone from business patrons and local convention-goers to families. Spacious and chic, they boast hand-printed wallpaper, luxurious fabrics, Philippe Starck bathrooms, superb beds and bedding, and state-of-the-art entertainment systems and kitchens. If you don't feel up to struggling out of bed to make breakfast yourself, you can order in a hamper. You can also order a "Grazing Pack" of luxury food items for your arrival, and room service is provided by a local Italian restaurant. At press time, a second Lawrance was slated to open in York.

Kings House, Kings Rd., Harrogate, North Yorkshire HG1 5JW. www.thelawrance.co.uk. ℰ **01423/503226.** 19 units. £85–£129 1-bed apartment; £129–£279 2-bed apartment. AE, MC, DC, V. Parking at most sites (free). **Amenities:** Cleaning (free every 5 days, or more often for fee); room service. *In room:* TV/DVD, MP3 docking station, kitchen.

INEXPENSIVE

There's a functional but entirely acceptable **Novotel** a 5-minute walk from the center of York, with a good swimming pool; doubles start at £69, rooms sleeping four (with a sofabed) at £85.

Knabb's Ash B&B ★★ ◢   This lovingly run guesthouse in quiet countryside 5½ miles west of Harrogate is an excellent budget base for exploring the Dales, with an amiable proprietess who goes out of her way to make you feel at home with little extras such as fluffy bathrobes and decanters of madeira wine in guest rooms. The three double rooms are prettily decorated and spankingly clean; one can be made into a twin for those with children 10 and over. The wonderful Yorkshire breakfasts, served in a bright and cheery dining room, include free-range eggs from the B&B's own hens, homemade jams, and local produce.

Skipton Rd. Felliscliffe, North Yorkshire HG3 2LT. www.knabbsash.co.uk. ℰ **01423/771-040.** 3 units. £70–£75 double. Rates include Yorkshire breakfast. No credit cards. Free parking. **Amenities:** Lounge with TV and terrace. *In room:* TV, minifridge, hair dryer, Wi-Fi (free).

COUNTY DURHAM

Durham: 270 miles N of London; 75 miles N of York; 140 miles S of Edinburgh

The countryside and coast around the famous—and exceedingly pleasant—university city of Durham don't get as many visitors as they deserve, eclipsed as they are by the close proximity of Yorkshire to the south and Northumberland to the north. The rolling hills and waterfalls of the Durham Dales in the North Pennines are particularly worthy of exploration, while the fascinating layers of local history are kept vividly alive at outstanding attractions such as the **North of England Lead Mining Museum** and **Beamish, the Living Museum of the North.**

Essentials

GETTING THERE Durham lies on the main London–York–Edinburgh rail line, with trains from London's King's Cross taking about 2¾ hours (at around £110 for a round-trip). There are also direct trains from Leeds (p. 633), Manchester (p. 562), and Birmingham (p. 466). Daily **National Express** (© **0871/781-8181;** www. nationalexpress.com) buses to Durham from London take 6 to 7½ hours. London to Durham by car is a straightforward 270-mile run up the M1, then the A1, taking you 4½ hours or more.

VISITOR INFORMATION **Durham Tourist Information Centre,** 2 Millennium Place (© **0191/384-3720;** www.thisisdurham.com), is open Monday to Saturday 9:30am to 5:30pm, Sunday and bank holidays 11am to 4pm.

  Durham Dales Centre, Castle Garden, Stanhope (© **01388/527650;** www. durhamdalescentre.co.uk), is open daily 10am–5pm.

SPECIAL EVENTS Durham's **Regatta** (www.durham-regatta.org.uk), dating back to 1834, attracts 600-plus crews to compete over a weekend in June, and also includes street theatre and a fireworks finale on the riverbanks.

Exploring the Area
DURHAM ★★

A pleasant stopover venue for those en route to Northumbria and a charming base for exploring the Durham Dales, this attractive university town is dominated by Britain's largest and best-preserved Norman stronghold, William the Conqueror's **Cathedral ★★** (© **0191/3864266;** www.durhamcathedral.co.uk). Breathtaking to view, this was the first English building with ribbed vault construction and also the first stone-roofed cathedral in Europe—this latter feature was an architectural necessity because it was not only a church and the final resting place of St. Cuthbert from nearby Lindisfarne but also "half Castle 'gainst the Scots." Within it you can see Cuthbert's shrine, cross, and coffin, plus the former monks' dorm with its hammerbeam oak roof. Young visitors are kept engaged by audio-visual displays; those over 1.3m (4 ft. 3 in.) tall can climb the tower for superb views. The cathedral's award-winning Undercroft restaurant champions local produce.

  The whole of Durham's city center is now a conservation area, home to more than 600 listed buildings. **Durham Castle** (© **0191/334-4099;** www.dur.ac.uk/university. college)—also Norman, and, like the cathedral, a UNESCO-listed World Heritage site—is now home to University College, part of the city's highly regarded university, and visitors can stay within its historic walls when the students have gone home for the holidays. There are also tours most afternoons in term time and every morning during vacations.

  Otherwise, Durham is a delightful and compact city to wander around, especially along the river (where you can boat in summertime). If you like Far Eastern and Islamic art, the **Oriental Museum** (© **0191/334-5694;** www.dur.ac.uk/oriental. museum) has an outstanding collection; its new children's trails, plus its program of family activities, means kids will enjoy it, too. If you are in the area with kids, head 6 miles outside Durham to Langley Park, where there's a **Diggerland** theme park.

DURHAM DALES, HERITAGE COAST & BEAMISH ★

Though coal- and iron-mining were the mainstays of the Durham Dales west of the city, the latter are now part of the **North Pennines Area of Outstanding Natural**

Beauty, which stretches into Northumberland and Cumbria (p. 668) and has been designated a UNESCO European Geopark for its outstanding geology. Don't miss **Teesdale** with its waterfalls—**High Force,** England's largest, drops 21m (70 ft). Also notable is **Weardale,** once the hunting ground of Durham's prince bishops; the **Weardale Museum** (© 01388/517433; www.weardalemuseum.co.uk) in Ireshopeburn has displays on local life and on Methodist John Wesley, who preached in the adjoining chapel several times.

This is good walking territory: The **Pennine Way** (p. 535) crosses the area, and there's the 90-mile **Teesdale Way** from Middlesborough in North Yorkshire across County Durham (via Barnard Castle) and into Cumbria, and the 77-mile **Weardale Way** along the River Wear from Roker on the coast near Newcastle. This latter takes you to **Killhope, the North of England Lead Mining Museum** (see below).

The market town of **Stanhope,** home to the Durham Dales Centre (p. 656) with its award-winning tearoom and crafts shops, is the starting point for a scenic ride on the heritage **Weardale Railway** (www.weardale-railway.org.uk) to Wolsingham. Or head to **Hamsterley Forest** (www.forestry.gov.uk) with its walking, cycling, and horse-riding routes, bike rental, visitor center, tearoom, and play park. Cyclists should also note that Stanhope is on the **C2C Cycle Route** (Coast to Coast or Sea to Sea national cycle route; www.c2c-guide.co.uk).

Travel 17 miles south of Stanhope to reach the town of **Barnard Castle,** named after its extensive ruined Norman **fortress** ★ (© 01833/690909; www.english-heritage.co.uk). High on a rock with stunning views over the Tees gorge, Barnard Castle has tactile gardens and a sensory garden with scented plants. Don't miss Richard III's boar emblem carved above the inner ward. It's open April to September daily 10am to 6pm and October to March Thursday to Monday 10am to 4pm, with entry £4.20 for adults, £2.10 for children. The town is also home to the **Bowes Museum** ★ (© 01833/690606; www.bowesmuseum.org.uk), housing northern England's best collection of European fine and decorative arts, including new Fashion & Textile and Silver & Metals galleries, within a magnificent mansion. Trails, activity sacks, and dressing-up areas make it accessible to kids. Open daily 10am to 5pm, the museum costs £8 for adults, free for kids.

Six miles from Barnard Castle on the way back up to Durham, medieval **Raby Castle** (© 01833/660202; www.rabycastle.com), surrounded by walled gardens and parkland in which fallow and roe deer roam free, has interesting medieval, Regency, and Victorian interiors containing European textiles and furniture from the 17th to the 20th centuries and artworks by Van Dyck, Reynolds, and others. Its coachhouse holds a display of carriages. The park and garden is open 11am to 5:30pm Sunday to Wednesday in May, June, and September; and Sunday to Friday in July and August. The castle can be visited between 1 and 4:30pm. Tickets for the castle, park, and gardens are £9.50 for adults, £4 for children 5 to 15.

The **Durham Heritage Coast** (www.durhamheritagecoast.org), despite being ravaged by mining in the 20th century (as well as impoverished by mine closures in the early 1990s), offers wild beaches, rugged cliffs, and imposing headlands blessed with rare plants and wildlife, best explored via the coastal path. Focal points are the **Castle Eden Dene National Nature Reserve** (© 0191/586-0004; www.natural england.org.uk), with 12 miles of footpaths through ancient woodlands, and the lively harbor of Seaham, with one of the U.K.'s oldest churches and—unexpectedly—a luxury hotel with a famous spa (see review for Seaham Hall & Serenity Spa, below).

The last sight in County Durham as you head north is **Beamish, the Living Museum of the North** deep in the countryside 12 miles northwest of Durham.

Beamish, the Living Museum of the North ★★★ ☺ MUSEUM   This vivid open-air re-creation of an early-19th-century pit village includes costumed interpreters acting out daily life in shops, houses, pubs, a farm, and so on. For kids, the stars are a ride on the Pockerley Waggonway-replica locomotives pulling re-created period carriages, the original carousel, and the coal-fired fish-and-chips shop.

Beamish. ℂ **0191/370-4000.** www.beamish.org.uk. Admission £16 adults, £10 children 5–16 high season; £7.50 adults, £6 children low season; £10 adults, £8 children at Christmas. Apr–Oct daily 10am–5pm; first 3 weeks. Nov and early Jan–Apr Sat–Sun and Tues–Thurs 10am–4pm, plus some days over Christmas.

Killhope, the North of England Lead Mining Museum ★ ☺ MUSEUM   Don hard hats to tour an old mine (ages 4 and up only), see displays about lead mining in the area, and walk in the surrounding woodland, complete with play park, picnic tables, and wildlife hides. The museum is a fun place to bring kids, with Sam Squirrel family backpacks available.

Near Cowshill. ℂ **01388/537505.** www.killhope.org.uk. Admission £7 adults, £4 children 4–16. Apr–Oct daily 10:30am–5pm.

Where to Eat

EXPENSIVE

For the White Room at Seaham Hall, see "Where to Stay," below.

Bistro 21 ★★ MODERN BRITISH/EUROPEAN   You won't regret venturing out of central Durham to this relaxed rustic-chic bistro, where mainly seasonal regional ingredients such as wild sea bass and vegetables grown in the restaurant's own courtyard are used to full effect in creative but comforting dishes such as local ham, French mushy peas, and slow-cooked egg; North Sea plaice with braised fennel, crushed potatoes, beetroot, and capers; and soft meringue roll with port and orange plums. Many dishes have a French or Spanish bias, but more global influences creep in, too, as do British classics such as fish and chips. There are good-value fixed-price menus plus a vegetarian menu.

Note that chef Terry Laybourne's protégé Paul O'Hara runs the **Bridge Inn Eating & Drinking House** ★★ (ℂ **01833/627341;** www.thebridgeinnrestaurant. co.uk) in the quaint village of Whorlton not far from Barnard Castle, where you can expect a similar style and quality of cooking.

Aykley Heads House, Aykley Heads, Durham. ℂ **0191/384-4354.** www.bistrotwentyone.co.uk. Reservations recommended. Main courses £15–£23. AE, DC, MC, V. Mon–Sat noon–2pm and 6–10pm.

Finbarr's ★★ MODERN BRITISH/EUROPEAN   Ranked by many as the best restaurant in town since opening in early 2010, this cozy inn-like building in Durham City's Conservation Area, on the edge of the Flass Vale nature reserve a short walk from the city center, conceals a haven of subtle modern chic. The contemporary rustic cooking with the odd, exotic touch features mainly regional produce—standouts are leek and potato soup with soft-poached egg and bacon crumbs, local pork "three ways" (belly, shoulder, and filet), and iced yogurt parfait with honey-roast figs. But the highlight is the wonderful Sunday lunches—a bargain at £18 for three courses, plus a £6 kids' menu or smaller portions from the main menu. Finbarr's is also open for breakfast daily.

Waddington St., Flass Vale, Durham. ✆ **0191/370-9999.** www.finbarrsrestaurant.co.uk. Reservations recommended. Main courses £11–£25. AE, DC, MC, V. Mon–Fri 7–9:30am, noon–2:30pm, and 6–9:30pm; Sat 7–10:30am, noon–2:30pm, and 6–9:30pm; Sun 7:30–10:30am and noon–9pm.

Riverside at the Swan ★★ BRITISH   Low-beamed ceilings, candles, joyful staff, and the smell of fabulously good local cooking will lure you into this award-winning restaurant overlooked by Barnard Castle, attracting food lovers from hundreds of miles away. Its Sunday lunches—both traditional and more experimental, and including kids' portions—are extremely popular with locals, while the chargrilled steaks from local farms are a big draw throughout the week, and the twice-cooked beef is a revelation. But you'll also find the irresistible likes of seared filet of sea bass with fresh leek tagliatelle, steamed Shetland mussels, crayfish and crab risotto, and savory Yorkshire blue cheese bread-and-butter pudding with thick-cut chips, sticky onion relish, and crisp dressed salad leaves.

Bridge End, Barnard Castle. ✆ **01833/637577.** www.riverside-restaurant.co.uk. Reservations recommended. Main courses £15–£21. MC, V. Tues–Sat noon–2pm (by reservation only Tues–Thurs) and 6–9:30pm; Sun noon–2pm.

MODERATE

The Church Mouse ★ ☺ BRITISH/PUB FOOD   Handy for Beamish, the Living Museum of the North (p. 658) this welcoming traditional pub in a former mining village has won awards for its cask-conditioned real ales but shouldn't be overlooked for its culinary offerings: Mediterranean-inspired sharing platters; Sunday roasts; "country pub classics" including beef, mushroom, and ale pie; and a great kids' menu, with main courses (averaging £4.50) including tomato *strozzapreti* (egg pasta tossed with a tomato garlic sauce), or rump steak with onion rings, plum tomato, peas, and chips. In winter there's a cozy log fire to warm your limbs, and in summer a garden where kids can stretch theirs. The interior melds original features such as beams and flagstone floors with dashes of low-key contemporary chic. Note that there's a Travelodge next door.

Waldridge, Chester-le-Street. ✆ **0191/3892628.** www.vintageinn.co.uk. Main courses £6.95–£16. MC, V. Mon–Sat noon–10pm, Sun noon–9:30pm.

INEXPENSIVE

The award-winning Undercroft restaurant at Durham Cathedral (p. 656) serves good cakes, scones, soups, sandwiches, salads, and main courses.

La Spaghettata ☺ 🔪 ITALIAN   The lines trailing down the stairs and out the door of this homey restaurant on the street leading up to Durham Cathedral testify to its superiority over the city's many other Italian restaurants in atmosphere, pricing, and portion size, though because it gets so busy, service can suffer. A favorite with Durham's students—perhaps for the penne with vodka, or the kitsch decor with its gaudy *trompe l'oeil* murals and plastic tablecloths—it's a great spot for a lively meal with kids, with meal deals keeping bills low. In addition to good pizzas and pasta dishes, there are intriguing main courses such as chicken breast with pesto and lime, or grilled salmon with chili, coriander, cherry tomatoes, ginger and scallions.

66 Saddler St., Durham. ✆ **0191/383-9290.** www.fabiosdurham.com/spag. Reservations recommended. Main courses £5.10–£13. MC, V. Mon–Thurs 5:30–10:30pm, Fri–Sun 11:30am–2pm and 5:30–10:30pm.

Penny's Tea Rooms   LUNCH/SNACKS/AFTERNOON TEA   This long-standing tearoom and restaurant is popular with locals and visitors for everything from tea and cakes to home-cooked meals written up on a chalkboard, amid murals picturing local landscapes. A typical day's offerings might include a soup, warm rolls, paninis, jacket potatoes, and the heartier likes of beef and mushroom cobbler, or shepherd's pie with vegetables. Whatever you choose, leave space for an indulgent dessert such as chocolate sponge or plum pie. Vegetarian and gluten- and dairy-free diets are catered for. The owners also offer B&B **rooms.**

4 Market Place, Barnard Castle. ⓒ **01833/637634.** www.pennys-tearooms.co.uk. Main courses £4.75–£6.50. MC, V. Mon–Sat 10am–7:30pm, Sun 10am–5pm.

Shopping

Durham is the county's shopping focus, notably the beautifully restored Victorian covered **Indoor Market;** its 50 traders selling local produce and goods (Mon–Sat 9am–5pm) include Humbies traditional candy shop, the award-winning Café Cenno bistro (with free Wi-Fi), and even a pipe and tobacco shop. The third Thursday of the month also sees the **City of Durham Farmers Market** in the Market Place, from 9am, and there's a twice-yearly Continental market, and a big Christmas market the first weekend of December. For information on all these, see www.durhammarkets. org.uk. There are also plenty of interesting one-off shops near the cathedral and around the city center; fashion mavens should make a bee-line for the fashion emporium **Van Mildert,** at 19–21 Elvet Bridge (ⓒ **0191/384-8508;** www.vanmildert. com), selling a huge range of desirable labels including Vivienne Westwood and Chloé.

Entertainment & Nightlife

Durham is also your best bet for lively nightlife in the county, with the student population ensuring that there's a healthy array of good pubs. On Old Elvet, the **Dun Cow Inn** (ⓒ **0191/386-9219**) is, in part, a 16th-century alehouse notorious for issuing the Dun Cow Challenge—to have a beer from every pump along the bar. The impossibly narrow 12th-century **Shakespeare Tavern** on Saddler Street (ⓒ **0191/384-3261**) lays claim to being England's most haunted pub.

Where to Stay

Great B&Bs are strangely hard to find in this neck of the woods. There's a new **Travelodge** (ⓒ **0871/559-1819;** www.travelodge.co.uk) by the Church Mouse (p. 659) at Chester-le-Street, with doubles and family rooms for around £50.

Durham Castle ★   Durham's famous fortress offers visitors the rare chance to stay in a UNESCO World Heritage site while its student residents are on vacation, offering accommodations in single and twin rooms, some with shared bathroom facilities and others in a medieval gatehouse. There are also two much grander state rooms available year-round, with en suite facilities—the two-room Chaplain's Suite is good for families, while the Bishop's Suite has incredible 17th-century tapestries and a four-poster. Breakfasts are served in the medieval Great Hall. Parking can be tricky: You can get a permit, subject to availability, to park overnight on Palace Green but must move by 9am. Guests get free castle tours.

Palace Green, Durham DH1 3RN. www.dur.ac.uk/university.college/conferences/bandb. ⓒ **0191/334-4106.** 177 units. £51–£70 double; £180–£240 suite. Rates include breakfast. MC, V. Free parking (night only, subject to availability). **Amenities:** Bar/lounge. *In room:* TV (in suites).

Durham Marriott Hotel Royal County 🍴 ☺ In a city oddly devoid of truly appealing hotels and B&Bs, this option has a helpful staff and good rates (some including breakfast) that make up for its shortcomings—bathrooms that fall far short of the standards of rooms themselves, and an uninspiring restaurant and bar. The hotel has a pleasant indoor pool. Rooms are divided between a huddle of older buildings—once the family home to the Queen Mother—and a more modern structure; the latter has the best guest rooms, with good views over the River Wear, but is a bit of a pain to reach because of the odd layout. Alternatively, some rooms have views up the cathedral and castle. Supreme Rooms with two double beds are great value for families, and connecting rooms are also available.

Old Elvet, Durham DH1 3JN. www.marriott.co.uk. © **01913/866821.** 150 units. £100–£145 double; from £180 suite. AE, DC, MC, V. Free parking. **Amenities:** 2 restaurants; bar/lounge; babysitting; exercise room; Jacuzzi; indoor pool; sauna, room service. *In room:* TV, hair dryer, Wi-Fi (£15 for 24 hr.).

Rockliffe Hall ★★ 🎁 This exciting addition to the northeast's luxury hotel scene opened to critical and public acclaim in late 2009, offering a large, state-of-the-art spa with a thermal bathing suite, an 18-hole championship golf course, and three restaurants—one with a Michelin-starred chef—on a vast riverside country estate. Within the 19th-century manor, stunning period features including carved stone pillars and fireplaces are beautifully enhanced by slick decor with a contemporary feel. Kids are allowed, but you'll feel more comfortable with older children than with energetic toddlers. As a family, you may also prefer to book one of the on-site Woodland Mews cottages, which sleep up to six.

Hurworth on Tees, Darlington, County Durham DL2 2DU. www.rockliffehall.com. © **01325/729999.** 61 units. AE, MC, DC, V. Free parking. £270–£430 double; £350–£430 suite. **Amenities:** 3 restaurants and bars; room service; spa; swimming pool; gym; golf course. *In room:* TV, hair dryer, kitchen (in cottages), Wi-Fi (free).

Seaham Hall & Serenity Spa ★ An unexpected oasis of luxury on the Durham Heritage Coast, this cliff-top boutique hotel lures people from far afield with an award-winning multimillion-pound spa that reliably makes it onto *Condé Nast Traveller*'s "Best U.K. Spas" list. Rooms and suites all have unique decor, layout, and views, so study the website before booking. Some have their own garden terrace, some freestanding two-person bathtubs, and others limestone fireplaces. As befits the house in which Lord Byron married Anabella Milbanke, Seaham Hall is best suited to a romantic break or a health spree, with boot camp and other exercise classes a specialty. That said, the **White Room Dining Room** (open evenings and Sun lunch), with its fine dining, won't help you keep off the weight. Think rolled terrine of Goosnargh duck with foie gras, olives, tarragon, chocolate, and coffee; pan-fried North Sea halibut with carrot, orange, and star anise; and red-wine poached pear with cinnamon foam and ginger ice cream.

Lord Byron's Walk, Seaham County Durham SR7 7AG. www.seaham-hall.co.uk. © **0191/516-1400.** 18 units. £180–£230 double, £280–£380 suite. Rates include breakfast. AE, DC, MC, V. Free parking. **Amenities:** Restaurant; bar; indoor swimming pool; room service; spa. *In room:* TV, Wi-Fi (free).

NEWCASTLE & GATESHEAD

Newcastle: 283 miles N of London; 145 miles NE of Manchester; 121 miles S of Edinburgh

Though distinctive, these cities are physically separated by the River Tyne alone. Seven bridges, including the iconic tilting Gateshead Millennium Bridge or "Winking

Eye," link them, and Newcastle and Gateshead are so closely bound that the local tourist board speaks of them as "NewcastleGateshead." Forming the core of the metropolitan county of Tyne & Wear, they have really only appeared on visitors' radars over the past few years, as major investment and development have brought new attractions in their wake.

Essentials

GETTING THERE   By direct train, Newcastle is about 3 hours from London King's Cross (around £110 for a round-trip). There are also direct trains from Manchester (p. 562), taking about 2½ hours, and from Edinburgh, taking about 1¾ hours. From Newcastle, trains take you directly to Gateshead's Metrocentre mall in less than 10 minutes, or there are ample city buses plus the city's efficient Metro light railway. Daily **National Express** buses (✆ **0871/781-8181;** www.nationalexpress.com) from London to Newcastle take 6½ hours and up.

From London, expect a drive of about 4¾ hours (283 miles), most of it up the main M1/A1.

Newcastle International Airport (www.newcastleairport.com), 8 miles outside the center (linked by Metro and buses) has links with many international and U.K. destinations. The city is also 42 miles north of Durham Tees Airport. The North Shields International Passenger Terminal, 8 miles east of the center, links Newcastle with the Netherlands.

VISITOR INFORMATION   **Newcastle Tourist Information Centre,** Central Arcade (✆ **0191/277-8000;** www.newcastlegateshead.com), is open Monday to Friday 9am to 5:30pm, Sat 9am to 5:30pm, Sun 11am to 5pm.

Gateshead Tourist Information Centre, Gateshead Heritage Centre at St. Mary's, (✆ **0191/478-4222;** www.newcastlegateshead.com), is open Tuesday to Sunday 10am to 4pm.

SPECIAL EVENTS   March sees the 6-day **Newcastle Science Fest** (www.newcastlesciencefest.co.uk), with events for all ages at several venues. In June and July, the city's annual 16-day **EAT! festival** (www.eatnewcastlegateshead.com) promotes local produce with special events.

Also in June, Sunderland (19 miles south of Newcastle, with Metro links) hosts the 2-day **Sunderland International Airshow** (www.sunderlandevents.co.uk), with spectacular flying displays over the coast.

Exploring the Area

NEWCASTLE

Tell a local you're on your way to this, one of Britain's most up-and-coming and hip cities, and they'll assume you have shopping or nightlife in mind. But Newcastle is more than the sum of its retail therapy opportunities. It was founded about 2,000 years ago as a stronghold along Hadrian's Wall (p. 669), the ruin of which you can see at **Segedunum Roman Fort, Baths & Museum** (**0191/236-9347;** www.twmuseums.org.uk) at Wallsend east of the center (accessible by Metro). If you head in that direction, carry on to the North Tyneside coast for the **Stephenson Railway Museum** at North Shields (✆ **0191/200-7146;** www.twmuseums.org.uk), home to George Stephenson's "Billy" and other engines from the great age of steam and occasionally offering rides pulled by heritage diesel engines. Entry is free; opening times are weekends and bank-holiday Mondays 11am to 4pm, daily in school holidays. Also

New Castle

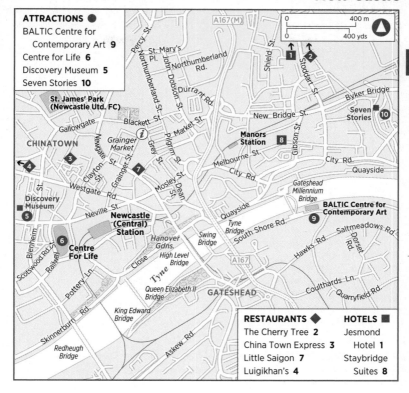

ATTRACTIONS ●
BALTIC Centre for
Contemporary Art **9**
Centre for Life **6**
Discovery Museum **5**
Seven Stories **10**

St. James' Park
(Newcastle Utd. FC)

CHINATOWN

Grainger
Market

RESTAURANTS ◆
The Cherry Tree **2**
China Town Express **3**
Little Saigon **7**
Luigikhan's **4**

HOTELS ■
Jesmond
Hotel **1**
Staybridge
Suites **8**

BALTIC Centre for
Contemporary Art

Seven
Stories **10**

Manors
Station **8**

Newcastle
(Central)
Station

Discovery
Museum **5**

Centre
For Life **6**

Gateshead
Millennium
Bridge

GATESHEAD

on the coast, on a rocky headland, **Tynemouth Castle and Priory** (✆ **0870/333-1181;** www.english-heritage.org.uk) is home to an interactive "Life in the Stronghold" exhibition about this site from its origins as an Anglo-Saxon settlement through its roles as an Anglican monastery, royal castle, artillery fort, and coastal defense. It's open daily 10am to 5pm in summer, to 4pm in winter, and costs £4.20 adults, £2.10 children 5 to 16.

Having grown from a Roman fort into a major port, Newcastle was a key player in the Industrial Revolution, after which, like many such places, it fell into a long decline. Part of its reawakening has come in the form of science—as well as a science fest (see "Special Events," above), it's home to the **Centre for Life** (see below) and the nearby **Discovery Museum.** A short walk north, by the university, the **Great North Museum ★**, Barras Bridge (✆ **0191/222-6765;** www.twmuseums.org.uk), opened in 2006 to bring together several pre-existing local collections in one £26-million museum. Highlights are the large-scale, interactive model of Hadrian's Wall (p. 669), and the interactive "Living Planet" gallery, with some live-animal tanks and aquariums.

To discover the best of the city itself, head for its historic heart, **Grainger Town,** north of Central Station. Here, classical streets built by Richard Grainger around

1840 contain some of Newcastle's finest buildings—Grainger Street, Clayton Street, and Grey Street are well worth a wander, with the latter voted Britain's finest street by BBC Radio 4 listeners in 2005. Southeast of Grainger Town stands the ruined Norman **Castle Keep** (ⓒ **0191/232-7938;** www.castlekeep-newcastle.org.uk), the "new castle"—after which the city was named—built in 1168–78 by Henry II on the site of an earlier castle by William the Conqueror's son, Robert Curthose. The site is open Monday to Saturday 10am to 5pm, Sunday noon to 5pm, with entry £4 adults, free for children 17 and under.

From here it's a pleasant stroll down to and along the quay-side, where you can truly get the measure of the city's transformation, with gleaming new architecture and riverside hotels and restaurants rubbing shoulders with industrial vestiges including Stephenson's High Level Bridge. The **Gateshead Millennium Bridge**—the world's only tilting bridge (to see it when it does, check times on www.gateshead.gov.uk)—allows walkers and cyclists quick access to Gateshead.

Centre for Life ★★ ☺ ENTERTAINMENT COMPLEX   Newcastle's cutting-edge science village is of most interest to visitors for its wonderful Science Centre, where well-thought-out interactive displays in themed areas, daily science and planetarium shows, and a motion ride make for a great family day out.

Discovery Square. ⓒ **0191/243-8210.** www.life.org.uk. Admission £8.25 adults, £6.45 children 5-17. Mon-Sat 10am-6pm, Sun 11am-6pm.

Discovery Museum ★ ☺ MUSEUM   A budget alternative to the Centre for Life, this venue includes a science maze, the new British Film Institute's Mediatheque, with more than 1,800 films and TV shows from the BFI's National Archive, and various hands-on displays about the history of Newcastle and Tyneside.

Blandford Square. ⓒ **0191/232-6789.** www.twmuseums.org.uk. Free admission. Mon-Sat 10am-5pm, Sun 2-5pm.

Seven Stories ★★ ☺ ENTERTAINMENT COMPLEX   About 20 minutes' walk outside the center, this unique establishment was set up in 2005 to celebrate children's literature through permanent and temporary exhibitions, as well as storytelling and other events. It also boasts one of the U.K.'s largest independent children's bookstores.

30 Lime St. ⓒ **0845/271-0777.** www.sevenstories.org.uk. Admission £6 adults, £5 children 3-16. Mon-Sat 10am-5pm, Sun and bank holidays 10am-4pm.

GATESHEAD

The Millennium Bridge brings you to the foot of the **BALTIC Centre for Contemporary Art,** stunningly set within a former red-brick flour mill on Gateshead Quays, looming over the river. It rather eclipses the nearby **Shipley Art Gallery,** Prince Consort Road (ⓒ **0191/477-1495;** www.twmuseums.org.uk), but the latter's excellent design and contemporary craft displays, plus its painting collection, make it well worth a visit. Also free, it's open Monday to Saturday 10am to 5pm, Sunday 2 to 5pm.

Though the Shipley has been around since 1907, this region's cultural renaissance is said to have been kickstarted by the building, in 1998, of the **Angel of the North,** or "Gateshead Flasher" as some locals have dubbed it—Antony Gormley's 20m-tall (60-ft.) steel sculpture of an angel on a hill at the southern edge of Low Fell, overlooking the A1 and A167 into Tyneside, as well as the main rail route. If you don't enter Gateshead via these means, the Angel Bus (www.simplygo.com/our-services/the-angel) can take you there.

Carry on down to Sunderland for more cutting-edge creativity at the **Northern Gallery for Contemporary Art,** Fawcett Street (✆ 0191/561-8407; www.ngca.co.uk), free to enter and open Monday and Wednesday 9:30am to 7:30pm; Tuesday to Friday 9:30am to 5pm; and Saturday 9:30am to 4pm. Sunderland is also home to the **National Glass Centre** (✆ 0191/515-5555; www.nationalglasscentre.com), with exhibitions, activities, and workshops about glassmaking. You can take a walk on its roof made of 6cm-thick (2½-in) glass. Open daily 10am to 5pm, it's free to visit.

Lastly, keen bird-spotters or those with kids should visit the **WWT Washington Wetland Centre** (✆ 0191/416-5454), between Gateshead and Sunderland, where wetlands, meadows, and woodlands house ducks, geese, waders, flamingos, cranes and herons, as well as frogs, bats, and goats. There are family activities galore; entry is £8.45 adults, £4.25 children 4 to 16; it's open daily 9:30am to 5:30pm (until 4:30pm Nov–Mar).

BALTIC Centre for Contemporary Art ★   This major international venue for contemporary visual art, which opened in 2002 and played host to the prestigious Turner Prize in 2011 (the first time it wasn't hosted by a Tate gallery), eschews a permanent collection in favor of an ever-changing roster of exhibitions and events. Arts showcased to date have included Antony Gormley, Anish Kapoor, and Sam Taylor-Wood.

Gateshead Quays, South Shore Rd. ✆ **0191/478-1810.** www.balticmill.com. Free admission. Daily 10am–6pm (from 10:30am Tues).

Where to Eat

Malmaison, Quayside (✆ 0191/245-0580), a brasserie celebrating Northumberland's "food heroes" in French-inflected dishes, plus a deli-style cafe. In the same area are the reliable Italians: **Café Vivo,** 27 Broad Chare (✆ 0191/232-1331; www.caffevivo.co.uk) and **Gusto,** Quayside (✆ 0191/260-2291; www.gustorestaurants.uk.com).

Amer's Restaurant is in the Jesmond Hotel (p. 667). For great fish and chips, head 12 miles east of Newcastle, to coastal South Shields, where **Colmans,** 182–186 Ocean Rd. (✆ 0191/456-1202; www.colmansfishandchips.com), is the proud holder of several national awards, served by four generations of the same family.

The Cherry Tree ★★★ ☺ MODERN BRITISH   Newcastle's foremost dining spot opened to critical acclaim in 2008 in the former telephone-exchange building in Jesmond, a 20-minute walk, or £5 taxi ride, north of the center. It's worth the detour. The space itself is clean, modern, buzzy, and family friendly; food is served from breakfast all through the day from a cafe menu, then there are fixed-price and a la carte lunches and dinners. Sunday lunch is a highlight, with traditional roasts sharing the menu with the likes of roast salmon with brown shrimps and caper butter, and goat's-cheese gnocchi with oregano, walnuts, and baby leeks. Kids get half-portions or their own menu. Desserts are sensational: Save room for blood-orange jelly with citrus salad and Earl Grey ice cream, or baked Alaska with stem-ginger ice cream and champagne rhubarb.

9 Osborne Rd., Newcastle. ✆ **0191/239-9924.** www.thecherrytreejesmond.co.uk. Reservations recommended for dinner. Main courses £15–£22. MC, V. Mon–Sat 9am–11:30pm, Sun 9am–9pm.

China Town Express ⚓ CHINESE   This is the best option in Newcastle's Chinatown—centered on Stowell Street and also hosting some Korean and Japanese restaurants and shops. As the name suggests, it's canteen-like and no-frills, but for quality, authenticity, and portion sizes, it blows the fancier places in the vicinity out of the water. The salt-and-pepper squid, stewed seafood udon, and Singapore vermicelli are particularly recommended; the chicken's feet are a more acquired taste. No alcohol is served, but there's free green tea in abundance. You may have to wait, as tables can't be booked; takeout is also available.

63–65 Stowell St., Newcastle. (C) **0191/233-1388.** Main courses £4.50–£8.50. No credit cards. Daily 11:30am–11pm.

Little Saigon ★ VIETNAMESE Ideally located for those going on to sample some of Newcastle's notoriously boisterous nightlife, or just those who love to people-watch, this is one of the best Asian restaurants in the Northeast, offering fresh-tasting, authentic Vietnamese fare at moderate prices, plus a few more elaborate specials. It's difficult to choose from the long menu of delicious-sounding treats, but sure-fire hits are the starter of grilled prawns, shredded papaya, and fresh herbs with chili vinaigrette, and the main course of simmered tamarind king prawn. Lunch, served to 5pm, is particularly good value.

6 Bigg Market, Newcastle. (C) **0191/233-0766.** www.littlesaigon.uk.com. Reservations recommended. Main courses £4.50–£17. MC, V. Sun–Wed 11am–11pm, Thurs–Sat noon–midnight.

Luigikhan's ★ 🍴 😊 INDIAN/ITALIAN The perfect solution for those who can't agree what kind of food they're in the mood for (or for parents who want something a little spicier than their offspring does), this restaurant offers mainly authentic Punjabi cuisine but also a smaller menu of Italian dishes and a few steaks and chicken dishes within the new Best Western Ryokan hotel, about a mile outside the center. The Indian food is stunning, so don't be tempted to play it safe unless you dislike exotic flavors—and even then, the likes of Tawa lamb chops in tomatoes, yogurt, and Asian fenugreek, with fresh coriander, bullet chili, and ginger, may convert you. The Italian menu includes pizzas and familiar pasta dishes but also some slightly more unusual combinations, such as pasta with tiger prawns and fresh asparagus. An interesting decor of leather banquettes, exposed brickwork, and empty picture frames add to the experience.

58 Westgate Rd., Newcastle. (C) **0191/272-4937.** www.luigikhans.com. Reservations recommended. MC, V. Main courses £3.95–£17. Daily 5:30–10:30pm.

Shopping

Newcastle's **Eldon Square** (www.eldon-square.co.uk), one of the U.K.'s biggest city-center shopping complexes, was rather eclipsed by the arrival of Gateshead's **Metrocentre** (www.metrocentre.uk.com), Europe's biggest indoor shopping and leisure center. Combined, they make "NewcastleGateshead" a major shopping destination—and that's not including the boutiques and independent stores of High-Bridge Street and Jesmond. Don't miss the beautifully preserved Edwardian Central Arcade in Grainger Town (p. 663), home to the Tourist Information Centre (p. 662).

If you're in the area for the art and feel inspired to invest, **The Biscuit Factory,** at 16 Stoddart St. ((C) **0191/261-1103;** www.thebiscuitfactory.com), is the U.K.'s biggest store for original art, selling paintings, drawings, prints, sculpture, photography, ceramics, jewelry, and glass by contemporary artists from around the globe. You can also buy contemporary art by the likes of Damien Hirst and Jake & Dinos Chapman at **Opus Art** ((C) **0191/232-7389;** www.opus-art.com), in the suburb of Gosforth to the north of the center, open by appointment only.

Entertainment & Nightlife

Newcastle and Gateshead are fantastic for music and theatre lovers. Newcastle's historic **Theatre Royal** (℃ **0844/811-2111**; www.theatreroyal.co.uk) is regional home to the Royal Shakespeare Company and hosts shows by the National Theatre, Opera North, Rambert Dance, West End musicals, comedy, and family shows. Also in Newcastle, the **Metro Radio Arena** (℃ **0844/493-6666,** www.metroradio arena.co.uk) attracts big-name rock, pop, and comedy acts. The iconic **Sage Gateshead** (℃ **0191/4434661;** www.thesagegateshead.org) hosts performances by its own chamber orchestra, the Northern Sinfonia, and visiting classical, pop, and jazz artists.

Newcastle is notorious for its social-drinking culture, especially around **Bigg Market** in the center. Other focal points are the Quayside and the area around Central Station with its "Diamond Strip" of upmarket bars. Jesmond is a mixture of the hip and studenty and more upmarket. The Pink Triangle, Newcastle's gay epicenter, is in the Centre for Life/Metro Radio Arena area.

Where to Stay

By far the best-located hotel in Newcastle is the **Malmaison** on the Quayside, with a stunning facade and views over the tilting bridge and toward BALTIC (£115–£135 double). Newcastle's **Hotel du Vin** is a 20-minute walk east of Quayside on City Road (℃ **0191/229-2200;** doubles about £120–£170).

Jesmond Hotel ★ ◢   Offering the personal touch in a smart suburb north of Newcastle's center, the Jesmond has small but clean and pleasant rooms furnished in a spare contemporary style at unbeatable rates that include an excellent breakfast (buffet and cooked). The on-site **Amer's Restaurant** (lunch Tues–Fri and Sun; dinner Tues–Sat), another great find, offers very good modern British cuisine such as pan-seared scallops with celeriac purée and lardons at more-than-reasonable prices, and the bar has a pleasant terrace for summer days and evenings. Check-in is a generous 1pm.

34 Osborne Rd., Newcastle NE2 2AJ. www.jesmondhotel.co.uk. ℃ **0191/281-5377.** 18 units. £80 double. Rates include breakfast. MC, V. Free parking (on street). **Amenities:** Restaurant; bar. *In room:* TV.

Souter Lighthouse Cottages ★ 🎒 ☺   Pretty as a picture, these National Trust holiday cottages are on the south side of a complex of buildings attached to the shore-based, cliff-top Souter Lighthouse just north of Sunderland (Cottage 1 was originally the lighthouse engineer's home). Available for 3 nights and up, each sleeps four plus a baby/toddler in a cot. Both are fairly modern yet homey in style, with touches of nautical and seabird imagery in the decor and furnishings. Kids love the Robinson Crusoe feel of it all, with the old boats on-site and the wild beach at hand, but they do need to be supervised on the grounds as this is a working lighthouse (cottage guests get free guided tours of it).

Whitburn, South Tyneside SR6 7EX. www.nationaltrustcottages.co.uk. ℃ **0844/800-2070.** 2 units. £186–£530 3 nights; £372–£884 7 nights. MC, V. Free parking. Amenities: Walled garden (shared). *In cottage:* TV, highchair, full kitchen (w/dishwasher and washing machine), travel cot.

Staybridge Suites ◢   Although billed as "extended stay hotels," Staybridge Suites—part of the giant Intercontinental Hotel Group that also embraces Holiday Inn—are just the ticket even if you're in Newcastle only for a night or two. They're a particular boon for families since all have full kitchens allowing you to eat in—the one-bedroom suites have a full bedroom and a reasonably spacious living room with a sofabed—and there are also laundry facilities. The location might seem a little dingy at first, but the Suites are just a 2-minute walk north of the Quayside with all its eating and drinking venues, and a 10-minute walk from the shopping heart of the city. There's also a small lobby grocery that should cover your basic needs. For a chain offering, the decor is pleasant and even quite luxurious for these prices.

Buxton St., Newcastle NE1 6NL. www.ichotelsgroup.com. ✆ **0191/238-7000.** 128 units. £79–£99 studio suite for 2; £104–£129 1-bedroom suite for up to 4. Rates include self-serve breakfast. AE, MC, DC, V. Parking £8. Amenities: Lounge; books/board games; fitness center; laundry facilities. In room: TV/CD/DVD, kitchen, Wi-Fi (free).

NORTHUMBERLAND ★★★

Newcastle: 283 miles N of London; 145 miles NE of Manchester; 121 miles S of Edinburgh

One of Britain's best-kept secrets, this northern county unfurling to the English border with Scotland attracts most visitors to its sections of **Hadrian's Wall** and the ruined Roman forts that dot its length. Few venture north of that historic line to experience the mysteries of the **Kielder Forest & Water Park** with its star-gazing facilities and modern open-air artworks, or to discover the breathtaking castles and beaches of a miraculously unspoilt and wild coastline.

Essentials

GETTING THERE   Newcastle (p. 662) is your major entry point for Northumberland, which is best explored by car (in winter, ideally a 4x4). From Newcastle, regular trains to Hexham take about a half-hour. At Hexham Station, local taxis take visitors to the main Hadrian's Wall sites about 15 miles to the northwest. A more economical option is the **Hadrian's Wall Bus** (AD122), which runs April to September between Newcastle and Carlisle, stopping at visitor attractions, towns, and villages en route (see www.northumberlandnationalpark.org.uk for details).

Kielder Water & Forest Park is 30 miles from Hexham, 52 miles from Newcastle; the Forest Drive is the most scenic way in but the surface is loose chip, and the route closes in winter and inclement weather.

Alnwick lies 35 miles (about 40 min.) north of Newcastle via the main A1, and Bamburgh Castle is another 17 miles (20 min.) north of Alnwick. For local buses, visit www.traveline.org.uk.

VISITOR INFORMATION   Hexham Tourist Information Centre, Wentworth Car Park, Wentworth Place (✆ **01434/652220;** www.visitnorthumberland.com), is open April to October Monday to Saturday 9:30am to 5pm, Sunday 11am to 4pm; November to March Monday to Saturday 11am to 4pm.

Once Brewed National Park Centre, Military Road, Bardon Mill (✆ **01434/344396;** www.northumberlandnationalpark.org.uk), is open April to October daily 9:30am–5pm.

Tower Knowe Visitor Centre (Kielder Water & Forest Park), Kielder (✆ **01434/251000;** www.visitkielder.com), is open April to June and September daily 10am to 5pm; July and August daily 10am to 6pm; October daily 10am to 4pm.

Alnwick Tourist Information Centre, 2 The Shambles (✆ **01665/511333;** www.visitnorthumberland.com), is open April to October Monday to Saturday 9:30am to 5pm, Sunday 10am to 4pm; November to March Monday to Saturday 9:30am to 4:30pm, Sunday 10am to 4pm.

Exploring the Area

NORTHUMBERLAND NATIONAL PARK

Covering almost 400 sq. miles of some of the least populated parts of England, this **National Park,** reaching up to the border with Scotland, is noted for its wild landscapes and weather and for its associations with the northern frontier of the ancient Roman Empire. A buffer zone between the warring English and Scots in the 13th and 14th centuries, these borderlands are most famously home to **Hadrian's Wall ★★★** (www.hadrians-wall.org), extending 73 miles across the north of England from the North Sea to the Irish Sea. It was built in A.D. 122 by legionnaires after the visit of Emperor Hadrian, who was inspecting far frontiers of the Roman Empire and wanted to construct a dramatic line between the Empire and the barbarians. The western end is accessible from Carlisle in Cumbria, while the eastern end can be reached from Newcastle, where relics include **Segedunum Roman Fort, Baths, & Museum** (p. 662).

The historic market town of **Hexham,** 24 miles west of Newcastle is a good jumping-off point for the Wall's most scenic section—the 10-mile stretch west of Housesteads, which itself lies 2¾ miles northeast of Bardon Mill with its National Park Centre. Only the lower courses of the wall were preserved intact; the rest were reconstructed in the 19th century using original stones. Sights concentrated in this area include **Housesteads Roman Fort & Museum** and **Roman Vindolanda** and its sister site, the **Roman Army Museum** (see below). Within easy walking distance of the museum, **Walltown Crags** (www.english-heritage.org.uk), free to visit, is one of the wall's highest-standing and most impressive sections.

The 84-mile coast-to-coast **Hadrian's Wall Path** (www.nationaltrail.co.uk/hadrians wall) takes you along sections of the wall as well as linking to more than 80 shorter walks, some within the National Park, and, near Housesteads, with the long-distance **Pennine Way** (p. 535), which takes you north into the Cheviot Hills along the Scottish border. Not for the faint-hearted walker, these hills—wrinkled by volcanic pressures, inundated by seawater, scoured by glaciers, silted over by rivers, and thrust upward during a series of geological events—are one of England's most tortuous landscapes.

Unless you're a hardened trekker, the area is best visited in the form of **Kielder Water & Forest Park ★★★** (*©* **01434/220616;** www.visitkielder.com), a huge natural playground with Europe's largest man-made lake, England's largest working forest, and activities galore including mountain-biking, watersports, forest walking trails, orienteering, and various adventure sports. There are visitor centers at Tower Knowe (see "Visitor Information," above), Kielder Castle, and Leaplish, plus an **Observatory ★** (*©* **07805/638469;** www.kielderobservatory.org) running star-gazing sessions—this area has the country's darkest night-skies—a salmon hatchery, and a birds-of-prey center. About half of England's native red squirrels hide out in this wildlife haven, where you may also spot otters, roe deer, and badgers, and the park is dotted with quirky modern art and architecture, including Silvas Capitalis, a wooden head you can climb in and peer out through the eyes.

Housesteads Roman Fort & Museum ★★ HISTORIC SITE

Britain's most complete Roman fort, set where Hadrian's Wall climbs to a dramatic escarpment, was a base for 800 soldiers, the remains of whose barracks blocks you can view, together with the commandant's house. The museum holds a model of what the intact fort would have looked like.

Housesteads Farm, Haydon Bridge. ℭ **0870/333-1181.** www.english-heritage.org.uk. Admission £5 adults, £3 children 5–16. Daily 10am–6pm (4pm in winter).

Roman Vindolanda & Roman Army Museum ★★ HISTORIC SITE The well-preserved fort of Vindolanda is believed to have been built around A.D. 85 and includes the excavated remains of a pre-Hadrian bathhouse, an officer's residence and some barracks, and a Romano-Celtic temple to an unknown god, plus a post-Roman mausoleum and Christian church. The museum, a sister site to Vindolanda a few miles to its west, added a 3-D film to its displays on Roman life and the wall's garrisons in 2011.

Vindolanda: southeast of Twice Brewed, just off the B6318; museum: west along the B6318, close to the village of Greenhead. ℭ **01434/344277.** www.vindolanda.com. Admission Vindolanda £5.90 adults, £3.50 children 5–18; museum £4.50 adults, £2.50 children. Daily 10am–4/6pm, depending on season (in bad weather call ahead to make sure Vindolanda is accessible).

ALNWICK, THE COAST & HOLY ISLAND

Spectacular, often-deserted beaches (some only accessible on foot), a landscape punctuated by truly breathtaking castles, and a relative lack of crowds make Northumberland's coast one of England's loveliest corners.

Heading up from Newcastle or Hexham, stop just inland to discover **Alnwick,** the gateway to the coast but with several attractions in its own right: Medieval **Alnwick Castle** (see below), **The Alnwick Garden** (see below), and **Barter Books** (ℭ **01665/604888;** www.barterbooks.co.uk), one of Europe's largest secondhand and antiquarian bookstores, set in the former railway station and boasting a model train doing the rounds of the shelves, a kids' room, and an honesty cafe in the old waiting room.

From the Coquet Estuary just southeast of Alnwick right up to Berwick-upon-Tweed, this coast is a designated Area of Outstanding Natural Beauty, with stunning beaches plus mud-flats that provide a home for waders, geese, and ducks. The **Northumberland Seabird Centre** ★ (ℭ **01665/710835;** www.rspb.org.uk) on the Quayside at Amble shows CCTV footage of the roseates and other terns and seabirds on Coquet Island itself, a bird sanctuary.

Starting at Cresswell, south of the Coquet Estuary, the **Northumberland Coast Path** is a 64-mile section of the North Sea Trail that also takes you as far as Berwick-upon-Tweed. The best-known beach on this stretch is Bamburgh, recognizable as the foreground for many photographs of the impossibly romantic **Bamburgh Castle** ★★★ (ℭ **01668/214-515;** www.bamburghcastle.com). Perhaps England's most impressive fortress of all, this seat of the kings of Northumbria sits proud on a volcanic outcrop overlooking the wave-battered coast. It's stunning enough from the outside, but you can go inside to explore 14 public areas (part of the castle houses private apartments). There are also live archeological excavations. The castle is open to visitors daily 10am to 5pm February to October, the rest of year Saturday and Sunday 11am to 4:30pm; adults pay £8.50, children £4.

Great beaches can be found at **Beadnell, Alnmouth,** and **Low Newton by the Sea.** The latter, a picturesque National Trust-owned 18th-century fishing village with cream-washed cottages, looks out to sea across the beach of Newton Haven and Embleton Bay to yet another wonderful fortress, **Dunstanburgh Castle**

(📞 **01665/576231;** www.english-heritage.org.uk). This impressive ruin is accessible only on foot from the pleasant little resort of Craster. It's open 10am to 4 or 5pm daily (except Tues–Wed Nov–Mar); admission is £4 adults, £2.40 for children.

Just to the south, **Howick Hall Gardens** (📞 **01665/577285;** www.howickhall gardens.org) is another highly rated spot for lovers of horticulture, with a Woodland Garden, a Bog Garden mostly planted from seed collected in the wild, and a new family trail in search of red squirrels, herons, and other wildlife. Howick is open mid-February to mid-November, daily noon to 6pm in summer and 10:30am to 4pm the rest of the year; children enter free, adults pay £6.

But the jewel in the crown of the Northumberland coast lies farther north, in the form of **Holy Island** or **Lindisfarne** (www.lindisfarne.org.uk), home to a monastery that was established by St. Aidan in 635 and became the main center of learning in Christendom under St. Cuthbert, until Viking raiders destroyed the community in 875 (Cuthbert's shrine is in Durham Cathedral; p. 656). Part of visiting Lindisfarne is the adventure of getting there—this is a tidal island, so check crossing times on the website before driving over the causeway. Once safely over, you have to leave your car in the parking lot to discover the village and the evocatively ruined **Lindisfarne Priory** (📞 **0870/333-1181;** www.english-heritage.org.uk)—not the original monastery but one built by Benedictine monks from Durham in the 12th century, with a visitor center recounting the site's history. It's open daily April to September 9:30am to 5pm (rest of year 10am–4pm), with admission £4.80 for adults, £2.90 for children. You can also visit the 16th-century **Lindisfarne Castle** (📞 **01289/389244;** www. nationaltrust.org.uk), a Tudor fort built to protect the harbor but converted into a private house by Sir Edwin Lutyens in 1903, with a walled garden by Gertrude Jekyll. Admission is £7.20 adults, £3.60 children 5 to 17; times vary according to tidal access to the island so check the website.

Lindisfarne and the other **Farne Islands** are a significant wildlife habitat for, among other creatures, gray seals and puffins. Boat trips (📞 **01665/720308;** www. farne-islands.com/boat-trips) from the little resort of Seahouses will take you to Inner Farne, the only inhabited island except Lindisfarne (and then only for part of the year, by National Trust bird wardens), and a couple of other islands.

Alnwick Castle ★★★ ☺ CASTLE Kids are thrilled to recognize this medieval castle from the first two Harry Potter movies, where it doubled as "Hogwarts." In addition to tours of the structure and grounds, the castle hosts events and activities aplenty, including Knight's Quest, when kids can dress as medieval knights, learn about dragons, and master the art of swordsmanship, archery, hands-on workshops, theatrical falconry, Harry Potter-themed magic and wizardry, and historical re-enactments. Combined tickets are available with The Alnwick Garden.

Alnwick. 📞 **01665/511100.** www.alnwickcastle.com. Admission £13 adults, £6 children 5-16. Daily 10am–6pm Apr-Oct.

The Alnwick Garden ★★★ ☺ GARDEN Set up just a decade ago by the lady of Alnwick Castle, the Duchess of Northumberland, one of the world's most exciting contemporary gardens occupies once-derelict terrain. Though boasting beautifully landscaped gardens and splendid architecture, it was conceived with families in mind, and younger visitors get lots of opportunities to engage in water-based play, including dodging the jets of the Grand Cascade, the largest water feature of its kind in the country. There's also a Bamboo Labyrinth, rope bridges leading to The

Treehouse restaurant (below), and a Poison Garden where you can hear tales of deadly plants (inspiration for the teen novel *The Poison Diaries*).

Denwick Lane, Alnwick. © **01665/511-350.** www.alnwickgarden.com. Admission £11 adults, £6 children 5-16. Summer daily 10am–6pm, winter Fri–Sun and public holidays 11am–3pm, but check for changes or weather-related disruptions.

Where to Eat
EXPENSIVE

Barn at Beal ★★ 🎁 ☺ SNACKS/AFTERNOON TEA/MODERN BRIT-ISH   Overlooking Lindisfarne National Nature Reserve with its sand dunes and mud-flats, this award-winning visitor center set up by a local farmer to educate visitors about agriculture and food fittingly promotes local produce in its restaurant and coffeeshop. You can come all day for cakes and snacks, or dinner is served two nights a week: Think seasonal dishes such as breaded local rabbit with black pudding and apple redcurrant sauce, Lindisfarne oysters grilled with a herb crust, or casserole of local game with colcannon root vegetables. There's a birds-of-prey center and a playground on-site, plus family-friendly walks and trails and a cycle track to the Lindisfarne causeway and beyond.

Beal Farm, Beal. © **01289/540044.** www.barnatbeal.com. Reservations recommended for dinner. Main courses £11–£17. MC, V. Daily 10am–5pm, Fri–Sat 7–11pm (closed Jan).

The Treehouse ★ ☺ MODERN BRITISH/EUROPEAN   For the sheer wow factor, this unique restaurant high in the treetops at The Alnwick Garden (p. 671) is reached via wooden bridges and has trees growing through the floor, plus a roaring fire in the cooler months. The food is surprisingly sophisticated, with the accent on organic Northumberland meats, crab, and other local seafood, and further regional specialties such as wood pigeon. Menus change seasonally but evening main courses might include plaice fillets with zucchini and fennel filling, ratte potatoes, and king prawn bisque. Lunch is substantially cheaper and includes snackier fare such as bacon sandwiches, risotto, and fish and chips, plus a kids' menu. There's also a more snacky bar menu. Sunday lunches include traditional roasts, and some evenings see performances of traditional Northumbrian music. You don't need a ticket to Alnwick Garden itself to visit the restaurant.

Denwick Lane, Alnwick. © **01665/511-852.** www.alnwickgarden.com. Reservations recommended. Main courses £14–£24 (dinner). MC, V. Daily 11:30am–2:45pm, also Thurs–Sun 7–11pm, and 6:30–9pm June–Sept and Mon when bank holiday.

MODERATE

The Olde Ship Inn TRADITIONAL BRITISH   A fine spot for real ales beside a warming log fire, this traditional pub by the tiny harbor of the resort town of Seahouses is about as nautical as they come. Its wooden floor is made from ships' decking, it has nautical artifacts galore (figureheads, diving helmets, pulling oars, fishbaskets, and branding irons), and there are model fishing boats and a replica of the lifeboat *The Grace Darling*, named after a local lighthousekeeper's daughter who saved 13 people from a shipwreck in Victorian times. There's a casual bar menu including homemade soup, sandwiches, and seafood, plus a lunch and evening menu with traditional favorites such as steak and ale pie and rich desserts including ginger trifle. Evenings, there's also a kids' menu; younger guests are welcome in the snug cabin or the beer garden with its harbor and Farne Island views. There are about 20 **guest rooms** and apartments on-site or nearby.

Seahouses. ✆ **01665/720200.** www.seahouses.co.uk. Main courses £9.50–£11. MC, V. Mon–Sat 11am–11pm, Sun noon–11pm.

The Pheasant Inn TRADITIONAL BRITISH   This down-to-earth country pub, handy for Kielder Water & Forest Park (p. 669), is another good spot for real ale and unpretentious English comfort-food favorites or more elaborate dishes, from a bar menu at lunchtime, or from bar and restaurant menus in the evening. There are also traditional Sunday lunches. Local-game pies, lamb, cheeses, and seafood are the highlights—we recommend the monkfish or sea bass, simply grilled with herb butter, or with a light cream sauce. The handful of **B&B rooms** include a family room for four to five; guests can order packed lunches to take out for the day.

Stannersburn. ✆ **01434/240382.** www.thepheasantinn.com. Main courses £6–£12. MC, V. Daily noon–2pm and 7–9pm.

INEXPENSIVE

In northern Northumberland, **Pinnacles in Seahouses,** 17–19 Main St. (✆ **01665/720-708**), serves very good fish and chips in basic surroundings.

Coastline   It's worth going out of your way to visit this huge fish-and-chips restaurant by the beach in the coastal town of Blyth in southern Northumberland (back toward Newcastle). Its award-winning cod and haddock are both locally caught and sustainably sourced where possible, as well as excellent value. Both are superb, but if you fancy something a little different, try the haddock and mozzarella fishcakes. Finish your meal in adjoining Caffè Sirena, an ice-cream parlor serving homemade Italian gelato in flavors ranging from classic vanilla to Turkish delight, as well as breakfasts, Italian coffee, cakes and pastries, and paninis and bruschetta.

Links Rd., Blyth. ✆ **01670/797428.** http://coastlinefishandchips.co.uk. Main courses £1–£3.80. MC, V. Summer Mon–Sat 11am–8pm, Sun 11am–6pm; winter Mon–Sat 11am–7pm, Sun 11–6pm.

Where to Stay
VERY EXPENSIVE

Langley Castle Hotel ★★   West of Hexham, England's only medieval fortified castle to welcome paying guests has atmosphere in spades, with its 14th-century spiral staircase, vast open hearths, and windows set into thick walls, many of which—in guest rooms and the bar—have been turned into quirky seating areas. All rooms are unique; some accommodate a family of five. The best, the Castle feature rooms, have unexpectedly luxurious modern bathrooms, some with a spa tub and sauna. Most rooms have a four-poster bed. The newer Castle View rooms, in a converted building, lack the atmosphere of the actual castle but might be preferred by families—Superior units have living rooms with sofabeds, affording some privacy for parents. Good food is available most of the day, including afternoon tea and an "Early Knight" menu (kids get their own menu). Guests can tour the turrets, weather permitting.

Langley-on-Tyne, Tynedale, Northumberland NE47 5LU. www.langleycastle.com. ✆ **01434/688888.** 27 units. £145–£265 double, from £185 suites. Rates include English breakfast. AE, MC, V. Free parking. **Amenities:** Restaurant; bar; babysitting; room service. *In room:* TV, hair dryer, minibar (some), spa bath and sauna (some), Wi-Fi (free).

Matfen Hall Hotel, Golf & Spa ★★ ☺   In countryside northeast of Hexham and also a handy option for those exploring Newcastle (p. 662) but not wishing to stay in the city, this stately home within its own parkland is home to a Go Ape! adventure course (www.goape.co.uk) for ages 10 and over, so it's a great place to bring active teens or pre-teens (though you don't have to stay on-site to use the course). There's also an indoor pool, children's prices (and lessons) on the golf estate, and a kids' menu in the Keeper's Lodge "pub restaurant" or family dining (6–7pm) in the Library Print Room Restaurant. But parents aren't forgotten—there's a very good spa. The rooms, some set up for families, come in a variety of guises, from fairly traditional in the old part of the hall to more contemporary in the newer part. If you feel like exploring, ask for a map of local routes, a Matfen Wildlife leaflet, and a packed lunch from the kitchen, or inquire about the Hadrian's Wall Adventure tour.

Matfen, Northumberland NE20 0RH. www.primahotels.co.uk/matfen. (C) **01661/880-6500.** 53 units. £130–£300 double. Rates include breakfast (half-board available). AE, DC. MC, V. Free parking. **Amenities:** 3 restaurants; bar; adventure course; golf estate; kids' book/DVD/games library; spa and leisure club with pool. *In room:* TV, DVD (by request), hair dryer.

EXPENSIVE

Chillingham Castle ☺   For those enraptured by the lovely castles that pepper the Northumberland coast, this 12th-century stronghold in Capability Brown-designed grounds 20 minutes' inland of Bamburgh offers several self-catering apartments (the largest sleeping seven or more), plus ghost tours on certain evenings. There are also daytime tours of the parkland, state rooms, dungeons, and torture chamber, and tours to see the world's only wild cattle (www.chillinghamwildcattle.com). You don't have to stay on-site to book a tour, but many visitors can't resist the chance to stay in a medieval castle or its former coaching rooms (rooms in the latter are larger but cheaper). The very private Guard Room, for couples, is where the relief watchmen slept. Furnishings are homey rather than plush, with a shabby-chic esthetic. Beware that some guests can find the castle a bit too spooky…

Chillingham, Northumberland NE66 5NJ. www.chillingham-castle.com. (C) **01668/215359.** £100–£170 apartment for 2, £200–£340 apartment for 4. MC, V. **Amenities:** Free access to parkland and garden; castle tours (extra charge). *In room:* TV, kitchen.

MODERATE

Coastal Retreats ★★ 🎒☺   The Northumberland coast is prime holiday cottage territory, but Coastal Retreats stands out, with all its cottages and beach apartments awarded the English Tourism Council's 5 Stars Self Catering accreditation. The contemporary interiors are professionally designed and include little luxuries such as woolen throws; some have wood-burning stoves. Kids are welcomed with dressing-up boxes, Wendy houses (playhouses), games rooms, trampolines, and more—the firm's own Starfish child-friendliness rating system helps find the best option for your family. Leisure club membership is included for those who'd like a swim or some pampering. There are sister country retreats, too (www.countryretreatsuk.com).

Northumberland coast (various addresses). www.coastalretreats.co.uk. (C) **0191/285-1272.** £470–£1,299 cottage for 4 per week (shorter stays available). MC, V. Free parking. **Amenities:** Vary by cottage but generally include games and toys; games room; health club membership. *In room:* TV/DVD/CD, books, kitchen, movie library, wood-burning stove (some), Wi-Fi (free).

Leaplish Waterside Park ★ ☺   For those who like to get away from it all, these Northumbrian Water-owned lodges (with adjoining caravan park) offer a great base for nature lovers and watersports enthusiasts visiting Kielder Water & Forest Park (p. 669). The relative isolation is compensated for with amenities including a sauna, indoor pool, play garden, mini-golf, birds-of-prey center, fishing, boat rental, and lakeside restaurant and bar. The four- and five-star Scandinavian-style lodges won the David Bellamy Gold Award for Conservation, boasting private verandas where you can sit and drink in the views over the lake and forest to the border hills. Sleeping from four to six, they include modern conveniences, plus, in some, whirlpool baths.

Kielder Water & Forest Park, Northumberland NE48 1BT. www.nwl.co.uk. © **01434/250232.** 32 units. £335–£1,145 per week (shorter stays available). MC, V. Free parking. **Amenities:** Restaurant; bar; boat rental; play area; indoor pool; mini-golf. *In room:* TV/DVD, baby equipment (extra charge), kitchen (w/ washer/dryer and dishwasher).

CARDIFF & THE SOUTH OF WALES

by Nick Dalton & Deborah Stone

This is a land of hills and history, of castles and sandy coves. Yet for every ancient site, there's a modern restaurant serving locally produced, organic food. Cardiff, the country's capital, is a vibrant destination, and Swansea, Wales's second city, is hot on its heels. What once was a heartland of the Industrial Revolution now welcomes tourists to the old mining towns as well as to the timeless and beautiful beaches of the Gower Peninsula and Pembrokeshire.

CITIES & TOWNS   Cardiff's old docks have been reinvented as the buzzing **Cardiff Bay.** The **Cardiff Bay Barrage** keeps the sea placid, and now the water laps against quaysides alive with restaurants and attractions. It's a perfect counterpoint to the city's fairytale castle, world-class museum, and extensive shopping. To the west is **Swansea,** a seafront city with its own revamped docks (the **Maritime Quarter**), cool hotels and beaches on **The Mumbles.** At Wales's westernmost point is **St. Davids,** Britain's smallest city, with a beautiful cathedral.

COUNTRYSIDE   The **Brecon Beacons National Park,** a wonderland of mountains, waterfalls, and stunning walks, is at the region's heart, but there is so much more. From the stark **Black Mountains** to the meandering valleys near **Rhayader** with their astonishing collection of **Victorian dams,** there's a beauty spot at every turn. There are walks along rivers, in forests, and up **Pen y Fan,** the south's highest peak.

EATING & DRINKING   This is a major food area, whether it's **Welsh lamb** grazed on lush hillsides or the **bounty of the sea.** Sophisticated restaurants are springing up all over, and boutique producers even extend to the **ice creams** of Cadwaladers, Gianni's, and Joe's. And **Welsh cakes,** a flat, sugary treat, are as good as ever.

COAST   The dazzling beaches on the west coast (**Newgale** near St. Davids is jaw-dropping) and the **Gower**'s fine sands get all the publicity, but there are special places all around the coastline; drive down a tiny lane and chances are you'll find a hidden spot. Resort towns are interspersed with extraordinary **castles,** and there are cliff-top walks and boat trips, watersports, and fishing villages. And the **Pembrokeshire Coast Path** offers a 186-mile walk from Amroth to Poppit.

THE best TRAVEL EXPERIENCES IN CARDIFF & THE SOUTH OF WALES

○ **Hitting the beach:** Here are some of the world's most stunning stretches of sand: Almost anywhere on the Gower Peninsula (especially Three Cliffs Bay; p. 703); Pembrokeshire (the desert island feel of lovely Barafundle Bay; p. 707); craggy cliff-backed Mwnt, near Cardigan, with its sandy beach and crystal-clear sea (p. 713); and the dunes and soft white sand of Dyfi National Nature Reserve (p. 714).

○ **Going underground:** You appreciate the hard life of the coal miner when you see the bleak mountainside entrance of the Big Pit, especially when it's covered in snow. The underground tour, a light strapped to your helmet, takes your breath away. Go down the pit, too, at Rhondda Heritage Park (also coal) and Dolaucothi gold mine. See p. 714.

○ **Storming the castle:** Whether it's Cardiff (a Victorian fairytale reconstruction of an ancient site; p. 680), Caerphilly (Britain's second largest castle; p. 683), the impressive Norman fortress of Pembroke (p. 707), or others, the castles here are all magnificent and wildly different from one another.

○ **Exploring the countryside:** It's easy to get away from it all here, up mountains, by lakes, on hills, in valleys, and on coastal cliffs. Stroll along rushing rivers, or drive down remote roads with jaw-dropping scenery around every turn of gently undulating pastures, magical forests, and picturesque peaks.

○ **Watching the wildlife:** Whether it's a relaxing trip out to spot dolphins in Cardigan Bay (p. 713), to see nesting cliff birds near Whitesands Bay (p. 711), or watching red kites circling overhead just about everywhere, there's plenty going on.

CARDIFF ★

155 miles W of London; 110 miles SW of Birmingham; 40 miles SE of Swansea

From the exciting, arty waterfront of **Cardiff Bay** to the growing number of smart shops in the heart of the city, and from the fairytale fantasy of **Cardiff Castle** to the Aladdin's cave of the **National Museum and Gallery,** this is a city that combines the new and old to great effect and demands to be enjoyed over several days. Once you take in the outskirts (the even more fairytale **Castell Coch,** the rural delights of **St. Fagans: National History Museum,** Newport's Roman remains, and the seaside of Penarth or Barry), you've got yourself a real holiday before even venturing farther afield. This is Europe's youngest capital city, designated as such only in 1955, although it has long been the country's most important urban center. Even though its roots can be traced back to 600 B.C., when the Celts invaded Europe, the Cardiff of today is vibrant. The Victorian indoor market rubs shoulders with the twin, upmarket malls of St. David's 1 and 2, traditional pubs sit next to modern bars, and you'll find some very cool hotels

Essentials

GETTING THERE Trains (First Great Western) from London arrive at Central Station on Wood Street every half-hour during the day, costing around £64 for a round-trip; the trip takes 2 hours. There are also regular services from cities such as Bristol, Birmingham, Edinburgh, and Glasgow.

National Express (℗ 0871/781-8181; www.nationalexpress.com) has frequent buses from London (a 3½-hr. journey) and from other cities.

Cardiff International Airport (℗ 01446/711111; www.tbicardiffairport.com) is 12 miles west of the city. **Flybe** (℗ 0871/700-2000; www.flybe.com) has five flights a week, and **Eastern Airways** (℗ 08703/669-100; www.easternairways. com) 11 flights a week from Newcastle. Flybe has up to eight flights a day from Glasgow and between them Flybe and **Bmibaby** (℗ 0905/8282828; www. bmibaby.com) have almost 30 flights a week from Edinburgh. Flybe also has up to four daily flights connecting Cardiff with Paris. **KLM** (℗ 0871/231-0000; www. klm.com) flies between Cardiff and Amsterdam; **Aer Lingus** (℗ 0871/718-5000 from U.K.; www.aerlingus.com) has a number of daily flights connecting Cardiff with Dublin (the latter has flights to and from New York, Chicago, Boston, and Orlando).

Cardiff Bus (℗ 0871/2002233; www.cardiffbus.com) operates bus no. X91, between the airport and bus station (in front of the rail station) hourly from 8:45am to 6:40pm Monday to Friday; Saturdays 6:25am to 6:40pm; and on Sundays, no. X5 and X91 operate from 10am to 7:30pm. A one-way trip is £3.70.

VISITOR INFORMATION **Cardiff Tourist Information Centre,** at the Old Library, the Hayes (℗ 029/2087-3573; www.visitcardiff.com), is in the heart of the city. Hours are Monday to Saturday 9:30am to 5:30pm, Sunday 10am to 4pm (July–Aug daily 9:30am–7pm). The Cardiff Bay office, the Tube, on Harbour Drive (℗ 029/2046-3833), is open daily 10am to 6pm.

GETTING AROUND As in most British cities, don't expect to use a car while you're here. Many of the places you'll want to visit are within walking distance of one another, and there's a good bus service, even to sights on the outskirts. One of your main journeys will be between city and Bay, which are connected by bus every few minutes. The **Valley Lines Day Explorer** rail ticket (www.arrivatrains.co.uk), available from any station, gives unlimited travel on lines around Cardiff, and up to Merthyr Tydfil for £9.10 adults, £4.55 children.

Buses cost £1.50 (children £1). The **Cardiff Bus** office (**Bws Caerdydd** in Welsh), across from the bus station in Wood Street (℗ 029/2066-6444; www. cardiffbus.com), has full route details. It's open Monday to Friday 8:30am to 5:30pm, Saturday 9am to 4:30pm. The service on Sunday morning is infrequent, and the last bus each day is at around 11pm.

Taxis are perhaps best reserved for getting home in the evening. Fares range from around £7 to £15. There are taxi stands at the rail and bus station and at St. David's Hall. Hotels and restaurants will call taxis for you, or contact **Capital Cabs** (℗ 029/2077-7777; www.taxinumber.com).

A good way to get an overall view of the city and its sights is a hop-on, hop-off open-top bus tour by **City Sightseeing** (℗ 029/2047-3432; www.city-sightseeing. com). Tours start outside Cardiff Castle. Adults pay £8.99, students and children ages 5 to 15 £3.99. Tour times change from month to month.

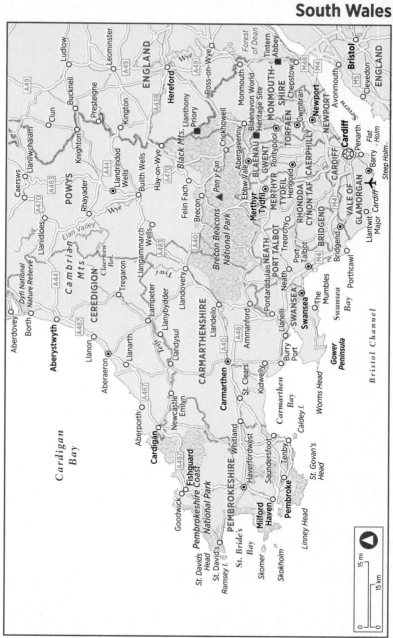

[FastFACTS] CARDIFF

Area Code   The area code for Cardiff is **029.**

Dentist   For emergencies, contact **Parade Dental Practice,** 23 The Parade (✆ **029/2048-1486**).

Doctor   For emergencies, dial ✆ **999** and ask for an ambulance. Doctors are on 24-hour call. A full list of doctors is posted at all post offices.

Drugstores   **Boots the Chemist** has various stores in town. The main prescription dispensing service is at 5 Wood St. (✆ **029/2037-7043;** www.boots.com), open Monday to Friday 8am to 6:30pm, Saturday 9am to 6pm.

Emergencies   For police, fire service, or ambulance, dial ✆ **999.**

Hospitals   The main hospital is the **University Hospital of Wales** (also known as the Heath Hospital), Heath Park (✆ **029/2074-7747**).

Internet Access   Wi-Fi is free in an increasing number of bars, coffee shops, and hotels. Or you can use **McDonald's,** 12–14 Queen St. (Sun–Thurs 5am–midnight; Fri–Sat open 24 hr.).

Maps   **Cardiff Tourist Information Centre,** the Old Library, The Hayes (✆ **029/2087-3573**), has a selection, and lots of free brochures.

Police   **Central Cardiff Police Station** is at King Edward VII Avenue, Cathays Park (✆ **029/2022-2111**).

Post Office   The main post office is at 45–46 Queens Arcade, Queen Street, (Mon–Sat 9am–5:30pm).

Exploring the City

Bute Park ★ PARK   Once the playground of the fabulously rich Bute family, this Capability Brown-designed park extends from the back of their former home, Cardiff Castle. There are flower gardens, an arboretum, open spaces, and the River Taff runs right through it.

Castle St./North Rd. ✆ **029/2068-4000.** Free admission. Daily dawn to dusk. Bus: 32 or 62.

Cardiff Castle ★★★ CASTLE   If you only have time for one thing, take a guided tour around this castle-cum-fantasyland. There's been a fort on the site since Roman times, and the 12th-century Norman keep is still intact, with fabulous views from its tower. But the building now known as Cardiff Castle was rebuilt in Victorian times in Gothic style by the third Marquess of Bute, reputedly the richest man in the world as owner of South Wales's coal mines, the railway that took the coal to the docks, and the docks themselves. Exquisite wall paintings depict fables, fairytales, and Biblical stories. Highlights include the banqueting hall with minstrels' gallery where the Queen and Prince Charles have dined; the ladies' sitting room, cheekily decorated like a harem; and the rooftop garden. But best of all is the day nursery with painted wall tiles depicting nursery rhymes and fairy stories. The last tour starts an hour before closing—although you have to stick with a guide for the castle itself, you can wander freely around the grounds, walls, keep, and military museum. The tours get busy so arrive, book, and then explore.

Castle St. ✆ **029/2087-8100.** www.cardiffcastle.com. Admission £11 adults, £9 students and seniors, £7.95 children 5–16. Mar–Oct daily 9am–6pm; Nov–Feb daily 9am–5pm. Last admission 1 hr. before closing. Closed Dec 25–26 and Jan 1. Bus: 32 or 62.

Cardiff

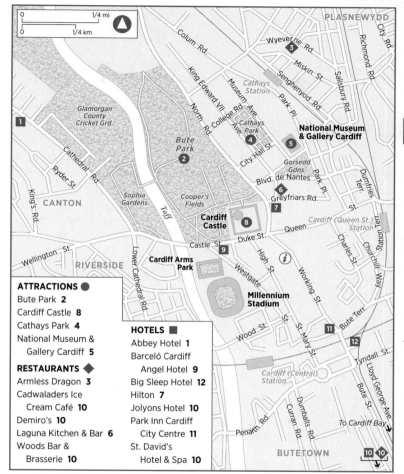

ATTRACTIONS ●

Bute Park **2**
Cardiff Castle **8**
Cathays Park **4**
National Museum &
　Gallery Cardiff **5**

RESTAURANTS ◆
Armless Dragon **3**
Cadwaladers Ice
　Cream Café **10**
Demiro's **10**
Laguna Kitchen & Bar **6**
Woods Bar &
　Brasserie **10**

HOTELS ■
Abbey Hotel **1**
Barceló Cardiff
　Angel Hotel **9**
Big Sleep Hotel **12**
Hilton **7**
Jolyons Hotel **10**
Park Inn Cardiff
　City Centre **11**
St. David's
　Hotel & Spa **10**

Cathays Park ★ PARK　Behind the National Museum and City Hall, this is a small oasis of calm, home to the Temple of Peace, which houses the Welsh Book of Remembrance. Within the park are Alexandra Gardens and the Welsh National War Memorial, a circular court of columns and sculptures dating from 1928.

Civic Centre. ✆ **029/2087-1847.** www.cardiff.ac.uk. Free admission. Daily, dawn to dusk. Bus: 32 or 62.

National Museum & Gallery Cardiff ★★ ☺ MUSEUM　In the grand tradition of British museums, this magnificent, domed building in Portland stone has a bit of everything: One of the biggest collections of Impressionist paintings outside Paris, a wealth of Monets, Manets, Van Goghs, and Cezannes; big names from other movements including the Pre-Raphaelites; and even a Rodin bronze. But this is a

18

CARDIFF & THE SOUTH OF WALES | Cardiff

681

festival CARDIFF

The **National St. David's Day Parade** (www.stdavidsday.org) is a March celebration of the national Welsh day featuring bands, choirs, and musical groups in national or historical dress as well as dance troupes and medieval re-enactments. The parade is in the afternoon, with a finale at the National Museum, but there are other events late into the evening. Cardiff Bay is host to many free festivals throughout the year (www.cardiff-festival.com) from **Cardiff**

International Food & Drink Festival, which snakes around the waterfront featuring the best of Welsh creations plus produce from the rest of the world, to **WOW on the Waterfront,** a celebration of dance and music (both in July). The **Harbour Festival** (Aug bank holiday) is one of the most popular, a weekend of family fun, food, and music along a nautical theme, with water-based activities and visits to tall ships at anchor.

full-fledged family attraction, with an "Evolution of Wales" section that takes you from the Big Bang to dinosaur skeletons, an animatronic woolly mammoth, the hands-on Clore Discovery Centre, and much more in galleries that have all been recently revamped.

Cathays Park, in the Civic Centre. ℂ **029/2039-7951.** www.museumwales.ac.uk. Free admission except for special exhibitions (prices vary). Tues–Sun 10am–5pm, plus bank holidays. Bus: 32 or 62.

Exploring Cardiff Bay

In 1999, the Barrage was built (basically a massive sea wall) across the bay, creating a vast freshwater lake accessible to vessels only via a lock. It is a mecca for sailing and other watersports, its shores full of attractions. **Cardiff Bay ★★**, the redeveloped area of the old dockland of Tiger Bay, is about 1½ miles from town. **Cardiff Bay Visitor Centre,** the Tube, Harbour Drive (ℂ **029/2046-3833;** www.visitcardiff. com), open 10am to 6pm, is an attraction in itself. It looks like a beached submarine and has films, exhibitions, a scale model of the city, as well as lots of free information. The **Waterbus** (ℂ **07940/142409;** www.cardiffcats.com) costs £3 one-way, £5 round-trip (children half-price) and leaves the city's Taff Mead Embankment every few minutes. It stops at Mermaid Quay for the Bay attractions, and at the Barrage for a walk to the beach resort of Penarth on its 30-minute tour. The Barrage (www.cardiff harbour.com) is open daily (free admission), for windy strolls and bicycle rides from the Bay attractions all the way to Penarth. There's even a windswept cafe.

Millennium Centre ENTERTAINMENT COMPLEX   The building that's the face of Cardiff Bay is an iconic arts hall with giant lines of poetry cut into its copper roof. The auditorium, like some jagged red-rock canyon from the American West, is even more stunning. Welsh stone, wood, metal, and glass have been used in construction, and Welsh artists have produced internal fixtures, fittings, and public art. There's often a free lunchtime concert in the lobby, which you can watch from the trendy cafe-bars, and a tour gets you among the giant sets, racks of costumes, and dressing rooms. See "Nightlife & Entertainment," below, for information on the performing arts here.

Bute Place. ℂ **08700/402000.** www.wmc.org.uk. Free admission to lobby; backstage tours £5.50 adults, £4.50 children 5–15. Daily from 10am. Bus: 6 Baycar, 7, 8, or 35.

Norwegian Church CHURCH   This white, clapboard church by the sea wall was built to serve the Norwegian seamen of the old docks; it's where *Charlie and the Chocolate Factory* author Roald Dahl, a local boy of Norwegian descent, was christened. Today it's a small arts center and cafe worth a swift look, and nice for a coffee at the outdoor tables gazing over the water.

Harbour Drive. ✆ **029-2045/4899.** Free admission. Daily 9am–5pm. Bus: 6 Baycar, 7, 8, or 35.

The Senedd ARCHITECTURE/GOVERNMENT BUILDING   This is the modernistic home of the Welsh Assembly, opened by the Queen in 2006. Visitors can take a free tour of the eco-friendly building (after airport-style security screening) and watch debates from the gallery under a wonderful, undulating wooden ceiling.

✆ **0845/0103300.** www.assemblywales.org. Free admission. Thurs–Tues times vary. Bus: 6 Baycar, 7, 8, or 35.

Exploring Beyond the City

Penarth is the delightful timewarp seaside resort across Cardiff Bay (walkable from the Barrage). The pretty high street dives down the hill to a mostly elegant promenade, and the beach (partly rocky, partly sandy). There's a small pier where the paddle steamers MV *Balmoral* and PS *Waverly* call in summer. You'll also find Decks selling chips (fries) with gravy, and Joe's ice cream from Swansea. The **Pierson** is a charming, old-style hotel with a modern flourish while **Mediterraneo,** in an old boat house, is a chic Italian seafood restaurant.

Caerleon Roman Baths & Amphitheatre HISTORIC SITE   One of the most important Roman sites in Britain, this is where the Second Augustan Legion (5,500 men) built a township, fortress, and barracks. The remains of the huge bathhouse are preserved in a modern, wooden hall, with walkways above the excavated hot and cold baths. Just along the road, on the site of the fortress, is the National Roman Legion Museum (free), full of pottery, coins, and artifacts. The amphitheatre, around the corner in the middle of a field, features stone banks encompassing the arena, once alive with pageantry and bloodlust. Now it's a great place to picnic, and in the summer there are often plays and living history enactments.

High St., Caerleon, Newport. ✆ **01633/422518.** www.cadw.cymru.uk. Admission to baths: £2.90 adults, £2.50 children 5–15. Apr–Oct daily 9:30am–5pm; Nov–Mar Mon–Sat 9:30am–5pm, Sun 11am–4pm. Amphitheatre: free, accessible all year.

Caerphilly Castle ★★ CASTLE   Crossing the bridge over the moat around the biggest medieval castle in Wales you are left breathless at the sheer size of the 12-hectare (30-acre) fortress. One tower leans at what looks like a dangerously drunken angle, but it only adds to the impressiveness of this 13th-century wonder built on three man-made islands and surrounded by artificial lakes created by damming the Nant y Gledr stream. It still looks as impregnable now as it did then with its concentric walls-within-walls design. You can wander into the Great Hall but there's no fancy interior, even though it was restored by the third Marquess of Bute.

On the A469, at Caerphilly. ✆ **029/2088-3143.** www.cadw.cymru.gov.uk. Admission £3.60 adults, £3.20 children 15 and under. Apr–May and Oct daily 9:30am–5pm; June–Sept daily 9:30am–6pm; Nov–Mar Mon–Sat 9:30am–4pm. Bus: 26 from Cardiff leaves for Caerphilly each hour (also bus no. 71 or 72). Caerphilly train with several departures daily from Central Station in Cardiff.

Castell Coch ★★★ CASTLE   The most beautiful castle in Wales looks like the fantasy fortress in *Chitty Chitty Bang Bang* in its tree-lined hillside position. You can even see it from the ramparts of Cardiff Castle, which is fitting as both were holiday homes for the fabulously rich third Marquess of Bute. He presided over the flamboyant Victorian rebuild of a medieval castle ruin to create a *Harry Potter*-esque fantasy that clings to the mountainside and is approached through a thick forest overlooking a gorge in the Taff Valley. Like its city cousin, the interior is a sumptuous Arts and Crafts-style interpretation of medieval decor. Scenes from Aesop's Fables decorate the walls and ceilings of the living rooms while the bedrooms are each an individual fantasy. There are spiral staircases and even a working portcullis and drawbridge.

Tongwynlais. ℘ **029/2081-0101.** www.cadw.cymru.gov.uk. Admission £3.70 adults, £3.50 children 15 and under. Daily generally 9:30am–5.30pm; slightly longer July–Aug, shorter Nov–Feb. Bus: 132 from Cardiff leaves every 30 min. (every 60 min. on Sun) for Tongwynlais, a half-mile away.

Dyffryn Gardens GARDEN   Only several miles from the city but deep in the Vale of Glamorgan, these Edwardian gardens cover 22 hectares (55 acres). Centrepoint is a collection of gardens, all clipped hedges, lovely brickwork, and formal planting, but there are also neat lawns, seasonal planting, and an arboretum with trees from around the world. There's been intensive effort to restore the 1906 glory of leading designer Thomas Mawson. A tearoom sits on the banks of a stream.

St. Nicholas, Vale of Glamorgan. ℘ **029/2059-3328.** www.dyffryngardens.org.uk. £6.50 adults (£3.25 winter), children 5–15 £2.50 (£1.25 winter). Daily Mar–Oct 10am–6pm; Nov–Feb 10am–4pm.

Llandaff Cathedral ★ CATHEDRAL   You can feel the history creeping up on you at one of the oldest Christian sites in Britain, where there was a community as far back as the 6th century. The current cathedral dates from the start of the 12th century, and accumulated classic features down the centuries. From the West Front (a medieval work of art) through Italian Temple touches from the 1700s to Sir Jacob Epstein's aluminum statue *Christ in Majesty,* part of the rebirth following a World War II bomb. The cathedral sits on the western edge of the city, on a green with a village atmosphere surrounded by timbered buildings.

Cathedral Rd. ℘ **029/2056-4554.** www.llandaffcathedral.org.uk. Free admission. Daily 7am–7pm. Call for times of services. Bus: 25, 33, 33A, or 62.

St. Fagans: National History Museum ★★ MUSEUM   This wonderful open-air museum has more than 40 historic Welsh buildings from around the country, restored to their former glory, on the 40-hectare (100-acre) grounds of St. Fagans Castle. It's so beautifully laid-out that you really do feel as though you're skipping down country lanes, walking down the high street of a century-old village, or being transported back to the Middle Ages. There's a farm, school, chapel, and ironmonger's, as well as Celtic huts with fires burning, and with shields and swords for children to wield. Traditional craftsmen, such as the potter, are at work and native breeds of farm animals graze in the fields. You'll find it to be less a museum than an exploration, before you return to the main building with its galleries devoted to history, textiles, agriculture, and costumes. The castle is actually a 16th-century mansion built inside a Norman castle wall, with formal gardens, now restored.

St. Fagans. ℘ **029/2057-3500.** www.museumwales.ac.uk. Free admission, but charge for parking lot. Daily 10am–5pm. Bus: 32 or 320, leaving from the bus station in Cardiff every hour during the day.

Where to Eat
MODERATE

Armless Dragon WELSH   About 1 mile north of the main streets, the Dragon is known for the best in Welsh produce. "Taste of Wales" dishes include an antipasto of cured ham, lava bread, quail egg, cockles, olives, and oatcakes. Starters include pan-fried pigeon breast with beetroot risotto, or homemade Glamorgan sausages with leeks and truffle oil. Among the mains are Welsh sirloin steak with field mushrooms and red-onion marmalade.

97 Wyeverne Rd. © **029/2038-2357.** www.armlessdragon.co.uk. Reservations recommended. Main courses £12–£17. MC, V. Tues–Fri noon–2pm; Tues–Thurs 7–9pm; Fri–Sat 7–9:30pm. Closed Dec 25–26.

Laguna Kitchen & Bar ★ INTERNATIONAL/WELSH   This place has a modern setting with the choice of a formal dining room or a laid-back bar featuring private booths. Local ingredients are turned into starters such as ham hock and parsley terrine, or the carpaccio of Welsh beef filet flavored with chili, ginger, and soy sauce. Grills are good—skate wing or rib-eye steaks. Other main courses include slow-cooked lamb shank with bubble and squeak.

Park Plaza hotel, Greyfriars Rd. © **029/2011-1111.** www.parkplaza.com/cardiffuk. Main courses £8.25–£18. AE, MC, V. Mon–Sat noon–2:30pm and 5–10:30pm; Sun noon–9pm.

Woods Bar & Brasserie ★ MODERN BRITISH/CONTINENTAL   In the old Pilotage Building down by the dock, this is a glass-fronted haven of modernity. For starters, try the pressed terrine of pig's brawn, pork jelly, sauce gribiche, and sourdough toasts. Main courses include pan-fried gilthead bream, boulanger potatoes with fennel, lava bread fritter, and cockle and lemon butter.

Pilotage Building, Stuart St., Cardiff Bay. © **029/2049-2400.** www.woods-brasserie.com. Reservations required. Main courses £12–£27; fixed-price 2-course lunch £15; fixed-price 2-course pre-opera dinner £18. AE, DC, MC, V. Mon–Sat noon–2pm and 5–10pm; Sun noon–3pm.

INEXPENSIVE
Cadwaladers Ice Cream Café BRITISH   Right on the quay-side at Cardiff Bay, this is one of a growing number of modern eateries from the family ice-cream company started in Criccieth, North Wales in 1927. The bright, lively place is where to come for that Willy Wonka moment, with wild concoctions such as Dragon's Breath and Chocolate Porridge. But there's plenty more, from coffee and cakes to attractive grilled bruschetta, brioche-style ham, leek pies (for lunch or a pre-theatre snack), and even alcoholic ice-cream cocktails.

Mermaid Quay, Cardiff Bay. © **029/2049-7598.** www.cadwaladersicecream.co.uk. Ice cream and dishes from £2–£8. MC, V. Daily from 10am; closing varies from 5pm in winter to 10pm in summer.

Demiro's ITALIAN/SPANISH/WELSH   This looks like a traditional Italian restaurant, all deep red with classical statues and big mirrors, but it actually has side-by-side Italian, Welsh, and Spanish menus. Will it be chicken cooked in the wood-burning oven or homemade faggots (an offal meatball) with peas and mash? At a basic level, there are great thin-crust pizzas but you can splash out on local steak and lamb. And there are nice views on to the Millennium Centre and over the Bay.

Mermaid Quay, Cardiff Bay. © **029-2049-1882.** www.demiros.com. Main courses £7–£20. AE, MC, V. Sun–Thurs noon–10pm; Fri–Sat until 10:30pm.

Shopping
Cardiff offers the joys of mainstream shopping on a grand scale. **Queen Street,** the main shopping thoroughfare (now car-free) has many major chain stores. A number of nearby streets are also part of the traffic-free zone, and include everything from sophisticated arcades to a traditional indoor market.

Of the varied arcades from Victorian and Edwardian times, the oldest is the Royal Arcade, connecting The Hayes and St. Mary Street. It dates from 1858 and still has some original Victorian store fronts. The Morgan Arcade, completed in 1899, runs parallel. Both are a wealth of elegant columns, flagstone floors, and mostly upmarket stores.

The extension to the St. David's indoor mall continues the arcade tradition with its limestone-rich Grand Arcade, which is 240 m (800 ft.) long, ending at the classic department store John Lewis, the biggest branch outside London. **St David's** (© 029/2036-7600; www.stdavidscardiff.com), with entrances on Queen Street, The Hayes, and various other streets, is the city's leading mall with more than 100 shops, plus its own restaurant quarter, East Side. The **Capitol Shopping Centre,** also on Queen Street, is another indoor complex.

Cardiff Central Market, St. Mary Street, is a classic Victorian indoor market, all iron pillars and glass roof with a wrought-iron balcony around the upper level. It's the place to buy local meat, cheese, laver bread (seaweed), and sugary Welsh cakes, as well as books, records, and much more. On Sunday mornings the Riverside Farmers' Market takes place on the embankment of the River Taff.

Cardiff's shopping streets are filled with grandiose buildings, many of them Edwardian; a good example is the **James Howell** department store on St. Mary Street (part of the upmarket House of Fraser chain), all designer fashion on the inside but Corinthian and Ionic columns on the exterior. **Spiller's Records** on The Hayes claims to be the world's oldest record shop, selling discs since 1894, and it's still a place to browse for music. **Jacob's Antiques Centre,** West Canal Wharf (© 029/2039-0939), near the rail station, is a four-floor red-brick warehouse with more than 50 stalls selling vintage clothes, bric-a-brac, furniture, and books. There are various other shops selling vintage clothes and accessories.

Entertainment & Nightlife
THE PERFORMING ARTS

The **Wales Millennium Centre ★★★** (© 029/2063-6464; www.wmc.org.uk), is a £100 million giant on the banks of Cardiff Bay with poetry in enormous letters cut out of its copper facade. Its 1,900-seat auditorium (along with the Weston Studio) is home to a clutch of arts groups, including the Welsh National Opera and the Dance Company of Wales. The Centre, opened by the Queen in 2004, attracts major international companies, but also puts on performances of everything from stand-up comedians to the musical *Mamma Mia!* Ticket prices vary, depending on the attraction. Tickets for some shows are below £10, others approaching £50.

St. David's Hall (or *Neuadd Dewi Sant* in Welsh), The Hayes (© 029/2087-8444; www.stdavidshall.co.uk), dates back to the early 1980s, and is a modernist venue that vies with the Millennium Centre for the title of Cardiff's leading concert hall. It is a constant host to ballets and orchestras, interspersed with more mainstream concerts. The adjoining **New Theatre** (© 029/2087-8889; www.new theatrecardiff.co.uk) actually dates from 1906 (it's hosted the likes of Sarah Bernhardt and Jelly Roll Morton) and puts on musicals and pantomimes. **Cardiff International Arena** (© 029/2022-4488; www.livenation.co.uk/cardiff) is a large indoor venue on Mary Ann Street and hosts major music and comedy acts.

LIVE MUSIC, COMEDY & NIGHTCLUBS

Clwb ifor Bach (the **Welsh Club**), 11 Womanby St. (© 029/2023-2199; www. clwb.net), focuses on home-grown acts, and still gets those who have made the leap

CARDIFF'S pubs

As a capital city, and one with docks and a working-class heritage, Cardiff has plenty of pubs, many of which are historic sites in themselves. The **City Arms,** 10 Quay St. (✆ **029/2022-5258**), is a warm, traditional place near the Millennium Stadium, which attracts rugby fans and anyone looking for the real Cardiff. The nearby **Horse & Groom,** on Womanby Street (✆ **08714/329005**), is Cardiff's smallest, oldest pub. The **Goat Major,** on the High Street (✆ **029/2033-7161**), is fabulously traditional, with beams on the outside and dark wood panels coating the inside, a backdrop to the black leather sofas. The **Owain Glyndwr,** 10 St. John's Square (✆ **029/2033-9303**), is near the castle and another small, friendly backstreet pub.

The Bay has glossy, modern bars such as **Salt,** with its balcony, on Mermaid Quay (✆ **029/2049-4375**; www. saltcardiff.com), home to a young,

cocktail-quaffing crowd. But look beneath the surface and you find the pubs of yesteryear, such as **The Packet,** on Bute Street (✆ **029/2046-5513**), a hotel for sailors in Victorian times, with its original rope-clad pillars and majestic mahogany-bar backdrop. The **White Hart**, 64 James St. (✆ **029/2047-2561**), is the oldest pub in the Docks area, dating back to 1855, and is a lively locals haunt.

Most of the pubs serve Cardiff-brewed Brains' beers, not least the **Yard Bar & Kitchen,** 42 St. Mary St. (✆ **029/2022-7577**; www.yard barkitchen.co.uk). It's a smart bar and restaurant in old brewery buildings on the edge of the Old Brewery Quarter, a traffic-free cluster of mostly chain eateries and bars. Visit www.sabrain.com for a full list of pubs selling delights such as SA amber ale and the rich dark Rev. James, named after a beer-brewing vicar from Victorian times.

to international stardom (such as Super Furry Animals) back for low-key shows. There are three floors and in addition to live music you'll also find hip-hop, dance, electronica, and more. Admission ranges from £3 to £10, and the club is open most nights, usually from 7:30pm to either 2 or 3am.

The Glee Club, Mermaid Quay (✆ **0871/472-0400**; www.glee.co.uk), at Cardiff Bay, is a large comedy club with acts generally appearing Thursday to Saturday. It can take up its seats to present the coolest of live music, both modern and from times past on most other evenings. Admission from £9 to £20. Entry varies, usually between 7:30 and 8pm.

The Globe, 125 Albany Rd. (✆ **029/2045-2151**; www.theglobecardiff.com), has live music 7 nights a week, from new names to established stars such as Colin Blunstone, singer with 1960s' heroes The Zombies. Tickets tend to be £10 to £15. Doors open around 7pm.

Oceana, Greyfriars Road (✆ **0845/2968588**; www.oceanaclubs.com), is Cardiff's biggest nightclub, with seven themed rooms, from Tahiti to New York to Monte Carlo, where you can dance, slump on sofas, or sip cocktails from 10 different bars. Prices start at £5, rising to £15 for special events. Hours are 9pm until 3 or 4am. The complex also features the Mordaith Bar and Grill (free entry), open 11am to 10pm, with deals such as a meal and drink for £4.50, and hosting Jongleurs comedy club nights, with free nightclub entry.

GAY CLUBS

Exit Club, 48 Charles St. (🕾 **029/2064-0102;** www.exitclubcardiff.com), is the city's longest-running gay club, with DJs 7 days a week for almost 20 years. At weekends it expands to two floors, split between pop and dance music, and there is also a beer garden. Prices vary. The club is open from 10pm until 2am, to 4am on Friday and 6am Saturday. **Club X,** 35 Charles St. (🕾 **07523/904775;** www.clubxcardiff. net) is the Exit's main contender with DJs playing house, club classics, and electronica. It's open Friday to Sunday until 6am; entry is free before 10pm, then £10.

Where to Stay

EXPENSIVE

Barceló Cardiff Angel Hotel ★   The elegant Victorian Angel Hotel, across from Cardiff Castle, was *the* place to stay in South Wales when it was first built. Over the years, it has attracted everybody from Greta Garbo to the Beatles to prime ministers. The Angel is still good—and it has regained some of its old prestige following a restoration. It's a world of neo-Doric decor, *trompe l'oeil* ceilings, Waterford crystal chandeliers, and hand-stippled faux-marble columns. As befits a hotel of this age, its guest rooms come in a wide variety of styles and sizes.

Castle St., Cardiff CF10 1SZ. www.barcelo-hotels.co.uk. 🕾 **029/2064-9200.** Fax 029/2039-6212. 102 units. £65–£200 double; £125–£300 suite. AE, DC, MC, V. Parking £5. **Amenities:** Restaurant; bar and lounge; babysitting; concierge; room service. *In room:* A/C, TV, hair dryer, Wi-Fi (£12 per 24 hr.).

Hilton ★★★ ☺   This is a delightful, friendly, and modern place in a perfect position across the road from the castle and museum, and around the corner from the shops. The rooms are large, sleek-but-comfy, and many have fantastic views. The stainless-steel swimming pool is a joy. The **Razzi restaurant,** serving modern British and Welsh cuisine (such as salt-marsh lamb with bubble and squeak), spills out into a glass extension opposite the castle, and manages to be both sophisticated and child-friendly, with an excellent children's menu.

Kingsway, Cardiff CF10 3HH. www.hilton.co.uk/cardiff. 🕾 **029/2064-9200.** 197 units. £99–£350 double; £159–£850 suite. AE, DC, MC, V. Valet parking £17. **Amenities:** Restaurant; 2 bars; room service; pool; gym; sauna; shop. *In room:* A/C, TV, hair dryer, Wi-Fi (£15 per 24 hr.).

St. David's Hotel & Spa ★★★ 📫   The iconic new face of Cardiff Bay is a stylish landmark on a promontory giving it watery views from every room. The glass atrium on the inside is as impressive as the sail-like roof. And there's five-star service to match. The rooms are big, stylishly furnished in a pale, interesting way, and have floor-to-ceiling windows leading on to balconies. The Marine Spa has been voted one of Britain's best, and there's a glorious pool. The **Tempus bar and restaurant** is a place for a sea-view cocktail, afternoon tea, or a meal, while the **Tides Grill** offers alfresco dining.

Havannah St., Cardiff Bay, Cardiff CF10 5SD. www.thestdavidshotel.com. 🕾 **029/2045-4045.** Fax 029/2048-7056. 132 units. £119–£190 double; £169–£570 suite. AE, DC, MC, V. Parking £8. **Amenities:** 2 restaurants; bar; babysitting; concierge; exercise room; indoor heated pool; room service; spa. *In room:* A/C, TV/DVD/CD player (in some), hair dryer, minibar.

MODERATE

Jolyons Hotel ★★ 📫   This former seamen's lodge on Cardiff Bay's oldest terrace has been turned into a delightful boutique hotel. There are only a few bedrooms, each individually furnished. The place is modern and stylish inside, but with a rustic, slate-floored bar with a log stove and red-leather sofas. Most of the bedrooms have views of the bay, and most come with king-size beds. Some of the bathrooms have whirlpool tubs and one has a "wet room."

5 Bute Crescent, Cardiff Bay, Cardiff CF10 5AN. www.jolyons.co.uk. ✆ **029/2048-8775.** Fax 029/2048-8775. 6 units. £75–£150 double. AE, MC, V. Rates include Welsh breakfast. **Amenities:** Bar; room service. *In room:* TV, hair dryer, Wi-Fi (free).

Park Inn Cardiff City Centre ★ ☺   Next to the Cardiff International Arena, the Park is stylish and classic. Spacious and well-furnished bedrooms are grouped around an atrium, which gives access to the smart public rooms. A few family rooms are available.

Mary Ann St., Cardiff CF10 2JH. www.cardiff-city.parkinn.co.uk. ✆ **888/201-1801** or 029/2034-1441. Fax 029/2022-3742. 146 units. £85–£165 double. Rates include breakfast. AE, DC, MC, V. Parking £8. **Amenities:** Restaurant; bar; babysitting; room service. *In room:* TV, hair dryer, Wi-Fi (£10 per day).

INEXPENSIVE

Abbey Hotel   Built in 1898 as a home for a wealthy sea captain and his family, this place has many of its original features and is one of the better and more reasonably priced B&Bs. Richard Burton once attended elocution lessons in the public lounge back when the hotel was a private school. Bedrooms are small but comfortable. A few have four-poster beds.

149–151 Cathedral Rd., Cardiff CF11 9PJ. www.bandb4u.co.uk. ✆ **029/2039-0896.** Fax 029/2023-8311. 26 units (shower only). £60–£75 double. MC, V. Free parking. **Amenities:** Restaurant; bar. *In room:* TV, hair dryer.

Big Sleep Hotel ★ 🔥   This place is part of a small chain of cool budget hotels partly owned by actor John Malkovich. What was a 1960s' office block is a great place to stay at great prices. Decor is sleek and modern, location is good (right by the St. David's shopping mall), there's a decent bar, and you even get a continental breakfast.

Bute Terrace, Cardiff CF10 2FE. www.thebigsleephotel.com. ✆ **029/2063-6363.** Fax 029/2063-6364. 81 units. Mon–Thurs £45–£69 double, £99 suite. Rates include continental breakfast. AE, MC, V. Parking £6. **Amenities:** Bar. *In room:* TV, hair dryer, Wi-Fi (£7.50 per day).

THE WELSH VALLEYS: THE WORLD OF COAL

165 miles W of London; 29 miles NE of Cardiff

The Welsh Valleys are the home of the coal industry. Or at least they were, until the ones that were left were closed in the 1980s. But despite the hardship that followed, the locals never gave up and have reinvented the brooding, often bleak, area as a mecca for industrial-heritage tourism. Pits have been turned into museums and even the most daunting landscape, littered with slag heaps and once-abandoned buildings, has risen in a new clanking, grinding glory. The area around **Blaenavon** (on the edge of the Black Mountains, southeast of Abergavenny) is one of the best. It's only a short drive from Cardiff but might as well be in another world, in another century. Tour the area, and you'll come across towns such as Merthyr Tydfil, which in 1845 had a population of 40,000 thanks to its iron and steel industry. Here the **Cyfarthfa Castle Museum** remembers the 1966 Aberfan disaster, when 20 houses and a school were buried in a slag-heap slide killing 144 people, mostly children.

Essentials

GETTING THERE   By rail, Abergavenny (45 mins, £11) and Merthyr Tydfil (1 hr., £5) have connections to Cardiff. Train times are irregular but frequent. The **Stagecoach** X43 bus from Brecon stops at both towns, but it's good to have a car and it's an easy drive from Cardiff and the M4.

VISITOR INFORMATION   There's an area tourist office at the Blaenavon Ironworks (© **01495/792615;** www.blaenavontic.com), which has seasonal opening, but the Blaenavon World Heritage Centre (see below) is best for information.

Exploring the Area

Big Pit ★★★ ☺ HISTORIC SITE   This is also called the National Coal Museum, but the Big Pit is truly what it is: a former coal mine that sits on a sweeping mountainside. It's what Wales was all about: hard work and dirt, and you can see it from the inside. After a multimedia presentation, you're given a hardhat and lamp and taken 92m (300 ft.) down the mineshaft in a real, clanking pit cage for a 50-minute tour. It's all authentic, and your guide is a real miner who remembers the place being closed by Prime Minister Margaret Thatcher in the 1980s. The tunnels, including underground stables for pit ponies, are dark and atmospheric. Above ground is a well-designed museum in the pithead baths, a number of old buildings to explore, and a cafe. It's all the more impressive in the bleak midwinter, with the landscape covered in snow. It's one of the country's must-see attractions, and it's free.

Blaenavon. © **01495/790311.** www.museumwales.ac.uk. Free admission. Daily 9:30am–5pm; tours 10:30am–3:30pm. From town follow museum signs.

Blaenavon Heritage Railway ★ ☺ RAILWAY   Built to transport coal from the Big Pit (see above), this is the highest and steepest standard-gauge railway in England and Wales reaching the countries' highest station, Whistle Halt (400m/1,307 ft.). It's not a long ride, but there is plenty to see: mountain ponies, peregrine falcons, red kites, and lots of hardy sheep. Five minutes from the main station Furnace Sidings are Garn Lakes, a lovely spot for picnics. The Whistle Inn at the end of the line has a beer garden. There are events throughout the year, including Santa Specials.

Blaenavon. © **01495/792263.** www.pontypool-and-blaenavon.co.uk. Tickets £5 adults, £3 children 5–15. Apr–Sept departures on weekends and some weekdays from around 11:30am–4:30pm, and other dates for events. From town follow signs.

Blaenavon World Heritage Site ★★★ HISTORIC SITE   This is the official name for one of the most impressive Industrial Revolution sites in Europe. The town of Blaenavon and its surroundings were awarded UNESCO World Heritage status in 2000. **Blaenavon World Heritage Centre,** in the restored St. Peter's School, gives an overview of the industrial landscape, with its interactive displays. It is also the start of various walks, and has a gift shop and cafe. The rather bleak valley setting is home to Europe's best-preserved 18th-century ironworks (which was fired by the local coal). Even seeing what's left of the five furnaces is enough to make you feel humbled. It wasn't even the biggest ironworks in Wales, but in 1789 it was the most advanced in the world. There are plenty of places to wander, such as the restored workers' cottages. The site includes the marvelous Big Pit museum and Pontypool and Blaenavon Railway, which are attractions in their own right (see reviews, above).

Church Rd., Blaenavon. © **01495/742333.** www.world-heritage-blaenavon.org.uk. Free admission. Centre Apr–Sept Tues–Sat 9am–5pm (until 4pm Oct–Mar). Ironworks daily Apr–Oct 10am–5pm;

Nov–Mar Fri–Sat 9:30am–4pm, Sun 11am–4pm. Follow signs from the A465 northwest of Cardiff, outside Pontypool.

Rhondda Heritage Park ☺ ENTERTAINMENT COMPLEX   In the Rhondda Valley, heart of Welsh coal mining, the former Lewis Merthyr Colliery at Trehafod has been transformed into a family history attraction. There's a reconstructed village street, including shops and homes, so you can see how life was lived from Victorian times up to the 1950s. Admission is free but you pay for the Black Gold Tour, an audio-visual presentation and tour of the pithead buildings followed by an underground trip. You get a helmet lamp but only go down a few feet, and the train ride finale is a Disney-esque vibrating carriage with runaway train film backdrop (great fun for children). There's also Energy Zone, a giant adventure playground, open April to September, a cafe, and a gift shop.

Coed Cae Rd., Trehafed, Pontypridd. ✆ **01443/682036.** www.rhonddaheritagepark.com. Free admission; Black Gold Tour £5.60 adults, £4.30 children 3–15. Daily 9am–4:30pm. Closed Dec 24–early Jan and Mon Oct–Easter. Btw. Pontypridd and Porth, just off the A470, near junction 32 of the M4.

Where to Eat

This is far from the most attractive part of Wales and therefore isn't a place to base yourself. Stay instead down in Cardiff, or up in the Brecon Beacons. For lunch, the **Heritage Café** (✆ **01495/742339**) at the BlaenavonWorld Heritage Centre, with its big windows and mountain views, is decent enough, with healthful options and some seasonal fare. And the **Whistle Inn** (✆ **01495/790403**) above Garn Lakes, by the railway, offers pub grub. There are also various cafes in Blaenavon.

ABERGAVENNY & THE BLACK MOUNTAINS

163 miles W of London; 31 miles NE of Cardiff

Traditionally viewed as the gateway to the Brecon Beacons (although it is outside the National Park), **Abergavenny** is more closely associated with the Black Mountains, an entity unto themselves that forms the eastern edge of the park. Sitting on the River Usk, Abergavenny is possibly the finest market town in Wales and increasingly a foodie destination. It is a popular weekend getaway. There's history, too, with a Norman castle tucked away in the backstreets, a classic Norman church, and a good museum. It's also a hub for mountain drives and walks. Outside town, the **Black Mountains** offer some of the most dramatic scenery in the Brecons, bald peaks, dizzying drives, and walks along the River Gavenny, River Usk, and Brecon and Abergavenny Canal.

Abergavenny is a good base for a range of **outdoor activities,** including pony trekking, hill walking and climbing, golfing, hang gliding, and fishing. You can also take a boat out for a day or longer on the canal, which passes near the town. To get a feel for the area's remoteness and hill farms, the single-lane roads, and the meandering river valleys, a car is essential.

Essentials

GETTING THERE   By rail, Abergavenny is linked to Newport (Arriva Trains Wales; £8), 19 miles to the southwest, from where there are connections to London (2½ hr.) and Cardiff. There are also trains from Abergavenny to Shrewsbury and

walking TALL

This area has more good hikes than you can shake a walking stick at. **Offa's Dyke Path** (www.offasdyke.demon. co.uk) is a 177-mile hike from Chepstow to Prestatyn on the north coast of Wales, but little more than a third follows the 8th-century earthwork, which protected the English from marauding Celts. There is, however, a particularly good stretch between the Llanthony Valley and Hay-on-Wye. Take the Offa's Dyke Flyer (linked to the Beacons Bus, p. 696) from Hay to Llanthony and walk back. The **Usk Valley Walk** (www.usk valleywalk.org.uk) is a 48-mile walk that starts at Brecon and mostly follows the Monmouthshire and Brecon Canal towpath, with diversions through woods and across fields, down to Abergavenny, where it follows the River Usk down to Caerleon, with occasional forays into the hills.

Hereford across the border. There are regular buses: No. 20 from Hereford, no. 21 from Brecon, and no. X4 from Cardiff.

Abergavenny is a short drive along the A4042 from the M4, which links Cardiff and London.

VISITOR INFORMATION   Abergavenny's Civic Society has laid out a **Town Trail,** marking buildings and other points of interest with brass plaques. The **Tourist Information Centre** is at the bus station on Monmouth Road (© **01873/853254;** www.visitabergavenny.co.uk). It's open daily 10am to 5pm.

Exploring Abergavenny

Abergavenny Castle, on Castle Street, is one of the best examples of a motte-and-bailey castle in Britain. Although much has disappeared, including the bailey (courtyard with outbuildings), the restored keep still sits on the motte (man-made mound), giving a good impression of what it would have been like in the 12th century. Admission is free, and it's open daily from dawn to dusk. **Abergavenny Museum** (© **01873/854282;** www.abergavennymuseum.co.uk) is in the castle keep, which was rebuilt as the Marquess of Abergavenny's hunting lodge in 1818. There are archeological finds (relics from the Roman fort of Gobannium) and lots of Welsh life, with displays housing the contents of a farmhouse kitchen, a saddler's, and a grocer's. Admission is free. The museum is open March to October, Monday to Saturday 11am to 1pm and 2 to 5pm, Sunday 2 to 5pm; and November to February, Monday to Saturday 11am to 1pm and 2 to 4pm.

St. Mary's Priory Church, Monk Street (© **01873/853168;** www.stmarys-priory.org), was the church to a priory set up by the first Norman lord of Abergavenny in the early 12th century. It's now one of the biggest parish churches in Wales. It has suffered much through the centuries: From (it is believed) Cromwell's rampaging troops, leaving the tombs wrecked, to injudicious restoration. There's still plenty to see, including the Norman font, carved 14th- and 15th-century monastic choir stalls, and some still outstanding tombs. It's open daily 9am to 7pm year-round.

Llanthony Priory (www.cadw.gov.uk; open daily; free admission) is a peaceful ruin in a quiet valley just north of Abergavenny in the foothills of the Black Mountains. It's an idyllic spot for a picnic or for a beer at the Llanthony Priory Hotel (see "Where To Eat & Stay," below). Talgarth, on the A479 at the northern edge of the

Black Mountains, is an attractive town where you can still catch a cattle market (some Tues and Fri), and where Tower House, one of only two fortified houses in Wales, serves as the **tourist office** (✆ **01874/712226**). Nearby is the **Pwll-y-Wrach Nature Reserve** with its waterfalls and springtime carpet of bluebells, where you may see otters, and the Woodland Trust's **Park Wood,** on a ridge above town.

Exploring Hay-on-Wye

For a small town Hay has a huge reputation, not least for its eccentricity: It is twinned with Timbuktu, and once declared independence from Britain. Hay (once half in England) is famed for having more secondhand bookstores than anywhere else in the world, but it was the **Hay Festival** (www.hayfestival.com), launched in 1987, that put the town on the international culture map. During the 10 days of the literary festival, starting the last week in May and attracting authors from around the globe, it becomes an arty city of 150,000. All the events and hotels get booked up fast, but you can still have a charming day here, thanks to the food marquees and setting. The rest of the time Hay is a leisurely delight with the bookstores interspersed with bric-a-brac emporia and organic food stores, and you can wander down to the River Wye for a gentle stroll. The Bailey Walk follows the river more than a mile on the town side to The Warren, a beauty spot where you can have a paddle and a picnic. Hay also has the remains of a Norman castle, now, predictably, a secondhand bookstore. The Offa's Dyke Path and easy Wye Valley Walk run through town; you can pick up a Walk Pack from the tourist office near the parking lot on Oxford Road.

Perhaps the biggest bookstore is the **Hay Cinema Bookshop,** Castle Street (✆ **01497/820071;** www.haycinemabookshop.co.uk), in the former cinema, with 200,000 volumes here, from 50p to £1,000 or more. Some of the most desirable volumes are found at **Boz Books,** 13A Castle St. (tel. **01497/821277;** www.boz books.demon.co.uk), which features many first editions by Charles Dickens and other 19th-century authors, as well as Dylan Thomas.

Drop in at **Old Black Lion,** Lion Street (✆ **01497/820841;** www.oldblacklion. co.uk), parts of which date back to the 1300s, near the Lion Gate of the old town wall. It's rated as one of Britain's best dining pubs and serves smart bar food as well as lunch and dinner in the oak-beamed restaurant dating from the 1600s. The cuisine is rather sophisticated: Everything from Moroccan lamb with couscous and an apricot-and-fig compote to peppered venison casserole. There are also 10 bedrooms, from £45 per person.

Hay-on-Wye is at the northeastern tip of the Black Mountains: Take the A40 north from Abergavenny, then the A479, turning onto the B4350 just before the English border.

Exploring Tintern

This is a small, rather lovely village a few miles southeast of Abergavenny, in a mystical wooded setting near Chepstow. Despite the antiques and bookstores, pubs and cafes, its real attraction is just down the hill and takes your breath away. **Tintern Abbey ★★** (✆ **01291/689251;** www.cadw.wales.gov.uk) is in ruins, but it's spine-tinglingly beautiful. Only the second Cistercian abbey in Britain, it was founded in 1131, became one of the most important monasteries in Wales, and survived until Henry VIII's dissolution of the monasteries. The towering remains are mostly from the 13th century, but you don't really need to go in. Parking is free (quite something

LIFE ON THE canal

The **Monmouthshire and Brecon Canal** is one of the most picturesque in Britain and follows the course of the River Usk for much of its 32 miles. Walking or cycling along the towpath is a rural delight, and you can spot herons, kingfishers, and buzzards. The canal starts in Brecon and heads southeast to Abergavenny and through or near other market towns—Talybont, Llangynidr, and Crickhowell. **Goytre Wharf** (© 01873/881069;** www.goytrewharf.com) at Llanover, just south of Abergavenny, off the A4042, combines a British Waterways Heritage Centre, aqueduct, shops, cafe, bar, children's play areas, woodland walk, canoe rental, and holiday narrowboat rental. At Llanfoist, just north of Abergavenny, **Beacon Park Boats** (© 01873/858277;** www.beaconparkboats.com) has luxury narrowboats for short breaks and longer, heading toward Brecon. *The Owl* canal boat has a four-poster bed, log fire, and hot tub plus a full-size rolltop bath.

at Welsh monuments), and you can walk freely along the river, and up into the surrounding hills, to see it in its full glory. That's what Wordsworth did when he wrote the poem *Composed A Few Miles Above Tintern Abbey*, and he knew a thing or two about views. Admission is £3.60 for adults and £3.20 for children 5 to 16. It's open March to May and October, daily 9:30am to 5pm; June to September, daily 9:30am to 6pm; and November to February, Monday to Saturday 9:30am to 4pm, Sunday 11am to 4pm; closed at all other times.

Shopping

Abergavenny is market heaven (© 01873/735811; www.abergavennymarket. co.uk): The Tuesday market has more than 200 stalls inside and outside the market hall, heaped with local produce and much more. But there's also an indoor-only market each Friday, a growing indoor/outdoor affair each Saturday, a big fleamarket each Wednesday (an excellent place to find vinyl records and old comic books), an antiques market, (3rd Sun each month), and a crafts market (2nd Sat each month). Apart from the high-street chains, visit **Rawlings**, 19 Market St. (© 01873/856773; www.rawlingsbutchers.co.uk), which is the place for sausages. Try Farmhouse Pork (voted best in Wales) or the hot, spicy Welsh Dragon. **M&D Cycles,** 36b Frogmore St. (© 01873/854980; www.mndcycles.co.uk) has cycles for hire.

Where to Eat & Stay

Llangoed Hall Hotel ★★★   This manor house dates back to 1632, and was revamped by Edwardian architect Clough Williams-Ellis into a grand country house in 1919. Its setting in the Wye Valley, overlooking the Black Mountains, is entrancing. The bedrooms, all very different, have a wealth of antiques and fine fabrics, eight with four-poster beds. Activities on the grounds include fly fishing, clay-pigeon shooting, and croquet, and there's a snooker table in the library. The **restaurant** is a divine space in pale blue, serving Welsh Black beef and Radnorshire lamb with vegetables from the gardens.

Llyswen, Brecon, Powys LD3 0YP. www.llangoedhall.com. © 01874/754525. Fax 01874/754545. 23 units. £210–£350 double; £385–£400 suite. Rates include breakfast. AE, DC, MC, V. On the A470, 2 miles northwest of Llyswen. **Amenities:** Restaurant; room service. *In room:* TV, hair dryer.

Llanthony Priory Hotel ★★ Staying here is a fabulous, fairytale experience. Originally part of the 12th-century priory, this unique and romantic hotel has four rooms in its tower, accessed by a stone spiral staircase. The rooms have no en suite bathroom facilities, but some have four-poster beds. The **dining room,** with vaulted ceiling and log fire, serves local produce (main courses from £9.50) and the Undercroft Bar, in the priory cellar, serves real ales. The Offa's Dyke Path passes by, and there is pony trekking nearby.

Llanthony, Abergavenny, Monmouthshire NP7 7NN. www.llanthonyprioryhotel.co.uk. ℰ **01873/890487.** 4 units. £80 (midweek), £175 (weekends) double. Rates include breakfast. AE, MC, V. Free parking. Head for Skirrid Mountain Inn, turn left just past inn and continue 5 miles. **Amenities:** Restaurant; bar. *In room:* No phone.

Skirrid Mountain Inn ★★ This is the oldest pub in Wales and arguably the oldest original pub building in Britain. The Skirrid was first noted in 1110 and has doubled as a courthouse with hangings taking place from the magnificent oak beamed stairs (wood believed to be salvaged from a Royal Navy ship). There are three antiques-filled bedrooms (two with four-posters), a simple menu (including Welsh steak and Hereford chicken), and a bar with regular guest beers.

Llanvihangel Crucorney, Abergavenny, Monmouthshire NP7 8DH. http://freespace.virgin.net/skirrid.inn. ℰ **01873/890258.** 3 units. £90 double. Rates include breakfast. AE, MC, V. Free parking. Just off the A465, 10 miles north of Abergavenny. **Amenities:** Restaurant; bar. *In room:* TV.

Walnut Tree Inn ★ The Walnut made a name for itself almost 40 years ago, before the great British food revival, then closed a few years ago and was rescued by Shaun Hill, whose countryside bounty at the Merchant House across the English border in Ludlow was renowned. The menu changes with each season but features partridge with chestnut stuffing, and hot pheasant pudding with bacon and sage, as well as a selection of fish dishes. It's open Tuesday to Saturday (main courses £12–£23). The inn has two cottages, Ivy Cottage and Old Post Office Cottage, accessible through the garden, each sleeping four guests, with king-size beds, terraces, and gardens. There are also links with Abergavenny's equally charming Angel hotel, whose proprietor is co-owner here.

Llandewi Skirrid, Abergavenny, Monmouthshire NP7 8AW. www.thewalnuttreeinn.com. ℰ **01873/852797.** Fax: 01873/859764. 2 units. £160 for 2 people, £200 for 3 people, £240 for 4 people. Rates include breakfast supplies. AE, MC, V. Free parking. On the B4521, 3 miles east of Abergavenny. **Amenities:** Restaurant. *In room:* TV, hair dryer, no phone.

BRECON BEACONS

140 miles W of London; 20 miles N of Cardiff

The Brecon Beacons is a **National Park,** but it isn't simply a rural wilderness as you might expect from the name; it's a lively region of villages and small towns—including the pretty town of Brecon itself—plus plenty of outdoor activities. The Brecon Beacons is the only U.K. National Park to include an area of such geological importance that it has been granted UNESCO Global Geopark status. And quite stunning it is, too: Open, grassy peaks and dense, forested valleys.

The Fforest Fawr Geopark (Fforest Fawr is Welsh for Great Forest) is the range of mountains between the central Beacons and the Black Mountain to the west and is home to stunning natural attractions such as the **National Showcaves Centre for Wales,** Craig-y-Nos Country Park, spectacular waterfalls, and brooding reservoirs, as well as the highest mountain in southern Britain (Pen y Fan, 886m/2,906 ft.) and the wilderness area of the Black Mountain.

However, the National Park extends farther to the west, taking in the mountain cliff-top castle of Carreg Cennon, near the market town of Llandeilo, and going as far east as the Black Mountains (different from the Black Mountain) between Abergavenny and Hay-on-Wye, and as far south as Pontypool, and the outskirts of Merthyr Tydfil.

The Brecons are the great outdoors, a place where you can not only walk but also cycle (there are plenty of places to rent bikes), go pony trekking, and explore the historic villages and towns that dot the area. You will be amazed by the different scenery around every twist and turn of the road.

Essentials

GETTING THERE   There is a daytime bus service (✆ **01443/692060;** www. sixtysixty.co.uk) between Cardiff and Brecon, via Merthyr Tydfil, which takes 1½ hours. On summer Sundays and bank holidays, the **Beacons Bus** network brings visitors from Cardiff (with a bike trailer) and other towns and cities such as Swansea and Hereford to Brecon, then tours the area before heading home (see www.brecon beacons.org). There are trains from Cardiff to Merthyr Tydfil, and connections from the Midlands to other stations. If you're driving from Cardiff, head north on the A470.

VISITOR INFORMATION   The **Tourist Information Centre,** in Brecon Cattle Market (✆ **01874/622485;** www.brecon-beacons.com), is open daily, summer 9:30am to 5:30pm; winter, Monday to Friday 9:30am to 5pm and weekends 9:30am to 4pm.

Exploring the Area

Brecon is a busy little market town at the meeting of the Usk and Honddu rivers, and the perfect base for exploring the area. Georgian buildings line the narrow streets, which are home to traditional butchers and greengrocers as well as more mode-ish cafes. The town was established around a castle and priory built by William the Conqueror's half-brother Bernard de Newmarch in 1093. The castle is now the Castle of Brecon hotel, and it's worth popping into the gardens where there are some ruins. The priory, on Priory Hill, was renamed **Brecon Cathedral** (✆ **01874/623857;** www.breconcathedral.org.uk) in 1923. It has an imposing tower, a heritage center in the tithe barn next door, and lovely **Pilgrim Tea Room** in the grounds. The cathedral is open daily 8am to 6:30pm (free). The **Brecknock Museum and Art Gallery,** Captain's Walk (✆ **01874/624121;** www.powys.gov.uk), is an old-fashioned museum in the former Shire Hall, still with Victorian courtroom, and with a collection including a 1,200-year-old canoe and contemporary Welsh art. It's open year-round Tuesday to Saturday 10am to 5pm (also Apr–Sept Sun–Mon noon–5pm); £1 adults, children free.

The **South Wales Borderers Museum** at The Barracks (✆ **01874/613310;** www.rrw.org.uk) is a real boys' toys place, with the finest collection of weapons in Wales. There's also the Zulu War Room, recounting the battles in which the regiment fought, including Rorke's Drift, which was turned into the 1964 movie *Zulu* with Michael Caine. It's open year-round Monday to Friday 10am to 5pm (also Apr–Sept Sat and bank holidays 10am–4pm); £4 adults, children free.

Brecon Beacons

Brecon Beacons National Park ★★★ NATIONAL PARK   Start at the **National Park Visitor Centre** (✆ **01874/623366;** www.breconbeacons.org), a few miles south of Brecon on the A470 at Libanus. It's an attraction in itself with a 3-D model of the area to help you get your bearings and remind you of the importance of getting a map if you're heading into the hills. There's a cafe with a Taste of Wales menu, a picnic area (with views of Pen y Fan), and walks on Mynydd Illtyd Common. The center is open year-round daily from 9am to 6pm (July–Aug), to 5:30pm (May–June), to 5pm (Mar–Apr and Sept–Oct), and to 4:30pm (Nov–Feb). There are also visitor centers in other towns.

While it's not a National Park in the same way as you'd find them in the U.S. (an area of wilderness with few developments), the 519 sq. miles of landscape is controlled and access is encouraged, although, if you didn't know you'd say it was simply an area of awe-inspiring countryside. Just driving through the scenery is a treat. Narrow, winding roads dip down beside rivers and then head up and over treeless ridges. Walking, however, gets you into the heart of things, and there are trails for all abilities. Note that it can be a harsh environment with weather changing quickly, so take care. A good way to explore is to sign up for one of the guided walks run by the Park authority.

Much of the Beacons is formed from limestone, creating some of the most outstanding caves in Europe. Most are hidden, open only to experts, but the **National Showcaves Centre for Wales,** Abercraf (© **01639/730801;** www.showcaves. co.uk), opens up this world to the public, including children. A series of caves winds through the hillside, revealing underwater rivers, pools, waterfalls, and stalactites and stalagmites. There's Cathedral Cave (two big waterfalls cascading into a lake to the sound of classical music), Bone Cave (a spooky place where 42 human Bronze Age skeletons were excavated), and the Dan-yr-Ogof caves, with their winding paths passing countless stalactites and stalagmites. You can easily spend a day here, particularly if you have children, who will love the life-size dinosaur models, museum, fossil collection, shire horses, special breeds farm, standing stones, play barn, and picnic area. Tours last about 2½ hours. The complex is open from Easter until October, daily from 10am to 3pm (later in high season); £14 adults, £7.50 children 3 to 16.

Waterfall Country is the area on the southern edge of the park, between the villages of Hirwaun, Ystradfellte, and Pontneddfechan. There are many walks, but opposite the tourist office in Pontneddfechan (with an exhibition on the area, maps, and hiking gear) is a path that climbs steeply up alongside the splashing river. The walk (a joy for energetic youngsters) takes you past a number of falls, until you emerge on a grassy plateau with picnic tables. Halfway up, follow the river Hepste a short distance to Sgwd Y Eira, the "waterfall of snow," a wide, low fall with a path behind the water. A few miles to the west is **Henrhyd** waterfall (follow the signs at Coelbren on the A4221), which, with its 24 m (80 ft.) drop, is the highest in South Wales. Again you can walk behind the water after an exciting walk from the parking lot taking you across the river Nant Llech, up steep steps, and along a narrow path. For good waterfalls information, visit the independent website www.brecon-beacons.com.

There are plenty of other attractions. Try the several-hour hike up **Pen y Fan** (from the parking lot at Storey Arms, on the A470). There's also the steam-powered narrow-gauge **Brecon Mountain Railway,** from Merthyr (© **01685/384854;** www.breconmountainrailway.co.uk). One of the most stunning sights is **Carreg Cennen Castle** (© **01558/822291;** www.cadw.wales.gov.uk), near Trapp at the park's western tip, sitting at the top of a limestone crag with a 90-m (295-ft.) drop on one side. Or explore the **Monmouthshire and Brecon Canal** from Brecon's canal basin, by hiring an electric boat (carries six passengers) from **Beacon Park Boats** (© **01873/858277;** www.beaconparkdayboats.com). Have lunch at a waterside pub then take your boat across the **Brynich Aqueduct.** For walkers and cyclists there's the 55-mile **Taff Trail** (www.tafftrail.org.uk), which links Brecon with Cardiff. It's mostly traffic-free, including a stretch along the canal and past Talybont Reservoir, and can be joined in many places for a short stroll.

Entertainment & Nightlife

The Brecon Beacons is all about the great outdoors, and apart from walking and cycling there's golf at Cradoc's 18-hole championship course with views over Pen y Fan. There's fly fishing for trout and salmon in the River Usk (see www.brecon beacons.org) and riding at stables such as **Cantref Riding Centre** (© **01874/665223;** www.cantref.com), off the A40 just east of Brecon, with options including day rides up into the hills. Or you could try pheasant shooting on the **Glanusk Estate** (© **01873/810414;** www.glanuskestate.com) and clay-pigeon shooting at **Woodland Park** (© **0781/1189413;** wpshoot.co.uk).

In the evening it's generally a restaurant or a pub, or both. **Theatr Brycheiniog** (✆ **01874/611622;** www.brycheiniog.co.uk) in Brecon is the region's arts hub with a rolling selection of music, dance, drama, and spoken word (sometimes in Welsh), and a bar-restaurant, Tipple 'n' Tiffin.

Where to Eat & Stay

Brecon Castle Hotel ★   This isn't a castle but an inn built in 1809, on the site of a Norman castle on a bluff in the midst of town, with views across the rooftops toward the mountains. Family-run and restored with care, it has an old-school charm. The rooms in the main hotel are charming and all different, and there is a more modern annex and self-catering accommodations. The oak-floored Regency-feel **Beacons View restaurant** looks as it might have 200 years ago. Food is modern Welsh, with dishes such as roast venison steak with roast beetroot, and a licorice and port jus, and a slow-cooked neck of lamb suet pudding.

Castle Square, Brecon, Powys LD3 9DB. www.breconcastle.co.uk. ✆**01874/624611.** Fax 01874/623737. 38 units. £75–£150 double. Rates include breakfast. AE, MC, V. Free parking. **Amenities:** Restaurant; bar. *In room:* TV, Wi-Fi (free) in main hotel.

Nant Ddu Lodge ★ ☺   This 19th-century shooting lodge is now a modern, bright hotel, bistro, and spa in the heart of the National Park, between Merthyr Tydfil and Brecon. The Lodge snuggles against a wooded hillside; the rooms (including family options) are full of country chic and have mountain views. The spa has an indoor pool, gym, and sauna. Food, proudly Welsh with lots of lamb, steak, and fish (main courses £13–£18), is served in the **bistro and bar.**

Cwm Taf, Merthyr Tydfil CF48 2HY. www.nant-ddu-lodge.co.uk. ✆ **01685/379111.** Fax 01685/377088. 31 units. £90–£100 double. Rates include buffet breakfast. AE, MC, V. Free parking. **Amenities:** Bistro; bar; spa; indoor pool; gym. *In room:* TV/DVD, hair dryer, Wi-Fi (free).

SWANSEA ★

190 miles W of London; 82 miles W of Bristol; 40 miles W of Cardiff

Walk or cycle around the 5-mile arch of Swansea Bay on a sunny day and you might think you've been transported to California, it's so beautifully laid-back. The sea is central to Wales's second city, from its early shipbuilding history and later prominence as a port to its newfound role as a major tourist attraction thanks to its newly developed (and quite superb) maritime quarter. That said, stand in Swansea on a murky day looking at rows of terraced housing climbing up its hillside and you can understand why the nation's greatest poet, Dylan Thomas, described it as an "ugly, lovely town." Whether you get sunshine or rain, there are a few must-dos: the **National Waterfront Museum** and the **Dylan Thomas Centre.** And do cycle or walk around the bay on the promenade, which follows an old tram route from the Marina to Mumbles pier.

Essentials

GETTING THERE   First Great Western trains arrive from London, via Cardiff, every hour. It's about 1 hour (£7) from Cardiff, 3 hours (£40 and up) from London. **National Express** (✆ **0871/781-8181;** www.nationalexpress.com) operates buses from London, Manchester, and Birmingham, and can involve a connection in Cardiff.

From Cardiff, it's an easy drive west along the M4.

VISITOR INFORMATION   The **Swansea Tourist Information Centre,** Plymouth Street (☏ **01792/468321;** www.visitswanseabay.com), is open year-round Monday to Saturday 9:30am to 5:30pm. From Easter to September, it's also open Sunday 10am to 4pm.

GETTING AROUND   Swansea has a good bus network, with buses leaving the bus station at the Quadrant Shopping Centre. Bus nos. 4, X12, X13, 25, and 404 go to the rail station. (Information: ☏ **0870/608-2608;** www.firstgroup.com).

Exploring the Area

The Maritime Quarter on South Dock is where historic buildings have found new glory, where yachts and old sailing ships bob happily, and where new apartments, shops, restaurants, and coffee bars have produced a vibrant area between the sea and the heart of town. The **National Waterfront Museum ★★** (☏ **01792/638950;** www.waterfrontmuseum.co.uk) is a state-of-the art building in which you could happily spend hours, a wonderful example of how a waterfront warehouse can be turned into a contemporary treasure trove. It explores how industrialization shaped Wales and the people who live here. Huge screens show what life used to be like, and there's a big collection of industrial equipment such as mine trucks, engines, carriages, and so forth. It is open daily 10am to 5pm, with free admission.

The **Dylan Thomas Centre,** Somerset Place (☏ **01792/463980;** www.dylanthomas.com), pays tribute to the poet who was born in the city with its free Man and Myth exhibition. It sells four "Dylan Thomas Trails" (£1.50 each), which direct you to his birthplace, at 5 Cwmdonkin Dr. (now available to rent: ☏ **01792/405331;** www.5cwmdonkindrive.com), as well as to spots farther afield. The center also holds many literary events. It is open daily 10am to 4:30pm, and has an excellent shop, cafe, and restaurant. The **Dylan Thomas Theatre,** Gloucester Place (☏ **01792/473238;** www.dylanthomastheatre.org.uk), is the modern home of Swansea Little Theatre, with which Thomas performed in the 1930s. Panels in the foyer tell his story. **Swansea Museum,** Victoria Road (☏ **01792/653763;** www.swansea.gov.uk), is irresistibly old-fashioned. It's the oldest public museum in Wales with glass cabinets full of artifacts, an Egyptian mummy, and countless other objects. **The Tramshed** features Swansea's last double-decker street tram, and there are boats (tug, lightship) in the dock behind. It's open Tuesday to Sunday 10am to 5pm, with free admission.

Glynn Vivian Art Gallery ★ 🎒 GALLERY   This unknown gem contains the work of 20th-century Welsh artists Augustus John, his sister Gwen John, and others. It was founded in 1911 by Richard Glynn Vivian, who made his fortune in copper, and was tireless in his travels and art collecting. One highlight is Alfred Janes's portrait of Dylan Thomas, from 1964.

Alexandra Rd. ☏ **01792/516900.** www.swansea.gov.uk. Free admission. Tues–Sun 10am–5pm.

Mumbles WALKWAY   Once a fishing village, then a Victorian seaside resort, and increasingly an upmarket haunt of the new breed of wealthy Welsh, Mumbles is a stirring 4-mile walk along Swansea Bay. It has half a dozen highly rated restaurants and several designer boutiques, but at heart it is still a jolly seaside village with gift shops, cafes, and pubs, as well as a pier and a wonderful, sandy beach. There's a branch of Swansea's finest, Joe's Ice Cream, award-winning stuff best sampled in

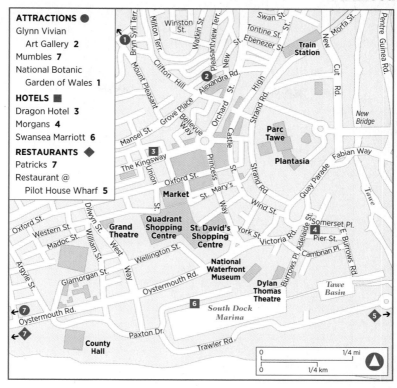

sundaes and knickerbocker glories. Oystermouth Castle stands guard over the area amid beautiful parkland. The park and woodland walks are open year-round while the castle, owned by the council (www.swansea.gov.uk), opens sporadically during the summer. On the way here you'll also find Clyne Gardens (daily, dawn to dusk with free admission), a park known for its rhododendron displays.

National Botanic Garden of Wales ★ GARDEN   This is a garden that is growing into itself; it only opened in 2000, transforming a 229-hectare (568-acre) Regency estate into a treasure trove of flowers and wildlife at a cost of £45 million. At its heart is a Great Glasshouse, the largest single-span greenhouse in the world, blending in naturally with the rolling Tywi Valley. It has the best collection of Mediterranean climate zone plants in the northern hemisphere. It's a full day out for visitors; after exploring the themed gardens you can stroll among the lakes, streams, marsh, semi-natural woodland, and meadows. The garden is 20 miles northwest of Swansea.

Middleton Hall, Llanarthne. ℂ **01558/668768.** www.gardenofwales.org.uk. Mar–Oct admission £8.50 adults, £7 seniors, £4.50 children 5–16, £21 family ticket. Daily Apr–Sept 10am–6pm (last admission 5pm); Oct–Mar 10am–4:30pm (last admission 3:30pm).

Where to Eat

Patricks ★ MODERN WELSH   This is what Mumbles is all about: A relaxed, airy seafront restaurant, with dishes, such as parsley-crusted hake filet with a cockle beurre blanc, that reflect the ethos of using local produce. They've even got a greenhouse and raised beds for micro herbs and fresh shoots. Lunch dishes (all £11) feature the likes of beer-battered pollock, pea purée, hand-cut chips, and tartare sauce. A children's menu offers slimmed-down versions of main dishes. This is a **"restaurant with rooms,"** 16 of them (£115–£175 double).

638 Mumbles Rd. ℂ **01792/360199.** www.patrickswithrooms.com. Main courses £17–£23. AE, MC, V. Daily noon–2:20pm, Mon–Sat 6:30–9:50pm.

Restaurant @ Pilot House Wharf ★ BRITISH/SEAFOOD   In the former pilot house at the marina, this seafood restaurant sits above a fishing tackle shop. Most of the dishes are solidly British, involving the catch of the day, but there are a few Mediterranean touches. There are also plenty of dishes other than fish.

Trawler's Rd. ℂ **01792/466200.** Main courses £15–£24. MC, V. Daily noon–2pm; Mon–Sat 6:30–9:30pm.

Entertainment & Nightlife

In addition to the **Dylan Thomas Theatre** (see above), there is the **Grand Theatre,** Singleton Street (ℂ **01792/475715;** www.swansea.gov.uk), next to the Quadrant Shopping Centre. It is a Victorian delight that has been refurbished and redeveloped into a multimillion-pound complex, and hosts international opera, ballet, and drama companies, along with dates from top touring entertainers.

   Wind Street (rhyming with "dined") is the nightlife hub, a cobbled street full of pubs, bars, and shops. Try **The Bank Statement,** 57–58 Wind St. (ℂ **01792/455477;** www.jdwetherspoon.co.uk), one of the chain of low-price, good-beer pubs that pride themselves on taking over unwanted old buildings; here it's in an ornate Victorian bank. More self-consciously trendy is the **No Sign Wine Bar,** 56 Wind St. (ℂ **01792/465300**).

   Other nearby streets (none as busy) also have decent offerings. The **Exchange,** 10 Strand (ℂ **01792/462896**), offers glimpses of Ireland, with live music and generous amounts of Celtic *joie de vivre.* The **Potters Wheel,** 85–86 Kingsway (ℂ **01792/465113;** www.jdwetherspoon.co.uk), a member of the same chain as the above-mentioned Bank Statement, offers food and drink in a setting that's nostalgically evocative of turn-of-the-20th-century Wales.

Where to Stay

Dragon Hotel   Right in the heart of the city, the Dragon has been around for 50 years and has just had a multimillion-pound revamp. It has understated, modern style in the rooms and the smart **brasserie** (2-course dinner £17). There are also excellent health facilities with an 18m (60 ft.) pool, gym, and beauty treatments. The first-floor lounge has its own snack menu. The breakfast buffet is £14.

The Kingsway, Swansea SA1 5LS. www.dragon-hotel.co.uk. ℂ **01792/657100.** Fax 01792/456044. 19 units. £78–£149 double. AE, DC, MC, V. Free parking. **Amenities:** Restaurant; bar; room service; indoor pool; gym. *In room:* AC, TV, hair dryer, Wi-Fi (£8.20 for 24 hr.).

Morgans ★★   This boutique hotel occupies the grandiose, Grade II-listed former Port Authority building. The decor really does use the setting well: Rich and heady with a sumptuous Morgans Bar and Champagne Bar, plus the upstairs **restaurant** with its high, curving ceiling and wood floor. Room prices are realistic, and even a 3-course dinner costs only £18 Monday to Friday, with £10 bottles of wine available. You can, however, choose to pay a lot more for the best rooms, which truly are huge, with 6-ft. beds and 42-in TVs. Across the road, next to the Dylan Thomas Centre, is Morgans Townhouse, a Georgian house converted into rooms (but without room service).

Somerset Place, Swansea SA1 1RR. www.morganshotel.co.uk. © **01792/484848.** 42 units. £65–£250 double. AE, DC, MC, V. Free parking. **Amenities:** Restaurant; bar; concierge; room service. *In room:* TV/DVD, hair dryer, Wii (in main hotel), Wi-Fi (free).

Swansea Marriott ★★ Right on the marina with panoramic views over the bay, this is the safe, international option. Even if it's not the most inspiring building to look at, inside it's everything you expect from the upmarket chain. Rooms are a decent size, and modern in a way that would never offend. There's a good pool, with views over the gardens, a gym, and **Abernethy's restaurant.**

Maritime Quarter, Swansea SA1 3SS. www.swanseamarriott.co.uk. © **800/228-9290** in the U.S. and Canada, or 01792/642020. Fax 01792/650345. 119 units. £101–£180 double. AE, DC, MC, V. Free parking. **Amenities:** Restaurant; bar; concierge; exercise room; Jacuzzi; indoor heated pool; room service; sauna. *In room:* A/C, TV, hair dryer, Wi-Fi (£7.50 per day).

GOWER PENINSULA

The Gower (in Wales it's often just "Gower") pokes out from South Wales at the edge of Swansea. Its coastline starts just past Mumbles, the seaside village at the end of Swansea Bay. Britain's first Area of Outstanding Natural Beauty, with a breathtakingly beautiful coastline, Gower is all about beaches. Some are huge (Rhossili is 3 miles long); some are almost exotically picturesque (Three Cliffs Bay is magical); others are simply unspoiled, clean, and sandy, providing everything you need for a beach vacation. There are plenty of outdoor activities here. Walking along the coast path is spectacular, or you can walk across the peninsula following the 35-mile Gower Way. There's also pony-trekking down to the sea, and watersports. Inland there are woods to tramp across, including **Park Wood,** near the **Gower Heritage Centre** at Parkmill (see below), and at **Millwood,** near Penrice, where wild daffodils grow. To the north, there's a huge network of dunes at **Whitford Burrows** and **Llanrhidian Sands.**

Essentials

GETTING THERE For train information see Swansea (above), because Gower starts just outside the city. By road, from Swansea follow Mumbles Road.

VISITOR INFORMATION The **Mumbles Tourist Information Centre,** on Mumbles Road (© **01792/361302;** www.mumblesinfo.org.uk), is open year-round, Monday to Saturday, 10am to 5pm (4pm winter).

GETTING AROUND Gower has a good bus network; the **Gower Explorer** will get you to Llangennith, Oxwich, Port Eynon, and Rhossili. **First Cymru** goes to Oystermouth, Mumbles, Bishopston, and Pennard. For details on both, call © **0871/2002233,** or visit www.traveline-cymru.info.

Exploring the Area

Three Cliffs Bay ★★★ is believed by many to be the most beautiful beach in Wales, and it certainly has everything: Fantastic sand, caves, rock pools, a ruined castle, and the unique three-pyramid rock formation (with its own natural arch), which gives it its name. It takes 20 to 30 minutes to walk from the Southgate parking lot, or with various paths you can scramble down the cliffs. Then there's the river (Pennard Pill) to cross at the start of the beach. There are stepping stones but once the tide starts racing in they are of little use, and swimming is too dangerous other than at low tide. This is a beach for those with a sense of adventure and who shun shops and cafes. You just need to time your visit so the tide is on its way out. If it's in, you can explore Pennard Warren, the sand dunes leading up to the unmanned ruins of Pennard Castle. **Tor Bay,** separated from Three Cliffs by the Great Tor headland, is another picturesque, sandy beach, with dunes filling the valley behind it. There's always sand, even at high tide. The best access is from Penmaen village, where there is parking and a 1-mile footpath.

Oxwich Bay lacks the magnificence of other Gower beaches, but is a lot easier to access. There's plenty of parking, plus beach shops and cafes to complement the 2½ miles of sand, safe swimming, and dunes to explore. Consequently it becomes crowded. If you want peace, walk east along the beach to Nicholaston Burrows; it's less crowded and the dunes are bigger. The ruins of Oxwich Castle are at Oxwich Point, to the west. It's really a 16th-century mock fortified manor.

Port Eynon Bay is another family spot, with parking at Horton, minutes from the beach. It was once smugglers' territory as you might guess from the Smugglers Gift Shop and Smugglers Haunt Restaurant. In summer there is also a surf shop and fish-and-chip shop. It has three beaches. **The Sands,** also known as Slade Bay, is farthest east, has rock pools and firm sand, and can be reached over the cliffs from Oxwich Bay. You can also walk 15 minutes across a field from the village of Slade, or via the coastal path from Horton. **The Cove,** also a mix of sand and rocks, is nearer the parking lot. To the far west the beach becomes rockier and near the Youth Hostel (see "Where to Stay," below) is **Salt House Mere,** a small, stony cove. Port Eynon also has the Smuggler's Haunt and Ship pubs.

Rhossili Bay ★★ can be reached by a wonderful 4-mile cliff walk from Port Eynon past Culver Hole, Paviland Cave, Mewslade, and Fall Bay, or you can park and walk down the cliff steps. Either way, the view over the majestic 3-mile sandy beach and the mighty Atlantic is quite something. **Worm's Head** is a rocky island (about a half-mile long) that has been shaped by the sea; if the tide's just gone out you'll have time to walk across the causeway. Rhossili is Gower's best surf beach, the power of the waves proved by the skeletons of two wrecked ships. Walk the length of the beach to Llangennith Burrows (big dunes), and at low tide you can walk out to Burry Holms, a tiny island with the ruins of a medieval monastic settlement.

Away from the coast (close to Parkmill on the A4118) you'll find **Parc le Breos (Giant's Grave)** burial chamber, a Stone Age legacy. The remains of at least four people have been found here. A central passage and four chambers are in a cairn about 21m (70 ft.) long. Parkmill, more a wooded valley than a village, is home to **Gower Heritage Centre** (✆ **01792/371206;** www.gowerheritagecentre.co.uk), a former mill, with animal park, museum, adventure playground, crafts workshops, and tearooms (adults £5.50, children 3 and older £4.50). Nearby is the **Gower Inn,** a stone pub with large garden, the **Parc-Le-Breos Riding Centre,** and several walks in Forestry Commission woods.

Where to Eat

Maes-yr-Haf ★ MODERN WELSH   This is a modern delight, perfectly placed at the end of the footpath down to Three Cliffs Bay (see above). Dishes such as a starter of carpaccio of truffled Welsh brie, pickled wild mushrooms, and caramelized walnut, and main courses such as rib-eye of Welsh Black pedigree beef, glazed Welsh rarebit, confit vine tomato, and duck-fat chips make the most out of local produce. The restaurant is cool and modern, using natural materials. It is also a **"restaurant with guest rooms"**: There are five bedrooms, with large TVs (from £140 with breakfast).

Parkmill, Gower. ✆ **01792/371000.** www.maes-yr-haf.com. Main courses £15–£22. AE, DC, MC, V. Tues–Sun noon–2:30pm; Tues–Sat 7–9:15pm. Follow the A4118 from Swansea.

The Welcome to Town MODERN WELSH   This "country bistro" is in a charming white-painted building in the heart of the Gower, but only 10 miles from Swansea. Chef proprietor Ian Bennett, who has worked at the feted Walnut Tree near Brecon, and for the Roux Brothers at the famed Waterside Inn in Bray, Berkshire, comes up with dishes such as roast best end of Welsh lamb with wild garlic polenta, glazed spring vegetables, and sauce caisson, and seared hand-dived scallops with curry salt, braised scallions, and crispy chicken skin.

Llanrhidian, Gower. ✆ **01792/390015.** www.thewelcometotown.co.uk. Lunch Tues–Sat 2 courses £14, 3 courses £16; Sun 2 courses £15, 3 courses £20; dinner 2 courses £27, 3 courses £33. AE, DC, MC, V. Tues–Sun noon–2pm; Tues–Sat 7–9:30pm. Follow the B4295 from Swansea.

Where to Stay

Fairyhill ★   This divine, stone-built 18th-century manor is set amid grounds with huge lawns, woods, lake, and a fishing stream. There's a splendid lounge with log fire and the rooms are bright, airy, and luxurious in a country style. The hotel has its own gardens, which supply seasonal vegetables to the kitchen to go with local seafood for dishes such as filet of Gower sea bass, green beans, crushed potatoes, laverbread, and lovage velouté (a white sauce with herbs). Two courses are £35, 3 courses £45.

Reynoldston, Gower, Swansea SA3 1BS. www.fairyhill.net. ✆ **01792/390139.** Fax 01792/391358. 8 units. £180–£280 double. Rates include breakfast. AE, MC, V. Outside Reynoldston, off the A4118 11 miles from Swansea. No children 7 and under. **Amenities:** Restaurant; bar; room service. *In room:* TV/DVD, CD, iPod docking station, Wi-Fi (free).

The Old Rectory ☺   The National Trust owns large areas of land here and also a number of cottages. The Old Rectory is the Trust at its best. It stands on a terrace above the dreamlike expanse of Rhossili Bay with uninterrupted views of golden sand and glorious sea all the way to Worm's Head. The main building is from 1850 with outbuildings that are possibly medieval. Inside it is warmly luxurious thanks to wood-burning stoves. There's a sitting room, study, dining room, big kitchen, and three double bedrooms (one king-size), a single, and a cot. It's great for families, and the village is only a 10-minute walk away.

Rhossili, Gower, Swansea SA3 1PL. www.nationaltrustcottages.co.uk. ✆ **01834/842881.** Sleeps 8. £510–£1,436 for 3 nights (3-night minimum). AE, MC, V. **Amenities:** TV, radio, washer/drier, pay phone.

Port Eynon Youth Hostel ★★ ☺ 🎒   If this were a boutique hotel it would cost a fortune to stay here in this beach-side setting. When the tide's in, it almost licks the back door of this old stone lifeboat station. When it's out you can jump onto the sands after your breakfast coffee behind the lounge's picture window. Like many Youth Hostels it's been given a makeover with en suite facilities, and has three double rooms, two family rooms, and a couple of small dorms.

Old Lifeboat House, Port Eynon, Swansea SA3 1NN. www.yha.org.uk. ✆ **0845/371-9135.** 28 beds. From £18 adults, £14 children 17 and under. Follow the hostel sign down an unpaved road behind the dunes. AE, MC, V. **Amenities:** Lounge, common room, self-catering kitchen.

LAUGHARNE TO PEMBROKE

Laugharne: 20 miles W of Swansea; Pembroke: 45 miles W of Swansea

To the west of the bright lights of Swansea and Cardiff you'll find a very different Wales. The coast gets wilder and you increasingly find yourself away from it all. **Laugharne** (pronounced *Larne*) is a peaceful estuary town, known mainly as the spot where Dylan Thomas lived and worked. **Pembroke** is a historic town, with an impressive castle. They are quaint and as charming as they come, albeit in a very different manner. But don't be fooled into thinking that this region is quiet and sparsely populated. Between Laugharne and Pembroke is the other face of coastal Wales, the jolly seaside experience of **Tenby** with busy beaches, shops selling beach toys, and ice-cream kiosks. Yet Tenby, Wales's busiest resort town, is a pretty place with brightly painted townhouses and historic buildings, including a fort. And it's handy for lots of natural coastal experiences. There's a big choice of caravan parks nearby, as well as great areas of beauty with smart hotels and cottages to stay in. Unspoiled beaches abound, from open expanses to hidden coves. There are plenty of festivals too: The Pembrokeshire Fish Week (www.fishweek.co.uk) takes place across the county each June, with cookery demonstrations and snorkeling safaris. Laugharne Weekend (www.thelaugharneweekend.com) is every March—you might find U.S. rocker Patti Smith reading her poetry here.

Essentials

GETTING THERE   From Swansea, there are trains to Tenby (Arriva Trains Wales, 1½ hr., £13) and Pembroke (which takes another 30 min.; £13); from Cardiff the journey takes another hour and is about £7 more.

VISITOR INFORMATION   **Tourist information offices** are in a number of towns, most open year-round with varying hours (see www.visitpembrokeshire for a list). The Tenby office is in the central Gateway Complex (✆ **01834/842402**); Pembroke, on Commons Road (✆ **01646/622388**); and Carmarthen, on Lammas Street (✆ **01267/231557;** www.discovercarmarthenshire.com).

GETTING AROUND   A car is really needed to explore, but there are other options. An 8-day **Explore Wales Pass** (www.arrivatrainswales.co.uk) gives rail travel for 4 days and bus travel for 8 days as far north as Aberystwyth for £57 (half-price for ages 5–25, free children 4 and under) and includes discounts for attractions. The **Coastal Cruiser** bus runs between Pembroke and several popular beaches, and there is a network of other services across to Carmarthenshire. A **West Wales Rover** ticket (£6 adults, £3 accompanied children), sold on buses, allows all-day travel in Pembrokeshire, Carmarthenshire, and up into Cardiganshire. Services are by varied companies, so local council websites are the best place for info (www.pembrokeshire.gov.uk and www.carmarthenshire.gov.uk). For times and routes see www.traveline-cymru.org.uk.

Exploring the Area

Laugharne sits on the River Taf estuary, with handsome Georgian buildings and pretty little cottages, a ruined castle, and the **Dylan Thomas Boathouse** ★ (✆ **01994/427420;** www.dylanthomasboathouse.com). This is where the poet and author spent the last 4 years of his life, before dying in 1953 during a visit to America. The boathouse itself is a museum with family rooms full of photos and information, and a little way along the river path you can peer through the windows of a shed where he wrote *Under Milk Wood,* and which gives the impression that he's likely to return from the pub at any moment. There is a neat little tearoom with homemade cakes and estuary views. Admission is £3.75 for adults, £2.95 for seniors, £1.75 for children 7 to 16, and free for children 6 and under. Hours are May to October, daily 10am to 5:30pm, and November to April, daily 10:30am to 3:30pm. Thomas is buried at the **Parish Church of St. Martin,** on the road into town, his grave marked by a wooden cross. **Laugharne Castle** (© **01443/336000;** www.cadw.wales.gov.uk) has a waterfront position; it's pleasing to walk among the ruins from Tudor times.

Tenby is a proper seaside town in the nicest possible way. It juts out into the sea with a quay in the middle and long beaches on either side: North Beach near the quay, and South Beach backed by sand dunes. The medieval town with its 13th-century walls, castle ruins, and narrow, winding streets rolls right down to the water. Up above are dolled-up hotels and guesthouses, smart shops, and restaurants that veer from the stylish to burger bars. By the quay there are stalls selling their catch, and places for a cup of coffee.

Tenby Museum & Art Gallery, Castle Hill (© **01834/842809;** www.tenby museum.org.uk), was founded in 1878 to display local naturalist and archeological collections, but now also features work by Augustus and Gwen John, and other prominent Welsh artists. It is open April to October, daily 10am to 5pm, and November to March, Monday to Friday 10am to 5pm. Admission costs £4 for adults, £2 for children 5 to 15. The **Tudor Merchant's House,** Quay Hill (© **01834/842279;** www.nationaltrust.org.uk), is a 15th-century home with Tudor furnishings. It's open April to October, Sunday to Friday 11am to 5pm. Admission costs £3 for adults and £1.50 for children 15 and under.

Boat trips leave the quay regularly for the 20-minute journey to **Caldy Island ★,** settled by Celtic monks in the 6th century. Once there you are free to wander among the trees and flowers or see the chapel, church, priory, and lighthouse. Children love the wild feel of the place. There is island-made perfume, chocolate, and shortbread to buy, and a Post Office selling specially franked covers. Relax in the tea gardens, or take a picnic to the big beach in Priory Bay. Boats run from Easter to late October, Monday to Friday 10am to 3pm, plus Saturdays from May to September. Round-trips are £11 adults, £6 children 14 and under. Call © **01834/844453,** or visit www. caldey-island.co.uk for information.

Just east of Tenby is the pretty village of **Saundersfoot,** with its central quay and beaches on either side, a lively place full of pubs and fish-and-chip shops. West of Tenby are a couple of the country's most enchanting beaches. **Manorbier** was home for a short time to playwright George Bernard Shaw, and novelist Virginia Woolf was a regular visitor. **Manorbier Castle** (© **01834/871394;** www.manorbier castle. co.uk) provides a backdrop (part of it is a holiday rental), and a stream runs down through the flat stones on the beach to the reddish sands.

Barafundle Bay, south of Pembroke, is one of Wales's natural wonders, like something out of *Pirates of the Caribbean,* a little beach backed by rocks and greenery, and only accessible by steep steps down after a cliff-top walk from Stackpole Quay, where there is a parking lot and cafe (© **01646/661359;** www.nationaltrust.org.uk/ stackpole).

Pembroke is a county town with shops, restaurants, and inns along one main charming street. It received its charter around 1090 and was built around **Pembroke Castle** (© **01646/681510;** www.pembrokecastle.co.uk), a fortress on a rocky spur above town. The town walls formed the castle's outer ward, and the 14-mile system

blue & GREEN

Bluestone is the new face of vacations in Wales: eco-friendly yet cutting-edge, luxurious, and nicely quaint. This village sweeps across two woodland vales in Pembrokeshire Coast National Park, just inland from Pembroke. More than 350 lodges, cottages, and studios (2–6 beds) are built from local, sustainable materials, have solar panels to heat water, and triple glazing. Yet the heart of the village looks like a historic hamlet, with little shops including a butcher's (with locally sourced meat) and a baker's. A pub rubs shoulders with a plush spa, plus restaurants and a sports club. There's a children's club, high ropes course, cycle hire, forest craft lessons, and more. Beaches are a short drive away. And then there's the Blue Lagoon, an indoor/outdoor water park designed to look like an upturned coracle (a small boat), with the U.K's largest indoor wave rider, flumes, rivers, pools, hot tubs, and wooden walkways, all heated by the same biomass plant that serves the main resort buildings. Bluestone guests get free access, but the **Blue Lagoon** (www.bluelagoonwales.com) is open to the general public. Bluestone, Canaston Wood Narberth, Pembrokeshire SA67 8DE (✆ **01834/ 888174;** www.bluestonewales.com), offers 3-night stays around weekends (from £225 double), 4-night stays midweek (from £225), among other options.

can still be viewed as a fortified town. The castle, on the banks of the River Pembroke, has been impressively restored. Its round keep is 23m (75 ft.) high with walls 5.5-m (18-ft.) thick, and topped by a dome. There are towers, battlements, passageways, and oak-beamed halls, which children love. The castle is where the Tudor dynasty began; it was the birthplace of Henry VII. Admission is £4.50 adults; £3.50 children 5 to 15. It is open March and October daily 10am to 5pm; April to September daily 9:30am to 6pm; and November to February daily 10am to 4pm.

Where to Eat

Lamphey Court Hotel ★ WELSH/BRITISH   This smart hotel, between Pembroke and the sea, has two options. The formal Georgian Restaurant is open on Friday and Saturday. The Conservatory is open daily for lunch, and is especially lovely when you can sit out on the patio. Both serve local food, including lobster from nearby Freshman Bay, River Teifi salmon, and lamb from Pembrokeshire's Preseli Hills. Main courses are accompanied by the fresh vegetables of the day and feature oven-baked rump of Welsh lamb on horseradish mash drizzled with honey, chili, and rosemary oil.

Lamphey Court Hotel, Lamphey. ✆ **01646/672272.** www.lampheycourt.co.uk. Reservations required. Main courses £16–£22. AE, DC, MC, V. Georgian Restaurant: Fri–Sat 7–9:30pm. Conservatory: daily noon–2:30pm.

Normandie INTERNATIONAL   Snuggled under the medieval walls, this old coaching inn is now a stylish, modern restaurant and bar. The main menu focuses on Tenby-caught fish and seafood, whether Welsh beer-battered cod or mussels in a cream sauce, plus local steaks. Also featured are pizza and baguettes stuffed with ingredients such as Carmarthenshire ham. There's a courtyard, and several **bedrooms** (£85 double).

Upper Frog St., Tenby. ✆ **01834/842227.** Fax 01834/844714. www.normandietenby.co.uk. Main courses £6.95–£16. AE, MC, V. Daily noon–9pm.

Stackpole Inn GASTROPUB This gastropub, a 15-minute walk from Barafundle Bay, has a restaurant run by head chef Andrew Griffith, a veteran of posh London eatery Gordon Ramsay at Claridges. The menu features dishes such as glazed pork belly with caramelized scallops, carrot purée and vinaigrette, and there are daily specials. The dining room has beamed ceilings, stone walls, and a wood-burning stove, and there are tables on the lawn. A selection of Welsh beer (including Double Dragon) is backed up by guest beers from around the U.K. Four soft, white **guest rooms** in a separate building offer a smart place to stay (£80 double).

Jasons Corner, Stackpole. ✆ **01646/672324.** www.stackpoleinn.co.uk. Main courses £12–£17. AE, MC, V. Mon–Fri noon–2pm and 6:30–9:30pm; Sun noon–2:30pm and 6:30–9pm (closed Sun evenings late Sept to spring).

Entertainment & Nightlife

Nightlife here isn't sophisticated. Tenby has more than a dozen pubs, such as the simple **Buckaneer Inn,** on Julian Street (✆ **01834/842273**) and the more boisterous **Sun,** on the High Street (✆ **01834/845941**). There are several brash nightclubs: **Sands,** in the adjoining resort of Saundersfoot (✆ **01834/813728**); and **Jammo's** (✆ **01834/845279**) and **DJ's** (✆ **01834/849400**) in Penally.

Where to Stay

Atlantic Hotel ☺ This grand old hotel looks out over the sea from Tenby's cliff-top seafront, with sweeping views of South Beach, Caldey Island, and Castle Hill. There are stylish but unfussy rooms, an indoor pool, the old-world charm of **Carrington's restaurant,** and a comfy lounge. There are sea-facing gardens from which you can descend to the beach.

The Esplanade, Tenby, Dyfed SA70 7DU. www.atlantic-hotel.uk.com. ✆ **01834/842881.** 42 units. £110–£180 double. Rates include breakfast. AE, MC, V. **Amenities:** Restaurant; bar; indoor pool; whirlpool bath; steam room. *In room:* TV, hair dryer, Wi-fi (free).

Lamphey Court Hotel ★ This Georgian mansion, amid landscaped gardens, has a formal country-house feel. You can stay in the house, where the rooms are more traditional, or in the adjoining Coach House, with 2-bedroom suites ideal for families. Its two **restaurants** (see "Where to Eat," above) are top class.

Lamphey, Pembrokeshire SA71 5NT. www.lampheycourt.co.uk. ✆ **01646/672273.** Fax 01646/672480. 37 units. £110–£150 double; £125–£160 studio. Rates include buffet breakfast. AE, DC, MC, V. Free parking. Take the A477 to Pembroke, turning left at Village Milton; Lamphey is signposted from there. **Amenities:** 2 restaurants; bar; babysitting; exercise room; indoor pool; room service; spa; outdoor tennis court (lit). *In room:* TV, hair dryer, Wi-Fi (free).

Manorbier Youth Hostel ☺ Wales has some wonderful Youth Hostels in idyllic locations, and this is one of the best, a striking modern building above Manorbier Beach. It's almost on the coastal path, with cliff walks over to other bays and beaches. The place is simple but classy with en suite rooms ideal for families, as well as the option of good meals and fair trade coffee, or self-catering.

Manorbier, Dyfed SA70 7TT. www.yha.org.uk. ✆ **0870/7705954.** 69 beds. From £16 adults, £12 children 17 and under. Free parking. Take the B4585 toward Manorbier, then follow YHA signs. **Amenities:** Restaurant; TV lounge.

Penally Abbey ★ Just outside Tenby, this country-house hotel sits next to a Norman church in the village of Penally. It comprises three buildings (St. Deiniol's Lodge, Coach House, and Abbey House) on the site of a 6th-century monastery and looks over the sea toward Tenby and the Gower Peninsula. The bedrooms are furnished with antiques and most have four-poster beds and sea or garden views. The **restaurant** is a romantic affair, candles twinkling beneath the chandelier.

Penally, Dyfed SA70 7PY. www.penally-abbey.com. ☎ **01834/843033.** Fax 01834/844714. 42 units. £189–£225 double; £270 suite. Rates include breakfast and dinner. AE, MC, V. **Amenities:** Restaurant; small indoor pool. *In room:* TV, hair dryer.

THE WILD SOUTHWEST

St. Davids: 95 miles NW of Cardiff, 60 miles W of Swansea

After Pembroke you find yourself in what is usually referred to as West Wales, the southern tip of the long west coast. This is the Pembrokeshire that has become the trendy holiday spot for Brits who race down the M4 from London, although the motorway ends just after Swansea and the rest of the journey can take as long again. Here you'll find Britain's smallest city, **St. Davids,** with its tiny, elegant cathedral. There's also the majestic sweep of St. Bride's Bay with its beaches, cliffs, and awesome sunsets. After St. David's, the coast wiggles northward past Fishguard (where the ferry boats arrive from Ireland) and gets ever more rugged until it reaches **Poppit Sands** at the mouth of the River Teifi, just across from Cardigan. All this is walkable on the Pembrokeshire Coastal Path, which is part of the **Pembrokeshire Coast National Park.** The region is dotted with smart holiday homes and cottages as well as hotels and guesthouses; it's a place full of visitors but also good for those who want to get away from it all. From the westernmost tip there really is nothing between you and the U.S., but the weather can be delightfully balmy: You're not far north of Cornwall down in England.

Essentials

GETTING THERE   Trains can get you as far as Haverfordwest (the region's hub), and Milford Haven, with occasional trains to Fishguard Harbour. The line runs along the south coast, via Swansea and Cardiff, with a line coming down from Birmingham and the Midlands. There's a Cardiff–Haverfordwest train (Arriva Trains Wales; about £20) every couple of hours and the shortest journey time is around 2 hours 20 minutes. By road, the A40 heads to Haverfordwest, with smaller roads radiating out.

VISITOR INFORMATION   The **National Park Visitor Centre** (Oriel y Parc) in High Street, St. Davids, (☎ **01437/720392;** www.pembrokeshirecoast.org.uk), is a modern gallery and exhibition space devoted to the area. It is open daily Easter to October 9:30am to 5:30pm, November to Easter, 10am to 4:30pm.

GETTING AROUND   See Laugharne to Pembroke "Essentials" for bus details (p. 706).

Exploring the Area

ST. BRIDE'S BAY   This great curve of coast, 30 miles from Wooltack Point, is southwest of Haverfordwest, stretching to St. Davids. Here you'll find attractive little seaside towns with hills rising up behind them, and beaches bookended by cliffs. There's picturesque **Little Haven** and busy **Broad Haven** with its wide beach, seafront shops, cafes, and pubs. The beach at **Druidston** is sandy and unspoiled, but parking is limited to the sides of the coast road, so arrive early. The only access is along two paths to the cliff-tops and then a steep climb down (there's an excellent hotel here, the Druidston: see "Where to Stay," below).

Access to sandy **Nolton Haven** is easier, with parking, shops, and cafes. And then you come to the pride of St Bride's: **Newgale ★★★**, a beach that will stay with you forever. It's where the A487 from Haverfordwest to St. Davids hits the coast, plunging down the hill into a heavenly vista with cliffs rising at either end. The flat, perfect sand stretches for 3 miles and the road squeezes between it and the Sands cafe, a pub, a couple of shops, and a busy campsite. There's pay parking (free for cafe users). No matter how many times you come, it's always different thanks to the undulating western light; sometimes in the morning the cliffs are shrouded in sea mist, sunlight filtering through the haze, but by late afternoon the skies can be awash with gold.

ST. DAVIDS   St. Davids is thought to be the birthplace of the patron saint of Wales. Dewi Sant (later St. David), a Celtic religious leader in the 6th century, set up a small monastic community here. The wooden church was burned or torn down several times until the Normans built one of stone. The town grew up around the church.

Today, with its ornately carved roof and a Norman nave, **St. Davids Cathedral** (*©* **01437/720199;** www.stdavidscathedral.org.uk) is a magnificent example of medieval religious architecture. It sits in a rural spot on the edge of town and contains what are said to be the bones of St. David. The nave is a place of medieval beauty, and the choir stalls, from the late 15th century, have lighthearted carvings. Entry is free, daily from 8:30am to 6:30pm. In July and August there are tours from volunteers (free, although a £4 donation is suggested).

The **Bishop's Palace** ruins (*©* **01437/720517;** www.cadw.wales.gov.uk) stand across the meadow and river, with gatehouse, battlements, and curtain walls. An outstanding sight is the elegant parapet that runs along both main walls. The site is open April to May and October daily 9:30am to 5pm, June to September daily 9:30am to 6pm, and November to March Monday to Saturday 9:30am to 4pm and Sunday 11am to 4pm. Admission is £3.10 for adults; £2.70 for seniors, students, and children 5 to 15; and £8.90 for a family ticket.

WHITESANDS ★★   This is a splendid beach, 2 miles northwest of St. Davids (take the A487, then the B4583). Access is free, but there's a £2 parking charge. Swimming is largely safe, and there are dunes to play in, beach shops, and cafes. Whitesands is also considered to have some of Britain's best surfing, and there are exhibitions with participants from as far away as California. From here you can take boat trips out to the RSPB reserve of Ramsey Island.

POPPIT SANDS ★   This is the final beach in Pembrokeshire before you cross into Cardigan (Ceredigion), and one of the few accessible beaches in the immediate area. It is a massive, flat expanse of sand, thanks to its position at the mouth of the River Teifi, backed by dunes, with striking views of Cardigan's cliffs. To find it, turn off the A487 just south of Cardigan onto the B4546 and meander through village lanes (including St. Dogmaels, where the Pembrokeshire Coast Path officially starts/ends) until you arrive at the shore where you'll find people cramming cars onto the verge to escape the parking fee. It is a wonderful, if windy, spot, and you might also see seals and dolphins. There's a cafe selling homemade cakes.

Where to Eat

Cwtch ★★★ 🎒 ☺ MODERN WELSH   Smart, hip, and family-friendly, Cwtch (pronounced *cutch*, which means snug) is a gem. It's a place that has a children's menu tempting older children rather than assuming everyone under 16 wants chicken nuggets. For £9 for 2 courses that means (give or take a dollop of chive and garlic butter) slimmed-down adult dishes such as lamb brochettes with couscous, or (for a £1.50 surcharge) a 4-oz. Welsh Black rib-eye, followed by white-chocolate and lemon curd cheesecake. The place is artily informal, the brainchild of a former ad exec, with slate and wood floors, and blackboards detailing fish specials. The grown-up menu is good value.

22 High St., St. Davids. © **01437/720491.** www.cwtchrestaurant.co.uk. £30 3-course menu. MC, V. Daily Apr–Oct from 6pm; Nov–Mar Tues–Sun from 6pm. Last sitting 9:30pm.

Sands Cafe ★ INTERNATIONAL   It's *the* place at big Newgale beach, smart and modern yet with the friendliness of a local cafe and a clientele that ranges from surfer dudes to parents with babies. Sands has a deck and even a lawn overlooking water meadows. Food includes fish and chips alongside baguettes (crab and so forth), and homemade hummus with pita bread. Ice cream is Gianni's, made with organic milk from Caerfai Farm, a renowned producer near St. Davids.

Newgale (where the A487 from Haverfordwest to St. Davids dips down to the sea), St. Bride's Bay. © **01437/729222.** www.newsurf.co.uk. Main courses £5–£10. MC, V. Daily 9:30am–5pm in winter, with extended hours in busier seasons.

Where to Stay

Druidstone ★★ 📖 ☺   This family haven sits in wild gardens on the cliff above Druidston Haven beach. It's part hotel, part holiday home; some of the rooms have en suite, some not. There are cottages converted from outbuildings that sleep 10. It's been run by the same couple since 1972 and has that post-hippie feel, sometimes with musical events (the owners are chummy with reformed pop-folk-rockers Stackridge, the first band George Martin worked with after The Beatles). Breakfast is a treat (St. Bride's Bay mackerel, organic black pudding); there's food served in the cellar bar, a restaurant with an ever-changing menu (main courses £13–£20); and children's high tea. A perfect place for a family get-together.

Broad Haven, Haverfordwest, Pembrokeshire SA62 3NE. www.druidstone.co.uk. © **01437/781221.** Fax 01437/720025. 18 units, inc. 7 cottages. £110–£180 double; cottages £400–£1,200 per week. Rates include breakfast. AE, MC, V. Free parking. **Amenities:** Restaurant; bar. *In room:* TV, hair dryer.

Warpool Court Hotel   The world's best views don't come cheap, and the panorama from this country house is enough to make you pay out. The Warpool sits high on the St. Davids' peninsula, just outside town, and its 6 hectares (15 acres) of gardens gaze loftily over sea and coast. The least expensive rooms are modest and don't benefit from the scenery outside. But for your money you do get secluded gardens and views over one of the most beautiful coastal stretches in Wales.

St. Davids, Pembrokeshire SA62 6BN. www.warpoolcourthotel.com. © **01437/720300.** Fax 01437/720676. 25 units. £200–£460 double. Rates include dinner and breakfast. AE, DC, MC, V. **Amenities:** Restaurant; bar; babysitting; covered heated pool (Easter–Oct only); outdoor tennis court (lit). *In room:* TV, hair dryer, Wi-Fi (free, in most rooms).

MID-WALES: COAST & COUNTRY

This isn't the best-known stretch of coast, but it does have its gems. Start at Cardigan and you pass the jolly seaside town of New Quay and the stylish fishing village of Aberaeron. As you edge into mid-Wales you reach the big town of Aberystwyth and eventually wind up on the dunes at the edge of the Dovey estuary, with views of the North Wales' mountains in the distance. Head inland and you quickly get into the wild country of hills and valleys and the little city of Lampeter with its university.

Essentials

GETTING THERE   There are hourly trains from Birmingham New Street Station to Aberystwyth (the Arriva Trains Wales service; from £20; trip around 3 hr.; a connecting service from London makes it nearly 5 hr.). **Arriva** (www.arrivabus.co.uk) operates the X40 Aberystwyth–Carmarthen bus service, roughly hourly, which takes around 2 hours. It passes through Aberaeron, from where the A550 service connects with New Quay. A few buses continue from Carmarthen to Cardiff, a total journey time of around 4 hours. Arriva also operates other buses in the area.

VISITOR INFORMATION   **Aberystwyth Tourist Information Centre,** Terrace Road (© **01970/612125;** www.ceredigion.gov.uk), is open year-round, generally 9:30am to 5:30pm. Offices are also at Aberaeron, New Quay, and Cardigan.

GETTING AROUND   The Arriva bus services (see "Getting There," above) are the best option. See p. 706 (Laugharne) for details of the Rover ticket.

Exploring the Area

MWNT ★★★   This is a classic Welsh beach, not least because of the tiny, meandering, hedge-lined lanes that lead to the cliff-top parking lot several miles north of Cardigan on the B4548. One person hauling a caravan can cause gridlock, and there's lots of standing around with hands on hips, cars reversing into farmers' fields. But when you get here the view from the grassy, windswept National Trust pay parking lot is awesome: A sandy beach with crashing waves, sheltered by rock faces on three sides. Steps descend past a snack kiosk (with homemade Welsh cakes) to the friendly, sometimes crowded, sands. Children adore the place, running into the water, playing beach cricket, dashing back up the steps (past people carrying canoes down) for an ice cream.

NEW QUAY ★   This quaint town tumbles down the hillside into a little quay, a lovely curving beach, and a traditional seaside resort: Ices, blow-up sunbeds, and pubs jostling for attention with green hills rising all around. Dylan Thomas lived in a cottage across the bay and his classic *Under Milk Wood* is believed to be based on the town and the people he met here. Thomas drank in the **Blue Bell,** and there's a Dylan Thomas Trail around places thought to feature in the book. The beach nestles between a stone slipway and stone pier. The beach gets busy but is soft, sandy, and safe. **Cardigan Bay Marine Wildlife Centre** (© **01545/560032;** www.cbmwc. org) occupies a listed, seafront building. It's free to enter and features information on bottlenose dolphins, gray seals, porpoises, and other local creatures. The charitable trust runs trips on its Dolphin Survey boat, which give a real insight into the bay's inhabitants. The center is open April to September, daily 10am to 5pm. Two-hour boat trips cost £18 for adults, £10 for children 11 and under. A path from town takes you onto the cliffs for spectacular views, especially from the National Trust spot Craig Yr Adar (Bird Rock). There you'll see many types of gulls, kestrels, and often seals and dolphins. Afterward there are plenty of fish-and-chip options, including the Mariner and Captain's Rendezvous, all within a few yards of one another.

ABERAERON   The main road runs through Aberaeron like many towns, but hidden away to one side is the delightful quay-side. It's like something in western France, but with gaily-painted Georgian buildings. There are friendly pubs, good fish-and-chip shops and the quay-side Harbourmaster Hotel (see "Where to Eat & Stay," below), which puts together the lively Cardigan Bay Seafood Festival each July.

ABERYSTWYTH　This respected university town has an oddly bohemian yet bookish feel to it. The little horseshoe-shaped North Beach is dark and shingly, hemmed in by tall Edwardian B&B-type places. A gentle seafront stroll takes you past the John Nash-designed college building and up to the ruins of the castle built by Edward I during his conquest of Wales (which is open at all times; free admission). There's a huge climbing frame in the little adjoining park, as well as a grassy area and picnic tables. As you round the small, rocky headland the view opens out with a long, blustery promenade and the more attractive South Beach, which ends at a little quay-side. The Cliff Railway, dating from 1896, creeps up the 130-m (465-ft.) Constitution Hill, at the far end of North Beach, to a cafe and picnic area. In town, the **Ceredigion** (Cardigan) **Museum** on Terrace Road (www.ceredigion.gov.uk) is housed in the Coliseum, a former Edwardian music hall. It's free and has an engaging collection of reconstructed rooms, farming implements, and other local bits and pieces. The **Ultracomida** deli, 31 Pier St. (✆ **01970/630686;** www.ultracomida.co.uk), has a Spanish-Welsh-French flavor, with lots of local cheese; the little restaurant behind the shop serves tapas/deli lunch dishes and on Friday and Saturday (7–9pm) there's a dinner menu with cross-cultural dishes such as Ceredigion lamb chops marinated in harissa and olive oil, with olive-oil mash (£11 for two courses, £15 with Welsh and French cheeses).

BORTH　A curious little seaside town just north of Aberystwyth (from where you can get a train), Borth features one long road running alongside the beach, although in some places the views are blotted out by the buildings. Leave the car at the parking area at the T-junction, and cross over to the 2-mile stretch of sand. When the tide's in it is a narrow strip of stones up against the sea wall, but when it's out it's really out. It's a trifle windswept but is a great place for games, and there are even donkey rides. Drive out the other side for one of the real delights of the coast. The road ends amid the giant, white sand dunes of the **Dyfi National Nature Reserve ★★★** at Ynyslas, at the mouth of the River Dyfi (Dovey), with Aberdyfi (Aberdovey) across the water. You can park on the hard sand, and the feel is California cool. There's a modern, wooden building across a meandering boardwalk with a cafe and toilets.

Dolaucothi Gold Mine

Arrive here and you know you're in a real mine, old buildings and discarded machinery in a quarry-like setting criss-crossed by narrow-gauge rail tracks. Children can pan for gold, play in the activity room, and generally run about, but the real action is below ground. Here you can tour some of the tunnels, which date back to Roman times, and which were used well into the last century. The underground tour is dark and fascinating. The mine is at Pumsaint, Llanwrda (✆ **01558/650177;** www.nationaltrust.org.uk). Admission is £3.60 adults, £1.80 children 5 to 15, and £9 family ticket; underground tour is £3.80 adults, £1.90 children, and £9.50 family ticket. Daily mid-March to October 11am to 5pm (6pm July–Aug).

LAMPETER It looks like an unassuming country town, but Lampeter boasts the oldest university college in Wales, the University of Wales Trinity St. David. After Oxford and Cambridge, it's the oldest degree-awarding institution in England and Wales. The student population adds an extra dimension to what has been a market town since medieval times, and which still has regular cattle markets and a horse fair.

Where to Eat & Stay

Gwesty Cymru MODERN WELSH   This restaurant with rooms is right on the seafront at North Beach. The old building is now awash with slate, chrome, and glass, and it serves up popular Welsh and other dishes with a contemporary touch. Starters include Llanilar wild rabbit pie, with bacon and rocket mash and a port sauce, while rump of Welsh lamb and a 10-oz. Welsh Black sirloin steak are tempting for a main course. The eight **guest rooms** feature handmade oak furniture, contemporary oil paintings on the walls, and luxury bathrooms.

19 Marine Terrace, Aberystwyth, Cardigan SY23 2AZ. ✆ **01970/612252.** www.gwestycymru.com. Main courses £13–£18. Rates include breakfast. AE, MC, V. Limited free parking. Daily noon–2pm and 6–9pm.

Harbourmaster Hotel ✦   The original Georgian harbormaster's house is now a smart hotel. There are seven rooms in the building, all reached by the original spiral staircase; a pair of doubles in a nearby cottage and four super-cool doubles (including the Aeron Queen with its Juliette balcony, and the John & Henry with its roof terrace, both overlooking the sea) in a converted warehouse next door. The bistro-style **restaurant and bar,** also in the warehouse with sea views, serves local lobster and spider crab, crab risotto, rib of Welsh beef, and local cheese (main course £9.50–£24). The restaurant is open noon to 2:30pm and 6:30 to 9pm; bar food (Welsh beef burgers, Welsh rarebit—a supercharged cheese on toast) is served all day. It's also open from 8am for breakfast.

Quayside, Aberaeron, Cardigan SA46 OBT. www.harbour-master.com. ✆ **01686/628200.** 13 units. Longhouse £110–£250 double. Rates include breakfast. AE, MC, V. Free parking on street. **Amenities:** Restaurant, bar. *In room:* TV/DVD, hair dryer.

Hive on the Quay MODERN WELSH   In an old stone wharf building, the Hive is a bright and breezy cafe and restaurant with a conservatory, and spills out onto brightly painted tables on the quay itself. At lunch it serves light fare: Ciabatta, salads, and tapas-style dishes. Come evening and you've got grilled sardines with salsa verde, salted cod cakes with rouille, and coca (a thick, crispy Catalan pizza). And then there's the Hive honey ice cream, a honey-sweetened delight in a number of varieties; there is a separate ice-cream counter outside.

Cadwgan Place, Aberaeron. ✆ **01545/570445.** www.hiveonthequay.co.uk. Main courses £8–£11. AE, MC, V. Daily 9am–9pm (lunch noon–3pm, dinner from 6pm).

ELAN VALLEY: WONDER OF THE DAMS

The Elan Valley, in the heart of Wales, is a beautiful spot. It twists and turns following the unobtrusive, gurgling River Elan. Hillsides rise up, layer upon layer; mostly they are open and littered with sheep, while forests roll into the hazy distance. It is an ancient and remote landscape, and yet it was tamed by the Victorians. More than 100 years ago they built a series of **mighty dams** to create a supply of drinking water for the multitudes toiling in England's industrial cities. Now, one moment you see a little river, but around the bend it becomes a vast lake, held in check by massive stone dams. They look brutal in their strength but are topped by delicate architecture such as little turrets like the decoration on a cake. The symmetry of man and nature here is astonishing, and quite beautiful.

Essentials

GETTING THERE   About half a dozen single-coach trains (Arriva Trains Wales; about £11) each day make their way up from Swansea to Llandrindod Wells, about 5 miles from Rhayader. The journey takes 2 to 4 hours. Buses (*C* **01597/852000;** www.veolia-transport.co.uk) connect with Rhayader roughly hourly and take about 30 minutes. By car, Rhayader is about 70 miles north of Brecon on the A470.

VISITOR INFORMATION   The **Elan Valley Visitor Centre** (*C* **01597/ 810880;** www.elanvalley.org.uk), off the B4518 3 miles southwest of Rhayader, is open late March to early November, 10am to 5:30pm.

GETTING AROUND   A car really is the best way to access the area of the Elan Valley. Walking is the only alternative, and hikers can take the Elan Valley Trail up from Rhayader.

Exploring the Area

Rhayader is the oldest town in mid-Wales, dating back to the 5th century. It's a small, pretty place, with tea shops, country stores, and a nice riverside picnic area. It's also a good base for exploring the Elan Valley. The **Rhayader Town Trail** (directions on www.rhayader.co.uk) takes you along the river, past the remains of a 12th-century wooden castle, past the Smithfield Market, where livestock sales still take place, and along the picturesque main street.

The **Elan Valley** is quite a remarkable place, a valley that has three enormous Victorian dams, creating five reservoirs, which were built so that there would be enough drinking water for the burgeoning city of Birmingham. **Elan Valley Visitor Centre** is signposted off the B4518 out of Rhayader. It's a Victorian pumping station, on the banks of the River Wye, which features a fascinating exhibition on the extraordinary nature of creating the reservoirs, a cafe, picnic area, and shop. There's also a big parking lot. The lowest dam, **Caban Coch,** appears like the gray wall of a science fiction citadel upriver from the visitor center. **Pen-y-Gareg** dam is equally impressive from downriver as you walk along the river, a sloping edifice of rock towering above the stream below. Farther on is **Craig Gogh** dam, perhaps the most impressive, a great curving edifice 317m (1,040 ft.) above sea level. It's topped with a narrow roadway that you can still drive across to a small parking lot; in the middle is a domed tower in "Birmingham Baroque" style, topped by a wind-vane in the shape of a fish. There are parking lots dotted along the road.

The **Elan Valley Trail** is a surfaced path that follows the old Elan Valley Railway route. It starts in Rhayader and goes 8 miles up the valley, but there are also a number of walks from the Visitor Centre. There is a selection of leaflets (30p) with maps. The Elan Valley Estate (managed by Wales Water) covers 70 sq. miles and has 80 miles of public rights of way.

Where to Eat & Stay

Rhayader has a number of pubs such as the **Lamb & Flag, Crown, Bear's Head,** and **Cornhill**, all of which serve food. The **Strand Bistro** on East Street (*C* **01597/810564;** www.strandbistro.org.uk) is smartly modern in an old, timbered building and serves dishes such as a duo of Welsh lamb (rack and shoulder), and organic chicken.

Elan Valley Cottages ✦ The Elan Valley Trust has three cottages in the area. The most attractive is the Llannerch y Cawr Longhouse overlooking the Dôl y Mynach reservoir. It's Grade II listed and dates back to the 16th century, when it would have housed people in one end and cattle in the other. Subtly restored, it still has original features such as the stone flooring, spiral staircase, and wooden beams. It is divided into two sections, one sleeping six, the other four.

Elan Valley Estate (check website for location/contact details). www.wales-holidays.co.uk. ✆ **01686/628200.** 3 units, each sleeping 4–6. Longhouse £211–£434 for 3 nights (minimum stay); other properties up to £698. AE, MC, V. **Amenities:** Firewood, central heating, pay phone.

Elan Valley Hotel ✦ This is a friendly, family-run hotel just half a mile from the Elan reservoirs. There are pretty rooms, which have views over the countryside or the large gardens. One of them has a four-poster bed and another, opening onto the grounds, is for families. The restaurant (main courses £11–£17) features dishes such as Welsh Black steak with a brandy and mushroom sauce, and Welsh lamb slowly cooked with red wine and rosemary.

Elan Valley, Rhayader, Powys LD6 5HN. www.elanvalleyhotel.co.uk. ✆ **01597/810448.** Fax 01597/810824. 11 units. From £48–£95. Rates include breakfast. AE, MC, V. **Amenities:** Restaurant; bar. *In room:* TV, hair dryer, Wi-Fi (free).

NORTH WALES

by Donald Strachan

I f the south is Wales's heart, the north keeps watch over its soul. North Wales is home to the country's most dramatic crags and mightiest castles, many within the boundary of the Snowdonia National Park. Along the shoreline of Anglesey and the Lleyn Peninsula, you'll find a coast that's perfect for leisure, but that can turn wild and windswept at a moment's notice. The sheltered valleys of Denbighshire hold top-class restaurants and relics of Wales's industrial past.

19

SIGHTSEEING Highlight of any trip to North Wales is a ride aboard one of the little steam trains. On the **Welsh Highland** and **Ffestiniog** narrow-gauge lines that once served the slate and copper mines, visitors ride old-fashioned, wood-paneled carriages through the heart of Snowdonia. At **Portmeirion,** architect Clough William-Ellis built a fantasy, pastel-colored village on a magical estuary, where you can roam—or even stay overnight. The once-fashionable Victorian resort of **Llandudno** is experiencing a comeback.

EATING & DRINKING The coasts and pastures of the Welsh North nurture everything from the Black breed of cattle that produces uniquely succulent **beef** to Menai **mussels** and **shellfish** caught in Cardigan Bay—all of which yields a superlative cuisine. Fine restaurants with rooms, such as Tyddyn Llan in Llandrillo and Venetia in Abersoch, are run by skillful chefs who know how to put the bounty to best use. Anglesey is also home of Halen Môn, the sea salt of choice for the world's top chefs.

OUTDOOR ACTIVITIES Mountain peaks, spectacular lakes and brooding cliffs, and valleys with tiny towns seemingly carved from granite—all these make up Snowdonia National Park. It's here that you'll find the best of the area's hiking trails, on **Snowdon** and **Cader Idris,** as well as through the gnarled **Aberglaslyn Gorge.** There's also serene coastal walking around Anglesey and the Lleyn, surfing at **Porth Neigwl,** and extreme mountain biking in the pine forests at **Coed y Brenin.** You need never sit down.

HISTORY It was in the North that many of the key 13th-century battles for Welsh independence were fought—and lost. Victorious English King Edward I subsequently built his "Iron Ring" of castles, the finest of which are mighty **Caernarfon** and **Beaumaris.** (Compare the ruinous state of native castles such as **Dolwyddelan.**) At **Conwy,** built around another of Edward's great castles, the fine Elizabethan townhouse **Plas**

Mawr testifies to the later wealth of the region's merchants. The servant's floor at stately home **Erddig** is like a domestic Victorian time capsule.

THE best TRAVEL EXPERIENCES IN NORTH WALES

○ **Hiking up the Aberglaslyn Gorge as the Welsh Highland Railway puffs past:** Between Beddgelert and Pont Croesor, the most famous stretch of this recently rebuilt narrow-gauge line cuts through terrain that's been a beauty spot since the 1800s. See p. 722.

○ **Standing on Yr Wyddfa, Mount Snowdon's 1,085-m (3,560-ft.) peak:** Whether you've arrived on the rack railway or hiked any of the marked trails to the summit, the view over the Snowdonia range and into the five countries of the British Isles is equally spectacular. See p. 720.

○ **Enjoying the tranquil comforts of 21st-century Beaumaris:** The more you encounter fragments of life here from centuries past, the more you discover that it wasn't always so genteel—although the contemporary cuisine at the Loft drags you right back to the present. See p. 732.

○ **Riding the "great little trains":** Originally built to carry slate and copper from mine to port, the Ffestiniog and Welsh Highland steam railways now rattle through some of Snowdonia's most breathtaking scenery. See p. 727 and 730.

○ **Driving and dining by the Ceiriog:** This little-visited valley twists an idyllic, 15-mile path from rolling terrain around Chirk to the Berwyn Mountains on the fringes of Snowdonia. The most beautiful stretch, around Llanarmon, is also home to one of Denbighshire's best eating spots. See p. 741.

SNOWDONIA ★★★

Llanberis: 105 miles SW of Manchester, 7 miles SE of Caernarfon; Betws-y-Coed: 16 miles E of Llanberis, 44 miles SW of Liverpool

More than just the roof of Wales and the tallest British peaks south of Scotland, the giant mountains of the 823-sq. mile **Snowdonia National Park** have also long been places of myth. Legend has it that dragons, faithful hounds, and even (in the original tales) King Arthur have all lived around here, but the principal attraction for visitors is the endless miles of hiking trails and epic scenery. Paths up **Mount Snowdon,** through the **Aberglaslyn Gorge,** and on the flanks **Cader Idris** are accessible to fit walkers of all experience levels.

Snowdonia also has a long history as a mining center, and the **National Slate Museum** in Llanberis and the **Llechwedd Slate Caverns** outside Blaenau Ffestiniog transport you back to an earlier, industrial era in the life of these beautiful but harsh mountains.

Essentials

GETTING THERE There's no sizable town in the National Park, just a collection of small places—including **Betws-y-Coed, Llanberis, Beddgelert,** and **Capel Curig**—any of which can be a base. There's also no major railway line that stops in Snowdonia itself. The nearest major station is Bangor, 9 miles north of Llanberis.

From Monday through Saturday, buses run frequently throughout the day from Bangor to Llanberis, taking about 40 minutes each way. The minor **Conwy Valley** rail line between Llandudno and Blaenau Ffestiniog passes through Betws-y-Coed and **Dolwyddelan,** but it runs just four trains each way daily. There are also regular buses from Llandudno and Porthmadog to towns in the park.

The best routes to Snowdonia by car from England are the A55 North Wales coastal road and the slower, but more scenic A5 from the Midlands, through Llangollen, a spectacular route first laid down by engineer Thomas Telford between 1815 and 1830.

VISITOR INFORMATION   The major information point for Snowdonia is the **Betws-y-Coed Information Centre,** Royal Oak Stables (✆ **01690/710426**), open from Easter to October, daily 9:30am to 5:30pm and in the off season, daily 9:30am to 4pm. There are smaller offices at Canolfan Hebog, Beddgelert (✆ **01766/890615;** daily Easter–Oct, Fri–Sun rest of the year); at Stryd Fawr, Harlech (✆ **01766/780658;** daily Easter–Oct, closed rest of the year); and at Stryd Fawr, Dolgellau (✆ **01341/422888;** daily Easter–Oct, Thurs–Mon rest of the year). The **Llanberis Tourist Information Centre,** 41B High Street (✆ **01286/870765;** www.visit snowdonia.info) is due to move in 2012 from 41B High Street to a unit in Padarn Country Park. Hours are subject to review, but currently it's open from Easter to the end of September, Saturday to Wednesday from 9:30am to 4:30pm. The official National Park website **www.eryri-npa.gov.uk** is packed with planning information.

Exploring Snowdonia

LLANBERIS ★ & ENVIRONS

The **Snowdon Mountain Railway** ★★ runs from Llanberis to within a few paces of Mount Snowdon's peak at 1,085m (3,560 ft.). The only rack-and-pinion train in Britain, it is also the country's steepest train ride. The final stretch affords views over classic glacial landscape features like U-shaped troughs and hanging valleys, as well as a frightening look down into the Llanberis Pass with the Glyderau peaks beyond. For information and schedules, call ✆ **0844/493-8120** or visit **www.snowdon railway.co.uk**. Trains run to the summit between May and October, costing £25 round-trip for adults and £18 round-trip for children 14 and under. You can get most of the way up between late March and the end of April. It's closed in winter. *Insider tip:* If you book by phone at least a day in advance for a 9am departure, ticket prices are £6 cheaper per person.

The romantic ruins of **Dolbadarn Castle,** subject of an iconic painting by Turner, overlook Llyn Padarn, a half-mile east of Llanberis; the castle is a relic of the time when the Llanberis Pass was crucial to any conquering army. You can take a look around the meager yet dramatic ruins for free; follow the marked trail opposite the parking-lot entrance.

Electric Mountain Visitor Centre, along the A4086 (✆ **01286/870636;** www.fhc.co.uk), is the gateway to one of the most technologically advanced power stations in Wales, Dinorwig. It incorporates a hydroelectric system harnessing the waters of a pair of nearby lakes, with its turbines concealed deep within the mountains so as not to spoil the natural beauty. Entrance to the visitor center is free, and 1-hour tours of the turbines run daily from Easter to October. Reservations are advised. Tickets cost £7.75 for adults, £3.95 for children 4 to 15, and £11 to £46 for a family ticket.

North Wales

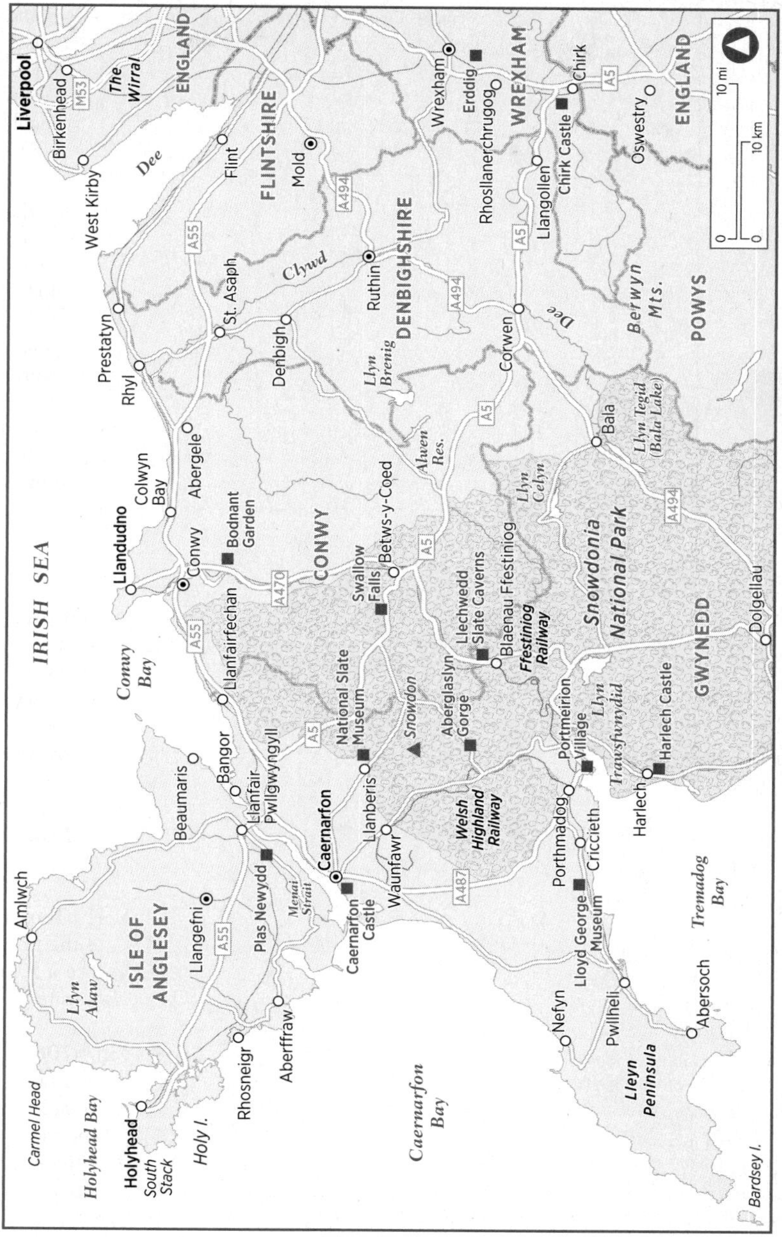
IRISH SEA
Liverpool
Birkenhead
M53
The Wirral
ENGLAND
West Kirby
Dee
Flint
FLINTSHIRE
Mold
A494
Wrexham
Erddig
Rhosllanerchrugog
WREXHAM
Chirk
Chirk Castle
Llangollen
A5
Oswestry
ENGLAND
10 mi
10 km
0
Prestatyn
Rhyl
St. Asaph
A55
Clywd
Denbigh
Ruthin
DENBIGHSHIRE
A494
Corwen
Dee
Berwyn Mts.
POWYS
Llyn Brenig
Alwen Res.
Abergele
Colwyn Bay
Llandudno
Conwy
Bodnant Garden
CONWY
A470
Betws-y-Coed
Swallow Falls
A5
Bala
Llyn Tegid (Bala Lake)
Llyn Celyn
A494
Snowdonia National Park
Llechwedd Slate Caverns
Blaenau Ffestiniog
Ffestiniog Railway
Dolgellau
GWYNEDD
Conwy Bay
Llanfairfechan
A55
National Slate Museum
Snowdon
Aberglaslyn Gorge
Portmeirion Village
Llyn Trawsfynydd
Harlech Castle
Harlech
Bangor
Beaumaris
Llanfair Pwllgwyngyll
A5
Llanberis
Caernarfon
Caernarfon Castle
Waunfawr
Welsh Highland Railway
A487
Porthmadog
Criccieth
Lloyd George Museum
Tremadog Bay
Amlwch
Llangefni
Plas Newydd
Menai Strait
ISLE OF ANGLESEY
A55
Llyn Alaw
Aberffraw
Rhosneigr
Carmel Head
Holyhead Bay
Holyhead
South Stack
Holy I.
Caernarfon Bay
Nefyn
Pwllheli
Abersoch
Lleyn Peninsula
Bardsey I.

As long as the weather's in your favor, make an attempt on the summit of **Mount Snowdon ★★★**—the peak so loved by such English Romantic poets as Wordsworth and Shelley remains literally the high-point of any trip to North Wales. On a clear day, you'll see every country of the British Isles, and every wrinkle and fold in the National Park below. Although there are trails that, given the wrong conditions, would challenge an experienced alpine hiker, summer months offer tracks that any fit traveler can attempt. The most popular route is the **Llanberis Path,** which slowly winds its way from Llanberis past cascades, across open sheep-grazing moorland, and then finally up to the peak via a dizzying view down into the Llanberis Pass. A fit child of 10 can handle the trail. The same goes for the **Rhyd Ddu Path** that rides Snowdon's western flank to the top. The best way to reach the trailhead is from Caernarfon for the first train of the day on the **Welsh Highland Railway** (p. 730). Get off at Rhyd Ddu station, just after one of the most glorious stretches of the line along the shore of Llyn Cwellyn. Check the timetable before setting off to confirm the time of the day's last return train. Both of these paths require about 5 hours for the return journey. Of course, the view from the top is the same if you ascend via the **Snowdon Mountain Railway** (see below); aim to get an early start so you encounter fewer people at the summit, and pay a cheaper ticket price. Whichever route you attempt (there are three further maintained trails), be sure to plan properly: The website **www.eryri-npa.gov.uk/hafan/visiting/walking/snowdon_paths.htm** should be your first stop. We recommend you pack Ordnance Survey 1:25,000 *Explorer* map OL17, which covers Snowdon and is available everywhere locally.

Our other favorite spot in Snowdonia is **Beddgelert ★★**. This well-kept little mountain village is the jumping-off point for some of Snowdonia's best gentle walks. Its name (literally, "Gelert's grave") comes from the faithful dog of 13th-century Prince Llywelyn, slain by his master for having been falsely suspected of killing his child. The classic local trek heads past **Gelert's Grave** (mythical rather than genuine) into the **Aberglaslyn Gorge ★★★**, a stunning steep-sided trail constantly sound-tracked with the rushing water of the River Glaslyn. The area was a favorite of well-to-do Victorians who first popularized Snowdonia as a leisure destination. Alternatively, a 2-hour circuit takes you northeast along the shores of **Llyn Dinas** and back to the village. With a little more time, you can link the two into a half-day hike by looping around Cwm Bychan. It's all relatively easy walking, but as with everywhere in Snowdonia you need to be fit and sure-footed.

The **Cader Idris ★★** range in Southern Snowdonia offers spectacular coastal views, particularly from the **Tŷ Nant Pony Path** that heads to the 893-m (2,927-ft.) summit of Pen y Gadair from the roadside Tŷ Nant parking lot, about 3 miles southwest of Dolgellau.

The less energetic can still get a taste of Snowdonia's majesty—from the car. The drive from Betws-y-Coed to Porthmadog passes through two of the most panoramic parts, along the shore of **Llyn Gwynant ★★★** and then through the Aberglaslyn Gorge. Take the A5 westbound from Betws, turning onto the A4086 at Capel Curig, then the A498 as the road divides at the foot of the Llanberis Pass. Driving time, at a relaxed pace with photo stops, is around an hour.

National Slate Museum ★ MUSEUM   While surrounded by so much tranquility and natural beauty, you could easily forget that Snowdonia was, until recently, a place of toil and hardship. The courtyard here once echoed to the industrial din of crushing, hammering, and splitting—this great gray building housed the workshops that kept nearby Dinorwic Quarry running. The impressive museum chronicles the methods, machinery, and men that dug 90,000 tons of slate a year from the mountainside. Particularly poignant are the relocated quarrymen's cottages, each dressed authentically at important moments in Snowdonia's industrial past, including 1969—when Dinorwic closed.

Llanberis. ℂ **01286/870630.** www.museumwales.ac.uk/en/slate. Free admission. Easter–Oct daily 10am–5pm. Closed Nov–Easter. In Padarn Country Park, ½ mile east of Llanberis.

BETWS-Y-COED TO BLAENAU FFESTINIOG

Betws-y-Coed was once an isolated Snowdonia village, surrounded by tumbling rivers, waterfalls, and mountains, nestled in the tree-lined valley of the River Conwy. There's still an alpine feeling about the place, but it gets busy in summer these days. However, as a base it's well located for exploring Snowdonia, and is well stocked with affordable B&Bs.

The town is known for its eight bridges, most notably **Waterloo Bridge** ★ at the village's southern end, the cast-iron construction of Thomas Telford in 1815. The most popular local beauty spot is the **Swallow Falls** ★, beside the A5, 2 miles west of the center. It comprises a series of waterfalls strung together, creating a mist. Drop a £1 coin into a tollbooth to get access to the path anytime you want, night or day.

Standing lonely on a ridge, **Dolwyddelan Castle,** about a mile south of the hamlet of Dolwyddelan (ℂ **01690/750366;** www.cadw.wales.gov.uk), was the birthplace in 1173 of Llewelyn the Great, according to tradition. It was certainly his royal residence, looking out on the rugged grandeur of Moel Siabod peak. A medieval road from the Vale of Conwy ran just below the west tower, which made this a strategic site to control passage. To enter, adults pay £2.70, children £2.30; a family ticket costs £7.70. It's open April to September, Monday to Saturday 10am to 5pm, Sunday from 11:30am to 4pm; off-season hours are Monday to Saturday 10am to 4pm, Sunday from 11:30am to 4pm.

The mining village of Blaenau Ffestiniog is the eastern terminus for the scenic, 13½-mile **Ffestiniog Railway** ★★, linking it with the slate port of Porthmadog. See p. 727.

Llechwedd Slate Caverns ★ ☺ HISTORIC SITE   There are 25 miles of tunnels and mine chambers buried in the great gray hill above Blaenau Ffestiniog, many of them still part of a working slate mine that opened in 1846. At Llechwedd, you can don hard hats to make two separate but complementary half-hour visits underground. The **Deep Mine** takes you 122m (400 ft.) below ground on a self-guided visit helped by eerie audio commentaries emanating from the darkness, and ends at a giant subterranean lake. The **Miners' Tramway** starts with a ride about a half-mile into the slate mountain, and continues with a more didactic talk on the geology of the mine and the working life of the 19th-century miner. On a wet day in high season, arrive early to minimize waiting times.

Blaenau Ffestiniog. ℂ **01766/830306.** www.llechwedd-slate-caverns.co.uk. One tour £10 adults, £9 seniors, £8 children 3–15; 2 tours £16 adults, £15 seniors, £12 children. Apr–Sept daily 10am–5:15pm, Oct–Mar daily 10am–4:15pm. Beside the A470, 1 mile north of Blaenau Ffestiniog.

SOUTHERN SNOWDONIA ★

Less visited than the heart of Snowdonia, the southern area of the park, where the mountains almost fall into Cardigan Bay, is no less dramatic. Quaint Dolgellau is the start of the **Mawddach Trail ★★**, a 9-mile cycle-and-walking path that follows an abandoned railway line along the most photogenic estuary in Wales, ending at the ¾-mile Barmouth railway bridge. The tiny town is also the jumping-off point for hiking on **Cader Idris ★★**; see "Snowdonia's Best Hikes," above.

Harlech Castle ★ If you were selecting a castle to live in, you'd be hard-pressed to find one with a view to match Edward I's great coastal pile. Built in the 1280s as one of the English king's imperial fortresses (p. 730), and despite brief occupation during Owain Glyndŵr's rebellion in 1404–09, its shell and gatehouse in particular are remarkably intact.

Castle Sq., Harlech. ℂ **01766/780552.** www.cadw.wales.gov.uk. Admission £3.60 adults, £3.20 children 5–15. Mar–Oct 9:30am–5pm (until 6pm July–Aug); Nov–Feb Mon–Sat 10am–4pm, Sun 11am–4pm.

Where to Eat & Stay

Among a glut of B&Bs in Betws-y-Coed, our favorite is **Oakfield House,** Pentre Du, Betws-y-Coed LL24 0BY (www.oakfieldhousebandb.co.uk; ℂ **01690/710450**), a handsome villa beside the A5 at the western fringe of the village. Completely refitted in 2011, rooms are comfortable and spacious, with flat-screen TVs (and DVD players) and free Wi-Fi. Doubles cost £70 per night.

Bryn Tyrch Inn ★ 🔥 A renovation project completed in 2011 has upgraded this cozy, informal roadside inn at the heart of Snowdonia to an ideal base for discerning hikers. Rooms, generally compact to midsize, are decked out with comfortable, traditional beds and light-wood furniture that gives them a slightly luxurious, Scandinavian feel. There are walking trails from (literally) the front door.

The **restaurant** is known for casting a wide net of culinary influence. Daily specials might include a Mediterranean tapas sharing plate, a chickpea risotto, or a pan-fried local sea bass with chive butter. Main courses range from £11 to £18.

Capel Curig, Conwy LL24 0EL. www.bryntyrchinn.co.uk. ℂ **01690/720223.** 12 units. £75–£85 double. Rates include Welsh breakfast. 2-night minimum stay at weekends (except Dec). MC, V. Free parking. **Amenities:** Restaurant; bar; bike rental. *In room:* TV, CD player, hair dryer, Wi-Fi (free).

Castle Cottage ★★ This elegant cottage/restaurant in a quiet corner of Snowdonia maintains consistently high standards. Rooms inside the petite, 400-year-old cottage are decorated in stylish, contemporary creams, with exposed wood beams, and come with the modern amenities you'd expect in a boutique hotel.

Eat-and-stay packages include dinner in the **award-winning restaurant,** which is also open to non-guests (reservations are essential). There's a determined focus on local ingredients—expect Welsh lamb and shellfish to appear on the menu—but with an open mind to combinations from farther afield. A three-course dinner costs £38 per person.

Y Lech, Harlech, Gwynedd LL46 2YL. www.castlecottageharlech.co.uk. ℂ **01766/780479.** 7 units. £125–£168 double. Extra bed £15–£25. Rates include Welsh breakfast. MC, V. Limited free parking. **Amenities:** Restaurant; bar; Wi-Fi (free). *In room:* TV/DVD, CD player/library, hair dryer, MP3 docking station, no phone.

Tan-y-Foel ★★ This converted 16th-century manor house is the best hotel around Betws-y-Coed, opening onto a panoramic sweep of Conwy Valley. Vibrant fabrics and modern paintings bring you into the 21st century, but the atmosphere is

Mountain bikers of all abilities will find riding to suit them in North Wales. The technical forest trails at **Coed y Brenin** ★ (☎ **01341/440747**), 6 miles north of Dol-gellau beside the A470, include the legendary, off-piste, expert-only Pink Heifer, as steep and wild as you'll find in the U.K. (and you won't find it on any official trail map; Google it). **Coed Llandegla Forest** ★ (www.coedllandegla.com), beside the A525, 9 miles west of Wrexham, has marked trails suited to all abilities, including family groups. Rent equipment locally from **One-Planet Adventure**, Ruthin Road, Llandegla (☎ **01978/751656**; www.oneplanetadventure.com). The essential website for mountain biking in Wales is **www.mbwales.com**.

still very much of yesteryear. Rooms are moderate to spacious, each individually furnished in markedly contrasting styles. Those with the best views open onto the front of the hotel.

In an intimate setting, chef and owner Janet Pitman takes her limited-choice, **three-course dinner** seriously. It costs £49 per person, and is an expertly assembled meal featuring such specialties as Welsh Black beef and produce from the hotel garden. Dinner reservations are essential, for both guests and non-guests, and note that vegetarian options are not available.

Capel Garmon, Llanrwst, Conwy LL26 ORE. www.tyfhotel.co.uk. ☎ **01690/710507.** Fax 01690/710681. 6 units. £115–£245 double. Rates include Welsh breakfast. MC, V. Free parking. From Betws-y-Coed, take the A5 onto the A470, heading north to Llanrwst, turning at the signpost for Capel Garmon. No children 11 and under. **Amenities:** Restaurant; lounge/bar. *In room:* TV/DVD, CD player/library, hair dryer, Wi-Fi (free).

Tŷ Gwyn ★   Laden with local artifacts, Tŷ Gwyn is a low-slung, 17th-century inn sitting opposite Waterloo Bridge in Betws-y-Coed. Inside, it's a world of old prints and chintz, time-darkened beams, and hanging copper pans. Bedrooms, often small, are comfortably furnished: Three come with a four-poster bed, and two have spa tubs in recently modernized bathrooms.

The **restaurant**'s menu of refined pub fare with an international twist features local produce such as mature Welsh filet of beef with sauce *au poivre*, as well as flavors from Thailand and elsewhere. Main courses range from £12 to £20.

Betws-y-Coed, Gwynedd LL24 OSG. www.tygwynhotel.co.uk. ☎ **01690/710383.** 13 units, 11 with bathroom. £56 double without bathroom, £78 double with bathroom, £98–£130 four-poster room. Rates include Welsh breakfast. MC, V. Free parking. **Amenities:** Restaurant; bar; Wi-Fi (free). *In room:* TV, no phone.

THE LLEYN PENINSULA ★

Porthmadog: 266 miles NW of London, 20 miles S of Caernarfon; Pwllheli: 14 miles W of Porthmadog; Abersoch: 28 miles SW of Caernarfon, 6 miles SW of Pwllheli

Separating Cardigan Bay and its northern arm, Tremadog Bay, from Caernarfon Bay, the gentle western **Lleyn Peninsula** thrusts out like a giant claw into the Irish Sea. The peninsula has a large Welsh-speaking population, and Welsh feeling is traditionally strong—Plaid Cymru, Wales's nationalist political party, was founded in Pwllheli in 1925. The main reasons to visit the Lleyn are great food and glorious solitude. Aside from small coastal centers like **Pwllheli, Criccieth,** and **Abersoch,** there's very little here—in an utterly splendid way. The peninsula is crisscrossed by small roads and walking trails, where out of season you'll be unlikely to meet anyone at all.

The Lleyn's main tourist center of **Porthmadog** is a terminus for two of Wales's "great little trains," the **Ffestiniog Railway** (see below) and the **Welsh Highland Railway** (p. 730).

Essentials

GETTING THERE A slow, local rail line connects Pwllheli, Porthmadog, and Criccieth with Aberystwyth (via Machynlleth) and Shrewsbury and Birmingham, in England. Buses also pull into Porthmadog every hour from Bangor. Porthmadog is well connected by road with Caernarfon and Snowdonia, via the A487. The main peninsula roads, the A499 and A497, converge at Pwllheli.

VISITOR INFORMATION The **Tourist Information Centre,** High Street, Porthmadog (© **01766/512981;** www.visitsnowdonia.info), is open from Easter to October, daily 9:30am to 5pm. Off-season hours are Monday to Saturday 10am to 3:30pm. In Pwllheli, there's a seasonal **Tourist Information Centre,** at Min y Don, Station Square (© **01758/613000**), usually open 5 days each week (currently closed Fri and Sun, but exact days change).

Exploring the Lleyn Peninsula

The peninsula takes its name from an Irish tribe, the Celtic Legine, or Laigin, who didn't have very far to go from home to invade the country of fellow Celts. They were followed by missionaries and pilgrims in the Christian era.

Now in ruins, **Criccieth Castle** (© **01766/522227**), built as a Welsh stronghold, commands a fine view of Tremadog Bay. During its years as an active fortress, it changed hands—Welsh to English and back and forth—until it was finally sacked and burned in 1404 by Owain Glyndŵr, never to rise again as a fortification. Admission is £3.10 for adults, £2.70 for seniors, students, and children 5 to 15. A family ticket goes for £8.90. It's open April through October, daily from 10am to 5pm, and November through March, Friday and Saturday 9:30am to 4pm and Sunday 11am to 4pm. Outside those hours, the castle exhibition is closed, but you can still enjoy the view from the site (10am to 4pm only).

About 2 miles west of Criccieth in Llanystumdwy, is **Highgate,** the boyhood home of David Lloyd George, prime minister of Britain between 1914 and 1918, and also the **Lloyd George Museum** (© **01766/522071**), designed by Clough Williams-Ellis of Portmeirion resort village fame (see below). The museum outlines the statesman's life, with displays illustrating his political career. Admission is £4 for adults, £3 for seniors and children 5 to 15, and £10 for a family. From May to September, it's open daily 10:30am to 5pm (closed weekends in May and Sun in June); in October, hours are Monday to Friday 11am to 4pm. Lloyd George's grave is nearby, on the banks of the River Dwyfor.

The pretty port-resort of **Abersoch** ★ is the best base for exploring the farther-flung, emptier reaches of the peninsula. Surfers should make straight for **Porth Neigwl,** "Hell's Mouth" beach; for a surf report, check **www.westcoastsurf.co.uk/surfreport.htm.** Serious bird-watchers and solitude-seekers, on the other hand, should book a day-trip to **Bardsey (Ynys Enlli)** ★. The tiny islet has been a place of pilgrimage since Christianity first came to North Wales in the 3rd or 4th century, and there was probably a monastery there by the 6th century. Today it is home to a thousands-strong colony of Manx shearwater and other species of coastal bird. Day-trips operated by **Bardsey Boat Trips** (✆ **07971/769895;** www.bardseyboattrips. com) depart from Porth Meudwy, Aberdaron, regularly in season. Trips cost £30 for adults, £20 children, and allow you about 3½ hours to roam Bardsey. For more about the island, see **www.enlli.org**.

Ffestiniog Railway ★★ RAILWAY   Ride near the front, with the window wedged down, for the full "age of steam" ambience (and odor) on Wales's most famous narrow-gauge heritage railway. The tiny steam engine pulls its wood-paneled carriages (with antique booth seating) the majestic 13½ miles from Portmadog to Blaenau Ffestiniog several times a day for most of the year. The Lleyn's main town, **Porthmadog,** was named after a "Celtification" of the English name of its builder, William Madocks, a mining mogul who built the town from scratch between 1808 and 1811. At its peak in 1873, 116,000 tons of Blaenau slate were shipped from this harbor across the empire and the world. (The railway was built in 1832 to carry Blaenau's slate down to the port.)

The route climbs quickly away from the Traeth Bach estuary, clinging to the hillside and winding through forests of pine and oak, past waterfalls and over picturesque uplands to Blaenau. Journey time is 1¼ hours each way.

Harbour Station, Porthmadog. ✆ **01766/516024.** www.festrail.co.uk. Day ticket £19 adults, £17 seniors; half-way round-trip £11 adults, £10 seniors; one child 3-15 travels free with each paying adult. See website for timetable.

Portmeirion Village ★ HISTORIC SITE   There's more than a whiff of Disney about this magical, multicolored village by the sea. It took architect Clough Williams-Ellis (1883–1978) over half a century to turn what was an original 1850 manor house and its abandoned estate into a "resort" like no other. His elaborate pastiche, with eclectic architectural influences both indigenous and foreign, wrapped in an Italianate sugar-coating and transplanted onto a wild Welsh estuary probably shouldn't work—but Williams-Ellis's understanding of how architecture and nature can function in harmony ensures that it just does. Wander buildings that veer between Arts and Crafts and neoclassical styles, or lose yourself in acres of subtropical garden walks and soak up a place that made a suitably surreal setting for *The Prisoner,* a cult 1960s' TV show. For the full Portmeirion effect, stay in the hotel here (see below).

Portmeirion (2½ miles southeast of Porthmadog). ✆ **01766/770000.** www.portmeirion-village.com. Admission £9 adults, £6 children 4-16 (£4.50 and £3, respectively, after 3:30pm). Daily 9:30am–7:30pm.

Where to Eat & Stay

Old-fashioned and a little timeworn, but also well located, friendly, and great value, the **Lion Hotel,** Y Maes, Criccieth, Gwynedd LL52 0AA (www.lionhotelcriccieth. co.uk; ✆ **01766/522460**), makes a practical overnight stop for touring visitors—especially those with children. Doubles cost £70 to £80, with two-room family suites going for around £100, depending on the season. There's hearty pub fare served downstairs in the restaurant and lively bar.

For a quarter-century, sophisticated foodies have been coming to **Plas Bodegroes** ★, Pwllheli, Gwynedd LL53 5TH (Ⓒ **01758/612363;** www.bodegroes.co.uk), an idyllic, 10-room Georgian manor house and gardens that was one of the country's original restaurants with rooms. A four-course, creative dinner menu costs £45 per person. Doubles cost between £130 and £180 per night. It's closed on Sunday and Monday. Reservations are, of course, essential.

Rhiwafallen (p. 730), outside Caernarfon, could also serve as a base for exploring the northern Lleyn.

Bron Eifion ★★ On 2 hectares (5 acres) of manicured gardens, this wood-paneled baronial mansion is the most elegant place to stay around Criccieth. The tended gardens evoke the South of France, and the interior looks like a good place to stage an Agatha Christie mystery. Rooms are spacious and traditionally furnished; some have four-poster beds. *Insider tip:* Check the website for off-season dinner, bed, and breakfast deals.

Dinner in the rarefied surrounds of the **Orangery Restaurant** is a refined affair, featuring such dishes as roast loin and confit shoulder of Welsh lamb with minted dauphinois potatoes. Main courses cost between £16 and £25.

Criccieth, Gwynedd LL52 0SA. www.broneifion.co.uk. Ⓒ **01766/522385.** Fax 01766/523796. 19 units. £135–£185 double. Rates include Welsh breakfast. AE; MC, V. Free parking. ½ mile outside Criccieth beside A497. **Amenities:** Restaurant; bar; babysitting; room service. *In room:* TV/DVD, hair dryer, Wi-Fi (free).

Gwesty Portmeirion ★★★ With one of the most idyllic settings in Wales, this hotel existed as an early Victorian villa before Clough Williams-Ellis converted it into an evocative resort from 1926 (see above). Writers such as H. G. Wells and George Bernard Shaw were habitués. The decor inside is exotic: fabrics from Kashmir, paintings from Rajasthan, tiles from Delft, and wallpaper from New York. About a dozen units are in the main house (the best having sea views), the rest in a cluster of "village houses." *Insider tip:* Check the website for special offers—especially out of season, which can get very affordable.

Portmeirion, Gwynedd LL48 6ER. www.portmeirion-village.com. Ⓒ **01766/770000.** Fax 01766/770300. 53 units. £95–£229 double; £189–£297 suite. Rates include Welsh breakfast. AE, DC, MC, V. Free parking. Off the A487, 2 miles southeast of Porthmadog. **Amenities:** 2 restaurants; bar; babysitting; outdoor pool; room service; outdoor tennis court. *In room:* TV (DVD in some), hair dryer, Wi-Fi (free).

Venetia ★★ 🎁 If you're seeking a sleek, chic seaside hideaway, there's nowhere better on the Lleyn than Venetia, in the pretty port-resort of Abersoch. Rooms inside the modernized Victorian villa are midsize and stylish, decorated in muted tones with flashes of exuberance, and dressed with Italian furniture and designer accoutrements. The best is Room no. 5, "Cinque," with a Jacuzzi big enough for two.

The cornerstone of Venetia's growing reputation is its **restaurant,** where locally sourced seafood is prepared expertly with a distinctive Italian accent. Try the likes of Cardigan Bay scallops with prosciutto and Grana Padano shavings, or Aberdaron crab linguine. Main courses range from £12 to £22. Reservations are essential for non-guests.

Lon Sarn Bach, Abersoch, Gwynedd LL53 7EB. www.venetiawales.com. Ⓒ **01758/713354.** 5 units. £80–£148 double. Rates include Welsh breakfast. 2-night minimum stay at weekends. AE, MC, V. Limited free parking. Closed Jan–mid-Feb, Tues all year, Mon Sept–May, and Sun Nov–Dec. **Amenities:** Restaurant; bar. *In room:* TV/DVD, hair dryer, MP3 docking station (in some), no phone, Wi-Fi (free).

CAERNARFON ★

249 miles NW of London; 68 miles W of Chester; 30 miles SE of Holyhead; 9 miles SW of Bangor

The principal reason to come to **Caernarfon,** at the mouth of the River Seiont, is to see **Caernarfon Castle.** In the 13th century, when King Edward I had defeated the Welsh after long and bitter fighting, he ordered the construction of a fortress on the site of an old Norman castle at the western end of the Menai Strait. From here, his sentinels could command a view of the land around, all the way to the mountains and far out across the bay. Caernarfon is also a great place to begin a journey into the heart of Snowdonia, aboard the historic **Welsh Highland Railway,** one of Wales's most scenic train rides.

The main downside to Caernarfon? Tourist buses can occasionally overrun the walled center in summer.

Essentials

GETTING THERE There's no regular rail link to Caernarfon; the nearest connection is through Bangor, to which Caernarfon is linked by bus. Buses run between Bangor and Caernarfon, a 25-minute ride, at least every 20 minutes throughout the day.

If you're driving from Bangor, head southwest along the A487; from Porthmadog, head north along the A487, or take a day-trip aboard the **Welsh Highland Railway** (see below).

VISITOR INFORMATION The **Caernarfon Tourist Information Centre** is at Oriel Pendeitsh, Castle Street (✆ **01286/672232**). From May through October, it's open daily 9:30am to 4:30pm; November through April, hours are Monday to Saturday 10am to 3:30pm.

Exploring Caernarfon

The Romans maintained a fort at **Segontium** for some 3 centuries. Excavations on the outskirts of Caernarfon beside the A4085 have disclosed foundations of barracks, bathhouses, and other remains. Finds from the excavations are displayed in the **museum** (✆ **01286/675625;** www.nationaltrust.org.uk) on the site, usually open year-round Tuesday to Sunday from 12:30 to 4:30pm. Admission is free. There are no outstanding relics here; allow about 30 minutes to walk around.

Caernarfon Castle ★ CASTLE The nearest thing Wales has to a royal palace was described by Dr. (Samuel) Johnson after a visit in 1774 as "an edifice of stupendous majesty and strength"—indeed, this may be the largest structure ever built in Wales. Based either on his firsthand observations (historians believe Edward I might have visited Constantinople during the Crusades) or on ancient drawings of Constantinople procured by Edward's architect, the Savoy-born James of St. George, the walls were patterned after those surrounding ancient Byzantium.

The walls between the Chamberlain Tower and Queen's Tower house the **Museum of the Royal Welch Fusiliers** (www.rwfmuseum.org.uk), which traces the history of the regiment's role in war across the globe since 1659. Allow 1½ hours total for your visit.

Caernarfon. ✆ **01286/677617.** Admission (includes museum) £5.25 adults, £4.85 seniors and children 5–15, £15 family ticket. Mar–Oct daily 9:30am–5pm; Nov–Feb Mon–Sat 10am–4pm, Sun 11am–4pm.

EDWARD'S iron RING

Although Edward I (1239–1307) was one of medieval England's most powerful kings, he had more than his share of problems with the Celts. Trouble flared up in the early 1280s when Llywelyn ap Gruffudd (1223–82)—still the only native prince a united Welsh nation has ever had—occupied Caernarfon. The Welsh appeared to have abandoned a tradition of internecine fighting in order to mount an effective insurrection against the English. However, Llywelyn was betrayed and killed in 1282 at the Battle of Orewin Bridge, near Builth Wells, and Edward moved quickly to eradicate his line and to establish an "Iron Ring" of castles designed to keep the locals in check forever. Flint and Rhuddlan, erected after lesser troubles in the 1270s, were strengthened. Progress at **Caernarfon** (see below) was so rapid that by 1284, Edward I's son, later Edward II, was born inside its Eagle Tower (a "native prince!" his father proclaimed). Coastal castles at **Conwy** (p. 736) and **Harlech** (p. 724) were designed to be equally impregnable, and when the Welsh revolted again, in 1294, Edward ordered Caernarfon's walls to be built even taller. The final link in his imperious chain, **Beaumaris** (p. 733), is the most elegant of royal master mason James of St. George's constructions. All have survived the centuries remarkably intact, and represent the pinnacle of medieval castle-building in Europe.

Welsh Highland Railway ★★★ 📷 RAILWAY Wales's most spectacular little steam railway plies a course from regal Caernarfon right into the heart of Snowdonia—and since early 2011, out the other side to Porthmadog, too. Historic carriages creek, rattle, and cough their way along the Gwyrfai Valley and the shores of Llyn Cwellyn before striking out into undiluted uplands suited only to sightseers, sheep, and the occasional hardy drover. A few trains a day make the return journey, so if you plan it right you can combine the train with some superlative hill walking: Get off at Rhyd Ddu or Snowdon Ranger for major paths up **Mount Snowdon** (p. 722), or at Beddgelert for the **Aberglaslyn Gorge** (p. 722), also the most memorable stretch of the rail line.

St. Helens Rd., Caernarfon. ℂ **01286/677018.** www.festrail.co.uk. Round-trip tickets £10–£28; one child travels free per adult. Apr–Oct 2–4 trains daily; see website for timetable.

Where to Eat & Stay

There's little reason to stay in Caernarfon itself—our favorite local accommodations are outside town—but if you're resolved on a room in the center, the **Celtic Royal Hotel,** Bangor Street, Caernarfon, Gwynedd LL55 1AY (www.celtic-royal.co.uk; ℂ **01286/674477**), combines some character with an outstanding array of amenities, including a heated indoor pool and health club. Double rooms cost £130 per night. For decent pub grub and a pint of local ale, your best bet is the **Black Boy Inn,** Northgate Street (ℂ **01286/673604;** www.black-boy-inn.com). Most main courses cost around £10.

Rhiwafallen ★★ 🏠 This cozy farmhouse-turned-restaurant with guest rooms is the boutique best-bet within range of Caernarfon. Rooms are dressed vibrantly to reflect contrasting themes; the best, Raspberry, has its own sundeck.

Chic wallpaper and light-wood furniture set off Rhiwafallen's **stylish, intimate dining room.** The three-course fixed-price menu (£35) changes seasonally, but diners are guaranteed the finest local produce combined with contemporary flair. Expect the likes of twice-cooked pork belly served with truffled potatoes and wilted greens. The restaurant is open for dinner Tuesday to Saturday, and on Sunday for lunch; advance reservations are essential.

Llandwrog, Caernarfon, Gwynedd LL54 5SW. www.rhiwafallen.co.uk. ✆ **01286/830172.** 3 units. £100–£150 double. Rates include Welsh breakfast. AE, MC, V. Free parking. No children under 16. **Amenities:** Restaurant. *In room:* TV/DVD, hair dryer.

Seiont Manor ★   Situated amid tranquil countryside between Caernarfon and Llanberis, this former farmstead of a Georgian manor house has been tastefully converted into a honeycomb of spacious guest rooms, each with a good-size bathroom, and all with views over 60 hectares (150 acres) of parkland. Not all the modern touches work, but the overall impression is of a place that guarantees seclusion, a sense of style, and some of the best leisure facilities in the area. Each of the rooms has a small balcony or a terrace; two are reserved for families.

Dining in the **Llwyn y Brain restaurant** guarantees classic local flavors and ingredients like Welsh Black beef and salmon. Set dinner menus cost £31.

Llanrug, Caernarfon, Gwynedd LL55 2AQ. www.handpickedhotels.co.uk. ✆ **01286/673366.** Fax 01286/672840. 28 units. £95–£165 double; from £145 suite. AE, DC, MC, V. Free parking. From Caernarfon, head east on the A4086 for 2 miles. **Amenities:** 2 restaurants; bar; babysitting; health club; indoor heated pool; room service. *In room:* TV/DVD, CD player/library, hair dryer, no phone, Wi-Fi (free).

THE ISLE OF ANGLESEY ★★

Holyhead: 27 miles NW of Caernarfon, 215 miles N of Cardiff; Beaumaris: 26 miles E of Holyhead

This is an island of many names: Ynys Môn to the Welsh, the Romans called it Mona, and these days it's usually just **Anglesey**—"Mother of Wales" and home in the 5th century of St. Dwynwen, Wales's patron saint of lovers, whose "alternative Valentine's" is celebrated each January 25. The scenery differs markedly from the mainland's, with undulating farmland interrupted by occasional crags and single-story whitewashed cottages. Then there's the 125 miles of silent coastline—with a marked circular coastal path for you to follow.

Its "capital," the little town of **Beaumaris**—named from a distinctly un-Welsh corruption of the French for "beautiful marsh"—is the natural first stop. Visit the **Castle,** then the **Court** and **Gaol,** to glimpse some unsavory but fascinating snapshots of life for those who got on the wrong side of this frontier town over the centuries—most of which were spent cut off from the rest of Wales by the narrow, tidal Menai Strait. More remote is **Holy Island,** home to Anglesey's westernmost point, **South Stack,** and the gateway to Ireland via the **Holyhead** ferry.

Essentials

GETTING THERE & AROUND   **Holyhead** is the terminus of the North Wales Coast rail line. Trains arrive regularly during the day from Cardiff, Bangor, Llandudno, Chester, and even London. **Llanfair PG** is the isle's other main rail halt. Transfer at Bangor for **Beaumaris:** Bus nos. 53, 56, 57, and 58 connect Bangor and Beaumaris approximately every 30 minutes during the day Monday to Saturday, less often on Sunday. The isle's major transport route, bus no. X4, runs regularly between Bangor and Holyhead via Llangefni.

Two ferry companies operate between Holyhead (pronounced *Holly*-head) and either the Irish port of Dun Laoghaire (a railway junction 7 miles south of Dublin) or Dublin Port itself. Both companies run a swift and a conventional service; journey time is around 2 hours for swift ferries (3½ hr. for conventional ones), with three to five departures daily. On **Stena Line** (*℗* **0844/770-7070; www.stenaline.co.uk**), only foot passengers are allowed on the swift ferry; passengers with cars must travel on conventional ferries. **Irish Ferries** (*℗* **0870/517-1717; www.irishferries.com**) carries passengers and cars on both services. Round-trips for passengers traveling or returning on the same day are £27 to £32 for adults, £14 to £19 for children 4 to 15, and £68 for a family day-trip ticket (Stena only). Fares for car passage vary with season and ticket type, but typically cost between £70 and £150 or more each way for a car and one passenger.

The A55 North Wales coastal road crosses the Menai Strait and is Anglesey's main arterial road, linking the Menai Bridge and Holyhead. It becomes a causeway as it approaches Holy Island; the Four Mile Bridge on the B4545 also links Holy Island to Anglesey. Aside from the A55, roads on the isle are slow going—but scenic.

VISITOR INFORMATION Anglesey's main **Tourist Information Centre,** Railway Station, Llanfair PG (*℗* **01248/713177;** www.visitanglesey.co.uk), is open Monday to Saturday 9:30am to 5:30pm, Sunday 10am to 5pm. It closes for lunch between 1 and 2pm.

Exploring Anglesey

Visitors cross the strait by one of the two bridges built by celebrated engineers of the 19th century: The **Menai Suspension Bridge** ★★, designed by Thomas Telford and completed in 1826, and the **Britannia Bridge,** originally only a railway bridge, which was the work of Robert Stephenson and opened 24 years later. The Britannia had to be rebuilt after a devastating 1970 fire that destroyed its pitch and timberwork; it now carries both trains and cars on two levels. The bridges are almost side-by-side west of Bangor.

BEAUMARIS ★★

The tiny town of **Beaumaris** is the site of the largest of Edward's "Iron Ring" of castles (p. 730). A small settlement grew up around the castle, developing into a major port and making Beaumaris a trading center until the arrival of the railway in the 1800s. Preserved just as it was in 1614, **Beaumaris Court,** Castle Street (*℗* **01248/811691**), hosts a fascinating, if slightly grim, exhibition that highlights the arbitrary and brutal nature of justice in centuries past. Although, timbered interior aside, it looks little different from a modern British courtroom, stories of "burning in the hand," hanging, and transportation thankfully belong to another era. It's open April through September Saturday to Thursday 10:30am to 5pm, and the same hours on October weekends. Admission costs £3 for adults, £2.25 for seniors and children. The town's squat Victorian **Gaol** ★, Steeple Lane (*℗* **01248/810921**), continues the penitentiary theme. You're free to explore its gloomy corridors and cells, many enhanced with detailed explanations of the prison's harsh regime. Grisly highlights include the prisoner-powered treadwheel (a punishment) and the "luxury" condemned man's cell—two public executions were staged here in the 1800s. Opening hours are the same as for the Court; admission costs £3.50 for adults, £2.75 for seniors and children.

Low-rise turrets and circumnavigating ducks give moated **Beaumaris Castle ★★** (✆ **01248/810361;** www.cadw.wales.gov.uk) a rather twee appearance. However, in the 14th century the last and most elegant of Edward I's maritime fortresses was a feared outpost of English might. Its formidable and largely intact concentric defenses give you an immediate sense of what it was used for—you'll quickly lose count of how many firing berths there are for defenders. In those days the sea came up to the southern walls, and on certain tides small ships could reach the castle directly; the dock is still visible. Visits are possible March to October, daily from 9:30am to 5pm; and November to February, Monday to Saturday from 10am to 4pm, Sunday 11am to 4pm. Admission is £3.80 for adults and £3.40 for seniors, students, and children 5 to 15; family tickets cost £11. Pause for an ice cream at **Red Boat,** 34 Castle St. (✆ **01248/810022;** www.redboatgelato.com), where flavors like New York lemon cheesecake and crème brûlée are handmade on the premises.

LLANFAIR PG

Its fame is its name: **Llanfairpwllgwyngyllgogerychwyrndrobwllllantysiliogogogoch,** or something like that. It translates as "St. Mary's Church in the Hollow of the White Hazel near a Rapid Whirlpool and the Church of St. Tysilio near the Red Cave." In the 1860s, a local tailor had the foresight to embellish the original (shorter) name as a tourist attraction—and the ruse worked. You can get the longest train-platform ticket in the world from the station here, giving the full name. (On maps and most references it is usually called just "Llanfair PG.") The first Women's Institute in Britain met here in 1915.

A short walk from the station is the **Marquess of Anglesey Column** (✆ **01248/714393**), standing 27m (90 ft.) high on a wooded mount 76m (250 ft.) above sea level. It has a statue of the marquess on top, to which visitors can climb—it's 115 steps up a spiral staircase. The marquess lost a leg while he was second in command to the Duke of Wellington at the Battle of Waterloo and was thereafter called "One Leg". The column is open year-round daily 9am to 5pm, charging £1.50 for adults, 75p for seniors and children.

About a mile southwest of the village with the long name, beside the A4080, is **Plas Newydd ★**, Llanfair PG (✆ **01248/715272;** www.nationaltrust.org.uk/plas newydd), standing on the shores of the Menai. An ancient manor house, it was converted between 1783 and 1809 into a splendid mansion in the Gothic and neoclassical styles. In the long dining room, there's a magnificent *trompe l'oeil* mural by Rex Whistler, and a military museum houses relics and uniforms of the Battle of Waterloo. The beautiful woodland garden and lawns have glorious Snowdonia panoramas. Plas Newydd can be visited only from Easter to October, Saturday to Wednesday 1 to 5pm. The gardens are open from 10am. A combined ticket for both the house and garden costs £8.45 for adults and £4.20 for children 15 and under; it's £21 for a family ticket.

Beyond Plas Newydd, a mile southwest of Brynsiencyn (follow signs for the Sea Zoo), is the home of family-run **Halen Môn Anglesey Sea Salt ★** (✆ **01248/430871;** www.halenmon.com). This prized natural salt is found in many of the world's most famous kitchens; it's used by Heston Blumenthal (p. 137), and goes into President Obama's favorite brand of chocolates, Fran's. You're free to taste the varieties, including salt smoked over local oak chippings, before you buy from the small shop at Halen Môn's tiny headquarters. It's open Monday to Friday 10am to 4:30pm.

HOLY ISLAND ★

The largest town on Anglesey, **Holyhead** is not actually on Anglesey at all but on **Holy Island.** However, the two islands have long been linked. Packet boats between Holyhead and Ireland were recorded as far back as 1573—and the town is now a functional place for those connecting with Dublin (see "To Ireland by Ferryboat," above).

Holyhead Mountain is the highest point in Anglesey, at 216m (710 ft.), from where you can see the Isle of Man, Ireland's Mourne Mountains, Snowdonia, and even Cumbria on a clear day. The summit is the site of an ancient hill fort and the ruins of an Irish settlement from the 2nd to the 4th century A.D. On the southwestern side of the mountain is **South Stack ★** (**℗ 01407/763207**), a lighthouse opened in 1809. The towering surrounding cliffs are home to colonies of razorbill, guillemot, and puffin, and gray seals breed in the caves below. The lighthouse is open Easter to September, daily from 10:30am to 5:30pm, charging £4 for adults and £2 for children—but, to reach it, be prepared to negotiate 400 steps there, and another 400 back. There's gentler, scenic coastal walking on the heathland nearby. Pack your binoculars.

Where to Eat & Stay

For a scenic seaside pint and a smoked salmon sandwich, the best spot on the island is **The Ship ★**, Red Wharf Bay (**℗ 01248/852568;** www.shipinnredwharfbay. co.uk), a whitewashed inn overlooking a sweeping bay 8 miles northwest of Beaumaris. It's signposted off the A5025.

Neuadd Lwyd ★★ Isolation was never so splendid as at this converted stone rectory stranded among the pastures of central Anglesey. Country house-style rooms are an elegant slice of yesteryear, with plush furnishings and antique furniture in keeping with the structure. It's open for bed and breakfast Wednesday through Saturday night.

To complement the sense of escape and regal splendor, dinner is a refined, intimate affair. Expect creative combinations such as carpaccio of Welsh Black beef with shavings of local goat's cheese and nasturtium flowers. The **restaurant** is open for dinner only Thursday to Saturday; a daily, no-choice, four-course menu costs £42 per person. Reservations—as far ahead as you can manage for non-guests—are essential.

Penmynydd, Llanfair PG, Anglesey LL61 5BX (off the B4520, 2½ miles north of Llanfair PG). www.neuadd lwyd.co.uk. **℗ 01248/715005.** 4 units. £150–£200 double. Rates include Welsh breakfast. MC, V. Free parking. Closed Dec–Jan. No children under 16. **Amenities:** Restaurant. *In room:* TV/DVD, hair dryer, no phone.

Anglesey's Best Beaches

The tiny resort of **Rhosneigr** has an unspoiled, sandy beach that's ideal for low-tide rockpooling (foraging for shells, crabs, and so forth). Strong currents make it a favorite haunt of water-sports fanatics. For swimming, especially with young children, you're better off on the sheltered eastern coast. The sands at **Benllech** and **Lligwy** are our favorite family spots.

The White Eagle ★ GASTROPUB Amid blissful seclusion in the southeastern corner of Holy Island, this landmark gastropub was completely redeveloped in 2007. Diners can choose between cozy, drawing room seating; a light-drenched, bustling modern bar area; or a glorious sundeck. The kitchen delivers gastropub fare with a flourish, including classics like a steaming bowl of Menai mussels served Flemish style with fries and crusty bread. There's a fine Anglesey and Welsh cheese menu to finish, and also usually six beers on tap, including offerings from the Conwy Valley's Great Orme brewery.

Rhoscolyn LL65 2NJ (off the B4545, 5 miles southeast of Holyhead). ☏ **01407/860267.** www.white-eagle.co.uk. No reservations. Main courses £10–£16. Mon–Fri noon–2:30pm and 6–9pm; Sat–Sun noon–9pm.

Ye Olde Bull's Head Inn & Townhouse ★★ This historic coaching inn has been the best address in Beaumaris for some time; it has welcomed such notables as Dr. (Samuel) Johnson and Charles Dickens. The well-decorated, characterful bedrooms come in an array of types and sizes, including traditional four-poster rooms. To match a different mood, units in the adjacent, contrasting Townhouse are sharp and contemporary.

You'll find Anglesey's most creative contemporary cooking in exclusive surroundings at the **Loft Restaurant,** under the eaves of the old inn. Expect the likes of crab and scallop lasagna followed by loin of Welsh lamb with creamed leek porridge and harissa spiced broad beans. It's open Tuesday through Saturday for dinner only. A three-course dinner costs £39.50. There's also a **Brasserie,** open daily for lunch and dinner, that features well-crafted, international bistro favorites like blackened Cajun spiced salmon. Main courses range from £9 to £14.

Castle St., Beaumaris, Anglesey LL58 8AP. www.bullsheadinn.co.uk. ☏ **01248/810329.** 26 units. £100–£160 double. Rates include Welsh breakfast. AE, MC, V. Limited free parking. **Amenities:** 2 restaurants; bar; room service. *In room:* A/C (in Townhouse), TV, hair dryer, MP3 docking station (in Townhouse), Wi-Fi (free).

CONWY ★★

241 miles NW of London; 37 miles E of Holyhead; 22 miles NE of Caernarfon

Pint-size and atmospheric, the market town of **Conwy** has a historical importance that punches well above the weight of its population of 15,000. The **castle, town walls,** and enclosed street-plan were laid down by English King Edward I in the 1200s, when Conwy was a crucial garrison town. Later history almost forgot this little trading port, until the Victorian era, when Telford's **Conwy Suspension Bridge** and Stephenson's **Tubular Railroad Bridge** spanned the estuary, bringing roads and the railway to its ancient town gates.

Essentials

GETTING THERE Trains run between Conwy and Chester, Bangor, northwest England, and London. Buses from Bangor heading for Llandudno pass through Conwy every 15 minutes during the day Monday to Saturday, and hourly on Sunday.

Motorists from England should head west along the main coastal route, the A55.

VISITOR INFORMATION Conwy Castle Visitor Centre, Castle Street (☏ **01492/592248**), dispenses information about the town and region, and is open the same hours as the castle (see below). A move is scheduled for 2012.

Exploring Conwy

Your first stop should be a walk to the apex of the almost-complete **town walls,** to gain some perspective over Conwy's near-perfect grid of streets.

The Conwy estuary is crossed by three bridges that all lead to Conwy. The handsome **Conwy Suspension Bridge** was built in 1826 by Thomas Telford, whom Romantic poet Robert Southey nicknamed the "Colossus of Roads" (on account of his feat of building the A5 road). It's closed to vehicular traffic now, but you can walk across it and marvel at how it served as the main entrance to the town for so long. Adjacent is Robert Stephenson's **Tubular Railroad Bridge,** built in 1848, and the only one of its kind still surviving. Completing the trio is the modern arched road bridge, completed in 1958.

St. Mary's, the parish church, stands inside the walls on the site of a 12th-century Cistercian abbey. It's the only structure in town to pre-date the medieval grid. The churchyard contains a marked but overgrown grave associated with William Wordsworth's poem, *We Are Seven.*

Aberconwy House HISTORIC SITE   The town's only medieval house still standing (and the oldest in Conwy), was completed sometime during the 14th century in the half-timbered English style—although it owes its survival to the stone construction of the first story. Rooms are dressed according to the house's various guises over 6 centuries: as a working base for a Tudor merchant placed strategically close to the quay; as the sometime home of an 18th-century sea captain; and as a temperance (i.e. alcohol-free) hotel in the 1890s.

Castle St. © **01492/592246.** www.nationaltrust.org.uk. Admission £3.40 adults, £1.70 children 5–16, £8.50 family ticket. Apr–Oct Wed–Mon (July–Aug daily) 11am–5pm.

Conwy Castle ★★ CASTLE   The entire town centers on Conwy Castle: Edward I had this masterpiece of medieval architecture built after he conquered the last native Prince of Wales, Llywelyn ap Gruffudd. More than any other fortress built for Edward, Conwy Castle provides insight into the clever military architecture of the king's master mason, James of St. George. Separated from the town by a massive ditch, with one entrance through two gates followed by the protection of Outer and Inner Wards, the castle would have been practically impossible to assault head-on—in fact, it was only ever taken by ruse or negotiation in its 700-year history. The wall-walk above the East Barbican is the place to head for the best view of Conwy's 19th-century bridges. Allow an hour to visit.

> ### Conwy's Combined Ticket
>
> The best-value way to see Conwy's two premier sights is with a combined ticket for the **Castle** and **Plas Mawr.** It costs £6.85 for adults; £5.85 for seniors, students, and children 5 to 15; and £20 for a family ticket.

Castle St. © **01492/592358.** www.cadw.wales.gov.uk. Admission £4.80 adults; £4.30 seniors, students, and children 5–15; £14 family ticket. Apr–June and Sept–Oct daily 9:30am–5pm; July–Aug daily 9:30am–6pm; Nov–Mar Mon–Sat 9:30am–4pm, Sun 11am–4pm.

Plas Mawr ★★ HISTORIC SITE   From its modest entrance, you get no sense of the scale of this immaculately preserved Elizabethan townhouse. The mansion and courtyard garden were built in the 1580s for Robert Wynn, a Tudor nobleman who fathered seven children in his seventies while simultaneously serving as the Member

Conwy

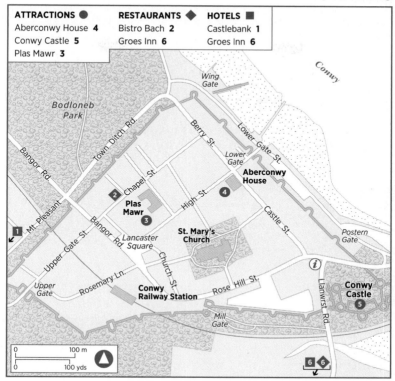

ATTRACTIONS ●
Aberconwy House **4**
Conwy Castle **5**
Plas Mawr **3**

RESTAURANTS ◆
Bistro Bach **2**
Groes Inn **6**

HOTELS ■
Castlebank **1**
Groes Inn **6**

of Parliament for Caernarvonshire, and as county sheriff. The kitchen, pantry, and dining hall are dressed as if the owner and staff had just stepped out—the former to hunt, and the latter to market.

High St. ℂ **01492/580167.** www.cadw.wales.gov.uk. Admission £4.95 adults; £4.60 seniors, students, and children 5–15; £15 family ticket. Apr–Sept Tues–Sun 9am–5pm; Oct Tues–Sun 9:30am–4pm. Closed Nov–Mar.

Where to Eat & Stay

If you want to stay in town, the best-value central hotel is **Castlebank ★**, Mount Pleasant, Conwy LL32 8NY (www.castlebankhotel.co.uk; ℂ **01492/593888**), where you'll find a home-away-from-home feel thanks to comfortable, traditional rooms and a can-do attitude from genial host-owners. A double costs between £75 and £90 depending on season.

Backstreet **Bistro Bach,** 26 Chapel St. (ℂ **01492/596326**), has an unshakable commitment to Welsh ingredients and a creative take on combining them. The short menu includes vegetarian options, alongside Llandudno-smoked fish and prize-winning meats. Main courses cost between £13 and £21.

Groes Inn ★   You can almost smell the 16th century at this roadside inn—it dates from 1573 and was the first licensed house in Wales. Although it has expanded over the years, the original core is still here, with log fires, antiques, and open-beamed, time-blackened ceilings, set amid rolling agricultural pastures. Rooms are in a separate wing away from the pub noise; Deluxe and Balcony units are a good size, comfortably furnished, and come with terraces.

Even if you don't stay, stop in for classic pub food cooked with the finest ingredients, which you can eat in the **restaurant** or an **informal bar.** There are plenty of local touches, like the Groes smokie (smoked haddock with Parmesan cheese), gammon steak served with a local farm egg, and Groes Ale, brewed specially for the inn. Main courses cost between £9 and £19.

Tyn-y-Groes, Conwy LL32 8TN. www.groesinn.com. ℰ **01492/650545.** Fax 01492/650855. 14 units. £115–£190 double. Rates include Welsh breakfast. AE, DC, MC, V. 3 miles south of Conwy on B5106. **Amenities:** Restaurant; bar; room service. *In room:* TV, hair dryer, Wi-Fi (free). Bus: 19.

LLANDUDNO

243 miles NW of London; 43 miles E of Holyhead

This once-fashionable seaside resort of **Llandudno** nestles in a crescent between the giant headlands of the **Great Orme** and the **Little Orme,** named by Vikings who thought they resembled sea serpents when shrouded in mist. The town was mostly built beginning around 1850 by the Mostyn family, after whom many local roads, avenues, and sites are named—and is forever linked with the Liddells, whose daughter Alice was the inspiration for Lewis Carroll's *Wonderland*. Although Llandudno has lost some of its prewar luster, its **Promenade** remains one of Britain's most handsome, and there are fine coastal views from **Marine Drive** and the **Great Orme Tramway.**

The resort's Victorian history lends it a certain cachet that's attracting a new generation of metropolitan weekend-breakers.

Essentials

GETTING THERE   **Virgin Trains** has services from London's Euston Station, frequently requiring a change of equipment in Chester, the gateway to the North Wales rail network. Three trains per day go direct from Euston to Llandudno Junction with no changes, taking 3 hours.

During the day, regular buses connect Llandudno with Bangor. Buses from Llandudno Junction Station to the center depart about every 10 minutes.

If you're driving from England, head across North Wales along the A55.

VISITOR INFORMATION   The **Llandudno Tourist Information Centre,** Mostyn Street (ℰ **01492/577577;** www.visitllandudno.org.uk), is open daily 9am to 5pm, but closed Sundays from November through March.

Exploring Llandudno

From the summit of the **Great Orme** ★ (206m/679 ft.), you get a panoramic view along the North Wales coast. You can walk up to the top if you're really energetic, but we prefer other means: Take the **Great Orme Tramway** ★ (ℰ **01492/879306;** www.greatormetramway.com), which has been carrying passengers to the summit since 1902. It operates every 20 minutes, daily from 10am to 6pm. The round-trip costs £5.80 for adults, £4 for children 3 to 16. It's closed between late October and

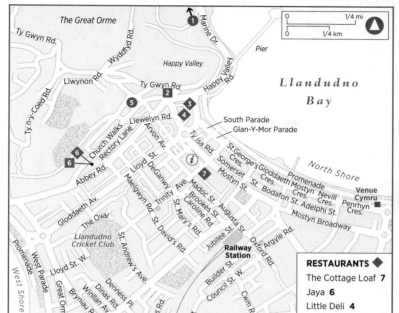

late March, during which period you can drive along a cliff-side road, the **Marine Drive,** which winds uphill in a circular route that reaches a point near the summit. Cars pay a toll of £2.50.

Just above Marine Drive is the ancient **Church of St. Tudno,** from which the town derives its name. The present stone building dates from the 12th century, but the church was founded 600 years earlier. Between April and October, it's open all day, and between June and September, there are open-air worship services every Sunday at 11am. For more information about the church and its services, call ✆ **01492/876624,** or visit **www.llandudno-parish.org.uk/sttudno.html**.

The resort has two beaches, the most famous on the northern edge of town, flanking a boardwalk and the Irish Sea, where you'll find the bandstand and traditional Punch and Judy shows in summer. Over on the quieter, west side of town, the beach opens onto more scenic views of Snowdonia and the Conwy Estuary. It's the place to head at sunset. At the end of the north-shore promenade, a fine Victorian **pier** was built in 1877, jutting 699m (2,295 ft.) into the bay at the base of the Great Orme. You'll get a fine view of it from **Happy Valley,** a former limestone quarry that was turned into lush pleasure gardens in the 1880s.

IN THE CONWY VALLEY

Bodnant Garden ★ 🏠 GARDEN   The 32-hectare (80-acre) hillside grounds of Bodnant Hall have been transformed into a charming mix of multi-tiered, labyrinthine formal gardens and managed wild spaces. Perfumed rose terraces have been carefully designed to afford views over the River Conwy to Snowdonia's foothills beyond. The garden is best known for its elegant laburnum arch and a unique, internationally important collection of rhododendrons, first planted here in 1909 (337 hybrids have been registered at Bodnant). April and May are particularly colorful.

Tal-y-Cafn, Conwy. 📞 **01492/650460.** www.nationaltrust.org.uk. Admission £7.70 adults, £3.90 children 5–16. Late Feb–Oct daily 10am–5pm; first half of Nov daily 10am–4pm. Closed mid-Nov–late Feb. Bus: 25 from Llandudno (35 min.).

Where to Eat

For lunch on the go, or a picnic, the **Little Deli** ★, 133 Mostyn Street (📞 **01492/ 872114;** www.thelittledeli.co.uk), offers tasty sandwiches and hot snacks, and sells homemade jams and chutneys. **The Cottage Loaf,** Market Square (📞 **01492/ 870762;** www.the-cottageloaf.co.uk), a tavern with a summer beer garden, serves the best pub grub in town, with main courses costing between £8 and £11. Food is served Monday to Friday 11:30am to 8pm, Saturday 11:30am to 7pm, and Sunday noon to 4pm. For an authentic taste of India's Punjab region, make a reservation at **Jaya,** inside Space (see "Where to Stay," below).

The Seahorse ★ SEAFOOD/INTERNATIONAL   Traditional, accomplished bistro cuisine and friendly service have brought this family-run restaurant a faithful list of habitués. The Seahorse has gained its reputation on the back of its excellent fish cooking. Dishes are catch dependent, but expect the likes of baked hake and crab thermidor or seared scallops with a lemon and saffron sauce. Lovers of land-roaming food are catered for with such dishes as crispy duck breast served with a Thai plum sauce.

7 Church Walks. 📞 **01492/875315.** www.the-seahorse.co.uk. Reservations recommended. Fixed-price menu £19 (1 course), £25 (2 courses), £29 (3 courses). AE, MC. Daily 4:30–11pm.

Entertainment & Nightlife

The seafront's most visible public monument is **Venue Cymru,** the Promenade (📞 **01492/872000;** www.venuecymru.co.uk). It's the place for everything from tours by the Welsh National Opera to plays and rock concerts. Most shows begin at 8pm; tickets usually cost £10 to £45.

Where to Stay

Llandudno is becoming increasingly popular with weekend visitors from the Northwest of England, so book hotels ahead on Friday and Saturday nights.

Bodysgallen Hall ★★★   This is the grandest address in the north of Wales, a dramatic 17th-century country house and spa with its own lookout tower, set on 80 hectares (200 acres) of parkland and manicured gardens. Skillfully restored, it offers architectural merit combined with 21st-century comfort. Each of the spacious and elegant bedrooms evokes a certain period in their styles and colors; some have four-poster beds. A few of the units, as good as those in the main house, are in converted cottages.

Llandudno LL30 1RS. www.bodysgallen.com. 📞 **01492/584466.** Fax 01492/582519. 33 units. £169–£349 double; £425 suite. Rates include continental breakfast. AE, MC, V. Free parking. 2 miles southeast of Llandudno along the A470. No children 5 and under. **Amenities:** 2 restaurants; bar; exercise room; indoor heated pool; spa; outdoor tennis court. *In room:* A/C (in some), TV/DVD, movie library, hair dryer, Wi-Fi (free).

Empire Hotel ★★ Behind a slightly incongruous neoclassical facade is the best full-service hotel in central Llandudno. Family managed, it is furnished with antiques and fine paintings in the Victorian tradition, but with a subtle contemporary edge. Bedrooms are midsize to spacious and luxuriously furnished. A Victorian annex, "No. 72," contains eight of the establishment's finest rooms, filled with period antiques, touches of silk, and a bathtub-cum-Jacuzzi. Book way ahead for a weekend stay.

Church Walks, Llandudno LL30 2HE. www.empirehotel.co.uk. ✆ **01492/860555.** Fax 01492/860791. 58 units. £99–£125 double. AE, DC, MC, V. Free parking. **Amenities:** 2 restaurants; bar; 2 heated pools (1 indoor, 1 outdoor); gym & spa; room service. *In room:* A/C (in some), TV/DVD, movie library, fridge, hair dryer, Wi-Fi (free).

Space ★ 🎁 The most peaceful—and the oldest—corner of Llandudno is the setting for this design-savvy "boutique B&B." The vibe is relaxed and personal. Rooms are midsize and based subtly on Indian elements, with color schemes and original, contemporary artwork carefully matched. Furniture in the public areas was designed by the owners and made in Malaysia.

The intimate on-site restaurant, **Jaya** ★ (www.jayarestaurant.co.uk), is open for dinner to non-guests Wednesday through Sunday. It specializes in home-cooked, authentic Punjabi dishes with an East African twist, like masala murgh (chicken cooked in a Kenyan style with masala sauce). Main courses cost £15 to £18.

36 Church Walks, Llandudno LL30 2HN. www.spaceboutique.co.uk. ✆ **01492/818198.** Fax 01492/550987. 11 units. £85–£95 double. Rates include full breakfast. AE, MC, V. Free parking. **Amenities:** Restaurant; bar. *In room:* TV, hair dryer, Wi-Fi (free).

DENBIGHSHIRE ★ & THE NORTHEAST BORDERLANDS

Llangollen: 65 miles SW of Manchester, 55 miles SE of Caernarfon; Wrexham: 34 miles S of Liverpool, 13 miles NE of Llangollen

Away from its developed northern coastline, the historic county of **Denbighshire** is a terrain of rolling, lush grazing pastures, misty hills, and wooded slopes. It's dotted with friendly, workaday market towns that are generally little troubled by tourists—and in sleepy, empty corners like the **Ceiriog Valley,** not even those. The exception is **Llangollen,** whose prime location at a bridge fording the River Dee has attracted visitors since the Regency era—when a trip to see the "Ladies of Llangollen" at their house, **Plas Newydd,** was all the rage. Castles such as the one at **Chirk** also testify that these Welsh borderlands haven't always been so far from the action.

Essentials

GETTING THERE & AROUND The closest rail hubs are at **Wrexham** and **Rhyl,** and a network of local buses serves the major market towns. However, the only practical way to explore the best of the region—particularly the countryside around the southern Denbighshire town of Llangollen—is by car.

VISITOR INFORMATION The main Denbighshire **Tourist Information Centre** is in Llangollen, at Y Capel, Castle Street (✆ **01978/860828;** www.northwales borderlands.co.uk). It's open daily 9:30am to 5pm, with a half-hour closure for lunch between 1 and 1:30pm.

Exploring Denbighshire & the Borderlands

The attractive little market town of **Llangollen** ★ has retained much of its Victorian character—the High Street straddling the River Dee is a pleasant place to stroll. It's easy to see why the so-called "Ladies of Llangollen," Miss Sarah Ponsonby (1755–1832) and Lady Eleanor Butler (1739–1829), loved their house and gardens at **Plas Newydd,** Hill Street (✆ **01978/862834**), perched on a hill above the town. The enviable location is complemented by the eccentric Tudor-Gothic house rich in stained glass and carved oak, in which they lived for nearly 50 years, beginning in 1778. Admission to the house costs £5.50 for adults, £4.50 for seniors and children. It's open between April and October Wednesday through Sunday 10am to 5pm.

The canal boat was the air freight of the Industrial Revolution—and 3½ miles east of Llangollen at Trevor, engineer Thomas Telford built the spectacular **Pontcysyllte Aqueduct** ★ between 1795 and 1805 to carry the Ellesmere (now Llangollen) Canal across the Dee Valley. Standing 39m (126 ft.) above the river, it's the tallest navigable aqueduct ever constructed; walk across it to get a sense of the dizzying height of its 18 piers, and drive the road below armed with a good camera. The aqueduct is still used to carry drinking water to Cheshire, across the border in England.

The most scenic Denbighshire drive follows the B4500 from Chirk up the idyllic, seemingly forgotten **Ceiriog Valley** ★★, as far as the **Pistyll Rhaeadr waterfall,** 4 miles northwest of Llanrhaeadr-ym-Mochnant. At 74m (240 ft.) high, it's the tallest single-drop waterfall in the U.K., and a good jumping off point for woodland and hill walking in the Berwyn Mountains.

Chirk Castle ★ CASTLE   Perched majestically and strategically on a knoll overlooking the lower Ceiriog Valley, the marcher fortress of Chirk was built around 1300 by Roger Mortimer (1287–1330), under the patronage (like so many castles in North Wales) of English King Edward I. Mortimer was a key player in the betrayal and killing of Llywelyn ap Gruffudd—still the only native Prince of Wales—in 1282, and Chirk was one of his rewards. The dungeon and Adam Tower date to this period, although the rest of the castle and courtyard have the genteel feel of an Oxford quadrangle, converted as it was to serve as the Myddleton family home for 400 years. Views back to the castle from the manicured formal gardens with box-cut yews are sublime.

Chirk (11 miles south of Wrexham). ✆ **01691/777701.** www.nationaltrust.org.uk. Admission castle, gardens, and tower: £8.70 adults, £4.35 children 5–16, £22 family; gardens and tower only: £6.15 adults, £3 children, £15 family. July–Oct daily 11am–5pm, mid-Mar–June Wed–Sun 11am–5pm; gardens and tower only also open Nov–mid-Dec and 3 weeks in Feb Sat–Sun 10am–4pm. Bus: 2 from Wrexham (45 min.). Train: Chirk.

Erddig ★★ HISTORIC SITE   A chance to glimpse how the other half—or, more precisely, the lower 95%—lived is the principal attraction of this stately Georgian home. Built in the 1680s, Erddig was the understated residence of the Yorke family for 2½ centuries from the 1720s, before being rescued from (literally) the brink of collapse by the National Trust. The restored outbuildings house the Yorke's 19th-century carriages, their 1907 family Rover motor-car, and a smithy, sawmill, and even working shire-horse stables—all of which were put to use during a massive restoration project in the 1970s that used only traditional materials and processes. Electricity never arrived at Erddig; it's as if the 20th-century didn't happen in the house's "below stairs" servants' area, with intact kitchen, pantry, scullery, and social rooms. Yet more unusual are portraits commissioned by the Yorke family (first paintings, later photographs) of the staff, each eulogized with its own substantial poem and hung proudly in the Servants' Hall.

Wrexham (2 miles south of the center off the A483, junction 3). © **01978/355314.** www.nationaltrust.org.uk/erddig. Admission house and gardens £9.35 adults, £4.70 children 5–16, £23 family; gardens and outbuildings only £6.10 adults, £3.05 children, £15 family. House mid-Mar–Oct daily 12:30–4:30pm (free tours also at 11:30am and noon); gardens and outbuildings Mar–Oct daily 11am–5:30pm, Nov–Dec daily 11am–4pm, Jan–mid-Feb Sat–Sun 11am–4pm. Bus: 2 from Wrexham to Felin Puleston (6 min.) then walk (1 mile) through park.

Where to Eat & Stay

The Hand at Llanarmon ★★   You'd be hard pressed to find a more peaceful setting than the tiny village of Llanarmon Dyffryn Ceiriog, in the upper reaches of the unspoiled Ceiriog Valley, where the Hand has established itself as a first-rate eat-and-stay destination for foodies and discerning walkers. All the hotel's simply decorated units have some pleasant rustic touches, but Character Rooms, with bigger beds and decor more in keeping with the traditions of this former coaching inn, are worth the extra £20.

The **restaurant's menu** sticks largely to gastropub classics, but delivers them with panache using the very best ingredients from local suppliers, including Ceiriog trout and pies from McArdles of Chirk. Main courses range from £9 to £20.

Llanarmon DC, Ceiriog Valley, Llangollen LL20 7LD. www.thehandhotel.co.uk. © **01691/600666.** 13 units. £90–£127 double. Rates include Welsh breakfast. MC, V. Free parking. **Amenities:** Restaurant; bar; Wi-Fi (free). *In room:* TV, hair dryer.

Tyddyn Llan ★★★   Set on the fringe of the Berwyn Mountains, this elegant manor with extensive private grounds has been converted into a restaurant along with accommodations that successfully combines Georgian exclusivity with modern hospitality. Rooms are traditionally and individually decorated, with leather seating and period furniture.

The fine-dining, **Michelin-starred restaurant** usually features an inventive menu stuffed with local ingredients such as Welsh Black beef, local organic pork, or foraged ceps; the two-course menu costs £42 (£50 for three courses), and is open to non-guests. Reservations are essential.

Llandrillo, Denbighshire LL21 0ST. www.tyddynllan.co.uk. © **01490/440264.** Fax 01490/440414. 13 units. £150–£240 double; £300 suite. Extra child bed £30. Rates include Welsh breakfast. MC, V. Free parking. **Amenities:** Restaurant; bar; babysitting; Wi-Fi (free). *In room:* TV/DVD, CD player, hair dryer, movie library. Tyddyn Llan Bus: X94 from Wrexham (70 min.).

PLANNING YOUR TRIP

by Nick Dalton, Deborah Stone & Donald Strachan

GETTING THERE
By Plane

England's main airport is **London Heathrow** (LHR; www.heathrow airport.com), 17 miles west of the city and boasting five hectic, bustling terminals (Terminals 1 to 5, although Terminal 2 is closed until 2014). This is the U.K. hub of most major airlines, including British Airways, Virgin Atlantic, Qantas, and the North American carriers. **London Gatwick** (LGW; www.gatwickairport.com) is the city's second major airport, with two terminals (North and South), 31 miles south of central London in the Sussex countryside. As with Heathrow, you can fly direct or with a connection to or from pretty much anywhere.

Increasingly, however, passengers are arriving at London's smaller airports—particularly as budget airlines have proliferated, and even come to dominate short-haul domestic and international routes. **London Stansted** (STN; www.stanstedairport.com), 37 miles northeast of the city, is the gateway to a vast array of short-haul destinations in the U.K., continental Europe, and parts of the Middle East. It's also a hub for major budget operator Ryanair. **London Luton** (LTN; www.london-luton.co.uk), anchoring a similarly diverse short-haul network, lies 34 miles northwest of London. Ryanair and easyJet are two of the main users. **London City** (LCY; www.londoncityairport.com), the only commercial airport actually in London itself, is used mainly by business travelers from nearby Docklands and the City, but does have some key intercity links—notably with regular direct flights to New York, Paris, Edinburgh, and Madrid. British Airways and Cityjet are the two major airlines at London City.

To find out which airlines travel to London, see "Airlines, Hotels, & Car Rental," p. 765.

England has a number of regional airports, some with direct flights from the U.S., and all with connections from London, the main ones being **Manchester** (MAN) and **Birmingham** (BHX). In Wales, **Cardiff** (CWL) is the main airport, although there is also one in **Swansea** (SWS).

GETTING INTO LONDON
Heathrow Airport

A journey to the heart of London via the Tube on the Piccadilly Line takes 45 to 50 minutes and costs between £2.70 and £5—it's cheapest if you travel after 9:30am and use an Oyster Card (p. 77). Trains leave every few minutes, but if you want to plan your connections, use the online journey planner at **www.tfl. gov.uk/journeyplanner**. For further Tube information see chapter 4. Although rail options (see below) are quicker to Paddington Station, unless that is your final destination you still have to continue (probably by Tube or cab), so the Tube can still be your best bet.

The **Heathrow Express** (✆ **0845/600-1515;** www.heathrowexpress.com) train service runs every 15 minutes daily from 5:10am until 11:40pm between Heathrow and Paddington Station, just west of London's West End. Tickets bought online in advance are £17 each way in economy class, rising to £18 if bought from one of the terminal ticket machines, and £23 on the train itself. First-class tickets are £26. Children 15 and under pay £8.20 standard, £13 in first class. The trip takes 15 minutes each way between Paddington and Terminals 1 and 3; 21 to 23 minutes from Terminals 4 or 5. The trains have special areas for wheelchairs. From Paddington, you can connect to the Tube, or hail a taxi outside.

A better-value, but slower, rail option is the **Heathrow Connect** (✆ **0845/678-6975;** www.heathrowconnect.com). A couple of trains an hour ply the route from Paddington Station via Ealing to Heathrow Terminals 1 and 3, where you make a quick change for a transfer to Terminals 4 or 5. Total journey time is about a half-hour for Terminals 1 and 3, 11 minutes more for Terminal 5, and an additional 6 minutes for Terminal 4. A single fare from Paddington is £7.90, with children 5 to 15 receiving a 50% discount.

Most expensive of the lot, a **taxi** hailed at one of the airport's official ranks is likely to cost anything from £60 to £85. You can save by booking a fixed-price minicab service in advance from **Addison Lee** (✆ **0844/800-6677;** www.addisonlee.com). Book online with a credit card.

Gatwick Airport

The fastest way to central London is via the **Gatwick Express** (✆ **0845/850-1530;** www.gatwickexpress.com), which departs every 15 minutes, daily between 5am and 12:35am. The round-trip fare between Gatwick and Victoria Rail Station is £29 for adults and £14 for children aged 5 to 15. (One-way fares cost £17 for adults and £8.45 for children.) If you book online, you can save 10% on ticket prices. The travel time each way is 30 minutes Monday to Saturday, and 35 minutes on Sunday. Check the website for regular pre-booking discounts, including 3-for-2 and 4-for-2 tickets that represent significant ticket savings for traveling groups.

Marginally cheaper local trains call at Gatwick several times an hour, connecting with Victoria; or London Bridge, City Thameslink, Blackfriars, Farringdon, and St. Pancras International. Journeys take 30 to 40 minutes. See **www.nationalrail. co.uk**.

Roughly hourly **National Express** (✆ **0871/781-8181;** www.nationalexpress. com) buses link Gatwick with London's Victoria Coach Station. The walk-up fare is £7.50 single, but that can fall to £4.50 if you book online in advance. Children aged 3 to 14 pay half-price.

A **taxi** from Gatwick to central London costs around £100.

London City Airport

Trains on the **Docklands Light Railway,** known locally as the "DLR," make runs at 10-minute intervals from City Airport to Bank Tube station in the heart of London's financial district. A **taxi** should cost £20 to £40.

Stansted Airport

The **Stansted Express** (© 08457/850-0150; www.stanstedexpress.com) train to Liverpool Street Station runs every 15 minutes from 6am to 11:45pm; the trip takes 45 minutes. If you book online, the cost is £19. Tickets cost an extra £1 from the station. If you're heading for the West End, get off at the Express's only interim stop, Tottenham Hale, and switch to the Tube's Victoria Line.

A slower rail route on **National Express East Anglia trains** (© 0845/600-7245; www.nationalexpresseastanglia.com) is no cheaper but does terminate at Stratford, ideal if you're heading to the Olympic Park or lodging in East London. Journey time is 1 hour, and trains leave hourly, Monday to Saturday.

By bus, you have several options depending on your final destination in the city. The **National Express A6 Airbus** (© 0871/781-8181; www.nationalexpress.com) heads for Victoria Station, via the West End 24 hours a day; tickets cost £10 one-way. The **National Express A9 Airbus** connects the airport with Stratford station, on the Tube's Jubilee and Central Lines. Tickets cost £8. **Easybus** (www.easybus.co.uk) connects Stansted with Baker Street, at bargain rates as low as £2 if you book ahead online. **Terravision** (© 01279/680-028; www.terravision.eu) runs two generally half-hourly services to Victoria and Liverpool Street Stations, respectively. One-way tickets cost £9. Note that because traffic conditions vary, any bus will take between 1 and 2 hours, at the lower end of that range for eastern destinations like Stratford and Liverpool Street.

For a ride to London's West End, a cab will charge around £100.

Luton Airport

Like Stansted, Luton Airport is well served by airbuses. **Greenline** (© 0844/801-7261; www.greenline.co.uk) service 757 links the airport with Victoria Station via Baker Street and Marble Arch. Fares are £15 for adults, £12 for children aged 5 to 13; a return costs £22 for adults, £17 for kids. (easyJet passengers can claim a significant discount by booking online ahead of time.) Buses leave half-hourly for most of the day. **Easybus** (www.easybus.co.uk) follows a similar route, with bargain one-way fares as low as £2 available if you book ahead online, though you're more likely to pay around £10. Buses depart every 20 minutes or thereabouts. The **National Express** (© 0871/781-8181; www.nationalexpress.com) airport bus runs a similar service, with similar frequency; tickets cost around £14 one-way; children get 50% off the full fare. All bus journey times are around 1½ hours, a little less if you get off at Baker Street.

It's quicker if you make for central London by train, although you first have to take the short shuttle bus to Luton Airport Parkway station (£1.50 each way; buses leave every 10 minutes). Both **First Capital Connect** (© 0845/026-4700; www.firstcapitalconnect.co.uk) and **East Midlands Trains** (© 08457/125-678; www.eastmidlandstrains.co.uk) run services to St. Pancras Station. Several direct trains leave every hour, taking between 27 and 33 minutes to reach St. Pancras. One-way tickets cost £12; half-price for children 5 to 15. See **www.nationalrail.co.uk** for timetables and service updates. Buy tickets for any of the bus or rail routes into town from the booths in the arrivals hall.

CHANGING AIRPORTS National Express (© 0871/781-8181; www.nationalexpress.com) buses leave from Heathrow, Gatwick, Stansted, and Luton, circumnavigating the M25 to each of these airports with varying frequencies. Gatwick to Heathrow, for example, costs £22 for adults and takes just over an hour. Between

Luton and Gatwick airports, the quickest and most frequent service is the train operated by **First Capital Connect** (📞 **0845/026-4700;** www.firstcapitalconnect.co. uk). A single fare is £25.

GETTING AROUND
By Train

Train travel in Britain is getting faster and more reliable. It is also a great way to get around, gliding through the countryside in a comfy seat with a coffee in your hand. There are two main lines north from London, the **East Coast Mainline,** which connects King's Cross with York, Newcastle, and Edinburgh; and the **West Coast Line,** which connects Euston Station with Birmingham, Manchester, the Lake District, and Glasgow. London Waterloo has trains to the south coast, Paddington to the west and Wales. Both also have many lines that serve the Midlands and the areas north of London. For more information on train connections from London stations see Chapter 4 "London," p. 67.

From **St. Pancras Station,** sandwiched between King's Cross and Euston, there are high-speed Eurostar services to Paris and Brussels via the **Channel Tunnel.** You can now reach Brussels in under 2 hours, and Paris in 2¼ hours, making them day-trip destinations. The station boasts Europe's longest champagne bar, all the Wi-Fi you'll ever need, plus dozens of stores. In Britain, make reservations for **Eurostar** by calling 📞 **0843/2186-186;** in North America, book online at **www.eurostar.com,** or contact **Rail Europe** (📞 **800/622-8600,** or 800/361-7245 in Canada; www. raileurope.com). U.S. visitors arriving from Continental Europe should remember that the validity of the Eurail pass ends at the English Channel. You'll need a separate BritRail pass if you plan to tour the U.K.

TRAVEL PASSES BritRail passes allow unlimited travel in England, Scotland, and Wales on any British Rail scheduled train over the whole of the network during the validity of the pass without restrictions. The passes are not available in England; you must buy them before you arrive. A **BritRail Consecutive Pass** allows you to travel for a consecutive number of days. In first class, adults pay $269 for 3 days, $339 for 4 days, $485 for 8 days, $725 for 15 days, $919 for 22 days, and $725 for 1 month. In second class, fares are $179 for 3 days, $225 for 4 days, $319 for 8 days, $485 for 15 days, $609 for 22 days, and $725 for 1 month. Seniors (60 and older) qualify for discounts in first-class travel and pay $229 for 3 days, $289 for 4 days, $409 for 8 days, $615 for 15 days, $779 for 22 days, and $925 for 1 month. Passengers 25 and younger qualify for a **Youth Pass.** In second class, rates are $145 for 3 days, $179 for 4 days, $259 for 8 days, $389 for 15 days, $489 for 22 days, and $925 for 1 month. One child (aged 14 and under) can travel free with each adult or senior pass when the **BritRail Family Pass** is requested while buying the adult pass. Additional children pay half the regular adult fare.

More versatile is the **BritRail FlexiPass,** allowing you to travel when you want during a 2-month period. In first class, it costs $339 for 3 days, $425 for 4 days, $619 for 8 days, and $925 for 15 days. In second class, it costs $229 for 3 days, $285 for 4 days, $619 for 8 days, and $625 for 15 days.

For information contact **BritRail** (📞 **866/BRIT-RAIL** [274-8724] in the U.S. and Canada; www.britrail.com). In Canada, also see www.britainontrack.com.

RAIL information

As baffling as rail travel in Britain can seem, with so many different train companies, getting information about times and routes is absurdly simple. **National Rail Enquiries** is a one-stop shop with everything you need to know. Go to the website w**ww.nationalrail.co.uk** and enter the names of two stations (or towns) and it will give you a list of trains, times, and routes. It will also show you fare options, of which there can be many, depending on when you travel and when you book. You can also get the information by phone (℡ **08457/484-950** in the U.K., or +44 20/7278-5240 from overseas). The site doesn't actually sell tickets but will connect you to one that does. If you are able to book in advance, **www.theTrain line.com** can bring significant savings on long-distance travel. You can collect tickets from your departure station. If you're fortunate, **MegaTrain** (www.mega train.com) may have a seat on your route at a big discount.

For Wales, the **Explore Wales Pass** gives unlimited access to all mainline rail services, and almost every bus. It also gives discounted entry to attractions and reduced rates at Youth Hostels. The pass costs £84 and gives 4 days of rail travel and 8 days of bus travel. If you're sticking to one part of the country there are South Wales and North & Mid-Wales Explorer passes that offer the same deal for £57. Children 5 to 15 are half-price, children 4 and under go free. Tickets can be bought at most rail stations and travel agents throughout Britain, or by calling ℡ **0870/9000-773.** For information, see www.arrivatrainswales.co.uk.

Train Travel from London to Principal Cities

TO	STATION	TRAINS	DAILY MILES	TRAVEL TIME
Bath	Paddington	25	107	1 hr. 11 min.
Birmingham Euston	Paddington	35	113	1 hr. 37 min.
Bristol	Paddington	46	119	1 hr. 26 min.
Cardiff	Paddington	24	148	2 hr.
Carlisle	Euston	10	299	3 hr. 40 min.
Chester	Euston	16	179	2 hr. 36 min.
Exeter	Paddington	17	174	1 hr. 55 min.
Leeds	King's Cross	19	185	2 hr. 12 min.
Liverpool	Euston	14	193	2 hr. 34 min.
Manchester	Euston	16	180	2 hr. 27 min.
Newcastle	King's Cross	26	268	2 hr. 50 min.
Penzance	Paddington	9	305	5 hr.
Plymouth	Paddington	14	226	2 hr. 35 min.
York	King's Cross	27	188	1 hr. 57 min.

By Bus

In Britain, a long-distance bus is called a "coach," and buses are local transport. Coaches are generally the cheapest way to get around the country, but also the slowest. Most sizable towns have a bus link with the capital, either direct

Getting Around

PLANNING YOUR TRIP

or via a connection, most run by **National Express** (© **0871/781-8181;** www.
nationalexpress.com), which uses coaches equipped with reclining seats and toilets.
A good alternative is super-budget **MegaBus** (© **0871/266-3333;** www.megabus.
com), with tickets costing as little as £1, plus £1 booking fee. Most buses terminate
at **Victoria Coach Station,** 164 Buckingham Palace Rd. (© **020/7730-3466**),
although many offer intermediate stops in the capital.

In Wales, **Arriva Buses Wales** (© **0844/800-4411;** www.arrivabus.co.uk) is
one of the main operators, with local buses in the north and faster services down to
the south. The area around Cardiff is covered by **Cardiff Bus** (© **029/2066-6444;**
www.cardiffbus.com). For a full list of bus companies, and other travel information,
see www.traveline-cymru.info.

By Plane

British Airways (© **800/AIRWAYS** [247-9297]; www.ba.com) flies to more than
20 cities outside London, including Manchester. To get to the heart of England
quickly, many visitors fly BA to Manchester, which is served by a dozen flights per day
from London's Heathrow, and seven flights per day from London's Gatwick. Other
airlines such as **Flybe, BMI,** and **easyJet** also have internal services to Manchester,
Newcastle, and other cities. **Air Southwest** (© **0870/241-8202;** www.air
southwest.com) has a number of flights each week between London Gatwick and
Newquay in Cornwall and Plymouth, Devon, which can be handy for cutting out the
long overland journey to the West Country.

By Car

This is the way to see the country at its best. Motorways, with a maximum speed of
70 mph, allow you to get from area to area swiftly and simply, then lesser roads and
eventually country lanes let you meander through villages, reach distant beaches,
experience glorious views, and generally see everything that's wonderful about
Britain.

Visitors from overseas should be aware that in Britain traffic travels on the left side
of the road, so steering wheels are on the "wrong" side. And most rental cars are
manual, so the gear shift will be on your left. Aside from motorways, other roads
outside urban areas have a 60 mph speed limit unless otherwise signposted, and 70
mph on a dual carriageway. The limit decreases depending on size of road, conditions,
and locality. Built-up areas generally have a 30 mph limit, although a number of towns
are now introducing a 20 mph limit in main streets. Road signs are clear and use
international symbols. The Highway Code gives full details of signs and driving
requirements. It is available from most service stations, many newsstands and bookstores, and can be read online at www.direct.gov.uk. See also "Car Rental" in "Fast
Facts," p. 754.

GETTING THE BEST DEAL ON YOUR RENTAL CAR The British car-
rental market is among the most competitive in Europe. Nevertheless, rentals are
expensive, although there are frequent promotional deals, often linked to airlines, and
mostly in the off season. It's always cheaper to arrange a car in advance through a
chain such as Hertz or Avis. You might also look into a fly/drive deal.

Car-rental rates vary even more than airline fares. What you pay depends not only
on the size of the car, but also where and when you pick it up and drop it off, length
of the rental period, where and how far you drive it, whether you get insurance, and
a host of other factors.

Most companies will rent only to people 23 years and older, and many will not rent to people aged 70 and older.

Rentals are available through **Avis** (℃ **800/331-1212;** www.avis.com), **Budget** (℃ **800/527-0700;** www.budget.com), and **Hertz** (℃ **800/654-3001;** www.hertz.com). **Kemwel Drive Europe** (℃ **877/820-0668;** www.kemwel.com) is among the cheapest and most reliable of the rental agencies. **AutoEurope** (℃ **888/223-5555** in the U.S., or **0800/223-5555** in London; www.autoeurope.com) acts as a wholesale company for rental agencies in Europe. For additional listings of the major car-rental agencies in England or Wales, see "Airlines, Hotels, & Car-Rental" (p. 765).

When booking your rental car, a few key questions could save you lots of money:

○ Are weekend rates lower than weekday? Ask if the rate is the same for pick-up Friday morning, for instance, as it is for Thursday night.

○ Is a weekly rate cheaper than a daily one? If you need the car for 4 days, it may be cheaper to rent it for 5, even if you don't need it for that long.

○ Is there a drop-off charge if you do not return the car to the pick-up location? Is it cheaper to pick up the car at the airport compared to a downtown location?

○ Are promotional rates available? If you see an advertised price in your local newspaper, ask for that specific rate; otherwise you may be charged the standard cost. The terms change constantly, and phone operators tend not to volunteer information.

○ Are discounts available for members of AARP, AAA, frequent-flier programs, or trade unions? If you belong to any of these, you are probably entitled to a discount of up to 30%.

○ What is the cost of adding an additional driver's name to the contract?

○ How many free miles are included in the price? Free mileage is often negotiable, depending on the length of rental.

○ How much does the rental company charge to refill your tank if you return with it less than full? Though most rental companies claim these prices are "competitive," fuel is almost always cheaper in town.

When you reserve a car, make sure you find out the total price, including the 20% value-added tax (VAT).

TIPS ON HOTELS

Make reservations as far in advance as possible, even in the quieter months from November to April. Travel to London peaks between May and October, and during that period, it's hard to come by a moderate or inexpensive hotel room. In a trendy spot such as Pembrokeshire in Wales it's nigh impossible to find an apartment or cottage to rent at short notice in the summer. And many of the smaller, boutique hotels around England and Wales can fill up year-round, especially at weekends. In older places guest rooms can be smaller than you might expect (if you base your expectation on a modern Radisson, for example), and each room is different, sometimes quirkily so. But this is part of the charm. Some rooms may only have a shower, not a bathtub, so if you

 Breakfast

Most hotels in Britain include breakfast in their rates, unlike the majority of hotels in the U.S. You might find that breakfast isn't included in big hotels that have a large business clientele, or very upmarket hotels that have an equally upmarket (and pricey) breakfast. Even then, there is often a rate offered that includes breakfast.

feel you can't exist without a tub, make that clear when booking. And don't look down on hotel restaurants any more. Many feature some of the finest places to eat, whether under the name of celebrity chefs such as Gordon Ramsay in London, or precocious chefs around the country.

Classification

British hotels are graded by stars. They are judged on standards, quality, and hospitality, and are rated "approved," "commended," "highly commended," and "deluxe." Five stars (deluxe) is the highest rating. A classification of "listed" refers to places that are, for the most part, very modest.

All establishments from two stars upward must have 100% en suite (private bathroom) facilities. In a one-star hotel, buildings are required to have hot and cold running water in all rooms, but in "listed" hotels, hot and cold running water in each room is not mandatory. Star ratings are posted outside the buildings. However, the system is voluntary, and many hotels do not participate.

Bed & Breakfasts

An English bed and breakfast (B&B) often used to be a glum place, little more than a house with rooms, and with guests banished from the premises during the day. Nowadays, though, most are reliable, with rooms that are at worst simple, or decorated to the owners' personal tastes. As in the U.S., a new breed has sprung up, with a boutique-hotel feel. Extravagant or quietly stylish rooms are offered, along with splendid breakfasts, and a decent lounge. Many are run with the sensibility of a small hotel; they simply don't serve lunch or dinner. **Bed & Breakfast Nationwide** (© **01255/672377;** www.bedandbreakfastnationwide.com) is an agency dealing in privately owned bed and breakfasts across the country, from cottages to castles, almost 700 of them.

Farmhouses

Farms often have rooms set aside for paying guests, sometimes in the main house, but increasingly in converted barns or cottages. You might still find some that simply offer a visitor a simple room for the night, but more and more they are expanding into full B&B territory, with breakfasts often sourced from the farm and its surroundings. Sometimes, also, you will find self-catering options. A growing number also offer evening meals, sometimes around a big kitchen table in front of a warming Aga. The settings are often wonderful, deep in the countryside.

Farm Stay UK (© **024/7669-6909;** www.farmstay.co.uk), set up in part by the Royal Agricultural Society of England, and still owned by a consortium of farmers, features more than 1,200 rural retreats including farms, B&Bs, and campsites. Most are open year-round.

Historic Properties

National Trust Holiday Cottages (© **0844/800-2070;** www.nationaltrust cottages.co.uk) is part of Britain's leading conservation group. The National Trust is mainly known for the castles, gardens, and historic homes that you can visit, but it also has 370 houses and cottages for rent in some of the most beautiful parts of England, Wales, and Northern Ireland. Some of these properties are in remote countryside, others are on the coast. They sleep from 2 to 12 guests, are self-catering, and mostly available year-round, for weekends, short breaks, and longer.

National Trust properties are also bookable from the Trust's U.S. affiliate, the **Royal Oak Foundation** (✆ **800/913-6565** or 212/480-2889; www.royal-oak.org). Annual membership is $55 (families $90), which gives admission to all National Trust sites and properties, plus discounts on air travel, train tickets, and bookings at National Trust cottages and houses.

The **Landmark Trust** (✆ **01628/825925**; www.landmarktrust.org.uk) is a charity that rescues historic buildings and turns them into places to stay. As well as cottages, you'll find castles, country houses, towers, and other odd buildings. There are around 180, such as the Gothic Temple, set in Capability Brown-designed grounds in Buckinghamshire, and Kingswear Castle, dating from 1502, on the water's edge near Dartmouth, Devon. Places sleep from 1 to 16 guests, and are ideal for family get-togethers.

Welsh Rarebits: Hotels of Distinction (✆ **01686/668030**; www.rarebits. co.uk) is a collection of 52 historic hotels across Wales, from Georgian country houses to the Italianate village of Portmeirion, all of them luxury, most of them small and personally run.

Holiday Cottages & Villages

Many companies around Britain have cottages for rent. **English Country Cottages** (✆ **0845/268-0785**; www.english-country-cottages.co.uk) focuses on four- and five-star properties the breadth of England and Wales. **Cottages 4 You** (✆ **0845/268-0760**; www.cottages4you.co.uk), part of the same company, deals in more modest options, and has 10,000 properties in the U.K. In Wales, **Coastal Cottages of Pembrokeshire** (✆ **01437/765765**; www.coastalcottages.co.uk), is a specialist in the busy southwestern getaway spot.

Holiday villages are traditionally jolly spots full of rows of mobile homes or simple chalets, along with bars, amusements, and restaurants. These still exist but more and more are moving upward in their ambitions, with smarter rooms, luxury mobile homes, and state-of-the-art water parks. **Hoseasons** (✆ **0844/847-1356**; www.hoseasons.co.uk) has mobile homes, timber lodges, and chalets in hundreds of parks across the country. Some are little more than camping sites, while others have swimming pools, children's clubs, and live entertainment in the evenings.

Butlins (✆ **0800/048-1002**; www.butlins.com) is one of the original holiday camp companies, popular well before international tourism took off, but which has reinvented itself. Butlins has three parks, at Minehead (Somerset), Skegness (Lincolnshire), and Bognor Regis (Sussex). The latter is the flagship resort; alongside the many comfortable apartments (all with TVs) and deluxe suites are two hotels, the Shoreline, and the modern-retro Ocean, which opened in 2009. There's an indoor water park, sports (archery and so forth), evening shows, and discos, all included in the price, and a beach outside the gates. Meal packages are available, and it is a great option for a short family break, especially if you take advantage of low off-season rates.

Center Parks (✆ **08448/267-723**; www.centerparcs.co.uk) is a more rural version of the holiday park. Each of the four (including Sherwood Forest in Nottinghamshire) is set in 400 acres of woodland, which visitors negotiate on foot or rental bike. At their heart is the Subtropical Swimming Paradise, a balmy, indoor water complex with wave machine, connected to outdoor pool and water chutes.

FROMMERS.COM: THE COMPLETE travel RESOURCE

Planning a trip or just returned? Head to **Frommers.com**, voted Best Travel Site by *PC Magazine*. We think you'll find our site indispensable before, during, and after your travels—with expert advice and tips; independent reviews of hotels, restaurants, attractions, and preferred shopping and nightlife venues; vacation giveaways; and an online booking tool. We publish the complete contents of more than 135 travel guides in our **Destinations** section, covering more than 4,000 places worldwide. Each weekday, we publish original articles that report on **Deals and News** via our free **Frommers.com Newsletters.** What's

more, **Arthur Frommer** himself blogs 5 days a week, with strong opinions about the state of travel in the modern world. We're betting you'll find our **Events** listings an invaluable resource; it's an up-to-the-minute roster of what's happening in cities everywhere—including concerts, festivals, lectures, and more. We've also added weekly **podcasts, interactive maps,** and hundreds of new images across the site. Finally, don't forget to visit our **Message Boards,** where you can join in conversations with thousands of fellow Frommer's travelers and post your trip report once you return.

Chain Hotels

Many U.S. chains, such as Best Western, Hilton, Sheraton, and Travelodge, are found throughout Britain. In addition, Britain has a number of leading chains. **Thistle Hotels** (www.thistle.com; ☎ **0871/376-9099** in the U.K., or 0845/305-8379) is a decent chain of moderate to upscale hotels. Increasingly, there are small chains of boutique hotels such as the discreetly stylish **Hotel du Vin** (www.hotelduvin.com; ☎ **0845/365-4438**) and the more outrageously stylish **Malmaison** (www.malmaison.com; ☎ **0845/365-4247**) whose properties include a former church and prison. Both are part of the same group. Von Essen (**www.vonessenhotels.co.uk**) is a superb group of some of the finest country-house hotels. At the other end of the scale **Premier Inn** (www.premierinn.com; ☎ **0870/242-8000**) is now the U.K.'s largest hotel chain, offering simple quality at low prices.

House Swapping

HomeLink International (www.homelink.org; ☎ 800/638-3841 or 954/566-2687), which costs $119 for a year's membership, is the oldest, largest, and best home-exchange holiday group in the world. A competitor is **Intervac International** (www.intervac-homeexchange.com; ☎ **800/756-HOME** [4663]), which costs $100 annually.

Youth Hostels

The **Youth Hostels Association** (www.yha.org.uk; ☎ **01629/592700**) has more than 200 hostels in cities, in the countryside, and along the coast. Hostels used to be known for their stark surroundings, dormitory rooms, and clientele of hardened hikers. However, in recent years they have widened their scope with new properties, family rooms, good food, and warm welcome. What haven't changed are the locations, many of which five-star hotels would kill for, not least in Snowdonia.

[FastFACTS] ENGLAND & WALES

Area Codes   The country code for Great Britain is **44.** Cities and towns within the country have their own area codes, all of which begin with **0.** The area code for London is **020;** Manchester is **0161.** A full local telephone number is then usually between 6 and 8 digits long.

Business Hours   With many exceptions, business hours are Monday to Friday 9am to 5pm. In general, retail stores are open Monday to Saturday 9am to 6pm, Sunday 11am to 5pm (sometimes noon–6pm). Thursday is usually late-night opening for central London's shops; until 8pm or later isn't unusual.

Car Rental   The main rental companies can be found at almost any airport, but you'll find it cheaper to book a car before you arrive. *Insider tip:* Don't go for a big car unless you need it. Gas/petrol at press time cost around £1.35 a liter (with 1 U.S. gallon equal to 3.785 liters, that makes it around $8 a gallon!). Do note, though, that any gallon prices mentioned in the U.K. are imperial gallons (4.546 liters). There are a number of price comparison websites such as **CarRentals.co.uk** and **travelsupermarket.com**, which can help you find a good deal if you are here and are planning a short trip. There are often good weekend offers, especially away from high season.

Cellphones   See "Mobile Phones," below.

Crime   See "Safety," below.

Customs   **Non-E.U. nationals aged 17 and over** can bring in, duty-free, 200 cigarettes, or 100 cigarillos, or 50 cigars, or 250 grams of smoking tobacco. You can also bring in 4 liters of wine and 16 liters of beer plus either 1 liter of alcohol more than 22% ("spirits") or 2 liters of "fortified" wine at less than 22%. Visitors may also bring in other goods, including perfume, gifts, and souvenirs, totaling £390 in value. (Customs officials tend to be lenient about these general merchandise regulations, realizing the limits are unrealistically low.) For **arrivals from within the E.U.,** there are no limits as long as goods are for your own personal use, or are gifts.

For specifics on what you can take home and the corresponding fees, U.S. citizens should download the free pamphlet *Know Before You Go* at **www.cbp.gov.** Alternatively, contact the **U.S. Customs & Border Protection (CBP),** 1300 Pennsylvania Ave. NW, Washington, DC 20229 (© **877/CBP-5511**), and request the pamphlet. For a clear summary of their own rules, Canadians should consult the booklet *Travelling Outside Canada,* issued by the **Canada Border Services Agency** (© **800/461-9999** in Canada, or 204/983-3500; www.cbsa-asfc.gc.ca). Australians need to read *Know Before You Go.* For more information, call the **Australian Customs Service** at © **1300/363263,** or download the PDF from **www.customs.gov.au.** For New Zealanders, most questions are answered under "Arriving in New Zealand" at **www.customs.govt.nz.** For more information, contact the **New Zealand Customs Service** (© **0800/428786** or 09/300-5399).

Disabled Travelers   The best group to consult for trip-planning advice is **Tourism for All UK,** Shap Road Industrial Estate, Shap Road, Kendal, Cumbria LA9 6NZ (© **0845/124-9971,** + 44/1539/814683 from overseas; www.tourismforall.org.uk). The website also has an invaluable list of relevant organizations to contact for advice relating to specific chronic complaints. The **Royal Association for Disability Rights (RADAR),** 12 City Forum, 250 City Rd., London EC1V 8AF (© **020/7250-3222;** www.radar.org.uk), campaigns on behalf of the disabled. RADAR also publishes a number of handy written resources and, for a small fee, sells a key that opens over 8,000 locked public disabled toilets countrywide (£3.50 includes U.K. P&P; £5.40 to anywhere in the world).

For visitors coming from North America, a number of travel agencies offer tours and itineraries for those with disabilities. **Flying Wheels Travel** (© 877/451-5006 or 507/451-5005; www.flyingwheelstravel.com) offers independent trips to London. **Accessible Journeys** (© 800/846-4537 or 610/521-0339; www.disabilitytravel.com) caters specifically for slow walkers and those in wheelchairs and their families and friends.

U.S. groups that offer assistance to people with disabilities include **MossRehab** (© 800/CALL-MOSS [2255-6677]; www.mossresourcenet.org), which provides a library of accessible-travel resources online; the **American Foundation for the Blind** (AFB; © 800/232-5463 or 212/502-7600; www.afb.org), a referral resource for the blind or visually impaired that includes information on traveling with Seeing Eye dogs; and **SATH** (**Society for Accessible Travel & Hospitality;** © 212/447-7284; www.sath.org), which offers a wealth of travel resources for people with all types of disabilities and informed recommendations on destinations, access guides, travel agents, tour operators, vehicle rentals, and companion services. You can also connect with SATH on Twitter and Facebook. The "Accessible Travel" link at **Mobility-Advisor.com** (www.mobility-advisor.com) offers a variety of travel resources to persons with disabilities. **Access-Able Travel Source** (www.access-able.com) offers extensive access information and advice for traveling the world with a disability. Quarterly magazine *Emerging Horizons* (www.emerginghorizons.com) is another handy resource.

Doctors If you need a non-emergency doctor, your hotel can recommend one, or contact your embassy or consulate. Failing that, try the general-practitioner finder at **www.nhsdirect.nhs.uk**. North American members of the **International Association for Medical Assistance to Travelers** (IAMAT; © 716/754-4883, or 416/652-0137 in Canada; www.iamat.org) can consult it for lists of local approved doctors. *Note:* U.S. and Canadian visitors who become ill while they're in London are eligible only for free *emergency* care. For other treatment, including follow-up care, you'll be asked to pay. See "Insurance," below, for details of how this affects you.

In any medical emergency, immediately call © **999,** or © 112.

Drinking Laws The legal age for buying alcohol is 18. Those 17 and over may have a glass of beer, wine, or cider with a meal in a pub or restaurant, if it is bought for them by a responsible adult. Children younger than 16 are allowed in pubs only if accompanied by a parent or guardian. Don't drink and drive: Penalties are stiff, not to mention the danger in which you're placing yourself and other road users. Drinking alcohol on London's **public transport network** is forbidden, and on-the-spot fines have been issued to transgressors.

Driving Rules See "Getting Around," earlier in this chapter.

Electricity British electricity operates at 240 volts AC (50 cycles), and most overseas plugs don't fit British wall outlets. Always bring suitable transformers and/or adapters, such as world multiplugs—if you plug some American appliances directly into a European electrical outlet without a transformer, for example, you'll destroy your appliance and possibly start a fire. Portable electronic devices such as iPods and mobile phones, however, recharge without problems via USB or using a multiplug. Many long-distance trains have plugs, for the charging of laptops and mobile phones only.

Embassies & Consulates The **U.S. Embassy** is at 24 Grosvenor Square, London W1A 1AE (© **020/7499-9000;** www.usembassy.org.uk; Tube: Bond St.). Standard hours are Monday to Friday 8am to 5:30pm. However, for passport and visa services relating to U.S. citizens, contact the **Passport and Citizenship Unit,** 55–56 Upper Brook St., London W1A 2LQ (same phone number as above). Most non-emergency inquiries require an appointment.

The **High Commission of Canada,** Canada House, 1 Trafalgar Square, London SW1Y 5BJ (*©* **020/7258-6600;** www.canadainternational.gc.ca/united_kingdom-royaume_uni/index.aspx; Tube: Charing Cross), handles passport and consular services for Canadians. Hours are Monday to Friday 9:30am to 1pm.

The **Australian High Commission** is at Australia House, Strand, London WC2B 4LA (*©* **020/7379-4334;** www.australia.org.uk; Tube: Charing Cross, Covent Garden, or Temple). Hours are Monday to Friday 9am to 5pm.

The **New Zealand High Commission** is at New Zealand House, 80 Haymarket (at Pall Mall), London SW1Y 4TQ (*©* **020/7930-8422;** www.nzembassy.com/uk; Tube: Charing Cross or Piccadilly Circus). Hours are Monday to Friday 9am to 5pm.

The **Irish Embassy** is at 17 Grosvenor Place, London SW1X 7HR (*©* **020/7235-2171;** www.embassyofireland.co.uk; Tube: Hyde Park Corner). Hours are Monday to Friday 9:30am to 5pm.

Emergencies Dial *©* **999** for police, fire, or ambulance. Give your name and state the nature of the emergency. Dialing *©* **112** also connects you to the local emergency services anywhere in the E.U.

Family Travel If you're renting a car, children 11 and under—and under 1.35m (4½ ft.) in height—must ride in an appropriate car seat. Consult your car-rental company in advance of arrival, but it's the driver's legal responsibility to ensure all child passengers comply (see **www.childcarseats.org.uk/law** for details). You'll also find babysitting available at most hotels; inquire at the concierge or reception desk.

The Web is chockfull of excellent family-travel resources. Recommended U.S. general family travel sites include **Family Travel Forum** (www.familytravelforum.com), a comprehensive site that offers customized trip planning; **Family Travel Network** (www.familytravelnetwork.com), an award-winning site that offers travel features, deals, and tips; and **Traveling Internationally with Your Kids** (www.travelwithyourkids.com), a comprehensive site offering sound advice for long-distance and international travel with children. The best family travel blogs with an international outlook are **Delicious Baby** (www.deliciousbaby.com) and **Travel Savvy Mom** (www.travelsavvymom.com). In the U.K., the mighty **Mumsnet** (www.mumsnet.com/travel) has plenty of holiday and travel advice and reviews. **Take the Family** (www.takethefamily.co.uk) has ideas and inspiration for England and Wales. For a list of more family-friendly travel resources, turn to the experts at **Frommers.com**.

To find hotels, restaurants, and attractions that are particularly child-friendly, refer to the "Kids" icon throughout this guide. *Frommer's London with Kids* ($17.99/£13.99) is the best specialist guidebook for families visiting the city.

Gasoline Please see "Car Rental," earlier in this chapter.

Health Visiting the U.K. doesn't pose any specific health risks. Common drugs widely available throughout the Western world are generally available over the pharmacy counter and in large supermarkets, although visitors from overseas should note the generic rather than brand names of any medicines they rely on. If you're flying into London, pack **prescription medications** in carry-on luggage and carry prescription medications in their original containers, with pharmacy labels—otherwise they won't make it through airport security. Also bring along copies of your prescriptions, in case you lose your pills or run out. Don't forget an extra pair of contact lenses or prescription glasses.

North American visitors can contact the **International Association for Medical Assistance to Travelers (IAMAT;** *©* **716/754-4883,** or 416/652-0137 in Canada; www.iamat.org) for tips on travel and health concerns. The United States **Centers for Disease Control and Prevention** (*©* **888/232-6348;** www.cdc.gov) provides up-to-date information on health hazards by region or country. If you suffer from a chronic illness, consult your doctor before your departure. All visitors with such conditions as epilepsy, diabetes, or heart problems, should consider wearing a **MedicAlert Identification Tag** (*✆* **888/633-4298** or 209/668-3333; www.medicalert.org; www.medicalert.org.uk in the U.K.), which will alert doctors to your condition should you become ill, and give them access to your records through MedicAlert's 24-hour hotline.

Deep vein thrombosis, or as it's known in the world of flying, "economy-class syndrome," is a blood clot that develops in a deep vein. It's a potentially deadly condition that can be caused by sitting in cramped conditions—such as an airplane cabin—for too long. During a flight (especially a long-haul flight), get up, walk around, and stretch your legs every 60 to 90 minutes to keep your blood flowing. Other preventative measures include frequent flexing of the legs while sitting, drinking lots of water, and avoiding alcohol and sleeping pills. If you have a history of deep vein thrombosis, heart disease, or another condition that puts you at high risk, some experts recommend wearing compression stockings or taking anticoagulants when you fly; always ask your family doctor about the best course for you. Symptoms of deep vein thrombosis include leg pain or swelling, or even shortness of breath.

It's always worth consulting the following official travel health websites before leaving home: In Australia, **www.smartraveller.gov.au**; in Canada, **www.hc-sc.gc.ca**; in the U.K., **www.nathnac.org**.

Hospitals The **NHS Choices** website (www.nhs.uk) has a search facility that enables you to locate your nearest Accident & Emergency department wherever you are in the U.K. In an emergency, you should dial *✆* **999.** Emergency care is free for all visitors, irrespective of country of origin.

Insurance **U.K. nationals** receive free medical treatment countrywide, but visitors from overseas only qualify automatically for free **emergency** care. **U.S. visitors** should note that most domestic health plans (including Medicare and Medicaid) do not provide coverage, and the ones that do often require you to pay for services upfront and reimburse you only after you return home. Try **MEDEX** (*✆* **410/453-6300;** www.medexassist. com) or **Travel Assistance International** (*✆* **800/821-2828;** www.travelassistance.com) for overseas medical insurance coverage. **Canadians** should check with their provincial health plan offices or call **Health Canada** (*✆* **866/225-0709;** www.hc-sc.gc.ca) to find out the extent of their coverage and what documentation and receipts they must take home in case they are treated overseas. **E.U. nationals** (and nationals of E.E.A. countries and Switzerland) should note that reciprocal health agreements are in place to ensure they receive free medical care while in the U.K. However, it is essential that visitors from those countries carry a valid **European Health Identity Card,** or EHIC. There are current bilateral agreements in place offering free healthcare to nationals of **New Zealand** and **Australia.** You should always double-check the latest situation before leaving home, with domestic health authorities or online at **www.dh.gov.uk/en/Healthcare/Entitlements andcharges/OverseasVisitors**.

For general travel insurance, it's wise to consult one of the price comparison websites before making a purchase. U.S. visitors can get estimates from various providers through **InsureMyTrip.com** (*✆* **800/487-4722**). Enter your trip cost and dates, your age, and other information, for prices from several providers. For U.K. travelers, **Moneysupermarket** (www.moneysupermarket.com) compares prices and coverage across a bewildering range of single- and multi-trip options. For all visitors, it's also worth considering trip-cancelation insurance, which will help retrieve your money if you have to back out of a trip or depart early. Trip cancelation traditionally covers such events as sickness, natural disasters, and travel advisories.

For information on traveler's insurance, trip cancelation insurance, and medical insurance while traveling, please visit **www.frommers.com/planning**.

Internet & Wi-Fi The availability of the Internet across the U.K. is in a constant state of development. How you access it depends on whether you've brought your own computer or smartphone, or if you're searching for a public terminal. Many hotels have computers for guest use, although pricing can vary from gratis to extortionate. To find a local Internet cafe, start by checking **www.cybercaptive.com** or **www.easyinternetcafe.com**. Although such places have suffered due to the spread of smartphones and free Wi-Fi (see below), they do tend to be prevalent close to popular tourist spots, especially ones frequented by backpackers. Aside from formal cybercafes, most **hostels** have Internet access, and some **public libraries** allow non-residents to use terminals.

If you have your own computer or smartphone, **Wi-Fi** makes access much easier. Always check before using your hotel's network—many charge exorbitant rates, and free or cheap Wi-Fi isn't hard to find elsewhere, in urban locations at least. Ask locally, or even Google "free Wi-Fi + [town]" before you arrive. To locate free Wi-Fi hotspots, it's worth using the hotspot locator at **www.jiwire.com**. National chains like **Welcome Break** motorway service stations (www.welcomebreak.co.uk) and **Wetherspoon** pubs (www.jdwetherspoon.co.uk), among many others, offer free Wi-Fi. There are also **BT Openzone** (www.btopenzone.com) hotspots in many cafes, hotels, and public places across the country (see http://btopenzone.hotspot-directory.com for a searchable directory and map). If you have a subscription to a global wireless ISP like **Boingo** (www.boingo.com), you can use these hotspots for free, or at a reduced rate depending on your subscription package. For example, unlimited global Wi-Fi access on your smartphone costs $7.95 a month from Boingo, or you can buy 5 days' access to BT Openzone from a smartphone or laptop for £27.

Savvy smartphone users from overseas may even find it cheaper and more practical to switch off 3G altogether and call using Wi-Fi in combination with a **Skype** (www.skype.com) account and mobile app.

The phone company 02 recently launched Wi-Fi hotspots in its stores, which are open to anyone (you have to give them your number to use it, and face being targeted by advertisers).

Legal Aid If you're visiting from overseas, contact your consulate or embassy (see "Embassies & Consulates," above). They can advise you of your rights and will usually provide a list of local attorneys (for which you'll have to pay if services are used), but they cannot interfere on your behalf in the English legal process. For questions about American citizens who are arrested abroad, including ways of getting money to them, telephone the **Citizens Emergency Center** of the Office of Special Consulate Services in Washington, D.C. (✆ **202/647-5225**).

If you're in some sort of substance-abuse emergency, call **Release** (✆ **0845/450-0215;** www.release.org.uk); the advice line is open Monday to Friday 11am to 1pm and 2 to 4pm. The **Rape and Sexual Abuse Support Centre** (✆ **0808/802-9999;** www.rapecrisis.org.uk) is open daily noon to 2:30pm and 7 to 9:30pm. **Alcoholics Anonymous** (✆ **0845/769-7555;** www.alcoholics-anonymous.org.uk) answers its helpline daily 10am to 10pm. For issues related to sexual health and sexually transmitted diseases, call the confidential **Sexual Health Line** at ✆ **0800/567123.**

LGBT Travelers **Gay News** (www.gayuknews.com) has a comprehensive database of the scene around the country. The **LGBT Tourist Information Office** (www.gaytouristoffice.co.uk) is another good place to find out what's on, or to seek advice on gay-friendly hotels and hostels. The **Lesbian and Gay Switchboard** (✆ **020/7837-7324;** www.llgs.org.uk) is open 10am to 11pm daily, providing information about gay-related activities in London and general advice. Their searchable online database (www.turingnetwork.org.uk) lists gay bars, clubs, and other services countrywide. London's best gay-oriented bookstore is **Gay's the Word,** 66 Marchmont St. (✆ **020/7278-7654;** www.gaystheword.co.uk;

Tube: Russell Sq.). July's annual **Pride London** march and festival (*(C)* **0844/884-2439;** www.pridelondon.org) is the highlight of London's LGBT calendar, while Pride Brighton & Hove (www.brightonpride.org) and Manchester Pride (www.manchesterpride.com) are the main events outside London, on different weekends in August. Manchester-based **Gaydio** (www.gaydio.co.uk) was the U.K.'s first radio station dedicated to lesbian, gay, bisexual, and trans listeners.

If you're planning to visit from the U.S., the **International Gay and Lesbian Travel Association** (**IGLTA;** *(C)* **800/448-8550** or 954/630-1637; www.iglta.org) is the trade association for the gay and lesbian travel industry, and offers an online directory of gay-and lesbian-friendly travel businesses. Many agencies offer tours and travel itineraries specifically for gay and lesbian travelers. **Above and Beyond Tours** (*(C)* **800/397-2681;** www.abovebeyondtours.com) is a gay and lesbian tour operator whose portfolio includes London. **Now, Voyager** (*(C)* **800/255-6951;** www.nowvoyager.com) is a well-known San Francisco-based gay-owned and operated travel service.

For more gay and lesbian travel resources, visit **Frommers.com.**

Mail   The British postal system is among the most reliable in the world, so you shouldn't need to depend on FedEx or some other courier service unless you're in a hurry. An air-mail letter to anywhere outside Europe costs 67p for up to 10g (⅓ oz.) and generally takes 5 to 7 working days to arrive; postcards also require a 67p stamp. Within the E.U., letters or postcards under 20g (⅔ oz.) cost 60p. Within the U.K, first class mail ought to arrive the following working day; second class mail takes around 3 days to reach its destination.

Medical Requirements   Unless you're arriving from an area known to be suffering from an epidemic (particularly cholera or yellow fever), inoculations or vaccinations are not required for entry into the U.K. Also see "Health," above.

Mobile Phones (Cell Phones)   The three letters that define much of the world's wireless capabilities are **GSM** (Global System for Mobiles), a seamless satellite network that makes for easy cross-border cellphone use throughout most of the planet, including England and Wales. If you own an unlocked GSM phone, simply pack it in your hand luggage and pick up a contract-free **SIM-only tariff** when you arrive in the U.K. The SIM card will cost very little, but you will need to load it up with credit to start making calls. Tariffs change constantly according to the market, but in general expect call charges of around 20p per minute, 10p for a text message, and a deal on data that might cap daily usage charges at about £2. There are phone and SIM card retailers on practically every major street in most cities, but not everywhere will sell SIM-only deals to non-residents. **Tesco Mobile** (www.tescomobile.com) sells SIMs for 99p that you can top-up in store with cash or an overseas credit card. Find a convenient branch at **www.tesco.com/storelocator.** **Three** (www.three.co.uk) sells SIMs for £1.99 that you can fill-up at Three stores, super-markets, and newsagents across the country. Three SIMs work only in 3G-compatible phones.

There are other options if you're visiting from overseas but don't own an unlocked GSM phone. For a short visit, **renting** a phone may be a good idea, and we suggest rent-ing the handset before you leave home. North Americans can rent from **InTouch USA** (*(C)* **800/872-7626** or 703/222-7161; www.intouchglobal.com) or **BrightRoam** (*(C)* **888/622-3393;** www.brightroam.com). However, handset purchase prices have fallen to a level where you can probably **buy a basic U.K. pay-as-you-go (PAYG) phone** for less than 1 week's handset rental. Prices at many cellphone retailers start from under £20 for an inexpensive model; there are now basic smartphones costing around £50. Expect out-going call charges of approximately 25p per minute to anywhere in the U.K., 10p for text messages (SMS); receiving calls on your local number is free. **Carphone Warehouse** (www.carphonewarehouse.com) has retail branches across the country, and stocks a reli-able range of cheap PAYG phones.

There are several U.K. networks offering a bewildering array of tariffs. Best for reliable nationwide voice and 3G reception are probably **O2** (www.o2.co.uk)—whose cell network is also used by Tesco Mobile—and **Vodafone** (www.vodafone.co.uk). **Orange** (www.orange.co.uk) tends to offer slightly better-value tariffs, and has performed well for us on trips to rural Wales. **Three** (www.three.co.uk) usually has the best deals for smartphone users who want data included in their rate. Unfortunately, per-minute charges for international calls can be high whatever network you choose, so if you plan to do a lot of calling home use a VoIP service like **Skype** (www.skype.com) or **Truphone** (www.truphone.com) in conjunction with a Web connection. See "Internet & Wi-Fi," above.

For advice on making **international calls,** see "Telephones," later in this section. Mobile coverage is usually very good, although there are still areas where you can't get a signal, and it's as likely to be in a rural area of Suffolk as a Welsh mountain.

Newspapers & Magazines England has some of the best newspapers in the world. Of the quality papers, *The Times* and *Daily Telegraph* generally lean right; the *Guardian* and *Independent* to the left of the political spectrum. All also issue Sunday editions: *The Sunday Times*, *Sunday Telegraph*, *Observer*, and *Independent on Sunday*, respectively. London has two daily papers, both of which are free and mostly available from rail stations: *Metro* appears in the morning (weekdays only), the *Evening Standard* from lunchtime onward, also weekdays only. For coverage of what's on, *Time Out* is London's major listings magazine, and also publishes editions elsewhere, such as Manchester.

Packing British weather is notoriously fickle, so although it rains in London much less than in the west of the British Isles, or Manchester—and nowhere close to the levels Britain's almost mythical reputation would have you believe—only the foolhardy visitor heads to the U.K. without some rainwear, even in high summer. On the plus side, winter temperatures rarely stay below freezing for long, and summers can be intermittently muggy but not as hot and humid as southern Europe or the U.S.

Whether you need to find room in your suitcase for formal eveningwear very much depends on where you plan to stay and (especially) dine. Traditional, upscale West End restaurants still largely expect you to arrive in a collared shirt, non-denim trousers, and "proper" shoes—and the equivalent attire for women—but any eatery with a contemporary edge, and any eatery period in the funkier east of the city, will welcome you as you are, even if that means jeans and sneakers.

For more helpful information on packing for your trip, download our Travel Tools app for your mobile device. Go to **www.frommers.com/go/mobile** and click on the Travel Tools icon.

Passports To enter the United Kingdom, all U.S. citizens, Canadians, Australians, New Zealanders, and South Africans must have a passport valid through their length of stay. No visa is required. A passport will allow you to stay in the country for up to 6 months. The immigration officer may also want to see proof of your intention to return to your point of origin (usually a round-trip ticket) and of visible means of support while you're in Britain. If you're planning to fly from the United States or Canada to the United Kingdom and then on to a country that requires a visa (India, for example), you should secure that visa before you arrive in Britain.

Passport Offices:

- **Australia** **Australian Passport Information Service** (✆ **131-232,** or visit www.passports. gov.au).
- **Canada** **Passport Office,** Department of Foreign Affairs and International Trade, Ottawa, ON K1A 0G3 (✆ **800/567-6868;** www.ppt.gc.ca).
- **Ireland** **Passport Office,** Setanta Centre, Molesworth Street, Dublin 2 (✆ **01/671-1633;** www.foreignaffairs.gov.ie).

- **New Zealand   Passports Office,** Department of Internal Affairs, P.O. Box 1658, Wellington, 6140 (ⓒ **0800/225050** in New Zealand or 04/474-8100; www.passports.govt.nz).
- **United States**   To find your regional passport office, check the U.S. State Department website (travel.state.gov/passport) or call the **National Passport Information Center** (ⓒ **877/487-2778**) for automated information.

Petrol   Please see "Car Rental" earlier in this chapter.

Police   Losses, thefts, and other criminal matters should be reported at the nearest police station immediately. You will be given a crime number, which your travel insurer will request if you make a claim. Dial ⓒ **999** or 112 if the matter is serious.

Safety   Britain has its share of crime, but in general it is one of the safest countries in the world for visitors. Pickpockets are a concern in London and the major cities, but violent crime is relatively rare. If you are in any doubt, ask the bar or restaurant you're leaving to phone you a minicab—never get into an unlicensed minicab, especially if you are female. Conceal your wallet or else hold on to your purse, and don't flaunt jewelry or cash. Personal electronic devices like smartphones and iPods are another obvious target. In short, it's the same advice you'd follow in your hometown.

Senior Travel   Britain offers many discounts to senior visitors. Many of the attractions recommended in this book list a separate, reduced entrance fee for seniors. However, even if discounts aren't posted, ask if they're available. Make sure you carry identification that shows your date of birth. Also, mention you're a senior when you make hotel reservations. Some offer discounts—but if you don't ask, they probably won't offer.

BritRail offers overseas seniors discounted rates on some rail passes around Britain. See **www.britrail.com**.

If you're heading to Britain from the U.S., members of **AARP,** 601 E St. NW, Washington, DC 20049 (ⓒ **888/687-2277;** www.aarp.org), can secure discounts on hotels, airfares, and car rentals. Anyone 50 or older can join.

Smoking   Smoking is banned in all indoor public places such as pubs, restaurants, and clubs across England and Wales. The regulations are almost universally observed and strictly enforced. If you wish to smoke, you will usually find temporary companions huddled close to the entrance door. Smoking is allowed in beer gardens and on terraces in bars, and the seats outside coffee shops, which generally means that the nice outdoor areas are effectively off-limits to non-smokers.

Student Travel   Never leave home without your student I.D. card. Visitors from overseas should arm themselves with an **International Student Identity Card (ISIC),** which offers local savings on rail passes, plane tickets, entrance fees, and much more. Each country's card offers slightly different benefits (in the U.S., for example, it provides you with basic health and life insurance and a 24-hour helpline). Apply before departing in your country of origin. In the U.S. or Canada, at **www.myisic.com**; in Australia, see **www. isiccard.com.au**; in New Zealand, visit **www.isiccard.co.nz**. U.K. students should carry their NUS card. If you're no longer a student but are still younger than 26, you can get an **International Youth Travel Card (IYTC),** which entitles you to a more limited range of discounts.

Taxes   All prices in the U.K. must be quoted inclusive of any taxes. Since January 1, 2011, the national value-added tax **(VAT)** has been 20%. This is included in all hotel and restaurant bills, and in the price of most items you purchase.

If you're permanently resident outside the E.U., VAT on goods can be refunded if you shop at stores that participate in the **Retail Export Scheme**—look for the window sticker or ask the staff. You need to fill out form VAT 407 in store, which the retailer will supply, and show your passport when you make the purchase. Show your receipt and form 407 to customs officials when you leave the U.K. (or at your point of departure from the E.U.)

and you then qualify for your refund. Each retailer is allowed to make its own arrangements for processing the refund—some require you to return the countersigned documents to them or an agent, others have an agreement in place with a booth at the airport. Details are posted online at **www.hmrc.gov.uk/vat/sectors/consumers/overseas-visitors.htm**.

Telephones   To make a call **within the U.K.,** the area codes found throughout this book all begin with "0"; you drop the "0" if you're calling from outside Britain, but you need to dial it along with the rest of the code if you're calling domestically. For calls within the same city or town, the local number is all you need, minus the area code. Dial just the **6- to 8-digit number.** Calling from a cellphone, you need to dial the full number including area code, *no matter where you're calling from.*

Phonecards are often the most economical method for visitors from overseas to make both international and national calls. They are available in several values, and are reusable until the total value has expired. Cards can be purchased from newsstands and small retailers nationwide, and offer call rates of a few pence per minute to English-speaking countries like Australia and the United States. Follow the instructions on the card to make a call from a public payphone. Most payphones now also take **credit cards,** but if your card doesn't have Chip and PIN technology embedded (see "Money & Costs," below), you may encounter problems.

For advice on using your **cellphone** in England and Wales, see "Mobile Phones," earlier in this section. If you intend to use your cellphone solely to call overseas, and it's unlocked and GSM-compatible, you may find purchasing a specialist **international SIM card** to be more convenient than phonecards. Calls to the U.S., for example, using a SIM card from either **Lyca** (✆ **020/7132-0322;** www.lycamobile.co.uk) or **Lebara** (✆ **0870/075-5588,** or 020/7031-0791; www.lebara-mobile.co.uk) cost 4p per minute. You can buy either at independent phone retailers on practically every urban street, and can fill up either brand with vouchers on sale at branches of Tesco, Sainsbury's, the Post Office, and hundreds of small retailers nationwide.

To make an **international call** from Britain, dial the international access code (**00),** then the country code, then the area code, and finally the local number. Common country codes are: USA and Canada, **1;** Australia, **61;** Ireland, **353;** New Zealand, **64;** and South Africa, **27.** For calling **collect** or if you need an international operator, dial ✆ **155.** Alternatively, call via one of the following long-distance access services: **AT&T USA Direct** (✆ **0800/890011** or 0500/890011), **Canada Direct** (✆ **0800/890016**), **Australia Direct** (✆ **0800/890061**), and **NZ Direct** (✆ **0800/890064**). For **directory assistance,** dial ✆ **118118.**

Callers beware: Many hotels routinely add outrageous surcharges onto phone calls made from your room. Inquire before you call. It may be a lot cheaper to use your own calling-card number or to find a phone card.

Time   Britain follows **Greenwich Mean Time** (GMT) between late October and late March. Daylight-saving **British Summer Time** (BST), 1 hour ahead of GMT, is in operation for the rest of the year. London is generally 5 hours ahead of U.S. Eastern Standard Time (EST), although because of different daylight-saving time practices in the two countries, there's a brief period (about a week) in autumn when Britain is only 4 hours ahead of New York or Toronto, and a brief period in spring when it's 6 hours ahead. Sydney is 10 or 11 hours ahead of U.K. time, Auckland 12 or 13 hours ahead.

For help with time translations download our convenient Travel Tools app for your mobile. Go to **www.frommers.com/go/mobile** and click the Travel Tools icon.

Tipping   Whether and how much to tip is not without controversy. Visitors from the U.S. in particular, tend to be more generous than locals—and indeed, some Brits resent a heavy tipping culture being "imported."

Tipping in **restaurants** is standard practice, as long as no automatic service charge is added to your bill. Leave 10% to 15% if you were happy with your server. However, be aware that a small number of places do not distribute these tips to staff as perks, but use them to pay their wages. This practice is only possible if you pay by credit or debit card, and unfortunately is perfectly legal. Ask who gets the tip, and if you're unhappy about paying the management's wage bill, have any automatic service charge removed and leave cash for your waiter or waitress to pick up. Earnings usually go into a communal pot to be shared among everyone from the kitchen porter to the sommelier, so no need to leave more than one tip per meal.

There's absolutely no need to tip the drivers of **black taxicabs:** They charge you extra for each item of luggage, and for standing in traffic. However, if the driver is especially helpful, add a pound or so to say thanks. Minicab drivers, on the other hand, generally earn less, and are always grateful if you are able to top up their rates, provided you're happy with the service.

Tipping in **bars** and **pubs** is practically unheard of, but if you receive table service in an upscale nightclub or wine bar, leave a couple of pounds.

In upscale **hotels**, porters expect around £1 per bag, even if you have only one small suitcase. Leave your maid £1 per day if you're happy with the cleaning, but only tip the concierge if they have performed something beyond the call of their regular work. In a bed-and-breakfast, you may ask that 10% be added to the bill and divided among the staff—but that certainly isn't expected.

Tour guides may expect £2 for a job well done, although it's not mandatory. Theatre ushers don't expect tips.

For help with tip calculations, and more, download our convenient Travel Tools app for your mobile device. Go to **www.frommers.com/go/mobile** and click on the Travel Tools icon.

Toilets Also known as "loos" or "public conveniences," these are marked by PUBLIC TOILET signs, and are usually free. You also find well-maintained lavatories in all larger public buildings, such as museums and art galleries, large department stores, and railway stations (although the latter generally impose a charge). It's not always acceptable to use the lavatories in restaurants and pubs if you're not a customer, but we can't say that we always stick to this rule.

VAT See "Taxes," above.

Visas No E.U. nationals require a visa to visit the U.K. Visas are also not required for travelers from Australia, Canada, New Zealand, or the U.S. For nationals of, or visitors from, other countries, see **www.ukvisas.gov.uk/en/doineedvisa**.

Visitor Information The U.K. has made huge investments in placing comprehensive, up-to-date, and inspirational visitor information online, so the Web is the place to begin your research. Try **www.enjoyengland.com**, **www.visitwales.co.uk,** and **www.visitlondon. com**, although almost any city or region has its own site. And, of course, there's plenty more—including features and updates—at **www.frommers.com/destinations/england**.

Wi-Fi See "Internet & Wi-Fi," above.

Women Travelers First and foremost, lone women should never ride in **unlicensed taxicabs,** especially at night. Recent high-profile cases have seen this method used by predatory sex attackers. **Journeywoman** (www.journeywoman.com) is the best source of tips and ideas for women travelers.

For general travel resources for women, go to **Frommers.com**.

MONEY & COSTS

UK£	Aus$	Can$	Euro (€)	NZ$	US$
£1	A$1.62	C$1.62	€1.17	A$2.06	$1.60

Frommer's lists exact prices in local currency. The currency conversions quoted above were correct at press. However, rates fluctuate, so before departing consult a website such as **www.oanda.com/currency/converter** to check up-to-the-minute rates.

While London is perceived as being the most expensive place in Britain, that is not always the case. As the countryside gentrifies, and smart hotels and Michelin-starred restaurants open up to well-heeled locals and equally well-off visitors, you might find yourself paying what we all call "London prices" for a meal, a room, even a beer. But there are still bargains to be had in more genuine parts of the country.

ATMs are everywhere in Britain—at banks, some gas stations, many supermarkets, and post offices. (Watch out for those inside small shops, however, as they charge users for withdrawing money.) These "cash machines" or "cashpoints" are the easiest way to get cash away from home. The **Cirrus** (www.mastercard.com) and **PLUS** (www.visa.com) networks span the globe; look at the back of your bank card to see which network you're on, then check online for ATM locations at your destination if you want to be ultra-organized. Be sure you know your personal identification number (PIN) and daily withdrawal limit before you depart. Note that U.K. machines use **4-digit PINs,** so if your bank issues a 6-digit number, contact them before you leave home. Credit cards are accepted just about everywhere, except for street markets and tiny independent retailers or street-food vendors. However, North American visitors should note that **American Express** is accepted much less in the U.K. than in the U.S. To be safe, bring a Visa or MasterCard as well.

Britain has been among the world's most aggressive countries in the fight against credit card fraud. Almost everywhere has moved from the magnetic strip credit card to the new system of **Chip and PIN** ("smartcards" with chips embedded in them). Most retailers ask for your 4-digit PIN to be entered into a keypad near the cash register. In restaurants, a waiter brings a hand-held device to your table to authorize payment. If you are visiting from a country where Chip and PIN is less prevalent (like the U.S.), it's possible retailers will be reluctant to accept your swipe cards. Be prepared to argue your case: Swipe cards are still legal, and the same machines that read the smartcard chips can also read your magnetic strip. However, do carry some cash with you, too.

If you're leaving your home country to visit the U.K., beware of hidden **credit- or debit-card fees.** Check with your card issuer to see what fees, if any, will be charged for overseas transactions. Recent reform legislation in the U.S., for example, has curbed some exploitative lending practices. But many banks have responded by increasing fees in other areas, including fees for customers who use credit and debit cards while out of the country—even if those charges were made in U.S. dollars. Fees can amount to 3% or more of the purchase price. Check with your bank before departing to avoid any surprise charges on your statement.

	UK£
Taxi from Heathrow to central London	60–85
Tube from Heathrow to Piccadilly Circus, using Oyster Card, off-peak	2.70
Double room at Claridge's, London (very expensive)	£500
Double room at Mandolay, Guildford, Surrey (expensive)	£120
Double room at Montague House, Sheringham, Norfolk (moderate)	£100
Double room at the Cathedral Gate Hotel, Canterbury, Kent (inexpensive)	£62
Lunch for one at the Box Tree, Ilkley, W. Yorks (expensive)	£35
Lunch for one at the Regency, Brighton, W. Sussex (inexpensive)	£20
Dinner for one, without wine, at Le Manoir aux Quat' Saisons (expensive)	£120
Dinner for one, without wine, at the Walnut Tree Inn, Abergavenny, Wales (moderate)	£50
Dinner for one, without wine, at Browns, Cambridge (inexpensive)	£25
Pint of beer	3–4
Cup of coffee	1.80–2.50
Admission to state museums	Free
Movie ticket	8–12
Theatre ticket	25–85

For help with currency conversions, tip calculations, and more, download Frommer's convenient Travel Tools app for your mobile device. Go to **www.frommers.com/go/mobile** and click on the Travel Tools icon.

AIRLINE, HOTEL & CAR-RENTAL WEBSITES

MAJOR U.S. AIRLINES
(all offer service to London)

American Airlines
www.aa.com

Continental Airlines
www.continental.com

Delta Air Lines
www.delta.com

United Airlines
www.united.com

US Airways
www.usairways.com

MAJOR INTERNATIONAL AIRLINES

Aer Lingus
www.aerlingus.com

Aeroméxico
www.aeromexico.com

Air Berlin
www.airberlin.com

Air Canada
www.aircanada.com

Air France
www.airfrance.com

Air India
www.airindia.com

Air New Zealand
www.airnewzealand.com

Air Transat
www.airtransat.com

Alitalia
www.alitalia.com

American Airlines
www.aa.com

Austrian Airlines
www.aua.com

BMI
www.flybmi.com

British Airways
www.british-airways.com

Cathay Pacific
www.cathaypacific.com

Continental Airlines
www.continental.com

Delta Air Lines
www.delta.com

Emirates Airlines
www.emirates.com

Finnair
www.finnair.com

Germanwings Airlines
www.germanwings.com

Iberia Airlines
www.iberia.com

Icelandair
www.icelandair.com
www.icelandair.co.uk (in U.K.)

Korean Airlines
www.koreanair.com

Lufthansa
www.lufthansa.com

Meridiana
www.meridiana.it

Monarch Flights
http://flights.monarch.co.uk

North American Airlines
www.flynaa.com

Norwegian Airlines
www.norwegian.no

Olympic Airlines
www.olympicairlines.com

Qantas Airlines
www.qantas.com

Qatar Airlines
www.qatarairways.com

Royal Dutch Airlines
www.klm.com

SAS (Scandinavian Airlines)
www.flysas.com

Singapore Airlines
www.singaporeair.com

South African Airways
www.flysaa.com

Swiss Air
www.swiss.com

Thai Airways International
www.thaiair.com

Tunisair
www.tunisair.com

Turkish Airlines
www.thy.com

United Airlines
www.united.com

US Airways
www.usairways.com

Virgin Atlantic Airways
www.virgin-atlantic.com

BUDGET AIRLINES

Aer Arann
www.aerarann.com

Aer Lingus
www.aerlingus.com

Air Berlin
www.airberlin.com

Aurigny
www.aurigny.com

BMI Baby
www.bmibaby.com

Brussels Airlines
www.brusselsairlines.com

Cimber Air
www.cimber.dk

Cirrus Airlines
www.cirrusairlines.de

Cityjet
www.cityjet.com

Condor
www.condor.com

Croatia Airlines
www.croatiaairlines.com

Czech Airlines
www.czechairlines.com

EasyJet
www.easyjet.com

Flybe
www.flybe.com

Ryanair
www.ryanair.com

Tap Airlines
www.flytap.com

Ted (part of United Airlines)
www.flyted.com

VLM
www.flyvlm.com

Wizz Air
www.wizzair.com

MAJOR HOTEL & MOTEL CHAINS

Accor Hotels
www.accorhotels.com

Best Western International
www.bestwestern.com

Britannia Hotels
www.britanniahotels.com

Carlson Hotels
www.carlson.com

Clarion Hotels
www.choicehotels.com

Comfort Inns
www.comfortinn.com

Courtyard by Marriott
www.marriott.com/courtyard

Crowne Plaza Hotels
www.ichotelsgroup.com

Holiday Inn Hotels
www.holidayinn.com

Days Inn Hotels
www.daysinn.com

Firmdale Hotels
www.firmdale.com

Four Seasons
www.fourseasons.com

Grange Hotels
www.grangehotels.com

Hilton Hotels
www1.hilton.com

Hotel du Vin
www.hotelduvin.com

Hotel Formule 1
www.hotelformule1.com

Hyatt
www.hyatt.com

Ibis Hotels
www.ibishotel.com

Imperial Hotels
www.imperialhotels.co.uk

InterContinental Hotels & Resorts
www.interconti.com

Leading Hotels of the World
www.lhw.com

Malmaison
www.malmaison.com

Marriott
www.marriott.com

Mercure Hotels
www.mercure.com

Millennium Hotels
www.millenniumhotels.com

Novotel Hotels
www.novotel.com

Preferred Hotels & Resorts
www.preferredhotels.com

Premier Inn Hotels
www.premierinn.com

Quality
www.choicehotels.com

Radisson Hotels & Resorts
www.radisson.com

Ramada Worldwide
www.ramada.com

Red Carnation Hotels
www.redcarnationhotels.com

Residence Inn by Marriott
www.marriott.com/residenceinn

Rocco Forte Collection
www.roccofortecollection.com

Shaftesbury Hotels
www.shaftesburyhotels.com

Sheraton Hotels & Resorts
www.starwoodhotels.com/sheraton

Small Luxury Hotels of the World
www.slh.com

Sol Melia Hotels & Resorts
www.solmelia.com

Thistle Hotels
www.thistle.com

Travelodge Hotels
www.travelodge.com

Von Essen Hotels
www.vonessenhotels.co.uk

Westin Hotels & Resorts
www.starwoodhotels.com/westin

CAR-RENTAL AGENCIES

Alamo
www.alamo.com

Auto Europe
www.autoeurope.com

Avis
www.avis.com

Budget
www.budget.com

Dollar
www.dollar.com

Enterprise
www.enterprise.com

Hertz
www.hertz.com

Kemwel (KHA)
www.kemwel.com

National
www.nationalcar.com

Thrifty
www.thrifty.com

Index